RETAILING MANAGEMENT

RETAILING TENTH EDITION
MANAGEMENT

Michael Levy, PhD
Babson College

Barton A. Weitz, PhD
University of Florida

Dhruv Grewal, PhD
Babson College

McGraw Hill Education

RETAILING MANAGEMENT

Published by McGraw-Hill Education, 2 Penn Plaza, New York, NY 10121. Copyright © 2019 by McGraw-Hill Education. All rights reserved. Printed in the United States of America. No part of this publication may be reproduced or distributed in any form or by any means, or stored in a database or retrieval system, without the prior written consent of McGraw-Hill Education, including, but not limited to, in any network or other electronic storage or transmission, or broadcast for distance learning.

Some ancillaries, including electronic and print components, may not be available to customers outside the United States.

This book is printed on acid-free paper.

1 2 3 4 5 6 7 8 9 LWI 21 20 19 18

ISBN 978-1-260-08476-4
MHID 1-260-08476-0

Cover Image: © *Jamie Grill/Getty Images*

ABOUT THE AUTHORS

Michael Levy
©Karen Rubin Photography

Michael Levy, PhD (Ohio State University), is the Charles Clarke Reynolds Professor of Marketing Emeritus at Babson College and CEO of RetailProf LLC. He received his PhD in business administration from Ohio State University and his undergraduate and MS degrees in business administration from the University of Colorado at Boulder. He taught at Southern Methodist University before joining the faculty as professor and chair of the marketing department at the University of Miami.

Professor Levy received the inaugural ACRA Academic Lifetime Achievement Award presented at the 2015 AMA/ACRA (American Marketing Association/American Collegiate Retailing Association) Triennial Conference, and was recognized for 25 years of dedicated service to the editorial review board of the *Journal of Retailing* in 2011. He won the McGraw-Hill Corporate Achievement Award for Grewal–Levy *Marketing 2e* with Connect in the category of excellence in content and analytics (2010); Revision of the Year for *Marketing 2e* (Grewal–Levy) from McGraw-Hill/Irwin (2010); the 2009 Lifetime Achievement Award, American Marketing Association, Retailing Special Interest Group (SIG); the Babson Faculty Scholarship Award (2009); and the Distinguished Service Award, *Journal of Retailing* (2009) (at winter AMA).

He was rated as one of the best researchers in marketing in a survey published in *Marketing Educator* (Summer 1997). He has developed a strong stream of research in retailing, business logistics, financial retailing strategy, pricing, and sales management. He has published over 50 articles in leading marketing and logistics journals, including the *Journal of Retailing, Journal of Marketing, Journal of the Academy of Marketing Science,* and *Journal of Marketing Research.* He has served on the editorial review boards of the *Journal of Retailing, Journal of the Academy of Marketing Science, International Journal of Physical Distribution and Materials Management, International Journal of Business Logistics, ECR Journal,* and *European Business Review,* and has been on the editorial advisory boards of *European Retail Research* and the *European Business Review.* He is coauthor of *Marketing 6e* (2018). Professor Levy was coeditor of the *Journal of Retailing* from 2001 to 2007. He cochaired the 1993 Academy of Marketing Science conference and the 2006 summer AMA conference.

Professor Levy has worked in retailing and related disciplines throughout his professional life. Prior to his academic career, he worked for several retailers and a housewares distributor in Colorado. He has performed research projects with many retailers and retail technology firms, including Accenture, Federated Department Stores, Khimetrics (SAP), Mervyn's, Neiman Marcus, ProfitLogic (Oracle), Zale Corporation, and numerous law firms.

Barton A. Weitz
Courtesy of Benjamin Simons, UF Warrington College of Business

Barton A. Weitz, PhD, received an undergraduate degree in electrical engineering from MIT and an MBA and a PhD in business administration from Stanford University. He has been a member of the faculty at the UCLA Graduate School of Business and the Wharton School at the University of Pennsylvania and is presently the JCPenney Emeritus Eminent Scholar Chair in Retail Management in the Warrington College of Business Administration at the University of Florida.

Professor Weitz is the founder of the David F. Miller Center for Retailing Education and Research at the University of Florida. The activities of the center are supported by contributions from 35 retailers and firms supporting the retail industry, including JCPenney, Macy's, Walmart, Office Depot, Walgreens, Home Depot, and the International Council of Shopping Centers. Each year, the center places more than 250 undergraduates in paid summer internships and management trainee positions with retail firms, and funds research on retailing issues and problems.

Professor Weitz has won awards for teaching excellence and made numerous presentations to industry and academic groups. He has published more than 50 articles in leading academic journals on channel relationships, electronic retailing, store design, salesperson effectiveness, and sales force and human resource management. His research has been recognized with two Louis Stern Awards for his contributions to channel management research and a Paul Root Award for the *Journal of Marketing* article that makes the greatest contribution to marketing practice. He serves on the editorial review boards of the *Journal of Retailing, Journal of Marketing, International Journal of Research in Marketing,* and *Journal of Marketing Research.* He is a former editor of the *Journal of Marketing Research.* Professor Weitz has been the chair of the American Marketing Association and a member of the board of directors of the National Retail Federation and the American Marketing Association. He was honored as the AMA/Irwin Distinguished Educator in recognition of his contributions to the marketing discipline. He was selected by the National Retail Federation as Retail Educator of the Year and been recognized for lifetime achievements by American Marketing Association Retailing, Sales, and Inter-Organizational Special Interests Groups.

Dhruv Grewal, PhD (Virginia Tech), is the Toyota Chair in Commerce and Electronic Business and a professor of marketing at Babson College. He is listed in The World's Most Influential Scientific Minds, Thomson Reuters 2014 (only 8 from the marketing field and 95 from economics and business are listed). He was awarded the 2013 university-wide Distinguished Graduate Alumnus from his alma mater, Virginia Tech, the 2012 Lifetime Achievement Award in Pricing (AMA Retailing & Pricing SIG), the 2010 Lifetime Achievement Award in Retailing (AMA Retailing SIG), the 2010 AMS Cutco/Vector Distinguished Educator Award, and the 2005 Lifetime Achievement in Behavioral Pricing Award (Fordham University, November 2005). He is a Distinguished Fellow of the Academy of Marketing Science. He was ranked first in the marketing field in terms of publications in the top-six marketing journals during the 1991–1998 period and again for the 2000–2007 period. He ranked eighth in terms of publications in the *Journal of Marketing* and the *Journal of Marketing Research* during the 2009–2013 period and ranked seventh in terms of publications in the *Journal of Public Policy & Marketing* for the period 1992–2001. He was also ranked first in terms of publications and third in citations for pricing research for the time period 1980–2010 in 20 marketing and business publications. He has served as VP, research and conferences, American Marketing Association Academic Council (1999–2001), and as VP, development for the Academy of Marketing Science (2000–2002). He was coeditor of *Journal of Retailing* from 2001 to 2007. He cochaired the 1993 Academy of Marketing Science Conference, the 1998 Winter American Marketing Association Conference, the 2001 AMA doctoral consortium, the American Marketing Association 2006 Summer Educators Conference, the 2011 DMEF research summit, and the 2012 and 2015 AMA/ACRA Retailing Conference.

Professor Grewal has published over 140 articles in journals such as the *Journal of Retailing, Journal of Marketing, Journal of Consumer Research, Journal of Marketing Research, Journal of Consumer Psychology, Journal of Applied Psychology,* and *Journal of the Academy of Marketing Science,* as well as other journals. He currently serves on numerous editorial and advisory review boards, such as the *Journal of Retailing, Journal of Marketing* (area editor), *Journal of Marketing Research, Journal of Consumer Psychology, Journal of the Academy of Marketing Science* (area editor), *Academy of Marketing Science Review, Journal of Interactive Marketing, Journal of Business*

Dhruv Grewal
©*Morse Photography*

Research, and *Journal of Public Policy & Marketing.* He has over 35,000 citations based on Google scholar.

Professor Grewal has won a number of awards for his teaching: 2005 Sherwin-Williams Distinguished Teaching Award, Society for Marketing Advances; 2003 American Marketing Association Award for Innovative Excellence in Marketing Education; 1999 Academy of Marketing Science Great Teachers in Marketing Award; Executive MBA Teaching Excellence Award (1998); School of Business Teaching Excellence Awards (1993, 1999); and Virginia Tech Certificate of Recognition for Outstanding Teaching (1989). He has won numerous awards for his research: 2016 *Journal of Marketing* Sheth Award; William R. Davidson *Journal of Retailing* Best Paper Awards 2010, 2012, and 2016; Luis W. Stern Awards 2011 and 2015 (AMA IO Sig); William R. Davidson *Journal of Retailing* Honorable Mention Awards 2010 and 2011; Babson College Faculty Scholarship Award (2010 and 2015); University of Miami School of Business Research Excellence Award for the years 1991, 1995, 1996, and 1998; Best Services Paper Award (AMA Services SIG 2002); Stanley C. Hollander Best Retailing Paper (AMS 2002 and 2008); and M. Wayne DeLozier Best Conference Paper (AMS 2002 and 2008). He also received Best Reviewer Awards (*Journal of Retailing* 2008, *Journal of Marketing* 2014), best area editor (*Journal of the Academy of Marketing Science* 2016), and a Distinguished Service Award (*Journal of Retailing* 2009).

Professor Grewal has taught executive seminars and courses and/or worked on research projects with numerous firms such as Dell, ExxonMobil, IRI, Radio Shack, Telcordia, Khimetriks, Profit-Logic, McKinsey, Ericsson, Motorola, Nextel, FP&L, Lucent, Sabre, Goodyear Tire & Rubber Company, Sherwin-Williams, and Asahi. He has delivered seminars in the United States, Europe, Latin America, and Asia. He has also served as an expert witness and worked as a consultant on numerous legal cases.

We are excited to bring you the tenth edition of *Retailing Management*. It has been four years since our last revision, and as you know, a lot has changed, and *Retailing Management* has changed with it.

This tenth edition of *Retailing Management* builds on the basic philosophy of the previous nine editions. We continue to focus on both strategic and tactical issues, with an emphasis on financial considerations and implementation through merchandise and store management.

NEW TO THE TENTH EDITION

Chapter 1, "Introduction to the World of Retailing," begins with discussion of two retail giants, Amazon and Walmart, and the struggle Walmart is facing in competing with the online retailer and its efficient supply chain and fulfillment capabilities, its vast inventory, and its recommendation algorithms. A new section on corporate social responsibility and conscious marketing's four overriding principles provides further insight into what makes a successful retailer. In addition, a new Retailing View highlights how innovative mobile payment systems are improving the lives of Africa's working poor.

Chapter 2, "Types of Retailers," opens with a brief vignette on the challenges faced by both Sam's Club and Walmart as they work to avoid cannibalizing upon one another. In addition, the newest trends in supermarket retailing are discussed, shedding light on food retailers' efforts to go above and beyond traditional store sales, including a new section on online grocery sales by traditional full-line discount stores, supermarkets that offer new, unexpected services, and the rise of limited-assortment and extreme-value food retailers. A new section on flash sale sites is also included, as are new Retailing Views about online grocery retailer FreshDirect; Macy's quest to combat sales declines and leverage both its existing advantages and new retail options; how Sephora has revolutionized the cosmetics industry; and McDonald's primary business model of franchising and the reciprocity of allegiance between the company and its franchisees.

Chapter 3, "Multichannel and Omnichannel Retailing," has been retitled to reflect the many ways in which retailing is available to consumers, and a revised set of learning objectives provides further ease of use and understanding of important chapter concepts. A new introduction looks at the way Rebecca Minkoff has integrated the in-store experience through the use of mobile devices. A new section elaborates on the types of retail channels that help define *omnichannel*, as well as each channel's benefits. New Retailing Views focus on Sephora's To Go app, Apple and the omnichannel experience; and retailer Warby Parker.

Chapter 4, "Customer Buying Behavior," opens with a short vignette about the many ways Macy's is wooing Millennials. In addition, new coverage of retailers' *and* consumers' reliance on mobile devices shows just how integral this technology has become—from checking inventory and creating virtual outfits to using apps that ease the purchasing of merchandise. New Retailing Views cover CVS's decision to ban the sale of cigarettes in its locations; H&M's effective segmentation strategy; how one regional Texas grocery chain attracts and retains customers; and the rise of fast fashion among Generation Z consumers.

Chapter 5, "Retail Market Strategy," opens with a discussion of the ways in which retailers are enticing customers to spend time in their stores to increase consumer spending by providing a range of unique in-store experiences. New sections on specific retailers' market strategies include those utilized by both Sephora and Lululemon.

New details are included about the various ways in which customer loyalty is achieved by retailers, as well as the opportunities and challenges of retail markets in India, China, and Russia. New Retailing Views include Whole Foods's efforts to promote sustainability and responsibility; the surprising success of Starbucks in Italy; Uniqlo's dual marketing strategy of quality and affordability.

Chapter 6, "Financial Strategy," begins with a discussion of the marketing and operations issues that impact financial performance for some of the world's best retailers. New sections provide easy-to-understand information on how the very different strategies of Nordstrom and Walmart translate into their financial performance, using the strategic profit model and its component financial ratios, net profit margin percentage, asset turnover, and return on assets. Further discussion on how other important financial ratios, such as gross margin, operating profit percentage, and inventory turnover, are used to make and evaluate both strategic and tactical decisions is presented. New examples throughout, combined with new and revised key terms written at a level students will understand, are designed to address these important, yet often difficult factors in measuring retailing success and failure. New Retailing Views discuss how Nordstrom and Walmart achieve success using differing retail strategies, how omnichannel retailers calculate profits of online and in-store sales, and the challenges of crowdfunding in retail operations.

Chapter 7, "Retail Locations," opens with a discussion of the challenges faced by malls and the ways in which malls are reinventing themselves to keep pace with customer demands. A new section on urban areas details the ways retailers address their customers' needs, and a new section on food deserts within inner cities discusses how retailers are addressing customers' basic needs. In addition, new content on the rise of nontraditional stores discusses how outlet centers, pop-up stores, and stores-within-stores have all become popular locations for retailers. A new Retailing View discusses how Apple is increasing mall foot traffic and becoming the new mall "anchors," and updates to existing Retailing Views provide critical new information about their respective topic.

Chapter 8, "Retail Site Location," begins with a discussion of Starbucks's perfection of Geographic Information Systems in planning new locations and expanding menu options worldwide. There is new content on how the increased importance of online and mobile impacts retail location decisions. A new Retailing View covers Lululemon and its location strategy, and an updated Retailing View discusses the importance of the "right" location for Speedway.

Chapter 9, "Information Systems and Supply Chain Management," opens with an example of fast fashion from retailer Zara and highlights how the company has thrived as a result. Updates underscore the role of the wholesaler in the supply chain; the benefits and limitations of vendor-managed inventory; and the flow of merchandise through a supply chain. The chapter ends with a discussion of system trends, with updated information on RFIDs and an example of their successful implementation, as well as customer store pickup through the use of mobile task management technology. New Retailing Views cover grocery giant Kroger's partnership with a particular supply chain for training purposes; how IKEA produces high-quality, low-cost furniture through its supply chain efficiency; and how robots are used to ensure that a store's products get to its intended customers.

Chapter 10, "Customer Relationship Management," begins with a look into grocery retailer Kroger's management of customer relationships, which has earned the chain the highest loyalty program participation rates in the grocery industry. New content on protecting customer privacy showcases the ways in which retailers can increase customers' confidence, as well as new information on the ways in which retailers are responding to unprofitable customers. New Retailing Views highlight how CVS uses customer loyalty data; how Whole Foods utilizes its loyalty program by offering personalized rewards; and how Staples is targeting the small-business owner with an app.

Chapter 11, "Managing the Merchandise Planning Process," has been retitled to be more descriptive of its content. The chapter begins with a discussion of the way in which Target and other stores are using nontraditional stocking techniques to increase sales. More explanation of GMROI is included, as well as the ways in which retailers perform market research. A new Retailing View covers Macy's use of predictive analytics in learning more about its customers and improving their online experience; updated Retailing Views elaborate on how the Weather Channel is marketing its weather analytics to retailers and how Saks Fifth Avenue learned from its price-cutting mistake following the most recent recession.

Chapter 12, "Buying Merchandise," opens with a discussion of how many national and worldwide chains use local appeal to attract customers. An updated section on how store-brand merchandise is developed and sourced is included, as well as updated content on how brands are taking legal action against counterfeiters and more examples of corporate social responsibility. A new Retailing View highlights the benefits of manufacturing in Africa.

Chapter 13, "Retail Pricing," begins with an overview of the "battle" in the pizza industry to keep prices low and increase sales and market share. In addition, an updated section on pricing techniques provides clear explanations of dynamic pricing and predatory pricing. New Retailing Views focus on Walmart's entry into the organic food market with its EDLP strategies, Disney and Universal's pricing plans, Amazon's daily price changes based on algorithms that provide insight into consumers' demands, and the unethical practice of deceptive reference pricing among some of the retail giants.

Chapter 14, "Retail Communication Mix," begins with a look at H&M's unconventional advertising as the company seeks to showcase its offerings in unique ways. A revised set of learning objectives provides further ease of use and understanding of important chapter concepts. New coverage of mobile marketing shows that these devices are being used by retailers. New Retailing Views cover the ways in which some European fashion multichannel retailers are appealing to their target markets using a combination of social media and print publishing, often including items they do not carry but which appeal and attract customers' attention; Domino's use of Snapchat as a marketing tool to entice customers; online versus print coupons and the rise of rebate apps; and the ways in which Hispanic consumers have become one of the most prominent, growing, and appealing targets for retailers.

Chapter 15, "Human Resources and Managing the Store," has been combined with the ninth edition's Chapter 9 on human resource management and retitled to reflect the inherent implementation issues associated with these two topics. A new introduction shows how Zappos's philosophy and strong leadership equals happy employees, and a revised set of learning objectives hones in on the most important chapter concepts. New material focuses on the benefits and drawbacks of using social media to research prospective employees, as well as the ways in which companies are rewarding and motivating their employees. New Retailing Views discuss the ways in which retailers are recruiting Millennials; one grocery chain's unique ownership structure that gives employees rewards for store performance; shifts in employee dress codes in response to changing cultural and social norms; and the laws that prohibit employers from altering employees' schedules without compensation.

Chapter 16, "Store Layout, Design, and Visual Merchandising," begins with the story of Bergdorf Goodman's New York City renovation and its quest to combine classical luxury and modern (social media) chic. New material on store design elements provides updated information on grid layout, how to attract supermarket shoppers to the center store, and the ways in which retailers are utilizing dressing rooms and the rising importance of virtual dressing rooms. New Retail Views cover the importance of function and experience for customers at Saks Fifth Avenue's new stores and its Off 5th outlet stores; the interesting ways in which retailers are catering to customers' impulse purchases; and retailers' use of scents to attract customers.

Chapter 17, "Customer Service," opens with the latest innovations by Rent the Runway to give customers perfectly fit clothing at affordable prices. New material is included on the ways in which retailers provide exceptional customer service, both in-store and online; the rise of standardized service; and the importance of social media in learning about customer expectations and perceptions. New Retailing Views focus on the ways in which Home Depot is renovating its stores to appeal to female consumers; grocery giant Kroger's use of analytics to reduce customers' wait time at registers; and Sprint's use of customer service robots in Japan.

A LETTER FROM THE AUTHORS

This text is organized around a model of strategic decision making outlined in Chapter 1. Each section and chapter relates back to that overarching strategic framework. To keep students engaged with this focus, we offer the following features:

- Introductory vignettes—Each chapter begins with an example of how a stellar retailer is particularly successful by excelling in the subject area for that particular chapter.

- Retailing Views—Each chapter contains new and updated "stories" that describe how particular retailers deal with the issues raised in each chapter. The majority of these Retailing Views are new in this edition.

- New cases—In Section 5, there are seven new cases and updates to existing cases.

- Graphics—Exhibits in each chapter provide critical, up-to-date information and lively visuals. Almost all of the photos are new to this edition.

- Streamlining—To facilitate student learning, we have streamlined the presentation, both visually and pedagogically. Based on reviewer comments, we have combined the chapters on human resource management and managing the store. In keeping with our goal of providing a "good read" for students, we continue to substantiate conceptual material with interesting, current, "real-world" retailing examples.

- Updating—Every example, fact, and key term has been checked, updated, and/or replaced.

In preparing this edition, we focused on five important factors that continue to delineate outstanding retailers:

- The use of big data and analytical methods for decision making.

- The application of social media and mobile for communicating with customers and enhancing their shopping experience.

- The issues involved in utilizing a mobile channel and providing a seamless multichannel experience for customers.

- The engagement in the overarching emphasis on conscious marketing and corporate social responsibility when making business decisions.

- The impact of globalization on the retail industry.

We realize that retailing is taught in a variety of formats, both face-to-face and online, so a comprehensive supplemental package for instructors is provided. In addition to the Connect materials described on the following pages and the comprehensive online Instructor's Manual with additional cases and teaching suggestions, we provide the following:

- **Get Out and Do It!** exercises at the end of each chapter. These exercises suggest projects that students can undertake by visiting local retail stores or surfing the Internet. A continuing assignment exercise is included so that students can engage in an exercise involving the same retailer throughout the course. The exercises are designed to provide a hands-on learning experience for students.

- **Authors' blog at theretailingmanagement.com** includes summaries and discussion questions of recent retailing articles from the business and trade presses. These articles are associated with specific chapters so that instructors can use them to stimulate class discussion.

We hope you and your students will enjoy the tenth edition of *Retailing Management*. Let us know what you think!

Michael, Bart, and Dhruv

 **connect**®

McGraw-Hill Connect® is a highly reliable, easy-to-use homework and learning management solution that utilizes learning science and award-winning adaptive tools to improve student results.

Homework and Adaptive Learning

- Connect's assignments help students contextualize what they've learned through application, so they can better understand the material and think critically.
- Connect will create a personalized study path customized to individual student needs through SmartBook®.
- SmartBook helps students study more efficiently by delivering an interactive reading experience through adaptive highlighting and review.

Connect's Impact on Retention Rates, Pass Rates, and Average Exam Scores

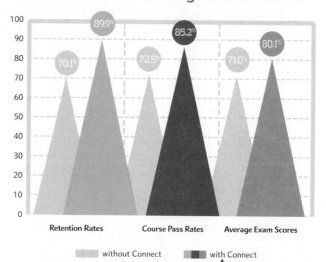

without Connect   with Connect

> Over **7 billion questions** have been answered, making McGraw-Hill Education products more intelligent, reliable, and precise.

> Using **Connect** improves retention rates by **19.8%**, passing rates by **12.7%**, and exam scores by **9.1%**.

> 73% of instructors who use **Connect** require it; instructor satisfaction **increases** by 28% when **Connect** is required.

Quality Content and Learning Resources

- Connect content is authored by the world's best subject matter experts, and is available to your class through a simple and intuitive interface.
- The Connect eBook makes it easy for students to access their reading material on smartphones and tablets. They can study on the go and don't need internet access to use the eBook as a reference, with full functionality.
- Multimedia content such as videos, simulations, and games drive student engagement and critical thinking skills.

Robust Analytics and Reporting

©Hero Images/Getty Images

- Connect Insight® generates easy-to-read reports on individual students, the class as a whole, and on specific assignments.

- The Connect Insight dashboard delivers data on performance, study behavior, and effort. Instructors can quickly identify students who struggle and focus on material that the class has yet to master.

- Connect automatically grades assignments and quizzes, providing easy-to-read reports on individual and class performance.

Impact on Final Course Grade Distribution

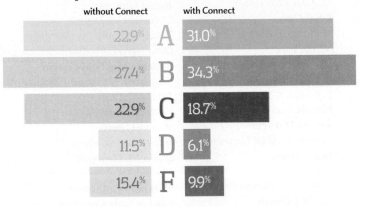

without Connect		with Connect
22.9%	A	31.0%
27.4%	B	34.3%
22.9%	C	18.7%
11.5%	D	6.1%
15.4%	F	9.9%

More students earn **As** and **Bs** when they use **Connect**.

Trusted Service and Support

- Connect integrates with your LMS to provide single sign-on and automatic syncing of grades. Integration with Blackboard®, D2L®, and Canvas also provides automatic syncing of the course calendar and assignment-level linking.

- Connect offers comprehensive service, support, and training throughout every phase of your implementation.

- If you're looking for some guidance on how to use Connect, or want to learn tips and tricks from super users, you can find tutorials as you work. Our Digital Faculty Consultants and Student Ambassadors offer insight into how to achieve the results you want with Connect.

ACKNOWLEDGMENTS

Throughout the development of this text, several outstanding individuals were integrally involved and made substantial contributions. First, we thank Elisabeth Nevins and Jenny Esdale for their important assistance in doing research for the book, writing examples, and preparing the manuscript for publication. Ancillary materials have become increasingly more integral to the success of any classroom experience. We are privileged to have had a superb team working with us on 10e: Shelly Kohan (Instructors' Manual), Nancy Murray (Test Bank/Quizzes and Connect Interactive Exercises), and Sue Sullivan (LearnSmart). The support, expertise, and occasional coercion from our product developer, Anne Ehrenworth, has always been helpful. Additionally, our production editor, Kelly Hart; our ever-diligent copyeditor and proofreader, Sharon O'Donnell; our eye-to-the-aesthetic and pedagogy photo editor, David Tietz; and our bridge to corporate intellectual property experts, content licensing specialist, Ann Marie Jannette, are greatly appreciated. We would also like to thank Meredith Fossel, executive brand manager, for her support and dedication to this project.

We would like to thank the following instructors who were instrumental in guiding this revision of ***Retailing Management***, as well as previous editions of our text.

Mark Abel
Kirkwood Community College

Nancy Abram
University of Iowa

Arthur Allaway
University of Alabama–Tuscaloosa

Steven J. Anderson
Austin Peay State University

Jill Attaway
Illinois State University

Sally Baalbaki
University of North Texas

Mary Barry
Auburn University

Lauren Beitelspacher
Babson College

Lance A. Bettencourt
Texas Christian University

David Blanchette
Rhode Island College

Jeff Blodgett
University of Houston–Victoria

Marjorie Bonavia
University of Maryland

George W. Boulware
Lipscomb University

Samuel Bradley
Alvernia University

Willard Broucek
Northern State University

Leroy M. Buckner
Florida Atlantic University

David J. Burns
Purdue University

Lon Camomile
Colorado State University

William J. Carner
West Minister College

Donald W. Caudill
Gardner-Webb University

James Clark
Southern Arkansas University

Sylvia Clark
St. John's University

Brad Cox
Midlands Technical College

Nicole Cox
University of Arkansas–Fayetteville

J. Joseph Cronin Jr.
Florida State University

Angela D'Auria
Stanton Radford University

Tracy Davis
University of Houston–Downtown

Sandy Dawson
Oregon State University

Irene J. Dickey
University of Dayton

Dina Dingman
Indiana University

Dawn DiStefano
Nassau Community College

Mary Anne Doty
Texas A&M University–Commerce

Patricia Doyle
University of Cincinnati

Ann DuPont
University of Texas

Chloe I. Elmgren
Minnesota State University

Richard L. Entrikin
George Mason University

David Erickson
Angelo University

Kenneth R. Evans
University of Missouri–Columbia

Richard Feinberg
Purdue University

Kevin Fertig
University of Illinois

Deborah Fowler
Texas Tech University

Rama Ganesan
University of Arizona

Trina Gannon
Ohio University–Athens

Stefanie Mayfield Garcia
University of Central Florida

Javier Garza
Cerritos College

Wayne Gawlik
Joliet Junior College

David M. Georgoff
Florida Atlantic University

Elizabeth Goldsmith
Florida State University

Peter Gordon
Southeast Missouri State University

Larry Gresham
Texas A&M University

Tom Gross
University of Wisconsin

Sejin Ha
University of Tennessee

Debra A. Haley
Southeastern Oklahoma State University

Jamey Halleck
Marshall University

Sally Harmon
Purdue University

Susan Harmon
Middle Tennessee State University

Michael D. Hartline
Florida State University

Tony L. Henthorne
University of Southern Mississippi

Kae Hineline
McLennan Community College

Cathleen Hohner
College of DuPage

Joshua Holt
Brigham Young University

Donna Hope
Nassau Community College

David Horne
California State University– Long Beach

Gary L. Hunter
Illinois State University

Fred Hurvitz
Pennsylvania State University

Brenda Jones
Northwest Missouri State University

Michael Jones
Auburn University

Eugene J. Kangas
Winona State University

Herbert Katzenstein
St. John's University

Seth Ketron
University of North Texas

Minjeong Kim
Indiana University– Bloomington

Stephen Kirk
East Carolina University

Shelley Kohan
Fashion Institute of Technology

Natalia Kolyesnikova
Texas Tech University

Terrence Kroeten
North Dakota State University

Archana Kumar
Montclair State University

Seung Hwan (Mark) Lee
Ryerson University

Dolly Loyd
University of Southern Mississippi

Ann Lucht
Milwaukee Area Technical College

Elizabeth Mariotz
Philadelphia University

Theresa Mastrianni
Kingsborough Community College

Tony Mayo
George Mason University

Harold McCoy
Virginia Commonwealth University

Michael McGinnis
Penn State

Phyliss McGinnis
Boston University

Kim McKeage
Hamline University

Barbara Mihm
University of Wisconsin– Stevens Point

Robert Miller
Central Michigan University

Mary Anne Milward
University of Arizona

Nancy Murray
University of Wisconsin– Madison

Ward Nefstead
University of Minnesota– Minneapolis

David Nemi
Niagara County Community College–Sanborn

Cheryl O'Hara
Kings College

Dorothy M. Oppenheim
Bridgewater State University

Michael M. Pearson
Loyola University–New Orleans

Janis Petronis
Tarleton State University

Linda Pettijohn
Missouri State University

Lucille Pointer
University of Houston– Downtown

John J. Porter
West Virginia University

Kathleen Richard
Madonna University–Livonia

Sue Riha
University of Texas–Austin

Rodney Runyan
Texas State University

Joan Ryan
Clackamas Community College

Amrut Sadachar
Auburn University

Melinda Salzer
Brookdale Community College

Nick Saratakes
Austin Community College

Ian J. Scharf
University of Miami–Coral Gables

Lisa Sciulli
Indiana University of Pennsylvania

Laura Scroggins
California State University– Chico

Rick Shannon
Western Kentucky University

Rob Simon
University of Nebraska–Lincoln

Rodger Singley
Illinois State University

Chuck Smith
Horry-Georgetown Technical College

Herschel Smith
College of DuPage

Jeffery C. Smith
Owens Community College

Steve Solesbee
Aiken Technical College

Rajesh Srivastava
Middle Tennessee State University

Roxanne Stell
University of Houston

Barbara Stewart
Northern Arizona University

Dan Stone
University of Kentucky

Shirley M. Stretch
California State University– Los Angeles

William R. Swinyard
Brigham Young University

Shelley R. Tapp
Wayland Baptist University

Amy Tomas
University of Vermont

Kathy Wachter
University of Mississippi

Janet Wagner
University of Maryland

Gary Walk
Lima Technical College

Anna Walz
Grand Valley State University

Mary Weber
University of New Mexico

Sandy White
Greenville Tech College

Fred T. Whitman
Mary Washington College

Kathleen Debevic Witz
University of Massachusetts– Amherst

Merv Yeagle
University of Maryland at College Park

Ron Zallocco
University of Toledo

BRIEF CONTENTS

CONTENTS

SECTION III MERCHANDISE MANAGEMENT

SECTION V   CASES

RETAILING
MANAGEMENT

The World of Retailing

The chapters in Section I provide background information about the types of retailers, the different channels they use, their customers and competitors— information that can be used to develop and implement an effective retail strategy.

Chapter 1 describes the importance of the retail industry to the U.S. economy and, more generally, to society as a whole. It also details the organization of this book, which revolves around the decisions that retailers make to satisfy their customers' needs.

Chapter 2 describes different types of food, merchandise, and service retailers, as well as their ownership structures.

Chapter 3 examines the channels that retailers use to satisfy the needs of their customers and the challenges they face in coordinating these multiple channels—stores, the Internet/mobile/ social, and catalogs—when interacting with their customers.

Chapter 4 discusses the process that consumers go through when choosing retail outlets and channels to buy merchandise and how retailers can affect this buying process.

The chapters in Section II focus on the decisions retailers make to develop strategic assets—assets that enable retailers to build sustainable competitive advantages.

The chapters in Sections III and IV explore more tactical execution decisions involving merchandise and store management.

© Chris Ratcliffe/Bloomberg/Getty Images

About 15 years ago, Walmart committed itself to Internet retailing. This year, it made the same commitment.[1] But the environments surrounding these similar announcements differ radically from each other. In particular, a couple of decades ago Amazon was just a small annoyance, totally dominated by Walmart's superior reach, sales, distribution capabilities, and revenue. Today, however, Amazon has overtaken Walmart in terms of its stock market value,[2] and it appears well positioned to compete in the digital marketplace, whereas Walmart continues to seek a firm toehold in the online realm.

Walmart certainly is not alone in struggling to compete with Amazon. Virtually every retailer in the world competes in some way with the online giant, because of what Amazon offers.[3] First, Amazon is incredibly convenient, available to meet shoppers' every product need, at any time. As a result, many shoppers use the site almost like a search engine. According to one recent survey, a remarkable 39 percent of consumers started looking for a product they wanted to buy by visiting Amazon first.[4] Second, it is increasing its remarkable availability even further, such as with its expansion into services and its introduction of new tools and channels to help customers interact with it more

often.[5] Third, just in case people want to interact personally, Amazon is gaining steam as a brick-and-mortar retailer as well.[6] But the direct comparison with Walmart offers the largest and most prominent example of how Amazon has transformed the retail landscape. In addition to its long-standing advantages—efficient supply chain, vast inventory unlimited by any reliance on square footage in stores, and an enviable recommendation algorithm—Amazon continues to invest heavily in its fulfillment capabilities. By achieving the ability to offer same-day and next-day delivery regularly,[7] Amazon has become a primary source that consumers rely on to meet their immediate consumption needs.

In contrast, Walmart's dominance has been predicated on its reputation for low prices and its excellent distribution network to stores. That is, Walmart's famed logistics capabilities have allowed it to get products from distribution centers onto store shelves more efficiently than virtually any other retailer. However, it lacks the skills and logistics ability to move those products from its online fulfillment centers to customers' homes. In contrast, Amazon's branded boxes are a frequent sight on consumers' front stoops. Amazon even got the U.S. Postal Service to deliver on Sundays—the first time the storied federal agency ever agreed to do so.[8]

Furthermore, Walmart's low price reputation is being challenged by Amazon too. Unscientific experiments show that the two retailers vary in which one offers the lowest price on any particular product. Amazon also changes its prices constantly, such that on any given day, 15 to 18 percent of the products for sale on its site feature different prices than the day before.[9] Thus, a direct price comparison is difficult. However, the overall notion that Walmart has long tried to develop—namely, that it would always be the place where consumers could find the lowest prices—no longer holds for many shoppers.[10] They might be able to find the lowest price at Walmart, but the substantial price transparency of the Internet means that they can always click around to see if they might find a better deal elsewhere—like Amazon. With its extensive infrastructure, Walmart also cannot change prices as flexibly and readily as an online competitor. When it considers doing so, it also has to address the potential cannibalization effects on its sibling company Sam's Club, such that if it competes too hard with its warehouse club, the corporation as a whole might suffer.[11]

In a sense, Walmart's dedication to online retail might be too little, too late. It spent years focused on ensuring its dominance in physical logistics channels, but in some ways, those investments have already grown outdated. By the same token, Walmart recognizes that it cannot simply ignore the online channel. It claims that shoppers actually want a hybrid offering, such that they can order online and pick up items in stores if need be. Beyond these benefits for consumers, Walmart is working to improve the contributions it makes to society more broadly, to ensure that it is a valuable member of the economy. Along these lines, it has committed to ambitious ecological standards in its operations, better animal welfare requirements for its supply chain, and hourly wages for employees that are higher than the mandated minimum wage.[12] By appealing to consumers along these lines, Walmart might be able to differentiate itself, such as by highlighting its role as a major employer in local areas. In that case, Walmart can leverage its existing advantages into the future as well. Yet Amazon is not going anywhere. If Walmart plans to continue to compete effectively with it, it needs to keep on committing to its online strategy.

Retailing is such a common part of our everyday lives that we often take it for granted. For most people, retailers simply are places to buy things. At a very young age, children know what stores have the things they want, and they expect to find the products they want when they visit a store or website. Sometimes consumers talk to a sales associate when they visit a store, and other times the only retail employees they interact with are cashiers collecting the money for purchases. Some college students work part time or over the holidays for retailers and have a somewhat deeper insight into what retailers do. But these limited exposures to retailing are just the tip of the iceberg. Behind the stores, websites, sales associates, and cashiers are an army of managers responsible for making sure that the products and services that people want are available when they want them, where they want them, and at a fair price.

To illustrate further just how big that iceberg below the surface can be, consider Walmart. It stocks and sells 120,000 different products, chosen from among the literally millions of potential options that inventory managers consider every year. Managers at Walmart must determine which subsets of these 120,000 items they will offer, in which stores, which include 11,545 locations all around the world, as well as on the Walmart website. Having selected which products to stock, managers must negotiate the prices that Walmart will pay to procure these products from more than 10,000 suppliers. Next they need to determine the prices they will charge their customers. Together with pricing decisions, Walmart managers determine how to present and display the 120,000 products in stores and on the retailer's website. In addition to selecting products, managers are responsible for selecting, training, and motivating the company's 2.3 million store employees to ensure that they work to keep shelves well stocked, display the merchandise attractively, and provide customers with the service they expect. Finally, perhaps most importantly, Walmart's managers develop and implement strategies to guide their decisions and provide good returns to stockholders, even while facing intense and increasing competition in retail markets.[13]

Working in this highly competitive, rapidly changing retail environment is both challenging and exciting, and it offers significant financial rewards. This book describes the world of retailing and offers key principles for effectively managing retail businesses. Knowledge of retailing principles and practices will help you develop management skills for many business contexts. For example, retailers are customers of many business-to-consumer (B-to-C) companies, such as Procter & Gamble (P&G) and Hewlett-Packard (HP). That means that even in B-to-C companies, which seemingly would focus mainly on consumers, brand managers need a thorough understanding of how retailers operate and make money so that they can encourage retailers to offer and promote their products. Financial and health care institutions use retail principles to develop their offerings; improve customer service; and provide convenient, easy access to their customers. Any student interested in professional B-to-C selling, marketing management, or finance should find this book useful.

WHAT IS RETAILING?

LO 1-1

Identify retailing activities.

Retailing is the set of business activities that adds value to products and services sold to consumers for their personal or family use. Often, people think of retailing only as the sale of products in stores, but retailing also involves the sale of services such as overnight lodging in a motel, a doctor's exam, a haircut, or a home-delivered pizza. Not all retailing is done in stores. Examples of nonstore retailing include ordering a T-shirt on your mobile phone app, buying cosmetics from an Avon salesperson, ordering hiking boots from an L.L.Bean catalog, and streaming a movie through Amazon Prime.

The Retailer's Role in a Supply Chain

A **retailer** is a business that sells products and/or services to consumers for their personal or family use. Retailers are a key component in a supply chain that links manufacturers to consumers. A **supply chain** is a set of firms that make and deliver goods and services to consumers. Exhibit 1–1 shows the retailer's position within a supply chain.

Retailers typically buy products from wholesalers and/or manufacturers and resell them to consumers. Why are retailers needed? Wouldn't it be easier and cheaper for consumers to cut out the intermediaries (i.e., wholesalers and retailers) and buy directly from manufacturers? The answer, generally, is no because retailers add value and are more efficient at adding this value than manufacturers or wholesalers.

Retailers Create Value

The value-creating activities undertaken by retailers include (1) providing an assortment of products and services, (2) breaking bulk, (3) holding inventory, and (4) providing services.

EXHIBIT 1–1   Example of a Supply Chain

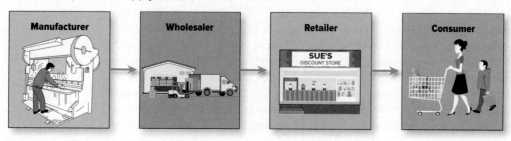

Providing Assortments   Conventional supermarkets typically carry about 30,000 different items made by more than 500 companies. Offering an assortment enables customers to choose from a wide selection of products, brands, sizes, and prices at one location. Manufacturers specialize in producing specific types of products. For example, Frito-Lay makes snacks, Yoplait makes yogurt, Skippy makes peanut butter, and Heinz makes ketchup. If each of these manufacturers had its own stores that sold only its own products, consumers would have to go to many different stores to buy the groceries needed to prepare a single meal.

Breaking Bulk   To reduce transportation costs, manufacturers and wholesalers typically ship cases of frozen dinners or cartons of blouses to retailers. Retailers then offer the products in smaller quantities tailored to individual consumers' and households' consumption patterns—an activity called **breaking bulk**. Breaking bulk is important to both manufacturers and consumers. It allows manufacturers to produce and ship merchandise efficiently and in larger quantities at one time, but it enables consumers to purchase the specific merchandise they want in smaller, more useful quantities.

Holding Inventory   A major value-providing activity performed by retailers is **holding inventory** so that products will be available when consumers want them. Thus, consumers can keep a smaller inventory of products at home because they know local retailers will have the products available when they need more. This activity is particularly important to consumers with limited storage space, such as families living in small apartments.

Providing Services   Retailers provide services that make it easier for customers to buy and use products. For example, retailers offer credit so that consumers can have a product now and pay for it later. They display products so that consumers can see and test them before buying. Some retailers employ salespeople in stores or maintain websites to answer questions and provide additional information about the products they sell.

© B2M Productions/Photodisc/Getty Images

Retailers add value by providing an assortment of products that customers can buy at one location when they want them.

Costs of Channel Activities

While the value-creating activities undertaken by channel members provide benefits to customers, they also increase the cost of products and services. Exhibit 1–2 illustrates the supply chain costs of getting a T-shirt from the manufacturer to the consumer. In this example, it costs the T-shirt manufacturer $10.00 to make and market the T-shirt. These costs include the design, raw materials, labor, production equipment, transportation to the wholesaler, and so on. The manufacturer sells the T-shirt to the wholesaler for $11.00 and makes $1.00 profit. The wholesaler incurs $2.00 in costs to handle and store the T-shirt and transport it to the retailers. The wholesaler sells the T-shirt to the retailers for $14.00, making a $1.00 profit. The retailer then incurs costs to fold the shirt, put price tags on it, store it, employ sales associates, light and air condition the store, and so on. The retailer sells the shirt to a customer for $19.95, making a profit of $1.95.

EXHIBIT 1–2
Costs of Value-
Added Activities in
the Distribution Channel
for a T-Shirt

Note that the costs in the supply chain, $8.95 ($19.95− $11.00), are almost as much as the cost to make the product. These costs are justified by the considerable value added by the wholesaler and retailers to the product. By providing assortments, breaking bulk, holding inventory, and providing services, retailers increase the benefits that consumers receive from their products and services.

Consider a T-shirt in a shipping crate in an Iowa manufacturer's warehouse. The T-shirt will not satisfy the needs of a student who wants to have something to wear at the basketball game tonight. The student finds the T-shirt more valuable and will pay more for it if it is available from a nearby department store that also sells pants, belts, and other items complementing the T-shirt and provides sales associates who can help the student find what she or he likes. If retailers did not provide these benefits, wholesalers or manufacturers would have to provide them, and they would typically not be as efficient as retailers in providing these benefits.

Retailers Perform Wholesaling and Production Activities

Wholesalers buy and store merchandise in large quantities from manufacturers and then resell the merchandise (usually in smaller quantities) to retailers. When manufacturers like Apple and Nike sell directly to consumers, they are performing the production, wholesaling, and retail business activities. Some large retailers, like Costco and Home Depot, function as both retailers and wholesalers: They perform retailing activities when they sell to consumers, but they engage in wholesaling activities when they sell to other businesses, such as restaurants or building contractors.

In some supply chains, the manufacturing, wholesaling, and retailing activities are performed by independent firms, but most supply chains feature some vertical integration. **Vertical integration** means that a firm performs more than one set of activities in the channel, as occurs when a retailer engages in wholesaling activities by operating its own distribution centers to supply its stores. **Backward integration** arises when a retailer performs some wholesaling and manufacturing activities, such as operating warehouses or designing private-label merchandise. **Forward integration** occurs when a manufacturer undertakes retailing and wholesaling activities, such as Apple operating its own retail stores.

Most large retailers such as Safeway, Walmart, and Lowe's manage their own distribution centers and perform activities undertaken by wholesalers. They buy directly from manufacturers, have merchandise shipped to their warehouses, and then distribute the merchandise to their stores. Other retailers, such as J.Crew and Victoria's Secret, are even more vertically integrated. They design the merchandise they sell and then contract with manufacturers to produce it exclusively for them. Stores like IKEA and Zara are almost completely vertically integrated since they manufacture and distribute most of the products they sell in their stores.

© VCG/Getty Images

IKEA is almost completely vertically integrated since it manufactures and distributes most of the products it sells in its stores.

Differences in Distribution Channels around the World

Some critical differences among the retailing and distribution systems in the United States, European Union, China, and India are summarized in Exhibit 1–3. As this exhibit suggests, the U.S. retail industry has the greatest retail density (retail stores per person) and concentration of large retail firms. Real estate in the United States is relatively inexpensive, and most consumers own automobiles. Thus, retailers often operate large stores in lightly populated areas. Many U.S. retailers have stores with more than 20,000 square feet. Due to their size, they have the scale economies to operate their own warehouses, eliminating the need for wholesalers. This combination of large stores and large firms in the United States results in a very efficient distribution system.

In contrast, the Indian distribution system is characterized by small stores operated by relatively small firms and a large independent wholesale industry. To make the daily deliveries to these small retailers efficiently, the merchandise often passes through several different wholesalers. In addition, the infrastructure to support modern retailing, especially the transportation and communication systems, is not as well developed in India as it is in more developed economies. These efficiency differences mean that a much larger percentage of the Indian labor force is employed in distribution and retailing than is the case in the United States, and the supply chain costs in India are higher.[14] Recent changes by the Indian government, however, have the potential to significantly modernize the retail landscape. For example, foreign retailers that

EXHIBIT 1–3   Comparison of Retailing and Distribution across the World

	United States	Northern Europe	India	China
Concentration (percentage of sales made by large retailers)	Highest	High	Lowest	Low
Retail density (square feet of retail space per person)	Highest	Modest	Lowest	Low
Average store size	Highest	Modest	Lowest	Modest
Role of wholesalers	Minimal	Modest	Extensive	Extensive
Infrastructure supporting efficient supply chain	Best	Good	Weakest	Weak
Restrictions on retail locations, store size, and ownership	Minimal	Extensive	Extensive	Modest

The retail industry in India is dominated by small, local retailers with few modern national chains.

© Dhruv Grewal

carry multiple brands, like Walmart, are now allowed to own up to 51 percent of joint ventures in India, and retailers that carry only their own brand, like adidas and Reebok, can now own 100 percent of their Indian businesses.[15]

China's retail industry is highly fragmented like the retail industry in India. It is composed of many small and medium-sized firms. The number of national and even regional chains is limited. However, China's retail distribution system is going through a period of rapid development. This development is spurred by the government's shifting interest away from a singular focus on exports and satisfying just basic consumer needs to finding ways to provide a higher quality of life. The government has removed most restrictions on direct foreign investments, and global retailers have flocked to this huge and growing market. As a result, China is the world's fastest-growing retail market, poised to hit the $8 trillion mark soon.[16] Walmart thus operates 425 stores in China, and Carrefour, the second-largest retailer in the world, operates 406. However, there is great disparity between the distribution system in the first-tier, eastern coastal cities—Beijing, Shanghai, and Guangdong—and the smaller western cities. The retail offering in the first-tier cities is very similar to the urban retail environment in U.S. cities such as New York and Chicago. In contrast, retailing in the smaller western cities is more similar to retailing in India.[17] The European distribution system falls between the U.S. and Indian systems on this continuum of efficiency and scale. In northern Europe, retailing is similar to that in the United States, with high concentration levels in some national markets.

ECONOMIC AND SOCIAL SIGNIFICANCE OF RETAILING

LO 1-2

Realize the importance of retailing in the U.S. and world economies.

Role in Developed Economies

Retail sales in 2015 were $5.3 trillion. More than 8 percent of the total U.S. gross domestic product (GDP) comes from retailing, almost as much as the contribution of the entire U.S. manufacturing industry sector.[18] But this sales level underestimates the impact of retailing on the U.S. economy because it does not include the sales and employment of many firms providing consumer services such as entertainment, home repairs, and health care.

Consumer spending plays a critical role in the economies of the United States and other developed countries. When consumers spend more money buying goods and services from retailers, a country's economy flourishes. Merchandise flies off the shelves, and retailers place orders for replacement merchandise. Manufacturers hire more employees, place orders for raw materials, and make more products. However, if consumers feel uncertain about their financial future and decide to refrain from buying new refrigerators or blue jeans, the economy slows down.

The retail sector plays a key role in developed economies, not only because consumer demand is an indication of a vibrant financial system but also because retailers are large employers. More than 14 million people were employed in retailing in 2015—approximately 10 percent of the U.S. workforce—and an additional 15 percent work for companies that either provide services to and/or sell products through retailers.[19]

Role in Developing Economies—The Bottom of the Pyramid

Retailers need to also focus on opportunities available by serving the needs of the 3 billion people living at the lowest end of the income distribution. This represents about 40 percent of the world's population that live on less than $2.50 per day.[20] Serving these customers also provides an important social benefit: reducing worldwide poverty.[21] Consumers in this low-income consumer segment, referred to as the **base of the pyramid** or **bottom of the pyramid (BoP)**, still have significant spending power. The sheer size and growth of the BoP markets, especially in countries with emerging economies such as China, India, and Brazil, together with the maturation of consumer goods and retail markets in developed economies is motivating firms to enter the BoP market.

Undertaking retailing activities for BoP markets is challenging, though. It is difficult to communicate and complete transactions with people in BoP markets because they often lack access to mass media, the Internet, mobile phones, or credit cards. Most people in BoP markets live in rural areas—remote villages that are not connected to the outside world through adequate roads. Limited local demand combined with the high cost of transporting goods to and from remote villages results in higher costs and prices for consumer goods. Thus, engagement at the BoP markets requires innovative approaches for doing business. Simply retrofitting business models used in the more developed markets will not work.[22] Retailing View 1.1 describes how some innovative mobile payment systems are helping improve the lives of people in Africa that are working, but whose incomes are below the poverty line.

Role in Society

In addition to providing goods and services to their customers, some retailers are realizing that their responsibility includes considering the needs and objectives of all of its **stakeholders**, which are the broad set of people who might be affected by a firm's actions, from current and prospective customers, to supply chain partners, to employees, to shareholders, to government agencies, to members of the communities in which the firm operates, and to a general view of society. For example, customers want low prices. Shareholders want high profits. Employees want high wages. Society wants firms to leave a low carbon footprint. As the recognition that attempting to satisfy the needs and objectives of multiple stakeholders has grown, some forward-thinking retailers are beginning to adopt the concept of conscious marketing.

These conscious marketing practices go beyond the traditional notion inherent in **corporate social responsibility (CSR)**, which involves an organization voluntarily engaging in business practices that meet or exceed the ethical and legal expectations of its stakeholders. **Conscious marketing** entails a sense of purpose for the firm higher than simply making a profit by selling products and services. It encompasses four overriding principles:[23]

1. **Recognition of the retailing firm's greater purpose.** When retailers recognize that its purpose should be more than just making profits—whether the purpose is

1.1 RETAILING VIEW   Retailing at the Bottom of the Pyramid

For people living in extreme poverty, basic, functional phones offer a vast opportunity for consumption. For retailers, they also offer access to a new segment of shoppers. In sub-Saharan Africa, for example, consumers rely on their mobile devices to access payment services that allow them to load as little as a dollar on their phones, which they can then use to pay for products and services that improve their quality of life. The ability to pay less than 50 cents daily meant that one consumer could receive electricity from a solar panel provider. In the past, taking such small daily payments would have been too much work and too inefficient for the service provider. By linking to a mobile payment system, neither the consumer nor the supplier needs to engage in additional effort. And if the consumer isn't able to load enough onto her phone on one day, she can go without electricity until she can reload her mobile account with funds, without the risk of harming her credit or losing access to her account.

Thus in Kenya, for example, 61 percent of mobile users rely on their devices to engage in money transfers. As one Kenyan investment firm, which helps poor consumers gain access to micro-insurance and savings plans, explains, "If you're taking a dollar off a million people, that's a reasonable revenue stream, but it wasn't possible to do that without the mobile phone."

Among these consumers bank accounts are unusual, so the mobile payment systems allow them to load funds with the assistance of agents that work in local gas stations and stores. Once the funds are loaded, they can pay for groceries at the point of sale by tapping their phones, or they can send funds electronically. This latter functionality is critical because for many Africans, making a trip to pay a bill might mean an entire day of lost labor due to travel times.

In sub-Saharan Africa, consumers rely on text messages to communicate with distant contacts because texts are less expensive than phone calls.

These benefits have turned Africa into the source of some astounding innovations, especially for microbusiness concepts. Sub-Saharan Africa accounts for about 70 percent of the world's poor population, but nearly 65 percent of these households have access to at least one mobile phone. In addition, Africa is the fastest-growing mobile market in the world.

Sources: Heidi Vogt, "Making Change: Mobile Pay in Africa," *The Wall Street Journal*, January 2, 2015; Pew Research Center, "Cell Phones in Africa: Communication Lifeline," April 15, 2015, http://www.pewglobal.org/2015/04/15/cell-phones-in-africa-communication-lifeline/.

providing free shoes for residents of poor nations, as TOMS does, or ensuring employment opportunities for local communities, or making strides toward more energy-efficient stores—the actions it undertakes change in focus.

2. **Consideration of stakeholders and their interdependence.** Retailers that embrace the notion of conscious marketing consider how their actions will affect the expansive range of potential stakeholders listed earlier. They realize that to serve as many stakeholders as possible but avoid inflicting severe damage on any others, they must give up their exclusive focus on maximizing profits.[24] Rather, they consider the broad implications of their actions. By considering these impacts as a foundation for any decision, these retailers achieve the most benefits for the largest numbers of stakeholders, while also ensuring that they avoid causing significant harm to any group. For example, when Walmart issued new standards for farms that supply it with livestock products, the effects were felt by the supply chain partners, who might need to adjust their practices; competitors that might need to adopt similar protections; consumers who can take more assurance that the animals raised for their food will not have been fed antibiotics; and animal welfare groups that call the new standards "a step in the right direction."[25]

3. **The presence of conscious leadership, creating a corporate culture.** A conscious marketing approach implies that the firm's leaders are dedicated to the proposition of being conscious at all levels of the business, throughout its entire

culture. The resulting conscious corporate culture stays in line with its higher purpose and in accordance with the leader's ideals. As a result, every member of the firm embodies the ideas of conscious marketing, and every stakeholder affected by that retailer can recognize the higher principles involved. The founder and CEO of Whole Foods Market, John Mackey, who is the subject of Retailing View 1.2, not only embraces the notion of conscious retailing, which he calls conscious capitalism, but also has written extensively, given speeches on the topic, and is a founder of consciouscapitalism.org.[26] Whole Foods's motto, "Whole Foods, Whole People, Whole Planet," emphasizes its goals of supporting the health and well-being of people and the planet.[27]

4. **The understanding that decisions are ethically based.** Retailers that are engaged in conscious marketing make decisions that are based on sound business **ethics**. Business ethics is concerned with distinguishing between right and wrong actions and decisions that arise in a business setting, according to broad and well-established moral principles. Examples of difficult situations that retail managers face include the following: Should a retailer sell merchandise that it suspects was made using child labor? Should a retailer advertise that its prices are the lowest available in the market, even though some are not? Should a retail buyer accept an expensive gift from a vendor? Should retail salespeople use a high-pressure sales approach when they know the product is not the best for the customer's needs? Should a retailer promote a product as being "on sale" if it never sold at a higher, nonsale price?

Although these retailers engage in conscious marketing because it is good for the long-term viability of their firms as well as its stakeholders, it just happens to be a good business practice in the near-term as well because it draws like-minded customers to the firm and makes them more engaged and loyal. When, after a major snowstorm, a customer shopping Trader Joe's forgot her wallet, the cashier paid the bill and told the customer to pay him the next time she came in. As a result of this act of kindness, which resulted in part from the retailer's allegiance to these conscious marketing and business practices, it created a customer for life.[28] Over time, customers like these may become champions for the retailer, identifying with its core values, and sharing those values with others.[29]

Trader Joe's recognizes that being good to its customers isn't just good business, it is also the right thing to do.

1.2 RETAILING VIEW   Whole Foods and John Mackey: The Birth of the Organic Supermarket

John Mackey had a relatively conventional, middle-class, suburban upbringing. But it was the 1970s, so Mackey quit college and embraced an alternative lifestyle (e.g., long beard, wild hair). After having worked in a vegetarian collective, he solicited money from family and friends so that he could open a new sort of co-op in 1978: an organic food store on the first floor, restaurant on the second floor, and living quarters on the top of the old Victorian house he had found.

A couple of years later, Mackey went further and opened the first Whole Foods store in a 10,000-square-foot space that had once been a nightclub. In keeping with its history, Mackey made sure his natural food store was no stodgy, boring site with just granola. He stocked beer, meat, and wine, and he "loved it. I loved retail. I loved being around food. I loved natural foods. I loved organic foods. I loved the whole idea of it. And a thought entered into my mind that maybe this is what I could do." This passion has not died down either. In 2014 Whole Foods began using a new rating system that took into account factors such as energy conservation, waste reduction, and the welfare of farmworkers, reflecting Mackey's sense that just being organic was not enough. Rather, he embraced the notion of "conscious capitalism." Although the rating system was met with much resistance from Whole Food suppliers, Mackey has not relented. Part of what has made Mackey so successful is his complete lack of fear of making people angry, when he believes he is making the right choices.

For example, being a grocer was not a particularly popular aspiration with his family. His mother, a former teacher, strongly discouraged his interest in Whole Foods. According to Mackey's account, on her deathbed in 1987, she asked him to promise to return to school to get his college degree; when he demurred, she complained, "I wish you'd just give up that stupid health-food store. Your father and I gave you a fine mind, and you're wasting it being a grocer."

He never did give up on his "stupid" store. Instead, the concept spread across the world, with over 435 stores in three countries. Mackey has adopted and adapted his ideas to fit local tastes. Through decentralized decision-making units, Whole Foods stores could choose to stock items specific to the preferences of the local markets, like live lobsters in Portland, Maine, or a kombucha bar in Venice, California. Through acquisitions, Whole Foods gained additional knowledge, too. In buying Wellspring Grocery, it learned about private-label options. The purchase of Mrs. Gooch's provided Whole Foods with insights

Whole Foods founder and CEO, John Mackey

into diet supplements. When it purchased Bread & Circus, it gained access to the Boston chain's famed seafood procurement expertise. By acquiring Allegro Coffee, it facilitated the development of in-store coffee bars that compete with Starbucks and Peet's, and provides a reason for customers to linger in its stores and hopefully buy more groceries.

Sources: John Mackey and Raj Sisodia, *Conscious Capitalism: Liberating the Heroic Spirit of Business* (Boston: Harvard Business School Press, 2014); Beth Kowitt, "John Mackey: The Conscious Capitalist," *Fortune,* August 20, 2015; "John Mackey: Co-Chief Executive Officer and Co-Founder," Whole Foods Market, http://media.wholefoodsmarket.com/experts/executives/john-mackey; www.wholefoodsmarket.com/company-info/whole-foods-market-history; Nick Paumgarten, "Food Fighter," *The New Yorker,* January 4, 2010.

THE GROWING IMPORTANCE OF RETAILING AND RETAILERS

LO 1-3

Analyze the changing retail industry.

Evolution of the Retail Industry

From a consumer's perspective, retailers are local businesses. Even though many consumers collect information and make purchases using the Internet or a mobile device, more than 90 percent of all retail sales are still made in stores—usually stores that are less than a 15-minute drive from the consumer's home or workplace. Thus, retail stores predominately compete against other stores that are located nearby.[30]

There has been a dramatic change in the structure of the retail industry over the past 50 years. Fifty years ago, Sears and JCPenney were the only retail firms that had chains of stores across the United States. The retail industry consisted of small, independent, local retailers competing against other small, independent retailers in the same community. Walmart, Home Depot, Staples, and Best Buy did not exist or were small companies with a few stores. Now, the retail industry is dominated by large, national, and even international retail firms. For example, though 2014 revenues for 250 of the world's top retailers approached $4.5 trillion, an estimated $100 billion of that amount went to just four massive retailers. About one-quarter of the retailers included in the top 250 list actually account for less than $5 billion in revenues total.[31] Home improvement centers in particular are highly concentrated; the two largest firms account for 45.6 percent of U.S. market share.[32] For department stores, there are six names that earn 62.9 percent of market share.[33] The two-store competition in the drugstore market shows varying market shares in different locations, such that CVS and Walgreens make up anywhere from between 50 and 75 percent of the market share in the largest cities in the United States.[34]

© Fotosearch/Getty Images

Fifty years ago, Sears was one of only a few retailers that had chains of stores across the United States.

The largest retailers in the world are shown in Exhibit 1–4. Nine of the top 20 retailers are headquartered in the United States; Germany has 5. Of these top 20 retailers, the U.S. retailers have fewer global operations than the non-U.S.-based retailers. The average number of countries in which these U.S.-based retailers operate is 7, compared with non-U.S.-headquartered retailers, which operate in an average of 18 countries. Four of the largest U.S.-based retailers operate in only one or two countries. Only 4 of the 11 non-U.S-based

EXHIBIT 1–4   The 20 Largest Retailers in the World

Rank	Name	Headquarters Location	Number of Countries	Stores in U.S.	Retail Revenue ($ millions)	Primary Format
1	Wal-Mart	U.S.	28	Yes	$485,651	Supercenter
2	Costco	U.S.	10	Yes	$112,640	Cash & Carry/Warehouse Club
3	The Kroger Co.	U.S.	1	Yes	$108,465	Supermarket
4	Schwarz Unternehmens Treuhand KG	Germany	26	No	$102,694	Discount Store
5	Tesco PLC	UK	13	Yes	$99,713	Supercenter
6	Carrefour SA	France	34	No	$98,497	Supercenter
7	Aldi Einkauf	Germany	17	Yes	$86,470	Discount Store
8	Metro Ag	Germany	32	No	$85,570	Cash & Carry/Warehouse Club
9	The Home Depot Inc.	U.S.	4	Yes	$83,176	Home Improvement
10	Walgreens Boots	U.S.	2	Yes	$76,392	Drugstore/Pharmacy
11	Target Corporation	U.S.	1	Yes	$72,618	Discount Department Store
12	Amazon.com Inc.	U.S.	14	Yes	$70,080	Nonstore
13	Groupe Auchan SA	France	13	No	$69,622	Supercenter
14	CVS	U.S.	3	Yes	$67,798	Drugstore/Pharmacy
15	Casino Guichard-Perrachon SA	France	29	No	$64,462	Supercenter
16	Aeon Co. Ltd.	Japan	11	No	$61,436	Supercenter
17	Edeka Group	Germany	1	No	$60,960	Supermarket
18	Lowe's Companies Inc.	U.S.	4	Yes	$56,223	Home Improvement
19	Seven & i Holdings Co. Ltd.	Japan	18	Yes	$53,839	Convenience/Forecourt Store
20	Rewe Combine	Germany	11	No	$51,168	Supermarket

Source: "2014 Global 250 Retailers," *Stores Magazine*, January 17, 2016.

© Mark Douet/Getty Images

The scanning of the onions at the POS terminal at the checkout counter of the grocery store launches a chain of activities that ensures that the store will not run out before the next order arrives.

retailers operate stores in the United States, the largest retail market in the world.

The development of information systems is one of the forces facilitating the growth of large retail firms—the shift from an industry dominated by small local retailers to large multinational chains. Prior to the development of these systems, it was difficult for someone other than the local store manager to track how merchandise in the store was selling—whether it was selling more than expected and needed to be reordered or if it was selling below expectations and needed to have its price reduced. It was also difficult to collect and consolidate the plans from a number of different stores so that a buyer could place large orders with vendors to get price discounts. Thus, before the availability of modern information systems, it was difficult for retailers to lower costs through scale economies, and larger retailers had limited advantages over small local or regional retailers.

Most consumers shopping in their local stores don't realize the sophisticated information systems used by retailers today to manage these large, complex supply chain systems. To illustrate the complexity of these systems, consider the following example. You go to Staples and find a tablet you are going to buy. When you decide to buy a tablet in a store, the point-of-sale (POS) terminal transmits data about the transaction to the retailer's distribution center and then on to the manufacturer. Data about your purchase are incorporated into a sophisticated inventory management system. When the in-store inventory level drops below a prespecified level, an electronic notice is automatically transmitted, authorizing the shipment of more units to the retailer's distribution center and then to the store. The retail buyer or a computer program analyzes the sales data to determine how many and which tablet models will be stocked in the retailer's stores and what price will be charged.

Role of Information Systems

Now, retailers are inundated with data about the thousands of transactions that take place each day. The challenge for retailers is to convert these raw data into information that managers can use to make better decisions. Many retailers now use customer data to identify their best customers and target customized promotions to them; use purchase data to determine how to place products in closer proximity when the data show that many customers buy the same products at the same time; and use location data to tailor the assortment of products in each store to match the needs of the store's local market.

MANAGEMENT AND ENTREPRENEURIAL OPPORTUNITIES

LO 1-4

Recognize the opportunities for you in retailing.

In addition to playing an important role in society in general, retailing provides personal opportunities to work for a company in an exciting, challenging environment or to start an entrepreneurial venture. These opportunities are discussed in this section.

Management Opportunities

To exploit these new technologies and systems and gain advantage in a highly competitive and challenging environment, retailers are hiring and promoting the best and brightest. Sherry Hollack, a former vice president of talent development at Macy's, emphasized this point: "One of the biggest challenges facing Macy's, and most other retail chains, is hiring and retaining managers to lead our company in the coming years. The changing demographics are working against us. Over the next ten years, a lot of our senior managers, members of the Baby Boomer generation, will be retiring. So we are going to be competing with other retailers and firms in other industries for a smaller pool of available managers in the generations behind the Boomers. In addition, retailing is becoming a much more sophisticated business. Our managers need to be comfortable with new technologies, information and supply chain management systems, and international business as well as managing a diverse workforce and buying merchandise."[35]

Students often view retailing as part of marketing because managing distribution (place) is one of the 4 Ps of marketing (price, product, promotion, and place). But retailers are businesses and, like manufacturers, undertake all the traditional business activities. Retailers raise capital from financial institutions; purchase goods and services; use accounting and management information systems to control their operations; manage warehouses and distribution systems; design and develop new products; and undertake marketing activities such as advertising, promotion, sales force management, and market research. Thus, retailers employ people with expertise and interests in finance, accounting, human resource management, supply chain management, and computer systems, as well as management and marketing.

Retail managers are often given considerable responsibility early in their careers. Retail management is also financially rewarding. Starting salaries are typically between $35,000 and $65,000 for college graduates entering management trainee positions. After completing a management training program, retail managers can double their starting salary in three to five years if they perform well. Senior buyers and others in higher managerial positions and store managers make between $120,000 and $300,000. (See Appendix 1A at the end of this chapter.)

Entrepreneurial Opportunities

Retailing also provides opportunities for people who wish to start their own business. Some of the world's most successful people are retailing entrepreneurs. Many are well known because their names appear over stores' doors; others you may not recognize. Retailing View 1.3 examines the life of one of the world's greatest entrepreneurs,

RETAILING VIEW   Jeff Bezos, Founder of Amazon   **1.3**

Jeffrey Bezos, founder and CEO of Amazon.com, is also the third-richest person in the world, with a net worth of $65.3 billion. After his own research uncovered that Internet usage was growing at a 2,300 percent annual rate in 1994, Bezos, the 30-year-old son of a Cuban refugee, quit his job on Wall Street and left behind a hefty bonus to start an Internet business. While his wife MacKenzie was driving their car across country, Jeff pecked out his business plan on a laptop computer. By the time they reached Seattle, he had rounded up the investment capital to launch the first Internet book retailer. The company, Amazon.com, is named after the river that carries the greatest amount of water, symbolizing Bezos's objective of achieving the greatest volume of Internet sales.

Under his leadership, Amazon developed technologies to make shopping on the Internet faster, easier, and more personal than shopping in stores by offering personalized recommendations and home pages. Amazon.com has become more than a bookstore. It is now one of the largest online retailers, with annual sales greater than $48 billion. Amazon also provides virtual stores and fulfillment services for many other retailers.

Those working with him say that "he has become a leader of leaders" empowering those around him, while stressing the importance of a customer focus and forward thinking. The sheer size of Amazon and the two other companies he runs necessitates this kind of leadership, though Amazon board members state that at the beginning he was in the center of

Jeff Bezos is the founder and CEO of Amazon.com.

© David McNew/Getty Images

everything and "the leadership was Jeff Bezos." Bezos also acquired the *Washington Post* in 2013 and has developed an aerospace company, Blue Origin, which launched its first rocket into suborbit in November 2015.

Sources: "Bezos Prime," *Fortune*, April 1, 2016; "Jeff Bezos," *Fortune*, July 29, 2016; "Amazon Boss Bezos Becomes World's Third Richest," BBC, July 29, 2016; Kelsey Lindsey, "Retail in a Slump? Not for These 6 Billionaires," *Retail Dive*, March 5, 2014; Tom Robinson, *Jeff Bezos: Amazon.com Architect* (Publishing Pioneers) (Edina, MN: Abdo Publishing, 2009); www.forbes.com/profile/jeff-bezos/.

Jeff Bezos. Some other innovative retail entrepreneurs include Sam Walton, Do Won and Jin Sook Chang, Ingvar Kamprad, and Howard Schultz. These entrepreneurs came from humble backgrounds and changed the way retailing is done.

Sam Walton (Walmart)   Sam Walton began working at an Iowa JCPenney store in 1940. After purchasing a Ben Franklin variety store franchise in Newport, Arkansas, he discovered that he could boost profits if he could find suppliers that would sell him merchandise at lower prices than it cost him to buy them from Ben Franklin. Walton lost his store in 1950, when the landlord refused to renew his lease, but the challenge pushed him to move and open a new Ben Franklin store with his younger brother. By 1960, the Waltons had 15 stores in Arkansas and Missouri, laying the foundation for what would become Walmart.

In 1962, Sam Walton brought his new ideas for the discount format to small southern towns, opening his first Walmart Discount City in Rogers, Arkansas. In 1991, the success of his concept and his efficient management practices had made Walton America's wealthiest person. He died of leukemia in 1992. His children and heirs still hold four spots on the list of the richest people in the world. Each Walton with a share benefits from the billions in sales earned by the world's largest retailer. In turn, they spread their wealth throughout various investments, charitable causes, and special interest groups.[36]

Do Won and Jin Sook Chang (Forever 21)   Do Won and Jin Sook Chang are self-made billionaires. In 1984, they cofounded the fast-fashion retail chain Forever 21. The pair emigrated from South Korea in 1981 and became naturalized American citizens, then opened their first store in 1984, focused on trendy, exciting clothing options. That year, sales grew from $35,000 to $700,000. Forever 21 has continued to experience explosive growth. It operates more than 600 stores worldwide with more than 35,000 employees and revenues of $4.4 billion. Forever 21 is a family operation: Do Won at the helm, Jin Sook in charge of merchandising, eldest daughter Linda runs marketing, and daughter Esther manages visuals.[37]

Forever 21 founder Do Won and his daughter Linda Chang (senior marketing manager) visiting their flagship store in Times Square.

© Jamie McCarthy/Getty Images

Ingvar Kamprad (IKEA)   Ingvar Kamprad, the founder of the Swedish-based home furnishing retailer chain IKEA, was always an entrepreneur. His first business was selling matches to neighbors from his bicycle. He discovered he could make a good profit by buying matches in bulk and selling them individually at a low price. He then expanded to selling fish, Christmas tree decorations, seeds, ballpoint pens, and pencils. By the time he was 17 years of age, he had earned a reward for succeeding in school. His father gave him the money to establish what is now IKEA. Like Sam Walton, the founder of Walmart, Kamprad is known for his frugality. He drives an old Volvo, flies economy class, and encourages IKEA employees to write on both sides of a sheet of paper. This thriftiness has translated into a corporate philosophy of cost cutting throughout IKEA so that the chain can offer quality furniture with innovative designs at low prices. Although Kamprad once was listed as the richest person in Europe, with an estimated net worth of around $33 billion,[38] he also continues to live up to his economic principles. Believing that the trappings of wealth are unimportant, he gave away most of his shares in IKEA—and thus much of his net worth—before stepping down and handing control of the company to his son in 2013. Even after doing so, because of the remarkable success of his ideas, he remains a billionaire.[39]

Howard Schultz (Starbucks)   In 1982, Howard Schultz, a salesperson for a plastic manufacturer, was hired as the new head of marketing for Starbucks, a coffee roaster with six cafés. Shortly after he was hired he went to Verona, Italy, to attend an international housewares show. He had his first latte in Verona, but he saw something more important than the coffee. The café patrons were enjoying themselves while sipping their coffees in the elegant surroundings. He had a vision of recreating the Old World magic and romance behind the Italian coffee bar. The owner wanted to focus on his plan to sell roasted whole beans, and eventually Schultz acquired Starbucks and began the company's march across the world. Schultz's father struggled at low-paying jobs with little to show for it when he died. "He was beaten down, he wasn't respected," Schultz said. "He had no health insurance, and he had no workers' compensation when he got hurt on the job." So with Starbucks, Schultz "wanted to build the kind of company that my father never got a chance to work for, in which people were respected."[40] Due to this childhood experience, Schultz initiated practices at Starbucks that are still uncommon in retailing, such as providing comprehensive health care for all employees working at least 20 hours a week, including coverage for unmarried spouses, and offering an employee stock-option plan. In 2016, Starbucks's sales were greater than $20 billion from the 24,000 stores it operates in 70 countries.[41]

In the next section, we discuss the decisions that retailers make to design and implement their retail strategy. This book is organized around this strategic decision-making process.

THE RETAIL MANAGEMENT DECISION PROCESS

This book is organized around the management decisions that retailers make to provide value to their customers and develop an advantage over their competitors. Exhibit 1–5 identifies the chapters in this book associated with each type of decision.

LO 1-5

Understand the strategic retail management decision process.

Understanding the World of Retailing—Section I

The first step in the retail management decision process, as Exhibit 1–6 shows, is understanding the world of retailing. Retail managers need to know the environment in which they operate before they can develop and implement effective strategies. The first section of this book therefore provides a general overview of the retailing industry and its customers.

EXHIBIT 1–5
Retail Management
Decision Process

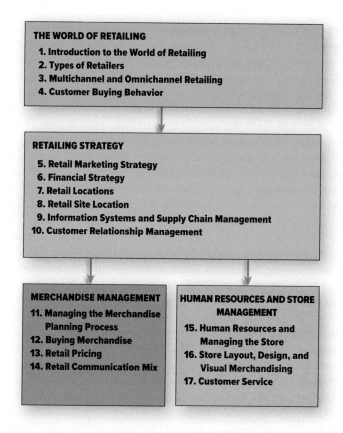

THE WORLD OF RETAILING
1. Introduction to the World of Retailing
2. Types of Retailers
3. Multichannel and Omnichannel Retailing
4. Customer Buying Behavior

RETAILING STRATEGY
5. Retail Marketing Strategy
6. Financial Strategy
7. Retail Locations
8. Retail Site Location
9. Information Systems and Supply Chain Management
10. Customer Relationship Management

MERCHANDISE MANAGEMENT
11. Managing the Merchandise Planning Process
12. Buying Merchandise
13. Retail Pricing
14. Retail Communication Mix

HUMAN RESOURCES AND STORE MANAGEMENT
15. Human Resources and Managing the Store
16. Store Layout, Design, and Visual Merchandising
17. Customer Service

The critical environmental factors in the world of retailing are (1) the macroenvironment and (2) the microenvironment. The impacts of the macroenvironment—including technological, social, and ethical/legal/political factors—on retailing are discussed throughout this book. For example, the influence of technology on the rise of multichannel and omnichannel retailing is reviewed in Chapter 3, the use of new information and supply chain technologies are examined in Chapter 9, customer relationship management systems are reviewed in Chapter 10, and new communication technologies are discussed in Chapter 14.

Competitors   The retailer's microenvironment focuses specifically on its competitors and customers. At first glance, identifying competitors appears easy: A retailer's primary competitors are other retailers that use the same retail approach. Thus, department stores compete against other department stores, and supermarkets compete with other supermarkets. This competition between the same type of retailers is called **intratype competition**.

EXHIBIT 1–6
The Retail Mix

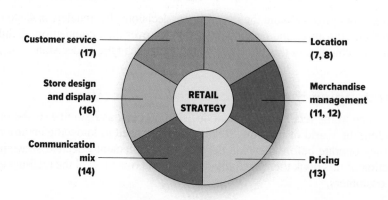

Customer service (17)

Store design and display (16)

Communication mix (14)

RETAIL STRATEGY

Location (7, 8)

Merchandise management (11, 12)

Pricing (13)

Yet to appeal to a broader group of consumers, many retailers are increasing the variety of merchandise they offer. By offering greater variety, retailers satisfy the needs of customers seeking a one-stop shopping experience. For example, Walgreens has added jewelry, accessories, and apparel to its already extensive health and beauty categories to meet the lifestyle needs of its customers. Amazon offers virtually any product, and many services, you might ever want to buy or rent. When retailers offer merchandise not typically associated with their type of store, such as clothing in a drugstore, the result is **scrambled merchandising**. Scrambled merchandising increases **intertype competition**, or competition among retailers that sell similar merchandise using different types of retail outlets, such as drugstores and department stores.

Scrambled merchandising is when a drugstore offers beauty products (left) and merchandise not typically associated with a drugstore, such as dairy products (right).

Management's view of competition also may differ depending on the manager's position within the retail firm. For example, the manager of the Saks Fifth Avenue women's sportswear department in Bergen County, New Jersey, views the other women's sportswear specialty stores in the Riverside Square mall as her major competitors. But the Saks store manager views the Bloomingdale's store in a nearby mall as her strongest competitor. These differences in perspective arise because the department sales manager is primarily concerned with customers for a specific category of merchandise, whereas the store manager is concerned with customers seeking the entire selection of all merchandise and services offered by a department store. The chief executive officer (CEO) of a retail chain, in contrast, views competition from a much broader perspective. For example, Nordstrom might identify its strongest competitor as Saks, Neiman Marcus, Bloomingdale's, and even Bluefly.com.

Chapter 2 discusses various types of retailers and their competitive strategies, and Chapter 3 concentrates on different types of channels that retailers use to complete transactions with their customers.

Customers   The second factor in the microenvironment is customers. Retailers must respond to broad demographic and lifestyle trends in our society, such as the growth in the senior and minority segments of the U.S. population or the importance of shopping convenience to the increasing number of two-income families. To develop and implement an effective strategy, retailers must understand why customers shop, how they select a store, and how they select among that store's merchandise—the information found in Chapter 4.

Developing a Retail Strategy—Section II

The next stages in the retail management decision-making process, formulating and implementing a retail strategy, are based on an understanding of the macro- and micro-environments developed in the first section of this book. Section II focuses on decisions related to developing a retail strategy, whereas Sections III and IV pertain to decisions surrounding the implementation of the strategy and building a long-term competitive advantage. The decisions discussed in Sections III and IV are more tactical.

Retail Strategy   The **retail strategy** identifies (1) the target market, or markets, toward which the retailer will direct its efforts; (2) the nature of the merchandise and services the retailer will offer to satisfy the needs of the target market; and (3) how the retailer will develop unique assets that enable it to achieve long-term advantage over its competitors.

Toys "R" Us focuses on toys and apparel for children, while Walmart's strategic focus is much broader.

© Chris Ratcliffe/Bloomberg/Getty Images

The nature of a retail strategy can be illustrated by comparing the strategies of Walmart and Toys "R" Us. Initially, Walmart identified its target market as small towns (fewer than 35,000 in population) in Arkansas, Texas, and Oklahoma. It offered name-brand merchandise at low prices in a broad array of categories, ranging from laundry detergent to girls' dresses, but offerings in each category were limited. Today, even as Walmart stores have expanded across the world, the selection in each category remains limited. A Walmart store might have only 3 models of flat-screen television sets, while an electronic category specialist like Best Buy might carry 30 models.

In contrast to Walmart, Toys "R" Us defines its primary target as consumers living in suburban areas of large cities. Rather than carrying many merchandise categories, Toys "R" Us stores specialize in toys and children's apparel and carry most types and brands currently available in the market. Walmart emphasizes self-service: Customers select their merchandise, bring it to the checkout line, and then carry it to their cars. But Toys "R" Us provides more customer service. It has salespeople to assist customers with certain types of merchandise.

Because Walmart and Toys "R" Us both emphasize competitive prices, they have made strategic decisions to sustain their low prices by developing a cost advantage over their competitors. Both firms have sophisticated distribution and management information systems to manage inventory. Their strong relationships with their suppliers enable them to buy merchandise at low prices.

Strategic Decision Areas   The key strategic decisions a retailer makes are defining its target market and its financial objectives. Chapter 5 discusses how the selection of a retail market strategy requires analyzing the environment and the firm's strengths and weaknesses. When major environmental changes occur, the current strategy and the reasoning behind it must be reexamined. The retailer then decides what, if any, strategy changes are needed to take advantage of new opportunities or avoid new threats in the environment. The retailer's market strategy must be consistent with the firm's financial objectives. Chapter 6 reviews how financial variables, such as return on investment, inventory turnover, and profit margin, can be used to evaluate the market strategy and its implementation.

The next set of strategic decisions involves the development of critical assets that enable retailers to build strategic advantages. These strategic assets are location, human resources, information and supply chain systems, supply chain organization, and customer loyalty.

Decisions regarding location (reviewed in Chapters 7 and 8) are important because location is typically consumers' top consideration when selecting a store. Generally, consumers buy gas at the closest service station and patronize the shopping mall that's most convenient to their home or office. In addition, location offers an opportunity to gain a long-term advantage over the competition. When a retailer has the best location, a competing retailer must settle for the second-best location.

Retail information and supply chain management systems also offer a significant opportunity for retailers to gain strategic advantage. Chapter 9 reviews how retailers are developing sophisticated computer and distribution technologies to monitor flows of information and merchandise from vendors to retail distribution centers to retail stores. These technologies are part of an overall inventory management system that enables retailers to (1) make sure desired merchandise is available when customers want it and (2) minimize the retailer's inventory investment.

Retailers, like most businesses, want to develop repeat purchases and loyalty in their best customers. Chapter 10 examines the process that retailers use to identify, design programs for, increase the share of wallet of, provide more value to, and build loyalty among their best customers. The implementation decisions are discussed in the next two sections.

Implementing the Retail Strategy—Sections III and IV

To implement a retail strategy, retailers develop a retail mix that satisfies the needs of its target market better than that of its competitors. The **retail mix** is a set of decisions retailers make to satisfy customer needs and influence their purchase decisions. Elements in the retail mix (Exhibit 1–6) include the types of merchandise and services offered, merchandise pricing, advertising and promotional programs, store design, merchandise display, assistance to customers provided by salespeople, and convenience of the store's location. Section III reviews the implementation decisions made by buyers, and Section IV focuses on decisions made by store managers.

Managers in the merchandise management area decide how much and what types of merchandise to buy (Chapter 11), what vendors to use and how to interact with them (Chapter 12), the retail prices to set (Chapter 13), and how to advertise and promote merchandise (Chapter 14). Store managers must determine how to recruit, select, and motivate sales associates (Chapter 15); where and how merchandise will be displayed (Chapter 16); and the nature of services to provide for customers (Chapter 17).

SUMMARY

LO 1-1 **Identify retailing activities.**

Retailing is defined as a set of business activities that add value to the products and services sold to consumers for their personal or family use. These value-added activities include providing assortments, breaking bulk, holding inventory, and providing services.

LO 1-2 **Realize the importance of retailing in the U.S. and world economies.**

Retailing plays an important role in the U.S. economy. One out of four workers in the United States works for a retailer or for a company selling products to a retailer, and the U.S. retail sector accounts for about the same percentage of the U.S. GDP as the entire manufacturing sector. Retailing also plays an important role in developing economies. Some business scholars feel that there is need for modern retail methods to be used to serve consumers at the bottom of the pyramid.

LO 1-3 **Analyze the changing retail industry.**

The retail industry has changed dramatically over the last 50 years. Many well-known national and international retailers were once small start-up companies; now the industry is dominated by large firms. The development of information systems is one of the forces facilitating the growth of large retailers. Before the availability of modern information systems, it was difficult for retailers to lower costs through economies of scale, and larger retailers had limited advantages over small local or regional retailers. With these information systems, retailers are able to efficiently and effectively manage millions of customer transactions with thousands of stores and suppliers across the globe.

LO 1-4 Recognize the opportunities for you in retailing.

Retailing offers opportunities for exciting, challenging careers, either by working for a retail firm or starting your own business. Aspects of retail careers are discussed in Appendix 1A.

LO 1-5 Understand the strategic retail management decision process.

The retail management decision process involves developing a strategy for creating a competitive advantage in the marketplace and then developing a retail mix to implement that strategy. The strategic decisions, discussed in the first half of this textbook, involve selecting a target market; defining the nature of the retailer's offering; and building a competitive advantage through locations, information and supply chain management systems, and customer relationship management programs.

The merchandise and store management decisions for implementing the strategy, discussed in the second half of this textbook, involve selecting a merchandise assortment, buying merchandise, setting prices, communicating with customers, managing the store, presenting merchandise in stores, and providing customer service. Large retail chains use sophisticated information systems to analyze business opportunities and make these decisions about how to operate their businesses in multiple countries.

KEY TERMS

backward integration, *8*	ethics, *13*	retail mix, *23*
base of the pyramid, *11*	forward integration, *8*	retail strategy, *21*
bottom of the pyramid (BoP), *11*	holding inventory, *7*	scrambled merchandising, *21*
breaking bulk, *7*	intertype competition, *21*	stakeholders, *11*
conscious marketing, *11*	intratype competition, *20*	supply chain, *6*
corporate social responsibility (CSR), *11*	retailer, *6*	vertical integration, *8*
	retailing, *6*	wholesaler, *8*

GET OUT AND DO IT!

1. **CONTINUING CASE ASSIGNMENT** In most chapters of this textbook, there will be a GET OUT AND DO IT! assignment that will give you an opportunity to examine the strategy and tactics of one retailer. Your first assignment is to select a retailer and prepare a report on the retailer's history, including when it was founded and how it has evolved over time. To ensure that you can get information about the retailer for subsequent Continuing Case Assignments, the retailer you select should:

   * *Be a publicly held company so that you can access its financial statements and annual reports.* Do not select a retailer that is owned by another company. For example, Bath & Body Works is owned by L Brands (formerly called Limited Brands), so you can get financial information about only the holding company and not the various, individual companies it owns, such as Victoria's Secret and The White Barn Candle Company.
   * *Focus on one type of retailing.* For example, Abercrombie & Fitch operates just one type of specialty store and thus would be a good choice. However, Walmart operates discount stores, warehouse club stores, and supercenters and would not be a good choice.
   * *Be easy to visit and collect information about.* Some retailers and store managers may not allow you to

   interview them about the store, take pictures of the store, talk with sales associates, or analyze the merchandise assortment in the store. Try to pick a retailer with a local store manager who can help you complete the assignments.

   Some examples of retailers that meet the first two criteria are Whole Foods Market, Dress Barn, Burlington Coat Factory, Ross Stores, Ann Taylor, Cato, Finish Line, Foot Locker, Brookstone, Claire's, Walgreens, Staples, Office Depot, American Eagle Outfitter, Pacific Sunwear, Abercrombie & Fitch, Tiffany & Co., Zales, Autozone, Pep Boys, Hot Topic, Wet Seal, Best Buy, Family Dollar, Dollar General, Michaels, PetSmart, Dillard's, Pier 1 Imports, Home Depot, Lowe's, Bed Bath & Beyond, Men's Wearhouse, Kroger, Kohl's, Radio Shack, Safeway, and Target.

2. **GO SHOPPING** Visit a local retail store, and describe each of the elements in its retail mix.

3. **INTERNET EXERCISE** Data on U.S. retail sales are available at the U.S. Bureau of the Census Internet site at: www.census.gov/retail/index.html. Under the heading "Monthly Retail Trade Report" there is a file titled "Retail and Food Services Sales" that lists sales by type of retailer. In which months are sales the highest? Which

kinds of businesses experience the greatest fluctuations in monthly sales? List reasons that help explain your findings.

4. **INTERNET EXERCISE** Go to the home pages of Macy's, Target, Walmart, Toys "R" Us, and the National Retail Federation Retail Careers Center (**www.nrf.com/RetailCareers/**) to find information about retail careers with these organizations. Review the information about the different positions described. In which positions would you be interested? Which

positions are not of interest to you? Which employer would interest you? Why?

5. **INTERNET EXERCISE** Choose one of the top 20 retailers (Exhibit 1–4). Go to the company's website and find out how the company started and how it has changed over time.

6. **INTERNET EXERCISE** Go online to the websites of Whole Foods or The Container Store. In a brief paragraph, describe how this retailer is taking steps to contribute to a social or ethical cause.

DISCUSSION QUESTIONS AND PROBLEMS

1. How do retailers add value to the products bought by consumers?

2. What is your favorite retailer? Why do you like this retailer? What would a competitive retailer have to do to get your patronage?

3. What are the benefits and limitations of purchasing a home entertainment system directly from a number of component manufacturers rather than from a retailer?

4. What retailers would be considered intratype competitors for a convenience store chain such as 7-Eleven? What firms would be intertype competitors?

5. How does Walmart contribute to and/or detract from the communities in which it operates stores?

6. The same brand and style of men's suits are sold at different prices at a department store like Macy's and at a specialty store like Men's Wearhouse. Why would a customer choose to buy the suit from one store rather than the other?

7. Compare and contrast the retail mixes of department stores and full-line discount stores. Use bullet points or a table to list the similarities and differences.

8. An entrepreneur approaches you about how to sell her new writing pens to consumers. The pens have a unique benefit—they are more comfortable to use than traditional pens. The entrepreneur is concerned the retailers she has approached want to buy the pens from her at $10 apiece and then sell the pens in their stores at $18 to consumers. The entrepreneur is dismayed at the extra $8 the retailers are getting and has decided to sell the product directly to consumers for $10. She wants to know your opinion. What do you think? Why?

9. From a personal perspective, how does retailing rate as a potential career compared with others you are considering? Why?

10. In this chapter, some socially responsible activities engaged in by retailers are described. Take the perspective of a stockholder in one of these companies. What effect will these activities have on the value of its stock? Why might they have a positive or negative effect?

APPENDIX 1A   Careers in Retailing

Retailing offers exciting and challenging career opportunities. Few other industries grant as many responsibilities to young managers. When students asked Dave Fuente, former CEO of Office Depot, what they needed to become a CEO someday, he responded, "You need to have profit and loss responsibility and the experience of managing people early in your career." Entry-level retail jobs for college graduates offer both these opportunities. Most college graduates begin their retail careers as assistant buyers, merchandise planners, or department managers in stores. In these positions, they are responsible for the profitability of a line of merchandise or an area of the store, and they manage people who work for them.

Even if you work for a large company, retailing provides an opportunity for you to do your own thing and be rewarded. You can come up with an idea, execute it almost immediately, and see how well it is doing by reviewing the sales data at the end of the day.

Retailing offers a variety of career paths, such as buying, store management, sales promotion and advertising, human resources, operations/distribution, real estate, loss prevention, and finance. In addition, retailing offers almost immediate accountability for talented people, so they can reach key management positions fairly quickly. Starting salaries are competitive, and the compensation of top management ranks among the highest in any industry.

CAREER OPPORTUNITIES

In retail firms, career opportunities are in merchandising/buying, store management, and corporate staff functions. Corporate positions are in accounting, finance, real estate, promotions and advertising, computer and distribution systems, and human resources.

The primary entry-level opportunities for a retailing career are in the areas of buying and store management. Buying positions are more numbers-oriented, whereas store management positions are more people-oriented. Entry-level positions on the corporate staff are limited. Retailers typically

© Xavier Arnau/E+/Getty Images

The typical entry-level position of college graduates interested in merchandise management is either assistant buyer or assistant planner in a merchandise category such as men's athletic shoes or consumer electronics.

want all of their employees to understand their customers and their merchandise. Therefore, most executives and corporate staff managers begin their careers in merchandise or store management.

Store Management

Successful store managers must have the ability to lead and motivate employees. They also need to be sensitive to customers' needs by making sure that merchandise is available and neatly displayed.

Store management involves all the discipline necessary to run a successful business: sales planning and goal setting, overall store image and merchandise presentation, budgets and expense control, customer service and sales supervision, human resource administration and development, and community relations.

Because store managers work in stores, they are often at quite a distance from the home office, which means they have limited direct supervision. Their hours generally mirror those of their store and can therefore include some weekends and evenings. In addition, they spend time during nonoperating hours tending to administrative responsibilities.

The typical entry-level store management position is a department manager with responsibility for merchandise presentation, customer service, and inventory control for an area of the store. The next level is an area or group manager with responsibility for executing merchandising plans and achieving sales goals for several areas, as well as supervising, training, and developing department managers. Beyond these positions, you might be promoted to store manager, then to district manager responsible for a group of stores, and then to regional manager responsible for a group of districts.

Merchandise Management

Merchandise management attracts people with strong analytical capabilities, an ability to predict what merchandise will appeal to their target markets, and a skill for negotiating

with vendors as well as store management to get things done. Many retailers have broken the merchandising management activities into two different yet parallel career paths: buying and merchandise planning.

Retail merchandise buyers are similar to financial portfolio managers. They invest in a portfolio of merchandise; monitor the performance (sales) of the merchandise; and on the basis of the sales, either decide to buy more merchandise that is selling well or get rid of (discount) merchandise that is selling poorly. Buyers are responsible for selecting the type and amount of merchandise to buy, negotiating the wholesale price and payment terms with suppliers, setting the initial retail price for the merchandise, monitoring merchandise sales, and making appropriate retail price adjustments. Thus buyers need to have good financial planning skills, knowledge of their customers' needs and wants and competitive activities, and the ability to develop good working relationships with vendors. To develop a better understanding of their customers, buyers typically stay in contact with their stores by visiting them, talking to sales associates and managers, and monitoring the sales data available through their merchandise management systems.

Planners have an even more analytical role than buyers. Their primary responsibility is to determine the assortment of merchandise sent to each store—how many styles, colors, sizes, and individual items. Once the merchandise is in the stores, planners closely monitor sales and work with buyers on decisions such as how much additional merchandise to purchase if the merchandise is doing well or when to mark down the merchandise if sales are below expectations.

The typical entry-level position of college graduates interested in merchandise management is either assistant buyer or assistant planner in a merchandise category such as men's athletic shoes or consumer electronics. In these positions, you will do the sales analysis needed to support the decisions eventually made by the planner or buyer for whom you work. From this entry-level position, you could be promoted to buyer and then divisional merchandise manager, responsible for a number of merchandise categories. Most retailers believe that merchandise management skills are not category-specific. Thus, as you are promoted in the buying organization, you will probably work in various merchandise categories.

Corporate Staff

The corporate staff positions in retail firms involve activities and require knowledge, skills, and abilities similar to those in comparable positions in nonretail firms. Thus, many managers in these positions identify with their profession rather than the retail industry. For example, accountants in retail firms view themselves as accountant, not retailers.

Management Information Systems (MIS)   Employees in this area are involved with applications for capturing data and developing and maintaining inventory, as well as the design of store systems such as POS terminals, self-checkout systems, and in-store kiosks.

Operations/Distribution   Operations employees are responsible for operating and maintaining the store's physical plant; providing various customer services; overseeing the receipt, ticketing, warehousing, and distribution of a store's inventory; and buying and maintaining store supplies and operating equipment. Students in operations typically major in production, operations, or computer information systems.

Promotion/Advertising   Promotion's many aspects include public relations, advertising, visual merchandising, and special events. This department attempts to build the retail firm's brand image and encourage customers to visit the retailer's stores and/or website. Managers in this area typically major in marketing or mass communications.

Loss Prevention   Loss prevention employees are responsible for protecting the retailer's assets. They develop systems and procedures to minimize employee theft and shoplifting. Managers in this area often major in sociology or criminology, although, as we discuss in Chapter 15, loss prevention is beginning to be viewed as a human resource management issue.

Finance/Accounting   Many retailers are large businesses involved in complicated corporate structures. Most retailers also operate with a tight net profit margin. With such a fine line between success and failure, retailers continue to require financial experts. The finance/accounting division is responsible for the financial health of the company. Employees in this division prepare financial reports for all aspects of the business, including long-range forecasting and planning, economic trend analysis and budgeting, shortage control and internal audits, gross and net profit, accounts payable to vendors, and accounts receivable from charge customers. In addition, they manage the retailer's relationship with the financial community. Students interested in this area often major in finance or accounting.

Real Estate   Employees in the real estate division are responsible for selecting locations for stores, negotiating leases and land purchases, and managing the leasehold costs. Students entering this area typically major in real estate or finance.

Store Design   Employees working in this area are responsible for designing the store and presenting merchandise and fixtures in the store. Talented, creative students in business, architecture, art, and other related fields will have innumerable opportunities for growth in the area of retail store design.

Human Resource Management   Human resource management is responsible for the effective selection, training, placement, advancement, and welfare of employees. Because there are seasonal peaks in retailing (such as Christmas, when many extra people must be hired), human resource personnel must be flexible and highly efficient.

ATTRACTIVENESS OF RETAILING CAREERS

Immediate Responsibility

Management trainees in retailing are given more responsibility more quickly than their counterparts in other industries. Buyers are responsible for choosing, promoting, pricing, distributing, and selling millions of dollars' worth of merchandise each season. The department manager, generally the first position after a training program, is often responsible for merchandising one or more departments, as well as managing 20 or more full- and part-time sales associates.

Many students and their parents think that people working in retailing have jobs as salesclerks and cashiers. They hold this view because, as customers in retail stores, they typically interact only with sales associates, not their managers. But as we have discussed in this chapter, retail firms are large, sophisticated corporations that employ managers with a wide variety of knowledge, skills, and abilities. Entry-level positions for college are typically management trainees in the buying or store organization, not sales associates.

While some employees are promoted on the basis of their retail experience, a college degree is needed for most retail management positions, ranging from store manager to CEO. More than 150 colleges and universities in the United States offer programs of study and degrees or majors in retailing.

Financial Rewards

Starting salaries for management trainees with a college degree range from $30,000 to $60,000 a year, and the compensation of top management ranks with the highest in any industry. For example, store managers with only a few years of experience can earn up to $100,000 or more, depending on their performance bonuses. A senior buyer for a department store earns from $50,000 to $90,000 or more. A big-box store manager can earn from $50,000 to $150,000; a discount store manager makes from $70,000 to $100,000 or more; and a specialty store manager earns from $35,000 to $60,000 or more.

Compensation varies according to the amount of responsibility. Specialty store managers are generally paid less than department store managers because their annual sales volume is lower. But advancements in this area can be faster. Aggressive specialty store managers often are promoted to district managers and run 8 to 15 units after a few years, so they quickly move into higher pay brackets.

Because information systems enable retailers to assess the sales and profit performance of each manager, and even each sales associate, the compensation of retail managers is closely linked to objective measures of their performance. As a result, in addition to their salaries, retail managers are generally given strong monetary incentives based on the sales they create.

A compensation package consists of more than salary alone. In retailing, the benefits package is often substantial and may include a profit-sharing plan, savings plan, stock options, medical and dental insurance, life insurance, long-term disability protection and income protection plans, and paid vacations and holidays. Two additional benefits of retailing careers are that most retailers offer employees valuable discounts on the merchandise they sell, and some buying positions include extensive foreign travel.

Opportunities for Advancement

While the growth rate of retail parallels the growth rate of the overall economy, many opportunities for rapid advancement exist simply because of the sheer size of the retail industry. With so many retail firms, there is always a large number of firms that are experiencing a high growth rate, opening many new stores, and needing store managers and support staff positions.

CHAPTER ENDNOTES

1. James B. Stewart, "Walmart Plays Catch Up with Amazon," *The New York Times*, October 22, 2015.

2. *"Amazon's Future: Looking beyond the Balance Sheet,"* Wharton School of Business, October 28, 2014, http://knowledge. wharton.upenn.edu/article/kw-radio-faderraff-amazon/.

3. Dan Berthiaume, "Three Reasons Amazon Is Everyone's Competitor," *Chain Store Age*, November 9, 2015.

4. Taylor Soper, "Amazon's Dominance of Online Shopping Starts with Product Searches, Study Shows," *GeekWire*, October 6, 2015.

5. "Amazon Rolls Out Devices That Fill Themselves," *Industry Week*, January 19, 2016.

6. Berthiaume, "Three Reasons"; Nick Wingfield, "Amazon Is Said to Be Planning an Expansion into Retail Bookstores," *The New York Times*, February 2, 2016.

7. Tom Ryan, "Amazon Rolls Out Free Same-Day Delivery," *RetailWire*, May 29, 2015; "Walmart Plans to Test Unlimited Shipping Service," Associated Press, May 13, 2015.

8. Ron Nixon, "Postal Service to Make Sunday Deliveries for Amazon," *The New York Times*, November 11, 2013.

9. Jenn Markey, "Three Things You Need to Know about Amazon's Price Strategy," *Retail Customer Experience*, April 21, 2014, http://www.retailcustomerexperience.com.

10. "In Amazon and Walmart's Battle for Dominance, Who Loses Out?," *Wharton School of Business*, November 13, 2013, http://knowledge.wharton.upenn.edu/article/amazon-walmarts-battle-dominance-future-retail-stake/.

11. Sarah Nassauer, "Sam's Club Aims to Be Less Like Wal-Mart," *The Wall Street Journal*, August 16, 2015.

12. Stephanie Strom, "Walmart Pushes for Improved Animal Welfare," *The New York Times*, May 22, 2015; Hiroko Tabuchi, "Walmart Raising Wage to at Least $9," *The New York Times*, February 18, 2015; Jessica Wohl, "Walmart Announces $50 Billion Buy American Campaign," *The Huffington Post*, January 15, 2013.

13. http://corporate.walmart.com/.

14. Preetika Rana, "IKEA's India Bet Runs into Thicket of Rules," *The Wall Street Journal*, February 23, 2016; Amol Sharma and Biman Mukherji, "Bad Roads, Red Tape, Burly Thugs Slow Walmart's Passage in India," *The Wall Street Journal,* January 12, 2013; Chitra Srivastava Dabas, Brenda Sternquist, and Humaira Mahi, "Organized Retailing in India: Upstream Channel Structure and Management," *Journal of Business & Industrial Marketing* 27, no. 3 (2012), pp. 176–195.

15. "Retail Industry in India," India Brand Equity Foundation, January 2016, http://www.ibef.org/industry/retail-india. aspx; Newley Purnell, "Apple Pushes to Bolster Market Share in India," *The Wall Street Journal*, January 20, 2016.

16. Marianne Wilson, "China Is Top Emerging Retail Market," *The New York Times*, June 1, 2015.

17. http://corporate.walmart.com/our-story/locations/china#/ china; http://www.carrefour.com/content/carrefour-stores-worldwide; Walmart China Fact Sheet, Alex Lawson, "Analysis: Retailing in China," *Retail Week,* April 20, 2012; Sheng Lu, "Understanding China's Retail Market," *China Business Review,* May–June 2010.

18. https://www.census.gov/retail/index.html.

19. "May 2015 National Occupational Employment and Wage Estimates United States," http://www.bls.gov/oes/current/ oes_nat.htm.

20. "11 Facts about Global Poverty," www.dosomething.org.

21. Stanley E. Fawcett and Matthew A. Waller, "Designing the Supply Chain for Success at the Bottom of the Pyramid," *Journal of Business Logistics* 36, no. 3 (2015), pp. 233–239; C. K. Prahalad, *The Fortune at the Bottom of the Pyramid: Eradicating Poverty through Profits,* revised and updated 5th anniversary edition (Philadelphia: Wharton School Publishing, 2009).

22. C. K. Prahalad, "Bottom of the Pyramid as a Source of Breakthrough Innovations," *Journal of Product Innovation Management* 29 (January 2012), pp. 6–12; A. Karamchandani and M. Kubzansky, "Is the Bottom of the Pyramid Really for You?," *Harvard Business Review,* March 2011, pp. 2–10.

23. Dhruv Grewal and Michael Levy, *Marketing,* 6th ed. (Burr Ridge, IL: McGraw-Hill Education, 2017); Dhruv Grewal, Anne L. Roggeveen, Rajendra Sisodia, and Jens Nordfalt, "Enhancing Customer Engagement through Consciousness," *Journal of Retailing* 93, no. 1 (March 2017), pp. 55–64. The first four principles draw on Raj Sisodia, "Conscious Capitalism: A Better Way to Win," *California Management Review* 53 (Spring 2011), pp. 98–108.

24. Gene R. Laczniak and Patrick E. Murphy, "Stakeholder Theory and Marketing: Moving from a Firm-Centric to a Societal Perspective," *Journal of Public Policy & Marketing* 31 (Fall 2012), pp. 284–292.

25. Stephanie Strom, "Walmart Pushes for Improved Animal Welfare," *The New York Times,* May 22, 2015.

26. John Mackey, "What Conscious Capitalism Really Is," *California Management Review* 53 (Spring 2011), pp. 83–90; John Mackey and Rajendra Sisodia, *Conscious Capitalism, with a New Preface by the Authors: Liberating the Heroic Spirit of Business* (Cambridge, MA: Harvard Business Review Press, 2014).

27. http://www.wholefoodsmarket.com/mission-values/core-values/declaration-interdependence.

28. Personal interview with former Trader Joe president Doug Rauch, 2016, found in Grewal et al., "Enhancing Customer Engagement through Consciousness."

29. C. B. Bhattacharya and Sankar Sen, "Consumer-Company Identification: A Framework for Understanding Consumers'

Relationships with Companies," *Journal of Marketing* 67 (April 2003), pp. 76–88.

30. Ibid.

31. National Retail Federation, "2016 Top 250 Global Powers of Retailing," January 2016, https://nrf.com/news/2016-top-250-global-powers-of-retailing.

32. Phalguni Son, "Home Improvement Retail: A Two-Horse Race for Supremacy," *Market Realist,* March 24, 2015.

33. Mazzone & Associates, "Market Share of Major Retail Companies in the United States in 2015," Statista: The Statistics Portal, October 2015, http://www.statista.com/statistics/473722/market-share-of-major-retail-companies-in-the-us/.

34. Corey Stern, "CVS and Walgreens Are Completely Dominating the US Drugstore Industry," www.businessinsider.com, July 29, 2015.

35. Personal conversation with author.

36. Kelsey Lindsey, "Retail in a Slump? Not for These 6 Billionaires," *Retail Dive*, March 5, 2014; Michael Bergdahl, *The Retail Revolution: How Wal-Mart Created a Brave New World of Business* (New York: Metropolitan Books, 2009).

37. "About Forever 21," http://newsroom.forever21.com/about; "America's Largest Private Companies 2016: #96 Forever 21," *Forbes*, July 20, 2016, http://www.forbes.com/companies/forever-21/; Andrea Chang, "To Forever 21, Big Stores Are a Good Fit," *Los Angeles Times*, May 25, 2011, p. B.1.

38. "The World's Billionaires 2007," *Forbes*, March 8, 2003.

39. "Ingvar Kamprad & Family," *Forbes*, July 2016, http://www.forbes.com/profile/ingvar-kamprad/.

40. Howard Schultz and Joanne Gordon, *Onward: How Starbucks Fought for Its Life without Losing Its Soul* (Emmaus, PA: Rodale Books, 2012).

41. "Starbucks Company Profile," http://www.starbucks.com/about-us/company-information/starbucks-company-profile; "The World's Biggest Public Companies 2016: # 389 Starbucks," *Forbes*, May 2016, http://www.forbes.com/companies/starbucks/; Schultz and Gordon, *Onward; How Starbucks Fought for Its Life without Losing Its Soul*; Howard Behar, Janet Goldstein, and Howard Schultz, *It's Not about the Coffee: Lessons on Putting People First from a Life at Starbucks* (New York: Portfolio Trade, 2009).

© Susana Gonzalez/Bloomberg/Getty Images

When it first entered the scene, Sam's Club had a specific and focused target market: small businesses that wanted to purchase bulk quantities of products to run their operations. But the popularity of the warehouse club has meant that over the years, its customers have increased in number and have grown far more diverse. With these developments, Sam's Club has also become a more competitive entrant in the retail market, adapting its strategic plan and positioning accordingly.

Unfortunately, this competitiveness has had some negative implications for its sibling company, the discount chain Walmart, which still promises the same thing it always has: low prices. Accordingly, it attracts a price-sensitive segment of shoppers who always are seeking the best deal. For a long time, these shoppers also enjoyed the warehouse options of Sam's Club, which enabled them to purchase large quantities at a lower price. In some cases, though, Sam's Club stocks smaller packages (e.g., a two-pack of toothpaste) that also would appear on Walmart's shelves. Furthermore, Walmart and other large discount retailers increasingly feature substantial packages of consumer products when they can get deals on them. Thus, the two sibling brands frequently cannibalize each other's sales.

In an effort to avoid that sort of competition, Sam's Club is looking to revise its image. Rather than a source of cheap, bulk goods, it wants to move up the ladder to become a semi-exclusive (based on the membership fee) environment, where high-end customers come to find reasonable deals on expensive items like televisions or jewelry. To achieve this shift, Sam's Club is expanding the assortment of organic goods it carries, adding more brand-name clothing labels, and dedicating a section to sheets with thread counts in the thousands. It also is running tests in a limited number of stores to see how offerings such as expensive furniture, luxury clothing, and prepared meals fare.

These experiments reflect Sam's Club's revised segmentation and targeting plan, which involves four main categories of members: large families with young children, "social couples" of various ages who like to entertain, families who live in close proximity to stores and regard the Club as a regular source for their grocery needs, and new moms shopping for their infants who offer strong loyalty potential over time. With these strategic considerations, Sam's Club clearly is going well beyond a traditional warehouse club model.

In addition to shifting its assortment and segmentation strategy, Sam's Club plans to leverage new technologies to differentiate itself from channel competitors and identify customers in proximity to its stores, then position those stores accordingly. For example, using zip code data, it learned that approximately 150 Sam's Club stores were located in high-income areas, yet high-income shoppers were not visiting those nearby stores. Furthermore, the ultimate goal of using digital technology is to make the shopping experience easier for its "exclusive" members, whether they visit stores or shop from home. By claiming leadership in digital uses in the warehouse club market, Sam's Club believes that "over time we'll have the best use of integrated technology in retail."[1]

You want to have a good cup of coffee in the morning, not instant, but you don't want to bother with grinding coffee beans, boiling water, pouring it through ground coffee in a filter, and waiting. Think of all the different retailers that could help you satisfy this need. You could get your cup of brewed coffee from the drive-through window at the local Starbucks, or you could decide to buy an automatic coffeemaker with a timer so that your coffee will be ready when you wake up. You could purchase the coffeemaker at a discount store like Walmart or Target, a department store such as Macy's, a drugstore like CVS, or a category specialist such as Best Buy. If you want to buy the coffeemaker without taking the time to visit a store, you could visit Google Shopping (**www.google. com/shopping**) or Shopzilla (**www.shopzilla.com**), search for "coffee and espresso maker," and review the details of thousands of options sold by hundreds of retailers.

All these retailers are competing against one another to satisfy your need for a hassle-free, good cup of coffee. Many are selling the same brands, but they offer different services, prices, environments, and convenience. For example, if you want to buy a low-priced, basic coffeemaker, you can go to a discount store. But if you are interested in a coffeemaker with more features and want to have someone explain the different features, you can visit a department store or a category specialist.

To develop and implement a retail strategy, retailers need to understand the nature of competition in the retail marketplace.[2] This chapter describes the different types of retailers and how they compete against one another by offering different benefits to consumers. These benefits are reflected in the nature of the retail mixes used by the retailers to satisfy customer needs: the types of merchandise and services offered, the degree to which their offerings emphasize services versus merchandise, and the prices charged.

RETAILER CHARACTERISTICS

The more than 1.1 million[3] retailers in the United States range from individual street vendors selling hot dogs to omnichannel retailers that offer thousands of products in their stores, through catalog and Internet channels. The different types of retailers offer unique benefits. The type of retailer a consumer chooses to patronize depends on the benefits the consumer is seeking. For example, if you are shopping for a gift, you might value the convenience of buying a shirt from a retailer's Internet channel so the retailer will ship it to a friend in another city. Alternatively, you might prefer to buy a shirt from a local store when making a purchase for yourself so that you can try it on. You might go to a discount store to buy an inexpensive shirt for a camping trip or a sporting goods specialty store to buy a shirt with the insignia of your favorite football team.

LO 2-1

List the different characteristics that define retailers.

All these retailers survive and prosper because they satisfy a group of consumers' needs more effectively than their competitors, and thus consumers patronize different retail types when they have different needs. As consumer needs and competition change, new retail formats are created and existing formats evolve.

Many retailers also are broadening their assortments, which means that their offerings overlap and competition increases. At eBay Motors, for example, consumers can buy cars and motorcycles from thousands of individual sellers and established dealers. When eBay sellers competed mainly with traditional automobile dealers that sell cars and motorcycles through conventional dealerships, the channel was vastly popular.

However, as the retail options for car buying have expanded—including not just Craigslist and CarMax online but also new retail services such as Vroom, Shift, and Beepi— eBay Motors has suffered from the increasing competition.[4]

The most basic characteristic used to describe the different types of retailers is their retail mix, or the elements retailers use to satisfy their customers' needs. Four elements of the retail mix are particularly useful for classifying retailers: the type of merchandise and/or services offered, the variety and assortment of merchandise offered, the level of customer service, and the price of the merchandise.

Type of Merchandise

The United States, Canada, and Mexico have developed a classification scheme, called the **North American Industry Classification System (NAICS)**, to collect data on business activity in each country. Every business is assigned a hierarchical, six-digit code based on the type of products and services it sells. The first two digits identify the firm's business sector, and the remaining four digits identify various subsectors.

The classifications for retailers selling merchandise, based largely on the type of merchandise sold, are illustrated in Exhibit 2–1. Merchandise retailers are in sectors 44

EXHIBIT 2–1   NAICS Codes for Retailers

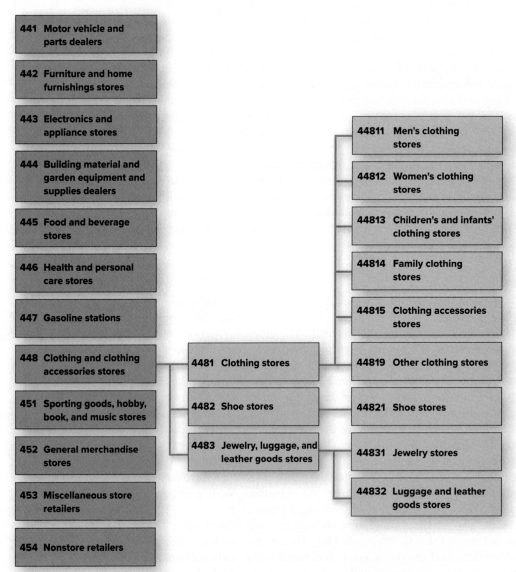

Source: "North American Industry Classification System (NAICS)," U.S. Census Bureau, www.census.gov/epcd/www/naics.html.

and 45. The next three digits provide a finer classification of merchandise retailers. For example, retailers selling clothing and clothing accessories are classified as 448, clothing stores as 4481, and men's clothing stores as 44811. The sixth digit, not illustrated in Exhibit 2–1, captures differences between the North American countries using the classification scheme.

Most services retailers are classified in sectors 71 (arts, entertainment, and recreation) and 72 (accommodation and food services). For example, food services and drinking places are in category 722, which is subdivided into full-service restaurants (722511) and limited-service eating places like fast-food restaurants (722513).

Variety and Assortment

Retailers can offer the same merchandise but differ in the variety and assortment of merchandise offered. **Variety** (also called **breadth**) is the number of merchandise categories a retailer offers. **Assortment** (also called **depth**) is the number of different items offered in a merchandise category. Each different item of merchandise is called a **stock-keeping unit (SKU)**. Some examples of SKUs include an original scent, 33-ounce box of Tide laundry detergent with bleach, or a blue, oxford cloth, long-sleeve, button-down-collar Ralph Lauren shirt, size medium.

Warehouse clubs, discount stores, and toy stores all sell toys, but warehouse clubs and full-line discount stores sell many other categories of merchandise in addition to toys (i.e., they have greater variety). Stores specializing in toys stock more types of toys (more SKUs) and thus offer a greater assortment (i.e., greater depth in the form of more models, sizes, and brands) than the full-line discount stores or warehouse clubs.

Variety and assortment can also be applied to a specific merchandise category rather than an entire store. Exhibit 2–2 shows the breadth and depth of bicycles, as well as the different price points and brands carried by three very different types of stores: Wheelworks, a bicycle specialty retailer with one store in Belmont, Massachusetts; Toys "R" Us, a toy big-box category killer; and Walmart, a full-line discount store. Toys "R" Us has a large variety of merchandise besides bicycles, but its bicycle assortment is narrow. Wheelworks has the smallest variety because it carries only bicycles, parts, and accessories, but its assortment is very deep. Walmart, trying to cater to a wide target market, has moderate variety and assortment.

One of the most interesting retailers, selling an amazing variety and assortment of merchandise, is Amazon, which is highlighted in Retailing View 2.1.

EXHIBIT 2–2   Variety and Assortment of Bicycles in Different Retail Outlets

	Adult Road	Adult Hybrid	Mountain	Child
Wheelworks	Bianci, Colnago, Peter Mooney, Serotta, Trek 150 SKUs $419.99–$7,999.99	Bianchi, Specialized, Trek 96 SKUs $349.99–$1,899.99	Salsa, Santa Cruz, Specialized, Trek 122 SKUs $299.99–$1,899.99	Electra, Gary Fisher, Haro, Kettler, Trek 56 SKUs $159.99–$429.99
Toys "R" Us	Mobo Triton Pro 3 SKUs $299.99–$359.99	—	Cycle Force, Huffy, Schwinn 4 SKUs $79.98–$135.99	Avigo, Cycle Force, Huffy, Mongoose, Pacific Cycle 228 SKUs $45.99–$499.99
Walmart	Cycle Force, Genesis, Kent, Mongoose 26 SKUs $99.97–$499.00	Cycle Force, Genesis, Schwinn, Tour De France 9 SKUs $179.00–$349.00	Havoc, Genesis, Schwinn, NEXT, Roadmaster 63 SKUs $88.00–$379.00	Huffy, Koxx, Micargi, Schwinn, Tour De France 195 SKUs $28.13–$675.00

Why do the three retailers' assortments differ from each other?

© Cultura RM/Alamy Stock Photo

Services Offered

Retailers also differ in the services they offer customers. Customers expect almost all retailers to provide certain services: displaying merchandise, accepting credit cards, providing parking, and being open at convenient hours. Some retailers charge customers for other services, such as home delivery and gift wrapping. However, retailers may differ on other services. For example, Wheelworks offers assistance in selecting the appropriate bicycle, as well as repairs. Walmart does not provide these services.

Prices and Cost of Offering Breadth and Depth of Merchandise and Services

Stocking a deep and broad assortment, like the one Wheelworks offers in bicycles, is appealing to customers but costly for retailers. When a retailer offers many SKUs, its inventory investment increases because the retailer must have backup stock for each and every SKU.

Similarly, services attract customers to the retailer, but they also are costly. More staff must be paid to provide information and assist customers, alter products to meet customers' needs, and demonstrate merchandise. Child care facilities, restrooms, dressing rooms, and coat check rooms take up valuable store space that could be used to stock and display merchandise. Offering delayed billing, credit, or installment payments requires a financial investment that could be otherwise used to buy more merchandise.

To make a profit, retailers that offer broader variety, deeper assortments, and/or additional services need to charge higher prices. For example, department stores have higher prices than discount stores partially because of their higher costs. Department stores stock more fashionable merchandise and have to reduce prices when they make a mistake in guessing what the popular styles will be. They also provide more personal sales service and have more expensive mall locations. In contrast, discount stores appeal to customers who are looking for lower prices. These consumers are less interested in the costly services provided by department

When it started out in 1994, Amazon simply promised more books than anyone else. It took a few years for the online retailer to grow large enough to threaten the big names—Borders, Barnes & Noble, and so on. But today, Borders has disappeared, and Amazon's competitive threat spreads far beyond bookstores: When it comes to competition among retailers, pretty much everyone in the United States competes with Amazon. From small sellers of personalized gifts to service retailers to massive consumer-goods providers, the retail market recognizes Amazon as a dominant actor, specialized in getting the products that customers want to them quickly, efficiently, and exactly when and where they want those items.

The reason has a lot to do with three key benefits that Amazon offers all retail customers. First, it is incredibly convenient, available to meet shoppers' every product need, at any time. Not only is Amazon's inventory unsurpassed, but it makes ordering easy with checkout tools such as one-click and automatic deliveries of repeated purchases on frequently bought items. With its Echo service, Amazon customers who pay for Prime Now service can place orders by calling out their grocery list to an artificial intelligence device installed in their homes. With records of prior purchases, Echo can also suggest alternative options and apply previously set shipping preferences. Then it gets these ordered products to customers quickly and conveniently. By paying a fee, many customers get the products on the same day, but even Amazon's free, standard shipping service is pretty fast.

Second, just in case people want to interact personally, Amazon is gaining steam as a brick-and-mortar retailer as well. Why does it need physical stores? It recognizes that some customers like to shop in an actual environment, rather than a virtual one. Accordingly, Amazon plans to apply its remarkable facility with integrating and leveraging customer data to make recommendations to its brick-and-mortar stores. In so doing, it appears poised to make a successful transition from a mainly online presence to a truly omnichannel source.

Third, retail isn't simply about physical goods. It also includes services, and on that front, Amazon is increasing its remarkable availability even further by expanding into new service offerings. It offers textbook rentals through its Kindle products to college students. It provides authors an easy route to self-publishing their work. Its cloud computing services are free for the first year—and its cloud offers enough storage for every person on the planet to store 82 books. It also has a roster of providers offering about 700 types of services to customers, from the conventional to the obscure (just what does a "silk aerialist" do?). Just as it has with products, it seeks to offer the widest selection of services possible, ensure speedy delivery, and provide highly competitive prices.

Amazon even functions as some users' primary search engine. Among 2,000 respondents, 44 percent indicated that when they began a product search, they started on Amazon rather than on traditional search engines such as Google or on specific retailers' own websites. When asked why they chose Amazon, most of these respondents noted that the retailer offered great personalization. When they enter a search term, Amazon knows how to suggest related and pertinent products that help them make good purchase decisions.

But its influence is not all threat. For small-business owners, the opportunity to sell through Amazon provides unparalleled exposure. Amazon actively seeks small retailers with

© franky242/Alamy Stock Photo

Amazon offers the largest variety and assortment of any retailer in the United States.

interesting products but insufficient resources to distribute those offerings widely. To them, Amazon is less a threat and more a golden opportunity. Still, as consumers invite Amazon in and solicit further services from it, the effect the retail giant has on the market appears destined to increase. For retailers seeking to compete with it—and by definition, that means pretty much every retailer in the world—paying attention to what Amazon is doing now is a necessary task. That is, because Amazon competes with literally every retailer, every retailer needs to understand what makes Amazon work so well if they are going to remain competitive and hold on to at least some of their market share.

Sources: Chantal Tode, "Amazon Makes Play for Greater Influence over In-Store Shoppers," *Mobile Commerce Daily*, July 3, 2012; Greg Bensinger, "Amazon's Tough Call," *The Wall Street Journal*, July 11, 2012; Molly McHugh, "Saving Cash on College Textbooks," *Digital Trends*, July 18, 2011; James Kendrick, "Amazon Debits Kindle Owner Lending Library," *ZDNet*, November 3, 2011; Vanchi Govind, "Amazon.com Offers Cloud Computing Services for Free," *InfoTech*, November 3, 2010; Jeffrey A. Trachtenberg, "Secret of Self-Publishing: Success," *The Wall Street Journal*, October 31, 2011; Zoe Fox, "How Amazon Became the World's Largest Retailer," *Mashable*, November 17, 2011; Hilary Stout, "Amazon, Google, and More Are Drawn to Home Services Market," *The New York Times*, April 12, 2015; Laura Lorenzetti, "Amazon's Handyman Service Is Expanding to 15 Cities," *Fortune*, July 22, 2015; Harriet Taylor, "Amazon, Google Move into On-Demand Home Services," *CNBC*, October 1, 2015; Taylor Soper, "Amazon's Dominance of Online Shopping Starts with Product Searches, Study Shows," *GeekWire*, October 6, 2015.

stores. Thus, a critical retail decision involves the trade-off between the costs and benefits of maintaining additional inventory or providing additional services. Chapters 6 and 12 address the considerations required in making this trade-off. In the next sections, we discuss the different types of food and general merchandise retailers.

FOOD RETAILERS

LO 2-2

Categorize the various types of food retailers.

The food retailing landscape is changing dramatically. Twenty years ago, consumers purchased food primarily at conventional supermarkets. Now conventional supermarkets account for less than 65 percent of food sales (not including restaurants).[5] Online sales of groceries have grown by 14.1 percent annually for the past five years.[6] Full-line discount stores like Walmart and Target offer full assortments of grocery items in their superstores, while traditional supermarkets are carrying more nonfood items. Many supermarkets offer pharmacies, health care clinics, banks, and cafés. An increasing number of them also are adding yoga classes, lounges for wine tastings, and pedicure services, in an effort to get customers to regard their local grocer as a place to hang out, not just pop in to grab the ingredients for dinner.[7] Exhibit 2–3 contains information about the size and growth rates for food retailers as well as many of the other types of retailers discussed in this chapter.

The world's largest food retailer, Walmart, attains more than $485 billion in sales of supermarket-type merchandise.[8] On this measure, it is followed by Costco (United States), Carrefour (France), Kroger (United States), Tesco (United Kingdom), Seven &

EXHIBIT 2–3
Sales and Growth Rate for Retail Sectors

	Estimated Sales, 2013 ($ millions)	Estimated Sales Growth 2008–2013 (%)
Food Retailers		
Conventional supermarkets	$622,896	3.3
Supercenters	354,905	7.1
Warehouse clubs	159,075	6.7
Convenience stores	748,186	3.0
General Merchandise Retailers		
Department stores	73,291	−0.9
Apparel and accessory specialty stores	210,236	4.5
Jewelry stores	36,848	3.4
Shoe stores	29,606	1.8
Furniture stores	66,262	2.2
Home furnishing stores	59,465	2.8
Office supply stores	26,404	2.2
Sporting goods stores	49,717	5.3
Bookstores	19,101	2.1
Building material, hardware, and garden supply stores	393,254	3.6
Consumer electronics and appliance stores	141,800	4.4
Drugstores	250,172	4.2
Full-line discount stores	126,385	0.0
Extreme-value stores	52,454	3.1
Nonstore Retailers		
Nonstore retailing	340,421	9.0
E-commerce	282,055	15.0

Sources: *Economic Forecast: Outlook to 2013 Food, Drug, Mass* (Columbus, OH: Retail Forward, November 2008); *Economic Forecast: Outlook to 2013 Homegoods* (Columbus, OH: Retail Forward, November 2008); *Economic Forecast: Outlook to 2013 Softgoods* (Columbus, OH: Retail Forward, November 2008).

EXHIBIT 2–4
Characteristics of Food Retailers

	Conventional Supermarket	Limited-Assortment Supermarket	Supercenter	Warehouse Club	Convenience Store
Percentage food	70–80	80–90	30–40	60	90
Size (000 sq. ft.)	35–40	7–10	160–200	100–150	3–5
SKUs (000)	30–40	1–1.5	100–150	20	2–3
Variety	Average	Narrow	Broad	Broad	Narrow
Assortment	Average	Shallow	Deep	Shallow	Shallow
Ambience	Pleasant	Minimal	Average	Minimal	Average
Service	Modest	Limited	Limited	Limited	Limited
Prices	Average	Lowest	Low	Low	High
Gross margin (%)	20–22	10–12	15–18	12–15	25–30

I (Japan), and Schwartz Group (Germany).[9] In North America specifically, the largest supermarket chains in order are Walmart, Kroger, Costco, Loblaw, Safeway, Publix, Ahold US, C&S Wholesale Grocers, Albertsons, and H-E-B.[10]

Despite their similarly large sizes, most of Walmart's food sales are generated from its supercenter format, whereas Carrefour garners most of its sales using the hypermarket format that it developed. The remaining larger food retailers primarily sell through conventional supermarkets. Exhibit 2–4 shows the retail mixes for different types of food retailers.

Supermarkets

A **conventional supermarket** is a large, self-service retail food store offering groceries, meat, and produce, as well as some nonfood items such as health and beauty aids and general merchandise.[11] Perishables, including meat, produce, baked goods, and dairy products, account for almost 54 percent of supermarket sales and typically have higher margins than packaged goods.[12]

Whereas conventional supermarkets carry about 30,000 SKUs, **limited-assortment supermarkets**, or **extreme-value food retailers**, stock only about 1,500 SKUs.[13]

Many conventional supermarkets have added services like a tea tasting counter to better compete with other food retailers.

Limited-assortment retailers like ALDI stock about 1,500 SKUs, compared to 30,000 SKUs for conventional supermarkets.

The two largest limited-assortment supermarket chains in the United States are Save-A-Lot and ALDI. Rather than carrying 20 brands of laundry detergent, limited-assortment supermarkets offer one or two brands and sizes, one of which is a store brand. Stores are designed to maximize efficiency and reduce costs. For example, merchandise is shipped in cartons on crates that can serve as displays so that no unloading is needed. Some costly services that consumers take for granted, such as free bags and paying with credit cards, are not provided. Stores are typically located in second- or third-tier shopping centers with low rents. By trimming costs, limited-assortment supermarkets can offer merchandise at prices 40 percent lower than those at conventional supermarkets.[14] These features have supported the substantial growth of such retailers, which appeal strongly to customers who are not loyal to national brands and more willing to try a store brand, especially if it means they pay lower prices.[15]

Trends in Supermarket Retailing   Although conventional supermarkets still sell the majority of food merchandise, they are under substantial competitive pressure on multiple sides: from supercenters, online retailers, warehouse clubs, extreme-value retailers, convenience stores, and even drugstores.[16] All these types of retailers have increased the amount of space (virtual or physical) that they devote to consumables.

Because consumers typically make three trips a week to buy food, but less than one trip a week to buy nonfood items, these competing retailers typically offer food merchandise to build the traffic in their stores and increase the sales of more profitable nonfood merchandise. They also have superior operating efficiencies and bargaining power with vendors that enable them to achieve low costs and offer low prices. These competing retailers have invested heavily in state-of-the-art supply chains, assortment planning, and pricing systems that reduce their inventories while increasing their sales and margins. These activities are discussed in more detail in Chapters 10 and 12.

To compete successfully against intrusions by other food retailing formats, conventional supermarkets are differentiating their offerings by (1) emphasizing fresh perishables; (2) targeting green, ethnic, and Millennial consumers; (3) providing better value with private-label merchandise; (4) adding new value-added services such as online ordering; and (5) providing a better shopping experience, such as by adding restaurant options or hosting social events.[17]

Supermarkets have expanded their assortments of fresh merchandise like sushi.

Fresh Merchandise   Fresh-merchandise categories are located in the areas around the outer walls of a supermarket, known as the **power perimeter**, and include the dairy, bakery, meat, florist, produce, deli, and coffee bar. These departments attract consumers and are very profitable. Conventional supermarkets are building on their strength in these categories and devoting more space and attention to them. They are promoting fresh merchandise with cooking exhibitions and "action" stations, such as store-made sushi and freshly grilled meat. In response to this consumer desire for more and better fresh merchandise, food retailers such as Fresh Fare (Kroger) and Fresh Market are opening food stores focusing on the power perimeter merchandise.

   Another example of the emphasis on "fresh" is the meal solutions offered to time-pressured consumers. A recent survey found that 64 percent of adult consumers have purchased ready-to-eat or heat-and-eat food from a grocery in the past month, creating an approximately $29 billion annual market.[18] The choices in the stores are as varied as the stores themselves, and growth in this category is approximately twice as great as that for traditional grocery store products. Despite the appearance of freshness, though, many of the items displayed for sale are actually prepared at a central location and then shipped to individual stores. Still, the variety of options available is immense: Market District offers smoothies; Buehler's Fresh Food sells crab cakes and beef burgundy; Safeway's Lifestyle stores have sandwich and sushi stations; Wegmans promotes its artichoke flan and coconut cream kale; and Whole Foods promises a range of tofu-based meals.[19]

Green Merchandise   Conventional supermarkets are offering more fair trade, natural, organic, and locally sourced foods for the growing segment of consumers who are health and environmentally conscious. **Fair trade** is the practice of purchasing from suppliers that pay workers a living wage, considerably more than the prevailing minimum wage, and offer other benefits such as onsite medical treatment. Organic food purchases have jumped in recent years, with sales increasing by nearly 20 percent annually. Consumers also are buying a wider range of organic products, provided by an ever-expanding array of organic providers, including staple items such as milk, eggs, and vegetables, as well as more food and nonfood options, such as ice cream and hair care products.[20]

In turn, traditional supermarket chains are offering more locally grown products, a trend brought about in response to environmental concerns and the increasing financial costs (e.g., fuel) of transporting food long distances. The **locavore movement** focuses on reducing the carbon footprint caused by the transportation of food throughout the world. Food miles are calculated using the distance that foods travel from the farm to the plate. Many Americans appreciate the idea of supporting local businesses, but they also want the variety of products they can find every day in their grocery store. It is difficult to maintain a balance between buying locally and maintaining such variety.

Ethnic Merchandise   Hispanics, who now constitute approximately 17 percent of the U.S. population, have significantly different shopping and eating patterns from those of the general population.[21] They are more likely to prepare meals from scratch, spend more on groceries, prefer stores with bilingual staff and signage, and place importance on fresh food. In addition to adding more ethnic merchandise in conventional supermarkets, retailers are opening supermarkets targeting Hispanic consumers.

For example, Northgate Markets in California cater to just Hispanic consumers. The chain's 42 stores, each approximately 50,000 square feet, feature both domestic and imported Latin American grocery items. Furthermore, they contain a dedicated tortilleria (where tortillas are made), prepared foods, and a well-stocked and staffed meat department.[22]

Private-Label Merchandise   Conventional supermarket chains are leveraging their quality reputation to offer more private-label merchandise. Private-label brands (discussed in Chapter 13) benefit both customers and retailers. The benefits to customers include having more choices and finding the same ingredients and quality as in national brands at a lower price or higher quality at a similar price to the national brands. The benefits of private-label brands to retailers include increased store loyalty, the ability to differentiate themselves from the competition, lower promotional costs, and higher gross margins compared with national brands.

Improving the Shopping Experience   Creating an enjoyable shopping experience through better store ambience and customer service is another approach that supermarket chains use to differentiate themselves from low-cost, low-price competitors. Supermarkets are increasingly incorporating "food as theater" concepts, such as in-store restaurants, open-air market designs, cooking and nutrition classes, demonstrations, baby-sitting services, and food and wine tasting. To appeal to on-the-go consumers, other supermarkets are offering self-service kiosks that are both fun and convenient. Among the offerings in place at both conventional supermarkets and limited-assortment stores are Coinstar, a change counting machine; Redbox, a movie rental kiosk; and Starbucks kiosks selling freshly ground and brewed coffee.[23]

Supercenters

Supercenters are large stores (160,000 to 200,000 square feet) that combine a supermarket with a full-line discount store. Walmart operates almost 3,500 supercenters in the United States.[24] Its leading competitors in the supercenter segment include Meijer, SuperTarget (Target), Fred Meyer (Kroger), and Super Kmart Center (Sears Holding)—though as we noted in the opener to this chapter, it also competes with retailers in other sectors, such as warehouse clubs. By offering broad assortments of grocery and general merchandise products under one roof, supercenters provide a one-stop shopping experience.

General merchandise (nonfood) items are often purchased on impulse when customers' primary reason for coming to the supercenter is to buy groceries. General merchandise has higher margins, enabling the supercenters to price food items more aggressively. However, supercenters are very large, so some customers find them inconvenient because it can take a long time to find the items they want.

Hypermarkets are also large, about the same size as supercenters.[25] Hypermarkets are not common in the United States, though they are similar to supercenters. Both hypermarkets and supercenters carry grocery and general merchandise categories, offer self-service, and are located in warehouse-type structures with large parking facilities. However, hypermarkets carry a larger proportion of food items than do supercenters and have a greater emphasis on perishables—produce, meat, fish, and bakery items. Supercenters, in contrast, have a larger percentage of nonfood items and focus more on dry groceries, such as breakfast cereal and canned goods, instead of fresh items. Hypermarkets also typically stock fewer SKUs than do supercenters— between 40,000 and 60,000 items. The world's second-largest retailer, Carrefour, operates hypermarkets, but none in the United States.

Both supercenters and hypermarkets face challenges in finding locations for new **big-box** (large, limited-service) **stores**. Although Brazil and China are promising emerging markets, many others are shrinking. In Europe and Japan, land for building large stores is limited and expensive.[26] New supercenters and hypermarkets in these areas often have to be multistory, which increases operating costs and reduces shopper convenience. Furthermore, some countries place restrictions on the size of new retail outlets. In the United States, there has been a backlash against large retail stores, particularly Walmart outlets. These opposing sentiments are based on local views that big-box stores drive local retailers out of business, offer low wages, provide nonunion jobs, have unfair labor practices, threaten U.S. workers through their purchase of imported merchandise, and cause excessive automobile and delivery truck traffic.

Warehouse Clubs

Warehouse clubs are retailers that offer a limited and irregular assortment of food and general merchandise with little service at low prices for ultimate consumers and small businesses. The largest warehouse club chains are Costco, Sam's Club (Walmart), and BJ's Wholesale Club (operating only on the East Coast of the United States). Customers are attracted to these stores because they can stock up on large packs of basics like paper towels, large-sized packaged groceries like a quart of ketchup, best-selling books and CDs, fresh meat and produce, and an unpredictable assortment of upscale merchandise and services at low prices. For example, at Costco you can buy a 5-carat diamond ring for $99,999.99 with an appraised value of $153,450. Heavy food sampling adds to the shopping experience.

Warehouse clubs like Costco are popular because they offer an unpredictable assortment of upscale merchandise at low prices.

© Justin Sullivan/Getty Images

Warehouse clubs are large (100,000 to 150,000 square feet) and typically located in low-rent districts. They have simple interiors and concrete floors. Aisles are wide so that forklifts can pick up pallets of merchandise and arrange them on the selling floor. Little service is offered. Warehouse clubs can offer low prices because they use low-cost locations, have inexpensive store designs, and offer little customer service; they further keep inventory holding costs low by carrying a limited assortment of fast-selling items. In addition, they buy merchandise opportunistically. For example, if Hewlett-Packard is introducing new models of its printers, warehouse clubs will buy the inventory of the older models at a significant discount and then offer them for sale until the inventory is depleted.

Warehouse clubs accordingly have had substantial influences on retailing and its structure. For example, the four biggest warehouse retailers accounted for approximately 8 percent of 2012 retail sales. That's nearly twice as much as e-commerce represented. Furthermore, between 1992 and 2013, warehouse club sales increased from $40 billion to $420 billion. The growth of warehouse clubs appears largely dependent on demand in more heavily populated areas, as the store locations move from distant suburbs into more city centers.[27]

Most warehouse clubs have two types of members: wholesale members who own small businesses and individual members who purchase for their own use. For example, many small restaurants are wholesale customers that buy their supplies, food ingredients, and desserts from a warehouse club rather than from food distributors. To cater to their business customers, warehouse clubs sell food items in very large containers and packages—sizes that also appeal to larger families. Typically, members pay an annual fee of around $50, which amounts to significant additional income for the chains.

Convenience Stores

Convenience stores provide a limited variety and assortment of merchandise at a convenient location in 3,000- to 5,000-square-foot stores with speedy checkout. Convenience stores enable consumers to make purchases quickly, without having to search through a large store and wait in a long checkout line. More than half the items bought are consumed within 30 minutes of purchase. 7-Eleven is the largest convenience store chain in North America, with more than 8,000 locations.[28] This type of retailer is the modern version of the neighborhood mom-and-pop grocery or general store.

Convenience stores like 7-Eleven provide a limited variety and assortment of merchandise at a convenient location in 3,000- to 5,000-square-foot stores with speedy checkout.

© Tim Boyle/Getty Images

Convenience stores generally charge higher prices than supermarkets for similar products like milk, eggs, and bread. These products once represented the majority of their sales, but now the majority of sales come from lower-profit products, such as gasoline and cigarettes, putting a strain on their profits.

Convenience stores also face increased competition from other formats. Supercenter and supermarket chains are attempting to appeal to customers by offering gasoline and tying gasoline sales to their frequent-shopper programs. For example, shoppers who spend at least $50 and swipe their Giant Eagle Advantage Card at any GetGo, Market District, Giant Eagle, or Giant Eagle Express location receive a 10-cent discount per gallon on their next fill-up.[29] Drugstores and full-line discount stores also have easily accessible areas of their stores filled with convenience store merchandise.

In response to these competitive pressures, convenience stores are taking steps to decrease their dependency on gasoline sales, tailor assortments to local markets, offer more fresh options, and make their stores even more convenient to shop. For example, to get gasoline customers to spend more on other merchandise and services, convenience stores are offering more food options that appeal to on-the-go consumers, especially women and young adults.[30] Finally, convenience stores are adding new services, such as financial service kiosks that give customers the opportunity to cash checks, pay bills, and buy prepaid telephone minutes, theater tickets, and gift cards.

To increase convenience, convenience stores are opening smaller stores close to where consumers shop and work. For example, 7-Eleven has stores in airports, office buildings, and schools. Easy access, storefront parking, and quick in-and-out access are key benefits offered by convenience stores. They also are exploring the use of technology to increase shopping convenience. Sheetz, a Pennsylvania-based convenience store chain, has touch-screen "Made-to-Order" kiosks at which customers can order customized deli sandwiches, wraps, salads, subs, and nachos while pumping gasoline.[31]

Online Grocery Retailers

Time-poor customers are willing to pay more to access options for ordering groceries online and having them delivered (e.g., for a gallon of organic milk, Safeway charges $5.99, and the delivery service Instacart charges $7.39). As a result, in the past five years, annual online sales of groceries have grown by 14.1 percent.[32] The set of retailers providing online capabilities continues to expand, with Amazon and Walmart joining the long-standing, online-only retailers such as Peapod and FreshDirect.[33] Furthermore, these retailers are joined by companies seeking to add value to the grocery channel by providing delivery services. That is, companies such as Instacart, Shipt, Postmates, and Google's delivery arm promise to allow customers to place online orders for items with their preferred grocers.[34]

Still, approximately 30 percent of the online orders placed with grocery retailers involve nonfood items, like paper products or cleaning items. In contrast, sales in stores generally feature only around 14 percent nonfood items. Consumers thus rely on online grocers for lower-profit-margin nonperishable items, rather than higher-margin fresh fruit or meats. As a result, slim margins continue to be a problem for both retailers and delivery services. For example, Instacart earns a profit only if the order is for more than around $68. Finally, even as customers call for grocery delivery services, and the industry has grown from 1.9 percent to 2.9 percent of total grocery sales, online grocery remains much smaller than other online retailing. Part of the reason may be the limited availability of grocery delivery services, which thus far remain accessible mainly in large cities. Delivery costs are also a factor even as the task is outsourced to relatively low-cost individual private contractors. This factor also might reflect a barrier to the industry's growth: Delivering perishable groceries to many customers is a lot easier and more feasible in dense, urban settings than across vast, rural distances.

Retailing View 2.2 describes how one online grocery retailer takes a specific approach to maintain its appeal and profitability.

2.2 RETAILING VIEW How FreshDirect Figures Out How and When Customers Order

FreshDirect first started delivering groceries to customers in the northeastern United States in 2002, with the notion that modern technology could facilitate "farm-to-table" shopping for customers. Underlying its appeal is the recognition that it can be hard for consumers to find and source a variety of high-quality groceries. Who has time to stop at the butcher shop for grass-fed beef, the bakery for fresh bread, and the farmer's market for vegetables, then run by the superstore for bulk packages of laundry detergent? Working with more than 60 local providers, FreshDirect has created an online resource for consumers in Philadelphia, Connecticut, New Jersey, and New York to get all these items, in one place.

But that "place" actually differs a little bit, even if it always involves the Internet. That is, the device that customers use makes a big difference in the items they order. Accordingly, FreshDirect acknowledges its need to understand where, when, and through which channels its customers are shopping during each interaction with the company.

As a simple example, the grocery delivery service has determined that when people place orders on Saturdays or Sundays, they are usually doing so on their mobile devices. During the workweek, though, they largely use computers, suggesting that they are ordering from their desks during their lunch breaks or in the midst of their workday. This difference means that the mobile site could promote more products that appeal to lazy weekend activities. But the traditional website likely needs to be quick, so that consumers can place their orders before their supervisors notice that they are on a shopping site during work hours.

The company's chief consumer officer offers a range of scenarios in which omnichannel and multidevice capabilities are critical for the retailer. In particular, she highlights questions about when and where consumers prefer to find recipes, as well as how they react to potential weather hazards, noting, "Let's say snow is coming. We don't know exactly which day. We need to figure out when's the last time we can fulfill orders this week. Are we going to need to shut down? We know people are panicked and they want their food. So we have to figure out where they are at that moment. Do we need to give a snow message on their mobile devices? And then coordinate it with what's on the desktop?"

As people's time spent interacting with online and mobile content increases, trends suggest that, conversely, their interactions with each individual seller are getting shorter. Online grocery retailers like FreshDirect have just a moment to

© Mario Tama/Getty Images

FreshDirect adjusts its online messages because customers' orders are different depending on the appliance they are using, as well as where, when, and through which channel they are shopping.

appeal to these quick-moving shoppers, and a key element of that appeal is understanding how they use their various devices in specific ways.

Sources: FreshDirect, "About Us," https://www.freshdirect.com/browse. jsp?id=about_overview&trk=snav; David Orgel, "FreshDirect Targets Multi-Device Strategies," *Supermarket News*, January 20, 2016.

GENERAL MERCHANDISE RETAILERS

LO 2-3

Identify the various types of general merchandise retailers.

The major types of general merchandise retailers are department stores, full-line discount stores, specialty stores, drugstores, category specialists, extreme-value retailers, off-price retailers, and outlet stores. Exhibit 2–5 summarizes the characteristics of general merchandise retailers that sell through stores.

EXHIBIT 2–5   Characteristics of General Merchandise Retailers

Type	Variety	Assortment	Service	Prices	Size (000 sq. ft.)	SKUs (000)	Location
Department stores	Broad	Deep to average	Average to high	Average to high	100–200	100	Regional malls
Discount stores	Broad	Average to shallow	Low	Low	60–80	30	Stand-alone, power strip centers
Category specialists	Narrow	Very deep	Low to high	Low	50–100	20–40	Stand-alone, power strip centers
Specialty stores	Narrow	Deep	High	High	4–12	5	Regional malls
Home improvement centers	Narrow	Very deep	Low to high	Low	80–120	20–40	Stand-alone, power strip centers
Drugstores	Narrow	Very deep	Average	Average to high	3–15	10–20	Stand-alone, strip centers
Off-price stores	Average	Deep but varying	Low	Low	20–30	50	Outlet malls
Extreme-value retailers	Average	Average and varying	Low	Low	7–15	3–4	Urban, strip

Department Stores

Department stores are retailers that carry a broad variety and deep assortment, offer customer services, and organize their stores into distinct departments for displaying merchandise. The largest department store chains in the United States include Sears, Macy's, Kohl's, JCPenney, and Nordstrom.[35]

Traditionally, department stores attracted customers by offering a pleasing ambience, attentive service, and a wide variety of merchandise under one roof. They sold both **soft goods** (nondurable or consumable goods that have a shorter life span, such as cosmetics, clothing, and bedding) and **hard goods**, also known as **durable goods** (manufactured items that are expected to last several years, such as appliances, furniture, and consumer electronics). But now, most department stores focus almost exclusively on soft goods. The major departments are women's, men's, and children's apparel; home furnishings; cosmetics; kitchenware; and small appliances. Each department within the store has a specific selling space allocated to it, as well as salespeople to assist customers. The department store often resembles a collection of specialty shops.

Department store chains can be categorized into three tiers. The first tier includes upscale, high-fashion chains with exclusive designer merchandise and excellent customer service, such as Neiman Marcus, Bloomingdale's (part of Macy's Inc.), Nordstrom, and Saks Fifth Avenue (part of Saks Inc.). Macy's and Dillards are in the second tier of traditional department stores, in which retailers sell more modestly priced merchandise with less customer service. The value-oriented third tier—Sears, JCPenney, and Kohl's—caters to more price-conscious consumers.

Department stores account for some of retailing's most cherished traditions—special events and parades (Macy's Thanksgiving parade in New York City), Santa Claus lands, and holiday decorations. But many consumers question the benefits and costs of shopping at department stores. Department stores are not as convenient as discount stores, such as Target, because they are located in large regional malls rather than local neighborhoods. JCPenney and Sears thus are following Kohl's lead by opening stores in nonmall locations.

To deal with their eroding market share, department stores are (1) increasing the amount of exclusive merchandise they sell, (2) increasing their use of private-label merchandise, and (3) expanding their omnichannel presence.

- *Increase exclusive merchandise.* To differentiate their merchandise offerings and strengthen their image, department stores are aggressively seeking **exclusive brands** in which national brand vendors sell them merchandise that is not available elsewhere. Ralph Lauren designed a line of casual apparel exclusively for JCPenney

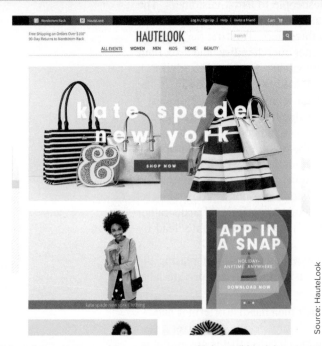

Nordstrom has a strong omnichannel presence with its traditional department stores (top), outlet Nordstrom Rack stores (middle), and its HauteLook Internet site (bottom).

called American Living. Furthermore, clothing is not the only category with exclusive lines: Customers looking for dinnerware collections can go to Macy's and get the Martha Stewart line or find the Rachael Ray collection at Sears.[36]

- *Increase private-label merchandise.* Department stores are placing more emphasis on developing their own **private-label brands**, or **store brands**. These items are developed and marketed by the retailer, available only in its stores. Macy's has been very successful in developing a strong image for its brands, including Alfani (women's fashion), Hotel Collection (luxury fabrics), and Tools of the Trade (housewares).[37]

- *Expand omnichannel and social media presence.* Finally, like most retailers, most department stores have become active participants in omnichannel retailing. At Macy's and Nordstrom, customers can buy or reserve products online and then pick them up at the store. Customers can also return online purchases to stores. At Macy's and JCPenney, sales associates can order out-of-stock merchandise online via their point-of-sale (POS) terminals and have it delivered directly to the customer. As Retailing View 2.3 describes, Macy's may be one of the most connected companies in the world.

Despite some suggestions that the era of the department store has come to an end, several retailers have introduced innovative ideas to appeal better to their existing target markets, as well as attract young consumers who tend to show preferences for smaller, specialty stores. As we discuss subsequently, Nordstrom has transformed its image as a high-end destination for only the wealthiest of shoppers by integrating an online flash sale site, HauteLook. There, shoppers can find famous name brands for substantially discounted prices. To make the varied, discounted merchandise available for hands-on buyers too, Nordstrom maintains its Rack stores, as an off-price arm of its retail empire. The number of Nordstrom Rack stores continues to

RETAILING VIEW   Making Macy's Meaningful in Multiple Channels   2.3

Faced with some surprising sales declines and threats to its status as the leading department store brand, Macy's has developed a strategy to leverage both its existing advantages and some new retail options. In particular, in its efforts to establish itself as an omnichannel retailer, the traditional department store is expanding its already strong online presence and simultaneously adopting some innovative in-store technologies.

For example, with large Look Book displays, consumers interact with a sort of digital catalog in the store, finding fashionable ideas, ways to extend their existing wardrobes, and images from forward-thinking fashion icons. Touching the screen enables them to check the availability of various colors and sizes, as well as receive more detailed information about items that are of interest. The POP (point-of-purchase) terminals in Macy's stores similarly are touch screens that provide extensive inventory information, though they are more functional than fashionable. These smaller kiosks indicate which colors and styles are available, as well as identifying which items have prompted the most Facebook likes or customer favorite rankings.

When it comes time to pay, Macy's is working to make the process easier and quicker by installing Apple Pay capabilities throughout its network of stores. As one of the earliest adopters of this new technology, Macy's is seeking to appeal to Apple fans who love to use their iPhones for nearly everything. With Macy's Wallet and the Shopkick app, customers have two methods to receive coupons and special offers. Once downloaded, the app requires people to opt in, and then, as they enter a Macy's store, reminds them to open it so that they can receive personalized notifications. It tracks their movements through the store, so that a shopper in the outerwear department receives a discount offer on gloves rather than cosmetics, for example. The Macy's Wallet program is similar, except that it is unique to this retailer and links to consumers' loyalty cards. A shopper who has earned a percentage-off offer, on the basis of her or his prior purchases, no longer needs to worry about forgetting the paper coupon at home.

Finally, with the recognition that modern consumers are happy to stay put and have products delivered to their doors, Macy's has sought ways to enhance its delivery systems and move beyond simple, centralized distribution methods. For example, workers in some stores receive online orders, pick the necessary items from store shelves, package them, and send them off to customers. However, the time demands associated with these tasks create significant concerns about efficiency; store clerks cannot both help customers in the store and pack items for shipping during the same shift. Therefore, Macy's assigned the order fulfillment process to merchandising teams that restock the stores before they open. It also uses a crowdsourced delivery service called Deliv, thus offering customers the option of making their purchases in the store, then having them delivered to their homes, so they no longer have to lug heavy packages through the mall.

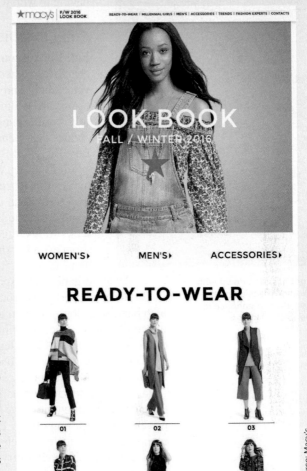

Source: Macy's

Macy's customers interact with large Look Book displays, which is a sort of digital catalog in the store, finding fashionable ideas, ways to extend their existing wardrobes, and images from forward-thinking fashion icons.

However, according to one analyst, the inventory in Macy's stores is often messy and seemingly overstocked, without sufficient on-duty personnel to keep the experience moving along nicely. Thus it might need to reorient its focus more on people and less on technology to maintain its high level of customer experience. To remain competitive, Macy's needs to leverage its multiple channels and exploit its omnichannel potential to its full extent.

Sources: Alexander Coolidge, "Hate Checkout Lines? Macy's Can Help," *Cincinnati Inquirer*, October 3, 2014; Ken Lonyai, "Rivals Need to Up Customer Experiences to Compete with Amazon," *RetailWire*, January 12, 2016; Shelly Banjo, Suzanne Kapner, and Paul Ziobro, "Retailers Bet on 'Omnichannel' Strategy to Fill Online Orders from Store Shelves," *The Wall Street Journal*, December 18, 2014.

Target has teamed up with well-known designers like Marimekko to enhance its "cheap chic" image.

grow. Furthermore, Nordstrom has created strong links between these two "alternative" channels, such that consumers who order the wrong size on HauteLook can return the products to Nordstrom Rack without having to worry about shipping it back.[38]

Full-Line Discount Stores

Full-line discount stores are retailers that offer a broad variety of merchandise, limited service, and low prices. Discount stores offer both private labels and national brands. The largest full-line discount store chains are Walmart, Target, and Kmart (Sears Holding). However, these full-line discount stores confront intense competition from category specialists that focus on a single category of merchandise, such as Staples, Best Buy, Bed Bath & Beyond, Sports Authority, and Lowe's.

In response, Walmart has taken several routes. First, it has converted many of its discount stores into supercenters,[39] which are more efficient than traditional discount stores because of the economies of scale that result from the high traffic generated by the food offering. Second, it seeks to leverage its existing capabilities in online settings and offer shoppers a hybrid option that enables them to order online and pick up items in stores.[40] Third, it is expanding its product range, including more organic and responsibly produced items on its store shelves.[41]

Target has experienced considerable growth because its stores offer fashionable merchandise at low prices in a pleasant shopping environment. It has developed an image of "cheap chic," continuously offering limited-edition exclusive apparel and cosmetic lines. In its GO International campaign, the retailer has teamed with such well-known designers as Missoni, Stefani, Harajuku Mini, Marimekko, Albertus Swanepoel, and Josie Natori.[42]

In contrast, Sears—and its Kmart brand—has struggled a bit in recent years and therefore is seeking innovative and unusual solutions. For example, it has expanded its private-label offerings (e.g., DieHard, Kenmore, Craftsman) of smart-technology-enabled products, including televisions, refrigerators, tool chests, and garage door openers.[43] But many observers worry about the long-term survival of this discount chain.[44]

Category Specialists

Category specialists are big-box stores that offer a deep assortment but narrow variety of merchandise. Exhibit 2–6 lists some of the largest category specialists in the United States.

Most category specialists predominantly use a self-service approach, but they offer assistance to customers in some areas of the stores. For example, Staples stores have a warehouse atmosphere, with cartons of copy paper stacked on pallets, plus equipment in boxes on shelves. But in some departments, such as computers and other high-tech products, it provides salespeople in the display area to answer questions and make

EXHIBIT 2–6
Category Specialists

Apparel/Shoes/Accessories	Furniture	Sporting Goods	Office Supply
DSW	IKEA	Bass Pro Shops Outdoor World	Office Depot
Men's Wearhouse	Pier 1	Cabela's	Staples
Books	**Home**	Dick's Sporting Goods	**Pet Supplies**
Barnes & Noble	Bed Bath & Beyond	Golfsmith	Petco
Consumer Electronics	The Container Store	L.L.Bean	PetSmart
Best Buy	World Market	REI	**Musical Instruments**
Crafts	**Home Improvement**	**Toys**	Guitar Center
Michaels	Home Depot	Toys "R" Us	
	Lowe's		

suggestions. Bass Pro Shops Outdoor World is a category specialist offering merchandise for outdoor recreational activities. The stores offer everything a person needs for hunting and fishing—from 27-cent plastic bait to boats and recreational vehicles costing $45,000. Sales associates are knowledgeable outdoors people. Each is hired for a particular department that matches that person's expertise. All private-branded products are field-tested by Bass Pro Shops's professional teams: the Redhead Pro Hunting Team and Tracker Pro Fishing Team.

By offering a complete assortment in a category, category specialists can

Category specialists, like Staples, offer a deep assortment of merchandise at low prices.

"kill" a category of merchandise for other retailers and thus are frequently called **category killers**. Using their category dominance and buying power, they buy products at low prices and are ensured of supply when items are scarce. Department stores and full-line discount stores located near category specialists often have to reduce their offerings in the category because consumers are drawn to the deep assortment and competitive prices at the category killer.

Although category specialists compete with other types of retailers, competition between them is intense. Competing category specialists such as Lowe's and Home Depot, or Staples and Office Depot, have difficulty differentiating themselves on most of the elements of their retail mixes. They all provide similar assortments because they have similar access to national brands, and they all provide a similar level of service. Primarily, then, they compete on price and location. Some category specialists are also experiencing intense competition from warehouse clubs like Sam's Club and Costco.

Therefore, many of them are attempting to differentiate themselves with customer service. For example, Home Depot and Lowe's hire experienced builders as sales associates to help customers with electrical and plumbing repairs. They also provide classes to train home owners in tiling, painting, and other tasks to give shoppers the confidence to tackle their do-it-yourself (DIY) projects on their own. Home Depot offers an integrated line of Martha Stewart brand products and an expanded inventory mix that includes more décor and convenience items for the household. The idea is that a trip to Home Depot can be a family event, because it carries items for parents of either gender, as well as small projects for kids.[45] Besides beefing up its sales associates' training to help customers purchase high-tech products like computers and printers, Staples has implemented "Easy Tech" in its stores to help people with computer and related problems and has installed Staples Copy and Print shops to compete with FedEx Office.

Specialty Stores

Specialty stores concentrate on a limited number of complementary merchandise categories and provide a high level of service. Exhibit 2–7 lists some of the largest specialty store chains.

Specialty stores tailor their retail strategy toward very specific market segments by offering a deep assortment but narrow variety, and sales associate expertise. Victoria's Secret is the leading specialty retailer of lingerie and beauty products in the United States. Using a multipronged location strategy that includes malls, lifestyle centers, and central business districts, the company conveys its message using supermodels and world-famous runway shows.[46]

EXHIBIT 2–7
Specialty Store Retailers

Apparel	Electronics/Software	Jewelry	GNC
Abercrombie & Fitch	Apple	Blue Nile	Kiehl's
Brooks Brothers	Ascend Acoustics	Tiffany & Co.	M.A.C.
The Buckle	Brookstone	Zales	MakeupMania.com
Forever 21	Crutchfield		Sephora
The Gap	GameStop	**Optical**	
H&M	Newegg	LensCrafters	**Shoes**
Indochino.com	Radio Shack	1-800 Contacts	ALDO
J.Crew	Tiger Direct	Pearle Vision	Allen Edmonds
Ralph Lauren		Sunglass Hut	FootLocker
Threadless	**Housewares**		Nine West
Urban Outfitters	Crate & Barrel	**Health/Beauty**	Steve Madden
Victoria's Secret	Pottery Barn	Aveda	The Walking Company
Zara	Sur la Table	Bath & Body Works	
	Williams-Sonoma	The Body Shop	Zappos

Sephora, France's leading perfume and cosmetic chain—a division of luxury-goods conglomerate LVMH (Louis Vuitton-Moet Hennessy)—is another example of an innovative specialty store concept. Sephora provides a cosmetics and perfume specialty store offering a deep assortment in a self-service format. It also maintains separate stores-within-stores at JCPenney. The approximately 15,000 SKUs and 200 brands, including its own private-label brand, are grouped by product category instead of by brand like in department stores, with brands displayed alphabetically so customers can locate them easily. Customers are free to shop and experiment on their own. Sampling is encouraged. Knowledgeable salespeople are available to assist customers. The low-key environment results in customers' spending more time shopping. Retailing View 2.4 examines how Sephora works to appeal to cosmetics consumers.

Specialty retailers have such great appeal that they rank among the most profitable and fastest-growing firms in the world. Apple stores sell a remarkable $4,798 per square foot on average. Lululemon's specialty is far less technical, involving yoga-inspired apparel and accessories, but it keeps opening its specialty stores at a remarkable rate of several per month. These stores earn an average of $1,675 per square foot. In contrast, department stores tend to average less than $200 per square foot.[47]

Many manufacturers, like Levi's, have opened their own specialty stores to keep control of its brand and provide a more complete assortment for its customers.

RETAILING VIEW   How Sephora Has Revolutionized
the Cosmetics Industry

There once was a gap in the cosmetics retail market. Shoppers could grab inexpensive, questionable-quality products at their local drugstore or grocer, or they could visit the high-end counters in department stores to purchase expensive, exclusive cosmetic brands. But that gap has rapidly and effectively been filled by specialty beauty brands such as Sephora. In dedicated stores, usually located conveniently in local shopping centers or malls, Sephora creates in-store experiences that allow consumers to play with the products, ranging from private-label to trendy national brands, inside store designs that are hip and fun.

Such retail options appeal greatly to Millennials, who tend to exhibit little brand loyalty. By visiting a Sephora store, they can review various options without having to visit separate stores or counters. They also can enjoy the potential of finding a unique, cutting-edge product that no one else is wearing; the stores' assortment strategies explicitly seek to stock lesser-known brands and items. This "treasure hunt" experience allows young beauty consumers to have fun in the process. Most of them have watched bloggers apply various makeup styles or read reviews of different products online, so they feel self-sufficient enough to search and try the cosmetics on their own.

As a result of these compelling appeals, Sephora, owned by the luxury French conglomerate LVMH, operates almost 1,800 stores worldwide, 360 of them in North America. JCPenney's agreement with the brand also puts more than 400 Sephora "store-within-a-store" operations in these department store outposts. Sephora's planned "Innovation Lab" will also work to develop new in-store and e-commerce technologies to ensure its continued growth.

For example, using in-store signage, Sephora promotes its loyalty program and mobile app, and new functions in the mobile app make it easier for consumers to shop both in-store and online. The Sephora To Go app makes the

Sephora creates in-store experiences that allow consumers to play with the products, ranging from private-label to trendy national brands, inside store designs that are hip and fun.

online and offline experience as seamless as possible. On the mobile site, customers can automatically create a Beauty Insider account, which loads a bar code that can be scanned at the point of sale to track customer purchases. Sephora also uses Passbook to promote its beauty card and loyalty program.

Thus, the offerings of this specialty retailer are as unique and interesting as the customers it hopes to attract to its stores and mobile and online channels.

Sources: Sarah Halzack, "The Sephora Effect: How the Cosmetics Retailer Transformed the Beauty Industry," *Washington Post,* March 9, 2015; Lauren Johnson, "Sephora Magnifies Mobile Ambitions via In-Store Signage, Updated App," *Mobile Commerce Daily,* August 23, 2013; Alix Strauss, "Sephora and the Upstarts," *The New York Times,* April 30, 2014.

Charming Charlie stores are not quite as well known as the preceding brands, but the small company's success confirms the appeal of specialty retailers. In just over a decade years, the accessories and jewelry chain has grown to more than 300 stores, spread over 42 U.S. states, 2 Canadian locations, and 2 stores in the United Arab Emirates. Its rapid growth is well matched by its influence: It was one of the first retailers to group merchandise by color instead of category. Furthermore, it works to maintain affordable prices ranging from less than $5 to no more than $50. That is, this specialty store specializes in helping customers update their wardrobes with new pieces, rather than forcing them to start all over again.[48]

In addition, many manufacturers have opened their own specialty stores. Consider, for instance, Levi's (jeans and casual apparel), Godiva (chocolate), Cole Haan (shoes and accessories), Lacoste (apparel), Coach (purses and leather accessories), Tumi (luggage), Wolford (intimate apparel), Lucky Brand (jeans and casual apparel), Samsonite (luggage), and Polo/Ralph Lauren (apparel and home). Tired of being at the mercy of retailers to purchase and merchandise their products, these manufacturers and specialty retailers can control their own destiny by operating their own stores.

Another growing specialty store sector is the resale store. **Resale stores** are retailers that sell secondhand or used merchandise. A special type of resale store is the **thrift store**, where merchandise is donated and proceeds go to charity. Another type of resale store is the **consignment shop**, a store that accepts used merchandise from people and pays them after it is sold. Resale stores earn national revenues of approximately $16 billion. They also have enjoyed stable growth rates of around 7 percent for the past few years.[49] Although the ambience of resale stores traditionally has been less appealing than that of other clothing or housewares retailers, the remarkable prices for used merchandise draws in customers.

Today, many resale stores also have increased their value by making their shopping space more pleasant and increasing levels of service.[50] With their lower cost of merchandise (in that they pay a relatively low price or take consigned goods), resale stores are moving into storefronts in higher-end locations that have been abandoned by traditional retailers.[51]

Perhaps the best-known and most widely expanded thrift shop is Goodwill Industries. In addition to its retail outlets, Goodwill runs an extensive job training and placement division, such that customers shopping at these outlets get a warm glow from knowing that their purchases help others. Unlike most other resale stores, Goodwill accepts all goods. The old stereotype of a cluttered, dark, odd-smelling Goodwill store has changed. The company has revamped and updated stores nationwide. Local stores seek to meet local needs, such that the New England–area Goodwill stores host annual bridal dress sales, and the Suncoast division in Florida maintains a catering department.[52]

Drugstores

Drugstores are specialty stores that concentrate on health and beauty care (HBC) products. Many drugstores have steadily increased the space devoted to cosmetics, but prescription pharmaceuticals still represent a substantial and growing portion of drugstore sales.[53]

The largest drugstore chains in the United States are CVS and Walgreens, Boots.[54] They are also virtually the only drugstore chains, due to increased concentration that has resulted from a string of mergers and acquisitions. For instance, CVS acquired Longs, Sav-On, and Osco (as well as Caremark, which manages the prescription drug aspect for many insurance plans). Walgreens acquired the British pharmacy chain Boots, and then the merged firm purchased Rite Aid, another prominent competitor.[55]

Drugstores face competition from pharmacies in discount stores and some food retailers and from pressure to reduce health care costs. In response, the major drugstore chains are offering a wider assortment of merchandise, including more frequently purchased food items, as well as services, such as the convenience of drive-through windows and curbside pickup for prescriptions, in-store medical clinics, and even makeovers and spa treatments.[56]

Walgreens hosts a café in its Chicago flagship store, where customers waiting to pick up a prescription can enjoy fresh coffee, breads, and pastries; munch on sushi or sandwiches; or visit the juice bar for a healthy smoothie or a nostalgic chocolate malted milkshake. But if they stop by later in the day, shoppers might prefer to browse the store's stock of 700 fine wines, artisanal cheeses, and gourmet chocolates.[57]

Although drugstores thus offer major advantages, especially in terms of convenience, they suffer from a price comparison when it comes to their grocery merchandise. A recent study indicated that the same selection of goods that cost $144.65 at a supermarket would run customers $168.96 at a nearby drugstore.[58]

Extreme-Value Retailers

Extreme-value retailers, also called **dollar stores**, are small discount stores that offer a broad variety but shallow assortment of household goods, health and beauty care (HBC) products, and groceries. The largest extreme-value retailers are Dollar General and Dollar Tree (which purchased the Family Dollar chain).[59] As noted in the discussion of

© Daniel Acker/Bloomberg/Getty Images

Dollar General is an extreme-value retailer that offers a broad variety but shallow assortment of household goods, health and beauty care products, and groceries.

trends in food retailing, these stores have been expanding their assortments to include more private-label options, food, tobacco, and impulse buys such as candy, magazines, and gift cards. Some extreme-value retailers, such as Dollar General, are adding refrigerated coolers and expanding their food offerings so that they can be known as the best destination store for a greater variety of household necessities. As a result, this retail model continues to attract significantly increasing numbers of shopper visits.[60]

Extreme-value retailers primarily target low-income consumers. These customers want well-known brands but cannot afford to buy the large-sized packages offered by full-line discount stores or warehouse clubs. Vendors such as Procter & Gamble often create special, smaller packages for extreme-value retailers. Because these stores appeal to low-income consumers, are located where they live, and have expanded their assortments while keeping their unit prices low, they have cut into other retailers' businesses, including Walmart.

Despite some of these chains' names, few just sell merchandise for a dollar. That is, their names imply a good value but do not limit customers to an arbitrary dollar price point. Dollar General sells merchandise for up to $20. Although Dollar Tree experimented with selling merchandise for more than a dollar, it is back to being a dollar purist.[61]

Off-Price Retailers

Off-price retailers offer an inconsistent assortment of brand-name merchandise at a significant discount off the manufacturer's suggested retail price (MSRP). America's largest off-price retail chains are TJX Companies (which operates TJ Maxx, Marshalls, Winners [Canada], HomeGoods, HomeSense [Canada]), Ross Stores, Burlington Coat Factory, Big Lots, and Overstock.com.

Off-price retailers are able to sell brand-name and even designer-label merchandise at 20 to 60 percent lower than the manufacturer's suggested retail price because of their unique buying and merchandising practices. Much of the merchandise is bought opportunistically from manufacturers that have overruns, canceled orders, forecasting mistakes causing excess inventory, closeouts, and irregulars. They also buy excess inventory from other retailers. **Closeouts** are end-of-season merchandise that will not be used in following seasons. **Irregulars** are merchandise with minor mistakes in construction. Off-price retailers can buy at low prices because they do not ask suppliers

Overstock.com is the largest Internet off-price retailer.

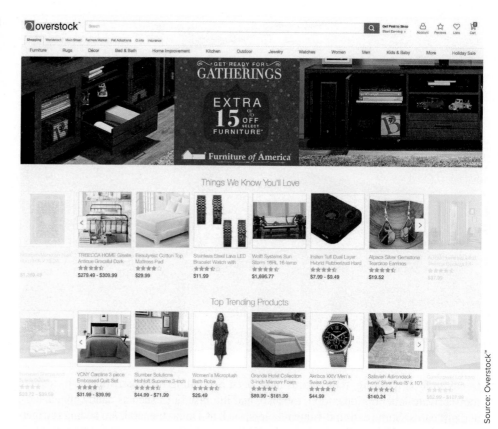

for advertising allowances, return privileges, markdown adjustments, or delayed payments. (These terms and conditions for buying merchandise are detailed in Chapter 13.)

Due to this opportunistic buying, customers cannot be confident that the same type of merchandise will be in stock each time they visit the store. Different bargains will be available on each visit. For many off-price shoppers, inconsistency is exactly why they like to go there. They enjoy hunting for hidden treasures. To improve their offerings' consistency, some off-price retailers complement their opportunistically bought merchandise with merchandise purchased at regular wholesale prices. Although not well known because few vendors to off-price retailers want to advertise their presence, the CEO of TJX asserts that the vast majority of merchandise in its stores is same-season items, purchased directly from manufacturers.[62] She also claims less than 5 percent of TJX merchandise is irregular.

A special type of off-price retailer is the outlet store. **Outlet stores** are off-price retailers owned by manufacturers or retailers. Those owned by manufacturers are also referred to as **factory outlets**. Manufacturers view outlet stores as an opportunity to improve their revenues from irregulars, production overruns, and merchandise returned by retailers. Others view it as simply another channel in which to sell their merchandise. Retailers with strong brand names such as Saks Fifth Avenue (Saks Fifth Avenue's Off 5th) and Williams-Sonoma operate outlet stores too. By selling excess merchandise in outlet stores rather than at markdown prices in their primary stores, these department and specialty store chains can maintain an image of offering desirable merchandise at full price.[63] For some retailers, their outlet stores are the wave of the future. Nordstrom thus has shifted gears, such that it maintains more Nordstrom Rack stores (around 200 in North America) than regular Nordstrom department stores (121 in the same area).[64] However, outlet stores can have an adverse effect on profits because they shift sales from full-price stores to the lower-priced outlets.

An online twist to off-price retailing comes from **flash sale sites** such as Gilt, Rue La La, and HauteLook. These sites send e-mails to registered members announcing the unique deals available for a limited, specific time. Although many flash sale sites started as independent operations, they have largely merged with existing department store retailers. For example, Gilt Groupe is now owned by Saks Fifth Avenue. Nordstrom owns Haute Look, and it has linked its nordstromrack.com site with the flash sale site.[65] Thus the flash sale sites provide an alternative outlet channel for department store retailers, yet they constitute a separate format and access point for consumers.

SERVICE RETAILING

The retail firms discussed in the previous sections sell products to consumers. However, **service retailers**, or firms that primarily sell services rather than merchandise, are a large and growing part of the retail industry. Consider a typical Saturday: After a bagel and cup of coffee at a nearby Einstein Bros. Bagels, you go to the Laundromat to wash and dry your clothes, drop off a suit at a dry cleaner, leave your computer to be serviced by the Geek Squad at Best Buy, and make your way to Jiffy Lube to have your car's oil changed. In a hurry, you drive through a Taco Bell so that you can eat lunch quickly and not be late for your 1:00 P.M. haircut. By midafternoon, you're ready for a workout at your health club. After stopping at home to change your clothes and meet the cleaning service that you hired through Amazon's online referral site to spiffy up your apartment, you're off to dinner, a movie, and finally clubbing with a friend. You end your day having interacted with a dozen different service retailers.

LO 2-4
Explain the differences between service and merchandise retailers.

Several trends suggest considerable future growth in service retailing. For example, the aging population will increase demand for health care services. Younger people are also spending more time and money on health and fitness. Busy parents in two-income families are willing to pay to have their homes cleaned, lawns maintained, clothes washed and pressed, and meals prepared so that they can spend more time with their families.

Exhibit 2–8 shows the wide variety of services, along with some national companies that provide these services. These companies are retailers because they sell goods

EXHIBIT 2–8
Service Retailers

Type of Service	Service Retail Firms
Airlines	American, Southwest, British Airways, JetBlue
Automobile maintenance and repair	Jiffy Lube, Midas, AAMCO
Automobile rental	Hertz, Avis, Budget, Enterprise
Banks	Citi, Wells Fargo, Bank of America
Child care centers	Kindercare, Gymboree
Dry cleaners	Zoots
Education	Babson College, University of Florida, Princeton Review
Entertainment	Disney World, Six Flags, Chuck E. Cheese, Dave & Busters
Express package delivery	FedEx, UPS, U.S. Postal Service
Fast food	Wendy's, McDonald's, Starbucks
Financial services	Merrill Lynch, Morgan Stanley, American Express, Visa
Fitness	Jazzercise, Bally's Total Fitness, Gold's Gym
Health care	Humana, HCA, Kaiser Permanente
Home maintenance	TruGreen, Mini Maid, Roto-Rooter
Hotels and motels	Hyatt, Sheraton, Marriott, Days Inn
Income tax preparation	H&R Block
Insurance	Allstate, State Farm, GEICO
Internet access/electronic information	Google, Internet Explorer, Mozilla Firefox, Safari
Movie theaters	AMC, Cineplex
Quick-service restaurants	Panera Bread, Red Mango, Pinkberry
Real estate	Century 21, Coldwell Banker
Restaurants	Applebee's, Cheesecake Factory
Truck rentals	U-Haul, Ryder
Video rental	Netflix
Vision centers	LensCrafters, Pearle Vision
Weight loss	Weight Watchers, Jenny Craig, Curves

EXHIBIT 2–9   Continuum of Merchandise and Service Retailers

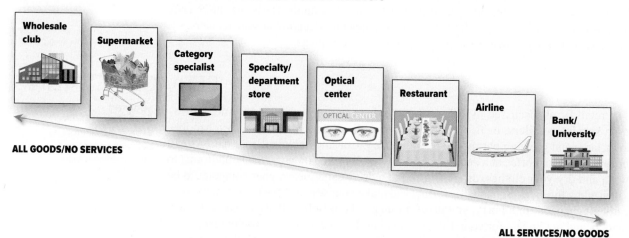

and services to consumers. However, some are not just retailers. For example, airlines, banks, hotels, and insurance and express mail companies sell their services to businesses as well as consumers.

Organizations such as banks, hospitals, health spas, legal clinics, entertainment firms, and universities that offer services to consumers traditionally have not considered themselves retailers. Yet due to increased competition, these organizations are adopting retailing principles to attract customers and satisfy their needs. For example, Zoots is a dry-cleaning chain in the Boston area.[66] Founded by a former Staples executive, Zoots has adopted many retailing best practices: It has convenient locations, and it offers pickup and delivery service. Zoots stores also provide extended hours, are open on weekends, and offer a drop-off option for those who cannot get to the store during operating hours. The stores are bright and clean. Customers can check their order status, schedule a pickup, and provide special instructions using the online MY ZOOTS service. Clerks are taught to welcome customers and acknowledge their presence, especially if there is a line.

Most retailers provide both merchandise and services for their customers. However, the emphasis placed on the merchandise versus the service differs across retail formats, as Exhibit 2–9 shows. On the left side of the exhibit are supermarkets and warehouse clubs. These retail formats consist of self-service stores that offer very few services, except perhaps cashing checks and assisting customers at checkout.

Moving along the continuum from left to right, department and specialty stores provide higher levels of service. In addition to providing assistance from sales associates, they offer services such as gift wrapping, bridal registries, and alterations. Optical centers and restaurants lie somewhere in the middle of the merchandise–service continuum. In addition to selling frames, eyeglasses, and contact lenses, optical centers provide important services like eye examinations and eyeglass fittings. Similarly, restaurants offer food plus a place to eat, music in the background, a pleasant ambience, and table service.

As we move to the right end of the continuum, we encounter retailers whose offerings are primarily services. However, even these retailers have some products associated with the services offered, such as a meal on an airplane or a checkbook at a bank.

Differences between Service and Merchandise Retailers

Four important differences in the nature of the offerings provided by service and merchandise retailers are (1) intangibility, (2) simultaneous production and consumption, (3) perishability, and (4) inconsistency of the offering to customers.

© Quique Garcia/AFP/Getty Images

A service provider like Uber is different than a merchandise retailer because it is intangible, there is simultaneous production and consumption, it is immediately perishable, and the service can be inconsistent from customer to customer.

Intangibility   Services are less tangible than products—customers cannot see or touch them. They are performances or actions rather than objects. For example, health care services cannot be seen or touched by a patient. Intangibility introduces several challenges for service retailers. Because customers cannot touch and feel services, it is difficult for them to evaluate services before they buy them or even after they buy and consume them. Due to the intangibility of their offerings, service retailers often use tangible symbols to inform customers about the quality of their services. For example, lawyers frequently have elegant, carpeted offices with expensive antique furniture. Service retailers also have difficulty evaluating the quality of services they are providing. For example, it can be hard for a law firm to evaluate how well its lawyers are performing their jobs. To determine the quality of their offerings, service retailers often solicit customer evaluations and scrutinize complaints. In addition, online evaluation systems such as Angie's List and Yelp compile reviews from other consumers. The summary reviews give a sense of how well the service provider performs, according to people who have already purchased the service.

Simultaneous Production and Consumption   Products are typically made in a factory, stored and sold by a retailer, and then used by consumers in their homes. Service providers, however, create and deliver the service as the customer is consuming it. For example, when you eat at a restaurant, the meal is prepared and consumed almost at the same time. The simultaneity of production and consumption also creates some special problems for service retailers. First, the customers are present when the service is produced, may even have an opportunity to see it produced, and in some cases may be part of the production process. For instance, customers at Build-A-Bear Workshop make their own teddy bears. Second, other customers consuming the service at the same time can affect the quality of the service provided. For example, an obnoxious passenger next to you on an airplane can make the flight very unpleasant. Third, service retailers often do not get a second chance to satisfy the needs of their customers. Whereas customers can return damaged merchandise to a store, customers who are dissatisfied with services have limited recourse. Thus, it is critical for service retailers to get it right the first time.

Because services are produced and consumed at the same time, it is difficult to reduce costs through mass production. For this reason, most service retailers are small, local firms. Some national service retailers are able to reduce costs by "industrializing" the services they offer. They make substantial investments in equipment and training to provide a uniform service.

Perishability   Services are perishable. They cannot be saved, stored, or resold. Once an airplane takes off with an empty seat, the sale is lost forever. In contrast, merchandise can be held in inventory until a customer is ready to buy it. Due to the perishability of services, service retailing must match supply and demand. Most service retailers have a capacity constraint, and their capacity cannot be changed easily. There are a fixed number of tables in a restaurant, seats in a classroom, beds in a hospital, and electricity that can be generated by a power plant. To increase capacity, service retailers need to make major investments, such as buying more airplanes or building an addition to increase the size of the hospital or restaurant. In addition, demand for service varies considerably over time. Consumers are most likely to fly on airplanes during holidays and the summer, eat in restaurants at lunch- and dinnertime, and use electricity for their homes in the evening rather than earlier in the day.

Service retailers use a variety of programs to match demand and supply. For example, airlines and hotels set lower prices on weekends, when they have excess capacity because businesspeople are not traveling. To achieve more capacity flexibility, health clinics stay open longer during flu season, and tax preparation services are open on weekends during March and April. Restaurants increase staffing on weekends, may not open until dinnertime, and use a reservation system to guarantee service delivery at a specific time. Finally, service retailers attempt to make customers' waiting time more enjoyable. For example, videos and park employees entertain customers while they wait in line at Disney theme parks.

Inconsistency   Products can be produced by machines with very tight quality control, so customers are reasonably assured that all boxes of Cheerios will be identical. But because services are performances produced by people (employees and customers), no two services will be identical. For example, tax accountants can have different knowledge and skills for preparing tax returns. The server at the Olive Garden can be in a bad mood and make your dining experience a disaster. Thus, an important challenge for service retailers is to provide consistent high-quality services. Many factors that determine service quality are beyond the control of retailers; however, service retailers expend considerable time and effort selecting, training, managing, and motivating their service providers.

Service retailing is such an important and growing retail sector that we devote Chapter 17 to the topic.

TYPES OF OWNERSHIP

LO 2-5

Explain the types of ownership for retail firms.

Previous sections of this chapter discussed how retailers may be classified in terms of their retail mix and the merchandise and services they sell. Another way to classify retailers is by their ownership. The major classifications of retail ownership are (1) independent, single-store establishments, (2) corporate chains, and (3) franchising.

Independent, Single-Store Establishments

Retailing is one of the few sectors in most countries in which entrepreneurial activity is extensive. Many retail start-ups are owner-managed, which means management has direct contact with customers and can respond quickly to their needs. Small retailers are also very flexible and can react quickly to market changes and customer needs. They are not bound by the bureaucracies inherent in large retail organizations.[67]

Consider Mackenzi Farquer, who opened her Lockwood shop to sell housewares, clothing, art, gifts, and children's books and clothing, in Queens, New York. The great success of the venture stems largely from Farquer's ability to connect with her customers and her vast knowledge of the local community. Having lived in the area for more than a decade, Farquer also runs the "We Heart Astoria" blog. She maintains constant interactions with customers to learn what they want and how the 1,300-square-foot store can ensure that it stocks décor that will complement the items those customers already have in their homes.[68] She also hosts events to provide added services to patrons, from children's cooking classes to artisanal food markets to the Astoria Art Festival.[69]

Whereas single-store retailers can tailor their offerings to their customers' needs, corporate chains can more effectively negotiate lower prices for merchandise and advertising because of their larger size. Corporate chains can and do invest in sophisticated analytical systems to help them buy and price merchandise. In addition, corporate chains have a broader management base, with people who specialize in specific retail activities. Single-store retailers typically must rely on their owner-managers' capabilities to make the broad range of necessary retail decisions.

To compete against corporate chains, some independent retailers join a **wholesale-sponsored voluntary cooperative group**, which is an organization operated by a wholesaler offering a merchandising program to small, independent retailers on a voluntary basis. The Independent Grocers Alliance (IGA), Tru Serv (supplier to True Value Hardware), and Ace Hardware are wholesale-sponsored voluntary cooperative groups. In addition to engaging in buying, warehousing, and distribution, these groups offer members services such as advice on store design and layout, site selection, bookkeeping and inventory management systems, and employee training programs.

Corporate Retail Chains

A **retail chain** is a company that operates multiple retail units under common ownership and usually has centralized decision making for defining and implementing its strategy. Retail chains can range in size from a drugstore with two stores to retailers with thousands of stores, such as Kroger, Walmart, Best Buy, and Macy's. Some retail chains are divisions of larger corporations or holding companies. For example, the Williams-Sonoma corporation actually consists of five brands: Williams-Sonoma, Pottery Barn, west elm, Mark and Graham, and Rejuvenation. Furthermore, its Pottery Barn branch features the PB teen and Pottery Barn kids lines and its Williams-Sonoma branch features the Williams-Sonoma Home line. Royal Ahold owns 14 retail chains, including Stop and Shop, Giant, and Peapod in the United States and ICA and Albert Heijn in Europe.

Franchising[70]

Franchising is a contractual agreement in which the franchisor (the company) sells the rights to use its business trademark, service mark, or trade name, or another commercial symbol of the company, to the franchisee for a one-time franchise fee and an ongoing royalty fee, typically expressed as a percentage of gross monthly sales. More than 40 percent of all U.S. retail sales are made by franchisees,[71] and this type of retail ownership is growing around the world.[72] Retailing View 2.5 describes how McDonald's is steadily growing its businesses and its franchises in the United States and the rest of the world.

When considering the franchise option, potential franchisees must understand the attractions and drawbacks of buying a franchise versus starting a retail business from scratch. There are many reasons to consider franchise ownership, including the success rate, which results partially from the proven business model that the franchisor offers. Success also results from the unique relationship between the franchisor and the franchisee, in which both parties benefit from the success of the franchisee. To get franchisees off to a good start, most franchisors provide offsite and onsite training, location analysis assistance, advertising, and sometimes a protected territory (i.e., no other franchise may open a store within a certain radius of the first store). Some franchisors even provide financing or offer third-party financing opportunities.

2.5   RETAILING VIEW   McDonald's, the Textbook Franchisor

McDonald's might be one of the largest, most well-known global brands in the world, but it also regards itself as a "collection of small businesses," each run by a unique franchise operator. As the company notes, more than 90 percent of its U.S. locations, and 80 percent worldwide, are owned and maintained by independent businesspeople—around 5,000 of them, mostly living and working in the same local community.

For all its storied history, McDonald's has always relied on franchising as its primary business model. This dedication to franchising in turn has earned McDonald's praise from analysts, who frequently rank it among the best franchise options available. It actively seeks to expand the ranks of female and minority franchisees to ensure diversity throughout the company. It also encourages successful franchisees to purchase additional restaurants, to extend their success and earnings potential. As a result of these activities, consumers can find more than 36,000 restaurants in more than 100 countries around the world. Together, McDonald's and its franchisees employ close to 2 million people.

Currently, purchasing a McDonald's franchise license costs a U.S. operator around $500,000, which functions as a down payment to ensure the stability of the potential franchisee. In turn, McDonald's provides franchisees with extensive training (including visits to the campus of its famous "Hamburger University," located outside Chicago) and ongoing support. For example, it offers advertising and marketing insights. It also assists franchisees with construction and real estate challenges, and it provides operations and purchasing recommendations to help the store owners perform optimally.

In return for these contributions, many franchisees express their close affiliation with and dedication to the company. Some of the fast-food chain's most famous products were innovated by franchise owners, including the Filet 'O Fish, Egg McMuffin, and Big Mac. Considering these close relations, the expansion of the menu to all-day breakfast offerings created some challenges. Some franchise owners complained that the expanded menu would require them to add new equipment to be able to meet demand for additional items simultaneously, as well as hire additional help to cook and serve up the food.

McDonald's has always relied on franchising as its primary business model. More than 90 percent of its U.S. locations, and 80 percent worldwide, are owned and maintained by independent businesspeople—around 5,000 of them, mostly living and working in the same local community.

These expensive investments could cut in to the franchisees' profits, as might the expanded sales of less expensive breakfast items that would replace purchases of lunch and dinner options.

But McDonald's corporate office insists that the move is a smart one, reflecting the company's responsiveness to customer demands. For decades, consumers had been clamoring for all-day breakfast. The press releases surrounding the launch signaled the corporation's expectation that breakfast will be the key to new growth and increased revenues. It has called on those franchisees to trust the move, with the promise that—as they have for years—they will be glad to have hooked up with the golden arches.

Sources: McDonald's, "Franchising," http://www.aboutmcdonalds.com/content/mcd/franchising.html; McDonald's, "Our Business Strategy," http://www.aboutmcdonalds.com/content/mcd/our_company/business-model.html; Hayely Peterson, "McDonald's Franchisees Say All-Day Breakfast Is a Nightmare," *Business Insider*, August 16, 2015; Robert Lara, "The True, Steamy Story of the Egg McMuffin Hockey Puck Breakfast Turns 40," *Adweek*, August 9, 2013.

There are also several drawbacks to franchise ownership. In addition to having to pay money to the franchisor, the franchisee needs financing for start-up costs, including rent or purchase price of office/retail space; modification of the space according to the guidelines of the franchisor (e.g., paint colors, flooring, lighting, layout); signage; opening inventory; and equipment. In addition to incurring the capital costs, the franchisee must adhere to the franchisor's rules and operating guidelines. In many cases, the franchisee is required to purchase operating materials from the franchisor, especially in fast-food franchises that rely on standardized products across franchises for the success of the brand. The franchisor also might require the franchisee to purchase the equipment needed to offer a new product, such as fryers at a McDonald's or beds at a Holiday Inn. The hours of operation and days of the year that the business is allowed to close also may be dictated by the franchisor.

SUMMARY

LO 2-1 **List the different characteristics that define retailers.**

To collect statistics about retailing, the federal government classifies retailers by the type of merchandise and services they sell. But this classification method may not be useful to determine a retailer's major competitors. A more useful approach for understanding the retail marketplace is to classify retailers on the basis of the retail mix, merchandise variety and assortment, services, location, pricing, and promotion decisions they make to attract customers.

LO 2-2 **Categorize the various types of food retailers.**

Food retailing has undergone substantial expansion. Whereas once supermarkets were nearly the only source for food shoppers, today they can choose among traditional supermarkets, hypermarkets or superstores, limited-assortment markets, warehouse clubs, online grocers, and convenience stores, to name a few.

LO 2-3 **Identify the various types of general merchandise retailers.**

General merchandise retailers come in various forms, each with its own offerings, benefits, and limitations. These formats include department stores, full-line discount stores, specialty stores, drugstores, category specialists, extreme-value retailers, off-price retailers, and outlet stores.

LO 2-4 **Explain the differences between service and merchandise retailers.**

The inherent differences between services and merchandise result in service retailers' emphasizing training of employees, whereas merchandise retailers emphasize inventory management issues. Retail institutions have changed in response to a changing marketplace, such that there is significant crossover between these types of retailers.

LO 2-5 **Illustrate the types of ownership for retail firms.**

Small, independent retailers are usually owned and managed by a single founder. In contrast, corporate retail chains involve vast organizations and operate multiple stores. Another option that allows individual entrepreneurs to enjoy the security of corporate chains is franchising, a growing type of retail organization.

KEY TERMS

assortment, *33*

big-box store, *41*

breadth, *33*

category killer, *49*

category specialist, *48*

closeout, *53*

consignment shop, *52*

convenience store, *42*

conventional supermarket, *37*

department store, *45*

depth, *33*

dollar store, *52*

drugstore, *52*

durable goods, *45*

exclusive brand, *45*

extreme-value food retailer, *37*

extreme-value retailer, *52*

factory outlet, *54*

fair trade, *39*

flash sale site, *54*

franchising, *59*

full-line discount store, *48*

hard goods, *45*

hypermarket, *41*

irregular, *53*

limited-assortment supermarket, *37*

locavore movement, *40*

North American Industry
   Classification System (NAICS), *32*

off-price retailer, *53*

outlet store, *54*

power perimeter, *39*

private-label brand, *46*

resale store, *52*

retail chain, *59*

service retailer, *55*

soft goods, *45*

specialty store, *49*

stock-keeping unit (SKU), *33*

store brand, *46*

supercenter, *40*

thrift store, *52*

variety, *33*

warehouse club, *41*

wholesale-sponsored voluntary
   cooperative group, *59*

GET OUT AND DO IT!

1. **CONTINUING CASE ASSIGNMENT: GO SHOPPING** The objective of this assignment is to have you take the retailer's, rather than the consumer's, perspective and think about the different strategies that the retailer you selected and another retailer might have, as well as how these strategies result in different retail mixes. The assignment is to conduct a comparison of the retail offerings for a specific merchandise category, such as tablets, men's suits, country/western CDs, women's athletic shoes, or house paint, for two different retailers. The other retailer selected might be a direct competitor using the same format or a retailer selling similar merchandise to a different target market with a different format.

   Your comparison should include the following:

   • The strategy pursued by the two retailers—each retailer's target market(s) and general approach to satisfying the needs of that target market.
   • The retail mixes (store location, merchandise, pricing, advertising and promotion, location of merchandise category in store, store design, customer service) used by each of the retailers.
   • With respect to the merchandise category, a detailed comparison of the variety and depth of assortment. In comparing the merchandise offerings, use a table similar to that in Exhibit 2–2.

   To prepare this comparison, you need to visit the stores, observe the retail mixes in the stores, and play the role of a customer to observe the service.

2. **GO SHOPPING** Go to an athletic footwear specialty store such as Foot Locker, a department store, and a discount store. Analyze their variety and assortment of athletic footwear by creating a table similar to that in Exhibit 2–2.

3. **GO SHOPPING** Keep a diary for two weeks of where you shop, what you buy, and how much you spend. Get your parents to do the same thing. Tabulate your results by type of retailer. Are your shopping habits significantly different from or are they similar to those of your parents? Do your and your parents' shopping habits coincide with the trends discussed in this chapter? Why or why not?

4. **GO SHOPPING** Describe how the supermarket where you shop is implementing organic, locally grown, ethnic, and private-label merchandise. If any of these categories of merchandise are missing, explain whether you believe it could be a potential opportunity for growth for this supermarket. Then describe any strategies or activities that you believe are providing a better shopping experience than its competition. If you believe that competing stores are providing a better shopping experience than your store, explain what they are doing, and evaluate whether or not these activities would benefit your supermarket.

5. **INTERNET EXERCISE** Data on U.S. retail sales are available from the U.S. Bureau of the Census Internet site at www.census.gov/retail/. Look at the unadjusted Retail and Food services monthly sales by NAICS (found in the Monthly Retail Trade Report section). Which categories of retailers have the largest percentage of sales in November and December (the holiday season)? Do your findings make sense to you? Why or why not?

6. **INTERNET EXERCISE** Three large associations of retailers are the National Retail Federation (www.nrf.com), the Food Marketing Institute (www.fmi.org), and the National Association of Convenience and Petroleum Stores (www.nacsonline.com). Visit these sites and report on the latest retail developments and issues confronting the industry.

7. **INTERNET EXERCISE** Go to *Entrepreneur* franchise zone web page at www.entrepreneur.com/franchise500 and view the top 500 franchises for the past year. How many of the retailers in the top 10 have you patronized as a customer? Did you know that they were operated as a franchise? Look at the lists from previous years to see changes in the rankings. Finally, what is the nature of the businesses that seem to lend themselves to franchising?

8. Best Buy is a category specialist with more than 1,400 store locations. It sells appliances (refrigerators, washers and dryers, small household appliances) and electronics (televisions, computers, cell phones, car electronics, wearable technology). What are the SIC and NAICS codes used by this retailer? What other retailers compete against Best Buy, and which store format is implemented by each competitor?

DISCUSSION QUESTIONS AND PROBLEMS

1. Distinguish between variety and assortment. Why are these important elements of the retail market structure?

2. What sorts of competitive pressures are confronting traditional grocery stores? What options do these stores have to ease the pressure?

3. What do off-price retailers need to do to compete against other formats in the future?

4. Compare and contrast the retail mixes of convenience stores, traditional supermarkets, supercenters, and warehouse stores. Can all of these food retail institutions be successful over the long run? How? Why?

5. Why is Walmart, the largest retailer in the world, facing slower growth than in the past? What can it do to accelerate its growth?

6. Why are retailers in the limited-assortment supermarket, online grocery retailing, and extreme-value discount store sectors growing so rapidly? From which retailers are they getting these additional sales?

7. The same brand and model of tablet is sold by specialty computer stores, discount stores, category specialists, online retailers, and warehouse stores. Why would a customer choose one retail format over the others?

8. Choose a product category that both you and your parents purchase (e.g., business clothing, casual clothing, music, electronic equipment, shampoo). In which type of store do you typically purchase this merchandise? What about your parents? Explain why there is, or is not, a difference in your store choices.

9. At many optical stores, you can get your eyes checked *and* purchase glasses or contact lenses. How is the shopping experience different for the service as compared to the product? Design a strategy to get customers to purchase both the service and the product. In so doing, delineate specific actions that should be taken to acquire and retain optical customers.

10. There are services and products involved when buying or renting a car, and in both cases, the customer drives away in a car. But buying a car focuses more on the product, whereas renting involves the service. Explain four ways in which marketing for a rental car company differs from marketing for an automobile dealership.

CHAPTER ENDNOTES

1. Sarah Nassauer, "Sam's Club Aims to Be Less Like Wal-Mart," *The Wall Street Journal,* August 16, 2015; George Anderson, "Will Sam's New Plan Lead to Sustainable Growth?," *Retail-Wire,* October 6, 2015; Bryan Roberts and Natalie Berg, *Walmart: Key Insights and Practical Lessons from the World's Largest Retailer* (Philadelphia: Koran Page, 2012).

2. Richard Hammond, *Smart Retail: Practical Winning Ideas and Strategies from the Most Successful Retailers in the World* (New York: FT Press, 2012).

3. U.S. Census Bureau, http://www.census.gov/prod/2011pubs/12statab/domtrade.pdf. Because the censuses for businesses are taken at varying intervals, data from 2008 are the most recent national statistics available.

4. Leena Rao, "As Used-Car Startups Take Off, eBay Motors Faces Uncertain Future," *Fortune,* January 15, 2016.

5. "Sales of Food at Home by Type of Outlet Table," USDA Economic Research Service, 2016.

6. Sarah Halzack, "The Staggering Challenges of the Online Grocery Business," *Washington Post,* January 20, 2015.

7. Heather Haddon, "Attention Shoppers: Yoga in Aisle 3," *The Wall Street Journal,* June 13, 2016.

8. "2016 Top 250 Global Powers of Retailing," *Stores,* January 2016, https://nrf.com/news/2016-top-250-global-powers-of-retailing#top10.

9. "Top 25 Global Food Retailers 2015," *Supermarket News,* 2015.

10. "2015 Top 75 U.S. & Canadian Food Retailers & Wholesalers," *Supermarket News,* 2015, http://supermarketnews.com/2015-top-75-us-canadian-food-retailers-wholesalers.

11. Conventional Supermarket, "TermWiki," http://en.termwiki.com/EN:conventional_supermarket (accessed April 27, 2016).

12. *Progressive Grocer,* "Share of Supermarket Sales in the United States in 2014, by Department," Statista—The Statistics Portal, July 2015, http://www.statista.com/statistics/240580/breakdown-of-us-supermarket-sales-by-department/.

13. Ashley Lutz, "Aldi's Secrets for Selling Cheaper Crockeries Than Wal-Mart or Trader Joe's," *Business Insider,* April 8, 2015, http://www.businessinsider.com/why-aldi-is-so-cheap-2015-4.

14. Ibid.

15. "No Limits on Small Grocers' Growth," *RetailWire,* February 2, 2011.

16. George Anderson, "Supermarkets Continue to Give Ground to Other Channels," *RetailWire,* February 19, 2014, http://www.retailwire.com/discussion/17340/supermarkets-continue-to-give-ground-to-other-channels.

17. Eliza Barclay, "Grocery Stores Are Losing You. Here's How They Plan to Win You Back," *NPR,* March 30, 2015, http://www.npr.org/sections/thesalt/2015/03/30/395774725/grocery-stores-are-losing-you-heres-how-they-plan-to-win-you-back.

18. www.packagedfacts.com/Prepared-Foods-Ready-2694891/; Katherine Hobson, "Supermarket Prepared Meals: What to Watch Out For," *Consumer Reports,* March 10, 2016, http://www.consumerreports.org/food-shopping/supermarket-prepared-meals-what-to-watch-out-for/.

19. Tim Carman, "Supermarket Customers Are Hot for Takeout," *Washington Post,* February 26, 2013.

20. Marie Clare Jalonick, "Consumers Buying More Organic Products, New Data Show," *NPBS Newshour,* April 15, 2015, http://www.pbs.org/newshour/rundown/consumers-buying-organic-products-new-data-show/.

21. U.S. Census, "Quick Facts Table," https://www.census.gov/quickfacts/table/PST045215/00.

22. Northgate Markets website, www.northgatemarkets.com; Northgate Markets Newsletter.

23. Nick Wingfield, "Thinking Outside the Redbox," *The New York Times,* February 17, 2012; George Anderson, "Kiosk Krazy," *RetailWire,* June 7, 2012.

24. http://corporate.walmart.com/our-story/locations/united-states#united-states.

25. Peter Child, Thomas Kilroy, and James Naylor, "Modern Grocery and the Emerging-Market Consumer: A Complicated Courtship," *McKinsey Quarterly,* August 2015, http://www.mckinsey.com/industries/retail/our-insights/modern-grocery-and-the-emerging-market-consumer-a-complicated-courtship; Greg Thain and John Bradley, *Store Wars: The Worldwide Battle for Mindspace and Shelfspace, Online and In-Store* (West Sussex, UK: Wiley, 2012).

26. Phil Wahba, "10 Big International Exits by Retailers," *Fortune,* January 16, 2015.

27. Sarah Halzack, "A Case for Costco and Other Warehouse Clubs Having Transformed Retail More Than Amazon," *Washington Post,* September 2, 2015.

28. "2016 Top 101 Convenience Stores," *CPS*, http://www.cspdailynews.com/industry-news-analysis/top-convenience-stores.

29. "Giant Eagle FAQ," Giant Eagle.com.

30. Elliot Zwiebach, "Fresh Enhances C-Store Ambiance," *Supermarket News*, February 29, 2016, http://supermarketnews.com/nga-show/fresh-enhances-c-store-ambience.

31. Tom Ryan, "C-Stores Morphing into QSRs," *RetailWire*, April 16, 2012.

32. Halzack, "The Staggering Challenges of the Online Grocery Business."

33. Tom Ryan, "Is Online Grocery Finally Ready for Launch?," *RetailWire*, January 23, 2014.

34. Joseph Pisani, "What's Better for Grocery Delivery: Google, Instacart, or Postmates?," *Mercury News Business*, June 19, 2014.

35. "Fortune 500," *Fortune*, http://fortune.com/fortune500/.

36. Stephanie Clifford, "To Stand Out, Retailers Flock to Exclusive Lines," *The New York Times*, February 14, 2011; Amy Verner, "How Department Stores Can Stay Relevant (and Chic)," *Globe and Mail* (Toronto), April 21, 2012.

37. "Private Brands and Exclusive Merchandise," Macy's Inc.

38. Kelly Tackett, "An Evolutionary Tale from Nordstrom," *RetailWire*, May 8, 2014; Robert Spector and Patrick McCarthy, *The Nordstrom Way to Customer Service Excellence: The Handbook for Becoming the "Nordstrom" of Your Industry* (Englewood Cliffs, NJ: Wiley, 2012).

39. "Our Stores," Walmart; Industry Outlook: Mass Channel.

40. James B. Stewart, "Walmart Plays Catch Up with Amazon," *The New York Times*, October 22, 2015.

41. Stephanie Strom, "Organic Farmers Object to Whole Foods Rating System," *The New York Times*, June 12, 2015; Stephanie Strom, "Walmart Pushes for Improved Animal Welfare," *The New York Times*, May 22, 2015.

42. Target, "Our Design Partnerships," https://corporate.target.com/about/design-innovation.

43. Michael Brown, "Sears Doubles Down on the Smart Home with New Kenmore, Craftsman, and DieHard Products," *TechHive*, June 16, 2016, http://www.techhive.com/article/3084689/connected-home/sears-doubles-down-on-the-smart-home-with-new-kenmore-craftsman-and-diehard-products.html.

44. Hayley Peterson, "Sears' Obsession with Wall Street Is Killing the Retailer for Good," *Business Insider*, June 16, 2016, http://www.businessinsider.com/sears-obsession-with-wall-street-2016-3.

45. Stephanie Clifford, "Revamping, Home Depot Woos Women," *The New York Times*, January 28, 2011; James M. Kerr, "How Appealing to Women Has Helped the Home Depot," ManagementIssues.com, October 3, 2014.

46. http://www.forbes.com/sites/greatspeculations/2015/12/09/how-victorias-secrets-stagnant-brand-image-might-dampen-l-brands-valuation/#c5a1d21eb395.

47. Brian Zajac, "The Most Profitable Stores in America," *Bloomberg Businessweek*, February 23, 2012; Phil Wahba, "Apple Extends Lead in U.S. Top 10 Retailers by Sales per Square Foot," *Fortune*, March 13, 2015.

48. Charming Charlie, "About," http://www.charmingcharlie.com/about/about-us/; Tanya Rutledge, "Charming Charlie: A Jewel of a Chain," *Houston Chronicle*, December 2, 2011.

49. The Association of Resale Professionals, "Industry Statistics & Trends," http://www.narts.org/i4a/pages/index.cfm?pageid=3285.

50. Patrice J. Williams, "V.I.P. Perks, Secondhand Stores," *The New York Times*, December 29, 2011.

51. Sandra M. Jones, "Resale Shops Remake Empty Retail Spaces as Consumers Reshape Buying Habits," *Chicago Tribune*, April 7, 2011; First Research, "Used Merchandise Stores Industry Profile," May 23, 2016, http://www.firstresearch.com/Industry-Research/Used-Merchandise-Stores.html.

52. www.goodwill.org/about-us/newsroom/press-kit/.

53. Thomas Lee, "Walgreens and CVS Up Their Game as Retail Drug Business Booms," *San Francisco Chronicle*, October 30, 2015.

54. Corey Stern, "CVS and Walgreens Are Completely Dominating the US Drugstore Industry," *Business Insider*, July 29, 2015, http://www.businessinsider.com/cvs-and-walgreens-us-drugstore-market-share-2015-7.

55. Dana Mattioli, Michael Siconolfi, and Dana Cimilluca, "Walgreens, Rite Aid Unite to Create Drugstore Giant," *The Wall Street Journal*, October 27, 2015.

56. Kate Taylor, "CVS Is Making an Unprecedented Move to Hook Millennial Moms," *Business Insider*, April 19, 2016, http://www.businessinsider.com/cvs-adds-curbside-pickup-service-2016-4; "12 New In-Store, Online, and Mobile Drugstore Services That Save You Time and Money," *Consumer Reports*, August 2014, http://www.consumerreports.org/cro/2014/08/new-pharmacy-services/index.htm.

57. Lydia Dishman, "Why Walgreens' Gamble on Glamming Up Drugstores Is a Winner," *Forbes*, January 20, 2012; Walgreens, "Walgreens Opens Flagship Drugstore in Iconic Wrigley Building," June 24, 2014, http://news.walgreens.com/press-releases/community-news/walgreens-opens-flagship-drugstore-in-iconic-wrigley-building.htm.

58. "Should You Buy Groceries at the Drug Store?," *Consumer Reports*, April 11, 2014, http://www.consumerreports.org/cro/news/2014/04/should-you-buy-groceries-at-the-drug-store/index.htm.

59. Jenna Martin, "Top 10 Stories of 2015: Family Dollar Completes Merger with Dollar Tree," *Charlotte Business Journal*, December 15, 2015, http://www.bizjournals.com/charlotte/news/2015/12/15/top-10-stories-of-2015-family-dollar-completes.html.

60. "Deconstructing the Dollar Stores' Dynamic Growth," RetailBuyers.net, September 17, 2015, http://retailbuyers.net/deconstructing-the-dollar-stores-dynamic-growth/; Maggie Lu and Warren Teichner, "Dollar Stores: The Next Wave of Growth in Consumer Healthcare and Beyond," *McKinsey Quarterly*, May 2013, http://www.mckinseyonmarketingandsales.com/dollar-stores-the-next-wave-of-growth-in-consumer-healthcare-and-beyond.

61. Jesse McKinley, "Bang for the Buck," *The New York Times*, January 11, 2012; Dollar General website.

62. Jayne O'Donnell, "Behind the Bargains at T.J. Maxx, Marshalls," *USA Today*, October 25, 2011.

63. Suzanne Kapner, "Retailers' Lines Blur on Outlet Stores," *The Wall Street Journal*, October 12, 2014.

64. Drew DeSilver, "Nordstrom Expanding through RackStores, Online," *Seattle Times*, June 13, 2012; Kapner, "Retailers' Lines Blur on Outlet Stores"; Nordstrom, "About Us,"

http://shop.nordstrom.com/c/about-us?cm_sp=
corp-_-corp_AboutUs-_-globalfooternav_aboutus%20.

65. Leena Rao, "Here's How Gilt Will Be Added to Saks Fifth
Avenue's Discount Retail Stores," *Fortune,* February 9, 2016;
Sara Ashley O'Brien, "Ultimate Flash Sale: Gilt Groupe Sells
for $250 Million," *CNN Money,* January 7, 2016, http://
money.cnn.com/2016/01/07/technology/gilt-groupe-
hudsons-bay-saks/.

66. www.zoots.com.

67. Robert Spector, *The Mom & Pop Store: True Stories from the
Heart of America* (New York: Walker & Co., 2009).

68. Nicole Leinbach-Reyhle, "Celebrating Independent Retailers:
Their Surprisingly Strong Future," *Forbes,* July 3, 2014.

69. Lockwood Shop, "About Us," http://lockwoodshop.com/
content/About-Us-/1002.

70. This section was prepared by Professor Tracy Meyer, University of North Carolina–Wilmington.

71. U.S. Census Bureau, "Census Bureau's First Release of Comprehensive Franchise Data Shows Franchises Make Up More
Than 10 Percent of Employer Business," September 14, 2010.

72. Dhruv Grewal, Gopalkrishnan Iyer, Rajshekhar G. Javalgi, and
Lori Radulovich, "Franchise Partnership and International
Expansion: A Conceptual Framework and Research Proposi-
tions," *Entrepreneurial Theory & Practice,* May 2011,
pp. 533–557.

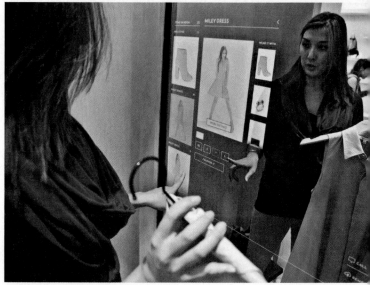

© Bebeto Matthews/AP Images

Even with all the talk about e-commerce and the spread of mobile shopping, studies show that around 80 percent of purchases continue to take place in physical locations. However, more than 90 percent of customers research their purchases online or through mobile sources before making them. Therefore, retailers cannot afford to ignore omnichannel retailing.[1]

Some prevalent retailing trends reinforce this warning. First, many retailers with physical stores are allowing consumers to check their in-store inventory on their mobile devices or make that information available on their websites. They are also using in-store signage that encourages consumers to consider omnichannel options, such as suggestions that they reserve a product online. Second, online offerings are diverse. A large percentage allow online purchases followed by in-store pickup services; free return shipping; and a "click to call" feature to connect online shoppers with service representatives. Third, a majority let shoppers begin their shopping, then save items in their digital shopping carts for purchase at some later time.[2]

These statistics and the accumulated evidence strongly suggest that omnichannel, rather than being a differentiator, is becoming a necessary capability for modern retailers. Consumers simply expect to be able to find retailers on multiple channels, in line with their daily practices, in which they switch seamlessly across physical, mobile, and online interactions.[3]

Accordingly, the popular designer brand Rebecca Minkoff has been on the forefront in the fashion industry in using these technologies. Its "connected store" concept was revealed in its flagship store in SoHo, New York City. This connected store features a "connected wall"—an interactive mirror display that shows the latest content from the brand, including fashion shows, photos, and virtually everything that is happening on social media that is related in any way to the brand. Furthermore, the connected wall allows customers to browse merchandise, request a fitting room, have clothing options sent to that fitting room, and even order drinks. Customers receive a text message when their dressing room is ready.[4]

Once they get to the dressing room, they encounter spaces that feature mirrored touch screens and radio frequency identification devices (RFIDs) that can recognize the products in the fitting room. Maybe one of the simplest, but most revolutionary, aspects of these fitting rooms is that customers can adjust the lighting, making it brighter to see details in the clothing or dimmer to avoid harsh reflections.

When they have finished trying on everything and are ready to make a purchase, customers can use the touch-screen display to send selected items directly to a checkout function.[5] Not only do the touch screens allow customers to access the entire store and its inventory, but they also offer a seamless connection to the Rebecca Minkoff app and mobile site. One option, "Save your fitting room session to your phone," means that customers can gain access to the clothes they tried on and make their purchases, through the app, later in the day, after they have had a chance to think it through or double-check that they don't already have something similar in their closet at home.[6]

The innovations are not just in stores, though; the brand also adopted a #seebuywear hashtag during a recent New York Fashion Week, with videos posted on the Rebecca Minkoff site featuring new fashions, together with clickable cards that viewers could use to visit the specific product pages. Or if they were watching the videos on a touch screen–enabled device, consumers could touch an accessory or clothing item as the model walked it down the runway in the videos, which would add that product to the user's shopping folder.[7] The stellar integration of mobile and in-store experiences have led to a nearly sevenfold increase in the sales of Rebecca Minkoff's "ready-to-wear" lines within just six months of the new introductions.[8]

A retail channel defines the way a retailer sells and delivers merchandise and services to its customers. The most common channel used by retailers is stores, but retailers also use a variety of nonstore channels, including the Internet, mobile, social media, and catalogs. This definition highlights the distinction between a channel and a medium, such as television advertising. A *channel* involves the opportunity to complete a transaction—to sell and deliver merchandise—while a *medium* is primarily used to communicate information to consumers. Although retailers certainly communicate some information through channels, their primary objective is to complete transactions. Still, the difference between a medium and a channel is starting to blur, especially as social media offer expanding options and means to buy goods and services.

LO 3-1

Understand the channels used by retailers.

Thus we can envision the progression of retailing as it has spread across channels. Retailers generally start their business with a single channel. Traditionally, it was a physical store (e.g., Walmart) but more recently, it also might have been a retail website (e.g., Amazon). **Single-channel retailing** is when retailers sell and deliver merchandise and services to their customers through only one channel. Over time and as they grow, many retailers spread to other channels, such as when brick-and-mortar retailers add an Internet presence to their stores or online retailers open a physical location. With this expansion they become multichannel retailers.

Multichannel retailing is when retailers offer more than one channel to sell and deliver merchandise and services to consumers. Channels operate without integrating operations between them. The birth of this form of retailing can be traced back to when Sears opened its first store in 1925, 33 years after it launched its catalog, which offered merchandise previously unavailable to the American masses.[9] Now, almost all large retailers that operate stores are multichannel retailers, with physical stores, an Internet channel that offers customers an opportunity to buy merchandise or services by accessing their website, and perhaps catalog orders.[10]

Having multiple channels in turn creates an opportunity for cross-channel retailing. With **cross-channel retailing**, customers actually use multiple channels to make purchases, such as when they receive an e-mailed coupon, download it onto their smartphone, and then go to a brick-and-mortar store to redeem the coupon and buy the product. Finally, this continued expansion of channels has led modern retailers to aspire to omnichannel retailing. **Omnichannel retailing** refers to a coordinated

EXHIBIT 3–1   Progression from Single-Channel to Omnichannel Retailing

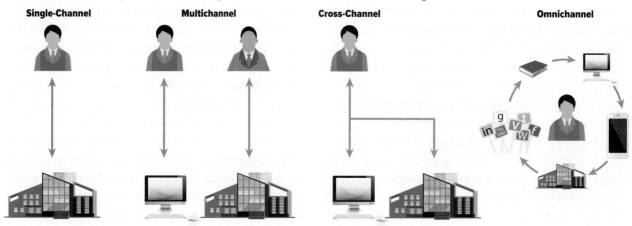

multichannel retail offering that provides a seamless and synchronized customer experience, using all of the retailer's shopping channels.[11] These various channels run in collaboration and effectively ensure that the customer (and customer data) is the center of the retail management processes. The progression from single-channel to omnichannel retailing is depicted in Exhibit 3–1.

In this chapter, we take a strategic perspective to examine the primary channels through which retailers sell merchandise and services to their customers: the store channel; Internet, mobile, and social retailing channels; and catalog and other nonstore channels. We briefly describe each of these retail channels in turn, in terms of the unique benefits they offer to consumers, as well as the benefits to retailers associated with offering a multichannel offering. We also describe the challenges that multichannel retailers face when using these channels synergistically, which helps clarify the path toward becoming an omnichannel retailer.

RELATIVE STRENGTHS OF RETAIL CHANNELS

LO 3-2

Compare the relative strengths of the major retail channels: stores; Internet, mobile, and social; and catalog and other nonstore channels.

In this section we discuss the relative strengths of three types of retail channels or retailing: in-store retailing; Internet, mobile, and social retailing; and catalog and other nonstore retailing.

In-Store Retailing

The different types of retailers, discussed in detail in Chapter 2, generally make most of their revenues through their brick-and-mortar or store channels. Stores offer several benefits to customers that they cannot get when they shop through other, nonstore channels (e.g., mobile, Internet, catalogs). The estimated percentage of annual retail sales (excluding motor vehicles and food services annual sales) made through each channel is shown in Exhibit 3–2. The vast majority of sales are a function of in-store retailing and occur through the store channel, but the Internet and catalog channels also account for significant sales, and the mobile channel shows the highest growth rate.

Touch and Smell of Products   Perhaps the greatest benefit offered by stores is the opportunity for customers to use all five senses—touching, smelling, tasting, seeing, and hearing—when examining and evaluating products. Although new technologies such as three-dimensional and 360-degree projections can enhance representations of products on a computer or mobile phone screen, these visual improvements do not provide the same level of information customers get when they actually try on a swimsuit or smell the fragrance of a candle.

Personal Service   Although consumers are often critical of the personal service they get in stores, sales associates still have the unique ability to provide meaningful, personalized information. They can tell customers if a suit looks good on them, suggest a tie to go with a dress shirt, or answer questions customers might have about what is appropriate to wear at a business-casual event.

Risk Reduction   The physical presence of the store reduces perceived risk and increases customers' confidence that any problems with a purchase will be corrected. Customers can easily access people in the store to resolve issues concerning defective or unsuitable merchandise or get additional information on how to use a product.

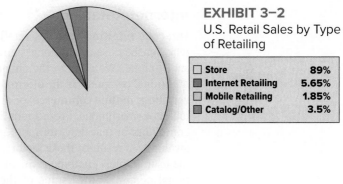

Sources: U.S. Census Bureau; www.internetretailer.com.

EXHIBIT 3–2
U.S. Retail Sales by Type of Retailing

☐ Store	89%
■ Internet Retailing	5.65%
☐ Mobile Retailing	1.85%
■ Catalog/Other	3.5%

Immediate Gratification   Customers can use merchandise immediately after they buy it in stores. Thus, when customers have a fever or need a last-minute gift, for example, they do not have to wait a day or two for the delivery of a prescription from Drugstore.com or a gift from Amazon.com.

Entertainment and Social Experience   In-store shopping can be a stimulating experience for some people, providing a break in their daily routine and enabling them to interact with friends. For retailers that emphasize the store experience, like Bass Pro Shops, the shopping trip is equivalent to a trip to a carnival, with a laser arcade, rock climbing, pistol shooting range, massive indoor waterfalls, and aquariums for fishing. By turning the store into an adventure, Bass Pro Shops affirms its reputation as an outdoorsy, rough-and-tumble brand, while still giving its customers a strong reason to visit their local store.[12]

Cash Payment   Stores are the only channel through which consumers can make cash payments. Some customers prefer to pay with cash because it is quicker, resolves the transaction immediately, and does not result in potential interest payments or excessive debt. Other customers are concerned about security and identity theft and thus prefer to use their credit card or debit card in person rather than electronically sending the payment information via the Internet.

© John Bohn/The Boston Globe/Getty Images

More than 116 million people annually visit Bass Pro Shops, compared with 20.5 million visitors to Disney World in Orlando. The excitement generated in a Bass Pro Shops store cannot be equaled by other channels.

Internet Retailing

Internet retailing involves retailers interacting with consumers via the Internet, whether they use a traditional computer or a laptop, a variety of sizes of tablets, or a smartphone. We refer to the channel that involves accessing the Internet through a traditional computer as the electronic channel. The mobile channel (also called **mobile retailing**, **mobile commerce**, or **m-commerce**) implies accessing the Internet using a tablet or smartphone. From a retailing perspective, smartphones differ from traditional computers in that they are more portable, have a smaller display, and are location-aware. As a result of these factors, they produce a different interface experience with the user. Tablets combine some of the advantages and disadvantages of using a traditional computer with some of the mobility benefits and problems associated with shopping with a mobile phone.

More and more traditional brick-and-mortar and catalog retailers of all sizes continue to add Internet channels to improve their ability to serve their customers and build a competitive advantage in several ways:

1. The addition of the Internet channels has the potential to offer a greater selection of products.

2. They allow retailers to provide more information.

3. They enable retailers to give customers more personalized information about products and services.

4. They offer sellers the unique opportunity to collect information about consumer shopping.

5. Internet channels provide an opportunity for retailers to enter new markets economically.

6. They provide information that they can use to improve the shopping experience across all channels.

7. Because of the information they gather, Internet channels also may increase consumer risk, which represents a potential threat that retailers must address to ensure their competitive advantage.

Deeper and Broader Selection   One benefit of adding Internet channels is the vast number of alternatives retailers can make available to consumers without crowding their aisles or increasing their square footage. Stores and catalogs are limited by their size. By shopping on the Internet, consumers can easily "visit" and select merchandise from a broader array of retailers. Individual retailers' websites typically offer deeper assortments of merchandise (more colors, brands, and sizes) than are available in stores or catalogs. This expanded offering enables them to satisfy consumer demand for less popular styles, colors, or sizes. Many retailers also offer a broader assortment (more categories) on their websites. Staples.com, for instance, offers soft drinks and cleaning supplies, which are not available in stores, so that its business customers will view it as a one-stop shop.

More Information for Evaluating Merchandise   An important service offered by retailers is providing information that helps consumers make better buying decisions. Retail channels differ in terms of how much information customers can access. The amount of information available through the store channel is limited by the number and training of sales associates and the space allocated to informative signage. Similarly, the information available through a catalog channel is limited by the number of pages in the catalog. In contrast, the information provided through Internet channels is unlimited. The vast amount of information available through these channels enables customers to solve problems, rather than just get information about specific products.

Personalization   Due to the Internet's interactive nature, the most significant potential benefit of Internet channels is their ability to personalize merchandise offerings and information, in an economical way, for each customer. Customers control some of this personalization by drilling down through web pages until they have enough information to make a purchase decision. In addition, when using Internet channels, customers can format the information so that they can use it effectively to compare alternatives. For example, online shoppers might open several pages of different retailers simultaneously and flip between them to compare prices. Retailers also facilitate this comparison prices with their website design. Office Depot provides information about alternatives selected by the customer in a side-by-side comparison format, for example. In contrast, customers in stores usually have to inspect each brand, one item at a time, and then remember the different attributes to make a comparison.

The retailer also can play a more proactive role in personalizing merchandise and information through Internet channels. For example, many retailers offer **live chats**: Customers can click a button at any time and have an instant messaging e-mail or voice conversation with a customer service representative. This technology also enables retailers to send a proactive chat invitation automatically to customers on the site. The timing of these invitations can be based on the time the visitor has spent on the site, the specific page the customer is viewing, or a product on which the customer has clicked. For example, Suitsupply.com has learned that reviewing several items in a short period implies the visitor has more than a passing interest in its offerings. Therefore, the site displays a pop-up window with a friendly face offering help.

The interactive nature of the Internet also provides an opportunity for retailers to personalize their offerings for each of their customers. For example, Amazon.com serves customers a personalized landing page with information about books and other products of interest based on the customer's past purchases and search behavior on the website. Amazon also sends interested customers customized e-mail messages that notify them that their favorite author or recording artist has published a new book or released a new CD. Amazon further personalizes customers' shopping experience by recommending complementary merchandise. Just as a well-trained salesperson would make recommendations to customers before checkout, an interactive web page can make suggestions to shoppers about additional items that they might like to consider.

Some multichannel and omnichannel retailers are able to personalize promotions and Internet home pages on the basis of several attributes tied to the shopper's current or previous web sessions, such as the time of day, time zone as determined by a computer's Internet address, and assumed gender.[13]

Expanded Market Presence   The market for customers who shop in stores is typically limited to consumers living in relatively close proximity to those stores. The market for catalogs is limited by the high cost of printing and mailing them and increasing consumer interest in environmentally friendly practices. By adding the Internet channel, retailers can expand their market without having to build new stores or incur the high cost of additional catalogs. Adding an Internet channel is particularly attractive to retailers with strong brand names but limited locations and distribution. For example, retailers such as Neiman Marcus, REI, IKEA, and L.L.Bean are widely known for offering unique, high-quality merchandise. If these retailers only had a store nearby, numerous customers would not have to travel vast distances to buy the merchandise they carry.

Information to Improve Shopping Experience across Channels   It is difficult for most store-based retailers to develop extensive purchase histories of their customers, because those retailers cannot link individual transactions to customers who pay cash or use third-party credit cards. In contrast, all transactions through the Internet have the customer identification information needed to send the product to the customer, as well as their search behavior. This information can be used to provide valuable insights into how and why customers shop and are dissatisfied or satisfied with their experiences.[14]

L.L.Bean has relatively few stores, but has a vast catalog and Internet presence that significantly expands its market.

The information is useful to retailers in several ways. First, it helps them design stores or websites. By knowing how people shop, a retailer can determine, for instance, whether a store or website should be laid out by brands, size, color, or price point. Second, it can help the retailer give suggestions about what items a customer might be interested in purchasing. For example, after a customer chooses a movie on Netflix, Netflix recommends additional movies that might be of interest to the customer using predictive analytic algorithms. Third, based on what customers clicked on or what they purchased in the past, retailers can provide unique promotions to individual customers that might encourage them to buy again or buy more.

Perceived Risks in Internet Shopping   Some consumers are concerned about buying products through an Internet channel. Specifically, some believe that the security of credit card transactions is greater in stores than online, and they also worry about the potential for privacy violations.

Although many consumers remain concerned about credit card security, extensive security problems have been rare. Almost all retailers use sophisticated technologies to encrypt communications. Also, all major credit card companies provide some consumer protection for retail transactions. Typically, customers are not liable for more than $50 as long as they report the unauthorized use in a timely manner. The consequences of security breaches can be far worse for the retailer from which the card number was stolen. Security breaches can ruin a retailer's reputation and possibly expose it to legal liability.[15]

Consumers also are concerned about the ability of retailers to collect information about their purchase history, personal information, and search behavior on the Internet without their knowledge.[16] They are worried about how this information will be used in the future. Will it be sold to other retailers, or will the consumer receive unwanted promotional materials online or in the mail? Issues related to privacy are discussed in more detail in Chapters 9 and 13.

Mobile Retailing

Due to the rapid growth of domestic and international broadband access through handheld devices, such as tablets and mobile phones, retailers are very interested in developing this channel's potential. Relative to stores, the mobile Internet channel offers the same benefits as computer-based electronic Internet channels, but it also has its own unique benefits and limitations. In particular, customers can easily carry the devices in their purses or pockets, so they can access retail sites from anywhere.

Another advantage of a mobile channel is that customer–retailer interactions can be location-sensitive. For example, a retailer can determine where a customer is located and send location-relevant information to the customer, such as promotions, to encourage customers to buy other products nearby the store or go to another area of the store.

The major disadvantage of a mobile channel, compared with a computer-based Internet channel, is the mobile device's smaller screen. To accommodate the smaller screen size, the software interface for interacting with mobile devices and computers is different. When using mobile channels, customers typically navigate using a touch screen with side scrolling, whereas a mouse or trackpad is used for an electronic channel. The smaller screen size and touch-screen navigation means that consumers using a mobile channel have to go through many more screens when browsing or trying to locate information.[17] Retailing View 3.1 highlights how Sephora has been using its app to pursue activities online that it would have struggled to achieve just through its stores.

The use of tablets may provide the best trade-off between the portability of mobile phones and the navigation ease of websites accessed by computers. Most retailers

RETAILING VIEW   Ensuring Mobile Dominance through In-Store Promotions

Some consumers rely on websites to reach their favorite retailers. Others like to head to the stores themselves to check out the options. Still others want a mobile app that enables them to shop quickly and on the go. Increasingly, today's customers demand that retailers offer them all of these options, consistently and constantly, so that they can pick and choose the channel they want to use at any specific time.

This demand is the impetus for the latest developments in the marketing strategy of Sephora, the specialty beauty products retailer. Although it has long maintained a good reputation for its interactive website, the company remains in constant pursuit of a strategy that enables it to reach all its customers through the most channels with the greatest frequency.

The 2 million users of the most recent version of its mobile app, Sephora to Go, can engage in any activities they would pursue in stores. The close alignment across these channels provides a seamless experience. In addition, the app encourages customers to sign up for the loyalty program and create a Beauty Insider account. Once they have done so, they gain a mobile version of their loyalty card. They can check their loyalty points at any time, as well as redeem them however they wish. Downloadable bar codes also are available, which can be scanned in stores.

Simultaneously, Sephora's in-store signage encourages shoppers to sign up for the loyalty program and create a Beauty Insider account. That is, both channels issue similar calls to action. Moreover, the in-store signs encourage brick-and-mortar shoppers to take advantage of the benefits they can gain from interacting with the retailer, either online or through mobile apps.

In its latest "flash" locations, Sephora stores feature selfie walls and cell phone chargers. But the biggest difference between a regular Sephora location and a flash location is the

Sephora can provide real-time, customized alerts to customers' phones, whether about updated loyalty program points, upcoming in-store events, or promotions for some frequently purchased items.

© Mark Metcalfe/Getty Images

provision of cards in the flash stores that function as customers' shopping carts. They just place the card and product in front of connected screens and the item is automatically added to their virtual cart.

Sephora is also innovating through the uses of beacon technology. By integrating beacons in its stores, Sephora can provide real-time, customized alerts to customers' phones, whether about updated loyalty program points, upcoming in-store events, or promotions for some frequently purchased items.

Sources: Lauren Johnson, "Sephora Magnifies Mobile Ambitions via In-Store Signage, Updated App," *Mobile Commerce Daily*, August 23, 2013; "Omnichannel Heroes: Sephora Leads the Way in Personalization," *Thriving Malls*, May 11, 2015; Marianna Wilson, "Sephora Makes Big Omnichannel Push," *Retailing Today*, March 6, 2015; Erika Childres, "Connected Store Spotlight: Sephora Flash," *Cloudtags*, March 3, 2016, http://omnichannel.me/connected-store-spotlight-sephora-flash/.

serve up the firm's website—that is, a specially designed mobile site—when a customer accesses an Internet channel. But retailers increasingly are designing distinct websites and apps for different devices. On Anthropologie's app, for example, consumers can browse items, clip pictures of the most appealing options to add to their social networks, and check out detailed, thumbnail views of the offerings. The collage option allows them to put together outfits, including accessories and jewelry, to buy as a set. The percentage of shoppers accessing Anthropologie's website through tablets tripled, to 6 percent, soon after it introduced the app; since that time, the retailer's sales growth has primarily been attributable to the expansion of its various e-commerce channels.[18]

Social Retailing

Social retailing, also known as **s-retailing**, involves conducting purchase transactions through a social media site. This expanded channel is steadily evolving and picking up steam. In particular, social media powerhouses such as Twitter, Pinterest, and Instagram have incorporated "buy buttons" that enable users to click on a featured post or picture to initiate a sales process. On Instagram, the button is similar in function to the Facebook buy button. That is, advertisers on the sites may include buy buttons in their ads. When users click, the button links them to an external website where they can complete their purchase. The process is a little different on Pinterest. The presence of "buyable" pins signals to users that they may click on the link to receive detailed information about available colors, sizes, and other information. If they choose to purchase, the order goes directly to the merchant, without ever taking the user off the Pinterest site. Such functionality seems likely to be successful; in a recent survey, 93 percent of Pinterest users—or pinners—noted that they would like to use the site to make their purchases.[19] Social retailing has grown from $3 billion in 2012 to an estimated $14 billion in 2015.[20] Currently, the largest number of social retailing orders comes from Facebook.[21]

Catalog and Other Nonstore Channels

The **catalog channel** is a nonstore retail channel in which the retail offering is communicated to customers through a catalog mailed to customers. About half of U.S. consumers shop through catalogs each year. The merchandise categories with the greatest catalog sales are drugs, beauty aids, computers, software, clothing, accessories, furniture, and housewares.[22] Similar to any other nonstore channel, catalogs provide safety and convenience benefits to customers, and they also continue to provide a few unique advantages over other nonstore formats. First, consumers can look at merchandise and place an order from almost anywhere, 24/7, without needing a computer, mobile device, or Internet connection. Second, consumers can refer to the information in a catalog anytime by simply picking it up from the coffee table. Third, catalogs can be easier to browse through than websites. However, the use of catalogs also has come under attack from consumer groups that believe they represent an unnecessary waste of natural resources.

In the past several years, IKEA has been using its website to augment its catalog channel. In particular, IKEA has dramatically improved the content and user experience associated with its widely distributed housewares catalog by including augmented reality. Shoppers can place their smartphones over selected pages to get additional content from the retailer's website, such as image galleries and videos. After downloading an app, customers can interact with a series of icons in the catalog to see more information about selected products. The information ranges from how-to videos to "X-ray" photographs of the inside of storage systems, to stories about the products and designers. Three-dimensional views of rooms, with and without textiles, even allow users to build in decorative elements and explore color options.[23]

Direct Selling   Another nonstore channel is direct selling. **Direct selling** is a retail channel in which salespeople interact with customers face-to-face in a convenient location, either at the customer's home or at work. Direct salespeople demonstrate merchandise benefits and/or explain a service, take an order, and deliver the merchandise. Direct selling is a highly interactive retail channel in which considerable information is conveyed to customers through face-to-face discussions and demonstrations. However, providing this high level of personalized information, including extensive demonstrations, is costly.

Annual U.S. sales through direct selling are more than $35 billion.[24] More than 60 percent of the products sold through the direct selling channel are home, family care, and home durables (cleaning products, cookware, cutlery, etc.); wellness (weight loss products, vitamins, etc.); and personal care (cosmetics, jewelry, skin care, etc.) items.[25]

Almost all of the over 20 million salespeople in the United States who work in direct sales are independent agents.[26] They are not employed by the direct sales firm but rather act as independent distributors, buying merchandise from the firms and then reselling it to consumers. In most cases, direct salespeople may sell their merchandise to anyone, but some companies, such as Avon, assign territories to salespeople who regularly contact households in their territory. Retailing View 3.2 describes how the direct selling channel is particularly effective in less developed countries.

Automated Retailing   **Automated retailing** is a retail channel in which merchandise or services are stored in a machine and dispensed to customers when they deposit

RETAILING VIEW   Avon's Direct Selling Channel in Brazil   3.2

Baixada Fluminense might be one of the toughest neighborhoods in Rio de Janeiro, but that doesn't mean its residents don't worry about lipstick colors. It might even mean they worry more. Thus, Heloisa Almada Contreira visits her 80 or so customers regularly in their homes, earning weekly sales of about $930 by selling Avon products. Spending 50 reais ($27) on cosmetics might seem like a lot for many low-income consumers, but, according to Almada Contreira, "For them, it's a necessity. Brazilian women can't go without their makeup."

Her impression might be anecdotal, but the statistics back up this claim, in that Brazil constitutes the world's third-largest market for beauty care products, behind only the United States and Japan. And whereas U.S. consumers of cosmetics increasingly head to a Sephora, Ulta, a department store, or even just the local drugstore, Brazil's consumers rely heavily on in-home access.

With its expansive coastline and warm climate, Brazil invites residents to visit beaches all year, though the approach of summer often finds millions of women initiating a diet and beauty regime that will enable them to live *verão sem kanga*—that is, as part of a robe-free summer on the beach. Such hot weather may be great for a beach day, but it also means that people often need at least a couple of showers. Thus, Brazilians use twice the shampoo, conditioner, and soap compared with residents of other countries. And then women need to apply their makeup a second time each day!

The constant demand for cosmetics and beauty products is no problem for Almada Contreira and her 1.1 million sales colleagues. Avon's Brazilian sales force sells door-to-door, whether the customers live in city slums, the Amazonian rainforest, or remote towns. In one recent year, more than half of Avon's $6.2 billion in revenues were generated in emerging markets, including its largest markets of Brazil, Mexico, Russia, and the Philippines. In these areas, direct sales can be particularly effective because the channel does not require a sophisticated

Avon's direct selling channel is particularly effective in developing countries such as Brazil.

or expensive infrastructure. Instead, salespeople handle distribution on their own. These independent agents not only sell and distribute the products to their customers, but they also take responsibility for ordering merchandise to restock their inventory. To reach customers in the Amazon, Avon salespeople might need to hire a small boat or plane, and the product delivery might be delayed for a week or more. But for those waiting for just the right color to apply to their cheeks, a week is not too long to wait.

Sources: Ciara Linnane, "Think the Avon Lady Is American? Think Again," *Market Watch*, August 3, 2016; Avon, Products, Inc., "Avon Reports Fourth-Quarter and Full-Year 2015 Results," PR Newswire, February 11, 2016; Christina Passariello and Emily Glazer, "Coty Knocks on Brazil's Door; Part of Avon's Allure to Fragrance Maker Is Its Sales Network in South America," *The Wall Street Journal*, April 5, 2012; Jenney Barchfield, "In Beauty-Obsessed Brazil, Clinics Offer Free Plastic Surgery to Poor," *Los Angeles Times*, March 25 2012, A.4; Jonathan Wheatley, "Beauty Business Turns Heads in Brazil," *Investor's Choice*, January 19, 2010.

EXHIBIT 3–3
Benefits Provided by
Major Channels

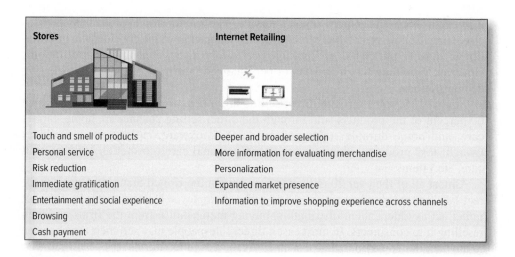

Stores	Internet Retailing
Touch and smell of products	Deeper and broader selection
Personal service	More information for evaluating merchandise
Risk reduction	Personalization
Immediate gratification	Expanded market presence
Entertainment and social experience	Information to improve shopping experience across channels
Browsing	
Cash payment	

cash or use a credit card. Automated retailing machines, also known as **vending machines**, are typically placed at convenient, high-traffic locations. About 80 percent of the automated retailing channel sales are from cold beverages, prepared food service, candy, and snacks. Annual U.S. sales in the channel exceed $6 billion.[27] Entrepreneurs also are reimagining the uses of vending machines, such that many of them are going high-tech.

Exhibit 3–3 summarizes the unique benefits of the different major retail channels. In the following section we discuss how retailers can provide a better customer shopping experience by integrating these channels into a true multichannel and omnichannel experience, even though doing so remains something of a challenge.

OPPORTUNITIES FACING MULTICHANNEL AND OMNICHANNEL RETAILERS

LO 3-3

Describe the opportunities associated with a true omnichannel strategy.

Retailers are using multiple channels to improve their offerings to their customers and build a competitive advantage. The typical examples of the evolution toward multichannel retailing are when store-based retailers and catalogers add Internet channels. But Amazon, which is famous for its Internet channels, already has opened a physical bookstore in Seattle, with plans to open a second store in San Diego. The store carries a limited selection of the best reviewed books available on Amazon. Just as on its online site, Amazon displays the books with their covers showing, instead of lining them up on shelves with just their spines displayed, to facilitate customer browsing. The store also features Amazon's Kindle, Fire TV, Fire Tablets, and Echo.[28]

Regardless of how they come to find a multichannel retailer, consumers want a seamless omnichannel experience: Whether they solicit a sales associate for help, seek out an in-store kiosk, call in to the call center, or log on to the website, they also like to be recognized. Once recognized, they also need the retailer to facilitate their ability to find and pick up their purchases, even if they want to buy

© George Rose/Getty Images

Internet retailer, Amazon, is opening stores.

RETAILING VIEW   Apple, the Gold Standard of Omnichannel   3.3

It should be no surprise that the most valuable brand in the world, Apple, has also become the gold standard in omnichannel. From in-store to online to mobile, Apple, its products, and even its product packaging create a single, seamless experience. For years Apple has been leading the way to omnichannel by using its stores as interactive experience zones that emphasize how using its products will feel. The store design, website design, product design, and packaging all reflect the clean, sleek simplicity that Apple has worked so hard to equate with its brand. Accordingly, customers feel as though their experiences at each of these touch points are integrated.

As is the case for any omnichannel retailer, Apple helps customers research its products online before coming in to the store to test out the different models. Once they reach the stores, customers can go online using one of the many products on display, schedule an appointment with a dedicated Genius representative, or sign up for a class to learn about the functionality of a new purchase. Furthermore, all Apple store associates are equipped with iPhones that allow them to assist and check out customers from anywhere in the store using a credit card or Apple Pay. If a customer has decided to purchase a customized Apple Watch, store associates can help him or her place an order online and have the product delivered to the customer's home. The introduction of iBeacon technology at Apple stores has enhanced its omnichannel capabilities even further, such that customers receive special

© Spencer Platt/Getty Images

Apple helps customers research its products online before coming in to the store to test out the different models and buy using Apple Pay.

offers and coupons as soon as they walk through the door to the store.

Sources: Sophie Loras, "Four Brands Leading the Way in Multichannel Marketing," *Clickz*, February 11, 2016; *Eyefaster*, "The Growth of Omni-Channel Retail: Integrating In-Store, Mobile and Desktop Shopping Channels," *Eyefaster*, August 11, 2015; Jillian Buttecali, "The Top 4 Omni-Channel Retailers," *ID.me*, January 15, 2015.

online and then pick up in the store, or vice versa. In addition, the various channels need to be consistent in the information they provide. Apple offers a prime example of a retailer that provides an effective omnichannel experience, as discussed in Retailing View 3.3.

Retailers also benefit by using the various channels synergistically. Multichannel and omnichannel retailers can use one channel to promote the services offered by other channels. For example, the URL of a store's website can be advertised on in-store signs, shopping bags, credit card billing statements, point-of-sale (POS) receipts, and the print or broadcast advertising used to promote the store. The physical stores and catalogs are also advertisements for a retailer's other channels. The retailer's channels can be used to stimulate store visits by announcing special store events and promotions.

Multichannel and omnichannel retailers can leverage their stores to lower the cost of fulfilling orders and processing returned merchandise. They can use their

© Jason Alden/Bloomberg/Getty Images

Multichannel and omnichannel retailers can use their shopping bags to promote their website.

stores as "warehouses" for gathering merchandise for delivery to customers. Customers also can be offered the opportunity to pick up and return merchandise at the retailer's stores rather than pay shipping charges. Many retailers will waive shipping charges when orders are placed online or through the catalog if the customer physically comes into the store.

CHALLENGES FACING MULTICHANNEL AND OMNICHANNEL RETAILERS

LO 3-4

Analyze the challenges facing multichannel and omnichannel retailers.

However, as illustrated in Exhibit 3–4, most multichannel retailers have yet to provide these seamless customer-facing processes. This apparent lack of progress should not be interpreted as a lack of interest. The results of a recent survey indicate that cross-channel coordination is extremely important to retailers, even if it has yet to reach its full cross-channel potential.[29]

Some of the challenges and trade-off decisions that confront multichannel and omnichannel retailers include multichannel and omnichannel supply chain and information system issues, a consistent brand image across channels, merchandise assortment trade-offs, pricing issues, and the challenge surrounding channel migration and showrooming.

Multichannel and Omnichannel Supply Chains and Information Systems

Multichannel and omnichannel retailers still struggle to provide an integrated shopping experience, because the various channels demand various skills as well as unique resources.[30] When retail distribution centers (DCs) support a store channel, they move merchandise, packed in cartons, off the suppliers' trucks, into the DC inventory, and then onto new trucks heading to retail stores. Some retailers use cross-docking DCs, described in Chapter 9, in which merchandise sits in the DC only briefly, often for less than a day. But DCs that supply the Internet, mobile, social, and catalog channels have other roles to fulfill as well: receive merchandise packed in cartons, then separate out the individual items to be repacked and shipped to individual end-customers. Handling individual items, rather than cartons, and shipping them to individual consumers, instead of retailers, requires unique packaging, a different type of storage and order picking system, different transportation systems, and intermediaries.

Due to these operational differences, many store-based retailers have a separate organization to manage their Internet and catalog operations. But as the multichannel and omnichannel operation matures and becomes more omnichannel, retailers tend to integrate all operations under one organization. Both Walmart and JCPenney initially had separate organizations for their Internet channel but subsequently integrated them with stores and catalogs.

EXHIBIT 3–4
Percentage of Multichannel Retailers Offering Cross-Channel Fulfillment

Cross-Channel Fulfillment Activities	High-Performance Retailers	Others
Buy online, return in store	70%	59%
Buy in store, fulfill through online	70	41
Buy online, pick up in store	50	52
Buy via mobile	35	48
Buy via social media source	30	11
Buy online, fulfill through any stop	30	30

Source: *Omni-Channel 2012: Cross-Channel Comes of Age, 2012 Benchmark,* RSR, June 2012.

© Susan Van Etten/PhotoEdit

Source: Patagonia

Consistent Brand Image across Channels

Retailers need to provide a consistent brand image of themselves and their merchandise across all channels. For example, Patagonia reinforces its image of selling high-quality, environmentally friendly sports equipment in its stores, its catalogs, and on its website. Each of these channels emphasizes function, not fashion in the descriptions of Patagonia's products. Patagonia's concerns about the environment are communicated by carefully lighting its stores and using recycled polyester in many of its clothes, as well as only organic, rather than pesticide-intensive, cotton. Its weblog, The Cleanest Line (**www.patagonia.com/blog**), is dedicated to essays and other features on environmental activism, innovative design, and sports.

Source: Patagonia

Emphasizing function, not fashion, Patagonia reinforces its image of selling high-quality, environmentally friendly sports equipment in its stores, its catalogs, and on its website.

Merchandise Assortment

Typically, different assortments are found for each of the channels. For example, multichannel and omnichannel retailers offer a broader and deeper merchandise assortment through their Internet channel than through their store channel. Because the Internet channel can have a much larger assortment, it can satisfy the needs of a larger variety of customer groups. For instance, multichannel and omnichannel apparel retailers can carry fringe sizes on their Internet channel, but it would be too expensive and space constricting to do so in their store channel. The channels also differ in terms of their effectiveness in generating sales for different types of merchandise. For example, the store channel is better suited for selling products with important "touch-and-feel" attributes such as the fit of a shirt, the taste of an ice cream flavor, or the smell of a perfume. On the other hand, an Internet channel might be just as effective as a store channel for selling products with important "look-and-see" attributes such as price, color, and grams of fat. Evaluating these products does not require senses beyond sight.

Pricing

Pricing represents another difficult decision for multichannel and omnichannel retailers. Many customers expect prices to be the same across channels. However, in some cases, retailers need to adjust their pricing strategy because of the competition they face in different channels. For example, BarnesandNoble.com offers lower prices through its Internet channels than through its stores to compete effectively against Amazon.com.

Retailers with stores in multiple markets often set different prices for the same merchandise to deal with differences in local competition. Most customers don't know about these price differences because they are exposed only to the prices in their local markets. However, multichannel and omnichannel retailers may have difficulties sustaining regional price differences when customers can easily check prices on the Internet.

Reduction of Channel Migration

An Internet channel helps customers search for information about products and prices. The most common multichannel and omnichannel usage involves an initial search online, followed by a purchase in stores. As long as the store and the Internet channel

---

3.4 RETAILING VIEW   Warby Parker, the Reverse Omnichannel Retailer

Warby Parker started as an exclusively online retailer before deciding to open physical retail locations. Some online retailers, such as Amazon and RentTheRunway, have experimented with brick-and-motor locations, but Warby Parker, with its trendy eyewear fashions and compelling brand image, is among the first to commit so strongly to this model, opening 34 locations across North America. Warby Parker stores have thus far been widely successful.

Furthermore, these stores actually enhance the profitability of its online channel. Part of Warby Parker's unique selling proposition is that it will send online customers up to five dummy frames for free, which they can try on, to see how they look, before making a purchase. The promise is central to the brand's success, but it also creates very high shipping costs, even before any sale is guaranteed. The presence of the store locations means that some customers can come in to find their perfect style, rather than receiving an expensive shipment at their homes.

Even as Warby Parker continues to embrace this traditional retail format, it maintains its innovative approach to retailing. In July 2016 it became one of the first retailers to sell on Snapchat. Customers could buy an exclusive pair of sunglasses, using a code that had been released on Warby Parker's Snapchat account. The glasses quickly sold out, especially after having been teased on the brand's Instagram account a week before. In this post, Warby Parker told customers to follow it on Snapchat for something exclusive.

© Kolasinski/BFA/REX/Shutterstock

Having stores enables customers to try on frames without having Warby Parker incur expensive shipping costs.

Although other companies have used Snapchat for marketing, this move marked a breakthrough for the app as a retailing channel.

Sources: www.warbyparker.com; Douglas MacMillan, "Warby Parker Adds Storefronts to Its Sales Strategy," *The Wall Street Journal*, November 17, 2014; Alyssa Hardy, "Warby Parker Sells Sunglasses on Snap-chat," *Teen Vogue*, July 21, 2016; Shannon Carlin, "Warby Parker Offers Limited-Edition Sunglasses on Snapchat," *Refinery29*, July 23, 2016.

represent the same retailer, the firm is happy. But if customers gather information from one of its channels, then buy from a channel hosted by a competitor, the retailer suffers from the frustrating problem of **channel migration**.[31] A particularly worrisome form of channel migration is called showrooming. **Showrooming** occurs when a consumer goes into a store to learn about different brands and products and then searches the Internet for the same product sold at a lower price. Three approaches that multichannel and omnichannel retailers can use to reduce showrooming are (1) providing better customer service, (2) offering uniquely relevant information based on proprietary data the retailer has collected about the customers, and (3) promoting private-label merchandise that can be purchased only from the retailer. These approaches are discussed in more detail in Chapter 5.[32] Retailing View 3.4 highlights how Warby Parker has successfully launched its store channel to complement its Internet retail channel in a way that helps it keep customers attached to the retailer.

SUMMARY

LO 3-1 Understand the channels used by retailers.

A retail channel is the way a retailer sells *and* delivers merchandise and services to its customers. The most common channel used by retailers is a store. Retailers also use a variety of nonstore channels, including the Internet, mobile, social, catalogs, direct mail, direct selling, and automated retailing (vending machines) to make sales to customers. Multichannel retailing is when retailers offer more than one channel to sell and deliver merchandise and services to consumers. But the channels operate without integrating operations between them. In a step beyond multichannel retailing, cross-channel retailing is when customers actually use multiple channels to make purchases. The most advanced type of selling channel, omnichannel retailing, is a coordinated multichannel retail offering that provides a seamless and synchronized customer experience, using all the retailer's shopping channels.

LO 3-2 Compare the relative strengths of the major retail channels: stores; Internet, mobile, and social; and catalog and other nonstore channels.

Stores offer several benefits to customers that they cannot get when they shop through nonstore channels. These benefits include touch and smell of products, personal service, risk reduction, immediate gratification, entertainment and social experience, and cash payment.

There are multiple advantages of Internet, mobile, and social channels. First, they can offer a wider selection of products. Second, they allow retailers to provide more information. Third, they enable retailers to inform customers, using more personalized details about products and services. Fourth, they offer sellers the unique opportunity to collect information about consumer shopping. Fifth, Internet and mobile channels provide an opportunity for retailers to enter new markets economically. Sixth, they provide information that the retailer can use to improve the shopping experience across all channels. However, some consumers are concerned about buying products through an Internet or mobile channel. In an adjunct to the Internet and mobile channels, social retailing involves conducting purchase transactions through a social media site, giving consumers yet another opportunity to buy.

The catalog channel, like all nonstore channels, provides safety and convenience benefits to customers. Using the catalog channel, consumers can look at merchandise and place an order from almost anywhere 24/7 without needing a computer, mobile device, or Internet connection. Consumers also can refer to the information in a catalog anytime by simply picking it up from the coffee table. Finally, catalogs can be easier to browse through than websites.

LO 3-3 Describe the opportunities associated with a true omnichannel strategy.

If retailers can devise an effective omnichannel strategy, they can achieve several benefits. In particular, consumers like the idea of a seamless experience, so an omnichannel approach appeals better to customers. Furthermore, omnichannel retailers can get their products to consumers more cost-efficiently and in the channel those consumers prefer. Good omnichannel retailers also use each channel to promote the others, such as highlighting their web address on bags that customers carry from their stores.

LO 3-4 Analyze the challenges facing multichannel and omnichannel retailers.

Multichannel retailers are still struggling to provide an integrated shopping experience across all their channels because of the unique skills and resources needed to manage each channel. A critical decision for multichannel retailers is the degree to which they should integrate the operations of their channels or rely on different organizations for each channel. The channels each offer unique sets of benefits, so customers who use the different channels are not using them for the same reasons. Retailers need to provide a consistent brand image of themselves and their merchandise across all channels. The degree to which merchandise assortments and pricing are similar across channels represents another difficult decision for a multichannel retailer. Finally, the availability of Internet and mobile channels enables customers to search easily for information about products and their prices during a shopping episode.

KEY TERMS

automated retailing, *75*

catalog channel, *74*

channel migration, *81*

cross-channel retailing, *67*

direct selling, *74*

Internet retailing, *70*

live chat, *71*

m-commerce, *70*

mobile commerce, *70*

mobile retailing, *70*

multichannel retailing, *67*

omnichannel retailing, *67*

retail channel, *67*

showrooming, *81*

single-channel retailing, *67*

social retailing, *74*

s-retailing, *74*

vending machine, *76*

GET OUT AND DO IT!

1. **CONTINUING CASE ASSIGNMENT: GO SHOP-PING** Assume that you are shopping on the Internet for an item in the same merchandise category you analyzed for the comparison shopping exercise in Chapter 2. Go to the retailer's website and compare the merchandise assortment offered, the prices, and the shopping experience in the store and on the store's website. How easy was it to locate what you were looking for? What were the assortment and pricing like? What was the checkout like? What are the categories and/or subcategories? How many SKUs were in each category and subcategory? What features of the sites did you like and dislike, such as the look and feel of the site, navigation, and special features?

2. **INTERNET EXERCISE** Go to the websites of J.Crew (www.jcrew.com), JCPenney (www.jcpenney.com), and American Eagle Outfitters (www.ae.com) and shop for a pair of khaki pants. Evaluate your shopping experience at each site. Compare and contrast the sites and your experiences on the basis of characteristics you think are important to consumers.

3. **INTERNET EXERCISE** Assume that you are getting married and planning your wedding. Compare and contrast the usefulness of www.theknot.com and www.mywedding.com for planning your wedding. What features of the sites do you like and dislike? Indicate the specific services offered by these sites that you would use.

4. **INTERNET AND SHOPPING EXERCISE** Pick a merchandise category like microwave ovens, power drills, digital cameras, blenders, or coffeemakers. Compare a retailer's offering in its local store and its Internet site. What are the differences in the assortments offered through its store, Internet, mobile, and social channels? Are the prices the same or different? What has the retailer done to exploit the synergies among the channels?

5. **INTERNET AND SHOPPING EXERCISE** Access the websites of Home Depot and Macy's using your mobile phone and computer. What are the differences in the ease of navigation when looking at the presentation of merchandise using the two methods of accessing the websites?

DISCUSSION QUESTIONS AND PROBLEMS

1. Why are store-based retailers aggressively pursuing sales through Internet channels?

2. What are the differences between a multichannel, cross-channel, and omnichannel retailer? Provide an example of each.

3. What aspects of omnichannel retailing would benefit you as a consumer?

4. Choose a retailer from whom you have purchased through multiple channels. Is it a multichannel, cross-channel, or omnichannel retailer? Justify your answer.

5. Using the same retailer that you chose in the previous question, how well have they integrated their operations across channels? How similar and different are their

assortments and prices? Should they do these things differently? Why or why not?

6. Do you participate in showrooming? Why or why not?

7. From a customer's perspective, what are the benefits and limitations of stores? Internet? Mobile? Social? Catalogs and other nonstore channels?

8. Which of the following categories of merchandise do you think could be sold most successfully through an Internet channel: jewelry; TV sets; computer software; high-fashion apparel; pharmaceuticals; health care products such as toothpaste, shampoo, and cold remedies? Why?

CHAPTER ENDNOTES

1. "McKinsey Minute: Omnichannel," *McKinsey on Marketing & Sales,* July 15, 2015, https://www.youtube.com/watch?v=P-rnrYPIRmA.

2. Dan Berthiaume, "Omnichannel Comes of Age with New Index," *Chain Store Age,* October 1, 2015.

3. Ibid.

4. Alicia Fiorletta, "Rebecca Minkoff Unveils Connected Store of the Future," *Retail Touch Points,* November 14, 2014; "Rebecca Minkoff Connected Store Demo," *eBay,* November 12, 2014, https://www.youtube.com/watch?v=6G3JIyG_GeY.

5. Ibid.

6. "Rebecca Minkoff Empowers Millennial Shoppers," *Think With Google,* August 26, 2015, https://www.youtube.com/watch?v=1i4KpNAY8uY.

7. Rachel Arthur, "Shoppable Content Rules Fashion Week Season, with Apple, Instagram, and More as Partners," *Forbes,* March 2, 2016.

8. Ibid.

9. "Multi-Channel Retail: A Strategic Overview for US and Canadian Retailers," a CDC eCommerce White Paper, January 20, 2011.

10. Nikki Baird and Brian Kilcourse, *Omni-Channel 2012: Cross-Channel Comes of Age, 2012 Benchmark Report* (Miami: Retail Systems Research, June 2012).

11. Brendan Witcher, Fiona Swerdlow, Diana Gold, and Laura Glazer, "Mastering the Art of Omnichannel Retailing," *Forrester Report,* December 22, 2015.

12. www.bassproshop.com; Tom Bailey Jr., "Bass Pro to Open 'Newest Generation' Megastore in Little Rock," *McClatchy–Tribune Business News,* June 15, 2012.

13. "Sponsored Supplement: Expanding the Reach of Personalization," *Internet Retailer,* March 2010.

14. Peter C. Verhoef, P. K. Kannan, and J. Jeffrey Inman, "From Multi-Channel Retailing to Omni-Channel Retailing: Introduction to the Special Issue on Multi-Channel Retailing," *Journal of Retailing* 91, no. 2 (2015), pp. 174–181; Kristina Melis, Katia Campo, Els Breugelmans, and Lien Lamey, "The Impact of the Multi-Channel Retail Mix on Online Store Choice: Does Online Experience Matter?," *Journal of Retailing* 91, no. 2 (2015), pp. 272–288; Scott A. Neslin, Dhruv Grewal, Robert Leghorn, Venkatesh Shankar, Marije L. Teerling, Jacquelyn S. Thomas, and Peter C. Verhoef, "Challenges and Opportunities in Multichannel Customer Management," *Journal of Service Research* 9, no. 2 (2006), pp. 95–112.

15. Riccardo Mangiaracina and Alessandro Perego, "Payment Systems in the B2C eCommerce: Are They a Barrier for the Online Customer?," *Journal of Internet Banking and Commerce* 14 (December 2009), pp. 1–17.

16. Elizabeth M. Aguirre, Dominik Mahr, Dhruv Grewal, Ko de Ruyter, and Martin Wetzels, "Unraveling the Personalization Paradox: The Effect of Information Collection and Trust-Building Strategies on Online Advertisement Effectiveness," *Journal of Retailing* 91, no. 1 (2015), pp. 34–49.

17. Adam S. Brasel and James Gips, "Tablets, Touchscreens, and Touchpads: How Varying Touch Interfaces Trigger Psychological Ownership and Endowment," *Journal of Consumer Psychology* 24, no. 2 (2014), pp. 226–233.

18. Ibid.; Urban Outfitters, Inc., "2015 Annual Report," March 31, 2016; Fareeha Ali, "Urban Outfitter's Focus Turns to Online-Offline Integration," *Internet Retailer,* March 8, 2016.

19. Matthew Stern, "Social Sites Move to Boost Retail Sales," *RetailWire,* June 5, 2015; "In-Tweet Purchases on Twitter," https://support.twitter.com/articles/20171947; Arthur, "Shoppable Content Rules Fashion Week Season."

20. Susannah Morris, "Where Social Commerce Revenue Comes From," HubSpot, January 14, 2015.

21. Ibid.

22. www.catalogs.com/info/b2b/catalog-merchandise.html; data from U.S. Census Bureau, http://blog.hubspot.com/marketing/social-ecommerce-revenue-infographic#sm.0000uabecras8eoetft106ewlww69.

23. http://www.ikea.com/ms/en_CA/catalogue/catalogue_index.html (see IKEA 2016 catalog); Tom Banks, "IKEA Catalogue Gets an Interactive Overhaul," *Design Week,* July 23, 2012; Victoria Thompson, "IKEA's Augmented Reality Catalogue Is a Step in the Right Direction," *Retail Week,* August 8, 2012.

24. *Fact Sheet: U.S. Direct Selling in 2015,* Washington, DC: Direct Selling Association, 2015.

25. Ibid.

26. Ibid.

27. https://www.census.gov/retail/index.html#arts.

28. Alexandra Alter and Nick Wingfield, "A Trip through Amazon's First Physical Store," *The New York Times,* March 10, 2016; Jennifer Van Grove and Shan Li, "Amazon to Open 2nd Physical Bookstore, This One in Southern California," *Los Angeles Times,* March 8, 2016.

29. *Omni-Channel 2012: Cross-Channel Comes of Age, 2012 Benchmark,* RSR, June 2012.

30. Witcher et al., "Mastering the Art of Omnichannel Retailing."

31. Verhoef et al., "From Multi-Channel Retailing to Omni-Channel Retailing."

32. Adam Rapp, Thomas L. Baker, Daniel G. Bachrach, Jessica Ogilvie, and Lauren Skinner Beitelspacher, "Perceived Customer Showrooming Behavior and the Effect on Retail Salesperson Self-Efficacy and Performance," *Journal of Retailing* 91, no. 2 (2015), pp. 358–369; Stephanie Clifford, "Luring Online Shoppers Offline," *The New York Times,* July 4, 2012; Stephanie Clifford, "Electronics Retailers Scramble to Adapt to Changing Market," *The New York Times,* June 18, 2012; Suzy Sandberg, "4 Ways Retailers Can Fight Showrooming," *Mobile Commerce Daily,* March 15, 2012; Sarah Mahoney, "Shoppers Mastering Art of Showrooming," *Marketing Daily,* March 2, 2012.

LEARNING OBJECTIVES

After reading this chapter, you should be able to:

LO 4-1 Describe the process that consumers go through when making retail patronage and buying decisions.

LO 4-2 Identify the different types of buying processes.

LO 4-3 Summarize how the economy and social factors affect customer purchase decisions.

LO 4-4 Determine why and how retailers group customers into market segments.

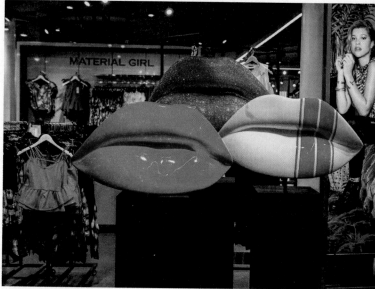

© Chris Goodney/Bloomberg/Getty Images

Just when retailers had figured out how to appeal to the huge target market of Baby Boomers, along came their children, the Millennials. This cohort, born between the 1980s and early 2000s, constitutes approximately one-quarter of the population (around 80 million people), and their annual spending appears likely to surpass $1.4 trillion—about one-third of all retail sales—within the next few years. But these shoppers behave differently than their parents did when they make purchases. Enticing this distinct generation of shoppers into stores, whether virtually or in person, and encouraging them to spend their limited funds thus requires a whole new set of approaches— a lesson retailers need to learn quickly if they hope to last until the next generation rolls around.[1]

For example, as Millennials increasingly enter the workforce, they are growing a bit more serious about their fashion choices and seeking some grown-up variety, especially when it comes to wardrobe basics. But they are the Millennials, so they are not visiting the same stores their parents did when they needed a pair of black pants or a new T-shirt. Instead, they prefer online retailers that offer them a range of

benefits, compared with traditional retailers, including easy ordering and delivery and low prices.[2]

In response, Macy's has committed to wooing Millennials and be there for "every major milestone in their lives": graduation, first interviews, bridal registry, baby registry, and everything that comes thereafter. Its overall goal is to cultivate loyal relationships with them now that might last over time, as this demographic group ages. In support of this effort, Macy's launched 13 new fashion lines and repositioned 11 of its private labels to appeal to the unique tastes of Millennials.[3]

It also implemented a $400 million renovation effort for its flagship New York City store, testing out various options that might attract more of the market of shoppers between the ages of 18 and 35 years. In that flagship store, the basement level is newly designated "One Below," and it offers a notably different shopping experience. In addition to merchandise designed to appeal to Millennials, it provides services such as blow drying stations, jean embroidering, and watch engraving. Shoppers can use a 3-D printer to create their own custom jewelry, and a touch-screen wall allows them to take high-quality selfies.[4]

With the recognition that young consumers tend to devote their spending more to personal or digital services than to apparel, suffer higher levels of debt (mostly due to student loans), and earn less on average than previous generations, Macy's is opening more off-price stores to offer lower-priced options. The expansions of its private-label brands seek similar outcomes. Furthermore, in its merchandising strategies, Macy's increasingly showcases furniture that can fit smaller homes (e.g., 650 square feet)—or maybe even their childhood bedrooms, considering that many younger Millennials are delaying moving out of their parents' homes for extended periods.[5]

Finally, in its communications, Macy's increasingly relies on social media, especially Facebook and Pinterest. Already a pioneer in using QR codes, Macy's also has added different kinds of mobile resources and platforms to its marketing mix. In a recent survey, the retailer discovered—to its surprise—that 40 percent of the responses came through mobile devices, so it has expanded its mobile ordering capabilities.[6] It also employs targeted product placement to reach Millennials: On *Pretty Little Liars*, the titular characters wear various Macy's private-label outfits. In partnership with fashion magazines such as *Glamour* and *Vogue*, Macy's hosts private back-to-school shopping events to appeal to the youngest members of this appealing shopping segment.

As Millennials grow up, some of the brands they or their parents have known and loved for years "haven't grown up with us." There's a lesson for every brand here: As times change, so must they, if they hope to remain relevant and interesting to new and emerging generations of shoppers.

As discussed in Chapter 1, an effective retail strategy satisfies customer needs better than do competitors' strategies. Successful retailers are customer-centric—their strategic and tactical decisions revolve around the experiences achieved by their present and potential customers. Thus, understanding customer needs and buying behavior is critical to formulating and implementing an effective retail strategy.

This chapter focuses on how customers process information and make decisions about what stores to patronize, what channels to use, and what products and services to buy.[7] It describes the stages customers go through when making purchase decisions and the factors that influence their buying process. Because typically it is not cost-efficient for retailers to develop unique offerings for individual customers, retailers target their offerings to groups of customers (market segments) with similar needs and buying processes. Thus, this chapter continues with a discussion of how market segments are formed. We use information about the buying process to discuss how retailers can identify the market segments that will be the target of their retail strategy. Appendix 4A, at the end of this chapter examines special aspects of consumer behavior that are of concern to retailers selling fashion merchandise.

THE BUYING PROCESS

LO 4-1

Describe the process that consumers go through when making retail patronage and buying decisions.

The following scenario illustrates the steps consumers go through when purchasing merchandise. Eva Mendoza, a student at the University of Washington, is beginning to interview for jobs. Eva planned to wear the blue suit her parents gave her several years ago to the interviews. But looking at her suit, she realizes that it's not very stylish and that the jacket is beginning to show signs of wear. Wanting to make a good first impression during her interviews, she decides to buy a new suit.

Eva surfs the Internet for tips on dressing for interviews and looks through some catalogs to see the styles and prices being offered. Eva surfs fashion blogs such as *Hello Fashion* and checks what her friends Like on Facebook, as well as what they have pinned on Pinterest. She goes to retailers' websites to examine and compare all their suits. She then decides to go to a store so that she can try on a suit and have it altered if necessary. She likes to shop at American Eagle Outfitters and Banana Republic, but neither sells business suits. Before going to the Northgate Mall in

Seattle, she issues a status update on her Facebook page, announcing her intentions to go to the mall and inviting friends to join her. Jenny responds to her Facebook posting, and they decide to meet at the mall entrance. Betsy also responds, but she has a cold and wants to rest.

Eva and Jenny first go to Macy's and are approached by a salesperson in the career women's department. After asking Eva what type of suit she wants and her size, the salesperson shows her three suits. Eva talks with Jenny about the suits, and they decide to get Betsy's opinion. So Eva takes photos of the suits with her mobile phone and uploads them on Instagram. Betsy likes all three, so Eva tries them on.

When Eva comes out of the dressing room, she is unsure which suit to select, but after sending Betsy some more photos, she, Jenny, and the salesperson decide the second suit is the most attractive and appropriate for interviewing. Eva is happy with the color, fit, fabric, and length of the suit, but she is concerned that it will require dry cleaning. It also costs more than she had planned to spend. Eva decides to buy the suit after another customer in the store, seeing her wearing the suit, tells her she looks very professional.

As Jenny and Eva are walking toward the door, they pass the shoe department. Jenny tells Eva, "You need to buy shoes that go with your suit." Eva finds a pair of Steve Madden pumps that are perfect. She tries on a few pairs to get the right size. Then Jenny tells her that she thinks the shoes are overpriced. Eva scans the UPC code for the shoes using her mobile phone's QRReader app and finds that Zappos is selling the shoes for $20 less and with no sales tax. So she orders the shoes from Zappos for delivery to her apartment the next day.

Consider Eva's shopping experience as we describe the customer buying process. The **buying process**—the steps consumers go through when buying a product or service—begins when customers recognize an unsatisfied need. Then they seek information about how to satisfy the need—what retailers, channels, and products or services might satisfy the need. Customers then evaluate the alternatives and choose a store or Internet site to visit or a catalog to review. Their encounter with a retailer provides more information and may alert customers to additional needs. After evaluating the retailer's offering, customers may make a purchase or go to another retailer to collect more information. Eventually, customers purchase a product, use the product, and then decide whether the retailer, channel, and product satisfy their needs during the postpurchase evaluation stage of the customer buying process.

Exhibit 4–1 outlines the buying process—the stages consumers go through to select a retailer and channel and to buy a specific item. The exhibit suggests that the buying process is linear. First, the channel and retailer are selected, and only then are the specific items selected. For each of these decisions, customers go through five stages, beginning with need recognition and ending with postpurchase. As we discuss the stages in the buying process, though, you should recognize that customers might not go through all the stages and/or might not go through the stages in the order shown in Exhibit 4–1. For example, Eva might have decided on the brand of suit she wanted before selecting a store, or she might have collected information about suits sold at Macy's and, on the basis of this information, decided to go to another store or to use another channel, such as the Internet, to buy the suit.

Retailers attempt to influence consumers as they go through the buying process to encourage consumers to buy merchandise and services from them. Each stage in the buying process is examined in the following sections.

Need Recognition

The buying process is triggered when consumers recognize they have an unsatisfied need. An **unsatisfied need** arises when customers' desired level of satisfaction differs from their present level of satisfaction. For example, Eva recognized that she had a need when she was faced with the prospect of interviewing for jobs in her blue suit. She needed a suit that would make a good impression and realized her worn, outdated blue suit would not satisfy this need. Need recognition can be as straightforward as realizing your hair has gotten too long and shaggy, feeling the desire for an uplifting experience after a final exam, receiving a message about something a friend bought, or getting a shipment from the sub-scription service you signed up for to receive monthly resupplies of your groceries.[8]

Types of Needs   The needs that motivate customers to go shopping can be classified as utilitarian or hedonic. When consumers go shop-ping to accomplish a specific task, such as Eva buying a suit for job interviews, they are seeking to satisfy **utilitarian needs**. When consumers go shopping for pleasure, they are seeking to satisfy their **hedonic needs**—their needs for entertain-ing, emotional, and recreational experiences. Thus, from the consumer's perspective, utilitar-ian needs are associated with work, whereas hedonic needs are associated with pleasure.[9]

Successful retailers attempt to satisfy both the utilitarian and the hedonic needs of their cus-tomers. Consumers motivated by utilitarian needs typically shop in a more deliberate and efficient manner. Thus, retailers need to provide adequate information and an effortless shopping experience for utilitarian shoppers. But shoppers with hedonic needs desire excitement, stimulation, status and power, recreation, and adventure.[10]

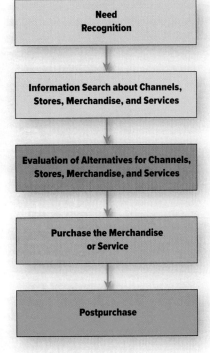

EXHIBIT 4–1
Stages in the Buying Process

The type of need may shift depending on the situation, the product category, and elu-sive shifts in consumer values. For example, the needs of male shoppers have been tradi-tionally more utilitarian when shopping for apparel.[11] Furthermore, men are not as interested in the "hunt" as women when it comes to shopping.[12] If he needs a new suit for a wedding, for example, he is likely to do a little research before going on a shopping out-ing. But then he will go to one or two stores, examine a few options, and make a decision.

Many retailers interested in attracting male shoppers thus have extended the size of the men's section in their stores and added new products. Nordstrom also came up with a new way to appeal to this market. Its online retail arm, Trunk Club, carries men's clothing from about 100 brands and attracts men who want to look good but are unfa-miliar with luxury clothing. In this unique retail model, men who sign up for the ser-vice undergo interviews with a stylist, then receive a trunk full of items each month. They pay for only what they do not return.[13] Thus, the shopping experience is hassle free, ensures that the clothing meets the customer's needs, and enables shoppers to look great, with the convenience of home delivery.

Some other examples of how retailers satisfy hedonic needs are listed next:

1. *Stimulation.* Retailers and mall managers use background music, visual displays, scents, and demonstrations in stores and malls to create a carnival-like, stimulating experience for their customers. (See Chapter 16.) Such environments encourage consumers to take a break from their everyday lives and visit stores. Retailers also attempt to stimulate customers with exciting graphics and photography in their catalogs and on their websites.

2. *Status and power.* Some people choose retailers based on the attention and respect they receive. For example, Canyon Ranch offers upscale health resorts in Tucson, Arizona, and Lenox, Massachusetts, as well as spa clubs in Las Vegas, Nevada, and on cruises, in collaboration with Celebrity Cruises, Oceania, and Regent Seven Seas or on the *Queen Mary 2*. All Canyon Ranch resorts and spas make the customer's experience the center of attention, offering spa services, medical and nutritional consultations, workshops, spiritual pursuits, and healthy gourmet cuisine.

Men who sign up for Nordstrom's online Trunk Club undergo interviews with a stylist, then receive a trunk full of items each month. They pay for only what they do not return.

3. *Adventure.* Often, consumers go shopping because they enjoy finding bargains, looking for sales, and finding discounts or low prices. They treat shopping as a game to be "won." Off-price retailers like Marshalls and Trader Joe's, warehouse clubs like Costco, and fast-fashion specialty retailers like Zara cater to this need by constantly changing their assortment so that customers never know what kind of treasure they will find.

Conflicting Needs   Most customers have multiple needs. Moreover, these needs often conflict. For example, Eva Mendoza would like to wear a DKNY suit, which would enhance her self-image and earn her the admiration of her college friends. But satisfying these hedonic needs might conflict with her utilitarian needs—the need to stay within her budget and the need to get a job. Employers might feel that she's not responsible if she wears a suit that is too expensive for an interview for an entry-level position. Later in this chapter, we discuss a model of how customers make trade-offs between conflicting needs.

The needs and decision-making processes may differ depending on the specific situation. For example, a skier may purchase expensive Spyder goggles but wear an inexpensive snowsuit from Target. A grocery shopper might buy an inexpensive store brand of paper towels and a premium national brand of orange juice. This pattern of buying both premium and low-priced merchandise or patronizing both expensive, status-oriented retailers and price-oriented retailers is called **cross-shopping.**[14]

Stimulating Need Recognition   Customers must first recognize unsatisfied needs before they are motivated to visit a store or go online to buy merchandise.

Sometimes these needs are stimulated by an event in a person's life, like Eva's impending interviews. But retailers use a variety of approaches to stimulate unmet needs. Advertising, e-mails, direct mail, publicity, and special events communicate the availability of new merchandise or special prices. Visits to WornOnTV (**www.wornontv.net**) can stimulate need recognition by showing products that celebrities or television characters have worn. In a social media campaign, Elephant Pants encouraged visitors to its website and Facebook page to consider a pant purchase by giving them a personality quiz that claimed to reveal which style best suited them.[15] Within a store, visual merchandising and salespeople can stimulate need recognition; for example, the display of shoes stimulated Eva's need for shoes to complement her new suit.

Source: Flayr

Flayr combines reviews and ratings from users' social networks with their own preferences to make accurate recommendations about products that a consumer might like and where to buy them.

Information Search

Once customers identify a need, they typically seek information about retailers, channels, or products to help them satisfy that need. Eva's search started on the Internet and then narrowed to the three suits shown to her by the salesperson at Macy's and the opinions of her friends. In other situations, Eva might have collected a lot more information by visiting several retailers and/or spending more time on the Internet getting information from fashion blogs like College Fashion, College Fashionista, and Her Campus.[16] New technologies, such as those available through Flayr, combine reviews and ratings from users' social networks with their own preferences to make accurate recommendations about products that a consumer might like and where to buy them.[17]

Sources of Information   Customers have two sources of information: internal and external. **Internal sources** are information in a customer's memory, such as names, images, and past experiences with different stores. The major source of internal information is the customer's past shopping experience. Even if they remember only a small fraction of the information to which they are exposed, customers have an extensive internal information bank to draw on when deciding where to shop and what to buy.

External sources consist of information provided by a host of sources. People search for products and information using search engines such as Google, visit the websites maintained by manufacturers and retailers, acquire information from traditional media (e.g., advertising), read blogs, watch product demonstrations on YouTube, and ask friends, in person and through social media.

When customers believe that they are not well enough informed or that their internal information is inadequate, they turn to external information sources. For example, Eva asked her friends, Betsy and Jenny, to help her make the purchase decision. To find out if the price of the shoes she liked was reasonable, she turned to an online shoe seller. Such external sources of information play a major role in the acceptance of fashions, as discussed in Appendix 4A.

Amount of Information Searched   In general, the amount of **information search** undertaken depends on the value customers believe they can gain from searching versus the cost of searching.[18] The value of the search stems from the degree to which the additional information improves the customer's purchase decision. Will the search help the customer find a lower-priced product or one that will give superior performance? The costs of the search include the customer's time and money. Traveling from store to store can cost money for gas and parking, but the major cost incurred is the customer's time.

Technology has dramatically reduced the cost of information search. For example, vast information about merchandise sold across the world is just a smartphone search away. Google indirectly facilitates consumer search by providing retailers with information about how shoppers search through its site. It even claims it can predict fashion trends better than most retailers, and it's willing to sell that information to them.[19]

The amount of information search also is affected by (1) characteristics of the individual customer and (2) aspects of the market and buying situation in which the purchase is made.[20] Some people search more than others. Shoppers seeking hedonic benefits typically spend more time collecting information and shopping because they enjoy the process. Customers who have prior experience purchasing and using the product or service tend to search less.

Two marketplace and situational factors affecting information search are (1) the number of competing brands and retail outlets and (2) the time pressure under which the purchase must be made.[21] When competition is greater and there are more alternatives to consider, the amount of information search increases. However, the amount decreases with greater time pressures.

Reducing Information Search   The retailer's objective for customers in the information search stage is to limit the customer's search to its store or website. One measure of a retailer's performance on this objective is the **conversion rate**, the percentage of customers who enter a store or access a website and then buy a product from that same store or website.

Each element of the retailing mix can be used to increase a retailer's conversion rate. Category specialists such as Best Buy provide a very deep assortment of merchandise, everything a customer might want to consider, so that the customer can collect all the information and make the necessary comparisons between products in their stores or on their websites. The H-E-B supermarket chain in Texas takes particular care to put its shoppers in a good mood to encourage them to stay there and buy, as Retailing View 4.1 describes. At Sephora, the fluid layout features products organized by brands and encourages customers to try products from different lines, which reduces their information search in other stores by giving customers a sense of the vast options available.[22] Many retailers also display items around the checkout area to encourage on-the-spot conversions.

Services provided by retailers can also limit the search once at the retailer's location. By offering credit and having informed salespeople, a retailer can convince consumers that they don't need to collect additional information from other retailers. Many retailers equip their floor staff with mobile devices to enable them to check inventory levels for customers on the spot or help them create virtual outfits by combining various apparel items available in the store. For example, the Macy's salesperson might have shown Eva how a nice scarf would help make her new suit look even more professional. However, such efforts still require old-fashioned attentiveness and training, such that employees have a sense of how to engage customers in the experience and encourage them to buy in the store.

Finally, with its **everyday low pricing (EDLP) strategy**, Walmart stresses the continuity of its retail prices at a level somewhere between the regular nonsale price and the deep-discount sale price of its competitors. This strategy reduces information search, because it helps assure customers that they won't find a lower price for these products at a different store the next time they go shopping. In addition, many stores offer money-back guarantees if a competitor offers the same merchandise at a lower price. These pricing policies tend to limit the customer information search to the retailer's offering.

RETAILING VIEW   The Supermarket That Gets Customers, and Also Gets Them to Stay

When it comes to consumer behavior, the research is clear: If they want to succeed, retailers need to attract customers' attention, affection, and commitment; put them in a great mood, perhaps by offering them something for nothing; and help people make their decisions easily and in a way that causes them to feel smart and informed. It may be clear, but few companies are applying these lessons as effectively as a regional grocery store chain in Texas, H-E-B.

The entire operation seeks to make it easier for consumers to buy the products they want and feel pleased with their purchases. H-E-B has avoided loyalty cards and instead simply offers all consumers in the store the same deals on the same items. Thus, shoppers do not need to remember to bring their store coupons or stick their loyalty cards in their wallets before they leave for their grocery run. The fresh food displays offer obvious highlights of their freshness: a constant smell of rotisserie chicken near the deli display, a guacamole prepping station featuring chefs carving out the avocados right in front of shoppers, sushi chefs working away in the center of the store.

Moreover, H-E-B gets its regional customers excited and entranced by playing on their shared identity of being from Texas. This option might be less effective in other regions with a weaker sense of identity, but in Texas, the idea that H-E-B is just like its consumers—big, brash, unafraid, and unabashed— garners it substantial attention and affection.

Once it has people in its stores, it gets them to engage and commit to actually buying by adding tear-off coupons to its displays. Rather than just seeing a sale sign, customers must undertake the action of tearing off a coupon. This action is not particularly strenuous of course, but the simple move increases the chances that shoppers will follow through on their already committed effort by completing the purchase.

In addition, H-E-B sets up an appealing and enjoyable atmosphere that seeks to put shoppers in a better mood. In particular, a plethora of coupons give buyers an additional

H-E-B is just like its consumers—big, brash, unafraid, and unabashed.

item for free after they purchase. People simply love things for free, so the constant reminder of how much they can get, seemingly at no cost, enhances their moods. As if that were not enough, H-E-B also gives away lots of free samples. In addition to food samples, to keep shoppers' blood sugar levels up it specializes in wine samples. Because alcohol releases dopamine in people's brains, just a small sip of a nice Zinfandel can leave shoppers in a better mood.

As a result, even though H-E-B remains a regional chain, with limited name recognition outside Texas, its ranking on a recent "consumer delight index" placed it on par with such well-known customer favorites as Trader Joe's and Whole Foods.

Source: Roger Dooley, "The Smartest Supermarket You Never Heard Of," *Forbes*, January 28, 2014, http://www.forbes.com.

Internet/Social Media/Mobile: Information Search and Price Competition

The Internet in general, social media, and the increasing applications for mobile devices have had a profound impact on consumers' ability to gather external information. In addition to placing their own information on their websites and apps, retailers encourage customers to post information such as product reviews, ratings, photos, and videos. Consumer reviews are emerging as a prime information source for shoppers as they collect information during the buying process.[23]

Apps, such as QRReader and Google's shopping feature,[24] that encourage **showrooming**—a practice in which consumers visit stores to gather information about the product, then buy online—enable consumers to find the best prices for any product quickly. Retailers and manufacturers are concerned that the ease of collecting this price information so easily through the Internet increases price competition. Traditionally, store-based retailers, offering the same merchandise, experienced limited price competition because of their geographic separation. The Internet, social media, and mobile apps mean that consumers' ability to compare prices no longer is limited by physical distance. Retailers like Best Buy and Walmart attempt to thwart the impact of showrooming by offering price matching guarantees.

© gpointstudio/iStock/Getty Images

Apps, such as QRReader and Google's shopping feature, that encourage showrooming—a practice in which consumers visit stores to gather information about the product, then buy online—enable consumers to find the best prices for any product quickly.

The Internet, social media, and mobile apps not only help online consumers collect price information but also give them information about the quality and performance of products, all at a low search cost. With more information about product quality, customers might be willing to pay more for high-quality products, which would mitigate the importance of price.[25]

Evaluation of Alternatives: The Multiattribute Model

The multiattribute attitude model provides a useful way to summarize how customers use the information they have collected to evaluate and select retailers, channels, and products. We discuss this model in detail because it offers a framework for developing a retailing strategy.[26]

The **multiattribute attitude model** is based on the notion that customers see a retailer, a product, or a channel as a collection of attributes or characteristics. The model is designed to predict a customer's evaluation of a product, retailer, or channel on the basis of (1) its performance on relevant attributes and (2) the importance of those attributes to the customer.

Beliefs about Performance   To illustrate this model, consider the store choice decision confronting a young, single, professional Milwaukee woman who needs groceries. She considers three alternatives: (1) a supercenter store in the next suburb, (2) her local supermarket, or (3) a grocer that operates only an Internet channel, such as FreshDirect. Her perception of the offerings provided by these retailers is shown in Exhibit 4–2.

EXHIBIT 4–2
Characteristics of Food
Retailers

A. INFORMATION ABOUT STORES SELLING GROCERIES			
Store Characteristics	**Supercenter**	**Supermarket**	**Internet Grocer**
Grocery prices	20% below average	Average	10% above average
Delivery cost ($)	0	0	10
Total travel time (minutes)	30	15	0
Typical checkout time (minutes)	10	5	2
Number of products, brands, and sizes	40,000	30,000	40,000
Fresh produce	Yes	Yes	Yes
Fresh fish	Yes	Yes	No
Ease of finding products	Difficult	Easy	Easy
Ease of collecting nutritional information about products	Difficult	Difficult	Easy

B. BELIEFS ABOUT STORES' PERFORMANCE BENEFITS*			
Performance Benefits	**Supercenter**	**Supermarket**	**Internet Grocer**
Economy	10	8	6
Convenience	3	5	10
Assortment	9	7	5
Availability of product Information	4	4	8

*10 = excellent, 1 = poor.

The customer mentally processes the "objective" information about each grocery retailer in part A of Exhibit 4–2 and forms an impression of the benefits each one provides. Part B of Exhibit 4–2 shows her beliefs about these benefits. Notice that some benefits combine several objective characteristics. For example, the convenience benefit combines travel time, checkout time, and ease of finding products. Grocery prices and delivery cost affect her beliefs about the economy of shopping at the various retail outlets.

The degree to which each retailer provides each benefit is represented on a 10-point scale: 10 means the retailer performs very well in providing the benefit; 1 means it performs very poorly. In this example, no retailer has superior performance on all benefits. The supercenter performs well on economy and assortment but is low on convenience. The Internet grocer offers the best convenience but is weak on economy and assortment.

Importance Weights The young woman in the preceding example forms an overall evaluation of each alternative on the basis of the importance she places on each benefit the retailers provide. The importance she places on a benefit can also be represented using a 10-point rating scale, with 10 indicating the benefit is very important to her and 1 indicating it's very unimportant. Using this rating scale, the importance of the retailers' benefits for the young woman and for a

The importance weights and performance beliefs for the young single woman (top) and the parent with children (bottom) are different, resulting in different grocery shopping choices.

parent with four children is shown in Exhibit 4–3, along with the performance beliefs previously discussed. Notice that the single woman values convenience and the availability of product information much more than economy and assortment. But to the parent, economy is very important and assortment is moderately important, whereas convenience and product information aren't very important.

EXHIBIT 4–3
Evaluation of Retailers

Characteristic	IMPORTANCE WEIGHTS*		PERFORMANCE BELIEFS		
	Young Single Woman	Parent with Four Children	Supercenter	Supermarket	Internet Grocer
Economy	4	10	10	8	6
Convenience	10	4	3	5	10
Assortment	5	8	9	7	5
Availability of product information	9	2	4	4	8
OVERALL EVALUATION					
Young single woman			151	153	221
Parent with four children			192	164	156

*10 = very important, 1 = very unimportant.

The importance of a retailer's benefits differs for each customer and also may differ for each shopping trip. For example, the parent with four children may stress economy for major shopping trips but place more importance on convenience for a fill-in trip.

In Exhibit 4–3, the single woman and parent have the same beliefs about each retailer's performance, but they differ in the importance they place on the benefits the retailers offer. In general, customers can differ in their beliefs about retailers' performances as well as in their importance weights.

Evaluating Retailers   Research has shown that a customer's overall evaluation of an alternative (in this situation, three retailers) is related to the sum of the performance beliefs multiplied by the importance weights. Thus, we calculate the young, single woman's overall evaluation or score for the supercenter as follows:

$$
\begin{aligned}
4 \times 10 &= 40 \\
10 \times 3 &= 30 \\
5 \times 9 &= 45 \\
9 \times 4 &= \underline{36} \\
&\ 151
\end{aligned}
$$

Exhibit 4–3 shows the overall evaluations of the three retailers using the importance weights of the single woman and the parent. For the single woman, the Internet grocer has the highest score, 221, and thus has the most favorable evaluation. She would probably select this retailer for most of her grocery shopping. On the other hand, the supercenter has the highest score, 192, for the parent, who'd probably buy the family's weekly groceries there.

When customers are about to select a retailer, they don't actually go through the process of listing store characteristics, evaluating retailers' performances on these characteristics, determining each characteristic's importance, calculating each store's overall score, and then patronizing the retailer with the highest score. The multiattribute attitude model does not reflect customers' actual decision process, but it does predict their evaluation of alternatives and their choice. In addition, the model provides useful information for designing a retail offering. For example, if the supermarket could increase its performance rating on assortment from 7 to 10 (perhaps by adding a bakery and a wide selection of prepared meals), customers like the parent might shop at the supermarket more often than at the supercenter.

The application of the multiattribute attitude model in Exhibit 4–3 deals with a customer who is evaluating and selecting a retailer. The same model can also be used to describe how a customer evaluates and selects which channel to use (store; Internet, mobile, and social; or catalog and other nonstore channels) or what merchandise to buy from a retailer. For example, the model could be used to describe Eva Mendoza's choice among the three suits she was considering.

Implications for Retailers   In this section, we describe how a retailer can use the multiattribute attitude model to improve customers' experience and encourage them to shop at the retailer more frequently. First, the model indicates what information customers use to decide which retailer to patronize or which channel to use. Second, it suggests tactics that retailers can undertake to influence customers' store, channel, and merchandise choices.

To develop a program for attracting customers, retailers need to do market research to collect the following information:

1. Alternative retailers that customers consider.
2. Characteristics or benefits that customers consider when evaluating and choosing a retailer.
3. Customers' ratings of each retailer's performance on the characteristics.
4. The importance weights that customers attach to the characteristics.

Armed with this information, the retailer can use several approaches to influence customers to patronize its store or Internet site.

Getting into the Consideration Set

Retailers need to be included in the customer's **consideration set**, or the set of alternatives the customer evaluates when making a choice of a retailer to patronize. To be included in the consideration set, retailers develop programs to increase the likelihood that customers will remember them when they're about to go shopping. Retailers can increase customer awareness through communication and location decisions. For example, search engine optimization techniques can help retailers land at the top of a page of organic results when customers search for products they sell, or they might purchase advertising space to ensure that they are the first source listed for a particular search term. They can also

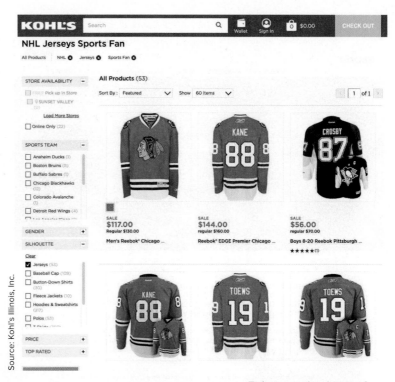

Source: Kohl's Illinois, Inc.

To increase the chance of getting into its potential customers' consideration set, Kohl's may have purchased a highly visible advertising position on Google to attract more shoppers and inform them that it carries NHL apparel.

develop communication programs that link categories and national brands they sell with their corporate name. Searching for "NHL apparel" on Google, for instance, leads a shopper to the NHL's site first, but the second ranking is held by Kohl's, which purchased the advertising position to attract more shoppers and inform them that it carries the gear. Starbucks locates several stores in the same area so that customers are exposed more frequently to the store name as they drive or walk through the area.

After ensuring that it is in consumers' consideration set, a retailer can use three methods to increase the chances that customers will select it for a visit:

1. Increase beliefs about the store's performance.
2. Change customers' importance weights.
3. Add a new benefit.

Changing Performance Beliefs   The first approach involves altering customers' beliefs about the retailer's performance by increasing the retailer's performance rating on a characteristic. For example, the supermarket in Exhibit 4–3 would want to increase its overall rating by improving its rating on all four benefits. The supermarket could improve its rating on economy by lowering prices and its assortment rating by stocking more gourmet and ethnic foods.

Because it can get costly for a retailer to improve its performance on all benefits, retailers must focus on improving their performance on those benefits that are important to customers in their target market. For example, Best Buy knows that an important benefit for its customers is not to be without their computers for lengthy amounts of time when repairs are needed. So through its Geek Squad, it offers around-the-clock support: online, over the phone, and in more than 1,100 stores. Best Buy also maintains a 240,000-square-foot "Geek Squad City" warehouse, with more than 700 employees. All of its Geek Squad agents are dedicated to reducing the time it takes to repair and return a computer. They fix more than 4,000 laptops per day.[27]

Changing Importance Weights   Altering customers' importance weights is another approach to influencing store choice. A retailer wants to increase the importance customers place on benefits for which its performance is superior and decrease the importance of benefits for which it has inferior performance.

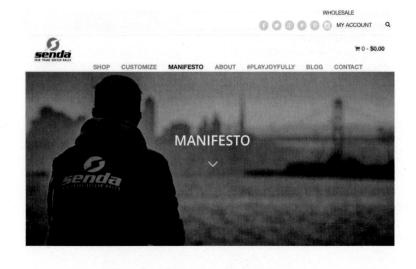

Senda was started with a clear goal: disrupt the industry by embracing Fair Trade, bringing back craftsmanship, promoting joyfully playing, and improving lives along the way.

We work to turn the current business model on its head. The model of major brands paying players millions for endorsements, while going to the developing world and making factories compete to offer them the lowest price (often at the expense of workers) is a broken model that needs to be changed.

Instead of paying producers the absolute lowest possible price, Senda is committed to Fair Trade certification to improve livelihoods.

Instead of cutting costs by lowering the quality of our products so we can spend that money on marketing, Senda uses only best-in-class materials and talented craftspeople.

Senda offers its customers a benefit not available from its competition—fair traded products.

© Senda Athletics

For example, if the supermarket in Exhibit 4–3 tried to attract families who shop at supercenters, it could increase the importance of convenience for them. Typically, changing importance weights is harder than changing performance beliefs, because importance weights reflect customers' personal values.

Adding a New Benefit   Finally, retailers might try to add a new benefit to the set of benefits customers consider when selecting a retailer. Senda (www.sendaathletics.com) does not just offer the typical assortment of athletic gear; it sells unusual items such as customizable soccer balls and training vests. It believes that by providing a deeper assortment than its competition, its customers will find it more attractive. Senda has also integrated an additional benefit not emphasized by its competition: It offers merchandise that is **fair trade** made by workers who are paid a fair wage, not just a minimum wage.[28] A fair wage means that workers are able to live relatively comfortably within the context of their local area. Offering fair trade merchandise is a benefit that is important to consumers who are concerned about the welfare of people in less developed countries.

Purchasing the Merchandise or Service

Customers don't always patronize a store or purchase a brand or item of merchandise with the highest overall evaluation. The product or service offering the greatest benefits (having the highest evaluation) may not be available from the retailer, or the customer may feel that its risks outweigh the potential benefits. Other consumers make purchase choices based on a single attribute, regardless of how well the offering performs on other characteristics. For example, Eva visited Macy's because the local store is convenient to her apartment, even though other department stores might have a wider selection of women's suits. One measure of retailers' success at converting positive evaluations into purchases is being able to minimize the number of real or virtual abandoned carts in the retailer's store or website.

Retailers use various tactics to increase the chances that customers will convert their positive evaluations into purchases. First, they attempt to make it easy to purchase merchandise by making it readily available on mobile devices. For example, Kohl's mobile app maintains a record of everything consumers have bought and the exact loyalty rewards they have earned, shows them the prices of items they select, and details exactly how the rewards and discounts they have earned will adjust those prices. Furthermore, Kohl's app enables customers to save items in their shopping carts and access them from multiple devices. For example, if a teen hopes that her parents will buy her a new pair of jeans that she found at Kohl's while browsing during lunch, she can add it to the shopping cart through her smartphone, then ask her parents to review the item on their tablet later that evening, when they get home from work.[29] In stores, retailers also can reduce the actual wait time for buying merchandise by having more checkout lanes open and placing them conveniently in the store or by equipping salespeople with mobile checkout terminals. In addition to reducing actual waiting time, they can reduce perceived wait times by installing digital displays to entertain customers waiting in line.[30] Many Internet retailers also send reminder e-mails to visitors about items in carts they have abandoned.[31]

Second, retailers' ability to turn a positive purchase intention into a sale can be increased by providing sufficient information that reinforces the customer's positive evaluation. For example, Eva's friend Jenny, the salesperson, and another potential customer also provided Eva with positive feedback to support her purchase decision.

Third, retailers can increase the chances of making a sale by reducing the risk of making a purchase mistake. For instance, retailers can offer liberal return policies, money-back guarantees, and refunds if customers find the same merchandise available at lower prices from another retailer.

Finally, retailers often create a sense of urgency or scarcity to encourage customers to make a purchase decision. Zappos.com and Overstock.com alert customers if an item in their shopping carts is about to sell out. The limited assortments offered by fast-fashion retailers like Zara and off-price retailers like TJX Corporation (TJ Maxx and Marshalls) have conditioned customers to buy when they see an item they like. Otherwise, it may be gone the next time they visit the store.

Postpurchase Evaluation

The buying process doesn't end when a customer purchases a product. After making a purchase, the customer uses the product and then evaluates the experience to determine whether it was satisfactory or unsatisfactory. **Satisfaction** is a postconsumption evaluation of how well a store or product meets or exceeds customer expectations. This **postpurchase evaluation** then becomes part of the customer's internal information and affects store and product evaluations and purchase decisions. Unsatisfactory experiences can motivate customers to complain to the retailer, patronize other stores, and select different brands in the future. Consistently high levels of satisfaction build store and brand loyalty, which are important sources of competitive advantage for retailers.[32]

To improve postpurchase assessments and satisfaction, retailers can take several steps. First, they must make sure to build realistic customer expectations, so they never let those shoppers down with their performance. Second, they should provide information about proper use and care of the items purchased. Third, as mentioned previously, guarantees and warranties reduce a negative feeling of risk, both before and after the purchase. Fourth, the best retailers make contact periodically with their customers to make sure they are satisfied, correct any problems, and remind customers of their availability. This last effort also can improve the chances that a customer puts the retailer in his or her consideration set for the next purchase occasion.

TYPES OF BUYING DECISIONS

LO 4-2

Identify the different types of buying processes.

In some situations, customers like Eva Mendoza spend considerable time and effort selecting a retailer and evaluating alternative products—going through all the steps in the buying process described in the preceding section. In other situations, buying decisions are made automatically with little thought. This section examines three types of customer decision-making processes: extended problem solving, limited problem solving, and habitual decision making.

Extended Problem Solving

Extended problem solving is a purchase decision process in which customers devote considerable time and effort to analyze their alternatives. Customers typically engage in extended problem solving when the purchase decision involves a lot of risk and uncertainty. **Financial risks** arise when customers purchase an expensive product or service. **Physical risks** are important when customers feel that a product or service may affect their health or safety. **Social risks** arise when customers believe a product will affect how others view them. Lasik eye surgery, for instance, involves all three types of risks: It can be expensive, potentially damage the eyes, and change a person's appearance.

Consumers engage in extended problem solving when they are making a buying decision to satisfy an important need or when they have little knowledge about the product or service. Due to the high risk in such situations, customers go beyond their internal knowledge to consult with friends, family members, or experts. They might also peruse online blogs; examine online reviews, both retailer-sponsored and independent review sites; and read reviews in publications like *Consumer Reports*. They may visit several retailers before making a purchase decision.

Retailers stimulate sales from customers engaged in extended problem solving by providing the necessary information in a readily available and easily understood manner and by offering money-back guarantees. For example, retailers that sell merchandise involving extended problem solving provide information on their websites describing the merchandise and its specifications, have informational displays in their stores (such as a sofa cut in half to show its construction), and use salespeople to demonstrate features and answer questions.

Limited Problem Solving

Limited problem solving is a purchase decision process involving a moderate amount of effort and time. Customers engage in this type of buying process when they have had some prior experience with the product or service and their risk is moderate. In such situations, customers tend to rely more on personal knowledge than on external information. They usually choose a retailer they have shopped at before and select merchandise they have bought in the past. The majority of customer purchase decisions involve limited problem solving.

Retailers attempt to reinforce this buying pattern and make it habitual when customers are buying merchandise from them. If customers are shopping elsewhere, however, retailers need to break this buying pattern by introducing new information or offering different merchandise or services. A common way to adjust the pattern is through coupons. Companies such as CVS and Walgreens often offer deep coupon discounts on commonly purchased products to get customers into their stores. Retailers are willing to give such steep discounts for two reasons. First, it breaks the established habit a customer may have of shopping elsewhere, and second, they know customers often buy many other, undiscounted items once they are in the store. After customers make these purchases, the retailers analyze their spending patterns and offer targeted coupons to encourage repatronage.[33]

Eva Mendoza's buying process illustrates both limited and extended problem solving. Her store choice decision was based on her knowledge of the merchandise in various stores she had shopped in and her search on *Hello Fashion*. Considering this information, she felt the store choice decision was not very risky; thus, she engaged in limited problem solving when deciding to visit Macy's. But her buying process for the suit was extended. This decision was important to her; thus, she spent time acquiring information from a friend, the salesperson, and another shopper to evaluate and select a suit.

One common type of limited problem solving is **impulse buying**, or **unplanned purchasing**, which is a buying decision made by customers on the spot after seeing the merchandise.[34] Retailers encourage impulse-buying behavior by using prominent point-of-purchase (POP) or point-of-sale (POS) displays to attract customers' attention. Retailers have long recognized that the most valuable real estate in the store is at the point of purchase. An increasing number of nonfood retailers (such as Forever 21) are looking to increase impulse buys from customers by offering gum, mints, beauty products, and other fun, hedonic items at their cash registers. Electronic shoppers are also stimulated to purchase impulsively when Internet retailers put special merchandise on their home pages and suggest complementary merchandise just before checkout.

Habitual Decision Making

Habitual decision making is a purchase decision process involving little or no conscious effort. Today's customers have many demands on their time. One way they cope with these time pressures is by simplifying their decision-making process. When a need arises, customers may automatically respond with, "I'll buy the same thing I bought last time from the same store." Typically, this habitual decision-making process occurs when decisions aren't very important to customers and involve familiar merchandise they have bought in the past. When customers are loyal to a brand or a store, they engage in habitual decision making.

© Jetta Productions/Getty Images

Retailers encourage impulse-buying behavior by using prominent point-of-purchase (POP) or point-of-sale (POS) displays to attract customers' attention.

Brand loyalty means that customers like and consistently buy a specific brand in a product category. They are reluctant to switch to other brands if their favorite brand isn't available. For example, loyal Coca-Cola drinkers won't buy Pepsi, no matter what. Thus, retailers can satisfy these customers' needs only if they offer the specific brands desired.

Brand loyalty creates both opportunities and problems for retailers.[35] Customers are attracted to stores that carry popular brands, but because retailers must carry these high-loyalty brands, they may not be able to negotiate favorable terms with the suppliers of the popular national brands. If, however, the high-loyalty brands are private-label brands (i.e., brands owned by the retailer), retailer loyalty is heightened.

Retailer loyalty means that customers like and habitually visit the same retailer to purchase a type of merchandise. All retailers would like to increase their customers' loyalty, and they can do so by selecting a convenient location (see Chapters 7 and 8), offering complete assortments of national and private-label brands (Chapter 12), reducing the number of stockouts (Chapter 12), rewarding customers for frequent purchases (Chapter 10), or providing good customer service (Chapter 17).

SOCIAL FACTORS INFLUENCING THE BUYING PROCESS

Exhibit 4–4 illustrates how customer buying decisions are influenced by four influential social factors: the economy, family, reference groups, and culture.

LO 4-3

Summarize how the economy and social factors affect customer purchase decisions.

The Economy

The state of the national and global economy has significant effects on the way people buy. When the global or national economies struggle or undergo recessions, consumers respond to the wider sense of uncertainty and risk by reducing their purchases or seeking more affordable options.[36] When the economy is flourishing, people often are willing to spend more on luxury or hedonic products, and retailers have less need to offer price discounts to move their merchandise. But sometimes the trends are less straightforward; for example, when faced with tight budgets, people often spend a little more on small luxuries, like cosmetics and wrapping paper. They may not be able to afford a brand-new outfit or a lavish gift, so they spend a little more on smaller purchases, to be able to enjoy splurging a little without guilt.[37]

EXHIBIT 4–4
Social Factors Affecting
Buying Decisions

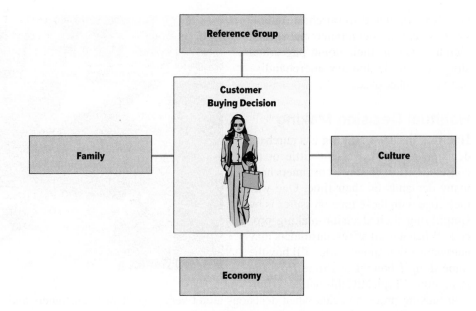

On an international level, the economy also is critical. National economies ebb and flow in their strength relative to one another. For example, many emerging economies, such as India and China, have opened their markets in ongoing processes of economic liberalization. Such moves allow retailers to sell to new segments of consumers, who previously lacked access to the kinds of retail offerings that are common in more developed economies. These consumers exhibit unique demands and behaviors, reflecting their economic history, as well as their growing purchasing power in their liberalizing economies.

Family

Many purchase decisions involve products that the entire family will consume or use. The previous discussion of the buying process focused on how one person makes a decision. When families make purchase decisions, they often consider the needs of all family members.[38]

In a tight economy, consumers may cut back on expensive purchases, but splurge on small luxuries like lipstick.

When choosing a vacation site, for example, all family members may participate in the decision making. In other situations, one member of the family may assume the decision-making role. For example, the husband might buy the groceries, which the wife then uses to prepare their child's lunch, which the child consumes in school. In this situation, the store choice decision might be made by the husband, but the brand choice decision might be made by the wife, though it likely is greatly influenced by the child.

Children play an important role in family buying decisions. Resort hotels now realize they must satisfy children's needs as well as those of adults. The Hyatt hotel chain thus cooperates with a mail-order baby supply company, Babies Travel Lite. After parents book a room, they can order all the diapers, formula, and organic baby food they will need for the trip. The items will be ready for them when they check in, which reduces the amount of baggage and increases convenience. For older children, Hyatt offers toys, available to be checked out from the front desk. In addition, working with the famous chef Alice Waters, it has revamped the children's menus in its hotel restaurants to offer nutritious, but also fun meal options.[39]

Retailers also can attract consumers who shop with other family members by satisfying the needs of all those family members. At Toys "R" Us, for example, recent store redesign efforts add more play areas to stores, designed to attract young consumers to enjoy the very experience of visiting a toy store. Interactive media throughout the new stores also seek to appeal to both children and their parents.[40] Many retailers are recognizing the benefits of getting the youngest members of the family on board, to influence older generations, as Retailing View 4.2 explains.

RETAILING VIEW   Pinning Consumption Choices on Online Reference Groups   4.2

According to one retail innovation analyst and "Generation Z expert," for young consumers today, "if it's not shareable, it didn't happen." That notion applies to everything in their lives, including the clothing they wear and the methods they use to purchase those products. Because of these developments, many of the clothing brands and retailers that dominated the market in previous decades are struggling, faced with a distinct lack of appeal to experience-focused, social media–addicted, young sharing consumers.

Stores like the Gap, J.Crew, and Abercrombie & Fitch still aim to target younger buyers with their clothing offerings, but those shoppers express little interest. Whereas previous generations might have accepted that they needed to keep a few staples in their wardrobe, today's buyers don't want to hold on to a good-old favorite pair of jeans. They want to snap up the latest style, take a picture of how it looks, and share it with their followers and friends. To be able to provide constant content updates on their social media sites, they need a constant flow of new items and clothing to highlight.

Such demands benefit the fast-fashion retailers that allow consumers to grab the latest styles the very moment that they fly off the design boards. In addition, because they sell products for low prices, even the most frugal young Gen Z buyer can afford to rotate his or her wardrobe nearly constantly. As a result, fast-fashion firms like Zara, H&M, Uniqlo, Mango, and Forever 21 are enjoying the market share that previously would have been held by traditional fashion companies such as the Gap.

The influences stemming from the preferences and practices of these young consumers also is spilling over to older generations and altering the way they shop. Consider the influence of social media usage, for example. By its very nature, Pinterest is aspirational, giving users something to aim for in the future. When it comes to clothing, that sort of dream approach means

Retailers targeting Generation Z customers turn to social media like Pinterest to get their attention. Their customers want to wear the latest styles, take pictures of how they look, and share them with their followers and friends.

that pinners readily have in mind what they want to wear next. Even older consumers thus are embracing the notion that they need the newest fashions, in constant rotation, so that they can live up to the dream they have pinned on their boards.

The idea of fashion, shopping, and consumption as an experience is a broad and seemingly unstoppable trend. It might have been largely sparked by the latest generation, the Gen Z teens of today, but it is expanding throughout the generational cohorts. Retailers thus have little choice but to find ways to ensure a shareable experience, not just a good product.

Source: Mallory Schlossberg, "Instagram and Pinterest Are Killing Gap, Abercrombie, & J. Crew," *Business Insider*, February 14, 2016.

© David Lees/Taxi/Getty Images

When considering athletic apparel, Eva turns to reference group member Serena Wiliams.

Reference Groups

A **reference group** includes one or more people whom a person uses as a basis of comparison for beliefs, feelings, and behaviors. A consumer might have a number of different reference groups, such as family, friends, celebrities, and opinion leaders. These reference groups affect buying decisions by (1) offering information, (2) providing rewards for specific purchasing behaviors, and (3) enhancing a consumer's self-image.

Reference groups provide information to consumers directly through conversation, either face-to-face or electronically, or indirectly through observation. For example, Eva received valuable information from her friend about the suits she was considering. On other occasions, Eva might look to women like tennis player Serena Williams or boxer Ronda Rousey to guide her selection of athletic apparel or to Demi Lovato and Katy Perry for casual fashion advice. The role of reference groups in creating fashion is discussed in Appendix 4A.

By identifying and affiliating with reference groups, consumers create, enhance, and maintain their self-image. Customers who want to be seen as members of an elite social class may shop at prestige retailers like Neiman Marcus, whereas others who want to create the image of an outdoor enthusiast might buy merchandise from L.L.Bean.

Retailers are particularly interested in identifying and reaching out to those in a reference group who act as store advocates and actively influence others in the group. **Store advocates** are customers who like a store so much that they actively share their positive experiences with friends and family. Consumers see so much advertising that they have become suspicious of the claims being made. Thus, they rely more on their own social networks for information about stores to patronize and merchandise to buy.

Culture

Culture is the meaning, beliefs, morals, and values shared by most members of a society. As the basis of the social factors that influence people's buying decisions, the culture or cultures in which each consumer participates often align with his or her reference groups. For example, Eva's cultural groups include her Latino heritage and the Pacific Northwest culture in which she lives. These cultural influences affect her consumer behavior. Because the culture at Eva's college is rather fashion conscious, she was immediately aware that her old suit was out of date and considered buying fashionable shoes a reasonable addition.

Many retailers, like Costco, have adjusted their strategies to appeal to different cultures and subcultures.

Many retailers and shopping center managers have recognized the importance of appealing to different cultures and subcultures.[41] For instance, the U.S. Hispanic population is expected to double by 2016, accounting for almost 20 percent of retail spending.[42] Many retailers, particularly supermarkets in areas with large Hispanic populations, have dedicated significant space to products that are indigenous to particular Spanish-speaking countries. The product mix will, however, differ depending on the region of the country. Merchandise should reflect that, for instance,

Miami has a large Cuban and Latin American population, whereas Los Angeles and Texas have more people from Mexico. Bilingual employees also are a critical success factor for stores catering to the Hispanic population. Accordingly, CVS has undertaken a new initiative to ensure it is serving Hispanic U.S. populations appropriately and effectively. It began by acquiring the largest Hispanic-owned drugstore chain, then moved forward by remodeling stores in Hispanic-dominant markets such as Miami. In accordance with these developments, CVS has announced it will start testing a new "CVC/pharmacy y mas" concept. In focal stores, all staff will be bilingual, and the shelves will stock brands familiar to Hispanic consumers, including Café la Llave, Creolina, Agustin Reyes, Suavitel, and Fabuloso. Cuban coffee will be brewed and served every day. In addition, stores that manifest the concept will provide a larger proportion of value- and family-sized products, along with competitive pricing positions.[43]

MARKET SEGMENTATION

LO 4-4

Determine why and how retailers group customers into market segments.

The preceding discussion focused on (1) how individual customers evaluate and select stores, channels, and merchandise and (2) the factors affecting their decision making. To be cost-effective, retailers identify groups of these customers (market segments) and target their offerings to meet the needs of typical customers in a segment rather than the needs of a specific customer. At one time, CVS sought to appeal to all consumers, but as Retailing View 4.3 shows, it has progressively focused its efforts on a particular group of shoppers: nonsmokers.

A **retail market segment** is a group of customers who are attracted to the same retail mix because they have similar needs. For example, Millennials have different needs than executives on business trips. Thus, Marriott offers hotel chains with different retail mixes for each of these segments—AC Hotels by Marriott for the young and hip and Marriott Hotels and Conference Centers for business executives and conferences.

The Internet enables retailers to target individual customers efficiently and market products to them on a one-to-one basis. This one-to-one marketing concept is discussed in Chapter 10 as it pertains to customer relationship management.

RETAILING VIEW   No More Smokes at CVS   4.3

When CVS announced that it would begin phasing out all sales of tobacco products, it noted the health harms these products produce, which did not align with the chain's position as a health care provider. The decision to eliminate tobacco products was simultaneous with the drugstore's rebranding as CVS Health, a broad-based provider of health care services, as well as its purchase of the pharmacy benefits company Caremark.

With these moves, CVS signaled its clear segmentation of customers into smokers and nonsmokers, as well as its clear goal to target only the latter. Excluding the segment of the population that uses tobacco was a risk; prior to the transition, CVS predicted that it would lose $2 billion in revenue by eliminating tobacco from its shelves. But it also claimed that, in the words of CVS Caremark's CEO, "This is the right decision at the right time as we evolve from a drugstore into a health-care company."

The choice was not solely driven by ethical considerations, though. By targeting nonsmokers, CVS Health gained a notable competitive advantage over competitors that continue to sell tobacco products, because it was able to develop partnerships with health care systems across the country. In these partnerships, CVS enjoys a position as the pharmacy of choice, such that the hospital systems send patients there for their follow-up prescriptions and treatments. Through Caremark, CVS Health encourages customers to patronize only pharmacies that refuse to sell tobacco (such as CVS outlets) and offers

discounted copayment charges for prescription medications obtained through those stores. Specifically, for people enrolled in Caremark pharmacy plans, the copayments for prescriptions obtained at non–tobacco outlets can be up to $15 less than the same purchases made through drugstores that also sell tobacco. Buying medications from competitors such as Walgreens and Rite Aid, which continue to sell tobacco, thus would leave consumers with a higher bill. By making it substantially more expensive for consumers to obtain their prescriptions from other chains, the Caremark division grants its affiliated CVS retail arm a powerful advantage.

At the store level, CVS also offers inducements to non-smokers and those who might like to quit. An in-store campaign featured "Ready to quit?" posters, in partnership with the American Lung Association. Furthermore, the company promised to continue working to expand its walk-in clinic services and pharmacy management practices. Its Minute Clinics, pharmacist counseling services, and vaccination offerings all drive toward a view of CVS as a partner, seeking to ensure consumers' health.

Sources: Timothy W. Martin and Mike Esterl, "CVS to Stop Selling Cigarettes," *The Wall Street Journal*, February 5, 2014; Tom Ryan, "Should CVS's Competitors Also Say Bye to Tobacco?," *RetailWire*, September 9, 2014; Ed Silverman and Paul Ziobro, "CVS Plays Hardball with Rival Drug Chains," *The Wall Street Journal*, October 20, 2014.

Criteria for Evaluating Market Segments

Customers can be grouped into segments in many different ways. There's no simple way to determine which method is best, though four criteria useful for evaluating whether a retail segment is a viable target market are as follows: actionable, identifiable, substantial, and reachable.

Actionable The fundamental criteria for evaluating a retail market segment are that (1) customers in the segment must have similar needs, seek similar benefits, and be satisfied by a similar retail offering; and (2) those customers' needs must differ from the needs of customers in other segments. **Actionable** means that the retailer should know what to do to satisfy needs for the consumers in the segment. According to this criterion, it makes sense for Banana Republic to segment the apparel market on the basis of the demographic characteristic of physical size. Customers who wear petite sizes have different needs than those who wear regular or large sizes, so they are attracted to a store offering a unique merchandise mix. In the context of the multiattribute attitude model discussed previously, people who wear small sizes place more importance on fit and customer service because it is generally more difficult for them to get the appropriate fit and because they need knowledgeable sales associates who know and can cater to their specific needs.

In contrast, it wouldn't make sense for a supermarket to segment its market on the basis of customer size. Large and small men and women probably have the same needs, seek the same benefits, and go through the same buying process for groceries. This segmentation approach wouldn't be actionable for a supermarket retailer because the retailer couldn't develop unique mixes for large and small customers. However, a segmentation scheme based on geography or demographics such as household income and ethnicity would be actionable.

Identifiable **Identifiable** means that the retailer is able to determine which customers are in the market segment. When customers are identifiable, the retailer can determine (1) the segment's size and (2) the consumers to whom the retailer needs to target its communications and promotions. For example, supermarket retailers use customer demographics to identify where they should put their stores and the merchandise that they should carry. More prepared and gourmet foods, fancy produce, and expensive cuts of meat would go into stores in neighborhoods with higher average incomes. Snack foods likely predominate in stores located near a college campus. It is equally important to ensure that the segments are distinct from one another, because too much overlap between segments means that distinct marketing strategies aren't needed. If, for example, a regional grocery store chain had stores located in neighborhoods containing people with similar demographics, there would be no need to vary its merchandise selection.

Substantial If a market is too small or its buying power insignificant (i.e., not **substantial**), it cannot generate sufficient profits to support the retailing mix activities. For example, the market for pet pharmaceuticals is probably not large enough in one local area to serve as a target market segment, but a national market could be served through the Internet channel.

Reachable **Reachable** means that the retailer can target promotions and other elements of the retail mix to consumers in the segment. For example, AutoZone targets men who repair their automobiles themselves. Potential customers in this segment are reachable because they read car magazines, watch NASCAR on TV, and have other distinct television viewing habits.

Approaches for Segmenting Markets

There are a wide variety of approaches for segmenting retail markets. No one approach is best for all retailers. Instead, they must explore various factors that affect customer buying behavior and determine which factors are most important for them.

Geographic Segmentation

Geographic segmentation groups customers according to where they live. A retail market can be segmented by countries (Japan, Mexico) or by areas within a country, such as states, cities, and neighborhoods.[44] Because customers typically shop at stores convenient to where they live and work, individual retail outlets usually focus on the customer segment reasonably close to the outlet.

Geographic segmentation would not be very effective for a product like raw denim jeans. A raw denim aficionado in Detroit probably seeks the same type of jeans as a denim enthusiast in Los Angeles.

Segments based on geography can be identifiable, substantial, and reachable. It's easy to determine who lives in a geographic segment, such as the Paris metropolitan area, and then determine how many potential customers are in that area. It is also relatively simple to target communications and locate retail outlets for customers in Paris and then determine if customers are being responsive to those communications. However, when customers in different geographic segments have similar needs, it is inefficient to develop unique retail offerings by geographic markets. For example, a raw denim aficionado in Detroit probably seeks the same type of jeans as a denim enthusiast in Los Angeles. Thus, it wouldn't be useful to segment the U.S. high-end denim market geographically.

Demographic Segmentation

Demographic segmentation groups consumers on the basis of easily measured, objective characteristics such as age, gender, income, and education. Demographic variables are the most common means of defining segments, because consumers in these segments can be easily identified, their size can be determined, and the degree to which they can be reached by and are responsive to media can be easily assessed. As Retailing View 4.4 reveals, demographic segmentation also can create several appealing markets for retailers.

However, demographics may not be useful for defining segments for some retailers because the motivations for purchasing transcend simple demographics. For example, demographics are poor predictors of users of athleisure clothing—athletic wear that you really aren't supposed to work out in because it looks so good and often costs so much.[45] At one time, retailers assumed that athletic clothing would be purchased exclusively by young athletic people, but the high-fashion nature of health and fitness clothing has led people of all ages to buy this merchandise. Relatively inactive consumers also find athleisure clothing to be stylish as well as comfortable.

Geodemographic Segmentation

Geodemographic segmentation uses both geographic and demographic characteristics to classify consumers. This segmentation scheme is based on the principle that "birds of a feather flock together." Consumers in the same neighborhoods tend to buy the same types of cars, appliances, and apparel and shop at the same types of retailers.[46]

4.4   RETAILING VIEW   Fashioning an Effective Segmentation Strategy

H&M, As one of the world's largest retailers specializing in fast fashion, needs to move quickly to keep its appeal to customers. Unlike its primary competitor Zara, H&M does not make most of its merchandise in-house, which means it also is more affected by changes and shifts in global markets. Some of those shifts have led to slowing growth, prompting H&M to expand its product offering, increase the number of stores it maintains, and penetrate new markets in countries with little competition. Along with its greater product breadth, H&M is implementing new strategies to target specific market segments: H&M Men, H&M Women, and H&M Children.

Both H&M Men and H&M Women target consumers between the ages of 15 and 30 years, such as students and young professionals living on a budget, for whom fashion is important. These product lines accordingly offer a wide array of merchandise—from party dresses to casual and business apparel to maternity wear for H&M Women, and then clothes perfect for the office, special occasions, and everyday necessities for H&M Men.

Although the men's market is growing and H&M has been expanding these lines, H&M Women had been the primary focus of one its most creative new targeting strategies. Specifically, the retailer has partnered with Lenanra Medine, a fashion blogger behind the successful *Man Repeller* blog. It also is seeking to connect with the next big name in fashion blogging, arranging for finalists in its blog competition to work with Medine at its headquarters in New York. The contest requires participants to create an outfit of H&M apparel that they could post. This digital visibility marks a new way that H&M has managed to reach customers in this segment.

Furthermore, its children's market is seeing huge growth, especially in Asia. H&M already ranks among the top 10 in its market share of children's apparel in this region, and this success seemingly comes from its decision not to target children directly. Rather, recognizing the geographic segmentation it is dealing with, H&M targets the parents of children, who are less interested in purely practical clothing and ready to buy children's fashions that reproduce adult styles.

H&M has specific segmentation strategies for men, women, and children.

Sources: Yehong Zhu, "Here's Why You Shouldn't Freak Out over H&M's Sales Growth Slowdown," *Forbes*, June 23, 2016; Simcon-Simsree Consulting Club, "Hennes & Mauritz Brand Analysis," *Simcon Blog*, December 19, 2015, https://simconblog.wordpress.com/2015/12/19/h-n-m-brand-analysis/; Bethany Biron, "H&M Is Trying to Find the Next Man Repeller," *Glossy*, May 19, 2016, http://glossy.co/modern-media/hm-is-trying-to-find-the-next-man-repeller; H&M, "Responsible Marketing," H&M, http://sustainability.hm.com/en/sustainability/commitments/be-ethical/responsible-marketing.html; Kate Abnett, "The Childrenswear Market Comes of Age," *Business of Fashion*, June 21, 2016, https://www.businessoffashion.com/articles/intelligence/the-childrenswear-market-comes-of-age.

One widely used tool for geodemographic market segmentation is the Tapestry Segmentation system developed and marketed by Environmental Systems Research Institute (ESRI).[47] Tapestry Segmentation classifies all U.S. residential neighborhoods into 65 distinctive segments based on socioeconomic and demographic characteristics.[48] The information in Exhibit 4–5 describes three Tapestry segments. These neighborhoods, with their similar demographics and buying behaviors, can be anyplace in the United States.

Geodemographic segmentation is particularly appealing for managing the store channel because customers typically patronize stores close to their neighborhoods.

EXHIBIT 4–5
Examples of Tapestry

	Segment 01 - *Top Rung*	Segment 18 - *Cozy and Comfortable*	Segment 52 - *Inner City Tenants*

LifeMode Summary Group	L1 *High Society*	L2 *Upscale Avenues*	L8 *Global Roots*
Urbanization Summary Group	U3 *Metro Cities I*	U8 *Suburban Periphery II*	U4 *Metro Cities II*
Household Type	Married-Couple Families	Married-Couple Families	Mixed
Median Age	44.6	41.7	28.8
Income	High	Upper Middle	Lower Middle
Employment	Prof/Mgmt	Prof/Mgmt	Srvc/Prof/Mgmt/Skilled
Education	Bach/Grad Degree	Some College	No HS Diploma; HS; Some Coll
Residential	Single Family	Single Family	Multiunit Rentals
Race/Ethnicity	White	White	White; Black; Hispanic
Activity	Participate in public/civic activities	Dine out often at family restaurants	Play football, basketball
Financial	Own stock worth $75,000+	Have personal line of credit	Have personal education loan
Activity	Vacation overseas	Shop at Kohl's	Go dancing
Media	Listen to classical, all-news radio	Listen to sporting events on radio	Read music, baby, fashion magazines
Vehicle	Own/Lease luxury car	Own/Lease minivan	Own/Lease Honda

Source: ESRI, "Tapestry Segmentation: The Fabric of America's Neighborhoods," www.esri.com.

Thus, retailers can use geodemographic segmentation to select locations for their stores and tailor the assortment in the stores to the preferences of the local community. In Chapter 8, we illustrate how geodemographic segmentation is used to make store location decisions.

Psychographic Segmentation   **Pschographic Segmentation** is method of segmenting customers based on how they spend their time and money, what activities they pursue, and their attitudes and opinions about the world in which they live. For example, a person might have a strong need to be physically fit and eat healthfully, which motivates him or her to seek opportunities to stay active and consume healthy foods, which in turn influences the stores in which he or she shops. Determining psychographics involves knowing and understanding three components: self-values, self-concept, and lifestyles.

   Self-values are goals for life, not just the goals one wants to accomplish in a day. They are the overriding desires that drive how a person lives his or her life. An example is the drive for self-improvement. This motivation causes people to develop self-images of how they want to be and then images of a way of life that will help them arrive at these ultimate goals. From a retailing point of view, self-values help determine the benefits the target market may be looking for from a store or the products it sells.

   Derived from self-values, people's **self-image**, or **self-concept**, is the image people ideally have of themselves.[49] A person who has a goal of being athletically fit based on their self-value of self-improvement for instance, may seek products and stores that are consistent with this self-concept, such as REI, Lululemon, or Patagonia. These retailers communicate the athletically fit image through their websites, stores, and products.

Lifestyles, the third component of people's psychographic makeup, are the way we live.[50] If values provide an end goal and self-concept is the way one sees oneself in the context of that goal, lifestyles are how we live our lives to achieve goals. Continuing with our example, people with a self-image of being physically fit will engage in sports, go to a health club, and possibly practice yoga, which requires purchasing athletic gear from stores that emulate that lifestyle.

One of the most widely used consumer segmentation tools is **VALS (values of lifestyle survey)**, from Strategic Business Insights. VALS examines the intersection of psychographics, demographics, and lifestyles. On the basis of responses to the VALS survey (**www.strategicbusinessinsights.com/vals/presurvey.shtml**) and a proprietary algorithm, individuals age 18 and older are classified into one of eight predetermined segments shown in Exhibit 4–7. The survey is for use in the United States and Canada only. Other countries require their own survey in consideration of both language and culture.

EXHIBIT 4–7
VALS

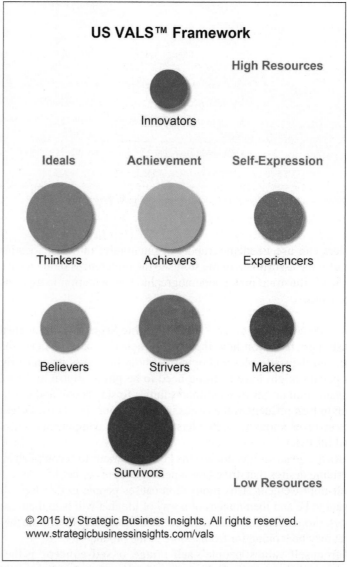

On the horizontal dimension, VALS segments reflect people's primary motivations based on their self-image. There are three primary motivations of U.S. consumers: ideals, achievement, and self-expression. People who are primarily motivated by ideals are guided by knowledge and principles. Those who are motivated by achievement look for products and services that provide personal benefits. Consumers who are primarily motivated by self-expression want physical activity, and have a desire to make an impact. On the vertical dimension, consumers' resources are measured, including income, education, health, and energy level, as well as leadership, variety, and information seeking. The segments on top have higher resources and a broader worldview than do segments on the bottom with lower resources and a narrower worldview.

Firms are finding that lifestyles are often more useful for predicting consumer behavior than are demographics alone. In particular, VALS explains why different consumer types exhibit different behaviors and why different consumer groups sometimes exhibit the same behaviors for different reasons. People who share demographics actually tend to have varying psychological traits. Two shoppers with similar demographic profiles still might have different levels of risk-taking propensity, social consciousness, or preferred benefits. College students and day laborers might earn similar incomes, but they spend that income quite differently because of their very different psychographics.

Lifestyle segmentation tools like VALS are useful when demographics like income are similar, but values and lifestyles are very different, as is the case with college students (top) and day laborers (bottom).

There are limitations to using most lifestyle segmentations, however. Lifestyles are not as objective as demographics, and it is harder to identify potential customers. With demographics, a firm like Nike can easily identify its customers as men or women and direct its marketing strategies to each group differently. For these reasons, lifestyle segmentation is often used in conjunction with other segmentation methods. Psychographics are more expensive as a means to identify potential customers but often have higher marketing utility than demographics. To identify and individual's membership in a VALS group, respondents must take the VALS survey. Behavioral data are available by asking additional questions in the survey, through VALS' national data partner GfK MRI, or through a linkage with a data set in which VALS was also included.

© PeopleImages/Digital Vision/Getty Images

Buying Situation Segmentation

The buying behavior of customers with the same demographics or lifestyle can differ depending on their buying situation. Thus, retailers may use **buying situations**, such as fill-in versus weekly shopping, to segment a market. For example, in Exhibit 4–3, the parent with four children evaluated the supercenter more positively than the Internet grocer or supermarket for weekly grocery purchases. But if the parent ran out of milk during the

© Mark Elias/Bloomberg/Getty Images

week, he or she would probably go to the convenience store rather than the wholesale club for this fill-in shopping. In terms of the multiattribute attitude model in Exhibit 4–3, convenience would be more important than assortment in the fill-in shopping situation. Similarly, an executive might stay at a convention hotel on a business trip and a resort during a family vacation.

Buying situation segmentation rates high among the criteria for evaluating market segments. The segments are actionable because it is relatively easy to determine what a marketer should do to satisfy the needs of a particular segment. They are identifiable and accessible because retailers or service providers can determine who the customers are on the basis of who has purchased the product or service and under what circumstances. Once they have identified the customer segment, they can assess its size.

Benefit Segmentation   Another approach for defining a target segment is to group customers seeking similar benefits; this method is called **benefit segmentation**. In the multiattribute attitude model, customers in the same benefit segment would have a similar set of importance weights for the attributes of a store or product. For example, customers who place high importance on fashion and style and low importance on price might form a fashion segment, whereas customers who place more importance on price would form a price segment. Hershey's has adopted this approach to segmentation: To appeal to hand-to-mouth munchers, it offers packages of bite-sized candy versions of its popular candy bars, such as Almond Joys, Reese's Peanut Butter Cups, and Hershey's Chocolate. It also tailors its packaging in international markets to offer the key benefits demanded by consumers. When its research showed that Chinese consumers prefer gold over silver, Hershey's changed the foil that wraps its Kisses candies in China.[51]

Benefit segments are very actionable. The benefits sought by customers in the target segment clearly indicate how retailers should design their offerings to appeal to those customers. But customers in benefit segments aren't easily identified or accessed; it's hard to look at a person and determine what benefits he or she is seeking. Typically, the audience for the media used by retailers is described by demographics rather than by the benefits they seek.

Composite Segmentation Approaches

No segmentation approach meets all the criteria. For example, segmenting by demographics and geography is ideal for identifying and accessing customers, but these characteristics often are unrelated to customers' needs. Thus, these approaches may not indicate the actions necessary to attract customers in these segments. In contrast, knowing what benefits customers are seeking is useful for designing an effective retail offering; the problem is identifying which customers are seeking these benefits. For these reasons, **composite segmentation** uses multiple variables to identify customers in the target segment according to their benefits sought, lifestyles, and demographics.

CVS uses what it calls the "CVS personalities" to target three composite segments. Each of these segments, referred to by a first name, is used to develop a retail strategy for the market segment.[52] "Caroline" is a segment composed of 18- to 24-year-old single or new moms who have a lower income but have the highest number of items purchased per trip. "Vanessa" targets a segment of 35- to 54-year-old women with children, at the peak of their income and generating the highest spending, frequency of purchases, and overall basket size. Finally, "Sophie" is a 55-plus empty nester woman with a median income and a health focus. These segments are useful in developing positioning messages that can be used in their ads, flyers, and displays. This information is also useful for manufacturers who sell their products through CVS. For example, for "Caroline," Dove bath products could be positioned as a convenient reenergizer. For "Vanessa," they could be positioned as an escape. Finally, for "Sophie," they could be touted as beneficial to health.

SUMMARY

LO 4-1 **Describe the process that consumers go through when making retail patronage and buying decisions.**

Consumers go through several stages when making a purchase decision: need recognition, information search, evaluation of alternatives, purchase, and postpurchase evaluation. It is important for retailers to understand how they can nudge their customers closer to a buying decision at each step of their buying process.

LO 4-2 **Identify the different types of buying processes.**

The importance of the stages depends on the nature of the customer's decision. When decisions are important and risky, the buying process is longer because customers spend more time and effort on the information search and evaluation of alternatives. When buying decisions are less important to customers, they spend little time in the buying process, and their buying behavior may become habitual.

LO 4-3 **Summarize how the economy and social factors affect customer purchase decisions.**

The buying process of consumers is influenced by their personal beliefs, attitudes, and values, as well as by their social environment. The primary social influences are provided by the economy, consumers' families, their reference groups, and culture.

LO 4-4 **Determine why and how retailers group customers into market segments.**

To develop cost-effective retail programs, retailers group customers into segments. Some approaches for segmenting markets are based on geography, demographics, geodemographics, lifestyle, usage situations, and benefits sought. Because each approach has its advantages and disadvantages, retailers typically define their target segment by several characteristics.

KEY TERMS

actionable, *104*
benefit segmentation, *110*
brand loyalty, *99*
buying process, *86*
buying situation, *109*
compatibility, *114*
complexity, *115*
composite segmentation, *110*
consideration set, *95*
conversion rate, *90*
cross-shopping, *88*
culture, *102*
demographic segmentation, *105*
everyday low pricing (EDLP) strategy, *90*
extended problem solving, *97*
external sources, *89*
fair trade, *96*
fashion, *113*

fashion leaders, *114*
financial risks, *97*
geodemographic segmentation, *105*
geographic segmentation, *105*
habitual decision making, *99*
hedonic need, *87*
identifiable, *104*
impulse buying, *98*
information search, *89*
innovators, *114*
internal sources, *89*
knockoff, *114*
lifestyle, *108*
limited problem solving, *98*
mass-market theory, *114*
multiattribute attitude model, *92*
observability, *115*
physical risks, *98*
postpurchase evaluation, *97*

psychographic segmentation, *107*
reachable, *104*
reference group, *102*
retailer loyalty, *99*
retail market segment, *103*
satisfaction, *97*
showrooming, *91*
social risks, *98*
store advocates, *102*
subculture theory, *114*
substantial, *104*
trendsetters, *114*
trialability, *115*
trickle-down theory, *114*
unplanned purchasing, *98*
unsatisfied need, *86*
utilitarian need, *87*
VALS (values of lifestyle survey), *108*

GET OUT AND DO IT!

1. **CONTINUING CASE ASSIGNMENT: GO SHOPPING** Visit the retail store operated by the target firm for your continuing assignment. Determine all the things that the store does to try to stimulate customers to buy merchandise at each stage of the buying process. In which types of buying decisions are most customers involved? Based on your observations and what you know about the target firm, what type(s) of market segmentation strategies are they involved in? Do you believe these are the best strategies for this firm?

2. **GO SHOPPING** Go to a supermarket and watch people selecting products to put in their shopping carts. How much time do they spend selecting products? Do some people spend more time than others? Why is this the case? Does consumer behavior vary in the store perimeter versus in the aisles? Explain your observations.

3. **INTERNET EXERCISE** To better understand the segmentation classification of consumers, Strategic Business Insights has developed the VALS tool, which uses psychology to segment people according to their distinct personality traits. Go to the firm's home page at www.strategicbusinessinsights.com/vals/presurvey.shtml, and take the survey to identify your VALS profile according to your values, attitudes, and lifestyle. According to the results, what is your VALS profile type? Do you agree with your consumer profile? Why or why not? How can retailers effectively use the results of this survey when planning and implementing their business strategies?

4. **INTERNET EXERCISE** Retailers want to segment the market on the basis of the geographic classification of customers to select the best sites for their businesses. Go to the ESRI Business Information Solutions "Explore Your Neighborhood" page at www.esri.com/data/tapestry/zip-lookup, type in the zip code for your hometown or your campus, and read the results. How would a retailer, such as a local restaurant, use the information in this report when making a decision about whether to open a location in this zip code?

5. **INTERNET EXERCISE** Go to the following Internet sites offering information about the latest fashions: *Vogue Magazine* at www.vogue.com/, *Allure Magazine* at www.allure.com/, *The Blonde Salad* fashion blog at www.theblondesalad.com, and *Crash Magazine* at www.crash.fr/. Write a brief report describing the latest apparel fashions that are being shown by designers. Which of these fashion trends do you think will be popular with college students? Why?

DISCUSSION QUESTIONS AND PROBLEMS

1. Does the customer buying process end when a customer buys some merchandise? Explain your answer.

2. Describe how service retailers, such as hotels, are using Twitter to provide information and answer questions about rates, services offered, and other amenities. How is this form of communication changing their expectations?

3. Considering the steps in the consumer buying process (Exhibit 4–1), describe how you (and your family) used this process to select your college or university. How many schools did you consider? How much time did you invest in this purchase decision? When you were deciding on which college to attend, what objective and subjective criteria did you use in the alternative evaluation portion of the consumer buying process?

4. In Exhibit 4–6, The Inner City Tenant is described. How should banks, restaurants, drugstores, and car dealers alter their retail mixes to meet the needs of this segment compared to the Top Rung segment?

5. Any retailer's goal is to get customers in its store so that they can find the merchandise that they are looking for

and make a purchase at this location. How could a sporting goods retailer ensure that the customer buys athletic equipment at its outlet?

6. A family-owned used bookstore across the street from a major university campus wants to identify the various segments in its market. What approaches might the store owner use to segment this market? List two potential target market segments based on this segmentation approach. Then contrast the retail mix that would be most appropriate for the two potential target segments.

7. How does the buying decision process differ when consumers are shopping on the Internet or mobile device compared with shopping in a store in terms of locations or sites visited, time spent, and brands examined?

8. Using the multiattribute attitude model, identify the probable choice of a local car dealer for a young, single woman and for a retired couple with limited income (see the accompanying table). What can the national retail chain do to increase the chances of the retired couple patronizing its dealership?

	IMPORTANCE WEIGHTS		PERFORMANCE BELIEFS		
Performance Attributes	Young, Single Woman	Retired Couple	Local Gas Station	National Service Chain	Local Car Dealer
Price	2	10	9	10	3
Time to complete repair	8	5	5	9	7
Reliability	2	9	2	7	10
Convenience	8	3	3	6	5

9. Think of a recent purchase that you made, and describe how economic and social environmental factors (e.g., reference group, family, and culture) influenced your buying decision. How are retailers using social media to affect your buying decisions?

10. Think about the merchandise sold at Office Depot/OfficeMax and Staples, and list three to four types of merchandise that fall into extended problem solving, limited problem solving, and habitual decision making for college students. Explain how the categories of merchandise would change for each type of buying decision if the customer was the owner of a medium-sized business.

APPENDIX 4A   Customer Buying Behavior and Fashion

Many retailers sell fashionable merchandise. To sell this type of merchandise profitably, retailers need to (1) understand how fashions develop and diffuse throughout the marketplace and (2) use operating systems that enable them to match supply and demand for this seasonal merchandise. This appendix reviews the consumer behavior aspects of fashion; the operating systems for matching supply of and demand for fashion merchandise are discussed in Chapter 11.

Fashion is a type of product or a way of behaving that is temporarily adopted by a large number of consumers because the product, service, or behavior is considered socially appropriate for the time and place.[53] For example, in some social groups it is or has been fashionable to have brightly colored hair or tattoos, wear a coat made from animal fur, or have a beard. Even though a wide range of activities and products go in and out of fashion, in many retail environments the term *fashion* is associated with apparel and accessories.

© Gary Gershoff/WireImage/Getty Images

Fashions help people manage their appearance, express their self-image and feelings, enhance their egos, make an impression on others, and overcome boredom.

CUSTOMER NEEDS SATISFIED BY FASHION

Fashion gives people an opportunity to satisfy many emotional and practical needs. Through fashions, people develop their own identity. They also can use fashions to manage their appearance, express their self-image and feelings, enhance their egos, and make an impression on others. Through the years, fashions have become associated with specific lifestyles or the roles people play. You wear different clothing styles when you are attending class, going out on a date, or interviewing for a job.

People use fashions to both develop their own identity and gain acceptance from others. These two benefits of fashion can be opposing forces. If you choose to wear something radically different, you will achieve recognition for your individuality but might not be accepted by your peers. To satisfy these conflicting needs, manufacturers and retailers offer customers designs that are fashionable but that still enable consumers to express their individuality.

Consumers also adopt fashions to overcome boredom. People get tired of wearing the same clothing and seeing the same furniture in their living rooms. They seek changes in their lifestyles by buying new clothes or redecorating their houses to meet their changing tastes, preferences, and income.

HOW DO FASHIONS DEVELOP AND SPREAD?

Fashions are not universal. A fashion might be accepted in one geographic region, country, or age group and not in another. Consider how your idea of "fashionable" differs from that of your parents. Many of you might have a hard time imagining them dressed in distressed, skinny jeans and a tight T-shirt. Well, they might have just as much trouble picturing you in a double-breasted business suit. One interesting sports fashion trend has been the uniforms for college and NBA basketball players. Forty years ago, they wore tight, short shorts, and Converse shoes. Now they have wear baggy shorts and Nike shoes.

The stages in the fashion life cycle are shown in Exhibit 4–8. The cycle begins with the creation of a new design or style. Then some consumers recognized as fashion leaders or innovators adopt the fashion and start a trend in their social group. The fashion spreads from the leaders to others and is accepted widely as a fashion. Eventually, the fashion is accepted by most people in the social group and can become overused. Saturation and overuse set the stage for that fashion's decline in popularity and the creation of new fashions. The time span of a fashion life cycle varies depending on the type of product and the market. The cycle for apparel fashions for young teenagers is measured in months or even weeks, whereas the fashion cycle for home furnishings may last several years.

EXHIBIT 4–8
Stages in the Fashion
Life Cycle

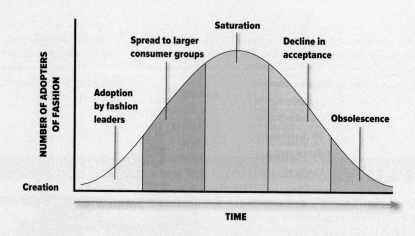

Creation

New fashions arise from a number of sources. Fashion designers are one source of creative inspirations, but fashions are also developed by creative consumers, celebrities, and even retailers. When high-profile actors, performers, and athletes wear the latest styles in television shows and movies, on stage, or on the red carpet, consumers interested in fashion often adopt and follow these trends.

Adoption by Fashion Leaders

The fashion life cycle really starts when the fashion is adopted by leading consumers. These initial adopters of a new fashion are called **fashion leaders**, **innovators**, or **trendsetters**, and they are the first people to display the new fashion in their social group or write about them in social media, like fashion blogs. If the fashion is too innovative or very different from currently accepted fashion, it might not be accepted by the social group, thereby prematurely ending its life cycle.

Three theories have been proposed to explain how fashion spreads within a society. The **trickle-down theory** suggests that fashion leaders are consumers with the highest social status—wealthy, well-educated consumers. After they adopt a fashion, the fashion trickles down to consumers in lower social classes. When the fashion is accepted in the lowest social class, it is no longer acceptable to the fashion leaders in the highest social class.

Manufacturers and retailers stimulate this trickle-down process by copying the latest styles displayed at designer fashion shows and sold in exclusive specialty stores. These copies, referred to as **knockoffs**, are sold at lower prices through retailers targeting a broader market. For example, designers at retailers like Forever 21 view fashion shows and interpret the designs for their market.[54] If the designers in Paris and Milan are showing turtlenecks, the Forever 21 designers determine what aspects of that fashion will appeal to their broader market and then have their designs manufactured in lower-cost countries like China. It is likely that the knockoff turtlenecks will be on the shelves at Forever 21 well before the higher-priced originals get to the high-end specialty and department stores.

The second theory, the **mass-market theory**, suggests that fashions spread across different peer groups. Each group has its own fashion leaders who play key roles in their own social networks. Fashion information trickles across groups rather than down from the upper classes to the lower classes.

Spain-based fast-fashion retailer Zara solicits new fashion advice from its store management all over the world. These managers funnel information to the corporate offices in Spain about fashion requests from its customers, what they are wearing, and how they are interpreting and changing off-the-rack apparel to adapt to their unique fashion senses. Zara's fashion designers synthesize the information and reinterpret this information into their own new fashions.

The third theory, the **subculture theory**, is based on the development of recent fashions. Subcultures of mostly young and less affluent consumers, such as urban youth, started fashions for such things as colorful fabrics, T-shirts, sneakers, jeans, black leather jackets, and surplus military clothing. Many times, fashions are started unintentionally by people in lower-income consumer groups and trickle up to mainstream consumer classes. For example, workers wear blue jeans that have holes in them and are distressed from manual labor, their T-shirts are faded from working in the sun, and people who paint houses are covered in splashes of paint. These looks have been adapted by manufacturers and sold to many different consumer groups. The more distressed, the more people are willing to pay.

These theories of fashion development indicate that fashion leaders can come from many different places and social groups. In our diverse society, many types of consumers have the opportunity to be the leaders in setting fashion trends.

Spread to Large Consumer Groups

During this stage, the fashion is accepted by a wider group of consumers referred to as early adopters. The fashion becomes increasingly visible, receives greater publicity and media attention, and is readily available in retail stores. The relative advantage, compatibility, complexity, trialability, and observability of a fashion affect the time it takes for that fashion to spread through a social group. New fashions that provide more benefits have a higher relative advantage compared with existing fashions, and these new fashions spread faster. Fashions are often adopted by consumers because they make people feel special. Thus, more exclusive fashions like expensive clothing are adopted more quickly in an affluent target market. On a more utilitarian level, clothing that is easy to maintain, such as wrinkle-free pants, will diffuse quickly in the general population.

Compatibility is the degree to which the fashion is consistent with existing norms, values, and behaviors. When new fashions aren't consistent with existing norms, the number of adopters and the speed of adoption are lower. Head-to-toe leather apparel is compatible only with a relatively small percentage of the public. Although this look may be moderately successful for a season or two, it will never achieve widespread acceptance.

Complexity refers to how easy it is to understand and use the new fashion. Consumers have to learn how to incorporate a new fashion into their lifestyles. For example, a platform, 6-inch, stiletto-heeled pump is difficult to walk in unless you are taking only a quick strut down the runway.

Trialability refers to the costs and commitment required to adopt the fashion initially. For example, consumers buying fashions through Internet channels or catalogs cannot examine the garments or try them on before making a purchase commitment—the trialability is low compared to shopping in stores. New size-matching machines are being used in several shopping centers around the United States. The machines take consumers' measurements and match them with specifications provided by clothing manufacturers, thus providing a proper fit and increasing trialability by reducing the risk associated with buying apparel that has not been tried on.[55]

Observability is the degree to which the new fashion is visible and easily communicated to others in the social group. Clothing fashions are very observable compared with fashions for the home, such as sheets and towels. It is therefore likely that a fashion in clothing will spread more quickly than a new color scheme or style for the bedroom.

Fashion retailers engage in many activities to increase the adoption and spread of a new fashion throughout their target market. Compatibility is increased and complexity is decreased by showing consumers how to coordinate a new article of fashion clothing with other items the consumer already owns. Trialability is increased by providing actual or virtual dressing rooms so that customers can try on clothing and see how it looks on them. Providing opportunities for customers to return merchandise also increases trialability because it reduces purchase risk. Retailers increase observability by displaying fashion merchandise in their stores, advertising it in the media, and facilitating coverage through social media like YouTube and fashion blogs.

Saturation

In this stage, the fashion achieves its highest level of social acceptance. Almost all consumers in the target market are aware of the fashion and have decided to either accept or reject it. At this point, the fashion has become old and boring to many people.

Decline in Acceptance and Obsolescence

When fashions reach saturation, they have become less appealing to consumers. Because most people have already adopted the fashion, it no longer provides an opportunity for people to express their individuality. Fashion creators and leaders thus are beginning to experiment with new fashions. The introduction of a new fashion speeds the decline of the preceding fashion.

CHAPTER ENDNOTES

1. Dionne Searcey, "Marketers Are Sizing Up the Millennials," *The New York Times,* August 21, 2014.

2. Kristina Monllos, "Millennials Are Flocking to Online Brands for Wardrobe Basics," *Advertising Age,* September 7, 2015.

3. Sandy Smith, "First Comes Love . . . Macy's Woos the Millennial Market," *Stores Magazine,* October 2013.

4. Marina Nazario, "Macy's Has a Master Plan to Capture the Most Difficult Customers," *Business Insider,* October 3, 2015.

5. Kelsey Lindsey, "It's the Age of the Millennial: What That Means for Retail," *Retail Dive,* April 8, 2014.

6. Sarah Mahoney, "Macy's Gets Face(book) Lift, Expands 'Ecosystem,'" *Marketing Daily,* February 29, 2012.

7. For detailed discussions of customer behavior, see J. Paul Peter and Jerry C. Olson, *Consumer Behavior,* 9th ed. (New York: McGraw-Hill, 2009); Michael R. Solomon, *Consumer Behavior: Buying, Having, and Being,* 12th ed. (Hoboken, NJ: Pearson, 2017); Delbert Hawkins, David L. Mothersbaugh, and Roger J. Best, *Consumer Behavior: Building Marketing Strategy,* 12th ed. (New York: McGraw-Hill/Irwin, 2012).

8. Stacy Cowley, "Want to Shop for a Surprise? Try a Subscription Box," *The New York Times,* August 12, 2015.

9. Ran Kivetz and Yuhuang Zheng, "The Effects of Promotions on Hedonic versus Utilitarian Purchases," *Journal of Consumer Psychology* 27, no. 1 (2017), pp. 59–68; Mark J. Arnold and Kristy E. Reynolds, "Approach and Avoidance Motivation: Investigating Hedonic Consumption in a Retail Setting," *Journal of Retailing* 88, no. 3 (September 2012), pp. 399–411.

10. Arnold and Reynolds, "Approach and Avoidance Motivation: Investigating Hedonic Consumption in a Retail Setting."

11. Ibid.

12. Ibid.

13. Ibid.

14. Jason M. Carpenter and Vikranth Balija, "Retail Format Choice in the US Consumer Electronics Market," *International Journal of Retail & Distribution Management* 38 (2010), pp. 258–274; Kåre Skallerud, Tor Korneliussen, and Svein Ottar Olsen, "An Examination of Consumers' Cross-Shopping Behaviour," *Journal of Retailing and Consumer Services* 16 (May 2009), pp. 181–189.

15. J. P. Misenas, "5 Examples of Brands Using Quizzes in Their Content Marketing," *OutBrain,* February 23, 2016, http://www.outbrain.com/blog/2016/02/5-examples-of-brands-using-quizzes-in-their-content-marketing.html.

16. "StudentAdvisor.com Celebrates Fashion Week with the Top 5 College Fashion Blogs," *Student Advisor,* http://www.studentadvisor.com/pages/top-5-college-fashion-blogs.

17. Serguei Netessine, Karan Girotra, and Christoph Pennetier, "Geolocation Is Changing the Retail Business Model Yet Again," *INSEAD Knowledge Blog,* November 3, 2014.

18. Moutusy Maity, Mayukh Dass, and Naresh K. Malhotra, "The Antecedents and Moderators of Offline Information Search: A Meta-Analysis," *Journal of Retailing* 90, no. 2 (2014), pp. 233–254.

19. Hiroko Tabuchi, "The Latest Fashion, Trending on Google," *The New York Times,* April 26, 2015.

20. Sungha Jang, Ashutosh Prasad, and Brian T. Ratchford, "How Customers Use Product Reviews in the Purchase Decision Process," *Marketing Letters* 23, no. 3 (2012), pp. 825–838.

21. Rebecca Jen-Hui Wang, Edward C. Malthouse, and Lakshman Krishnamurthi, "On the Go: How Mobile Shopping Affects Customer Purchase Behavior," *Journal of Retailing* 91, no. 2 (2015), pp. 217–234; Jordan Etkin, Ioannis Evangelidis, and Jennifer Aaker, "Pressed for Time? Goal Conflict Shapes How Time Is Perceived, Spent, and Valued," *Journal of Marketing Research* 52, no. 3 (2015), pp. 394–406.

22. Lauren Sherman, "Inside Sephora's Branded Beauty Strategy," *Business of Fashion,* September 24, 2013, https://www.businessoffashion.com/articles/intelligence/marc-jacobs-sephora-lvmh-branded-beauty-strategy.

23. Josh Chasin, "The Impact of Digital on Path to Purchase," Measurable Marketing in the Path-To-Purchase Conference, New York University, September 28, 2012; "Consumers Rely on Online Reviews and Price Comparisons to Make Purchase Decisions," *Lightspeed Research,* April 13, 2011; Spencer E. Ante, "How Amazon Is Turning Opinions into Gold," *BusinessWeek,* October 26, 2009, p. 47; Tim Sander, "Business Venues Find User Reviews Have a Growing Impact on Guests," *New Media Age,* October 22, 2009, p. 9.

24. Jennifer Bergen, "The 10 Best Shopping Apps to Compare Prices," PCMag.com, November 25, 2011; Geoffrey A. Fowler and Yukari Iwatani Kane, "Price Check: Finding Deals with a Phone," *The Wall Street Journal,* December 16, 2009; Philipp Broeckelmann and Andrea Groeppel-Klein, "Usage of Mobile Price Comparison Sites at the Point of Sale and Its Influence on Consumers' Shopping Behaviour," *International Review of Retail, Distribution and Consumer Research* 18 (May 2008), pp. 149–158.

25. John Lynch and Dan Ariely, "Wine Online: Search Costs Affect Competition on Price, Quality, and Distribution," *Marketing Science* 19 (Winter 2008), pp. 83–104.

26. Tammo H. A. Bijmolt and Michel van de Velden, "Multiattribute Perceptual Mapping with Idiosyncratic Brand and Attribute Sets," *Marketing Letters* 23, no. 3 (2012), pp. 585–601; William L. Wilkie and Edgar D. Pessimier, "Issues in Marketing's Use of Multi-Attribute Attitude Models," *Journal of Marketing Research,* November 1973, pp. 428–441.

27. Tyler Mathisen, "In Geek Squad City, Dead PCs Come to Life," CNBC, January 19, 2012; "Geek Squad," http://www.bestbuy.com/site/electronics/geek-squad/pcmcat138100050018.c?id=pcmcat138100050018.

28. https://sendaathletics.com/manifesto/.

29. Aaron Pressman, "The Department Store App That Outpaced Uber, Tinder, and Nike," *Yahoo Finance,* May 1, 2015.

30. Ruby Roy Dholakia and Miao Zhao, "Retail Web Site Interactivity: How Does It Influence Customer Satisfaction and Behavioral Intentions?," *International Journal of Retail & Distribution Management* 37 (2009), pp. 821–838.

31. Brad Tuttle, "The Passive-Aggressive Way to Haggle Online: Abandon Your Shopping Cart," *Time Moneyland,* September 27, 2012; Claire Cain Miller, "Closing the Deal at the Virtual Checkout Counter," *The New York Times,* October 12, 2009.

32. Deborah J. C. Brosdahl and Jason M. Carpenter, "U.S. Male Generational Cohorts: Retail Format Preferences, Desired Retail Attributes, Satisfaction and Loyalty," *Journal of Retailing and Consumer Services* 19, no. 6 (2012), pp 545–552; Jason M. Carpenter, "Consumer Shopping Value, Satisfaction and Loyalty in Discount Retailing," *Journal of Retailing and Consumer Services* 15 (September 2008), pp. 358–363; Dhruv Grewal, Ram Krishnan, and Joan Lindsey-Mullikin, "Building

Store Loyalty through Service Strategies," *Journal of Relationship Marketing* 7, no. 4 (2008), pp. 341–358.

33. Charles Duhigg, "How Companies Learn Your Secrets," *The New York Times,* February 16, 2012.

34. Piyush Sharma, Bharadhwaj Sivakumaran, and Roger Marshall, "Impulse Buying and Variety Seeking: A Trait-Correlates Perspective," *Journal of Business Research* 63 (March 2010), pp. 276–283; David H. Silvera, Anne M. Lavack, and Fredric Kropp, "Impulse Buying: The Role of Affect, Social Influence, and Subjective Well-being," *Journal of Consumer Marketing* 25, no. 1 (2008), pp. 23–33; Ronan De Kervenoael, D. Selcen, O. Aykac, and Mark Palmer, "Online Social Capital: Understanding E-Impulse Buying in Practice," *Journal of Retailing and Consumer Services* 16 (July 2009), pp. 320–328.

35. Lars Meyer-Waarden, "Effects of Loyalty Program Rewards on Store Loyalty," *Journal of Retailing and Consumer Services* 24 (2015), pp. 22–32; Dhruv Grewal, Michael Levy, and Britt Hackmann, "Making Loyalty Programs Sing," working paper, Babson College, 2016.

36. Donald F. Sacco, Aaron Bermond, and Steven G. Young, "Evidence for the Lipstick Effect at the Level of Automatic Visual Attention," *Evolutionary Behavioral Sciences* 10, no. 3 (2016), pp. 213–218; Yu Ma, Kusum L. Ailawadi, Dinesh Gauri, and Dhruv Grewal, "An Empirical Investigation of the Impact of Gasoline Prices on Grocery Shopping Behavior," *Journal of Marketing* 75 (March 2011), pp. 18–35; Lisa Bannon and Bob Davis, "Spendthrift to Penny Pincher: A Vision of the New Consumer," *The Wall Street Journal,* December 17, 2009.

37. Ma et al., "An Empirical Investigation of the Impact of Gasoline Prices on Grocery Shopping Behavior"; Christina C. Berk, "Gas Crunch Slams Brands—But Not the Ones You Think," CNBC.com, March 10, 2011; Stephanie Clifford and Andrew Martin, "In Time of Scrimping, Fun Stuff Is Still Selling," *The New York Times,* September 23, 2011; Brad Tuttle, "Smart Spending: Consumer Phrase of the Day: 'Lipstick Effect,'" *Time,* April 19, 2011.

38. Pierre Chandon and Brian Wansink, "Is Food Marketing Making Us Fat? A Multi-disciplinary Review," *Foundations and Trends in Marketing* 5, no. 3 (2011), pp. 113–196; Melissa G. Bublitz, Laura A. Peracchio, and Lauren G. Block, "Why Did I Eat That? Perspectives on Food Decision Making and Dietary Restraint," *Journal of Consumer Psychology,* 20 (2012), pp. 239–258; Juliano Laran, "Goal Management in Sequential Choices: Consumer Choices for Others Are More Indulgent Than Personal Choices," *Journal of Consumer Research* 37, no. 2 (August 2010), pp. 304–314; R. K. Srivastava and Beverlee B. Anderson, "Gender Roles and Family Decision Making: A Study of Indian Automobile Purchases," *International Journal of Services, Economics and Management* 2, no. 2 (2010), pp. 109–120.

39. "Hyatt Announces Groundbreaking Children's Menu 'For Kids by Kids' and Three-Course Organic Menu Developed by Alice Waters," press release, July 16, 2012; "Hyatt Hotels & Resorts and Babies Travel Lite Help Families Lighten Their Load by Offering Convenient Alternatives to Packing and Traveling with Baby Supplies," press release, September 22, 2008.

40. George Anderson, "Toys 'R' Us Transformation to Be Built on Fun," *RetailWire,* April 17, 2015; Bryan Pearson, "Run on Fun: Toys 'R' Us Playing Customer Experience to Win against Walmart, Amazon," *Forbes,* April 16, 2015.

41. Shivendra Pandey, Arpita Khare, and Preshth Bhardwaj, "Antecedents to Local Store Loyalty: Influence of Culture, Cosmopolitanism and Price," *International Journal of Retail & Distribution Management* 43, no. 1 (2015), pp. 5–25; JungKun Park, Frances Gunn, and Sang-Lin Han, "Multidimensional

Trust Building in e-Retailing: Cross-Cultural Differences in Trust Formation and Implication for Perceived Risk," *Journal of Retailing and Consumer Services* 19 (May 2012), pp. 304–312; Vishag Badrinarayanan, Enrique Beceerra, Chung-Hyun Kim, and Sreedhar Madhavaram, "Transference and Congruence Effects on Purchase Intentions in Online Stores of Multi-Channel Retailers: Initial Evidence from the U.S. and South Korea," *Journal of Academy of Marketing Science* 40 (August 2012).

42. Sarah Mahoney, "McKinsey: Retailers Need to Evolve Faster," *Marketing Daily,* November 7, 2013.

43. George Anderson, "CVS Is Muy Serio about Engaging Hispanics," *RetailWire,* June 4, 2015.

44. James M. Gladden, George R. Milne, and Mark A. McDonald, "Biases in Self-Reports of Zip Codes and Zip+ 4 in Geodemographic Segmentation," in *Proceedings of the 1997 World Marketing Congress* (Springer International Publishing, 2015); Bodo B. Schlegelmilch, "Segmenting Targeting and Positioning in Global Markets," in *Global Marketing Strategy* (Springer International Publishing, 2016), pp. 63–82.

45. Kristin Tice Studeman, "From Alexander Wang to Beyonce, Everyone's Doing It: A Look at How Gym-to-Street Became the New Uniform," *Vogue,* October 28, 2014.

46. Jakob Peterson, Maurizio Gibin, Paul Longley, Pablo Mateos, Philip Atkinson, and David Ashby, "Geodemographics as a Tool for Targeting Neighbourhoods in Public Health Campaigns," *Journal of Geographical Systems* 13 (June 2011), pp. 173–192; Óscar González-Benito, César A. Bustos-Reyes, and Pablo A. Muñoz-Gallego, "Isolating the Geodemographic Characterisation of Retail Format Choice from the Effects of Spatial Convenience," *Marketing Letters* 18, no. 1–2 (2007), pp. 45–59; Richard Harris, Peter Sleight, and Richard Webber, *Geodemographics, GIS and Neighbourhood Targeting* (Hoboken, NJ: Wiley, 2005); Michael J. Weiss, *The Clustered World* (Boston: Little, Brown, 2000).

47. ESRI, "Tapestry Segmentation Reference Guide" and "Tapestry Segmentation: The Fabric of America's Neighborhood," www.esri.com.

48. ESRI, "Lifestyles—ESRI Tapestry Segmentation."

49. Rosellina Ferraro, Amna Kirmani, and Ted Matherly, "Look at Me! Look at Me! Conspicuous Brand Usage, Self-Brand Connection, and Dilution," *Journal of Marketing Research* 50, no. 4 (2013), pp. 477–88; Keith Wilcox and Andrew T. Stephen, "Are Close Friends the Enemy? Online Social Networks, Self-Esteem, and Self-Control," *Journal of Consumer Research* 40, no. 1 (2013), pp. 90–103.

50. Michael R. Solomon, *Consumer Behavior: Buying*, Having, and Being, 10th ed. (Upper Saddle River, NJ: Prentice Hall, 2012).

51. John Luciew, "Hershey Learns at Retail Stores How to Get Its Candy into Your Head," February 16, 2010.

52. Personal interviews with Helena Faulkes and Robert Price of CVS.

53. Patrik Aspers, *Orderly Fashion: A Sociology of Markets* (Princeton, NJ: Princeton University Press, 2016); Annemarie Iverson, *In Fashion: From Retail to the Runway, Everything You Need to Know to Break into the Fashion Industry* (New York: Clarkson Potter, 2010).

54. Jenna Sauers, "How Forever 21 Keeps Getting Away with Designer Knockoffs," *Jezebel,* July 20, 2011.

55. John Riccio, "Virtual Dressing Rooms Will Become Reality Sooner Than You Imagined," *Digital Pulse,* July 27, 2015, https://www.digitalpulse.pwc.com.au/virtual-dressing-rooms/.

Retailing Strategy

Section I described the decisions that retail managers make when formulating and implementing their strategy; the different types of retailers; the multiple channels—stores; Internet, mobile, and social; and catalogs and other nonstore channels—that retailers use to interact with and sell merchandise to their customers; and factors that affect consumers' choices of retailers, channels, and merchandise. This broad overview of retailing provides the background information needed to develop and implement an effective retail strategy.

The chapters in Section II discuss specific strategic decisions made by retailers:

> Chapter 5 describes the development of a retail market strategy.
>
> Chapter 6 examines the financial strategy associated with the market strategy.
>
> Chapters 7 and 8 discuss the location strategy for retail outlets.
>
> Chapter 9 examines systems used to control the flow of information and merchandise.
>
> Chapter 10 details approaches that retailers take to manage relationships with their customers.

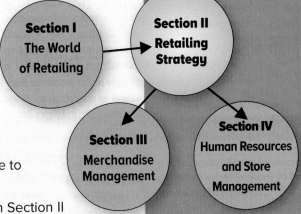

As outlined in Chapter 1, the decisions discussed in Section II are more strategic than tactical because they involve committing significant resources to developing long-term advantages over the competition in a target market segment.

Sections III and IV review the more tactical decisions, regarding merchandise and store management, that are involved in implementing the retail strategy. These implementation decisions affect a retailer's efficiency, but their impact is shorter term than the strategic decisions reviewed in Section II.

CHAPTER 5 | Retail Market Strategy

© Gareth Cattermole/Getty Images

If modern buyers can get everything they need, delivered to their door quickly and efficiently, without having to leave home, what's to prompt them to visit stores? This question, and its answers, appear to underlie some of the latest retail market strategies adopted by creative retailers seeking to encourage consumers to embrace the beauty of "slow shopping."

Rather than prioritizing efficiency, speed, or moving of customers through their stores, these retailers design their stores and their retail formats to provide inducements for shoppers to linger, spend time leisurely making their way around the store, and test various product options. For example, dozens of Origins stores now feature sinks in stores, with open jars of the brand's skin care products waiting next to them. Consumers can lather up with the various options, determining which scent they like best or which version feels nicest on their skin. With the recognition that these shoppers are interested in organic and sustainable options, Origins lists all the ingredients in its products, then displays some of them featured in jars on nearby shelves. Although no one can purchase the displayed ginger or mushrooms, they provide insights into what goes in to the products.

Other retailers devote considerable, and valuable, square footage to such non-revenue-inducing offerings such as libraries, performance spaces, expansive seating, and selfie walls. Rather than packing more products into a space, these retailers consciously are reducing the number of products available in stores, in the hope that the in-store experience will be so appealing that more customers will visit and spend more time there.

In support of this rationale, research studies consistently show that the more time people spend in a store, the more they buy. In the past, high-end department stores embodied this concept, providing fancy restaurants and tea rooms that allowed shoppers to take a break halfway through an all-day visit to the stores. Even local drugstores encouraged people to linger, offering soda fountains or lunch counters.

Modern anecdotal evidence affirms the idea, too. When Club Monaco added nonretail offerings to its various stores, with locally specific offerings (e.g., a farmers' market in Hong Kong) and décor, shoppers started asking salesclerks if the apparel company provided home decorating services too. They also started buying the furniture and artwork on display. In turn, the retailer has initiated a renewed concept of inventory rotation, such that its in-store decorations change every few months, depending on what shoppers have purchased.

The appealing in-store experience also can attract people who have never shopped with the brand before. Urban Outfitters thus seeks to extend its reputation as a funky retailer of unusual items by hosting concerts to get music fans in its shops. The shows, similar to some of the retailer's products, are not available anywhere else, so people must visit Urban Outfitters to enjoy these offerings.

When it opened a lunch counter in a Chicago-area store, Restoration Hardware attracted a shopper who had never been there before but needed a quick bite during the workday. By recognizing what this shopper needed (i.e., a quick lunch near her office) but also offering a retail format that encouraged her to shop a bit, the retailer was able to appeal to her enough that she purchased several towel sets and rugs that she normally would have bought online.[1]

The retailers described in this chapter's opener are taking a long-term strategic perspective to cope effectively with the growing intensity of retail competition, as well as the emergence of new channels, technologies, and globalization. The retail strategy indicates how a retailer will deal effectively with its environment, customers, and competitors.[2] As the retail management decision-making process (discussed in Chapter 1) indicates, the retail strategy (Section II) is the bridge between understanding the world of retailing (Section I) and more tactical merchandise management and store operations activities (Sections III and IV) undertaken to implement the retail strategy.

The first part of this chapter defines the term *retail strategy* and discusses three important elements of retail strategy: (1) the target market segment, (2) the retail format, and (3) the retailer's bases of sustainable competitive advantage. Then we outline approaches that retailers use to build a sustainable competitive advantage. After reviewing the various growth opportunities, including international expansion, that retailers can pursue, the chapter concludes with a discussion of the strategic retail planning process.

WHAT IS A RETAIL STRATEGY?

LO 5-1

Define retail strategy.

The term *strategy* is frequently used in retailing. For example, retailers talk about their merchandise strategy, promotion strategy, location strategy, channel strategy, or branding strategy. The term is used so commonly that it might appear that all retailing decisions are strategic decisions, but *retail strategy* isn't just another synonym of *retail management*.

Definition of Retail Market Strategy

A **retail strategy** is a statement identifying (1) the retailer's target market, (2) the format and resources the retailer plans to use to satisfy the target market's needs, and (3) the bases on which the retailer plans to build a sustainable competitive advantage.[3] The **target market** is the market segment(s) toward which the retailer plans to focus its resources and retail mix. A **retail format** describes the nature of the retailer's operations—its retail mix (type of merchandise and services offered, pricing policy, advertising and promotion programs, store design and visual merchandising, typical locations, and customer services)—that it will use to satisfy the needs of its target market. A **sustainable competitive advantage** is one the retailer maintains over its competition that is not easily copied by competitors and thus can last over a long period of time. The following are a few examples of retail strategies:

- *Sephora*. Rather than visiting their local drugstore to grab inexpensive, questionable quality cosmetics or heading to a department store to visit high-end makeup counters, customers shopping at Sephora encounter fun in-store environments that encourage them to play with the products, which include both store brands and famous names. They can consider various options, without having to visit separate stores or counters.

Lululemon's retail strategy is selling merchandise that appeals to consumers seeking spiritual enrichment through yoga.

© Luis Sinco/Los Angeles Times/Getty Images

They also enjoy the potential of finding a unique, cutting-edge product that no one else is wearing; the stores' assortment strategies explicitly seek to stock lesser-known brands and items. The "treasure hunt" experience created allows young beauty consumers, most of whom have watched bloggers apply various makeup styles or read reviews of different products online, have fun searching and trying the cosmetics on their own. Sephora operates almost 1,800 stores worldwide, 360 of them in North America. Its "Innovation Lab" is tasked with developing new in-store and e-commerce technologies to ensure its continued growth. JCPenney even has acknowledged the dominance of Sephora's strategy, entering into an agreement to locate more than 400 Sephora "store-within-a-store" operations in its outposts.[4]

- *Lululemon Athletica.* Lululemon is a Canadian specialty store chain selling apparel and accessories that support the practice of yoga. The products it sells include headbands, bamboo blocks, and yoga mats printed with encouraging healthy-living slogans like "Drink fresh water." One of its signature items is the Groove Pant, cut with special gussets and flat seams to create a feeling of a drop of water free from gravity. Lululemon's apparel is made with special materials, Silverescent and Luon, enabling customers to engage in vigorous yoga exercises and still look attractive. Lululemon has also recently started targeting male customers with its first men's store, located in SoHo, New York. The men's products extend beyond yoga attire to merchandise for all types of athletes, including runners and customers who practice Crossfit. Lululemon stores are a community hub where people can learn about and discuss the physical aspects of healthy living, from yoga and diet to running and cycling, as well as the spiritual aspects of life. To create this community, the company recruits local ambassadors before opening a store. These ambassadors, usually popular yoga teachers, are featured on Lululemon's website and on bulletin boards in the store.[5]

- *Save-A-Lot.* From a single store in 1977, Save-A-Lot, a wholly owned subsidiary of SuperValu, has grown to more than 1,300 stores, making it the nation's 13th-largest U.S. supermarket chain. Save-A-Lot stores offer a limited assortment of 3,000 SKUs, compared with 20,000 to 30,000 SKUs in a conventional supermarket. By offering only the most popular items in each category, most of which are private-label merchandise, Save-A-Lot reduces its costs and is able to price its merchandise 40 percent lower than the prices at conventional supermarkets. Due to its buying power, Save-A-Lot also is able to develop customized product specifications that provide high-quality, private-label merchandise at low prices. Because the stores generally do not feature grocery store–style shelving, items instead are available in specially printed, cut-out shipping containers. Finally, most customers bring their own bags; the stores charge those customers who forget their own and need to obtain bags from the retailer.[6]

CENTRAL CONCEPTS IN A RETAIL MARKET STRATEGY

LO 5-2

Illustrate how retailers build a sustainable competitive advantage.

Each of the retail strategies described in the preceding section involves (1) the selection of target market segment(s), (2) the selection of a retail format (the elements in the retailer's retail mix), and (3) the development of a sustainable competitive advantage that enables the retailer to reduce the level of competition it faces. Now let's examine these central concepts of a retail strategy.

Bebe is a specialty store that targets a fashion-forward customer.

© Fernando Leon/WireImage/Getty Images

Target Market and Retail Format

A **retail market segment** is a group of consumers with similar needs and a group of retailers that satisfy those needs using similar retail channels and format.[7] The matrix in Exhibit 5–1 describes the battlefields on which women's apparel retailers compete— that is, the set of retail market segments for women's clothing. It lists various retail formats in the left-hand column. Each format offers a different retail mix to its customers.

EXHIBIT 5–1   Retail Market Segments for Women's Apparel

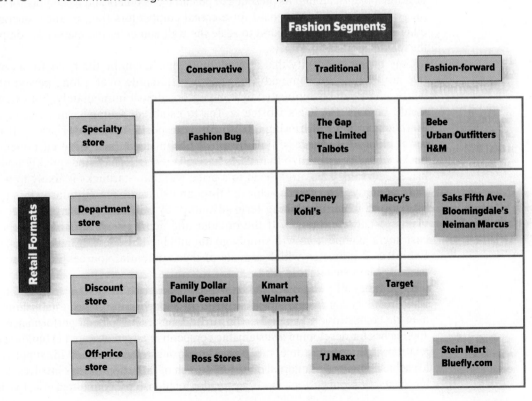

	Fashion Segments		
	Conservative	**Traditional**	**Fashion-forward**
Specialty store	Fashion Bug	The Gap The Limited Talbots	Bebe Urban Outfitters H&M
Department store		JCPenney Kohl's Macy's	Saks Fifth Ave. Bloomingdale's Neiman Marcus
Discount store	Family Dollar Dollar General Kmart Walmart	Target	
Off-price store	Ross Stores	TJ Maxx	Stein Mart Bluefly.com

Retail Formats

Market segments are listed in the exhibit's top row. As mentioned in Chapter 4, these segments could be defined in terms of the customers' geographic location, demographics, lifestyle, buying situation, or benefits sought. In the exhibit we divide the market into three fashion-related segments: (1) conservative—consumers who place little importance on fashion; (2) traditional—those who want classic styles; and (3) fashion-forward—those who want the latest fashions.

Each square of the matrix in Exhibit 5–1 describes a potential retail market in which retailers battle for consumers with similar needs. For example, Walmart and Kmart stores in the same geographic area fight each other by offering a full-line discount store format that targets conservative customers. Bloomingdale's and Neiman Marcus compete using a department store format and targeting fashion-forward segments. The position on each battlefield (cell in the matrix) indicates the first two elements of a retailer's strategy: the fashion segment (the x-axis) and the retail format (the y-axis).

Consider the situation confronting Target as it refines its battle plan (i.e., retail strategy) for the women's clothing market. Should Target compete on all 12 fronts (i.e., retail markets) in Exhibit 5–1, or should it focus on a limited set of targets? If Target decides to focus on a limited set of markets, which should it pursue? Target's answers to these questions define its retail strategy and indicate how it will focus its resources.

The women's clothing market in Exhibit 5–1 is just one of several representations that we could have used. For example, the retail formats might be expanded to include off-price stores and category specialists. But this exhibit and the battlefield analogy help illustrate how retail market segments can be defined in terms of retail format and customer market segments.

Building a Sustainable Competitive Advantage

After selecting a target market and a retail mix, the final element in a retail strategy is the retailer's approach to building a sustainable competitive advantage.[8] Establishing a competitive advantage means that the retailer, in effect, builds a wall around its battle position—that is, around its present and potential customers and its competitors. When the wall is high, it will be hard for external competitors (i.e., retailers operating in other markets or entrepreneurs) to scale the wall and enter the market to compete for the retailer's target customers.

Any business activity that a retailer engages in can be the basis for a competitive advantage. But some advantages are sustainable over a long period of time, while others can be duplicated by competitors almost immediately. For example, it would be hard for Peets Coffee & Tea to establish a long-term advantage over Starbucks by simply offering the same coffee specialties at lower prices. If Peets's lower prices were successful in attracting a significant number of customers, Starbucks would soon realize that Peets had lowered its prices and quickly match the price reduction. This might lead to a price war that Starbucks is likely to win, because it enjoys lower costs achieved through its larger size. Similarly, it is unusual for retailers to develop a long-term advantage by offering broader or deeper assortments of national brands. If the broader and deeper assortment attracts a lot of customers, competitors will simply go out and buy the same branded merchandise. Exhibit 5–2 indicates which aspects of these potential sources of advantage are more and less sustainable.

Over time, all advantages erode due to competitive forces, but by building high walls, retailers can sustain their advantage for a longer time. Thus, establishing a sustainable competitive advantage is the key to long-term financial performance. Three approaches for developing a sustainable competitive advantage are (1) building strong relationships with customers, (2) building strong relationships with suppliers, and (3) achieving efficient internal operations. Each of these approaches involves developing an asset—loyal customers, strong vendor relationships, committed effective human

EXHIBIT 5–2
Approaches for
Developing a
Sustainable
Competitive
Advantage

Sources of Advantage	SUSTAINABILITY OF ADVANTAGE	
	Less Sustainable	**More Sustainable**
Customer loyalty (Chapters 10 and 15)	Habitual repeat purchasing because of limited competition in the local area	Building of a brand image with an emotional connection with customers; use of databases to develop and utilize a deeper understanding of customers
Location (Chapters 7 and 8)		Convenient locations
Human resource management and managing the store (Chapter 15)	More employees	Committed, knowledgeable employees
Distribution and information systems (Chapter 9)	Bigger warehouses; automated warehouses	Shared systems with vendors
Unique merchandise (Chapters 11 and 12)	More merchandise; greater assortment; lower price; higher advertising budgets; more sales promotions	Exclusive merchandise
Vendor relations (Chapter 12)	Repeat purchases from vendor due to limited alternatives	Coordination of procurement efforts; ability to get scarce merchandise
Customer service (Chapter 17)	Hours of operation	Knowledgeable and helpful salespeople

resources, efficient systems, and attractive locations—that is not easily duplicated by competitors. Let's look at each of these approaches.

Relationships with Customers—Customer Loyalty

Customer loyalty means that customers are committed to buying merchandise and services from a particular retailer. Loyalty is more than simply liking one retailer over another. It means that customers will be reluctant to switch and patronize a competitive retailer. For example, loyal customers will continue to have their car serviced at Jiffy Lube, even if a competitor opens a store nearby and charges slightly lower prices. Approaches for developing loyalty include building a strong brand image, creating a unique positioning in the target market, offering unique merchandise, providing excellent customer service, implementing a customer relationship management program, and building a retail community.

Brand Image   Retailers build customer loyalty by developing a well-known, attractive image of their brands and of the name over their doors. For example, when most consumers think about fast food or hamburgers or French fries, they immediately think of McDonald's. Their image of McDonald's may include many favorable beliefs, such as fast service, consistent quality, and clean restrooms. If their image of the McDonald's is less favorable, though, they may prefer and exhibit loyalty to Burger King, which they regard as more innovative or entertaining in its brand image. In these cases, customers are unlikely to visit the other chain and perhaps even would drive a little farther to get to their preferred source of burgers.

Strong brand images facilitate customer loyalty because they reduce the risk associated with purchases. They assure customers that they will receive a consistent level of quality and satisfaction from the retailer. The retailer's image can also create an emotional tie with a customer that leads the customer to trust the retailer.

Positioning   A retailer's brand image reflects its positioning strategy. **Positioning** is the design and implementation of a retail mix to create an image of the retailer in the customer's mind relative to its competitors. A **perceptual map** is frequently used to represent the customer's image and preferences for retailers.

EXHIBIT 5–3   Hypothetical Perceptual Map of Women's Apparel Market

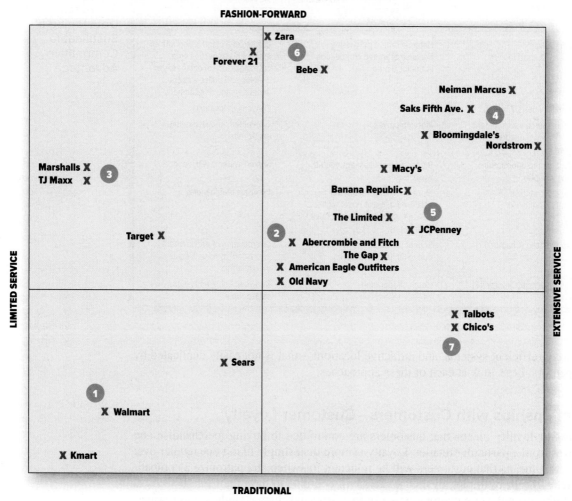

Exhibit 5–3 offers a hypothetical perceptual map of retailers selling women's clothing. The two dimensions in this map, fashion and service, represent two important characteristics that consumers in this example use in forming their images of retailers.

Perceptual maps are developed such that the distance between two retailers' positions on the map indicates how similar those stores appear, according to consumers. For example, Neiman Marcus and Saks Fifth Avenue are very close to each other on the map, because consumers in this illustration anticipate that they offer similar services and fashion. In contrast, Nordstrom and Marshalls are far apart, indicating that consumers believe they are quite different. Note that stores close to each other compete vigorously because consumers feel they provide similar benefits and have similar images. In this example, Macy's has an image of offering moderately priced, fashionable women's clothing with good service. TJ Maxx offers slightly less fashionable clothing with considerably less service. Sears is viewed as a retailer offering women's clothing that is not very fashionable and that provides moderate customer service.

The ideal points (marked by red dots on the map) indicate the characteristics of an ideal retailer for consumers in different market segments. For example, consumers in segment 3 prefer a retailer that offers high-fashion merchandise with low service, while consumers in segment 1 want more traditional apparel and are less concerned about service. The ideal points are located so that the distance between a retailer's position, or image (marked with a blue X), and the ideal point indicates how consumers in the segment will evaluate the retailer. Retailers that are closer to an ideal point are evaluated more favorably by the consumers in the segment than are retailers located farther away.

Thus, consumers in segment 6 prefer Forever 21 and Bebe to Neiman Marcus because these retailers are more fashion-forward and their target customers do not require such high service levels. Retailers strive to develop an image desired by customers in their target segment and thus develop loyalty among those customers.

Unique Merchandise   It is difficult for a retailer to develop customer loyalty through its merchandise offerings, because most competitors can purchase and sell the same popular national brands. Specialty stores such as Victoria's Secret, Apple, and Lululemon create loyalty by offering specific items that customers cannot find anywhere else; they also reinforce that appeal by providing dedicated in-store experiences that match the unique products.[9] Many retailers thus develop **private-label brands** (also called **store brands** or **own brands**) that are marketed by and available only from that retailer to keep customers loyal.[10] Costco's highly regarded private-label brand, Kirkland Signature, engenders a strong brand image and generates considerable loyalty toward Costco. The strong quality image of these private-label products also make significant contributions to enhance the image of Costco. Additional issues pertaining to the development of store brand merchandise are discussed in Chapter 12.

© Michael Stewart/FilmMagic/Getty Images

Specialty stores such as Victoria's Secret create loyalty by offering specific items that customers cannot find anywhere else.

Customer Service   Retailers also can develop customer loyalty by offering excellent customer service.[11] Consistently offering good service is difficult because retail employees will always be less consistent than machines. Machines can be programmed to make every box of Cheerios identical, but employees will never provide a completely consistent level of service, because they vary in their training, motivation, and mood.

It takes considerable time and effort to build a tradition and reputation for customer service. But once a retailer has earned a service reputation, it can sustain this advantage for a long time because it's hard for a competitor to develop a comparable reputation. For example, Ritz-Carlton hotels are renowned for providing outstanding customer service. It is the only hotel chain and the first service company to win the annual Malcolm Baldrige

© Oliver Strewe/Lonely Planet Images/Getty Images

Ritz-Carlton's outstanding service builds customer loyalty.

National Quality Award, and then win it multiple times.[12] Employees at the Ritz gather daily for a 15-minute staff meeting, during which they share accounts of how they or their peers have gone above and beyond the call for conventional customer service, also known as "WOW stories." A great example involved a chef in a Balinese Ritz-Carlton who learned that a guest had extensive food allergies and responded by having special eggs and milk flown in from a small grocery store located in another country. Such WOW stories help maintain employees' focus on customer service and give them recognition for the efforts they make.[13] Chapter 17 discusses how retailers can develop a customer service advantage.

Customer Relationship Management Programs   **Customer relationship management (CRM) programs**, also called **loyalty** or **frequent-shopper programs**, are activities that focus on identifying and building loyalty with a retailer's most valued customers.[14] These programs typically involve offering customers rewards based on the amount of services or merchandise they purchase. For example, airlines offer free tickets to travelers who have flown a prescribed number of miles, and local sandwich shops might give customers a free sandwich for each 10 they purchase.

The discounts offered by these programs may not create loyalty. Customers may join loyalty programs of competing retailers and continue to patronize multiple retailers. However, the data collected about customer shopping behavior by these programs can provide insights that enable retailers to build and maintain loyalty. For instance, CVS Caremark's CRM program gives the drugstore retailer extensive information about each of its customers, which it uses to increase sales. For example, if customers shop just once a month to fill their prescriptions, CVS Caremark may provide incentives that expire in a week to encourage more frequent visits. Alternatively, if customers buy frequently but spend less than $20 per visit, CVS Caremark offers incentives to increase each visit's purchases to, say, $25. It may provide incentives to get customers who are purchasing only national brands to purchase more private-label merchandise. CVS also uses the loyalty data to determine if a household is purchasing less of a category than it should based on usage in similar households, in which case it will offer a "buy one, get one free" coupon. Thus, the data developed through the loyalty program enable a retailer to develop a personal relationship with customers that builds loyalty. CRM programs are discussed in detail in Chapter 10.

Building a Retail Community Using Social Media   Some retailers use their websites and social media to develop retail communities. A **retail community** is a group of consumers who have shared involvement with a retailer. The members of the community share information with respect to the retailer's activities. Involvement in the community can range from simply becoming a fan of a retailer's Facebook page to meeting face-to-face with community members to share experiences. Increased involvement in the community by its members leads to a greater emotional feeling and loyalty toward the retailer.[15]

Starbucks started building a community in 2008 when it launched My Starbucks Ideas (http://mystarbucksidea.force.com). The website was initially a hub for Starbucks customers to share their ideas, suggestions, and even frustrations on this social network. As Starbucks customers started enjoying their time

SHARE.
VOTE.
DISCUSS.
SEE.

Share your ideas, tell us what you think of other people's ideas and join the discussion.

my STARBUCKS IDEA

Source: Starbucks

http://mystarbucksidea.force.com has created a community of Starbucks customers. It enables customers to make suggestions, vote on ideas, and check out the results.

interacting with other customers, the website evolved into a community. Now the online community gives customers the ability to see what others are suggesting, vote on ideas, and check out the results. Starbucks actually implements the most popular ideas, giving customers the feeling that they have a say in what their favorite coffee brand does.[16]

Relationships with Suppliers

A second approach for gaining a competitive advantage is to develop strong relationships with companies that provide merchandise and services to the retailer, such as real estate developers, advertising agencies, and transportation companies. Of these relationships with suppliers, the most important are relationships with vendors. For example, the relationship between Walmart and Procter & Gamble initially focused on improving supply chain efficiencies. Today, the partners in this relationship share sensitive information with each other so that Walmart is better able to plan for the introduction of new P&G products and even develop some unique packaging for P&G's national brands exclusively available at Walmart. Walmart shares its sales data with P&G so that P&G can better plan its production and use a just-in-time inventory management system to reduce the level of inventory in the system. By strengthening relationships with each other, both retailers and vendors can develop mutually beneficial assets and programs that give the retailer–vendor pair an advantage over competing pairs.[17]

Relationships with vendors, like relationships with customers, are developed over a long time and may not be easily offset by a competitor. Chapter 12 examines how retailers work with their vendors to build mutually beneficial, long-term relationships.

Efficiency of Internal Operations

In addition to strong relationships with external parties, customers, and suppliers, retailers can develop competitive advantages by having more efficient internal operations. Efficient internal operations enable retailers to have a cost advantage over competitors or offer customers more benefits than competitors at the same cost.

Larger companies typically have greater internal operations efficiency. Larger retailers can invest in developing sophisticated systems and spread the fixed cost of these systems over more sales. In addition to size, other approaches for improving internal operating efficiencies are human resource management and information and supply chain management systems.

Human Resource Management   Retailing is a labor-intensive business, in which employees play a major role providing services to customers and building customer loyalty. Some retailers view employees as an expense that needs to be reduced over the long run. But highly successful retail chains, such as Costco, actually invest heavily in their store employees while still achieving low prices, solid financial performance, and better customer service than their competitors. They recognize that underinvesting in employees makes their operations more inefficient and therefore much less profitable. Knowledgeable and skilled employees committed to the retailer's objectives are critical assets that support the success of these retailers. The retail landscape thus is increasingly dominated by retailers such as Wegmans and Costco that have adapted to this new reality.[18] Chapter 15 examines how retailers can increase employee productivity and retention through recruiting, training, and leadership.

Distribution and Information Systems   The use of sophisticated distribution and information systems offers an opportunity for retailers to reduce operating costs—the costs associated with running the business—and make sure that the

Starbucks creates a competitive advantage by saturating an area with stores, which makes it difficult for competitors to find good locations.

© Rob Crandall/Alamy Stock Photo

right merchandise is available at the right time and place.[19] Information flows seamlessly from Walmart to its vendors to facilitate quick and efficient merchandise replenishment and reduce stockouts. Walmart's distribution and information systems have enabled it to have a cost advantage that its competitors cannot overcome. This component of competitive advantage is discussed in Chapter 9.

In addition to using information systems to improve supply chain efficiency, purchase data collected by information systems provide an opportunity for retailers to tailor store merchandise assortments to the market served by each of its stores and to tailor promotions to the specific needs of individual customers. These data about its customers' buying behavior are valuable assets, offering an advantage that is not easily duplicated by competitors. These information systems applications are discussed in more detail in Chapter 9.

Location

Committed relationships with customers and vendors and efficient internal operations are important sources of advantage, but location is perhaps the most pervasive form of advantage in retailing. The classic response to the question "What are the three most important things in retailing?" is "Location, location, location." Location is a critical opportunity for developing competitive advantage for two reasons: First, location is the most important factor determining which store a consumer patronizes. For example, most people shop at the supermarket closest to where they live. Second, location is a sustainable competitive advantage because it is not easily duplicated. Once Walgreens has put a store at the best location at an intersection, CVS is relegated to the second-best location.

Starbucks has developed a strong competitive advantage with its locations. As it expanded across the United States, it saturated each market before entering a new market. For example, there were more than 100 Starbucks outlets in the Seattle area before the company expanded to a new region. Starbucks frequently opens several stores close to one another. It has two stores on two corners of the intersection of Robson and Thurlow in Vancouver. By having such a high density of stores, Starbucks makes it very difficult for a competitor to enter a market and find good locations. Approaches for evaluating and selecting locations are discussed in Chapters 7 and 8.

Multiple Sources of Advantage

To build an advantage that is sustainable for a long period of time, retailers typically cannot rely on a single approach, such as good locations or excellent customer service. Instead, they use multiple approaches to build as high a wall around their position as possible. For example, McDonald's long-term success is based on providing customers with a good value that meets their expectations, having efficient customer service, possessing a strong brand name, and offering convenient locations. By building strategic assets in all of these areas, McDonald's has developed a strong competitive position in the quick-service restaurant market.

In addition to the unique products and associated customer loyalty, customers loyal to IKEA appreciate its strong and quirky brand image and the stimulating shopping experience it provides in stores. Walmart complements its size advantage with strong

RETAILING VIEW   The Meaning of Best Value: Whole Foods's Purpose-Based Marketing

From its earliest days, starting out as a single store in Austin, Texas, Whole Foods has enjoyed its reputation as "America's Healthiest Grocery Store," a source of organic and local produce, as well as packaged foods that promise to exclude preservatives. It also is known for its high prices. Facing some dwindling sales numbers and decreased earnings, some observers recommended that the grocery chain would have no choice but to lower its prices so that consumers would consider it more valuable. Whole Foods rejects that notion, arguing instead that value means far more than prices. To sustain its advantages, it cannot simply cut its prices and risk offering lower-quality products. Instead, it has a few other ideas in mind to prove that its competitive advantages are actually diverse, valuable, and sustainable.

To start, it has introduced a new Responsibly Grown rating program, which identifies all fresh produce and flowers according to their environmental impact. The program is stringent in its demands. When vendors exert minor environmental impacts, they are rated "good"; those producers that go further, such as minimizing wasteful plastic usage or ensuring conservation areas for bees, earn a ranking of "better." The producers identified as the "best" address a vast range of responsibility initiatives, from working conditions for farmers to conservation efforts to clean energy to renewable resources and so on. For example, one criterion asks farmers how many earthworms live in the soil on their farms.

This produce-oriented initiative follows Whole Foods's existing efforts, such as the proprietary eco-scale it applies to rate cleaning products and separate programs to determine the sustainability and responsibility associated with animal and fish products. Furthermore, by 2018 it plans to introduce labels that indicate whether every single food item on its shelves contains any genetically modified ingredients.

In parallel with these new initiatives, Whole Foods has developed a revised advertising campaign, with a prominent tagline that reminds shoppers that "Values matter." The

Whole Foods's proprietary eco-scale determines the sustainability and responsibility associated with animal and fish products.

commercials emphasize that by shopping at Whole Foods, consumers can be confident that their food has been sourced responsibly and fairly. For example, any beef purchased in the stores has been raised by responsible ranchers who give the cows "room to roam."

By promoting the idea that "value is inseparable from values," Whole Foods seeks to remind shoppers of the advantages that it provides to them, in exchange for a somewhat higher price point. In particular, it promises that they can make their food choices confidently, buoyed by a range of information that Whole Foods will make available to them at all times.

Sources: Stephanie Strom, "Whole Foods to Rate Its Produce and Flowers for Environmental Impact," *The New York Times*, October 15, 2014; Stuart Elliot, "Whole Foods Asks Shoppers to Consider a Value Proposition," *The New York Times*, October 19, 2014, http://www.nytimes.com; "Whole Foods Market," https://en.wikipedia.org/wiki/Whole_Foods_Market.

vendor relationships and the clear positioning of a retailer that offers superior value. Starbucks combines its location advantage with unique products, committed employees, a strong brand name, and strong relationships with coffee growers to build an overall advantage that is very difficult for competitors to erode. Retailing View 5.1 describes how Whole Foods has built and continues to expand the sources of its sustainable competitive advantages.

GROWTH STRATEGIES

LO 5-3

Classify the different strategic growth opportunities retailers pursue.

In the preceding sections, we focused on a retailer's strategy, its target market and retail format, and the approaches that retailers take to build a sustainable competitive advantage and defend their position from competitive attacks. When retailers develop these competitive advantages, they have valuable assets. In this section, we discuss how retailers leverage these assets to expand their businesses.

EXHIBIT 5–4
Growth Opportunities

TARGET MARKETS

Growth Opportunities

Four types of growth opportunities that retailers may pursue—market penetration, market expansion, retail format development, and diversification—are shown in Exhibit 5–4.[20] The vertical axis indicates the synergies between the retailer's present markets and the growth opportunity—whether the opportunity involves markets the retailer is presently pursuing or new markets. The horizontal axis indicates the synergies between the retailer's present retail mix and the retail mix of the growth opportunity—whether the opportunity exploits the retailer's skills and knowledge in operating its present format or requires new capabilities to operate a new format.

Market Penetration   A **market penetration growth opportunity** is a growth opportunity directed toward existing customers using the retailer's present retailing format. Such opportunities involve either attracting new consumers from the retailer's current target market who don't patronize the retailer currently or devising approaches that get current customers to visit the retailer more often and/or buy more merchandise on each visit.

Market penetration approaches include opening more stores in the target market and/or keeping existing stores open for longer hours. Other approaches involve displaying merchandise to increase impulse purchases and training salespeople to cross-sell. **Cross-selling** means that sales associates in one department attempt to sell complementary merchandise from other departments to their customers. For example, a sales associate who has just sold a Blu-ray player to a customer might walk the customer over to the accessories department to sell special cables to improve the performance of the player.

Market Expansion   A **market expansion growth opportunity** involves using the retailer's existing retail format in new market segments. For example, Dunkin' Donuts has been opening new stores outside its traditional target market in the northeastern United States. When Chico's acquired White House Black Market, it engaged in a market expansion growth opportunity. Chico's and White House Black Market have similar retail formats. They are both mall-based specialty apparel stores. But Chico's targets women over 30 years old, while White House Black Market targets a younger age segment. In contrast, Chico's acquisition of Soma, a mall-based specialty store chain offering lingerie for women between 35 and

Chico's (top) acquisition of White House Black Market (middle) is a market expansion growth opportunity. But its acquisition of Soma (bottom) was a market penetration opportunity.

(top): © Rosalrene Betancourt/Alamy Stock Photo; (middle): © Marc Dimov/ Patrick McMullan/Getty Images; (bottom): © John Crowe/Alamy Stock Photo

55 years of age, was a market penetration opportunity—same market and similar operations, but Chico's and Soma offer different products. Retailing View 5.2 highlights Starbucks's expansion in Italy.

Retail Format Development   A **retail format development growth opportunity** is an opportunity in which a retailer develops a new retail format—a format with a different retail mix—for the same target market. The UK-based retailer Tesco has employed a retail format development growth strategy by operating several different food store formats that all cater to essentially the same target market. The smallest is Tesco Express, with formats up to 3,000 square feet. These stores are located close to where customers live and work. Tesco Metro stores are 7,000 to 15,000 square feet, bring convenience to city center locations, and specialize in offering a wide range of ready-to-eat meals. Tesco Superstores, up to 50,000 square feet, are the oldest format. Finally, Tesco Extra stores, more than 60,000 square feet, are designed to be a one-stop destination, with the widest range of food and nonfood products, from housewares and clothing to garden furniture.[21]

Diversification   A **diversification growth opportunity** is one in which a retailer introduces a new retail format directed toward a market segment that's not currently served by the retailer. Diversification opportunities are either related or unrelated.

5.2   RETAILING VIEW   Starbucks's Expansion in Italy

The 74th country in which Starbucks will open shops is also the first place that anyone ever had the idea for Starbucks. As the chain's well-known origin story has noted, Howard Schultz loved the espresso culture in Italy and sought to bring it to the United States. But the version of this culture and experience that has made Starbucks into a global juggernaut is quite different from the traditional version of espresso consumption in Italy, raising questions about just how successful this specific international expansion will be.

In particular, in Italy an espresso break means heading over to a small bar, where consumers receive small cups, with saucers, of the strong coffee, consumed quickly while standing up. They might chat for a few moments about the weather, the football league, or politics, but after a few minutes, the bar owner will shoo them out the door to make room for the next consumers.

The experience at Starbucks is totally different, of course, and for some traditionalists, the expectation that Italians would linger over sweetened drinks with made-up names, served in paper cups, is not just absurd but also a little horrifying. Paper cups!

However, some evidence suggests that there is room for both traditional bars and third space venues like Starbucks. Arnold Coffee is a four-store chain that has adopted the Starbucks model, offering free wi-fi, bagels and brownies, and cinnamon caffe lattes. Even its motto highlights its distinction, laying claim to offering "The American Coffee Experience." Especially for younger consumers, as one student explained, "The experience at the traditional Italian bar, downing an espresso in two seconds, isn't what I'm looking for. I need a place like this to study or meet friends or just relax."

That is precisely what Starbucks offers, so the company expresses confidence in the expansion. At the same time, it is

Who is selling what to whom? Starbucks brought an Italian coffee experience to the United States and is now attempting to repatriate the idea back to Italy. At the same time, the Italian chain, Arnold Coffee, pictured here is offering "The American Coffee Experience" to Italians.

making some nods to local preferences. Starting in its first Milan store, Starbucks will emphasize espresso more than it does in other international locations, where coffee drinkers prefer something a little lighter. It also will rely on local farmers to source milk and some of its food options. Although further expansions have not been announced yet, it seems like only a matter of time before the mermaid logo will appear on corners of cities throughout Italy, next to the espresso bars that line the streets today.

Source: Dan Liefgreen and Chiara Albanese, "Can Starbucks Sell Espresso Back to Italians?," *Bloomberg*, June 16, 2016.

Related versus Unrelated Diversification   In a **related diversification growth opportunity**, the retailer's present target market and retail format share something in common with the new opportunity. This commonality might entail purchasing from the same vendors, operating in similar locations, using the same distribution or management information system, or advertising in the same newspapers to similar target markets. In contrast, an **unrelated diversification growth opportunity** has little commonality between the retailer's present business and the new growth opportunity.

Through acquisition, Home Depot built a wholesale building supply business, called HD Supply, which had generated more than $3 billion in annual sales. Management felt that this growth opportunity would be synergistic with the firm's retail business, because its stores were already selling similar merchandise to contractors. Thus, Home Depot viewed this growth opportunity as a related diversification because the targeted customers (i.e., contractors) would be similar, and the new large contractor market could be served using a retail mix similar to Home Depot's present retail mix. In addition, Home Depot would realize cost savings by placing larger orders with vendors because it would be selling to both retail and wholesale large and small customers.

In hindsight, though, HD Supply actually was an unrelated diversification. The large contractor market served by HD Supply sold primarily pipes, lumber, and concrete—products with limited sales in Home Depot's retail stores. Selling these supplies to large contractors involved competitive bidding and transporting large, bulky orders to job sites—skills that Home Depot lacked. So Home Depot sold this unrelated diversification to concentrate on its core retail, small-contractor business.[22]

Vertical Integration   **Vertical integration** describes diversification by retailers into wholesaling or manufacturing. For example, some retailers go beyond designing their private-label merchandise to owning factories that manufacture the merchandise. When retailers integrate backward and manufacture products, they are making risky investments, because the requisite skills to make products are different from those associated with retailing them. In addition, retailers and manufacturers have different customers. The immediate customers for a manufacturer's products are retailers, while a retailer's customers are consumers. Thus, a manufacturer's marketing activities are very different from those of a retailer. Note that designing private-label merchandise is a related diversification because it builds on the retailer's knowledge of its customers, whereas actually making the merchandise is an unrelated diversification.

Growth Opportunities and Competitive Advantage

Typically, retailers have the greatest competitive advantage and most success when they engage in opportunities that are similar to their present retail operations and markets. Thus, market penetration growth opportunities have the greatest chances of succeeding because they build on the retailer's present bases of advantage and don't involve entering new, unfamiliar markets or operating new, unfamiliar retail formats.

When retailers pursue market expansion opportunities, they build on their advantages in operating a retail format and apply this competitive advantage in a new market. A retail format development opportunity builds on the retailer's relationships and loyalty of present customers. Even if a retailer lacks experience or skills operating in the new format, it hopes to attract its loyal customers to it. Retailers have the least opportunity to exploit a competitive advantage when they pursue diversification opportunities.

GLOBAL GROWTH OPPORTUNITIES

LO 5-4

Identify issues that arise as domestic retailers become global retailers.

In this section, we provide a more detailed discussion of one type of growth opportunity: expanding operations to international markets. This growth opportunity is particularly attractive to large retailers as they saturate their domestic market. Of the 20 largest retailers in the world, only 3 operate in one country.[23] By expanding internationally, retailers can increase their sales, leverage their knowledge and systems across

5.3 RETAILING VIEW   Uniqlo: The Brand without Borders

The Japanese clothing retailer Uniqlo started with just one store; it now has locations in 18 different countries and continues to expand, planning to add about 100 stores per year in the near future. The foundation of the company is its ability to produce quality clothing that is affordable. Uniqlo also aims to keep its designs simple but fashionable and with the times. Therefore, it constantly releases new fashions and produces its own clothing, prompting some observers to lump Uniqlo in with other fast-fashion retailers such as Zara. But Uniqlo's founder seeks to avoid being known solely as a fashion company, even as it functions within the fashion industry.

Rather, Uniqlo takes a unique approach to targeting its market segments. Instead of focusing on one specific market, Uniqlo hopes to become a "truly global brand" that transcends different segments across global markets. It seeks to produce clothes that can be worn by fashionistas, professionals, and anyone in between, not just another brand that consumers can go to for the basics. Creating a brand that speaks to everyone in a single country is difficult; the challenge increases exponentially when the goal is to branch out to reach global markets.

To find the appropriate balance between local and global appeal, Uniqlo partners with local designers whose products appeal to a broad audience. The strategy seemingly is working: By 2016, Uniqlo had opened nearly 800 stores outside its

Uniqlo uses an antisegmentation strategy by creating a global brand that attempts to appeal to everyone, everywhere.

home market of Japan, and it forecast that in 2017 it would have more stores outside Japan that in it, for the first time in its history.

Sources: Marianne Wee-Slater, "Uniquely Uniqlo: Creating a 'Borderless' Apparel Brand," *Today*, July 1, 2016; "UNIQLO Business Strategy," *UNIQLO*, http://www.fastretailing.com/eng/group/strategy/tactics.html; http://www.uniqlo.com/us/company/about-uniqlo.html; UNIQLO, "Annual Report 2015," *UNIQLO*, February 26, 2016.

a greater sales base, and gain more bargaining power with vendors. But international expansion is risky because retailers must deal with different government regulations, cultural traditions, consumer preferences, supply chains, and languages. As Retailing View 5.3 describes, it also can be challenging as retailers like Uniqlo seek to balance the local and global needs of their customers.

We first discuss the attractiveness of different opportunities for global expansion and then the keys to success for expanding globally. Finally, we review the approaches that retailers can take to enter international markets.

Attractiveness of International Markets

Three factors that are often used to determine the attractiveness of international opportunities are (1) the potential size of the retail market in the country, (2) the degree to which the country does and can support the entry of foreign retailers engaged in modern retail practices, and (3) the risks or uncertainties in sales and profits. Some indicators of these factors are shown in Exhibit 5–5. The (+) or (−) indicates whether the indicator is positively or negatively related to the factor.

Note that the importance of some country characteristics depends on the type of retailer evaluating the country for entry. For example, a retailer of video games, such as Gamestop, would find a country with a large percentage of people under 19 years of age to be more attractive than a country with a large percentage of people over 65 years. High-fashion retailers that sell expensive merchandise, such as Neiman Marcus and Cartier, would find a country that has a significant percentage of the population with high incomes to be more attractive than a country that has a large percentage of people in poverty.

Most retailers considering entry into foreign markets are successful multinational retailers that use sophisticated management practices. Thus, they would find countries

EXHIBIT 5–5   Indicators of the Potential, Support, and Risk in International Markets

Country Potential	Country Support	Country Risk
Population (+)	Market share of modern retailing (+)	Political stability (+)
Population growth rate (+)	Quality of infrastructure (roads, trains, etc.) (+)	Business-friendly laws and regulations (+)
GDP (+)	Urban population (+)	Access to bank financing (+)
GDP growth rate (+)	Market share of domestic retailers (+)	National debt (−)
GDP per capita (+)	Market share of international retailers (+)	Crime (−)
Retail sales (+)	Market share of largest retailers (+)	Violence (−)
Retail sales growth rate (+)		Corruption (−)
Retail sales per capita (+)		
Population (+)		
Income distribution (+ or −)		
Age (+ or −)		

that have modern retailing, more advanced infrastructures, and significant urban populations to be more supportive. In addition, countries that lack strong domestic retailers but have stable economic and political environments would be more appealing.

The factors outlined in Exhibit 5–5 are weighted to develop an index that can score each country on the attractiveness dimensions. One index ranking the 20 most attractive international retail markets on market potential (country potential and support) and risk is shown in Exhibit 5–6. Of the top 20 countries in this ranking, 10 are emerging economies. The emerging international markets that receive the most attention from global retailers are Brazil, Russia, India, and China, collectively referred to as the BRIC nations. However, in this analysis Russia is not in the top 20 because of its high risk. India and China both may be large and deeply attractive retail markets, but they offer different opportunities and challenges for retailers contemplating entry.[24]

EXHIBIT 5–6   Country Attractiveness

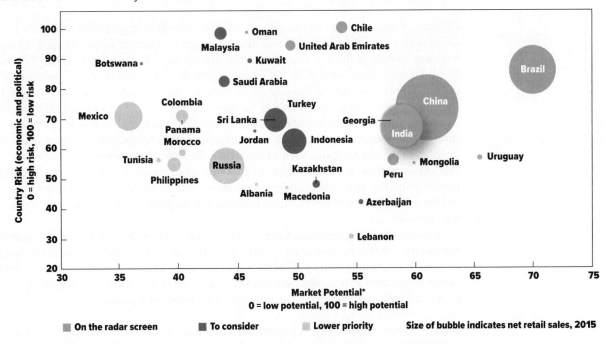

*Based on weighted score of market attractiveness, market saturation, and time pressure of top 30 countries

© Erica Simone Leeds

In India, most consumers shop at small, independent retail outlets.

India In India and most emerging economies, the retail industry is divided into organized and unorganized sectors. The **unorganized retailing** sector includes small independent retailers—local *kirana* (small neighborhood) shops, owner-operated general stores, *paan/beedi* shops, convenience stores, and handcart and street vendors. Most Indians shop in open markets and the millions of independent *kirana*. Less than 5 percent of India's retail sales are through organized retail channels.[25] Yet India's growing, well-educated, aspirational middle class wants a more sophisticated retail environment and global brands—a demand that international retailers are struggling to meet.

As the world's largest pluralistic democracy, with myriad cultures and 22 official languages, India actually is a conglomeration of discrete markets. Previously, government regulations greatly restricted foreign investments in retailing; today, though some of the restrictions have been relaxed, foreign retailers still must comply with a myriad of regulations before opening stores and shipping merchandise. For example, there are taxes for moving goods to different states and even within states. But companies no longer are required to partner with Indian companies, so familiar international retailers such as IKEA, Apple, and Walmart have attempted to enter. A new rule instead requires retailers to ensure that 30 percent of the products they sell have been produced locally, a challenging mandate that has prompted IKEA to petition for more time to reach the threshold. Apple has enjoyed some success in urban areas, but it continues to struggle to penetrate rural areas as well. And even with the relaxed laws, Walmart was forced to abandon its expansion into the Indian market.[26]

China When it comes to retailing at least, government regulations are much less onerous in China than in India, and direct foreign investment is encouraged. China thus was ranked at the top emerging retail market in A.T. Kearney's annual Global Retail Development Index (GRDI). Even as growth in its gross domestic product has slowed, China maintains a thriving retail market, likely to reach the $8 trillion mark soon and surpass the United States as the world's largest.[27] Seven global food retailers (Auchan, Carrefour, Ito-Yokado, Metro, Tesco, Walmart, and Seven & I) maintain strong operations in China, though much of this retail development has taken place in large, eastern, coastal cities such as Shanghai, Beijing, Guangzhou, and Shenzhen.[28] The infrastructure needed to support modern retailing also continues to develop: Highway density in China is approaching levels similar to those in the United States, and the country already has multiple high-quality airports and a rapidly growing railroad network.

However, doing business in China is challenging. Operating costs are increasing, managerial talent is becoming more difficult to find and retain, and an underdeveloped and inefficient supply chain predominates. Companies such as Walmart, 7-Eleven, and Home Depot have experienced significant closure rates or left the country altogether, even as Carrefour and Metro have increased their expansion plans.[29]

Brazil Brazil has the largest population and strongest economy in Latin America. It is a country of many poor people and a few very wealthy families. Brazilian retailers have developed some very innovative practices for retailing to low-income families, including offering credit and installment purchases. The very wealthy Brazilians provide a significant market for luxury goods and retailers. Even though these wealthy Brazilians are approximately 10 percent of the population, this equates to approximately 20 million people, a market just a little smaller than all of Australia.

Russia   In Russia, the impediments to market entry are less visible but more problematic. In 2015 it ranked as one of the top countries in terms of retail growth; even though economic and political issues challenge its retail growth prospects, the market simply is too big for most retail firms to ignore.[30] Yet corruption is rampant, and various administrative authorities can impede operations if they do not receive what they regard as appropriate bribe payments.

Retailers also encounter severe logistical challenges in supporting their operations in Russia, including long delays at borders and ports and a scarcity of containers. More than 70 percent of international container shipments come through the St. Petersburg port, which is very congested. But the quality of domestic products made in Russia tends to be poor, so retailers cannot rely on local suppliers. A solution might come in the form of Russia's booming e-commerce, which attracts retailers such as Amazon and Alibaba.[31] In particular, Russia's Internet market, which presently includes 83 million customers, making it Europe's largest,[32] is growing at a rate of approximately 10 percent annually.[33]

In addition, international sanctions on Russia, in response to its aggressive international involvements, combined with fluctuations in oil prices, threaten to push it into a financial crisis.[34] Uncertain international relations can create further challenges for retailers; some McDonald's outlets allege that they have been subjected to suspicious inspections by Russian agencies that find questionable code violations, seemingly in response to the strained relations between the Russian and U.S. governments.[35] Yet McDonald's continues to expand, including a plan to open 20 new restaurants in remote Siberian regions.[36]

Keys to Success in Global Retailing

Four characteristics of retailers that have successfully exploited international growth opportunities are (1) a globally sustainable competitive advantage, (2) adaptability, (3) a global culture, and (4) financial resources.

Globally Sustainable Competitive Advantage   Entry into nondomestic markets is most successful when the expansion opportunity builds on the retailer's core bases of competitive advantage. For example, Walmart and ALDI enjoy significant cost advantages that can facilitate their success in international markets in which price plays an important role in consumer decision making. However, they also require those markets to offer a distribution infrastructure that enables them to exploit their advantageous logistical capabilities. For H&M and Zara, success instead is more likely in international markets that value lower-priced, fashionable merchandise.

Some U.S. retailers have a competitive advantage in global markets because American culture is emulated in many countries, particularly by young people. Due to rising prosperity and increasing access to the Internet, social media like Facebook, and networks such as MTV, fashion trends in the United States have spread to young people in emerging countries. The global MTV generation prefers Coke to tea, Nikes to sandals, Chicken McNuggets to rice, and credit cards to cash. China's major cities have American stores and restaurants, including KFC, Pizza Hut, and McDonald's. Shanghai and Beijing have almost 400 Starbucks stores, even though coffee had never been the drink of choice before Starbucks came to town.[37] But Chinese urban dwellers go to Starbucks to impress a friend or because it is a symbol of a new kind of lifestyle. Although Western products and stores have gained a reputation for high quality and good service in China, in some ways it is the American culture that many Chinese consumers want.

China's major cities have American stores and restaurants, including McDonald's.

© In Pictures Ltd./Corbis/Getty Images

Adaptability   Although successful global retailers build on their core competencies, they also recognize cultural differences and adapt their core strategy to the needs of local markets. Retailing View 5.4 illustrates how 7-Eleven changed its retail offering to be more appealing in Indonesia.

Peak selling seasons also vary across countries. In the United States, many stores experience a sales increase in August, when families stock up on back-to-school supplies and apparel. However, this month is one of the slowest sales periods in Europe because most people are on vacation. Back-to-school season in Japan occurs in April.

Store designs and layouts often need to be adjusted in different parts of the world. In the United States, for instance, supercenters are usually quite large and on one level, except in a few urban areas. In other parts of the world, such as Europe and parts of Asia, where space is at a premium, stores must be designed to fit smaller footprints and are often housed in multiple levels. In some cultures, social norms dictate that men's and women's clothing cannot be displayed next to each other.

Government regulations and cultural values can also affect store operations. Some differences, such as holidays, hours of operation, and regulations governing part-time employees and terminations, are easy to identify. Other factors require a deeper understanding. For example, Latin American culture is very family oriented, so traditional U.S. work schedules would need to be adjusted so that Latin American employees could have more time with their families during family meals. Boots, a UK drugstore chain owned by Walgreens, has the checkout clerks in its Japanese stores stand up because it discovered that Japanese shoppers found it offensive to pay money to a seated clerk, but retailers have to provide seating for checkout clerks in Germany. Retailers in Germany also must recycle packaging materials sold in their stores. Also in Germany, seasonal sales can be held only during specific weeks and apply only to specific product categories, and the amount of the discounts are limited. Spanish and French retailers work under government-controlled operating hours and must mind policies prohibiting midseason sales.[38]

Global Culture   To be global, retailers must think globally. It is not sufficient to transplant a home-country culture and infrastructure to another country. In this regard, Carrefour is truly global. In the early years of its international expansion, it started in each country slowly, an approach that reduced the company's ethnocentrism. Further enriching its global perspective, Carrefour has always encouraged the

RETAILING VIEW   7-Eleven Is a Trendy Hangout in Indonesia   **5.4**

In a local hangout in Jakarta, hipsters gather to drink iced coffee, gossip, eat nachos, listen to a live band, and text their friends. This sort of hanging out is so popular and common among young Indonesians that their language includes a word to describe sitting around, chatting, and generally doing nothing productive: *nongkrong*. For years, the most popular gathering spots were food stalls, located along the sides of roads, known as *warung*. But the *warung* are giving way to another popular *nongkrong* location: local 7-Eleven stores.

This shift is exactly the response that 7-Eleven hoped to achieve when it instituted a new strategy in Indonesia: adding seating to its existing small supermarkets and offering inexpensive, ready-to-eat meals, such as fried rice and pillow bread (i.e., small cheese- or chocolate-filled sandwiches). 7-Eleven also offers a delivery service to get these homemade meals to customers who would rather eat in; such meals and drinks make up approximately 90 percent of store sales. Jakarta is notably lacking in outdoor recreation space, so the little hangouts effectively attract social customers. Although there are only 176 location in Indonesia, the stores have been so successful that 7-Eleven has plans to expand, not just in Jakarta but also in nearby cities, bringing the total number of stores in Indonesia to 2,500. Many of these new locations will be inside malls and office buildings, such as one recently opened inside the Indonesian Stock Exchange.

The strategy also means that the franchise mainly targets young customers, who constitute 65 percent of its market. These Millennials make use of the 24/7 access that 7-Eleven offers, surfing the Internet at all hours, before or after gathering with their friends. In Indonesia, one of the most electronically connected nations in the world, customers constantly update their social networks to alert them about when a band is about to start playing at the local 7-Eleven, for example.

7-Eleven is a trendy place for young Indonesians to hang out with their friends.

Among this generational cohort, the store appeals to a wide range of economic classes, such that the parking lots fill with Mercedes-Benzes interspersed with rusted-out motor bikes.

Despite these unique offerings, 7-Elevens are still 7-Elevens: They sell Big Gulps, flavored Slurpees, doughnuts, and hot coffee. But in locations in the world's most populous Muslim country, 7-Eleven sells alcohol only after conducting neighborhood surveys to obtain community approval.

Sources: Wataru Suzuki, "Indonesia Holds Promise, Pitfalls for 7-Eleven," *Nikkei Asian Review*, October 16, 2014; Hannah Adulla, "Indonesia: 7-Eleven Operator Outlines Expansion Plans," *Just-Food*, April 28, 2014; Sara Schonhardt, "7-Eleven Finds a Niche by Adapting to Indonesian Ways," *The New York Times*, May 28, 2012; Anthony Deutsch, "7-Eleven Becomes Indonesia's Trendy Hangout," *Financial Times*, September 13, 2011.

rapid development of local management and retains few expatriates in its overseas operations. Carrefour's management ranks are truly international. One is just as likely to run across a Portuguese regional manager in Hong Kong as a French or Chinese one. Finally, Carrefour discourages the classic overseas "tour of duty" mentality often found in U.S. firms. International assignments are important in themselves, not just as stepping stones to ultimate career advancement in France. The globalization of Carrefour's culture is perhaps most evident in the speed with which ideas flow throughout the organization. A global management structure of regional committees, which meet regularly, advances the awareness and implementation of global best practices. The proof of Carrefour's global commitment lies in the numbers: It has had more than 30 years of international experience in more than 30 countries, both developed and developing.[39]

Financial Resources   Expansion into international markets requires a long-term commitment and considerable up-front planning. Retailers find it very difficult to generate short-term profits when they make the transition to global retailing. Although firms such as Walmart, Carrefour, Office Depot, and Costco often initially have difficulty achieving success in new global markets, these large firms generally are in a strong financial position and therefore have the ability to keep investing in projects long enough to become successful.

Entry Strategies

Four approaches that retailers can take when entering nondomestic markets are direct investment, joint venture, strategic alliance, and franchising.[40]

Direct Investment   **Direct investment** occurs when a retail firm invests in and owns a retail operation in a foreign country. This entry strategy requires the highest level of investment and exposes the retailer to the greatest risks, but it also has the highest potential returns. A key advantage of direct investment is that the retailer has complete control of the operations. For example, McDonald's chose this entry strategy for the UK market, building a plant to produce buns when local suppliers could not meet its specifications.

Joint Venture   A **joint venture** is formed when the entering retailer pools its resources with a local retailer to form a new company in which ownership, control, and profits are shared. A joint-venture entry strategy reduces the entrant's risks. In addition to sharing the financial burden, the local partner provides an understanding of the market and has access to local resources, such as vendors and real estate. Many foreign countries require that foreign entrants partner with domestic firms. Problems with this entry approach can arise if the partners disagree or the government places restrictions on the repatriation of profits.

Strategic Alliance   A **strategic alliance** is a collaborative relationship between independent firms. For example, a retailer might enter an international market through direct investment but use independent firms to facilitate its local logistical and warehousing activities.

Franchising   **Franchising** offers the lowest risk and requires the least investment but also has the lowest potential return on investment. The retailer has limited control over the retail operations in the foreign country, and any potential profits must be split with the franchisee. Once the franchise is established, there is also the threat that the franchisee will break away and operate as a competitor under a different name. In this case, the expanding retailer runs the risk of creating its own local competitor. Still, the agreement can work to everyone's benefit: The UK-based Marks & Spencer, for example, has franchised stores in more than 50 countries.[41]

THE STRATEGIC RETAIL PLANNING PROCESS

LO 5-5

Know the steps retailers go through to develop a strategic plan.

In the previous sections, we reviewed the elements in a strategy statement, the approaches for building a sustainable competitive advantage, the growth opportunities that retailers consider, and the factors they consider when evaluating and pursuing a global growth opportunity. In this section, we outline the process retailers use to review their present situation and decide on a strategy to pursue.

The **strategic retail planning process** is the set of steps a retailer goes through to develop a strategy and plan[42] (see Exhibit 5–7). It describes how retailers select target market segments, determine the appropriate retail format, and build sustainable competitive advantages. As indicated in Exhibit 5–7, it is not always necessary to go through the entire process each time a strategy and plan are developed (step 7). For instance, a retailer could evaluate its performance and go directly to step 2 to conduct a SWOT analysis.

The planning process can be used to formulate strategic plans at different levels within a retail corporation. For example, the corporate strategic plan of Tesco indicates how to allocate resources across the corporation's various divisions, such as Tesco, Tesco Extra, Tesco Express, Tesco Metro, Tesco Homeplus, Dotcom Only, One Stop, and Dobbies. Each division, in turn, develops its own strategic plan.

As we discuss the steps in the retail planning process, we will apply each step to the planning process for a hypothetical retailer owned by Kelly Bradford. Kelly owns Gifts To Go, a small, two-store chain in the Chicago area. One of her 1,000-square-foot stores is located in the downtown area; the other is in an upscale suburban mall. The target

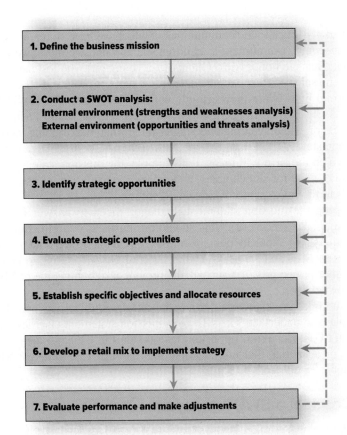

EXHIBIT 5–7
Stages in the Strategic
Planning Process

1. Define the business mission

2. Conduct a SWOT analysis:
   Internal environment (strengths and weaknesses analysis)
   External environment (opportunities and threats analysis)

3. Identify strategic opportunities

4. Evaluate strategic opportunities

5. Establish specific objectives and allocate resources

6. Develop a retail mix to implement strategy

7. Evaluate performance and make adjustments

market for Gifts To Go is upper-income men and women looking for gifts in the $50 to $500 price range. The stores have an eclectic selection of merchandise, including hand-made jewelry and crafts, fine china and glassware, perfume, watches, writing instruments, and a variety of one-of-a-kind items. Gifts To Go also has developed a number of loyal customers whom the sales associates contact when family anniversaries and birthdays come up. In many cases, customers have close relationships with a sales associate and enough confidence in the associate's judgment that they tell the associate to pick out an appropriate gift. The turnover of Gifts To Go sales associates is low for the industry because Kelly treats associates as part of the family. The company pays for health insurance for all associates, and the associates share in the profits of the firm.

Step 1: Define the Business Mission

The first step in the strategic retail planning process is to define the business mission. The **mission statement** is a broad description of a retailer's objectives and the scope of activities it plans to undertake.[43] The mission statement attempts to answer two main questions: What type of business are we? What do we need to do to accomplish our goals and objectives? These fundamental business questions must be answered at the highest corporate levels. While the principle objective of a publicly held firm is to maximize its stockholders' wealth, firms also are concerned about their impact on society.

For example, Maxine Clark, founder and chief executive bear at Build-A-Bear Workshop, in discussing her goals for the company, says, "We also believe strongly

© Adam Bettcher/Getty Images

As part of **Build-A-Bear Workshop's ongoing commitment to children's health and wellness, it introduced a series of Nicki Bears to honor Nicki Giampolo, a young girl who lost her life to cancer. A portion of the sales is donated to support programs that help children maintain normal lives while they struggle with health issues.**

that we need to give back to the communities in which we have stores. For example, as part of our on-going commitment to children's health and wellness, we introduced a series of Nicki Bears to honor Nicki Giampolo, a young girl who lost her life to cancer. A portion of the sales of each Nicki is donated to support programs that help children maintain normal lives while they struggle with difficult health issues."[44] Owners of small, privately held firms frequently have other objectives, such as achieving a specific level of income and avoiding uncertainty rather than maximizing income.

The mission statement defines the general nature of the target segments and retail formats on which the firm will focus. For example, the mission statement "Serve the customer, build value for shareholders, and create opportunities for associates" is too broad. It fails to provide a sense of strategic direction.

In developing the mission statement, managers need to answer five questions: (1) What business are we in? (2) What should our business be in the future? (3) Who are our customers? (4) What are our capabilities? (5) What do we want to accomplish? Gifts To Go's mission statement is "The mission of Gifts To Go is to be the leading retailer of higher-priced gifts in Chicago and provide a stable income of $100,000 per year for the owner."

Because the mission statement defines the retailer's objectives and the scope of activities it plans to undertake, Gifts To Go's mission statement clarifies that its management won't consider retail opportunities outside the Chicago area, selling low-priced gifts, or activities that might jeopardize its ability to generate $100,000 in annual income.

Step 2: Conduct a SWOT Analysis

After developing a mission statement and setting objectives, the next step in the strategic planning process is to conduct a **SWOT analysis**. A SWOT analysis involves an analysis of the retailer's internal environment (**s**trengths and **w**eaknesses) and external environment (**o**pportunities and **t**hreats).

Internal Environment   The internal analysis identifies the retailer's *strengths and weaknesses*—the retailer's unique strategic capabilities relative to its competition. These unique capabilities are the assets, knowledge, and skills that the retailer possesses, such as the loyalty of its customers and the quality of its relationships with its vendors. These capabilities reflect the retailer's ability to develop a strategic advantage as an opportunity it is considering. Exhibit 5–8 outlines some issues to consider in performing a **strengths and weaknesses analysis**.

EXHIBIT 5–8
Elements in a Strengths and Weaknesses Analysis

Management capability	Capabilities and experience of top management
	Depth of management—capabilities of middle management
	Management's commitment to firm
Financial resources	Cash flow from existing business
	Ability to raise debt or equity financing
Operations	Overhead cost structure
	Quality of operating systems
	Distribution capabilities
	Management information systems
	Loss prevention systems
	Inventory control systems
Merchandising capabilities	Knowledge and skills of buyers
	Relationships with vendors
	Capabilities in developing private brands
	Advertising and promotion capabilities
Store management capabilities	Management capabilities
	Quality of sales associates
	Commitment of sales associates to firm
Locations	
Customers	Loyalty of customers

EXHIBIT 5–9   Gifts To Go's Strengths and Weaknesses

Management capability	Limited—Two excellent store managers and a relatively inexperienced person helped Kelly buy merchandise. An accounting firm kept the financial records for the business but had no skills in developing and utilizing customer databases.
Financial resources	Good—Gifts To Go had no debt and a good relationship with a bank. Kelly had saved $255,000 that she had in liquid securities.
Operations	Poor—While Kelly felt Gifts To Go had relatively low overhead, the company did not have a computer-based inventory control system or management and customer information systems. Her competitors (local department stores, catalog, and Internet retailers) certainly had superior systems.
Merchandising capabilities	Good—Kelly had a flair for selecting unique gifts, and she had excellent relationships with vendors providing one-of-a-kind merchandise.
Store management capabilities	Excellent—The store managers and sales associates were excellent. They were very attentive to customers and loyal to the firm. Employee and customer theft were kept to a minimum.
Locations	Excellent—Both of Gifts To Go's locations were excellent. The downtown location was convenient for office workers. The suburban mall location was at a heavily trafficked juncture.
Customers	Good—While Gifts To Go did not achieve the sales volume in gifts done in department stores, the company had a loyal base of customers.

Kelly Bradford's analysis of Gifts To Go's strengths and weaknesses is outlined in Exhibit 5–9.

External Environment   The external analysis identifies the retailer's opportunities and threats—the aspects of the environment that might positively or negatively affect the retailer's performance. These factors associated with the market, competition, and environment dynamics are typically beyond the retailer's control. Exhibit 5–10 outlines some issues to consider when doing an **opportunities and threats analysis**.

Market Factors   The attractiveness of a target market in which a retailer is involved or considering is affected by the size of the market, market growth, cyclicality of sales, and seasonality. Market size is important because it indicates a retailer's opportunity to generate revenues to cover its investment.

Growing markets are typically more attractive than mature or declining markets. For example, retail markets for limited-assortment, extreme-value retailers are growing faster than are those for department stores. Typically, the return on investment may be higher in growing markets because competition is less intense than in mature markets. Because new customers are just beginning to patronize stores in growing markets, they may not have developed strong store loyalties and thus might be easier to attract to new retail offerings.

Firms are often interested in minimizing the business cycle's impact on their sales. Thus, retail markets for merchandise that is affected by economic conditions (such as cars and major appliances) are less attractive than retail markets that are less affected by economic conditions (such as food). In general, markets with highly seasonal sales are unattractive because a lot of resources are needed to accommodate the peak season, and then the resources go underutilized the rest of the year. Retailers can take steps to reduce seasonality; for instance, ski resorts can promote summer vacations.

To conduct an analysis of the market factors for Gifts To Go, Kelly Bradford went on the Internet to get information about the size, growth, and cyclical and seasonal nature of the gift market in general and, more specifically, in Chicago. On the basis of her analysis, she concluded that the market factors were attractive. The market for more expensive gifts was large, growing, and not vulnerable to business cycles. The

Market Factors	Competitive Factors	Environmental Dynamics
Market size	Barriers to entry	Technological changes
Market growth	Bargaining power of vendors	Economic/consumer/social changes
Cyclicality of sales	Competitive rivalry	Regulatory changes
Seasonality		

EXHIBIT 5–10
Opportunities and Threats

only negative aspect was the high seasonality of gifts, with peaks at Valentine's Day, June (due to weddings), Christmas, and other holidays.

Competitive Factors   The nature of the competition in retail markets is affected by barriers to entry, the bargaining power of vendors, and competitive rivalry.[45] Retail markets are more attractive when barriers to entry are high. **Barriers to entry** are conditions in a retail market that make it difficult for other firms to enter the market. Some of these conditions are (1) scale economies, (2) customer loyalty, and (3) the availability of great locations.

Scale economies are cost advantages due to a retailer's size. Markets dominated by large competitors with scale economies are typically unattractive because the dominant firms have sustainable cost advantages. For example, an entrepreneur would view the drugstore market as unattractive because it is dominated by two large firms: Walgreens and CVS. These firms have considerable cost advantages over an entrepreneur because they have significant bargaining power over suppliers and can buy merchandise at lower prices. They have the resources to invest in the latest technology and can spread the fixed costs of such investments across more outlets.

Retail markets dominated by a well-established retailer that has developed a loyal group of customers also are unattractive. For example, Home Depot's high customer loyalty in Atlanta, where it has its corporate offices, makes it hard for a competing home improvement center like Lowe's to compete effectively in the Atlanta market.

The availability of locations may impede competitive entry. Staples, for instance, attributes part of its success over its rivals in the northeastern United States to its first-mover advantage. The Northeast has a preponderance of mature but stable retail markets, so finding new locations is more difficult there than it is in most of the rest of the United States. Because Staples started in the Northeast, it was able to open stores in the best available locations.

Entry barriers are a double-edged sword. A retail market with high entry barriers is very attractive for retailers presently competing in that market, because those barriers limit competition. However, markets with high entry barriers are unattractive for retailers not already in the market.

Another competitive factor is the **bargaining power of vendors**. Markets are less attractive when only a few vendors control the merchandise sold in the market. In such

It is difficult to enter the cosmetics industry because two suppliers, Estée Lauder (left) and L'Oréal (right) provide most of the desirable premium brands.

(left): © Diane Langlume/Bloomberg/Getty Images; (right): © Adam Berry/Bloomberg/Getty Images

situations, vendors have the opportunity to dictate prices and other terms (like delivery dates), reducing the retailer's profits. For example, the market for retailing fashionable cosmetics is less attractive because two suppliers, Estée Lauder (Estée Lauder, Clinique, Prescriptives, Aveda, Jo Malone London, Bumble and Bumble, Tommy Hilfiger, MAC, and Origins) and L'Oréal (Maybelline, Giorgio Armani, Redken, Lancôme, Garnier, and Ralph Lauren) provide most of the desirable premium brands. Because department stores need these brands to support a fashion image, the vendors have the power to sell their products to retailers at high prices.

The final competitive factor is the level of competitive rivalry in the retail market. **Competitive rivalry** is the frequency and intensity of reactions to actions undertaken by competitors. When rivalry is high, price wars erupt, retailers attempt to "steal" employees from one another, advertising and promotion expenses increase, and profit potential falls. Conditions that may lead to intense rivalry include (1) a large number of competitors that are all about the same size, (2) slow growth, (3) high fixed costs, and (4) a lack of perceived differences between competing retailers. For example, Home Depot and Lowe's have an intense rivalry in many markets.

When Kelly Bradford started to analyze the competitive factors for Gifts To Go, she realized that identifying her competitors wasn't easy. Although there were no gift stores carrying similar merchandise at the same price points in the Chicago area, there were various other retailers from which a customer could buy gifts. She identified her primary competitors as department stores, craft galleries, catalogs, and Internet retailers. Kelly felt there were some scale economies in developing customer databases to support gift retailing. The lack of large suppliers meant that vendors' bargaining power was not a problem, and competitive rivalry was minimal because the gift business was not a critical part of a department store's overall business. In addition, merchandise carried by the various retailers offered considerable differentiation opportunities.

Environmental Dynamics   Environmental dynamics that can affect market attractiveness include technological, economic/consumer/social and regulatory changes. When a retail market is going through significant changes in technology, existing competitors are vulnerable to new entrants that are skilled at using the new technology. Many traditional store-based retailers were slow to develop their omnichannel strategies fully.

But paying attention to these dynamics can be a strong strategy. Hot Topic initially differentiated itself from other mall-based retailers targeting the Generation Y segment by offering an edgier alternative, with goth-themed merchandise and sales associates sporting tattoos, multiple piercings, spiked hair, and all-black clothing. Over time, though, as the tastes of fickle teens changed and mall traffic declined, sales stagnated. In analyzing the situation, Hot Topic determined that its advantage among teens came not from its goth image but rather its connection to pop culture and the indie music scene. Thus it expanded its stock of t-shirts featuring small, avant-garde bands. Licenses allow it to produce unusual fashions inspired by the characters featured in *Suicide Squad*. The stores are filled with loud music, dark walls, and bulletin boards crammed with concert flyers and staff music picks, as well as free acoustic shows, called Local Static, featuring bands chosen by salespeople in its local stores.[46]

Hot Topic's advantage among teens comes from its connection to pop culture and the indie music scene, so it features free acoustic shows, called Local Static, featuring bands chosen by salespeople in its local stores.

© ZUMA Press Inc./Alamy Stock Photo

Paying attention to economic, consumer, and social dynamics in the external environment is also important when determining the attractiveness of a retail market. Many local and regional governments try to stop Walmart from entering their markets in an attempt to protect locally owned retailers. It even has been blocked from opening a store in New York City by the mayor and city council, who cite the potentially negative effect Walmart may have on small businesses and employee wages. This argument was weakened when Walmart announced its plans to raise the minimum wage earned by its sales associates. But as of 2016, there still were not any Walmart locations in any of the five boroughs of the city, despite customer demand.[47]

When it comes to the various environmental factors they encounter, retailers need to answer three main questions:

1. What new developments or changes might occur, such as new technologies and regulations or different social factors and economic conditions?

2. What is the likelihood that these environmental changes will occur? What key factors affect whether these changes will occur?

3. How will these changes affect each retail market, the firm, and its competitors?

Kelly Bradford's primary concern when she did an environmental analysis was the potential growth of Internet gift retailers such as Uncommon Goods. Gifts seem ideal for an electronic channel, because customers can order the item over the Internet and have it shipped directly to the gift recipient. Kelly also recognized that the electronic channel could effectively collect information about customers and then target promotions and suggestions to them when future gift-giving occasions arose.

Step 3: Identify Strategic Opportunities

After completing the SWOT analysis, the next step is to identify opportunities for increasing retail sales. Kelly Bradford presently competes in gift retailing using a specialty store format. The strategic alternatives she is considering are defined in terms of the growth opportunities in Exhibit 5–4. Note that some of these growth strategies involve a redefinition of her mission.

Step 4: Evaluate Strategic Opportunities

The fourth step in the strategic planning process is to evaluate opportunities that have been identified in the SWOT analysis. The evaluation determines the retailer's potential to establish a sustainable competitive advantage and reap long-term profits from the opportunities being evaluated. Thus, a retailer must focus on opportunities that utilize its strengths and its competitive advantage.

Both the market attractiveness and the strengths and weaknesses of the retailer need to be considered in evaluating strategic opportunities. The greatest investments should be made in market opportunities for which the retailer has a strong competitive position. Kelly's informal analysis is shown in Exhibit 5–11:

EXHIBIT 5–11
Gifts To Go's Evaluation of Strategic Opportunities

Growth Opportunity	Market Attractiveness	Competitive Position
Increase size of present stores and amount of merchandise in stores	Low	High
Open additional gift stores in Chicago area	Medium	Medium
Open gift stores outside the Chicago area (new geographic segment)	Medium	Low
Sell lower-priced gifts in present stores or open new stores selling low-priced gifts (new benefit segment)	Medium	Low
Sell apparel and other nongift merchandise to same customers in same or new stores	High	Medium
Sell similar gift merchandise to same market segment using the Internet	High	Low
Open apparel stores targeted at teenagers	High	Low
Open a category specialist selling low-priced gifts	High	Low

Step 5: Establish Specific Objectives and Allocate Resources

After evaluating the strategic investment opportunities, the next step in the strategic planning process is to establish a specific objective for each opportunity. The retailer's overall objective is included in the mission statement; the specific objectives are goals against which progress toward the overall objective can be measured. Thus, these specific objectives have three components: (1) the performance sought, including a numerical index against which progress may be measured; (2) a time frame within which the goal is to be achieved; and (3) the level of investment needed to achieve the objective. Typically, the performance levels are financial criteria such as return on investment, sales, or profits. Kelly's objective is to increase profits by 20 percent in each of the next five years. She expects she will need to invest an additional $25,000 in her apparel and other nongift merchandise inventory.

Step 6: Develop a Retail Mix to Implement the Strategy

The sixth step in the planning process is to develop a retail mix for each opportunity in which an investment will be made and control and evaluate performance. Decisions related to the elements in the retail mix are discussed in Sections III and IV.

Step 7: Evaluate Performance and Make Adjustments

The final step in the planning process is to evaluate the results of the strategy and implementation program. If the retailer is meeting or exceeding its objectives, changes aren't needed. But if the retailer fails to meet its objectives, reanalysis is required. Typically, this reanalysis starts with reviewing the implementation programs, but it may indicate that the strategy (or even the mission statement) needs to be reconsidered. This conclusion would result in starting a new planning process, including a new SWOT analysis.

Strategic Planning in the Real World

The planning process in Exhibit 5–7 suggests that strategic decisions are made in a sequential manner. After the business mission is defined, the SWOT analysis is performed, strategic opportunities are identified, alternatives are evaluated, objectives are set, resources are allocated, the implementation plan is developed, and, finally, performance is evaluated and adjustments are made. But actual planning processes have interactions among the steps. For example, the SWOT analysis may uncover a logical alternative for the firm to consider, even though this alternative isn't included in the mission statement. Thus, the mission statement may need to be reformulated. The development of the implementation plan might reveal that the resources allocated to a particular opportunity are insufficient to achieve the objective. In that case, the objective would need to be changed, the resources would need to be increased, or the retailer might consider not investing in the opportunity at all.

SUMMARY

LO 5-1   **Define retail strategy.**

A retail strategy is a statement that identifies (1) the retailer's target market, (2) the format and resources the retailer plans to use to satisfy the target market's needs, and (3) the bases on which the retailer plans to build a sustainable competitive advantage. The target market is the market segment(s) toward which the retailer plans to focus its resources and retail mix. A retail format describes the nature of the retailer's operations—its retail mix. A sustainable competitive advantage is an advantage the retailer has over its competition that is not easily copied by competitors and thus can be maintained over a long period of time.

LO 5-2 Illustrate how retailers build a sustainable competitive advantage.

Three approaches for developing a sustainable competitive advantage are (1) building strong relationships with customers, (2) building strong relationships with suppliers, and (3) achieving efficient internal operations. Each of these approaches involves developing an asset—loyal customers, strong vendor relationships, committed effective human resources, efficient systems, and attractive locations—that is not easily duplicated by competitors. To build an advantage that is sustainable for a long period of time, retailers typically cannot rely on a single approach, such as good locations or excellent customer service. Instead, they use multiple approaches to build as high a wall around their position as possible.

LO 5-3 Classify the different strategic growth opportunities retailers pursue.

Four types of growth opportunities that retailers may pursue are market penetration, market expansion, retail format development, and diversification. Success in pursuing these growth opportunities is defined by synergies between the retailer's present markets and the growth opportunity—whether the opportunity involves markets the retailer is presently pursuing or new markets—and the synergies between the retailer's present retail mix and the retail mix of the growth opportunity—whether the opportunity exploits the retailer's skills and knowledge in operating its present format or requires new capabilities to operate a new format.

LO 5-4 Identify issues that arise as domestic retailers become global retailers.

By expanding internationally, retailers can increase their sales, leverage their knowledge and systems across a greater sales base, and gain more bargaining power with vendors.

But international expansion is risky because retailers must deal with different government regulations, cultural traditions, consumer preferences, supply chains, and languages. The attractiveness of international opportunities is assessed by (1) the potential size of the retail market in the country, (2) the degree to which the country does and can support the entry of foreign retailers engaged in modern retail practices, and (3) the risks or uncertainties in sales and profits. The most attractive international markets include India, China, and Brazil.

LO 5-5 Know the steps retailers go through to develop a strategic plan.

Strategic planning is an ongoing process. Every day, retailers audit their situations, examine consumer trends, study new technologies, and monitor competitive activities. But the retail strategy statement does not change every year or every six months; the strategy statement is reviewed and altered only when major changes in the retailer's environment or capabilities occur.

When a retailer undertakes a major reexamination of its strategy, the process for developing a new strategy statement may take a year or two. Potential strategic directions are generated by people at all levels of the organization and then evaluated by senior executives and operating personnel to ensure that the eventual strategic direction is profitable in the long run and can be implemented.

The strategic planning process consists of a sequence of steps: (1) define the business mission, (2) conduct a SWOT analysis, (3) identify strategic opportunities, (4) evaluate strategic opportunities, (5) establish specific objectives and allocate resources, (6) develop a retail mix to implement the strategy, and (7) evaluate performance and make adjustments.

KEY TERMS

bargaining power of vendors, *146*

barriers to entry, *146*

competitive rivalry, *147*

cross-selling, *132*

customer loyalty, *125*

customer relationship management (CRM) program, *128*

direct investment, *142*

diversification growth opportunity, *134*

franchising, *142*

frequent-shopper program, *128*

joint venture, *142*

loyalty program, *128*

market expansion growth opportunity, *132*

market penetration growth opportunity, *132*

mission statement, *143*

opportunities and threats analysis, *145*

own brand, *127*

perceptual map, *125*

positioning, *125*

private-label brand, *127*

related diversification growth opportunity, *135*

retail community, *128*

retail format, *121*

retail format development growth opportunity, *134*

retail market segment, *123*

retail strategy, *121*

scale economies, *146*

store brand, *127*

strategic alliance, *142*

strategic retail planning process, *142*

strengths and weaknesses analysis, *144*

sustainable competitive advantage, *121*

SWOT analysis, *144*

target market, *121*

unorganized retailing, *138*

unrelated diversification growth opportunity, *135*

vertical integration, *135*

GET OUT AND DO IT!

1. **CONTINUING CASE ASSIGNMENT** Prepare an analysis of the company you selected for the continuing assignment. Identify its direct competitors, its target market and positioning, its strategy with respect to its competitors, its retail format (the elements in its retail mix—merchandise variety and assortment, pricing, locations), and its bases for developing a competitive advantage relative to its competitors. Outline the retailer's strengths, weaknesses, opportunities, and threats relative to its competitors. Pick a specific country in which the firm does not operate and make a recommendation about whether the retailer should enter the country and, if so, how it should do so.

2. **INTERNET EXERCISE** Visit the websites for IKEA (**www.ikea.com**) and Starbucks (**www.starbucks.com**).

Are the look and feel of these Internet sites consistent with the in-store experience of these retailers?

3. **INTERNET EXERCISE** Go to the websites for Walmart (**www.walmartstores.com**), Carrefour (**www.carrefour.fr**), Royal Ahold (**www.ahold.com**), and Metro AG (**www.metro.de**). Which chain has the most pervasive global strategy? Justify your answer.

4. **GO SHOPPING** Visit two stores that sell similar merchandise categories and cater to the same target segment(s). How are their retail formats (the elements in their retail mixes) similar? Dissimilar? On what bases do they have a sustainable competitive advantage? Explain which you believe has a stronger position.

DISCUSSION QUESTIONS AND PROBLEMS

1. For each of the three retailers discussed at the beginning of the chapter (Sephora, Lululemon, and Save-A-Lot), describe its strategy and the basis of its competitive advantage.

2. Choose a retailer and describe how it has developed a competitive strategic advantage.

3. Give an example of a market penetration, a retail format development, a market expansion, and a diversification growth strategy that a store called Performance Bicycle might use.

4. Choose your favorite retailer. Draw and explain a positioning map, like that shown in Exhibit 5–3, that includes your retailer, retailers that sell the same types of merchandise, and the target customer segments (ideal points).

5. Do a SWOT analysis for McDonald's. What is its mission? What are its strengths and weaknesses? What opportunities and environmental threats might it face over the next 10 years? How could it prepare for these threats?

6. What are Neiman Marcus's and PetSmart's bases for sustainable competitive advantage? Are they really sustainable, or are they easily copied?

7. Assume you are interested in opening a restaurant in your town. Go through the steps in the strategic planning process shown in Exhibit 5–7. Focus on conducting a

SWOT analysis of the local restaurant market, identifying and evaluating alternatives, and selecting a target market and a retail mix for the restaurant.

8. The Gap owns several chains, including Old Navy, Banana Republic, INTERMIX, and Athleta. What type of growth opportunity was the Gap pursuing when it opened each of these retail concepts? Which is most synergistic with the original Gap chain?

9. Identify a store or service provider that you believe has an effective loyalty program. Explain why it is effective.

10. Choose a retailer that you believe could be, but is not yet, successful in other countries. Explain why you think it could be successful.

11. Amazon.com started as an Internet retailer selling books. Then it pursued a variety of growth opportunities, including expanding to groceries, DVDs, apparel, software, and travel services; introducing e-readers (Kindle); operating the Internet channel for other retailers; and hosting virtual stores for small, independent retailers. Evaluate these growth opportunities in terms of the probability that they will be profitable businesses for Amazon.com. What competitive advantages does Amazon.com bring to each of these businesses?

CHAPTER ENDNOTES

1. Ellen Byron, "The Slower You Shop, the More You Spend," *The Wall Street Journal,* October 20, 2015; Tom Ryan, "Should Retailers Slow Down Shopping?," *RetailWire,* October 30, 2015.

2. See Robert W. Palmatier and Shrihari Sridhar, *Marketing Strategy: Based on First Principles and Data Analytics* (New York: Palgrave Macmillan, 2017); Robert M. Grant, *Contemporary Strategy Analysis,* 9th ed., (Hoboken, NJ: Wiley, 2016); Arthur Thompson, Margret Peteraf, John Gamble, and A. J. Strickland III, *Crafting and Executing Strategy: The Quest for Competitive Advantage: Concepts and Cases,* 20th ed. (New York: McGraw-Hill, 2015); David Aaker, *Strategic Market Management,* 10th ed. (New York: Wiley, 2013).

3. Michael E. Porter and Mark R. Kramer, "Strategy and Society: The Link between Competitive Advantage and Corporate Responsibility," *Harvard Business Review,* December 2006; Michael Porter, *On Competition* (Boston: Harvard Business School Press, 1998); Michael Porter, "What Is Strategy?," *Harvard Business Review,* November–December 1996, pp. 61–78.

4. Sarah Halzack, "The Sephora Effect: How the Cosmetics Retailer Transformed the Beauty Industry," *Washington Post,* March 9, 2015.

5. www.lululemon.com; Dana Mattioli, "Lululemon's Secret Sauce," *The Wall Street Journal,* March 22, 2012; Adrianne Pasquarelli, "Lululemon Tries New Store Concept in Efforts to Woo Shoppers," *Advertising Age,* November 17, 2015; Mallory Schlossberg, "Lululemon Has Unveiled Its New Store of the Future," *Business Insider,* November 18, 2015; Matthew Stern, "Will Cross-Gender Stores Mean More for Lululemon or Nike?," *RetailWire,* December 18, 2014; John Kell, "Lululemon for Men—Not Just Yogis," *Forbes,* November 2014.

6. www.savealot.com, Jon Springer, "Save-A-Lot Files for Potential Spin-Off," *Supermarket News,* January 7, 2016.

7. Jorge A. Vasconcellos e Sá, Fátima Olão, and Magda Pereira, "From Levitt to the Global Age: One More Time, How Do We Define Our Business?," *Management Decision* 49, no. 1 (2011), pp. 99–115; Anthony Boardman and Aidan Vining, "Defining Your Business Using Product-Customer Matrices," *Long Range Planning* 29 (February 1996), pp. 38–48.

8. A. Thompson, M. Peteraf, J. Gamble, A. J. Strickland III, and A. K. Jain, *Crafting & Executing Strategy: The Quest for Competitive Advantage: Concepts and Cases,* 19th ed. (Burr Ridge, IL: McGraw-Hill/Irwin, 2013); S. D. Hunt, "The Theoretical Foundations of Strategic Marketing and Marketing Strategy: Foundational Premises, RA Theory, Three Fundamental Strategies, and Societal Welfare," *AMS Review* 5, nos. 3–4 (2013), pp. 61–77; Jay Barney, David J. Ketchen Jr., and Mike Wright, "The Future of Resource-Based Theory Revitalization or Decline?," *Journal of Management* 37 (September 2011), pp. 1299–1315.

9. Tom Ryan, "Do Vertical Retailers Have a Customer Engagement Edge?," *RetailWire,* March 16, 2016.

10. S. Seenivasan, K. Sudhir, and D. Talukdar, "Do Store Brands Aid Store Loyalty?," *Management Science 62,* no. 3 (2015), pp. 802–816; N. Koschate-Fischer, J. Cramer, and W. D. Hoyer, "Moderating Effects of the Relationship between Private Label Share and Store Loyalty," *Journal of Marketing* 78, no. 2 (2014), pp. 69–82; Michael S. Pepe, Russell Abratt, and Paul Dion, "The Impact of Private Label Brands on Customer Loyalty and Product Category Profitability," *Journal of Product & Brand Management* 20, no. 1 (2011), pp. 27–36.

11. Simon Clatworthy, "Bridging the Gap between Brand Strategy and Customer Experience," *Managing Service Quality* 22, no. 2 (2012), pp. 108–127; Bo Edvardsson, Bård Tronvoll, and Thorsten Gruber, "Expanding Understanding of Service Exchange and Value Co-Creation: A Social Construction Approach," *Journal of the Academy of Marketing Science* 39 (2011), pp. 327–339.

12. http://patapsco.nist.gov/Award_Recipients/index.cfm.

13. Carmine Gallo, "How the Ritz-Carlton Inspired the Apple Store," *Forbes,* April 10, 2012; Carmine Gallo, "Employee Motivation the Ritz-Carlton Way," *BusinessWeek,* February 29, 2008.

14. J. H. Schumann, N. V. Wünderlich, and H. Evanschitzky, "Spillover Effects of Service Failures in Coalition Loyalty Programs: The Buffering Effect of Special Treatment Benefits," *Journal of Retailing* 90, no. 1 (2014), pp. 111–118; J. Pelser, K. de Ruyter, M. Wetzels, D. Grewal, D. Cox, and J. van Beuningen, "B2B

Channel Partner Programs: Disentangling Indebtedness from Gratitude," *Journal of Retailing* 91, no. 4 (2015), pp. 660–678; P. K. Kopalle, Y. Sun, S. A. Neslin, B. Sun, and V. Swaminathan, "The Joint Sales Impact of Frequency Reward and Customer Tier Components of Loyalty Programs," *Marketing Science* 31, no. 2 (2012), pp. 216–235.

15. E. Aguirre, A. L. Roggeveen, D. Grewal, and M. Wetzels, "The Personalization-Privacy Paradox: Implications for New Media," *Journal of Consumer Marketing* 33, no. 2 (2016), pp. 98–110; D. Grewal, Y. Bart, M. Spann, and P. P. Zubcsek, "Mobile Advertising: A Framework and Research Agenda,"*Journal of Interactive Marketing* 34 (2016), pp. 3–14; Constance Elise Porter, Naveen Donthu, William H. Macelroy, and Donna Wydra, "How to Foster and Sustain Engagement in Virtual Communities," *California Management Review* 53, no. 4 (2011), pp. 80–110.

16. http://mystarbucksidea.force.com/; Hesham, "My Starbucks Idea [Case Study]."

17. http://www.industryweek.com/supplier-relationships/how-sharing-data-drives-supply-chain-innovation; http://www.wsj.com/articles/wal-mart-and-p-g-a-10-billion-marriage-under-strain-1465948431.

18. Zeynep Ton, "Why 'Good Jobs' Are Good for Retailers," *Harvard Business Review,* January–February 2012; T. Russell Crook, Samuel Y. Todd, James G. Woehr, and David J. Ketchen Jr., "Does Human Capital Matter? A Meta-Analysis of the Relationship between Human Capital and Firm Performance," *Journal of Applied Psychology* 96, no. 3 (2011), pp. 443–456.

19. Petra Schubert, Susan P. Williams, and Ralf Woelfle, "Sustainable Competitive Advantage in E-Commerce and the Role of the Enterprise System," *International Journal of Enterprise Information Systems* 7 (April–June 2011), pp. 1–17; Richard Cuthbertson, Gerd Islei, Peter Franke, and Balkan Cetinkaya, "What Will the Best Retail Supply Chains Look Like in the Future?," *European Retail Digest,* Summer 2006, pp. 7–15; "Competitive Advantage through Supply-Chain Innovation," *Logistics & Transport Focus,* December 2004, pp. 56–59.

20. Igor Ansoff, "Strategies for Diversification," *Harvard Business Review* 35 (September–October 1957), pp. 113–124.

21. http://www.tesco-careers.com/stores/.

22. Andrew Sorkin and Michael De La Merced, "Home Depot Sells a Unit That Never Fit," *The New York Times,* June 20, 2007, p. C1; Andrew Sorkin and Michael De La Merced, "Home Depot Supply Unit May Be Sold," *The New York Times,* February 13, 2007, p. C1.

23. "Global Powers of Retailing 2016," *Deloitte,* January 2016, p. 12.

24. Nyshka Chandran, "Next Largest Retail Market: Take a Wild Guess," *CNBC,* February 13, 2015.

25. Deepika Jhamb and Ravi Kiran, "Emerging Trends of Organized Retailing in India: A Shared Vision of Consumers and Retailers Perspective," *Middle-East Journal of Scientific Research* 11, no. 4 (2012), pp. 481–490.

26. Malavika Sharma, "With Wal-Mart Locked Out, India's Billionaires Rush In," *Bloomberg Businessweek,* July 5, 2012; Newley Purnell, "Apple Pushes to Bolster Market Share in India," *The Wall Street Journal,* January 20, 2016; Preetika Rana, "IKEA's India Bet Runs into Thicket of Rules," *The Wall Street Journal,* February 23, 2016.

27. https://www.atkearney.com/consumer-products-retail/global-retail-development-index; Marianne Wilson, "China Is Top Emerging Retail Market," *The Chain Store Age,* June 1, 2015.

28. Alex Lawson, "Analysis: Retailing in China," *Retail Week,* April 20, 2012; Robert A. Rogowsky, "China Retail Market Booming and Evolving," *China Daily,* August 3, 2012, pp. 2–12.

29. Li Jiaboa and Li Woke, "Foreign Companies Adapt to China's Changing Retail Landscape," *China Daily,* May 31, 2013.

30. Wilson, "China Is Top Emerging Retail Market."

31. James Marson, "At E-Commerce Firms, Russia Rises," *The Wall Street Journal,* November 12, 2013.

32. eMarketer, "Number of Internet Users in Russia from 2013 to 2019 (in Millions)," *Statista,* February 4, 2016, http://www.statista.com/statistics/251818/number-of-internet-users-in-russia/.

33. "Russia," Internet Live Stats, http://www.internetlivestats.com/internet-users/russia/.

34. Paul Gregory, "A Russian Crisis with No End in Sight, Thanks to Low Oil Prices and Sanctions," *Forbes,* May 14, 2015, http://www.forbes.com/sites/paulroderickgregory/2015/05/14/a-russian-crisis-with-no-end-in-sight-thanks-to-low-oil-prices-and-sanctions/3/#5502e1f66d5e.

35. "For First Time Ever, McDonald's Closes a Restaurant in Russia," *The Moscow Times,* April 14, 2015, http://www.themoscowtimes.com/business/article/for-first-time-ever-mcdonalds-closes-a-restaurant-in-russia/519066.html.

36. Olga Razumovskaya, "McDonald's Extends Reach in Russia," *The Wall Street Journal,* August 21, 2015, http://www.wsj.com/articles/mcdonalds-extends-reach-in-russia-1440174904.

37. Quartz, "Cities with the Largest Number of Starbucks Stores Worldwide as of May 2014," *Statista,* May 2014, http://www.statista.com/statistics/306896/cities-with-the-largest-number-of-starbucks-stores-worldwide.

38. "Working in Spain," https://www.internations.org/spain-expats/guide/working-in-spain-15498; "What Their Sunday Trading Laws Say about the French," *The Telegraph,* September 24, 2015.

39. www.carrefour.com.

40. Michael R. Czinkota and Ilkka A. Ronkainen, *International Marketing,* 9th ed. (Mason, OH: Thomson South-Western, 2009).

41. www.marksandspencer.com.

42. Donald Lehman and Russell Winer, *Analysis for Marketing Planning,* 7th ed. (Burr Ridge, IL: McGraw-Hill/Irwin, 2007).

43. Linda Stallworth Williams, "The Mission Statement," *Journal of Business Communication* 45, no. 2 (2008), pp. 94–119.

44. Maxine Clark, founder and chief executive bear at Build-A-Bear Workshop.

45. Michael Porter, "Strategy and the Internet," *Harvard Business Review,* March 2001, pp. 63–78; Michael Porter, *Competitive Strategy* (New York: Free Press, 1980).

46. Brandon Davis, "Full Suicide Squad Fashion Collection Debuts at Hot Topic," *ComicBook.com,* June 30, 2016, http://comicbook.com/dc/2016/06/30/full-suicide-squad-fashion-collection-debuts-at-hot-topic/; Schuyler Velasco, "How 'The Hunger Games' Scored a Marketing Win," *Christian Science Monitor,* March 2012, p. 10; Nivedita Bhattacharjee, "Hot Topic Gets Hunger Games Lift but May Not Last," Reuters, March 2012, http://community.hottopic.com/content/about-hot-topics.

47. Al McClain, "Consumers to NYC: We (Still) Want Walmart!," *RetailWire,* August 13, 2015.

CHAPTER 6 | Financial Strategy

© Ron Antonelli/Bloomberg/Getty Images

When we try to identify the "best" member of a category, like the best retailer or best brand, one of the biggest challenges is picking which criteria to use to define what "best" means. According to one annual report of the top 100 retailers, a key factor is whether the companies function as omnichannel actors. Some started online and spread to gain a physical presence; others took the opposite route. Some leveraged an existing catalog channel to expand their mobile capacity. Regardless of the path of their evolution, these successful firms are available in whatever channel customers prefer to use.

It may sound like an easy prescription for success—be omnichannel!—but it's a lot harder than that. As one analyst explains, "Today's demanding omni-shoppers know what they want: They want retailers to offer whatever, wherever, whenever they want. And when it comes to value, they want their cake and eat it too—they don't expect to pay more for convenience."[1]

Facing such challenging and conflicting demands, top retailers develop effective financial strategies to ensure that they earn a profit, even as they meet customers' expanding demands. For example, they work to manage their inventory to avoid ever being out of stock on a highly demanded item or overstocking other items. Such errors invoke some pretty remarkable costs: According to one recent analysis, revenue losses due to overstocks, out-of-stock events, and returns add up to a staggering $1.75 trillion every year. When it comes to overstocks, omnichannel retailers, with their extensive inventories of items available on websites, often have too much inventory on hand. Because the inventories are so vast, some individual items get lost in the shuffle, such that consumers might not even recognize that they are available. Accounting for about $123 billion in lost revenue, these overstocks generally imply inefficient uses of analytics and forecasting software. As a partial solution, some retailers are making better use of alternative channels, such as when Nordstrom moves unsold merchandise quickly into its Nordstrom Rack stores.[2]

In the Omnichannel Retail Index by the National Retail Federation and the FitforCommerce digital consultancy, BJ's Warehouse Club, GameStop, Lowe's, PetSmart, and Staples take top positions on measures related to which stores do the best job of providing information about in-store availability on their websites and mobile apps.[3] This strategy helps these retailers achieve their inventory goals while also avoiding customer annoyance that can arise due to stockouts or misplaced merchandise. For Walmart alone, insufficient inventory led to estimated losses of $3 billion in one year, even as the total amount of inventory it offered for sale increased.

Finally, it might be impossible to eliminate all returns, but better operations could help retailers avoid those that stem from their own mistakes. A retail group recently held a contest in which it asked consumers to send in pictures of online orders they received that they had to return. Many of these photographs reflected needless errors, such as a purse sent without its strap or a red hat sent when the customer's order clearly indicated a preference for the blue version. Such unnecessary returns (i.e., those that are not due to the customer's preferences or choices) represent $246 billion in losses to retailers. For customers who need to return items they have purchased, though, the top-ranked retailers are Aldo, Cabela's, and Target.[4]

Thus, whether the stated goal is to be omnichannel or to serve customers most effectively, success and being the "best" still might come down to the same thing: Design a strategy that appeals to carefully defined target markets, wherever the retailer encounters them, and pursue it efficiently and with the fewest mistakes, to ensure that its profits are not only sufficient but among the best in the industry.

Financial objectives and goals are an integral part of a retailer's market strategy. In Chapter 5, we examined how retailers develop their strategy and build a sustainable competitive advantage to generate a continuing stream of profits. In this chapter, we look at how financial analysis is used to assess the retailer's market strategy—to monitor the retailer's performance, assess the reasons its performance is above or below expectations, and provide insights into appropriate actions that can be taken if performance falls short of expectations.

For example, Kelly Bradford, the owner of Gifts To Go, whom we described in Chapter 5, needs to know how well she is doing because she wants to stay in business, be successful, increase the profitability of her company, and realize her goal of generating an annual income of $100,000. To assess her performance, she can add up the receipts at the end of each day. But this simple measure, sales, doesn't provide a complete assessment of how she is doing financially, and it may even be misleading. For instance, she might find that sales meet expectations and her accountant confirms that her business is profitable, but she doesn't have the cash to buy new merchandise or pay her employees. When this happens, Kelly needs to analyze her business to determine the cause of the problem and what can be done to overcome it.

In this chapter, we first review the types of objectives that retailers have. Then we introduce the strategic profit model and use it to discuss the two paths for achieving the desired financial performance. To illustrate the use of this model, we examine and compare the factors affecting the financial performance of Walmart and Nordstrom, two very successful retailers with different retail strategies. Then we demonstrate how the model can be used to evaluate one of the growth opportunities Kelly Bradford is considering. In the last part of this chapter, we examine productivity measures that assess the performance of merchandise management and store operations decisions.

OBJECTIVES AND GOALS

Review the strategic objectives of a retail firm.

As we discussed in Chapter 5, the first step in the strategic planning process involves articulating the retailer's objectives and the scope of activities it plans to undertake. These objectives guide the development of the retailer's strategy and the specific performance goals the retailer plans to achieve. When the goals are not being achieved, the retailer knows that it must take corrective actions. Three types of objectives that a retailer might have are (1) financial, (2) societal, and (3) personal.

Financial Objectives

When assessing the financial performance of a firm, most people focus on profits: What were the retailer's profits or profit as a percentage of sales last year, and what will they be this year and into the future? But the appropriate financial performance measure is not profits but return on assets. **Return on assets (ROA)** is the profit generated by the assets possessed by the firm. A retailer might set a financial objective of making a profit of at least $1 million a year, but the retailer really must consider the assets it needs to employ to make the desired $1 million. The retailer would be delighted if it made $1 million and needed only $5 million in assets (a 20 percent ROA) but would be disappointed if it had to use $40 million in assets to make a $1 million profit (a 2.5 percent ROA).

6.1 RETAILING VIEW   One for One to Achieve TOMS Shoes's Societal Objectives

In 2006, after competing on the second season of *The Amazing Race,* Blake Mycoskie visited Argentina, where he was struck by the poverty—including the number of children walking around without shoes. Because the traditional Argentine alpargata shoe offers a simple, revolutionary solution for providing footwear, he set out to provide footwear for poor families by reinventing the alpargata for the U.S. market. To make the connection, Mycoskie committed to providing one new pair of shoes to a child living in poverty for every pair of shoes that consumers purchased from the One for One website. As he recounted, "I was so overwhelmed by the spirit of the South American people, especially those who had so little. And I was instantly struck with the desire—the responsibility—to do more."

The success of the initial idea pushed Mycoskie to move beyond just the Argentinean-styled classic alpargata shoes. Thus, TOMS today sells Cordones for wear with or without laces; Botas for both women and men; Stitchouts which are only for men; Wedges and Wrap Boots for women; and of course, Youth and Tiny TOMS for children and toddlers. It also has added lines of vegan and recycled shoes. Then it expanded into sunglasses, where its One for One philosophy dictates that for every pair sold, TOMS provides eye care, such as medicines, glasses, or surgery, to someone else in the world at risk of losing his or her sight. TOMS has also included coffee, bags, and backpacks among its offerings. When a customer makes a purchase from the TOMS line of coffee, a week's worth of safe water goes to someone in need. For each bag purchased, TOMS helps provide the materials and training that health care providers require to help mothers give birth safely. Backpack purchases help prevent bullying because TOMS provides teachers, school counselors, and other school staff with bullying prevention and intervention training in return for the purchases.

This socially responsible business model appeals particularly to Millennial consumers in developed economies who want to be able to shop, socialize, and save the world, simultaneously. Wearing TOMS shoes is a fashion statement that also provides a public proclamation of their own social responsibility. Through their social media networks, these TOMS aficionados, many of whom belong to the thousands of TOMS university clubs, affirm their love for TOMS and encourage others to join the movement. With annual sales estimated at greater than $250 million, TOMS has provided more than

Achieving societal objectives is important to Blake Mycoskie, founder, CEO, and chief giving officer of TOMS Shoes.

60 million pairs of new shoes to children in more than 70 countries—including the United States.

Sources: www.toms.com; Ed Hammond and Elizabeth Paton, "Shoemaker Toms Put Up for Sale," *Financial Times,* June 9, 2014; Ricardo Lopez, "It's Doing Well by Doing Good," *Los Angeles Times,* January 25, 2012, p. B.1; Gregory Ferenstein, "TOMS Shoes Generation Y Strategy," *Fast Company,* June 9, 2010.

Societal Objectives

Societal objectives are related to broader issues that make the world a better place to live. For example, retailers might be concerned about providing employment opportunities for people in a particular area or for minorities or for people with disabilities. Other societal objectives might include offering people unique merchandise, such as environmentally friendly products; providing an innovative service to improve personal health, such as weight reduction programs; or sponsoring community events. Retailing View 6.1 describes a retail entrepreneur offering shoes and other products whose sale leads to notable benefits for disadvantaged people throughout the world.

Compared with financial objectives, societal performance objectives are more difficult to measure. But explicit societal goals can be set, such as specific reductions in energy usage and excess packaging, increased use of renewable resources, and support for nonprofit organizations such as the United Way and Habitat for Humanity.

Personal Objectives

Many retailers, particularly owners of small, independent businesses, have important personal objectives, including self-gratification, status, and respect. For example, the owner-operator of a bookstore may find it rewarding to interact with others who like reading and authors who visit the store for book-signing promotions. By operating a popular store, a retailer might become recognized as a well-respected business leader in the community.

While societal and personal objectives are important to some retailers, all retailers need to be concerned about financial objectives or they will fail. Therefore, the remaining sections of this chapter focus on financial objectives and the factors affecting a retailer's ability to achieve financial goals.

STRATEGIC PROFIT MODEL

The **strategic profit model (SPM)**, illustrated in Exhibit 6–1, is a method for summarizing the factors that affect a firm's financial performance, as measured by ROA. Return on assets is an important performance measure for a firm and its stockholders because it measures the profits that a firm makes relative to the assets it possesses. Two retailers that each generate profits of $1 million on $20 million in net sales, at first glance, might look like they have comparable performance. But the performance of the retailers looks quite

LO 6-2

Contrast the two paths to financial performance using the strategic profit model.

EXHIBIT 6–1
Strategic Profit Model

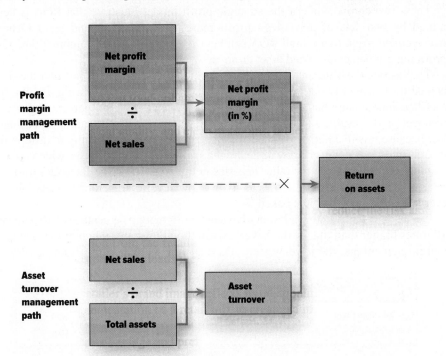

La Chatelaine Bakery (left) is a low-profit-margin/high-turnover operation, whereas Lehring Jewelry (right) is a high-profit-margin/low-turnover operation. But both stores have the same return on assets (ROA).

different if one has $10 million in assets and the other has $25 million. The performance of the first would be higher because it needs fewer assets to earn its profit than does the other. Thus, a retailer cannot concern itself only with making a profit. It must make a profit efficiently by balancing both profit and the assets needed to make the profit.

The **net profit margin (in %)** refers to how much profit (after taxes, interest income, and extraordinary gains and losses) a firm makes divided by its net sales. Thus, it reflects the profits generated from each dollar of sales. If a retailer's net profit margin percentage is 5 percent, it generates income of $0.05 for every dollar of merchandise or services it sells.

Asset turnover is the retailer's net sales divided by its assets. This financial measure assesses the productivity of a firm's investment in its assets. It indicates how many sales dollars are generated for each dollar of assets. If a retailer's asset turnover is 3.0, it generates $3 in sales for each dollar invested in the firm's assets.

The retailer's ROA is determined by multiplying the two components together:

$$\text{Net profit margin (in \%)} \times \text{Asset turnover} = \text{Return on assets (ROA)(in \%)}$$

$$\frac{\text{Net profit margin}}{\text{Net sales}} \times \frac{\text{Net sales}}{\text{Total assets}} = \frac{\text{Net profit margin}}{\text{Total assets}}$$

These two components of the strategic profit model illustrate that ROA is determined by two sets of activities—profit margin management and asset turnover management—and that a high ROA can be achieved by various combinations of net profit margin percentages and asset turnover levels.

To illustrate the different approaches for achieving a high ROA, consider the financial performance of two very different hypothetical retailers, as shown in Exhibit 6–2. La Chatelaine Bakery has a net profit margin percentage of only 1 percent and an asset turnover of 10, resulting in an ROA of 10 percent. Its net profit margin percentage is low because it is in a highly competitive market with little opportunity to differentiate its offering. Consumers can buy basically the same baked goods from a wide variety of retailers, as well as from the other bakeries in the area. However, its asset turnover is relatively high because the firm has a very low level of inventory assets—it sells everything the same day it is baked.

On the other hand, Lehring Jewelry has a net profit margin percentage of 10 percent—10 times higher than that of the bakery. Even though it has a much higher net profit margin percentage, the jewelry store has the same ROA because it has a very low

EXHIBIT 6–2

Different Approaches for Achieving an Acceptable ROA

	Net Profit Margin	×	Asset Turnover	=	Return on Assets
La Chatelaine Bakery	1%		10 times		10%
Lehring Jewelry	10%		1 time		10%

asset turnover of 1. Lehring's asset turnover is low compared with the bakery's because Lehring has a high level of inventory and stocks a lot of items that take many months to sell.

In the following sections, we take a closer look at these two components of ROA. We examine the relationship between these ratios and a firm's retail strategy and describe how these financial measures can be used to assess performance with traditional accounting information. To illustrate the financial implications of different retail strategies, we compare the financial performance of Walmart and Nordstrom. The retail strategies of these two retailers are described in Retailing View 6.2.

RETAILING VIEW   Nordstrom and Walmart: Successful Retailers Using   **6.2**
Different Retail Strategies

Nordstrom

Nordstrom, Inc. has transformed from a small shoe seller in Seattle to the leading fashion specialty retailer that it is today. Its central goal—to help "customers possess style, not just buy fashion"—has made the chain famous for its excellent customer service. Nordstrom encourages its employees to connect with customers and empowers them to help customers as best as they can. Furthermore, it goes above and beyond by sending thank-you cards, offering home deliveries and personal appointments, and issuing personal calls to educate shoppers about upcoming sales. The emphasis on customer service has influenced every aspect of the company, even down to its return policy, which states, "We do not have a formal return policy at our Nordstrom full-line stores or online at Nordstrom.com. Our goal is to take care of our customers, which includes making returns and exchanges easy, whether in stores or online, where we offer free shipping and free returns." This customer-centric model combined with its impressive assortment has helped make Nordstrom America's favorite retailer for three consecutive years.

Walmart

Walmart's founder Sam Walton opened the first store in Arkansas in 1962. Now Walmart is one of the biggest and best-known retail chains in the world, with over 11,500 stores in almost 30 countries; its e-commerce website is available in 11 countries. In 2016 Walmart's revenue reached almost $500 billion, based on its four-pronged strategy focused on price, access, experience, and assortment. As the retail giant notes, "We understand not only what our customers want and need, but also where they want it and how they want to experience it." A cornerstone of this strategy is Walmart's everyday low pricing (EDLP) model, which stresses continuity of retail prices at a level somewhere between the regular nonsale price and the deep-discount sale price of its competitors. Selling products for such low prices, such that it earns relatively low profit margins, Walmart maintains a vast assortment that ensures it is a one-stop shopping destination for consumers. Furthermore, Walmart is fanatical about keeping its costs down, which it does by having mastered the art of operational excellence through its private fleets of trucks and modern distribution and fulfillment centers.

Walmart also operates Sam's Club, which competes with companies like Costco, for customers who prefer to buy in bulk. When Sam Walton originally opened Sam's Club, its target market was small business owners and the goal was to help them save on buying merchandise. However, wholesale

Nordstrom (top) and Walmart (bottom) have very different retail strategies and financial performance measures.

clubs like Sam's Club also have become increasing popular for consumers with families, even as this retail arm continues to appeal to entrepreneurs and serve about half a million business owners each day.

Sources: "Nordstrom, 'About Us,'" http://shop.nordstrom.com/c/about-us?origin=breadcrumb; Nordstrom, Inc., "Annual Report," 2014; Christian Conte, "Nordstrom Built on Customer Service," *Jacksonville Business Journal*, September 7, 2012, http://www.bizjournals.com/jacksonville/print-edition/2012/09/07/nordstrom-built-on-customer-service.html?page=all; Andrés Cardenal, "How America's Favorite Retailer Is Crushing the Competition," *The Motley Fool*, April 14, 2015, http://www.fool.com/investing/general/2015/04/14/how-americas-favorite-retailer-is-crushing-the-com.aspx; *Dallas Business Journal*, October 17, 2014; http://corporate.walmart.com.

EXHIBIT 6–3
Income Statements for
Nordstrom and Walmart

	Nordstrom Income Statement (FY 1/30/2016)	Walmart Income Statement (FY 1/31/2016)
	Values in Millions	**Values in Millions**
Net sales	$14,437	$482,130
Less cost of goods sold (COGS)	9,168	360,984
Gross margin	5,269	121,146
Less operating expenses (SG&A)	4,168	97,041
Operating profit margin	1,101	24,105
Less other income (expense), interest, taxes	501	9,411
Net profit margin	600	14,694
Ratios		
Gross margin as a percentage of sales	36.50%	25.13%
Operating expenses as a percentage of sales	28.87%	20.13%
Operating profit margin as a percentage of sales	7.63%	5.00%
Net profit margin as a percentage of sales	4.16%	3.05%

Sources: Walmart 10K, filed March 30, 2016; Nordstrom, Inc. 10K, filed March 14, 2016.

Profit Margin Management Path

The information used to examine the profit margin management path comes from the retailer's **income statement**, also called the **statement of operations** or **profit and loss (P&L) statement**. The income statement summarizes a firm's financial performance over a period of time, typically a quarter (three months) or year. Exhibit 6–3 shows income statements adapted from the annual reports of Walmart and Nordstrom Inc. The components in the profit margin management path portion of the strategic profit model are summarized for both retailers in Exhibit 6–4.

Components in the Profit Margin Management Path   The components in the profit margin management path are net sales, cost of goods sold (COGS), gross margin, operating expenses, interest and taxes, and net profit margin. These factors have some unique characteristics when a retailer uses multiple channels to sell its goods, as Retailing View 6.3 explains. **Net sales** are the total revenues received by a retailer that are related to selling merchandise during a given time period minus returns, discounts, and credits for damaged merchandise.

EXHIBIT 6–4
Profit Margin
Management Path of
Strategic Profit Model

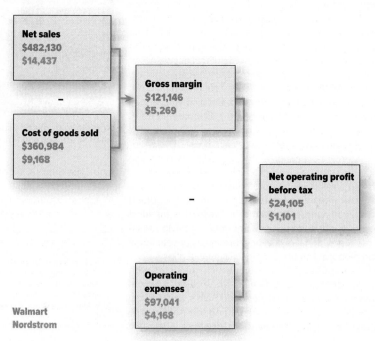

RETAILING VIEW   Calculating the Costs and Profits of Online Channels   6.3

Modern retailers are turning to an omnichannel strategy to remain competitive. And if all they needed to worry about were sales levels, the channels used would not matter. But the margins are different among the channels. For omnichannel retailers, the different profit implications between online and in-store sales can be substantial: According to a recent survey, only 16 percent of omnichannel retailers earn a profit on their operations, and 67 percent of them anticipate further rising costs.

The reason has to do with the very nature of the sales channels. In brick-and-mortar stores, the costs to sell to 20 customers are approximately the same as those to sell to 50 customers. That is, the store is already open, staffed, and stocked, no matter how many people enter through its doors. Thus, each additional sale increases the profit that the retailer earns, after paying all its costs. In contrast, each product sold online induces new, unique costs to pick, pack, and ship the item. If 50 people buy pairs of jeans, the costs to the retailer shipping them are much higher than if 20 people buy those jeans.

Omnichannel operations increase the costs of not just shipping but also handling, returns, and decision making. For example, for each order received, the retailer needs to determine which channel to use to source it. Should it send an employee in the local store into the aisles to pick the item, pack it up, and ship it? Should it procure it from a centralized distribution center? Should it require the manufacturer to ship it directly to the customer? In addition, retailers do not know where they will receive each return, and because Internet shoppers cannot touch or feel products before they buy, returns are far more frequent for online purchases. Therefore, retailers must deal with the costs of returns, including additional shipping, labor to restock, and potential losses if the returned items cannot be resold.

Thus at Kohl's, the profits earned from online sales are approximately half those earned for the same products sold in stores. Both Target and Best Buy announced that their predicted profits would continue to diminish as their online

The retailer's cost to sell a pair of jeans online is higher than in a store because of shipping, handling, and returns.

channels grew. Yet as Kohl's chief executive Kevin Mansell explained, "I don't care if customers buy online or in store. We're focused on sales." This focus may be necessary because customers demand the convenience of online ordering. Even if companies earn less, they likely need a web presence. Not everyone agrees, though: The European discount retailer Primark has pulled itself off the Internet, noting that despite a lot of demand, it could never earn a profit on its online sales.

In response, retailers must find ways to enhance their omnichannel performance, including their logistics, transportation, and inventory capabilities. If retailers must create omnichannel environments to stay competitive, they also must engage in intelligence gathering and data analysis that can reveal the most efficient strategies and the most appropriate trade-offs to make in their operations.

Sources: Suzanne Kapner, "Internet Drags Down Some Retailers' Holiday Profit," *The Wall Street Journal*, December 1, 2014; Tom Ryan, "Omnichannel Puts Retailers in the Red," *RetailWire*, April 20, 2015.

The **cost of goods sold (COGS)** is the amount a retailer pays to vendors for the merchandise the retailer sells plus transportation costs. **Gross margin**, also called **gross profit**, is the net sales minus the cost of the goods sold. It is an important measure in retailing because it indicates how much profit the retailer is making on merchandise sold, without considering the expenses associated with operating the store and corporate overhead expenses.

Some retailers have additional revenue sources related to merchandise sales, such as payments from vendors. For example, grocery retailers often charge vendors for space in their stores, known as a **slotting fee** or **slotting allowance**. Retailers may also require that vendors pay a **chargeback fee** if merchandise bought from the vendor does not meet all the terms of the purchase agreement, such as if the delivery is late. Such payments from vendors are typically incorporated into the income statement as a reduction in the COGS.

Gross margin = Net sales − Cost of goods sold

Operating expenses, also called **selling, general, and administrative (SG&A) expenses**, are the overhead costs associated with normal business operations, such as salaries for sales associates and managers, advertising, utilities, office supplies, depreciation, amortization, transportation from the retailer's warehouses to its stores, and rent.

Operating profit margin is the gross margin minus the operating expenses. In retailing management decisions we usually focus on the operating profit margin because it reflects the performance of retailers' fundamental operations, not the financial decisions retailers make with regard to nonoperating income/expense, interest, and taxes.

Operating profit margin = Gross margin − Operating expenses

Finally, **net profit margin**, or **net income**, is the operating profit margin minus other income or expenses not associated with the retailers' fundamental operation, such as the cost of opening or closing stores, acquisitions, and credit card programs. Interest and taxes are also subtracted from the operating profit to get the net profit margin. The net profit margin is used to calculate ROA.

Net profit margin = Operating profit margin − Other income or expenses − Interest − Taxes

Analyzing Performance in the Profit Margin Management Path   The level of sales, gross margin, operating profit margin, and net profit margin in Exhibit 6–4 provide some useful information about the financial performance of the two retailers. However, it is difficult to compare the performance of the retailers when they differ in size. If Nordstrom were interested in comparing its performance with Walmart, it would expect that Walmart would have a much greater gross margin and operating profit margin because the latter retailer has nearly 35 times greater sales than Nordstrom. Thus, some of the differences in the income statement numbers are due to differences in size, not the retailers' performance. It is therefore useful to use ratios with net sales in the denominator when evaluating a retailer's performance and comparing it with other retailers'. Three useful ratios in the profit margin management path are gross margin percentage, operating expenses as a percentage of sales, and operating profit margin percentage of sales.

Gross margin (in %) is gross margin divided by net sales. Retailers use this ratio to compare (1) the performance of various types of merchandise and (2) their own performance with that of other retailers with higher or lower levels of sales.

$$\frac{\text{Gross margin}}{\text{Net sales}} \times 100 = \text{Gross margin (in \%)}$$

$$\text{Walmart:} \quad \frac{\$121,146}{\$482,130} \times 100 = 25.13\%$$

$$\text{Nordstrom:} \quad \frac{\$5,269}{\$14,437} \times 100 = 36.50\%$$

Even though Walmart has almost 35 times the sales of Nordstrom, Nordstrom has a higher gross margin percentage. This difference in gross margin percentage can be traced back to the retail strategies of the companies. Department stores, especially high-end department stores like Nordstrom, generally have higher gross margin percentages than full-line discount stores because they target less price-sensitive customers who are interested in luxury branded fashion merchandise and personal service and are willing to pay for it. That is, customers are willing to pay a premium price for a high-fashion dress by a famous designer at Nordstrom, but they expect very competitive and low prices for a six-pack of plain white T-shirts or a pound of Great Value coffee at Walmart.

Like the gross margin, **operating expenses (in %)** can facilitate comparisons among firms. It is important for department stores to achieve relatively high gross margins because their operating expenses tend to be higher than those of other retail formats like discount stores. Nordstrom spends proportionally more on customer service and selling expenses, more to maintain the appearance of its stores, and more on rental expenses per square foot because most of its stores are located in premium malls. Discount stores instead operate with relatively fewer administrative staff than do department stores. Walmart's buying expenses are comparatively lower because it needs fewer buyers to complete the simpler buying process associated with the relatively few SKUs for commodity-type merchandise, like packaged foods and fresh meat and produce. Nordstrom instead faces more complex, and more expensive, buying processes for the fashion apparel it stocks, including the expenses of sending its buyers to fashion markets around the world. Walmart has little need to make such expenditures. But then why is Walmart's operating expenses as a percentage of sales (20.1 percent) significantly lower than the value for Nordstrom (28.9 percent)? Part of the reason comes from Walmart's strategic choice to have lower-cost store locations compared to Nordstrom.

$$\frac{\text{Operating expenses}}{\text{Net sales}} \times 100 = \text{Operating expenses (in \%)}$$

Walmart: $\dfrac{\$97,041}{\$482,130} \times 100 = 20.13\%$

Nordstrom: $\dfrac{\$4,168}{\$14,437} \times 100 = 28.87\%$

Similar to the gross margin and operating expenses, **operating profit margin (in %)**, expressed as a percentage of net sales, facilitates comparisons across firms. It is calculated as operating profit margin divided by net sales.

Nordstrom's operating profit margin percentage is 50 percent larger than Walmart's. The reason is that Nordstrom's gross margin percentage is much higher than Walmart's even though its operating expenses percentage is also higher. Thus, the profit margin management path of the strategic profit model suggests that Nordstrom is outperforming Walmart. But the asset turnover management path tells a different story.

$$\frac{\text{Gross margin} - \text{Operating expenses}}{\text{Net sales}} \times 100 = \text{Operating profit margin (in \%)}$$

Walmart: $\dfrac{\$121,146 - \$97,041}{\$482,130} \times 100 = 5.00\%$

Nordstrom: $\dfrac{\$5,269 - \$4,168}{\$14,437} \times 100 = 7.63\%$

Finally, net profit margin percentage also facilitates comparisons across firms. It is calculated as net profit divided by net sales.

$$\frac{\text{Net profit margin}}{\text{Net sales}} \times 100 = \text{Net profit margin (in \%)}$$

Walmart: $\dfrac{\$14,964}{\$482,130} \times 100 = 3.05\%$

Nordstrom: $\dfrac{\$600}{\$14,437} \times 100 = 4.16\%$

Asset Turnover Management Path

The information used to analyze a retailer's asset turnover management path comes primarily from the retailer's balance sheet. Whereas the income statement summarizes financial performance over a period of time (usually a year or quarter), the balance sheet summarizes a retailer's financial position at a given point in time, typically the end of its fiscal year. Nordstrom and Walmart balance sheets are shown in Exhibit 6–5, and the asset turnover management path components in the strategic profit model are shown in Exhibit 6–6.

EXHIBIT 6–5
Balance Sheets for
Nordstrom and Walmart

	Nordstrom Income Statement (FY 1/30/2016)	Walmart Income Statement (FY 1/31/2016)
	Values in Millions	Values in Millions
Cash and cash equivalents	595	8,705
Merchandise inventory	1,945	44,469
Other current assets	474	7,065
Total current assets	3,014	60,239
Property & equipment (net)	3,735	110,171
Intangible assets	435	23,040
Other noncurrent assets	514	66,370
Total noncurrent assets	4,684	139,342
Total assets	7,698	199,581
Inventory turnover (cost of goods sold ÷ inventory at cost)	4.71	8.12
Asset turnover (sales ÷ total assets)	1.88	2.42
ROA (net profit margin ÷ total assets) or net profit margin percentage × asset turnover	7.79%	7.36%

Sources: Walmart 10K, filed March 30, 2016; Nordstrom, Inc. 10K, filed March 14, 2016.

EXHIBIT 6–6
Asset Turnover
Management Path in
Strategic Profit Model

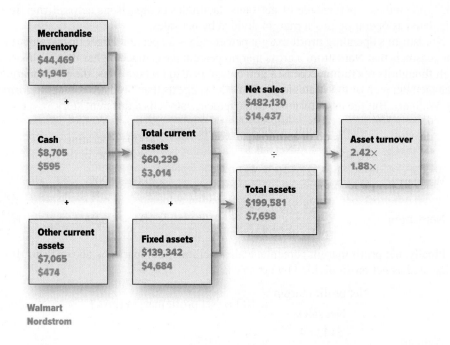

Components in the Asset Turnover Management Path   **Assets** are economic resources (e.g., inventory, buildings, computers, store fixtures) owned or controlled by a firm. There are two types of assets, current and noncurrent. We examine examples of these assets and how they play into the financial pictures of Nordstrom and Walmart.

Current Assets   Assets that can normally be converted to cash within one year are considered **current assets**. For retailers, current assets are primarily cash, merchandise inventory, and other assets such as accounts receivable. **Cash and cash equivalents** include currency, checks, short-term bank accounts, and investments that mature within three months or less.[5] Traditional retailers require some minimal amount of cash and cash equivalents to conduct their day-to-day business.

Merchandise inventory is a retailer's lifeblood; the primary reason the retailer exists is to sell its merchandise inventory. Getting the right merchandise in the right quantities at the right time and place is critical. Stocking more merchandise enhances sales because it increases the chances that customers will find something they want. But it also increases the investments that retailers must make in this asset. Retailing View 6.4 describes how crowdfunding can subvert traditional inventory models, allowing retailers to maintain a bare minimum of inventory on hand.

Inventory turnover, which measures how effectively retailers utilize their investment in inventory, is another important ratio for assessing retail performance. **Inventory turnover** shows how many times, on average, inventory cycles through the store during a specific period of time (usually a year). It is calculated as the COGS during a time period, typically a year, divided by the average level of inventory (expressed at cost) during the time period. Some retailers use an equivalent inventory turnover calculation using retail values, i.e., net sales (at retail) divided by average inventory (also at retail). A surrogate measure for average inventory is the inventory value at the end of the fiscal year reported on the balance sheet. Note that the inventory level reported on the balance sheet is the level on the last day of the

RETAILING VIEW   Basing Inventory Levels on Crowdfunding Campaigns   6.4

Crowdfunding raises money to support a particular project by convincing a large group of people to donate money, often in relatively small amounts. It has enabled filmmakers to produce their movies, musicians to get their albums recorded, and candidates to run political campaigns. In some recently emerging examples, it also has given retail entrepreneurs a means to get their innovative products to customers, without forcing them to incur the risk and cost of massive inventories.

Fashion retailers always confront the inherent gap between when they purchase their inventory and when the demand for that inventory becomes evident. As a result, inventory management is especially challenging for them, often leaving retail shelves bare of popular fashions but weighted down with unpopular options. With crowdfunding, retail entrepreneurs can avoid starting production until they have actual orders in hand. They also know exactly how much fabric to purchase or how many buttons they will need, which helps reduce their supply chain costs.

On Kickstarter, the vintage-inspired lingerie brand Blackbird Underpinnings raised more than $40,000 before it even found a factory that could handle full production runs of its products. The 10-Year Hoodie planned to raise $50,000, but it proved so popular to Kickstarter users that it took in more than $1 million beyond its goal.

The men's denim brand Gustin also relied on Kickstarter for its first crowdfunding campaign, after deciding that a traditional retail fashion model was too costly, both for the company and for customers. Its premium denim products were selling in local retail boutiques for $205. Through Kickstarter at first, and now through its own proprietary crowdfunding site (www.weargustin.com), Gustin instead waits until it has sufficient orders for each style to initiate a production run. With this approach, it can sell raw selvedge denim jeans for as low as $81. In addition to the price benefits, Gustin highlights how its innovative strategy reduces waste overall, which is more sustainable. It also offers guarantees of high quality because it remains in close contact with its customers every time they order directly from the retail site.

Source: Gustin

If you want a good deal on jeans and you don't mind waiting a couple of months to get them, try Gustin. It uses a crowdfunding model to keep its costs low.

Examples of successes are still relatively rare, though. Without a compelling appeal to crowdfunders, basic fashion brands tend to get overlooked. Fashion customers generally don't like to wait the 60 to 90 days to get their apparel. Unlike a movie or political campaign, selling fashion through crowdfunding also creates challenges in terms of returns, which can be more problematic since the normal business model is "buy and pay now, but wait to receive."

Sources: Rachel Brown, "Kickstarter Fashion: Retail Disrupter, or Oxymoron?," *San Francisco Chronicle*, January 27, 2016; Ellen Huet, "Crowdfunding Might Be Right Fit for Fashion Startups," *SFGate*, January 3, 2014; Christina Desmarais, "How 3 Kickstarter Projects Beat the Odds," *Inc.*, May 8, 2013; https://www.weargustin.com.

fiscal year, not the average level. To measure the average inventory level more accurately, retailers measure the inventory level on each day of the year and divide by 365 (see Chapter 10).

$$\frac{\text{COGS}}{\text{Average inventory at cost}} = \text{Inventory turnover}$$

Walmart: $\dfrac{\$360,984}{\$44,469} = 8.12$

Nordstrom: $\dfrac{\$9,168}{\$1,945} = 4.31$

Walmart's inventory turnover is almost two times faster than Nordstrom's. Walmart's higher inventory turnover is to be expected, considering the nature of its retail strategy and the merchandise it sells. That is, most items in Walmart are low-cost staples such as food, batteries, housewares, and basic apparel items. Unlike apparel fashions that are the mainstay for Nordstrom, these staples can be replenished quickly. Walmart stores typically have relatively few SKUs in a particular product category, such as men's dress shirts. Nordstrom, in contrast, may stock 500 SKUs of men's dress shirts (different colors, sizes, styles, and brands). Larger assortments, like those in department stores, require relatively higher inventory investments, which slows inventory turnover.

Noncurrent Assets   Assets that are not likely to be converted to cash within one year represent **noncurrent assets**. For retailers, noncurrent assets primarily include fixed assets and intangible assets. In retailing, the principal **fixed assets** are buildings, distribution centers, fixtures (e.g., display racks), and equipment (e.g., computers, delivery trucks). **Intangible assets** include nonphysical assets such as patents and goodwill. Notice that the balance sheet does not include most of the critical assets used by retailers to develop a sustainable competitive advantage (discussed in Chapter 5) such as brand image, customer loyalty, customer service, information and supply chain systems, human resources (committed, knowledgeable employees), and a database of customer buying behaviors and preferences. These factors are critical assets, but because they cannot be valued by accountants, they are not included on the balance sheet (unless they are the result of an acquisition). So while these assets are important for generating long-term financial performance, they are *not* included in the calculation of return on assets.

$$\frac{\text{Net sales}}{\text{Total assets}} = \text{Asset turnover}$$

Walmart: $\dfrac{\$482,130}{\$199,581} = 2.42$

Nordstrom: $\dfrac{\$14,437}{\$7,698} = 1.88$

Analyzing the Performance of the Asset Turnover Management Path   Asset turnover is used to assess the performance of the asset management component in the strategic profit model. It is net sales divided by total assets. Walmart's asset turnover is 25 percent greater than that of Nordstrom. The difference in their asset turnovers is due to Walmart's higher inventory turnover and the lower cost of the fixed assets in its stores. As we noted earlier, retailers like Walmart that sell basic merchandise at low prices typically have higher inventory turnover than fashion apparel sold by retailers like Nordstrom. Also, Nordstrom stores include much more expensive fixed assets, such as fixtures, lighting, mannequins, and flooring, than does a typical Walmart store.

Combining the Profit Margin and Asset Turnover Management Paths

In terms of the profit margin management path, Nordstrom has a higher operating profit margin percentage and thus performs better than Walmart on profits. But Walmart has a higher asset turnover. Although this type of performance is expected, given their overall strategy and retail formats, both retailers strive to increase their performance on these key ratios. For example, department stores like Nordstrom are working to develop supply chains and buying systems that mimic those of successful fast-fashion retailers like Zara and H&M that allow less merchandise to be delivered more often—more closely matching supply and demand. This lower average inventory and total assets, while also potentially increasing sales, results in higher inventory and asset turnovers. Discount stores like Walmart instead are attempting to increase their gross margins by carrying more fresh and organic produce, meat, and prepared foods. Although most experts have been underwhelmed by its efforts to offer more fashionable apparel, Walmart regards this merchandising strategy as a way to increase its profit margins.[6]

The two retailers' overall performance, measured by ROA, can be determined by considering the effects of both paths—that is, by multiplying the net profit margin by asset turnover. Nordstrom had a significantly higher operating profit margin percentage than Walmart, and its net profit margin was also much higher. Yet Nordstrom's performance on asset turnover was inferior to Walmart's. As a result, the two retailers' overall performance, as measured by ROA, are remarkably similar!

	Asset turnover	×	Net profit margin (in %)	=	Return on assets (in %)
Walmart:	2.42	×	3.05%	=	7.38%
Nordstrom:	1.88	×	4.16%	=	7.82%

Implications for Improving Financial Performance

The profit margin management and asset turnover management paths in the strategic profit model suggest different approaches for improving financial performance. Focusing on the profit margin management path, the operating profit margin could be increased by increasing sales or reducing COGS or operating expenses. For example, Walmart could increase its sales by increasing promotions to attract more customers. The increase in sales will have a positive effect on Walmart's operating profit margin percentage and its ROA as long as the increase in promotional expenses generates more gross margin dollars than they cost. In addition, the increase in sales will increase Walmart's asset turnover because sales will increase but assets will remain the same. The net effect will be a positive impact on ROA.

Looking at the asset turnover management path, Nordstrom could increase its asset turnover by decreasing the dollar amount of inventory in its stores. However, decreasing the level of inventory could actually decrease sales because customers might not find the products they want to buy, causing them to shop elsewhere. If they tell their friends, post negative online reviews, or use social media like Twitter to voice their discontent, the lack of salable inventory could have a cascading deleterious impact on sales and profits.

The strategic profit model illustrates two important issues. First, retailers and investors should consider both operating and net profit margin and asset turnover when evaluating their financial performance. Firms can achieve high performance (high ROA) by effectively managing both profit margin and asset turnover. Second, retailers need to consider the implications of their strategic decisions on both components of the strategic profit model. For example, increasing prices might increase the gross margin and operating profit margin in the profit margin management path. However, increasing prices could also result in fewer sales, with negative impacts on both total gross margin and net operating profit margin dollars. At the same time, assuming the level of assets stays the same, asset turnover will decrease. Thus, a simple change in one strategic variable, such as pricing, has multiple repercussions on the strategic profit model, all of which need to be considered when determining the impact on ROA.

EVALUATING GROWTH OPPORTUNITIES

LO 6-3

Illustrate the use of the strategic profit model for analyzing growth opportunities.

To illustrate the use of the strategic profit model for evaluating a growth opportunity, let's look at the opportunity that Kelly Bradford, from Chapter 5, is considering. Recall that Kelly Bradford owns Gifts To Go, a two-store chain in the Chicago area. She's considering several growth options, one of which is to open an Internet channel called www.Gifts-To-Go.com. She has determined that the market size for this channel is large but very competitive. Now she needs to conduct a financial analysis for the proposed online channel, compare the projections with Gifts To Go stores, and determine the financial performance of the combined businesses. We'll first look at the profit margin management path, followed by the asset turnover management path. Exhibit 6–7 shows income statement information for Kelly's Gifts To Go stores, her estimates for Gifts-To-Go.com, and the combined businesses.

Profit Margin Management Path

Kelly thinks she can develop Gifts-To-Go.com into a business that will generate annual sales of $440,000. She anticipates some cannibalization of her store sales by the Internet channel; some customers who would have bought merchandise at Gifts To Go will no longer go into her stores to make their purchases. She also thinks the Internet channel will stimulate some store sales; customers who see gift items on her website will visit the stores and make their purchases there. Thus, she decides to perform the analysis with the assumption that her store sales will remain the same after the introduction of the Internet channel.

Gross Margin   Kelly plans to charge the same prices and sell basically the same merchandise, with an extended assortment, on Gifts-To-Go.com as in her stores. Thus, she expects the gross margin percentage for store sales will be the same as the gross margin percentage for Gifts-To-Go.com sales.

$$\frac{\text{Gross margin}}{\text{Net sales}} \times 100 = \text{Gross margin (in \%)}$$

$$\text{Stores:} \quad \frac{350,000}{\$700,000} \times 100 = 50\%$$

$$\text{Gifts-To-Go.com:} \quad \frac{220,000}{\$440,000} \times 100 = 50\%$$

Operating Expenses   Initially, Kelly thought that her operating expenses as a percentage of sales would be lower for Gifts-To-Go.com because she would not need to pay rent or have highly trained salespeople. But she discovered that her operating

EXHIBIT 6–7
Income Statement Information of Analysis of Gifts To Go Growth Opportunities

Income Statements	Gifts To Go Stores	Gifts-To-Go.com (projected)	Businesses Combined
Net sales	$700,000	$440,000	$1,140,000
Less cost of goods sold	350,000	220,000	570,000
Gross margin	350,000	220,000	570,000
Less operating expenses	250,000	150,000	400,000
Operating profit	100,000	70,000	170,000
Less interest expenses and taxes	40,000	24,000	64,000
Net profit margin	$60,000	$46,000	$106,000
Ratios			
Gross margin as a % of net sales	50.0%	50.0%	50.0%
Operating expense as a % of net sales	35.7%	34.1%	35.1%
Operating profit as a % of net sales	14.3%	15.9%	14.9%
Net profit margin as a % of net sales	8.6%	10.5%	9.3%

expenses as a percentage of sales will be only slightly lower for Gifts-To-Go.com because she needs to hire a firm to maintain the website, process orders, and get orders ready for shipment. Also, Gifts To Go stores have an established clientele and highly trafficked locations with good visibility. Although some of her current customers will learn about the website from her in-store promotions, Kelly will have to invest in advertising and promotions to create awareness for her new channel and inform people who are unfamiliar with her stores.

$$\frac{\text{Operating expenses}}{\text{Net sales}} \times 100 = \text{Operating expenses (in \%)}$$

Stores: $\dfrac{\$250,000}{\$700,000} \times 100 = 35.7\%$

Gifts-To-Go.com: $\dfrac{\$100,000}{\$440,000} \times 100 = 34.1\%$

Net Operating Profit Margin   Because the gross margin and operating expenses as a percentage of sales for the two operations are projected to be about the same, Gifts-To-Go.com is expected to generate a slightly higher operating profit margin percentage.

$$\frac{\text{Net profit}}{\text{Net sales}} \times 100 = \text{Net profit (in \%)}$$

Stores: $\dfrac{\$100,000}{\$700,000} \times 100 = 14.3\%$

Gifts-To-Go.com: $\dfrac{70,000}{\$440,000} \times 100 = 15.9\%$

Net profit margin percentage, expressed as a percentage of net sales, is calculated as net profit margin (or net profits) divided by net sales. Gifts-To-Go.com generates a much better net profit margin as a percentage of sales.

$$\frac{\text{Net profit margin}}{\text{Net sales}} \times 100 = \text{Net profit margin (in \%)}$$

Stores: $\dfrac{\$60,000}{\$700,000} \times 100 = 8.6\%$

Gifts-To-Go.com: $\dfrac{\$46,000}{\$440,000} \times 100 = 10.5\%$

Asset Turnover Management Path

Now let's compare the two operations using the asset turnover management path with the balance sheet information in Exhibit 6–8. Kelly estimates that Gifts-To-Go.com

Balance Sheets	Gifts To Go Stores	Gifts-To-Go.com (projected)	Businesses Combined
Cash	175,000	131,000	306,000
Merchandise inventory	175,000	70,000	245,000
Total current assets	350,000	201,000	551,000
Fixed assets	30,000	10,000	40,000
Total assets	380,000	211,000	591,000
Ratios			
Inventory turnover	2.00	3.14	2.33
Asset turnover	1.84	2.09	1.93
ROA	15.8%	21.8%	17.9%

EXHIBIT 6–8
Balance Sheet Information of Analysis of Gifts To Go Growth Opportunities

will have a higher inventory turnover than Gifts To Go stores because it will consolidate the inventory at one centralized distribution center that serves a large sales volume, as opposed to Gifts to Go, which has inventory sitting in two stores each with relatively lower sales volumes. Additionally, Gifts-To-Go.com will have relationships with several of its vendors in which they "drop ship," or send merchandise directly from the vendor to the customer. In these situations, Gifts-to-Go.com has no inventory investment.

$$\frac{\text{Cost of goods}}{\text{Average inventory}} = \text{Inventory turnover}$$

Stores: $\dfrac{350,000}{\$175,000} = 2.0$

Gifts-To-Go.com: $\dfrac{220,000}{\$70,000} = 3.1$

Gifts To Go's store space is rented. Thus, Kelly's fixed assets consist of the fixtures, lighting, and other leasehold improvements for her stores, as well as equipment such as point-of-sale terminals. Kelly also has invested in assets that make her stores aesthetically pleasing. Gifts-To-Go.com is outsourcing the fulfillment of orders placed on its website, so it has no warehouse assets. Thus, its fixed assets are its website and order-processing computer system.

As she expects, Gifts-To-Go.com's projected asset turnover is higher than that of Gifts To Go's stores because Kelly estimates that Gifts-To-Go.com will have a higher inventory turnover, and its other assets are lower.

$$\frac{\text{Net sales}}{\text{Total assets}} = \text{Asset turnover}$$

Stores: $\dfrac{700,000}{\$380,000} = 1.84$

Gifts-To-Go.com: $\dfrac{440,000}{\$211,000} = 2.09$

Because Kelly's estimates for the net profit margin and asset turnover for Gifts-To-Go.com are higher than those for her stores, Gifts-To-Go.com achieves a higher ROA. Thus, this strategic profit model analysis indicates that Gifts-To-Go.com is a financially viable growth opportunity for Kelly.

	Asset turnover	×	Net profit margin (in %)	=	Return on assets (in %)
Stores:	1.84	×	8.6%	=	15.8%
Gifts-To-Go.com:	2.09	×	10.5%	=	21.8%

Using the Strategic Profit Model to Analyze Other Decisions

Another investment that Kelly might consider is installing a computerized inventory control system that would help her make better decisions about which merchandise to order, when to reorder merchandise, and when to lower prices on merchandise that is not being bought.

If she buys the system, her sales will increase because she will have a greater percentage of merchandise that is selling well and fewer stockouts. Her gross margin percentage will also increase because she won't have to mark down as much slow-selling merchandise.

Looking at the asset turnover management path, the purchase of the computer system will increase her fixed assets by the amount of the system, but her inventory turnover will increase and the level of inventory assets will decrease because she is able to buy more efficiently. Thus, her asset turnover will probably increase because sales will increase at a greater percentage than will total assets. Total assets may actually decrease if the additional cost of the inventory system is less than the reduction in inventory.

SETTING AND MEASURING PERFORMANCE OBJECTIVES

In the previous sections, we discussed the measures used to evaluate the overall financial performance of a retailer, including ROA and its components. In this section, we review some measures used to assess the performance of specific assets possessed by a retailer—its employees, real estate, and merchandise inventory. Retailers use these measures to evaluate their firm's performance and set objectives.

LO 6-4

Review the measures retailers use to assess their performance.

Setting performance objectives is a necessary component of any firm's strategic management process. Performance objectives should include (1) a numerical index of the performance desired against which progress may be measured, (2) a time frame within which the objective is to be achieved, and (3) the resources needed to achieve the objective. For example, "earning reasonable profits" isn't a good objective. It doesn't provide specific goals that can be used to evaluate performance. What's reasonable? When do you want to realize the profits? A better objective would be "earning $100,000 in profit during calendar year 2018 on a $500,000 investment in store displays, computer equipment, and inventory."

Top-Down versus Bottom-Up Process

Setting objectives in large retail organizations entails a combination of the top-down and bottom-up approaches to planning. **Top-down planning** means that goals get set at the top of the organization and are passed down to the lower operating levels. In a retailing organization, top-down planning involves corporate officers developing an overall retail strategy and assessing broad economic, competitive, and consumer trends. With this information, they develop performance objectives for the corporation. These overall objectives are then broken down into specific objectives for each buyer and merchandise category and for each region, store, and even department within stores and the sales associates working in those departments.

The overall strategy determines the merchandise variety, assortment, and product availability, plus the store size, location, and level and type of customer service. Then performance goals are established for each buyer and merchandise manager. This process is reviewed in Chapter 11.

Similarly, the company's performance objectives are broken down into objectives for the store managers. The process then trickles down to department managers in the stores and individual sales associates. The process of setting objectives for sales associates in stores is discussed in Chapter 14.

This top-down planning is complemented by a bottom-up planning approach. **Bottom-up planning** involves lower levels in the company developing performance objectives that are aggregated up to develop overall company objectives. Buyers and store managers estimate what they can achieve, and their estimates are transmitted up the organization to the corporate executives. Frequently there are disagreements between the goals that have trickled down from the top and those set by lower-level employees of the organization, which are resolved through negotiations. For example, a store manager may not be able to achieve the 10 percent sales growth set for his or her region because a major employer in the area has announced plans to lay off 2,000 employees. If the operating managers aren't involved in the objective-setting process, they won't accept the objectives and thus will be less motivated to achieve them.

Who Is Accountable for Performance?

At each level of the retail organization, the business unit and its manager should be held accountable only for the revenues, expenses, cash flow, and contribution to ROA that they can control. Thus, expenses that affect several levels of the organization (e.g., labor and capital expenses associated with operating a corporate headquarters) shouldn't be arbitrarily assigned to lower levels. In the case of a store, for example, it may be appropriate to set performance objectives based on sales, sales associate productivity, store inventory shrinkage due to employee theft and shoplifting, and energy costs. If the buyer makes poor decisions and has to lower prices to get rid of merchandise and therefore profits suffer, it is not fair to assess a store manager's performance on the basis of the resulting decline in store profit.

Performance objectives and measures can be used to pinpoint problem areas. The reasons that performance may be above or below planned levels must be examined. Perhaps the managers involved in setting the objectives aren't very good at making estimates. If so, they may need to be trained in forecasting. Also, buyers may misrepresent their business unit's ability to contribute to the firm's financial goals to get a larger inventory budget than is warranted and consequently earn a higher bonus. In either case, investment funds would be misallocated.

Actual performance may differ from what the plan predicts due to circumstances beyond the manager's control. For example, there may have been a recession. Assuming the recession wasn't predicted, or was more severe or lasted longer than anticipated, there are several relevant questions: How quickly were plans adjusted? How rapidly and appropriately were pricing and promotional policies modified? In short, did the manager react to salvage an adverse situation, or did the reaction worsen the situation?

Performance Objectives and Measures

Many factors contribute to a retailer's overall performance, and this makes it hard to find a single measure to evaluate performance. For instance, sales are a global measure of a retail store's activity level. However, as illustrated by the strategic profit model, a store manager could easily increase sales by lowering prices, but the profit realized on that merchandise (gross margin) would suffer as a result. An attempt to maximize one measure may lower another. Managers must therefore understand how their actions affect multiple performance measures.

The measures used to evaluate retail operations vary depending on (1) the level of the organization at which the decision is made and (2) the resources the manager controls. For example, the principal resources controlled by store managers are space and money for operating expenses (such as wages for sales associates and utility payments to light and heat the store). Thus, store managers focus on performance measures like sales per square foot, employee costs, and energy costs as percentages of sales.

Types of Measures

Exhibit 6–9 breaks down a variety of retailers' performance measures into three types: input measures, output measures, and productivity measures. **Output measures** assess the results of a retailer's investment decisions. For example, sales revenue, gross margin, and net profit margin are all output measures and ways to evaluate a retailer's input or resource allocation decisions. A **productivity measure** (the ratio of an output to an input) determines how effectively retailers use their resources—what return they get on their investments in inputs.

Input measures are the resources or money allocated by a retailer to achieve outputs, or results. For example, the amount and selection of merchandise inventory, the number of stores, the size of the stores, the employees, advertising, markdowns, store hours, and promotions all require managerial decisions about inputs.

EXHIBIT 6–9   Measure for Assessing the Performance of Retailers

Level of Organization	Output	Input	Productivity (output/input)
Corporate (measures for entire corporation)	Net sales Net profits Growth in sales, profits, comparable-store sales	Square feet of store space Number of employees Inventory Advertising expenditures	Return on assets Asset turnover Sales per employee Sales per square foot
Merchandise management (measures for a merchandise category)	Net sales Gross margin Growth in sales	Inventory level Markdowns Advertising expenses Cost of merchandise	Gross margin return on investment (GMROI) Inventory turnover Advertising as a percentage of sales* Markdown as a percentage of sales*
Store operations (measures for a store or department within a store)	Net sales Gross margin Growth in sales	Square feet of selling areas Expenses for utilities Number of sales associates	Net sales per square foot Net sales per sales associate or per selling hour Utility expenses as a percentage of sales* Inventory shrinkage*

*These productivity measures are commonly expressed as an input–output ratio.

In general, because productivity measures are ratios of outputs to inputs, they are very useful for comparing the performance of different business units. Suppose Kelly Bradford's two stores are different sizes: One has 5,000 square feet, and the other has 10,000 square feet. It's hard to compare the stores' performances using just output or input measures because the larger store will probably generate more sales and have higher expenses. But if the larger store has lower space productivity because it generates $210 net sales per square foot and the smaller store generates $350 per square foot, Kelly knows that the smaller store is operating more efficiently, even though it's generating lower sales.

Corporate Performance   At a corporate level, retail executives have three critical resources (inputs)—merchandise inventory, store space, and employees—that they can manage to generate sales and profits (outputs). Thus, effective productivity measures of the utilization of these assets include asset and inventory turnover, sales per square foot of selling space, and sales per employee.

As we have discussed, ROA is an overall productivity measure combining the operating profit margin percentage and asset turnover. Another commonly used measure of overall performance is **comparable-store sales growth** (also called **same-store sales growth**), which compares sales growth in stores that have been open for at least one year. Growth in sales can result from increasing the sales generated per store or by increasing the number of stores. Growth in comparable-store sales assesses the first component in sales growth and thus indicates how well the retailer is doing with its core business concept. New stores do not represent growth from last year's sales but rather new sales created where no other sales existed the year before. Thus, a decrease in comparable-store sales indicates that the retailer's fundamental business approach is not being well received by its customers, even if overall sales are growing because the retailer is opening more new stores.

Merchandise Management Measures   The critical resource (input) controlled by merchandise managers is merchandise inventory. Merchandise managers also have the authority to set initial prices and lower prices when merchandise is not selling (i.e., take a markdown). Finally, they negotiate with vendors over the price paid for merchandise.

Inventory turnover is a productivity measure of the management of inventory; higher turnover means greater inventory management productivity. Gross margin percentage indicates the performance of merchandise managers in negotiating with vendors and buying merchandise that can generate a profit. Discounts (markdowns) as a percentage of sales are also a measure of the quality of the merchandise buying decisions. If merchandise managers have a high percentage of markdowns, they may not be buying the right merchandise or the right quantities, because they weren't able to sell some of it at its original retail price. Note that gross margin and discount percentages are productivity measures, but they are typically expressed as an input divided by an output, as opposed to typical productivity measures that use outputs divided by inputs.

Store Operations Measures   The critical assets controlled by store managers are the use of the store space and the management of the store's employees. Thus, measures of store operations productivity include sales per square foot of selling space and sales per employee (or sales per employee per working hour, to take into account that some employees work part time). Store management is also responsible for controlling theft by employees and customers (referred to as inventory shrinkage), store maintenance, and energy costs (lighting, heating, and air conditioning). Thus, some other productivity measures used to assess the performance of store managers are inventory shrinkage and energy costs as a percentage of sales.

Assessing Performance: The Role of Benchmarks

As we have discussed, the financial measures used to assess performance reflect the retailer's market strategy. For example, because Walmart has a different business strategy than Nordstrom, it has a lower profit margin. But it earns an acceptable ROA because its inventory and asset turnovers are relatively high, due to its strategy of stocking a more limited merchandise assortment of less fashionable, staple items. In contrast,

Nordstrom offers a broad and deep merchandise assortment in fashionable apparel and accessories. Thus, it has lower inventory and asset turnover. Its operating profit margin and net profit margin are relatively high, resulting in an ROA that is similar to Walmart's. In other words, the performance of a retailer cannot be assessed accurately simply by looking at isolated measures, because they are affected by the retailer's strategy. To get a better assessment of a retailer's performance, we need to compare it against a benchmark. Two commonly used benchmarks are (1) the performance of the retailer over time and (2) the performance of the retailer compared with that of its competitors.

To assess performance over time, the retailer would compare its own recent performance with its performance in preceding months, quarters, or years. Then it needs to determine the reasons for any differences. For example, if ROA increases, is that because the retailer improved its asset turnover or its operating profit percentage? And, if there was a change, why did it occur?

To benchmark performance against competitors, the retailer would consider how direct competitors for its customers have performed. That is, Nordstrom would not benchmark against Walmart because they are not direct competitors. Instead, it would likely consider how well Macy's performed recently, while Walmart might benchmark against Target or Amazon.

SUMMARY

LO 6-1 **Review the strategic objectives of a retail firm.**

This chapter explains some basic elements of the retailing financial strategy and examines how retailing strategy affects the financial performance of a firm. The strategy undertaken by retailers is designed to achieve financial, societal, and personal objectives. However, the financial objectives are of greatest importance to large, publicly owned retailers.

LO 6-2 **Contrast the two paths to financial performance using the strategic profit model.**

The strategic profit model is used as a vehicle for understanding the complex interrelations between financial ratios and retailing strategy. Different types of retailers have different financial operating characteristics. Specifically, department store chains like Nordstrom generally have higher profit margins and lower turnover ratios than full-line discount stores like Walmart. Yet when margin and turnover are combined into return on assets, it is possible to achieve similar financial performance.

LO 6-3 **Illustrate the use of the strategic profit model for analyzing growth opportunities.**

In addition to helping retailers understand the financial implications of the trade-offs they face in developing a retail strategy, this chapter illustrates how the strategic profit model can be used to evaluate growth and investment opportunities.

LO 6-4 **Review the measures retailers use to assess their performance.**

Various financial performance measures are used to evaluate different aspects of a retailing organization. Although the return-on-assets ratio in the strategic profit model is appropriate for evaluating the performance of the retail executives responsible for managing the firm, other measures are more appropriate for more specific activities. For instance, inventory turnover and gross margin are appropriate for buyers, whereas store managers should be concerned with sales or gross margin per square foot or per employee.

KEY TERMS

assets, *164*

asset turnover, *158*

bottom-up planning, *171*

cash and cash equivalents, *164*

chargeback fee, *161*

comparable-store sales growth, *173*

cost of goods sold (COGS), *161*

crowdfunding, *165*

current assets, *164*

fixed assets, *166*

gross margin, *161*

gross margin (in %), *162*

gross profit, *161*

income statement, *160*

input measure, *172*

intangible assets, *166*

inventory turnover, *165*

merchandise inventory, *165*

net income, *162*

net profit margin, *162*

net profit margin (in %), *158*

net sales, *160*

noncurrent assets, *166*

operating expenses, *161*

operating expenses (in %), *162*

operating profit margin, *162*

operating profit margin (in %), *163*

output measure, *172*

productivity measure, *172*

profit and loss (P&L) statement, *160*

return on assets (ROA), *156*

same-store sales growth, *173*

selling, general, and administrative (SG&A) expenses, *161*

slotting allowance, *161*

slotting fee, *161*

statement of operations, *160*

strategic profit model (SPM), *157*

top-down planning, *171*

GET OUT AND DO IT!

1. **CONTINUING CASE ASSIGNMENT** Evaluate the financial performance of the retailer you have selected for the Continuing Case Assignment and of another store that sells similar merchandise categories but to a very different target market. If yours is a high-margin/low-turnover store, compare it with a low-margin/high-turnover store. You can get this information from your chosen store's latest annual report, available in the "investor relations" area of its website, at Hoovers Online, or in the Edgar files at www.sec.gov. Explain why you would expect the gross margin percentage, operating expenses as a percentage of sales, operating profit margin percentage, inventory turnover, asset turnover, and return on assets to differ between the two stores. Which retailer achieves better overall financial performance?

2. **INTERNET EXERCISE** Go to the latest annual reports and use the financial information to update the numbers in the net profit margin management model and the asset turnover management model for Nordstrom and Walmart. Have there been any significant changes in their financial performance? Why are the key financial ratios for these two retailers so different?

3. **GO SHOPPING** Go to your favorite store and interview the manager. Determine how the retailer sets its performance objectives. Evaluate its procedures relative to the procedures presented in the text.

DISCUSSION QUESTIONS AND PROBLEMS

1. What are the key productivity ratios for measuring the retailer as a whole, its merchandise management activities, and its store operations activities? Why are these ratios appropriate for one area of the retailer's operation and inappropriate for others?

2. What are examples of the types of objectives that entrepreneurs might have for a retail business they are launching?

3. Buyers' performance is often measured by the gross margin percentage. Why is this measure more appropriate than the operating or net profit percentage?

4. A supermarket retailer is considering the installation of self-checkout POS terminals. How would the replacement of cashiers with these self-checkouts affect the elements in the retailer's strategic profit model?

5. Macy's and Costco have targeted different customer segments. Which retailer would you expect to have a higher gross margin? Higher operating expenses as a percentage of sales? Higher operating profit margin percentage? Higher inventory turnover and asset turnover? Higher ROA? Why?

6. Why do investors place more weight on comparable-store sales than growth in sales?

7. Blue Nile is a jewelry retailer than uses only an Internet channel for interacting with its customers. What differences would you expect in the strategic profit model and key productivity ratios for Blue Nile and Zales, a multichannel jewelry retailer?

8. Using the following information taken from the 2016 balance sheet and income statement for Urban Outfitters, develop a strategic profit model. (Figures are in millions of dollars.)

Net sales	$2,473.8
Cost of goods sold	$1,316.2
Operating expenses	$ 575.8
Inventory	$ 250.1
Accounts receivable	$ 36.7
Other current assets	$ 68.9
Fixed assets	$ 690.0

9. A friend of yours is considering buying some stock in retail companies. Your friend knows that you are taking a course in retailing and asks for your opinion about Costco. Your friend is concerned that Costco is not a good firm to invest in because it has such a low net operating profit. What advice would you give your friend? Why?

CHAPTER ENDNOTES

1. David P. Schulz, "Top Retailers 2015," *Stores Magazine,* July 2015.
2. Sandy Smith, "Lost and Found," *Stores Magazine,* July 2015.
3. Dan Berthiaume, "And the Top Omnichannel Retailers Are . . . ," *Retailing Today,* October 2, 2015.
4. Ibid.
5. See www.accountingcoach.com/blog/item-in-cash-and-cash-equivalents.
6. Andrew Martin, "Wal-Mart Promises Organic Food for Everyone," *Bloomberg,* November 6, 2014, http://www.bloomberg.com/news/articles/2014-11-06/wal-mart-promises-organic-food-for-everyone; Ravi Vij, "How Walmart Makes Money: Understanding Walmart Business Model," *Revenues & Profits,* November 6, 2015, http://revenuesandprofits.com/how-walmart-makes-money-understanding-walmart-business-model/.

© mbbirdy/iStock/Getty Images

When shoppers with smartphones can access virtually any retail store they want from their homes, offices, or schools, getting them to visit brick-and-mortar stores is more challenging, as every retailer knows. Getting them to drive further, deal with parking challenges, and trudge through a mall may be even more difficult. Furthermore, malls are suffering from increased competition from other brick-and-mortar locations, outside their enclosed spaces. Building booms in previous decades have a "glut of stores in many parts of the country."[1] When there is more retail space than retailers to fill it, stores can pick and choose their locations. For many, the prominence of a stand-alone outlet is more appealing than a location in a fading mall. Thus some observers suggest that, after a run of several decades, the traditional mall is dead.[2]

But rather like a character on *Game of Thrones*, being dead might not be the end for the mall. Rather, the changed situation offers new opportunities for unique concepts. Some new malls harken back to older notions of communities and downtowns.[3] Others embrace modern technology and entertainment

options to lure people across distances, then keep them there.[4] Still others seek to redefine what it means to be a mall and which type of retailers should reside within them.[5] Let's consider each of these solutions and responses in turn.

First, many young consumers today seek the convenience and entertainment aspects offered by downtown locations, thus leaving behind the suburban living that their parents' generation sought. But malls are mostly located far outside city centers because they need expansive land for their buildings and parking facilities. If consumers have to drive to a mall, they demand expansive offerings, giving them opportunities for entertainment and socializing rather than just shopping. Modern versions of malls therefore look like Main Streets of yore, with service providers (e.g., barbers, dog groomers, dry cleaning) intermingled with retailers selling a range of goods, from clothing to food to children's train rides. These versions tend to be referred to by names such as "lifestyle centers" or "town centers," reflecting their role as a replacement of a traditional neighborhood focus or downtown location. Many of the facilities feature at least some outdoor elements, including sidewalks to facilitate strolling, as well as attractive installments such as fountains that allow people to enjoy nice weather when it is available and interact with others.[6]

Second, malls can go in another direction and embrace the latest technology, instead of nostalgia, to get people to visit. Consider the Mall of America, a massive attraction that brings tourists from everywhere in the world to visit Minnesota—a place that frequently endures temperatures of negative 40 degrees. Its overall strategy is to supply an "Enhanced Service Portal," or ESP. For example, during a recent snowstorm it offered free passes to its theme park and rides through social media channels, thereby convincing approximately 100,000 shoppers to brave terrible road conditions and get to the shops. When Twitter exploded with news that a popular band would be visiting one of its stores, mall management recognized that the influx of fans would be more than the individual store could handle, so it transformed a vacant space into a meet-and-greet site, then tweeted the location in the mall where fans could find their adored boy band, thus avoiding potential conflicts or overcrowding. If shoppers agree to allow mall personnel to access their locations, employees can provide valuable information, including reminders of where they parked, maps to preferred stores, or the location of the nearest nursing station for new moms. The ESP employees also can help shoppers make restaurant reservations, hours before they even get to the wing of the mall that houses the restaurant. A planned expansion even will allow out-of-town tourists to check their luggage for a few hours so that they can shop while waiting to take a shuttle to the Minneapolis–St. Paul airport.[7]

Third, faced with competition and declining tenancy rates—including the loss of their traditional anchor stores—some malls have changed the definition of what an anchor store is, to include a broader range of retail providers. Many mall properties have started to feature grocery stores in prominent locations. Similar to traditional anchor stores, grocers sell products that most shoppers need, offer familiar brand names, and account for a significant portion of the mall's total real estate; they also enhance the one-stop shopping convenience offered to consumers and promise benefits for other tenants. Consumers who need to stop by the mall anyway to pick up a few groceries are more likely to take a few extra steps to check in on the latest fast fashions. Another option features fitness centers and gyms as anchors, such that the mall becomes a routine site that many shoppers visit regularly. Because they are so familiar with the location they visit for every workout, they also may be more likely to revisit it when they need to find a tux or a gift for a friend.[8]

The challenges for malls are clear in some summary statistics: In the United States alone, recent years have seen the closure of approximately 25 enclosed malls, and 60 others appear at risk of closure. Among the survivors, around one-fifth of them suffer vacancy rates of at least 10 percent, and 3 percent of them are "dying," as signaled by their vacancy percentages that exceed 40 percent.[9] But even as traditional versions of malls seemingly have become largely a thing of the past, the malls that appear in the marketplace today, and those slated to come in the future, are finding ways to leverage their locational advantages. As one retail analyst notes, "If you had told a developer or landlord 15 years ago that they would be putting grocery stores or fitness centers in malls, they might have looked at you sideways. Not only are they doing it now, but [they] are finding success in its application."[10]

The often-referenced response to the question "What are the three most important things in retailing?" is "Location, location, location." Why is store location such an important decision for a retailer? First, location is typically one of the most influential considerations in a customer's store choice. For instance, when choosing where you're going to have your car washed, you usually pick the location closest to your home or work. Most consumers similarly shop at the supermarket closest to them.

Second, location decisions have strategic importance because they can be used to develop a sustainable competitive advantage. If a retailer has the best location—that is, the location that is most attractive to its customers—competitors can't copy this advantage. Competitors are relegated to occupying the second-best location.

Third, location decisions are risky. Typically, when retailers select a location, they either must make a substantial investment to buy and develop the real estate or must commit to a long-term lease with developers. Retailers often commit to leases for 5 to 15 years.

In the first part of this chapter, we discuss the types and relative advantages of three types of locations available to retailers—unplanned, planned, and nontraditional. We then examine how the location decision fits into the retailer's strategy. For example, the best locations for a 7-Eleven convenience store are not the best locations for a category specialist such as a Best Buy. We end this chapter by discussing the societal and legal considerations affecting a retailer's location decisions. In the next chapter, we discuss the issues involved in selecting areas of the country in which to locate stores and how to evaluate specific locations and negotiate leases.

TYPES OF RETAIL LOCATIONS

LO 7-1

Describe the types of retail locations available to retailers.

Many types of locations are available for retail stores, each with benefits and limitations. The two basic types of location are unplanned (freestanding and urban sites) and planned (shopping centers). **Unplanned locations** do not have any centralized management that determines what stores will be in a development, where the specific stores will be located, or how they will be operated. In **planned locations**, a shopping center developer and/or manager makes and enforces policies that govern store operations, such as the hours that a store must be open. Such managers also are responsible to maintain common facilities such as the parking area—an arrangement referred to as **common area maintenance (CAM)**—and provide security, parking lot lighting, outdoor signage for the center, advertising, special events to attract consumers, and so on.

In the United States, about 47 percent of the gross leasable square feet of retail space is in planned locations, with remainder in unplanned locations.[11] **Gross leasable area (GLA)** is the real estate industry's term for the total floor area designed for the retailer's occupancy and exclusive use, including any basements, mezzanines, or upper floors.

When choosing a particular location type, retailers evaluate a series of trade-offs involving the size of the trade area, the occupancy cost of the location (rent, maintenance, energy cost, etc.), the pedestrian and vehicle customer traffic associated with the location, the restrictions placed on store operations by shopping center management, and the convenience of the location for customers. The **trade area** is the geographic area that encompasses most of the customers who would patronize a specific retail site. The following sections describe the characteristics of each type of location.

UNPLANNED LOCATIONS

LO 7-2

Review the types of unplanned locations.

The three types of unplanned retail locations are freestanding sites, urban locations, and Main Street locations.

Freestanding Sites

Freestanding sites are retail locations for an individual, isolated store unconnected to other stores; however, they might be near other freestanding stores or near a shopping center. The advantages of freestanding locations are their convenience for customers (easy access and parking); high vehicular traffic and visibility to attract customers driving by; modest occupancy costs; and fewer restrictions on signs, hours, or merchandise that might be imposed by the managers of planned locations.

There are several disadvantages to freestanding sites. First, their trade area might be limited if there are no other nearby retailers to attract customers interested in conveniently shopping for multiple categories of merchandise on one trip. In addition, freestanding locations typically have higher occupancy costs than shopping centers because they do not have other retailers to share the common area maintenance costs. Finally, freestanding locations generally have little pedestrian traffic, limiting the number of customers who might drop in because they are walking by.

Some retailers are shifting from planned locations to freestanding locations to offer their customers a better shopping experience. The major drugstore chains (CVS, Walgreens Boots) have shifted their emphasis from strip malls to freestanding locations because they want accessible drive-through windows for pharmacies, more floor space, and better access for receiving merchandise.

Outparcels are freestanding stores that are not connected to other stores in a shopping center but are located on the premises of a shopping center, typically in a parking area. Some advantages of outparcels compared with other freestanding locations are that they can offer customers the convenience of a drive-through window, extensive parking, and clear visibility from the street. These locations are popular for fast-food restaurants and banks.

CVS has shifted its location emphasis from strip malls to freestanding locations to provide better access to its pharmacy drive-through windows, for more floor space, and for better access for receiving merchandise.

Urban Locations

Urban areas offer three main types of locations: the central business district, inner city, and gentrified residential areas. Across these areas, retailers are revising their offerings to reflect the restrictions associated with these locations. When selecting a store to patronize, urban consumers, unlike suburban consumers, typically place more importance on reducing their shopping time rather than finding a broad and deep assortment. For example, Office Depot's urban stores are 5,000 square feet, about one-fifth the size of a suburban store. The shelves are about 6 feet high, much shorter than in a suburban store, so visitors can navigate quickly. The signs above the aisles are simplified so customers do not waste time interpreting them. A suburban Office Depot store has 9,000 SKUs for sale, while its urban stores have half that number. The merchandise offered focuses on immediate-replacement items (a pen) versus stock-up items (a ream of paper).[12]

Retailers with urban locations also recognize the unique consumer needs within these markets. Consider two proximal Walgreens stores, for example. The one in New York City's Union Square attracts commuters and tourists using the subway; the store a few blocks north draws mostly local residents. The Union Square site thus carries lots of products such as umbrellas for the unprepared tourists, along with cosmetics and snacks; the other store is more heavily stocked with household-cleaning items and toothpaste.[13] People living and working in urban areas are likely to use public transportation or walk when they go shopping, so they are reluctant to buy bulky items like a 24-pack of toilet paper, and they are active users of Internet retail channels and home delivery services.

Cleveland's East Fourth Street development attracts consumers to the CBD.

Central Business District   The **central business district (CBD)** is the traditional downtown financial and business area in a city or town. Due to its daily activity, it draws many people and employees into the area during business hours. There is a high level of pedestrian traffic, but shopping flow in the evening and on weekends is slow in many CBDs. Vehicular traffic is limited due to congestion in cities, and parking problems reduce consumer convenience. Many CBDs have a large number of residents living in nearby areas.

Risk-taking entrepreneurial developers working with forward-thinking urban planners and city leaders are slowly attracting more people to many CBDs at

night and during weekends. For example, coal and steel are no longer the backbone of Cleveland's economy. City leaders and local developers reinvented the CBD using an entertainment-focused strategy to redevelop East Fourth Street. Retail stores occupy about one-third of the 600,000-square-foot, $110 million, historic redevelopment project. The rest is housing. The area is spectacularly designed with art, flowers, decorative paving, planters, outdoor seating, and special overhead lighting. To increase the foot traffic, two new stadiums for the city's football and baseball teams, a new arena for its (World Champion) basketball team, and the Rock and Roll Hall of Fame were built. Today, city residents and suburbanites flock to East Fourth Street before and after sports and entertainment events, as well as for an interesting afternoon or evening "on the town."[14]

Inner City   During the 1970s and 1980s, many U.S. and some European cities experienced urban decay. **Urban decay** is the process of a previously functioning city, or part of a city, falling into disrepair. The **inner city** is a low-income residential area within a large city. Empty lots, buildings, and condemned houses attract criminal activity, making living in the inner city relatively dangerous. One of the major causes of urban decay is when businesses relocate from urban settings to suburbs.

Some U.S. retailers avoid opening stores in the inner city because they think these stores are riskier and produce lower returns than other areas. Although income levels are lower in inner cities than in other neighborhoods, inner-city retailers often achieve a higher sales volume and higher margins, resulting in higher profits.

But these profits also can be ethically troubling. Inner-city residents and public policy advocates frequently express concerns about the offerings, or lack thereof, at inner-city grocery stores. Instead of fresh meat and produce, they tend to feature lower-priced, less-healthy packaged foods that have longer shelf lives. As a result, many inner-city consumers face **food deserts**, defined as areas that lack ready access to affordable fresh fruits, vegetables, dairy, whole grains, and other healthful foods, as might be provided by grocery stores or farmers' markets.[15] Even as government agencies work with retailers to address this challenge, access to healthy food remains a challenge for lower-income residents of inner cities. For example, though the top U.S. grocery store chains opened more than 10,000 new inner-city locations in the first half of the 2010s, only about 250 of them were full-service supermarkets; the others were convenience or dollar stores that do not offer fresh food options.[16] Nonprofit organizations such as Philadelphia's Food Trust continue to lobby for loans and government subsidies to encourage the entry of supermarkets into lower-income areas.[17]

Retailing thus has an important role to play in inner-city locations. In addition to providing needed consumer services and jobs for inner-city residents, the presence of retailers raises property taxes to support redevelopment efforts. However, inner-city redevelopments also can be controversial. Often local governments will use the right of eminent domain to buy buildings and land and then sell it to developers at an attractive price. Furthermore, as more people move into previously underdeveloped areas, the existing residents may be displaced by the rising prices; even if they are not, they must confront increased traffic and parking challenges.

Gentrified Residential Areas   As the description of inner-city locations suggests, they may go through a process of **gentrification**—the renewal and rebuilding of offices, housing, and retailers in deteriorating areas—coupled with an influx of more affluent people that displaces the former, lower-income residents. Young professionals and retired empty-nesters are moving into these areas to enjoy the convenience of shopping, restaurants, and entertainment near where they live. Well-known retailers like Nordstrom Rack, Whole Foods, Target, Walmart, Office Depot, Home Depot, and Costco, which usually locate in the suburbs, in turn are opening outlets in cities, typically with smaller stores.[18] In some sense, the arrival of an appealing retailer can be the culmination of the process. For example, when Whole Foods opened a Los Angeles location in a new Eighth & Grand apartment complex, "the gentrification [was]

© John Tlumacki/The Boston Globe/Getty Images

Newbury Street in Boston is the center of a gentrified residential area and contains many fashionable shops.

complete."[19] Several stores preceded it, as did most of the residents of the new complex, located in the heart of downtown LA. But Whole Foods, with its vast selection of artisanal cheeses, organic wines, and bicycle delivery services, represents a notable step in the overall gentrification of the area. Whether people who lived there before the redevelopment can afford such options remains an open question.

Main Street

Main Street refers to the traditional downtown shopping area in smaller towns and secondary shopping areas in large cities and their suburbs. Over the past 30 years, many downtowns in small U.S. towns have experienced decay similar to that of inner cities. When Walmart and other big-box retailers opened freestanding stores on

© Craig McCausland/Getty Images

Boulder, Colorado, has a thriving Main Street retail scene.

the outskirts of these towns, local retailers could not compete effectively and went out of business. In response, smaller towns are undertaking redevelopment programs to draw residents back to their downtown areas, and retailers play a major role in these efforts.

To attract consumers and retailers, these Main Street redevelopment efforts focus on providing a better shopping experience than big-box retailers do. Instead of streets, they develop pedestrian walkways. Next to major crosswalks, pedestrian shelters equipped with benches provide shady resting spots for shoppers, helping them extend their visits and prolong their shopping excursions. Property owners can also receive grants if they agree to maintain and enhance their shops' appearance with necessary repairs, new signage, attractive entrances, attention-grabbing windows, and nice awnings. Furthermore, the town administrations work to improve downtown aesthetics with landscaping, which surrounds repaved sidewalks and updated (and functioning) street lights.[20]

Main Street locations share most of the characteristics of locations in gentrified urban areas, but their occupancy costs are generally lower. Main Street locations do not draw as many people as the CBD because fewer people work in the area, and the fewer stores generally mean a smaller overall draw to the area. In addition, Main Streets typically don't offer the range of entertainment and recreational activities available in the more successful primary CBDs. Finally, the planning organization for the town or redevelopment often imposes some restrictions on Main Street store operations.

SHOPPING CENTERS AND PLANNED RETAIL LOCATIONS

LO 7-3

Analyze the characteristics of the different types of shopping centers.

In this section, we discuss the different types of shopping centers and planned locations, as summarized in Exhibit 7–1. A **shopping center** is a group of retail and other commercial establishments that are planned, developed, owned, and managed as a single property. By combining many stores at one location, developments attract more consumers to the shopping center than would be the case if the stores were at separate locations. The developer and shopping center management carefully select a set of retailers that are complementary to provide consumers with a comprehensive shopping experience at one, convenient location.

EXHIBIT 7–1   Characteristics of Different Retail Locations

	Size (000 sq. ft.)	Trading Area (miles)	Annual Occupancy Cost ($ per sq. ft.)	Shopping Convenience	Pedestrian Traffic	Vehicular Traffic	Restrictions on Operations	Typical Tenants
Shopping Centers								
Neighborhood and community shopping centers	30–350	3–6	8–20	High	Low	High	Medium	Supermarkets, discount stores
Power centers	250–600	5–10	10–20	Medium	Medium	Medium	Limited	Category specialists
Regional and super-regional enclosed malls	400–1,000	5–25	10–70	Low	High	Low	High	Department and specialty apparel stores
Lifestyle centers	150–800	5–15	15–35	Medium	Medium	Medium	Medium to high	Specialty apparel and home stores, restaurants
Outlet centers	50–400	25–75	8–15	Low	High	High	Limited	Off-price retailers and factory outlets
Theme/festival centers	80–250	N/A	20–70	Low	High	Low	Highest	Specialty stores and restaurants

Source: Personal communications with industry executives.

Lease agreements typically require that retailers in the center pay a portion of the common area maintenance (CAM) costs for the center according to the size of their store's space and/or sales volume and a retail fee based on sales. The shopping center management group can place restrictions on the operating hours, signage, and even the type of merchandise sold in the stores.

Most shopping centers have at least one or two major retailers, referred to as **anchors**, such as Macy's, Walmart, or Kroger. These retailers are courted by the center's developer because they attract a significant number of consumers and consequently make the center more appealing for other retailers. To get these anchor retailers to locate in a center, developers frequently give them special deals, such as reduced lease costs.

Shopping centers are generally managed by a **shopping center property management firm**, which is a company that specializes in developing, owning, and/or managing shopping centers. Management of these shopping malls entails selecting and negotiating leases with retail tenants, maintaining the common areas, marketing the centers to attract consumers, and providing security.

Convenience, Neighborhood, and Community Shopping Centers

Convenience, **neighborhood**, and **community shopping centers** (also called **strip shopping centers**) are attached rows of open-air stores, with onsite parking usually located in front of the stores. The most common layouts are linear, L-shaped, and inverted U-shaped. Historically, the term *strip center* has applied to the linear configuration.

Smaller centers (convenience and neighborhood centers) are 10,000 to 60,000 square feet and are typically anchored by a supermarket. They are designed for convenience shopping. These centers typically have 10 to 15 smaller retailers such as a bakery, dollar store, dry cleaner, florist, laundry center, barber shop, and mail service. The larger centers (community centers) are typically 25,000 to 50,000 square feet and are anchored by at least one big-box store such as a full-line discount store, an off-price retailer, or a category specialist.

The primary advantages of these centers are that they offer customers convenient locations and easy parking, and they have relatively low occupancy costs. The primary disadvantage is that smaller centers have a limited trade area due to their size, and they lack entertainment and restaurants to keep customers in the center for a longer time. In addition, there is no protection from the weather. As a result, neighborhood and community centers do not attract as many customers as do larger, enclosed malls.

National chains such as The Children's Place, Kohl's, and Marshalls compete effectively against their rival mall-based retailers by offering the convenience of a neighborhood or community center. In these locations, they can offer lower prices, partly because of the lower occupancy cost, and their customers can drive right up to the door.[21]

Power Centers

Power centers are shopping centers that consist primarily of collections of big-box retail stores, such as full-line discount stores (Target), off-price stores (Marshalls), warehouse clubs (Costco), and category specialists (Lowe's, Staples, Michaels, Barnes & Noble, Best Buy, Dick's Sporting Goods, and Toys "R" Us). Although these centers are open air, unlike traditional strip centers, power centers often consist of a collection of free-standing (unconnected) "anchor" stores and only a minimum number of smaller specialty store tenants. Many power centers are located near an enclosed shopping mall.

Power centers offer low occupancy costs and modest levels of consumer convenience and vehicular and pedestrian traffic. The growth in power centers reflects the growth of category specialists. Many power centers are now larger than regional malls and have trade areas as large as regional malls.

Power centers are shopping centers that consist primarily of collections of big-box retail stores.

Enclosed Shopping Malls

Enclosed shopping malls have several advantages over alternative locations. First, shopping malls attract many shoppers and have a large trade area because of the number of stores and the opportunity to combine shopping with an inexpensive form of entertainment. Older citizens get their exercise by walking the malls, and teenagers hang out and meet their friends, though some malls are restricting their admittance in the evenings. Thus, malls generate significant pedestrian traffic inside the mall, especially if they include an Apple Store, as Retailing View 7.1 notes. Second, customers don't have to worry about the weather, thus malls are appealing places to shop during cold winters and hot summers. Third, mall management ensures a level of consistency that benefits all the tenants. For instance, most major malls enforce uniform hours of operation.

However, malls also have disadvantages. First, mall occupancy costs are higher than those of strip centers, freestanding sites, and most central business districts. For example, the occupancy cost (rent, common area maintenance, and taxes) for an enclosed mall is almost 140 percent greater than that for an open-air shopping center ($50 compared with $28 per square foot).[22] Second, some retailers may not like mall management's control of their operations, such as strict rules governing window displays and signage. Third, competition within shopping centers can be intense. Several specialty and department stores might sell very similar merchandise and be located in close proximity. Fourth, freestanding locations, strip centers, lifestyle centers, and power centers are more convenient because customers can park in front of a store, go in and buy what they want, and go about their other errands. Fifth, some malls were built more than 50 years ago and have not been subject to any significant remodeling, so they appear rundown and unappealing to shoppers. Furthermore, these older malls are often located in areas with unfavorable demographics because the population has shifted from the near suburbs to outer suburbs. Sixth, the consolidation in the department store sector has decreased the number of potential anchor tenants and diminished the drawing power of enclosed malls. Finally, the growing sales through the Internet channel is cannibalizing sales in the store channel.

For these reasons, mall traffic and sales are declining.[23] Most malls that close are razed; however, mall managers and developers are trying to redevelop some sites. Some redevelopment projects become mixed-used spaces, incorporating

RETAILING VIEW   How Apple Stores Transform the Mall Equation

To locate their stores in popular malls, retailers pay mall operators rent, which usually reflects the sales per square foot. But the companies running the mall also understand that different tenants have different effects on mall traffic, so they vary the rents they demand from various stores. A small, specialty retailer that benefits mainly from spillover customers from other stores might pay up to 15 percent of its sales per square foot. The department stores that anchor malls and draw most of their customers sometimes pay nothing at all.

But all this conventional wisdom is starting to shift due to the simple presence of about 450 Apple Stores worldwide (256 of them in the United States). Because Apple fans are so eager to visit the well-designed, comforting stores, Apple can draw crowds to a mall like no other retailer has done in the past. Specifically, some estimates suggest that adding an Apple Store increases a mall's average foot traffic by about 10 percent. On average, each Apple Store earns a sizable $6,000 per square foot per year, and the most popular stores reach as high as $10,000 per square foot, compared to the average for the most productive mall in the United States, the Bal Harbour Shops in South Florida, which earns about $3,000 per square foot.

Noting its value to the mall and the other tenants, Apple has demanded substantial breaks on the rents it pays, such that it refuses to go higher than 2 percent of its sales per square foot. Although these rates are much lower than other retailers', they do not quite get the nearly free ride that malls offer to department stores. That is because visitors to Apple Stores often head straight for the technology retailer and its

Apple Stores are so popular that Apple can get substantial breaks on the rents it pays.

Genius Bar, without stopping to shop with other tenants in the mall. Department stores instead act like feeders to the rest of the mall, so their value overall is generally greater. Moreover, the presence of an Apple Store enables mall operators to turn to their other tenants, point to the increased foot traffic, and demand higher rents from them.

Sources: Suzanne Kapner, "Apple Gets Sweet Deal from Mall Operators," *The Wall Street Journal*, March 10, 2015; Krystina Gustafson, "Malls That Rake in the Most Sales per Square Foot," CNBC, June 8, 2015.

unconventional tenants like government offices, churches, medical clinics, and satellite university campuses. Others, such as the Arcade, which was the oldest enclosed mall in the United States, convert their space into residential "micro-apartments."[24] Still others seek to become one-stop sources for various services, not just fashionable apparel. A busy working mother visiting The Westside Pavilion mall in Los Angeles can thus drop off her kids for piano lessons at Music Stars & Masters on the second floor. During their lesson, she also can send an overnight package, get a haircut, have her purse repaired, and check out some books for the kids from the public library. If the kids do well with their lessons, mom might treat them to ice cream, too.[25]

Another approach for dealing with aging malls and the changing demographics in their trade areas is to tailor the offerings to the markets that do exist today. Older shopping centers such as Northridge Mall in northern California (built in 1972) can be repositioned to appeal to immigrant populations. In recent decades, the demographics of Monterey County have changed, producing a rich Latino culture in which approximately 75 percent of the population in the mall's trade area is of Latino heritage. Property managers thus are trying to lure Latinos with a combination of live entertainment, children's rides, and a mix of food and retail options. The courtyard at the entryway to the mall hosts mariachi bands on weekend afternoons, while clowns and dancers provide family-friendly entertainment underneath colorful piñatas that have been suspended from the ceiling. To appeal to the large Roman Catholic population, the mall also offers services with religious themes, such as celebrations on Día de los Santos Reyes and shrines to the Virgen de Guadalupe Las Posadas. The idea is that the mall

Some aging malls in areas with changing demographics are being repositioned to appeal to immigrant populations.

can be so welcoming that the local community views it more like a weekend home than a retail destination.[26]

Influxes of exciting new tenants in some malls such as Forever 21, Sephora, and H&M have drawn customers, and anchors such as Macy's and Nordstrom are enjoying improved performance. Furthermore, discount retailers such as Ross and TJ Maxx have taken advantage of closures by some traditional mall tenants such as Radio Shack and moved their operations to these appealing locations, which the mall operators are eager to fill and thus might offer for a relatively lower rental rate.[27] These redevelopment efforts and new tenants have improved the overall health of some enclosed malls.

Lifestyle Centers

Lifestyle centers are shopping centers that have an open-air configuration of specialty stores, entertainment, and restaurants, with design ambience and amenities such as fountains and street furniture. Lifestyle centers resemble the main streets in small towns, where people stroll from store to store, have lunch, and sit for a while on a park bench talking to friends. Thus, they cater to the "lifestyles" of consumers in their trade areas. Lifestyle centers are particularly attractive to specialty retailers.

People are attracted to lifestyle centers not only because of their shops and restaurants but also because of their outdoor attractions such as a pop-up fountain, ice cream carts, stilt walkers, balloon artists, magicians, face painters, concerts, and other events. Because some lifestyle centers have limited auto access, customers can be dropped off right in front of a store.

Lifestyle centers are open air, so bad weather can be an impediment to traffic. But some centers, like the Easton Town Center in Columbus, Ohio, thrive despite the climate.[28] When the weather is bad, tough Ohioans simply bundle up and take a stroll.

Due to the ease of parking, lifestyle centers are very convenient for shoppers, and the occupancy costs, like those of all open-air developments, are considerably lower than those for enclosed malls. But they typically have less retail space than enclosed

© Ty Wright/Bloomberg/Getty Images

Resembling main streets in small towns, lifestyle centers like the Easton Town Center in Columbus, Ohio, are shopping centers that have an open-air configuration of specialty stores, entertainment, and restaurants, with design ambience and amenities such as fountains and street furniture.

malls and thus may attract fewer customers than enclosed malls. Many lifestyle centers are located near higher-income areas, so the higher purchases per visit compensate for the fewer number of shoppers. Finally, many lifestyle centers are part of larger, mixed-use developments, which are described in the next section.

Mixed-Use Developments

Mixed-use developments (MXDs) combine several different uses into one complex including retail, office, residential, hotel, recreation, or other functions. They are pedestrian-oriented and therefore facilitate a live-work-play environment.[29] They appeal to people who have had enough of long commutes to work and the social fragmentation of their neighborhoods and are looking for a lifestyle that gives them more time for the things they enjoy and an opportunity to live in a genuine community. In addition, MXDs are popular with retailers because they bring additional shoppers to their stores. They are also popular with governments, urban planners, developers, and environmentalists because they provide a pleasant, pedestrian environment and are an efficient use of space. For instance, land costs the same whether a developer builds a shopping mall by itself or an office tower on top of the mall or parking structure.

The Boca Mall, a 430,000-square-foot regional shopping mall in Boca Raton, Florida, opened in 1974. Decades later, the mall was plagued by two trends: population growth occurring elsewhere and competing malls that were attracting most of its patrons. The original anchors and many of the specialty stores departed. The Boca Mall was demolished and replaced with a mixed-use development called Mizner Park. Mizner Park has commercial office space located above the ground-floor retail space on one side of the street, and residential units sit above the retail space on the opposite side of the street.[30]

Outlet Centers

Outlet centers are shopping centers that contain mostly manufacturers' and retailers' outlet stores.[31] Some outlet centers have a strong entertainment component, including movie theaters and restaurants to keep customers on the premises longer. For example, the Outlets at Orange, in Orange, California, has a multiplex theater, with an IMAX movie theater; a children's play area; and Thrill It Fun Center.[32] Furthermore, increasing numbers of high-end fashion brands and designers are opening shops in outlet centers, seeking to gain access to entry-level consumers who might be willing to pay a little less to get last season's Alexander McQueen designs.[33]

Typically, outlet centers are in remote locations. These remote locations offer lower costs and reduce the competition between the outlet stores and department and specialty stores offering the branded merchandise at full price. But as outlet centers have grown more common, consumers have grown to expect ready access to them, such that operators are opening more proximal centers: 70 percent of the outlet centers that opened in one recent year were in metropolitan areas that contained at least 1 million residents.[34]

Tourism represents a majority of the traffic generated for many outlet centers. Thus, many are located with convenient interstate access and close to popular tourist attractions. Some center developers actually organize bus tours to bring people hundreds of miles to their malls. As a result, the primary trade area for some outlet centers is 50 miles or more. Outlet centers are also very popular in Europe, Japan, and China. Retailing View 7.2 describes an upscale outlet center with a unique theme in China.

7.2   RETAILING VIEW   For China's High-End Fashion Consumers, "Italy" Is Now Just a Bullet Train Away

Between Beijing and Tijanjin, you can find an Italian village—or at least a themed outlet mall that seeks to recreate one. With its more than 200 luxury-brand offerings, Florentia Village drew over 4.3 million visitors in 2014, most of whom came to check out the reproduced sixteenth-century Italian village, with its narrow streets and piazzas. Once they experienced the trip back in history, they could indulge in purchases of Italian luxury brands, including Armani, Ferragamo, Prada, Fendi, Bulgari, and Moncler. Near the "Colosseum," Tod's, Tory Burch, Marc by Marc Jacobs, and Brooks Brothers maintain their storefronts, whereas customers move through the "Grand Canal Promenade" to find Fendi, Burberry, and Prada.

China is both the largest source of counterfeits in the world and one of the biggest markets for luxury goods—valued at $17 billion in 2015. The visitors who arrive at Florentia Village in the morning come by train. Wearing Western clothes, they are mostly young, evidently wealthy, and obviously Chinese. Later in the day, wealthy women wearing designer clothing drive their SUVs into the parking lots; they actively avoid the crowds of visitors on the weekends.

Although Chinese-owned outlet malls have existed for more than a decade, their success has been limited by their failure to attract top brands. These top brands worried about the effect of outlet sales on their brand images. The lesson learned is that an outlet mall's quality image is crucial; it must look like a location that sells luxury. Florentia Village thus has created an environment that is unique: Customers can enjoy "foreign" architecture, cafés, and luxury brands, all while still saving about 70 percent off the conventional prices of the designer products.

Buoyed by this success, the RDM Group, which owns Florentia Village, has opened two more locations, in Shanghai and Guangfo, and seeks to open another four locations within the next year or so. In turn, the growing success of these local

The Florentia Village outlet center in China draws young and evidently wealthy customers from around the country.

luxury outlets has affected the global luxury market: In 2015, spending on luxury goods by Chinese tourists abroad fell for the first time in 15 years. Although overall tourist spending in Europe might have declined due to other global factors too, the dip in Chinese customer spending is notable and troublesome, especially considering that China accounts for about one-third of the global luxury market.

Sources: http://www.florentiavillage.com/jj-en/aboutus.html; Yanie Durocher, "Discount-Chic in China: Florentia Village Brings Italian Glamour to Outlet Shopping," *Jing Daily*, February 11, 2015; Cherry Cao, "Italian Retailer Eyes 5 More Outlets," ShanghaiDaily.com, January 23, 2015; Christopher Horton, " When It Comes to Luxury, China Still Leads," *The New York Times*, April 5, 2016; "Luxury Goods Spending by Chinese Tourists Down 24 PCT in March," *Reuters*, April 15, 2016; Christopher Carothers, "A New Outlet for China's Consumerism," *The Wall Street Journal*, March 8, 2012; Peter Foster, "China Builds Replica of Italian Town Called Florentia Village," *The Telegraph*, June 27, 2011.

© David Wall Photo/Getty Images

The Grand Canal Shops at the Venetian Hotel in Las Vegas is a theme/festival center with a unifying theme.

Theme/Festival Centers

In **theme/festival centers**, a unifying theme generally is reflected in each individual store, both in their architecture and the merchandise they sell. Theme/festival centers are a relatively new type of shopping center. In the late 1970s, a private developer took Boston's historic Faneuil Hall and reconceived it as a "festival marketplace." The goal was to attract multitudes of tourists and local visitors by being more fun and interesting than a basic suburban mall. The Faneuil Hall Marketplace resonates with a colonial history theme. Subsequent applications of the idea have included Baltimore's Inner Harbor and the Grand Canal Shops at the Venetian Hotel in Las Vegas.

When they first opened, some of these festival locations were successful at drawing visitors and reinvigorating urban centers suffering from crime and an exodus of population. But now, with invented themes, generic stores, and vigorous competition from other nearby retailers, such centers are viewed by many as tourist traps and are avoided by many locals. In 1985, the themed shopping center that opened on Pier 17 in Lower Manhattan promised to reinvigorate the South Street Seaport. After decades of disappointment though, new owners tore down the three-story building and sought to replace it with a controversial mixed-use development hosting retail, residential, and commercial space.[35]

Larger, Multiformat Developments

New shopping center developments are combining enclosed malls, lifestyle centers, and power centers. Although centers of this type do not have an official name, they reasonably might be referred to as **omnicenters**.

Omnicenters represent a response to several trends in retailing, including the desire of tenants to lower CAM charges by spreading the costs among more tenants and to function inside larger developments that generate more pedestrian traffic and longer shopping trips. In addition, they reflect the growing tendency of consumers to **cross-shop**, which is a pattern of buying both premium and low-priced merchandise or patronizing expensive, status-oriented retailers and price-oriented retailers, as occurs when a customer shops at both Walmart and Nordstrom. Time-scarce customers are also attracted to omnicenters because they can get everything they need in one place. For example, the 1.3 million-square-foot St. John's Town Center in Jacksonville, Florida, is divided into three components: a lifestyle center with a Dillard's department store anchor, a mini–power center anchored by Dick's Sporting Goods and a Barnes & Noble bookstore, and a Main Street with Cheesecake Factory and P.F. Chang's restaurants as anchors.[36]

NONTRADITONAL LOCATIONS

LO 7-4

Discuss nontraditional retail locations.

Pop-up stores, stores within a store, and kiosks are other location alternatives for many retailers. Retailing View 7.3 describes some of Subway's nontraditional locations and the accommodations it needed to make to secure those locations.

Pop-Up Stores and Other Temporary Locations

Pop-up stores are stores in temporary locations that focus on new products or a limited group of products. These "stores" have been around for centuries as individuals sold merchandise on city streets and at festivals or concerts, such as the Newport Jazz Festival, weekend craft fairs, or farmers' markets. For instance, in New York's Columbus Circle, 100 vendors sell a variety of gifts from yogawear to handmade glass jewelry. Cities around the United States generally welcome these temporary retailers because they bring people and money to areas, creating excitement. Local retailers, who pay high rents, aren't necessarily so enthusiastic because some of the temporary retailers sell competing merchandise.

Since shopping center vacancies have increased and occupancy costs have decreased, retailers and manufacturers are opening pop-up stores in these vacant locations. Pop-up stores are particularly attractive to retailers with highly seasonal

---

7.3 RETAILING VIEW   Subway Goes to Church

In 2011, Subway Restaurants passed McDonald's to become the largest restaurant chain in the world, in terms of number of locations. It has continued on this pace, such that Subway's 44,000 locations far surpass McDonald's 36,000. Subway has achieved this rapid growth partly by opening stores in nontraditional locations: an appliance store in Brazil, an automobile showroom in California, a Goodwill store in South Carolina, a riverboat in Germany. One of the more remarkable locations was its One World Trade Center construction site in New York City, where the restaurant got hoisted up to the next level as each floor of the 105-story building was completed. As the chain's chief development officer puts it, "We're continually looking at just about any opportunity for someone to buy a sandwich, wherever that might be. The closer we can get to the customer, the better." Noting the more than 10,500 Subways in unusual locations, he adds, "The non-traditional is becoming traditional."

With its menu of sandwiches, Subway has an easier time opening in unusual venues because it has a simpler kitchen than traditional fast-food restaurants, which require frying and grilling equipment. Hospitals and religious facilities have a favorable attitude toward Subway because it promotes its sandwiches as a fresher, healthier alternative to traditional fast food.

Subway often has to make special accommodations when opening stores in nontraditional locations, though. For example, the first of many kosher Subway stores opened in the Jewish Community Center of Cleveland in 2006, and Subway is now the largest kosher chain in the United States. The kosher stores still have steak and cheese subs, except the cheese is a soy-based product. In observance of the Jewish Sabbath, these restaurants are closed on Friday afternoon and all day Saturday.

When a Subway opened in the True Bethel Baptist Church of Buffalo, New York, in a low-income area of town,

To maintain growth, Subway has opened outlets in nontraditional locations like this one at a Baptist church in Buffalo, New York.

the franchisee worked closely with church leaders. To support the congregation and create jobs, church leaders had approached several fast-food franchisers about opening a franchise in a corner of the church. Subway was the only chain that was flexible enough toward the space available and the operating hours to accommodate the church. The chain agreed to waive its requirement of a Subway sign on the outside of the building and created a parking pattern to keep restaurant traffic from displacing churchgoers during services.

Sources: http://www.subway.com/en-us/aboutus/history; http://www.aboutmcdonalds.com/content/mcd/investors.html; Subway Restaurants, "Subway Restaurant Goal to Add More Than 2,500 Locations Worldwide in 2015," PR Newswire, May 17, 2015; Jonathan Maze, "How Much Bigger Can Subway Get?," *Restaurant Finance Monitor*, May 6, 2014; Julie Jargon, "Unusual Store Locations Fuel Subway's Growth," *The Wall Street Journal*, March 10, 2011; Alan J. Liddle, "10 Non-Traditional Subway Restaurants," *Nation's Restaurants*, July 26, 2011.

sales such as Toys "R" Us. Toys "R" Us has been experimenting with pop-ups for several years, starting with separate Express stores and then expanding its options by opening smaller, temporary stores within Macy's stores in the months leading up to the holiday season (see the next section on stores-within-a-store).[37] Other pop-up experiments are even more creative, including a pop-up store in Manhattan's trendy Meatpacking district to present a new Volvo model,[38] temporary stores selling buttons prompting the Republican or Democratic Parties in the weeks leading into their national conventions, or Life of Pablo shops that Kanye West has opened in various cities around the world.[39]

Birchbox's pop-up store is in a temporary location and focuses on a limited selection of products.

Cities have adopted the pop-up store concept to revitalize their neighborhoods too. In Oakland, California, the Pop-Up Hood concept grants six months' worth of rent-free space to independent retailers if they agree to test their innovative retail concepts in designated parts of the inner city.[40] On the other end of the spectrum, pop-up stores thrive in the summer months in the Hamptons, where wealthy New Englanders often spend their vacations. With relatively less investment, high-end boutiques can introduce their offerings to clientele who might be ready to spend immediately or else could recall the brand later, even after they return home.[41]

Store-within-a-Store

Store-within-a-store locations involve an agreement in which a retailer rents a part of the retail space in a store operated by another independent retailer. The host retailer basically "sublets" the space to the store-within retailer.[42] The store-within retailer manages the assortment, inventory, personnel, and systems and delivers a percentage of the sales or profits to the host. Grocery stores have been experimenting with the store-within-a-store concept for years with service providers such as coffee bars, banks, film processors, and medical clinics. Starbucks operates cafés in many retail stores.

Department stores in the United States have traditionally leased some space to other retailers, such as retailers of beauty salons, fine jewelry, and furs. Macy's experiments with a wealth of partners, including Toy "R" Us, as we noted in the previous section, and Best Buy. Mini–Best Buys in select Macy's locations take up about 300 square feet of space and offer tablets, smartphones, smartwatches, audio devices, and accessories. As it does in traditional Best Buy stores, Samsung has a strong presence. Staffing the in-store stores, Best Buy personnel are ready to answer shoppers' questions about high-tech devices. Macy's customers seek more variety in the items available to them, whether to purchase for themselves or as gifts. By adding the latest and coolest electronics gadgets, Macy's ensures that it is a shopping destination for virtually anyone.[43]

Macy's has an Apple store-within-a store at its flagship location in New York.

Macy's is notable in the States, but most department stores in Europe, Japan, and China are a collection of store-within-a-store retailers. For example, Modern Plaza, a luxury department store in Beijing, "rents" all of the space in its store to a set of luxury brands, and the brands operate a store within Modern Plaza. Thus, Modern Plaza performs the role of mall manager rather than a retail store.[44]

Stores-within-a-store can be mutually beneficial to the store within and the host retailer. For example, Ace Hardware recently announced plans to work with local grocers and small chains to create combined storefronts that offer greater convenience for consumers. For Ace, the new initiative enables it to grow in a new direction. For the local grocers, many of whom own both the grocery store and the Ace franchise, the retail innovation should help drive more traffic into their stores. For customers, the collaboration means they can pick up both groceries and the lug nuts they've been needing in a single trip.[45] In general, the inserted store within gets an excellent location with high pedestrian traffic of customers in its target market. The host retailer generates increased revenue from the space and enhances its brand image. However, there are risks associated with this arrangement. Over time, the host or store within could have conflicting, rather than synergistic, target markets and/or brand images.

Merchandise Kiosks

Merchandise kiosks are small selling spaces, typically located in the walkways of enclosed malls, airports, college campuses, or office building lobbies. Some are staffed and resemble a miniature store or cart that could be easily moved. Others are twenty-first-century versions of vending machines, such as the Apple kiosks that sell iPods and other high-volume Apple products.

For mall operators, kiosks are an opportunity to generate rental income in otherwise vacant space and offer a broad assortment of merchandise for visitors. They also can generate excitement from retailers like national cell phone provider Sprint to smaller niche products like Israeli Dead Sea cosmetics, leading to additional sales for the entire mall. Moreover, mall kiosks can be changed quickly to match seasonal demand.

When planning the location of kiosks in a mall, operators are sensitive to their regular mall tenants' needs. They are careful to avoid kiosks that block any storefronts, create an incompatible image, or actually compete directly with permanent tenants by selling similar merchandise.

LOCATION AND RETAIL STRATEGY

Match the locations to the retailer's strategy.

The selection of a location type reinforces the retailer's strategy. Thus, the location-type decision is consistent with the shopping behavior and size of the target market and the retailer's positioning in its target market. Each of these factors is discussed next.

Shopping Behavior of Consumers in Retailer's Target Market

A critical factor affecting the type of location that consumers select to visit is the shopping situation in which they are involved. Three types of shopping situations are convenience shopping, comparison shopping, and specialty shopping.

Convenience Shopping   When consumers are engaged in **convenience shopping** situations, they are primarily concerned with minimizing their effort to get the product or service they want. They are relatively insensitive to price and indifferent about which brands to buy. Thus, they don't spend much time evaluating different brands or retailers; they simply want to make the purchase as quickly and easily as possible. Examples of convenience shopping situations are getting a cup of coffee during a work break, buying gas for a car, or buying milk for breakfast in the morning.

Retailers targeting customers involved in convenience shopping, such as quick-service restaurants, convenience stores, and gas stations, usually locate their stores close to where their customers are and make it easy for them to access the location, park, and find what they want. Thus, convenience stores, drugstores, fast-food restaurants, supermarkets, and full-line discount stores are generally located in neighborhood strip centers and freestanding locations. Both CBDs and Main Street locations are prime locations for convenience shopping for people who are on the move, going to and from work or other errands.

Comparison Shopping   Consumers involved in **comparison shopping** situations are more involved in the purchase decision. They have a general idea about the type of product or service they want, but they do not have a well-developed preference for a brand or model. Because the purchase decisions are more important to them, they seek information and are willing to expend effort to compare alternatives. Consumers typically engage in this type of shopping behavior when buying furniture, appliances, apparel, consumer electronics, and hand tools.

Furniture retailers, for instance, often locate next to one another to create a "furniture row." In New York City, a number of retailers selling houseplants and flowers are all located in Chelsea between 27th and 30th Streets on 6th Avenue, and diamond dealers are located on West 47th Street between 5th and 6th Avenues. These competing retailers locate near one another because doing so facilitates comparison shopping and thus attracts many customers to the locations.

Enclosed malls offer the same benefits to consumers interested in comparison shopping for fashionable apparel. Thus, department stores and specialty apparel retailers locate in enclosed malls for the same reason that houseplant retailers locate together on 6th Avenue in New York City. By co-locating in the same mall, they attract more potential customers interested in comparison shopping for fashionable apparel. Even though the enclosed mall might be inconvenient compared with a freestanding location, comparison shopping is easier after the customers have arrived.

Category specialists offer the same benefit of comparison shopping as a collection of co-located specialty stores like those described previously. Rather than going to a set of small hardware stores when comparison shopping for an electric drill, consumers know they can get almost anything they need to fix or build a house in either Home Depot or Lowe's.

Convenience stores (top) usually locate close to where their customers are and make it easy for them to access the location, park, and find what they want. Shopping stores (middle) usually locate in close proximity to other shopping stores selling the same type of merchandise. It doesn't matter as much where a specialty store (bottom) is located because its customers will seek it out.

Thus, category specialists are **destination stores**, places where consumers will go even if it is inconvenient, just like enclosed malls are destination locations for fashionable-apparel comparison shopping. Category specialists locate in power centers, primarily to reduce their costs and create awareness of their location and secondarily to benefit from multiple retailers that attract more consumers and the resulting potential for cross-shopping. Basically, power centers are a collection of destination stores.

Specialty Shopping   When consumers go **specialty shopping**, they know what they want and will not accept a substitute. They are brand and/or retailer loyal and will pay a premium or expend extra effort, if necessary, to get exactly what they want. Examples of these shopping occasions include buying organic vegetables, a luxury automobile, or a high-end road or mountain bike. The retailers they patronize when specialty shopping also are destination stores. Thus, consumers engaged in specialty shopping are willing to travel to an inconvenient location. Having a convenient location is not as important for retailers selling unique merchandise or services.

Density of Target Market

A second, but closely related, factor that affects the retailer's choice of location type is the density of the retailer's target market in relation to the location. A good location has many people in the target market who are drawn to it. Thus, a convenience store located in a CBD can be sustained by customers living or working in fairly close proximity to the store. Similarly, a comparison shopping store located next to a Walmart is a potentially good location because Walmart draws lots of customers from a very large area. It is not as important to have high customer density near a store that sells specialty merchandise because people are willing to search out this type of merchandise. A Porsche dealer, for instance, need not be near other car dealers or in close proximity to its target market, because those seeking this luxury car will drive to wherever the dealer may be. However, Tesla purposefully locates its innovative dealerships in high-traffic areas because its goal is to introduce the brand and its offerings to as wide an audience as possible, even if passersby might not immediately be ready to buy a $120,000 electric vehicle.[46]

Uniqueness of Retail Offering

Finally, the convenience of their locations is less important for retailers with unique, differentiated offerings than for retailers with an offering similar to other retailers. For example, Bass Pro Shops stores provide a unique merchandise assortment and store atmosphere. Customers will travel to wherever the store is located, and its location will become a destination.

SOCIETAL AND LEGAL CONSIDERATIONS

LO 7-6

Review the societal and legal considerations in selecting locations.

Societal and legal considerations often restrict where retailers can locate and operate their stores. These restrictions reflect the general concern that many communities have with urban sprawl, and more specifically with the opening of big-box retail stores in their communities. These restrictions on store location are often implemented through local zoning ordinances.

While there are relatively few restrictions on where stores can be located in the United States, location decisions are more restricted in other areas of the world. For example, western Europe and Asia have higher population densities and more people living and shopping in urban environments. Thus, less space is available for retailing, and the space that is available is costly. In addition, many western European countries restrict retailing to specific areas and then restrict the sizes of the stores that can be built.

In this section, we discuss the nature of the restrictions, reasons communities impose these restrictions, and the impact of these restrictions on society.

Urban Sprawl

Urban sprawl is the increased expansion of residential and shopping center development in suburban and rural areas outside of their respective urban centers. Before World War II, the downtown urban area was a community's commercial hub. Consumers shopped at local businesses downtown. The presence of offices, banks, and libraries guaranteed traffic in the downtown center. Downtown also was an important part of an area's social life. On weekends, people met to window shop, eat at restaurants, and go to the movies.

The interstate highway system and growth of the suburbs changed the way Americans live and work. With improved transportation, people could travel longer distances to work or shop. As a result, many downtown retailers went out of business. As customers and sales dwindled, property values and tax revenues dropped. Historic buildings were neglected and storefronts boarded up, reinforcing the decline of downtown areas.

In addition to the decline of the downtown, some other negative consequences of urban sprawl are congestion and air pollution due to increased automobile travel, loss of farmland, concentrated poverty, and racial and economic segregation. On the other hand, some desirable outcomes of this migration to the suburbs are better housing opportunities, public schools, and less crime.[47]

The European Union is very concerned about urban sprawl and the effects of big-box retailers locating outside the city limits. The EU is trying to restrain the growth of big-box retailers, limiting their size and subsidizing the redevelopment of the inner city (called the High Street in the United Kingdom) to help local retailers compete. Europe has greater population density and less space than the United States, and stricter planning and greenbelt laws provide a sharp division between town and country. Suburbs are few, thus minimizing urban sprawl. But preserving the environment comes at a cost for Europe. The limits on out-of-town, big-box retailing reduce competition and retailing efficiency, causing higher prices.[48]

Opposition to Big-Box Retailers

Retailers that operate big-box stores like Walmart, Target, Costco, and Home Depot often meet with a great deal of resistance when they plan to build a store in a community. Many people vehemently oppose big-box stores entering their community. The opponents of the store openings argue that these retailers sell merchandise at lower prices that drive local retailers out of business; do not provide a living wage for employees; hire part-time workers to avoid providing health insurance benefits; and achieve their low prices by manufacturing merchandise outside the United States, thus contributing to the decline of U.S. jobs.

Discussions between big-box stores and local communities continue to occur throughout the United States and other countries. Some communities have allowed for the building of such stores when the retailers agree to pay employees a set wage or fund low-cost housing for employees. Zoning, discussed in the following section, is one method used by local communities to restrict big-box retailers.

Zoning

Local governments in the United States use **zoning** to regulate land uses in specific areas to prevent any interference with existing uses by residents or businesses, as well as encourage the preservation of a community's sense of identity. Thus, zoning ordinances might keep McDonald's from opening a franchise in a residential neighborhood. In other nations, such as France and Germany, zoning regulations and planning are enforced at national or state levels instead of locally.

In urban areas, zoning ordinances often specify five categories of activities that are acceptable in a certain region or on a particular site: residential, commercial, mixed residential and commercial, industrial, or special. In addition, most zoning regulations include detailed density limitations, such as those indicating whether an area may host high-density high rises or instead is limited to low-density, single-family housing. Noting that exceptions can exist, most ordinances denote the conditions—usually hardship-related—that must be met for variances to be granted.

EXHIBIT 7–2 Zoning Map of Superior, Wisconsin

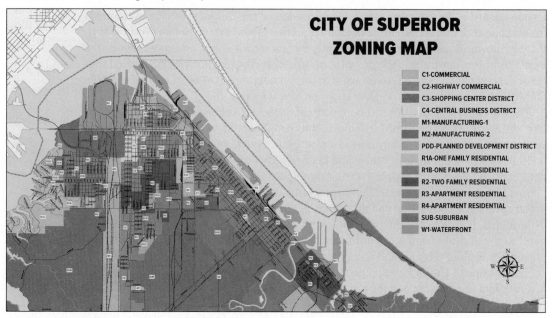

Source: City of Superior, Wisconsin.

Exhibit 7–2 describes the zoning restrictions in Superior, Wisconsin. These zoning maps are typically developed by a planning commission and approved by the city council. Note that the areas dedicated for retailing shown in red are adjacent to the two major highways. Some areas (shown in green) are dedicated open spaces and residential areas are shown in yellow.

Building Codes

Building codes are legal restrictions that specify the type of building, signs, size and type of parking lot, and so forth that can be used at a particular location. Some building codes require a certain-sized parking lot or a particular architectural design. In Santa Fe, New Mexico, for instance, building codes require that buildings keep a traditional mud stucco (adobe) style.

Building codes in Santa Fe, New Mexico, require that buildings keep a traditional mud stucco (adobe) style.

Signs Restrictions on the use of signs can affect a particular site's desirability. Sign sizes and styles may be restricted by building codes, zoning ordinances, or even the shopping center management group. At the Bal Harbour Shops in North Miami Beach, for example, all signs (even sale signs) must be approved by the shopping center management group before implementation by each individual retailer.

Licensing Requirements Licensing requirements may vary in different parts of a region. For instance, some Dallas neighborhoods are dry, meaning no alcoholic beverages can be sold; in other areas, only wine and beer can be sold. Such restrictions can affect retailers other than restaurants and bars. For instance, a theme/festival shopping center that restricts the use of alcoholic beverages may find its clientele limited at night.

SUMMARY

LO 7-1 **Describe the types of retail locations available to retailers.**

Store location decisions are important decisions for a retailer because location is typically one of the most influential considerations in a customer's store-choice decision. Location decisions also have strategic implications because they can be used to develop a sustainable competitive advantage and location decisions are risky.

LO 7-2 **Review the types of unplanned locations.**

Two basic types of location are unplanned (freestanding and urban sites) and planned (shopping centers). Unplanned locations do not have centralized management that determines what stores will be in a development, where the specific stores will be located, and how they will be operated. The three types of unplanned retail locations are freestanding sites, urban, and Main Street locations. Freestanding locations are convenient for customers and have high vehicular traffic and visibility, modest occupancy costs, and few restrictions. But freestanding sites are higher in cost and have smaller trade areas. In general, urban locations have lower occupancy costs than enclosed malls; vehicular traffic is limited, and parking problems reduce consumer convenience. Many central business districts, inner-city, and Main Street locations have become more viable options than they were in the past because of gentrification of the areas, tax incentives, and lack of competition.

LO 7-3 **Analyze the characteristics of the different types of shopping centers.**

By combining many stores at one location, shopping centers attract more consumers to the center than would be the case if the stores were at separate locations. The developer and shopping center management carefully select a set of retailers that are complementary to provide consumers with a comprehensive shopping experience at one, convenient location.

There are a wide variety of shopping center types for retailers. They can locate in a strip or power center; an enclosed mall; or a lifestyle, theme/festival, or outlet center.

LO 7-4 **Discuss nontraditional retail locations.**

Pop-up stores, stores-within-a-store, and kiosks are other location alternatives for many retailers. Pop-up stores are particularly attractive to retailers with highly seasonal sales. Store-within-a-store locations involve an agreement in which a retailer rents a part of the retail space in a store operated by another independent retailer. These locations are mutually beneficial to the host and store within. Kiosks are small selling spaces, typically located in walkways. They offer retailers a selling opportunity at a relatively low cost due to the small size. But when located in a mall, they can be detrimental to the more permanent retailers.

LO 7-5 **Match the locations to the retailer's strategy.**

The selection of a location type reinforces the retailer's strategy. Thus, the location-type decision is consistent with the shopping behavior and size of the target market and the retailer's positioning in its target market. Different shopping locations are more appropriate for consumers engaged in three types of customer shopping situations: convenience shopping, comparison shopping, and specialty shopping.

LO 7-6 **Review the societal and legal considerations in selecting locations.**

Societal and legal considerations often restrict the locations and operations of stand-alone stores and shopping centers. These restrictions reflect the general concern that many communities have with urban sprawl and, more specifically, with the opening of big-box retail stores in their communities. Shopping center developers and retailers often need to deal with zoning ordinances and building codes before they open stores in a community.

KEY TERMS

anchor, *183*

building codes, *196*

central business district (CBD), *179*

common area maintenance (CAM), *178*

community shopping center, *183*

comparison shopping, *193*

convenience shopping, *192*

convenience shopping center, *183*

cross-shop, *189*

destination store, *194*

food desert, *180*

freestanding site, *178*

gentrification, *180*

gross leasable area (GLA), *178*

inner city, *180*

lifestyle center, *186*

Main Street, *181*

merchandise kiosk, *192*

mixed-use development (MXD), *187*

neighborhood shopping center, *183*

omnicenter, *189*

outlet center, *187*

outparcel, *179*

planned location, *178*

pop-up store, *190*

power center, *183*

shopping center, *182*

shopping center property management firm, *183*

specialty shopping, *194*

store-within-a-store, *191*

strip shopping center, *183*

theme/festival center, *189*

trade area, *178*

unplanned location, *178*

urban decay, *180*

urban sprawl, *195*

zoning, *195*

GET OUT AND DO IT!

1. **CONTINUING CASE ASSIGNMENT** Interview the manager of the shopping center that contains the retailer you selected for the Continuing Case Assignment. Write a report summarizing which retailers the shopping center manager thinks are his or her best tenants and why they are valued. How does the manager rate the retailer you have selected? What criteria does he or she use?

2. **INTERNET EXERCISE** Go to the web page for Faneuil Hall Marketplace at **www.faneuilhallmarketplace.com** and the online site for CocoWalk at **www.cocowalk.net**. What kinds of centers are these? List their similarities and differences. Who is the target market for each of these retail locations?

3. **GO SHOPPING** Go to your favorite shopping center and analyze the tenant mix. Do the tenants appear to complement one another? What changes would you make in the tenant mix to increase the overall performance of the center?

4. **GO SHOPPING** Visit a lifestyle center. What tenants are found in this location? Describe the population characteristics around this center. How far would people drive to shop at this lifestyle center? What other types of retail locations does this lifestyle center compete with?

5. **INTERNET EXERCISE** Go to the home page of your favorite enclosed mall and describe the mall in terms of the following characteristics: number of anchor stores, number and categories of specialty stores, number of sit-down and quick-service restaurants, and types of entertainment offered. What are the strengths and weaknesses of this assortment of retailers? What are the unique features of this particular mall?

6. **GO SHOPPING** Visit a power center that contains a Target, Staples, Dick's Sporting Goods, Home Depot, or other category specialists. What other retailers are in the same location? How is this mix of stores beneficial to both shoppers and retailers?

7. **INTERNET EXERCISE** Review the research summarized at **http://www.accessmagazine.org/articles/spring-2015/the-first-big-box-store-in-davis/**. How did Target opening a store in Davis, California, affect the town? Summarize the benefits and harms. Are you surprised by the study findings? Why or why not?

DISCUSSION QUESTIONS AND PROBLEMS

1. Why is store location such an important decision for retailers?

2. Pick your favorite store. Describe the advantages and disadvantages of its current location, given its store type and target market.

3. Home Depot typically locates in either a power center or a freestanding site. What are the strengths of each location for this home improvement retailer?

4. As a consultant to 7-Eleven convenience stores, American Eagle Outfitters, and Porsche of America, what would you say is the single most important factor in choosing a site for these three very different types of stores?

5. Retailers are locating in urban areas that have suffered decay. As a result, these areas are rejuvenating, a process known as gentrification. Some people have questioned the ethical and social ramifications of this process. Discuss the benefits and detriments of gentrification.

6. Staples and Office Depot/OfficeMax have strong multi-channel strategies. How do competition and the Internet affect their strategies for locating stores?

7. In many malls, quick-service food retailers are located together in an area known as a food court. What are the advantages and disadvantages of this location for the food retailers?

8. Why would a Payless ShoeSource store locate in a neighborhood shopping center instead of a regional shopping mall?

9. How does the mall near your home or university combine the shopping and entertainment experiences?

10. Consider a big city that has invested in an urban renaissance. What components of the gentrification project attract both local residents and visiting tourists to spend time shopping, eating, and sightseeing in this location?

CHAPTER ENDNOTES

1. Nelson D. Schwartz, "The Economics (and Nostalgia) of Dead Malls," *The New York Times,* January 3, 2015.

2. Sandy Smith, "Reinventing the Mall," *Stores,* June 2014; Schwartz, "The Economics (and Nostalgia) of Dead Malls"; Barbara Thau, "Retail's Dirty Open Secret: Store Traffic Declines Are Shaking Up the Shopping Experience," *Forbes,* June 24, 2016.

3. Bernice Hurst, "Stepping Back in Time to Re-Imagine the Future of Malls," *RetailWire,* April 17, 2015.

4. Smith, "Reinventing the Mall."

5. Krystina Gustafson, "What's Different about Tomorrow's Mall: You Never Have to Leave," CNBC.com, April 22, 2014.

6. Hurst, "Stepping Back in Time to Re-Imagine the Future of Malls."

7. Smith, "Reinventing the Mall."

8. Gustafson, "What's Different about Tomorrow's Mall."

9. Schwartz, "The Economics (and Nostalgia) of Dead Malls."

10. Gustafson, "What's Different about Tomorrow's Mall."

11. eData, International Council of Shopping Centers.

12. Stephanie Clifford, "Retailers' Idea: Think Smaller in Urban Push," *The New York Times,* July 25, 2012.

13. Ibid.

14. http://www.clevelandgatewaydistrict.com/history/; Keith Schneider, "Cleveland Turns Uptown into New Downtown," *The New York Times,* November 2011, p. B.7; Sue Halpern, "Mayor of Rust," *The New York Times Magazine,* February 13, 2011, pp. 30–35

15. Mari Gallagher, "USDA Defines Food Deserts," *Nutrition Digest* 38, no. 1 (2010), http://americannutritionassociation.org/newsletter/usda-defines-food-deserts.

16. Andrew Soergel, "Millions of Food Desert Dwellers Struggle to Get Fresh Groceries," *US News and World Report,* December 7, 2015; Kelly Brooks, "Research Shows Food Deserts More Abundant in Minority Neighborhoods," *Johns Hopkins Magazine,* Spring 2014, http://hub.jhu.edu/magazine/2014/spring/racial-food-deserts/.

17. David Bornstein, "Conquering Food Deserts with Green Carts," *The New York Times,* April 18, 2012; Terry Pristin, "With a Little Help, Greens Come to Low-Income Neighborhoods," *The New York Times,* June 17, 2009, p. B6.

18. Stephanie Clifford, "Retailers' Idea: Think Smaller in Urban Push," *The New York Times,* July 25, 2012; Shan Li, "Target Plans Another Urban-Format Store for Los Angeles," *Los Angeles Times,* May 1, 2012.

19. S. Irene Virbila, "Whole Foods Opening Downtown at 8th and Grand, with Roy Choi's Chego," *Los Angeles Times,* November 3, 2015.

20. Matthew E. Kures and William F. Ryan, "Challenges of an Organizational Approach to Downtown Market Analysis," *Applied Geography* 32, no. 1 (January 2012), pp. 80–87; Kent A. Robertson, "The Main Street Approach to Downtown Development: An Examination of the Four-Point Program," *Journal of Architectural and Planning Research* 21, no. 1 (Spring 2004), pp. 55–78.

21. A. D. Pruitt, "A Strip-Mall Revival," *The Wall Street Journal,* September 26, 2012, p. C11.

22. Robert J. Gibbs, *Principles of Urban Planning and Development* (New York: Wiley, 2011); Brandon Rogoff, "The Performance of U.S. Shopping Centers," *ICSC Research Review* 16, no. 1 (2009), pp. 8–10.

23. Kate Murphy, "Revitalizing a Dead Mall (Don't Expect Shoppers)," *The Wall Street Journal,* October 30, 2012; Kris Hudson, "The Malaise Afflicting America's Malls," *The Wall Street Journal,* March 1, 2012.

24. Thau, "Retail's Dirty Open Secret."

25. Kris Hudson, "Malls Make Way for Grocers," *The Wall Street Journal,* August 5, 2012; Andrea Chang, "Malls Are Morphing into One-Stop Shops," *Los Angeles Times,* November 12, 2011.

26. Miriam Jordan, "Mall Owners Woo Hispanic Shoppers," *The Wall Street Journal,* August 13, 2013; Jeff Mitchell, "Northridge Mall in Salinas Aims to Capture Latino Customers," *The Californian,* March 9, 2012; David Ferry, "Land Battle Stirs Richmond," *The Wall Street Journal,* June 16, 2011.

27. Tim McLaughlin, "Bargain Retail Lifts U.S. Shopping Centers as Big Names Stumble," *Reuters,* March 16, 2014; Shelley DuBois, "The American Mall: Back from the Dead," *Fortune,* February 15, 2011.

28. Maria Matzer Rose, "Easton Shuffle," *Columbus Dispatch,* January 31, 2010; Tim Feran, "Easton Town Center Has Become Such a Popular Fixture, It's Hard to Remember That Its Concept Was a Risky Decision," *Columbus Dispatch,* July 5, 2009.

29. www.icsc.org/srch/lib/Mixed-use_Definition.pdf.

30. www.miznerpark.com/.

31. Sascha M. Pardy, "Outlet Centers Rise to the Top during Recession," *COStar Group News,* September 30, 2009.

32. http://www.simon.com/mall/the-outlets-at-orange.

33. Tiffany Hsu, "With Luxury Brands, Outlet Centers Give Malls a Run for Their Money," *Los Angeles Times,* April 26, 2014.

34. Suzanne Kapner, "Retailers' Lines Blur on Outlet Stores," *The Wall Street Journal,* October 12, 2014.

35. Eliot Brown, "As Urban Centers Rebound, Some Themed Marketplaces Appear Generic and Dated," *The Wall Street Journal,* March 9, 2012; Charles V. Bagli, "Despite Amenities, South Street Seaport Redevelopment Plans Stall over a High-Rise," *The New York Times,* February 16, 2015; Konrad Putzier, "Howard Hughes to Self-Fund Seaport Development," *The Real Deal,* May 10, 2016, http://therealdeal.com/2016/05/10/howard-hughes-to-self-fund-seaport-development/.

36. www.simon.com/mall/default.aspx?id=857.

37. Stephanie Clifford and Peter Lattman, "Toys 'R' Us, in a Box," *The New York Times,* April 7, 2012, p. B.1; Peter Evans, "Pop-Up Shops Go Mainstream," *The Wall Street Journal,* September 3, 2012; Tiffany Hsu, "Toys R Us to Open Holiday Pop-Up Shops in Macy's," *Los Angeles Times,* October 10, 2012; David Kaplan, "A Permanent Trend of Pop-Up Shops," *McClatchy-Tribune Business News,* December 3, 2011.

38. Peter Gareffa, "2017 Volvo S90 Showcased at Manhattan Pop-Up Store," Edmunds.com, June 28, 2016.

39. Alyssa Bailey and Sarah Lindig, "Kanye's 'Life of Pablo' Pop-Up Was as Insane as You Could've Guessed," *Elle,* March 19, 2016.

40. http://www.popuphood.com/consulting.html.

41. "Pop-Up Shops Proliferate in the Hamptons," *Crain's New York Business,* July 7, 2016, http://www.crainsnewyork.com/article/20160707/REAL_ESTATE/160709943/how-the-hamptons-became-a-pop-up-breeding-ground.

42. "The Economic Incentives of the 'Store-within-a-Store' Retail Model," *Knowledge@Wharton,* September 2, 2009.

43. George Anderson, "Best Buy to Open Shops Inside of Macy's Stores," *RetailWire,* September 9, 2015.

44. Xing Chen, "Modern Plaza Beijing," *GoShop Beijing,* January 3, 2012, http://goshopbeijing.com/modern-plaza-beijing-310.html.

45. Ian Ritter, "Ace Hardware Partners with Regional Supermarkets to Create One-Stop Shopping," *SCT,* August 25, 2014.

46. Nurun, "Tesla Motors: A Retail Experience That Reinvents the Way Cars Are Sold," http://www.nurun.com/en/case-studies/tesla-motors-retail-kiosks/.

47. PBS, "Store Wars: When Wal-Mart Comes to Town," www.pbs.org/itvs/storewars/.

48. "Nation of Shop Critics," *The Economist,* January 21, 2012.

CHAPTER 8 | Retail Site Location

LEARNING OBJECTIVES

After reading this chapter, you should be able to:

LO 8-1 Summarize the factors considered in locating a number of stores.

LO 8-2 Review the characteristics of a particular site.

LO 8-3 Understand how retailers analyze the trade area for a site.

LO 8-4 Determine the forecasted sales for a new store location.

LO 8-5 Illustrate the site selection process.

LO 8-6 Explain the different types and terms of leases.

© Alex Wong/Getty Images

By now, nearly everyone on the planet recognizes the green mermaid logo that proudly sits atop every Starbucks sign, poster, and cup. The ubiquitous coffee giant maintains more than 24,000 locations in over 70 countries, providing a third place (in addition to their homes and workplaces) where people can linger.[1] To ensure that this third place is one that appeals to consumers, Starbucks relies on a range of data, data analytical tools, and insights from its partners (i.e., employees).

The need for extensive insights from a variety of sources became clear when, in the last decade, hundreds of newly opened stores had to be closed because of their poor performance.[2] In analyzing how the company got to that point, Starbucks's manager of global market planning, Patrick O'Hagan, explained that many of the stores never should have opened. However, the staff in charge of location choices had been inundated with so many data, they were unable to use them to make profitable decisions.

Although Starbucks began using ESRI's geographic information system (GIS) technology as far back as the 1990s, it has perfected its applications of the GIS-provided predictive analytics more recently.[3] It uses the information gleaned from the technology to plan new locations, as well as consider expanded menu options in particular sites. With the system's ArcGIS Online tool, Starbucks obtains a graphical summary of the GIS data in map form. These data include location information and demographic details, which the software analyzes according to pertinent criteria. So for example, it can determine where a new office building is going up in a small city in China, then predict where the workers will be arriving from to identify where the new shop should appear. Starbucks also feeds these data into its proprietary Atlas application, which it refers to as the "destination for our GIS."[4]

Not only does the GIS technology help Starbucks determine the ideal locations for new stores, but it also can enable the company to decide which kinds of stores to open. For example, many planned new stores will feature drive-through windows; others will be smaller stores, strategically placed to provide the greatest customer convenience. The data further define what to include on the menus, including more pastry options in locations where consumers tend to have a sweet tooth. Because the GIS technology is accessible across various platforms, location experts in the field can combine the high-tech insights with their real-world observations. The Atlas system even has suggested that Starbucks consider adding wine to its menus at some locations that function as evening destinations. The new approach already has been proving effective, according to results that show that the most recent newly opened stores, particularly those in the Americas, consistently are producing great returns.

Beyond these demographic data, Starbucks relies heavily on its mobile app as a source of information. For example, it can determine who orders what and where, as well as where adoption rates of its app are high. A recent analysis identified some areas with low smartphone ownership that also contained pockets where lots of people carried mobile devices. It immediately sought to add stores in those locations and reach out to the local consumers through its mobile app.

Once the correct type of Starbucks store is opened in the right location, all these tools also help drive traffic. For example, available software integrates weather patterns and news into the map. When a heat wave is about to hit a particular city, it can promote cold Frappuccinos for the week before the temperature spikes, putting the frosty treats right in the path of thirsty patrons at the moment they need to cool down.

Chapter 5 emphasized the strategic importance of location decisions. Although location decisions can create strategic advantages, like all strategic decisions, they are also risky because they involve a significant commitment of resources. Opening a store at a site often involves committing to a lease of five years or more or purchasing land and building a store. If the store's performance is below expectations, the retailer may not be able to recover its investment easily by having another party move in and assume the lease or buy the building.

Chapter 7 reviewed the different types of locations available to retailers and why certain types of retailers gravitate toward particular locations. This chapter takes a closer look at how retailers choose specific sites to locate their stores.

Selecting retail locations involves the analysis of a large amount of data and the use of sophisticated statistical models. Because most retailers make these decisions infrequently, it is not economical for them to employ full-time real estate analysts with state-of-the-art skills. Small retailers often use firms that provide the geographic and demographic data and consulting services needed to evaluate specific sites. Even massive chains like Starbucks might turn to experts to help them deal with the vast amounts of data available to inform their new store placements. Yet even with all these advanced technologies, there continues to be an element of art in making these location decisions.

This chapter reviews the steps retailers go through in selecting their store locations and negotiating leases. The first part of the chapter examines the factors retailers consider when selecting a general area for locating stores and determining the number of stores to operate in each area. Then it reviews different approaches used to evaluate specific sites and estimate the expected sales if and when a store is located at that site. Finally, the chapter looks at the various terms that are negotiated when a retailer commits to leasing space for its store.

EVALUATING AREAS FOR LOCATIONS AND DETERMINING THE NUMBER OF STORES IN AN AREA

The first part of this section discusses the areas retailers typically analyze when making location decisions, and the second part reviews factors retailers consider when evaluating these areas for locating stores and determining the number of stores to put in an area.

LO 8-1

Summarize the factors considered in locating a number of stores.

Metropolitan Statistical Area

Areas that retailers consider for locating stores might be countries, areas within a country such as a state in the United States, particular cities, or areas within cities. In the United States, retailers often focus their analysis on a **metropolitan statistical area (MSA)** because consumers tend to shop within an MSA, and media coverage and demographic data for analyzing location opportunities often are organized by MSA.

An MSA is a core urban area containing a population of more than 50,000 inhabitants, together with adjacent communities that have a high degree of economic and social integration with the core community. For example, many people in an MSA commute to work in the central business district but live in the surrounding areas. An MSA can consist of one or several counties and usually is named after the major urban area in the MSA. For example, the Cincinnati-Middletown MSA consists of 17 counties (3 in Indiana, 8 in Kentucky, and 6 in Ohio) with a population of 2,157,719; the Missoula, Montana, MSA consists of one county with a population of 114,181.

In contrast, a **micropolitan statistical area (µSA)** is somewhat removed from larger U.S. cities, often by up to 100 miles. Although they lack big cities' pull and economic significance, these notable population centers often are responsible for substantial production capabilities and provide reasonable housing accommodations for many residents. The designation refers to the core population of a central town, so regardless of its name, a micropolitan area could be larger than a metropolitan area. The largest µSA is Claremont-Lenanon, New Hampshire-Vermont, with a population of 217,510.[5]

Considerations in Evaluating Store Locations

The best areas for locating stores are those that generate the highest long-term profits for a retailer. Some factors affecting the long-term profit generated by stores that should be considered when evaluating an area include (1) the economic conditions, (2) competition, (3) the strategic fit of the area's population with the retailer's target market, and (4) the costs of operating stores (see Exhibit 8–1). Note that these factors are similar to those that retailers consider when evaluating an investment in a new business growth opportunity or entry into a foreign market, as discussed in Chapter 5.

Economic Conditions   Because locations involve a commitment of resources over a long time horizon, it is important to examine an area's level and growth of population and employment. A large, fully employed population means high purchasing power and high levels of retail sales.

EXHIBIT 8–1
Factors Affecting the Attractiveness of an Area for Locating Stores

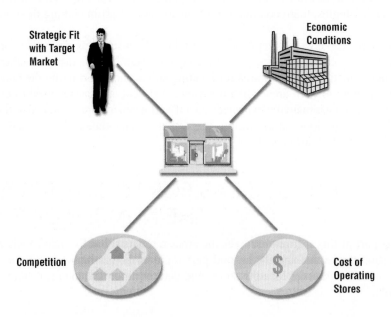

Strategic Fit with Target Market

Economic Conditions

Competition

Cost of Operating Stores

But population and employment growth alone aren't enough to ensure a strong retail environment in the future. Retail location analysts need to determine how long such growth will continue and how it will affect demand for merchandise sold in the stores. For instance, if growth is not diversified in various industries, the area may be unattractive because of extreme cyclical trends. The economies of some Rust Belt cities like Detroit, Michigan, experience greater peaks and valleys because of their dependence on specific industries such as automobiles.

Also, it is useful to determine which areas are growing quickly and why. For instance, the east side of Seattle, Washington, has become a desirable retail location because of its proximity to Microsoft's corporate headquarters. But the performance of these retail locations is linked to the financial performance of Microsoft.

In most cases, areas where the population is large and growing are preferable to those with declining populations. However, some retailers, such as Subway, often go into new strip shopping centers with few nearby households with the anticipation that the surrounding suburban area will eventually be built up enough to support the stores.

Competition   The level of competition in an area affects the demand for a retailer's merchandise. Walmart's early success was based on a location strategy of opening stores in small towns with little competition. It offered consumers in small towns quality merchandise at low prices. Previously, rural consumers either shopped in small stores with limited assortments or drove to larger towns.

Although they once were viewed as undesirable areas, inner-city neighborhoods today host many full-service restaurant chains, including Chili's, Denny's, IHOP, and so forth. For such casual restaurants, underserved urban locations offer some strong attractions, including minimal competition levels; a large, readily accessible labor force; and, in some neighborhoods, a surrounding market of customers with high disposable incomes.

Retailing View 8.1 describes the success realized by Stage Stores targeting small towns with limited competition for fashionable apparel.

RETAILING VIEW   Big Payoff from Small Towns   8.1

Even though Stage Stores is a billion-dollar retail chain operating in about 850 locations, it is relatively unknown because most of its stores are located in small towns and operate under different store names. Being outside the big city has advantages, though. "The beauty of our business model is that we have no natural competitor," said Andy Hall, former president and CEO of Stage Stores. "Most small towns are not big enough for two stores like ours. The first one in wins." Typically, the nearest thing to competition for Stage Stores's small-town locations are regional malls 40 miles away and online sites.

Among the 850 stores, more than 550 are in small markets (small MSAs and larger μSAs), mostly in strip centers in towns with less than 50,000 people within a 10-mile radius. Another approximately 150 locations are in mid-sized communities with populations between 50,000 and 150,000 people. Stage Stores operates under the names Palais Royal, Bealls, Goody's, Peebles, and Stage. For all these store names, the retailer strategically seeks to locate close to grocery stores, drugstores, and major discount stores, such as Walmart. Customers buy their groceries and hard goods at Walmart and their apparel at Stage Stores. Name brands, such as Lee, Levi's, Calvin Klein, Izod, Nike, Nautica, Dockers, Nine West, Clinique, and Estée Lauder, account for 85 percent of sales.

Bealls, a subsidiary of Stage Stores, focuses on small towns where it faces little competition for its assortment of designer fashion apparel and accessories.

A downside of being small-town-focused is being overlooked by many investors, according to Hall. "Most city dwellers don't understand the vibrancy of small markets. It's an amazing culture in small markets," Hall said. Sales associates and customers there are more likely to know each other, and their relationships in the stores are often warm.

Source: www.stagestores.com; David Kaplan, "Stage Stores' Strategy Pays Off Big in Small Towns," *Houston Chronicle,* August 1, 2011.

Retailers like La Curacao target their assortment of electronics, appliances, and home goods to Hispanics by locating their stores in trade areas where they live.

© Aurelia Ventura/La Opinion/Newscom

Strategic Fit   Economic conditions and competition alone don't tell the whole story. The area needs to have consumers who are in the retailer's target market—who are attracted to the retailer's offerings and interested in patronizing its stores. Thus, the area must have the right demographic and lifestyle profile. The size and composition of households in an area can be an important determinant of success. For instance, the electronics, appliance, and home goods store La Curacao focuses on Hispanic consumers. It has 11 locations in Southern California and Arizona—all locations are areas with at least 250,000 Hispanics.[6] The ethnic composition of the trade area instead is not a particularly critical issue for Toys "R" Us, which is interested more in locations with heavy concentrations of families with young children.

Operating Costs   The cost of operating stores can vary across areas. For example, store rental and advertising costs in the Missoula, Montana, MSA are significantly lower than those in the Cincinnati-Middletown MSA. But the potential sales and profits from stores located in the Cincinnati-Middletown MSA are substantially greater, due to its larger and denser population.

Operating costs are also affected by the proximity of the area being considered to other areas in which the retailer operates stores. For example, if a store is located near other stores and the retailer's distribution centers, the cost of shipping merchandise to the store is lower, as is the cost and travel time spent by the district manager supervising the stores' operations.

The local and state legal and regulatory environment can have a significant effect on operating costs. Some retailers may be reluctant to locate stores in California, for example, because they worry that the state and local governments, the political process of voter-initiated referendums, and a legal environment that fosters class-action lawsuits result in higher operating costs.[7]

Number of Stores in an Area

Having selected an area in which to locate its stores, a retailer's next decision is how many stores to operate in the area. At first glance, you might think that a retailer should choose the one best location in each MSA, but clearly, larger MSAs can support more stores than smaller MSAs. It may therefore be more advantageous to locate several stores in one MSA and none in others. But there is a limit to how many stores can be operated in even the largest MSAs. When making the decision about how many stores to open in an area, retailers must consider the trade-offs between lower operating costs and potential sales cannibalization from having multiple stores in an area.

Economies of Scale from Multiple Stores   Most retail chains open multiple stores in an area to lower promotion and distribution costs by realizing economies of scale. A retailer's total promotional costs are the same for newspaper advertising that promotes 20 stores in an MSA or only 1 store. Multiple stores in an MSA can be serviced by the same distribution center. Thus, chains like Walmart expand into areas only where they have a distribution center in place to support the stores.[8] When Kohl's entered the Florida market, it opened 14 stores in Jacksonville and Orlando on the same day.

Cannibalization   Although retailers gain scale economies from opening multiple locations in an MSA, they also suffer diminishing returns associated with locating too many additional stores in an area. For example, suppose the first four stores opened in an MSA by a specialty store retailer generate sales of $2 million each. Because they are located far apart from one another, customers consider patronizing only the store nearest to them, and there is no cannibalization. When the retailer opens a fifth store close to one of the existing stores, it hopes for a net sales increase for the area of $2 million; the new store should generate the same sales level as the four existing stores. Instead, the increase in incremental sales might be only $1.5 million because the sales in the nearest existing store's sales drop to $1.7 million, and sales from the new store are only $1.8 million because its location is only the fifth best in the area. Thus, because the new store cannibalizes sales from the closest store, it contributes sales of only $1.5 million.

Because a primary retailing objective is to maximize profits for the entire chain, retailers should continue to open stores only as long as profits continue to increase or, in economic terms, as long as the marginal revenues achieved by opening a new store are greater than the marginal costs. Exhibit 8–2 shows the location of customers that

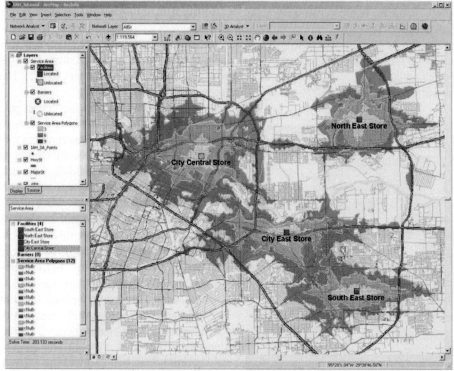

EXHIBIT 8–2
Location of Customers Patronizing a Retailer's Store

Source: Environmental Systems Research Institute (ESRI)

are 3 (yellow), 6 (pink), and 9 (blue) minutes from a retailer's four stores in an area. Note how there is very little overlap, thus little cannibalization except for the City East and the South East stores.

For franchise retail operations the objectives of the franchisor and franchisee differ, therefore disputes can arise over the number of locations in an area. The franchisor is interested in maximizing the sales of all stores because it earns a royalty based on total store sales. The franchisee is interested in just the sales and profits from its store(s). Thus, the franchisor is not as concerned about cannibalization as the franchisee is. To reduce the level of conflict, most franchise agreements grant franchisees an exclusive territory to protect them from another franchisee cannibalizing their sales.

EVALUATING SPECIFIC SITES

LO 8-2

Review the characteristics of a particular site.

Having decided to locate stores in an area, the retailer's next step is to evaluate and select a specific site. In making this decision, retailers consider three factors: (1) the characteristics of the site, (2) the characteristics of the trading area for a store at the site, and (3) the estimated potential sales that can be generated by a store at the site. The first two sets of factors are typically considered in an initial screening of potential sites. The methods used to forecast store sales, the third factor, can involve a more complex analytical approach. Each of these factors is discussed in the following sections.

Site Characteristics

Some characteristics of a site that affect store sales and thus are considered in selecting a site are (1) the traffic flow past the site and accessibility to the site, (2) parking, (3) visibility, (4) adjacent tenants, and (5) restrictions and costs.

Traffic Flow and Accessibility   One of the most important factors affecting store sales is the **traffic flow**—the number of vehicles and pedestrians that pass by the site. When the traffic is greater, more consumers are likely to stop in and shop at the store. Thus, retailers often use traffic count measures to assess a site's attractiveness. Traffic counts are particularly important for retailers offering merchandise and services bought on impulse or on frequent trips such as grocery and convenience stores, and car washes. In contrast, traffic flow is not as important for destination retailers such as The Container Store.

Airports are an appealing location for some retailers because there are lots of potential customers with time to shop.

© EyesWideOpen/Getty Images

Airports increasingly are leveraging their substantial traffic flows to sell or lease retail space to various retailers that are assured a nearly constant stream of appealing consumers, including international and business travelers who normally are too busy to shop.[9] Today's passengers often leave a little extra time to make sure they can get through security and still make their flight, so they are left with a "golden hour" before they board, when they can browse various offerings and pick up gifts for their families waiting at home. Accordingly, retail sales in airports are expected to grow by 73 percent by 2019.[10]

In other transportation settings, though, more traffic flow is not always better, and traffic volume counts for roadways, used to assess the attractiveness of a retail site, can be misleading. They give a reasonable estimate of the level of activity in an area, but they do not provide any indication of how much of that volume actually stops and shops at a particular retail location. Most shopping centers are located along roads and highways that are heavily traveled by drivers commuting to and from work or carrying out daily errands that might not include shopping. As such, daily traffic counts are skewed during rush hours, which creates congestion that impedes access to the stores. Also, traffic volume counts are collected over a 24-hour period, and average rates are reported, whereas retail properties are typically open for only 8 to 12 hours each day.

The **accessibility** of the site, which can be as important as traffic flow, is the ease with which customers can get into and out of the site. Accessibility is greater for sites located near major highways, on uncongested highways, and at streets with traffic lights and lanes that enable turns into the site. Retailing View 8.2 describes the importance of being on the right side of the road.

RETAILING VIEW   It Pays to Locate on the Right Side of the Road   8.2

For U.S. drivers, businesses and stores located on the right side of the road, rather than on the left, are the ones they see most readily on their commutes home from work or school. That is, if we were to measure the volume of traffic on a road, we would find that the right-hand side of the yellow lines takes up far more afternoon volume. Accordingly, for many businesses, a location on that right-hand side can be highly desirable because it is easy for customers to make a quick right turn into their properties, then an easier right turn out of the retail parking area, without having to cross many lanes of traffic.

In the morning, a right-side location might be ideal for a coffee shop or newspaper stand. But most commuters have little time to spare in the mornings, so they reserve their stops to fill up on gas, grab a cup of coffee, or perhaps sneak in an afternoon candy bar for their rides home.

For Speedway gas stations and convenience stores, locating on the right-hand side for afternoon commuters is a priority. Its 2,770 stores in 22 states makes it the second-largest company owned and operated convenience store chain in the United States. Speedway maintains a staff that evaluates the location of stores it is considering to build or acquire. When evaluating locations, it looks at all the numbers—the size and characteristics of the store's trading area, the demographics and geodemographics of the customers that drive by the location and live in the area. However, the most important factors for them are visibility and access—that is, can customers see the signage for our stores and easily make a right turn into the location on their way home? While the data on a location are useful, taking a look at it in person to assess its visibility and access is critical.

Right turns into and out of Speedway locations are particularly important for its customers, who demand a maximum of convenience from their convenience stores. For many drivers, being required to cross multiple lanes of traffic (and hold up frustrated drivers behind them) to make a left turn simply isn't worth the hassle. If they also need to make a left turn out of the parking lot to continue their commute, their quick pit stop could turn into an extended chore as they wait for gaps in the heavy rush hour traffic to enter the flow of cars.

© Kiichiro Sato/AP Images

Speedway likes to locate its gas stations on the right-hand side of the road because of its easy in-and-out access.

Locations on the left-hand side of the road, from commuters' perspective, also have grown increasingly problematic with the expansion of "access control" policies by local, county, and state transportation agencies. Such controls include the installation of medians and curbing that limit left turns, as well as prohibitions on U-turns at traffic signals.

As a result of these consumer preferences and governmental policies, being on the "wrong" side of the road can result in a 5 to 20 percent decrease in customer transactions, depending on the road's specific traffic volume patterns.

The bottom line is that it is no longer just "location, location, location" that matters for retail sales. Location questions must be evaluated in the context of "access, access, access," especially for customers seeking convenience. Any retailer evaluating locations for stores therefore should think carefully about the traffic patterns whizzing by. Are you on the right side, or the wrong side, of the road?

Sources: www.speedway.com/about/; "It Pays to Be on the Right Side of the Road," TSImaster, 2011.

Natural barriers, such as rivers or mountains, and **artificial barriers**, such as railroad tracks, divided or limited-access highways, or parks, may also affect accessibility. These barriers' impact on a particular site primarily depends on whether the merchandise or services will appeal to customers so strongly that they cross the barrier. For example, a supermarket on one side of a divided highway with no convenient crossover point will appeal only to consumers going in one direction.

A more accurate measure of traffic, which can be obtained from several specialized companies, is the number of consumers entering the shopping center, collected at store entrances within the shopping center. This measure provides a more accurate picture of the number of consumers actually patronizing the shopping center. Additionally, the measure is available for every day of the year individually, rather than the annual averages provided by firms specializing in traffic counts. This allows for more detailed and targeted analyses based on seasonal or week-to-week comparisons.

In the United States, most consumers drive to shopping centers, thus vehicular traffic can be an important consideration when evaluating a site. However, pedestrian traffic flow and access by public transportation are more important for analyzing sites in countries such as China, where consumers do not drive to shop, or for evaluating urban sites and sites within an enclosed mall.

Parking   The amount and quality of parking facilities are critical for evaluating a shopping center. On the one hand, if there aren't enough spaces or the spaces are too far from the store, customers will be discouraged from patronizing the site and the store. On the other hand, if there are too many open spaces, the shopping center may be perceived as having unpopular stores. A standard rule of thumb is 5.5:1,000 (5.5 spaces per 1,000 square feet of retail store space) for a shopping center and 10 to 15 spaces per 1,000 square feet for a supermarket.

Retailers need to observe the shopping center at various times of the day, week, and season. They also must consider the availability of employee parking, the proportion of shoppers using cars, parking by nonshoppers, and the typical length of a shopping trip.

An issue closely related to the amount of available parking facilities but extended into the shopping center itself is the relative congestion of the area. **Congestion** is an

The parking around this Best Buy store contributes to the quality of this location.

© Michael Neelon/Alamy Stock Photo

excess level of traffic that results in customer delays. There is an optimal level of congestion for customers. Too much congestion can make shopping slow, irritate customers, and generally discourage sales. However, a relatively high level of activity in a shopping center creates excitement and can stimulate sales.

Visibility   **Visibility** refers to customers' ability to see the store from the street. Good visibility is less important for stores with a well-established and loyal customer base, but most retailers still want a direct, unimpeded view of their store. In an area with a highly transient population, such as a tourist center or large city, good visibility from the road is particularly important.

To some extent, this location criterion has shifted due to consumers' increasing uses of mobile devices. When shoppers have smartphones in hand, they can readily search for the location of a store they want to find and receive detailed, step-by-step or turn-by-turn directions to reach it. As long as the store is something of a destination or can get customers to search their phones to find it—possibly by using technology that identifies potential customers walking in the nearby area and sends solicitations to them at that very moment—it might be able to deemphasize the traditional visibility criterion. Because the meaning of visibility changes somewhat in the modern mobile era, the definitions of the best locations might change for some retailers too.

Adjacent Tenants   Locations with complementary, as well as competing, adjacent retailers have the potential to build traffic. Complementary retailers target the same market segment but have a different, noncompeting merchandise offering. For example, stores like Save-A-Lot, a limited-assortment supermarket targeting price-sensitive consumers, might prefer to be co-located with other retailers targeting price-sensitive consumers, such as Big Lots, Family Dollar, or even Walmart.

Have you ever noticed that competing fast-food restaurants, automobile dealerships, antique dealers, or even shoe and apparel stores in a mall are located next to one another? Consumers looking for these types of merchandise are involved in convenience or comparison shopping situations, as we described in Chapter 7. They want to be able to make their choice easily in the case of convenience shopping, or they want to have a good assortment so that they can "shop around," in the case of shopping goods. This grouped location approach is based on the principle of **cumulative attraction**, which states that a cluster of similar and complementary retailing activities will generally have greater drawing power than isolated stores that engage in the same retailing activities.[11]

Restrictions and Costs   As we learn later in this chapter, retailers may place restrictions on the type of tenants that are allowed in a shopping center in their lease agreement. Some of these restrictions can make the shopping center more attractive for a retailer. For example, a specialty men's apparel retailer may prefer a lease agreement that precludes other men's specialty apparel retailers from locating in the same center. A florist in a strip center may specify that if the grocery anchor tenant vacates the center, it can be released from its lease since the amount of people frequenting the center would be significantly diminished. Retailers would look unfavorably on a shopping center with a sign size restriction that prevented easy visibility of the store's name from the street. At the end of the chapter, we discuss some other restrictions and cost issues involved in negotiating a lease.

Locations within a Shopping Center

While the previous discussion focused on factors affecting the attractiveness of a shopping center location, the location within a shopping center has a significant effect on both sales and occupancy costs. The better locations have higher

Based on the principle of cumulative attraction, stores selling similar merchandise to similar target markets, such as Rolex and Piaget, should locate in close proximity to one another to increase the appeal of the location to its customers.

occupancy costs. In a strip shopping center, the locations closest to the supermarket are more expensive because they attract greater foot traffic. So a flower shop or sandwich shop that may attract impulse buyers would want to be close to the supermarket. But a shoe repair store, which does not cater to customers shopping on impulse, could be in a lower-traffic location farther away from the supermarket because customers in need of this service will seek out the store. In other words, it is a destination store.

The same issues apply to evaluating locations within a multilevel, enclosed shopping mall. Stores that cater to consumers engaging in comparison shopping (e.g., buyers of fashionable apparel) benefit from being in more expensive locations near the department store anchors, which are destinations for comparison apparel shoppers. As apparel shoppers enter and leave the department store, they walk by and may be attracted to neighboring specialty store retailers. In contrast, a retailer such as Foot Locker, another destination store, need not be in the most expensive location because many of its customers know they are in the market for its type of product before they even go shopping.

Another consideration is how to locate stores that appeal to similar target markets. In essence, customers want to shop where they will find a good assortment of merchandise. The principle of cumulative attraction applies to both stores that sell complementary merchandise and those that compete directly with one another.[12]

DEFINING TRADE AREAS

LO 8-3

Understand how retailers analyze the trade area for a site.

After identifying several sites that have acceptable traffic flow, accessibility, and other location characteristics, the next step is to collect information about the trade area that can be used to forecast sales for a store located at the site. The retailer first needs to define the trade area for the site. Once the trade area is defined, the retailer can use several different information sources to develop a detailed understanding of the nature of consumers in the site's trade area.

Trade Area Definition

A **trade area** is a contiguous geographic area that accounts for the majority of a store's sales and customers. Trade areas can be divided into three zones, as shown in

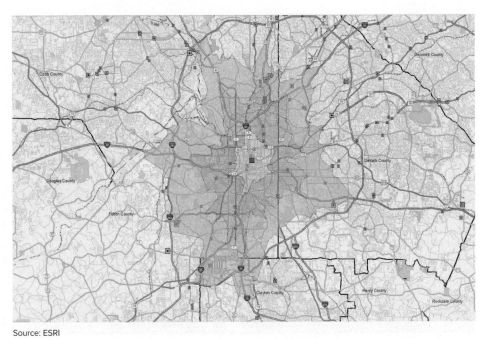

Source: ESRI

EXHIBIT 8–3
Zones in a Trade Area

Exhibit 8–3. The exhibit shows the trade area zones for a shopping center located at the red square: the 5-minute drive-time zone (light brown), the 10-minute zone (blue), and the 15-minute zone (green).

Furthermore, trade area zones are not just concentric circles based on distance from the store. Exhibit 8–3 depicts irregular polygons based on the location of roads, highways, and natural barriers, like rivers and valleys, that affect the driving time to the store. The location of competitive stores can also affect the actual trade area configuration.

The **primary trading area** is the geographic area from which the shopping center or store site derives 50 to 70 percent of its customers. The **secondary trading area** is the geographic area of secondary importance in terms of customer sales, generating about 20 to 30 percent of the site's customers. The **tertiary trading area**, or **fringe trading area** (the outermost area), includes the remaining customers who shop at the site but come from widely dispersed areas. These customers might travel an unusually long distance because they do not have comparable retail facilities closer to home, or they may drive near the store or center on their way to or from work.

The best way to define the three zones is based on driving time rather than distance. Thus, the primary trading area might be defined as customers within 5 minutes' driving time of the site; the secondary trading area, as customers with a 10-minute drive; and the tertiary zone, as customers more than 15 minutes away from the site by car. The exact definitions of the zones also depend on the type of retailer, such that people might drive 16 minutes to get to a general store but only 12 minutes to access their gym or yoga studio. They are willing to travel farther to find a wedding retailer (23 minutes) or medical provider, such as a dentist or doctor (21 minutes). Demographics also can affect trade areas and drive-time choices. Younger customers express a greater willingness to travel farther to wedding-related stores, whereas older ones would drive more miles to visit their accountant. Women consistently express willingness to go farther to meet their retail needs, such as 5 more minutes to visit a hair salon or 3 more minutes to get to a yoga class, compared with their male counterparts.[13]

Although driving time is the best way to define a trade area, it is much easier to collect information about the number of people and their characteristics in the

Bass Pro Shops has a large trade area because its huge stores have lots of merchandise and an entertaining environment.

© Danita Delimont/Alamy Stock Photo

different zones by geographic distance than by driving time. Thus, retailers often define the zones by distance—such as 3, 5, and 10 miles from the site—rather than driving time.

Factors Affecting the Size of the Trade Area

The actual boundaries of a trade area are determined by the store's accessibility, natural and physical barriers, level of competition, nature of the merchandise sold, the assortment offered, and the location of alternative sources for the merchandise.

A Starbucks in a central business district, for example, may have a trade area of only two or three blocks. A category specialist like Michaels may draw customers from 10 miles away. The Container Store, which is the only store of its kind in a city, might draw customers from 30 miles away. Bass Pro Shops even claims that its customers drive an average of more than 50 miles to get to one of its fun, experiential locations.[14] Category specialists offer a large choice of brands and products for which customers are engaged in comparison shopping. Thus, customers generally drive some distance to shop at these stores. In general, destination stores have a large trade area—people are willing to drive farther to shop there.

Measuring the Trade Area for a Retail Site

Retailers can determine the trade area for their existing stores by customer spotting. **Customer spotting** is the process of locating the residences of customers for a store on a map and displaying their positions relative to the store location. The addresses for locating the customers' residences usually are obtained by asking customers, recording the information from a check or Internet channel purchase, collecting the information from customer loyalty programs, or gathering mobile data from dedicated app users. The data collected from customer spotting can be processed in two ways: manually plotting the location of each customer on a map or using a geographic information system (GIS), similar to the one Starbucks uses, as detailed in the opener to this chapter. We discuss GIS further in subsequent sections.

Multichannel and omnichannel retailers use their catalog and Internet sales data to spot customers and use that information to identify potential store locations. The number of catalog and Internet channel customers in an area can be used to predict the sales of a store placed in the area.

It is more challenging to estimate the trade area for a new store location than for existing locations. To do so, retailers use information about the trade areas for existing stores to estimate the trade areas for new stores. For example, if Marshalls knows the trade areas of several stores with similar characteristics, including their locations or customers, it can readily predict the trade area of a new store that shares those traits.

Sources of Information about Trade Areas

To analyze the attractiveness of a potential store site, retailers use information about both the consumers and the competitors in the site's trade area. Two widely used sources of information about the nature of consumers in a trade area are (1) data published by the U.S. Census Bureau, based on the Decennial Census of the United States; and (2) data from geographic information systems, provided by several commercial firms.

Demographic Data from the U.S. Census Bureau   Every 10 years, **census** takers gather demographic information (sex, age, ethnicity, education, marital status, etc.) from every household in the United States. The decennial census is more than just a head count; it provides a snapshot of the country's demographic, social, and economic characteristics. The U.S. Census Bureau prepares periodic reports summarizing the data. There are 8 million **census blocks** in the United States, each containing the residences of about 40 people. The smallest unit of analysis is the **block group**, a collection of adjacent blocks that contain between 600 and 3,000 people.[15]

Although the data from the U.S. Census Bureau can be used to develop a better understanding of the nature of consumers in a region or trade area, these data have several limitations. First, because they are based on information collected every 10 years, they are not very current, though the projections are reasonably accurate. Second, the data are not particularly user-friendly. It is difficult to utilize census data to examine the trade areas for various locations for specific products or services. Thus, most retailers rely on the geographic information system data offered by a number of companies to examine trade areas for potential stores.

Geographic Information System Suppliers   A **geographic information system (GIS)** is a system of hardware and software used to store, retrieve, map, and analyze geographic data. The key feature of GIS data is that they are identified with a coordinate system (latitude and longitude) that references a particular place on Earth. The data in the systems include spatial features such as rivers and roads, as well as descriptive information associated with the spatial features, such as the street address and the characteristics of the household at the address.

Firms such as Environmental Systems Research Institute (ESRI) (www.esri.com), Nielsen, which purchased Claritas (www.claritas.com/sitereports/Default.jsp), and Pitney Bowes, which purchased MapInfo (www.pitneybowes.com/us/location-intelligence/gis-data-sets.html), offer services that combine updated demographic census data with data from other sources that describe consumer spending patterns and lifestyles in a geographic area. In addition, they provide a user-friendly interface so that the data can be accessed and analyzed easily. Frequently, the outputs from the system are maps that enable retailers to visualize the implications of the data quickly. For example, the map in Exhibit 8–4 shows the trade areas for three branch banks that a retailer has in an MSA and a fourth branch it is considering, as well as the residences of its customers relative to the branch at which they bank. This map suggests that people bank near their work and that the new location might cannibalize from the other branches.

EXHIBIT 8–4
GIS Map for the Trade Area of a Bank

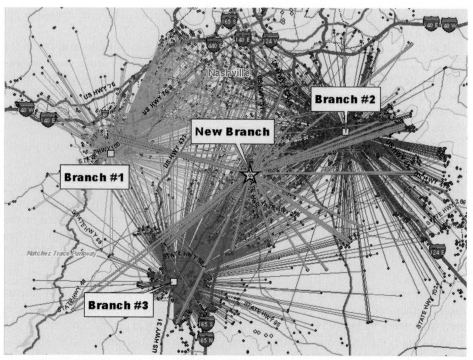

Source: ESRI

Retailers interested in developing a deeper understanding of their trade areas for several sites can provide one of these firms with the street addresses for the sites under consideration. The system then provides the projected data shown in Exhibit 8–5 for current year estimates and five-year projections pertaining to people living within a 3-, 5-, and 10-mile radius of the sites. In addition, these GIS firms can provide data on the lifestyles of consumers, consumer spending potential, and the locations of competitive retailers. An example of a report on the retail goods and services purchased by residents in a trade area is shown in Exhibit 8–5.

Tapestry Segmentation   ESRI and other GIS suppliers have developed schemes for classifying geographic areas in the United States by combining census and survey data about people's lifestyles and purchasing behavior with the mapping capabilities of GIS. The analysis is based on the premise that "birds of a feather flock together." Specifically, people who live in the same neighborhoods tend to have similar lifestyles and consumer behavior patterns. As Retailing View 8.3 notes, Lululemon relies on such flocking tendencies in making its store location decisions.

The ESRI Tapestry Segmentation system classifies all U.S. residential neighborhoods into 67 distinctive segments, based on demographic and socioeconomic characteristics.[16] Exhibit 8–6 is a hypothetical report for the area within a 1.5-mile radius of 100 S. Wacker Drive in Chicago. Each segment provides a description of the typical

EXHIBIT 8–5
Information Provided by GIS Report

Gender	Occupation
Income	Travel time to work
Disposable income	Transportation mode to work
Net worth	Household composition
Education	Household expenditures by NAICS categories
Age	Geodemographic market segment
Race/ethnicity	Market potential index
Employment status	Spending potential index

Source: ESRI

8.3

RETAILING VIEW   How Lululemon's Flagship Store Summarizes Its Location Strategy

The newly opened, flagship, Manhattan-area Lululemon store does more than sell exercise clothing and yoga equipment. It leverages the retailer's knowledge of what consumers in this area want to devise an innovative community space, targeted directly at the shoppers who live and work nearby. Approximately one-third of the store is not devoted to selling merchandise. Instead, concierge services, available to recommend a nearby gym or help shoppers book class time, take up part of the facility. On another floor, the Hub Seventeen space is used for yoga classes, demonstrations, concerts, and other community-building events.

The new store opened in the Flatiron District in New York City, which was the perfect match for Lululemon, because that area already features a broad range of top fitness studios, such as Pure Barre and SoulCycle, as well as other athletic retailers, includ-

Lululemon locates its stores where its customers live, and lures them in by offering much more than yoga clothing—a concierge service, yoga classes, demonstrations, concerts, and other community-building events.

ing Athleta and Sweaty Betty. In this sense, it has collaborators to which it can refer customers who want to plié or pedal for an hour. The presence of competitors also is informative because it implies that a good target market already exists. Despite the increased competition, Lululemon believes that it can set itself apart from other athletic gear retailers in the same area with its concierge service and dedication to a sense of community. Concierges on staff also might suggest places in any local area where shoppers could find a healthy meal. In invoking this sense of community, Lululemon hopes to become a new "third place" for its consumers and fans after their home and work, such that they might feel comfortable stopping by to have a cup of tea and relax in the store, even if they are not going to make a purchase.

Although the Hub Seventeen space might not be an appropriate addition to all stores, the concept implies the company's overall service-oriented efforts to make its stores more than just retail outlets. In particular, with the offer of yoga classes, Lululemon gives its customers what they clearly want, namely, a space to practice the type of exercise for which they already have purchased the gear. By embracing the unique community surrounding every store, Lululemon allows its locations to inform its strategies.

Sources: Adrianne Pasquarelli, "Lululemon Tries New Store Concept in Efforts to Woo Shoppers," *Advertising Age*, November 17, 2015; Mallory Schlossberg, "Lululemon Has Unveiled Its New Store of the Future," *Business Insider*, November 18, 2015; Nicole Santos, "Grand Opening for Lululemon Draws Crowds to Fig Garden," *Fresno Bee*, July 3, 2015; Teresa Novellino, "What to Expect from Lululemon's Largest-Ever Retail Store, Opening in N.Y.C.," *New York Business Journal*, November 17, 2015.

person in that segment. The largest segment in the trade area report in Exhibit 8–6 is Metro Renters. According to ESRI, residents of Metro Renters neighborhoods are young (with a median age of 31.8 years), well-educated singles beginning their professional careers in some of the largest U.S. cities such as New York City, Los Angeles, and Chicago. The median household income is $52,000. Most rent apartments in high-rise buildings, living alone or with a roommate. They travel, prefer environmentally conscious products, participate in actives such as yoga and downhill skiing, and are highly connected, using tablets to read magazines and newspapers while streaming television shows and movies on their computers. They also are politically liberal.

Exhibit 8–7 shows the location of customers who have the desired geodemographic profile on a trade area map for a shopping center. Note that most of the retailer's desirable customers are not even in the tertiary trade area; thus, this shopping center would not be a desirable location. (The shopping center is designated by the red star. The primary trade area is green; the secondary trade area is lavender; and the tertiary trade area is turquoise.)

EXHIBIT 8–6   GIS Data for Retail Expenditures in a Trade Area

esri

Retail Goods and Services Expenditures
Sample Report

Proposed Location
100 S Wacker Dr, Chicago, IL 60606-4006
Ring: 1 mile radius

Latitude: 41.8805
Longitude: -87.63715

Top Tapestry Segments:		Demographic Summary	2010	2015
Metro Renters	68.4%	Population	45,534	50,151
Laptops and Lattes	23.4%	Households	24,338	26,808
City Strivers	2.7%	Families	7,223	7,843
Main Street, USA	1.8%	Median Age	35.7	35.8
Metropolitans	1.6%	Median Household Income	$81,441	$100,632

	Spending Potential Index	Average Amount Spent	Total
Apparel and Services	120	$2,873.94	$69,945,928
Men's	112	$512.65	$12,476,953
Women's	104	$861.55	$20,968,522
Children's	121	$485.96	$11,827,277
Footwear	84	$349.13	$8,497,153
Watches & Jewelry	173	$335.43	$8,163,589
Apparel Products and Services[1]	352	$329.21	$8,012,434
Computer			
Computers and Hardware for Home Use	169	$324.62	$7,900,647
Software and Accessories for Home Use	169	$48.15	$1,171,788
Entertainment & Recreation	155	$4,996.06	$121,594,105
Fees and Admissions	155	$960.54	$23,377,534
Membership Fees for Clubs[2]	155	$253.65	$6,173,216
Fees for Participant Sports, excl. Trips	145	$154.42	$3,758,358
Admission to Movie/Theatre/Opera/Ballet	172	$260.56	$6,341,578
Admission to Sporting Events, excl. Trips	149	$88.77	$2,160,410
Fees for Recreational Lessons	147	$201.16	$4,895,736
Dating Services	257	$1.98	$48,236
TV/Video/Audio	161	$2,003.60	$48,763,617
Community Antenna or Cable TV	157	$1,130.81	$27,521,629

Source: ESRI

EXHIBIT 8–7
Location of Target
Customers in a Shopping
Center Trade Area

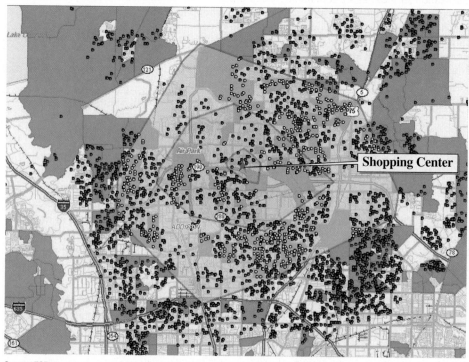

Source: ESRI

Spending Potential Index   Data in ESRI's consumer spending database are reported by product or service; variables include total expenditures, average amount spent per household, and a **Spending Potential Index (SPI)**. The SPI compares the local average expenditure by product to the national average amount spent. An index of 100 is average. For example, an SPI of 120 shows that average spending by local consumers is 20 percent above the national average; an SPI of 80 means that average local spending is 20 percent below the national average. (See Exhibit 8–6.)

Competition in the Trade Area

In addition to needing information about the residents in a trade area, retailers need to know about the amount and type of competition in the trade area. Although GIS vendors provide data on the location of competitive retailers, there are also other sources for this information. For example, most retailer websites list not only all current store locations but future sites as well. A more traditional method of accessing competitive information is to look through the Yellow Pages of the telephone book, or companies might look up the ratings of competitors listed on Yelp using its map function. Other sources of competitive information include directories published by trade associations, chambers of commerce, Chain Store Guide (published by CSG Information Services, www.csgis.com), and municipal and county governments.

ESTIMATING POTENTIAL SALES FOR A STORE SITE

Two approaches for using information about the trade area to estimate the potential sales for a store at the location are (1) regression analysis and (2) the analog method.

LO 8-4

Determine the forecasted sales for a new store location.

Regression Analysis

The **regression analysis** approach is based on the assumption that factors that affect the sales of existing stores in a chain will have the same impact on stores located at new sites being considered. When using this approach, the retailer employs a technique called multiple regression to estimate a statistical model that predicts sales at existing store locations. The technique can consider the effects of the wide range of factors discussed in this chapter, including site characteristics, such as visibility and access, and characteristics of the trade area, such as demographics and lifestyle segments represented.

Consider the following example: A chain of sporting goods stores has analyzed the factors affecting sales in its existing stores and found that the following model is the best predictor of store sales (the weights for the factors, such as 275 for the number of households, are estimated using multiple regression):

Stores sales = 275 × Number of households in trade area (15-minute drive time)
+ 1,800,000 × Percentage of households in trade area with children under 15 years of age
+ 2,000,000 × Percentage of households in trade area in Tapestry segment Aspiring Young
+ 8 × Shopping center square feet
+ 250,000, if visible from street
+ 300,000, if Walmart in center

The sporting goods retailer is considering the following two locations: Using the regression model, the forecasted sales for location A are:

Stores sales at location A = $7,635,000 = 275 × 11,000
+ 1,800,000 × 0.7
+ 2,000,000 × 0.6
+ 8 × 200,000
+ 250,000 × 1
+ 300,000 × 1

and forecasted sales for location B are:

$$\text{Store sales at location B} = \$6{,}685{,}000 = 275 \times 15{,}000$$
$$+ 1{,}800{,}000 \times 0.2$$
$$+ 2{,}000{,}000 \times 0.1$$
$$+ 8 \times 250{,}000$$
$$+ 250{,}000 \times 0$$
$$+ 300{,}000 \times 0$$

Note that location A has greater forecasted sales, even though it has fewer consumers in its trading area and shopping center size, because the profile of its target market fits the retailer's target market (families with children under 15 and in the Aspiring Young Tapestry segment) better.

Analog Approach

To estimate a regression model to predict sales from a site, a retailer needs data about the trade area and site characteristics from a large number of stores. Because small chains cannot use the regression approach, they use the similar but more subjective analog approach. When using the **analog approach**, the retailer simply describes the site and trade area characteristics for its most successful stores and attempts to find a site with similar characteristics. The use of this approach is described in the following illustration.

ILLUSTRATION OF SITE SELECTION: EDWARD BEINER PURVEYOR OF FINE EYEWEAR

LO 8-5

Illustrate the site selection process.

Edward Beiner Purveyor of Fine Eyewear is a 12-store Florida retailer specializing in upper-end, high-fashion eyewear. Its store in South Miami lacks the entertainment and recreation found in shopping centers. Other problems with the location are a lack of protection against the heavy rains that characterize the area's subtropical climate, security, and parking. However, some positive features of the location are the relatively low rent, high pedestrian traffic, few restrictions, and no other high-quality and fashion optical stores in the area, though there are other optical stores in the general area.

Edward Beiner Purveyor of Fine Eyewear wants to open a new location. Because the South Miami site is its best store, it would like to find a location whose trade area has similar characteristics. It has identified several potential locations that it is evaluating.

Using the analog approach, Edward Beiner undertakes the following steps:

1. Conduct a competitive analysis.
2. Define the present trade area.
3. Analyze the trade area characteristics.
4. Match characteristics of the present trade area with potential sites.

Step 1: Conduct a Competitive Analysis

The competitive analysis of the four potential sites being considered by Edward Beiner is shown in Exhibit 8–8. To perform the analysis, Edward Beiner first estimated the number of eyeglasses sold per year per person (column 2), obtained from industry sources. Then the area population was taken from U.S. Census data (column 3). Column 4 is an estimate of the trade area potential reached by multiplying column 2 by column 3.

The estimates of the number of eyeglasses sold in the trade areas, column 5, are based on visits to competitive stores. Column 6 represents the unit sales potential for eyeglasses in the trade areas, or column 4 minus column 5. Then the trade area potential penetration is calculated by dividing column 6 by column 4. For instance, because the total eyeglass potential for the South Miami store trade area is 17,196 pairs and an additional 9,646 pairs

Edward Beiner Purveyor of Fine Eyewear specializes in high-fashion eyewear and targets affluent customers.

EXHIBIT 8–8   Competitive Analysis of Potential Locations

(1) Trade Area	(2) Eyeglasses/ Year/ Person	(3) Trade Area Population	(4) Total Eyeglasses Potential	(5) Estimated Eyeglasses Sold	(6) Trade Area Potential Units	(7) Trade Area Potential Percentage	(8) Relative Level of Competition
South Miami	0.2	85,979	17,196	7,550	9,646	56.09%	Low
Site A	0.2	91,683	18,337	15,800	2,537	13.83	Medium
Site B	0.2	101,972	20,394	12,580	7,814	38.32	Low
Site C	0.2	60,200	12,040	11,300	740	6.15	High
Site D	0.2	81,390	16,278	13,300	2,978	18.29	Medium

could be sold in that trade area, 56.1 percent of the eyeglass market in this area remains untapped. The bigger the number, the lower the competition.

Column 8, the relative level of competition, is subjectively estimated on the basis of column 7. Unlike other optical stores in the trade area, Edward Beiner carries a very exclusive merchandise selection. In general, however, the higher the trade area potential, the lower the relative competition will be.

On the basis of the information in Exhibit 8–8, Edward Beiner should locate its new store at site B. The trade area potential is high, and competition is relatively low. Of course, relative competition is only one issue to consider. Later in this section, we'll consider competition along with other issues to determine which is the best new location for Edward Beiner.

Step 2: Define the Present Trade Area

On the basis of customer spotting data gathered from Beiner's data warehouse of current customers, the trade area map in Exhibit 8–9 was generated using ESRI's GIS software. The zones are based on drive times: 5 minutes for the primary trade area (red), 10 minutes for the secondary trade area (purple), and 20 minutes for the tertiary

EXHIBIT 8–9   Trade Area for Edward Beiner Purveyor of Fine Eyewear

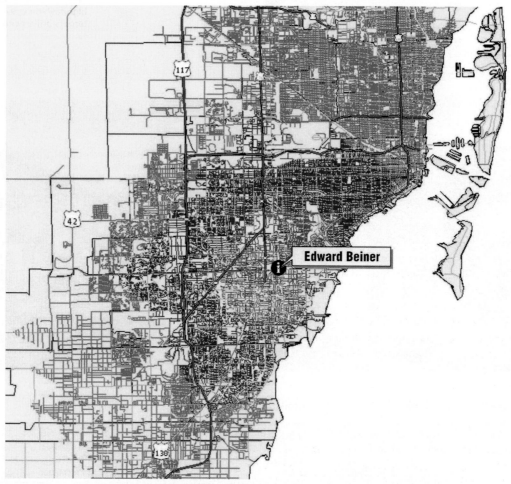

Source: ESRI

trade area (green). Note that the trade area boundaries are oblong because the major highways, especially U.S. 1, run north and south. Not only do the north–south highways bring traffic to the area, but heavy traffic often makes them difficult to cross. Biscayne Bay also limits the trade area on the east.

Because Edward Beiner has a Main Street location, its trade area is smaller than it would be if the store were located in a regional shopping mall. However, Edward Beiner is one of several optical shops in this business district. Having similar shopping goods stores in the same vicinity expands its trade area boundaries; more people are drawn to the area to shop because of its expanded selection. In addition, Edward Beiner's trade area is limited on the south by a large regional shopping center that has several stores carrying similar merchandise.

Step 3: Analyze the Trade Area Characteristics

Having defined its trade area, Edward Beiner reviewed a number of reports describing the characteristics of its trade area. Some of interesting findings from these reports were:

- The average household income is $92,653.

- 27.6 percent of the households have incomes between $75,000 and $149,000, and 13.7 percent have incomes greater than $150,000. The 3-mile ring surrounding Edward Beiner thus is very affluent.

- The area surrounding Edward Beiner has a population that is more than 50 percent Hispanic.

EXHIBIT 8–10 Four Potential Locations for a New Store

Store Location	Average Household Income	White-Collar Occupations	Percentage Residents Age 45 and Over	Predominant Geodemographic Segments	Level of Competition
Edward Beiner					
Optical	$100,000	High	37%	Top One Percent	Low
Site A	60,000	High	25	Young Immigrant Families	Medium
Site B	70,000	Low	80	Gray Power	Low
Site C	100,000	High	30	Young Literati	High
Site D	120,000	High	50	Upper-Income Empty-Nesters	Medium

Step 4: Match Characteristics of the Present Trade Area with Potential Sites

Edward Beiner believes that the profile of its current trade area is high income, predominantly white-collar occupations, a relatively large percentage of older residents, upscale geodemographic segments, and relatively low competition for expensive, high-fashion eyewear. Exhibit 8–10 compares Edward Beiner's current location with four potential locations on these five factors.

Although the potential customers of site A typically have white-collar occupations, they also have relatively low incomes and are comparatively young. Young Immigrant Families also tend to have young families, so expensive eyewear may not be a priority purchase. Finally, there's a medium level of competition in the area.

The Gray Power residents surrounding site B have moderate incomes and are mostly retired. Even though competition would be low and most residents need glasses, these customers are more interested in value than in fashion.

Site C has strong potential because the Young Literati residents in the area are young and have a strong interest in fashion. Although working, they are busy furnishing their first homes and apartments and paying off college loans. They probably would appreciate Edward Beiner's fashionable assortment, but they won't appreciate the high prices. Also, other high-end optical stores are entrenched in the area.

Site D is the best location for Edward Beiner. The residents are older professionals or early retirees with high incomes. Upper-Income Empty-Nesters are sophisticated consumers of adult luxuries like high-fashion eyewear. Importantly, this geodemographic segment is similar to a large segment in Edward Beiner's current location.

Unfortunately, finding analogous situations isn't always as easy as in this example. The weaker the analogy, the more difficult the location decision will be. When a retailer has a relatively small number of outlets (say, 20 or fewer), the analog approach is often best. As the number of stores increases, it becomes more difficult for the analyst to organize the data in a meaningful way. More analytical approaches, such as regression analysis, then are necessary.

NEGOTIATING A LEASE

Once a particular site is chosen, retailers still face a multitude of decisions, including the types and terms of the lease.

LO 8-6

Explain the different types and terms of leases.

Types of Leases

There are two basic types of leases: percentage and fixed rate.

Percentage Leases Although there are many combinations within each type of lease, the most common form is a **percentage lease**, in which the rent is based on a percentage of sales. In addition to the percentage of sales, retailers typically pay a common area maintenance (CAM) fee based on a percentage of their gross leasable square footage. Most malls use some form of percentage lease. Because retail leases typically run for 5 to 10 years, they appear equitable to both parties if rents go up (or down) with sales and inflation.

A **percentage lease with a specified maximum** is a lease that pays the shopping center manager a percentage of sales up to a maximum amount. This type of lease rewards good retailer performance by allowing the retailer to hold rent constant above a certain level of sales. A similar variation, the **percentage lease with a specified minimum**, specifies that the retailer must pay a minimum rent, no matter how low sales are.

Another type of percentage lease is a **sliding scale lease**, in which the percentage of sales paid as rent decreases as the sales go up. For instance, a retailer may pay 4 percent on the first $200,000 in sales and then 3 percent on sales greater than $200,000. Similar to the percentage lease with a specified maximum, the sliding scale rewards high-performing retailers.

Fixed-Rate Leases   The second basic type of lease is a **fixed-rate lease**, most commonly used by community and neighborhood centers. A retailer pays a fixed amount per month over the life of the lease. With a fixed-rate lease, the retailer and shopping center management know exactly how much will be paid in rent, but this type of lease is not as popular as the various forms of percentage leases.

A variation of the fixed-rate lease is the **graduated lease**, in which rent increases by a fixed amount over a specified period of time. For instance, rent may be $1,000 per month for the first three years and $1,250 for the next five years.

Terms of the Lease

Although leases are formal contracts, they can be changed to reflect the relative power of the retailer and shopping center management and specific needs of the retailer. In addition to the rent, some other negotiable aspects of the lease are cotenancy, prohibited-use, and exclusive-use clauses.

Cotenancy Clause   Some retail leases contain **cotenancy clauses**. These clauses may require that a certain percentage of a shopping center be leased or that specified stores be in the center. For example, if The Gap goes into a mall, it doesn't want to be by itself. In all likelihood it has a group of retailers that it views as complements. These may include Banana Republic, Old Navy (both of which are owned by The Gap), Aeropostale, American Eagle Outfitters, Ann Taylor, and bebe, among others. It would not be uncommon to see a lease requirement where The Gap will sign only if at least three of these six retailers just listed are also in the development.

If these terms are violated, the retailers with the cotenancy clauses may demand rent reductions or leave altogether. Cotenancy clauses have become particularly important in the past few years because many retailers, including several large chains like Circuit City, Borders, and Linens 'N Things, have created vacancies as a result of their bankruptcies.[17]

Prohibited-Use Clause   A **prohibited-use clause** limits the shopping center management from leasing to certain kinds of tenants. Many retailers don't want the shopping center space to be leased to establishments that take up parking spaces but do not bring in shoppers, such as a bowling alley, skating rink, meeting hall, dentist, or real estate office. Retailers may also wish to restrict the use of space from those establishments that could harm the shopping center's image. Prohibited-use clauses often specify that bars, pool halls, game parlors, off-track betting establishments, massage parlors, and pornography retailers are unacceptable.

Exclusive-Use Clause   An **exclusive-use clause** prohibits the shopping center management from leasing to retailers that sell competing products. For example, a discount store's lease may specify that the landlord cannot lease to other discount stores, variety stores, or limited-assortment value retailers.

6. Retailers have a choice of locating on a mall's main floor or second or third level. Typically, the main floor offers the best, but most expensive, locations. Why would specialty stores such as The Body Shop or Foot Locker choose the second or third floor?

7. What kind of lease should a new retail enterprise, opening its first store in an urban location that is experiencing gentrification and growth, seek to negotiate with the building owner?

8. If you were considering the ownership of a Taco Bell franchise, what would you want to know about the location in terms of traffic, population, income, employment, and competition? What else would you need to research about a potential location?

CHAPTER ENDNOTES

1. "About Us," http://www.starbucks.com/about-us/company-information/starbucks-company-profile.

2. Barbara Thau, "How Big Data Helps Chains Like Starbucks Pick Store Locations—An (Unsung) Key to Retail Success," *Forbes*, April 24, 2014, http://www.forbes.com.

3. Malcolm Wheatley, "Data-Driven Location Choices Drive Latest Starbucks Surge," *Data Informed*, January 10, 2013, http://data-informed.com/-data-driven-location-choices-drive-latest-starbucks-surge/.

4. ESRI Australia, "Coffee Beans and Business Strategy," https://esriaustralia.com.au/retail.

5. http://www.census.gov/population/metro/.

6. www.icuracao.com.

7. Wendell Cox and Steven Malanga, "California—Toxic for Business," *Los Angeles Times*, November 14, 2011.

8. Thomas J. Holmes, "The Diffusion of Wal-Mart and Economies of Density," *Econometrica* 79, no. 1 (January 2011), pp. 253–302.

9. Lauren K. Ohnesorge, "How Retail Fits into RDU's Terminal 2 Plans," *Triangle Business Journal*, June 22, 2016, http://www.bizjournals.com/triangle/blog/techflash/2016/06/how-retail-fits-into-rdus-terminal-2-plans.html.

10. Celia Brown, "Airport Retail: The Golden Hour and 4 Missed Opportunities," *Forbes*, August 8, 2014.

11. Christopher Teller and Jonathan R. Elms, "Urban Place Marketing and Retail Agglomeration Customers," *Journal of Marketing Management* 28, no. 5–6 (2012), pp. 546–567; Ellen Sewell, "Competition and Dealership Agglomeration in New Car Markets," *Applied Economics Letters* 18, no. 13 (2011), pp. 1279–1283.

12. "Directory," https://www.mallofamerica.com/shopping/map.

13. Tom Ryan, "17 Minutes Defines Local," *RetailWire*, June 2, 2014.

14. Ibid.

15. https://www.census.gov/geo/reference/gtc/gtc_bg.html.

16. http://www.esri.com/landing-pages/tapestry.

17. "Top Ten Issues in Co-Tenancy Provisions in Retail Lease," www.coxcastle.com/publications/article.cfm?id=44.

© Abdelhak Senna/AFP/Getty Images

Fast-fashion retailers offer fashion-conscious customers inexpensive, fashionable merchandise early in the fashion life cycle. These shoppers, who simply must have the latest looks but are also on a very limited budget, buy new fashionable apparel every few weeks instead of purchasing a few higher-priced items every few months. The strategy was pioneered by Zara, a global specialty apparel chain located in La Coruña, Spain, and it demands timely flows of information and merchandise across the supply chain. For example, in Zara stores, managers always have reporting devices literally in hand. The handheld devices are linked directly to the company's corporate office in Spain, so they can issue daily reports about exactly what customers are asking for in each store.[1]

For example, customers might want a purple version of a pink shirt that they see on the shop floor. Managers immediately pass on the information to the designers in Spain. Those designers communicate electronically with the factory that produces fabric for shirts. The factory starts up its automated equipment, run by assemblers who live in close proximity to the factory. (The undyed fabric comes from Asia, where Zara finds inexpensive sources, and then bulk fabric ships to Spain and Portugal to be manufactured into apparel.) The robots in the company's 23 highly automated factories start cutting out shirts and mixing purple dye. For final construction, a network of 300 or so small assemblers, located near the factories in Galicia, Spain, and northern Portugal, take responsibility for the final product. Finally, to ensure timely delivery, the shirts get shipped by truck to stores in Europe and by air express to stores in the rest of the world.

Zara's main advantage over its competitors has resulted from its highly responsive and tightly organized supply chain. Zara selects factory locations that are in close geographic proximity to the company's headquarters in Spain. Although this approach increases labor costs, it also improves communication, reduces shipping costs and time, and reduces the time before new fashions appear in stores. It also gives Zara the flexibility to modify its operations in one supply chain function to expedite processes in another, such as pricing or tagging. It might hang merchandise on racks in the warehouse so that store employees can move apparel directly from delivery to the sales floor.

Furthermore, instead of shipping new products a few times a season, as many of its competitors do, Zara makes deliveries to every one of its stores every few days. The purple shirts would be in stores in two weeks—compared with the several months it would take for most department stores and other specialty apparel stores to accomplish the same feat. Because its fast-fashion system also ensures shorter lead times, it's less likely that any Zara store will be out of stock before the next sweater shipment arrives. By producing and shipping in these small quantities, Zara can quickly recover from its (rare) fashion faux pas. The efficiency of its supply chain means Zara rarely has to discount merchandise that is not selling; the number of items that end up marked down is about half the industry average. Yet Zara still manages to introduce around 10,000 new designs and 40,000 new SKUs each year, as well as strong annual growth rates.

This massive scale means that Zara's average shipping total has reached nearly 2.5 million items per week, all coming from the company's distribution center. Its legendary supply chain efficiency thus was in danger of a clogged artery. By their very nature, fashion trends change rapidly and constantly, and so must the merchandise on Zara's shop floors. Faced with disappointed customers, some sales managers ordered extra quantities of hot items to avoid stock-outs, but then they might receive fewer units than they had ordered because the overall (inflated) demand exceeded inventory levels. For some items, Zara even confronted perhaps the most frustrating scenario in a supply chain: Inventory sat unused, eating up storage costs, at one location, even as another store desperately pleaded for the same inventory to meet its customers' demand.

In response, Zara has adopted some new mathematical processes that turn human experience and mountains of data into actionable information. These models factor in store managers' unique requests for merchandise replenishments, together with historical trends in the sales of the same item. Merchandise display practices have been altered, such as removing all sizes of a garment from the sales floor if a popular size is not available. This practice helps reduce customer frustration, in that they never see an item that might not be available in their size. It also diminishes shipping; if the medium size is unavailable, the small and large sizes do not get shipped either. Instead, these remaining sizes head toward the stores that still have all sizes in stock, so they can be available to customers there.

J oe Jackson wakes up in the morning, takes a shower, dresses, and goes to his kitchen to make a cup of coffee and a bagel. He slices the bagel and puts it in his toaster oven, but to his dismay, the toaster oven is not working. He reviews his e-mails as he is eating his untoasted bagel with his coffee and notices an electronic coupon from Target for home appliances. He reviews the toaster ovens sold by Target on its website, decides he likes a Michael Graves toaster oven best, and sees it available at a store near his apartment. So on his way home from work, he stops at a Target store. He finds the Michael Graves model his likes on the shelf and buys it.

Joe expected to find the Michael Graves toaster oven, as well as other models, available at Target, but he probably didn't realize that a lot of behind-the-scenes activities were going on to get those toaster ovens to the store. Target uses sophisticated information and supply chain management systems to make sure that the Michael Graves toaster ovens and other brands are available in its stores and online whenever Joe and other customers want them. When Joe bought the toaster oven, the information about his transaction was automatically forwarded by the information systems to Target's regional distribution center (DC), the home appliance planner at Target's corporate headquarters in Minneapolis, and the toaster oven manufacturer in China. A **distribution center (DC)** is a facility for the receipt, storage, and redistribution of goods to company stores. It may be operated by retailers, manufacturers, or distribution specialists.[2] A computer information system also monitors all toaster oven sales and inventory levels in every Target store and online and indicates when to have toaster ovens shipped from the manufacturer in China to the regional distribution and fulfillment centers (FCs) and then from the centers to the stores or to individual customers. Although they are similar to DCs, instead of shipping to stores, **fulfillment centers (FCs)** ship directly to customers. Shipments to DCs, FCs, and stores all get monitored using a satellite tracking system that locates the ships and trucks transporting the toaster ovens.

Of course, Target could ensure the availability of toaster ovens and other merchandise by simply keeping a huge inventory of units in the stores and at the FCs at all times. But stocking a large number of each model would require much more space to store the items and a significant investment in additional inventory. So the challenge for Target is to limit its inventory and space investment but still make sure products are always available when customers want them.

This chapter begins by outlining how retailers can gain a strategic advantage through supply chain management and information systems. Then it describes the flows of information and merchandise in the supply chain. Finally, the chapter outlines some of the decisions and trends that retailers make to determine the structure of the supply chain, such as whether to use DCs or direct store deliveries and whether to outsource some supply chain functions.

CREATING STRATEGIC ADVANTAGE THROUGH SUPPLY CHAIN MANAGEMENT AND INFORMATION SYSTEMS

LO 9-1

Understand the strategic advantage generated by a supply chain.

As discussed in Chapter 1, retailers are the connection between customers and manufacturers. It is the retailer's responsibility to gauge customers' wants and needs and work with the other members of the supply chain—wholesalers, vendors, and transportation companies—to make sure the merchandise that customers want is available when they want it. **Wholesalers** are firms that buy products from manufacturers and resell them to retailers. A simplified supply chain is illustrated in Exhibit 9–1. The

EXHIBIT 9–1
Illustration of a
Supply Chain

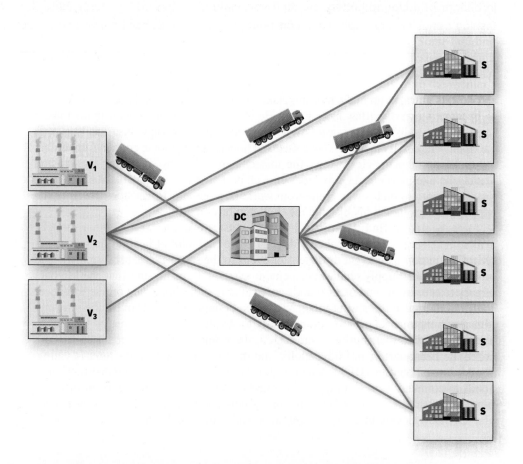

exhibit would be much more complicated—and harder to read—if we included all the various suppliers of materials to manufacturers; all the various manufacturers, wholesalers, and stores in a typical supply chain; and electronic channels through which customers order products and receive them directly with the assistance of delivery providers such as UPS, FedEx, or the U.S. Postal Service.

Instead, in this simplified supply chain, vendors ship merchandise either to a distribution center (DC) (as is the case for vendors V_1 and V_3) or directly to stores (as is the case for vendor V_2). The factors considered in deciding to ship directly to stores versus to DCs are discussed later in this chapter.

Supply chain management is a set of activities and techniques firms employ to efficiently and effectively manage these flows of merchandise from the vendors to the retailer's customers. These activities ensure that the customers are able to purchase merchandise in the desired quantities at a preferred location and appropriate time.[3]

Retailers are increasingly taking a leadership role in managing their supply chains. When retailers were predominantly small businesses, larger manufacturers and distributors dictated when, where, and how merchandise was delivered. But with the consolidation and emergence of large, global retail chains, retailers often play a dominant role in coordinating supply chain management activities. They often work closely with their suppliers to educate and protect is customers, as described in Retailing View 9.1. As we discuss later in the chapter, retailers also are sharing their data on shopping behaviors with suppliers to plan production, promotions, deliveries, assortments, and inventory levels. Efficient supply chain management is important to retailers because it can provide a strategic advantage from increases in product availability and inventory turnover and produces a higher return on assets.

RETAILING VIEW   Kroger's Communications with Suppliers Benefits Customers

9.1

As customers become more environmentally and health conscious, smart grocers are finding ways to collaborate with their supply chains to meet their needs. When customers ask questions and demand information about the origin of their food, providing answers requires input from the entire food supply chain, from the farmers to manufacturers to grocers. Such collaboration is especially important when things go wrong.

Accordingly, the food supplier Cargill promises visibility to its retail partners and consumers, all the way back to the practices on the farms from which it sources its raw materials. When Kroger stores suffered challenges due to an outbreak of bird flu among some suppliers, Cargill helped the chain find new sources of turkey for its deli operations.

Customers at Kroger also want sales associates to be able to answer specific questions about the products that they carry. But each Kroger location has 50,000–60,000 items, sourced from thousands of suppliers, which makes it very difficult to ensure that each sales associate has all the knowledge needed to address these varied customer concerns. In its attempt to provide the most information it can, though, Kroger works with some suppliers. For example, part of its 10-year partnership with Murray's Cheese includes the provision of extended training for Kroger associates. Over a two- to three-week training program, the grocery retailer's dairy department employees learn about where the various cheeses supplied by Murray's actually gets made. Part of this program even involves field trips and visits to the farms that

Murray's Cheese provides extended training to Kroger associates about its cheeses.

are home to the cows whose milk gets used to produce the final product.

Sources: Eric Schroeder, "Driving Partnership across the Food Supply Chain," *Food Business News*, May 20, 2016; Marcel Smits, Don Mulligan, Mike Schlotman, Kelly Bania, and Ken Zaslow, "Cargill Inc., General Mills and The Kroger Co at BMO Capital Markets Farm to Market Conference (Keynote Panel)," May 19, 2016, http://www6.lexisnexis.com/publisher/EndUser?Action=UserDisplayFullDocument&orgId=2430&topicId=100010172&docId=l:2591728624&Em=7&start=3; Ken Roseboro, "Organic Food Companies Collaborating to Increase Organic Grain Supply," *The Organic & Non-GMO Report*, March 27, 2015.

Strategic Advantage

As we discussed in Chapter 5, strategic advantages are unique, and sustainable advantages enable retailers to realize a higher-than-average return on their assets. Of course, all retailers strive to develop a competitive advantage, but not all retailers can develop a competitive advantage from their information and supply chain systems.[4] However, if they do develop such an advantage, the advantage is sustainable because it is difficult for competitors to duplicate.

For example, a critical factor in Walmart's success is its information and supply chain management systems. Even though competitors recognize this advantage, they have difficulty achieving the same level of performance as Walmart's systems for four reasons. First, Walmart has made substantial initial and continuing investments in developing its systems over a long time period. Second, it has the size and scale economies to justify these investments. Third, its supply chain activities take place within the firm and are not easily known and copied by competitors. Its systems are not simply software packages that any firm can buy from a software supplier. Through its continuous learning process, Walmart is always refining its systems to improve its performance. Fourth, the coordinated effort of employees and functional areas throughout the company is supported by Walmart's top management and organization culture.

Yet even with these remarkable advantages, Walmart reported sales losses of about $3 billion in a recent year, due solely to out-of-stock events.[5] The reason may have to do with the many and varied activities that retailers undertake to keep merchandise in stock, including the following:

- Accurately forecast sales and needed inventory levels for each category and SKU at the DCs, FCs, and stores.
- Replenish merchandise from DCs with the right quantities when the stores need it.
- Monitor sales to detect deviations from the forecast.
- Transport the right amount of merchandise from the DCs to each store.
- Make sure that accurate information is available that indicates where the merchandise is—in the vendor's warehouse, the DCs or FCs, the stores, sold to customer, or in transit.
- Place accurate, timely orders with vendors.
- Ensure that buyers and marketing managers coordinate merchandise delivery with special sales and promotional materials.
- Collect and process returned merchandise.

Improved Product Availability

Efficient supply chain management provides two benefits to retailers and their customers: (1) fewer stockouts and (2) tailored assortments. These benefits translate into greater sales, lower costs, higher inventory turnover, and lower markdowns for retailers.

Fewer Stockouts   A **stockout** occurs when an SKU that a customer wants is not available. What would happen if Joe went to the Target store and the store did not have the Michael Graves toaster oven he wants because the DC did not ship enough to the store? The store would give Joe a **rain check** so that he could come back and still pay the sale price when the store receives a new shipment. But Joe would not be pleased because he would have made a wasted trip to the store. As a result of the stockout, Joe might decide to buy another model, or he might go online to Amazon to buy a toaster oven. While at Amazon, he could buy other items in addition to the toaster oven. He also might be reluctant to shop at Target in the future and might tell his friends about the negative experience he had or post a negative review on Yelp or Twitter. This bad experience could have been avoided if Target had done a better job of managing its supply chain.

© Phil Walter/Getty Images

Efficient supply chain management reduces stockouts.

In general, stockouts have significant negative short- and long-term effects on sales and profits. Data from apparel shoppers show that when experiencing a stockout, 17 percent of consumers will switch to another brand, 39 percent will go to another store to buy the product, and the remaining 44 percent will just stop shopping. In addition, when experiencing multiple stockouts, customers typically switch to another retailer.[6] Accordingly, stockouts cost U.S. retailers approximately $130 billion in lost revenue each year.[7]

Tailored Assortments   Another benefit provided by information systems that support supply chain systems is making sure that the right merchandise is available at the right store. Most national retail chains adjust assortments in their stores on the basis of climate—stocking more wool sweaters in northern stores and cotton sweaters in southern stores during the winter. Some retailers are now using sophisticated statistical methods to analyze sales transaction data and adjust store assortments for a wide range of merchandise on the basis of the characteristics of customers in each store's local market. (See Chapter 11 for more information on assortment planning.)

Higher Return on Assets

From the retailer's perspective, an efficient supply chain and information system can improve its return on assets (ROA) because the system increases sales and net profit margins, without increasing inventory. Net sales increase because customers are offered more attractive, tailored assortments that are in stock. Consider Joe Jackson's toaster oven purchase. Target, with its information systems, could accurately estimate how many Michael Graves toaster ovens each store and online would sell during the special promotion. Using its supply chain management system, it would make sure sufficient stock was available at Joe's store so that all the customers who wanted to buy one could.

Net profit margin is improved by increasing the gross margin and lowering expenses. An information system that coordinates buyers and vendors allows retailers to take advantage of special buying opportunities and obtain the merchandise at a lower cost, thus improving their gross margins. By effectively forecasting sales, retailers can

By effectively forecasting sales, retailers can reduce the overstock situations that result in markdowns, which also improves gross margins.

© Peter Scholey/Alamy Stock Photo

reduce the overstock situations that result in markdowns, which also improves gross margins. One estimate suggests that U.S. retailers lose $123 billion in annual earnings, which they would have received had they not had to cut prices to move their excess inventory.[8] Retailers also can lower their cost of goods sold by coordinating deliveries, thus reducing transportation expenses. With more efficient DCs and FCs, merchandise can be received, prepared for sale, and shipped to stores or customers with minimum handling, further reducing expenses.

By efficiently managing their supply chains, retailers can carry less backup inventory yet still avoid stockouts. Thus, inventory levels are lower, and with a lower inventory investment, total assets are also lower, so the asset and inventory turnovers are both higher.

THE FLOW OF INFORMATION THROUGH A SUPPLY CHAIN

LO 9-2

Describe how information flows in a supply chain.

Information flows from the customer to stores, to and from DCs and FCs, to and from wholesalers, to and from product manufacturers, and then on to the producers of any components and the suppliers of raw materials. To simplify our discussion—and because information flows are similar in other marketing channel links, such as through the Internet and catalogs—we again shorten the supply chain in this section to exclude wholesalers, as well as the link from suppliers to manufacturers. Exhibit 9–2 illustrates the flow of information that starts when Joe Jackson bought his toaster oven at Target. The flow follows these steps:

- **Flow 1 (Customer to Store):** At the **point-of-sale (POS) terminal**, the associate scans the **universal product code (UPC)** tag on the toaster oven packaging, and the customer receives a receipt. The UPC tag is the black-and-white bar code found on most merchandise. It contains a 13-digit code that indicates the manufacturer of the item, a description of the item, information about special packaging, and special promotions.[9] In the future, RFID tags, discussed later in this chapter, may replace UPC tags.

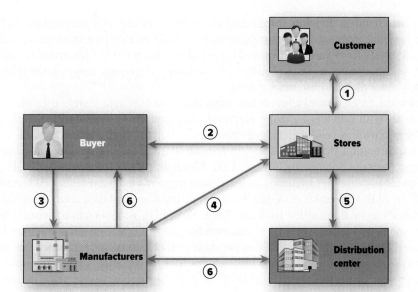

EXHIBIT 9–2
Information Flows

- **Flow 2 (Store to Buyer):** The POS terminal records the purchase information and electronically sends it to the buyer at Target's corporate office. The sales information is incorporated into an inventory management system and used to monitor and analyze sales and decide to reorder more toaster ovens, change a price, or plan a promotion. Buyers also send information to stores about overall sales for the chain, ways to display the merchandise, upcoming promotions, and so on.

- **Flow 3 (Buyer to Manufacturer):** The purchase information from each Target store and its online operation is typically aggregated by the retailer as a whole, which creates an order for new merchandise and sends it to the toaster oven manufacturer. The buyer at Target may also communicate directly with the manufacturer to get information and negotiate prices, shipping dates, promotional events, or other merchandise-related issues.

- **Flow 4 (Store to Manufacturer):** In some situations, the sales transaction data are sent directly from the store to the manufacturer, and the manufacturer decides when to ship more merchandise to the DCs, FCs, and the stores. In other situations, especially when merchandise is reordered frequently, the ordering process is done automatically, bypassing the buyers. By working together, the retailer and manufacturer can better satisfy customer needs.

- **Flow 5 (Store to Distribution Center):** Stores also communicate with the Target distribution centers to coordinate deliveries and check inventory status. When the store inventory drops to a specified level, more toaster ovens are shipped to the store, and the shipment information is sent to the Target computer system.

- **Flow 6 (Manufacturer to Distribution Center and Buyer):** When the manufacturer ships the toaster ovens to the Target DCs or FCs, it sends an advanced shipping notice to them. An **advance shipping notice (ASN)** is an electronic document that the supplier sends the retailer in advance of a shipment to tell the retailer exactly what to expect in the shipment. The center then makes appointments for trucks to make the delivery at a specific time, date, and loading dock. When the shipment is received at the distribution center, the buyer is notified and authorizes payment to the vendor.

Data Warehouse

Purchase data collected at the point of sale (information flow 2 in Exhibit 9–2) goes into a huge database known as a **data warehouse**. Using the data warehouse, executives can learn how the corporation is generally doing. They also can look at the data for a merchandise division, a region of the country, or the total corporation. A buyer may be more interested in a particular manufacturer in a certain store on a particular day. Analysts from various levels of the retail operation extract information from the data warehouse to make a plethora of marketing decisions about developing and replenishing merchandise assortments.

In some cases, manufacturers also have access to this data warehouse. They communicate with retailers by using electronic data interchange (EDI) and supply chain systems known as vendor-managed inventory.

In information flows 3, 4, and 6 in Exhibit 9–2, the retailer and manufacturer exchange business documents through EDI. **Electronic data interchange (EDI)** is the computer-to-computer exchange of business documents from a retailer to a vendor and back. In addition to sales data, purchase orders, invoices, and data about returned merchandise can be transmitted back and forth. With EDI, vendors can transmit information about on-hand inventory status, vendor promotions, and cost changes to the retailer, as well as information about purchase order changes, order status, retail prices, and transportation routings. Thus EDI enables channel members to communicate more quickly and with fewer errors than in the past, ensuring that merchandise moves from vendors to retailers more quickly.

Vendor-Managed Inventory and Collaborative Planning, Forecasting, and Replenishment

Vendor-managed inventory (VMI) is an approach for improving marketing channel efficiency, in which the manufacturer is responsible for maintaining the retailer's inventory levels in each of its stores.[10] By sharing the data in the retailer's data warehouse and communicating that information via EDI, the manufacturer automatically sends merchandise to the retailer's store, DC, or FC when the inventory at the store reaches a prespecified level.[11]

In ideal conditions, the manufacturer replenishes inventories in quantities that meet the retailer's immediate demand, reducing stockouts with minimal inventory. In addition to providing a better match between retail demand and supply, VMI can reduce the vendor's and the retailer's costs. Manufacturer salespeople no longer need to spend time generating orders on items that are already in the stores, and their role shifts to selling new items and maintaining relationships. Retail buyers and planners no longer need to monitor inventory levels and place orders.

The use of VMI is not a new approach. Frito-Lay and other snack food, candy, and beverage vendors have used VMI combined with direct store delivery to manage the inventory of their products on supermarket shelves for a long time. However, technological advances like EDI have increased the sophistication of VMI.

Although it is a more advanced level of collaboration, VMI still has its limitations. The vendor coordinates the supply chain for its specific products, but it does not know what other actions the retailer might be taking that could affect the sales of its products in the future. For example, Pepsi might not know that a supermarket will be having a big promotion in three weeks for a new beverage introduced by Coca-Cola. Without this knowledge, Pepsi would ship too much merchandise. To overcome the lack of two-way communications that is inherent in traditional VMI systems, **collaborative planning, forecasting, and replenishment (CPFR)** relies on shared forecasts and related business information and collaborative planning between retailers and vendors to improve supply chain efficiency and product replenishment. Although retailers share sales and inventory data when using a VMI approach, the vendor remains responsible for managing the inventory. In contrast, CPFR is a more advanced form of retailer–vendor collaboration that involves sharing proprietary information such as business strategies, promotion plans, new product developments and introductions, production schedules, and lead-time information.

For example, in its efforts to enhance the sustainability of its operations, Walmart works with its vendors to plan hauling and shipping operations more carefully, and has doubled its fleet efficiency in the United States since 2005. It has also eliminated over 650,000 metric tons of greenhouse gas and reduced 75 percent of its global waste from landfills.[12]

THE FLOW OF MERCHANDISE THROUGH A SUPPLY CHAIN

Exhibit 9–3 illustrates the merchandise flow steps for a large retailer that relies largely on its physical store operations, such as Target. The merchandise flows and pertinent decision variables in an Internet channel are similar, except that orders arrive from customers one at a time and go out in relatively small quantities, so the facility used to store and process these orders—that is, the fulfillment center (FC)—works a little differently. In general, the merchandise flow steps are:

LO 9-3

Consider the flow of merchandise through a supply chain.

1. Toaster oven manufacturer to Target's distribution centers, or

2. Manufacturer directly to Target's stores.

3. If the merchandise goes through distribution centers, it is then shipped to stores,

4. and then the customer buys it.

EXHIBIT 9–3   Merchandise Flows

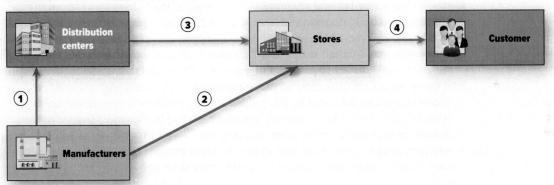

Making merchandise flow involves first deciding whether the merchandise will go from the manufacturer to a retailer's DC or directly on to stores. Once in a DC, multiple activities take place before it is shipped to a store. These activities might vary across different supply chains.

Distribution Centers versus Direct Store Delivery

As indicated in Exhibit 9–3, manufacturers can ship merchandise directly to a retailer's stores—**direct store delivery (DSD)** (flow 2)—or to their DCs (flow 1). Although manufacturers and retailers may collaborate, the ultimate decision is usually up to the retailer and depends on the characteristics of the merchandise and the nature of demand.

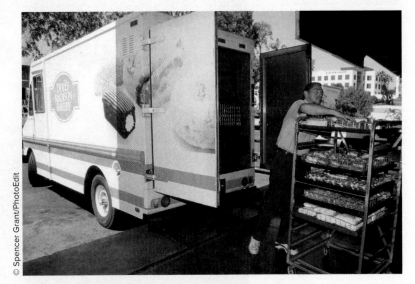

© Spencer Grant/PhotoEdit

Dolly Madison's baked goods are delivered directly to the retailer's store, bypassing the DC, ensuring that customers can get the freshest merchandise.

To determine which distribution system—DCs centers or direct store delivery—is better, retailers consider the total cost associated with each alternative and the customer service criterion of having the right merchandise at the store when the customer wants to buy it.

There are several advantages to using a distribution center:

- More accurate sales forecasts are possible when retailers combine forecasts for many stores serviced by one DC rather than doing a forecast for each store. Consider a set of 50 Target stores, serviced by a single DC that each carries Michael Graves toaster ovens. Each store normally stocks 5 units for a total of 250 units in the system. By carrying the item at each store, the retailer must develop individual forecasts, each with the possibility of errors that could result in either too much or too little merchandise. Alternatively, by delivering most of the inventory to a DC and feeding the stores merchandise as they need it, the effects of forecast errors for the individual stores are minimized, and less backup inventory is needed to prevent stockouts.

- Distribution centers enable the retailer to carry less merchandise in the individual stores, which results in lower inventory investments systemwide. If the stores get frequent deliveries from the DC, they need to carry relatively less extra merchandise as backup stock.

- It is easier to avoid running out of stock or having too much stock in any particular store because merchandise is ordered from the DC as needed.

- Retail store space is typically much more expensive than space at a DC, and DCs are better equipped than stores to prepare merchandise for sale. As a result, many retailers find it cost-effective to store merchandise and get it ready for sale at a DC rather than in individual stores. But DCs aren't appropriate for all retailers. If a retailer has only a few outlets, the expense of a DC is probably unwarranted. Also, if many outlets are concentrated in metropolitan areas, merchandise can be consolidated and delivered by the vendor directly to all the stores in one area economically. Direct store delivery gets merchandise to the stores faster and thus is used for perishable goods (meat and produce), items that help create the retailer's image of being the first to sell the latest product (e.g., video games), or fads. Finally, some manufacturers provide direct store delivery for retailers to

Direct store delivery gets merchandise to the stores faster and thus is used for perishable goods like produce.

ensure that their products are on the store's shelves, properly displayed, and fresh. For example, employees delivering Frito-Lay snacks directly to supermarkets replace products that have been on the shelf too long and are stale, replenish products that have been sold, and arrange products so they are neatly displayed.

The Distribution (or Fulfillment) Center

The DC performs the following activities: managing inbound transportation; receiving and checking; storing and cross-docking; getting merchandise floor-ready; ticketing and marking; preparing to ship merchandise to stores; and shipping merchandise to stores. Fulfillment centers perform the same functions, but because they deliver directly to customers rather than to stores, they do not have to get merchandise floor ready. To illustrate these activities being undertaken in a DC, we'll continue our example of toaster ovens being shipped to a Target DC.

Managing Inbound Transportation   Traditionally, buyers focused their efforts, when working with manufacturers, on developing merchandise assortments, negotiating prices, and arranging joint promotions. Now, buyers and planners are much more involved in coordinating the physical flow of merchandise to stores. **Buyers** are generally responsible for the purchase and profitability of merchandise, whereas **planners** are responsible for the financial planning and analysis of merchandise and its allocation to stores.

The buyer arranges for a truckload of toaster ovens to be delivered to a DC at a specific time because the distribution center has all of its 100 receiving docks allocated throughout the day, and much of the merchandise on this particular truck is going to be shipped to stores that evening. Unfortunately, the truck was delayed in a snowstorm. The **dispatcher**—the person who coordinates deliveries to the distribution center—reassigns the truck delivering the toaster ovens to a Wednesday morning delivery slot and charges the firm several hundred dollars for missing its delivery time. Although many manufacturers pay transportation expenses, some retailers negotiate with their vendors to absorb this expense. These retailers believe they can lower their net merchandise cost and better control merchandise flow if they negotiate directly with trucking companies and consolidate shipments from many vendors.

Receiving and Checking Using UPC or RFID   **Receiving** is the process of recording the receipt of merchandise as it arrives at a distribution center. **Checking** is the process of going through the goods upon receipt to make sure they arrived undamaged and that the merchandise ordered was the merchandise received.

In the past, checking merchandise was a very labor-intensive and time-consuming process. Today, however, many distribution systems using EDI are designed to minimize, if not eliminate, these processes. The advance shipping notice (ASN) tells the distribution center what should be in each carton. A UPC label or radio frequency identification (RFID) tag on the shipping carton that identifies the carton's contents is scanned and automatically counted as it is being received and checked. **Radio frequency identification (RFID) tags** are tiny computer chips that automatically transmit to a special scanner all the information about a container's contents or individual products.

Storing and Cross-Docking   After the merchandise is received and checked, it is either stored or cross-docked. When merchandise is stored, the cartons are transported by a conveyor system and forklift trucks to racks that go from the distribution center's floor to its ceiling. Then, when the merchandise is needed in the stores, a forklift driver or a robot goes to the rack, picks up the carton, and places it on a conveyor system that routes the carton to the loading dock of a truck going to the store.

Using a **cross-docking distribution center**, merchandise cartons are prepackaged by the vendor for a specific store. The UPC or RFID labels on the carton indicate the

No hands are needed to cross-dock merchandise. The automated conveyor systems move merchandise from the unloading area for a vendor's inbound truck to the loading area for a retailer's outbound truck going to its store.

© Carla Gottgens/Bloomberg via Getty Images

store to which it is to be sent. The vendor also may affix price tags to each item in the carton. Because the merchandise is ready for sale, it is placed on a conveyor system that routes it from the unloading dock at which it was received to the loading dock for the truck going to the specific store—hence the name *cross-docked.* The cartons are routed on the conveyor system automatically by sensors that read the UPC or RFID label on the cartons. Cross-docked merchandise is in the DC for only a few hours before it is shipped to the stores.

Merchandise sales rate and degree of perishability or fashionability typically determine whether cartons are cross-docked or stored. For instance, because the toaster ovens sell so quickly, it is in Target's interest not to store them in a DC. Similarly, cross-docking is preferable for fashion apparel or perishable meat or produce.

Getting Merchandise Floor-Ready   For some merchandise, additional tasks are undertaken in the distribution center to make the merchandise floor-ready. **Floor-ready merchandise** is merchandise that is ready to be placed on the selling floor. Getting merchandise floor-ready entails ticketing, marking, and, in the case of some apparel, placing garments on hangers (or maybe attaching RFID chips). For the UK-based grocery chain Tesco, it is essential that products ship in ready-to-sell units so that it has little manipulation or sorting to do at the distribution center or in the stores. To move the store-ready merchandise it receives from suppliers quickly into the store, Tesco demands that products sit on roll cages rather than pallets. Then, store employees can easily wheel them onto the retail floor. The stores' backrooms have only two or three days' worth of backup inventory, and it is important to keep inventory levels low and receive lots of small, accurate deliveries from its suppliers—which also helps cut costs.[13] Retailing View 9.2 provides more detail about how IKEA's unique and innovative supply chain leads to a whole new definition of what floor-ready can mean.

Ticketing and Marking   **Ticketing and marking** refers to affixing price and identification labels to the merchandise. It is more efficient for a retailer to perform these activities at a DC than in its stores. In a DC, an area can be set aside and a process implemented to efficiently add labels and put apparel on hangers. Conversely, getting merchandise floor-ready in stores can block aisles and divert sales people's attention from their customers. An even better approach from the retailer's perspective is to get

IKEA, a global retailer headquartered in Sweden, offers a wide range of well-designed, functional home furnishing products at low prices. It's easy to make high-quality products and sell them at a high price or make low-quality products to sell at a low price. But IKEA seeks to be cost-effective and innovative, such that it sells relatively high-quality products at low prices. In its efforts to provide "affordable solutions for better living," IKEA has radically changed the way many people furnish and decorate their homes. As the chain has grown and spread, from its single-operation origins in Sweden to a global presence of more than 350 stores in nearly 50 countries, it has prompted millions of customers to regard furniture as something they can put together on their own, rather than items they should purchase preassembled. To be ready for sale, furniture needs only to be packed in a box that consumers can take home. It does not necessitate labor in distribution centers or stores to put the items together.

IKEA's unique approach starts on the factory floor. Product developers and designers work closely with suppliers to use production equipment and raw materials efficiently and keep waste to a minimum. Early on, an IKEA product developer learned about board-on-frame construction while touring a door factory. This cost-effective, environmentally friendly technique layers sheets of wood over a honeycomb core to provide a strong, lightweight structure with minimal wood content. IKEA engineers similarly have replaced solid table legs with hollow ones, reducing both the weight of the tables being shipped and the amount of raw materials required to make them. It has redesigned a popular sofa to be sold in pieces, instead of a single unit, which allows the retailer to fit all the pieces into a much smaller box, without any dead air in the box. As the CEO of IKEA asserts, "We hate air," because eliminating dead spaces anywhere in its packaging and shipping containers allows the company to fit more units onto trucks, reducing the number of trips required to restock stores—and significantly cutting transportation costs. In turn, it passes on the cost savings to customers, encouraging more people to purchase the lighter-weight, but otherwise similar, products.

IKEA's furniture is packed in a box that its customers can take home and put together. It designs furniture to fit in boxes without dead space to reduce waste and transportation expenses.

With these various moves, IKEA is determined to keep existing customers loyal, constantly attract new customers, and meet ambitious growth goals of $56.2 billion by 2020, which would require nearly 10 percent growth every year until then, compared to an average of around 5 percent in recent years. It strongly believes that its supply chain efficiency efforts ultimately lead to better products, at better prices, that are not available anywhere else. Thus it hopes to put the right products in the right place, with the lowest cost and the least damage to the environment. That's a nearly irresistible recipe for growth.

Sources: IKEA, "Flat Packs, Stacks and How We Ship Them," http://www.ikea.com/ms/en_US/the_ikea_story/working_at_ikea/work_areas_logistics.html; "IKEA," https://en.wikipedia.org/wiki/IKEA; Matt McCue, "IKEA: For Delighting Customers at Each and Every Turn," *Fast Company,* February 9, 2015, http://www.fastcompany.com/3039598/most-innovative-companies-2015/ikea; Saabira Chaudhuri, "IKEA's Favorite Design Idea: Shrink the Box," *The Wall Street Journal,* June 18, 2015; Deniz Caglar, Marco Kesteloo, and Art Kleiner, "How IKEA Reassembled Its Growth Strategy," *Strategy1Business,* May 2012; Yongquan Hu and Huifang Jiang, "Innovation Strategy of Retailers: From the View of Global Value Chains," *6th International Conference on Service Systems and Service Management,* 2009, pp. 340–345.

vendors to ship floor-ready merchandise, totally eliminating the expensive, time-consuming ticketing and marking process.

Preparing to Ship Merchandise to a Store At the beginning of the day, the computer system in the DC generates a list of items to be shipped to each store on that day. For each item, a pick ticket and shipping label is generated. The **pick ticket** is a document or display on a screen in a forklift truck indicating how much of each item to get from specific storage areas. The forklift driver goes to the storage area, picks up the number of cartons indicated on the pick ticket, places UPC shipping labels on the cartons that indicate the stores to which the items are to be shipped, and puts the cartons on the conveyor system, where

Ticketing and marking are often done in the DC so that the merchandise is floor-ready—that is, ready to put on the sales floor when the carton is opened at the store.

When it is not economical to send a full carton of a single item to a store, the multiple items are picked from the shelves and put into another carton for shipment to the store.

they are automatically routed to the loading dock for the truck going to the stores. In some distribution and fulfillment centers, these functions are performed by robots.

Shipping Merchandise to Stores

Shipping merchandise to stores from a DC has become increasingly complex. Most DCs run 50 to 100 outbound truck routes in one day. To handle this complex transportation problem, the centers use sophisticated routing and scheduling computer systems that consider the locations of the stores, road conditions, and transportation operating constraints to develop the most efficient routes possible. As a result, stores are provided with an accurate estimated time of arrival, and vehicle usage is maximized.

Inventory Management through Just-in-Time Inventory Systems

Marketing channel management today offers some cutting-edge solutions to the various distribution problems faced by firms. As recently as the early 1990s, even the most innovative firms needed 15 to 30 days—or even more—to fulfill an order from the warehouse to the customer. The typical order-to-delivery process had several steps: order creation, usually using a telephone, fax, or mail; order processing, using a manual system for credit authorization and assignment to a warehouse; and physical delivery. Things could, and often did, go wrong. Ordered goods were not available. Orders were lost or misplaced. Shipments were misdirected. These mistakes lengthened the time it took to get merchandise to customers and potentially made the entire process more expensive.

Faced with such predicaments, firms began stockpiling inventory at each level of the supply chain (retailers, wholesalers, and manufacturers), but keeping inventory where it is not needed becomes a huge and wasteful expense. If a manufacturer has a huge stock of items stuck in a warehouse, it not only is not earning profits by selling those items but also must pay to maintain and guard that warehouse.

Therefore, many firms, such as Zara, Mango, Uniqlo, H&M, and Forever 21, have adopted a practice developed by Toyota in the 1950s. **Just-in-time (JIT) inventory systems**, also known as **quick response (QR) inventory systems** in retailing, are inventory management systems that deliver less merchandise on a more frequent basis than traditional inventory systems. The firm gets the merchandise just in time for it to be used in the manufacture of another product or for sale when the customer wants it. The benefits of a JIT system include reduced **lead time** (the amount of time between the recognition that an order needs to be placed and the arrival of the needed merchandise at the seller's store and is available for sale), increased product availability, and lower inventory investment.

Reduced Lead Time   By eliminating the need for paper transactions, the EDI in the JIT systems reduces lead time. Even better, the shorter lead times further reduce the need for inventory because the shorter the lead time, the easier it is for the retailer to accurately forecast its demand.

Increased Product Availability and Lower Inventory Investment   In general, as a firm's ability to satisfy customer demand by having stock on hand increases, so does its inventory investment; that is, it needs to keep more backup inventory in stock. But with JIT, the ability to satisfy demand can actually increase while inventory decreases. Because a firm like H&M can make purchase commitments or produce merchandise closer to the time of sale, its own inventory investment is reduced. H&M needs less inventory because it's getting less merchandise in each order but receiving those shipments more often.

The ability to satisfy customer demand by keeping merchandise in stock also increases in JIT systems as a result of the more frequent shipments. For instance, if an H&M store runs low on a medium-sized, red T-shirt, its JIT system ensures a shorter lead time than those of more traditional retailers. As a result, it is less likely that the H&M store will be out of stock for its customers before the next T-shirt shipment arrives.

Costs of a JIT System   Although firms achieve great benefits from a JIT system, it is not without its costs. The distribution function becomes much more complicated with more frequent deliveries. With greater order frequency also come smaller orders, which are more expensive to transport and more difficult to coordinate. Therefore, JIT systems require a strong commitment by the firm and its vendors to cooperate, share data, and develop systems.

SYSTEM DESIGN ISSUES AND TRENDS

This section reviews some of the various issues and considerations that currently affect supply chain decisions, including outsourcing options and defining the type of supply chain to use. It also addresses the final steps in the supply chain, namely, getting merchandise to consumers and possibly taking it back when needed.

LO 9-4

Review the considerations and trends in the design of supply chains.

Outsourcing Supply Chain Functions

To streamline their operations and make more productive use of their assets and personnel, some retailers **outsource** supply chain functions. Many independent companies are very efficient at performing individual activities or all the supply chain activities. There are a large number of companies that can transport merchandise from the vendor to DCs, from the centers to the retailer's stores, or from the FCs to individual consumers. Rather than owning warehouses to store merchandise, retailers can use **public warehouses** that are owned and operated by an independent company. Rather than outsource specific activities, retailers can use freight forwarders to arrange for the storage and shipping of their merchandise. **Freight forwarders** provide a wide range of services: tracking transportation routes, preparing export and shipping documentation, booking cargo space (or warehousing items until the cargo space is needed), negotiating the charges for and consolidating freight, and insuring the cargo or filing insurance claims as necessary.[14]

Advantages and Disadvantages of Outsourcing Supply Chain Activities
The primary benefit of outsourcing is that the independent firms can perform the activity at a lower cost and/or more efficiently than the retailer. Independent firms typically have a lower cost because they perform the activity for many retailers and thus realize scale economies. For example, independent trucking firms have more opportunities to fill their trucks on the return trip (**backhaul**) with merchandise for other retailers after delivering merchandise to one retailer's stores. In addition, when there are many independent firms available to undertake the activity, retailers can have the firms bid against each other to undertake the activity and thus drive down the costs.

However, when retailers outsource a supply chain activity they can no longer develop a competitive advantage based on the performance of this activity. If the retailer's competitor discovers that the retailer is significantly reducing its costs or improving its efficiency by using an independent firm, the competitor can match the performance improvement by contracting with the same provider.

Pull and Push Supply Chains

Another supply chain decision retailers make is determining whether merchandise will be pushed from the DCs to the stores or pulled from the DCs to the stores. Information and merchandise flows such as those described in Exhibit 9–2 illustrate a **pull supply chain**—a supply chain in which requests for merchandise are generated at the store level on the basis of sales data captured by POS terminals. Basically, in this type of supply chain, the demand for an item pulls it through the supply chain. An alternative is a **push supply chain**, in which merchandise is allocated to stores on the basis of forecasted demand. Once a forecast is developed, specified quantities of merchandise are shipped (pushed) to DCs and stores at predetermined time intervals.

In a pull supply chain, there is less likelihood of being overstocked or out of stock because the store requests for merchandise are based on customer demand. A pull approach increases inventory turnover and is more responsive to changes in customer demand, and it becomes even more efficient than a push approach when demand is uncertain and difficult to forecast.[15]

Although generally more desirable, a pull approach is not the most effective in all situations. First, a pull approach requires a more costly and sophisticated information system to support it. Second, for some merchandise, retailers do not have the flexibility to adjust inventory levels on the basis of demand. For example, commitments must be made months in advance for fashion and private-label apparel. Because these commitments cannot be easily changed, the merchandise has to be allocated to the stores at the time the orders are formulated.

Radio Frequency Identification Devices[16]

In support of a pull supply chain, item-level RFID can benefit both retailers and vendors. For retailers, RFID provides an accurate, affordable, real-time measure of item inventory levels. As discussed earlier, radio frequency identification devices are tags that transmit identifying information and are attached to individual items, shipping cartons, and containers. They then transmit data about the objects in which they are embedded. These devices have two advantages over traditional bar codes. First, they can hold more data and update the data stored. For instance, the device can keep track of where an item has been in the supply chain and even where it is stored in a DC. With these data, retailers can dramatically reduce inventory levels and stockouts. Second, the data on the devices can be acquired without a visual line of sight. Thus, RFID enables the accurate, real-time tracking of every single product, from manufacturer to checkout in the store. It eliminates the manual point-and-read operations needed to get data from UPC bar codes.[17] Walmart, Macy's, Marks & Spencer, Dillard's, JCPenney, and others have implemented large-scale, item-level RFID initiatives.[18]

Assume one of GameStop's stores has just received a shipment of 10 units of the hottest new video game. The store sold 5 units and 5 units were stolen by an employee. GameStop's inventory control systems thinks there are still 5 units on the shelf at the store and thus does not send more replenishment units of the video game to the store. Customers trying to buy the game are frustrated and may think that GameStop is not a good place to buy the hottest video games. To correct this problem, GameStop needs to frequently have its employees count up the number of units on the shelf for each SKU, compare the physical count with the number of units indicated by

Radio frequency identification (RFID) devices are tags that transmit identifying information and are attached to individual items, shipping cartons, and containers.

© Yoshikazu Tsuno/AFP/Getty Images

the inventory control system, and make a correction when there is a difference. If the video games had RFID tags, each unit on the shelf would be sending out a radio signal. There would be no signals from the stolen items, and the inventory control system would have accurate, real-time data. Stockouts would be reduced, and sales associates would have more time to provide customer service instead of counting inventory. Another benefit of item-level RFID is to reduce theft. The technology can track products throughout the supply chain and identify their locations at all times. This helps reduce theft in transportation, at DCs, or in stores.

The main stumbling block with RFID implementation is its cost.[19] Tags add 5 to 30 cents per item shipped. In addition, there are one-time costs for readers and implementation costs such as retraining staff and IT integration.

Supply Chain for Fulfilling Catalog and Internet Orders

The supply chain and information systems for supporting catalog and Internet channels tend to be distinct from those that support the traditional store channel. For example, a typical retail DC supporting a store channel is designed to receive a relatively small number of cartons from vendors and ship about the same number of cartons to its stores. In contrast, FCs supporting nonstore channels are designed to receive about the same number of cartons from vendors but ship a very large number of small packages to customers. In addition, the information system for supporting a store channel focuses on products—making sure that the right number of products are delivered to each store—while information systems supporting nonstore channels are focused on the customer—making sure that the right customer receives the right product.

Because completely different warehouse designs are required for supporting the different channels, when a store-based retailer adds nonstore channels, it has to outsource fulfillment of the nonstore sales, designate separate areas within the present DCs for shipments to individual consumers, build different FCs for the new channels, or fulfill orders by picking and packing merchandise in their stores.

Instead of building FCs for nonstore sales fulfillment, Macy's is using many of its stores as FCs because, as one executive noted, "We've spent the last 153 years building warehouses. We just called them stores."[20] These centers should facilitate inventory management; a store with too much inventory can ship the extra to the fulfillment site. Orders placed online can get filled by the nearest stores, which should reduce shipping costs and time.

Yet because filling orders by hand using store employees is relatively inefficient, there is some debate about whether retailers should operate separate warehouses to deal with store and nonstore channels, use stores instead of or in conjunction with FCs, or use the same DCs for both. Synergies between the channels can be exploited if the same centers are used for all channels. For example, less inventory is needed to support distribution for all channels from one center. However, these potential synergies might be limited, and the difference between the operations of each area might cause inefficiencies.

For Walmart, with its reputation for efficiency, a delivery-based supply chain for online orders represents one of its most recent introductions. The ShippingPass service, available in limited areas, costs $49 per year and promises members free delivery of millions of popular products, in under two days. In contrast, nonmembers must wait up to six days for delivery and are required to pay the shipping costs for any orders that total less than $50. To support these promises, Walmart is relying on its excellent distribution network, including eight e-commerce-dedicated warehouses that coordinate with its more than 150 distribution centers. Furthermore, Walmart plans to leverage its existing stores, which number more than 4,600, and its fleet of more than 6,000 trucks to increase consumers' access to products they order online.[21]

In contrast, Amazon already has a strong supply chain in place for orders that come in to its site. Its Prime service is well established, having been around for more than a decade. Also promising two-day, free delivery in most cases, it costs more, $99 per year, but it includes immediate access to digital content, including select television shows, movies, music, and books. Amazon lacks its own stores or trucking fleet, but it has existing agreements with various delivery services to get packages onto consumers' doorsteps quickly and accurately.

Drop Shipping

Drop shipping, or **consumer direct fulfillment**, is a system in which retailers receive orders from customers and relay these orders to vendors; the vendors then ship the merchandise ordered directly to the customer. Such systems are especially popular among companies that need to ship products made from bulky or heavy materials (e.g., lumber, iron). Retailing View 9.3 describes another option for this form of delivery: robot services.

From the retailer's perspective, drop shipping reduces the retailer's supply chain costs and investment because the vendor, rather than the retailer, assumes the costs and risks of supplying merchandise to customers. The vendor has to build and operate the DCs, hire and pay for employees (or robots) to pick and pack individual orders, and manage inventory. Drop shipping is particularly attractive for retailers that do not have DCs capable of fulfilling individual orders from customers. However, drop shipping can lengthen delivery times and increase costs, particularly for customers who order multiple items from different vendors. In addition, retailers do not have control over an aspect of their offering that is of importance to their customer—how and when orders are delivered. Finally, defining the process for handling returns is an issue.

9.3   RETAILING VIEW   A Robotic Supply Chain, All the Way from the Warehouse to Customers' Doors

Almost invariably, discussions about robots spark fantastic visions of a future in which no one has to do housework anymore, and the daily commute is as easy as plugging in a destination. But the realistic applications of robots are both more detailed and potentially more meaningful in terms of their implications for how consumers access the daily products they buy.

Consider Tally, for example. This prototype robot moves automatically through the aisles of grocery stores, taking pictures and scanning approximately 15,000 items each hour. With this information, it can alert the grocer to misplaced products, unstocked shelves, and messy displays. It also checks prices. Beyond the immediate alerts of problems, Tally uploads and aggregates these data, producing summary reports that grocery retailers can use to adjust their practices and improve their presentations.

Tally has a cute name; another innovation for retailers evokes a different image. Starship Technologies sounds like it belongs on a television screen, but the company is already testing the use of robots that can cover the last leg in the delivery process. These delivery vehicles—about the same size as a mini-refrigerator, with sturdy wheels that enable them to get up and over short flights of stairs—will carry small purchases from a retailer to a customer's home. They rely on cameras, radar, and location software to navigate, such that most of the time, they are moving without any direct human intervention. Currently being tested in just a few cities, the robots might soon be a common sight on sidewalks around the world.

The Tally robot moves through grocery stores, taking pictures and scanning items. With this information, it can alert the grocer to misplaced products, unstocked shelves, and messy displays. It also checks prices.

In the near future, whether consumers prefer to make a visit to their local grocery store or order their supplies for the week online, they are likely to encounter autonomous robots, busy doing their jobs to ensure that products get to the people who want to purchase them.

Source: Jim Rock, "Autonomous Robots Are Changing the Way We Build and Move Products around the World," *TechCrunch*, January 10, 2016.

© Simbe Robotics/REX/Shutterstock

© Kristoffer Tripplaar/Alamy Stock Photo

Retailers like Walmart offer customer pickup of online purchases, which if done effectively, can enhance the customer experience.

Customer Store Pickup

Rather than shipping orders directly to customers, retailers can enable them to make a purchase online and then pick up the merchandise in stores. Retailers that can offer this option drive additional sales, as customers who come into the store to pick up online orders are more likely to make additional purchases while in store. For retailers to be successful with the buy-online/pick-up-in-store option, they need to invest in technology that enables order allocation systems to locate every item in stock to fulfill the order in a timely manner. They also must be omnichannel retailers that function consistently across channels. That is, to be successful, retailers must ensure that the products that show up as being available online actually are available in stock and ready for pickup, which requires a high level of accuracy in the inventory management system.

The notification of sales to stores quickly and accurately also is crucial. Retailers thus must equip themselves with mobile task management technology. **Mobile task management** technology is a wireless network and a mobile device that receives demand notification and enables a speedy response. This solution allows the associate closest to the ordered item to physically pull it and verify its availability.

If the retailer can move a product along its supply chain smoothly, effectively, and efficiently, to ensure that each order by an individual customer is available in the store on time, it can deliver an outstanding in-store pickup experience, which likely encourages the customer to return to the store in the future.[22]

Reverse Supply Chain

Finally, even after customers have taken possession of merchandise, retailers still must make decisions about their supply chains. **Reverse Supply Chain** is the process of capturing value from and/or properly disposing of merchandise returned by customers and/or stores. A reverse supply chain system processes merchandise that is returned because it is damaged, has been recalled, is no longer sold to customers because its selling season has ended, the merchandise was incorrectly sent to a store or directly to a customer, the product has been discontinued, or there is excessive inventory in stores or DCs.[23] The returned merchandise might involve returns from a customer to a retail store or FC, from a retail store to a DC, or from a DC to a vendor.[24]

When customers return items to retail stores, the stores collect the items and send them to DCs or centralized returns centers. Sophisticated retailers enter information about each item into their information systems so that it can be used to evaluate

Customer returns are expensive for retailers and can be frustrating for customers.

products, vendors, and the returns process. When the product arrives at the center, the retailer needs to examine the product and decide what do with it. Some of the potential dispositions are return it to the vendor for a refund, repair and/or repackage it and sell it as new, sell it to an outlet store or broker, donate it to charity, or recycle it. In general, retailers prefer to return items to the vendor for a refund. Due to the high cost of refurbishing and transporting small quantities, some vendors negotiate with retail buyers to offer a percentage of sales discount for returns and have the retailers dispose of the merchandise, either giving it to charity or throwing it away.

Reverse supply chain systems are challenging. Some differences between the forward flow of merchandise, shown in Exhibit 9–3, and the reverse flow include the forms of consolidation, product quantities, the distribution patterns, and cost transparency. First, a forward process sends goods from a few DCs or FCs to a vast number of stores or customers, whereas with a reverse process, goods come from all over and must be consolidated in one or a few receiving centers. Second, the goal of the forward process is consistent quality; the reverse process exists inherently because of the lack of consistency in the products involved. Third, a distribution plan in a forward process is designed carefully and set in advance. For a reverse process, the ad hoc distribution pattern can take a variety of unpredictable patterns. Fourth, the forward process constantly seeks more cost transparency in its standardized cost structures, but such a goal is not pertinent to the reverse process, for which none of the cost-imposing processes are likely to be standardized.[25]

Two reasons more attention is being directed toward reverse supply chain systems are the growth of sales through Internet channels and the increasing interest in environmental sustainability. First, the percentage of returned merchandise is much greater for purchases made through the Internet channel compared to the store channel.[26] Because the percentage of merchandise returns bought through the Internet channel is as much as four times greater than for merchandise bought through the store channel, the growth in Internet sales is going to significantly increase the number of returns and the cost of processing them through the reverse supply chain system.

Second, the efficiency of reverse supply chain systems affects environmental sustainability because packaging and shipping materials are processed through the reverse supply chain system. When retailers reduce transportation costs by consolidating shipments to stores, DCs, and FCs and optimize the disposal of returned merchandise, they reduce harmful emissions, energy usage, and their costs.[27] Green supply chain systems are becoming a standard business practice.

SUMMARY

LO 9-1 Understand the strategic advantage generated by a supply chain.

Supply chain management is a set of activities and techniques firms employ to efficiently and effectively manage the flow of merchandise from the vendors to the retailer's customers. These activities ensure that the customers are able to purchase merchandise in the desired quantities at a preferred location and appropriate time. Efficient supply chain management provides three benefits to retailers: (1) fewer stockouts, (2) tailored assortments, and (3) higher return on assets.

LO 9-2 Describe how information flows in a supply chain.

A retailer's information system tracks the flow of merchandise through distribution centers to retail stores and from fulfillment centers to their customers. Most communications between vendors and retailers occur via electronic data interchange over the Internet. Most multistore retailers operate their own DCs and FCs. Sometimes merchandise is temporarily stored at the DC; other times it just passes directly through the center from an inbound to an outbound truck. Retailers have developed data warehouses that provide them with intimate knowledge of who their customers are and what they like to buy. In some cases, retailers share this information with their vendors to improve the merchandise flow through the supply chain.

LO 9-3 Consider the flow of merchandise through a supply chain.

Most large retailers own and operate their own DCs. Some of the activities performed by the center are managing inbound and outbound transportation, receiving and checking merchandise shipments, storing and cross-docking merchandise, and getting merchandise floor-ready. Some merchandise flows directly from manufacturers to stores. In the case of the electronic and catalog channels, merchandise flows from fulfillment centers directly to customers. Many retailers are adopting a quick response inventory system that is characterized by smaller, more frequent shipments from manufacturers.

LO 9-4 Review the considerations and trends in the design of supply chains.

In designing their supply chain management systems, retailers make decisions about what activities to outsource; when to use a push and pull system for replenishing stores; whether the benefits of radio frequency identification devices outweigh the costs; how to handle merchandise shipped through DCs to stores versus FCs to customers; whether to have manufacturers ship merchandise directly to customers; whether to offer customers the opportunity to pick up merchandise ordered through the electronic channel at stores; and how to handle returned merchandise.

KEY TERMS

advance shipping notice (ASN), *233*

backhaul, *241*

buyer, *237*

checking, *237*

collaborative planning, forecasting, and replenishment (CPFR), *234*

consumer direct fulfillment, *244*

cross-docking distribution center, *237*

data warehouse, *233*

direct store delivery (DSD), *235*

dispatcher, *237*

distribution center (DC), *227*

drop shipping, *244*

electronic data interchange (EDI), *234*

floor-ready merchandise, *238*

freight forwarders, *241*

fulfillment center (FC), *228*

just-in-time (JIT) inventory system, *240*

lead time, *240*

mobile task management, *245*

outsource, *241*

pick ticket, *239*

planner, *237*

point-of-sale (POS) terminal, *232*

public warehouse, *241*

pull supply chain, *242*

push supply chain, *242*

quick response (QR) inventory system, *240*

radio frequency identification (RFID) tag, *237*

rain check, *230*

receiving, *237*

reverse supply chain, *245*

stockout, *230*

supply chain management, *229*

ticketing and marking, *238*

universal product code (UPC), *232*

vendor-managed inventory (VMI), *234*

wholesaler, *228*

GET OUT AND DO IT!

1. **CONTINUING ASSIGNMENT** Interview the store manager working for the retailer you have selected for the Continuing Case assignment. Write a report that describes and evaluates the retailer's information and supply chain systems. Use this chapter as a basis for developing a set of questions to ask the manager. Some of the questions might be these: Where is the store's DC? Does the retailer use direct store delivery from vendors? How frequently are deliveries made to the store? Does the merchandise come in ready for sale? What is

the store's percentage of stockouts? Does the retailer use a push or pull system? Does the store get involved in determining what merchandise is in the store and in what quantities? Does the retailer use VMI, EDI, CPFR, or RFID?

2. **INTERNET EXERCISE** Go to Barcoding Incorporated's web page at **www.barcoding.com/** and search for *retail, warehouse management,* and *RFID.* How is this company using technology to support retailers with information systems and supply chain management?

3. **INTERNET EXERCISE** Go to the home page of *RFID Journal* at **www.rfidjournal.com/** and search for *supply chain* in the current issue. Summarize one of the recent articles, and explain how the key concept(s) described could make the shopping experience better for consumers and improve efficiency in the supply chain.

DISCUSSION QUESTIONS AND PROBLEMS

1. Retail system acronyms include DSD, VMI, EDI, CPFR, and RFID. What do these terms mean and how are they related to one another?

2. Explain how an efficient supply chain system can increase a retailer's level of product availability and decrease its inventory investment.

3. This chapter presents some trends in supply chain and information systems that benefit retailers. How do vendors benefit from these trends?

4. What type of merchandise is most likely to be cross-docked at retailers' DCs? Why is this often the case?

5. Why haven't more fashion retailers adopted an integrated supply chain system similar to Zara's?

6. Explain the differences between pull and push supply chains.

7. Consumers have five key reactions to stockouts: buy the item at another store, substitute a different brand, substitute the same brand, delay the purchase, or do not purchase the item. Consider your own purchasing behavior, and describe how various categories of merchandise would result in different reactions to a stockout.

8. Abandoned purchases as a result of stockouts can mean millions of dollars a year in lost sales. How are retailers and manufacturers using technology to reduce stockouts and improve sales?

9. What is a universal product code (UPC)? How does this code enable manufacturers, distributors, and retailers to track merchandise throughout the supply chain?

10. Why are some retailers switching from UPC codes to RFID?

CHAPTER ENDNOTES

1. Ben Latham, "How Retailers Can Learn from Fast Fashion to Beat the Weather," *Retail Week,* April 20, 2016; Seth Stevenson, "Polka Dots Are In? Polka Dots It Is! How Zara Gets Fresh Styles to Stores Insanely Fast—within Weeks," *Slate,* June 21, 2012; Suzy Hansen, "How Zara Grew into the World's Largest Fashion Retailer," *The New York Times,* November 9, 2012; Greg Petro, "The Future of Fashion Retailing—The Zara Approach," *Forbes,* October 25, 2012; Vertica Bhardwaj and Ann Fairhurst, "Fast Fashion: Response to Changes in the Fashion Industry," *International Review of Retail, Distribution and Consumer Reearch* 20 (February 2010), pp. 165–173; Felipe Caro et al., "Zara Uses Operations Research to Reengineer Its Global Distribution Process," *Interfaces* 40 (2010), pp. 71–84; Carmen Lopez and Ying Fan, "Case Study: Internationalisation of the Spanish Fashion Brand Zara," *Journal of Fashion Marketing and Management* 13, no. 2 (2009), pp. 279–296.

2. See http://www.marketingpower.com/_layouts/Dictionary.aspx.

3. Paige Baltzan, *M: Information Systems,* 3rd ed. (New York: McGraw-Hill Education, 2014); Donald Bowersox, David Closs, and M. Bixby Cooper, *Supply Chain Logistics Management,* 4th ed. (New York: McGraw-Hill, 2013).

4. Bob Trebilcock, "Creating Competitive Advantage," *Supply Chain Management Review* 16, no. 6 (November 2012), pp. S61–S67.

5. Sandy Smith, "Lost and Found," *Stores Magazine,* June 2015.

6. T. Wu, S. Huang, J. Blackhurst, X. Zhang, and S. Wang, "Supply Chain Risk Management: An Agent-Based Simulation to Study the Impact of Retail Stockouts," *IEEE Transactions on Engineering Management* 60, no. 4 (2013), pp. 676–686; Dhruv Grewal, Praveen Kopalle, Howard Marmorstein, and Anne L. Roggeveen, "Does Travel Time to Stores Matter? The Role of Merchandise Availability," *Journal of Retailing* 88, no. 3 (2012), pp. 437–444; Walter Zinn and Peter C. Liu, "A Comparison of Actual and Intended Consumer Behavior in Response to Retail Stockouts," *Journal of Business Logistics* 29, no. 2 (2011), pp. 141–159.

7. Smith, "Lost and Found."

8. Ibid.

9. http://www.marketingpower.com/_layouts/Dictionary.aspx.

10. http://www.vendormanagedinventory.com.

11. G. P. Kiesmüller and R. A. C. M. Broekmeulen, "The Benefit of VMI Strategies in a Stochastic Multi-Product Serial Two Echelon System," *Computers and Operations Research* 37, no. 2 (2010), pp. 406–416; Dong-Ping Song and John Dinwoodie, "Quantifying the Effectiveness of VMI and Integrated Inventory Management in a Supply Chain with Uncertain Lead-Times and Uncertain Demands," *Production Planning & Control* 19, no. 6 (2008), pp. 590–600.

12. *2016 Global Responsibility Report,* Walmart, Bentonville, Arkansas; Andrew Winston, "How Walmart's Green Performance Reviews Could Change Retail for Good," *HBR Blog,* October 2, 2012; Stephanie Rosenbloom, "Wal-Mart Unveils Plan to Make Supply Chain Greener," *The New York Times,* February 25, 2010.

13. Kevin Scarpati, "Tesco Big Price Drop Helped by Supply Chain Management," *Supply Chain Digital,* September 23, 2011, http://www.supplychaindigital.com; Michael Garry, "Supply Chain Systems Seen Boosting Tesco's U.S. Stores," *Supermarket News* 55, no. 43 (2007).

14. www.businessdictionary.com/definition/freight-forwarder. html.

15. John Hagel III and John Brown, "From Push to Pull: Emerging Models for Mobilizing Resources," *Journal of Service Science,* 2011, pp. 93–110; Huaqin Zhang and Guojie Zhao, "Strategic Selection of Push-Pull Supply," *Modern Applied Science* 2, no. 1 (2008).

16. Dan Berthiaume, "TechBytes: Five Hot Tech Trends from NRF 2015," *Chain Store Age,* January 20, 2015, http://www. chainstoreage.com/article/techbytes-five-hot-tech-trends-nrf-2015.

17. "Increasing Adoption of RFID Technology Will Significantly Propel the Global Inventory Management Software Market in the Retail Sector until 2020, Says Technavio," *Business Wire,* July 13, 2016, http://www.businesswire.com/news/home/20160713005033/en/Increasing-Adoption-RFID-Technology-Significantly-Propel-Global; Cleopatra Bardaki, Panos Kourouthanassis, and Katerina Pramatari, "Deploying RFID-Enabled Services in the Retail Supply Chain: Lessons Learned toward the Internet of Things," *Information Systems Management* 29, no. 3 (2012), pp. 233–245; Massimo Bertolini, Eleonora Bottani, Gino Ferretti, Antonio Rizzi, and Andrea Volpi, "Experimental Evaluation of Business Impacts of RFID in Apparel and Retail Supply Chain," *International Journal of RF Technologies: Research and Applications* 3, no. 4 (2012), pp. 257–282; Philip Trocchia and Thomas Ainscough, "Consumer Attitudes toward RFID Tracking in the Retail Environment," *Review of Business Information Systems* 16, no. 2 (2012), pp. 67–72.

18. "RFID Use Reaching a 'Tipping Point,'" *RetailWire,* March 30, 2015, http://www.retailwire.com/discussion/rfid-use-reaching-a-tipping-point/; "Retailers' RFID Programs Have Major Implications for Relationships with Suppliers," *Chain-Link Research,* February 8, 2013; Bill McBeath, "What Retailer Mandates Mean for Suppliers," *ChainLink Research,* February 6, 2013.

19. George Anderson, "Will RFID Take Off Now That Tag and Hardware Prices Have Dropped?," *RetailWire,* April 19, 2013.

20. Phil Mahba, "Macy's CEO Sees Stores Borrowing Ideas from Online," *Bloomberg Businessweek,* April 12, 2012.

21. Tom Ryan, "Walmart Tests Matching Prime Delivery Speed, *RetailWire,* May 17, 2016.

22. Jen Mosscrop, "The Fulfillment Option That Brings Customers Back in Store," *Chain Store Age,* March 25, 2014.

23. Tom Ryan, "The True Cost of Returns," *RetailWire,* January 4, 2016.

24. Hing Kai Chan, Shizhao Yin, and Felix Chan, "Implementing Just-in-Time Philosophy to Reverse Logistics Systems: A Review," *International Journal of Production Research* 48, no. 21 (2010), pp. 6293–6313; Eric Jack, Thomas Powers, and Lauren Skinner, "Reverse Logistics Capabilities: Antecedents and Cost Savings," *International Journal of Physical Distribution & Logistics Management,* 40, no. 3 (2010), pp. 228–246; Michael Bernon, Silvia Rossi, and John Cullen, "Retail Reverse Logistics: A Call and Grounding Framework for Research," *International Journal of Physical Distribution & Logistics Management* 41, no. 5 (2011), pp. 484–510.

25. V. G. Venkatesh, "Reverse Logistics: An Imperative Area of Research for Fashion Supply Chain," *IUP Journal of Supply Chain Management,* March 2010, pp. 77–89.

26. Shelly Banjo, "Rampant Returns Plague E-Retailers," *The Wall Street Journal,* December 22, 2013.

27. Remy Le Moigne, "Why Reverse Logistics Is an Essential Part of the Circular Economy," *Circulate,* June 8, 2016, http://circulatenews.org/2016/06/why-corporations-will-have-to-invest-in-their-reverse-logistics/.

CHAPTER 10 | Customer Relationship Management

© Daniel Acker/Bloomberg via Getty Images

Kroger is the second-largest grocery retailer in the United States (following Walmart), with more than $109 billion in sales.[1] It is also the third-largest retailer in the world.[2] Its impressive status is largely the result of a strategic decision it made to build a competitive advantage by collecting and analyzing customer data, then to use such data to manage its customer relationships. As a result, Kroger has the highest loyalty program participation rates in the grocery industry.

It began working with the UK-based consulting firm Dunnhumby in 2001. Since then, the partners have developed a joint venture called Dunnhumby USA that is responsible for converting all the data that Kroger collects from its customers when they swipe loyalty cards or enter their phone numbers at the point of sale into viable information that can help Kroger make decisions. As discussed in Chapter 4, retailers frequently segment their market using demographic variables such as age, income, and education, but they are poor predictors of sales. Dunnhumby USA's analyses instead enable Kroger to develop a better segmentation scheme, based on actual purchase behavior rather than demographics. With these analyses, Kroger can identify different segments of its customers who have, for example, newborn babies, like to cook, or entertain frequently.

Similar to most supermarkets, Kroger's primary communication tool is a weekly newspaper circular featuring sale products. Category managers nominate products to include in the circular, and space is allocated according to the importance of the product category, any special promotions offered by vendors, and the margin Kroger earns on the advertised item. But the way it chooses items for the circulars is more sophisticated than many of its competitors. By analyzing which items customers purchase in each trip, Dunnhumby USA has been able to improve this method and increase the effectiveness of the weekly circular. In particular, the purchase data identify complementary products, such that Kroger can prompt the sale of other items. For example, when customers purchase sliced deli roast beef, they also tend to purchase other deli meats, cheese, mustard, mayonnaise, and a loaf of fresh rye bread. But when they buy deli turkey, they don't buy these additions. Thus, roast beef is a better candidate for the circular because it will tend to trigger the purchase of other items.

Kroger sends more than 55 million loyal customer mailings to its frequent-shopper cardholders every quarter. These mailings offer promotions on products that customers normally buy, as well as on products that Kroger predicts they would like, based on its analyses of what similar customers buy. So, for instance, if Kroger can predict that a customer is part of a young family based on the purchase of hot dogs, Kellogg's Cocoa Krispies, and a lot of animal crackers, it can provide that family with a coupon for milk.

Such precise segmentation capabilities not only help Kroger appeal appropriately to customers, encouraging their loyalty, but they also enable better decisions about in-store assortments, merchandise locations, store locations, and promotional designs. Beyond its loyalty program, Kroger also offers excellent customer service to maintain its close relationships with customers. After a recent hurricane, Kroger opened its doors even though the store was flooding. Even as they sought to clean up water from the floor, Kroger's employees recognized that their customers needed supplies; the store was the only one open in the area. The employees willingly connect with their customers because Kroger embraces the ideal that happier employees provide better service and works to retain knowledgeable employees who can provide information about the store and its products. For example, Kroger pays its employees significantly more than the industry average, leading to better, happier employees who continue to work for Kroger longer and can develop close relationships with customers.

Sources: Hayley Peterson and Ashley Lutz, "Why Kroger Is America's Most Underrated Grocery Store," *Business Insider,* March 6, 2015; Jack Neff, "Tesco Splits with Kroger on Dunnhumby to Form New Marketing Shop," *Advertising Age,* April 27, 2015; Dhruv Grewal, Michael Levy, and Britt Hackmann, "Making Loyalty Programs Sing," Working Paper, Babson College, 2013; Josh Pichler, "Firm Remakes Retailers' Knowledge of Shoppers," *Cincinnati Enquirer,* January 31, 2013; Josh Pichler, "DunnhumbyUSA Combs through Data to Help Retailers Reward Their Most Loyal Customers," *Cincinnati Enquirer,* January 31, 2013.

The business press and retailers are talking a lot about the importance of becoming more customer-centric and managing their customer experiences and relationships better. Retailers spend millions of dollars on computer systems to collect and analyze data about their customers. With all this buzz, you would think that the customer is a popular new kid in the neighborhood. However, the customer is more like an old friend who's been taken for granted—until now.

Consider the following: Shari Ast is on her third business trip this month. She takes a cab from Boston's Logan Airport to the Ritz-Carlton, her favorite hotel in Boston. As the door attendant opens the car door for her, he greets her with, "Welcome back to the Ritz-Carlton, Ms. Ast." When she goes to the registration desk, the receptionist gives her a room key. Then she goes to her room and finds just what she likes—a room with a view of the Boston Common, a single king-sized bed, an extra pillow and blanket, a printer with a wireless connection for her laptop, and a basket with her favorite fruits and snacks.

Shari Ast's experience is an example of Ritz-Carlton's customer relationship management program. A **customer relationship management program** is the set of activities designed to identify and build the loyalty of the retailer's most valuable customers. Also called loyalty program or frequent-shopper program. With CRM, retailers can develop a base of loyal customers and increase their **share of wallet**—the percentage of the customers' purchases made from that retailer.

Traditionally, retailers have focused their attention on encouraging more customers to visit their stores, look through their catalogs, or visit their websites. To accomplish this objective, they have used mass-media advertising and sales promotions to attract visits from customers. This approach treats all existing and potential customers the same way. They would all receive the same messages and the same promotions.

The Ritz-Carlton provides personalized service for its preferred customers.

© Jim Cummins/Taxi/Getty Image

Today, retailers are concentrating on developing customer loyalty and increasing the share of wallet by providing more value to their best customers using targeted, personalized merchandise, services, and promotions. Mindy Grossman, CEO of HSN, believes "it would take 10 new customers to replace one 'best' customer."[3] Her perspective is supported by research indicating that retailers are more profitable when they focus on retaining and increasing sales to their best customers rather than attempting to generate sales from new customers or less profitable existing customers.[4] In the following sections of this chapter, we discuss in more depth the objective of CRM programs and the elements of the CRM process.

THE CRM PROCESS

The objective of the CRM process is to develop loyalty and repeat purchase behavior among a retailer's best customers. Simply leaving customers satisfied and ready to make repeat visits is not sufficient. For example, a customer might exclusively patronize a local supermarket because it is the only supermarket convenient to her house, but she still might not be loyal to it. If another supermarket opened with a somewhat better offering, the customer might immediately switch to the new supermarket, even though she was a repeat customer at her present supermarket.

Instead **customer loyalty** means that customers are committed to purchasing merchandise and services from the retailer and will resist the activities of competitors attempting to attract their patronage. Thus, if our preceding consumer were truly loyal, she would not switch to the new supermarket, even though its offering was somewhat better.

Loyal customers develop a bond with the retailer that is based on an emotional connection, more than a just having a positive feeling about the retailer. This emotional bond is a personal connection. Customers feel that the retailer is a friend. Their goodwill toward the retailer encourages them to make repeat purchases and recommend it to their friends and family.

All elements in the retail mix contribute to the development of customer loyalty and repeat purchase behavior.[5] Customer loyalty can be enhanced by creating an appealing brand image, offering exclusive merchandise, establishing convenient locations, and providing an engaging shopping experience. However, personal attention and customer service are two of the most effective methods for developing loyalty. For example, many small, independent restaurants build loyalty by functioning as neighborhood cafés, where servers recognize customers by name and know their preferences. Nordstrom invites its best customers to grand-opening celebrations, pampers them during private shopping parties, and provides concierge services and free alterations. Such practices are more effective than discounts because when a retailer develops a personal connection with customers, it is difficult for any competitors to attract them away. The CRM programs and activities discussed in this chapter use information systems and customer data to personalize a retailer's offering and increase the value that its best customers receive. Personalized value also can be provided by employees in face-to-face interactions with customers. These forms of personalization are discussed in more detail in Chapter 17.

Overview of the CRM Process

Exhibit 10–1 illustrates that CRM is an iterative process that turns customer data into customer loyalty and repeat purchase behavior through four activities: (1) collecting customer shopping data, (2) analyzing customer data and identifying target customers, (3) developing CRM through frequent-shopper programs, and (4) implementing CRM programs. The process begins with the collection and analysis of data about a retailer's customers and the identification of its best customers. The analysis translates the customer data into information and activities that offer value to these targeted customers. Then these activities are executed through personalized communications with customers.

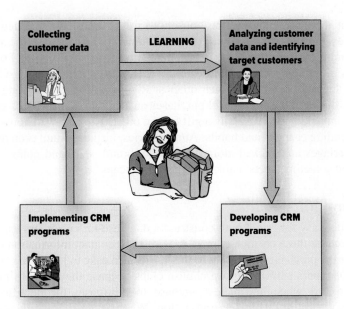

EXHIBIT 10–1
The CRM Process Cycle

COLLECTING CUSTOMER SHOPPING DATA

The first step in the CRM process is to construct a data warehouse. This database is part of the data warehouse described in Chapter 9. It contains all the data the firm has collected about its customers and is the foundation for subsequent CRM activities.

LO 10-2

Understand how customer shopping data are collected.

Data Warehouse

Ideally, the data warehouse should contain the following information:

- *Transactions.* A complete history of the purchases made by the customer, including the purchase date, the SKUs purchased, the price paid, the amount of profit, and whether the merchandise was purchased in response to a special promotion or marketing activity.

- *Customer contacts.* A record of the interactions that the customer has had with the retailer, including visits to the retailer's website, inquiries made through in-store kiosks, comments made on blogs and Facebook pages, merchandise returns, and telephone calls made to the retailer's call center, plus information about contacts initiated by the retailer, such as catalogs and e-mails sent to the customer.

- *Customer preferences.* What the customer likes, such as favorite colors, brands, fabrics, and flavors, as well as apparel sizes.

- *Descriptive information.* Demographic and psychographic data describing the customer that can be used in developing market segments.

© Ingram Publishing

Customer transactions are collected from a POS terminal and stored in a customer database.

Different members of the same household might also have interactions with a retailer. Thus, to get a complete view of the customer, retailers need to be able to combine individual customer data from each member of a household. For example, Richards is a family-owned apparel chain in Westport and Greenwich, Connecticut. Spouses often buy presents for each other at Richards. The chain's data warehouse keeps track of both household-level purchases and individual purchases so that sales associates can help one spouse buy a gift for the other. The data warehouse also keeps track of spending changes and habits. Anniversaries, birthdays, and even divorces and second marriages are tracked along with style, brand, size, and color preferences, hobbies, and sometimes pets' names and golf handicaps.[6]

Identifying Information

It is relatively easy for retailers to construct a database for customers using nonstore channels because these customers must provide their contact information (e.g., name, address) for the purchases to be sent to them. It is also easy to keep track of purchases made by customers patronizing warehouse clubs because they need to present their membership cards when they make a purchase. In these cases, the identification of the customer is always linked to the transaction. When retailers issue their own credit cards, they also can collect the contact information for billing when customers apply for the card. However, identifying most customers who are making in-store transactions is more difficult because they often pay for the merchandise with cash, a third-party credit card such as Visa or MasterCard, or their mobile wallets (e.g., Apple Pay).

Four approaches that store-based retailers use to overcome this problem are to (1) ask customers for identifying information, (2) connect Internet and store purchasing data, (3) offer frequent-shopper programs, or (4) place RFID chips on merchandise.

Ask for Identifying Information   Some retailers have their sales associates ask customers for identifying information, such as their phone number, e-mail address, or name and home address, when they process a sale. This information is then used to link all the transactions to the customer. However, some customers may be reluctant to provide the information because they feel that the sales associates are violating their privacy.

Connect Internet and Store Purchasing Data   When customers use third-party credit cards such as Visa or MasterCard to make a purchase in a store, the retailer cannot identify the purchase by the customer. However, if the customer used the same credit card while shopping at the retailer's website and provided shipping information, the retailer could connect the credit card purchases through its store and electronic channels.

Offer Frequent-Shopper Programs   **Frequent-shopper programs**, also called **loyalty programs**, are programs that identify and provide rewards to customers who patronize a retailer. Customer transaction data are automatically captured when the card is scanned at the point-of-sale terminal. Customers are enticed to enroll in these programs and provide some descriptive information about themselves by offering them discounts if they use the cards when making purchases from the retailer. These frequent-shopper programs are discussed in more depth in following section of this chapter.

Place RFID Chips on Merchandise   Perhaps RFID provides the most convenient approach, from the customer's perspective, for customers to make purchases. An RFID reader in the store can acquire the customer's personal information from small devices carried by customers and RFID tags on the merchandise they want to purchase. In addition, using a global satellite tracking system, the store reader could also collect information about where the customer has been in the store.

Privacy and CRM Programs

The collection and analysis of data about customer attitudes, preferences, and shopping behaviors enables retailers to target information and promotions and provide greater value to their customers. However, many customers are concerned that retailers violate their privacy when they collect detailed personal information. Even if customers trust a retailer, they are concerned that the data may not be secure and/or may be sold to other businesses.

Privacy Concerns   Although there is no clear consensus about the definition of personal information, the degree to which consumers feel their privacy has been violated depends on:

- *Their control over their personal information when engaging in marketplace transactions.* Do they feel they can decide the amount and type of information that is collected by the retailer?
- *Their knowledge about the collection and use of personal information.* Do they know what information is being collected and how the retailer will be using it or sharing it with other parties?[7]

These concerns are particularly acute for online customers, because of the extensive amount of information that can be collected without their knowledge, using cookies. **Cookies** are small files stored on a customer's computer that identify customers when they return to a website. Because of the data in cookies, customers do not have to identify themselves or use passwords every time they visit a site. However, cookies also can enable the collection of data about what pages people have viewed, other sites the people have visited, how they spend money online, and their interactions on social networking sites.

Protecting Customer Privacy   In the United States, existing consumer privacy legislation is limited to the protection of information associated with government functions and with practices in credit reporting, video rentals, banking, and health care. Thus, the privacy of most consumer data is not protected, though Congress continues to consider new legislation that would mimic regulatory oversights in other sectors, such as health care, and require similar privacy protections. Proactive retailers also can increase customers' confidence by[8]

- Adopting a strategic "privacy by design" approach that requires input from various departments, including marketing, legal, human resources, and IT, before making any choices that might affect customers' privacy.
- Retaining customer data only for as long as they are being used, then destroying them.
- Undertaking explicit legal reviews to determine what personal information consumers may access and edit.
- Buying better security measures.
- Appointing privacy advocates to communicate privacy concerns throughout the organization and ensure the firm is adhering to its privacy policies.

The European Union (EU), Australia, New Zealand, and Canada have more stringent consumer privacy laws. Some of the provisions of the EU directive on consumer privacy include the following:

- Businesses can collect consumer information only if they have clearly defined the purpose, such as completing the transaction.
- The purpose must be disclosed to the consumer from whom the information is being collected.
- The information can be used only for that specific purpose.
- The business can keep the information only for the stated purpose. If the business wants to use the information for another purpose, it must initiate a new collection process.

Basically, the EU perspective is that consumers own their personal information, so retailers must get consumers to agree explicitly to share this personal information. This agreement is referred to as **opt in**. In contrast, personal information in the United States is generally viewed as being in the public domain, and retailers can use it any way they desire. American consumers must explicitly tell retailers not to use their personal information—they must explicitly **opt out**.[9] Considering the growing consensus that personal information must be collected fairly and purposefully, and that the data should be relevant, accurate, and secured, retailers should find ways to assure customers that information about them is held securely and not passed on to other companies without the customers' permission.

ANALYZING CUSTOMER DATA AND IDENTIFYING TARGET CUSTOMERS

LO 10-3

Explain the methods used to analyze customer data and identify target customers.

The next step in the CRM process (see Exhibit 10–1) is to analyze the customer data and convert them into information that will help retailers develop programs for increasing the value they offer to their best customers, or those customers whose loyalty and repatronage will add significantly to the retailer's bottom line. Two objectives for analyzing the customer database are (1) identifying the retailer's best customers and (2) using analytical methods to improve decisions made by retail managers. These two objectives are discussed in this section.

Identifying the Best Customers

One of the goals of CRM is to identify and cater to the retailer's most valuable customers. Retailers often use information in their customer databases to determine how valuable each customer is to their firm. The value of a customer, called **customer lifetime value (CLV)**, is the expected contribution from the customer to the retailer's profits over their entire relationship with the retailer. Retailers typically use past behaviors to forecast their CLV. To illustrate some of the factors considered in developing a measure of CLV, consider the purchase histories of two customers during the last 12 months shown here:

	December	January	February	March	April	May	June	July	August	September	October	November	Total
Shirley	$400	0	0	0	0	0	0	0	0	0	0	0	$400
Marcia	$ 10	$10	$25	$25	$15	$25	$40	$20	$35	$35	$50	$65	$355

Which woman has the highest CLV—that is, who would be the most valuable customer for the retailer in the future? If the retailer considered only the purchases made by the two women over the past 12 months, the retailer might conclude that Shirley is most valuable because she has bought the most merchandise during the last 12 months ($400 versus $355). But Shirley's purchase history might reflect her visit to the United States from Brazil, when she made a one-time purchase, such that she is unlikely to patronize the retailer again. As the retailer digs deeper into the data, it might decide that Marcia is the most valuable customer because she purchases merchandise both more frequently and more recently. In addition, her monthly purchases are trending up. Even though Shirley might have bought more in the last 12 months, Marcia's purchase pattern suggests she will buy more in the future.

The CLV in the example is based on sales, not on the profitability of the customers. The use of sales to identify a retailer's best customers can be misleading, however. For example, airlines assign rewards in their frequent-flyer programs on the basis of miles flown. These programs provide the same rewards to customers who take low-cost, less profitable flights as to those who make a larger contribution to the airline's profit by flying first class and paying full prices. Sophisticated statistical methods are typically used to estimate the CLV for each customer, like Shirley and Marcia.[10] These deeper analyses consider the gross margin from the customer's purchases and the costs associated with the purchase, such as the cost of advertising and promotions used to acquire the customers, and the cost of processing merchandise that the customer returned. For example, customers who pay full price and buy the same amount of merchandise have a higher CLV than customers who buy only items on sale. Customers who return 30 percent of the merchandise they purchase have a lower CLV than customers who rarely return merchandise.

Retail Analytics

Retailers can use data they have collected about their customers to measure each customer's CLV. In the remaining portion of this section, we explain how the availability of a data warehouse provides a resource that retailers can use to develop strategies and make better decisions. Retailing View 10.1 describes how the drugstore chain CVS derives insights by analyzing its extensive customer database.

RETAILING VIEW   How CVS Uses Loyalty Data to Define Coupons   10.1

In general, loyalty programs offer an effective means to provide more value to customers. In particular, the CVS ExtraCare program represents a flagship loyalty program, as one of the oldest and largest in the United States. The program has been running for nearly 20 years; one in every three people in the United States has an ExtraCare card. Thus, more than 90 million households use it in a typical year.

The primary focus of the ExtraCare program has been to provide personalized offers that are relevant to and appreciated by customers, while also encouraging their consistent shopping behavior. In recent developments, the program has spread across multiple channels, allowing customers to connect with offers in print, online, or through a mobile app. For example, customers can access the newly launched, omnichannel MyWeeklyAd program online or from a mobile device, or they can visit coupon kiosks in stores to scan their loyalty program cards and print coupons on the spot.

To support a unique, relevant, and well-appreciated shopping experience that encourages these customers to interact with the program and undertake additional sales, CVS relies heavily on customer data analytics. It collects vast amounts of data on the purchases that each ExtraCare member makes, and then it analyzes those data to uncover interesting or unexpected relationships among the items purchased. For example, customers who buy skin and hair products also purchase cosmetics, though not always at CVS. Furthermore, CVS discovered notable and helpful purchase timing patterns, such as its recognition that people typically buy toothpaste every five weeks.

By using the established relationships among the items that appear together in market baskets, CVS can obtain valuable insights, which in turn inform the personalized offers it sends to customers in an effort to adjust their behaviors. Thus, if an ExtraCare member buys face wash or conditioner, she might receive a coupon for lipstick. If another customer hasn't bought toothpaste in four and a half weeks, he will receive a coupon that provides him with a special incentive to purchase a high-end brand of toothpaste. CVS also uses these analytics

CVS's ExtraCare loyalty program provides personalized offers that are relevant to and appreciated by customers, while also encouraging their consistent shopping behavior.

to encourage customers to buy more each trip, such that a customer who typically spends $20 may receive a special offer if she spends $30 the next time she shops. Finally, the data analytics give CVS important insights into which types of loyalty program offers are most successful—as well as which ones are not. For example, it determined that brand-specific coupons (e.g., for Pantene shampoo) were less effective than promotions geared toward the whole category (i.e., shampoos of various brands).

Sources: Elyse Dupré, "CVS/Pharmacy Devotes ExtraCare to Its Loyalty Program," *DM News* 36, no. 8 (2014), pp. 19–22; Stephanie Clifford, "Using Data to Stage-Manage Paths to the Prescription Counter," *The New York Times*, June 19, 2013, http://bits.blogs.nytimes.com.

© Fuse/Getty Images

Market basket analysis is a data mining tool that determines which products appear in the market basket that a customer purchases during a single shopping trip. It is used to suggest merchandise that should be placed and promoted together.

Retail analytics are applications of statistical techniques and models that seek to improve retail decisions through analyses of customer data.[11] **Data mining** is an information processing method that relies on search techniques to discover new insights into the buying patterns of customers, using large databases.[12] Three of the most popular applications of data mining are market basket analysis, targeting promotions, and assortment planning.

Market Basket Analysis   In a **market basket analysis**, the data mining tools determine which products appear in the market basket that a customer purchases during a single shopping trip. This analysis can suggest where stores should place merchandise and which merchandise to promote together based on merchandise that tends to show up in the same market basket.

To perform a market basket analysis, a computer program counts the number of times two products get purchased at the same time. An often-used example of market basket analysis is the discovery by a supermarket chain that on Friday evenings between 6:00 and 7:00 p.m., many market baskets, particularly those bought by men, contained both beer and baby diapers. This relationship between beer and baby diapers arises because diapers come in large packages, so wives, who do most of the household shopping, leave the diaper purchase to their husbands. When husbands buy diapers at the end of the workweek, they also want to get some beer for the weekend. When the supermarket discovered this shopping pattern, it put a premium beer display next to the diapers. Because the premium beer was so conveniently placed next to the diapers, men tend to be up-sold and buy the premium brands rather than spend time going to the beer aisle for lower-priced brands.

Some other examples of how market basket analyses have revised product locations are as follows:

- Bananas are the most common item in Americans' grocery carts, so supermarkets often place bananas both in the cereal aisle and in the produce section.

- Tissues are in the paper goods aisle but also mixed in with cold medicine.

- Measuring spoons appear in the housewares section and also hang next to baking supplies, such as flour and shortening.

- Flashlights are placed in the hardware aisle and with a seasonal display of Halloween costumes.

- Snack cakes appear in the bread aisle, but they also are available next to the coffee.

- Bug spray is merchandised with hunting gear and with household cleaning supplies.

Targeting Promotions   Beyond aiding decisions about where to place products in a store, market basket analysis can help provide insights into assortment decisions and promotions. For example, retailers might discover that customers typically buy a specific brand of conditioner and shampoo at the same time (in the same market basket). With this information, the retailer might offer a special promotion on the conditioner, anticipating that customers will also buy the (higher margin) shampoo at its full price.

Assortment Planning   Managers have to make decisions about what merchandise to carry in each category. Customer data also can be mined to help with these assortment decisions. By analyzing which products the retailer's most valued customers purchase, the manager can ensure that they are available in the store at all times. For example, an analysis might discover that customers in its highest CLV segment are very loyal to a brand of gourmet mustard. However, this brand of mustard is only the tenth best seller in the retailer's mustard category across all customers. Due to its relatively low sales, the retailer might consider dropping the mustard brand from its assortment. But based on this analysis, the retailer would decide to continue offering the mustard, fearing that these high CLV customers would defect to another retailer if the gourmet brand was no longer stocked in its stores.

DEVELOPING CRM THROUGH FREQUENT-SHOPPER PROGRAMS

As mentioned earlier, frequent-shopper or loyalty programs are marketing efforts that reward repeat buying behavior. Two objectives of these programs are to (1) build a data warehouse that links customer data to their transactions and (2) encourage repeat purchase behavior and loyalty. The implications of the first objective are discussed in a preceding section of this chapter; the implications of the second objective are reviewed in the following section.

LO 10-4

Outline how retailers develop their frequent-shopper programs.

Effectiveness of Frequent-Shopper Programs

Although frequent-shopper programs are useful for building data warehouses, they are not particularly useful for building long-term customer loyalty.[13] The perceived value of these programs by consumers is low because consumers perceive little difference among the programs offered by competing retailers. Most programs simply offer customers price discounts that are available to all customers that register for the programs. These discounts are appealing to price-conscious shoppers but not necessarily to the high-CLV shoppers. In addition, competitive advantages based on frequent-shopper programs are rarely sustainable. The programs are very visible, so they can be easily duplicated by competitors. They also are very expensive in most cases.[14] A 1 percent price discount might cost large retailers around $100 million—and that is only after they invest up to $30 million to get the loyalty program up and running. Over time, they must continue to invest, up to $10 million annually, to maintain the program, including IT costs, marketing efforts, and training. As Retailing View 10.2 shows, Whole Foods's new loyalty program thus goes above and beyond just providing discounts.

Finally, loyalty programs are difficult to revise or correct. Once they become part of customers' shopping experience, retailers have to inform customers about even the smallest changes. If those changes imply that customers are losing some of the benefits of the programs, a strong negative reaction is likely, even from customers who exhibit relatively little loyalty in the first place.

Frequent-shopper programs have limited effectiveness because consumers join all of the programs offered by competing programs.

Making Frequent-Shopper Programs More Effective

Frequent-shopper programs seek to encourage repeated purchases and develop customer loyalty. To build true loyalty, retailers need an emotional connection with consumers, as well as a sense of commitment from them. When a Starwood Hotels representative helped a frequent customer find a car when she was stranded in Chicago, then called the woman's husband to let him know she was fine, that associate earned the traveler's loyalty.[15] Therefore, to move frequent-shopper programs beyond simple data collection and short-term sales effects, retailers might (1) create tiered rewards, (2) treat frequent shoppers as VIPs, (3) incorporate charitable activities, (4) offer choices, (5) reward all transactions, and (6) make the program transparent and simple.[16]

© David De Lossy/Getty Images

10.2 RETAILING VIEW　Whole Foods's Loyalty Program Goes Beyond Other Grocers'

Many grocery retailers maintain loyalty programs that offer discounts on certain items or cash back on related fuel purchases. But these programs—nearly identical in their structure and offers, providing undifferentiated discounts and benefits—often cost more to manage than they benefit the store in increased revenues. Research shows that they fail to achieve their basic, named objective, that is, to make customers more loyal.

Whole Foods has always been a little distinct from other grocers, and its perspective on loyalty programs is no different. While others are shutting down or scaling back their programs, Whole Foods has just initiated its first program, though currently only as a pilot program. The rationale for launching the program may not seem surprising. As more competitors consider the benefits of stocking local produce or organic options, the competitive advantages that enabled Whole Foods to charge price premiums have started to collapse. Thus, it has needed to take steps to retain its competitive position.

With the introduction of its loyalty program, Whole Foods is looking to establish a new means to differentiate itself and justify its price points. The loyalty program goes well beyond coupons or free gifts. Instead, it features personalized rewards based on each shopper's purchase history, including experience-based rewards. For example, it might offer meetings with a nutritionist to a shopper who prefers low-calorie options or cooking classes with the sushi chef to a loyal buyer who buys raw fish once a week.

The program members can register their purchases by handing their identification card to the clerk or by downloading and using the mobile app. Both channels will integrate seamlessly with Apple Pay, reflecting Whole Foods's

Source: Whole Foods Market IP, LP

Whole Foods's loyalty program features personalized rewards based on each shopper's purchase history.

predictions about the expansion of that convenient payment method.

Source: Fred Thompson, "Why Luxury Retailers Should Watch Whole Foods' New Loyalty Rewards Pilot," *Luxury Daily*, December 8, 2014.

Offer Tiered Rewards　Many frequent-shopper programs contain cascading tier levels, such as silver, gold, and platinum. The higher the tier, the better the rewards. This reward structure provides an incentive for customers to consolidate their purchases with one retailer to reach the higher tiers. Some programs combine both discounts and points. For example, a retailer might offer a $5 discount on purchases between $100 and $149.99, $10 off purchases from $150 to $249.99, and $15 off purchases of $250 or more. Then beyond $250, customers accumulate points that can be redeemed for special, unique rewards, such as a free shirt or tickets to a local baseball game.

A key requirement for a tiered program is to design tiers that consumers perceive as attainable. Frequent shoppers can calculate the tier level they can achieve with their usual spending pretty easily. They may be less inclined to shop at a retailer or participate in its frequent-shopper program if the tiers are impossibly distant. Although Neiman Marcus has a reward tier for customers who make $600,000 in annual purchases, a similar reward tier would be vastly inappropriate for a grocery store loyalty program.

Treat High CLVs as VIPs　Consumers respond to being treated as if they are someone special. Effective programs therefore go beyond discounts on purchases to offer unique rewards. For example, in its PowerUp Rewards program, GameStop

RETAILING VIEW   InCircle Builds Neiman Marcus's Share of Wallet   10.3

Neiman Marcus targets the top 2 percent of consumers, in terms of their income, which generally means that people in its stores are well educated and well traveled. These sophisticated shoppers are attracted to the retailer's InCircle frequent-shopper program, widely considered a CRM best practice.

The InCircle program is linked to the store credit card and offers six levels of benefits, based on annual purchases at Neiman Marcus. Circle 1 indicates purchases less than $1,000; the President's Level means the customer has spent $75,000 to $600,000 that year.

Depending on their tier, customers receive from 2 to 5 InCircle points for every dollar charged on their credit cards. For every 10,000 points earned, the members receive a $100 gift card. In addition, they accrue other benefits, depending on their spending level: discounts on in-store dining, free alterations, store delivery, hassle-free parking, fur storage, free repair and cleaning of jewelry, engraving, shoe and handbag repair, monogramming, and discounts at salons, to name a few. For example, a customer who spends $75,000 in a year receives help from a concierge who can locate an item that the customer might have seen on a fashion runway, make a reservation at an exclusive restaurant, and run errands; and a wardrobe consultation.

InCircle members can quickly look up their point balance on the InCircle website. They receive e-mails announcing special events and notifications when they are approaching a new tier level. They also get *Entrée* magazine, a publication produced by Time Warner exclusively for Neiman Marcus. In turn, Neiman Marcus asks for feedback about how it can help improve its value for InCircle members.

At the store level, sales associates unobtrusively gather insights about customers, using their prior purchases and behaviors in the store. Once they have struck up a relationship, the sales associates contact customers directly when a new shipment of their favorite brand has arrived, for example. The sales associates also move freely throughout the store to find whatever items their InCircle members want at the time or to encourage them to make use of the services available, such as gift wrap and travel advice.

The program thus offers great value for customers, which means that it benefits Neiman Marcus too. InCircle members spend 11 times more than nonreward member customers, accounting for approximately 40 percent of the retailer's overall revenue.

Sources: Sarah Jones, "Effective Loyalty Programs Hinge on Engaging Consumers Beyond Sign-Up," *Luxury Daily,* January 13, 2016; Adele Chapin, "More Than 40% of Neiman Marcus Shoppers Are Millionaires," *Racked,* August 5, 2015; www.incircle.com; www.neimanmarcus.com; 10K 2015 Neiman Marcus annual report.

encouraged its target customers to spend more on racing and fantasy video games by offering tickets to NASCAR races or backstage access to Comic-Con.[17] The rewards accordingly should match the retailer's target market to make customers feel really special: A private shopping night might be important for a high-spending Nordstrom shopper, whereas an exclusive tour of the company's facility might be more interesting for Apple customers. These events also should be promoted in advance to encourage more customers to enroll and pursue enough points to be invited to attend the events. Retailing View 10.3 describes how the Neiman Marcus InCircle program actively appeals to its best customers.

Incorporate Charitable Contributions   Many programs are linked to charitable causes. For example, participants in Pampers's Rewards program can redeem their points by offering them as charitable donations to a charity devoted to children's health.[18] Although these altruistic rewards can be an effective element of a frequent-shopper program, they probably should not be the focal point of the program.

Offer Choices   Not all customers value the same rewards, so the most effective frequent-shopper programs provide choices. Sainsbury, a UK supermarket chain, allows customers to use their Nectar points for vouchers at a variety of retail partners. Caesars Entertainment has different programs for guests who live close to one of its properties and for customers who must fly to its casinos or resorts. It also introduced

Source: Procter and Gamble

Pampers's Rewards program allows customers to redeem their points by offering them as charitable donations to a charity devoted to children's health.

Total Rewards Member Pricing, which enables loyalty program members to get better pricing than nonmembers at Caesars property restaurants, as well as the opportunity to purchase presale show tickets.[19]

Starwood Hotels (which owns the Westin, W, Sheraton, and Four Points chains, among others) maintains a program within its Starwood Preferred Guest program, called Moments, that gives point-holders chances to bid in an auction for spectacular experiences. Participants use their earned points to bid on the right to attend a variety of exclusive access events: meeting Coldplay backstage before a concert, playing golf with pro Lorena Ochoa, or meeting the chef while having dinner at the famous Per Se restaurant.[20]

Reward All Transactions   To ensure that the retailer collects all customer transaction data and encourages repeat purchases, programs need to reward all purchases, not just purchases of selected merchandise or those made through certain channels (e.g., in-store versus online). Customers should gain entry to an introductory tier with nearly their first purchase, to encourage them to join. Accordingly, Sephora designates customers as Beauty Insiders the moment they sign up for a card. Once they earn 100 points, they qualify to receive a free sample-sized product.[21]

Make the Program Transparent and Simple   Effective programs are transparent in that they make it easy for customers to keep track of their spending and available rewards. When they are both transparent and convenient, loyalty programs can quickly become integral to shoppers' consumption choices. Thus, there is an increasing use of smartphone-linked programs that let customers earn and redeem rewards through a mobile app, instead of requiring them to remember their cards or coupons. With a push of a button, shoppers can recall their point totals, how much more they need to spend to reach a desired prize, or whether they can redeem points for something great today.

When loyalty programs also are simple, their effectiveness increases even more. A program with a confusing maze of rules and regulations has little appeal to consumers. Some airlines have suffered from accusations that their confusing blackout dates and redemption rules make their loyalty programs virtually useless. Instead, simple, straightforward programs can succeed just by offering a few options consistently and dependably.

IMPLEMENTING CRM PROGRAMS

LO 10-5

Explain various ways to implement effective CRM programs.

Having developed CRM through frequent-shopper programs, the last step in the CRM process is to implement those programs (see Exhibit 10–1).

Customer Pyramid

For most retailers, a relatively small number of customers account for the majority of their profits. This condition is often called the **80–20 rule**—80 percent of the sales or profits come from 20 percent of the customers. Thus, retailers could group their customers into two categories on the basis of their CLV scores. One group would be the 20 percent of the customers with the highest CLV scores, and the other group would be the rest. However, this two-segment scheme, "best" and "rest," does not consider important differences among the 80 percent of customers in the "rest" segment. Many of the customers in the "rest" category are potentially "best," or at least, good customers. A commonly used segmentation scheme divides customers into four segments, as illustrated in Exhibit 10–2. This scheme allows retailers to develop more effective strategies for each of the segments. Different CRM programs are directed toward customers in each of the segments. Each of the four segments is described next.[22]

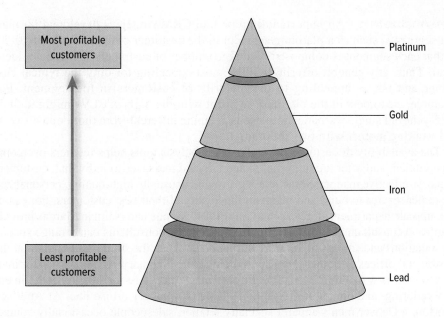

EXHIBIT 10–2
The Customer Pyramid

Platinum Segment   This segment is composed of the customers with the top 25 percent CLVs. Typically, these are the most profitable and loyal customers who, because of their loyalty, are typically not overly concerned about prices. Customers in this quartile buy a lot of the merchandise sold by the retailer and often place more value on customer service than price.

Gold Segment   The next quartile of customers, in terms of their CLVs, make up the gold segment. Even though they buy a significant amount of merchandise from the retailer, they are not as loyal as platinum customers and patronize some of the retailer's competitors. The profitability levels of the gold-tier customers are less than those of the platinum-tier customers because price plays a greater role in their decision making. An important objective of any CRM program is to provide incentives to move gold-tier customers to the platinum level.

Iron Segment   The customers in this quartile purchase a modest amount of merchandise, but their spending levels, loyalty, and profitability are not substantial enough for special treatment. Although it could be possible to move these people up to higher tiers in the pyramid, for reasons such as limited income, price sensitivity, or shared loyalties with other retailers, additional expenditures on them may not be worth it.

Lead Segment   Customers with the lowest CLVs can make a negative contribution to the firm's income. They often demand a lot of attention but do not buy much from the retailer. When they do buy from the retailer, they often buy merchandise on sale or abuse return privileges. They may even cause additional problems by complaining about the retailer to others. As a result, retailers should not direct any attention to these customers.

   In the following sections, we discuss programs retailers use to retain their best customers, convert good customers into high-CLV customers, and get rid of unprofitable customers.

Customer Retention

Two approaches that retailers use to retain customers and increase the share of wallet are personalization and community.

Personalization   An important limitation of CRM strategies developed for market segments, such as a platinum segment in the customer pyramid (Exhibit 10–2), is that each segment is composed of a large number of customers who are not identical. Thus, any general offering will be most appealing for only the typical customer and not as appealing to the majority of customers in the segment. For example, customers in the platinum segment with the highest CLVs might include a 25-year-old single woman whose needs are quite different from those of a 49-year-old working mother with two children.

The availability of customer-level data and analysis tools helps retailers overcome this problem and offer unique benefits and targeted messages to individual customers in a cost-effective manner. Some retailers provide unusually high-quality, personalized customer service to build and maintain the loyalty of their best customers. For example, upscale department stores such as Saks Fifth Avenue and Neiman Marcus provide wardrobe consultants for their best customers. These consultants can arrange special presentations and fittings in the store during hours when the store is not open or at the customers' offices or homes. Nordstrom holds complimentary private parties for invitees to view new clothing lines. Saks Fifth Avenue offers free fur storage, complimentary tailoring, and dinner at the captain's table on a luxury cruise line. At Andrisen Morton, a Denver men's apparel specialty retailer, salespeople occasionally contact customers directly; if the store receives a new shipment of Brioni suits, they call customers who have purchased Brioni in the past. If a customer has been relatively inactive, the associates might offer him a $100 certificate for something he has not bought in a while.

Developing retail programs for small groups or individual customers is referred to as **1-to-1 retailing**. Many small, local retailers have always practiced 1-to-1 retailing. They know each of their customers, greet them by name when they walk into the store, and then recommend merchandise they know the customers will like. These local store owners do not need customer data warehouses and data mining tools because they can keep the information in their heads. But most large retail chains and their employees lack such intimate knowledge of their customers. Thus, CRM enables larger retailers to develop relationships similar to those that many small local retailers have with customers.

Upscale retailers like Saks Fifth Avenue provide unique personalized benefits and targeted messages to its best customers.

Another aspect of personalization is to involve the best customers in the retailer's business decisions. Some retailers ask their best customers to participate in focus groups to evaluate alternatives the retailer is considering. Loyalty increases when customers feel valued for not just the money they have spent but for their opinions as well. TAG/Burger and Bar at Madison Street in Denver creates a sense of community by encouraging customers to send in original hamburger combination recipes through e-mail, Facebook, and Twitter. Every month, management chooses the best one and offers it for sale for a month. The winner gets as many as he or she wants for the month that it is featured.

Personalized rewards or benefits that customers receive thus can be based on unique information possessed by the retailer and its sales associates. This information, in the retailer's customer data warehouse, cannot be accessed or used by competitors. Thus, it provides an opportunity to develop a sustainable competitive advantage.

The effective use of this information creates the positive feedback cycle in the CRM process (see Exhibit 10–1). Increasing repeat purchases from a retailer increases the amount of data collected from the customer, which enables the retailer to provide more personalized benefits, which in turn increases the customer's purchases from the retailer.

Community   A second approach for building customer retention and loyalty is to develop a sense of community among customers. A **retail brand community** is a group of customers who are bound together by their loyalty to a retailer and the activities the retailer sponsors and undertakes. Community members identify themselves with other members and share a common interest and participation in activities related to the retailer. They also feel an obligation to attract new members of the community and help other members of the community by sharing their experiences and product knowledge. By participating in such a community, customers become more reluctant to leave the "family" of other people patronizing the retailer.[23] Retailing View 10.4 describes how Staples has worked to build community with its small business customers.

Customer Conversion: Making Good Customers into Best Customers

In the context of the customer pyramid (Exhibit 10–2), increasing the sales made to good customers can be referred to as customer alchemy—converting iron and gold customers into platinum customers.[24] A way to achieve customer alchemy is through

---

RETAILING VIEW   Staples's App-Based Small Business Community   10.4

With its Quick Wins app, Staples is hoping to reach out to the small business owners who shop at its retail stores, providing them with not just office supplies but also ideas on how to run their offices. The app tracks their performance on a range of measures, including social media engagement, website traffic, and financial metrics, all in one place.

The introduction is a clear response to customer demand. Through its research, Staples determined that approximately 41 percent of its small business customers expressed their need for help with these measures of performance, but they also did not know which metrics were most important, nor did they have a clear sense of how to measure them accurately. Worried about their ability to keep up with the information, respondents to Staples's surveys also noted that they would prefer for all the data to be available in one, easy-to-read dashboard.

By helping these business customers track key data regularly, Staples also promises to develop customized, specific suggestions for how the business customers can expand and increase their firms. Furthermore, through the Quick Wins app, users can interact with other small business owners, seeking answers and support from their peers.

Overall, Staples gathered feedback from customers and acted to provide them the benefits they requested. In so doing, it makes sure that they receive personalized information, not just from Staples itself but also from other small businesses that might form a community around the app. By implementing all these best practices, Staples creates conditions for loyalty that make it invaluable to small business customers.

Source: Mike Troy, "Staples' New Digital Tool to Help Small Biz," *Retailing Today,* January 4, 2016.

add-on selling, which involves offering and selling more products and services to existing customers to increase the retailer's share of wallet with these customers.

A retailer's customer data warehouse reveals opportunities for add-on selling. Many retailers use their data on customers' shopping histories to suggest products to them. For example, if a supermarket discovers that customers are buying cat food and not kitty litter, it might distribute coupons for kitty litter to the customers. These coupons could be provided to the customers when they enter the store and swipe their frequent shopper cards, when they log on to the retailer's website, or through messages sent to the customers' mobile phones.

Amazon.com is a master at generating add-on sales through its recommendations. Personalized recommendations, based on past purchases, are made when consumers first visit the website. If they scroll down to get more information about a book, the site recommends other books that have been bought by customers who purchased the book being examined. Then a bundle of two books, the one being examined and a complementary book, is offered at a discounted price.

Dealing with Unprofitable Customers

In many cases, the bottom tier of customers actually has a negative CLV. Retailers lose money on every sale they make to these customers. For example, catalog retailers have customers who repeatedly buy three or four items and return all but one of them. The cost of processing two or three returned items is much greater than the profits coming from the one item that the customer kept. The National Retail Federation estimates that return fraud accounts for $9 billion in losses for retailers annually.[25] In response, Saks notes in its policies that any customer who has been flagged with an unreasonable return pattern may be refused or restricted on a future purchase.[26]

Customers in the bottom tier may also be there because they stopped buying from the retailer for a period of time and then resumed patronizing the retailer. For example, customers may vanish because a competitor is offering a more attractive offer, or they are dissatisfied and then return months or years later as a new customer. The costs of their (re)acquisition make them unprofitable. The process of no longer selling to these unprofitable customers can be referred to as "getting the lead out," in terms of the customer pyramid.[27]

Approaches for getting the lead out are (1) offering less costly services to satisfy the needs of lead customers and (2) charging customers for the services they are abusing. For example, a retailer might get 70,000 daily calls, about three-quarters of which go to automated systems that cost the company less than $1 each. The remaining calls are handled by call center agents that cost $13 per call. The retailer could contact 25,000 lower-tier customers who placed a lot of calls to agents and tell them they must use the website or automated calls for simple account and price information. Each name could be flagged and routed to a special representative who would direct callers back to automated services and tell them how to use it.

SUMMARY

LO 10-1 **Describe the customer relationship management process.**

A **customer relationship management program** is the set of activities designed to identify and build the loyalty of the retailer's most valuable customers. Also called loyalty program or frequent-shopper program. Loyal customers are committed to patronizing a retailer and are not prone to switch to competitors. In addition to building loyalty by increasing customer value, CRM programs are designed to increase the share of wallet that a retailer earns from its better customers.

Customer relationship management is an iterative process that allows the retailer to encourage increased loyalty through its efforts to (1) collect customer data, (2) analyze the customer data and identify target customers, (3) develop CRM and frequent-shopper programs, and (4) implement CRM programs.

LO 10-2 **Understand how customer shopping data are collected.**

Retailers collect extensive data about customers, which they store in their data warehouses. To gather these data, retailers might ask for it at the point of sale, obtain it through online channels, or gather it from applications that customers submit to a loyalty program. Although it can be challenging to ensure that all collected data are accurately connected with each customer transaction, the collection and analysis of data about customer attitudes, preferences, and shopping behaviors enables retailers to closely target their promotions and provide more value to their customers.

However, many customers are concerned that retailers might violate their privacy when they collect detailed personal information. There is a growing consensus that personal information must be fairly collected, that the collection must be purposeful, and that the data should be relevant and kept reasonably secure. Anticipating increasing data privacy regulations, many retailers are working proactively to establish secure methods that can guarantee the privacy of their customers' data.

LO 10-3 **Explain the methods used to analyze customer data and identify target customers.**

Once retailers have collected sufficient data, they must analyze them to derive actionable information. A common measure for describing shoppers is their customer lifetime value (CLV). More sophisticated retail analytics also include market basket analysis, which provides information about the products most commonly purchased together. Such information can inform retail decisions about which assortment to

maintain in a store to appeal best to valuable customers, as well as which merchandise items to promote together to increase sales.

LO 10-4 **Outline how retailers develop their frequent-shopper programs.**

Frequent-shopper programs serve two main purposes: (1) build a customer data warehouse that links customers to transactions and (2) encourage repeat purchase behavior and loyalty. Frequent-shopper programs can be effective for building a customer data warehouse, but they are not very useful for ensuring long-term customer loyalty. To enhance their loyalty effects, frequent-shopper programs should seek to (1) create tiered rewards, (2) treat frequent shoppers as VIPs, (3) incorporate charitable activities, (4) offer choices, (5) reward all transactions, and (6) make the rewards program transparent and simple.

LO 10-5 **Explain various ways to implement effective CRM programs.**

Using this information about customers, retailers can develop programs to build loyalty in their best customers, increase their share of wallet with better customers (e.g., convert gold customers into platinum customers), and deal with unprofitable customers (getting the lead out). Four approaches that retailers use to build loyalty and retain their better customers are (1) launch frequent-shopper programs, (2) offer special customer services, (3) personalize the services they provide, and (4) build a sense of community. To deal with unprofitable customers identified by their CRM data, retailers need to develop lower-cost approaches to serve them, or else exclude those customers altogether from the retail offer.

KEY TERMS

add-on selling, *266*	data mining, *258*	opt in, *256*
cookies, *255*	80–20 rule, *262*	opt out, *256*
customer lifetime value (CLV), *256*	frequent-shopper program, *254*	retail analytics, *258*
customer loyalty, *252*	loyalty program, *254*	retail brand community, *265*
customer relationship management (CRM), *251*	market basket analysis, *258*	share of wallet, *251*
	1-to-1 retailing, *264*	

GET OUT AND DO IT!

1. **CONTINUING ASSIGNMENT** Interview the store manager working for the retailer you have selected for the continuing assignment. Ask the manager if the store offers a frequent-shopper or loyalty program and how effective it is in terms of increasing the store's sales and profits. Find out why the manager has these views and what could be done to increase the effectiveness of the program. Then talk to some customers in the store. Ask them why they are or are not members. Find out how membership in the program affects their shopping behavior and relationship with the retailer.

2. **INTERNET EXERCISE** Go to the home page of a retailer that you frequent and review its privacy policy. How is this retailer protecting its customers' information? Which policies, or lack of policies, raise your concern? Why? Which policies give you comfort that your private information is being protected? Why?

3. **INTERNET EXERCISE** Go to the website of the Electronic Privacy Information Center (www.epic.org) and review the issues raised by the organization. What does this watchdog organization feel are the most

important retailers' consumer privacy issues? How will these issues evolve in the future?

4. **INTERNET EXERCISE** Go to the 1-800-Flowers Fresh Rewards Landing page at www.1800flowers.com/ fresh-rewards and read about the Fresh Rewards program. How does this company's CRM program help it track its better customers, grow its business, and increase customer loyalty?

DISCUSSION QUESTIONS AND PROBLEMS

1. What is a customer relationship management (CRM) program? Describe one CRM program that you have participated in as a customer.

2. Why do retailers want to determine the lifetime value of their customers? How does past customer behavior help retailers anticipate future customer retention?

3. Why do some customers have a low or negative CLV value? What approach can retailers take with these customers to minimize their impact on the bottom line?

4. Why do customers have privacy concerns about the frequent-shopper programs that supermarkets offer, and what can supermarkets do to minimize these concerns?

5. Why are most frequent-shopper programs ineffective in terms of building loyalty? What can be done to make them more effective?

6. Which of the following types of retailers do you think would benefit most from instituting a CRM program: (a) supermarkets, (b) banks, (c) automobile dealers, or (d) consumer electronics retailers? Why?

7. Develop a CRM program for a local store that sells apparel and gifts with your college's or university's logo. What type of information would you collect about your customers, and how would you use this information to increase the sales and profits of the store?

8. What are the different approaches retailers can use to identify customers by their transactions? What are the advantages and disadvantages of each approach?

9. A CRM program focuses on building relationships with a retailer's better customers. Some customers who do not receive the same benefits as the retailer's best customers may be upset because they are treated differently. What can retailers do to minimize this negative reaction?

10. Think of one of your favorite places to shop. How does this retailer create customer loyalty and satisfaction, encourage repeat visits, establish an emotional bond between the customer and the retailer, know the customer's preferences, and provide personal attention and memorable experiences to its best customers?

CHAPTER ENDNOTES

1. Kroger—2015 Annual Report, I Kroger, 2016, http://eproxy-materials.com/interactive/kr2015/.

2. "2014 Global 250 Retailers," *Stores Magazine,* January 17, 2016.

3. Interview reported in Dhruv Grewal, Michael Levy, and Britt Hackmann, "Making Loyalty Programs Sing," Working Paper, Babson College, 2016.

4. Scott A. Neslin, "Customer Relationship Management," in *The History of Marketing Science,* Russell S. Winer and Scott A. Neslin, eds. (Hackensack, NJ: World Scientific Publishing, 2014), pp. 289–318; V. Kumar and Werner Reinartz, *Close Customer Relationship Management: Concept, Strategy and Tools* (New York: Springer, 2012); Francis Buttle, *Customer Relationship Management* (Hungary: Routledge, 2012).

5. V. Kumar, Ankit Anand, and Hyunseok Song, "Future of Retailer Profitability: An Organizing Framework," *Journal of Retailing* 93, no. 1 (March 2017), pp. 96–119; Bernhard Swoboda, Bettina Berg, Hanna Schramm-Klein, and Thomas Foscht, "The Importance of Retail Brand Equity and Store Accessibility for Store Loyalty in Local Competition," *Journal of Retailing and Consumer Services* 20, no. 3 (May 2013), pp. 251–262.

6. Jack Mitchell, *Hug Your Customers: The Proven Way to Personalize Sales and Achieve Astounding Results* (New York: Hyperion, 2003).

7. Elizabeth M. Aguirre, Dominik Mahr, Dhruv Grewal, Ko de Ruyter, and Martin Wetzels, "Unraveling the Personalization Paradox: The Effect of Information Collection and Trust-Building Strategies on Online Advertisement Effectiveness,"

Journal of Retailing 91, no. 1 (2015), pp. 34–49; Jeff Chester, "Cookie Wars: How New Data Profiling and Targeting Techniques Threaten Citizens and Consumers in the 'Big Data' Era," in *European Data Protection,* Serge Gutwirth, Ronald Leenes, Paul De Hert, and Yves Poullet, eds. (New York: Springer, 2012), pp. 53–77; Jodie Ferguson, "Consumer Attitudes toward Sharing Personal Health and Shopping Information: A Hierarchical Model to Understanding Privacy Concerns," *Marketing Theory and Applications,* 2012, pp. 140–149.

8. Marc Roth, "The Retailer's Guide to Big Data," *CSN,* March 30, 2015; Federal Trade Commission, *Protecting Consumer Privacy in an Era of Rapid Change* (Washington, DC: Author, March 26, 2012).

9. https://www.ftc.gov/tips-advice/business-center/guidance/how-comply-privacy-consumer-financial-information-rule-gramm.

10. V. Kumar and Werner Reinartz, "Creating Enduring Customer Value," *Journal of Marketing* 80, no. 6 (November 2016), pp. 36–68; Yao Zhang, Eric T. Bradlow, and Dylan S. Small, "Predicting Customer Value Using Clumpiness: From RFM to RFMC," *Marketing Science* 34, no. 2 (2014), pp. 195–208; V. Kumar, Lerzan Aksoy, Bas Donkers, Thorsten Wiesel, Rajkumar Venkatesan, and Sebastian Tillmanns, "Undervalued Customers: Capturing Total Customer Engagement Value," *Journal of Service Research* 13 (2010), pp. 297–310; V. Kumar, "Customer Lifetime Value-Based Approach to Managing Marketing in the Multichannel,

Multimedia Purchasing Environment," *Journal of Interactive Marketing* 25, no. 2 (2010), pp. 71–81.

11. Emmitt Cox, *Retail Analytics: The Secret Weapon* (Hoboken, NJ: Wiley, 2011).

12. Charu C. Aggarwal, *Data Mining:* The Textbook (New York: Springer, 2015); Gordon S. Linoff and Michael J. Berry, *Data Mining Techniques: For Marketing, Sales, and Customer Relationship Management,* 3rd ed. (Hoboken, NJ: Wiley, April 2011); Alexander Tuzhilin, "Customer Relationship Management and Web Mining: the Next Frontier," *Data Mining and Knowledge Discovery,* 2012, pp. 1–29.

13. Lindsay Kolowich, "7 Customer Loyalty Programs That Actually Add Value," *HubSpot,* July 1, 2015; Marie-Claude Nideau and Marc Singer, "The Secret to Creating Loyalty Programs That Actually Work," *Business Insider,* March 21, 2014; Matilda Dorotic, Tammo H. A. Bijmolt, and Peter C. Verhoef, "Loyalty Programmes: Current Knowledge and Research Directions," *International Journal of Management Reviews* 14, no. 3 (2012), pp. 217–237.

14. Don Peppers, "When Loyalty Programs Are a Waste of Money," *Fast Company,* March 2, 2012.

15. Alexandra Berzon, "Starwood Perks Up Loyalty Program," *The Wall Street Journal,* February 1, 2012.

16. Kolowich, "7 Customer Loyalty Programs That Actually Add Value"; Nideau and Singer, "The Secret to Creating Loyalty Programs That Actually Work"; Bryan Pearson, "How to Create Loyalty Programs Consumers Will Actually Get Excited About," *Fast Company,* January 11, 2013; Erdener Ortan, "How to Implement a Customer Loyalty Program?," *Erdener Ortan's blog,* October 20, 2012; Don Peppers, "5 Best Practices for Loyalty Programs," *Fast Company,* July 8, 2012.

17. Pearson, "How to Create Loyalty Programs Customers Will Actually Get Excited About."

18. http://www.pampers.com/en-us/rewards/make-a-donation-to-the-march-of-dimes; Bryan Pearson, "How to Align Your Loyalty Program with Your Company's Charitable Works," *Retail Customer Experience,* December 5, 2014.

19. Pearson, "How to Create Loyalty Programs Customers Will Actually Get Excited About."

20. https://auction.starwoodhotels.com/about-moments.

21. https://www.sephora.com/profile/beautyInsider/.

22. Valarie Zeithaml, Roland Rust, and Katherine Lemon, "The Customer Pyramid: Creating and Serving Profitable Customers," *California Management Review* 43 (Summer 2001), p. 124.

23. Brian J. Baldus, Clay Voorhees, and Roger Calantone, "Online Brand Community Engagement: Scale Development and Validation," *Journal of Business Research* 68, no. 5 (2015), pp. 978–985; Gianluca Marzocchi, Gabriele Morandin, and Massimo Bergami, "Brand Communities: Loyal to the Community or the Brand?," *European Journal of Marketing* 47, no. 1 (2013), pp. 93–114.

24. Roland Rust, Valerie Zeithaml, and Katherine Lemon, *Driving Customer Equity* (New York: Free Press, 2002), chap. 13; Zeithaml et al., "The Customer Pyramid."

25. Amy Martinez, "REI Is Now Limiting Returns to One Year," *Seattle Times,* June 3, 2013.

26. Tom Ryan, "Should Chronic Returners Be Banned?," *Retail-Wire,* August 12, 2014.

27. "Find the 'Keepers': Identify Your Most Profitable Customers and Grow Your Share of Business," *Dragnet Solutions,* June 29, 2015; Michael Haenlein and Andreas Kaplan, "The Impact of Unprofitable Customer Abandonment on Current Customers' Exit, Voice, and Loyalty Intentions: An Empirical Analysis," *Journal of Services Marketing* 26, no. 6 (2012), pp. 458–470.

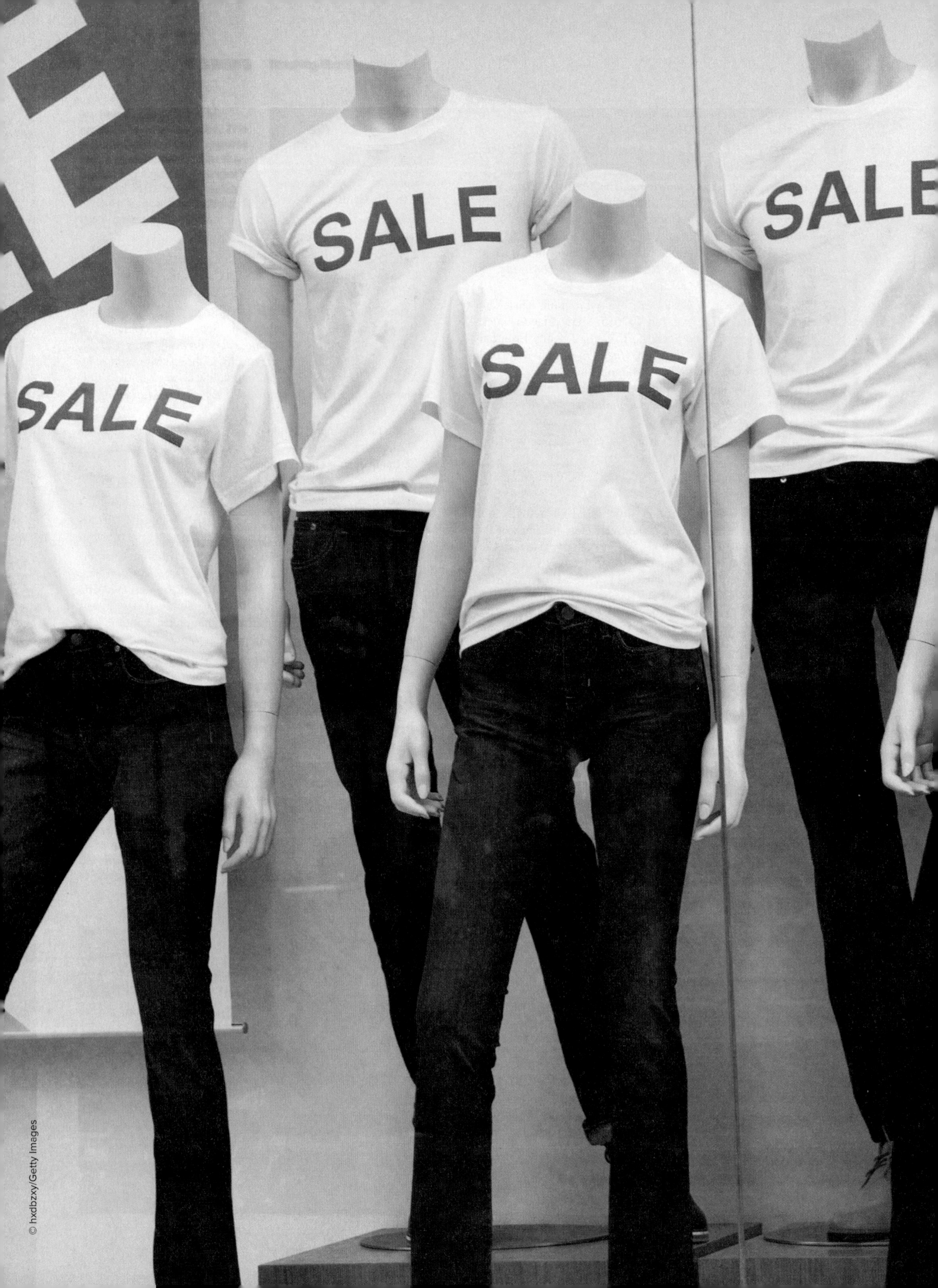

© hxdbzxy/Getty Images

Merchandise Management

Section II reviewed the strategic decisions made by retailers—the development of their retail market strategy, their financial strategy associated with the market strategy, their store location opportunities, factors affecting the selection of a specific site, the systems they use to control the flow of information and merchandise, and the approaches they take to manage relationships with their customers. These decisions are more strategic than tactical, in that they involve committing significant resources to develop long-term advantages over the competition in a target retail market segment.

This section, Section III, examines the more tactical merchandise management decisions undertaken to implement the retail strategy.

Chapter 11 provides an overview of how retailers manage their merchandise inventory—how they organize the merchandise planning process, evaluate their performance, forecast sales, establish an assortment plan, determine the appropriate service levels, allocate merchandise to stores, and monitor the performance of the merchandise inventory control activities.

Chapter 12 explores how retailers buy merchandise from vendors— their branding options, negotiating processes, and vendor relationship-building activities.

Chapter 13 addresses the question of how retailers set and adjust prices for the merchandise and services they offer.

Chapter 14 looks at the approaches that retailers take to build their brand image and communicate with their customers.

The subsequent section, Section IV, focuses on store management decisions.

CHAPTER 11 | Managing the Merchandise Planning Process

© iStockphoto/Getty Images

It may seem like a contrast, but for some retailers, keeping more inventory on their physical shelves and widening the product assortment in brick-and-mortar stores might be the answer to increasing online sales. That claim might not make much sense at first glance, but as our previous discussions of omnichannel retailing have revealed, in ever-changing markets, retailers face the constant need to reconsider and reconceive of the best ways to get the products that their customers want in their hands, at exactly the time and place that they want those items.

In a traditional model, more inventory on store shelves reduces the chances that a retailer might find itself out of stock of some product that a shopper wants to buy. But it also increases the costs associated with running a store, so finding a balance traditionally has entailed identifying the exact amount of product to hold so that the store is never out of important items but also never overstocked with too much of something. In an online sales model, some of these costs were supposed to nearly disappear. The idea was that online retailers would not have to worry about putting products on display in a store and hiring sales associates to take care of customers. Instead, they could hold them relatively inexpensively in a warehouse and just ship them out to each customer for each order as it occurred.

But in the new omnichannel environment, these two models blend, creating a far more complicated algorithm for retailers. Target has sought to resolve the challenges by establishing a new balance. It keeps more products on shelves in its stores, but it also relies on these stocks to supply its online orders. Therefore, it can afford to increase its inventory because it is using those stocks to support its online sales supply as well as its in-store sales.[1]

The strategy has provoked a lot of questions, but Target appears quite pleased with the results. In recently released data, it noted that it had improved its in-stock performance by about 20 percent. Furthermore, it was able to fulfill approximately 30 percent of its online orders with products taken from local store shelves, which also minimized shipping distances. Many online buyers volunteered to pay online and then pick up their orders in stores. In perhaps its happiest statistic, Target noted that its online sales grew by 34 percent in a recent quarter and surpassed the sales achieved by its main rival, Walmart. To achieve these outcomes, though, Target increased its in-store inventory levels by about 4 percent.

Although these moves have been successful thus far, Target also is confronting new sources of competition, as retailers that previously dedicated their merchandise assortments to specific products expand and broaden their offerings. As a general merchandise retailer, Target stocks a little bit of everything, both products that people often purchase online (e.g., books) and those that they tend to prefer to pick up in person from the store (e.g., toilet paper). But as U.S. consumers reduce their number of shopping trips by an average of 3.8 percent, more retailers similarly are promoting themselves as viable options that will enable shoppers to cover all their needs in a single trip.[2]

In particular, many retailers are expanding their merchandise selections to include seemingly mismatched items. For example, Home Depot now stocks laundry detergent and charcoal—products that have little in common with its do-it-yourself home improvement image. But by paying attention to what consumers were actually buying, the big-box retailer realized that shoppers sought charcoal to go along with the new grills they had just bought, and laundry detergent to use with their new washer/dryer combo.

Other retailers have gone even further afield. Staples stocks coffee pods because office employees and home-based workers rely on their single-serving machines for a caffeine boost. But it also provides personal deodorant and shaving cream. By stocking such items, Staples hopes that people popping in for toner will also appreciate the convenience of purchasing some basic necessities in the same store, rather than visiting another retailer to gather such items.

Another driver of an expanded product assortment is the potential these assortments offer for increasing repeat visits. For example, Best Buy pushes personal soda machines such as Soda Stream, because a customer who buys the machine from this retailer is likely to return to the same store to refill the CO_2 cartridges that the machines require. Such return visits further encourage more impromptu purchases of the latest DVD or a new set of headphones.

Not to be outdone in these expansion efforts, Target has announced plans to extend its grocery assortment, especially when it comes to organic, gluten-free, and natural options in seven key categories: produce, granola/yogurt, snacks, fresh meat, beer/wine, candy, and tea/coffee.[3] In this case, rather than being a "warehouse" that people visit to grab toilet paper (which they might be getting at Home Depot anyway), Target hopes to position itself as a meaningful source of delicious food options too.

Merchandise management activities are undertaken primarily by buyers and their superiors, divisional merchandise managers (DMMs) and general merchandise managers (GMMs). Many people view these jobs as very exciting and glamorous. They think that buyers spend most of their time trying to identify the latest fashions and trends, attending designer shows replete with celebrities in Paris and Milan, and going to rock concerts and other glamorous events to see what the trendsetters are wearing. But in reality, the activities of retail buyers are more like those of Wall Street investment analysts than globe-trotting trend spotters.

Investment analysts manage a portfolio of stocks. They buy stocks in companies they think will increase in value and sell stocks in companies they believe do not have a promising future. They continuously monitor the performance of the stocks they own to see which are increasing in value and which are decreasing. Sometimes, they make mistakes and invest in companies that do not perform well. So they sell their stock in

© Martin Leissl/Bloomberg via Getty Images

Retail inventory management is similar to managing an investment portfolio.

these companies and lose money, but they use the money from the sold stocks to buy more attractive stocks. Other times, the stocks they buy increase dramatically in price, and they wish they had bought more shares.

Rather than managing a portfolio of stocks, retail buyers manage a portfolio of merchandise inventory. They buy merchandise they think will be popular with their customers. Like investment analysts, they use an information system to monitor the performance of their merchandise portfolio—to see what is selling and what is not. Retail buyers also make mistakes. When the merchandise they bought is not selling well, they get rid of it by putting it on sale so that they can use the money to buy better-selling merchandise. However, they also might take a chance and buy a lot of a new merchandise item and be rewarded when it sells well, while competitors, who were more conservative, don't have enough of the product.

Chris Manning, a former swimwear buyer at Macy's, draws an analogy between surfing and buying merchandise:

> My job is like surfing. Sometimes you catch a big wave (trend) and it's exhilarating, and sometimes you think you've caught a good wave and brown turns out not to be the color this season. But the real fun is getting the most out of the wave you can. Let me give you an example of how I worked a big wave. Vendors started to show tankinis—women's bathing suits with bikini bottoms and tank tops. My customers were women in their 40s that had a couple of kids. I thought they would really go for this new style because it had the advantages of a two-piece bathing suit, but wasn't much more revealing than a one-piece suit. I bought a wide color assortment—bright reds, yellows, pink, and black—and put them in our fashion-forward stores in January for a test. The initial sales were good, but our customers thought they were a little too skimpy. Then I started to work the wave. I went back to the vendor and got them to recut the top so that the suit was less revealing, and I placed a big order for the colors that were selling best. Sales were so good that the other Macy's divisions picked up on it, but we rode the wave the longest and had the best swimwear sales of all of the divisions.[4]

Merchandise management is the process by which a retailer attempts to offer the appropriate quantity of the right merchandise, in the right place, and at the right time, so that it can meet the company's financial goals. Buyers need to be in touch with and anticipate what customers will want to buy, but this ability to sense market trends is just one skill needed to manage merchandise inventory effectively. Perhaps an even more important skill is the ability to analyze sales data continually and make appropriate adjustments in prices and inventory levels.

The first part of this chapter provides the background needed to understand the merchandise management process. In this introduction, we discuss how the process is organized, who makes the merchandise decisions, and how merchandise management performance is evaluated. The last part of the chapter examines the steps in the merchandise management process—forecasting sales, formulating an assortment plan, determining the appropriate inventory level, developing a merchandise management plan, allocating merchandise to stores, and monitoring performance. Appendix 11A at the end of this chapter provides a more detailed discussion of the steps used to develop a merchandise budget plan. Other activities involved in merchandise management are reviewed in subsequent chapters: buying merchandise (Chapter 12) and pricing (Chapter 13).

MERCHANDISE MANAGEMENT OVERVIEW

This section provides an overview of the merchandise management process, including the organization of a retailer's merchandise management activities and the objectives and measures used to evaluate merchandise management performance. In the following section, we review the differences in the process for managing fashion and seasonal merchandise versus basic merchandise and each of the steps in the merchandise management process.

LO 11-1

Explain the merchandise management organization and performance measures.

The Buying Organization

Every retailer has its own system for grouping categories of merchandise, but the basic structure of the buying organization is similar for most retailers. Exhibit 11–1 illustrates this basic structure by depicting the organization of the merchandise division for a department store chain such as Macy's, Belk, or Dillard's. Exhibit 11–1 shows the organization of buyers in the merchandise division. A similar structure for planners parallels the structure for buyers.

The highest classification level is the **merchandise group**. The organization chart in Exhibit 11–1 has four merchandise groups: (1) women's apparel; (2) men's, children's, and intimate apparel; (3) cosmetics, shoes, jewelry, and accessories; and (4) home and kitchen. Each of the four merchandise groups is managed by a general

EXHIBIT 11–1   Illustration of Merchandise Classifications and Organization

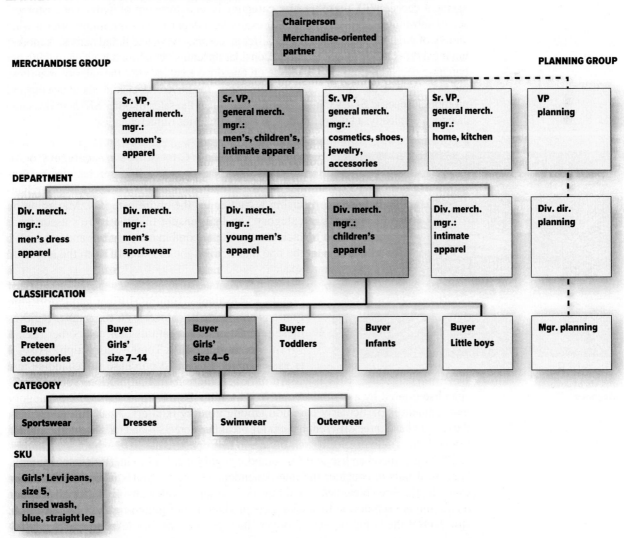

merchandise manager (GMM), who is often a senior vice president in the firm. Each of the GMMs is responsible for several departments. For example, the GMM for men's, children's, and intimate apparel makes decisions about how the merchandise inventory is managed in five departments: men's dress apparel, men's sportswear, young men's apparel, children's apparel, and intimate apparel.

The second level in the merchandise classification scheme is the **department**. Departments are managed by divisional merchandise managers (DMMs). For example, the DMM highlighted in Exhibit 11–1 manages the buyers responsible for six children's apparel merchandise departments.

The **classification** is the third level for categorizing merchandise and organizing merchandise management activities. A classification is a group of items targeting the same customer type, such as girls' sizes 4 to 6. Categories are the next lower level in the classification scheme. Each buyer manages several merchandise categories. For example, the girls' sizes 4 to 6 buyer manages the sportswear, dresses, swimwear, and outerwear categories for girls who wear sizes 4 to 6.

A **stock-keeping unit (SKU)** is the smallest unit available for inventory control. In soft-goods merchandise, for instance, a SKU usually means a particular brand, size, color, and style—for example, a pair of size 5, rinsed wash, blue, straight-legged Levi jeans is a SKU.

Merchandise Category—The Planning Unit

The merchandise category is the basic unit of analysis for making merchandising management decisions. A **merchandise category** is an assortment of items that customers see as substitutes for one another. For example, a department store might offer a wide variety of girls' dresses sizes 4 to 6 in different colors, styles, and brand names. A mother buying a dress for her daughter might consider the entire set of dresses when making her purchase decision. Lowering the price on one dress may increase the sales of that dress but also decrease the sales of other dresses. Thus, the buyers' decisions about pricing and promoting specific SKUs in the category will affect the sales of other SKUs in the same category. Typically, a buyer manages several categories of merchandise.

The chilled drink department consists of several categories.

© Aardvark/Alamy Stock Photo

Ways to Manage Categories   A **category management** approach to managing merchandise assigns one buyer or category manager to oversee all merchandising activities for the entire category. Managing by category can help ensure that the store's assortment includes the "best" combination of sizes and vendors—the one that will get the most profit from the allocated space.[5]

Some retailers instead define categories in terms of brands. For example, Tommy Hilfiger and Polo/Ralph Lauren each might be categories if the retailer believes these brands are not substitutes for each other (i.e., a "Tommy" customer buys Tommy, not Ralph). Also, it is easier for one buyer to purchase merchandise and coordinate distribution and promotions for the merchandise offered by a national-brand vendor. This brand-based approach to category management is particularly common among grocery retailers. A supermarket chain thus might have three different buyers for breakfast cereals—one for Kellogg's, one for General Mills, and one for General Foods.

Managing merchandise within a brand category can lead to inefficiencies, though, because it fails to consider the interdependencies among SKUs in the category. For example, the three breakfast cereal buyers for a supermarket chain, one for each major brand, might each decide to stock a new product line of gluten-free breakfast cereals. However, if the brand-organized buyers had taken a category-level perspective, they would have realized that the market for gluten-free cereals was limited and that their company (i.e., the supermarket) could have generated more sales by stocking just one brand of gluten-free cereals. Then it could have used some of the space set devoted to all those gluten-free cereal brands to stock a locally produced cereal that has a strong following among other customers.

Category Captain Some retailers select a vendor, such as General Mills or Kellogg's, to help them manage a particular category. The vendor, known as the **category captain**, works with the retailer to develop a better understanding of consumer shopping behaviors, create assortments that satisfy consumer needs, and improve the profitability of the merchandise category.

Selecting vendors as category captains has several advantages for retailers. It makes merchandise management tasks easier and can increase profits. Vendors are often in a better position to manage a category than are retailers because they have superior information about the specific category. The vendor's entire focus is on that category; buyers instead are typically responsible for several categories. In addition, the insights that vendors acquire from managing the category for other retailers can be applied to a current problem.

A potential problem with establishing a vendor as a category captain is that the vendor could take advantage of its position. It is somewhat like "letting the fox into the henhouse." Suppose, for example, that Frito-Lay chose to maximize its own sales, rather than the retailer's sales, in managing the salty snack category. It could suggest an assortment plan that included most of its SKUs and exclude SKUs that are more profitable to the retailer, such as high-margin, private-label SKUs. Thus, retailers are becoming increasingly reluctant to turn over these important decisions to their vendors. Working closely with vendors and carefully evaluating their suggestions offers a much more prudent approach.

Finally, there are some antitrust considerations associated with category captains. For example, a vendor's category captain could collude with the retailer to fix prices or block other brands, particularly smaller ones, from gaining access to valuable shelf space.[6]

Evaluating Merchandise Management Performance

As we discussed in Chapter 6, a good performance measure for evaluating a retail firm is return on assets (ROA). ROA is composed of two components, asset turnover and net profit margin percentage. But ROA is not a good measure for evaluating the performance of merchandise managers because they do not have control over all of the retailer's assets or all the expenses that the retailer incurs. Merchandise managers have control only over what merchandise they buy (i.e., their merchandise inventory, but not the cost of other assets such as cash, accounts receivable, or fixtures). They also control the cost of the merchandise and the price at which it is sold, which results in the gross margin. They do not, however, have control over operating expenses, such as store operations, human resources, real estate, and logistics and information systems.

GMROI A financial ratio that assesses a buyer's contribution to ROA is gross margin return on inventory investment (GMROI). It measures how many gross margin dollars are earned on every dollar of inventory investment. GMROI combines gross margin percentage (expressed as a decimal) and the sales-to-stock ratio, which is related to inventory turnover.

$$\text{GMROI} = \text{Gross margin percentage} \times \text{Sales-to-stock ratio}$$

$$= \frac{\text{Gross margin}}{\text{Net sales}} \times \frac{\text{Net sales}}{\text{Average inventory at cost}}$$

$$= \frac{\text{Gross margin}}{\text{Average inventory at cost}}$$

The reason we use the sales-to-stock ratio to calculate GMROI instead of inventory turnover is that GMROI is a type of return on investment measure, so the investment in inventory is expressed at cost. Inventory turnover and sales-to-stock ratios are very similar in concept, but they are calculated slightly differently.

The difference between the sales-to-stock ratio and inventory turnover is the numerator of the equation. When you are calculating the sales-to-stock ratio, the numerator is net sales. When you are calculating inventory turnover, the numerator is the cost of goods sold. To convert the sales-to-stock ratio to inventory turnover, simply multiply the sales-to-stock ratio by (1 − Gross margin percentage). Thus, if the sales-to-stock ratio is 9.0 and the gross margin percentage (expressed as a decimal) is 0.40, the inventory turnover for the category is 5.4:

$$\text{Inventory turnover} = (1 - \text{Gross margin percentage}) \times \text{Sales-to-stock}$$
$$5.4 = (1 - 0.4) \times 9.0$$

Buyers have control over both components of GMROI. The gross margin component is affected by the prices they set and the prices they negotiate with vendors when buying merchandise. The sales-to-stock ratio is affected by the popularity of the merchandise they buy. If they buy merchandise that customers want, it sells quickly and the sales-to-stock ratio is high.

Like the profit and asset management paths to assess ROA, there are two paths to achieving high GMROI: gross margin and inventory turnover (sales-to-stock ratio). For instance, within a supermarket, some categories (e.g., gourmet canned food) are high-margin, low-turnover while other categories (e.g., fresh bakery bread) are low-margin, high-turnover. If the gourmet canned food category's performance were compared with that of fresh bakery bread using inventory turnover alone, the contribution of gourmet canned food to the supermarket's performance would be undervalued. In contrast, if only gross margin were used, gourmet canned food's contribution would be overvalued.

Consider the situation in Exhibit 11–2, in which a supermarket wants to evaluate the performance of these two categories: fresh bakery bread and gourmet canned food. If evaluated on gross margin percentage alone, gourmet canned food is certainly the winner, with a 50 percent gross margin, compared with fresh bakery bread's gross margin of 20 percent. Yet gourmet canned food's sales-to-stock ratio is only 4, whereas fresh bakery bread has a sales-to-stock ratio of 10. Using GMROI, both categories achieve a GMROI of 200 percent and so are equal performers from a return on investment perspective.

Note that even though fresh bakery bread had five times the amount of sales (i.e., $1,000,000 versus $200,000) and twice the amount of gross margin dollars (i.e., $200,000 versus $100,000), neither the amount of sales nor gross margin dollars affect GMROI in this example. Thus, GMROI, like other financial ratios, should

EXHIBIT 11–2
Illustration of GMROI

PLANNING DATA			
		Fresh Bakery Bread	**Gourmet Canned Food**
Sales		$1,000,000	200,000
Gross margin		200,000	100,000
Average inventory		100,000	50,000

CALCULATIONS						
	GMROI =	$\dfrac{\text{Gross margin}}{\text{Net sales}}$	×	$\dfrac{\text{Net sales}}{\text{Average inventory}}$	=	$\dfrac{\text{Gross margin}}{\text{Average inventory}}$
Fresh Bakery Bread	GMROI =	$\dfrac{200,000}{1,000,000}$	×	$\dfrac{1,000,000}{100,000}$	=	$\dfrac{200,000}{100,000}$
	=	20%	×	10	=	200%
Gourmet Canned Food	GMROI =	$\dfrac{100,000}{200,000}$	×	$\dfrac{200,000}{50,000}$	=	$\dfrac{100,000}{50,000}$
	=	50%	×	4	=	200%

The bakery department in a supermarket typically has a high sales-to-stock ratio and a low gross margin.

not be used in isolation. Buyers, categories, and SKUs that generate more sales and profits are obviously outperforming those with lower sales and profits, all other things held equal.[7]

Measuring Sales-to-Stock Ratio   Retailers normally express inventory turnover (sales-to-stock) ratios on an annual basis rather than for part of a year. If the sales-to-stock ratio for a three-month season equals 2.3, the annual sales-to-stock ratio will be four times that number (9.2). Thus, to convert a sales-to-stock ratio based on part of a year to an annual figure, multiply it by the number of such time periods in the year.

The most accurate way to measure average inventory is to measure the inventory level at the end of each day and divide the sum by 365. Most retailers can use their information systems to get accurate average inventory estimates by collecting and averaging the inventory in stores and distribution centers at the end of each day. Another method is to take the end-of-month (EOM) inventories for several months and divide by the number of months. For example,

Month	End-of-Month Inventory
January	$22,000
February	35,000
March	38,000
Total	$93,000
Average (Total/3)	$31,000

Improving GMROI

There are two paths that buyers can take to increase GMROI: (1) improve inventory turnover (sales-to-stock ratio) or (2) increase gross margin.

Improve Inventory Turnover (Sales-to-Stock Ratio)   To improve the inventory turnover (sales-to-stock ratio), buyers can either reduce the level of inventory or increase sales. One approach that buyers take to increase inventory turnover is to reduce the number of SKUs within a category. Buyers need to provide backup stock for each SKU so that the products will be available in the sizes and colors that customers are seeking. Fewer SKUs means that less backup stock is needed. However, reducing the number of SKUs could reduce sales because customers will be less likely to find what they want. Even worse, if they continually can't find the brand or product line at all, customers might start shopping at a competitor and also urge their friends to do the same.[8] As Retailing View 11.1 describes, it is for this very reason that Macy's uses such advanced data analytics to predict consumers' preferences.

A second approach for reducing the level of inventory is to keep the same number of SKUs but reduce the backup stock for each SKU. This approach has the same problem as reducing the number of SKUs. Less backup stock increases the chances that customers will not find the size and color they want when visiting a store or website.

A third approach for increasing inventory turnover is to buy merchandise more often but in smaller quantities, which reduces average inventory without reducing sales. But buying smaller quantities can decrease the gross margin because buyers can't take advantage of quantity discounts and transportation economies of scale. It also requires the buying staff to spend more time placing orders and monitoring deliveries.

A fourth approach is to increase sales and not increase inventory proportionally. For example, buyers could increase sales by reducing prices. While inventory turnover would increase in this situation, gross margin would also decrease, which could have a negative impact on GMROI.

Increasing inventory turnover can have positive impacts on sales by attracting more customer visits, improving sales associate morale, and providing more resources to take advantage of new buying opportunities. Higher inventory turnover increases sales because new merchandise is continually available to customers. New merchandise attracts customers to visit the store more frequently because they know they will be seeing different merchandise each time they visit the store. When inventory turnover is low, the merchandise begins to look **shopworn**—slightly damaged from being displayed and handled by customers for a long time. Salespeople are excited about and more motivated to

11.1 RETAILING VIEW   How Macy's Manages Its Merchandise

Macy's uses predictive analytics to gain more insight into its customers, create an appealing merchandise assortment, and improve buying experiences across all channels. For years, Macy's has been collecting data to create a customer-centric in-store experience. In particular, it collects detailed data about out-of-stock rates, price promotions, and sell-through rates, then combines those data with stock-keeping unit (SKU) information from each location to segment customers and create personalized store assortments.

As sales continue to shift to digital platforms, Macy's also uses predictive analytics to create an engaging online experience through Macys.com. The company analyzes visit frequency, style preferences, and shopping motivations in its website data, then seeks to apply the insights to ensure that every customer has an enjoyable, effortless shopping experience. But Macys.com does more than just use predictive analytics to create personalized purchase suggestions. It calculates the likelihood that each customer will spend a specific amount in a particular product category, then uses that information to present the customer with personalized offers on the checkout page. Furthermore, analytics enable Macy's to send registered users of Macys.com even more personalized e-mail offers. For example, it can send up to 500,000 unique versions of the same mailing.

For the future, Macy's plans to improve its online and mobile shopping experiences even further while enhancing the integration of these various shopping platforms to create a seamless experience, with just the right product mix.

Macys.com analyzes visit frequency, style preferences, and shopping motivations in its website data to develop promotions like the one pictured.

Sources: Mark van Rijmenam, "Macy's Is Changing the Shopping Experience with Big Data Analytics," *DataFloq*, March 14, 2014, https://datafloq.com/read/macys-changing-shopping-experience-big-data-analyt/286; Nicole Marie Melton, "Macy's Boosts Web Sales, Email Marketing with Predictive Analytics," *FierceRetail*, May 14, 2014, http://www.fierceretail.com/retailit/story/macys-boosts-web-sales-email-marketing-predictive-analytics/2014-05-14; Joe Keenan, "Customer Retention: Macy's Uses Predictive Analytics to Grow Customer Spend," *Retail Online Integration*, August 2014, http://www.retailonlineintegration.com/article/macys-uses-predictive-analytics-grow-customer-spend/1.

sell the new merchandise, and thus sales increase, increasing inventory turnover even further. Finally, when inventory turnover increases, more money is available to buy new merchandise. Having money available to buy merchandise late in a fashion season can open up profit opportunities. For instance, buyers can take advantage of special prices offered by vendors that have too much inventory left over at the end of the season.

Increase Gross Margin   Three approaches to increasing the gross margins are increasing prices, reducing the cost of goods sold, or reducing customer discounts. Increasing prices increases gross margin, but it can also decrease sales and inventory turnover because price-sensitive customers buy less. Buyers usually attempt to lower the cost of goods sold by negotiating for better prices from vendors, though they also might increase the percentage of private-label merchandise in a category's assortment, because private-label merchandise is generally less costly than similar merchandise made by national-brand vendors (see Chapter 12). Finally, buyers can increase gross margins by reducing the customer discounts needed to sell unwanted merchandise or merchandise left over at the end of the season. To minimize these discounts, buyers need to do a better job of buying products that customers want and accurately forecasting sales.

In summary, when attempting to increase GMROI, buyers need to strike a balance to determine appropriate levels of inventory turnover and gross margins. Some approaches for improving inventory turnover have secondary effects that can lower GMROI by lowering sales volume or reducing gross margins. As we discussed in Chapter 9, several steps can be taken to improve supply chain efficiency, such as improved vendor relationships, VMI, and CPFR, which increase inventory turnover without negative side effects.

EXHIBIT 11–3
Merchandise Planning Process

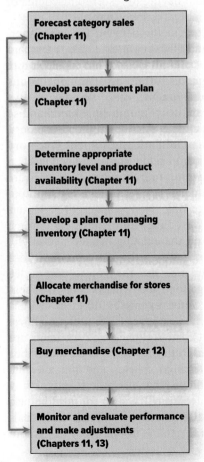

MERCHANDISE PLANNING PROCESSES

As shown in Exhibit 11–3, the merchandise management process involves buyers forecasting category sales, developing an assortment plan for merchandise in the category, and determining the amount of inventory needed to support the forecasted sales and resulting assortment plan. Then buyers develop a plan outlining the sales expected for each month, the inventory needed to support the sales, and the money that can be spent on replenishing sold merchandise and buying new merchandise. Along with developing the plan, the buyers or planners decide what type and how much merchandise should be allocated to each store. Having developed the plan, the buyer negotiates with vendors and buys the merchandise. Merchandise buying activities are reviewed in Chapter 12.

Finally, buyers continually monitor the sales of merchandise in the category and make adjustments. For example, if category sales are less than forecasted in the plan and the projected GMROI for the category falls below the buyer's goal, the buyer may decide to dispose of some merchandise by putting it on sale and then use the money generated to buy merchandise with greater

LO 11-2

Contrast the merchandise management processes for staple and fashion merchandise.

sales potential or to reduce the number of SKUs in the assortment to increase inventory turnover.

Although Exhibit 11–3 suggests that these decisions follow each other sequentially, in practice, some decisions may be made at the same time or in a different order. For example, a buyer might first decide on the amount of inventory to invest in the category, and this decision might determine the number of SKUs that can be offered in the category.

Types of Merchandise Management Planning Systems

Retailers use different types of merchandise planning systems for managing (1) staple and (2) fashion merchandise categories. **Staple merchandise** categories, also called **basic merchandise** categories, are those categories that are in continuous demand over an extended time period. While consumer packaged-goods companies introduce many "new products" each year, the number of "new to the world" product introductions each year in staple categories is limited. Some examples of staple merchandise categories include most categories sold in supermarkets, white paint, copy paper, and basic casual apparel such as T-shirts and men's underwear.

Because sales of staple merchandise are fairly steady from week to week, it is relatively easy to forecast demand, and the consequences of making mistakes in forecasting are not great. For example, if a buyer overestimates the demand for canned soup and buys too much, the retailer will have excess inventory for a short period of time. Eventually the canned soup will be sold without having to resort to discounts or special marketing efforts.

Because the demand for staple merchandise is very predictable, merchandise planning systems for staple categories often involve **continuous replenishment**. These systems involve continuously monitoring merchandise sales and generating replacement orders, often automatically, when inventory levels drop below predetermined levels.

Fashion merchandise categories are in demand only for a relatively short period of time. New products are continually introduced into these categories, making the existing products obsolete. In some cases, the basic product does not change but the colors and styles change to reflect what is "hot" that season. Some examples of fashion merchandise categories are athletic shoes, tablets, smartphones, and women's apparel. Retailing View 11.2 describes how Mango creates and manages its fashion merchandise assortments.

Forecasting the sales for fashion merchandise categories is much more challenging than doing so for staple

Staple merchandise categories are those categories that are in continuous demand over an extended time period (top), whereas fashion merchandise categories are in demand only for a relatively short period of time (bottom).

© Jay Laprete/Bloomberg via Getty Images

© Donato Sardella/Getty Images

RETAILING VIEW   Fast Fashion at Mango   11.2

Mango is a specialty apparel fast-fashion retailer headquartered in Barcelona, Spain, though its more than 2,700 stores are spread across 105 countries. Mango places more emphasis on the "fashion" rather than the "fast" element in its fast-fashion retail concept—as pioneered by Spain's Zara, Sweden's H&M, and the United States' Forever 21.

Mango's Hangar Design Center, the biggest design center in Europe, spreads over more than 100,000 square feet and houses around 550 sharply dressed professionals, creating fashion garments and accessories, predominately for women. The design, purchasing, and quality departments are also located in the Hangar. More than 86 percent of the company's employees are women, with an average age of 29 years. The work environment is very casual, in that suits or ties are rare, but fashion creativity is abundant, with employees expressing themselves through the way they dress. Mango headquarters also includes 1,800 employees representing 37 nationalities, communicating in several languages.

Mango's merchandise planning cycle begins every three months, when designers meet to discuss important new trends for each of its main collections, each of which contains five or six mini-collections. Shops receive a near-constant stream of new merchandise, ranging from clingy short dresses and party frocks to casual everyday attire. New items get sent to stores once a week, roughly six times as often as typical apparel clothing chains.

To get ideas for each collection, designers attend traditional fashion shows and trade fairs. But they also stay close to the customer. They take photos of stylish young women and note what people are wearing on the streets and in night-clubs. "To see what everyone's going to do for next season is very easy," says David Egea, Mango's merchandising director, "but that doesn't mean this is the thing that is going to catch on." Hoping to stay *au courant,* design teams meet each week to adjust to ever-changing trends.

Mango describes each of its stores and clothing designs according to a set of traits: trendy, dressy, suitable for hot weather, and so on. When collection designs are set, a proprietary computer program then matches the new products' traits with compatible stores.

© Robert Marquardt/Getty Images

Mango is a specialty apparel fast-fashion retailer headquartered in Spain. Its merchandise planning cycle begins every three months and contains five or six mini-collections. How does this planning system impact inventory turnover?

In addition, Mango stores display only a limited merchandise assortment. On each rack, only one item per size hangs. This policy encourages a sense of urgency by playing on customers' worst fear: Maybe your size is going to run out.

Sources: www.mango.com; Manuel Baigorri, "Mango Mirroring Zara Challenges Europe's Wealthiest Man," *Bloomberg,* March 24, 2013; Jennifer Overstreet, "Mango Executive Shares Global Expansion Insights," *NRF Blog,* January 3, 2013; Kim Bhasin, "There Has Been a Changing of the Guard at Mango," *The Guardian,* November 24, 2012; Vertica Bhardwaj and Ann Fairhurst, "Fast Fashion: Response to Changes in the Fashion Industry," *International Review of Retail, Distribution and Consumer Research* 20 (February 2010), pp. 165–173.

categories. Buyers for fashion merchandise categories have much less flexibility in correcting forecasting errors. For example, if the tablet buyer for Best Buy purchases too many units of a particular model, the excess inventory cannot be easily sold when a new upgraded model is introduced. Due to the short selling season for most fashion merchandise, buyers often do not have a chance to reorder additional merchandise after an initial order is placed. So if buyers initially order too little fashion merchandise, the retailer may not be able to satisfy the demand for the merchandise and will develop a reputation for not having the most popular merchandise in stock. If buyers order too much fashion merchandise, they will have to put it on sale at a discount or dispose of it in some other way at the end of the season. Thus, an important objective of merchandise planning systems for fashion merchandise categories is to be as close to out of stock as possible at the same time that the SKUs move out of fashion.

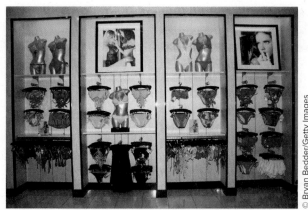

Swimwear (left) is a fashion goods category, whereas snow shovels (right) are staple merchandise. But both of these categories are seasonal merchandise.

Seasonal merchandise categories consist of items whose sales fluctuate dramatically depending on the time of year. Some examples of seasonal merchandise are Halloween candy, Christmas ornaments, swimwear, and snow shovels. Both fashion and more basic merchandise can be seasonal categories. For example, swimwear is fashionable and snow shovels are more basic.

However, from a merchandise planning perspective, retailers buy seasonal merchandise in much the same way that they buy fashion merchandise. Retailers could store unsold snow shovels at the end of the winter season and sell them the next winter, but it is typically more profitable to sell the shovels at a steep discount near the end of the season rather than incur the cost of carrying this excess inventory until the beginning of the next season. Thus, plans for seasonal merchandise, like fashion merchandise, hope to zero out inventory at the end of the season.

These two different merchandise planning systems, staple and fashion, affect the nature of the approaches used to forecast sales and manage inventory. The following section describes each of the steps in the merchandise management process for staple and fashion merchandise.

FORECASTING CATEGORY SALES

LO 11-3

Describe how to predict sales for merchandise categories.

As indicated in Exhibit 11–3, the first step in merchandise management planning is to develop a forecast for category sales. The methods and information used for forecasting staple and fashion merchandise categories are discussed in this section.

Forecasting Staple Merchandise

The approach for forecasting sales of staple merchandise is to project past sales trends into the future, while making adjustments for any anticipated factors, such as promotions and weather, that may affect future sales.

Use of Historical Sales   The sales of staple merchandise are relatively constant from year to year. Thus, forecasts are typically based on extrapolating historical sales. Because there are substantial sales data available, sophisticated statistical techniques can be used to forecast future sales for each SKU. However, these statistical forecasts are based on the assumption that the factors affecting item sales in the past will be the same and have the same effect in the future. Thus, even though sales for staple merchandise categories are relatively predictable, controllable and uncontrollable factors can have a significant impact on sales.

Adjustments for Controllable and Uncontrollable Factors   Controllable factors include the opening and closing of stores, the price set for the merchandise in the category, special promotions for the category, the pricing and promotion of complementary categories, and the placement of the merchandise categories in the stores. Some factors beyond the retailer's control are the weather; general economic conditions; special promotions or new product introductions by vendors; and new product, pricing, and promotional activities by competitors.[9] Thus, buyers need to adjust the forecast on the basis of statistical projections to reflect the effects of these controllable and uncontrollable factors. Retailing View 11.3 illustrates how retailers use long-range weather forecasts to improve their forecasts.

Forecasting Fashion Merchandise Categories

Forecasting sales for fashion merchandise is challenging because buyers typically need to place orders and commit to buying specific quantities between three to six months before the merchandise will be delivered and made available for sale.[10] In addition, for

---

RETAILING VIEW   Weather's Effects on Retail Sales   11.3

Home improvement centers know that when hurricane season comes, they need to be ready with bottled water, batteries, flashlights, plywood, and generators. However, subtler weather conditions, like a warmer-than-normal holiday season, can have a significant impact on retail sales as well. As the weather becomes warmer in the summer, some obvious categories increase sales, such as ice, bottled water, and sports drinks. A hot summer results in consumers seeking out air-conditioned spaces. Big-box retailers and movie theaters offer a chilly respite from the sweltering heat. A warm winter stimulates sales of lawn tools, barbeque grills, and garden equipment in February and March rather than April, May, or June.

One category that thrives particularly during extended summer seasons is fashion. Retailers typically roll out their summer collections well before consumers can comfortably wear the clothes outside, but if the weather is already warm, it will ignite sales early. If the summer stays warmer longer, retailers can delay sales discounts, thus improving their margins.

To incorporate weather effects into their forecasts, many retailers subscribe to long-range weather forecasting services. Merchandise managers use the information provided by these services to make decisions about the timing of merchandise deliveries, promotions, and price discounts. One year, Planalytics (a company that offers long-range weather forecasts) informed a Canadian men's clothing retailer that the spring would be colder than normal, but the summer temperatures would be higher than normal. In turn, the retailer made a few strategic moves. First, it delayed taking markdowns on shorts for sale. Second, it moved nearly 10,000 pairs of shorts to stores along the west coast, which was predicted to be even hotter than the east. Third, it adjusted its sales staff to match the weather-related demands. As a result, it earned an additional $250,000 in revenues, beyond its expectations.

Noting these trends in the retail world, the Weather Channel has transformed itself into Weather Co. and now sells its highly sophisticated forecasts and weather trend analyses to retailers around the world. For example, it tells Pantene and drugstore retailers that stock the hair care products that customers who check the weather app on their phones in the morning probably should receive a coupon for anti-frizz shampoo on days when the humidity levels is high but volumizing spray if humidity is low.

Merchandise managers incorporate the effects of weather to make decisions about the timing of merchandise deliveries, promotions, and price discounts.

© Andy Katz/Pacific Press/LightRocket via Getty Images

For the craft goods retailer Michaels, Weather Co. suggested advertising its assortment in any location for which the forecast for three days later was for rain, because on rainy days, customers like to do projects indoors. To be ready for rainy days, parents and babysitters need to stock up on craft supplies, so Michaels should be ready and waiting to remind them.

In addition, the data provided by Weather Co. take the time of year into account. If consumers experience a sunny, 75-degree day in October, it puts them in a great mood. The same type of day in mid-July is less compelling because it seems more expected. Retailers of hedonic, "pick-me-up" products thus have learned that the best time to advertise might be in the midst of a long spell of cold, dreary weather, when consumers need something to get them out of their rain-induced funk.

Sources: www.planalytics.com; Katherine Rosman, "Weather Channel Now Also Forecasts What You'll Buy," *The Wall Street Journal*, August 14, 2013; Sydney Ember, "Nike Embraces Weather App in Campaign to Sell Gear Suited to Local Conditions," *The New York Times*, October 29, 2015; Catherine Valenti, "More Companies Use Weather to Forecast Sales," *ABC News*, March 12, 2013; "How Does Hot Weather Affect People's Buying Patterns?," *CBC*, July 2012; Cecilia Sze and Paul Walsh, "How Weather Influences the Economy," *ISO Review*, www.iso.com/Research-and-Analyses/ISO-Review/How-Weather-Influences-the-Economy.html.

BEST SELLERS   PreOwned Games

SAVE WHEN YOU TRADE

© Patrick T. Fallon/Bloomberg via Getty Images

Retailers like GameStop use previous sales data of older games to predict the sales of similar, but new video games.

fashion items there often is no opportunity to increase or decrease the quantity ordered before the selling season has ended. Suppliers of popular merchandise usually have orders for more merchandise than they can produce and excess inventory of unpopular items. Finally, forecasting fashion merchandise sales is particularly difficult because some or all of the items in the category are new and different from units offered in previous seasons or years. Some sources of information that retailers use to develop forecasts for fashion merchandise categories are (1) previous sales data, (2) market research, (3) fashion trend services, and (4) vendors.

Previous Sales Data   Although items in fashion merchandise categories might be new each season, many items in a fashion category are often similar to items sold in previous years. Thus, accurate forecasts might be generated by simply projecting past sales data. For example, football video games, such as Madden NFL, might change from season to season with new editions, but while the SKUs are different each season, the total number of football video games sold each year might be relatively constant and predictable. Such predictability enables retailers such as GameStop to maintain appropriate levels of inventory, even for trendy products, and keep customers informed about where and when they can find their favorite titles.[11]

Market Research   Buyers for fashion merchandise categories undertake a variety of market research activities to help them forecast sales. These activities range from informal, qualitative research about trends affecting the category to more formal experiments and surveys.

To find out what customers are going to want in the future, buyers immerse themselves in their customers' world. For example, buyers look for information about trends by going to Internet chat rooms and blogs, attending soccer games and rock concerts, and visiting hot spots around town like restaurants and nightclubs to see what people are talking about and wearing. Buyers are information junkies and read voraciously. What movies are hits at the box office, and what are the stars wearing? Who is going to see them? What books and albums are on the top 10 lists? What magazines are consumers purchasing? Are there themes that keep popping up across these sources of information?

Social media sites are important sources of information for buyers. Buyers learn a lot about their customers' likes, dislikes, and preferences by monitoring their past purchases and by monitoring their interactions with social network sites such as Facebook, Pinterest, and Twitter. Customers appear keen to submit their opinions about their friends' purchases, interests, and blogs.

Retailers also use traditional forms of marketing research such as in-depth interviews and focus groups. The **in-depth interview** is an unstructured personal interview in which the interviewer uses extensive probing to get individual respondents to talk in detail about a subject. Buyers can gather customer data from the retailer's database, then call specific shoppers to find out what they like, or don't like, about the merchandise in the store.

A more informal method of interviewing customers is to require that buyers spend some time (e.g., one day per week) on the selling floor waiting on customers. Buying offices for Target and The Gap are in Minnesota and northern California, respectively, yet their stores are located throughout the United States. It becomes increasingly hard for buyers in such large chains to be attuned to local customer demand. Frequent store visits help resolve the situation. They also can inform strategy decisions; when Target realized that its core shopper changed, the CEO decided that the company needed to get to know its shoppers again. Therefore he and several other top executives traveled the United States, talking with new typical customers, such as single women and Hispanic moms, and visiting their homes to understand their needs better.[12]

In a **focus group**, a small group of respondents submits to be interviewed by a moderator who uses a loosely structured format. Participants are encouraged to express their views and comment on the views of others in the group. To keep abreast of the youth market for example, some stores have teen boards consisting of opinion leaders who meet to discuss merchandising and other store issues.

The UK-based supermarket Tesco has long used such customer insights to inform many aspects of its business. It created "Tesco Families"—in-depth focus groups that provide the retailer with information about what to buy and stock in stores.[13] Furthermore, Tesco holds a forum every year in which 12,000 customers share their views on products, price, quality, and Tesco's service to the community.[14]

Finally, many retailers have a program for conducting merchandise sales experiments. For example, retailers continually run experiments to determine whether new merchandise concepts will produce adequate sales. They introduce the new merchandise into a representative sample of stores, then measure the sales generated by those items. Multichannel retailers often run similar experiments by offering new items on their websites before making a decision to stock them in their stores.

Fashion Trend Services   There are many services that buyers—particularly buyers of apparel categories—can subscribe to that forecast the latest fashions, colors, and styles. For example, Doneger Creative Services (http://www.doneger.com/) offers various forecasting services, describing the color trends it anticipates for men's, women's, and children's apparel, lifestyle products, and accessories. Its color forecast service provides color direction for each season using dyed-to-specification color standards, plus suggested color combinations and applications for specific categories. Its online clipboard reports present actionable information and style news, from the runways to the streets.

Vendors   Vendors have proprietary information about their marketing plans, such as new product launches and special promotions that can have a significant impact on retail sales for their products and the entire merchandise category. In addition, vendors tend to be very knowledgeable about market trends for particular merchandise categories, because they typically specialize in fewer merchandise categories than do retailers. Thus, information from vendors about their plans and market research about merchandise categories is very useful to buyers as they develop category sales forecasts.

Sales Forecasting for Service Retailers

Due to the perishable nature of services, service retailers face an even more extreme problem than fashion retailers. Their offering perishes at the end of the day, not at the end of the season. If there are empty seats when a plane takes off or a rock concert ends, the revenue that might have been generated from these seats is lost forever. Likewise, if more people are interested in dining at a restaurant than there are tables available, a revenue opportunity also is lost. So service retailers have devised approaches for managing demand for their offering so that it meets but does not exceed capacity.

Some service retailers attempt to match supply and demand by taking reservations or making appointments. Physicians often overbook their appointments, so many patients have to wait. They do this so that they will always fill their capacity and not have unproductive, non-revenue-generating time. Restaurants take reservations so that customers will not have to wait for a table. In addition, the reservations indicate the staffing levels needed for the shift. Another approach is to sell advance tickets for a service, such as arenas do for concerts.[15]

DEVELOPING AN ASSORTMENT PLAN

LO 11-4

Summarize the trade-offs for developing merchandise assortments.

After forecasting sales for the category, the next step in the merchandise management planning process is to develop an assortment plan (see Exhibit 11–4). An **assortment plan** is the set of SKUs that a retailer will offer in a merchandise category in each of its stores and from its website.

Category Variety and Assortment

The assortment plan reflects the breadth and depth of merchandise that the retailer plans to offer in a merchandise category. In the context of merchandise planning, the **variety**, or **breadth**, of a merchandise category is the number of different merchandising subcategories offered, and the **assortment**, or **depth**, of merchandise is the number of SKUs within a subcategory.

Determining Variety and Assortment

The process of determining the variety and assortment for a category is called **editing the assortment**. An example of an assortment plan for girls' jeans, as shown in Exhibit 11–4, includes 10 types or varieties (skinny or boot-cut, distressed denim or rinsed wash, and three price points reflecting different brands). For each type there are 81 SKUs (3 colors × 9 sizes × 3 lengths). Thus, this retailer plans to offer 810 SKUs in girls' jeans.

When editing the assortment for a category like jeans, the buyer considers the following factors: (1) the firm's retail strategy, (2) the effect of assortments on GMROI, (3) the complementarities among categories, (4) the effects of assortments on buying behavior, and (5) the physical characteristics of the store.[16]

Retail Strategy   The number of SKUs offered in a merchandise category is a strategic decision. For example, Costco supermarkets focus on customers who are looking for low prices and do not care much about brands, so they offer very few SKUs in a

EXHIBIT 11–4   Assortment Plan for Girls' Jeans

Styles	Skinny	Skinny	Skinny	Skinny	Skinny	Skinny
Price levels	$20	$20	$35	$35	$45	$45
Fabric composition	Distressed	Rinsed wash	Distressed	Rinsed wash	Distressed	Rinsed wash
Colors	Light blue	Light blue	Light blue	Light blue	Light blue	Light blue
	Indigo	Indigo	Indigo	Indigo	Indigo	Indigo
	Black	Black	Black	Black	Black	Black
Styles	**Boot-Cut**	**Boot-Cut**	**Boot-Cut**	**Boot-Cut**		
Price levels	$25	$25	$45	$45		
Fabric composition	Distressed	Rinsed wash	Distressed	Rinsed wash		
Colors	Light blue	Light blue	Light blue	Light blue		
	Indigo	Indigo	Indigo	Indigo		
	Black	Black	Black	Black		

Costco offers a limited assortment at low prices, increasing its inventory turnover and lowering its costs.

category. With limited SKUs, Costco can increase its inventory turnover, lower costs, and charge lower prices. In contrast, Best Buy's target customers are interested in comparing many alternatives, so the retailer must offer several SKUs in each consumer electronics category.

The breadth and depth of the assortment in a merchandise category can affect the retailer's brand image too. Retailers might increase the assortment in categories that are closely associated with their image. For example, Staples sells coffee pods, as we noted in the opener to this chapter, but it carries only a few SKUs because coffee is not part of the core office supply assortment for which it is known. It carries a much broader and deeper assortment of paper products because its customers expect to find such options when they visit the office supplier.

Assortments and GMROI   In developing the assortment plan, buyers need to be sensitive to the trade-off of increasing sales by offering greater breadth and depth but at the same time potentially reducing inventory turnover and GMROI because of the increased inventory investment. Increasing assortment breadth and depth also can decrease gross margin. For example, the more SKUs offered, the greater the chance of **breaking sizes**—that is, stocking out of a specific size or color SKU. If a stockout occurs for a popular SKU in a fashion merchandise category and the buyer cannot reorder during the season, the buyer will typically discount the entire merchandise type, thus reducing gross margin. The buyer's objective is to remove the merchandise type from the assortment altogether so that customers will not be disappointed when they don't find the size and color they want.

Complementary Merchandise   When buyers develop assortment plans, they need to consider the degree to which categories in a department complement each other. For instance, 3-D Blu-ray players may have a low GMROI, suggesting that the retailer carry a limited assortment. But customers who buy a 3-D Blu-ray player might also buy complementary products and services such as accessories, cables, and warranties that have a high GMROI. Thus, the buyer may decide to carry more 3-D Blu-ray player SKUs to increase the more profitable accessory sales.

Effects of Assortment Size on Buying Behavior   Offering large assortments provides a number of benefits to customers. First, increasing the number of SKUs that customers can consider increases the chance they will find the product that best satisfies their needs. Second, large assortments are valued by customers because they provide a more informative and stimulating shopping experience due to the complexity associated with numerous products and the novelty associated with unique items. Third, large assortments are particularly appealing to customers who seek variety—those who want to try new things. However, offering a large assortment can make the purchase decision more complex and time-consuming and potentially overwhelms the consumer, which could reduce sales.

Research indicates that customers' perceptions of assortments are not based simply on the number of SKUs offered in a product category. Instead, assortment perceptions are affected by the similarity of the SKUs in the category, the size of the category's display, and the availability of the customer's favorite SKU. Perceived assortment is greater when the items in the assortment are different, the category occupies more space, and the customer's favorite product is available. In one study, customer perceptions of the assortment offered by a retailer did not change when a retailer decreased the number of SKUs by 54 percent but kept the category display size, similarity of the products, and availability of the favorite product the same. In another study, the perceived assortment actually increased by 25 percent when the actual assortment decreased but the display of the most popular brands increased, because customers could more easily locate their favorite brand. Other studies show that customers perceive assortments to have more variety when they are presented with a horizontal display, rather than a vertical one. In turn, when customers see having more options as a positive benefit, they are more satisfied with their purchases. Other factors affecting how customers perceive assortments are discussed in Chapter 16.[17]

Many retailers have initiated **SKU rationalization programs** in their efforts to analyze the benefits they might gain from deleting, adding, or keeping certain items in their assortments. The objective of such a program is to increase inventory turnover by reducing the number of SKUs without reducing sales. Of the 40,000 SKUs offered by a typical supermarket, the average household annually uses only 350 SKUs. Because typically 20 percent of the SKUs account for 80 percent of sales, eliminating the bottom 15 percent of the SKUs should have limited effect on sales.

Physical Characteristics of the Store   Buyers need to consider how much space to devote to a category. More space is needed to display categories with large assortments. In addition, a lot of space is needed to display individual items in some categories, and this limits the number of SKUs that can be offered in stores. For example, furniture takes up a lot of space, thus furniture retailers typically display one model of a chair or sofa and then have photographs and cloth swatches or a virtual display on a computer to show how the furniture would look with different upholstery.

Multichannel retailers address space limitations in stores by offering a greater assortment through their Internet and catalog channels than they do in stores. For example, Staples offers more types of laptop computers and printers on its Internet site than it stocks in its stores. If customers do not find the computer or printer they want in the store, sales associates direct them to the company's Internet site and can even order the merchandise for them on the spot from a POS terminal.

SETTING INVENTORY AND PRODUCT AVAILABILITY LEVELS

LO 11-5

Illustrate how to determine the appropriate inventory levels.

Model Stock Plan

The **model stock plan**, illustrated in Exhibit 11–5, is the number of each SKU in the assortment plan that the buyer wants to have available for purchase in each store. For example, the model stock plan in Exhibit 11–5 includes nine units of size 1, short, which represent 2 percent of the 429 total units for girls' skinny $20 denim jeans in light blue. Note that there are more units for more popular sizes.

		Size								
LENGTH		**1**	**2**	**4**	**5**	**6**	**8**	**10**	**12**	**14**
Short	%	2	4	7	6	8	5	7	4	2
	units	9	17	30	26	34	21	30	17	9
Medium	%	2	4	7	6	8	5	7	4	2
	units	9	17	30	26	34	21	30	17	9
Long	%	0	2	2	2	3	2	2	1	0
	units	0	9	9	9	12	9	9	4	0
Total 100%										
429 units										

EXHIBIT 11–5
Model Stock Plan for
Girls' Jeans

Retailers typically have model stock plans for the different store sizes in a chain. For example, retailers typically classify their stores as A, B, and C stores on the basis of their sales volume. The basic assortment in a category is stocked in C stores. For the larger stores, because more space is available, the number of SKUs increases. The larger A and B stores may have more brands, colors, styles, and sizes.

Product Availability

The number of units of **backup stock**, also called **buffer stock** or **safety stock**, in the model stock plan determines product availability. **Product availability** is defined as the percentage of the demand for a particular SKU that is satisfied. For instance, if 100 people go into a PetSmart store to purchase a small Great Choice portable kennel but only 90 people can make the purchase before the kennel stock is depleted, the product availability for that SKU is 90 percent. Product availability is also referred to as the **level of support** or **service level**.

More backup stock is needed in the model stock plan if a retailer wants to increase product availability—that is, increase the probability that customers will find the product they want when they visit the retailer's store or website. Choosing an appropriate amount of backup stock is critical to successful assortment planning. If the backup stock is too low, the retailer will lose sales and possibly customers as well when they find that the products they want are not available from the retailer. If the level is too high, scarce financial resources will be wasted on needless inventory, which lowers GMROI, rather than being more profitably invested in increasing variety or assortment.

Exhibit 11–6 shows the trade-off between inventory investment and product availability. Although the actual inventory investment varies in different situations, the general relationship shows that extremely high levels of product availability result in a prohibitively high inventory investments.

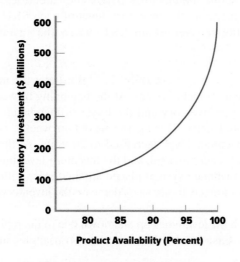

EXHIBIT 11–6
Inventory Investment
and Product Availability

The trade-off among variety, assortment, and product availability is a crucial issue in determining a retailer's merchandising strategy. Buyers have a limited budget for the inventory investments they can make in a category. Thus, they are forced to sacrifice breadth of merchandise if they opt to increase depth, or they must reduce both depth and breadth to increase product availability.

Retailers often classify merchandise categories or individual SKUs as A, B, or C items, reflecting the product availability the retailer wants to offer. The A items are best-sellers bought by many customers. For example, white paint is an A item for Sherwin-Williams, and copy paper is an A item for Office Depot. A retailer rarely wants to risk A-item stockouts because running out of these very popular SKUs would diminish the retailer's brand image and customer loyalty. On the other hand, lower product availability is acceptable for C items, which are purchased by a small number of customers and are not readily available from other retailers. The greater the fluctuations in demand, the lead time for delivery from the vendor, and the fluctuations in vendor lead time, the greater the backup stock levels required to maintain a particular product availability level. However, less backup stock is needed to maintain a particular product availability level with more frequent store deliveries.

ESTABLISHING A CONTROL SYSTEM FOR MANAGING INVENTORY

LO 11-6

Analyze merchandise control systems.

The first three steps in the merchandise planning process—forecasting SKU and category sales, determining the assortment plan, and establishing the model stock plan (see Exhibit 11–3)—quantify the buyer's sales expectations and service level. The fourth step in the merchandise management process is to establish a control system for how the orders, deliveries, inventory levels, and merchandise sales will evolve over time. The objective of this control system is to manage the flow of merchandise into the stores so that the amount of inventory in a category is minimized but the merchandise will still be available when customers want to buy it. The differences between the control systems for staple and fashion merchandise are discussed in the following sections.

Control System for Managing Inventory of Staple Merchandise

The SKUs in a staple merchandise category are sold month after month, year after year. Lowe's sales of purple paint this month will be about the same as they were during the same month a year ago. If the sales of purple paint are below forecast this month, the excess inventory of purple paint can be sold during the following month. Thus, an automated continuous replenishment control system is used to manage the flow of staple merchandise SKUs and categories. The continuous replenishment system monitors the inventory level of each SKU in a store and automatically triggers the reorder of an SKU when the inventory falls below a predetermined level.

Flow of Staple Merchandise   Exhibit 11–7 illustrates the merchandise flow in a staple merchandise management system. At the beginning of week 1, the retailer had 150 units of the SKU in inventory and the buyer or merchandise planner placed an order for 96 additional units. During the next two weeks, customers purchased 130 units, and the inventory level decreased to 20 units. At the end of week 2, the 96-unit order from the vendor arrived, and the inventory level jumped up to 116 units. The continuous replenishment system placed another order with the vendor that will arrive in two weeks, before customer sales decrease the inventory level to zero and the retailer stocks out.

Inventory for which the level goes up and down due to the replenishment process is called **cycle stock** or **base stock** (shown in the two triangles in Exhibit 11–7). The

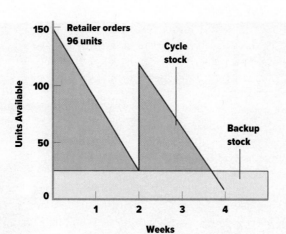

EXHIBIT 11–7
Merchandise Flow of a
Staple SKU

retailer hopes to reduce the cycle stock inventory to keep its inventory investment low. One approach for reducing the cycle stock is to reorder smaller quantities more frequently. But more frequent, smaller orders and shipments increase administrative and transportation costs, and reduce quantity discounts.

Because sales of each SKU and on-time deliveries of orders from vendors cannot be predicted with perfect accuracy, the retailer has to carry backup stock, as a cushion, so that it doesn't stock out before the next order arrives. Backup stock is shown in the horizontal numbered bar at the bottom of Exhibit 11–7. Backup stock is the level of inventory needed to ensure merchandise is available in light of these uncertainties.

Determining the Level of Backup Stock   Several factors determine the level of backup stock needed for an SKU. First, the level depends on the product availability the retailer wants to provide. As discussed previously, more backup stock is needed when the retailer wants to reduce the chances of a stockout and increase the availability of the SKU. Thus, if Lowe's views white paint as an A item and rarely wants to stock out of it, a higher level of backup stock is needed. However, if melon paint is a C item and 75 percent product availability is acceptable, the level of backup stock can be lowered.

Second, the greater the fluctuation in demand, the more backup stock is needed. Suppose a Lowe's store sells an average of 30 gallons of purple paint in two weeks. Yet in some weeks sales are 50 gallons, and in other weeks they are only 10 gallons. When sales are less than average, the store ends up carrying a little more merchandise than it needs. But when sales are much more than average, there must be more backup stock to ensure that the store does not stock out. Note in Exhibit 11–7 that during week 4, sales were greater than average, so the retailer had to dip into its backup stock to avoid a stockout.

Third, the amount of backup stock needed is affected by the lead time from the vendor. **Lead time** is the amount of time between the recognition that an order needs to be placed and the point at which the merchandise arrives in the store and is ready for sale. If it took two months to receive a shipment of purple paint, the possibility of running out of stock is greater than it would be if the lead time was only two weeks. The shorter lead times inherent in collaborative supply chain management systems like CPFR (collaborative planning, forecasting, and replenishment, described in Chapter 9) result in a lower level of backup stock required to maintain the same level of product availability.

Fourth, fluctuations in lead time also affect the amount of backup stock needed. If Lowe's knows that the lead time for purple paint is always two weeks, plus or minus one day, it can more accurately plan its inventory levels. But if the lead time is 1 day on one shipment and then 10 days on the next shipment, the stores must

Lowe's carries more backup
stock of its popular white
paint than its specialty colors
like melon.

© Scott Eells/Bloomberg via Getty Images

carry additional backup stock to cover this uncertainty in lead time. Many retailers using collaborative supply chain management systems require that their vendors deliver merchandise within a very narrow window—sometimes two or three hours—to reduce the fluctuations in lead time and thus the amount of required backup stock.

Fifth, the vendor's fill rate affects the retailer's backup stock requirements. The percentage of SKUs received complete on a particular order from a vendor is called the **fill rate**. For example, Lowe's can more easily plan its inventory requirements if the vendor normally ships every item that is ordered. If, however, the vendor ships only 75 percent of the ordered items, Lowe's must maintain more backup stock to be certain that the paint availability for its customers isn't adversely affected.

Automated Continuous Replenishment   Once the buyer sets the desired product availability and determines the variation in demand and the vendor's lead time and fill rate, the continuous replenishment systems for staple SKUs can operate automatically. The retailer's information system determines the inventory level at each point in time, the **perpetual inventory**, by comparing the sales made through the POS terminals with the shipments received by the store. When the perpetual inventory level falls below the predetermined level, the system sends an EDI reorder to the retailer's distribution center and the vendor. When the reordered merchandise arrives at the store, the level of inventory is adjusted up.

However, it is difficult to achieve fully automated continuous replenishment of staple merchandise because of errors in determining the actual inventory. For example, the retailer's information system might indicate that 10 Gillette Fusion razors are in the store when, in fact, 10 razors were stolen by a shoplifter and there are actually 0 razors in the store. Because there are no razors in the store, there are no sales, and the automated continuous replenishment system will never reorder razors for the store. Such inaccuracies also can arise when an incorrect number of units is input into the information system about a shipment from the distribution center to the store when it is delivered. To address these problems, store employees need to periodically check the inventory recorded in the system with an actual inventory of the store by physically counting all inventory.

EXHIBIT 11–8   Inventory Management Report for Rubbermaid SKUs

In-Season Management - Worksheet: Inventory Mangement - Rubbermaid (Business View: "Inventory Management : Global")

Worksheet   In-Season Management

Plan   Edit   View   Tools   Help

Skip To   Style

	Quantity On Hand	Quantity On Order	Sales Last 4 Wks	Sales Last 12 Wks	Forecast Next 4 Wks	Forecast Next 8 Wks	Product Availability	Backup Stock	Turnover Planned	Turnover Actual	Order Point	Order Quantity
RM- Bath												
RM Bath Mat - Avocado	30	60	72	215	152	229	99	18	12	11	132	42
RM Bath Mat - Blue	36	36	56	130	115	173	95	12	9	10	98	26
RM Bath Mat - Gold	41	72	117	325	243	355	99	35	12	13	217	104
RM Bath Mat - Pink	10	12	15	41	13	25	90	3	7	7	13	0

Inventory Management Report   The inventory management report provides information about the inventory management for a staple category. The report indicates the decision variables set by the buyer, such as product availability, the backup stock needed to provide the product availability, the order points, and quantities, plus performance measures such as planned and actual inventory turnover, the current sales rate or velocity, sales forecasts, inventory availability, and the amount on order. Exhibit 11–8 is an inventory management report for Rubbermaid bath mats.

The first five columns of Exhibit 11–8 contain the descriptions of each item, how many items are on hand and on order, and sales for the past 4 and 12 weeks. The first-row SKU is a Rubbermaid bath mat in avocado green. There are 30 units on hand and 60 on order. Thus, the quantity available of this SKU is 90. Sales for the past 4 and 12 weeks were 72 and 215 units, respectively.

Sales forecasts for the next 4 and 8 weeks are determined by the system using a statistical model that considers the trends in past sales and the seasonal pattern for the SKU. However, in this case, the buyer made an adjustment in the forecast for the next 4 weeks to reflect an upcoming special promotion on avocado, blue, and gold bath mats.

The product availability is a decision variable that is input by the buyer. For the avocado bath mat SKU, the buyer wants 99 out of every 100 customers to find it in stock (99 percent product availability). But the buyer is less concerned about stocking out of pink bath mats and thus sets its product availability at 90 percent (on average, 90 out of 100 customers will find it in stock). The system then calculates the necessary backup stock for the avocado bath mat based on a predetermined formula—18 units. This number is determined by the system on the basis of the specified product availability, the variability in demand, the vendor delivery lead time, and the variability in the lead time.

The planned inventory turnover for the SKU, 12 times, is a decision variable also set by the buyer on the basis of the retailer's overall financial goals; it drives the inventory management system. For this SKU, the system determined that the actual turnover, based on the cost of goods sold and average inventory, is 11.

Order Point   The **order point** is the amount of inventory below which the quantity available shouldn't go or the item will be out of stock before the next order arrives. This number tells the buyer that when the inventory level drops to this point, additional merchandise should be ordered. For this SKU, the buyer needs to place an order if the quantity in inventory falls to 132 or fewer units to produce the desired product availability.

Order Quantity   When inventory reaches the order point, the buyer, or system, needs to order enough units to ensure product availability before the next order arrives. Using the avocado bath mats in Exhibit 11–8 as an example, the order quantity is 42 units.

EXHIBIT 11–9   Six-Month Merchandise Budget Plan for Men's Casual Slacks

	Spring	April	May	June	July	August	September
1. Sales % Distribution to Season	100.00%	21.00%	12.00%	12.00%	19.00%	21.00%	15.00%
2. Monthly Sales	$130,000	$27,300	$15,600	$15,600	$24,700	$27,300	$19,500
3. Reduc % Distribution to Season	100.00%	40.00%	14.00%	16.00%	12.00%	10.00%	8.00%
4. Monthly Reductions	$16,500	$6,600	$2,310	$2,640	$1,980	$1,650	$1,320
5. BOM Stock to Sales Ratio	4.00	3.60	4.40	4.40	4.00	3.60	4.00
6. BOM Inventory	$98,280	$98,280	$68,640	$68,640	$98,800	$98,280	$78,000
7. EOM Inventory	$65,600	$68,640	$68,640	$98,800	$98,280	$78,000	$65,600
8. Monthly Additions to Stock	$113,820	$4,260	$17,910	$48,400	$26,160	$8,670	$8,420

Control System for Managing Inventory of Fashion Merchandise

The control systems for managing fashion merchandise categories are the merchandise budget plan and the open-to-buy.

Merchandise Budget Plan   The **merchandise budget plan** specifies the amount of merchandise in dollars (not units) that needs to be delivered during each month, based on the sales forecast, the planned discounts to employees and customers, and the level of inventory needed to support the sales and achieve the desired GMROI objectives.

Exhibit 11–9 shows a six-month merchandise budget plan for men's casual slacks at a national specialty store chain. Appendix 11A describes in detail how the plan is developed. Most retailers use commercially available software packages to develop merchandise budget plans.

Inventory turnover, GMROI, and the sales forecast are used for both planning and control. Buyers negotiate GMROI, inventory turnover, and sales forecast goals with their superiors, the GMMs and DMMs. Then merchandise budgets are developed to meet these goals. Well before the season, buyers purchase the amount of merchandise specified in the last line of the merchandise budget plan to be delivered in those specific months—the monthly additions to stock.

After the selling season, the buyer must determine how the category actually performed compared with the plan. If the actual GMROI, inventory turnover, and forecast are greater than those in the plan, performance is better than expected. However, performance evaluations should not be based solely on any one of these measures. Several additional questions should be answered to evaluate the buyer's performance: Why did the performance exceed or fall short of the plan? Was the deviation from the plan due to something under the buyer's control? For instance, was too much merchandise purchased? Did the buyer react quickly to changes in demand by either purchasing more or having a sale? Was the deviation instead due to some external factor, such as a change in the competitive level (e.g., new competitors' stores opened in the area) or economic activity (e.g., recession)?

Open-to-buy is similar to keeping track of the checks you write. Buyers need to keep track of the merchandise they purchase and when it is to be delivered so they don't buy more (overbuy) or less (underbuy) than they have money in their budget to spend each month.

© jwohlfeil/iStockphoto/Getty Images

Every attempt should be made to discover answers to these questions. Later in this chapter we will examine several additional tools used to evaluate merchandise performance.

Open-to-Buy System   After the merchandise is purchased on the basis of the merchandise budget plan, the **open-to-buy** system is used to keep track of the actual merchandise flows—what the present inventory level is, when purchased merchandise is scheduled for delivery, and how much has been sold to customers. In the same way that you must keep track of the checks you write, buyers need to keep track of the merchandise they purchase and when it is to be delivered so they don't buy more (overbuy) or less (underbuy) than they have money in their budget to spend each month. Without the open-to-buy system keeping track of merchandise flows, merchandise could be delivered when it isn't needed or be unavailable when it is needed.

The open-to-buy system compares the planned end-of-month inventory to the actual end-of-month inventory. Differences between actual and planned levels may arise because an order was shipped late or sales deviated from the forecast. When sales are greater than planned, the system determines how much merchandise to buy, in terms of dollars the buyer has available, to satisfy the increased customer demand.

ALLOCATING MERCHANDISE TO STORES

After developing a plan for managing merchandise inventory in a category, the next step in the merchandise management process is to allocate the merchandise purchased and received to the retailer's stores (see Exhibit 11–3). Research indicates that these allocation decisions have a much bigger impact on profitability than does the decision about the quantity of merchandise to purchase.[18] In other words, buying too little or too much merchandise has less impact on a category's profitability than does making mistakes in allocating the right amount and type of merchandise to stores. Allocating merchandise to stores involves three decisions: (1) how much merchandise to allocate to each store, (2) what type of merchandise to allocate, and (3) when to allocate the merchandise to different stores.

LO 11-7

Describe how multistore retailers allocate merchandise to stores.

Amount of Merchandise Allocated

Retail chains typically classify each of their stores on the basis of annual sales. Thus, A stores would have the largest sales volume and typically receive the most inventory, while C stores would have the lowest sales volume and receive the least inventory for a category. In addition to the store's sales level, when making allocation decisions for a category, allocators consider the physical characteristics of the merchandise and the depth of assortment and level of product availability that the firm wants to portray for the specific store.

Type of Merchandise Allocated

The geodemographics of a store's trading area (discussed in Chapter 8) are considered in making allocation decisions. Consider the allocation decision

Assortment allocation decisions for grocery stores are different depending on the customer characteristics in the trade area.

© Katrina Wittkamp/Getty Images

EXHIBIT 11–10
Examples of
Geodemographic
Segments

Laptops and Lattes: The Most Eligible and Unencumbered Marketplace	Rustbelt Retirees
Laptops and Lattes are affluent, single, and still renting. They are educated, professional, and partial to city life, favoring major metropolitan areas such as New York, Boston, Chicago, Los Angeles, and San Francisco. Median household income is more than $87,000; median age is 38 years. Technologically savvy, the Laptops and Lattes segment is the top market for notebook PCs and PDAs. They use the Internet on a daily basis to trade stocks and make purchases and travel plans. They are health conscious and physically fit; they take vitamins, use organic products, and exercise in the gym. They embrace liberal philosophies and work for environmental causes.	Rustbelt Retirees can be found in older, industrial cities in the Northeast and Midwest, especially in Pennsylvania and other states surrounding the Great Lakes. Households are mainly occupied by married couples with no children and singles who live alone. The median age is 43.8 years. Although many residents are still working, labor force participation is below average. More than 40 percent of the households receive Social Security benefits. Most residents live in owned, single-family homes, with a median value of $118,500. Unlike many retirees, these residents are not inclined to move. They are proud of their homes and gardens and participate in community activities. Some are members of veterans' clubs. Leisure activities include playing bingo, gambling in Atlantic City, going to the horse races, working crossword puzzles, and playing golf.

of a national supermarket for its ready-to-eat cereal assortment. Some stores are located in areas dominated by segments called "Rustbelt Retirees," and other areas are dominated by the "Laptops and Lattes" segment, as described in Exhibit 11–10.

The ready-to-eat breakfast cereal planner would offer different assortments for stores in these two areas. Stores with a high proportion of Rustbelt Retirees in their trading areas would get an assortment of lower-price, well-known brands and more private-label cereals. Stores in areas dominated by the Laptops and Lattes geodemographic segment would get an assortment with higher-price brands that feature low sugar, organic ingredients, and whole wheat. Private-label cereals would be deemphasized.

Even the sales of different apparel sizes can vary dramatically from store to store in the same chain. Exhibit 11–11 illustrates this point. Notice that store X sells significantly more large sizes and fewer small sizes than is average for the chain. If the planner allocated the same size distribution of merchandise to all stores in the chain, store X would stock out of large sizes, have an oversupply of small sizes, and be out of some sizes sooner than other stores in the chain. Retailing View 11.4 provides a glimpse of how Saks Fifth Avenue allocates merchandise to stores on the basis of customer characteristics.

Timing of Merchandise Allocation

In addition to the need to allocate different inventory levels and types of merchandise across stores, differences in the timing of category purchases across stores need to

EXHIBIT 11–11
Apparel Size Differences
for the Average and
Specific Store in a Chain

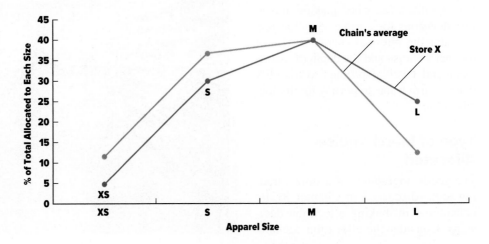

RETAILING VIEW   Customer-Centric Merchandise Allocation at Saks Fifth Avenue

11.4

Having the right merchandise in the right stores at the right time is the key to merchandising success for fashion retailers like Saks Fifth Avenue. For instance, Saks considers its core shopper at its New York flagship store in Manhattan to be a woman, between 46 and 57 years of age, with a largely "classic" style, especially when it comes to work clothes, and a taste for slightly more modern looks when she goes out with friends on weekends. But it also recognizes that the merchandise selections for stores located elsewhere needs to be less New York–centric. Even stores close to New York City attract different types of shoppers. A Greenwich, Connecticut, Saks caters to a slightly older shopper than does the Saks in Stamford, Connecticut, about five miles away. Stamford shoppers tend to be women who work in town, whereas Greenwich attracts a higher proportion of women who are at home full-time. Online Saks shoppers are 7 years younger than a regular Saks customer, but they seek out specific items, whereas in-store shoppers are looking to be outfitted from head to toe during a single shopping trip.

To better match its assortments with its stores, Saks has developed a nine-box grid. On one side of the matrix are style categories: "Park Avenue," or classic; "Uptown," or modern; and "Soho," meaning trendy or contemporary. On the other axis are pricing levels, from "good" (brands such as Dana Buchman, Real Clothes [Saks's private label], and Eileen Fisher) to "better" (Piazza Sempione and Armani Collezioni) to "best" (Chanel, Gucci, and Yves Saint Laurent). By cross-referencing the preferred styles and spending levels for each assortment at each location, the grid charts the best mix of clothes, brands, and accessories to stock at the store.

Following the recession in the first decade of this century, Saks implemented price cuts across the board to get customers—any and all of them—into stores. But the strategy backfired because it ran contrary to the customer-centricity that had set Saks apart. It also allowed for a lower-quality image to sneak in, manifested in bland and boring merchandise. Such perceptions could never appeal to the stylish women of various ages that Saks truly wants to attract. Therefore, by 2014, Saks had reversed course, making sure to stock high-end, exciting fashion merchandise by up-and-coming designers. The "wow" looks, with their complex designs and exotic fabrics, are again tailored to local markets, appealing more precisely to the shoppers who are coming back through the doors.

Sources: Eileen Rojas, "Saks Fifth Avenue Switches to Edgier and Pricier Designs in Its Stores," *The Motley Fool,* April 13, 2014; Elizabeth Lippman, "The Woman behind the Saks Fifth Avenue Revamp," *The Wall Street Journal,* April 2, 2014; Elizabeth Holmes, "At Saks, It's Full Price Ahead as CEO Pares Back Discounts," *The New York Times,* September 12, 2011; Stephanie Rosenbloom, "As Saks Reports a Loss, Its Chief Offers a Plan," *The New York Times,* February 26, 2009; Vanessa O'Connell, "Park Avenue Classic or Soho Trendy?," *The Wall Street Journal,* April 20, 2007, p. B1; www.saks.com.

© Thomas Concordia/WireImage/Getty Images

© Victor Virgile/Gamma-Rapho via Getty Images

Saks Fifth Avenue provides different assortments to different stores depending on its clientele. More "Uptown" fashions (top) go to some stores, while "Soho" fashions (bottom) go to others.

EXHIBIT 11–12
Sales of Capri Pants
by Region

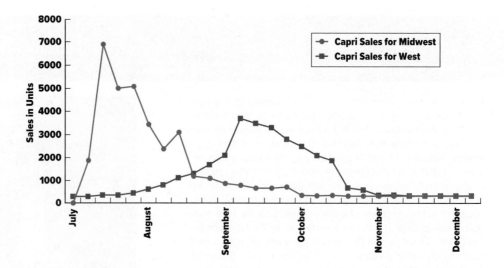

be considered. Exhibit 11–12 illustrates these differences by plotting sales data over time for capri pants in different regions of the United States. Comparing regions shows that capri sales peak in late July in the Midwest and at the beginning of September in the West, due to seasonality differences and differences in consumer demand. To increase inventory turnover in the category, buyers need to recognize these regional differences and arrange for merchandise to be shipped to the appropriate regions when customers are ready to buy.

Retailers also consider the "paycheck cycle" when making merchandise allocation and promotion decisions, particularly in difficult economic times. Cash-strapped consumers tend to make their largest purchases when they get their paychecks at the beginning of the month, but cut back on purchases as that money runs out toward the end of the month. As a result, some supermarket chains devote more shelf space and promote larger-package sizes at the beginning of the month and smaller sizes at the end of the month.[19]

ANALYZING MERCHANDISE MANAGEMENT PERFORMANCE

LO 11-8

Review how retailers evaluate the performance of their merchandise management decisions.

The next step in the merchandise planning process (see Exhibit 11–3) is to analyze the performance of the process and make adjustments, such as ordering more or less merchandise, lowering prices to increase sales, allocating different assortments to specific stores, or changing the assortment and model stock plans. Three types of analyses related to the monitoring and adjustment step are (1) sell-through analysis, (2) ABC analysis of assortments, and (3) multiattribute analysis of vendors. The first analysis provides an ongoing evaluation of the merchandise management plan compared with actual sales. The remaining two analyses offer approaches for evaluating and altering the assortment plan using the specific SKUs in the plan and the vendors that provide the merchandise to support the plan.

Evaluating the Merchandise Plan Using Sell-Through Analysis:

A **sell-through analysis** compares actual and planned sales to determine whether more merchandise is needed to satisfy demand or whether price reductions (markdowns) are required. Exhibit 11–13 shows a sell-through analysis for blouses for the first two weeks of the season.

These blouses are high-fashion items that experience significant uncertainty in sales. Thus, after two weeks in the stores, the buyer reviews sales and determines if adjustments are needed. Buyers would use a longer review period for merchandise with an extended fashion cycle. The need to make adjustments depends on a variety of factors, including experience with the merchandise in the past, plans for featuring the merchandise in advertising, and the availability of **markdown money** from

EXHIBIT 11–13
Example of Sell-Through
Analysis

Stock Number		Description	WEEK 1			WEEK 2		
				Actual-to-Plan			Actual-to-Plan	
			Plan	Actual	Percentage	Plan	Actual	Percentage
1011	Small	White silk V-neck	20	15	−25%	20	10	−50%
1011	Medium	White silk V-neck	30	25	−16.6	30	20	−33
1011	Large	White silk V-neck	20	16	−20	20	16	−20
1012	Small	Blue silk V-neck	25	26	4	25	27	8
1012	Medium	Blue silk V-neck	35	45	29	35	40	14
1012	Large	Blue silk V-neck	25	25	0	25	30	20

vendors (funds that a vendor gives a retailer to cover lost gross margin dollars that result from markdowns).

In this case, the white blouses are selling significantly less well than planned. Therefore, the buyer makes an early price reduction to ensure that the merchandise isn't left unsold at the end of the season. The decision regarding the blue blouses isn't as clear. The small blue blouses are selling slightly ahead of the plan, and the medium blue blouses are also selling well, but the large blue blouses start selling ahead of plan only in the second week. In this case, the buyer decides to wait another week or two before taking any action. If actual sales stay significantly ahead of planned sales, a reorder might be appropriate.

Evaluating the Assortment Plan Using ABC Analysis

An **ABC analysis** identifies the performance of individual SKUs in the assortment plan. It is used to determine which SKUs should be in the plan and how much backup stock and resulting product availability are provided for each SKU in the plan. In an ABC analysis, the SKUs in a merchandise category are rank-ordered by several performance measures, such as sales, gross margin, inventory turnover, and GMROI. Typically, this rank order reveals the general 80–20 principle; namely, approximately 80 percent of a retailer's sales or profits come from 20 percent of the products. This principle suggests that retailers should concentrate on the products that provide the biggest returns.

After rank-ordering the SKUs, the next step is to classify the items. On the basis of the classification, the buyer determines whether to maintain the items in the assortment plan and, if so, what level of product availability to offer. For example, a men's dress shirt buyer might identify the A, B, C, and D SKUs by rank-ordering them by sales volume.

Which of these shirts is an A item? Which is a B item?

© demidoffaleks/iStock/Getty Images

The A items account for only 5 percent of the SKUs in the category but represent 70 percent of sales. The buyer decides that these SKUs should never be out of stock and thus plans to maintain more backup stock for A items, such as keeping more units for each SKU of long- and short-sleeved white and blue dress shirts, than of the B and C items.

The B items represent 10 percent of the SKUs and 20 percent of sales. These items include some of the other better-selling colors and patterned shirts and contribute to the retailer's image of having fashionable merchandise. Occasionally, the retailer will run out of some SKUs in the B category because it does not carry the same amount of backup stock for B items as it does for A items.

The C items account for 65 percent of SKUs but contribute to only 10 percent of sales. The planner may plan to carry some C items only in the most popular sizes of the most basic shirts, with special orders used to satisfy customer demand.

Finally, the buyer discovers that the remaining 20 percent of the SKUs, D items, have virtually no sales until they are marked down. Not only are these items excess merchandise and an unproductive investment, but they also distract from the rest of the inventory and clutter the store shelves. The buyer decides to eliminate most of these items from the assortment plan.

Evaluating Vendors Using the Multiattribute Method

The **multiattribute analysis** method for evaluating vendors uses a weighted-average score for each vendor.[20] The score is based on the importance of various issues and the vendor's performance on those issues. This method is similar to the multiattribute approach that can be used to understand how customers evaluate stores and merchandise, as we discussed in Chapter 4.

To better understand the multiattribute method of evaluating vendors, either current or proposed, consider the example in Exhibit 11–14 for vendors of men's casual slacks.

A buyer can evaluate vendors using the following five steps:

1. Develop a list of issues to consider in the evaluation (column 1).

2. In conjunction with the GMM, determine the importance weights for each issue in column 1 on a 1-to-10 scale (column 2), where 1 equals not important and 10 equals very important. For instance, the buyer and the merchandise manager

EXHIBIT 11–14
Multiattribute Method for Evaluating Vendors

Issue (1)	Importance Evaluation of Issues (I) (2)	PERFORMANCE EVALUATIONS OF INDIVIDUAL BRANDS ACROSS ISSUES			
		Brand A (P_a) (3)	Brand B (P_b) (4)	Brand C (P_c) (5)	Brand D (P_d) (6)
Vendor reputation	9	5	9	4	8
Service	8	6	6	4	6
Meets delivery dates	6	5	7	4	4
Merchandise quality	5	5	4	6	5
Markup opportunity	5	5	4	4	5
Country of origin	6	5	3	3	8
Product fashionability	7	6	6	3	8
Selling history	3	5	5	5	5
Promotional assistance	4	5	3	4	7
Overall evaluation a $\sum_{i=1}^{n} I_i \times P_{ij}$		280	298	212	341

$\sum_{i=1}^{n}$ = Sum of the expression.

I_i = Importance weight assigned to the ith dimension.

P_{ij} = Performance evaluation for jth brand alternative on the ith issue.

I = Not important.

10 = Very important.

believe that vendor reputation should receive a 9 because it's very important to the retailer's image. Merchandise quality receives a 5 because it's moderately important. Finally, a vendor's selling history is less important, so it could be rated 3.

3. Make judgments about each individual brand's performance on each issue (remaining columns). Note that some brands have high ratings on some issues but not on others.

4. Develop an overall score by multiplying the importance of each issue by the performance of each brand or its vendor. For instance, vendor reputation importance (9) multiplied by the performance rating for brand A (5) is 45. Promotional assistance importance (4) multiplied by the performance rating (7) for vendor D is 28. This type of analysis illustrates an important point: It doesn't pay to perform well on issues that retailers don't believe are very important. Although vendor D performed well on promotional assistance, the buyer didn't rate this issue highly in importance, so the resulting score was still low.

5. To determine a vendor's overall rating, add the scores for each brand for all issues. In Exhibit 11–14, brand D has the highest overall rating (341), so D is the preferred vendor.

SUMMARY

LO 11-1 **Explain the merchandise management organization and performance measures.**

Merchandise is broken down into categories for planning purposes. Buyers and planners manage these categories, often with the help of their major vendors. The key performance measures used to assess merchandise management are GMROI and its components; sales-to-stock ratio, which is similar to inventory turnover; and gross margin. High inventory turnover is important for a retailer's financial success, but if the retailer attempts to push inventory turnover to its limit, stockouts and increased costs may result.

LO 11-2 **Contrast the merchandise management processes for staple and fashion merchandise.**

Retailers use different types of merchandise planning systems for managing (1) staple and (2) fashion merchandise categories. Staple merchandise categories, also called basic merchandise categories, are categories that are in continuous demand over an extended time period. Fashion merchandise categories are in demand only for a relatively short period of time. New products are continually introduced into these categories, making the existing products obsolete. Seasonal merchandise categories consist of items whose sales fluctuate dramatically depending on the time of year.

The steps in the merchandise management planning process are (1) forecast category sales, (2) develop an assortment plan, (3) determine appropriate inventory levels and product availability, (4) develop a plan for managing inventory, (5) allocate merchandise to stores, and (6) monitor and evaluate performance and make adjustments.

LO 11-3 **Describe how to predict sales for merchandise categories.**

The first step in merchandise management planning is to develop a forecast for category sales. The approach for forecasting sales of staple merchandise is to project past sales trends into the future, making adjustments for anticipated factors affecting future sales.

Forecasting sales for fashion merchandise is challenging because buyers typically need to place orders and commit to buying specific quantities between three and six months before the merchandise will be delivered and made available for sale. Some sources of information that retailers use to develop forecasts for fashion merchandise categories are (1) previous sales data, (2) market research, (3) fashion trend services, and (4) vendors.

LO 11-4 **Summarize the trade-offs for developing merchandise assortments.**

After forecasting sales for the category, the next step in the merchandise management planning process is to develop an assortment plan. An assortment plan is the set of SKUs that a retailer will offer in a merchandise category in each of its stores and from its website. When determining the assortment for a category, buyers consider the following factors: the firm's retail strategy, the effect of assortments on GMROI, the complementarities between categories, the effects of assortments on buying behavior, and the physical characteristics of the store.

LO 11-5 **Illustrate how to determine the appropriate inventory levels.**

After developing the assortment plan, the third step in the merchandise planning process is to determine the model stock plan for the category. The model stock plan is the number of units of backup stock for each SKU. Retailers typically have different model stock plans for the different store sizes in a chain.

The first three steps in the merchandise planning process—forecast SKU and category sales, determine the assortment plan, and establish the model stock plan—quantify the buyer's sales expectations and service level.

LO 11-6 Analyze merchandise control systems.

The fourth step in the merchandise management process is to establish a control system for how the orders, deliveries, inventory levels, and merchandise sales will evolve over time. The objective of this control system is to manage the flow of merchandise into the stores so that the amount of inventory in a category is minimized but the merchandise will still be available when customers want to buy it.

Buying systems for staple merchandise are very different from those for fashion merchandise. Because staple merchandise is sold month after month and the sales levels are predictable, an automated continuous replenishment system is often used to manage staple merchandise categories. By definition, SKUs within a fashion category change rapidly, so fashion merchandise categories are managed in dollars (i.e., how much money is spent on each category), rather than in units as is staple merchandise.

LO 11-7 Describe how multistore retailers allocate merchandise to stores.

Allocating merchandise to stores involves three decisions: (1) how much merchandise to allocate to each store, (2) what type of merchandise to allocate, and (3) when to allocate the merchandise to different stores. Retail chains typically classify each of their stores on the basis of annual sales. Thus, A stores would have the largest sales volume and typically receive the most inventory, while C stores would have the lowest sales volume and receive the least inventory for a category. In addition to the store's sales level, when making allocation decisions for a category, allocators consider the physical characteristics of the merchandise and the depth of assortment and level of product availability that the firm wants to portray for the specific store.

LO 11-8 Review how retailers evaluate the performance of their merchandise management decisions.

Three different approaches for evaluating aspects of merchandise management and planning performance are sell-through analysis, ABC analysis, and the multiattribute model. The sell-through analysis is useful for examining the performance of individual SKUs in the merchandise plan. The buyer compares actual with planned sales to determine whether more merchandise needs to be ordered or whether the merchandise should be put on sale. In an ABC analysis, merchandise is rank-ordered from highest to lowest. The merchandising team uses this information to set inventory management policies. The multiattribute analysis method for evaluating vendors uses a weighted-average score for each vendor based on the importance of various issues and the vendor's performance on those issues. Buyers choose the vendor with the highest weighted score.

KEY TERMS

ABC analysis, *301*
assortment, *288*
assortment plan, *288*
backup stock, *291*
base stock, *292*
basic merchandise, *282*
breadth, *288*
breaking sizes, *289*
buffer stock, *291*
category captain, *277*
category management, *276*
classification, *276*
continuous replenishment, *282*
cycle stock, *292*
department, *276*

depth, *288*
editing the assortment, *288*
fashion merchandise, *282*
fill rate, *294*
focus group, *287*
in-depth interview, *286*
lead time, *293*
level of support, *291*
markdown money, *300*
merchandise budget plan, *296*
merchandise category, *276*
merchandise group, *275*
merchandise management, *274*
model stock plan, *290*
multiattribute analysis, *302*

open-to-buy, *297*
order point, *295*
perpetual inventory, *294*
product availability, *291*
safety stock, *291*
seasonal merchandise, *284*
sell-through analysis, *300*
service level, *291*
shopworn, *280*
shrinkage, *307*
SKU rationalization program, *290*
staple merchandise, *282*
stock-keeping unit (SKU), *276*
stock-to-sales ratio, *307*
variety, *288*

GET OUT AND DO IT!

1. **CONTINUING ASSIGNMENT** Go to a store of the retailer you selected for the continuing assignment, and audit the variety and assortment for a specific merchandise category. Record the breadth and depth of the assortment and the level of support (average number of items for the SKUs in each category). Compare the variety, assortment, and support for the same category in a competing retail store. Evaluate both stores' assortment on that category. Which is better?

2. **INTERNET EXERCISE** Go to the home page of Merchandise Management Company (MMC) at www. merchmanco.com. Read the posted information (read

section on "news") on this website. How does this service provider support vendors to manage merchandise sold at this discount department store (read section on "Our Services")?

3. **IN-STORE OR INTERNET EXERCISE** Go to the store location or home page of a craft store such as Michaels Stores, Jo-Ann Fabric and Craft Stores, or A.C. Moore Arts & Crafts (www.michaels.com, www.joann. com, or www.acmoore.com). How does this retailer organize its merchandise in terms of merchandise group, department, category, and stock-keeping unit? Select two categories of merchandise: one that you would expect to have a high inventory turnover and the other, a low inventory turnover. Explain your reasoning for each selection.

4. **GO SHOPPING** Visit a big-box office supply store and then a discount store to shop for school supplies.

Contrast the variety and assortment offered at each. What are the advantages and disadvantages of breadth versus depth for each retailer? What are the advantages and disadvantages from the consumer's perspective?

5. **INTERNET EXERCISE** Go to the home pages of the following retail trade publications: *Chain Store Age* at www.chainstoreage.com and *Retailing Today* at www.retailingtoday.com. Find an article in each that focuses on managing merchandise. How can these articles assist retailers with merchandise planning decisions?

6. **INTERNET EXERCISE** Go to www.sas.com/en_us/ industry/retail/integrated-merchandise-planning. html, the SAS Merchandise Planning website. How does its system provide retailers with information to support merchandising planning, forecasting, and measurement?

DISCUSSION QUESTIONS AND PROBLEMS

1. How and why would you expect variety and assortment to differ between JCPenney's store and Internet site?

2. Simply speaking, increasing inventory turnover is an important goal for a retail manager. What are the consequences of turnover that's too low? Too high?

3. Assume you are the grocery buyer for canned fruits and vegetables at a five-store supermarket chain. Del Monte has told you and your boss that it would be responsible for making all inventory decisions for those merchandise categories. Del Monte will now determine how much to order and when shipments should be made. It promises a 10 percent increase in gross margin dollars in the coming year. Would you take Del Monte up on its offer? Justify your answer.

4. A buyer at Old Navy has received a number of customer complaints that he has been out of stock on some sizes of men's T-shirts. The buyer subsequently decides to increase this category's product availability from 80 percent to 90 percent. What will be the impact on backup stock and inventory turnover? Would your answer be the same if the product category were men's fleece sweatshirts?

5. Variety, assortment, and product availability are the cornerstones of the merchandise planning process. Provide examples of retailers that have done an outstanding job

of positioning their stores on the basis of one or more of these issues.

6. The fine jewelry department in a department store has the same GMROI as the small appliances department, even though characteristics of the merchandise are quite different. Explain this situation.

7. Calculate the GMROI and inventory turnover given annual sales of $20,000, average inventory (at cost) of $4,000, and a gross margin of 45 percent.

8. As the athletic shoe buyer for Dick's Sporting Goods, how would you go about forecasting sales for a new Nike running shoe?

9. Using the 80–20 principle, how can a retailer make certain that it has enough inventory of fast-selling merchandise and a minimal amount of slow-selling merchandise?

10. A buyer at a sporting goods store in Denver receives a shipment of 400 ski parkas on October 1 and expects to sell out by January 31. On November 1, the buyer still has 350 parkas left. What issues should the buyer consider in evaluating the selling season's progress?

11. A buyer is trying to decide from which vendor to buy a certain item. Using the information in the accompanying table, determine from which vendor the buyer should buy.

		VENDOR PERFORMANCE	
	Importance Weight	Vendor A	Vendor B
Reputation for collaboration	8	9	8
Service	7	8	7
Meets delivery dates	9	7	8
Merchandise quality	7	8	4
Gross margin	6	4	8
Brand-name recognition	5	7	5
Promotional assistance	3	8	8

APPENDIX 11A Merchandise Budget Report and Open-to-Buy System for a Fashion Merchandise Category

MERCHANDISE BUDGET PLAN

In this appendix, we describe the steps in developing the merchandise budget plan for a fashion merchandise category. These steps are taken to develop the bottom line—line 8, "Monthly Additions to Stock" also known as "Monthly Additions to Inventory—in Exhibit 11–15. The figures on this line tell the buyer how much merchandise in retail dollars he or she needs to have, on average, at the beginning of each month for the retailer's financial goals to be met. Note that Exhibit 11–15 is the same as Exhibit 11–9 in the chapter.

Monthly Sales Percentage Distribution to Season (Line 1)

Line 1 of the plan projects what percentage of the total sales is expected to be sold in each month. In Exhibit 11–15, 21 percent of the six-month sales are expected to occur in April.

	Six-Month Data	SPRING			SUMMER		
		April	May	June	July	August	September
Line 1: Monthly sales % distribution to season	100.00%	21.00%	12.00%	12.00%	19.00%	21.00%	15.00%

Historical sales data provide the starting point for determining the percentage distribution of sales by month. The percentage of total category sales that occurs in a particular month doesn't vary much from year to year. However, the buyer might adjust the historical percentages to reflect changes in buying patterns and special promotions. For instance, the buyer might feel that the autumn selling season for men's casual slacks continues to be pushed further back into summer and thus increase the percentages for July and decrease the percentages for August and September. The buyer might also decide to hold a special Easter sale promotion, increasing the April percentage and decreasing the other percentages.

Monthly Sales (Line 2)

Monthly sales are the forecasted total sales for the six-month period in the first column ($130,000) multiplied by each monthly sales percentage (line 1). In Exhibit 11–15, monthly sales for April = $130,000 × 21 percent = $27,300.

	Six-Month Data	SPRING			SUMMER		
		April	May	June	July	August	September
Line 2: Monthly sales	$130,000	$27,300	$15,600	$15,600	$24,700	$27,300	$19,500

Monthly Reductions Percentage Distribution to Season (Line 3)

To have enough merchandise every month to support the monthly sales forecast, the buyer needs to consider other factors that reduce the inventory level in addition to sales made to customers. Although sales are the primary reduction, the value of the inventory is also reduced by markdowns (sales discounts), shrinkage, and discounts to employees. The merchandise budget planning process builds these additional reductions into the planned purchases. If these reductions were

EXHIBIT 11–15 Six-Month Merchandise Budget Plan for Men's Casual Slacks

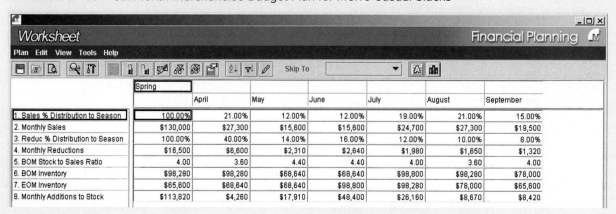

	Spring						
		April	May	June	July	August	September
1. Sales % Distribution to Season	100.00%	21.00%	12.00%	12.00%	19.00%	21.00%	15.00%
2. Monthly Sales	$130,000	$27,300	$15,600	$15,600	$24,700	$27,300	$19,500
3. Reduc % Distribution to Season	100.00%	40.00%	14.00%	16.00%	12.00%	10.00%	8.00%
4. Monthly Reductions	$16,500	$6,600	$2,310	$2,640	$1,980	$1,650	$1,320
5. BOM Stock to Sales Ratio	4.00	3.60	4.40	4.40	4.00	3.60	4.00
6. BOM Inventory	$98,280	$98,280	$68,640	$68,640	$98,800	$98,280	$78,000
7. EOM Inventory	$65,600	$68,640	$68,640	$98,800	$98,280	$78,000	$65,600
8. Monthly Additions to Stock	$113,820	$4,260	$17,910	$48,400	$26,160	$8,670	$8,420

not considered, the category would always be understocked. Note that in Exhibit 11–15, 40 percent of the season's total reductions occur in April as a result of price discounts (markdowns) during end-of-season sales as well.

Markdowns also can be forecasted from historical records. However, changes in markdown strategies—or changes in the environment, such as competition or general economic activity—must be taken into consideration when forecasting markdowns as well.

Discounts to employees are like markdowns, except that they are given to employees rather than to customers. The level of the employee discount is tied fairly closely to the sales level and number of employees. Thus, employee discounts also can be forecasted from historical records.

		SPRING			SUMMER		
	Six-Month Data	April	May	June	July	August	September
Line 3: Reductions % distribution to season	100.00%	40.00%	14.00%	16.00%	12.00%	10.00%	8.00%

Shrinkage refers to inventory losses caused by shoplifting, employee theft, merchandise being misplaced or damaged, and poor bookkeeping. Retailers measure shrinkage by taking the difference between (1) the inventory's recorded value based on merchandise bought and received and (2) the physical inventory actually in stores and distribution centers. Shrinkage varies by department and season, but typically it varies directly with sales as well. So if sales of men's casual pants increase by 10 percent, then the buyer can expect a 10 percent increase in shrinkage.

Monthly Reductions (Line 4)

Monthly reductions are calculated by multiplying the total reductions by each percentage in line 3. The total reductions for this example are based on historical data. In Exhibit 11–15, April reductions = $16,500 × 40 percent = $6,600.

		SPRING			SUMMER		
	Six-Month Data	April	May	June	July	August	September
Line 4: Monthly reductions	$16,500	$6,600	$2,310	$2,640	$1,980	$1,650	$1,320

BOM (Beginning-of-Month) Stock-to-Sales Ratio (Line 5)

The **stock-to-sales ratio**, listed in line 5, specifies the amount of inventory that should be on hand at the beginning of the month to support the sales forecast and maintain the inventory turnover objective for the category. Thus, a stock-to-sales ratio of 2 means that the retailer plans to have twice as much inventory on hand at the beginning of the month as there are forecasted sales for the month. Both the BOM stock and forecasted sales for the month are expressed in retail sales dollars.

		SPRING			SUMMER		
	Six-Month Data	April	May	June	July	August	September
Line 5: BOM stock-to-sales ratio	4.0	3.6	4.4	4.4	4.0	3.6	4.0

Rather than specifying the stock-to-sales ratio, many retailers specify a related measure, weeks of inventory. A stock-to-sales ratio of 4 means there are 16 weeks of inventory, or approximately 112 days, on hand at the beginning of the month. A stock-to-sales ratio of 1/2 indicates a two-week supply of merchandise, or enough for approximately 14 days. The stock-to-sales ratio is determined so the merchandise category achieves its targeted performance—its planned GMROI and inventory turnover. The steps in determining the stock-to-sales ratio for the category are shown next.

Step 1: Calculate Sales-to-Stock Ratio   The GMROI is equal to the gross margin percentage times the sales-to-stock ratio. The sales-to-stock ratio is conceptually similar to inventory turnover except the denominator in the stock-to-sales ratio is expressed in retail sales dollars, whereas the denominator in inventory turnover is the cost of goods sold (sales at cost). The buyer's target GMROI for the category is 123 percent, and the buyer feels the category will produce a gross margin of 45 percent. Thus,

$$GMROI = \text{Gross margin percentage} \times \text{Sales-to-stock ratio}$$

$$\text{Sales-to-stock ratio} = GMROI/\text{Gross margin percentage} = 123/45 = 2.73$$

Because this illustration of a merchandise budget plan is for a six-month period rather than a year, the sales-to-stock ratio is based on six months rather than annual sales. So for this six-month period, sales must be 2.73 times the inventory cost to meet the targeted GMROI.

Step 2: Convert the Sales-to-Stock Ratio to Inventory Turnover

Inventory turnover is

$$
\begin{array}{llll}
\text{Inventory} & \text{Sales-to-stock} & (1.00 - \text{Gross margin} \\
\text{turnover} & = \text{ratio} & \times & \%/100) \\
& = 2.73 & \times (1.00 - 45/100) \\
1.50 & = 2.73 & \times 0.55
\end{array}
$$

This adjustment is necessary because the sales-to-stock ratio defines sales at retail and inventory at cost, whereas inventory turnover defines both sales and inventory at cost. Like the sales-to-stock ratio, this inventory turnover is based on a six-month period.

Step 3: Calculate Average Stock-to-Sales Ratio

The average stock-to-sales ratio is

$$
\text{Average stock-to-sales ratio} = 6 \text{ months/Inventory turnover}
$$
$$
4 = 6/1.5
$$

If preparing a 12-month plan, the buyer divides 12 by the annual inventory turnover. Because the merchandise budget plan in Exhibit 11–15 is based on retail dollars, it's easiest to think of the numerator as BOM retail inventory and the denominator as sales for that month. Thus, to achieve a six-month inventory turnover of 1.5, on average, the buyer must plan to have a BOM inventory that equals four times the amount of sales for a given month, which is equivalent to four months, or 16 weeks of supply.

One needs to be careful when thinking about the average *stock-to-sales ratio*, which can be easily confused with the *sales-to-stock ratio*. These ratios are not the inverse of each other. Sales are the same in both ratios, but stock in the sales-to-stock ratio is the average inventory at cost over all days in the period, whereas stock in the stock-to-sales ratio is the average BOM inventory at retail. Also, the BOM stock-to-sales ratio is an average for all months. Adjustments are made to this average in line 5 to account for seasonal variation in sales.

Step 4: Calculate Monthly Stock-to-Sales Ratios

The monthly stock-to-sales ratios in line 5 must average the stock-to-sales ratio calculated previously to achieve the planned inventory turnover. Generally, monthly stock-to-sales ratios vary in the opposite direction of sales. That is, in months when sales are larger, stock-to-sales ratios are smaller, and vice versa.

To make this adjustment, the buyer needs to consider the seasonal pattern for men's casual slacks in determining the monthly stock-to-sales ratios. In the ideal situation, men's casual slacks would arrive in the store the same day and in the same quantity that customers demand them. Unfortunately, the real-life retailing world isn't this simple. Note in Exhibit 11–15 (line 8) that men's casual slacks for the spring season start arriving slowly in April ($4,260 for the month), yet demand lags behind these arrivals until the weather starts getting warmer. Monthly sales then jump from 12 percent of annual sales in May and June to 19 percent in July (line 1). But the stock-to-sales ratio (line 5) decreased from 4.4 in May and June to 4.0 in July. Thus, in months when sales increase (e.g., July), the BOM inventory also increases (line 6) but at a slower rate, which causes the stock-to-sales ratios to decrease. Likewise, in months when sales decrease dramatically, like in May (line 2), inventory also decreases (line 6), again at a slower rate, causing the stock-to-sales ratios to increase (line 5).

When creating a merchandise budget plan for a category such as men's casual slacks with a sales history, the buyer also examines previous years' stock-to-sales ratios. To judge how adequate these past ratios were, the buyer determines if inventory levels were exceedingly high or low in any months. Then the buyer makes minor corrections to adjust for a previous imbalance in inventory levels, as well as for changes in the current environment. For instance, assume the buyer is planning a promotion for Memorial Day. This promotion has never been done before, so the stock-to-sales ratio for the month of May should be adjusted downward to allow for the expected increase in sales. Note that monthly stock-to-sales ratios don't change by the same percentage that the percentage distribution of sales by month is changing. In months when sales increase, stock-to-sales ratios decrease but at a slower rate. Because there is no exact method of making these adjustments, the buyer must make some subjective judgments.

BOM Inventory (Line 6)

The amount of inventory planned for the beginning-of-month (BOM) inventory for April equals

$$
\begin{array}{lll}
\text{BOM inventory} = & \text{Monthly sales} & \times \text{BOM stock-to-sales} \\
& \text{(line 2)} & \text{ratio (line 5)} \\
\$98,280 & = \$27,300 & \times 3.6
\end{array}
$$

| | Six-Month Data | SPRING | | | SUMMER | | |
		April	May	June	July	August	September
Line 6: BOM inventory	$98,280	$98,280	$68,640	$68,640	$98,800	$98,280	$78,000

EOM (End-of-Month) Inventory (Line 7)

The BOM inventory for the current month is the same as the EOM (end-of-month) inventory in the previous month. That is, BOM inventory in line 6 is simply EOM inventory in line 7 from the previous month. Thus, in Exhibit 11–15, the EOM inventory for April is the same as the BOM inventory for May, $68,640. Forecasting the ending inventory for the last month in the plan is the next step in the merchandise budget plan. Note that EOM inventory for June is high, which indicates planning for a substantial sales increase in July.

		SPRING			SUMMER		
	Six-Month Data	April	May	June	July	August	September
Line 7: EOM inventory	$65,600	$68,640	$68,640	$98,800	$98,280	$78,000	$65,600

Monthly Additions to Stock (Inventory) (Line 8)

The monthly additions to stock needed is the amount to be ordered for delivery in each month to meet the inventory turnover and sales objectives.

Additions to stock = Sales (line 2) + Reductions (line 4) + EOM inventory (line 7) – BOM inventory (line 6)

Additions to stock (April) = $27,300 + 6,600 + 68,640 – 98,280 = $4,260

At the beginning of the month, the inventory level equals BOM inventory. During the month, merchandise is sold, and various inventory reductions affecting the retail sales level occur, such as markdowns and theft. So the BOM inventory minus monthly sales minus reductions equals the EOM inventory if nothing is purchased. But something must be purchased to get back up to the forecast EOM inventory. The difference between EOM inventory if nothing is purchased (BOM inventory – sales – reductions) and the forecast EOM inventory is the additions to stock.

		SPRING			SUMMER		
	Six-Month Data	April	May	June	July	August	September
Line 8: Monthly additions to stock	$113,820	$4,260	$17,920	$48,400	$26,160	$8,670	$8,420

OPEN-TO-BUY SYSTEM

The open-to-buy system is used after the merchandise is purchased and is based on the merchandise budget plan or staple merchandise management system. The merchandise management systems discussed previously provide buyers with a plan for purchasing merchandise. The open-to-buy system keeps track of merchandise flows while they are occurring. It keeps a record of how much is actually spent purchasing merchandise each month and how much is left to spend.

In the same way that you must keep track of the checks you write, buyers need to keep track of the merchandise they purchase and when it is to be delivered. Without the open-to-buy system keeping track of merchandise flows, buyers might buy too much or too little. Merchandise could be delivered when it isn't needed and be unavailable when it is needed. Thus, sales and inventory turnover would suffer. For consistency, we will continue with our example of an open-to-buy system using the merchandise budget plan previously discussed. The open-to-buy system is also applicable to staple goods merchandise management systems.

To make the merchandise budget plan successful (i.e., meet the sales, inventory turnover, and GMROI goals for a category), the buyer attempts to buy merchandise in quantities with delivery dates such that the actual EOM stock for a month will be the same as the forecasted EOM stock. For example, at the end of September, which is the end of the spring/summer season, the buyer would like to be completely sold out of spring/summer men's casual slacks so there will be room for the fall styles. Thus, the buyer would want the projected EOM stock and the actual EOM stock for this fashion and/or seasonal merchandise to both equal zero.

Calculating Open-to-Buy for the Current Period

Buyers develop plans indicating how much inventory for the merchandise category will be available at the end of the month. However, these plans might be inaccurate. Shipments might not arrive on time, sales might be greater than expected, and/or reductions (price discounts due to sales) might be less than expected.

The open-to-buy is the difference between the planned EOM inventory and the projected EOM. Thus, open-to-buy for a month is:

Open-to-buy = Planned EOM – Projected EOM
inventory inventory

If open-to-buy is positive, then the buyer still has money in the budget to purchase merchandise for that month. If the open-to-buy is negative, then the buyer has overbought, meaning he or she has spent more than was in the budget.

The planned EOM inventory is taken from the merchandise budget plan, and the projected EOM inventory is calculated as follows:

Projected EOM inventory = Actual BOM inventory
+ Monthly additions actual (received new merchandise)
+ On order (merchandise to be delivered)
– Sales plan (merchandise sold)
– Monthly reductions plan

Exhibit 11–16 presents the six-month open-to-buy for the same category of men's casual slacks discussed in the fashion merchandise planning section of this chapter. Consider May as the current month. The BOM stock (inventory) actual level is $59,500, but there is no EOM actual inventory yet because the month hasn't finished. When calculating the open-to-buy for the current month, the projected EOM stock plan comes into play. Think of the projected EOM stock plan as a new and improved estimate of the planned EOM stock from the

EXHIBIT 11–16   Six-Month Open-to-Buy System Report

open to buy Ex. 13-4.bmp						

In-Season Planning - Worksheet: Mens department (Business View: 'OTB : Global')

Worksheet   In-Season Management

Plan Edit View Tools Help

Skip To Month

Loc - 10 / Merch - Aged Soft	Spring April	May	June	July	August	September
EOM Stock Plan	$68,640	$68,640	$98,800	$98,280	$78,000	$65,600
EOM Actuals	$69,950					
BOM Stock Plan	$98,280	$68,640	$68,640	$98,800	$98,280	$78,000
BOM Stock Actual	$95,000	$59,500				
Monthly Additions Plan	$4,260	$17,910	$48,400	$26,160	$8,670	$8,420
Monthly Additions Actuals	$3,500	$7,000				
OnOrder	$45,000	$18,000	$48,400			
Sales Plan	$27,300	$15,600	$15,600	$24,700	$27,300	$19,500
Sales Actuals	$26,900					
Monthly Reductions Plan	$6,600	$2,310	$2,640	$1,980	$1,650	$1,320
Monthly Reductions Actuals	$1,650					
Projected EOM Stock Plan	$59,500	$66,590	$96,750	$70,070	$41,120	$20,300
Projected BOM Stock Plan	$24,570	$59,500	$66,500	$96,750	$70,070	$41,120
OTB	$0.00	$2,050	$2,050	$28,210	$36,860	$45,300

merchandise budget plan. This new and improved version takes information into account that wasn't available when the merchandise budget plan was made. The formula for projected EOM inventory for the category is

Projected	= Actual BOM inventory	$59,500
EOM inventory	+ Monthly additions actual	7,000
	+ On order	18,000
	− Sales plan	15,600
	− Monthly reductions plan	2,310
	=	$66,590

The open-to-buy for the current month is:

Open-to-buy plan = EOM inventory − Projected EOM
                        planned   inventory

$2,050   = $68,640   − $66,590

Therefore, the buyer has $2,050 left to spend in May to reach the planned EOM stock of $68,640. This is a relatively small amount, so we can conclude that the buyer's plan is right on target. But if the open-to-buy for May were $20,000, the buyer could then go back into the market and look for some great buys. If one of the vendors had too much stock of men's casual slacks, the buyer might be able to use the $20,000 to pick up some bargains that could be passed on to customers.

If, however, the open-to-buy was a negative $20,000, the buyer would have overspent the budget. Similar to overspending your checkbook, the buyer would have to cut back on spending in future months so the total purchases would be within the merchandise budget. Alternatively, if the buyer believed that the overspending was justified because of changes to the marketplace, a negotiation could take place between the buyer and the divisional merchandise manager to get more open-to-buy.

CHAPTER ENDNOTES

1. Loretta Chao, "Target Says Online Sales Surge Tied to Store Inventories," *The Wall Street Journal,* February 24, 2016.

2. Shelly Banjo and Serena Ng, "Home Depot: The Place to Go for Toilet Paper?," *The Wall Street Journal,* June 6, 2014.

3. Paul Ziobro, "Target Revamps Groceries for Millennials," *The Wall Street Journal,* March 3, 201.

4. Personal communication.

5. Jonathan O'Brien, *Category Management in Purchasing: A Strategic Approach to Maximize Business Profitability* (London: Kogan Page, 2015); Deborah Fowler and Ben Goh, *Retail Category Management* (Englewood Cliffs, NJ: Prentice Hall, 2011).

6. Richard Gooner, Neil Morgan, and William Perreault Jr., "Is Retail Category Management Worth the Effort (and Does a Category Captain Help or Hinder)?," *Journal of Marketing* 75, no. 5 (2011), pp. 18–33; Joseph Hall, Praveen Kopalle, and Aradhna Krishna, "Retailer Dynamic Pricing and Ordering Decisions: Category Management versus Brand-by-Brand Approaches," *Journal of Retailing* 86, no. 2 (2010), pp. 172–183; Mümin Kurtulu and Beril Toktay, "Category Captainship vs. Retailer Category Management under Limited Retail Shelf Space," *Production and Operations Management* 20, no. 1 (2011), pp. 47–56; Joshua D. Wright, "Antitrust Analysis of Category Management: Conwood v United Tobacco," *Supreme Court Economic Review* 17, no. 1 (2009), pp. 27–35.

7. Michael Levy and Charles A. Ingene, "Residual Income Analysis: A Method of Inventory Investment Allocation and Evaluation," *Journal of Marketing* 48 (Summer, 1984), pp. 93–104.

8. Kyuseop Kwak, Sri Devi Duvvuri, and Gary J. Russell, "An Analysis of Assortment Choice in Grocery Retailing," *Journal of Retailing* 91, no. 1 (2015), pp. 19–33; Martin Eisend, "Shelf Space Elasticity: A Meta-Analysis," *Journal of Retailing* 90,

no. 2 (2014), pp. 168–181; Justin Beneke, Alice Cumming, and Lindsey Jolly, "The Effect of Item Reduction on Assortment Satisfaction—A Consideration of the Category of Red Wine in a Controlled Retail Setting," *Journal of Retailing and Consumer Services* 20, no. 3 (2013), pp. 282–291; Walter Zinn and Peter Liu, "A Comparison of Actual and Intended Consumer Behavior in Response to Retail Stockouts," *Journal of Business Logistics* 29, no. 2 (2011), pp. 141–159.

9. Stephan Kolassa, "Retail Analytics: Integrated Forecasting and Inventory Management for Perishable Products in Retailing," *Journal of the Operational Research Society* 66, no. 12 (2015), pp. 2103–2104; Patrik Appelqvist, Flora Babongo, Valérie Chavez-Demoulin, Ari-Pekka Hameri, and Tapio Niemi, "Weather and Supply Chain Performance in Sport Goods Distribution," *International Journal of Retail & Distribution Management* 44, no. 2 (2016), pp. 178–202.

10. Mijeong Noh and Pamela Ulrich, "Querying Fashion Professionals' Forecasting Practices: The Delphi Method," *International Journal of Fashion Design, Technology and Education* 6, no. 1 (2013), pp. 1–8; Yong Yu, Tsan-Ming Choi, and Chi-Leung Hui, "An Intelligent Fast Sales Forecasting Model for Fashion Products," *Expert Systems with Applications* 38, no. 6 (2011), pp. 7373–7379.

11. Dan Berthiaume, "And the Top Omnichannel Retailers Are . . . ," *Retailing Today,* October 2, 2015.

12. Hayley Peterson, "Target's CEO Is Visiting Customers' Homes to Succeed Where Walmart Failed," *Business Insider,* January 21, 2016.

13. Tesco PLC, "Business Model," 2014, https://www.tescoplc.com/files/pdf/reports/ar14/download_business_model.pdf; D. Cushman and Jamie Burke, *The 10 Principles of Open Business: Building Success in Today's Open Economy* (London: Palgrave Macmillan, 2014); Joel Alden, Hana Ben-Shabat, Bobby Wehmeyer, Basil Wuson, and A. T. Kearney, "Organizing for Insight: How Retailers Can Collect and Gain Advantage from Meaningful Consumer Insights," *Chain Store Age,* April 23, 2012.

14. "Tesco—Every Little Helps," *Loyalty Square,* http://www.loyaltysquare.com/tesco.php.

15. Soo-Haeng Cho and Christopher S. Tang, "Advance Selling in a Supply Chain under Uncertain Supply and Demand," *Manufacturing & Service Operations Management 15,* no. 2 (2013), pp. 305–319.

16. Dhruv Grewal, Michael Levy, Anuj Mehrotra, and Arun Sharma, "Planning Merchandising Decisions to Account for Regional and Product Assortment Differences," in J. Zhu (Ed.), *Data Envelopment Analysis* (New York: Springer Science+Business Media, 2016), pp. 469–990; Murali Mantrala, Michael Levy, Barbara Kahn, Edward Fox, Peter Gaidarev, Bill Dankworth, and Denish Shah, "Why Is Assortment Planning So Difficult for Retailers? A Framework and Research Agenda," *Journal of Retailing* 85, no. 1 (2009), pp. 71–83.

17. Xiaoyan Deng, Barbara Kahn, H. Rao Unnava, and Hyojin Lee, "A 'Wide' Variety: Effects of Horizontal versus Vertical Display on Assortment Processing, Perceived Variety, and Choice," *Journal of Marketing Research* 53, no. 5 (2016), pp. 682–698; Susan Broniarczyk and Wayne Hoyer, "Retail Assortment: More Is Better," in M. Krafft and M. Mantrala (Eds.), *Retailing in the 21st Century,* 2nd ed. (New York: Fairchild Books, 2010), pp. 271–284; Christopher Miller, Stephen Smith, Shelby McIntyre, and Dale Achabal, "Optimizing and Evaluating Retail Assortments for Infrequently Purchased Products," *Journal of Retailing* 86, no. 2 (2010), pp. 159–171; Mümin Kurtulu and Alper Nakkas, "Retail Assortment Planning Under Category Captainship," *Manufacturing & Service Operations Management* 13, no. 1 (2011), pp. 124–142; Alexander Hübner and Heinrich Kuhn, "Retail Category Management: State-of-the-Art Review of Quantitative Research and Software Applications in Assortment and Shelf Space Management," *Omega* 40, no. 2 (2012), pp. 199–209.

18. Murali Mantrala, P. Sinha, and A. Zoltners, "Impact of Resource Allocation Rules on Marketing Investment-Level Decisions and Profitability," *Journal of Marketing Research* 29, no. 2 (May 1992), pp. 162–175.

19. Anjali Cordeiro, "Consumer-Goods Makers Heed 'Paycheck Cycle,'" *The Wall Street Journal,* February 23, 2009.

20. William Ho, Xiaowei Xu, and Prasanta Dey, "Multi-Criteria Decision Making Approaches for Supplier Evaluation and Selection: A Literature Review," *European Journal of Operational Research* 202, no. 1 (2010), pp. 16–24.

LEARNING OBJECTIVES

After reading this chapter, you should be able to:

LO 12-1 Identify the branding options available to retailers.

LO 12-2 Describe how retailers buy national brands.

LO 12-3 List the issues retailers consider when developing and sourcing store-branded merchandise internationally.

LO 12-4 Understand how retailers prepare for and conduct negotiations with their vendors.

LO 12-5 Determine why retailers build strategic relationships with their vendors.

LO 12-6 Indicate the legal, ethical, and social responsibility issues involved in buying merchandise.

© Earth Photography/Alamy Stock Photo

Even retailers with a national presence like to make customers feel as if the local store is "their" store, with dedicated, unique, and targeted products and familiar personnel. Balancing the merchandise assortment across well-known national brands, local producers, and specific store-brand offerings is a perpetual challenge, leading various retailers to take some innovative approaches to make it work. They recognize that localization enables them to match the needs and preferences of the clientele who enter their stores on a regular basis. But retailers also gain economies of scale by stocking the same items in all their outlets. Such consistency also reassures customers that they can always find their favorite products, regardless of the store they visit.

At Whole Foods, a portion of the products it carries are consistent in all its stores. But store managers also are responsible for selecting local products and items that will appeal to their regional shoppers, as well as for customizing the look and feel of their individual stores. The purpose of assigning these responsibilities to local store managers—who already have a lot of other responsibilities to address—is to make sure that each store has a local, homey feel. In Detroit, for example, Whole Foods uses vinyl records to mark the aisles, emphasizing the Motown connection. Artistic graffiti covers the dairy department, and the products produced by a Detroit-area salsa company receive a prime location. Therefore, consumers sense that the store is their own, likely enhancing their loyalty and patronage to it.[1]

Still, even for local or small-batch producers, the standards are the same. Whole Foods maintains a long list of prohibited ingredients for its suppliers; even if a product is natural in all other respects, if it contains any bleached flour, it will not make the Whole Foods grade. It also has encouraged some small firms to change their names to ensure greater appeal among Whole Foods's vast market.[2] Local producers might enter their products in just a few stores, but Whole Foods still demands that they offer the same quality that it demands from the big national brands—a requirement that might benefit the big manufacturers that already have their production practices and efficiencies established.

But retail trends are not all good news for the national-brand manufacturers. As grocery retailers and customers increasingly demand more organic, small-batch, and local products, the massive brands that have long dominated grocery store shelves are the odd ones out. For example, since its inception in 1988, Amy's Kitchen has sold frozen and packaged meals, such as organic enchiladas and a natural macaroni and cheese offering, at small retailers. But in recent years, as consumers have demanded more and more natural and organic options, major national retail chains have approached Amy's as well. To be able to supply national chains such as Piggly Wiggly, Amy's expanded to a second production facility—which it purchased, rather ironically, from H.J. Heinz. Whereas once the national brands like Heinz and Kraft could count on receiving preferential treatment and the best placement from their retail partners, those relationships are changing. Retailers apparently have determined that their first priority needs to be stocking what consumers want to buy, not what their suppliers want to place in their stores.

But when retailers are focused strongly on efficiency as a competitive advantage, buying unique merchandise for different stores and consumers can be impossible. In this case, an alternative option arises, in which retailers sell items designed to create customized versions of the standard product. For example, IKEA furniture has a standardized look, so companies such as Bemz sell coverings for the standard couches, chairs, and beds. By providing unique merchandise that can create individual versions of mass-market products, Bemz recently earned US$8 million in annual revenue. In Sweden, Prettypegs also makes alternative legs for IKEA furniture, and Superfront sells facings and tops for the cabinets. Mykea, which is based in Amsterdam, produces stickers that customers can apply to customize their IKEA furniture. In Melbourne, Comfort Works manufactures slipcovers too.[3] In addition to the local benefits, these products enable customers to change the look of their homes frequently, without having to buy new furniture.

In some cases, the retailers even proactively seek out alternative options that might appeal to their shoppers. For example, Kroger worked with a small, local pancake mix manufacturer from Colorado to develop its product and packaging. After allowing FlapJacked to test various marketing strategies and flavors in its Colorado-area stores, Kroger added the products to more than 500 of its stores across the country. Of course, the big manufacturers are not just ignoring these trends. Many well-known brands have introduced organic or all-natural product lines, including Campbell's organic soups and Kellogg's Origins granola. But the size and long-standing reputation of these companies—once among their most valuable assets—may be liabilities in this altered market space. As one observer noted, no one is ever going to accept the notion of "organic Velveeta."[4]

Such trends are widespread. Target might be a nationwide chain, but its customers increasingly look for local appeal too, so the retailer has undertaken a new form of designer collaboration to leverage local pride and encourage sales. That is, Target has initiated multiple collaborations with well-known designers. But the latest interaction with designer Todd Snyder is a little different. Rather than introducing an element of his existing clothing offerings, the "Local Pride by Todd Snyder" line will feature a greatly expanded assortment, specific to various cities and locales.

The first collection focuses on Boston. Snyder has designed T-shirts that play on locals' accents and self-esteem, proclaiming their wearers "Wicked Smaht." The collection also features offerings of Marshmallow Fluff to make Fluffernutter sandwiches (i.e., a local favorite, made with peanut butter and marshmallow fluff between two pieces of bread) and Topps's baseball cards. Other cities will have their own unique product lines. For Chicago, for example, Snyder anticipates offerings of Old Style beer and various items featuring Mike Ditka. Plans for additional cities include Los Angeles and San Francisco, though depending on the success of the assortments, the collaboration could extend further. For now, only local stores will carry these items. The products also might be available for sale on Target.com eventually, but only after it has ensured the local consumers that it really understands them—even when they speak in strong Boston accents.[5]

The preceding chapter outlined the merchandise management process and the steps in the process that buyers go through to determine what and how much merchandise to buy. After creating an assortment plan for the category, forecasting sales, and developing a plan outlining the flow of merchandise (how much merchandise needs to be ordered and when it needs to be delivered), the next step in the merchandise management process is to acquire the merchandise.

Buying merchandise isn't easy.[6] At a grocery chain like Kroger, for instance, the soup category manager must decide on the mix between purchasing well-known national brands like Campbell's or Progresso or developing store brands like Wholesome@Home. Whether offering national or store brands, the category manager negotiates many issues, such as prices, delivery dates, payment terms, and financial support for advertising and markdowns. The buying process for store brands is often more complex than that for national brands, because the store takes an active role in developing the products.

This chapter begins with a description of the different merchandise branding alternatives. Then we review the issues involved in buying national and store brands, including negotiating with vendors. Next, the development of strategic partnering relationships between retailers and their suppliers is discussed. The chapter concludes with an examination of the legal, ethical, and social responsibility issues surrounding the buying of merchandise.

BRAND ALTERNATIVES

LO 12-1

Identify the branding options available to retailers.

Retailers and their buyers face a strategic decision about the mix of national brands and private-label brands offered in a category. Three types of brands discussed in this section are national, store, and generic brands.

National Brands

National brands, also known as **manufacturer's brands**, are products designed, produced, and marketed by a vendor and sold to many different retailers. The vendor is responsible for developing the merchandise, producing it with consistent quality, and undertaking a marketing program to establish an appealing brand image. Examples of national brands are Tide detergent, Ralph Lauren polo shirts, and Hewlett-Packard printers.

In some cases, vendors use an **umbrella** or **family brand** associated with their company and a **subbrand** associated with the product, such as Kellogg's (family brand) Raisin Bran (subbrand) or Ford (family brand) F-Series trucks (subbrand). In other cases, vendors use individual brand names for different product categories and do not associate the brands with their companies. For example, most consumers probably don't know that Unilever makes Q-tips, Dove soap, Lipton Tea, Hellmann's mayonnaise, Pond's cold cream, and many others.

Some retailers organize their buying activities around national-brand vendors that cut across merchandise categories. Thus, buyers in department stores may be responsible for all cosmetic brands offered by Estée Lauder (Estée Lauder, Origins, Clinique, and Prescriptives) rather than for a product

National brands like Kellogg's use subbrands like Raisin Bran.

© Daniel Acker/Bloomberg via Getty Images

category (such as skin care or eye makeup). Managing merchandise by vendor rather than by category gives retailers more clout when dealing with vendors. However, as indicated in Chapter 11, there are inefficiencies associated with managing merchandise at the brand or vendor level rather than the category level.

Store Brands

Store brands, also called **private-label brands**, **house brands**, or **own brands**, are products developed by retailers. In many cases, retailers develop the design and specifications for their store-brand products, then contract with manufacturers to produce those products. In other cases, national-brand vendors work with a retailer to develop a special version of its standard merchandise offering to be sold exclusively by the retailer. In these cases, the national-brand vendor or manufacturer is responsible for the production of the merchandise.

Unilever uses individual brands for different product categories like Q-tips, Dove, and Lipton.

In the past, sales of store brands were limited. National brands had the resources to develop customer loyalty toward their brands through aggressive marketing. It was difficult for smaller local and regional retailers to gain the economies of scale in design, production, and promotion that were needed to develop well-known brands. In recent years, though, as the size of retail firms has increased, more retailers have obtained sufficient scale economies to develop store brands and use this merchandise to establish a distinctive identity. Now retailers offer a broad spectrum of store brands, ranging from lower-price, lower-quality products to products that offer superior quality and performance compared with national brands.[7] Three examples of store brands are premium store brands, exclusive brands, and copycat brands.

Tesco Finest (UK) is its premium store brand, comparable to a manufacturer's brand quality.

Premium Store Brands   **Premium store brands** offer the consumer a product that is comparable to a manufacturer's brand quality, sometimes with modest price savings. Examples of premium store brands include Kroger's Private Selection, Tesco Finest (UK), "The Men's Collection" at Saks Fifth Avenue, and Bloomingdale's Aqua. Safeway, a leading grocery chain, earns a substantial portion of its $45 billion in sales from its premium store brands. Not only is its main store brand, Safeway Select, recognized for its high quality, but it also stocks various other strong store brands, such as Signature Café (fresh food), Primo Taglio (premium cheese and cold cuts), Eating Right (healthy foods), Snack Artist (nuts and snacks), and Open Nature (natural foods).[8]

Exclusive Brands   An **exclusive brand** is a brand that is developed by a national-brand vendor, often in conjunction with a retailer, and sold exclusively by the retailer. The simplest form of an exclusive brand occurs when a national-brand manufacturer assigns different model numbers and has different exterior features for the same basic product sold by different retailers, but

TESCO *Finest*

SWISS 72% PLAIN CHOCOLATE

* Chocolate made from premium grade cocoa beans sourced from South America and Africa. Smooth intense chocolate flavour.

SWISS	Two squares contain				WEIGHT
	Calories	Sugar	Fat	Saturates	Salt	
🇨🇭	113	5.4g	9.1g	5.5g	trace	100g
	6%	6%	13%	28%	<1%	e
	of your guideline daily amount				

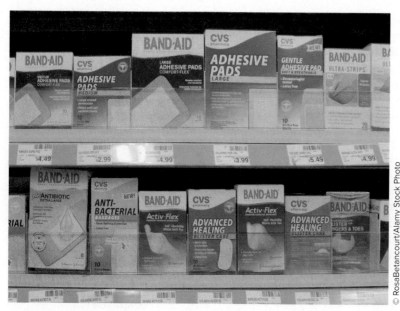

© RosaBetancourt/Alamy Stock Photo

CVS places its copycat brand of adhesive bandages next to the Band-Aid national brand.

the product is still marketed under the manufacturer's brand. For example, a Canon digital camera sold at Best Buy might have a different model number than a Canon digital camera with similar features available at Walmart. These exclusive models make it difficult for consumers to compare prices for virtually the same camera sold by different retailers.

A more sophisticated form of exclusive branding occurs when a retailer develops a store brand with its own unique identity. At Macy's, for example, customers do not often realize that the brands they purchase are its store brands. Thus, its American Rag brand has reached a significant market share in the young men's category, without ever communicating to this brand-conscious customer segment that the brand is produced by Macy's. In this case, it becomes difficult to distinguish Macy's brands, such as American Rag and INC, from national brands such as Levi's—except that consumers can find American Rag and INC only in Macy's stores.

Copycat Brands   **Copycat brands** imitate the manufacturer's brand in appearance and packaging, generally are perceived as lower quality, and are offered at lower prices. Copycat brands abound in drugstores and grocery stores. For instance, CVS or Walgreens brands are placed next to the manufacturer's brands and often look like them.

Generic Brands

In a sense, a generic brand isn't actually a brand at all and, as such, is neither a store nor a national brand. **Generic brands** are labeled with the name of the commodity and thus actually have no brand name distinguishing them. These products target a price-sensitive segment by offering a no-frills product at a discount price. They are used typically for prescription drugs and commodities like milk or eggs. Except for prescription drugs, where the use of generics has increased significantly over the last few decades, the sales of generics have declined significantly.

National Brands or Store Brands?

When determining the mix between national versus store brands, retailers consider the effect on their overall assortment, profitability, and flexibility.

Store Brands Enhance and Expand Assortments   Retailers examine their assortments to make sure they are providing what their customers want. They may introduce an innovative new store-branded product that isn't being offered by their national-brand vendors or a product that can be offered at a better value—or both. Staples, for example, carries a large number of shredders, produced by many different manufacturers. But the company's market researchers found that people tend to sort through their mail in their kitchens. Thus, it produces, under its store brand, the MailMate, a small shredder that fits on a kitchen counter and is less expensive than the national-brand options. Staples filled a key gap in its assortment by producing an innovative, yet value-oriented product for families tired of stacks of junk mail but also worried about their privacy.

Many categories contain a market-leading national brand, such as Tide or All in the laundry detergent category. There may be opportunities for store brands in these categories, but the greatest potential appears in categories where there is no national-brand domination, such as with organic products in grocery stores. Whole Foods largely pioneered the concept in grocery retailing, but competitors such as SuperValu (which owns the Shaw's and Albertsons chains) have rapidly increased the number of products offered under its organic labels, such as Wild Harvest. At the wholesale club retailer BJ's, shoppers choose between the basic Elias store-brand frozen pizza and the premium organic store-brand Earth's Pride.

Many store brands today extend assortments by creating multiple price tiers, often referred to as low cost, value, and premium. The low-cost and value tiers have long been in place; the premium option is relatively newer. Such premium options offer consumers quality that is comparable to that of national brands, sometimes (but not always) at a modest price savings. Retailing View 12.1 examines how Kroger uses price tiers in its store brands to enhance and expand its assortments.

Profitability   Stocking national brands is a double-edged sword for retailers. Many customers have developed loyalty to specific national brands. They patronize only retailers selling these national-brand merchandise. This loyalty toward the national brand develops because customers know what to expect from the products and like them. They trust the brand to deliver consistent quality. Every bottle of Chanel No. 5 will have the same fragrance, and every pair of Levi's 501 jeans will have the same fit.

RETAILING VIEW   Kroger's Store Brands Have It All   12.1

Kroger runs its own store brands as if they were separate vendors, demanding high-quality standards and price competitiveness. The grocer even demands that its store brands earn 50 percent higher rankings than national brands in taste tests. In response, customers express their loyalty to the store brands, which translates to loyalty loyal to the store. The retailer can even brag that among the customers it cares most about, "99.5 percent of our loyal and our premium loyal customer segments are buying our corporate brands."

In the 1990s, Kroger first started playing around with store brands, developing its high-end Private Selection line, and a Value label. In more recent years, it has further expanded its store brands to include Simple Truth (an all-natural line of products), Check This Out (for paper and cleaning products), P$$t (canned goods), and Heritage Farm (fresh foods) brands. In addition, it chose to phase out the line of Value brand products.

Yet Kroger also takes a broad perspective on its use of store brands. It acknowledges that "our stores would go away if we didn't have national brands. And our stores would go away if we didn't have our own brand. And there is a lot of upside for both of them."

Kroger's vision for its store brands is to build loyalty among customers, with strong store brands that are exclusive to the retailer. It pursues a multiple-tier store-brand strategy to provide Kroger products to all customer segments. In the ice cream category, for instance, it offers the "Banner Brand," which is geared to the customer who wants ice cream comparable to Breyers. At the higher end is the "Private Selection" brand, which competes with Dove and Häagen Dazs. Developing products for all these customer segments means that Kroger closes any gaps in the ability of its current assortment to meet customers' needs.

Not all tiers appear in every product category, though. For commodities with minimal differentiation (sugar is sugar), it limits the assortment to two store brands, Banner and organic. The flower selection in stores consists of only the "Private Selection" label. Figuring that flowers must be alive and attractive if they are to sell, Kroger assumes it can target mainly upscale or aspirational customers willing to spend money simply to make their homes more beautiful. Similarly, homemade breads, pies, and cookies are branded by "Private Selection," whereas in the bread aisle, packaged bread carries the Banner brand label.

Coordinating store brands within and across categories is difficult. At Kroger, in the past the category managers had control of the store brands within their category. For example, the category manager for canned soup bought national brands like Campbell's and Progresso and managed the store brands. The category manager would control the store brand's packaging, pricing, promotion, and even the brand's name. Because of this relative autonomy, Kroger had more than 40 store-brand names. Because there was little synergy between the brands, each brand had relatively low customer recognition. Through an extensive editing process, Kroger developed a structure that stresses a consistent vision for each brand. Customers have come to recognize and demand these store brands, resulting in synergies across categories. So, if a customer likes Kroger's "Private Selections" ice cream, he or she will likely be drawn to its "Private Selections" angus beef or artisan breads.

Source: Alexander Coolidge, "Kroger Using House Brands to Power Growth," *Cincinnati Inquirer*, September 20, 2014; personal communication with Linda Severin, Kroger.

In addition, the availability of national brands can affect customers' image of the retailer. For example, the fashion image of JCPenney increased when it added Liz Claiborne and Sephora to its assortment. If a retailer does not offer the national brands, customers might view its assortment as lower in quality, with a resulting loss of profits.

On the other hand, the consistency of national brands means that it is easy to compare the retailer's prices for national brands. Thus, the same national brands offered by competing retailers can be differentiated only on price, which means retailers often have to offer significant discounts on some national brands to attract customers to their stores, further reducing their profitability.

Store brands instead offer an opportunity for retailers to differentiate their products and reduce price competition, though the retailer incurs additional costs designing and marketing store brands, which reduces its profitability. In addition, the retailers assume the risk associated with uncertain sales.[9] If, for instance, a product doesn't sell, the retailer can negotiate to either send the merchandise back to the vendor, have the vendor pay for the difference in lost gross margin if the merchandise has to be marked down, or sell the inventory to an off-price retailer. Retailers have no such cushions for their store brands. Because private-label products are specific to the store, there are few alternative options for getting rid of excess inventory.

The potential profitability for exclusive store brands is stronger, however. Customers can't compare prices for these products because they are, in fact, exclusive to one retailer. Because the retailers are less likely to compete on price when selling exclusive brands, the profitability potential for exclusive store brands is higher, and they are motivated to devote more resources toward selling them than they would for similar national brands.[10]

Flexibility   National brands can limit a retailer's flexibility. Vendors of strong brands can dictate how their products are displayed, advertised, and priced. Ralph Lauren, for instance, tells retailers exactly when and how its products should be advertised.

BUYING NATIONAL-BRAND MERCHANDISE

LO 12-2

Describe how retailers buy national brands.

In this section, we review how retail buyers of national brands meet with vendors, review the merchandise they have to offer at wholesale markets, and place orders.

Meeting National-Brand Vendors

A **wholesale market** for retail buyers is a concentration of vendors within a specific geographic location, perhaps even under one roof or over the Internet. Wholesale markets may be permanent wholesale market centers, annual trade shows, or trade fairs. Retailers also interact with vendors at their corporate headquarters. News about various trade shows is readily available on the Trade Show News network (www.tsnn.com). Its database features more than 25,000 trade shows and 137,000 registered users.[11]

Wholesale Market Centers   For many types of merchandise, particularly fashion apparel and accessories, buyers regularly visit with vendors in established market centers. Wholesale market centers have permanent vendor showrooms that retailers can visit throughout the year. At specific times during the year, these wholesale centers host **market weeks**, during which buyers make appointments to visit the various vendor showrooms. Vendors that do not have permanent showrooms at the market center lease temporary space to participate in market weeks.

Probably the world's most well-known wholesale market center for many merchandise categories is in New York City. The Fashion Center, also known as the

The International Consumer Electronics Show (CES) in Las Vegas is the world's largest trade show for consumer technology.

Garment District, is located from Fifth to Ninth Avenues and from 34th to 41st Streets. Thousands of apparel buyers visit every year for five market weeks and numerous annual trade shows. The Garment District hosts thousands of showrooms and factories.[12] There are also major wholesale market centers in London, Milan, Paris, and Tokyo. The United States also has various regional wholesale market centers—like the Dallas Market Center (positioned as the world's most complete wholesaler) or the Atlanta Merchandise Mart—that smaller retailers rely on to view and purchase merchandise.

Trade Shows   **Trade shows** provide another opportunity for buyers to see the latest products and styles and interact with vendors. Vendors display their merchandise in designated areas and have sales representatives, company executives, and sometimes even celebrities available to talk with buyers as they walk through the exhibit area. For example, consumer electronics buyers always make sure that they attend the annual Consumer Electronics Show (CES) in Las Vegas, the world's largest trade show for consumer technology (**www.cesweb.org**). The most recent show was attended by 165,000 people (representing more than 150 countries), such as vendors, developers, and suppliers of consumer technology hardware, content, technology delivery systems, and related products and services.[13] Nearly 3,700 vendor exhibits take up close to 2 million square feet of exhibit space, showcasing the very latest products and services. Vendors often use CES to introduce new products, including the first camcorder (1981), high-definition television (HDTV, 1998), Internet protocol television (IPTV, 2005), 3D printers (2014), and virtual reality (2015).[14] In addition to providing an opportunity for retail buyers to see the latest products, the CES conference program features prominent speakers from the technology sector.

Trade shows are typically staged at convention centers not associated with wholesale market centers. McCormick Place in Chicago (the nation's largest convention complex, with more than 2.6 million square feet) has about 3 million visitors a year attending meetings and trade show.[15] Vendors from outside the United States and store-brand manufacturers attend trade shows to learn about the market and pick up on trend information. Some store-brand manufacturers attend and display at trade shows, but most participants are national-brand vendors.

National-Brand Buying Process

When attending market weeks or trade shows, buyers and their supervisors typically make a series of appointments with key vendors. During these meetings, the buyers discuss the performance of the vendors' merchandise during the previous season, review the vendors' offerings for the coming season, and possibly place orders for the coming season. These meetings take place in conference rooms in the vendors' showrooms at wholesale market centers. During trade shows, these meetings typically are less formal. The meetings during market weeks offer an opportunities for an in-depth discussion, whereas trade shows provide the opportunity for buyers to see a broader array of merchandise in one location and gauge reactions to the merchandise by observing the level of activity in the vendor's display area.

Often, buyers do not negotiate with vendors or place orders during the market week or trade show. They typically want to see what merchandise and prices are available from all the potential vendors before deciding what items to buy. So, after attending a market week or trade show, buyers return to their offices, review requested samples of merchandise sent to them by vendors, meet with their supervisors to review the available merchandise, make decisions about which items are most attractive, and then negotiate with the vendors before placing an order. The issues involved in negotiating the purchase of national-brand merchandise are discussed later in this chapter.

DEVELOPING AND SOURCING STORE-BRAND MERCHANDISE

LO 12-3

List the issues retailers consider when developing and sourcing store-branded merchandise internationally.

Retailers use a variety of different processes to develop and buy store brands.

Developing Store Brands

Larger retailers that offer a significant amount of store-brand merchandise, such as Kroger (discussed in Retailing View 12.1), J.Crew, H&M, IKEA, and Walgreens, have large divisions with people devoted to the development of their store-brand merchandise. Employees in these divisions specialize in identifying trends, designing and specifying products, selecting manufacturers to make the products, maintaining a worldwide staff to monitor the conditions in which the products are made, and managing facilities to test the quality of the manufactured products. For example, MGF Sourcing maintains joint ventures and manufacturing operations in dozens of countries, where it fulfills contracts for manufacturing, importing, and distributing various products. In addition to being the major store-brand supplier of L Brands (Victoria's Secret and Bath & Body Works), it provides store-brand merchandise for Express, Chico's, and Betsey Johnson. However, most retailers do not own and operate or have ownership stakes in manufacturing facilities.[16]

Smaller retail chains can offer store brands without making a significant investment in the supporting infrastructure. Smaller retailers often ask national-brand or store-brand suppliers to make minor changes to products they offer and then provide the merchandise with the store's brand name or a special label copyrighted by the national brand. Alternatively, store-brand manufacturers can sell to them from a predetermined stock selection. Hollander thus makes more than 30 million pillows for companies such as Beautyrest, Ralph Lauren, and Simmons. It also makes store-brand versions for various retailers (e.g., Walmart, JCPenney).[17]

Sourcing Store-Brand Merchandise

Once the decision has been made about which and how much store-brand merchandise will be acquired, the designers develop a complete specification plan and work with the sourcing department to find a manufacturer for the merchandise. For example, JCPenney has sourcing and quality assurance offices in 10 countries. These offices

RETAILING VIEW   The Search for Cheaper Garment Factories Leads to Africa

Global clothing supply chains are complex, varied entities. But they all have several needs in common: for raw materials, such as cotton; for inexpensive labor that can sew the clothing, so that they can keep their retail prices low enough to appeal to consumers; and a means to transport materials from production sites to retail markets.

Considering these demands, Africa is rapidly emerging as a location of great interest for clothing companies. First, many areas in Africa are able to grow their own cotton, so the raw material is available and locally sourced for factories that transform the cotton into clothing. In contrast, Asian locations that currently are among the most prominent sites for manufacturing, such as Vietnam and China, lack the proper environmental conditions for growing cotton.

Second, due to shifting trends and social norms, many Asian countries have implemented minimum wages and required safety protections for unskilled labor forces. For example, in Bangladesh, the site of several tragic factory incidents in recent years, a $67 monthly minimum wage has been instituted, along with stricter requirements for factory safety. In China, with its reputation for efficient and effective manufacturing, minimum wages range around $200 per month. But in Ethiopia, for example, there is no minimum wage, so clothing companies can hire workers for far less.

Third, unlike several Asian nations, many African countries have free trade agreements in place with several Western nations, including the United States. These agreements facilitate trade across their geographic boundaries. In Ethiopia, the national government also has invested in manufacturing facilities in an attempt to attract more companies to locate there. However, Ethiopia lacks a port, and in much of Africa, the

© brianafrica/Alamy Stock Photo

Africa is emerging as a great location to source apparel because it grows its own cotton, it has implemented minimum wages and required safety protections for unskilled laborers, and it has free trade agreements with several Western countries.

infrastructure, including roads, remains underdeveloped. In this sense, it lags behind most Asian sites for manufacturing.

Although Africa appears poised to emerge as a much more popular location for manufacturing than in the past, it still has some ground to make up when it comes to competing with the locations that already are popular with clothing companies.

Source: Christina Passariello and Suzanne Kapner, "Search for Ever Cheaper Garment Factories Leads to Africa," *The Wall Street Journal*, July 12, 2015.

take the specification developed by the designer, negotiate a contract to produce the item with manufacturers, and monitor the production process.[18] As barriers to international trade continue to fall, retailers can consider more sources for merchandise, anywhere in the world, as described in Retailing View 12.2. In this section, we examine the cost factors and managerial issues that influence global sourcing.

Costs Associated with Global Sourcing Decisions   Retailers use production facilities located in developing economies for much of their private-label merchandise because of the very low labor costs in these countries. However, counterbalancing the lower acquisition costs are other expenses that can increase the costs of sourcing private-label merchandise from other countries. These costs include the relative value of foreign currencies, tariffs, longer lead times, and increased transportation costs.[19]

© Rex Wholster/iStock/Getty Images

The rise of the value of the U.S. dollar against the euro and other important world currencies in recent years has made imports to the United States less expensive and exports from the United States more expensive.

Retailers can hedge against short-term foreign currency fluctuations by buying contracts that lock the retailer into a set price, regardless of how the currency fluctuates. But in the longer term, the relative value of foreign currencies can have a strong influence on the cost of imported merchandise. For example, if the Indian rupee has a sustained and significant increase relative to the U.S. dollar, the cost of store-brand merchandise produced in India and imported for sale into the United States will increase. **Tariffs**, also known as **duties**, are taxes collected by a government on imports. Import tariffs have been used to shield domestic manufacturers from foreign competition. Inventory turnover also is likely to be lower when purchasing from foreign suppliers. Because lead times are longer and more uncertain, retailers using foreign sources must maintain larger inventories to ensure that the merchandise is available when the customer wants it. Larger inventories mean larger inventory carrying costs. Finally, transportation costs are higher when merchandise is produced in foreign countries.

Managerial Issues Associated with Global Sourcing Decisions   Whereas the cost factors associated with global sourcing are easy to quantify, some more subjective issues include quality control, time to market, and sociopolitical risks. When sourcing globally, it is harder to maintain consistent quality standards than it is when sourcing domestically. Quality control problems can cause delays in shipment and adversely affect a retailer's image.

The collaborative supply chain management approaches described in Chapter 9 are more difficult to implement when sourcing globally. Collaborative systems are based on short and consistent lead times. Vendors provide frequent deliveries of smaller quantities. For a collaborative system to work properly, there must be a strong alliance between the vendor and the retailer that is based on trust and shared information. These activities are more difficult to perform globally than domestically.

Another issue related to global sourcing is the problem of policing potential violations of human rights and child labor laws (as discussed in Retailing View 12.2). Many retailers have had to publicly defend themselves against allegations of human rights, child labor, or other abuses involving the factories and countries in which their goods are made. Due to the efforts of U.S. retailers and nonprofit organizations, fewer imported goods are produced in sweatshop conditions today. Some retailers are quite proactive in enforcing the labor practices of their suppliers. L Brands, for instance, was one of the first U.S. apparel manufacturers to develop and implement policies requiring that vendors and their subcontractors and suppliers observe core labor standards as a condition of doing business. Among other things, this requirement ensures that each supplier pays minimum wages and benefits; limits overtime to local industry standards; does not use prisoners, forced labor, or child labor; and provides a healthy and safe environment.[20] Other companies that rely on firms in low-wage countries for their production also pursue self-policing to avoid unpleasant surprises and reputational risks.

Resident Buying Offices   Many retailers purchasing private-label merchandise use **resident buying offices**, which are organizations located in major market centers that provide services to help retailers buy merchandise. As retailers have become larger and more sophisticated, these third-party, independent resident buying offices have become less important. Now, many large retailers have their own buying offices in other countries.

To illustrate how buying offices operate, consider how David Smith of Pockets Men's Store in Dallas uses his when he goes to market in Milan. Smith meets with market representative Alain Bordat of the Doneger Group. Bordat, an English-speaking Italian, knows Smith's store and his upscale customers, so before Smith's visit, he sets up appointments with Italian vendors that he believes will fit Pockets's image.

When Smith is in Italy, Bordat accompanies him to the appointments and acts as a translator, negotiator, and accountant. Bordat informs Smith of the cost of importing the merchandise into the United States, taking into account duty, freight, insurance, processing costs, and so forth.

Once the orders are placed, Bordat writes the contracts and follows up on delivery and quality control. The Doneger Group also acts as a home base for buyers like Smith, providing office space and services, travel advisers, and emergency aid. Bordat and his association continue to keep Smith abreast of what's happening on the Italian fashion scene through reports and constant communication. Without the help of a resident buying office, it would be difficult, if not impossible, for Smith to access the Italian wholesale market.

Reverse Auctions Rather than negotiating with a specific manufacturer to produce the merchandise, some retailers use reverse auctions to get quality private-label merchandise at low prices.[21] In traditional auctions like those conducted on eBay, there is one seller and many buyers. Auctions conducted by retailer buyers of private-label merchandise are called **reverse auctions** because there is one buyer (the retailer) and many potential sellers (the manufacturing firms). In a reverse auction, the retail buyer provides a specification for what it wants to a group of potential vendors. The competing vendors then bid on the price at which they are willing to sell until the auction is over. However, the retailer is not required to place an order with the lowest bidder. The retailer can choose to place an order at the offered price from whichever vendor the retailer feels will provide the merchandise in a timely manner and with the specified quality.

The most common use of reverse auctions is to buy the products and services used in retail operations rather than merchandise for resale. Some operating materials that are frequently bought through reverse auctions are store carpeting, fixtures, and supplies. However, reverse auctions also are being used by several retailers to procure store-brand merchandise, such as commodities and seasonal merchandise like lawn furniture.

Reverse auctions are not popular with vendors. Few vendors want to be anonymous contestants in bidding wars where price alone, not service or quality, seems to be the sole basis for winning the business. Strategic relationships are also difficult to nurture when the primary interactions with vendors are through electronic auctions.

NEGOTIATING WITH VENDORS

When buying national brands or sourcing private-label merchandise, buyers and firm employees responsible for sourcing typically enter into negotiations with suppliers. To understand how buyers negotiate with vendors, consider a hypothetical situation in which Carolyn Swigler, women's jeans buyer at Bloomingdale's, is preparing to meet with Dario Carvel, the salesperson from Juicy Couture, in his office in New York City. Swigler, after reviewing the merchandise during the women's wear market week in New York, is ready to buy Juicy Couture's spring line, but she has some merchandising problems that have yet to be resolved from last season.

LO 12-4

Understand how retailers prepare for and conduct negotiations with their vendors.

Knowledge Is Power

The more Carolyn Swigler knows about her situation and Juicy Couture's, as well as the trends in the marketplace, the more effective she will be during the negotiations. First, Swigler assesses the relationship she has with the vendor. Although Swigler and Carvel have met only a few times in the past, their companies have had a long, profitable relationship. A sense of trust and mutual respect has been established, which Swigler feels will lead to a productive meeting.

Although Juicy Couture jeans have been profitable for Bloomingdale's in the past, three styles sold poorly last season. Swigler plans to ask Carvel to let her return some merchandise. Swigler knows from past experience that Juicy Couture normally doesn't allow merchandise to be returned but does provide **markdown money**—funds vendors give retailers to cover lost gross margin dollars due to the markdowns needed to sell unpopular merchandise.

Vendors and their representatives are excellent sources of market information. They generally know what is and isn't selling. Providing good, timely information about the market is an indispensable and inexpensive marketing research tool. So Swigler plans to spend at least part of the meeting talking to Carvel about market trends.

Just as Carvel can provide market information to Swigler, she can provide information to him. For example, on one of her buying trips to Japan, she found jeans in a great new wash made by a small Japanese firm on old selvage looms. She bought a pair and gave them to Carvel, who passed it along to Juicy Couture's designers. They used the jeans to develop a new wash that was a big success.

Swigler also knows that Carvel will want her to buy some of the newest and most avant-garde designs in Juicy Couture's spring product line. Carvel knows that many U.S. buyers go to market in New York and that most stop at Bloomingdale's to see what's new, what's selling, and how it's displayed. Thus, Carvel wants to make sure that Juicy Couture is well represented at Bloomingdale's.

Negotiation Issues

In addition to taking care of last season's leftover merchandise, Swigler is prepared to discuss six issues during the upcoming meeting: (1) prices and gross margin, (2) additional markup opportunities, (3) terms of purchase, (4) exclusivity, (5) advertising allowances, and (6) transportation.

Prices and Gross Margin   Of course, Swigler wants to buy the merchandise at a low price so that she will have a high gross margin. In contrast, Carvel wants to sell the jeans at a higher price because he is concerned about Juicy Couture's own margins. Two factors that affect the price and gross margin are margin guarantees and slotting allowances.

Margin Guarantees by Providing Markdown Money   Swigler, like most buyers, has a gross margin goal for each merchandise category that is quantified in her merchandise budget plans (see Appendix 11A at the end of Chapter 11). The wholesale price Swigler negotiates for the Juicy Couture merchandise might enable her to achieve her gross margin goal. However, if the merchandise does not sell as expected, Swigler might have to put the items on sale, and she will not make her margin goal. Faced with this uncertainty, Swigler, and other buyers, may seek a commitment from Juicy Couture to "guarantee" that she will realize her gross margin goal on marked-down merchandise by providing Bloomingdale's with markdown money to make up the lost margin due to the markdown.

Carvel, like many vendors, might be willing to provide this gross margin guarantee. However, Carvel is concerned that Swigler might not aggressively promote Juicy Couture's merchandise if she knows that her gross margin is guaranteed. Thus, Carvel will offer the guarantee only in exchange for a commitment from Swigler that she will feature Juicy Couture merchandise in the store and advertise the product line.

Slotting Fees   In addition to negotiating the wholesale price, supermarket buyers often negotiate slotting fees. **Slotting fees**, or **slotting allowances**, are charges imposed by a retailer to stock a new item. When a vendor agrees to pay that fee, the retailer will stock the product for a period of time, assess its sales and margin, and, if it is successful, continue to offer the product after the trial period. For example, when Kraft wants to introduce a new product, supermarket chains might charge between $1 million and $2 million for a national rollout to stock the product. The fee varies, depending on the nature of the product and the relative power of the retailer. Products with low brand loyalty pay the highest slotting allowances. Likewise, large supermarket chains can demand higher slotting allowances than can small, independent retailers.

Vendors may view slotting allowances as extortion, and small vendors believe these fees preclude their access to retail stores. However, retailers and most economists argue that slotting allowances are a useful method for retailers to determine which new products merit inclusion in their assortment. The vendor has more information than the retailer about the quality of its new product. Thus, the slotting fee is a method for getting the vendor to reveal this private information. If the new product is good, the vendor will be willing to pay the fee because the vendor knows that the product will sell and generate adequate margins during the trial period. However, a vendor promoting a poor product will be reluctant to pay the fee.[22]

Additional Markup Opportunities   At times in the past, Juicy Couture has offered Swigler discounted prices to take excess merchandise. The excessive merchandise arises from order cancellations, returned merchandise from other retailers, or simply an overly optimistic sales forecast. Although Swigler can realize higher-than-normal gross margins on this merchandise or put the merchandise on sale and pass the savings on to customers, Bloomingdale's has to preserve its image as a fashion leader, and thus Swigler is not very interested in any excess inventory that Juicy Couture has to offer.

Terms of Purchase   Swigler would like to negotiate for a long period in which to pay for merchandise. A long payment period improves Bloomingdale's cash flow, lowers its liabilities (accounts payable), and can reduce its interest expense if it is borrowing money from financial institutions to pay for its inventory. But Juicy Couture also has its own financial objectives it wants to accomplish and thus would like to be paid soon after it delivers the merchandise.

Exclusivity   Retailers often negotiate with vendors for an exclusive arrangement so that no other retailer can sell the same item or brand. Through an exclusive arrangement, the retailer can differentiate itself from competitors and realize higher margins due to reduced price competition. In some cases, vendors also benefit by making sure that the image of retailers selling their merchandise is consistent with their brand image. For example, Prada might want to give exclusive rights for its apparel to only one store in a major market, such as Neiman Marcus. In addition, an exclusive arrangement offers a monopoly to the retailer and thus a strong incentive to promote the item.

In fashion merchandise categories, being the first retailer in a market to carry certain products helps that retailer hold a fashion-leader image and achieve a differential advantage. Swigler wants her shipment of the new spring line to arrive as early in the season as possible and would like to have some jeans styles and washes that won't be sold to competing retailers. In contrast, Juicy Couture wants to have its products sold by many different retailers to maximize its sales.

Advertising Allowances   Retailers often share the cost of advertising through a cooperative arrangement with vendors known as **cooperative (co-op) advertising**— a program undertaken by a vendor in which the vendor agrees to pay for all or part of a pricing promotion. As a fashion leader, Bloomingdale's advertises heavily. Swigler would like Juicy Couture to support an advertising program with a generous advertising allowance.

Transportation   Transportation costs can be substantial, though this concern is less prominent for Juicy Couture jeans because its merchandise has a high unit price and low weight. Nonetheless, the question of who pays to ship merchandise from the vendor to the retailer remains a significant negotiating point.

Now that some of the issues involved in the negotiation between Juicy Couture and Bloomingdale's are on the table, the next section presents some tips for effective negotiations.

Tips for Effective Negotiating[23]

Have at Least as Many Negotiators as the Vendor   Retailers have a psychological advantage at the negotiating table if the vendor is outnumbered. At the very least, retailers want the negotiating teams to be the same size. Swigler plans to invite her divisional merchandise manager (DMM) to the discussion if Carvel comes with his sales manager.

Choose a Good Place to Negotiate   Swigler may have an advantage in the upcoming meeting because it will be in her office. She'll have ready access to information, plus secretarial and supervisory assistance. From a psychological perspective, people generally feel more comfortable and confident in familiar surroundings. However, Swigler also might get more out of the negotiation if Carvel feels comfortable. In the end, selecting the location for a negotiation is an important decision.

Be Aware of Real Deadlines   Swigler recognizes that Carvel must go back to his office with an order in hand because he has a quota to meet by the end of the month. She also knows that she must get markdown money or permission to return the unsold jeans by the end of the week or she won't have sufficient open-to-buy funds to cover the orders she wishes to place. Recognizing these deadlines will help Swigler come to closure quickly in the upcoming negotiation.

Separate the People from the Problem   Suppose Swigler starts the meeting with, "Dario, you know we've been friends for a long time. I have a personal favor to ask. Would you mind taking back $10,000 in shirts?" This personal plea puts Carvel in an uncomfortable situation. Swigler's personal relationship with Carvel isn't the issue here and shouldn't become part of the negotiation. An equally detrimental scenario would be for Swigler to say, "Dario, your line is terrible. I can hardly give the stuff away. I want you to take back $10,000 in jeans. After all, you're dealing with Bloomingdale's. If you don't take this junk back, you can forget about ever doing business with us again." Threats usually don't work in negotiations. They put the other party on the defensive. Threats may actually cause negotiations to break down, in which case no one wins.

Insist on Objective Information   The best way to separate the people from the business issues is to rely on objective information. Swigler must know exactly how many jeans need to be returned to Juicy Couture or how much markdown money is necessary to maintain her gross margin. If Carvel argues from an emotional perspective, Swigler will stick to the numbers. For instance, suppose that after Swigler presents her position, Carvel says that he'll get into trouble if he takes back the merchandise or provides markdown money. With the knowledge that Juicy Couture has provided relief in similar situations in the past, Swigler should ask what Juicy Couture's policy is regarding customer overstock problems. She should also show Carvel a summary of Bloomingdale's buying activity with Juicy Couture over the past few seasons. Using this approach, Swigler forces Carvel to acknowledge that providing assistance in this overstock situation—especially if it has been done in the past—is a small price to pay for a long-term profitable relationship.

Invent Options for Mutual Gain   Inventing multiple options is part of the planning process, but knowing when and how much to give, or give up, requires quick thinking at the bargaining table, and, as such, should be decided in advance, whenever possible. Consider Swigler's overstock problem. Her objective is to get the merchandise out of her inventory without significantly hurting her gross margin. Carvel's objective is to maintain a healthy, yet profitable, relationship with Bloomingdale's. Thus, Swigler must invent options that could satisfy both parties, such as offering to buy some of Juicy Couture's most avant-garde jeans in return for markdown money for her excess inventory.

Let Them Do the Talking   There's a natural tendency for one person to continue to talk if the other person involved in the conversation doesn't respond. If used properly, this phenomenon can work to the negotiator's advantage. Suppose Swigler asks Carvel for special financial support for Bloomingdale's Christmas catalog. Carvel begins with a qualified no and cites all the reasons he can't cooperate. But Swigler doesn't say a word. Although Carvel appears nervous, he continues to talk. Eventually, he comes around to a yes. In negotiations, those who break the silence first lose.

Know How Far to Go   There's a fine line between negotiating too hard and walking away from the table without an agreement. If Swigler negotiates too aggressively for the markdown money, better terms of purchase, and a strong advertising allowance, the management of Juicy Couture may decide that other retailers are more worthy of early deliveries and the best styles. Carvel may not be afraid to say no if Swigler pushes him beyond a legal, ethical, profitable relationship.

Don't Burn Bridges   Even if Swigler gets few additional concessions from Carvel, she shouldn't be abusive or resort to threats. Bloomingdale's may not want to stop doing business with Juicy Couture on the basis of this one encounter. From a personal perspective, the world of retailing is relatively small. Swigler and Carvel may meet at the negotiating table again, possibly both working for different companies. Neither can afford to be known in the trade as unfair, rude, or worse.

Don't Assume   Many issues are raised and resolved in any negotiating session. To be certain there are no misunderstandings, participants should orally review the outcomes at the end of the session. Swigler and Carvel should both summarize the session in writing as soon as possible after the meeting.

STRATEGIC RELATIONSHIPS

Chapter 5 emphasized that maintaining strong vendor relationships is an important way to develop a sustainable competitive advantage. Chapters 9 and 11 discussed some of the ways partnering relationships can improve information exchange, planning, and the management of supply chains. For example, a vendor-managed inventory system cannot operate effectively without the vendor and retailer making a commitment to work together and invest in the relationship.[24] In this section, we examine how retailers develop strategic relationships and the characteristics of successful long-term relationships.

LO 12-5

Determine why retailers build strategic relationships with their vendors.

Defining Strategic Relationships

Traditionally, relationships between retailers and vendors have focused on haggling over how to split up a profit pie.[25] The relationships were basically win–lose encounters because when one party got a larger portion of the pie, the other party got a smaller portion. Both parties were interested exclusively in their own profits and unconcerned about the other party's welfare. These relationships continue to be common, especially when the products being bought are commodities and have limited impact on the retailers' performance. In these situations, there is no benefit to the retailer from entering into a strategic relationship.

A **strategic relationship**, also called a **partnering relationship**, emerges when a retailer and vendor are committed to maintaining the relationship over the long term and investing in opportunities that are mutually beneficial to both parties. In this relationship, it is important for the partners to take risks to expand the profit pie to give the relationship a strategic advantage over other companies. In addition, the parties have a long-term perspective: They are willing to make short-term sacrifices because they know that they will get their fair share in the long run.[26]

The Danish design firm Marimekko has a strategic partnership with Target. They work together on their exclusive branding program.

© Neil Rasmus/BFA/REX/Shutterstock

Strategic relationships are win–win relationships. Both parties benefit because the size of the profit pie increases. Both the retailer and the vendor increase their sales and profits, because the parties in strategic relationships work together to develop and exploit joint opportunities. They depend on and trust each other heavily. They share goals and agree on how to accomplish those goals, and they thus reduce the risks of investing in the relationship and sharing confidential information. Even as the power in supply chains has shifted from large manufacturers to large retailers such as Walmart and Target, the relationships are generally not adversarial. Instead, these supply chain partners share point-of-sale data and collaborate and cooperate on issues such as which items to buy, how much, and when. As a result of these collaborative efforts, financial performance throughout the supply chain has been enhanced.[27]

For example, when the Danish design firm Marimekko embarked on an exclusive branding program with Target, it worked together with its merchandising team to determine its customers' needs, likes, and dislikes.[28] Then it jointly developed an assortment and pricing strategy that is expected to be much more successful than would have been possible if the two sides had worked separately and just negotiated a quantity and price. To sustain their successful momentum, they will need to share trends in the market and agree to respond quickly when a change occurs or when a product should be produced in a short time.

A strategic relationship is like a marriage. When businesses enter strategic relationships, they're wedded to their partners for better or worse. For example, Spain-based fast-fashion retailer Zara manufactures about 40 percent of its finished garments with the help of about 450 independently owned workshops located near the corporate headquarters that sew precut fabric into finished garments. Most of these relatively small workshops have had long-term relationships with Zara. Zara provides them with technology, logistics, and financial support, as well as other types of assistance. In return, the workshops support Zara's mission of being able to quickly provide women and men in 88 countries with relatively inexpensive fashion apparel. Like any supplier, these small workshops sometimes miss a deadline or make a mistake on a garment. But as in a marriage, Zara doesn't dump them and move on to someone else. It works with them to make things work.[29] Another company that works closely with its vendors, Zappos, is discussed in Retailing View 12.3.

RETAILING VIEW   Zappos Values Relationships with Its Vendors, the Merchandise Experts   **12.3**

Founded in 1999, and acquired by Amazon in 2009, Zappos is best known as an online shoe retailer. Through its emphasis on customer service, it has grown into the largest shoe retailer in the world. It may sell shoes, clothing, and more, but the "secret sauce" that has led to its blockbuster success has less to do with the products Zappos sells and more to do with the relationships it builds—with customers, employees, and every supplier with which it deals. Its customer service and resulting customer satisfaction are legendary. For employees, its emphasis on relationships is evidenced by Zappos's consistent rating as one of the best companies to work for, buoyed by its offerings of benefits such as onsite "laughter yoga" classes and opportunities for every employee to pitch new business ideas.

Strong vendor relations may be even more key to the success of Zappos. Vendors feel valued, respected, and appreciated in all aspects of the business relationship. When vendors come to visit, a Zappos representative picks them up at the airport using the corporate shuttle, and snacks and drinks await them when they arrive. New vendors receive a tour of the facilities. If a vendor contacts Zappos, the company either calls back the same day or responds to e-mails within a few hours. When they dine out together, Zappos always picks up the bill. Its signals of appreciation don't stop with one-on-one visits; Zappos hosts appreciation events for its vendors year-round. The last Friday of every month, Zappos hosts a golf tournament for vendors, and once a year, it hosts a lavish vendor appreciation party.

Cleary, Zappos is interested in strong vendor relationships. But what exactly does the company get out of it? What's the return on its investment? Normally, retailers seek to beat vendors in negotiations, to get the lowest prices and best terms. Zappos believes, instead, that strong relationships lead to better partnerships. Instead of adversarial negotiations, it embraces transparency. Vendors gain access to information on Zappos's inventory, sales, and profitability. With these collaborative efforts, it seeks to encourage shared risks and rewards, and thus shared goals. With shared goals also come greater accountability and, at the end of the day, more committed vendors.

In a time when most retailers are trying to reduce their costs by cutting back on employee and vendor benefits, Zappos has taken the opposite strategy. As a top online retailer, its emphasis on building strong relationships with its vendors has resulted in a unique competitive advantage. Instead of buyers needing to wrestle with its vendors, Zappos has converted them into advocates for the company.

Sources: "About Us," Zappos, about.zappos.com; Tom Rogers, "How Zappos Gets More from Its Vendors," *VendorCentric*, April 23, 2015; Tom Ryan, "Zappos Makes Nice with Vendors," *RetailWire*, March 2, 2011; Tony Hsieh, "A Lesson from Zappos: Follow the Golden Rule," *HBR Blog*, June 4, 2010; Aida Ahmed, "Zappos Ranks No. 11 on List of Best Companies to Work For," *VegasInc*, January 19, 2012.

Building Partnering Relationships

Although not all retailer–vendor relationships should or do become strategic partnerships, the development of strategic partnerships tends to go through a series of phases characterized by increasing levels of involvement: (1) awareness, (2) exploration, (3) expansion, and (4) commitment.

Awareness   In the awareness stage, no transactions have taken place. This phase might begin with the buyer seeing some interesting merchandise at a retail market or an ad in a trade magazine. The reputation and image of the vendor can play an important role in determining if the buyer moves to the next stage.

Exploration   During the exploration phase, the buyer and vendor begin to explore the potential benefits and costs of a partnership. At this point, the buyer may make a small purchase and try to test the demand for the merchandise in several stores. In addition, the buyer will get information about how easy it is to work with the vendor.

Expansion   Eventually, the buyer has collected enough information about the vendor to consider developing a longer-term relationship. The buyer and the vendor determine if there is the potential for a win–win relationship. They begin to work on joint promotional programs, and the amount of merchandise sold increases.

Commitment   If both parties continue to find the relationship mutually beneficial, it moves to the commitment stage and becomes a strategic relationship. The buyer and vendor then make significant investments in the relationship and develop a long-term perspective toward it.

It is difficult for retailer–vendor relationships to be as committed as some supplier–manufacturer relationships. Manufacturers can enter into monogamous (sole-source) relationships with other manufacturers. However, an important function of retailers is to provide an assortment of merchandise for their customers. Thus, they must always deal with multiple, sometimes competing suppliers.

Maintaining Strategic Relationships

The four foundations of successful strategic relationships are (1) mutual trust, (2) common goals, (3) open communication, and (4) credible commitments.

Mutual Trust   The glue in a strategic relationship is trust. **Trust** is a belief that a partner is honest (reliable and stands by its word) and benevolent (concerned about the other party's welfare).[30] When vendors and buyers trust each other, they are more willing to share relevant ideas, clarify goals and problems, and communicate efficiently. Information shared between the parties becomes increasingly comprehensive, accurate, and timely. There is less need for the vendor and buyer to constantly monitor and check up on each other's actions, because each believes the other will not take advantage, even when given the opportunity.[31] If Walmart's sustainability initiatives described in Retailing View 12.4 are to be achieved, it is important for Walmart to trust its vendors, and vice versa.

Common Goals   Vendors and buyers must have common goals for a successful relationship to develop.[32] Shared goals give both members of the relationship an incentive to pool their strengths and abilities and exploit potential opportunities between them. They also create an assurance that the other partner will not do anything to hinder goal achievement within the relationship.

For example, Walmart and its vendors have recognized that it was in their common interest to develop and sell products that have a positive impact on the environment. Walmart cannot demand that its vendors take on sustainability programs that are so expensive that they won't make money, and its vendors must try to accommodate the

---

12.4 RETAILING VIEW   It Isn't Easy to Sell to Walmart

Walmart is known for its low prices—and for driving its vendors to tears to get them. Now it is pressuring its vendors to also supply it with environmentally friendly merchandise, with labels to prove it. Suppliers who have taken steps to become more sustainable now carry a "sustainability leader" badge on Walmart's website. To measure how a vendor's products are doing, Walmart uses its sustainability index that simultaneously takes several issues into consideration.

Walmart has laid out three goals that it aspires to achieve: to use 100 percent renewable energy, to reduce its waste production to zero, and to market products that will sustain both customers and the environment. These are very lofty aspirations that have resulted in multiple, concrete goals.

Walmart is also requiring its top 200 factories to become 20 percent more energy efficient, a feat that many experts believe may be impossible, even with Walmart's help. Initial results are promising, though. For example, Jiangsu Redbud Dyeing Technology in China has cut its coal consumption by one-tenth and is attempting to cut its toxic emissions to zero.

But Walmart hasn't always been touted as such a good corporate citizen. In the 1990s, it came to light that workers at some factories producing clothing for Walmart were subjected to inhumane conditions. More recently, two government organizations accused Walmart of buying from 15 factories that engage in abuse and labor violations, including child labor, 19-hour shifts, and below-subsistence wages. Walmart and other companies have also been accused of dumping hazardous waste in Oklahoma City.

Some wonder why Walmart is attempting to position itself as the retail industry's sustainability leader. Certainly, initiatives that show that it is a good corporate citizen enhance its image. But Walmart expects that these initiatives will be good for business as well. Its customers, especially those born between 1980 and 2000, are increasingly concerned about how the products they use affect the environment and the people who produce them. Also, Walmart believes that many of these initiatives will help streamline supply chain processes and, therefore, provide additional financial benefits to its suppliers and customers.

Sources: Lauren Hepler, "How Walmart's Green Label Aims to Drive Supplier 'Race to the Top,'" *GreenBiz*, February 25, 2015; "Beyond 50 Years: Building a Sustainable Future," *Walmart 2012 Global Responsibility Report*; http://sustainabilitycases.kenexcloud.org/about; http://corporate.walmart.com/global-responsibility/environment-sustainability/sustainability-index.

demands of its biggest customer. With a common goal, Walmart and its suppliers have an incentive to cooperate because they know that by doing so, both can achieve their common sustainability goals and still make profits.

Common goals also help sustain the relationship when goals are not realized according to plan. If, for instance, a vendor fails to reach an acceptable score on Walmart's sustainability index but has made significant progress, Walmart won't suddenly call off the whole arrangement. Instead, Walmart is likely to work harder to help the vendor raise its score and remain in the relationship because Walmart knows that it and the vendor are committed to the same goals in the long run.

Open Communication   To share information, develop sales forecasts together, coordinate deliveries, and achieve their sustainability common goals, Walmart and its vendors must have open and honest communication. This requirement may sound easy in principle, but most businesses don't like to share information with their business partners. They believe it is none of the other's business. But open, honest communication is a key to developing successful and profitable relationships.[33] Buyers and vendors in a relationship need to understand what is driving each other's business, their roles in the relationship, each firm's strategies, and any problems that arise over the course of the relationship. The CPFR (collaborative planning, forecasting, and replenishment) systems described in Chapter 9 in which retailers and their vendors share forecasts and collaborate on replenishment issues are an example of open communications.

Credible Commitments   Successful relationships develop because both parties make credible commitments. Credible commitments are tangible investments in the relationship. They go beyond just making the hollow statement "I want to be your partner." Credible commitments involve spending money to improve products or services and, in the case of Walmart and its vendors, taking mutual steps to improve the sustainability index. For example, the goal of reducing Jiangsu Redbud Dyeing Technology's toxic emissions in China is a joint effort and investment by Walmart and Jiangsu.

Regardless of how strong the relationships between retailers and their vendors are, they are always complicated. And in any complicated business relationship, legal, ethical, and social responsibility issues can arise. These issues are discussed in the next section.

LEGAL, ETHICAL, AND SOCIAL RESPONSIBILITY ISSUES FOR BUYING MERCHANDISE

Legal and Ethical Issues

This section reviews some practices that arise in buyer–vendor negotiations that may have legal and/or ethical implications, and it looks at some ways that retailers are becoming more socially responsible in their buying practices.

LO 12-6

Indicate the legal, ethical, and social responsibility issues involved in buying merchandise.

Counterfeit Merchandise   Selling counterfeit merchandise can negatively affect a retailer's image and its relationship with the vendor of the legitimate brand. **Counterfeit merchandise** includes goods made and sold without the permission of the owner of a trademark or copyright. Trademarks and copyrights are **intellectual property**, that is, intangible and created by intellectual (mental) effort as opposed to physical effort. A **trademark** is any mark, word, picture, device, or nonfunctional design associated with certain merchandise (e.g., the crown on a Rolex watch, the red Levi's tag on the back pocket of a pair of jeans). A **copyright** protects the original work of authors, painters, sculptors, musicians, and others who produce works of artistic or intellectual merit. This book is copyrighted, so these sentences cannot be used by anyone without the consent of the copyright owners.

It is illegal for this "street retailer" to sell counterfeit watches because it violates the watch manufacturers' rights to control the use of their trademarks.

© Spencer Platt/Getty Images

The nature of counterfeiting has changed over time. Counterfeit name-brand merchandise, such as women's handbags or dresses, has improved in quality, making these items more expensive and difficult to distinguish from the real merchandise. In response, some luxury brands have begun taking legal action against the online retailers that they believe facilitate the selling of counterfeit goods. For example, in 2015 Gucci and several other luxury brands filed a lawsuit against the Chinese e-commerce giant Alibaba for selling counterfeit merchandise. These charges come after Alibaba promised luxury brands that if they open a store on TMall, its vendor-supplied site, it would actively work to crack down on counterfeits. Although the suit was dismissed in court, the Chinese government has still found that Alibaba has not done enough to fight counterfeits.[34]

Also, there is a thriving business in counterfeit information products such as music, software, and Blu-rays. This type of merchandise is attractive to counterfeiters because it has a relatively high unit value, is easy to duplicate and transport, and prompts high consumer demand. The ease of illegally downloading and distributing music means that neither the record label nor the artist receives any money for their investment, work, or talent, and thus both may be less motivated to develop and produce music. Although the music isn't counterfeit, illegal downloading represents an illegal theft of intellectual property. In 2016 a study found that about 57 million Americans download music illegally.[35]

Gray-Market, Diverted, and Black-Market Merchandise   **Gray-market goods**, also known as **parallel imports**, involve the flow of merchandise through distribution channels, usually across international borders, other than those authorized or intended by the manufacturer or producer.[36] In the perfume category, designer fragrance suppliers in the United States sell their brands such as Davidoff, Dolce & Gabbana, or Calvin Klein perfumes directly to department stores and other high-end retailers. They do not sell to Walmart, CVS, or Target. However, in Europe and Asia, most suppliers sell their wares to distributors and wholesalers, which can earn profits by selling some of these fragrances to mass retailers in the United States. Thus the perfumes go from U.S. suppliers to international distributors, then back to U.S. mass merchandisers before reaching U.S. consumers. Still, the pricing system generally allows the prices for these products to remain lower than the prices charged by department stores and perfumeries for the luxury brands. Retailers vigorously assert that they have done nothing wrong in procuring the products, and they enjoy the nice bump in sales they can earn from selling a bottle of Hugo Boss perfume for something like $30—less than it would cost at Bloomingdale's, but a high-ticket item for a discount retailer. If shoppers see a famous luxury brand for sale at Target or Walmart, however, they may start to perceive the brand as common or conventional, rather than high-end or premium. Thus, for example, Procter & Gamble, which owns the rights to Hugo Boss, Gucci, and Dolce & Gabbana perfumes, has threatened to stop selling to distributors that turn around and provide the fragrances they receive to unauthorized retailers. Davidoff perfumes even sued CVS to stop it from selling gray-market versions of its Cool Water perfumes in tampered packaging.[37]

Diverted merchandise is similar to gray-market merchandise except there need not be distribution across international borders. Suppose, for instance, that the fragrance manufacturer Givenchy grants an exclusive scent to Saks Fifth Avenue. The Saks buyer has excess inventory and sells it at a low price to a discount retailer in the United States, such as an off-price retailer. In this case, the merchandise has been diverted from its legitimate channel of distribution, and Saks would be referred to as the diverter.

While Saks may benefit from diverting its excess inventory to an off-price retailer, the fragrance manufacturer is concerned about gray markets and diversions. Making the product available at discount stores at low prices may reduce the vendor's brand image and the service normally provided with the brand. So, though such practices are usually legal, vendors seek to minimize gray-market and diverted merchandise.

Vendors engage in other activities to avoid gray-market/diversion problems, though. They require that all of their retail and wholesale customers sign a contract stipulating that they will not engage in gray marketing. If a retailer is found in violation of the agreement, the vendor will refuse to deal with it in the future. Another strategy is to produce different versions of products for different markets. For instance, McGraw-Hill sells a different version of this textbook in India than it sells in the United States.

A **black market** occurs when consumer goods are scarce, such as water or gasoline after a natural disaster; heavily taxed, such as cigarettes or alcohol; or illegal, such as drugs or arms. We rarely see black-market merchandise sold through legitimate channels in the United States.

Terms and Conditions of Purchase   The Robinson-Patman Act, passed by the U.S. Congress in 1936, potentially restricts the prices and terms that vendors can offer to retailers. The act makes it illegal for vendors to offer different terms and conditions to different retailers for the same merchandise and quantity. Sometimes called the Anti-Chain-Store Act, it was passed to protect independent retailers from chain-store competition. Thus, if a vendor negotiates a good deal on the issues discussed in the previous section (price, advertising allowance, markdown money, transportation), the Robinson-Patman Act requires that the vendor offer the same terms and conditions to other retailers.

However, vendors can offer different terms to retailers for the same merchandise and quantities if the costs of manufacturing, selling, or delivery are different. The cost of manufacturing is usually the same, but selling and delivery could be more expensive for some retailers. For example, vendors may incur larger transportation expenses due to smaller shipments to independent retailers.

Different prices can also be offered if the retailers are providing different functions. For example, a large retailer can get a lower price if its distribution centers store the merchandise or its stores provide different services valued by customers. In addition, lower prices can be offered to meet competition and dispose of perishable merchandise.[38]

Commercial Bribery   **Commercial bribery** occurs when a vendor or its agent offers or a buyer asks for "something of value" to influence purchase decisions. Say a salesperson for a ski manufacturer takes a sporting goods retail buyer to lunch at a fancy private club and then proposes a ski weekend in Vail. These gifts could be construed as bribes or kickbacks, which are illegal unless the buyer's manager is informed of them. To avoid such problems, many retailers forbid employees to accept any gifts from vendors. Other retailers have a policy that it is fine to accept limited entertainment or token gifts, such as flowers or wine for the holidays. As we discussed in Retailing View 12.3, Zappos stops potential commercial bribery in its tracks by bestowing free lunches and other favors on its vendors, rather than accepting anything from vendors. In any case, retailers want their buyers to decide on purchases solely on the basis of what is best for the retailer.

Chargebacks   A **chargeback** is a practice used by retailers in which they deduct money from the amount they owe a vendor. Retailers often use a chargeback when a vendor did not meet the agreed-on terms, for example, if it improperly applied labels to shipping containers or merchandise or sent shipments that had missing items or were late. Chargebacks are especially difficult for vendors because once the money is deducted from an invoice and the invoice is marked "paid," it is difficult to dispute the claim and get the amount back. Vendors sometimes feel that the chargebacks retailers take are not justifiable and thus are unethical.

Buybacks   Similar to slotting allowances, **buybacks**, also known as **stocklifts** or **lift-outs**, are activities engaged in by vendors and retailers to get old products out of retail stores and new products in their place. Specifically, in a buyback situation, either a retailer allows a vendor to create space for its merchandise by "buying back" a competitor's inventory and removing it from the retailer's system, or the retailer forces a vendor to buy back slow-moving merchandise. A vendor with significant market power can violate federal antitrust laws if it stocklifts from a competitor so often that it shuts the competitor out of a market, but such cases are difficult to prove.

Exclusive Dealing Agreements   **Exclusive dealing agreements** occur when a vendor restricts a retailer to carrying only its products and nothing from competing vendors. For example, Ford may require that its dealers sell only Ford cars and no cars made by General Motors. The effect of such arrangements on competition is determined by the market power of the vendor. For example, it may be illegal for a market leader like Coca-Cola to sell its products to a small supermarket chain only if the chain agrees not to sell a less popular cola product like RC Cola.

Tying Contract   A **tying contract** exists when a vendor requires that a retailer take a product it doesn't necessarily desire (the tied product) to ensure that it can buy a product it does desire (the tying product). Tying contracts are illegal if they substantially lessen competition or tend to create a monopoly. But the complaining party has the burden of proof. Thus, it is typically legal for a vendor to require that a buyer buy all items in its product line. For example, if a gift store sued a postcard manufacturer for requiring that it purchase as many "local view" postcards (the tied product) as it did licensed Disney character postcards (the tying product), the court would probably dismiss the case because the retailer would be unable to prove a substantial lessening of competition.

Refusal to Deal   The practice of refusing to deal (buy or sell to) can be viewed from both vendors' and retailers' perspectives. Generally, both vendors and retailers have the right to deal or refuse to deal with anyone they choose. But there are exceptions to this general rule when there's evidence of anticompetitive conduct by one or more firms that wield market power. A vendor may refuse to sell to a particular retailer, but it cannot do so for the sole purpose of benefiting a competing retailer. For example, Mattel decided not to offer certain popular Barbie packages to wholesale clubs. This action in itself would not have been illegal. However, it was determined that Mattel agreed to do so as part of a conspiracy among 10 toy manufacturers orchestrated by Toys "R" Us to prevent wholesale clubs from underselling the same toy packages that Toys "R" Us sold. The refusal to deal then became an illegal group boycott.[39]

Corporate Social Responsibility

Corporate social responsibility (CSR) describes the voluntary actions taken by a company to address the ethical, social, and environmental impacts of its business operations. Retailers act socially responsibly in many ways, from giving to charity to donating time to philanthropic community activities to supporting the rights of minority groups to adopting responsible marketing and sales practices. Recently, however, retailers have been increasing their efforts to buy merchandise in a socially responsible way.

Whole Foods considers local to be anything produced within the same state as one of its stores. In larger states, like California, Whole Foods also breaks the state into specific areas, such as The Bay Area. It requires that all its stores buy from at least four local farmers. It gives $25 million a year in low-interest loans to help small, local farmers and producers of grass-fed and humanely raised meat, poultry, and dairy animals.[40]

Some retailers are getting involved in **fair trade**, a socially responsible movement that ensures that producers receive fair prices for their products. Peet's Coffee offers a fair trade blend. Walmart is investing heavily in fair trade coffee, partially in response to its corporate philosophy that goes beyond "everyday low prices" to "doing well by doing good." Bono, the U2 lead singer and an activist, is selling his high-priced fair trade apparel line, Edun, to stores such as Saks Fifth Avenue and Nordstrom. Starbucks has made huge strides in fair trade production, such that in 2015, 99 percent of its coffee was either fair trade or CAFÉ (Coffee and Farmer Equity) certified, and it aims to reach 100 percent ethical sourcing.[41]

Home Depot is encouraging its suppliers to include their products in its Eco Options marketing campaign. Some products are obviously attractive to green customers, such as organic gardening products and high-efficiency light bulbs. But a number of less obvious products are also good for the environment. Home Depot also has introduced some new environmentally sensitive products into its assortment, including solar-powered landscape lighting, biodegradable peat pots, and paints that discharge fewer pollutants. Home Depot encourages its vendors to use

Home Depot is encouraging its suppliers to include their products in its Eco Options marketing campaign.

recyclable plastic or cardboard packaging.[42] Other retailers are demanding smaller, eco-friendly packages from their suppliers. Smaller packages save not only materials but also energy. Because more packages can be transported on a truck, the transportation cost per unit goes down. Several other manufacturers (Patagonia and Timberland), retailers (e.g., Walmart, JCPenney, H&M), and organizations involved in the supply chain (e.g., Environmental Protection Agency, Environmental Defense Fund) are cooperating to create the Sustainable Apparel Coalition. One of the coalition's key objectives is to create a database that summarizes the environmental issues associated with each manufacturer and its processes, such that ultimately the coalition can provide a score or ranking for each garment that consumers may consider.[43]

These initiatives and many others suggest a complicated business model. Are socially responsible activities good for business? Some are more expensive than traditional products and initiatives. Are consumers interested in or willing to pay the higher prices? Are firms really interested in improving the environment, or are they **greenwashing** (doing a green whitewash) or practicing **green sheen**, which is the disingenuous practice of marketing products or services as being environmentally friendly with the purpose of gaining public approval and sales rather than actually improving the environment. Consumers should question whether a firm is spending significantly more money or time advertising that it is **green** or that it operates with consideration for the environment rather than spending resources on environmentally sound practices.

SUMMARY

LO 12-1 Identify the branding options available to retailers.

Retailers can purchase national, store (private-label), and generic brands. Each type has its own relative advantages. Choosing appropriate brands and a branding strategy is an integral component of a firm's merchandise and assortment planning process.

LO 12-2 Describe how retailers buy national brands.

Buyers of manufacturer's brands attend trade shows and wholesale market centers to meet with vendors, view new merchandise, and place orders. Virtually every merchandise category has at least one annual trade show at which retailers and vendors meet.

LO 12-3 List the issues retailers consider when developing and sourcing store-branded merchandise internationally.

Buying merchandise sometimes is facilitated by resident buying offices. Market representatives of the resident buying offices facilitate merchandising purchases in foreign markets. The process for buying store brands or private-label merchandise can be more complicated than that for buying national brands because the retailer takes on some of the responsibilities that a national-brand manufacturer normally would have, such as designing and specifying products and selecting manufacturers to make the products. A large percentage of private-label merchandise is manufactured outside the United States. The cost, managerial, and ethical issues surrounding global sourcing decisions must be considered.

LO 12-4 Understand how retailers prepare for and conduct negotiations with their vendors.

Buyers of both national brands and store brands engage in negotiating a series of issues with their vendors, including prices and gross margin, additional markup opportunities, terms of purchase, exclusivity, advertising allowances, and transportation. Successful vendor relationships depend on planning for and being adept at negotiations.

LO 12-5 Determine why retailers build strategic relationships with their vendors.

Retailers that can successfully team up with their vendors can achieve a sustainable competitive advantage. There needs to be more than just a promise to buy and sell on a regular basis. Strategic relationships require trust, shared goals, strong communications, and a financial commitment.

LO 12-6 Indicate the legal, ethical, and social responsibility issues involved in buying merchandise.

Buyers need to be aware of ethical and legal issues that can guide them in their negotiations and purchase decisions. There are also problems associated with counterfeit and gray-market merchandise and issues that vendors face when selling to retailers, such as exclusive territories and tying contracts. Care should be taken by vendors when placing restrictions on which retailers they will sell to, what merchandise, how much, and at what price. Some retailers are taking giant steps toward being more socially responsible.

KEY TERMS

black market, *333*

buyback, *334*

chargeback, *334*

commercial bribery, *333*

cooperative (co-op) advertising, *325*

copycat brand, *316*

copyright, *331*

corporate social responsibility (CSR), *335*

counterfeit merchandise, *331*

diverted merchandise, *333*

duty, *322*

exclusive brand, *315*

exclusive dealing agreement, *334*

fair trade, *335*

family brand, *314*

generic brand, *316*

gray-market goods, *332*

green, *336*

green sheen, *336*

greenwashing, *336*

house brand, *315*

intellectual property, *331*

lift-out, *334*

manufacturer's brand, *314*

markdown money, *323*

market weeks, *318*

national brand, *314*

own brand, *315*

parallel imports, *332*

GET OUT AND DO IT!

1. **CONTINUING ASSIGNMENT** Go visit the retailer you have selected for the continuing assignment and perform an audit of its manufacturer's and store brands. Ask the manager to comment on the store's philosophy toward manufacturer's versus store brands. Why does it use store brands? Does it offer different store brands to appeal to different customer segments? Select three different merchandise categories. Compare the price of the same item for store versus manufacturer's brand. Has the percentage of store brands increased or decreased during the past five years? On the basis of what you see and hear, assess its branding strategy.

2. Go to the home page for the Private Label Manufacturers Association (PLMA), and read the "What Are Store Brands?" page, which can be found at http://plma.com/storeBrands/facts13.html. What are store-brand products? Who purchases store brands? Who makes store brands? What store brands are you purchasing on a regular basis?

DISCUSSION QUESTIONS AND PROBLEMS

1. Assume you have been hired to consult with Forever 21 on sourcing decisions for sportswear. What issues would you consider when deciding whether you should buy from Mexico or China or find a source within the United States?

2. What are the differences among counterfeit, gray-market, and black-market merchandise? Is the selling of this type of merchandise legal? Do you believe that selling these types of merchandise should be allowed? Provide a rationale for your position. Would you purchase a counterfeit wallet? What about a counterfeit car part or prescription medication?

3. What are the advantages and disadvantages of manufacturer's brands versus store brands? Consider both the retailer's and customer's perspectives.

4. Does your favorite clothing store have a store-brand strategy? If yes, how does it build store loyalty? If no, how could a store brand create loyalty?

5. Explain why a grocery store, such as Kroger, offers more than one tier of store brands within a particular product category.

6. Why have retailers found exclusive store brands to be an appealing branding option? Choose a department store, a discount store, and a grocery store. What exclusive store brands do they offer? How are they positioned in relation to their national-brand counterparts?

7. When you go shopping, in which product categories do you prefer store brands or national brands? Explain your preference.

8. What are retailers doing to be more socially responsible in buying merchandise? Why are they becoming more socially responsible? Do you buy products that you believe were produced in a socially responsible manner, even if they cost more?

9. You have decided that you don't want to take the final in this class. Explain how you would negotiate this request with the instructor. Consider place, deadlines, past relationship, possible objections, options for mutual gain, and how to maintain a professional relationship.

CHAPTER ENDNOTES

1. Steve Rowan, "Local Approach Works for Whole Foods," *RetailWire,* March 6, 2015.

2. Annie Gasparro and Leslie Josephs, "Whole Foods Calls the Shots for Startups," *The Wall Street Journal,* May 7, 2015.

3. Katarina Gustafsson, "Ikea Couches with Added Bling Boost Furniture Startups," *Bloomberg Businessweek,* February 18, 2014.

4. Leslie Josephs and Annie Gasparro, "Balance of Power Shifts in Groceries," *The Wall Street Journal,* March 26, 2015.

5. Christina Binkley, "Target Goes for Local Cool," *The Wall Street Journal,* July 15, 2015.

6. Jay Diamond, *Retail Buying,* 9th ed. (Upper Saddle River, NJ: Pearson, 2012).

7. Peter J. Boyle and E. Scott Lathrop, "The Value of Private Label Brands to U.S. Consumers: An Objective and Subjective Assessment," *Journal of Retailing and Consumer Services* 20 (January 2013), pp. 80–86.

8. www.plstorebrands.com/plmag-article-safeway_selective-3689.html.

9. Keith Lincoln and Lars Thomassen, *Private Label: Turning the Retail Brand Threat into Your Biggest Opportunity* (London: Kogan, 2009); John A. Quelch, "Brands vs. Private Labels: Fighting to Win," *Harvard Business Review,* March 3, 2009.

10. Phil Wahba, "J.C. Penney's Secret Comeback Sauce? Its Own Brands," *Fortune,* December 22, 2014.

11. Trade Show News Network (TSNN), www.tsnn.com.

12. The Fashion Center, www.fashioncenter.com.

13. Andrew Mach, "10 Cutting Edge Gadgets from the 2016 Consumer Electronics Show," *PBS NewsHour,* January 9, 2016.

14. "CES 2016 Fact Sheet," https://mms.businesswire.com/bwapps/mediaserver/ViewMedia?mgid=502407&vid=1.

15. McCormick Place, www.mccormickplace.com.

16. http://www.mgfsourcing.com/our-company/; Leonie Barrie, "US: Limited Brands Spins Off Mast Apparel Sourcing Unit," *Just-Style,* November 3, 2011.

17. "Hollander Home Fashions, LLC," Answers, www.answers.com/topic/hollander-home-fashions-corp.

18. JCPenney, 2016 10-K Report, filed with the Securities and Exchange Commission.

19. Bernice Hurst, "Turning Points 2008: Global Sourcing Not Always a Sure Winner," *RetailWire,* December 16, 2008.

20. "Annual Highlights—2015: A Year of Giving Back," https://www.lb.com/responsibility/community/annual-highlights.

21. Len Kaplan, "Is e-Sourcing for You," *InShare3,* November 2012; Marjolein C. J. Caniëls and Erik M. van Raaij, "Do All Suppliers Dislike Electronic Reverse Auctions?," *Journal of Purchasing and Supply Management* 15, no. 1 (March 2009), pp. 12–23; Alberto A. Gaggero, "Retailers Curtail Rising Costs through Private Label Procurement," *Internet Wire,* August 16, 2011; Cigdem A. Gumussoy and Fethi Calisir, "Understanding Factors Affecting E-Reverse Auction Use: An Integrative Approach," *Computers in Human Behavior* 25, no. 4 (2009), pp. 975–988.

22. Ravi S. Achrol, "Slotting Allowances: A Time Series Analysis of Aggregate Effects over Three Decades," *Journal of the Academy of Marketing Science* 40 (September 2012), pp. 673–694; Oystein Foros, Hans Jarle Kind, and Jan Yngve Sand, "Slotting Allowances and Manufacturers Retail Sales Effort," *Southern Economic Journal* (Southern Economic Association) 76, no. 1 (2009), pp. 266–282; David Hoffman, "Vendor Allowances in Retail Industry, Not Cut and Dry," *Chain Store Age,* July 29, 2009.

23. These guidelines are based on Roger Fisher, William Ury, and Bruce Patton, *Getting to Yes: Negotiating Agreements without Giving In* (New York: Penguin, 2011); Gavin Kennedy, *Negotiation: An A–Z Guide (Economist A–Z Guide)* (London: Economist Books, May 2009).

24. A. Parmigiani and M. Rivera-Santos, "Clearing a Path through the Forest: A Meta-Review of Interorganizational Relationships," *Journal of Management* 37 (2011), pp. 1108–1136; Stephen Samaha, Robert W. Palmatier, and Rajiv P. Dant, "Poisoning Relationships: Perceived Unfairness in Channels of Distribution," *Journal of Marketing* 75 (May 2011), pp. 99–117; Todd Arnold, Eric Fang, and Robert W. Palmatier, "The Effects of Customer Acquisition and Retention Orientations on Radical and Incremental Innovation Performance," *Journal of the Academy of Marketing Science* 39 (April 2011), pp. 234–251.

25. Matthew Hudson, "10 Tips to Negotiate Prices in Retail," *The Balance,* June 15, 2016, https://www.thebalance.com/how-to-negotiate-prices-and-more-2890063; Robert Johnston and Roy Staughton, "Establishing and Developing Strategic Relationships: The Role for Operations Managers," *International Journal of Operations & Production Management* 29, no. 6 (2009), pp. 564–590; Thomas Powers and William Reagan, "Factors Influencing Successful Buyer–Seller Relationships," *Journal of Business Research* 60 (December 2007), pp. 1234–1242.

26. Alicia Fiorletta, "Collaboration Becomes Key to Success for Retailers and Suppliers," *Retail Touch Points,* September 2, 2014; Gary L. Frazier, Elliot Maltz, Kersi D. Antia, and Aric Rindfleisch, "Distributor Sharing of Strategic Information with Suppliers," *Journal of Marketing* 73, no. 4 (2009), pp. 31–43; G. T. M. Hult, J. A. Mena, O. C. Ferrell, and L. K. Ferrell, "Stakeholder Marketing: A Definition and Conceptual Framework," *AMS Review* 1, no. 1 (2011). doi:10.1007/s13162-011-0002-5; Bill Donaldson and Tom O'Toole, *Strategic Market Relationships: From Strategy to Implementation,* 2nd ed. (Indianapolis: Wiley, 2007).

27. Christian Hofer, Yao Jin, Rodger Swanson, Matthew Waller, and Brent Williams, "The Impact of Key Retail Accounts on Supplier Performance: A Collaborative Perspective of Resource Dependency Theory," *Journal of Retailing* 88, no. 3 (2012), pp. 412–420.

28. https://corporate.target.com/article/2016/03/marimekko-for-target.

29. https://www.inditex.com/brands/zara; Zeynep Ton, Elena Corsi, and Vincent Dessain, "Zara: Managing Stores for Fast Fashion," Harvard Business School Publications, January 19, 2010.

30. Robert W. Palmatier, Mark Houston, Rajiv P. Dant, and Dhruv Grewal, "Relationship Velocity: Towards Developing a Theory of Relationship Dynamics," *Journal of Marketing* 77, no. 1 (2013) pp. 13–30; Robert W. Palmatier, *Relationship Marketing* (Cambridge, MA: Marketing Science Institute, 2008).

31. Plexus Consulting Group, *The Power of Partnership: Principles and Practices for Creating Strategic Relationships among Nonprofit Groups, For-Profit Organizations, and Government Entities* (Washington, DC: ASAE & The Center for Association Leadership and U.S. Chamber of Commerce, June 25, 2008).

32. Palmatier et al. "Relationship Velocity."

33. Hofer et al., "The Impact of Key Retail Accounts on Supplier Performance."

34. Nate Raymond, "U.S. Judge Dismisses Part of Alibaba Counterfeit Goods Lawsuit," Reuters, August 4, 2016; Carlos Tejada, "China Raps Alibaba for Fakes," *The Wall Street Journal,* January 28, 2015; Kathy Chu and Joanne Chiu, "Alibaba Cleans Up 'Gray Market' for Some Prestigious Brands," *The Wall Street Journal,* August 10, 2014.

35. James Geddes, "57 Million Americans Are Downloading Music Illegally: Study," *Tech Times,* February 29, 2016.

36. For a review, see David R. Sugden, *Gray Markets: Prevention, Detection and Litigation* (New York: Oxford University Press, 2009).

37. Serena Ng, "Luxury Perfume Makers Turn to Wal-Mart, Target," *The Wall Street Journal,* September 26, 2015.

38. Jane P. Mallor, A. James Barnes, Thomas Bowers, and Arlen W. Langvardt, *Business Law: The Ethical, Global, and E-Commerce Environment,* 15th ed. (New York: McGraw-Hill/ Irwin, 2013).

39. *In re Toys R Us AntiTrust Litigation,* 191 F.R.D. 347 (E.D.N.Y. 2000).

40. "Locally Grown: List of Vendor Profiles," Whole Foods, http://wholefoodsmarket.com/locally-grown; "Local Producer Loan Program," Whole Foods, http://wholefoodsmarket.com/mission-values/caring-communities/local-producer-loan-program; Julie Schmit, "'Locally Grown' Food Sounds Great, but What Does It Mean?," *USA Today,* October 27, 2008; Carol Ness, "Whole Foods, Taking Flak, Thinks Local," *San Francisco Chronicle,* July 26, 2006; "Retailers Push Packagers to Think 'Green,'" Reuters, September 4, 2007.

41. "Ethical Sourcing: Coffee," http://www.starbucks.com/responsibility/sourcing/coffee; Margaret Badore, "Starbucks Says It Now Serves '99 Percent Ethically Sourced Coffee.' So What Does that Mean?," *Tree Hugger,* April 9, 2015.

42. www.ecooptions.homedepot.com/; www6.homedepot.com/earthday/L105066_GreenGuide_Book.pdf.

43. Tom Zeller, "Clothes Makers Join to Set 'Green Score,'" *The New York Times,* March 1, 2011.

LEARNING OBJECTIVES

After reading this chapter, you should be able to:

LO 13-1 Explain the difference between a high/low pricing strategy and an everyday low-pricing strategy.

LO 13-2 Identify the factors retailers consider when pricing their merchandise.

LO 13-3 Examine how and why retailers take markdowns.

LO 13-4 Identify the pricing techniques retailers use to increase sales and profits.

LO 13-5 Indicate the legal and ethical issues retailers should consider when setting prices.

© Kevork Djansezian/Getty Images

For most consumers, "pizza wars" mean a fight over which toppings to put on a shared pie. But in truth, the pizza industry is in the midst of a battle, for which the weapons of choice are mainly pricing tactics. In addition to the small, local pizzerias that appear in nearly every town, there are four major chains that pursue pizza-loving consumers in the United States, a massive market in which approximately 1 in 8 people eat pizza on any particular day.[1] Running the gamut from a low-price promise to a higher-price and higher-quality appeal, these four chains all seek to price their offerings in ways that promise to increase their sales and market share. How exactly are they doing so?

With its well-known spokespeople, from Peyton Manning and J.J. Watt to the founder himself, "Papa" John Schnatter, Papa John's is a familiar name to many advertising viewers, even though it accounts for only about 6 percent of the national market. Along with these recognizable faces, Papa John's has established a motto and tagline that most consumers can repeat from memory: "Better Ingredients, Better Pizza." In accordance with this focus on quality, Papa

John's rarely tries to offer the lowest price in a market. Constantly lowering of prices means, according to Schnatter, that "you are either serving ingredients that are not high quality or you're putting less on."[2] Papa John's says that it will never seek to reach the $5 pizza threshold that many of its national competitors offer. But to gain ground, it cannot just ignore the price interests of its consumers. In response, Papa John's promises that if consumers order one large pizza at the regular price, they can get a second for just $0.50.[3] The combined deal still remains above that $5 threshold, but it brings the overall cost to consumers more in line with competitors' prices. Papa John's also seeks to introduce various innovations to get people calling. For example, during a recent one-month promotional run, it offered the Brookie—a combination chocolate chip cookie and brownie—for $6 with the order of any pizza.[4]

Little Caesars also has a well-known tagline ("Pizza! Pizza!"), but its offer is premised almost completely on convenience. With a different business model than any of the other big players in the market, the restaurant chain promises that its food is "hot and ready": At the moment consumers walk in to a store, the pizza will be ready for them to take, for just about $5. For a little more, they can upgrade their pie, such as selecting the cheese-stuffed crust or bacon-wrapped deep-dish versions.[5] The chain likes to play with its "underdog," overlooked status, despite its prominence.[6] In one promotion, it promised an even lower price—free—if any team that was seeded sixteenth in the men's college basketball tournament won in the first round, which would mean that it would have unseated the top-ranked team in its division.[7] The risk was relatively low, considering that no team has ever done so. Still, it put the idea in people's minds and offered the chance of a free Hot-N-Ready lunch if the upset occurred. (It didn't.)

In the past, Domino's was known for its promise to deliver pizzas in 30 minutes or less, though it ultimately removed the guarantee for safety reasons. Still, it built its reach throughout the market by promising to make it easy for people at home to get their pizza fix. That reputation continues to inform its approach to growth today. By "utilizing mobile better than their competitors,"[8] Domino's restaurants make it easy for tech-savvy consumers to gain access to the offerings. For example, its well-developed Pizza Tracker app, which is available on all the major mobile platforms, gives users one-touch ordering functions and constantly updated delivery times.[9] Yet these mobile innovations have not led Domino's to alter its pricing strategy substantively. As one spokesperson noted, Domino's does not "play the price or product-of-the-month gimmick game others seem to. The limited-time-only tactic is something we left behind years ago."[10] Instead, since about 2010, Domino's has continued to offer the same baseline: medium cheese pizzas for around $5.99 each. Increasing the size or adding more toppings increases the price, but the pricing is clearly transparent and mostly consistent over time and geographic locations.

Finally, Pizza Hut, the world's largest pizza chain, started the most recent pizza pricing war by creating a new initiative. As long as consumers bought at least one other item (e.g., breadsticks, wings, another pizza), they could get a medium, one-topping pizza for just $5.[11] The promotion is part of the launch of a wider, $5 "flavor menu" that includes multiple options. Similar to single-price menus in other fast-food settings, this approach allows consumers to decide which items they prefer to purchase for their set budget. One consumer might want the variety of wings and pizza, another might need a couple of pizzas to feed multiple people, and yet another could want both a meal and a dessert. With its more than 15,000 stores, Pizza Hut enjoys vast reach, excellent brand awareness, and a market-leading position. It also asserts that it has been "serving the same great-tasting pizza, at a great value" for its entire history.[12] Yet for several quarters, the performance of the chain had not met the expectations of either investors or its corporate brand owner, Yum! Brands. To address these concerns, Pizza Hut not only introduced its new price promotion but also adopted a "focused emphasis on making it easier to get a better pizza."[13]

So what have the results been? In recent quarters, Papa John's announced a 5 percent growth rate.[14] Little Caesars's sales increased from $2.9 million to $3.4 million over a two-year period.[15] Domino's enjoyed 13 percent revenue growth. Pizza Hut reported flat sales.[16] Will the outcome of the pizza battle change these trends?

The decisions examined in this textbook are directed toward facilitating exchanges between retailers and their customers. As discussed in Chapter 1, retailers offer a number of benefits to their customers, including making merchandise available to customers when they want it, at a convenient location, and in the quantities they want. In addition, retailers provide services, such as the opportunity for customers to see and try out merchandise before buying it. In exchange for these benefits, customers pay money for the merchandise and services provided by retailers.

The importance of pricing decisions is growing because today's customers have more alternatives to choose from and are better informed about the alternatives available in the marketplace. Thus, they are in a better position to seek a good value when they buy merchandise and services. **Value** is the ratio of what customers receive (the perceived benefit of the products and services offered by the retailer) to what they have to pay for it:

$$\text{Value} = \frac{\text{Perceived benefits}}{\text{Price}}$$

Retailers can increase value and stimulate more sales (exchanges) by either increasing the perceived benefits offered or reducing the price. To some customers, a good value means simply paying the lowest price, because other benefits offered by retailers are not important to them. Others are willing to pay extra for additional benefits as long as they believe they're getting their money's worth in terms of product quality or service. In its effort to provide more value options to its customers, Wendy's has expanded its pricing options. If a fast-food patron wants a smaller item on a particular visit, he or she can purchase from the 99-cent menu. But if he or she is much hungrier or in the mood for a fresher option, this consumer can jump up to a $1.99 menu items. Each option provides value, but the value is perceived differently by different people and in different situations. Similarly, few dollar stores still limit themselves to only $1 options, because doing so limited the depth of their offerings and made them less appealing to consumers, who sought a great deal, not just a way to get rid of all their single dollar bills.[17]

Wendy's provides value to its customers by providing 99-cent options.

© Tim Boyle/Getty Images

If retailers set prices higher than the benefits they provide, sales and profits will decrease. In contrast, if retailers set prices too low, their sales might increase but profits might decrease because of the lower profit margin. In addition to offering an attractive value to customers, retailers need to consider the value proposition offered by their competitors and legal restrictions related to pricing. Thus, setting the right price can be challenging.

The first section of this chapter examines two very different pricing strategies used by retailers. The factors and techniques retailers use to set retail prices are then reviewed, followed by the reasons that retailers reduce their prices when taking markdowns, as well as some other pricing techniques that retailers use to increase their sales and profits. This chapter concludes with a discussion of the legal and ethical issues that retailers must consider when making pricing decisions.

PRICING STRATEGIES

LO 13-1

Explain the difference between a high/low pricing strategy and an everyday low-pricing strategy.

Retailers use two basic retail pricing strategies: high/low pricing and everyday low pricing. Each of these strategies and its advantages and disadvantages is discussed in this section.

High/Low Pricing

Retailers using a **high/low pricing strategy** frequently—often weekly—discount the initial prices for merchandise through sales promotions. However, some customers learn to expect frequent sales and simply wait until the merchandise they want goes on sale and then stock up at the low prices.

Everyday Low Pricing

Many retailers, particularly supermarkets, home improvement centers, and discount stores, have adopted an **everyday low-pricing (EDLP) strategy**. This strategy emphasizes the continuity of retail prices at a level somewhere between the regular nonsale price and the deep-discount sale price of high/low retailers. Although EDLP retailers

The retailer on the left is using a high/low pricing strategy, whereas the retailer on the right is using an everyday low pricing strategy.

(left): © Mark Lennihan/AP Images; (right): © Jin Lee/Bloomberg via Getty Images

embrace their consistent pricing strategy, they occasionally have sales, just not as frequently as their high/low competitors.

The term *everyday low pricing* is somewhat misleading because low doesn't mean "lowest." Although retailers using EDLP strive for low prices, they aren't always the lowest prices in the market. Walmart is renowned for its everyday low prices, and it is so effective in its approach that it even can promise relatively lower prices on traditionally higher-priced goods such as organic produce, as Retailing View 13.1 explains. Still, at any given time, a sale price at a high/low retailer may be the lowest price available in

RETAILING VIEW   Walmart Offers Low-Priced Organic Foods   13.1

One word can strike fear into the heart of any small retailer: Walmart! Because it enjoys massive economies of scale, Walmart's entry into a market can cause tremors for even other large retailers, because somehow it always seems to manage to underprice everyone else with the everyday low-pricing (EDLP) strategy for which it has become famous. Long a consumer-goods giant, the Arkansas-based behemoth also has turned its massively successful EDLP practices to the grocery industry, where it quickly became the country's largest grocer as well.

Not satisfied with being just the largest grocer, Walmart aims to gain a substantial share of the lucrative organic food market. In true Walmart fashion, it intends to do so using its well-known EDLP strategies. Organic products typically feature premium prices, but at Walmart "there will be no premium for the customer to purchase organic products," according to the executive vice president of grocery at Walmart U.S. "They will be able to purchase organic at non-organic prices." In-house research indicated that consumers would overwhelmingly purchase organic products if they cost less, so Walmart responded.

But how can Walmart be the only retailer to offer organic products at nonorganic prices? It will deliver organic items through an atypical "bigger is better" mentality. That is, organic foods typically come from small farms, which send their products out to be processed at facilities that simultaneously process conventional foods. The switches from organic to conventional processing and back again require a great deal of labor, which increases costs and thus prices. Because of their economies of scale, Walmart can work with larger farms and processing plants that cater only to organic food production, saving time, labor, and money—by a margin of as much as 20 to 30 percent.

Walmart has extended its everyday low-pricing strategy to include traditionally higher-priced goods such as organic produce.

© Joe Raedle/Getty Images

As is also its habit, Walmart is thinking long term and locking its suppliers into agreements that will enable it to meet the enormous requirements associated with its lofty organic goals.

Sources: Elizabeth A. Harris and Stephanie Strom, "Walmart to Sell Organic Food, Undercutting Big Brands," *The New York Times*, April 10, 2014, http://www.nytimes.com; Dan Charles, "Can Wal-Mart Really Make Organic Food Cheap for Everyone?," *NPR*, April 19, 2014, http://www.wbur.org/npr/; Steven Overly, "Wal-Mart Plans to Bring Its Compete-on-Price Approach to Organic Food: Here's How," *The Washington Post*, April 10, 2014, http://www.washingtonpost.com.

a market. To reinforce their EDLP strategy, many retailers have adopted a **low-price guarantee policy** that guarantees customers that the retailer will have the lowest price in a market for products it sells. The guarantee usually promises to match or beat any lower price found in the market and might include a provision to refund the difference between the seller's offer price and the lower price. Target has expanded the number of competitors whose prices it will beat to 29 online and brick-and-mortar competitors, including CVS, Kohl's, Amazon, Walmart, and Office Depot.[18]

Advantages of the Pricing Strategies

The high/low pricing strategy has the following advantages:

- **Increases profits.** High/low pricing allows retailers to charge higher prices to customers who are not price-sensitive and will pay the "high" price while charging lower prices to price-sensitive customers who will wait for the "low" sale price.

- **Creates excitement.** A "get them while they last" atmosphere often occurs during a sale. Sales draw a lot of customers, and a lot of customers create excitement. Some retailers augment low prices and advertising with special in-store activities, such as product demonstrations, giveaways, and celebrity appearances.

- **Sells slow-moving merchandise.** Sales allow retailers to get rid of slow-selling merchandise by discounting the price.

The EDLP approach has its own advantages, as follows:

- **Assures customers of low prices.** Many customers are skeptical about initial retail prices. They have become conditioned to buying only on sale—the main characteristic of a high/low pricing strategy. The EDLP strategy lets customers know that they will get the same low prices every time they patronize the EDLP retailer. Customers do not have to read the ads and wait for items they want to go on sale.

- **Reduces advertising and operating expenses.** The stable prices caused by EDLP limit the need for the weekly sale advertising used in the high/low strategy. In addition, EDLP retailers do not have to incur the labor costs of changing price tags and signs and putting up sale signs.

- **Reduces stockouts and improves inventory management.** The EDLP approach reduces the large variations in demand caused by frequent sales with large markdowns. As a result, retailers can manage their inventories with more certainty. Fewer stockouts mean more satisfied customers, resulting in higher sales. In addition, a more predictable customer demand pattern enables the retailer to improve inventory turnover by reducing the average inventory needed for special promotions and backup stock.

SETTING RETAIL PRICES

LO 13-2

Identify the factors retailers consider when pricing their merchandise.

Five factors that retailers must consider when setting retail prices are (1) the price sensitivity of consumers; (2) competition; (3) the pricing of services; (4) analytical factors such as cost, break-even points, pricing software, and Internet, mobile, and social; and (5) legal and ethical issues. We cover the first four elements in this section; legal and ethical issues are discussed at the end of the chapter.

Customer Price Sensitivity

Generally, as the price of a product increases, the sales for the product will decrease because fewer and fewer customers feel the product is a good value. The price sensitivity of customers determines how many units will be sold at different price levels. If customers in the target market are very price-sensitive, sales will decrease significantly when prices increase. If customers are not very price-sensitive, sales will not decrease significantly if the prices are increased.

One approach that can be used to measure the price sensitivity of customers is a price experiment. Consider the following situation: A restaurant chain wants to determine the best price for a new item, a riblet basket. It selects restaurants in the chain with very similar trade areas and sets prices at different levels in each of the restaurants for a week. Assume that the variable cost of the riblets is $5 per plate and the fixed cost of operating the restaurant for a week, the cost for rent, labor, and energy, is $8,000.

The results of this experiment are shown in Exhibit 13–1. Notice in Exhibit 13–1A that as prices increase, the fixed costs remain the same, sales and variable costs both decrease, but sales decrease at a faster rate than variable costs (Exhibit 13–1B). So the highest profit level occurs at a $7 price (Exhibit 13–1C). If the restaurant considers

© Greg Blomberg/Alamy Stock Photo

To determine the most profitable price for a riblet basket, a restaurant chain may set different prices at different locations.

Data from Price Experiment   **EXHIBIT 13–1A**

(1) Restaurant	(2) Price	(3) Quantity Sold	(4) Column (2) × Column (3) = Revenue	(5) Column (3) × $5 Variable Cost per Riblet Basket = Variable Cost	(6) Fixed Cost	(7) Column (4) — Column (5) — Column (6) = Contribution to Profit
1	$6.00	9,502	$57,012	$47,510	$8,000	$1,502
2	6.50	6,429	41,789	32,145	8,000	1,644
3	7.00	5,350	37,450	26,750	8,000	2,700
4	7.50	4,051	30,383	20,255	8,000	2,128
5	8.00	2,873	22,984	14,365	8,000	619
6	8.50	2,121	18,029	10,605	8,000	−577

EXHIBIT 13–1B
Quantity Sold at Different Prices

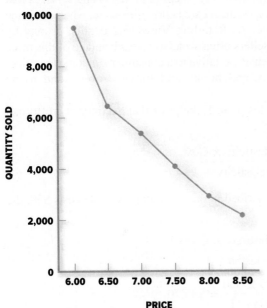

EXHIBIT 13–1C
Profit at Different Prices

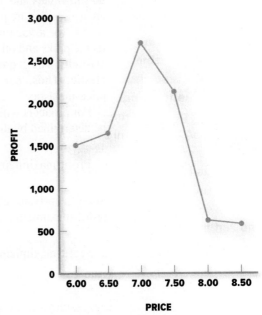

only customers' price sensitivity and cost in setting prices, it would set the price for the riblet basket with these demand characteristics at $7 to maximize profits.

Price Elasticity A commonly used measure of price sensitivity is **price elasticity**, or the percentage change in quantity sold divided by the percentage change in price:

$$\text{Elasticity} = \frac{\text{Percentage change in quantity sold}}{\text{Percentage change in price}}$$

Assume that a retailer originally priced a private-label DVD player at $90 and then raised the price to $100. Before raising the price, the retailer was selling 1,500 units a week. When the price increased, sales dropped to 1,100 units per week. The calculation of the price elasticity is as follows:

$$\text{Elasticity} = \frac{\text{Percentage change in quantity sold}}{\text{Percentage change in price}}$$
$$= \frac{(\text{New quantity sold} - \text{Old quantity sold}) \div (\text{Old quantity sold})}{(\text{New price} - \text{Old price}) \div (\text{Old price})}$$
$$= \frac{(1,100 - 1,500)/1,500}{(10 - 9)/9} = \frac{-0.2667}{0.1111} = -2.4005$$

Because the quantity sold usually decreases when prices increase, price elasticity is a negative number.

The target market for a product is generally viewed to be price-insensitive (referred to as **inelastic**) when its price elasticity is more positive than −1.0 (e.g., −0.50)—that is, when a 1 percent decrease in price results in a 1/2 percent increase in quantity sold. The target market for a product is price-sensitive (referred to as **elastic**) when the price elasticity is more negative than −1 (e.g., −2.0), that is, when a 1 percent decrease in price produces a 2 percent increase in quantity sold. The price elasticity for a product can be estimated by conducting an experiment as described previously or by using statistical techniques to analyze how sales have changed in the past when prices changed.

Various factors affect the price sensitivity for a product. First, the more substitutes a product or service has, the more likely it is to be price-elastic (sensitive). For example, there are many alternatives for a riblet basket at a restaurant like Applebee's, and thus fast-food prices are typically price-elastic, but branded luxury goods have almost no substitutes and are price-inelastic (insensitive). Second, products and services that are necessities are price-inelastic. Thus, medical care is price-inelastic, whereas airline tickets for a vacation are price-elastic. As Retailing View 13.2 details, pricing by theme parks and other entertainment sellers often seeks to take advantage of this price elasticity. Third, products that are expensive relative to a consumer's income are price-elastic. Thus, cars are price-elastic, and books and movie tickets tend to be price-inelastic.

For products with price elasticities less than 1, the price that maximizes profits can be determined by the following formula:

$$\text{Profit-maximizing price} = \frac{\text{Price elasticity} \times \text{Cost}}{\text{Price elasticity} + 1}$$

So, if the private-label DVD player described in the preceding example costs $50, the profit-maximizing price would be:

$$\text{Profit-maximizing price} = \frac{\text{Price elasticity} \times \text{Cost}}{\text{Price elasticity} + 1}$$
$$= \frac{-2.4005 \times \$50}{-2.4005 + 1} = \$85.70$$

RETAILING VIEW The Increasing Costs of Play: New Offers and Pricing by Disney and Universal Theme Parks — **13.2**

The price to get into Disneyland in Anaheim, California, or Disney World in Orlando, Florida, keeps increasing. At Universal Studios Hollywood, a one-day pass is $80. But instead of just raising its prices to match Disney, Universal has introduced a new pricing plan that offers greater access to those willing to pay more—quite a lot more.

The VIP service at Universal allows park visitors to bypass every line in the park, after having their car parked by a valet. They get free breakfast and lunch in a luxury lounge, serving scallops and short ribs, for example. Then they can access the backlots while toting their free gift bags with mints, hand sanitizer, and a poncho to wear on water rides. All this at a cost of $299 per ticket. For those who don't worry about their breath or eating fancy meals, a $149 option instead offers just line-jumping privileges.

Such benefits raise some questions about the economic stratification Universal is promoting, such that only the wealthy get to enjoy all the perks. For Disney, concerns about damage to its "magical" image have halted it from classifying different price points for tickets based on different levels of access. Yet as a recent controversy—in which wealthy families hired people with disabilities to join their trips so that they could skip lines—showed, demand for such special treatment exists.

Even though theme parks are enjoying record attendance and revenue levels, they keep looking for ways to increase their appeal. New rides and attractions are expensive, and in many cases, they seem out of date pretty quickly. In this case, the magic may be in the pricing.

Sources: Brooks Barnes, "At Theme Parks, a V.I.P. Ticket to Ride," *The New York Times*, June 9, 2013; "Ticket to Disneyland: Now $92," *The Wall Street Journal*, June 3, 2013; https://www.universalorlando.com/Theme-Park-Tickets/Vip-Experience.aspx.

Competition

Consumers have lots of choices for goods and services, and they typically search for the best value. Retailers therefore need to consider competitors' prices when setting their own. The previous discussion about setting price on the basis of customer price sensitivity (elasticity) ignores the effects of competitors' prices. For example, assume the restaurant chain that conducted the experiment had a $7.50 price for the riblet basket and, following the results of its experiment, dropped its price to $7.00 to increase sales and profits. If the increased sales occurred, other restaurant chains would see a decline in their sales and react by dropping their prices to $7.00, and the experimenting restaurant chain might not realize the sales and profit increases it anticipated.

Retailers can price above, below, or at parity with the competition. The chosen pricing policy must be consistent with the retailer's overall strategy and its relative market position. Consider, for instance, Walmart and Tiffany and Co. Walmart tries to price the products it sells below its competition. Tiffany, in contrast, offers significant benefits to its customers beyond just the merchandise. Its brand name and customer service assure customers that they will be satisfied with the jewelry they purchase. Due to the unique nature of its offering, Tiffany is able to set its prices higher than those of competitors.

Most retailers routinely collect price data about their competitors to see if they need to adjust their prices to remain competitive. Competitive price data are typically collected using store personnel, but pricing data also are available from business service providers such as the Nielsen Company and SymphonyIRI.

Pricing of Services

Additional issues need to be considered when pricing services relative to products, including the need to match supply and demand and the difficulties that customers have in determining service quality.[19]

Matching Supply and Demand Services are intangible and thus cannot be inventoried. When retailers are selling products, if the products don't sell one day, they can be stored and sold the next day. However, when a plane departs with empty seats or a play is performed without a full house, the potential revenue from the unused capacity is lost forever. In addition, most services have limited capacity. For example, restaurants are limited in the number of customers that can be seated. Due to capacity constraints, service retailers might encounter situations in which they cannot realize as many sales as they could make. For example, airlines' dynamic pricing techniques, described later in the chapter, monitor reservations and ticket sales for each flight and adjust prices according to capacity utilization. Prices are lowered on flights when sales are below forecasts and there is significant excess capacity. As ticket sales approach capacity, prices are increased.[20]

Other service retailers use less sophisticated approaches to match supply and demand. For example, more people want to go to a restaurant for dinner or see a movie at 7:00 p.m. than at 5:00 p.m. Restaurants and movie theaters thus might not be able to satisfy the demand for their services at 7:00 p.m. but have excess capacity at 5:00 p.m. Therefore, restaurants and movie theaters often price their services lower for customers who use them at 5:00 p.m. rather than 7:00 p.m. in an effort to shift demand from 7:00 p.m. to 5:00 p.m. Accordingly, service providers such as OpenTable seek to help retailers leverage these demand shifts through surge pricing. When the desired product is more desirable, such as a 7:00 reservation at the hottest restaurant in town, Open-Table offers Premium Reservations that allow diners to pay an extra fee to book the best seats in the house. Surrogate taxi service Uber relies on similar pricing strategies to balance the demand for its services.[21]

Determining Service Quality   Due to the intangibility of services, it is often difficult for customers to assess service quality, especially when other information is not available.[22] Thus, if consumers are unfamiliar with a service or service provider, they may use price to make quality judgments. For example, most consumers have limited information about lawyers and the quality of legal advice they offer. They may, therefore, base their assessment of the quality of legal services offered on the fees they charge. They may also use other nondiagnostic cues to assess quality, such as the size and décor of the lawyer's office.

Another factor that increases the dependence on price as a quality indicator is the risk associated with a service purchase. Customers are reticent to entrust their medical or legal problems to low-cost providers. The risk need not be expensive. Some customers may find the risk associated with inexpensive hair salons or tattoo parlors to be too much as well.

Because customers depend on price as a cue of quality and because price creates expectations of quality, service prices must be determined carefully. In addition to being chosen to manage capacity, prices must be set to convey the appropriate quality signal. Pricing too low can lead to inaccurate inferences about the quality of the service. Pricing too high can set expectations that may be difficult to match in service delivery.

Using Analytical Tools to Set Prices

Many retailers need to set prices for more than 50,000 SKUs and make thousands of pricing decisions each month. From a practical perspective, they cannot conduct experiments or do statistical analyses to determine the price sensitivity for each item. Therefore, they rely on some standard analytical approaches, such as those based on cost or break-even points, which they adopt by relying on pricing software and Internet, mobile, and social capabilities.

Setting Prices Based on Costs   Many retailers set prices by marking up the item's cost to yield a profitable gross margin. Then, this initial price is adjusted on the basis of insights about customer price sensitivity and competitive pricing.

Retail Price and Markup   When setting prices on the basis of merchandise cost, retailers start with the following equation:

Retail price = Cost of merchandise + Markup

The **markup** is the difference between the retail price and the cost of an item. Thus, if a sporting goods retailer buys a tennis racket for $75 and sets the retail price at $125, the markup is $50. The appropriate markup is the amount that covers all of the retailer's operating expenses (labor costs, rent, utilities, advertising, etc.) incurred to sell the merchandise and produces a profit for the retailer.

The **markup percentage** is the markup as a percentage of the retail price:

$$\text{Markup percentage} = \frac{\text{Retail price} - \text{Cost of merchandise}}{\text{Retail price}}$$

Thus, the markup percentage for the tennis racket is:

$$\text{Markup percentage} = \frac{\$125 - \$75}{\$125} = 40\%$$

The retail price based on the cost and markup percentage is:

$$\begin{aligned}
\text{Retail price} &= \text{Cost of merchandise} + \text{Markup} \\
&= \text{Cost of merchandise} + (\text{Retail price} \times \text{Markup percentage}) \\
&= \frac{\text{Cost of merchandise}}{1 - \text{Markup percentage (as a fraction)}}
\end{aligned}$$

Thus, if a buyer for an office supply category specialist purchases calculators at $14 and needs a 30 percent markup to meet the financial goals for the category, the retail price needs to be:

$$\text{Retail price} = \frac{\text{Cost}}{1 - \text{Markup percentage}} = \frac{\$14.00}{1 - 0.30} = \$20.00$$

For instance, if an apparel retailer used a 50 percent markup, an approach referred to as **keystoning**, the retail price would be double the cost.

Initial Markup and Maintained Markup   The previous discussion is based on the assumption that the retailer sells all items at an initially set price. However, retailers rarely sell all items at the initial price. They frequently reduce the price of items for special promotions or to get rid of excess inventory at the end of a season. In addition, discounts are given to employees, and some merchandise is lost to theft and accounting errors (**inventory shrinkage**). These factors that reduce the actual selling price from the initial sales price are called **reductions**. Thus, there is a difference between the initial markup and the maintained markup.

The **initial markup** is the retail selling price initially set for the merchandise minus the cost of the merchandise. The **maintained markup** is the actual sales realized for the merchandise minus its costs. It is the amount of profit realized from merchandising decisions.

Thus, the maintained markup is conceptually similar to the gross margin, but slightly different. Some retailers have workroom costs, such as alterations of a suit or assembly of a bicycle, that would reduce the maintained markup compared with the gross margin. Retailers often receive cash discounts from vendors for paying invoices early, which increase the maintained markup compared with the gross margin. Because workroom costs and cash discounts are not typically under the buyer's control, they are accounted for separately. To summarize:

$$\text{Gross margin percentage} = \frac{\text{Maintained markup} - (\text{Workroom costs} + \text{Cash discounts})}{\text{Net sales}}$$

The difference between the initial and maintained markups is illustrated in Exhibit 13–2. The item illustrated costs $0.60, and the initial price for the item is $1.00, so the initial markup is $0.40 and the initial markup percentage is 40 percent. However, the average actual sale price for the item is $0.90. The reductions are $0.10, so

EXHIBIT 13–2

Difference between Initial Markup and Maintained Markup

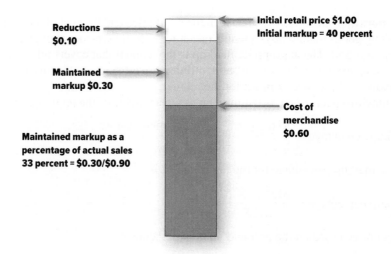

Reductions $0.10

Initial retail price $1.00
Initial markup = 40 percent

Maintained markup $0.30

Cost of merchandise $0.60

Maintained markup as a percentage of actual sales 33 percent = $0.30/$0.90

the maintained markup is $0.30 and the maintained markup percentage is 33 percent (0.30/0.90).

The relationship between the initial and maintained markup percentages is:

$$\text{Initial markup percentage} = \frac{\begin{array}{c}\text{Maintained markup percentage} \\ \text{(as a percentage of planned} \\ \text{actual sales)}\end{array} + \begin{array}{c}\text{Percent reductions} \\ \text{(as a percentage of planned} \\ \text{actual sales)}\end{array}}{100\% + \begin{array}{c}\text{Percent reductions} \\ \text{(as a percentage of planned} \\ \text{actual sales)}\end{array}}$$

Thus, if the buyer setting the price for the item shown in Exhibit 13–2 planned on reductions of 10 percent of actual sales and wanted a maintained markup of 33 percent, the initial markup should be:

$$\text{Initial markup percentage} = \frac{33\% + (\$0.10/\$0.90 = 11.111\%)}{100\% + 11.111\%} = 40\%$$

and the initial retail price should be:

$$\text{Initial retail price} = \frac{\text{Cost}}{1 - \text{Initial markup percentage}} = \frac{\$0.60}{1 - 0.40} = \$1.00$$

Setting Prices Using Break-Even Analysis   Retailers often want to know the number of units they need sell to begin making a profit. For example, a retailer might want to know:

- Break-even sales to generate a target profit.
- Break-even volume and dollars to justify introducing a new product, product line, or department.
- Break-even sales change needed to cover a price change.

A useful analytical tool for making these assessments is **break-even analysis**, which determines, on the basis of fixed and variable costs, how much merchandise needs to be sold to achieve a break-even (zero) profit.

The **break-even point quantity** is the quantity at which total revenue equals total cost, and then profit occurs for additional sales.

The formula for calculating the sales quantity needed to break even is:

$$\text{Break-even quantity} = \frac{\text{Total fixed costs}}{\text{Actual unit sales price} - \text{Unit variable cost}}$$

The following examples illustrate the use of this formula in determining the break-even volume of a new private-label product and the break-even change in volume needed to cover a price change.

Calculating Break-Even for a New Product   Hypothetically, PetSmart is considering an introduction of a new private-label, dry dog food targeting owners of older dogs. The cost of developing this dog food is $700,000, including salaries for the design team and costs of testing the product. Because these costs do not change with the quantity of product produced and sold, they're known as **fixed costs**. PetSmart plans to sell the dog food for $12 a bag—the unit price. The **variable cost** is the retailer's expenses that vary directly with the quantity of product produced and sold. Variable costs often include direct labor and materials used in producing the product. PetSmart will be purchasing the product from a private-label manufacturer. Thus, the only variable cost is the dog food's cost, $5, from the private-label manufacturer.

$$\text{Break-even quantity} = \frac{\text{Fixed costs}}{\text{Actual unit sales price} - \text{Unit variable cost}}$$

$$= \frac{\$700,000}{\$12 - \$5} = 100,000 \text{ bags}$$

Thus, PetSmart needs to sell 100,000 bags of dog food to break even, or make zero profit, and for every additional bag sold, it will make $7 profit.

Now assume that PetSmart wants to make $100,000 profit from the new product line. The break-even quantity now becomes:

$$\text{Break-even quantity} = \frac{\text{Fixed costs}}{\text{Actual unit sales price} - \text{Unit variable cost}}$$

$$= \frac{\$700,000 + \$100,000}{\$12 - \$5} = 114,286 \text{ bags}$$

Calculating Break-Even Sales   An issue closely related to the calculation of a break-even point is determining how much unit sales would have to increase to make a profit from a price cut or how much sales would have to decline to make a price increase unprofitable. Continuing with the PetSmart example, assume the break-even quantity is 114,286 units, based on the $700,000 fixed cost, the $100,000 profit, a selling price of $12, and a cost of $5. Now PetSmart is considering lowering the price of a bag of dog food to $10. How many units must it sell to break even if it lowers its selling price by 16.67 percent, to $10? Use the following formula:

$$\text{Break-even quantity} = \frac{\text{Fixed costs}}{\text{Actual unit sales price} - \text{Unit variable cost}}$$

$$= \frac{\$700,000 + \$100,000}{\$10 - \$5} = 160,000 \text{ bags}$$

So, if PetSmart decreases its price by 16.67 percent, from $12 to $10, unit sales must increase by 40 percent: $(160,000 - 114,286) \div 114,286$.

Setting Prices Using Optimization Software   Since the early 2000s, many retailers have taken a more comprehensive approach to setting prices, combining various methods by implementing **pricing optimization software**. The software programs use a set of algorithms that analyze past and current merchandise sales and prices, as well as competitors' prices; estimate the relationship between prices and sales generated; and then determine the optimal (most profitable) initial price for the merchandise and the appropriate size and timing of markdowns. Optimization can be accomplished at the store level and even at the individual customer level using the dynamic pricing techniques described later in the chapter.

To set initial prices, the software uses historical sales data from its own and competitors' stores. It determines the price–sales relationship of complementary items—those that have a similar sales pattern, such as Pepsi and Lay's Potato Chips. Thus, not only can the software tell buyers the best price for Pepsi, but it also suggests a price for the chips. Buyers can also determine how much Pepsi they will sell at a given price if they lower the price of Coke or their private-label (or store) brand. The software can incorporate other factors, such as the store's image (e.g., inexpensive or premium price), where the nearest rival is located, seasonal factors (e.g., soft drinks sell better in the summer than in the winter), or whether an item is featured in coupons or other promotions. It can set decision rules, such as optimizing the regular price to never be more than a nickel above a competitor's price. Or the software might suggest offering a very competitive price on products for which customers are very sensitive, such as milk or diapers, but take a larger margin on less price-sensitive items, such as baby accessories and store brands.[23]

Merchandising optimization software can be expensive, but its use can have an impressive impact on bottom-line profitability. For instance, the Walgreens-owned and New York City–based Duane Reade pharmacy chain used merchandising optimization software to boost its sales of diapers.[24] The chain had tried discounts and coupons, but the category was losing ground to the competition. The software indicated that the markup should be a function of the age of the child for whom parents were buying diapers. For newborn sizes, Duane Reade raised prices, but once the child got to the training pants stage, it offered lower unit prices. A year later, Duane Reade's revenues in the baby care category had jumped 27 percent, with gross margin increases of 2 percent. With a traditional analysis, the chain was unlikely to ever guess that brand-new parents exhibit little price sensitivity, compared with parents who have been at it awhile.

Setting Prices by Relying on Internet, Mobile, and Social Capabilities The growth of the electronic channel, the popularity of social media, and the adoption of smartphones has greatly changed the way consumers get and use information to make purchasing decisions based on price. Traditionally, price competition between store-based retailers offering the same merchandise was reduced by geography because consumers typically shop at the stores and malls closest to where they live and work. However, Internet sites such as Shopzilla, RedLaser, and ShopStyle allow customers to compare prices across a range of retailers.

Today, growing numbers of consumers are opting into services provided by various mobile firms and their applications (e.g., Foursquare, LocalResponse) to receive mobile offers. The latest generation of price promotional offers takes into account the consumers' geographic location that is accessed from their phone location or locational coding via certain sites and offers them localized promotions for retailers who are in close proximity. This concept is called **geofencing**. As a consequence, these mobile offers are increasingly relevant, and the redemption of online coupons is growing at an astronomical rate.[25]

These mobile offers can be delivered by a host of different methods. For example, Meijer supermarkets has created applications for its consumers.[26] This application has a host of interesting features from providing customers the ability to create shopping lists, access Meijer perks (Mperks coupons and sale items), and find the merchandise in a given store. Sensors in the store allow such apps to offer appropriate coupons and to constantly organize the list by the user's location in the store.[27]

Although consumers shopping electronically can collect price information with little effort, they also can get a lot of other information about the quality and performance of products, thus making them less sensitive to price. For instance, an Internet site that offers custom-made Oriental rugs can clearly show real differences in the patterns and materials used for construction. Electronic grocery services offered by Safeway allow customers to sort cereals by nutritional content, thus making it easier to use that attribute in their decision making. If a customer wants to make an egg dish for

© ekkasit919/Shutterstock

breakfast, the site can also recommend numerous recipes that include eggs, as well as providing the nutritional information. The additional information about product quality might lead customers to pay more for high-quality products, thus decreasing the importance of price.

MARKDOWNS

LO 13-3

Examine how and why retailers take markdowns.

The preceding section reviewed how retailers initially set prices on the basis of the merchandise cost and desired maintained margin. However, retailers also take **markdowns** by reducing the initial retail price. This section examines why retailers take markdowns, how they optimize markdown decisions, how they reduce the amount of markdowns, and how they liquidate markdown merchandise.

Reasons for Taking Markdowns

Retailers' reasons for taking markdowns can be classified as either clearance (to dispose of merchandise) or promotional (to generate sales). Clearance markdowns are examined in this section, while promotional markdowns are discussed later in this chapter as a method of increasing sales and profits.

When merchandise is selling at a slower rate than planned and will become obsolete at the end of its season, or is priced higher than competitors' goods, buyers generally mark it down for clearance purposes. As discussed in Chapter 11, slow-selling merchandise decreases inventory turnover; prevents buyers from acquiring new, better-selling merchandise; and can diminish the retailer's image for selling the most current styles and trends.

Markdowns are part of the cost of doing business, and thus buyers plan for them. They tend to order more fashion merchandise than they forecast actually selling because they are more concerned about underordering and stocking out of a popular item before the end of the season than about overordering and having to discount excess merchandise at the end of the season. Stocking out of popular merchandise can have a detrimental effect on a fashion retailer's image, whereas discounting merchandise at the end of the season just reduces maintained markup.

Thus, a buyer's objective isn't to minimize markdowns. If markdowns are too low, the buyer is probably pricing the merchandise too low, not purchasing enough merchandise, or not taking enough risks with the merchandise being purchased. Thus,

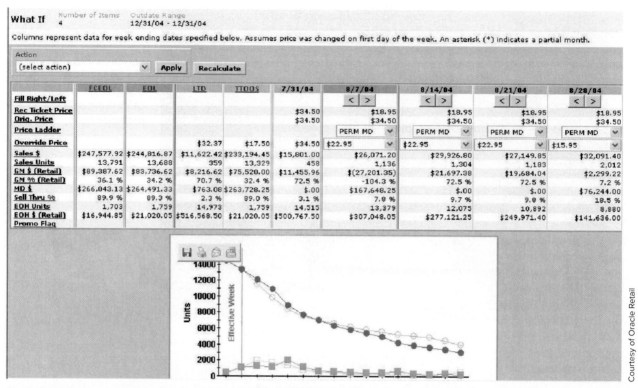

What If	Number of Items 4	Outdate Range 12/31/04 - 12/31/04								
Columns represent data for week ending dates specified below. Assumes price was changed on first day of the week. An asterisk (*) indicates a partial month.										

Action (select action) ▼   Apply   Recalculate

	FCEOL	EOL	LTD	TTOOS	7/31/04	8/7/04	8/14/04	8/21/04	8/28/04
Fill Right/Left						< >	< >	< >	< >
Rec Ticket Price					$34.50	$18.95	$18.95	$18.95	$18.95
Orig. Price					$34.50	$34.50	$34.50	$34.50	$34.50
Price Ladder						PERM MD ▼	PERM MD ▼	PERM MD ▼	PERM MD ▼
Override Price			$32.37	$17.50	$34.50	$22.95 ▼	$22.95 ▼	$22.95 ▼	$15.95 ▼
Sales $	$247,577.92	$244,816.87	$11,622.42	$233,194.45	$15,801.00	$26,071.20	$29,926.80	$27,149.85	$32,091.40
Sales Units	13,791	13,688	359	13,329	458	1,136	1,304	1,183	2,012
GM $ (Retail)	$89,387.62	$83,736.62	$8,216.62	$75,520.00	$11,455.96	$(27,201.35)	$21,697.38	$19,684.04	$2,299.22
GM % (Retail)	36.1 %	34.2 %	70.7 %	32.4 %	72.5 %	-104.3 %	72.5 %	72.5 %	7.2 %
MD $	$266,043.13	$264,491.33	$763.08	$263,728.25	$34.50	$167,648.25	$.00	$.00	$76,244.00
Sell Thru %	89.9 %	89.3 %	2.3 %	89.0 %	3.1 %	7.8 %	9.7 %	9.8 %	18.5 %
EOH Units	1,703	1,759	14,973	1,759	14,515	13,379	12,075	10,892	8,880
EOH $ (Retail)	$16,944.85	$21,020.05	$516,568.50	$21,020.05	$500,767.50	$307,048.05	$277,121.25	$249,971.40	$141,636.00
Promo Flag									

Courtesy of Oracle Retail

Oracle Retail features a price optimization software tool. This example output indicates that the model's recommended markdown of $18.95 will result in more than $5,000 greater profit than the buyer's planned markdown of $22.95.

buyers set the initial markup price high enough that even after markdowns and other reductions have been taken, the planned maintained markup is still achieved.

Optimizing Markdown Decisions   Retailers have traditionally created a set of arbitrary rules for taking markdowns to dispose of unwanted merchandise. One retailer, for instance, identifies markdown candidates when its weekly sell-through percentages fall below a certain level. Another retailer cuts prices on the basis of how long the merchandise has been in the store—marking down products by 20 percent after 8 weeks, then by 30 percent after 12 weeks, and finally by 50 percent after 16 weeks. Such a rule-based approach, however, is limiting because it does not consider the demand for the merchandise at different price points or in different locations and thus produces less-than-optimal profits.

The optimization software described previously in this chapter, used to set initial retail prices, can also indicate when to take markdowns and how much they should be in different locations.[28] It works by continually updating its pricing forecasts on the basis of actual sales throughout the season and factoring in differences in price sensitivities. For example, the software recognizes that in early November, a winter item's sales are better than expected in Colorado, so it delays taking a markdown that had been planned but takes the markdown

© Mark Lennihan/AP Images

Pricing optimization software recognizes when sales for winter coats are slower than expected and suggests both the timing and amount of markdowns.

in New England. Each week, as new sales data become available, it readjusts the forecasts to include the latest information. It computes literally thousands of scenarios for each item—a process that is too complicated and time-consuming for buyers to do on their own. It then evaluates the outcomes on the basis of expected profits and other factors and selects the action that produces the best results across all regions.

Reducing the Amount of Markdowns   Retailers have several options for reducing the amount of markdowns. They can work closely with vendors to choose merchandise and coordinate deliveries to help reduce the financial burden of taking markdowns. They can also buy smaller quantities to make it easier to forecast demand for a shorter time period and create a feeling of scarcity. Finally, retailers can strive to offer a good value.

Vendors have a partnering relationship with their retailers and thus a vested interest in their success. Vendors that are knowledgeable about the market and competition can help with stock selections. Of course, a retailer must also trust its own taste and intuition; otherwise, its store will have the same merchandise as all other stores. As discussed in Chapter 12, buyers can often obtain **markdown money**—funds a vendor gives the retailer to cover lost gross margin dollars that result from markdowns and other merchandising issues.

Another method of reducing markdowns is to buy smaller quantities.[29] By adopting a just-in-time inventory policy, in which small amounts of merchandise arrive just in time to be sold, customers perceive a scarcity and purchase at full price. (See Chapter 12 for more on this strategy.) Creating a feeling of scarcity among customers is an excellent method of reducing markdowns. Even if there are adequate quantities of merchandise available in the stockroom or in a distribution center, displaying just a few items on the sales floor sends a signal to the customer to "buy them now, while they last!" If retailers simply change their displays frequently, customers will perceive that the merchandise is new and available in limited quantities.

When customers believe that a particular retailer offers them a good value, they will be less likely to wait for markdowns. An everyday low-price strategy implies that a retailer's products are already at low prices and therefore will not be further discounted. Zara and H&M don't need to advertise their low prices. Loyal customers return time after time to look for low-priced treasures. A few retailers, like Apple, focus on quality and image and therefore simply don't have sales! It is an enviable position to which most retailers can only aspire.

Liquidate Markdown Merchandise   Even with the best planning, some merchandise may remain unsold at the end of a season. Retailers use one of six strategies to liquidate this unsold merchandise.

Sell to Another Retailer   Selling the unsold merchandise to another retailer is a very popular strategy among retailers. For instance, off-price retailers such as TJX Corporation (owners of TJ Maxx and Marshalls), Nordstrom Rack, and Ross Stores purchase end-of-season merchandise from other retailers and sell it at deep discounts. However, this approach for liquidating unsold merchandise enables retailers to recoup only a small percentage of the merchandise's cost—often a mere 10 percent.

Consolidate Unsold Merchandise   Markdown merchandise can be consolidated in a number of ways. First, the consolidation can be made into one or a few of the retailer's regular locations. Second, markdown merchandise can be consolidated into another retail chain or an outlet store under the same ownership. Saks Fifth Avenue OFF Fifth, Nordstrom Rack, and Neiman Marcus Last Call Clearance Center each use this approach. Third, unsold merchandise can be shipped to a distribution center or a rented space such as a convention center for final sale. However, consolidation sales can be complex and expensive due to the extra transportation and record keeping involved.

Sell on the Internet   The Internet is increasingly useful for liquidating unsold merchandise. For example, an electronics store might utilize eBay to sell goods it has received from trade-ins. Many retailers have separate areas of their websites for clearance merchandise.

Return to Vendor   Some large retailers have enough clout to negotiate an agreement that some merchandise be returned to vendors. Although an outstanding option, it is not generally viable unless the balance of power rests solidly with the retailer.

Donate to Charity   Donating clearance merchandise to charities is a common practice. Charitable giving is always a good corporate practice. It is a way of giving back to the community and has strong public relations benefits. Also, the cost value of the merchandise can be deducted from income, thus reducing the firm's tax liability.

Carry Over the Merchandise to the Next Season   The final liquidation approach—to carry over merchandise to the next season—is used with relatively high-priced nonfashion merchandise, such as traditional men's clothing and furniture. Generally, however, it is not profitable to carry over merchandise because of excessive inventory carrying costs and the potential of having the merchandise look "shopworn" or outdated.

PRICING TECHNIQUES FOR INCREASING SALES AND PROFITS

LO 13-4

Identify the pricing techniques retailers use to increase sales and profits.

This section reviews several pricing techniques used by retailers to increase sales and profits.

Dynamic Pricing

Dynamic pricing, also known as **individualized pricing**, refers to the process of charging different prices for goods or services based on the type of customer, time of the day, week, or even season, and level of demand. Ideally, retailers could maximize their profits if they charged each customer as much as the customer was willing to pay.

Dynamic pricing has always been popular in some retail sectors, such as automobile and antique dealers, in which customers are used to haggling over prices. And it is very popular with some services such as airlines and Uber, to match supply and demand, as discussed earlier in this chapter. But it is not very practical in the brick-and-mortar arena for consumer products such as detergents or cereals. First, it is difficult to assess each customer's willingness to pay. Second, these retailers cannot change the posted prices in stores as customers with different willingness to pay enter the store. Finally, customers might feel they are being treated unfairly if they realize that they are being charged a higher price than other customers.

Internet retailers have, however, increased their use of dynamic pricing techniques due their ability to process the vast amount of purchase information that is available. Amazon is remarkable in its dynamic pricing capabilities, as Retailing View 13.3 recounts.

Promotional Markdowns

Retailers employ promotional markdowns to promote merchandise and increase sales. Markdowns can increase customer traffic flow. Retailers plan promotions in which they take markdowns for holidays, for special events, and as part of their overall promotional program. Retailers hope that customers will purchase other products at regular prices while they're in the store. Another opportunity created by promotional markdowns is to increase the sale of complementary products. For example, a supermarket's markdown on hotdog buns may be offset by increased demand for hotdogs, mustard, and relish—all sold at regular prices.

RETAILING VIEW   Changing Once, Changing Twice, Changing 3 Million Times: How Amazon Prices to Win

On a recent Black Friday (i.e., the day after Thanksgiving, when many retailers make enough profit for the year to exceed their costs, known as getting in the black), Amazon actively changed the prices of one-third of the products in its seemingly endless supply. Try to imagine what that means. Amazon, the marketplace for virtually everything, engaged in literally millions of price changes, on what would already be probably its busiest shopping day. Why?

Here's the thing: It isn't all that unusual for Amazon. It changes the prices of 15–18 percent of its products every single day. With its famous algorithms and remarkable data warehouses, Amazon evidently believes it has better insights into what consumers will pay at any particular moment for a vast range of products.

Some product categories come in for more changes than others. Some are subject to change every day, others undergo price alterations every third day, another set shifts once a week, and still others experience changes only once or twice a month. Perhaps unsurprisingly, considering its investment in the Kindle, the most frequently changed product category is tablets, for which Amazon changes the prices of 15 percent of its stock every one to two days.

But the really remarkable transitions are the ones that take place around the holidays. Reports from holiday trends indicate that Amazon literally changed more than 3 million prices each and every day in November—of course, with the previously mentioned jump in activity on the day after Thanksgiving. Pleased with how well these changes have worked, Amazon promises to continue making them, and perhaps even ramp up its efforts.

Source: Jenn Markey, "Three Things You Need to Know about Amazon's Price Strategy," *Retail Customer Experience*, April 21, 2014, http://www.retailcustomer-experience.com.

Amazon changes prices of at least 15 percent of its stock every day. Note that the Apple iPad Air 2 9.7 inch is $395.00 one day (top) and to $359.00 on another day (bottom).

(both): Source: Amazon.com

McDonald's uses price bundling when it combines a sandwich, French fries, and a soft drink in an Extra Value Meal.

© Ted Pink/Alamy Stock Photo

Clearance Markdowns for Fashion Merchandise

While the discussion of clearance markdowns earlier in the chapter focused primarily on how retailers get rid of unwanted merchandise, this merchandise can also be used to attract different market segments based on their degree of price sensitivity. Fashion-conscious customers who have a high willingness to pay because they want to be the first to wear the latest fashions self-select to pay higher prices. More price-sensitive customers wait to buy the merchandise at the end of the season when prices are lower.

Coupons

Coupons offer a discount on the price of specific items when they're purchased. Coupons are issued by manufacturers and retailers in newspapers, on products, on the shelf, at the cash register, over the Internet and mobile devices, and through the mail. Retailers use coupons because they are thought to induce customers to try products for the first time, convert first-time users to regular users, encourage large purchases, increase usage, instill loyalty, and protect market share against the competition. Coupons are an attractive way to target price-sensitive customers because they will likely expend the extra effort to collect and redeem coupons, whereas price-insensitive customers will not.

Price Bundling

Price bundling is the practice of offering two or more different products or services for sale at one price. For instance, McDonald's offers a bundle of a sandwich, French fries, and a soft drink in an Extra Value Meal at a discount compared with buying the items individually. Price bundling increases both unit and dollar sales by increasing the amount of merchandise bought during a store visit.

Quantity Discounts

Quantity discounts, also called **multiple-unit pricing**, refers to the practice of offering two or more similar products or services for sale at one lower total price. For example, a convenience store may sell three one-liter bottles of soda for $2.39 when the price for a single one-liter bottle is 99 cents—a saving of 58 cents. Like price bundling, this variable-pricing approach is used to increase sales volume. Depending on the type of product, however, customers may stockpile the items for use at a later time, thus having no impact on sales over time.

Zone Pricing

Zone pricing is the practice of charging different prices in different stores, markets, regions, or zones. Retailers generally use zone pricing to address different competitive situations in their various markets. For example, some multichannel retailers implement zone pricing by asking customers to enter their zip code if they want a price quote. A single city might comprise five or so pricing zones, categorized by its proximity to a Walmart versus a less economical regional grocery chain, for example. Although widely considered unethical, many retailers have charged higher prices in stores located in lower-income or urban areas because these customers, including older retirees, have less access to alternatives. Furthermore, the cost of operating businesses in those areas can be more expensive than in others.

Leader Pricing

Leader pricing is the practice of pricing certain items lower than normal to increase customers' traffic flow or boost sales of complementary products. Some retailers call these products **loss leaders**. In a strict sense, loss leaders are sold below cost and would therefore be considered predatory pricing, which is discussed in the next section. But a product doesn't have to be sold below cost for the retailer to use a leader-pricing strategy.

The best items for leader pricing are frequently purchased products like white bread, milk, and eggs or well-known brand names like Coca-Cola and Kellogg's Corn Flakes. Customers take note of ads for these products because they're purchased weekly. The retailer hopes consumers will also purchase their entire weekly grocery list while buying the loss leaders.

One problem with leader pricing is that it might attract shoppers referred to as **cherry pickers**, who go from one store to another buying only items that are on special. These shoppers are clearly unprofitable for retailers.[30]

Price Lining

Retailers frequently offer a limited number of predetermined price points within a merchandise category, a practice known as **price lining**. For instance, because Kroger's vision for its store brands is to build loyalty among customers, with strong store brands that are exclusive to the retailer, it pursues a price lining store-brand strategy to provide Kroger products to all customer segments (refer to Retailing View 12.1). Developing products for all these customer segments means that Kroger closes any gaps in the ability of its current assortment to meet customers' needs.

Odd Pricing

Odd pricing refers to the practice of using a price that ends in an odd number, typically a 9. Odd pricing has a long history in retailing. In the nineteenth and early twentieth centuries, odd pricing was used to reduce losses due to employee theft. Because

The practice of offering odd prices—a price that ends in an odd number, typically a 9—is more than 100 years old. Although empirical studies have mixed results, many retailers believe that the practice can increase profits.

© Bettmann/Getty Images

merchandise had an odd price, salespeople typically had to go to the cash register to give the customer change and record the sale, making it more difficult for salespeople to keep the customer's money. Odd pricing was also used to keep track of how many times an item had been marked down. After an initial price of $20, the first markdown would be $17.99, the second markdown $15.98, and so on.

The results of empirical studies in this area are mixed;[31] however, many retailers believe that odd pricing can increase profits. The theory behind odd pricing is the assumption that shoppers don't notice the last digit or digits of a price, so that a price of $2.99 is perceived as $2.00. An alternative theory is that "9" endings signal low prices. Thus, for products that are believed to be sensitive to price, many retailers will round down the price to the nearest 9 to create a positive price image. If, for example, the price would normally be $3.09, many retailers will lower the price to $2.99.

LEGAL AND ETHICAL PRICING ISSUES

LO 13-5

Indicate the legal and ethical issues retailers should consider when setting prices.

Retailers consider certain legal and ethical issues when setting prices.

Deceptive Reference Prices

A **reference price** is the price against which buyers compare the actual selling price of the product, and thus it facilitates their evaluation process. Typically, the retailer labels the reference price as the "regular price" or "original price." When consumers view the "sale price" and compare it with the provided reference price, their perceptions of the value of the product or service will likely increase.[32]

If the reference price is bona fide, the advertisement is informative. If the reference price has been inflated or is just plain fictitious, however, the advertisement is deceptive and may cause harm to consumers. But it is not easy to determine whether a reference price is bona fide. What standard should be used? If an advertisement specifies a "regular price," just what qualifies as regular? How many units must the store sell at this price for it to be a bona fide regular price—half the stock? A few? Just one? Finally, what if the store offers the item for sale at the regular price but customers do not buy any? Can it still be considered a regular price? In general, if a seller is going to label a price as a regular price, the Better Business Bureau suggests that at least 50 percent of the sales should have occurred at that price.[33] Retailing View 13.4 highlights the ethical issues associated with advertised discounts.

Predatory Pricing

Predatory pricing arises when a dominant retailer sets prices below its costs to drive competitive retailers out of business. Eventually, the predator hopes to raise prices when the competition is eliminated and earn back enough profits to compensate for its losses. For instance, independent booksellers have accused Walmart, Target, and Amazon of pricing best-selling books below their cost, thus claiming an illegal predatory pricing practice, which they believe is damaging to the book industry and harmful to consumers.[34] However, retailers generally may sell merchandise at any price as long as the motive isn't to eliminate competition, and this motive is very difficult to prove.

Resale Price Maintenance

Vendors often encourage retailers to sell their merchandise at a specific price, known as the manufacturer's suggested retail price (MSRP). Vendors set MSRPs to reduce retail price competition among retailers and stimulate retailers to provide complementary services. Vendors enforce MSRPs by withholding benefits such as cooperative

When a retailer advertises the price of an item as a sale price, it generally anchors that promotion on a higher, regular price. So a sweater on sale for $20 is anchored, using a percentage or a numerical comparison, as 50 percent off its regular price of $40, for example. But who decides what the regular prices are? If that product line of sweaters has literally never sold at $40 but instead has always been available at some lower price (whether $30, or the current sale price of $20, or maybe even $10), is $40 still the regular price?

Legally, the practice of setting such deceptive reference prices is questionable, because it misleads consumers into thinking they are getting a deal. A recent class-action lawsuit brought claims against JCPenney, arguing that the sale prices the retailer promotes are actually just its regular prices, with "sale" stickers on them. They might list a higher price, but the retailer never earned those prices from consumers. Without admitting any guilt, JCPenney agreed to pay the plaintiffs $50 million to make the case go away.

The broader issue is that retailers frequently engage in a misleading practice by which they mark prices higher than they ever expect to sell the products, then immediately discount them to what they consider a reasonable price point. In this case, consumers are fooled into thinking that they have gotten a deal, when really they are just paying the retailer's low prices. Other retailers similarly have been accused of using such deceptive reference prices, such as Kohl's, Sears, Macy's, and Men's Wearhouse.

Macy's and Sears both contest these accusations, noting that their pricing strategies are complex and dynamic, such that prices change daily, depending on a multitude of factors, including seasonal trends, customer responses, and product characteristics. Their pricing tactics also are purposefully designed to enable them to offer discounts competitively and differently, such as special online-only or in-store-only deals or member pricing for loyalty program members. Finally, they emphasize that they believe all their pricing methods are clearly and firmly in compliance with all applicable laws.

Yet when retailers engage in unethical "sale" pricing practices, they often do so in relation to their private-label or exclusive products. For example, at JCPenney, the Liz Claiborne blouses at the heart of the lawsuit were not available for sale anywhere else. Thus, consumers had no means to compare the prices with the costs they faced elsewhere.

Sources: Daphne Howland, "Are Department Store Prices Phony?," *Retail Dive*, June 25, 2015; Hiroko Tabuchi, "J.C.Penney Settles Shoppers Suit over False Advertising," *The New York Times*, November 11, 2015.

advertising or even refusing to deliver merchandise to noncomplying retailers. The latest U.S. Supreme Court ruling suggests that the ability of a vendor to require that retailers sell merchandise at MSRPs would be decided on a case-by-case basis, depending on the individual circumstances.[35]

Horizontal Price Fixing

Horizontal price fixing involves agreements between retailers that are in direct competition with each other to set the same prices. This practice clearly reduces competition and is illegal. As a general rule of thumb, retailers should refrain from discussing prices or terms and conditions of sale with competitors. If buyers or store managers want to know competitors' prices, they can look at a competitor's advertisements, its websites, or check out its stores.

Bait-and-Switch Tactics

A **bait and switch** is an unlawful, deceptive practice that lures customers into a store by advertising a product at a lower-than-normal price (the bait) and then, once they are in the store, induces them to purchase a higher-priced model (the switch). Bait and switch usually involves the store either having inadequate inventory for the advertised product or pushing salespeople to disparage the quality of the advertised model and emphasize the superior performance of a higher-priced model. To avoid disappointing customers and risking problems with the Federal Trade Commission (FTC), the retailer should have sufficient inventory of advertised items and offer customers rain checks if stockouts occur. A **rain check** is a promise to customers to sell currently out-of-stock merchandise at the advertised price when it arrives.

SUMMARY

LO 13-1 Explain the difference between a high/low pricing strategy and an everyday low-pricing strategy.

Setting prices is a critical decision in implementing a retail strategy because price is a critical component in customers' perceived value. Retailers use two basic retail pricing strategies: high/low pricing and everyday low pricing (EDLP). Each of these strategies has its advantages and disadvantages. The high/low strategy increases profits through price discrimination, creates excitement, and provides an opportunity to sell slow-moving merchandise. The EDLP approach assures customers of low prices, reduces advertising and operating expenses, reduces stockouts, and improves supply chain management.

LO 13-2 Identify the factors retailers consider when pricing their merchandise.

In setting prices, retailers consider the price sensitivity of customers in their target market, the pricing of services, analytical factors, competitive prices, and legal and ethical issues. Theoretically, retailers maximize their profits by setting prices on the basis of the price sensitivity of customers and the cost of merchandise. However, this approach does not consider the prices being charged by competitors. Another problem with attempting to set prices on the basis of customer price sensitivity is the implementation challenges associated with the large number of pricing decisions a retailer must make. Additional challenges arise when pricing services, due to the need to match supply and demand and the difficulties customers have in determining service quality. Most retailers set price by marking up the item's cost to yield a profitable gross margin. Then this initial price is adjusted on the basis of insights about customer price sensitivity and competitive pricing. To determine the initial retail price, retailers apply a markup as a percentage of the retail price.

Retailers often do not sell merchandise at the initial retail price. The average initial price is reduced by markdowns, discounts given to employees, and theft. Planning for these so-called reductions is important when determining the initial retail price so that the planned profit for the merchandise is obtained. Break-even analysis is also useful for determining how much a retailer needs to sell to begin making a profit. Retailers use dynamic pricing techniques to match supply and demand for services. The increased access to the Internet and the use of social media and smartphones has resulted in consumers having greater access to product and price information as they go about making purchasing decisions.

LO 13-3 Examine how and why retailers take markdowns.

Initial prices are adjusted over time using markdowns and for different market segments using variable-pricing strategies. Retailers take markdowns to either dispose of merchandise or generate sales. Markdowns are part of the cost of doing business, and thus buyers plan for them.

LO 13-4 Identify the pricing techniques retailers use to increase sales and profits.

Retailers use a variety of techniques to maximize sales and profits by charging different prices to different customers. These techniques include dynamic pricing, promotional markdowns, clearance markdowns for fashion merchandise, coupons, price bundling, quantity discounts, zone pricing, leader pricing, price lining, and odd pricing.

LO 13-5 Indicate the legal and ethical issues retailers should consider when setting prices.

There are several legal and ethical issues retailers consider when setting prices. These include deceptive reference prices, predatory pricing, resale price maintenance, horizontal price fixing, and bait-and-switch tactics.

KEY TERMS

bait and switch, *361*

break-even analysis, *350*

break-even point quantity, *350*

cherry picking, *359*

coupons, *358*

dynamic pricing, *356*

elastic, *346*

everyday low-pricing (EDLP) strategy, *342*

fixed costs, *351*

geofencing, *352*

high/low pricing strategy, *342*

horizontal price fixing, *361*

individualized pricing, *356*

inelastic, *346*

initial markup, *349*

inventory shrinkage, *349*

keystoning, *349*

leader pricing, *359*

loss leader, *359*

low-price guarantee policy, *344*

maintained markup, *349*

markdown, *353*

markdown money, *355*

markup, *349*

markup percentage, *349*

multiple-unit pricing, *358*

odd pricing, *359*

predatory pricing, *360*

price bundling, *358*

price elasticity, *346*

price lining, *359*

pricing optimization software, *351*

quantity discount, *358*

rain check, *361*

reductions, *349*

reference price, *360*

value, *341*

variable costs, *351*

zone pricing, *358*

GET OUT AND DO IT!

1. **CONTINUING ASSIGNMENT** Go shopping at the retailer you have selected for the continuing assignment. Does the retailer use high/low pricing or an EDLP strategy? Ask the store manager how markdown decisions are made and how the store decides how much a markdown should be. What rule-based approaches are used to make markdowns, or does the retailer use markdown optimization software? Does the retailer use techniques for stimulating sales such as price lining, leader pricing, bundling, or multiple-unit and odd pricing? Are the prices on its website the same as those in the store? Evaluate your findings. Do you believe the retailer is using the best pricing strategies and tactics for its type of store? What, if anything, could it do to improve?

2. Go to the web page of Overstock.com (www.overstock.com) and look at its top-selling merchandise. Select a few key items, and compare the price of each product at other online retail sites such as Target.com, Amazon.com,

Sears.com, and Macys.com. How do the prices at this Internet outlet compare to those at a discount store, online retailer, and department store? Are the results what you expected, or were you surprised? Explain your reaction.

3. Go to the website of Sandals (www.sandals.com) and see what you can get for an all-inclusive price. Describe how bundling services and products provides vacationers with value. Find an example of price bundling outside the travel industry. Which method, bundling or nonbundling, do you believe provides the customer with the best value? Which makes the retailer or service provider more profits?

4. Go to your favorite food store and your local Walmart to find their prices for the market basket of goods listed in the accompanying table. What was the total cost of the market basket at each store? How did the prices compare? Did Walmart live up to its slogan of "Always lower prices"?

Item	Size	Brand	Grocery	Walmart	Price Difference	Percent Savings
Grocery						
Ground coffee	11.5-oz can	Folgers				
Raisin Bran	25.5-oz box	Kellogg's				
Pet Supplies						
Puppy Chow	4.4-lb bag	Purina				
Cleaning						
Liquid laundry detergent	100-oz bottle	All				
Dryer sheets	80 count	Bounce				
Liquid dish detergent	25-oz bottle	Palmolive				
Health and beauty						
Shampoo	12-oz bottle	Dove				
Toothpaste	4.2-oz tube	Colgate Total				
Total cost of the market basket of goods						

DISCUSSION QUESTIONS AND PROBLEMS

1. What types of retailers often use a high/low pricing strategy? What types of retailers generally use an everyday low-pricing strategy? How would customers likely react if a retailer switched its pricing strategy from one to the other? Explain your response.

2. Why would sewing pattern manufacturers such as Simplicity (www.simplicity.com/patterns/) and Butterick (https://butterick.mccall.com/) ask $12.95 (or more) on each pattern and then two times a year offer patterns for sale at $1.99 each? How could this markdown influence demand, sales, and profits?

3. What is the difference between bundled pricing and multiple-unit pricing?

4. A department store's maintained markup is 38 percent, reductions are $560, and net sales are $28,000. What's the initial markup percentage?

5. Maintained markup is 39 percent, net sales are $52,000, and reductions are $2,500. What are the gross margin in dollars and the initial markup as a percentage? Explain why initial markup is greater than maintained markup.

6. The cost of a product is $150, markup is 50 percent, and markdown is 30 percent. What's the final selling price?

7. Men's Wearhouse purchased black leather belts for $15.99 each and priced them to sell for $29.99 each. What was the markup on the belts?

8. Answer the following questions:

(a) J.Crew is planning a new line of jackets for fall. It plans to sell the jackets for $100. It is having the jackets produced in the Dominican Republic. Although J.Crew does not own the factory, its product development and design costs are $400,000. The total cost of the jacket, including transportation to the stores, is $45. For this line to be successful, J. Crew needs to make $900,000 profit. What is its break-even point in units and dollars?

(b) The buyer has just found out that The Gap, one of J.Crew's major competitors, is bringing out a similar jacket that will retail for $90. If J.Crew wants to match The Gap's price, how many units will it have to sell?

CHAPTER ENDNOTES

1. Hollis Johnson, "We Taste-Tested Pizzas from Papa John's, Pizza Hut, and Domino's—Here's Who Does It Best," *Business Insider*, November 13, 2015.

2. Aamer Madhani, "Papa John's Tries New Tack to Challenge Pizza Hut, Domino's for Pizza Supremacy," *USA Today*, January 30, 2016.

3. Fast Food, "2016 Pizza Wars: Who Will Win," February 12, 2016, http://www.fastfoodmenuprices.com/2016-pizza-war-who-will-win/.

4. Fast Food, "Papa John's Rings 2016 with the Launching of Its New Dessert," February 12, 2016, http://www.fastfoodmenuprices.com/2016-pizza-war-who-will-win/.

5. Erik Oster, "Barton F. Graf Hypes Little Caesars Stuffed Crust Deep! Deep! Dish with 'Faces,'" *Ad Week*, March 25, 2016, http://www.adweek.com/agencyspy/barton-f-graf-hypes-little-caesars-stuffed-crust-deep-deep-dish-with-faces/105328.

6. Jonathan Maze, "The Most Underappreciated Growth Restaurant in the Country," *Nation's Restaurant News*, July 22, 2015, http://nrn.com/blog/most-underappreciated-growth-restaurant-country.

7. Brian Manzullo, "Little Caesars Will Give You Free Lunch If No. 16 Seed Scores an Upset," *Detroit Free Press*, March 16, 2016.

8. Rebecca Borison, "Domino's Earns Customer Loyalty with Mobile at the Forefront," *Mobile Commerce Daily*, October 21, 2013, http://www.mobilecommercedaily.com/domino's-leads-the-mobile-way-for-pizza-chains.

9. Seb Joseph, "Domino's Says Its Snapchat Test Led to a 'Surprising' Surge in Pizza Orders," *Business Insider*, February 18, 2016.

10. Chris Isidore, "Pizza War! Pizza Hut and Papa John's Slash Prices," *CNN Money*, January 4, 2016.

11. Ibid.

12. Aamer Madhani, "Papa John's Tries New Tack to Challenge Pizza Hut, Domino's for Pizza Supremacy," *USA Today*, January 30, 2016.

13. Monica Watrous, "Pizza Hut's Performance Warms Up," *Food Business News*, February 5, 2016, http://www.foodbusiness-news.net/articles/news_home/Financial-Performance/2016/02/Pizza_Huts_performance_warms_u.aspx?ID=%7B406380A3-B93E-4EAA-A162-97E225B69B2E%7D&cck=1.

14. Isidore, "Pizza War!"

15. Maze, "The Most Underappreciated Growth Restaurant in the Country."

16. Isidore, "Pizza War!"

17. Maureen Morrison and Matthew Creamer, "How P&G, Ford, and Wendy's Are Redefining Value," *Advertising Age,* April 22, 2013.

18. George Anderson, "Target Takes Price Matching to a Whole New Level," *RetailWire*, October 1, 2015.

19. Valarie A. Zeithaml, Mary Jo Bitner, and Dwayne Gremler, *Service Marketing: Integrating Customer Focus across the Firm,* 6th ed. (New York: McGraw-Hill, 2012).

20. "A Look Back: How Predictive Analytics Transformed the Airline Industry," Cusotra, https://www.custora.com/university/for-marketers/predictive-analytics/basic/predictive-analytics-and-the-airline-industry; "Price Trends & Tips Explanation," Kayak, 2015, http://www.kayak.com.

21. George Anderson, "Will Surge Pricing Become the New Normal?," *RetailWire*, October 1, 2015.

22. Zeithaml et al., *Service Marketing.*

23. Susan Reda, "Pricing Transparency," *Stores*, February 2012.

24. Bergstein, "Pricing Software Could Reshape Retail."

25. Dhruv Grewal, Yakov Bart, Martin Spann, and Peter Pal Zubcsek, "Mobile Advertising: A Framework and Research Agenda," *Journal of Interactive Marketing* 34 (May 2016), pp. 3–14.

26. https://www.meijer.com/content/content.jsp?pageName=mobile_app.

27. Ibid.; Dan Mattioli and Miguel Bustillo, "Can Texting Save Stores?," *The Wall Street Journal,* May 8, 2012.

28. Praveen K. Kopalle, "Editorial: Modeling Retail Phenomena," *Journal of Retailing* 86, no. 2 (2010), pp. 117–124; Michael Levy, Dhruv Grewal, Praveen K. Kopalle, and James D. Hess, "Emerging Trends in Retail Pricing Practice: Implications for Research," *Journal of Retailing* 80, no. 3 (2004), pp. xiii–xxi.

29. Steve McKee, "How to Discount (If You Insist)," *BusinessWeek,* August 14, 2009; Teri Evans, "An Expert's Guide to Discounting," *BusinessWeek,* April 3, 2009.

30. Debabrata Talukdar, Dinesh K. Gauri, and Dhruv Grewal, "An Empirical Analysis of Extreme Cherry Picking Behavior of Consumers in the Frequently Purchased Goods Market," *Journal of Retailing* 86, no. 4 (2010), pp. 336–354; Leigh McAlister, Edward I. George, and Yung-Hsin Chien, "A Basket-Mix Model to Identify Cherry-Picked Brands," *Journal of Retailing* 85, no. 4 (2009), pp. 425–436.

31. Sandrine Mace, "The Determinants of Nine-Ending Effects: An Empirical Analysis Using Store-Level Scanner Data," *Journal of Retailing* 88, no. 1 (2012), pp. 115–130; Traci H. Freling, Leslie H. Vincent, Robert Schindler, David M. Hardesty, and Jason Rowe, "A Meta-Analysis of Just-Below Pricing Effects: Separating Reality from the 'Magic,'" Working paper, 2012; R. M. Schindler, "Patterns of Price Endings Used in U.S. and Japanese Price Advertising," *International Marketing Review* 26, no. 1 (2009), pp. 17–29; R. M. Schindler, "The 99-Price Ending as a Signal of a Low-Price Appeal," *Journal of Retailing* 82, no. 1 (2006), pp. 71–77.

32. Dhruv Grewal, Anne L. Roggeveen, and Joan Lindsey-Mullikin, "The Contingent Effects of Semantic Price Cues," *Journal of Retailing* 90, no. 2 (2014), pp. 198–205; Abhijit Biswas, Sandeep Bhowmick, Abhijit Guha, and Dhruv Grewal, "Consumer Evaluation of Sale Price: Role of the Subtraction Principle," *Journal of Marketing* 77 (July 2013), pp. 49–66; Dhruv Grewal and Larry Compeau, "Consumer Responses to Price and Its Contextual Information Cues: A Synthesis of Past Research, a Conceptual Framework, and Avenues for Further Research," in *Review of Marketing Research,* vol. 3, Naresh Malhotra, ed. (Armonk, NY: M.E. Sharpe, 2006), pp. 109–131; Larry D. Compeau and Dhruv Grewal, "Comparative Price Advertising: An Integrative Review," *Journal of Public Policy & Marketing* 17 (Fall 1998), pp. 257–274.

33. https://www.bbb.org/atlanta/for-businesses/code-of-advertising/.

34. Steven W. Beattie, "Stephen King's New Face of Evil: Predatory Pricing," *Quill & Quire,* October 26, 2009.

35. Gregory T. Gundlach, Joseph P. Cannon, and Kenneth C. Manning, "Free Riding and Resale Price Maintenance: Insights from Marketing Research and Practice," *Antitrust Bulletin* 55, no. 2 (Summer 2010), pp. 381–422; Gregory T. Gundlach, "Overview of the Special Issues: Antitrust Analysis of Resale Price Maintenance after *Leegin*," Special Issue, Part II, *Antitrust Bulletin* 55, no. 2 (2010), pp. 271–276; Gregory T. Gundlach, "Overview and Contents of the Special Issues: Antitrust Analysis of Resale Price Maintenance after *Leegin*," Special Issue, Part I, *Antitrust Bulletin* 55, no. 1 (2010), pp. 1–24.

© Andrew H. Walker/Getty Images

For H&M, fashion may be fast, but to be appealing, it also has to spread the message about its offerings far and wide. Accordingly, the retailer uses a mix of creative media and new and traditional communication channels to reach consumers.

For example, for its Times Square flagship store, H&M posts advertising banners on the nearest subway platform, encouraging commuters to stop by before they head home or during their lunch break. On the sides of the building, a more modern form of billboard advertising runs constant videos of the available fashions on huge, 30 × 200-foot LED screens. Even the store windows communicate the retail offering, with interactive features that seek to draw customers into the retail venue, where they can interact further with in-store communications, including light boxes that highlight deals and specials and revolving mannequins that model the latest fashions.[1]

Such options signal H&M's efforts to put a modern spin on traditional communications methods, such as billboards, in-store signage, and displays. In its print advertising campaigns, it similarly seeks to push the boundaries. For example, a campaign features high-end portraits of artists and muses, including Iman, Chloë Sevigny, Chance the Rapper, and Rosario Dawson, all shot by the famous photographer Jean-Paul Goude. Thus H&M uses the traditional medium of print advertising, yet it does so in a way that is unconventional, featuring faces that might be a bit different than the conventional models depicted in fashion advertising.[2]

With televised spots, H&M also aims to ensure its international appeal, featuring dancers and actors from across the world, all interpreting an original composition by M.I.A. titled "Rewear It." The combination advertisement–music video features a song in English but also provides subtitles in various languages, all while encouraging consumers to recycle their clothing rather than simply disposing of the fast-fashion options.[3]

In addition, the fast-fashion retailer embraces less traditional methods to reach shoppers using a very creative approach. For example, it noted the popularity of the funny, sharp, and personal *Man Repeller* blog—a site dedicated to the proposition that fashion is about expressing an individual preference and style, not attracting potential romantic partners. With 1.4 million followers on Instagram and 360,000 on

Twitter, as well as approximately 1 million daily visits to the blog, the witty site has quickly became a force to be reckoned with in the fashion world.[4] Rather than depending on the dictates of fashion editors and designers, consumers increasingly turn to bloggers, seemingly regular people who can put together an outfit and have an eye for color.

Noting these shifts, H&M has actively sought to work with *Man Repeller* to encourage promotions on that blog, and then to identify other influential people who might want to link with H&M. Thus the blogger behind *Man Repeller,* Leandra Medine, functioned as a judge and mentor in a contest on the Bloglovin' blog network that sought to find the best fashion blogger available. The contest drew some 3,500 applicants, each of whom had to post some of her previous work, as well as create a new outfit for others to critique.[5] The outfit had to contain at least one H&M piece, reflecting the retailer's sponsorship of the contest.

The winner of the contest was named the "Breakthrough Fashion Blogger of the Year," leading to vastly increased exposure for the blogger, as well as suggestions from Medine as a mentor. For H&M, its participation in the contest also gave it access to a whole range of fashion bloggers, whom it considers "instrumental to everything we do. We admire their passion and love that they showcase how H&M products can work for anyone and everyone."[6] In this modern world, finding new and creative ways to showcase the retail offering is often the key to success.

The preceding chapters in this section on merchandise management described how retailers develop an assortment and merchandise budget plans, then buy and price the merchandise. The next step is to develop and implement a communication program that will attract customers to retail locations (whether in stores or online) and encourage them to buy the merchandise available. The communication program informs customers about the retailer, describes the merchandise and services offered, helps develop the retailer's brand, and plays a critical role in encouraging repeat visits and customer loyalty.

At the end of the twentieth century, most retail communication programs were fairly simple. Local newspaper advertising was the primary medium, and the message was typically oriented toward providing incentives—usually a special price—to motivate customers to visit the store. **Advertising** is paid communications delivered to customers through nonpersonal mass media such as newspapers, television, radio, direct mail, and the Internet. Today, successful retailers utilize an **integrated marketing communication (IMC) program** in which they integrate a variety of communication elements to deliver a comprehensive, consistent message to all customers over time, across all elements of their retail mix and across all delivery channels.

For example, CVS certainly uses traditional media, such that it includes advertising in newspapers,

The myWeekly Ad initiative creates specific digital circulars that are e-mailed to each consumer who registers, featuring products that they might be interested in and encouraging them to expand their purchases at CVS.

Source: CVS.com

EXHIBIT 14–1   Elements of an Integrated Marketing Communication Strategy

Media/Characteristics	Personalizations	Interactivity	Message Control	Information	Cost per Exposure
New Media					
• Online	Depends	Depends	High	High	Depends
• Mobile	High	Depends	Depends	Low	Low
• Social	High	High	Depends	Depends	Low
Traditional Media					
• Mass advertising	None	None	High	Low	Very low
• Sales promotions	Depends	Depends	High	Low	Low
• In-store marketing/design elements	Depends	Depends	High	Depends	Low
• Personal selling	High	High	Medium	High	Very high
• Public relations	None	None	Depends	Medium	Low

television, and billboards. But it also has developed advanced tools to personalize people's shopping experience, including the marketing communications they receive. The myWeekly Ad initiative, part of CVS's loyalty program, creates specific digital circulars that are e-mailed to all consumers who register, featuring products that they might be interested in and encouraging them to expand their purchases at CVS. In addition to customized coupons, the myWeekly Ad communication is specific to the customers' local store, so shoppers can use the link while in stores to find the aisle location of the promoted product.[7] Coordination across these channels is critical; if CVS focuses solely on its friendly and helpful pharmacists in its television advertising, but then pursues a low-cost image in its circulars, customers are likely to sense some confusion.

For any communications campaign to succeed, the retailer must deliver the right message to the right audience through the right media at the right time, with the ultimate goal of profiting from long-term customer relationships, as well as short-term sales. Reaching the right audience is becoming more difficult as the media environment grows more complicated. No single type of media is necessarily better than another. The goal of a retail communication strategy is to plan all of the elements to work together so the sum exceeds the total of the individual media parts.

We now examine the individual elements of a retail communication strategy and the way each contributes to a successful communication campaign (see Exhibit 14–1). These elements are divided into new and traditional media. The new media elements include online (websites, e-mail, mobile) and social media (YouTube, Facebook, blogs, and Twitter). Traditional media elements include mass advertising, sales promotions, in-store marketing/design elements, personal selling, and public relations. These media elements vary on five dimensions: personalization, interactivity, message control, extent of information provided, and the cost per exposure.

NEW MEDIA ELEMENTS

Identify the new media elements.

Over the past decade or so, the use of newer forms of media, such as online (e.g., websites, e-mail, and mobile), and social media (e.g., YouTube, Facebook, blogs, and Twitter) has exploded. Each of these new media elements is discussed next.

Online Media

Websites   Retailers are increasing their emphasis on communicating with customers through their websites, which are used to build their brand images; inform customers of store locations, special events, and the availability of merchandise in local stores; and sell merchandise and services. Many retailers also devote areas of their websites to community building. These sites offer an opportunity for customers with similar interests to learn about products and services that support their hobbies and to share information with others. Visitors can also post questions seeking information and/or

Source: Recreational Equipment, Inc.

REI creates a community of customers through its adventure planning division that engages its customers and encourages them to buy its merchandise.

comments about issues, products, and services. For example, REI, an outdoor apparel and equipment retailer, offers adventure travel planning resources for hiking trips, bike tours, paddling, adventure cruises, and other trips. By doing so, REI creates a community of customers who engage in activities using the merchandise that REI sells. The community thus reinforces REI's brand image.

Many retailers encourage customers to post reviews of products they have bought or used on their websites. Research has shown that these online product reviews increase customer loyalty and provide a competitive advantage for sites that offer them.[8] In a further effort to appeal to consumers and encourage them to interact with the retailer in various ways, some websites provide editorial content and fashion advice, rather than being dedicated solely to selling products to users, as Retailing View 14.1 explains.

Depending on how customers use retailers' websites, they can experience a very personalized and interactive experience. The message can contain lots of information and is easily controlled. The cost per exposure is comparatively moderate because the cost of maintaining and operating a website can be expensive.

Retailers are actively using **search engine marketing (SEM)** to improve the visibility of their websites in searches. One SEM method is to use **search engine optimization (SEO)**, which is creating and adjusting website content to show up closer to the top of a **search engine results page (SERP)**. These SERPs list the results that a search engine provides, in response to a user's keyword query. Thus, SEO is used to enhance unpaid or organic searches. Another SEM method is using paid search through Google's sponsored link advertising program. These results are placed above and to the right of natural or organic search results.[9]

E-mail   **E-mail** involves sending messages over the Internet to specific individuals. Retailers use e-mail to inform customers of new merchandise and special promotions, confirm the receipt of an order, and indicate when an order has been shipped. The increased use of customer databases has enabled retailers to identify and track consumers over time and across purchase situations (see Chapter 10). As a result, e-mail can be highly personal and the message very controlled. However, when the same message is

14.1   RETAILING VIEW   Getting Shoppers to Stop at the Site, Even If Just for a Quick Read

Similar to the way that the distinction between online and offline channels have blurred, the latest developments in fashion-oriented multichannel retailing are eliminating the differences between commercial and editorial content. In publications offered both online and offline, retailers tout modern trends and cutting-edge fashions, sometimes without any consideration of whether their shopping channels offer those self-same items.

The European retailer Asos exemplifies this emerging development. Its Fashion Finder site combines new product information with fashion tips and style innovations, presented with a mix of visual content and magazine-like articles and features. In addition, it publishes a glossy paper magazine with a circulation of nearly half a million readers, then also makes this content available as digital versions adapted to U.S., French, German, and Australian markets.

By integrating retailing, social media, and publishing operations, Primark manifests a unique growth approach. It does not have an online channel, and it does not advertise in a traditional sense. Rather, its Primania social media site is populated by exuberant fans of the retailer's offerings, who post selfies that feature their recent purchases, along with commentary and price information. The approximately 300,000 weekly visitors to Primania are mostly young women, who check their social media profiles with remarkable frequency and demand interpersonal interactions with their favorite brands. Furthermore, more than half of this target market initiates a purchase by browsing offerings through a smartphone or other mobile device. Thus the central goal for retailers is to attract their attention, which means giving them interesting content. Even if the retailer does not carry the skirt worn by a popular celebrity to a recent event, it may run a story about

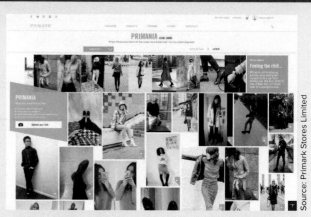

Source: Primark Stores Limited

Primark's social media site Primania posts selfies of its fans' recent purchases, along with commentary and price information.

her fashion choices to ensure that potential customers at least stop for a quick read.

Although some more traditional retailers are following suit, their efforts may be less successful, according to the segments of customers they generally attract. For example, Marks & Spencer has expanded its website to include a style and living section that provides magazine-style content and information. But perhaps because most of its clientele tends to be older women who visit the website to make efficient purchases rather than learn about lip gloss trends, its online sales have lagged.

Source: Sarah Butler, "Love the Dress: Sharing Websites Are the Latest Must-Have for Fashion Retailers," *The Observer*, June 28, 2014.

To promote its World Burger Tour, the Hard Rock Café used geotargeted rich mobile ads directed at customers within a specific radius of the restaurant.

© Aaron Davidson/Getty Images

delivered electronically to all recipients, e-mails more closely resemble the more impersonal medium, mass advertising. Because e-mail recipients can respond back to the retailer, it is considered an interactive medium. Finally, the cost per exposure is low.

Mobile Marketing   **Mobile marketing**, also called **mobile commerce**, **M-commerce**, or **mobile retailing**, is marketing through wireless handheld devices such as cellular telephones.[10] Smartphones have become far more than tools to place calls; they offer a kind of mobile computer with the ability to obtain sports scores, weather, music, videos, and text messages as well as purchase merchandise. Marketing success rests on integrating marketing communications with fun, useful apps that are consistent with these consumer attitudes toward mobile devices. In response, firms are steadily improving customers' potential experience with their mobile interface.

Retailers use applications to communicate with mobile phone users and send them messages on the basis of their location, as determined by GPS technology. With the GPS-based application, users also can recommend nearby retailers to friends in the area. Furthermore, the app's data analytic capabilities allow retailers to track the impact of mobile marketing campaigns. To promote its World Burger Tour, the Hard Rock Café used geotargeted rich mobile ads directed at customers within a specific radius of the restaurant. The Hard Rock was also able to access customer information that helped identify vacationers who would be more likely to be eating out. The campaign was a huge success, leading to a 220 percent increase in traffic.[11] But even when the communications have less of an analytical component, they can be meaningful, as the example in Retailing View 14.2 suggests. Retailers also use mobile channels to deliver coupons or other promotional offers, such as free shipping to customers who

---

RETAILING VIEW   Analyzing the Unmeasured: A Snapchat Experiment by Domino's to Test the Channel's Effectiveness   **14.2**

Most marketing communications and advertising campaigns start with an idea, and then the appropriate channel to share it is chosen. But in a recent Snapchat campaign by the UK arm of Domino's Pizza, the pattern was reversed: Domino's wanted to experiment with using Snapchat, so it chose the channel first, and then developed an idea that would enable it to test the success of the campaign.

The unique approach was necessary because Snapchat—as a primarily creative, rather than informative, messaging channel—lacks the analytical tools available in most other sources. Unlike other social media sites, for example, it does not provide users with measures of reach or consumer responses. Yet it is an organic and popular social media application, with great promise for reaching and appealing to young and savvy consumers.

Therefore, Domino's decided to undertake an experimental test in which it posted a series of videos. The storyline featured a delivery driver beset by an alien invasion over multiple video uploads. Each entry in the series gave viewers a portion of a code; once they had the entire code, they could use it to receive a purchase voucher. Thus, the number of vouchers redeemed offered a good estimate of reach, because it signaled how many people were willing to watch the entire video series. After the 24-hour experiment, Domino's was pleasantly surprised by how many additional orders it received. As another measure of the campaign's success, Domino's also determined how far the video spread among various consumers.

Noting the gaps in its analytical capabilities, Snapchat is rumored to be working on developing better measurement and assessment tools. Some reports also suggest it might begin offering e-commerce capabilities and group messaging. Yet part of the appeal of Snapchat is the creativity it invokes. Other competitors already offer group messaging services, so expanding the services it offers could move Snapchat into more direct competition with new rivals, as well as disrupting its reputation as a fun site, not a commercial one.

The Domino's test remains just that; the pizza chain has not determined exactly how it will continue to use Snapchat in its marketing communications. But the promising results give it a good reason to continue experimenting. As Domino's head of digital marketing suggested, using Snapchat alongside other social media and traditional communications channels seemed like the way to go, such that "Our anticipation is

Source: Domino's Pizza

To test Snapchat's effectiveness as a promotional channel, Domino's posted a series of videos featuring a delivery driver beset by an alien invasion. Each video contained a hidden code that allowed viewers to receive a discount. Domino's tracked code redemption to gauge the reach of the campaign.

that Snapchat will become a tool we add to our toolkit, rather than being the one that we use for everything."

Source: Seb Joseph, "Domino's Says Its Snapchat Test Led to a 'Surprising' Surge in Pizza Orders," *Business Insider,* February 18, 2016.

purchase online from the retailer while in its brick-and-mortar store. Finally, retailers might use the related location-based technology to deliver tailored, local messages to customers to drive them into their stores.

Social Media

Social media include various forms of electronic communication, which users can employ to create online communities in which they share ideas, information, their interpersonal messages, and other content (e.g., videos). Three major online facilitators of social media are YouTube, Facebook, and Twitter. As another online vehicle that encourages word-of-mouth communications, online forums enable consumers to review, communicate about, and aggregate information about products, prices, and promotions. These forums also allow users to interact among themselves (e.g., form a community).[12] Such online communities enable users to provide other like-minded consumers and retailers with their thoughts about and evaluations of a retailer's products or services.

Retailers use social media to engage their customers in proactive dialogue.[13] When a retailer provides content in a social media website, people often begin sharing and commenting on it. The retailer then must monitor the feedback and respond if necessary—especially if the commentary is negative. For example, **sentiment analysis** is the process of analyzing data posted on social media sites to assess customers' overall valence (positive, neutral and negative) and their intensity of their sentiments and can be used to understand overall attitudes and preferences for products and advertising campaigns. Scouring millions of sites by combining automated online search tools with text analysis techniques, sentiment mining yields qualitative data that provide new insights into what consumers really think. Retailers plugged into this real-time information can become more nimble allowing for quick changes in a product rollout or a new advertising campaign.

As these various examples of social media indicate, they can be very personal and interactive. When the message is produced by the retailer, it can be controlled, but when customers are involved, as is the case with reviews, there is little control over the message whatsoever. Likewise, the level of information content is dependent on who is doing the communications. The cost per exposure for social media is relatively low compared to traditional media.

YouTube   On this video-sharing social media platform, users upload, share, view, and comment on videos. This medium gives retailers a chance to express themselves in a different way than they have before. A retailer such as the television home shopping company HSN, discussed in Retailing View 14.3, can broadcast its own channel, that is, a YouTube site that contains content relevant only to the company's own products.[14]

YouTube also provides an effective medium for hosting contests and posting instructional videos. Home Depot has attracted more than 18,000 subscribers and racked up more than 41 million views with an array of videos detailing new products available in stores, as well as instructional do-it-yourself videos, like "How-to Tips for Mowing Your Lawn" or "How to Repair a Toilet."[15] These videos maintain the core identity of the Home Depot brand, while also adding value for consumers, who learn useful ways to improve their homes.

Home Depot fosters its identity with instructional do-it-yourself videos on YouTube.

Source: Home Depot

Facebook   This social media platform with more than 1.5 billion active users[16] gives companies a forum to interact with fans. Retailers have access to the same features that regular users do, including a "wall" where they can post company updates, photos, and videos or participate in a discussion board.

RETAILING VIEW   YouTube and HSN   14.3

Begun as a local cable channel in 1982, Home Shopping Network (HSN) offered consumers a central location from which to buy through their televisions. As competition in this field increased, HSN tailored its communication strategy to reach more shoppers. For example, HSN.com is one of the most visited e-commerce sites. But perhaps the most powerful tool HSN has added to its communication strategy is YouTube.

By reaching 40 to 50 percent of the company's target market, YouTube gives HSN a way to interact differently with customers and further increase its share of wallet with its current customers. The video format humanizes the connection and provides additional information about products.

For consumers, YouTube offers a seamless experience. Products promoted on HSN, such as Serena Williams's fashion line, are available on YouTube almost immediately after they appear on television. The YouTube channel also provides fun and related content, such as reality shows that follow Williams's experiences at New York's Fashion Week, then makes the fashions available immediately. In turn, HSN can use the information gathered from YouTube to target direct mail campaigns. For example, it could send promotions for a sweater to households that viewed the YouTube video clip for the collection of knitwear from Serena Williams. Consumer responses get monitored 24/7 and measured against hourly

Source: HSN, Inc.

Products promoted on HSN, such as Serena Williams's fashion line, are available on YouTube almost immediately after they appear on television.

sales goals. There's never a dull moment—it's like the CNN of shopping.

Sources: www.gstatic.com/youtube/engagement/platform/autoplay/advertise/downloads/YouTube_InTheKnow.pdf; www.gstatic.com/youtube/engagement/platform/autoplay/advertise/downloads/YouTube_BrandChannels.pdf; www.gstatic.com/youtube/engagement/platform/autoplay/advertise/downloads/YouTube_Insight.pdf; https://www.youtube.com/watch?v=5TynMOILW6I&list=PLhTr_-xYVr2j2jEFWh_L48ZQVOojy4vsA&index=1.

For Macy's, Facebook has long been a promising communication outlet, so it also became one of the first retailers to adopt the Facebook Page format. Furthermore, the Facebook timeline format has worked well in highlighting its events. Macy's has started to advertise more on Facebook, using more targeted ads to communicate with current and potential fans. Adapting along with the social media site represents just one facet in its broader plan to revamp its social media initiatives to attract more 25- to 54-year-old female consumers, along with some Millennial fashionistas. It believes that Facebook is a great way to get the right message in front of the right people.[17]

Facebook also provides an appealing means to target local groups of consumers for smaller retailers. For example, PCC Natural Markets in Seattle engages customers in social media dialogue on Facebook about local products. To encourage participation in local events, such as its "Taste PCC: A Local Food Celebration" or "Deli Throw Down" contest, it spreads vast word-of-mouth communication with minimal investment by relying on postings and tweets through Facebook and Twitter.[18]

Retailers like PCC Natural Markets use Facebook to communicate with customers and create a sense of community.

Blogs   On a **blog (weblog)**, an individual blogger or a group of users regularly post their opinions and various topical information on a web page. The administrator of the blog can either be an independent person, a retailer, or another type of firm. A well-received blog can communicate trends, announce special events, and create **word of mouth**, which is

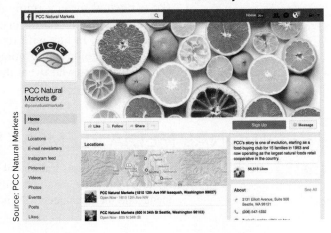

Source: PCC Natural Markets

communication among people about an entity such as a retailer or a product or service.[19] Blogs connect customers by forming a community, allowing a retailer to respond directly to customers' comments, and facilitate long-term relationships between customers and the retailer. By their very nature, blogs are supposed to be transparent and contain authors' honest observations, which can help customers determine their trust and loyalty levels. If, however, the blog is created or sponsored by a retailer, the information may be positively biased. Also, retailers have limited control over the content posted on blog; thus the information posted can be negative or incorrect. Many retailers use blogs as part of their communication strategy. On the *Canopy* blog, the community of registered members identify the best products available for purchase on Amazon, with the acknowledgment that it is "Amazon-curated." The link to the retailer is part of its appeal; visitors know that they can access these products quickly and easily.[20]

Twitter   In discussions of social media, Facebook and Twitter often get mentioned in the same breath, but they differ in some critical ways. Twitter is a **microblog**—a short version of a blog—in which users are limited to 140-character messages. The use of 140-character messages forces retailers to post short, timely, and relevant posts. The 140 characters no longer include @names and images, thus stretching the potential length of the tweet.[21] Where retailers may use Facebook to encourage discussions of their brand, promotions, or even ask their "friends" to post videos, they are more likely to use Twitter to announce up-to-date or fast-changing information to excite consumers. Twitter is actively used by both small and large retailers. Smaller retailers with limited marketing budgets love the response they can induce by sending a promotional message immediately. Before the 2013 blizzard Nemo, a local food truck tweeted at the beginning of the day, "Headed to @dumbofoodtrucks Front St & Main St! Come get Korilla before Nemo does!" allowing its customers to know both where to find them and create a sense of urgency before the storm—a huge captive audience for a local entity.[22]

Large retailers may have enough funds to mass-market through national campaigns, but Twitter provides them with a way to stay in personal touch with customers. The well-reputed Wegmans grocery store chain posts the dates and times on which it receives its produce deliveries, so customers who prize the very freshest produce can show up just as the vegetables are getting unloaded. Along with these delivery details, Wegmans tweets grower and farmer information, as well as available stock. Wegmans also uses social media to answer customer questions.

Twitter has also changed the way customers get product or service information and register praise and complaints. Whereas once customers with questions about a product or service had to call up the retailer's customer service line and sit through prerecorded voice prompts, today they can turn to Twitter to get immediate feedback. Retailers measure Twitter customer service success by the quality, accuracy, and timeliness of their response to customers' service issues. For example, the Penske car rental agency implemented its Twitter customer service program after spending an entire year observing how customers were using Twitter for customer service issues. In line with its findings, it trained its call-center employees to use the new technology and monitor the Twitter feed from 7:00 a.m. to 11:00 p.m. daily. Customers who tweet their car rental questions receive nearly instantaneous responses.[23]

TRADITIONAL MEDIA ELEMENTS

LO 14-2

Identify the traditional media elements.

Retailers use various traditional media elements: mass media advertising, promotions, in-store marketing, personal selling, and public relations. Each of these five media elements and their subcategories is discussed next.

Mass Media Advertising

Advertising   This form of mass media entails the placement of announcements and persuasive messages purchased by retailers and other organizations that seek to inform and/or persuade members of a particular target market or audience about their products, services, organizations, or ideas.[24] After automobile manufacturers, retailers are the second-largest group of national advertisers, spending more than $15 billion annually on online and mobile advertising. Amazon, Apple, Best Buy, Walt Disney, McDonald's, Sears Holding, Macy's, Target, and Home Depot are among the largest advertisers.[25]

Mass advertising is typically used to generate awareness in the need recognition stage of the buying process (see Chapter 4) because of its low cost per exposure and the control retailers have over content and the timing of the communication. But it is not as effective for helping consumers search for information because the amount of information that can be transmitted is limited. By its very nature, it is impossible to personalize messages or interact directly with customers. But it is a cost-effective method for announcing sales or new store openings. Traditionally, mass advertising has been limited to newspapers, magazines, direct mail, TV, radio, and billboards.

Newspapers   Retailing and newspaper advertising grew up together over the past century. But the growth in newspaper advertising by retailers has slowed recently as retailers have begun using other media. Still advertisers, mostly retailers, spend over $53 billion on newspaper ads annually, representing approximately a fifth of newspaper revenue.[26] In addition to displaying ads with their editorial content, newspapers distribute freestanding inserts. A **freestanding insert (FSI)**, also called a **preprint**, is an advertisement printed at the retailer's expense and distributed as an insert in the newspaper. Although popular with advertisers, there are so many FSIs in some newspapers that readers can become overwhelmed. As a result, some retailers have reduced the number of FSIs they use because of the clutter and because younger readers, who may be their primary target market, don't regularly read newspapers.

This FSI, appearing in a Sunday newspaper, highlights deals that are being offered at Central Market.

Most newspapers, except for a select few national newspapers like *The Wall Street Journal* and *USA Today*, are distributed in well-defined local market areas, so they are effective for targeting specific retail markets. Newspaper readers can go through an advertisement at their own pace and refer to the part of the advertisement when they want. But newspaper ads aren't effective for showing merchandise, particularly when it is important to illustrate colors, because of the relatively poor reproduction quality.

Finally, the cost of developing newspaper ads is relatively low. However, the cost of delivering the message may be high if the newspaper's circulation is much broader than the retailer's target market, requiring the retailer to pay for exposure that won't generate sales.

Source: H-E-B, Central Market Division

Magazines   Advertising in national magazines is mostly done by national retailers such as Target and Sephora. With the growth of local magazines, regional editions of national magazines, and specialized magazines, local retailers can take advantage of this medium. Many magazines either offer both a print and an online version, or have transitioned to online only. This change in the business model for some magazines from print to online (or both) enables retailers to reach potential customers at a lower cost per exposure. Retailers tend to use it for image advertising because the reproduction quality is high.

Direct Mail   **Direct mail** includes any brochure, catalog, advertisement, or other printed marketing material delivered directly to the consumer through the mail or a private delivery company.[27] Retailers have communicated with their customers through the mail for as long as the mail has existed. The vast majority of direct mail goes to customers or the current resident of the household on a nonpersonalized basis. With the advent of loyalty and CRM programs, retailers are now able to personalize their direct mail to all customers, to a subset of the customers according to their previous purchases, or even on a personalized basis to individual customers. Although relatively expensive on a per-customer basis (because of printing, mail costs, and a relatively low response rate), direct mail is still extensively used by many retailers because people respond favorably to personal messages.

Television   Television commercials can be placed on a national network or local station. Retailers typically use TV for image advertising, to take advantage of the high production quality and the opportunity to communicate through both visual images and sound. Television ads can also demonstrate product usage. For example, TV is an excellent medium for car, furniture, and consumer electronics dealers. TV is also used extensively to promote sales, particularly at a local level.

In addition to its high production costs, broadcast time for national TV advertising is expensive. **Spots**, which are ads in local markets as opposed to national ads, have relatively small audiences, but they may be economical for local retailers. To offset the high production costs, many vendors provide modular commercials in which the retailer can insert its name or a "tag" after information about the vendor's merchandise.

Radio   Many retailers use radio advertising because messages can be easily targeted to a specific segment of the market.[28] Some radio stations' audiences are highly loyal to their announcers, especially in a "talk radio" format. When these announcers promote a retailer, listeners are impressed. The cost of developing and broadcasting radio commercials is relatively low.

One disadvantage of radio advertising, however, is that listeners generally treat the radio broadcast as background, which limits the attention they give the message. Consumers must get the information from a radio commercial when it is broadcast; they cannot refer back to the advertisement for information they didn't hear or don't remember.

Billboards   **Billboards** are outdoor advertisements that are generally large and appear adjacent to and above roads or highways. Retailers typically use billboards to attract customers to a specific store location. Since everyone who drives or walks by sees them, exposure is high. A potential disadvantage, however, is that everyone is exposed but potentially few are in a retailer's target market. Given the relatively high price of creating and posting a billboard, as well as the relatively long-term commitment for and cost of displaying it, exposing everyone who drives by it can be an inefficient use of scarce promotional dollars. A billboard on an interstate highway indicating the location of a Cracker Barrel is relatively more efficient than one for a fine jewelry store because everyone driving by the Cracker Barrel billboard is a potential customer; relatively few people on the Interstate would be in the market for fine jewelry at that moment. Billboards may become more attractive to retailers as they embrace new digital billboard technology.

Sales Promotions

Sales promotions are special incentives or excitement-building programs that encourage consumers to purchase a particular product or service. Some sales promotions have become integral components of retailers' long-term customer relationship management programs, which they use to build customer loyalty. The ability to personalize messages and interact directly with customers depends on the type of sales promotion retailers use. Generally, however, sales promotions provide relatively little information. But on the positive side, the ability to control the message is high and the cost per exposure is low. The tools used in sales promotions, such as coupons, rebates, and premiums, are discussed next.

Coupons   **Coupons** offer a discount on the price of specific items when they are purchased. Coupons are issued by manufacturers and retailers in newspapers, on products, on the shelf, at the cash register, over the Internet, on mobile devices, and through the mail. The range of options for providing coupons keeps expanding, as Retailing View 14.4 describes. Retailers use coupons because they are thought to induce customers to try products for the first time, convert first-time buyers into regular users, encourage large purchases, increase usage, and protect market share against competition. Some retailers have linked coupons directly to their loyalty programs. Using detailed consumer behavior data collected through its loyalty cards, Safeway offers very personalized bargains. If one consumer buys several of the store's private-label products, such as paper towels and glass cleaner for example, she will receive an enticing coupon for the store's private-label dishwashing detergent too. Another customer might receive a coupon for the same item, but if his behavior indicates he is less likely to buy the store brand (because he has purchased name brand paper towels in the past), that coupon will be worth much less.[29]

Rebates   **Rebates** provide another form of discounts for consumers. In this case, however, the manufacturer, instead of the retailer, issues the refund as a portion of the purchase price returned to the buyer in the form of cash. Retailers generally welcome rebates from vendors because they generate sales in the same way that coupons do, but the retailers incur no handling costs, similar to the Ibotta app described in Retailing View 14.4. Vendors can offer generous rebates because the likelihood that consumers will actually apply for the rebate is low because of the hassle involved in doing so. But some retailers offer "instant rebates" that can be redeemed at the point-of-purchase. Staples and Apple have simplified the rebate redemption process with "Easy Rebates" and Apple.com/promo.[30]

Premiums   A **premium** offers an item for free or at a bargain price to reward some type of behavior, such as buying, sampling, or testing. Such rewards build goodwill among consumers, who often perceive high value in them. Premiums can be distributed in a variety of ways: They can be included by the manufacturer in the product packaging, such as the toys inside cereal boxes; placed visibly on the package, such as a coupon for free milk on a box of Cheerios; handed out in the store; or delivered in the mail, such as the free perfume offers that Victoria's Secret mails to customers.

When customers sign up for its loyalty card, they also agree to let Safeway track their purchases. With this information, Safeway can offer coupons that are likely to appeal to each customer.

Source: Safeway Inc.

14.4 RETAILING VIEW Does the Future of Couponing Look Different Than Its Past?

The practice of couponing is alive and well; it even is bigger and better than traditional forms of coupons that required people to clip the paper inserts in newspapers. Millennials, with their massive student debt and relatively low incomes, embrace the appeal of couponing. They are also redefining what a coupon is and how it is used. To start, for most young consumers, a coupon can take a variety of forms. It might still be a slip of paper promising a discount on packaged goods at the grocery store. But retailers also tend to lump rebates and promotions into their couponing practices. Thus customers use their loyalty card at the drugstore, purchase a piece of clothing from a flash sale site, join cash-back shopping programs, input discount codes to retail websites, or refer a friend to get a discount on a service offering; it all seems like variations on the basic couponing theme. Considering the wide range of these promotional options available, one assessment suggests that nearly 9 out of every 10 Millennials use coupons.

The variety of couponing options also continues to expand. For example, Valpak still sends blue envelopes to consumers' mailboxes, and the circulation rates for these hard copy coupons has remained steady at about 39 million households. But it also offers local online and mobile search functions that enable users to find businesses that are offering relevant coupons. As a result, it notes that 2 million coupons were printed from electronic links in a recent year.

The notion that customers would need to print physical copies of coupons or continue to use the versions published in newspapers may seem anachronistic in the modern Internet and mobile era. But thus far, digital coupons have remained diverse and uncoordinated, failing to offer a "seamless experience." It quickly becomes confusing to determine which app to download or which box to click to receive the coupon discount when each retailer has a different process. Therefore, customers looking to ensure that they receive their discount from a coupon still like to print out a hard copy that they can present wherever they choose to shop. In this environment, one app claims that it can address the confusion and still enable young users to avoid extra pieces of paper. Ibotta is a rebate app on

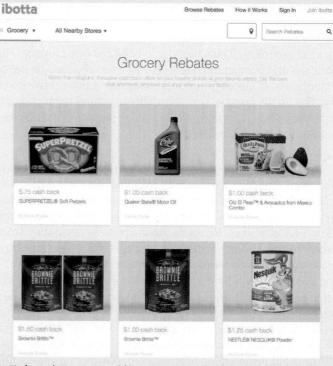

Ibotta is a rebate app on which users upload their receipts to demonstrate that they have purchased a particular item or visited a certain store. They then receive refunds of the promised discount.

which users upload their receipts to demonstrate that they have purchased a particular item or visited a certain store. They then receive refunds of the promised discount; users report an average of $10–$12 in savings each month. In addition to appealing to consumers by putting the entire process on one app, Ibotta promises some notable benefits to the brands and retailers that offer coupons. In particular, they pay only for discounts that get redeemed. Rather than providing money upfront, the companies know that each discount represents an actual sale of their product. Furthermore, Ibotta helps its client companies collect extensive, aggregated data about who is buying, when, where, and in response to which coupon offer.

Source: Penny Mosendz, "Penny-Pinching Millennials Are Keeping the Coupon Alive," *Bloomberg, Businessweek,* June 16, 2016.

In-Store Marketing/Design Elements

Retailers and their vendors are focusing considerable attention on in-store marketing design elements and activities. As we discussed in Chapter 4, customers often make purchase decisions while in the store. So store environmental elements, such as eye-catching point-of-purchase displays, and in-store activities, such as providing merchandise samples and special events, can increase customers' time in the store and their propensity to purchase. These in-store marketing/design elements are discussed next. Chapter 16 examines other store design and visual merchandising techniques that influence customers' purchase behavior.

Point-of-purchase displays stimulate impulse purchases while customers are waiting to pay for their purchases.

Point-of-Purchase Displays   **Point-of-purchase (POP) displays** are merchandise displays located at the point of purchase, such as at the checkout counter in a supermarket. Retailers have long recognized that the most valuable real estate in the store is at the POP. Customers see products like a magazine or a candy bar while they are waiting to pay for their items and impulsively purchase them. POP displays can't be personalized to each customer because the message is the same to everyone. Interactivity is low. Information content can range from minimal to high. Finally, the cost per exposure is low.

Samples   **Samples** offer potential customers the opportunity to try a product or service before they make a buying decision. Distributing samples is one of the most costly sales promotion tools, but it is also one of the most effective. Retailers of cosmetics and fragrances, as well as grocery stores, frequently employ sampling. For instance, Whole Foods provides samples of products to customers. Costco uses so many samples that customers can have an entire meal during their shopping trip. In the case of cosmetics and fragrances, sampling can be highly personal because the sales associate can easily switch to a sample a customer might want or need; but this is generally not the case for food stores because everyone typically receives the same sample. Sampling can also be highly interactive, the message can be controlled, and the information provided can be high because the sales associate can adapt based on the situation and the customer. Cost per exposure, however, is relatively high.

Special Events   A **special event** is a sales promotion program comprising a number of sales promotion techniques built around a seasonal, cultural, sporting, musical, or some other type of activity.[31] Special events can generate excitement and traffic to the store. Apparel and department stores do trunk shows, made-to-measure events, and fashion shows. Sporting goods stores offer demonstrations of equipment, while grocery stores might have cooking classes. Bookstores hold readings and book signings. Car dealerships can have rallies or shows of new or vintage models. Even if the sales registered during the event aren't significant, the long-term effect can be quite beneficial.

Although it does not always take place in stores, **event sponsorship** occurs when retailers support various activities (financially or otherwise), usually in the cultural or

© Mark Cunningham/Getty Images

The Little Caesar's Pizza Bowl is an example of event sponsorship.

sports and entertainment sectors. Some retailers sponsor sporting events such as the Little Caesars Pizza Bowl in Detroit. Others buy naming rights to a sporting venue, such as Target Field, which is home to MLB's Minnesota Twins, and HSBC Arena, home to the NHL's Buffalo Sabres. McDonald's and Dick's Sporting Goods sponsored the 2016 Olympics in Rio.[32] Special events can't be personalized, but they are highly interactive. The message and information can be controlled, and the cost per exposure is low.

Personal Selling

Personal selling is a communication process in which sales associates help customers satisfy their needs through face-to-face exchanges of information. Salespeople can personalize every message to fit the customers' needs and provide as much information as needed. It is highly interactive, and to the extent that the salespeople are well trained, the message can be controlled. Yet, the cost of communicating directly with a potential customer is quite high compared with other forms of promotion. Customers can buy many products and services without the help of a salesperson, but salespeople simplify the buying process by providing information and services that save customers time and effort. The impact of personal selling on customer service is examined further in Chapter 17.

Public Relations

Public relations (PR) involves managing communications and relationships to achieve various objectives, such as building and maintaining a positive image of the retailer, handling or heading off unfavorable stories or events, and maintaining positive relationships with the media. In many cases, public relations activities support other promotional efforts by generating "free" media attention and general goodwill. PR activities cannot be personalized and are not interactive. To the extent that the media

© LM Otero/AP Images

A recent Neiman Marcus Christmas catalog features Arizona football player Brady White as Santa Claus, left, and model Roxana Redfoot, as well as a Limited-Edition Masarati Ghiblis Q4 for just $95,000.

interprets the message the way the retailer has intended and disseminates it, the message can be somewhat controlled, and the information content is modest. The cost per exposure is relatively low. The types of PR campaigns retailers use are as varied as the retailers themselves. We examine several different ways in which retailers employ public relations in their communications strategy.

Neiman Marcus and Its Christmas Catalog   The Neiman Marcus Christmas book is perhaps the nation's best-known retail catalog. Its reputation is largely due to its annual tradition of ultra-extravagant his-and-hers gifts. The unique merchandise generates free publicity as journalists and style watchers are astonished at what the retailer came up with each year.

The Christmas book was first distributed in 1915 as a Christmas card, inviting Neiman Marcus customers to visit the store during the holiday season. In the late 1950s, customers were asking Neiman Marcus about unique gifts and merchandise not available in the store or from other catalogs. A recent Neiman Marcus Christmas catalog features Arizona football player, Brady White as Santa Claus, and model Roxana Redfoot, as well as a Limited-Edition Masarati Ghiblis Q4 for just $95,000. Running close to 200 pages, the book is mailed to nearly 2 million customers and is also available on the Neiman Marcus website.

Macy's and Cause-Related Marketing   Macy's has partnered with many charities in a successful **cause-related marketing campaign** (i.e., commercial activity in which businesses and charities form a partnership to market an image, product, or service for their mutual benefit). In addition to providing a benefit for society, its Shop for a Cause campaign generates a lot of publicity. The program allows partnering charities to sell coupons, at $5 each, that give the purchaser a 25 percent discount at Macy's on a specific day. As long as they were nonprofit organizations, charities were eligible to participate, leading to a wide range of partnerships, from Autism Speaks to Food Banks to YMCAs to animal rescues to the Alliance for Lupus Research. Meanwhile, Macy's sells coupons in its stores to benefit the March of Dimes. Each charity retains all proceeds from the coupon sales, and Macy's benefits from increased sales.

Rick's Hyundai Tuscon on *The Walking Dead* is an example of product placement in which retailers and vendors pay to have their product included in nontraditional situations.

Source: Hyundai

Retailers and Product Placement   When retailers and vendors use **product placement**, they pay to have their product included in nontraditional situations, such as in a scene in a movie or television program.[33] The product placement of Rick's Hyundai Tucson on *The Walking Dead* seems to be the only item that zombies haven't torn to shreds.

PLANNING THE RETAIL COMMUNICATION PROGRAM

LO 14-3

List the steps involved in developing a communication program.

Exhibit 14–2 illustrates the four steps involved in developing and implementing a retail communication program: establish objectives, determine a budget, allocate the budget, and implement and evaluate the program. The following sections detail each of these steps.

Establish Objectives

Retailers establish objectives for their communication programs to provide direction for people implementing the program, and a basis for evaluating its effectiveness. As discussed at the beginning of this chapter, some communication programs can have a long-term objective, such as creating or altering a retailer's brand

EXHIBIT 14–2   Steps in Developing a Retail Communication Program

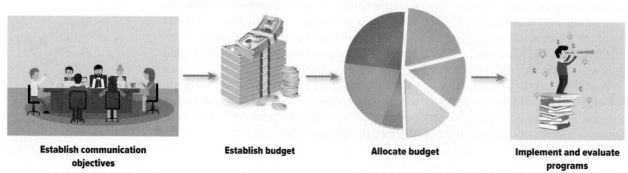

Establish communication objectives   Establish budget   Allocate budget   Implement and evaluate programs

RETAILING VIEW Retailing Communications and Comunicaciones
Venta al Por Menor   14.5

In the United States, the cohort of Hispanic consumers has emerged as one of the most prominent, growing, and appealing targets for marketers, and perhaps especially for retail brands that span the nation. Three familiar brands—Target, JCPenney, and Macy's—are taking some similar approaches to appeal to Hispanic shoppers, as well as adding some unique elements to set their image apart.

For example, all three chains have expanded the amount of in-store signage that appears in both English and Spanish. They also have translated some of their advertising campaigns into Spanish, and all three retailers seek to connect with Hispanic shoppers through social media.

Some of the differences are instructive too. Rather than simply translating existing English-language advertising into Spanish, Target has developed specific ads to appeal to Hispanic consumers. The advertising campaign, titled "Sin Traducción" ("Without Translation"), highlights terms without direct translations into English and references that only Hispanic consumers are likely to understand. This campaign, combined with other communications devoted to Hispanic shoppers, account for $51.5 million of Target's advertising budget, which is equivalent to approximately 3 percent of its total spending.

At JCPenney, the director of multicultural marketing asserted that Latina women are the primary targets of its assortment and merchandising mix. To support these offers, JCPenney launched an advertising blitz tied to the World Cup, which prompted notable improvements in consumers' perceptions of the brand.

For Macy's, a dedicated line, with the imprint of the singer Thalia Sodi, is the largest exclusive collection that it carries. Both the merchandising and the related marketing were designed expressly with the goal of appealing to Hispanic

In an effort to capture the fastest-growing populations in the United States, some retailers, including Target, are tailoring more of their stores to better reach the Hispanic market.

women. Macy's spends approximately $36.6 million on advertising in Hispanic-oriented media, including live-streamed fashion shows and other social media tactics.

The reasons for these moves are unsurprising: As the Hispanic population in the United States continues to grow, so does the buying power of this vast and diverse demographic group. According to some estimates, it has reached $1.5 trillion—making investments of a few million dollars to appeal to these shoppers seem quite reasonable.

Source: Ashley Rodriguez, "Retailers Duke It Out for Hispanic Shoppers' Dollars," *Advertising Age*, April 6, 2015.

image. As Retailing View 14.5 reveals, they also might target specific consumer markets to establish a long-term appeal. But other communication programs focus on improving short-term performance, such as increasing store traffic on a specific weekend.

Although retailers' overall objective is to generate long- and short-term sales and profits, they often use communication objectives rather than sales objectives to plan and evaluate their communication programs. **Communication objectives** are specific goals related to the retail communication mix's effect on the customer's decision-making process.

Exhibit 14–3 shows some hypothetical information about customers in the target market for a Safeway supermarket. This information illustrates the goals related to the stages in the consumer decision-making process outlined in Chapter 4. Note that 95 percent of the customers are aware of the store (the first stage in the decision-making process) and 85 percent know the type of merchandise it sells. But only 45 percent of the customers in the target market have a favorable attitude toward the store. Thirty-two percent intend to visit the store during the next few weeks, 25 percent actually visit the store during the next two weeks, and 18 percent regularly shop at the store.

EXHIBIT 14–3
Communication
Objectives and Stages
in Consumers' Decision-
Making Process

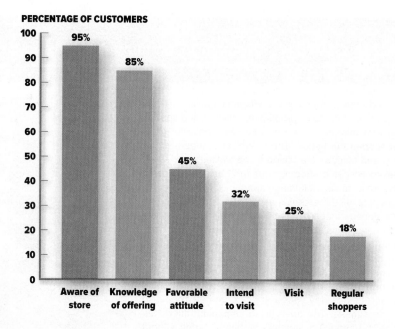

PERCENTAGE OF CUSTOMERS

Stage	Percentage
Aware of store	95%
Knowledge of offering	85%
Favorable attitude	45%
Intend to visit	32%
Visit	25%
Regular shoppers	18%

In this hypothetical example, most people know about the store and its offering. The major problem confronting Safeway is the big drop between knowledge and favorable attitudes. Thus, the store should develop a communication program with the objective of increasing the percentage of customers with a favorable attitude toward it.

To effectively implement and evaluate a communication program, its objectives must be clearly stated in quantitative terms. The target audience for the communication mix needs to be defined, along with the degree of change expected and the time period during which the change will be realized.

For example, a communication objective for a Safeway program might be to increase the percentage of customers within a five-mile radius of the store who have a favorable attitude toward the store from 45 to 55 percent within three months. This objective is clear and measurable. It indicates the task that the program should address. The people who implement the program thus know what they're supposed to accomplish.

Safeway's communication objectives should be to increase the number of people with a favorable attitude toward it.

The communication objectives and approaches used by vendors and retailers differ, and the differences can lead to conflicts. Some of these points of conflict are as follows:

- Long-term versus short-term goals. Most communications by vendors are directed toward building a long-term image of their products. In contrast, retailer communications typically are used to announce promotions and special sales that generate short-term revenues.

- Product versus location. When vendors advertise their branded products, they aren't concerned about where customers buy them as long as they buy their brands. In contrast, retailers aren't concerned about what brands customers buy as long as they buy them in their stores.

- Breadth of merchandise. Typically, because vendors have a relatively small number of products to promote, they can devote a lot of attention to developing consistent communication programs for each brand they make. Retailers have to develop communication programs that promote a much wider range of products.

Determine the Communication Budget

The second step in developing a retail communication program is to determine a budget (see Exhibit 14–2). The economically correct method for setting the communication budget is marginal analysis (discussed shortly). Even though retailers usually don't have enough information to perform a complete marginal analysis, the method shows managers how they should approach budget-setting programs. The marginal analysis method for setting a communication budget is the approach that retailers should use when making all of their resource allocation decisions, including the number of locations in a geographic area (Chapter 8), the allocation of merchandise to stores (Chapter 12), the staffing of stores (Chapter 15), and the floor and shelf space devoted to merchandise categories (Chapter 16).

An important source of the communication budget is cooperative (co-op) advertising programs. A **cooperative (co-op) advertising** program is a promotional program undertaken by a vendor and a retailer working together. The vendor pays for part of the retailer's promotion but dictates some conditions. For example, Best Buy might pay half of the expenses for ads that feature Sony digital TVs. In addition to lowering costs, co-op advertising enables a retailer to associate its name with well-known national brands and use attractive artwork created by the national brands.

Marginal Analysis Method   **Marginal analysis** is based on the economic principle that firms should increase communication expenditures as long as each additional dollar spent generates more than a dollar of additional contribution. To illustrate marginal analysis, consider Diane West, the owner and manager of a specialty store selling women's business clothing. Exhibit 14–4 shows her analysis to determine how much she should spend next year on her communication program.

For 21 different communication expense levels (column 1), West estimates her store sales (column 2), gross margin (column 3), and other expenses (columns 4 and 5). Then she calculates the contribution, excluding expenses on communications (column 6), and the profit when the communication expenses are considered (column 7). To estimate the sales generated by different levels of communications, West can simply rely on her judgment and experience, or she might analyze past data to determine the relationship between communication expenses and sales. Historical data also provide information about the gross margin and other expenses as a percentage of sales.

Notice that at low levels of communication expenses, an additional $5,000 in communication expenses generates more than a $5,000 incremental contribution. For example, increasing the communication expense from $15,000 to $20,000 increases the contribution by $10,800 (or $48,400 − $37,600). When the communication expense reaches $65,000, further increases of $5,000 generate less than $5,000 in additional

EXHIBIT 14–4   Marginal Analysis for Setting Diane West's Communication Budget

Level	Communication Expenses (1)	Sales (2)	Gross Margin Realized (3)	Rental Expense (4)	Personal Expense (5)	Contribution before Communication Expenses (6) = (3) – (4) – (5)	Profit after Communication Expenses (7) = (6) – (1)	
1	$ 0	$240,000	$ 96,000	$44,000	$52,200	$ (200)	$ (200)	
2	5,000	280,000	112,000	48,000	53,400	10,600	5,600	
3	10,000	330,000	132,000	53,000	54,900	24,100	14,100	
4	15,000	380,000	152,000	58,000	56,400	37,600	22,600	
5	20,000	420,000	168,000	62,000	57,600	48,400	28,400	
6	25,000	460,000	184,000	66,000	58,800	59,200	34,200	
7	30,000	500,000	200,000	70,000	60,000	70,000	40,000	Last year
8	35,000	540,000	216,000	74,000	61,200	80,800	45,800	
9	40,000	570,000	228,000	77,000	62,100	88,900	48,900	
10	45,000	600,000	240,000	80,000	63,000	97,000	52,000	
11	50,000	625,000	250,000	82,500	63,750	103,750	53,750	
12	55,000	650,000	260,000	85,000	64,500	110,500	55,500	Chosen budget
13	60,000	670,000	268,000	87,000	65,100	115,900	55,900	
14	65,000	690,000	276,000	89,000	65,700	121,300	56,300	Best profit
15	70,000	705,000	282,000	90,500	66,150	125,350	55,350	
16	75,000	715,000	286,000	91,500	66,450	128,050	53,050	
17	80,000	725,000	290,000	92,500	66,750	130,750	50,750	
18	85,000	735,000	294,000	93,500	67,050	133,450	48,450	
19	90,000	745,000	298,000	94,500	67,350	136,150	46,150	
20	95,000	750,000	300,000	95,000	67,500	137,500	42,500	
21	100,000	750,000	300,000	95,000	67,500	137,500	37,500	

contributions. For example, increasing the budget from $65,000 to $70,000 generates only an additional $4,050 in contribution ($125,350 − $121,300).

In this example, West determines that the maximum profit would be generated with a communication expense budget of $65,000. But she notices that expense levels between $55,000 and $70,000 all result in about the same level of profit. Thus, West makes a conservative decision and establishes a $55,000 budget for her communication expenses.

In most cases, it's very hard to perform a marginal analysis because managers don't know the relationship between communication expenses and sales. Note that the numbers in Exhibit 14–4 are simply West's estimates, and they may not be accurate.

Sometimes retailers perform experiments to get a better idea of the relationship between communication expenses and sales. Say, for example, a catalog retailer selects several geographic areas in the United States with the same sales potential. The retailer then distributes 100,000 catalogs in the first area, 200,000 in the second area, and 300,000 in the third. Using the sales and costs for each distribution level, it could conduct an analysis like the one in Exhibit 14–4 to determine the most profitable distribution level. (Chapter 13 described the use of experiments to determine the relationship between price and sales.)

Some other methods that retailers use to set communication budgets are the objective-and-task and rules-of-thumb methods, which include the affordable budgeting method, percentage-of-sales, and competitive parity methods. These methods are easy to use but do not result in the optimal level of communication expenditures.

Objective-and-Task Method   The **objective-and-task method** determines the budget required to undertake specific tasks to accomplish communication objectives. To use this method, the retailer first establishes a set of communication objectives and

Objective: Increase the percentage of target market (working women) who know of our store's location and who purchase business attire from 25 percent to 50 percent over the next 12 months.	
Task: 480, 30-second radio spots during peak commuting hours	$12,000
Task: Sign with store name near entrance to mall	5,000
Objective: Increase the percentage of target market who indicate that our store is their preferred store for buying their business wardrobe from 5 percent to 15 percent in 12 months.	
Task: Develop TV campaign to improve image and run 50, 30-second commercials	24,000
Task: Hold four "Dress for Success" seminars followed by a wine-and-cheese party	8,000
Objective: Sell merchandise remaining at end of season.	
Task: Special event	6,000
Total budget	$55,000

EXHIBIT 14–5

Illustration of Objective-and-Task Method for Setting a Communication Budget

then determines the necessary tasks and their costs. The total of all costs incurred to undertake the tasks is the communication budget.

Exhibit 14–5 illustrates how Diane West could use the objective-and-task method to complement her marginal analysis. West establishes three objectives: to increase awareness of her store, to create a greater preference for her store among customers in her target market, and to promote the sale of merchandise remaining at the end of each season. The estimated communication budget she requires to achieve these objectives is $55,000.

In addition to defining her objectives and tasks, West rechecks the financial implications of the communication mix by projecting the income statement for next year using the communication budget (see Exhibit 14–6). This income statement includes an increase of $25,000 in communication expenses compared with last year. But West believes this increase in the communication budget will boost annual sales from $500,000 to $650,000. According to West's projections, the increase in communication expenses will raise store profits. The results of both the marginal analysis and the objective-and-task methods suggest a communication budget between $55,000 and $65,000.

Rule-of-Thumb Methods　The previous two methods set the communication budget by estimating communication activities' effects on the firm's future sales or communication objectives. The **rule-of-thumb methods** discussed in this section use the opposite logic. They use past sales and communication activities to determine the present communication budget.[34]

Affordable Budgeting Method　When using the **affordable budgeting method**, retailers first forecast their sales and expenses, excluding communication expenses, during the budgeting period. The difference between the forecast sales and expenses plus the desired profit is then budgeted for the communication mix. In other words, the affordable method sets the communication budget by determining what money is available after operating costs and profits are subtracted.

Percentage-of-Sales Method　The **percentage-of-sales method** sets the communication budget as a fixed percentage of forecast sales. Retailers use this method to

	Last Year	Next Year
Sales	$500,000	$650,000
Gross margin (realized)	200,000	260,000
Rental, maintenance, etc.	−70,000	−85,000
Personnel	−60,000	−64,500
Communications	−30,000	−55,000
Profit	$ 40,000	$ 55,500

EXHIBIT 14–6

Financial Implications of Increasing the Communication Budget

determine the communication budget by forecasting sales during the budget period and then applying a predetermined percentage to set the budget. The percentage may be the retailer's historical percentage or the average percentage used by similar retailers.

Competitive Parity Method   Under the **competitive parity method**, the communication budget is set so that it is equal to the communication expenditure of the firm's most significant competitor(s). It is based on an absolute dollar amount used by a competitor, rather than a percentage. For example, consider Roots, a well-established restaurant in a small town. A new restaurant opens down the block called Linger. Roots estimates that Linger's communication budget is $5,000 per year, so Roots sets its budget similarly.

Relative Advantages and Problems with Rule-of-Thumb Methods   The major problem with these methods is they don't assume that communication expenses stimulate sales and profit. Communication expenses are just a cost of business, like the cost of merchandise. When retailers use these methods, they typically cut "unnecessary" communication expenses if sales fall below the forecast rather than increasing communication expenses to increase sales.

None of these methods allow retailers to exploit the unique opportunities or problems they confront in the market. Roots has been around for many years, and is therefore well known and maintains a loyal customer base. Its communication needs are different from and probably less expensive than Linger. These methods also ignore the differential abilities of different retailers to create and implement their communication strategies. Just because two retailers spend the same amount on communications or use the same percentage of sales doesn't mean their programs are equally effective.

The percentage-of-sales and competitive parity method also assumes that the copied competitor has an equally appealing retail format (i.e., product offering, location, price, etc.). Yet Roots, for instance, has a superior location and many believe that its food offerings are tastier, healthier, and offered at a lower price. So, it may not have to spend as much on communications as Linger to get the same sales impact. Despite the shortcomings of these rule-of-thumb methods, taken together they can provide some insight into what is its best course of action for setting a communication budget.

One advantage of both the affordable method and the percentage-of-sales method for determining a communication budget is that the retailer won't spend beyond its means. Because the level of spending is determined by sales, the budget will go up only when sales go up and as the retailer generates more sales to pay the additional communication expenses. When times are good, these methods work well because they allow the retailer to communicate more aggressively with customers. But when sales fall, communication expenses are cut, which may accelerate the sales decline.

Allocate the Promotional Budget

After determining the size of the communication budget, the third step in the communication planning process is to allocate the budget (see Exhibit 14–2). In this step, the retailer decides how much of its budget to allocate to specific communication elements, merchandise categories, geographic regions, or long- and short-term objectives. For example, Dillard's must decide how much of its communication budget to spend in each area it has stores: Southeast, Mid-Atlantic, Southwest, Midwest, and West Coast. Michaels decides how much to allocate to merchandise associated with different crafts. The sporting goods store owner-manager must decide how much of the store's $2,250 communication budget to spend on promoting the store's image versus generating sales during the year and how much to spend on advertising and special promotions.

Research indicates that allocation decisions are more important than the decision about the amount to spend on communications.[35] In other words, retailers often can realize the same objectives by reducing the size of the communication budget but allocating it more effectively.

An easy way to make such allocation decisions is to spend about the same in each geographic region or for each merchandise category. But this allocation rule probably won't maximize profits, because it ignores the possibility that communication programs might be more effective for some merchandise categories or for some regions than for others. Another approach is to use rules of thumb, such as basing allocations on the sales level or contributions for the merchandise category.

Allocation decisions, like budget-setting decisions, should use the principles of marginal analysis. The retailer should allocate the budget to areas that will yield the greatest return. This approach for allocating a budget is sometimes referred to as the **high-assay principle**. Consider a miner who can spend his time digging on two claims. The value of the gold on one claim is assayed at $20,000 per ton, whereas the assay value on the other claim is $10,000 per ton. Should the miner spend two-thirds of his time at the first mine and one-third of his time at the other mine? Of course not! The miner should spend all of his time mining the first claim until the assay value of the ore mined drops to $10,000 a ton, at which time he can divide his time equally between the claims.

Similarly, a retailer may find that its customers have a high awareness and very favorable attitude toward its women's clothing but do not know much about its men's clothing. In this situation, a dollar spent on advertising men's clothing might generate more sales than a dollar spent on women's clothing, even though the sales of women's clothing are greater than the sales of men's clothing.

Implement and Evaluate Communication Programs—Three Illustrations

The final stage in developing a retail communication program is its implementation and evaluation (see Exhibit 14–2).[36] This final section of the chapter illustrates the implementation and evaluation process for three communication programs: a traditional advertising campaign, a Facebook campaign, and a Google AdWords campaign by a small specialty retailer.

Advertising Campaign   Hypothetically, imagine Fabulous Fromage is a specialty import cheese shop, located just outside New York City. The store's appearance combines the ambiance of a French café with the conveniences of a modern retailer; most of its merchandise is imported from France and a few other renowned cheese-making regions around the world.

Harry Owens, the owner, realizes that his communication budget is considerably less than the budget of the local Whole Foods store, which also sells gourmet cheeses. He therefore decides to concentrate his limited budget on a specific segment and use

© Chuck Place/Alamy Stock Photo

Effective communication with their customers, great products, and knowledgeable employees help specialty import cheese stores thrive.

very creative copy and distinctive artwork in his advertising. His target market is knowledgeable, sophisticated consumers of gourmet foods and kitchenwares. His experience indicates the importance of personal selling for these seasoned shoppers because they (1) make expensive purchases but (2) seek considerable information before making their decisions. Thus, Owens spends part of his communication budget on training his sales associates.

The advertising program Owens develops emphasizes his store's distinctive image. He uses the newspaper as his major vehicle. Whereas the ads issued by Whole Foods tend to highlight price promotions on specialty cheeses, the advertising for Fabulous Fromage emphasizes French country imagery, including off-the-beaten-path scenes of French pastures and unusual art objects. This theme is also reflected in the store's atmosphere.

To evaluate his communication program, Owens needs to compare the results of his program with the objectives he has developed during the first part of the planning process. To measure his campaign's effectiveness, he conducts an inexpensive tracking study. Telephone interviews are performed periodically with a representative sample of customers in his store's trading area. Communication objectives are assessed using the following questions:

Communication Objectives	Questions
Awareness	What stores sell imported cheese?
Knowledge	Which stores would you rate outstanding on the following characteristics (e.g., sales assistance)?
Attitude	On your next shopping trip for imported cheese, which store would you visit first?
Visit	Which of the following stores have you been to?

Here are the survey results for one year:

Communication Objective	Before Campaign	6 Months After	One Year After
Awareness (% mentioning store)	38%	46%	52%
Knowledge (% giving outstanding rating for sales assistance)	9	17	24
Attitude (% first choice)	13	15	19
Visit (% visited store)	8	15	19

The results show a steady increase in awareness, knowledge of the store, and choice of the store as a primary source of fine imported cheeses. This research thus provides evidence that the advertising is conveying the intended message to the target audience.

Facebook Marketing Campaign   Owens is developing a Facebook marketing campaign for a new product line he plans to import from Italy using the steps outlined in Exhibit 14–2.[37]

1. Establish objectives. Owens must determine the objectives he hopes to achieve through his campaign. Is it designed to increase awareness of the product line? Is he hoping more potential customers might visit and Like his Facebook page? Is his focus mainly on increasing sales of the product line? Depending on what he aims to achieve, he might focus on developing a Facebook Page, creating a Facebook App, or hosting a Facebook Event.

   As part of his objectives, he also needs to determine whom Fabulous Fromage is targeting. Facebook enables Owens to perform targeting based on location, language, education, gender, profession, age, relationship status, likes/dislikes, and friends or connections. Owens's aim is to find a big enough audience to reach those who might buy the new product line without being so big that he ends up trying to appeal to someone way outside of his target audience. A Facebook targeting example is depicted in Exhibit 14–7.

2. Develop the budget. Budgeting is key. Facebook allows advertisers to set a daily budget: Once the costs (usually per click) reach a certain level, the ad disappears for the rest of the day. Of course, this option can be risky if the retailer is getting great feedback, and all of a sudden, a compelling ad disappears. Therefore, similar to the campaign content, budgets demand nearly constant review. For example, if a competitor lowers its price significantly, it might be necessary to follow suit to avoid being excluded from customers' consideration sets.

3. Allocate budget (develop the campaign). Now that Owens knows who he is targeting and what his budget is for the campaign, the next step is to develop the communication, including the copy and images. Here again, the process is not very different from any other marketing communications campaign. There should be a call to action that is clear and compelling. Strong, eye-catching images and designs are important. And the campaign must appeal to the right customers. However, an aspect that is more critical with social media than other forms of marketing communications is that the images and messages need to be updated almost constantly. Because people expect changing content online, it would be inappropriate to run the same campaign for several months, as the shop might if it were advertising on television, for example.

4. Implement and evaluate the program. The final step is to implement and review the success of the campaign and make changes as necessary. Facebook's Ad Manager offers various metrics and reports, such as number of clicks on ads, audience demographics, and ad performance for specific time periods.

Google AdWords Campaign   Fabulous Fromage's target market is young, well-educated men and women aged 30 to 40 years interested in food and wine. The owner's experience indicates the importance of personal selling for his sophisticated target market because the marketed customers (1) make large purchases and (2) seek information

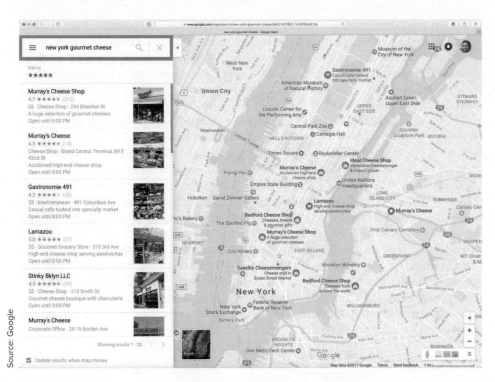

Advertisers pay Google to show up in the ad section column of this screen grab based on the keywords customers use in their searches.

EXHIBIT 14–7   Example Facebook Targeting Choices

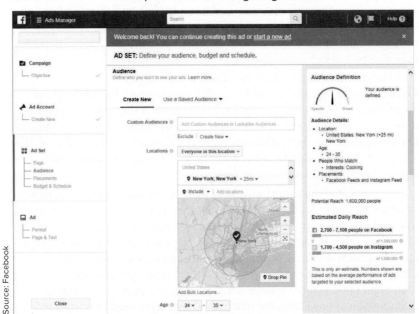

Source: Facebook

about gourmet products before making a decision. Owens has, therefore, decided to concentrate his limited budget on a specific segment and use electronic media in his IMC program to generate business through his new website.

To reach new customers, Owens is actively using search engine marketing. In particular, he is using Google AdWords, a search engine marketing tool offered by Google that allows advertisers to show up in the ad section of the search results page based on the keywords potential customers use (see the ad section column of the Google screen grab shown above). Owens is also using what he has learned from his interactions with Google consultants and is rewriting content on his website to achieve search engine optimization (as we discussed earlier in the chapter). Thus, Owens is experimenting with both paid search through Google's advertising program and organic search through his revised website content.

Owens must determine the best keywords to use for his sponsored-link advertising program. Some potential customers might search using the keywords "New York Gourmet Cheese," "Imported Cheese," or other such versions. Using Google AdWords, Owens can assess the effectiveness of his advertising expenditures by measuring the reach, relevance, and return on advertising investment for each of the keywords that potential customers used during their Internet searches.

To estimate reach, Owens uses the number of **impressions** (the number of times the ad appears in front of the user) and the **click-through rate (CTR)**. To calculate CTR, he takes the number of times a user clicks on an ad and divides it by the number of impressions.[38] For example, if a sponsored link was delivered 100 times and 10 people clicked on it, then the number of impressions is 100, the number of clicks is 10, and the CTR would be 10 percent. The **relevance** of the ad describes how useful an ad message is to the consumer doing the search. Google provides a measure of relevance through its AdWords system using a proprietary metric known as a Quality Score.[39] The Quality Score uses multiple factors to measure the keyword's relevance to the ad text or a user's search. A high Quality Score generally implies that the keyword will result in ads that appear higher on the page, with a lower cost per click.[40] In a search for "Gourmet Cheese," the Fabulous Fromage ad showed up fourth, suggesting high relevance.

Using the following formula, Owens also can determine an ad's **return on advertising investment (ROAI)**:

$$ROAI = \frac{\text{Net sales } - \text{ Advertising cost}}{\text{Adertising cost}}$$

EXHIBIT 14–8 ROAI Assessment for Two Google AdWords

(1) Keyword	(2) Clicks	(3) Cost	(4) Sales	(5) Revenue – Cost (Col. 4 – Col. 3)	(6) ROAI (Col. 5/Col. 3) × 100)
New York Gourmet Cheese	110	$10/day	$35/day	$25	250%
Imported Cheese	40	$25/day	$40/day	$15	60%

For the two keyword searches in Exhibit 14–8, Owens finds how much the advertising cost him (column 3), the sales produced as a result (column 4), and the ROAI (column 6). For "New York Gourmet Cheese," the website had a lot more clicks (110) than the clicks received from "Imported Cheese" (40) (see column 2, Exhibit 14–8). Even though the sales were lower for the keywords "New York Gourmet Cheese" at $35 per day, versus $40 per day for the keywords "Imported Cheese," the ROAI was much greater for the "New York Gourmet Cheese" keyword. In the future, Owens should continue using this keyword, in addition to producing others that are similar to it, in the hope that he will attain an even greater return on investment.

SUMMARY

LO 14-1 Identify the new media elements.

In the past decade or so, retailers have embraced several new media elements. The online elements include websites, e-mail, mobile, and social media. Examples of the social media elements embraced by retailers are YouTube, Facebook, blogs, and Twitter.

LO 14-2 Identify the traditional media elements.

Retailers communicate with customers using a variety of traditional media elements. These include mass media advertising, sales promotions, in-store marketing/design elements, personal selling, and public relations.

LO 14-3 List the steps involved in developing a communication program.

Retailers go through four steps to develop and implement their communication program: establish objectives, determine a budget, allocate the budget, and implement and evaluate the program. Marginal analysis is the most appropriate method for determining how much should be spent to accomplish the retailer's objectives because it maximizes the profits that could be generated by the communication mix. Because marginal analysis is difficult to implement, however, many retailers use rule-of-thumb methods to determine the size of the promotion budget.

KEY TERMS

advertising, *367*
affordable budgeting method, *387*
billboard, *376*
blog (weblog), *373*
cause-related marketing campaign, *381*
click-through rate (CTR), *392*
communication objectives, *383*
competitive parity method, *388*
cooperative (co-op) advertising, *385*
coupons, *377*
direct mail, *376*
e-mail, *369*
event sponsorship, *379*
freestanding insert (FSI), *375*
high-assay principle, *389*
impressions, *392*
integrated marketing communication (IMC) program, *367*
marginal analysis, *385*
m-commerce, *370*
microblog, *374*
mobile commerce, *370*
mobile marketing, *370*
mobile retailing, *370*
objective-and-task method, *386*
percentage-of-sales method, *387*
personal selling, *380*
point-of-purchase (POP) display, *379*
premium, *377*
preprint, *375*
product placement, *382*
public relations (PR), *380*
rebate, *377*
relevance, *392*
return on advertising investment (ROAI), *392*
rule-of-thumb method, *387*
sales promotion, *377*
sample, *379*
search engine marketing (SEM), *369*
search engine optimization (SEO), *369*
search engine results page (SERP), *369*
sentiment analysis, *372*
social media, *372*
special event, *379*
spot, *376*
word of mouth, *373*

GET OUT AND DO IT!

1. **CONTINUING ASSIGNMENT** Evaluate the communication activities undertaken by the retailer you have selected for the continuing assignment. Briefly explain how your retailer uses each of the following elements of its communication program: direct marketing, online marketing, personal selling, sales promotions, direct mail and e-mail, mobile marketing, advertising (media used?), social media, public relations, website, and events. What communication elements would you change? Why?

2. Go to the home page for Interbrand (http://interbrand.com/best-brands/best-global-brands/2016/) and select the Top 100 Global Brands. On the basis of this ranking, list the top 20 global retail brands. In two or three paragraphs, describe what makes a strong retail brand. How were brand equity and financial performance used to measure brand value for these retailers?

3. Retailers and manufacturers deliver coupons through the Internet in addition to delivering them by mail or as inserts. Go to retailmenot.com for coupons offered over the Internet. How does this coupon distribution system compare with the other two distribution systems?

4. Trader Joe's is a gourmet grocery store offering items such as health foods, organic produce, and nutritional supplements. Go to www.traderjoes.com and see how the firm uses its Internet site to promote its retail stores and merchandise. Why does this retailer include recipes and a seasonal guide on its website? Does the information provided on the web page reinforce the store's upscale grocery image? Explain why or why not.

5. Go to the social media site for a retailer that you have shopped at during the last few weeks. How was social media used as an element in the retailer's communication program? What audience is being reached with social media? Is the social media message consistent or inconsistent with other communication elements? Is this a strong or weak strategy? Please explain.

6. Go to the home page for Target's Pressroom at https://corporate.target.com/. How does this retailer use public relations to communicate with investors and customers? Is this an effective communication tool for this retailer? Provide support for your response.

7. Go to www.facebook.com/business to see how to build pages, ads, and sponsored stories, as well as how to take advantage of mobile applications. What are some of the steps that Facebook suggests a person consider when marketing using ads?

DISCUSSION QUESTIONS AND PROBLEMS

1. What are the positive and negative aspects of direct marketing from the customer's perspective?

2. What types of sales promotions have been successful with you as a consumer? Which ones have not been successful? Explain your responses.

3. What factors should be considered in dividing up the advertising budget among a store's different merchandise areas? Which of the following should receive the highest advertising budget: staple, fashion, or seasonal merchandise? Why?

4. Outline some elements in a communication program that can be used to achieve the following objectives: (a) Increase store loyalty by 20 percent. (b) Build awareness of the store by 10 percent. (c) Develop an image as a low-price retailer. How would you determine whether the communication program met each of these objectives?

5. A retailer plans to open a new store near a university. It will specialize in collegiate merchandise such as apparel, accessories, and school supplies. Consider the pros and cons of each of the following media: TV, radio, city newspaper, university newspaper, local magazine, website, blog, and event sponsorship for this retailer to capture the university market.

6. Why do some online retailers include editorials and customer reviews along with product information on their websites? Explain how this may influence the consumer's buying behavior.

7. Assume you work for a large consumer packaged-goods firm that has learned its latest line of snack foods is selling very slowly in retail stores. Recommend a strategy for listening to what consumers are saying on blogs, review sites, and the firm's website. Describe how your strategy might provide insights into consumers' sentiments about the new product line.

8. As an intern for Dunkin' Donuts, you have been asked to develop a social media campaign for a new glazed muffin. The objective of the campaign is to increase awareness and trial of the new line of muffins. How would you go about putting together such a campaign?

CHAPTER ENDNOTES

1. Sharon Edelson, "H&M Opening High-Tech Flagship in Times Square," *Women's Wear Daily,* November 12, 2013.

2. Sarah Mahoney, "Iman, Chloe Sevigny Star in New H&M/Kenzo Campaign," *MediaPost,* September 12, 2016.

3. Tracy Chan, "H&M TVC Calls for Recycling of Clothes," *Marketing Interactive,* April 15, 2016.

4. Bethany Biron, "H&M Is Trying to Find the Next *Man Repeller,*" *Glossy,* May 10, 2016.

5. "Olivia Culpo, Chelsea Leyland, and Leandra Medine Celebrate Winners of the 2016 Bloglovin' Awards Presented by H&M," PR Newswire, September 13, 2016.

6. Biron, "H&M Is Trying to Find the Next *Man Repeller.*"

7. Stuart Elliott, "For CVS Regulars, Ads Tailored Just for Them," *The New York Times,* October 10, 2013.

8. Ludwig Stephan, Ko de Ruyter, Mike Friedman, Elisabeth C. Brüggen, Martin Wetzels, and Gerard Pfann, "More Than Words: The Influence of Affective Content and Linguistic Style Matches in Online Reviews on Conversion Rate," *Journal of Marketing* 77 (January 2013), pp. 87–103; Peter De Maeyer, "Impact of Online Consumer Reviews on Sales and Price Strategies: A Review and Directions for Future Research," *Journal of Product & Brand Management* 21, no. 2 (2012), pp.132–139; Yue Pan and Jason Q. Zhang, "Born Unequal: A Study of the Helpfulness of User-Generated Product Reviews," *Journal of Retailing* 87, no. 4 (December 2011), pp. 598–612.

9. www.wordstream.com/sponsored-links-google.

10. Panos E. Kourouthanassis and George M. Giaglis, "Introduction to the Special Issue Mobile Commerce: The Past Present, and Future of Mobile Commerce Research," *International Journal of Electronic Commerce* 16, no. 4 (Summer 2012), pp. 5–18.

11. Brielle Jaekel, "Top 10 Mobile Advertising Campaigns of 2015," *Mobile Marketer,* January 5, 2016, http://www.mobilemarketer.com.

12. Colin Campbell, Leyland F. Pitt, Michael Parent, and Pierre R. Berthon, "Understanding Consumer Conversations around Ads in a Web 2.0 World," *Journal of Advertising* 40, no. 1 (Spring 2011), pp. 87–102.

13. Adam Rapp, Lauren Bietelspacher, Dhruv Grewal, and Doug Hughes. "Understanding Social Media Effects across Seller, Retailer, and Consumer Interactions," *Journal of the Academy of Marketing Science* 41 (September 2013), pp. 547–566.

14. "Brand Channels," YouTube, www.gstatic.com/youtube/engagement/platform/autoplay/advertise/downloads/YouTube_BrandChannels.pdf

15. The Home Depot Branded Channel, www.youtube.com/user/homedepot.

16. We Are Social and IAB Singapore, "Leading Social Networks Worldwide as of March 2015, Ranked by Number of Active Users (in Millions)," Statista—The Statistics Portal, http://www.statista.com/statistics/272014/global-social-networks-ranked-by-number-of-users/ (accessed March 19, 2015).

17. Ashley Rodriguez, "Macy's Embraces a 'Digital' World," *Advertising Age,* May 13, 2015; http://www.adweek.com/news/technology/how-macys-will-target-its-facebook-and-instagram-ads-holidays-168243; Sarah Mahoney, "Macy's Gets Face(book) Lift; Expands 'Ecosystem,'" *Marketing Daily,* February 29, 2012.

18. https://www.facebook.com/search/top/?q=pcc%20natural%20markets.

19. Bin Gu, Jaehong Park, and Prabhudev Konana, "The Impact of External Word-of-Mouth Sources on Retailer Sales of High-Involvement Products," *Information Systems Research* 23, no. 1 (March 2012), pp. 182–196; Jillian C. Sweeney, Geoffrey N. Soutar, and Tim Mazzarol, "Word of Mouth: Measuring the Power of Individual Messages," *European Journal of Marketing* 46, no. 1/2 (2012), pp. 237–257; Robert East, Kathy Hammond, and Malcolm Wright, "The Relative Incidence of Positive and Negative Word of Mouth: A Multi-Category Study," *International Journal of Research in Marketing* 24, no. 2 (2007), pp. 175–184.

20. https://canopy.co.

21. David Goldman, "Twitter Will Stretch Its 140-Character Limit," *CNN Money,* May 24, 2016.

22. https://twitter.com/DUMBOFoodTrucks.

23. Katie Wagner, "Listening Online Is Essential for Customer Service," *Katie Wagner Social Media,* October 9, 2015, http://katiewagnersocialmedia.com/listening-online-is-essential-for-customer-service/; https://techcrunch.com/2016/09/15/twitter-rolls-out-new-features-for-businesses-running-customer-service-accounts/; Alex Schmidt, "Twitter Lets Customers Skip Recordings, and Make Choices," *NPR,* August 15, 2012.

24. American Marketing Association, *Dictionary of Marketing Terms* (Chicago: American Marketing Association).

25. "The US Top 100 Advertisers in 2015 by Expenditure," http://www.adbrands.net/us/top_us_advertisers.htm; "Retail Will Continue to Outspend Other Industries on Digital Advertising," *eMarketer,* May 16, 2016.

26. Suzanne Kapner, "Retailers Can't Shake the Circular Habit," *The Wall Street Journal,* March 11, 2015; "Inserts Still Deliver for Retailers," *Mansi Media,* http://mansimedia.com/our-expertise/industry-news/article/2015/03/26/inserts-still-deliver-for-retailers.

27. Sebastian Feld, Heiko Frenzen, Manfred Krafft, Kay Peters, and Peter C. Verhoef, "The Effects of Mailing Design Characteristics on Direct Mail Campaign Performance," *International Journal of Research in Marketing* (2012). doi: 10.1016/j.ijresmar.2012.07.003.

28. "Why Radio," *RadioAdvertising,* http://radioadvertising.co.nz/Site/Why/Default.aspx.

29. Stephanie Clifford, "Shopper Alert: Price May Drop for You Alone," *The New York Times,* August 9, 2012.

30. www.stapleseasyrebates.com/img/staples/paperless/pages/Landing.html.

31. www.marketingpower.com/_layouts/Dictionary.aspx?dLetter=S.

32. http://www.teamusa.org/sponsors.

33. S. Chin and B. Wilson, "Product Placement in the Digital World: A Conceptual Framework," in *Proceedings of the Changing Roles of Advertising Conference,* Charles R. Taylor, Patrick De Pelsmacker, Scott Koslow, and Peter Neijens, eds. (Stockholm, Sweden, June 29–30, 2012); Eva A. van Reijmersdal, Peter C. Neijens, and Edith G. Smit, "A New Branch of Advertising: Reviewing Factors That Influence Reactions to Product Placement," *Journal of Advertising Research* 49, no. 4 (December 2009), pp. 429–449; Pamela Mills Homer, "Product Placement: The Impact of Placement Type and Repetition on Attitude," *Journal of Advertising* 38, no. 3 (Fall 2009).

34. Murali Mantrala, "Allocating Marketing Resources," in *Handbook of Marketing,* Barton Weitz and Robin Wensley, eds. (London: Sage, 2002), pp. 409–435.

35. V. Shankar and Gregory S. Carpenter, *Handbook of Marketing Strategy* (Northhampton, MA: Edward Elgar, 2012), chap. 9.

36. Marshall Sponder, *Social Media Analytics: Effective Tools for Building, Interpreting, and Using Metrics* (New York: McGraw-Hill, 2011).

37. Andy Shaw, "How to Create a Facebook Ad Campaign," *Social Media Tips,* September 23, 2011.

38. "Clickthrough rate (CTR): Definition," Google, https://support.google.com/adwords/answer/2615875?hl=en.

39. "Quality Score: Definition," https://support.google.com/adwords/answer/140351?hl=en.

40. "Things You Should Know about Ads Quality," https://support.google.com/adwords/answer/156066#QSvAR.

Human Resources and Store Management

Section IV focuses on the implementation issues associated with human resources and store management, including managing store employees and controlling costs (Chapter 15), presenting merchandise (Chapter 16), and providing customer service (Chapter 17).

Traditionally, the issues pertaining to merchandise management were considered the most important retail decisions, and buying merchandise was considered the best career path for achieving senior retail management positions. Today, developing a strategic advantage through merchandise management is becoming more difficult because competing firms often have similar assortments of national-brand merchandise.

Because customers can find the same assortments in a number of conveniently located retail stores and through the Internet, effective store management has become a critical basis for developing strategic advantages. Retailers are increasing their emphasis on differentiating their offering from those of competitors on the basis of the customers' experiences in the retailers' stores and websites, including the service they get from store employees and the quality of the shopping environment.

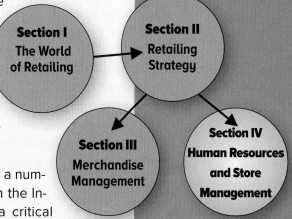

© Gina Ferazzi/Los Angeles Times via Getty Images

When it comes to raising and testing radical ideas for retailing, Zappos ranks among the most active firms. Consider some of its best-known and unique policies. If new hires, after undergoing training, decide the company is not for them, Zappos pays them a substantial amount, rather than trying to hold on to dissatisfied employees. It was among the first to offer free return shipping and even to encourage customers to order multiple sizes of their preferred shoe styles, then send back the ones that didn't fit. Zappos is big on employee empowerment as a way to achieve customer satisfaction too. It allows and encourages customer service representatives to find the products that customers want, even if that means sending them to another retail site.

Its latest creative idea is similarly revolutionary, though the success of the initiative is yet to be determined. Noting the criticisms that hierarchical corporate cultures can stifle creativity and effectiveness, Zappos dismantled anything resembling a hierarchical structure. There are no job titles, and job roles are fluid and shifting, according to what needs to be done at any particular moment. Rather than "bosses,"

the holocracy system relies on networks of self-managing teams that overlap in their responsibilities and interactions.[1]

In keeping with Zappos's philosophy that it is less expensive to pay a fee to those who don't want to stay than to force them to remain on staff, it offered severance packages to any employees who chose to leave rather than work in the holocracy. The packages offered at least three months' pay, or one month of pay for every year the employee had been with the company, whichever amounted to more.

In response to this relatively generous offer, an estimated 18 percent of the company's staff chose to leave, which is slightly lower than the firm's average annual turnover of about 20 percent.[2] Furthermore, Zappos's charismatic CEO Tony Hsieh argues that most of these departures did not constitute indications that people were unhappy with the holocracy. Rather, he asserts that it implies that the severance offer was so good, they could not pass up the opportunity to have a few months' salary in the bank, as a cushion while they "pursued their dreams."

Hsieh also notes that transformations to radically new forms of organization always lead to a dip in productivity and other metrics, while the staff reorients to the new normal.[3] In the boss-less offices at Zappos, some of the remaining employees concur with this prediction. For example, one human resource manager noted that her long-term goal had been to become a vice president, and in the new Zappos, that goal would not be possible because there were no vice presidents. But once she stopped "freaking out" about the loss of conventional power, she embraced the notion of self-management and devised her own, new responsibilities in the holocracy.

Still, some reports suggest that the new structure increases inefficiencies, such that it leaves decision-making authority unclear. It also requires substantial resources to implement, considering that it represents an untried and unfamiliar way of working. One anonymous call-center worker complained that the launch of the holocracy involved a wealth of time-consuming, unproductive meetings, as the company worked to explain the new concept and ensure that it was functioning as intended.

According to John Bunch, the holocracy implementation at Zappos might be challenging, but it also is the best way to interact with and manage modern employees, including young workers whose views of their workspace differ from those of their predecessors. But he also promises that a holocracy can work for everyone because it allows for distinct forms of working for all the "different types of people within the organization. There are some people who really enjoy being able to flexibly move across different work assignments and try to find new areas. And there are other people that just want something stable, they just want to come in every day and do what they're accustomed to and know what that is. And both types of those people can work in this environment."[4]

Retailers achieve their financial objectives by effectively managing five critical assets: location, merchandise inventory, channels, employees, and customers. This chapter focuses on managing employees—building a human resource competitive advantage. Sam Walton, founder of Walmart, famously warned that if employee support was not the top priority for members of his management team, they would no longer be part of that team. To ensure company success, he believed that the workforce had to be inspired to contribute their ideas actively, as well as engage with their job and the company.[5] Howard Schultz, founder, former CEO, and current executive chair of Starbucks, supporting this perspective said, "The relationship that we have with our people and the culture of our company are our most sustainable competitive advantages."[6] As this chapter's opener expounds, Zappos also believes that a happy employee is a productive one.

Human resource management (HRM) is responsible for aligning the capabilities and behaviors of employees with the short- and long-term goals of the retail firm. Effective management of HRM can build a competitive advantage by lowering costs and/or increasing differentiation. In particular, as the largest controllable expense for most retailers, labor might take up around 10 percent of revenues earned, which means that effective HRM also has an opportunity to produce a cost advantage.[7] In addition, employees can play a major role in differentiating a retailer's offering by enhancing a customer's experience through the information and assistance they provide. The differentiating advantages gained through HRM are difficult for competitors to duplicate. For example, as we note in this chapter's opener, Zappos's sales associates are known for providing outstanding customer service. However, most retailers are not able to develop Zappos's customer-oriented culture in their own firms.

This chapter focuses on the broad strategic issues involving acquiring and retaining employees. It also focuses on leadership and cost-control issues. Finally, organization structure and legal issues associated with human resource management are discussed.

ACQUIRE AND RETAIN HUMAN RESOURCES

LO 15-1

Describe how to acquire and retain employees.

Exhibit 15–1 illustrates the activities retail managers engage in to acquire and retain productive employees.[8] These activities do not represent a linear process. The recruiting step occurs only once with each employee; whereas the remaining activities are ongoing. Each of these activities is discussed in this section.

Recruit Retail Employees

Step 1 in the process for acquiring and retaining employees (Exhibit 15–1) is to recruit competent employees. This step entails preparing a job description, finding potential applicants with the desired capabilities, and screening the best candidates to interview.[9] (Appendix 1A of Chapter 1 describes the recruiting and selection process from the perspective of people interested in pursuing retail careers and applying for management trainee positions.) Retailing View 15.1 describes some revised considerations that retailers address when seeking to recruit young workers.

Develop the Job Description   The **job description** identifies essential activities to be undertaken and is used to determine the qualifications of potential employees. It influences responses of job seekers or applicants.[10] The retailer's or employer's brand or reputation has a large influence on the applicant pool.[11] It includes specific activities the employee needs to perform and the performance expectations expressed in quantitative terms. Retail salespeople's responsibilities vary from company to company and department to department within a store. Retail employees in self-service stores such as supermarkets and full-line discount stores typically help customers find merchandise, bring out and display merchandise, and ring up sales. In contrast, employees who work in jewelry stores, high-end apparel department stores, or furniture stores typically get involved in a more extensive selling process that begins with determining the customer's needs, then proposing solutions, overcoming objections, closing the sale, and providing after-sale support.[12] The skill level required for employees engaged in selling high-involvement merchandise such as jewelry or home entertainment systems are much greater than the skills needed for employees who have limited interactions with customers. Exhibit 15–2 lists some questions that managers use when undertaking a job description of store employees.

Locate Prospective Employees   Some creative approaches being used by retailers to recruit applicants, in addition to placing ads on Craigslist and posting job openings on websites such as LinkedIn and TweetMyJobs, are working with the American Association of Retired Persons (AARP) to match seniors with job openings at their companies. Other options include partnering with government agencies to recruit unemployed individuals, veterans, and former welfare recipients, or using employees as talent scouts. Retailers often ask their own employees if they know someone the company could hire.[13] When Starbucks store managers receive exceptional service from other providers, they give the associate a business card, inviting him or her to drop into Starbucks, have a free latte, and discuss employment opportunities. Some employers provide employees rewards, such as $500 for every full-time hire and $200 for every part-timer.

EXHIBIT 15–1
Activities for Acquiring and Retaining Employees

Recruit

Train & Acculturate

Motivate

Evaluate

Reward and Compensate

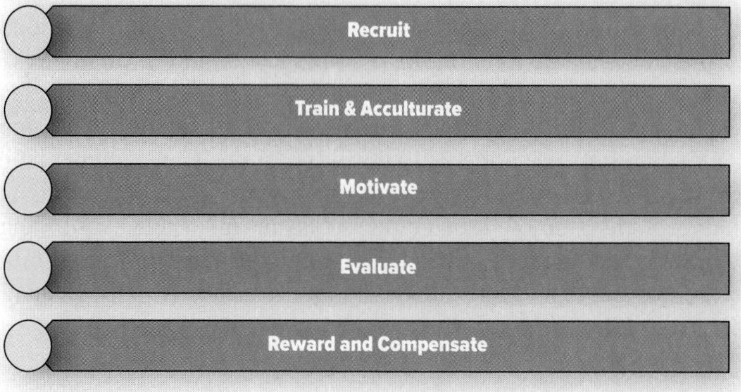

RETAILING VIEW   How Can Retailers Best Recruit Millennial Employees?   15.1

When it comes to appealing to Millennials, retailers have to consider more than just young consumers; they need to think about the job applicants that present themselves to fill the many jobs available in the retail sector. Although the strategies to find and hire the best applicants might not be totally different based on generational cohorts, some aspects of the process could require adjustment to appeal to Millennials, who currently account for approximately one-third of the workforce and will constitute the majority of workers by around 2025.

In particular, some studies suggest that a key practice is to engage in dialogue, to find out what each individual applicant seeks in terms of job goals, responsibilities, and future prospects. With this information, a Millennial job candidate can affirm whether she or he will fit with the retailer's corporate culture, which constitutes an important criterion for young workers. Other reports suggest that working in a team setting that enables them to receive training on the job is important to most Millennials.

Although such tactics might be optimal for getting individual employees to commit, hiring firms appear to hold somewhat poor views of Millennials as a group. For example, 74 percent of hiring managers surveyed in one study indicated their sense that Millennials had a poor work ethic, compared with previous generations of workers.

Part of the source of these conflicting notions might stem from a basic difference in perspective about what employment should mean. Many previous generations might have sought to obtain a job and stay with that same company for their entire careers, and people with that attitude likely are the ones doing the hiring. But Millennials instead might respond better to a strategy that encourages them to develop

Millennials and their older supervisors may have different perspectives about what employment should mean.

© Erik Isakson/Blend Images/Getty Images

their skills and talents by leveraging the resources available in the company at that time. By helping them cultivate these skills, in line with their own preferred job trajectory, the retailer can ensure that it prepares them to perform well in the future. From a traditional view, the challenge of such an approach is that the Millennial might find more opportunities with another company. But that might be the price modern retailers need to pay to attract the best talent among the current generation of workers.

Source: Matthew Stern, "Should Retailers Consider New Recruiting Strategies for Millennials?," *RetailWire,* January 13, 2016.

Screen Applicants to Interview   The screening process matches applicants' qualifications with the job description. Many retailers use automated prescreening programs as a low-cost method of identifying qualified candidates. Applicants initially apply in the store using a traditional paper application or through a web-enabled store kiosk. They can also apply online or call a toll-free telephone number.

Application Forms   **Job application forms** contain information about the applicant's employment history, previous compensation, reasons for leaving his or her previous

- How many salespeople will be working in the department at the same time?
- Do the salespeople have to work together in dealing with customers?
- How many customers will the salesperson have to work with at one time?
- Will the salesperson be selling on an open floor or working behind the counter?
- How much and what type of product knowledge does the salesperson need?
- Does the salesperson need to sell the merchandise or just ring up the orders and provide information?
- Is the salesperson required to make appointments with customers and develop a loyal customer base?
- Does the salesperson have the authority to negotiate price or terms of the sale?
- Does the salesperson need to demonstrate the merchandise?
- Will the salesperson be expected to make add-on sales?
- Is the salesperson's appearance important? How should an effective salesperson look?
- Will the salesperson be required to perform merchandising activities such as stocking shelves and setting up displays?
- Whom will the salesperson report to?
- What compensation plan will the salesperson be working under?

EXHIBIT 15–2
Questions for Undertaking a Job Description

employment, education and training, and references. This information enables the manager to determine whether the applicant has the minimum qualifications, and it also provides information that is useful when the manager interviews the applicant. Today, many large retailers have found that having a nationwide centralized recruiting process reduces costs considerably and improves the quality of candidates that are eventually hired.

Reference Checking   Most retailers verify the information given on an application form by contacting the applicant's references and doing an online search. Because people are more likely to be honest in conversations, managers often talk to the references, rather than relying on written opinions. Due to potential legal problems, however, many companies have a policy of not commenting on prior employees. A Google search can also be useful for finding out information that may not appear on the job application or emerge through contacts with references.

Retail managers generally expect to hear favorable comments from an applicant's references or previous supervisors, even if they may not have thought highly of the applicant. One approach to reduce this positive bias is to ask the reference to rank the applicant relative to others in the same position. For example, the manager might ask, "How would you rate Pat's customer service skills in relation to other retail sales associates you have worked with?"

Social media such as Twitter, Facebook, and LinkedIn are excellent sources of information on prospective employees. These sites often reveal more about the person than a face-to-face interview. While social media platforms can provide employers with a wealth of information about job candidates, there is a risk of relying too heavily on this information for selecting employees. Much of the information on social media sites—such as ethnicity, age, religion, marital status, and sexual orientation—is sensitive and protected by law. The use of sensitive, protected information could expose an employer to discrimination claims, especially if it is not relevant for the employee's eventual job performance.[14]

Test Applicants   Some retailers use intelligence, ability, personality, and interest tests to gain insights about candidates. Tests also can be used to match applicants with job openings and to develop training programs. However, tests must be scientifically and legally valid. They can be used only when the scores have been shown to be related to job performance. It is illegal to use tests that assess factors that are not job-related or discriminate against specific groups.

Many retailers require that applicants take drug tests. Some retailers also use tests to assess applicants' honesty and ethics. Paper-and-pencil honesty tests include questions designed to find out if an applicant has ever thought about stealing and if he or she believes other people steal ("What percentage of people take more than $1 from their employer?").

Preview the Job   Turnover, employees who leave the job, declines when applicants understand both the attractive and unattractive aspects of the job. For example, PetSmart, a pet supply category specialist, shows each applicant a 10-minute video that begins with the advantages of being a company employee and continues with scenes of employees dealing with irate customers and cleaning up animal droppings. Using job previews like this typically screens out many applicants who would most likely have quit due to the job requirements within three months if hired.

Conduct a Personal Interview   After screening applicants, the selection process typically involves a personal interview. Because the interview is usually the critical factor in the hiring decision, the manager needs to be well prepared and have complete control over the interview.

The objective of the interview is to gather relevant information, not simply to ask a lot of questions. The most widely used interview technique, called the **behavioral interview**, asks candidates how they have handled actual situations they have encountered in the past, especially situations requiring the skills outlined in the job description. For example, applicants applying for a job requiring that they handle customer

EXHIBIT 15–3   Interviewing Questions

EDUCATION	**PREVIOUS EXPERIENCE**	**QUESTIONS THAT SHOULD NOT BE ASKED PER EQUAL EMPLOYMENT OPPORTUNITY GUIDELINES**
What were your most and least favorite subjects in college? Why?	What's your description of the ideal manager? Subordinate? Coworker?	Do you have plans for having children/a family?
What types of extracurricular activities did you participate in? Why did you select those activities?	What did you like most/least about your last job?	What are your marriage plans?
	What kind of people do you find it difficult/easy to work with? Why?	What does your husband/wife do?
If you had the opportunity to attend school all over again, what, if anything, would you do differently? Why?	What has been your greatest accomplishment during your career to date?	What happens if your husband/wife gets transferred or needs to relocate?
How did you spend the summers during college?	Describe a situation at your last job involving pressure. How did you handle it?	Who will take care of your children while you're at work?
Did you have any part-time jobs? Which of your part-time jobs did you find most interesting? What did you find most difficult about working and attending college at the same time? What advice would you give to someone who wanted to work and attend college at the same time?	What were some duties on your last job that you found difficult?	(Asked of men) How would you feel about working for a woman?
	Of all the jobs you've had, which did you find the most/least rewarding?	How old are you?
	What is the most frustrating situation you've encountered in your career?	What is your date of birth?
	Why do you want to leave your present job?	How would you feel about working for a person younger than you?
What accomplishments are you most proud of?	What would you do if . . . ?	Where were you born?
	How would you handle . . . ?	Where were your parents born?
	What would you like to avoid in future jobs?	Do you have any disabilities?
	What do you consider your greatest strength/weakness?	As a person with a disability, what help are you going to need to do your work?
	What are your responsibilities in your present job?	How severe is your disability?
	Tell me about the people you hired on your last job. How did they work out? What about the people you fired?	What's your religion?
		What church do you attend?
	What risks did you take in your last job, and what were the results of those risks?	Do you hold religious beliefs that would prevent you from working on certain days of the week?
	Where do you see yourself in three years?	Do you feel that your race/color will be a problem in your performing the job?
	What kind of references will your previous employer give?	Are you of _____ heritage/race?
	What do you do when you have trouble solving a problem?	

complaints would be asked to describe a situation in which they were confronted by someone who was angry about something they had done. Candidates might be asked to describe the situation, what they did, and the outcomes of their actions. These situations also can be used to interview references for the applicants. Exhibit 15–3 lists some questions that manager might ask.

Train and Acculturate Employees

Having hired employees with the required skills or potential to develop these skills, retailers need to train them to do their jobs and introduce them to the firm's policies, values, and strategies (step 2 in Exhibit 15–1). This acculturation process affects the degree to which newcomers become involved, engaged contributors to the firm's successful performance. Overcoming the shock of starting a new job can be a problem for even the most knowledgeable and mature new employees. College students who accept management trainee positions often find significant differences between their role as students and employees.

The training and acculturation program for new employees might be limited to several hours during which they learn the retailer's policies and procedures and how to use the point-of-sale (POS) terminal. Other retailers, like The Container Store, have a much more intensive training program. At this retailer, one of *Fortune* magazine's best places to work, new employees go through a week of foundation training.[15] Before employment begins, they receive a handbook and assignments to complete. The first day of Foundation Week begins with the company philosophy and a visit from store managers. Days 2–5 continue with hands-on, on-the-floor training, including interaction with and instruction about various positions in the store. The culmination of Foundation Week is a ceremony during which the new employees receive their aprons, signifying their membership in this elite organization. The orientation process also continues past Foundation Week; every first-year, full-time salesperson receives about 263 hours of training, compared with 8 hours in the retail industry, on average. Training continues throughout an employee's career.[16]

To be effective, new employee training should feature a blended approach that includes both structured and more informal, on-the-job lessons. Managers should continue to work with employees by helping them analyze their successes and failures.[17]

Provide a Structured Program

A **structured training program** helps new employees acquire the basic skills and knowledge that they need to be able to do their jobs. For example, sales associates learn what the company policies are, how to use the POS terminal, and basic selling skills. Stockroom employees learn procedures for receiving merchandise.

Some retailers find that providing structured training over the Internet offers benefits compared to the on-the-job training. There is greater consistency, because the same material is presented rather than having material presented by different trainers or supervisors. Costs are lower; once the system is set up, there is no need for instructors or travel, and employees can undertake the training whenever they want.

Many retailers are now using online training systems. These systems often combine one-way video with two-way audio and data exchange capability, which allows instructors to chat online with students during training programs. Often, along with presentations from instructors, the trainings include pre-class and post-class testing to measure comprehension levels. Furthermore, many retailers also now use training applications that employees can access on their smartphone or mobile device.[18]

Offer On-the-Job Training

Structured training programs need to be combined with **on-the-job training** in which new employees work in specific jobs under the direct supervision of their managers. New employees can learn about company policies and skills needed to perform their jobs through structured programs, but they must be able to apply the information they have learned from training programs on the job. The best way to learn is to practice what is being taught. New employees learn by engaging in activities, making mistakes, and then learning how not to make those mistakes again.

New employees at the outdoor equipment retailer Recreational Equipment Inc. (REI) work "buddy shifts" with senior sales associates to learn successful sales techniques. Although this is a time-consuming type of on-the-job training, it helps salespeople engage in productive selling interactions and provides a pleasant experience for customers.[19] The training is so effective that many REI salespeople, when given the opportunity to move up the corporate ladder, choose to remain on the selling floor, where they enjoy the work–life balance and workplace satisfaction, along with their relatively high compensation.[20]

Use a Blended Approach

Because of the relative advantages of structured and on-the-job training, many firms use a blended approach. Teams of Best Buy associates attend monthly, nearly three-hour-long training sessions led by qualified instructors, focused on new products and services or specific departmental concerns. Furthermore, employees role-play to practice customer interactions. In online training sessions, available through the retailer's proprietary learning management system, associates complete courses that enable them to use virtual versions of the products they sell or play interactive video games to practice challenging interactions with virtual customers. As a result, Best Buy often is ranked among the top 30 firms for employee training.[21]

Analyze Successes and Failures   Every new employee makes mistakes. Effective managers provide an atmosphere in which sales associates can try out different approaches for providing customer service and selling merchandise. Managers need to recognize that some of these new approaches are going to fail, and when they do, effective managers do not criticize the individual sales associate. Instead, they talk about the situation, analyze why the approach didn't work, and discuss how the sales associate could avoid the problem in the future. Managers also work with employees to help them understand and learn from their successes. For example, salespeople shouldn't consider a large, multiple-item sale to occur simply due to luck. They should be encouraged to reflect on the sale, identify their key behaviors that facilitated the sale, and then remember these sales behaviors for future use.

It's important to help sales associates assign the right kinds of reasons for their performance. For example, some sales associates take credit for successes and blame the company, the buyers, or the merchandise for their failures. Managers can help sales associates constructively analyze their successes and failures by asking "why" questions that force them to analyze the reasons for effective and ineffective performance. To encourage learning, managers get salespeople to recognize that they could have satisfied the customer if they had used a different approach or been more persistent. When sales associates accept such responsibility, they'll be motivated to search for ways to improve their sales skills.[22]

Motivate Employees

The third activity involved in acquiring and retaining is to motivate them (see Exhibit 15–1). High-performance employees work hard, and the activities they work on should be consistent with the retailer's strategy and goals. Motivating employees to perform up to their potential may be managers' most important and challenging task. The implementation of the retailer's evaluation, rewards, and compensation schemes, discussed in this section, together affect the motivation of employees and the effort they expend. We use the following hypothetical situation to illustrate some issues pertaining to employee motivation.

After getting an associate's degree at a local community college, Jim Taylor was hired for a sales position at a department store. Taylor was told that if he did well in this assignment, he could become a management trainee. After observing Taylor on the sales floor, his manager, Jennifer Chen, evaluated Taylor's performance as average. She felt he was effective only when interacting with customers like himself: young, career-oriented men and women. To encourage Taylor to sell to other types of customers, Chen reviewed Taylor's performance goals with him. She reduced the portion of his compensation composed of a fixed salary and increased his commission rate. Taylor now feels a lot of pressure to increase his sales level. He's beginning to dread coming to work in the morning and is thinking about getting out of retailing and working for a bank.

In this hypothetical situation, Chen focused on increasing Taylor's motivation by providing some feedback and more incentive-based compensation. In discussing this illustration, we'll examine the appropriateness of this approach versus other approaches for improving Taylor's performance.

Set Goals to Motivate Employees   To effectively motivate employees, managers need to set goals for their employees and provide feedback on the employees' performance relative to those goals. Employee performance improves when employees feel that (1) their efforts will enable them to achieve the goals set for them by their managers and (2) they'll receive rewards they value if they achieve their goals. Thus, managers can motivate employees by setting realistic goals and offering rewards that employees want.[23]

Another option, as highlighted in Retailing View 15.2, is to motivate employees by becoming part owners of the retail establishment.

For example, Jennifer Chen set specific selling goals for Jim Taylor when he started to work in her department. Taylor, like other store sales associates, has goals in five selling

15.2   RETAILING VIEW   Motivated by Ownership at Publix

At Publix, a regional grocery store chain that started in Florida and is prominent throughout the southeastern United States, a key differentiator is its ownership structure. That might seem like a strange thing to use as a strategic advantage, considering that grocery shoppers are unlikely to take the time to think about who owns the store where they pick up their milk and bread. But according to the company's CEO, because employees account for a substantial portion of ownership shares—around 30 percent of the total shares available—the owners are what makes Publix different from any other chain.

In particular, the CEO cites the improved service that employees provide because they have "skin in the game." This effect has been in place since the start of the firm. Its original founder believed that employees would be more conscientious and careful in their work if they could also earn profits from improved store performance. As a result, Publix frequently appears in lists of the best places to work; one survey showed that 78 percent of its employees would recommend it as an employer.

These positive reviews affect the stores' performance in the consumer market too. In various polls, it ranks as the best grocer in the south, as well as second in the nation, behind only Trader Joe's. Thus it appears that the founder was right: Giving employees a vested interest in the company's

© JeffG/Alamy Stock Photo

Publix frequently appears in lists of the best places to work, at least partially because its employees account for a substantial portion of ownership shares.

performance leads to better performance, both at the bottom line and in the store aisles.

Source: George Anderson, "For Publix, Success Comes Down to Its Owners," *RetailWire*, May 13, 2015.

areas: sales per hour, average amount per transaction (size of average sale), percentage multiple transactions (percentage of sales with add-on items), number of preferred customers, and number of preferred customer appointments made. This retailer defines preferred clients as customers who have a high CLV (customer lifetime value; see Chapter 10). In addition, sales associates like Taylor are often evaluated on the overall department inventory loss due to stolen merchandise (departmental shrinkage), the errors they make in using the POS terminal (system errors), and their contribution to maintaining the department's appearance (merchandise presentation). Chen also designed a program for Taylor's development as a sales associate. The activities she outlined over the next six months required Taylor to attend in-house classes to improve his selling skills.

Chen needs to be careful in setting goals for Taylor. If she sets the goals too high, he might become discouraged, feel the goals are unattainable, and thus not be motivated to work harder. However, if she sets the goals too low, Taylor can achieve them easily and won't be motivated to work to his full potential.

Goals are most effective at motivating employees when they're based on the employee's experience and confidence. Experienced salespeople have confidence in their abilities and should have "stretch" goals (high goals that will make them work harder). New salespeople need lower goals that they have a good chance of achieving. The initial good experience of achieving and surpassing goals builds new salespeople's confidence and motivates them to improve their skills.

Although young employees have traditionally made up the majority of the retail labor force, retailers have realized that what these employees want out of their jobs and work environments is quite different from what their older supervisors want. As a result, different goals and approaches are necessary to manage and motivate younger employees. Specifically, they want more flexibility, meaningful jobs, professional freedom, and a better work–life balance than older employees. They readily switch jobs if their expectations aren't met, making employee turnover high.[24] Retailing View 15.3 highlights one of these differences, when it comes to corporate dress codes.

Whether it is the desire to show off their latest tattoo or a preference to wear black pants instead of khakis, retail employees often find themselves limited in their expressions, especially if they work for national retailers such as Starbucks or Walmart. Rules prohibiting visible displays of tattoos or piercings have long been in place for many stores, and dress codes often mandate exactly what colors and styles of clothing are acceptable. But some of these regulations are softening, evidently in response to changing cultural and social acceptance of a more casual, individualistic approach to dressing. Following its competitor Peet's, Starbucks has begun to allow visible tattoos on baristas, though it mandates that they cannot contain any offensive content (e.g., nudity, obscene language). Employees who once might have worn long-sleeved shirts all year long now might be able to display their inked arms.

Walmart is becoming both more lenient and stricter in its dress code. It still prohibits visible tattoos and piercings, but rather than only khaki pants, employees may now wear black pants as well. But with those black pants, they must still wear the blue Walmart vests that mark them as available to help shoppers. Such vests are effective signals in large stores such as Walmart and Home Depot, where customers might be relieved to find the brightly dressed employees who can help them find the right drill bit or paint roller.

For Walmart, though, the shift in the dress code created a resurgence of the conversation about how it treats employees. One store clerk complained, in a letter to company headquarters, that buying new clothes to match the dress code, even at Walmart, was more than his salary would cover.

© Waring Abbott/Getty Images

In response to changing cultural and social mores, many local coffee shops and some national chains including Starbucks allow employees to have visible tattoos.

Retailers legally may impose virtually any dress code they want, but the pushback from employees might not be worth it. Many young employees consider their tattoos or piercings part of their self-expression, and this cohort is unlikely to agree to cover those artistic renderings for such a vast portion of their daily lives.

Sources: John Kell, "Corporate Dress Codes Relax in an Age of Tattoos, Piercings," *Fortune*, September 17, 2014; "What Employers Should Learn from Wal-Mart's Dress Code Controversy," *Knowledge@Wharton*, September 22, 2014.

Evaluate Employees

The fourth activity involved in acquiring and retaining employees is to evaluate them (see Exhibit 15–1). The objective of the evaluation process is to identify the employees who are performing well and those who aren't. On the basis of the evaluation, high-performing employees should be rewarded and considered for positions with greater responsibility. Plans need to be developed to increase the productivity of employees performing below expectations. Should poor performers be terminated? Do they need additional training? If yes, what kind of training do they need?[25]

Who Should Do the Evaluation?
In large retail firms, the evaluation system is usually designed by the human resource department. But the evaluation itself is done by the employee's immediate supervisor—the manager who works most closely with the employee. For example, in a discount store the department manager is in the best position to observe a sales associate in action and understand the reasons for the sales associate's performance. The department manager also oversees the recommendations that come out of the evaluation process. Inexperienced supervisors are often assisted by a senior manager in evaluating employees.

How Often Should Evaluations Be Made?
Most retailers evaluate employees annually or semiannually. Feedback from evaluations is the most effective method for improving employee skills. Thus, evaluations should be done more frequently when managers are developing inexperienced employees. However, frequent formal evaluations are time-consuming for managers and may not give employees enough time to respond to

EXHIBIT 15–4   Factors Used to Evaluate Sales Associates at a Specialty Store

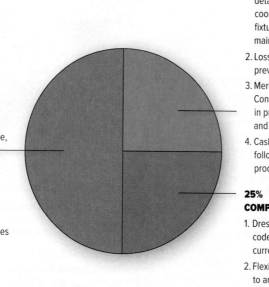

50%
SALES/CUSTOMER RELATIONS

1. Greeting. Approaches customers within 1 to 2 minutes with a smile and friendly manner. Uses open-ended questions.

2. Product knowledge. Demonstrates knowledge of product, fit, shrinkage, and price and can relay this information to the customer.

3. Suggests additional merchandise. Approaches customers at fitting room and cash/wrap areas.

4. Asks customers to buy and reinforces decisions. Lets customers know they've made a wise choice and thanks them.

25%
OPERATIONS

1. Store appearance. Demonstrates an eye for detail (color and finesse) in the areas of display, coordination of merchandise on tables, floor fixtures, and wall faceouts. Takes initiative in maintaining store presentation standards.

2. Loss prevention. Actively follows all loss prevention procedures.

3. Merchandise control and handling. Consistently achieves established requirements in price change activity, shipment processing, and inventory control.

4. Cash/wrap procedures. Accurately and efficiently follows all register policies and cash/wrap procedures.

25%
COMPLIANCE

1. Dress code and appearance. Complies with dress code. Appears neat and well groomed. Projects current fashionable store image.

2. Flexibility. Able to switch from one assignment to another, open to schedule adjustments. Shows initiative, awareness of store priorities and needs.

3. Working relations. Cooperates with other employees, willingly accepts direction and guidance from management. Communicates to management.

suggestions before the next evaluation. Effective managers supplement formal evaluations with frequent informal ones. For example, Jennifer Chen should work with Jim Taylor informally and not wait for the formal six-month evaluation. The best time for Chen to provide this informal feedback is immediately after she has obtained, through observations or reports, positive or negative information about Taylor's performance.

What Format Should Be Used for Evaluations?   Evaluations are meaningful only if employees know what they're required to do, the expected level of performance, and how they'll be evaluated. Exhibit 15–4 shows a specialty retailer's criteria for evaluating sales associates.

In this case, the employee's overall evaluation is based on subjective evaluations made by the manager and assistant managers. It places equal weight on individual sales/customer relations activities and activities associated with overall store performance. By emphasizing overall store operations and performance, the assessment criteria motivate sales associates to work together as a team.

The criteria used at the department store to evaluate Jim Taylor are objective sales measures based on POS data, not subjective measures like those used by the specialty store. Exhibit 15–5 summarizes Taylor's formal six-month evaluation. The evaluation form lists results for various factors in terms of both what's considered average performance for company salespeople and Taylor's actual performance. His department has done better than average on shrinkage control, and he has done well on system errors and merchandise presentation. However, his sales performance is below average, even though he made more than the average number of presentations to preferred customers. These results suggest that Taylor's effort is good, but his selling skills may need improvement.

How Can Managers Avoid Evaluation Errors?   Managers can make evaluation errors when they first form an overall opinion of the employee's performance and then allow this opinion to influence their ratings of each performance factor. For example,

	Average Performance for Sales Associates in Department	Actual Performance for Jim Taylor
Sales per hour	$75	$65
Average amount per transaction	$45	$35
Percentage multiple transactions	55%	55%
Number of preferred customers	115	125
Number of preferred customer appointments	95	120
Departmental shrinkage	2.00%	1.80%
Systems errors	10	2
Merchandise presentation (10-point scale)	5	8

EXHIBIT 15–5
Summary of Jim Taylor's Six-Month Evaluation

a store manager might feel that a salesperson's overall performance is below average and then rate the salesperson as below average on selling skills, punctuality, appearance, and stocking. When an overall evaluation casts such a negative halo on multiple aspects of a salesperson's performance, the evaluation is no longer useful for identifying specific areas that need improvement.

In making evaluations, managers are often unduly influenced by recent events and their evaluations of other salespeople. For example, a manager might remember a salesperson's poor performance with a customer the day before and forget the salesperson's outstanding performance over the past three months. Similarly, a manager might be unduly harsh in evaluating an average salesperson just after completing an evaluation of an outstanding salesperson. Finally, managers have a natural tendency to attribute performance (particularly poor performance) to the salesperson and not to the environment in which the salesperson is working. When making evaluations, managers tend to underemphasize effects of external factors on the department, such as merchandise and competitors' actions.

The department store's approach for evaluating sales associates avoids many of these potential biases because most of the ratings are based on objective data. In contrast, the specialty store's evaluation approach (Exhibit 15–4) considers a wider range of activities but uses more subjective performance measures. Because subjective information about specific skills, attitudes about the store and customers, interactions with coworkers, enthusiasm, and appearance aren't used in the department store's evaluation, performance on these factors might not have been explicitly communicated to Jim Taylor. The subjective characteristics in the specialty store evaluation are more prone to bias, but they also might be more helpful to salespeople as they try to improve their performance. To avoid bias when making subjective ratings, managers need to observe performance regularly, record their observations, avoid evaluating many salespeople at one time, and remain conscious of the various potential biases. They also can rely on some specific performance measures.

HRM Performance Measures   Three measures that retailers frequently use to assess HRM performance are employee productivity, turnover, and **engagement**.

Productivity   **Productivity** is the sales generated per employee calculated as follows:

$$\text{Employee productivity} = \frac{\text{Net sales}}{\text{Number of full-time equivalent employees (FTEs)}}$$

A full-time equivalent is the number of hours worked by an employee divided by the number of hours considered to be a full-time workweek for an employee. Thus, a sales associate who worked 12 hours for a retailer with a standard workweek of 36 hours would be considered a one-third FTE. Employee productivity can be improved by increasing the sales generated by employees, reducing the number of employees, or both.

Turnover   Another HRM performance measure is turnover. Employee **turnover** is calculated as follows:

$$\text{Employee turnover} = \frac{\text{Number of employees who leave their jobs during a year}}{\text{Number of positions}}$$

Thus, if a store owner had five sales associate positions but three employees left their jobs and were replaced during the year, the turnover would be 3/5 = 60 percent. Note that turnover can be greater than 100 percent if a substantial number of people are replaced more than once during the year. In our example, if the replacements for the three employees who left also left during the same year, the turnover would be 6/5 = 120 percent.

Engagement   Engagement is an emotional commitment by an employee to the organization and its goals. It goes beyond employee happiness and satisfaction.[26] Employees might be happy at work, but that doesn't necessarily mean they are working hard to make sure the retailer achieves its goals. Similarly satisfied employees might not expend extra effort on their own. Engaged employees care about their work and their company. They don't just work for a paycheck, or just for the next promotion, but they also work to enable the retailer to achieve its goals. They are more motivated to support the retailer in its efforts to improve the satisfaction of customers and build customer loyalty. Engaged employees also are less likely to leave the company. Typically, retailers use employee surveys to measure employee engagement.[27]

Reward and Compensate Employees

Employees receive two types of rewards from their job: extrinsic and intrinsic.[28] The largest and typically most important form of extrinsic reward from both the retailer's and employee's perspective is monetary compensation.

Extrinsic Rewards: Compensation Programs   **Extrinsic rewards** are rewards provided by either the employee's manager or the firm (i.e., external to the employee, such as compensation, promotion, and recognition). Employees don't all seek the same rewards. For example, some salespeople want more compensation; others strive for a promotion in the company or public recognition of their performance. Jim Taylor wants a favorable evaluation from his manager so that he can enter the management training program. Managers can offer a variety of extrinsic rewards, such as compensation, as discussed next, to motivate employees.

The objectives of a compensation program are to attract and keep good employees, motivate them to undertake activities consistent with the retailer's strategy, and strike a balance between controlling labor costs and providing enough compensation to keep high-quality employees. A compensation plan is most effective for motivating and retaining employees when the employees feel that the plan is fair and that their compensation is related to their efforts. Retail firms typically use one or more of the following compensation plans: straight salary, straight commission, salary plus commission, and quota bonus.

Straight Salary Compensation   With **straight salary compensation**, salespeople receive a fixed amount of compensation for each hour or week they work. For example, a salesperson might be paid $24 an hour or a department manager $2,000 a week. Typically, market conditions determine the amount of compensation. Walmart upped the minimum wages it pays salespeople, above the nationally mandated minimum wage, in part to compete better for good employees with other retail chains.[29]

This plan is easy for the employee to understand and for the store to administer. Under a straight salary plan, the retailer has flexibility in assigning salespeople to different activities and sales areas. For example, salaried salespeople will undertake nonselling activities, such as stocking shelves, and won't be upset if they're transferred from a high-sales-volume department to a low-sales-volume department.

The major disadvantage of the straight salary plan is employees' lack of immediate incentives to improve their productivity. They know their compensation won't change in the short run, regardless of whether they work hard or slack off. Another disadvantage is that a straight salary becomes a fixed cost that the firm incurs even if sales decline, which means a greater loss of profits during hard economic times.

Incentive Compensation   **Incentive compensation plans** reward employees on the basis of their productivity.[30] With some incentive plans, a salesperson's income is based entirely on commission—called a **straight commission**. A salesperson thus might be paid a commission based on a percentage of sales made minus merchandise returned. Normally, the percentage is the same for all merchandise sold (e.g., 7 percent of sales). But some retailers use different percentages for different categories of merchandise (e.g., 4 percent for low-margin items and 10 percent for high-margin items). Different percentages provide additional incentives for salespeople to sell specific items. Typically, the compensation of salespeople selling high-priced items such as jewelry, men's suits, cars, furniture, and appliances is based largely on their commissions.

Incentive compensation is most effective when a salesperson's performance can be measured easily and precisely. It's difficult to measure individual performance when salespeople work in teams or must perform a lot of nonselling activities. Retailers can easily measure a salesperson's actual sales, but it's hard to measure her or his customer service or merchandising performance. Salespeople who are compensated totally by commission generally are less willing to perform nonselling activities, such as stocking shelves, and they tend to concentrate only the most expensive, fast-moving merchandise.

For the retailer, another issue is that salespeople compensated primarily by incentives don't develop loyalty to their employer. The employer doesn't guarantee them an income, so they feel no obligation to the firm. Finally, incentives are less effective with inexperienced salespeople, who are less confident in their skills, because they inhibit learning and also can cause excessive stress. Because compensation plans based (almost) exclusively on sales incentives generally fail to promote good customer service, some plans include a fixed salary plus a commission on total sales or a commission on sales over quota.

Under a straight commission plan, salespeople's incomes can fluctuate from week to week, depending on their sales. Because retail sales are seasonal, salespeople might earn most of their incentive income during the Christmas season but much less during the summer months. To provide a steadier income for salespeople who are paid by high-incentive plans, some retailers offer a drawing account. With a **drawing account**, salespeople receive a weekly check based on their estimated annual income, and commissions earned are credited against the weekly payments.

Quotas are often used with compensation plans. A **quota** is a target level used to motivate and evaluate performance. Examples might include sales per hour for salespeople or maintained margin and inventory turnover for buyers. For department store salespeople, selling quotas vary across departments due to differences in sales productivity levels.

Quota Bonus Compensation   A **quota bonus plan** provides sales associates with a bonus when their performance exceeds their quota. A quota bonus plan's effectiveness depends on setting reasonable, fair quotas, but this can be hard to do. Usually, quotas are set at the same level for everyone in a department, yet salespeople in the same department may have different abilities or face different selling environments. For example, salespeople in the suit area have much greater sales potential than salespeople in the accessories area. Newly hired salespeople might have a harder time achieving a quota than more experienced salespeople. Thus, a quota based on average productivity may be too high to motivate the new salesperson and too low to motivate experienced salespeople. Quotas should be developed for each salesperson based on their experience and abilities.

To encourage employees in a department or store to work together, some retailers provide additional **team incentives**. For example, salespeople might be paid a commission based on their individual sales and then receive additional compensation according to the amount of sales generated by all salespeople in the department. The group incentive encourages salespeople to work together in their nonselling activities and while handling customers so that the department sales target will be achieved.[31]

Intrinsic Rewards   **Intrinsic rewards** are rewards that employees get personally from doing their job well. For example, salespeople often like to sell because they think it's challenging and fun. Of course they want to be paid, but they also find it rewarding to help customers and make sales.[32] Most managers focus on extrinsic rewards to motivate employees.[33] However, an emphasis on extrinsic rewards can make employees lose sight of their job's intrinsic rewards. Employees can begin to feel that their only reason for working is to earn money and that the job isn't fun. Note that Jennifer Chen tried to motivate Jim Taylor by using extrinsic rewards when she linked more of his compensation to how much he sold. This increased emphasis on extrinsic financial rewards may be one reason Taylor now dreads coming to work in the morning. He might not think his job is fun anymore.

When employees find their jobs intrinsically rewarding, they're motivated to learn how to do their job better. This is similar to a person who runs a marathon or climbs a mountain simply for the pride and joy he or she gets from accomplishing it. Some managerial actions that affect intrinsic rewards are contests and job enrichment.

Contests   An approach to making work fun is to hold contests with relatively small prizes. Contests are most effective when everyone has a chance to win. Contests in which the best salespeople always win aren't exciting and may even be demoralizing. For example, consider a contest in which a playing card is given to salespeople for each men's suit they sell during a two-week period. At the end of two weeks, the best poker hand wins. This contest motivates all salespeople during the entire period of the contest. A salesperson who sells only four suits can win with four aces on cards he or she got on the last day of the contest. Contests should be used to create excitement and make selling challenging for everyone, not to pay the best salespeople more money.[34]

Job Enrichment   Experienced employees often lose interest in their jobs. Extrinsic rewards, such as pay or promotion, may not be particularly motivating because the employees might be satisfied with their present income and job responsibilities. But these employees can be motivated by intrinsic rewards presented as job enrichment. **Job enrichment** is the redesign of a job to include a greater range of tasks and responsibilities, including skill variety, task significance, autonomy, and job feedback.[35] For example, an experienced sales associate who has lost some interest in his or her job could be given responsibility for merchandising a particular area, training new salespeople, or planning and managing a special event.

LEADERSHIP

LO 15-2

Illustrate effective leadership strategies of a retail manager.

Leadership is the process by which a person attempts to influence others to accomplish a common goal or task. Managers are leaders of their group of employees. They use a variety of motivational techniques to increase productivity by helping employees achieve professional goals consistent with their firm's objectives.[36]

Leader Decision-Making Style

Managers vary in how much they involve employees in making decisions. **Autocratic leaders** make all decisions on their own and then announce them to employees. They use the authority of their position to tell employees what to do. For example, an autocratic manager determines who will work in each area of the store, when they'll take breaks, and what days they'll have off.

In contrast, **democratic leaders** seek information and opinions from employees and base their decisions on this information. Democratic managers share their power and information with their employees. They ask employees where and when they want to work and make schedules to accommodate those employee desires as much as possible. Effective managers use different leadership styles, selecting the one that is most appropriate for each situation. For example, a manager might be autocratic with an insecure new trainee but democratic with an effective, experienced employee.

The best managers (leaders) go beyond influencing employee behaviors. **Transformational leaders** get people to transcend their personal needs for the sake of the group or organization. They are engaged and generate excitement. They revitalize organizations. Transformational managers create this enthusiasm in their employees through their personal charisma. They are self-confident and have a clear vision that grabs employees' attention. They communicate this vision through words and symbols. Finally, transformational leaders delegate challenging work to subordinates, have free and open communication with them, and provide personal mentoring to develop subordinates.

Maintaining Morale

Managers play an important role in improving the work atmosphere and its effect on the performance of employees. Typically, morale goes up when things are going well and employees are highly motivated. But when sales aren't going well, morale tends to decrease, and employee motivation declines. Effective managers build morale by doing small but meaningful things for employees like throwing a party when goals are met or dividing the charity budget by the number of employees and inviting them to suggest how their "share" should be used. One store manager used real-time sales data collected in her firm's information system (see Chapter 9) to build excitement among her employees. On the first day of the Christmas season, she wrote $4,159 on a white board in the store. That was the store's sales during the first day of the Christmas season last year. She told her sales associates that beating that number was not enough; she wanted to see a 25 percent increase, the same sales increase the store achieved over the previous Christmas season. By setting financial objectives and keeping sales associates informed of up-to-the-minute results, managers can convert an eight-hour shift of clock watchers into an excited team of racers. All day, as customers come and go, sales associates take turns consulting the backroom computer that records sales from the store's POS terminals.

CONTROLLING COSTS

LO 15-3

Explore the various strategies retail managers can undertake to control costs.

Retailers must control their expenses if they are to be profitable. To control costs, retailers often hire people with little or no experience to work as sales associates, bank tellers, and food servers. High turnover, absenteeism, and poor performance often result from this use of inexperienced, low-wage employees. Such results of a lack of experience and motivation among retail employees are particularly troublesome because these employees are often in direct contact with customers. Poor appearance, manners, and attitudes can have a negative effect on sales and customer loyalty. Research has shown that in some types of retail operations, a modest investment in hiring more staff will result in a significant increase in sales.[37] If customers can't find a particular product on their own, or if they can't get an explanation of how it works or how it is used, they are not likely to buy the product.

Other options for controlling costs thus might be more effective. Labor scheduling, store maintenance, and inventory shrinkage offer three opportunities to reduce store operating expenses.

Labor Scheduling

Labor scheduling (determining the employees assigned to each area of the store during each hour) is difficult because customer traffic varies greatly during the day and the week. In addition, multiple shifts are required to staff stores up to 24 hours a

Labor scheduling software ensures that there are enough associates to take care of customers when it is busy (left), but not so many that the associates have little to do when business is slow (right).

day, seven days a week. Poor labor scheduling can result in long checkout lines, sales associates with nothing to do, and lower labor productivity. For example, if 6 percent of a store's sales volume and 9 percent of the total labor-hours occur between 2:00 and 3:00 p.m., the store might be overstaffed during this time period and under-staffed in others.

Retailers' needs for store employees vary depending on the time of day, day of week, time of year, and promotion schedule. These complexities drive many retailers to utilize computer software to schedule workers. By analyzing sales, transactions, and customer traffic for each time period, the software determines the appropriate number of employees to have in each area of the store during each time period and develops a work schedule for each employee.[38] In turn, retailers can control their costs, as well as improve their service provision, because they can match their staffing to customer demand on an hourly basis. The systems account for special events in the surrounding area (e.g., a downtown ice cream shop increases its staffing during the annual town fair), the timing of marketing promotions, and weather and seasonal patterns to make staffing recommendations.

To minimize costs, the systems often suggest that retailers complement their full-time (40 hours per week) store employees with part-time workers. Part-time employees are less expensive than comparable full-time employees and usually are not offered any health or retirement benefits and little job security. However, part-time employees are typically less engaged than full-time employees.[39]

Although these scheduling systems benefit both retailers and customers, they can have an adverse impact on employees. The schedules suggested by this software often recommend irregular work hours, which can burden sales associates with requirements that they remain "on call" on their days off—though such practices are coming more to the attention of policy makers, as Retailing View 15.4 explains. While some employees prefer part-time work because it fits in with their lifestyle, many others prefer to work full time.[40]

Store Maintenance

Store maintenance entails the activities involved with managing the exterior and interior physical facilities associated with the store. The exterior facilities include the parking lot, entrances to the store, and signs on the outside of the store. The interior facilities include the walls, flooring, ceiling, bathrooms, HVAC systems, and displays and signs. Store maintenance affects both the sales generated in the store and the cost of running the store. A store's cleanliness and neatness affect consumer perceptions of the quality of its merchandise, but this maintenance is costly. Poor maintenance short-ens the useful life of air-conditioning units, floors, and fixtures.

In New York and several other states, laws in place require that employers provide their workers with advance notice of their schedules and pay them for a minimum of four hours, even if they send those workers home to limit their labor costs. But did you know that? It seems that few employees are aware of the rules, such that many employers might not be complying with the mandates. In noting this potential problem, the New York attorney general issued cautionary letters to dozens of large retailers, asking for more information about how they handle their on-call staffing practices.

The issue has become more prominent with the expansion of immediate connectivity. It is easy for managers to send quick text messages to employees, moments before they are scheduled to start a shift, and tell those workers that their labor is not needed for the day. Other companies establish an on-call system that requires workers to initiate the contact, shortly before their scheduled shift, to find out if they are needed or not. Such moves can benefit the company, because if business is slow or the schedule is overstaffed, it can reduce its labor costs by telling some workers to stay home.

For the workers, though, these last-minute changes are expensive and frustrating. Especially for workers with families, who have arranged for child care or other logistics, the loss of a shift means that they have wasted efforts. In addition, it means the loss of that day's wages, which may be severely detrimental for many retailer workers.

The retail companies that received the warning letters were well-known names: Target, Gap, Abercrombie & Fitch, Burlington, Crocs, JCPenney, J.Crew, L Brands, Sears, TJX, Urban Outfitters, and Williams-Sonoma. Several of the companies responded immediately to the letters, asserting that they do not require workers to function on-call, nor do they cancel shifts at the last minute. For example, Target noted that it uploads workers' schedules to the company website at least 10 days prior to each shift.

These questions are particularly prominent for retailers because of their vast reliance on less skilled, hourly workers, whose efforts can be limited or extended relatively easily. They also have gained some salience in the modern labor framework, where critics increasingly are demanding improved working conditions. The drive for an increase in the minimum wage is closely related to questions about scheduling. In both cases, the goal must be to find a way to compensate employees fairly for their work, without putting the retailer at a competitive disadvantage.

Source: Lauren Weber, "Retailers Are under Fire for Work Schedules," *The Wall Street Journal*, April 12, 2015.

Inventory Shrinkage

Shrinkage is the inventory loss due to employee theft, shoplifting, mistakes, inaccurate records, and vendor errors. It is the difference between the recorded value of inventory (at retail prices) based on merchandise bought and received and the value of the actual inventory (at retail prices) in stores and distribution centers, divided by retail sales during the period. For example, if accounting records indicate that inventory should be $1,500,000, the actual count of the inventory reveals $1,236,000, and sales were $4,225,000, the shrinkage is 6.2 percent [($1,500,000 − $1,236,000) ÷ $4,225,000].

Reducing shrinkage is an important store management issue because retailers' annual loss from shrinkage averages about 1.4 percent of total sales. In the United States, retail theft costs retailers more than $45 billion in 2015.[41]

A recent survey attributes 34.5 percent of inventory shrinkage to employee theft, 38 percent to shoplifting, 16.5 percent to mistakes and inaccurate records (e.g., failing to ring up an item, miscounting merchandise during physical inventories), and 6.8 percent to vendor fraud (e.g., when vendor shipments contain less than the amount indicated on the packing slip and the retailer fails to recognize it), with an unaccounted for 6.1 percent.[42]

Employee theft has become an increasingly sophisticated, high-tech activity. For example, in collaboration with criminal accomplices, retail employees accept fake merchandise returns and put the "refund" onto gift cards. The employee might use the card himself or herself or hand it to the accomplice. Later, they redeem the card at another store or sell it online. The Internet makes it easy to convert such gift cards into cash. In response, many retailers have hired loss prevention specialists who spend most of their time searching auction sites for suspicious gift card offerings, such as those for much below face value or sales of dozens of cards from the same retailer.[43]

In their efforts to combat shoplifting by customers, retailers confront a trade-off between providing shopping convenience and imposing monitoring systems to prevent losses. The key to an effective loss prevention program is determining the most effective way to protect merchandise while preserving an open, attractive store atmosphere. Loss prevention thus requires coordination among store management, visual merchandising, and store design.

Whether the goal is to reduce employee theft or prevent shoplifting, the best solution is to create a trusting, supportive work environment. When employees feel they're respected members of a team, they identify their goals with the retailer's goals. Stealing from their employer thus becomes equivalent to stealing from themselves or their family, and they go out of their way to prevent others from stealing from the "family." Thus, retailers with a highly committed workforce and low employee turnover typically have low inventory shrinkage.

THE ORGANIZATION STRUCTURE FOR A RETAIL FIRM

LO 15-4

Summarize how retailers are typically organized.

The **organization structure** identifies the activities to be performed by specific employees and determines the lines of authority and responsibility in the firm. The first step in developing an organization structure is to determine the tasks that must be performed. Exhibit 15–6 shows tasks that are typically performed in a retail firm.

These tasks are divided into four major categories in retail firms: strategic management, administrative management (operations), merchandise management, and store management. Note that this textbook is organized around these tasks and the managers who perform them. Section II of this text focuses on strategic and administrative tasks. Strategic marketing and financial decisions (Chapters 5 and 6) are undertaken primarily by senior management. Administrative tasks (Chapters 7 through 10) are performed by corporate managers who have specialized skills such as location analysts (Chapters 7 and 8), information and supply chain managers (Chapter 9), and CRM managers (Chapter 10). Category managers, buyers, and merchandise planners are involved in merchandise management (Section III), and store managers and the regional managers above them are involved in the management of the stores (Section IV). These managers implement the strategic plans and make the day-to-day tactical decisions that directly affect the retailer's performance.

To illustrate the connection between the tasks performed in Exhibit 15–6 and the organization structure presented in the following sections, the tasks are color-coded. Green is used for the strategic tasks, orange for the administrative tasks, yellow for the merchandising tasks, and blue for the store management tasks.

Organization of a Single-Store Retailer

Initially, the owner-manager of a single store may be the entire organization. When he or she goes to lunch or heads home, the store closes. As sales grow, the owner-manager may hire employees. Coordinating and controlling employee activities is easier in a small store than in a large chain of stores. The owner-manager simply assigns tasks to each employee and watches to see that these tasks are performed properly. Because the number of employees is limited, single-store retailers have little specialization. Each employee may perform a wide range of activities, while the owner-manager is responsible for all strategic decisions.

EXHIBIT 15–6   Tasks Performed by the Typical Multichannel Retail Firm

STRATEGIC MANAGEMENT
- **Develop overall retail strategy**
- **Identify the target market**
- **Determine the retail format**
- **Design organization structure**
- **Develop private-label merchandise**
- **Develop Internet/catalog strategy**
- **Develop global strategy**
- **Coordinate multichannel offering**

MERCHANDISE MANAGEMENT
- **Buy merchandise**
  - **Select, negotiate with, and evaluate vendors**
  - **Select merchandise**
  - **Place orders**
- **Control merchandise inventory**
  - **Develop merchandise budget plans**
  - **Allocate merchandise to stores**
  - **Review open-to-buy and stock positions**
- **Price merchandise**
  - **Set initial prices**
  - **Adjust prices**

STORE MANAGEMENT
- **Recruit, hire, and train store personnel**
- **Plan labor schedules**
- **Evaluate store and personnel performance**
- **Maintain store facilities**
- **Locate and display merchandise**
- **Sell merchandise to customers**
- **Repair and alter merchandise**
- **Provide services such as gift wrapping and delivery**
- **Handle customer complaints**
- **Take physical inventory**
- **Prevent inventory shrinkage**

ADMINISTRATIVE MANAGEMENT
- **Marketing**
  - **Promote the firm, its merchandise, and its services**
  - **Plan communication programs including advertising**
  - **Plan special promotions and events**
  - **Manage public relations**
  - **Coordinate social media programs**
- **Manage human resources**
  - **Develop policies for managing store personnel**
  - **Recruit, hire, and train managers**
  - **Keep employee records**
- **Manage supply chain**
  - **Receive merchandise**
  - **Store merchandise**
  - **Ship merchandise to stores**
  - **Return merchandise to vendors**
- **Manage financial performance**
  - **Provide timely information on financial performance**
  - **Forecast sales, cash flow, and profits**
  - **Raise capital from investors**
  - **Select and manage locations (real estate)**
- **Visual merchandising**
  - **Develop and coordinate displays in stores and windows**
- **Management information systems**
  - **Work with all functional areas to develop and operate information systems for merchandising, marketing, accounting, finance, etc.**
- **General counsel (legal)**
  - **Work with all functional areas to be in compliance with laws and regulations**

Legend:
- Strategic management
- Store management
- Merchandise management
- Administrative management

As sales continue to increase, specialization in management may occur when the owner-manager hires additional management employees. Exhibit 15–7 illustrates the common division of management responsibilities into merchandise and store management. The owner-manager continues to perform strategic management tasks. The store manager may be responsible for administrative tasks associated with receiving and shipping merchandise and managing the employees. The merchandise manager or

EXHIBIT 15–7   Organization Structure for a Small Retailer

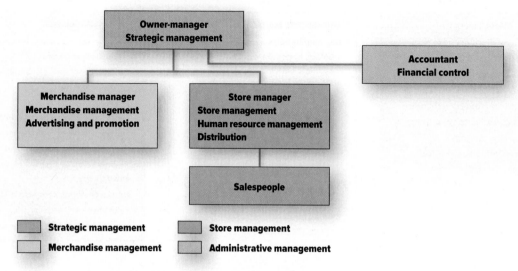

buyer may handle the advertising and promotion tasks, as well as merchandise selection and inventory management tasks. Often the owner-manager contracts with an accounting firm to perform financial control tasks for a fee.

Organization of a National Retail Chain

In contrast to the management of a single store, the management of a retail chain is complex. Managers must supervise units that are geographically diverse. In the following sections we discuss the organization structure of a typical retail chain.

Exhibit 15–8 shows the organization chart of a typical department store. The **chief executive officer (CEO)** is responsible for overseeing the entire organization. Reporting to the CEO are the presidents of global operations, the Internet channels, and private-label management and the senior vice presidents of merchandising, stores, and administration.

Merchandising   Looking at the merchandising division, the senior vice president (SVP) of merchandising works with buyers and planners to develop and coordinate the management of the retailer's merchandise offering and ensure that it is consistent with the firm's strategy (see Chapters 11 through 14 of this textbook).

The buyers in the merchandise division are responsible for determining the merchandise assortment, pricing, and managing relationships and negotiating with vendors. Most retail chains have a set of planning positions parallel to the buying positions supervised by a senior vice president of planning. **Merchandising planners** are responsible for allocating merchandise and tailoring the assortment of several categories for specific stores in a geographic area.

As shown in Exhibit 15–8, there are several levels of management in the merchandise division—general merchandise managers (GMMs), divisional merchandise managers (DMMs), and buyers. Most large retailers have several GMMs who are responsible for several merchandise classifications. Similarly, several DMMs report to each GMM and a number of buyers report to each DMM.

Stores   The senior vice president (SVP) of stores supervises all activities related to stores, including working with the regional managers, who supervise district managers, who supervise the individual store managers.

Store managers in large stores have several assistant store managers who report to them (not depicted in Exhibit 15–8). Typically, one assistant manager is responsible for administration and manages the receiving, restocking, and presentation of the

EXHIBIT 15–8   Organization of a Typical Department Store Chain

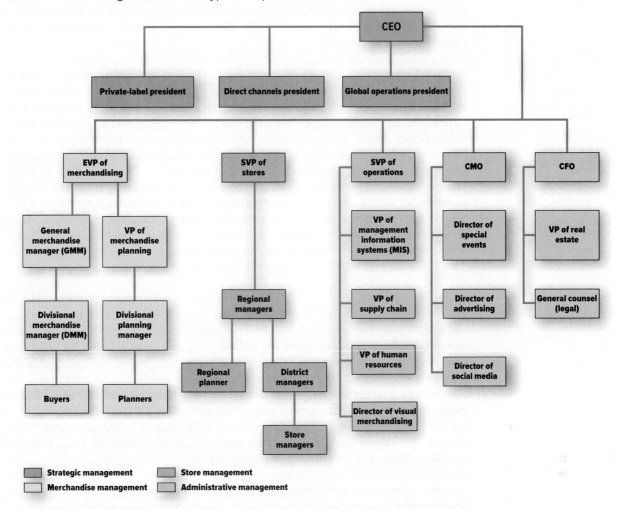

merchandise in the store. Another is responsible for human resources, including selecting, training, and evaluating employees. A third is responsible for operations such as store maintenance and store security.

Each region often has regional planners who work as liaisons between stores in their region and the corporate planners to ensure that the stores have the right merchandise, at the right time, in the right quantities. The stores division also works closely with the real estate division (under the chief financial officer) to plan new stores and with those in charge of visual merchandising, layout, and store design.

Operations   The executive vice president (EVP) of operations oversee managers in charge of management information systems (MIS), supply chain, human resources, and visual merchandising. The EVP of operations is also in charge of shrinkage and loss prevention and the operation and maintenance of the physical assets of the firm, such as stores, offices, distribution and fulfillment centers, and trucks (not reflected in Exhibit 15–8).

Marketing   The **chief marketing officer (CMO)** works with staff to develop advertising, promotion, and social media programs. Managers in charge of public relations, annual events, credit marketing, and cause-related marketing initiatives also report to the CMO.

Finance   The **chief financial officer (CFO)** works with the CEO on financial issues such as equity-debt structure and credit card operations. In addition, the real estate division and general counsel (legal) divisions, headed by vice presidents, report to the CFO.

Retailers vary considerably on how they organize their private-label development activities, direct channels, and global operations. Exhibit 15–8 shows these activities as being performed by wholly owned subsidiaries with the presidents of three subsidiaries reporting to the CEO.

Private Label The private-label president is responsible for the conceptualization, design, sourcing, quality control, and marketing of private-label and exclusive merchandise. When the private-label organization is a separate division, as in Exhibit 15–8, buyers in the merchandising division often evaluate the private-label merchandise offering as they would any other vendor, and they are therefore free to accept or reject the private-label merchandise presented. In some retail organizations, decisions on what private-label merchandise is included in the retailer's assortment are strategic decisions made by senior managers. In these cases, the buyers are required to carry private-label merchandise, and the sourcing and quality control are done by a VP of private-label development. In either case, the managers involved with private-label merchandise work closely with buyers and planners to ensure that the merchandise offered in each category is coherent and meets the needs of the retailer's target market. (See Chapter 12 for more on how private labels are purchased.)

Direct Channels The president of direct channels is responsible for the selection and pricing of the merchandise assortment offered through the Internet, mobile, social, and catalog and other nonstore channels, the maintenance and design of the retailer's website, customer call centers, and the fulfillment centers that fill orders for individual customers. However, many multichannel retailers are integrating the operation of the Internet, mobile, social, and catalog and other nonstore channels with their store channel. At these retailers, the selection and management of the merchandise offered in all channels (stores; Internet, mobile, and social; and catalog and other nonstore) for a category are handled by the same buying team, rather than by separate buyers for each channel. The buying team might include specialists in direct channels and a financial analyst in addition to associate and assistant buyers.

Global The global operations president oversees retailing operations outside the home country. The size and complexity of this operation are determined by the number of countries served and the number of stores within each country. Regardless of size, many of the functions performed by the home-country operation are duplicated in the global operations. For instance, the global organization typically has merchandising, administration, stores, and operations divisions for each country or region.

HUMAN RESOURCE MANAGEMENT LEGAL ISSUES

LO 15-5

Identify the legal issues involved with human resource management.

The proliferation of laws and regulations affecting employment practices in the 1960s was a major reason for the emergence of human resource management as an important organization function. Managing in this complex regulatory environment requires expertise in labor laws, as well as skills in helping other managers comply with those laws. The major legal and regulatory issues involving the management of retail employees are (1) equal employment opportunity, (2) compensation, (3) labor relations, (4) employee safety and health, (5) sexual harassment, and (6) employee privacy.

Equal Employment Opportunity

The basic goal of equal employment opportunity regulations is to protect employees from unfair discrimination in the workplace. **Illegal discrimination** refers to the actions of a company or its managers that result in members of a protected class being treated unfairly and differently from others. A **protected class** is a group of individuals who share a common characteristic as defined by the law. Companies cannot treat employees differently simply on the basis of their race, color, religion, sex, national origin, age, or disability status. There is a very limited set of circumstances in which employees can be treated differently. For example, it is illegal for a restaurant to hire young, attractive servers because that is what its customers prefer. Such discrimination must be absolutely necessary, not simply preferred.[44]

Title VII of the Civil Rights Act prohibits discrimination on the basis of race, national origin, gender, or religion in company personnel practices. Discrimination is specifically prohibited in the following human resource decisions: recruitment, hiring, firing, layoffs, discipline, promotion, compensation, and access to training. The expansion of this act in 1972 led to the creation of the **Equal Employment Opportunity Commission (EEOC)**, which allows employees to sue employers that violate the law. Several major retailers have been successfully sued because they discriminated in hiring and promoting minorities and women.

Compensation

The **Fair Labor Standards Act** of 1938 set minimum wages, maximum hours, child labor standards, and overtime-pay provisions. Enforcement of this law is particularly important to retailers because they hire many low-wage employees and teenagers and ask their employees to work long hours.

The **Equal Pay Act**, now enforced by the EEOC, prohibits unequal pay for men and women who perform equal work or work of comparable worth. Equal work means that the jobs require the same skills, effort, and responsibility and are performed in the same working environment. Comparable worth implies that men and women who perform different jobs of equal worth should be compensated the same. Differences in compensation are legal when compensation is determined by a seniority system, an incentive compensation plan, or market demand.

Labor Relations

Labor relations laws describe the process by which unions can be formed and the ways in which companies must deal with the unions. They precisely indicate how negotiations with unions must take place and what the parties can and cannot do. Walmart has vigorously challenged attempts by unions to represent its employees. Supermarket chains, in contrast, are typically unionized and, therefore, believe they have a labor cost disadvantage that makes it difficult for them to compete effectively with Walmart.

Employee Safety and Health

The basic premise of **health and safety laws** is that the employer is obligated to provide each employee with an environment that is free of hazards that are likely to cause death or serious injury. Compliance officers from the Occupational Safety and Health Administration (OSHA) conduct inspections to ensure that employers are providing such an environment for their workers. OSHA even gets involved in ensuring the safety of customers in stores.[45] For instance, it provides guidance to retailers on how to control crowds on Black Friday, the busy shopping day after Thanksgiving. The guidelines include using a bullhorn to manage crowds, setting up barricades or rope lines, and clearing the entrances of shopping carts and other potentially dangerous obstacles.

Sexual Harassment

Sexual harassment includes unwelcome sexual advances, requests for sexual favors, and other inappropriate verbal or physical conduct. Harassment is not confined to requests for sexual favors in exchange for job considerations such as a raise or promotion. Simply creating a hostile work environment can be considered sexual harassment. For example, actions considered sexual harassment include lewd comments, joking, and graffiti, as well as showing obscene photographs, staring at a coworker in a sexual manner, alleging that an employee got rewards by engaging in sexual acts, and commenting on an employee's moral reputation.

Customers can engage in sexual harassment as much as supervisors and coworkers. For example, if a male customer is harassing a female server in a restaurant and the restaurant manager knows about it and does nothing to stop the harassment, the employer can be held responsible for that sexual harassment.

Employee Privacy

Employees' privacy protection is very limited. For example, employers can monitor e-mail and telephone communications, search an employee's workspace and handbag, and require drug testing. However, employers cannot discriminate among employees when undertaking these activities unless they have a strong suspicion that specific employees are acting inappropriately.

SUMMARY

LO 15-1 Describe how to acquire and retain employees.

Managers can improve the abilities of their employees through effective recruiting, socializing, and training. To recruit skillful, or potentially skillful, employees, managers prepare a job description, find potential applicants with the desired capabilities, and screen the best candidates to interview. Having hired employees with the required skills or potential to develop these skills, retailers need to introduce the new employees to the firm and its policies, values, and strategies. This acculturation process affects the degree to which newcomers become involved, engaged contributors to the firm's successful performance. In addition, acculturation helps newly hired employees learn about their job responsibilities and the company they've decided to join. Effective training for new employees includes both structured and on-the-job learning experiences.

High-performance employees work hard, and the activities they work on are consistent with the retailer's strategy and goals. Motivating employees to perform up to their potential may be managers' most important and challenging task. To effectively motivate employees, managers need to set goals for the employees and provide feedback on the employee's performance relative to these goals. Employees receive two types of rewards from their job: extrinsic and intrinsic. Extrinsic rewards include compensation, promotion, and recognition. Intrinsic rewards are rewards employees get personally from doing their job well. For example, salespeople often like to sell because they think it's challenging and fun. The compensation program is the strongest motivator. It attracts and keeps good employees, motivates them to undertake activities consistent with the retailer's strategy, and strikes a balance between controlling labor costs and providing enough compensation to keep high-quality employees.

LO 15-2 Illustrate effective leadership strategies of a retail manager.

Leadership is the process by which a person attempts to influence others to accomplish a common goal or task. Managers are leaders. The best managers (leaders) go beyond influencing employee behaviors. There is no one best leadership style.

Effective managers use all styles, selecting the style most appropriate for each situation. Transformational leaders get people to transcend their personal needs for the sake of the group or organization so they are engaged and excited about their job.

LO 15-3 Explore the various strategies retail managers can undertake to control costs.

Labor scheduling, store maintenance, and inventory shrinkage offer three opportunities to reduce store operating expenses. Using employees efficiently is an important and challenging problem. Although store employees provide important customer service and merchandising functions that can increase sales, they also are the store's largest operating expense. An important issue facing store management is reducing inventory losses due to employee theft, shoplifting, mistakes, inaccurate records, and vendor errors. In developing a loss prevention program, retailers confront a trade-off between providing shopping convenience and a pleasant work environment on the one hand, and preventing losses due to shoplifting and employee theft on the other. The key to an effective loss prevention program is determining the most effective way to protect merchandise while preserving an open, attractive store atmosphere and a feeling among employees that they are trusted. Loss prevention requires coordination among store management, visual merchandising, and store design.

LO 15-4 Summarize how retailers are typically organized.

The organization structure defines supervisory relationships and employees' responsibilities. The four primary groups of tasks performed by retailers are strategic decisions, administrative tasks by the corporate staff, merchandise management by the buying organization, and store management.

LO 15-5 Identify the legal issues involved with human resource management.

The human resource department is also responsible for making sure that its firm complies with the laws and regulations that prevent discriminatory practices against employees and making sure that employees have a safe and harassment-free work environment.

KEY TERMS

autocratic leader, *412*	health and safety laws, *421*	productivity, *409*
behavioral interview, *402*	illegal discrimination, *420*	protected class, *420*
buyer, *418*	incentive compensation plan, *411*	quota, *411*
chief executive officer (CEO), *418*	intrinsic reward, *412*	quota bonus plan, *411*
chief financial officer (CFO), *419*	job application form, *401*	sexual harassment, *421*
chief marketing officer (CMO), *419*	job description, *400*	shrinkage, *415*
democratic leader, *413*	job enrichment, *412*	store maintenance, *414*
drawing account, *411*	labor relations laws, *421*	straight commission, *411*
engagement, *409*	labor scheduling, *413*	straight salary compensation, *410*
Equal Employment Opportunity Commission (EEOC), *421*	leadership, *412*	structured training program, *404*
Equal Pay Act, *421*	merchandising planner, *418*	team incentive, *412*
extrinsic reward, *410*	on-the-job training, *404*	transformational leader, *413*
Fair Labor Standards Act, *421*	organization structure, *416*	turnover, *410*

GET OUT AND DO IT!

1. **CONTINUING CASE ASSIGNMENT** Go to the store you have selected for the continuing case assignment, and meet with the person responsible for personnel scheduling. Report on the following:
   - Who is responsible for employee scheduling?
   - How far in advance is the schedule made?
   - How are breaks and lunch periods planned?
   - How are overtime hours determined?
   - On what is the total number of budgeted employee hours for each department based?
   - How is flexibility introduced into the schedule?
   - How are special requests for days off handled?
   - How are peak periods (hours, days, or seasons) planned for?
   - What happens when an employee calls in sick at the last minute?
   - What are the strengths and weaknesses of the personnel scheduling system from the manager's and employees' perspectives?

2. **CONTINUING CASE ASSIGNMENT** Go to the store you have selected for the continuing case assignment, and talk to the person responsible for human resource management to find out how sales associates are compensated and evaluated for job performance.

   - How are sales associates trained? What are the criteria for evaluation?
   - How often are they evaluated?
   - Do salespeople have quotas? If they do, how are they set? What are the rewards of exceeding quotas? What are the consequences of not meeting these objectives?
   - Can sales associates make a commission? If yes, how does the commission system work? What are the advantages of a commission system? What are the disadvantages?
   - If there is no commission system, are any incentive programs offered? Give an example of a specific program or project used by the store to boost employee morale and productivity.

   Evaluate each of the answers to these questions, and make recommendations for improvement where appropriate.

3. **INTERNET EXERCISE** Find an article that describes a case of a retailer violating Title VII in either its hiring or promotion practices. Summarize the case and court decision. What should this retailer do differently in the future to improve its employment policies?

DISCUSSION QUESTIONS AND PROBLEMS

1. How do on-the-job training, Internet training, and classroom training differ? What are the benefits and limitations of each approach?

2. Give examples of a situation in which a manager of a McDonald's fast-food restaurant should utilize different leadership styles.

3. Using the interview questions in Exhibit 15–3, role-play with another student in the class as both the interviewer and the applicant for an assistant store manager position at a store of your choice.

4. Name some laws and regulations that affect the employee management process. Which do you believe are the easiest for retailers to adhere to? Which are violated the most often?

5. What's the difference between extrinsic and intrinsic rewards? What are the effects of these rewards on the behavior of retail employees? Under what conditions would you recommend that a retailer emphasize intrinsic rewards over extrinsic rewards?

6. What are the advantages and disadvantages of the different forms of compensation programs described in this chapter? Considering the disadvantages only, how can department managers lessen the effects of the disadvantages?

7. When evaluating retail employees, some stores use a quantitative approach that relies on checklists and numerical scores similar to the form in Exhibit 15–5. Other stores use a more qualitative approach, similar to that in Exhibit 15–4, whereby less time is spent checking and adding and more time is devoted to discussing strengths and weaknesses in written form. What are the advantages and disadvantages of quantitative versus qualitative evaluation systems?

8. Some staff pharmacists working for retail chains refuse to dispense the Plan B "morning after" contraceptive pill because of their religious beliefs. In another situation, Muslim and Jewish checkout clerks working for supermarket chains refused to touch, scan, or bag products that contained any pork because of their religious beliefs. Do managers have the right to force employees to take actions that are contrary to their beliefs? Should customers be unable to buy products they want because of an employee's beliefs? Should employees be required to ignore their religious beliefs? What would you do if you were faced with these or similar ethically sensitive situations?

9. Discuss how retailers can reduce shrinkage from shoplifting and employee theft.

10. Drugstore retailers such as CVS place diabetic test strips and perfume behind locked glass cabinets and nearly all over-the-counter medicines behind Plexiglas panels. What are the pros and cons of these locked glass cabinets from the retailer's perspective? From the customer's perspective?

CHAPTER ENDNOTES

1. Matthew Stern, "Not Everyone at Zappos Loves Holocracy," *RetailWire,* January 19, 2016.

2. Gregory Ferenstein, "The Zappos Exodus Wasn't about Holocracy, Says Tony Hsieh," *Fast Company,* January 19, 2016.

3. Jennifer Reingold, "The Zappos Experiment," *Fortune,* March 15, 2016.

4. Curt Nickisch, "The Zappos Holacracy Experiment," *Harvard Business Review,* July 28, 2016.

5. Kevin Ready, "What Sam Walton and China's Lao Tzu Can Teach You about Team Building," *Forbes,* June 11, 2012.

6. Susan Jackson and Randall Schuler, *Managing Human Resources through Strategic Relationships,* 11th ed. (Mason, OH: South-Western, 2011).

7. Zeynep Toy, "Why Good Jobs Are Good for Retailers," *Harvard Business Review,* January–February 2012.

8. Raymond Andrew Noe, John R. Hollenbeck, Barry Gerhart, and M. Wright, *Fundamentals of Human Resource Management,* 5th ed. (New York: McGraw-Hill, 2013); H. John Bernardin, *Human Resource Management,* 6th ed. (New York: McGraw-Hill, 2013); Scott Carbonara, *Manager's Guide to Employee Engagement* (New York: McGraw-Hill, 2013).

9. James Breaugh, "Employee Recruitment: Current Knowledge and Suggestions for Future Research," *The Oxford Handbook of Personnel Assessment and Selection* (New York: Oxford University Press, 2012), pp. 68–87.

10. Matthias Baum, Anke Sterzing, and Neslim Alaca, "Reactions towards Diversity Recruitment and the Moderating Influence of the Recruiting Firms' Country-of-Origin," *Journal of Business Research* 69, no. 10 (2016), pp. 4140–4149; David Kraichy and Derek Chapman, "Tailoring Web-Based Recruiting Messages: Individual Differences in the Persuasiveness of Affective and Cognitive Messages," *Journal of Business and Psychology* 29, no. 2 (2013), pp. 253–268.

11. Jean Phillips and Stanley Gully, "Multilevel and Strategic Recruiting: Where Have We Been, Where Can We Go from Here?," *Journal of Management* 41, no. 5 (2015), pp. 1416–1445; Tara Behrend, Becca Baker, and Lori Foster Thompson, "Effects of Pro-Environmental Recruiting Messages: The Role of Organizational Reputation," *Journal of Business and Psychology* 2, no. 3 (2009), pp. 341–350; Rhett Brymer, Janice Molly, and Brett Gilbert, "Human Capital Pipelines Competitive Implications of Repeated Interorganizational Hiring," *Journal of Management* 40, no. 2 (2013), pp. 483–508; Valentina Franca, "The Strength of the Employer Brand: Influences and Implications for Recruiting," *Journal of Marketing and Management,* May 2012, pp. 78–122.

12. Stephan Castleberry and John Tanner, *Personal Selling: Building Relationships,* 8th ed. (New York: McGraw-Hill, 2011).

13. UK Commission for Employment and Skills, "Employer Perspectives Survey 2014: UK Results," November 2014, https://www.gov.uk/government/uploads/system/uploads/attachment_data/file/373770/14.11.11._EPS_2014_-_Executive_Summary_full.pdf; Priyanka Prabhu, "Role of Employee Referrals—Industry Perspective," *Recruiter,* July 30, 2014, https://www.recruiter.com/i/role-of-employee-referrals-industry-perspective/; Kathleen Keeling, Peter McGoldrick, and Henna Sadhu, "Staff Word-of-Mouth (SWOM) and Retail Employee Recruitment," *Journal of Retailing* 89, no. 1 (2013), pp. 88–104.

14. "TMI? The Risks of Recruiting Using Social Media Profiles," *HRNews Daily,* December 16, 2012.

15. The Container Store, "The Container Store Jumps to #14 on Fortune's List of 100 Best Companies to Work For®," *The Container Store Investor Relations,* March 3, 2016, http://investor.containerstore.com/press-releases/press-release-details/2016/The-Container-Store-Jumps-to-14-on-Fortunes-List-of-100-Best-Companies-to-Work-For/default.aspx; www.containerstore.com/careers/faqs.html#question14.

16. www.containerstore.com/careers/faqs.html#question14.

17. Lora Kolodny, "The Latest Approach to Employee Training," *The Wall Street Journal,* March 13, 2016; Heather Huhman, "4 Ways to Train Employees Effectively," *Entrepreneur,* November 23, 2015.

18. Huhman, "4 Ways to Train Employees Effectively."

19. Amy Lyman, "REI—Working Together for a Better World: Best Company for 25 Years," *Great Place to Work Institute,* https://www.rei.com/pdf/jobs/2009-Best-Company-for-25-Years-REI-for-REI.pdf.

20. Tom Ryan, "Perks/Culture Make Happy REI Employees," *RetailWire,* January 3, 2013.

21. Ed Stych, "Best Buy's Employee Training Ranked among Best in Nation," *Minneapolis/St. Paul Business Journal,* February 14, 2012; Lorri Freifeld, "Focus on Retail: Best Buy Connects with Customers," *Sales and Marketing Management,* August 1, 2007.

22. Robert Porter and Gary Latham, "The Effect of Employee Learning Goals and Goal Commitment on Departmental Performance," *Journal of Leadership & Organizational Studies* 20, no. 1 (2013), pp. 62–68; Jean-Francois Coget, "Performance

Orientation or Learning Orientation: Which Helps Salespeople Better Adapt to Organizational Change?," *The Academy of Management Perspectives* 24, no. 3 (2010), pp. 106–108; Simon Bell, Bülent Mengüç, and Robert E. Widing II, "Salesperson Learning, Organizational Learning, and Retail Store Performance," *Journal of the Academy of Marketing Science* 38, no. 2 (2010), pp. 187–201.

23. Marc Bishop, "How Can I Boost Employee Performance?," *Strategic HR Review* 12, no. 2 (2013), p. 8; Frank Q. Fu, Keith A. Richards, and Eli Jones, "The Motivation Hub: Effects of Goal Setting and Self-Efficacy on Effort and New Product Sales," *Journal of Personal Selling and Sales Management*, 29 (Summer 2009), pp. 277–292; C. Fred Miao and Kenneth R. Evans, "The Impact of Salesperson Motivation on Role Perceptions and Job Performance—A Cognitive and Affective Perspective," *Journal of Personal Selling & Sales Management* 27, no. 1 (2007), pp. 89–101.

24. Samuel Bacharach, "Gen-Y Employees: How to Motivate Them," *Inc.*, August 14, 2012; Leslie Kwoh, "More Firms Bow to Generation Y's Demands," *The Wall Street Journal*, August 22, 2012; David Solnet, Anna Kralj, and Jay Kandampully, "Generation Y Employees: An Examination of Work Attitude Differences," *Journal of Applied Management and Entrepreneurship* 17, no. 3 (2012), pp. 36–45.

25. Dhruv Grewal, Anne L. Roggeveen, Nancy M. Puccinelli, and Charles Spence, "Retail Atmospherics and In-Store Nonverbal Cues: An Introduction," *Psychology & Marketing* 31, no. 7 (2014), pp. 469–471.

26. Kevin Kruse, "What Is Employee Engagement?," *Forbes*, June 26, 2012; Scott Sonenshein and Utpal Dholakia, "Explaining Employee Engagement with Strategic Change Implementation: A Meaning-Making Approach," *Organization Science* 23, 1 (2012), pp. 1–23; Catherine Baumgardner and Jennifer L. Myers, "Employee Engagement, and Why It Is Important," *The Encyclopedia of Human Resource Management: HR Forms and Job Aids*, 2012, pp. 202–204; Amanda Shantz, Kerstin Alfes, Catherine Truss, and Emma C. Soane, "The Role of Employee Engagement in the Relationship between Job Design and Task Performance, Citizenship and Deviant Behaviours," *International Journal of Human Resource Management*, 2012; Timothy D. Ludwig and Christopher B. Frazier, "Employee Engagement and Organizational Behavior Management," *Journal of Organizational Behavior Management* 32, 1 (2012), pp. 75–82.

27. Emma Soane, Katie Truss, and Alfes Kerstin, "Development and Application of a New Measure of Employee Engagement: The ISA Engagement Scale," *Human Resource Development International*, 2012; Emma Soane, K. Alfes, K. Truss, C. Rees, and M. Gatenby, "Employee Engagement: Measure Validation and Associations with Individual Level Outcomes," *Human Resource Development International*, 2013.

28. Sebastian Hohenberg and Christian Homburg, "Motivating Sales Reps for Innovation Selling in Different Cultures," *Journal of Marketing* 80, no. 2 (2016), pp. 101–120; C. Fred Miao, Kenneth Evans, and Zou Shaoming, "The Role of Salesperson Motivation in Sales Control Systems—Intrinsic and Extrinsic Motivation Revisited," *Journal of Business Research* 60 (2007), pp. 417–425; Michael Lee, Robyn Raschke, and Robert Louis, "Exploiting Organizational Culture: Configurations for Value through Knowledge Worker's Motivation," *Journal of Business Research* 69, no. 11 (2016), pp. 5442–5447; Xiao-Hau Wang, Tae-Yeol Kim, and Lee Deog-Ro, "Cognitive Diversity and Team Creativity: Effects of Team Intrinsic Motivation and Transformational Leadership," *Journal of Business Research* 69, no. 9 (2016), pp. 3231–3239.

29. Hiroko Tabuchi, "Walmart Raising Wage to at Least $9," *The New York Times*, February 18, 2015.

30. Rachel Dodes and Dana Mattioli, "Theory & Practice: Retailers Try on New Sales Tactics," *The Wall Street Journal*, April 19, 2010.

31. Christopher Barnes, John Hollenbeck, Dustin Jundt, D. Scott DeRue, and Stephen Harmon, "Mixing Individual Incentives and Group Incentives: Best of Both Worlds or Social Dilemma?," *Journal of Management* 37, no. 6 (2011), pp. 1611–1635; James P. Guthrie and Elaine C. Hollensbe, "Group Incentives and Performance: A Study of Spontaneous Goal Setting, Goal Choice and Commitment," *Journal of Management* 30, no. 2 (2004), pp. 263–285.

32. Donald Barnes, Nicole Ponder, and Christopher Hopkins, "The Impact of Perceived Customer Delight on the Frontline Employee," *Journal of Business Research* 68, no. 2 (2015), pp. 433–441; Bove et al., "Exploring the Effects of Different Reward Programs on In-Role and Extra-Role Performance of Retail Sales Associates"; Brooks, "I Love My Work"; Fleming and Asplund, *Human Sigma: Managing the Employee–Customer Encounter.*

33. Walter Tymon, Stephen Stumpf, and Jonathan Doh, "Exploring Talent Management in India: The Neglected Role of Intrinsic Rewards," *Journal of World Business* 45, no. 2 (2010), pp. 109–121.

34. William Murphy and Peter A. Dacin, "Sales Contest Research: Business and Individual Difference Factors Affecting Intentions to Pursue Contest Goals," *Industrial Marketing Management* 38, no. 1 (2009), pp. 109–118.

35. Fred C. Lunenburg, "Motivating by Enriching Jobs to Make Them More Interesting and Challenging," *International Journal of Management, Business, and Administration* 15, no. 1 (2011), pp. 1–11.

36. Chiung-Wen Tsao, Shyh-Jer Chen, and Yi-Hsien Wang, "Family Governance Oversight, Performance, and High Performance Work Systems," *Journal of Business Research* 69, no. 6 (2016), pp. 2130–2137; Lale Gumusluoglu, Zahide Karakitapoğlu-Aygün, and Giles Hirst, "Transformational Leadership and R&D Workers' Multiple Commitments: Do Justice and Span of Control Matter?," *Journal of Business Research* 66, no. 11 (2013), pp. 2269–2278; Christian Schmitzx, Lee You-Cheong, and Gary Lilien, "Cross-Selling Performance in Complex Selling Contexts: An Examination of Supervisory- and Compensation-Based Controls," *Journal of Marketing* 78, no. 3 (2014), pp. 1–19; Annie McKee, Richard Boyatzis, and Fran Johnston, *Becoming a Resonant Leader: Develop Your Emotional Intelligence, Renew Your Relationships, Sustain Your Effectiveness* (Boston: Harvard Business School Press, 2008).

37. Marshall L. Fisher and Ananth Raman, *The New Science of Retailing: How Analytics Are Transforming the Supply Chain and Performance* (Cambridge, MA: Harvard Business School Press, 2010).

38. Steven Greenhouse, "A Part-Time Life, as Hours Shrink and Shift," *The New York Times*, October 27, 2012.

39. Ibid.

40. Dave Jamieson, "Walmart-Contracted Workers Strike ahead of Black Friday," *The Huffington Post*, November 14, 2012.

41. Richard Hollinger, "2016 National Retail Security Survey Key Findings," *LPM Magazine*, July 12, 2016.

42. Bob Moraca, Richard Hollinger, and Vicki Cantrell, *The 2015 National Retail Security Survey* (Gainesville: University of Florida, 2015).

43. Ibid.

44. "Is Pre-Employment Screening (Slowly?) Being 'Outlawed'?," *HR.com blog*, February 2013.

45. "Crowd Management Safety Guidelines for Retailers," OSHA Fact Sheet, 2012.

© Ben Gabbe/Getty Images

Retailers often establish landmark, flagship locations that epitomize what their stores "mean" to shoppers. Altering those locations and their designs can have serious implications (as Macy's learned when it bought Chicago's Marshall Fields department store chain and changed the iconic State Street store, sparking angry backlash from shoppers). But store designs also have to be updated and refreshed occasionally to keep the stores interesting, exciting, and appealing. So how do retailers find a balance?

At Bergdorf Goodman, the latest renovation to its New York City store was the first one in nearly 30 years. Its driving goal was to give luxury shoppers an enjoyable, memorable experience by highlighting the beautiful antique architecture of its 114-year-old building and also integrating some of the staples of modern luxury.[1] In particular, as Internet sales of luxury items have increased, the brick-and-motor retailer seeks to create an experience for customers that bring them into the store.[2]

The renovation has restored the main chandelier, which not only brings the piece back to its original glory

but also brightens the store and highlights the intricate, sculpted decorations along the ceiling. Bergdorf also has added marble flooring, handcrafted cases, and an expansive window with a view of Central Park.

Together with these classical signals of luxury and experience, the redesign also suggests that the space is pretty modern and chic.[3] For example, the new layout relies on an "open sell" model, in which there is no designated front or back to any of the counters. Nor do those counters still feature glass doors that must be opened by a sales associate. Instead, sales associates are free to walk around the store, assisting customers where they need it; customers are free to explore the store and the merchandise on display. According to Bergdorf's president, with the new layout "the product is much more accessible."[4]

Even if the goal of the redesign is to create a valuable experience for customers that they cannot get by shopping online, most of today's shoppers rely on the Internet and mobile channels for something. Thus, Bergdorf sought ways to link with them through its stores as well. For example, the newly available view of the Pulitzer Fountain and Central Park may help make the New York store into an Instagram hotspot in the city. If the social media connection becomes strong enough, Bergdorf even might become synonymous with these famous landmarks, offering a popular destination for shoppers who want hip New York selfies.[5]

The environment in a store, the design of the store, and the presentation and location of merchandise in the store have significant impacts on shopping behavior. The design of a store or website attracts customers to visit the location, increases the time they spend in the store or on the site, and increases the amount of merchandise they purchase. Store design also has long-term effects on building customer loyalty toward the retailer by enhancing the retailer's brand image and providing rewarding shopping experiences that encourage repeat visits.

This chapter is part of the store management section because store managers are responsible for implementing the design and visual merchandising developed by specialists at the retailer's corporate headquarters. They adapt the prototype plans to the unique characteristics of their stores, then make sure the image and experience provided by the design are consistent over time. However, as discussed in this chapter, store design and visual merchandising are also elements of a retailer's communication mix and play an important role in creating and reinforcing a retailer's brand image.

The chapter begins with a discussion of store design objectives. Next, the elements of store design are discussed. The decisions about how much space to allocate to different merchandise categories and departments and where they should be located in the store are reviewed. The chapter concludes with an examination of how retailers use store design elements, such as color, lighting, and music, to enhance the customer's shopping experience.

STORE DESIGN OBJECTIVES

Some store design objectives are to (1) implement the retailer's strategy, (2) build loyalty by providing a rewarding shopping experience, (3) increase sales on a visit, (4) control costs, and (5) meet legal requirements.

LO 16-1

Identify the critical issues retailers need to consider when designing a store.

Implement the Retail Strategy

The primary objective for store design is to implement the retailer's strategy. The design must be consistent with and reinforce the retailer's strategy by meeting the needs of the target market and building a sustainable competitive advantage. Starbucks's store designs are inspired by the Italian coffee bars that not only have great coffee but also serve as a place to meet friends, socialize, and relax. Soft lighting, wood tables, comfortable seating, free wi-fi, and clean bathrooms make Starbucks a place where people just want to hang out and have a good cup of coffee.

Build Loyalty

When customers consistently have rewarding experiences when patronizing a retailer's store or website, they are motivated to visit repeatedly and develop loyalty toward the retailer. Store design plays an important role in making shopping experiences rewarding. Customers seek two types of benefits when shopping—utilitarian and hedonic benefits.[6]

Store design provides **utilitarian benefits** when it enables customers to locate and purchase products in an efficient and timely manner with minimum hassle. Such

utilitarian benefits are becoming increasingly important in today's time-poor society. Therefore, drugstore retailers such as CVS and Walgreens have designed their stores to include drive-through pharmacies and have invested in various technologies to augment customer convenience associated with these store design elements. They have developed mobile apps to help people refill their prescriptions; they then pick them up through the drive-through. These design elements and connected apps are further speeding up customers' shopping trips.

Store design provides **hedonic benefits** by offering customers an entertaining and enjoyable shopping experience. They then want to spend more time in the store or on the website because the visit itself is rewarding. For example, Cabela's, a chain of stores catering to outdoor enthusiasts, provides an educational and entertaining experience that mixes museum-quality dioramas of wildlife on display, massive huge aquariums featuring native fish, a restaurant where diners can order wild-game sandwiches, and a shooting gallery that teaches basic shooting and safety lessons while also providing a fun experience. These shopping and tourism destinations draw customers from the local area certainly, but they also can attract travelers from hundreds of miles away.

Of course, few retailers can offer only utilitarian or hedonic benefits, as Retailing View 16.1 explains. Most need to use both routes to ensure customer loyalty. Wegmans has applied a more utilitarian look and feel in some sections, to welcome price-sensitive customers and reassure its existing shoppers that it recognizes their economic constraints.[7] But the supermarket chain also explicitly designs its stores to make the chore of grocery shopping more fun: Instead of linoleum floors, harsh fluorescent lights, and narrow aisles, shoppers experience the feel of an open-air market. Wegmans also offers various eat-in options, an exotic tea bar, a trail mix bar, and gourmet chef-prepared meals to take home. This unique experience for customers has helped Wegmans's 91 stores earn nearly $8 billion in sales annually.[8]

Increase Sales on Visits

A third design objective is to increase the sales made to customers on any particular visit. Store design has a substantial effect on which products customers buy, how long they stay in the store, and how much they spend during a visit. Because most consumers spend very little time and thought on shopping and selecting items in supermarkets, these purchase decisions are greatly influenced by what products customers see

RETAILING VIEW   Saks: Luxury Shopping as Both Functional and Experiential

Luxury retailers offer high-end experiences and stellar service, which may or may not be what modern shoppers seek. In response, Saks Fifth Avenue is adopting various methods to meet the demands of its hedonic shoppers, who want to be pampered and enjoy their day of luxury shopping, as well as its utilitarian shoppers, who want to snap up a high-quality wardrobe essential quickly and easily.

At its new flagship location in Toronto, the store feels more like an art gallery than a department store, in line with the retailer's goals. Saks wanted to incorporate the artistic history of the city carefully into its design, so each entrance features a dramatic exhibit; the furniture and merchandise are laid out to appear like they are part of the art and sculptures placed strategically throughout the store. It also features three distinct landscapes: serene rain, forest, and storm. Even the floor plan feels like a gallery, with lots of open space that encourages customers to wander slowly through the store. Similarly, its latest New York store, across the street from the World Trade Center, takes inspiration from museums and hosts rotating "installations" of different designers.

But the new downtown Manhattan store (only the second one in New York City) also offers functional benefits. With its "Power Lunch" service, it promises shoppers that they can get a beauty treatment, style consultation, and lunch, all within 60 minutes. If they encounter a zipper that won't zip or break a heel on their shoes, they also can call the "Saks Save Me" hotline.

Then, in its Off 5th outlet stores, Saks works to appeal to bargain hunters by looking "a little more unkempt." Rather than being artfully arranged on sculptures, apparel gets stacked in piles; shoes are organized by size rather than by brand, as is more common in discount retailers. The "mess" helps customers feel comfortable really digging in to find the bargains and enhances the perception of a treasure hunt. As retail analysts have long indicated, the more packed with merchandise a store is, the more customers think that it offers value. The retailer continues to expand the number of Off 5th locations.

Finally, in its effort to leverage both the hedonism of the in-store experience with the convenience of online shopping, Saks is experimenting with a new omnichannel initiative that adopts a store design intended to mimic a website, while also training salesclerks to answer consumers' questions electronically. In the first experimental store, which is smaller than most stores, the circular layout leads shoppers to walk laps around the store, with the implication that they can always find new things (as they would by clicking on a new link). The product displays are arranged by brand, rather than separated in different departments, and they appear laid out on tables, similar to the "flat shots" that an online consumer might see. In addition Saks lowered the fixtures in the store, which helps shoppers survey the entire space easily. But the fitting rooms are clearly high end, with plush carpets and gentle lighting. Here, the goal is to leverage one of the most appealing benefits of online shopping: being able to try on the clothing at home, in a natural environment.

To help build brand loyalty through store design, Saks Fifth Avenue offers both utilitarian (top) and hedonic (bottom) benefits.

The salesclerks in the experimental store similarly span the gap between in-store and online, enjoyment and convenience. Saks's research showed that most customers prefer to shop alone, but those who receive help from salesclerks tend to spend more. Therefore, it hired employees for the new store by interviewing them about their digital savvy. It expects them to join the ranks of its personal shoppers, who are available for consumers in various markets. Using e-mailed requests, live chats, or shopping appointments, consumers can get personal recommendations and assistance from employees in nearby stores. Thus they receive the personalized attention of a lengthy visit to the store, but they can remain in their homes or offices and have the chosen products shipped to them. Combining these tools has led to a reported 50 percent increase in the average size of consumers' purchases.

Sources: Elizabeth Holmes, "Why Can't a Store Be More Like a Website?," *The Wall Street Journal,* September 27, 2016; Phil Wahba, "Saks Fifth Avenue Opens Store in Manhattan's New Luxury Battleground," *Fortune,* September 8, 2016; Jenny Rebholz, "Saks Opens New Flagship Store in Toronto," *Design:Retail,* August 18, 2016; Tom Ryan, "Saks Outlets to Get Sloppier," *RetailWire,* February 4, 2014.

during their visit. What they see in turn is affected by the store layout and how the merchandise is presented. Thus, retailers attempt to design their stores in a manner that motivates unplanned purchases. As discussed later in this chapter, retailers use the cash wrap area (where people pay for merchandise) to display and therefore stimulate the sale of impulse items such as candy at a supermarket checkout terminal or jewelry at a women's apparel store.

Control Costs to Increase Profits

The fourth design objective is to control the cost of implementing the store design and maintaining the store's appearance. Although the types of lighting that Neiman Marcus shines on its expensive jewelry and crystal use more electricity and are less ecologically friendly than rows of bare fluorescent bulbs, the retailer considers such costs necessary to highlight these high-ticket items. In contrast, other retailers have embraced the notion of gaining efficiency in their energy use; for several years, Walmart has designed new stores expressly to ensure their energy efficiency by reducing the amount of energy and other natural resources required for store operations, minimizing the raw materials used to construct each facility, and using renewable materials whenever possible.[9]

Store designs can also affect labor costs and inventory shrinkage. Some stores are organized into isolated departments, which provides an intimate, comfortable shopping experience that can result in more sales. However, the design prevents sales associates from observing and covering adjacent departments, which makes it necessary to have at least one sales associate permanently stationed in each department to provide customer service and prevent shoplifting.

Another design consideration related to controlling cost is flexibility. Retailing is a very dynamic business. Competitors enter a market and cause existing retailers to change the mix of merchandise offered. As the merchandise mix changes, so must the space allocated to merchandise categories and the layout of the store. Thus, store designers attempt to design stores with maximum flexibility.

Flexibility is an important design consideration for college bookstores because they need to expand and contract their spaces to accommodate the large seasonal fluctuations inherent in the college-bookstore business. At the beginning of a semester, considerable space needs to be allocated to textbooks. But after the first week of the semester, the demand for textbooks decreases quickly, and space allocated to textbooks needs to be reallocated to apparel and consumer electronics. The key to providing this flexibility often lies in innovative fixture and wall systems that portion off the textbook area.

Meet Legal Considerations—Americans with Disabilities Act

All store design and redesign decisions must comply with the 1990 Americans with Disabilities Act (ADA) and its 2008 amendments.[10] This law protects people with disabilities from discrimination in employment, transportation, public accommodations, telecommunications, and activities of state and local governments. It affects store design because the act calls for "reasonable access" to merchandise and services in retail stores built before 1993; stores built after 1993 must be fully accessible.

The act also states that retailers should not have to incur "undue burdens" to comply with ADA requirements. Although retailers are concerned about the needs of their customers with disabilities, they are also worried that making merchandise completely accessible to people in a wheelchair or a motorized cart will result in less space available to display merchandise and thus will reduce sales. However, providing for wider aisles and more space around fixtures can result in a more pleasant shopping experience for all customers.

The ADA does not clearly define critical terms such as "reasonable access," "fully accessible," or "undue burden." So the actual ADA requirements are being defined through a series of court cases in which plaintiffs who are disabled have filed class-action suits against retailers.[11] On the basis of these court cases, retailers are typically required to (1) provide 32-inch-wide pathways in the main aisle, to bathrooms, dressing rooms, and elevators, and around most fixtures; (2) lower most cash wraps (checkout stations) and fixtures so that they can be reached by a person in a wheelchair; (3) create disability-accessible checkout aisles; (4) provide bathrooms with handrails or grab bars; and (5) make dressing rooms fully accessible. Nor does the ADA stop at the store exit. Very clear guidelines establish the number of accessible parking spaces that stores must provide for people with disabilities.[12] Some of these accessibility requirements are somewhat relaxed for retailers in very small spaces and during peak sales periods such as the Christmas holidays.

© Arterra/UIG via Getty Images

The Americans with Disabilities Act (ADA) requires retailers to provide "reasonable access" to merchandise and services.

Design Trade-Offs

Few store designs can achieve all of these objectives, so any store design involves trade-offs among the objectives. Home Depot's traditional warehouse design can efficiently store and display a lot of merchandise with long rows of floor-to-ceiling racks, but this design is not conducive for a pleasant shopping experience. This trade-off led many female shoppers to avoid the home improvement big-box store, so it is rebalancing its approach to appeal better to this important segment. For example, rather than a construction site aesthetic, newly renovated stores feature better lighting, cleaner product displays, and space set aside for greeters at the front doors, who can help shoppers find what they need.[13]

Retailers often make trade-offs between stimulating impulse purchases and making it easy to buy products. For example, supermarkets place milk, a commonly purchased item, at the back of the store to make customers walk through the entire store, thus stimulating more impulse purchases. Realizing that some customers may want to buy only milk, some drugstores place its milk at the front of the store, enabling it to compete head-to-head with convenience stores.

The trade-off between making it easy to find merchandise and providing an interesting shopping experience is determined by the customer's shopping needs. For example, supermarket and drugstore shoppers typically focus on utilitarian benefits and want to minimize the time they spend shopping, so the design of supermarkets emphasizes the ease of locating merchandise (there are exceptions, such as Wegmans). In contrast, customers shopping for specialty goods like a computer, a home entertainment center, or furniture are more likely to spend time in the store browsing, comparing, and talking with the salesperson. Thus, specialty store retailers that offer this type of merchandise place more emphasis on providing hedonic benefits and encouraging exploration than on making it easy to find merchandise.

Another trade-off is the balance between giving customers adequate space in which to shop and productively using this scarce resource for merchandise. Customers are attracted to stores with wide aisles and fixtures whose primary purpose is to display rather than hold the merchandise. Also, shoppers do not like it when a store is so cramped that they touch one another, a phenomenon known as the "butt-brush effect."[14] However, a spacious design reduces the amount of merchandise that can be available to buy and thus may also reduce impulse purchases and the customers' chances of finding what they are looking for. But too many racks and displays in a store can cause customers to feel uncomfortable and even confused. There must be a compromise between having a store that is too spacious and one that is overcrowded.

This section examined the various objectives retailers seek to satisfy when designing their stores. The next section explores important elements of design.

STORE DESIGN ELEMENTS

LO 16-2

List the advantages and disadvantages of alternative store layouts.

Four elements in the design of stores are the (1) layout, (2) signage and graphics, (3) feature areas, and (4) store exteriors. Each of these elements is discussed in this section.

Layouts

Retailers use three general types of store layout design: grid, racetrack, and free-form. Each of these layouts has advantages and disadvantages.

Grid Layout   The **grid layout**, illustrated in Exhibit 16–1, has parallel aisles with merchandise on shelves on both sides of the aisles. Cash registers are located at the entrances/exits of the stores.

The grid layout is well suited for customers who are primarily interested in the utilitarian benefits offered by the store. They are not interested in the hedonic benefits provided by a visually exciting design. They want to easily locate products they want to buy, and they make their purchases as quickly as possible. Most supermarkets and full-line discount stores use the grid layout because this design enables their customers to easily find the product they are looking for and minimizes the time spent on a shopping task that most don't enjoy.

EXHIBIT 16–1
Grid Store Layout

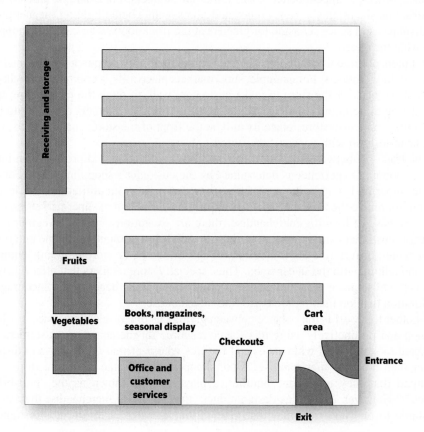

The grid layout is also cost-efficient. There's less wasted space with the grid layout than with other layouts because the aisles are all the same width and designed to be just wide enough to accommodate shoppers and their carts. The use of high shelves for merchandise enables more merchandise to be on the sales floor compared with other layouts. Finally, because the fixtures are generally standardized, the cost of the fixtures is low.

One limitation of the grid layout, from the retailer's perspective, is that customers typically aren't exposed to a lot of the merchandise in the center store, which limits unplanned purchases. The **center store** refers to the middle of each aisle, where most grocers and other retailers using a grid layout stock seemingly less compelling or exciting products, though ones that consumers still require. Imagine, for example, the cereal or detergent aisle in your local grocer. Unless a particular item is on promotion and displayed prominently on the end cap, these products are lined up with all their competitors, with little to set them apart.

By equipping shopping carts with GPS locators, researchers have found that supermarket shoppers enter a supermarket, turn right, go along the periphery of the store looking down the aisles, and occasionally walk into the center store with their carts or leave the cart at the end of the aisle and walk down the aisle to select a specific item and return to the cart. The periphery is popular because it contains appealing displays of fresh, perishable merchandise categories such as meat, seafood, dairy, poultry, baked goods, and produce. A path taken by a typical customer is shown in Exhibit 16–2.[15]

According to one recent study, grocery shoppers spend an average of 13 minutes in stores, and only 18 percent of that time involves the center store. However, center store products account for approximately 73 percent of grocers' total dollar sales.[16]

So retailers are experimenting to increase center store sales. For example, both Kraft and Kellogg's have recommended organizing stores by types of meals, such as a "breakfast aisle," linking the perimeter better to the center store, and engaging shoppers in the middle of the aisle.[17] Another way to extend shopping time in the center store of a grid layout is to make customers' shopping path less efficient by altering the straight aisles to form a zig-zag pattern, an approach that likely is familiar to IKEA shoppers who enter into a challenging maze every time they visit, forcing them to stroll by multiple displays—at least one of which is likely to prompt them to pick up a few items they had not planned on buying. Another approach locates power brands—those with high awareness and market share such as Coca-Cola and Tide—and eye-attracting displays in the middle of the aisle rather than at the ends. The power brands appear from the top to the bottom, creating a swath of color

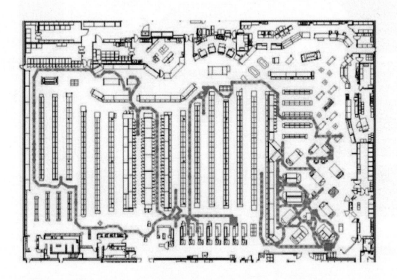

EXHIBIT 16–2
Example of a Traffic Pattern in a Grid Layout Supermarket

that captures the attention of customers as they peek down the aisle.[18] Other methods to increase such engagement might include staggered aisles, the use of recessed shelves, pyramid-shaped displays, focused lighting, more in-aisle sampling kiosks, or innovative signage.

Racetrack Layout   The **racetrack layout**, also known as a **loop layout**, is a store layout that provides a major aisle that loops around the store to guide customer traffic around different departments within the store. Point-of-sale terminals are typically located in each department bordering the racetrack.

The racetrack layout facilitates the goal of getting customers to see the merchandise available in multiple departments and thus encourages unplanned purchasing. As customers go around the racetrack, their eyes are forced to take different viewing angles rather than looking down one aisle, as in the grid design. Low fixtures are used so that customers can see merchandise beyond the products displayed on the racetrack.

Exhibit 16–3 shows the layout of a department store. Because the store has multiple entrances, the racetrack layout places all departments on the main aisle by drawing customers through the store in a series of major and minor loops. To entice customers through the various departments, the design places some of the more popular departments, like juniors, toward the rear of the store. The newest items also are featured on the aisles to draw customers into departments and around the loop.

The racetrack usually is wider than other aisles and defined by a change in flooring surface or color. For instance, the aisle flooring might be marblelike tile, whereas the department floors vary in material, texture, and color, depending on the desired ambience.

EXHIBIT 16–3   Racetrack Layout

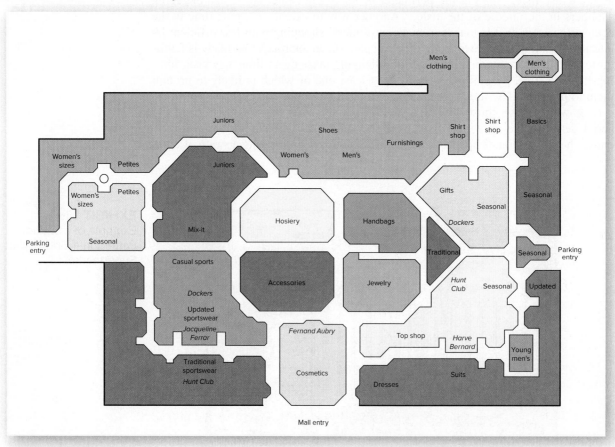

EXHIBIT 16–4
Free-Form Store Layout

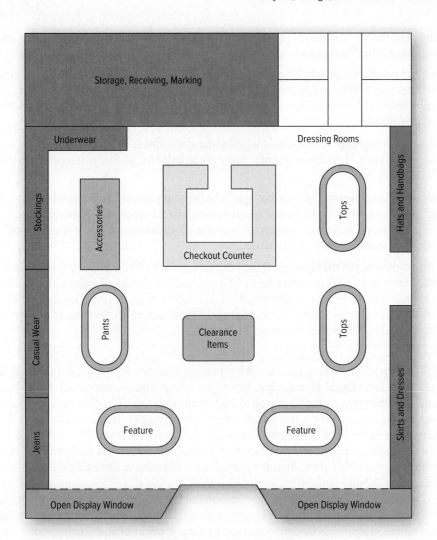

Free-Form Layout

A **free-form layout**, also known as **boutique layout**, arranges fixtures and aisles in an asymmetric pattern (Exhibit 16–4). It provides an intimate, relaxing environment that facilitates shopping and browsing. It appears most commonly in specialty stores or as departments within department stores.

However, creating such pleasing shopping environments is costly. Because there is no well-defined traffic pattern, as there is in the racetrack and grid layouts, customers aren't naturally drawn around the store or department, and personal selling becomes more important to encourage customers to explore merchandise offered in the store. In addition, the layout reduces the amount of merchandise that can be displayed.

Signage and Graphics

Signage and graphics inside the store help customers locate specific products and departments, provide product information, and suggest items or special purchases. Graphics, such as photo panels, can reinforce a store's image. Signage is used to identify the location of merchandise categories within a store and the types of products offered in the category. The signs are hung typically from the ceiling to enhance their visibility. Frequently, icons rather than words are used to facilitate communication with customers speaking different languages. For example, a red and yellow circus tent icon identifies the area for children's toys more effectively than a black and white, worded rectangular sign. Smaller signs are used to identify sale items and provide more information about specific products. Finally, retailers may use images, such as pictures of people and places, to create moods that encourage customers to buy products. Some different types of signs are:

- **Call-to-action signage**. Placed in strategic locations in the store can convey how, where, and why to engage with the retailer via QR (quick response) codes on customers' cell phones, via e-mail, short-message services, Facebook, or other digital channels.

- **Category signage**. Used within a particular department or sector of the store to identify types of products offered. They are usually located near the goods to which they refer.

- **Promotional signage**. Describes special offers and found within the store or displayed in windows to entice the customer into the store. For instance, value apparel stores for young women often display large posters in their windows of models wearing new or sale items.

- **Point-of-sale (POS) signage**. Point-of-sale signs are placed near the merchandise they refer to so that customers know its price and other detailed information. Some of this information may already be on product labels or packaging. However, POS signage can quickly identify for the customer those aspects likely to be of greater interest, such as whether the product is on sale.

Digital Signage   Many retailers are replacing traditional signage with digital signage systems.[19] **Digital signage** includes signs whose visual content is delivered electronically through a centrally managed and controlled network, distributed to servers in stores, and displayed on flat-panel screens. The content delivered can range from entertaining video clips to simple price displays.

Digital signage provides a number of benefits over traditional static-print signage. Due to their dynamic nature, digital signs are more effective in attracting the attention of customers and helping them recall the messages displayed. Digital signage also offers the opportunity to enhance a store's environment by displaying complex graphics and videos to provide an atmosphere that customers find appealing.[20] Because the content is delivered digitally, it can easily be tailored to a store's market and remain consistent in every store, displayed at the right time and right place. Furthermore, by overcoming the time-to-message hurdle associated with traditional print signage, digital signage enables the content to be varied within and across stores at different times of the day or days of the week—without incurring the expense of printing, distributing, and installing new static signs or hiring labor to post them. If the temperatures rise, digital in-store signage might automatically advertise cold drinks; if the forecast continues to be warm and sunny, it might promote sunscreen. Of course, there is a drawback too. The initial cost of the display devices and the system that supports the delivery of signage can be quite high.

Recent research shows customers spend $1.52 more per trip at grocery stores when digital displays are used. Less than $2.00 might not seem like that much, but the overall effect is huge in the grocery sector, with its tight margins and high volume of shoppers.[21] The effect of digital signage on sales is not limited to grocers. Lord & Taylor has added digital signage to its flagship store in Manhattan and plans to expand its use. The store reports the addition of digital signage

In-store digital displays highlight key product features and experiential elements at the point of purchase.

© Dhruv Grewal

in its fragrance department paid for itself in less than a year, and digital technology in the men's suit department led to double-digit sales increases.[22]

Feature Areas

In addition to using layout and signage, retailers can guide customers through stores and influence buying behavior through the placement of feature areas. **Feature areas** are the areas within a store that are designed to get customers' attention. They include freestanding displays, mannequins, end caps, promotional aisles or areas, walls, dressing rooms, and cash wraps.

Freestanding Displays

Freestanding displays are fixtures that are located on aisles and designed primarily to attract customers' attention and bring them into a department. These fixtures often display and store the newest, most exciting merchandise in the particular department.

Mannequins

A **mannequin** is a life-sized representation of the human body, used for displaying apparel. In the past, mannequins were often plain and boring. Twenty-first-century retailers have begun to realize that mannequins don't need to be hairless, featureless, blindingly white, skinny space holders. They can help personify a brand, push customers to enter their stores, and perhaps even offer an ideal image that encourages shoppers to buy a little something extra that looks great on display.[23] At the Disney Store, children are enchanted as whimsical mannequins swoop down from the ceiling or execute a perfect princess curtsy.

Whimsical mannequins attract the attention of children in Disney stores.

© Gustavo Caballero/Getty Images

End-cap displays that end in a disorganized dump bin (left) encourage more purchases than an organized bin (right).

(both photos): © Jens Nordfält

End Caps

End caps are displays located at the end of an aisle in stores using a grid layout. Due to the high visibility of end caps, sales of a product increase dramatically when that merchandise is featured on an end cap. End-cap displays that end in a disorganized dump bin encourage more purchases than an organized bin.[24] Thus, retailers use end caps for higher-margin, impulse, and sale merchandise. In the supermarket industry, vendors often negotiate for their products to be on end-cap displays when they are offering special promotional prices.

Promotional Aisle or Area

A **promotional aisle** or **promotional area** is a space used to display merchandise that is being promoted. Drugstores, for instance, use promotional aisles to sell seasonal merchandise, such as lawn and garden products in the summer and Christmas decorations in the fall. Specialty stores and department stores tend to locate a promotional area at the back of the store or department. To get to the items on sale, customers must pass through all the full-price merchandise, which makes it more likely that something will catch their eye.

Lacoste uses the upper wall space to creatively display merchandise by color, and wall shelves for effective, yet spacious merchandise storage.

© Thos Robinson/WireImage/Getty Images

Walls

Because retail floor space is often limited, many retailers increase their ability to store extra stock, display merchandise, and creatively present a message by utilizing wall space. Merchandise can be stored on shelving and racks and coordinated with displays, photographs, or graphics featuring the merchandise. At the French clothier Lacoste, for instance, merchandise is spaciously displayed by color relatively high on the wall. Wall shelves store merchandise in an aesthetically pleasing, yet efficient manner. Not only does this allow the merchandise to "tell a story," but it also helps customers feel more comfortable because they aren't crowded by racks or by other people, and they can get a perspective on the merchandise by viewing it from a distance.

Dressing Rooms   Dressing rooms are critical spaces where customers often decide whether to purchase an item. Large, clean, and comfortable dressing rooms put customers in the mood to buy. In recent years, retailers have even begun to compete aggressively on the basis of the quality of their dressing rooms. Rebecca Minkoff's store in SoHo, New York City, features a "connected wall"—an interactive mirror display that shows the latest content from the brand, including fashion shows, photos, and virtually everything that is happening on social media that is related in any way to the brand. The connected wall allows customers to browse merchandise, request a fitting room, have clothing options sent to that fitting room, and even order drinks. Customers receive a text message when their dressing room is ready.[25] Once they get to the dressing room, they encounter spaces that feature mirrored touch screens and RFID (radio frequency identification device) technology that can recognize the products in the fitting room. Maybe one of the simplest, but most revolutionary, aspects of these fitting rooms is that customers can adjust the lighting, making it brighter to see details in the clothing or dimmer to avoid harsh reflections. The Rebecca Minkoff app and mobile site contains the option "Save your fitting room session to your phone" in which customers can gain access to the clothes they tried on and make their purchases, through the app, later.[26]

Virtual dressing rooms are becoming more important and interesting to online shoppers. People cannot try on clothes displayed on a website, but the spread of webcams embedded in laptops, tablets, and desktop computers is making it possible for programmers to create "virtual dressing rooms" that could permit Internet customers to "try on" clothing and accessories, simply by standing in front of their webcams.[27]

Cash Wraps   **Cash wraps**, also known as **point-of-purchase (POP) counters** or **checkout areas**, are places in the store where customers can purchase merchandise. Because many customers go to these areas and wait in line to make a purchase, retailers often use them to display impulse purchase items. For example, in supermarkets, batteries, candy, gum, and magazines are often shelved at the checkout counter. But as shopping habits change, these traditionally valuable spaces have become less effective, as Retailing View 16.2 notes.

RETAILING VIEW   Finding Ways to Get Modern Shoppers to Buy Candy, Gum, and Magazines   **16.2**

Grocery customers continue to demand more convenience and ease in their shopping. Grocery retailers have responded in various ways: self-checkout stations, real-time adjustments to long queues, and so forth. But these efforts to improve the customer experience have had some unintended and worrisome consequences for grocers.

Traditionally, when customers had to stand in line for several minutes to check out, they encountered a familiar range of candies, gum, tabloid magazines, and small convenience items. Although these offerings account for only about 1 percent of stores' total floor space, the impulse purchases they prompt often can provide up to 4 percent of the grocers' overall sales. Impulse buying is therefore a valuable and necessary element for supermarkets that survive on razor thin margins.

But when customers do not wait in line, whether because the grocer is quick to open new checkouts or because the customers can check themselves out, they also do not have the enforced downtime to consider impulse purchases of some candy or gum. Thus, grocers are seeing significant declines in their traditional impulse purchase sales.

Neither the retailers nor the affected manufacturers are ready to give up on this lucrative market though. Hershey's is testing a menu board for candy at stores that offer customers the opportunity for curbside pickups. New versions of vending machines might provide access to packs of gum at self-checkout lines. Another proposed idea would try to reach customers elsewhere: Grocery customers might be able to speed through checkout, but people pumping gas still have to stand there and wait for their tanks to fill, so some new vending machines might appear alongside gas pumps.

Source: Susan Reda, "Impulse under Siege?," *Stores,* March 18, 2015.

UK-based Jigsaw carried its unique window treatment into the store. The funnel form made from thin pieces of wood surrounds the windows and opens up into the store, becoming part of the display space.

(first and second): © Checkland Kindleysides Ltd.

Store Exteriors

Before shoppers even get within the store, retailers need to attract their attention with an appealing exterior that invites them in and leads them to walk or drive to access that particular retail location. The exterior includes not just the physical store (e.g., windows, entrances) but also signage, parking, and landscaping. Stores with varying types of locations face different opportunities and limitations on how they can use their exteriors. For example, stores in malls have only the front face to leverage, and the mall operator may dictate some aspects of their exterior designs, whereas stand-alone stores might be subject to certain height restrictions or limits on the types of lighting they can use.

Windows   Window displays draw customers into the store and provide a visual message about the type of merchandise offered in the store and the type of image the store wants to portray. Research suggests that storefront window displays are an effective tool for building the store image, particularly with new customers who are unfamiliar with the store.[28]

Effective window displays are not easy to achieve, however. They take time, creativity, and thought to be effective and coordinate with stores' current assortments. Having great windows without the merchandise to support them is a wasted opportunity. Window ideas can come from an upcoming event like the Boston Marathon, or from a color or pattern being featured in the store. They should tell a story—how a product is used or how apparel should be worn. Like many forms of promotion, stores cannot directly measure windows' effects on sales. But an effective window can attract customers who are walking by to come in and shop.[29]

When the UK-based women's clothing store Jigsaw opened its first mall location, it needed to figure out how to create a unique environment and differentiate itself from the other retailers in the location. It therefore created a funnel form made from thin pieces of wood, which surrounds the windows and opens up into the store. The funnel form brings customers into the store and also acts as display space. This unique design creates a natural flow of movement throughout the store while also evoking a sense of femininity that appeals to its customers.[30]

Entrances   The entryway also is critical because it determines whether consumers believe they can and should enter and affects the customer's image of the store. Whether they locate in malls or stand alone, Apple Stores effectively signal their reputation for technological innovation because the entryways are wide open, showcasing the sleek interiors and available products. Customers can view the open floor plan from the entrance and vast windows, enticing them to come in and "play" with the merchandise.[31]

Although technically not external to the store, the entry area also plays a prominent role in drawing customers into the selling area and reinforcing an image. Often referred to as the "decompression zone," the first 10 feet or so within the store allows customers to adjust to the new environment: escaping from the noisy street or mall, taking off their sunglasses, closing their umbrellas, and developing a visual impression of the entire store. Customers are not prepared to evaluate merchandise or make purchase decisions in the decompression zone, so retailers try to keep this area free of merchandise, displays, and signage.[32]

© Smith Collection/Gado/Getty Images

Apple stores effectively use entryways to showcase their sleek interiors and available products, enticing customers to come in and "play" with the merchandise.

Exterior Signage and Store Design   The signs that appear on the exterior are the primary means for shoppers to find the retail location. Famous signs can even bring the retail offer to mind nearly automatically: The Golden Arches are a bright and prominent feature that alerts consumers to the presence of hamburgers and fries at that particular location, and the Starbucks mermaid appears everywhere one of the brand's coffee shops does.

Much like Apple, IKEA has built a brand around simplicity, so its entire blue and yellow store exteriors essentially serve as part of its signage. The colors make it easy to spot an IKEA store from the highway.[33] Unlike IKEA's simple, yet colorful store designs, Louis Vuitton's store design is consonant with the high-fashion merchandise inside. It's asymmetrical "crystal pavilion" flagship store in Singapore embodies fashion itself. The store, located on the water, features steel frames and windows from ceiling to floor. The Louis Vuitton symbol appears in white lights on the top left corner. White linen hung from the interior over the windows not only provides UV protection for the high-end products but also offers a nautical feel, evoking sails. With this combination, the exterior complements the natural setting while also mirroring the brand's high-fashion image.[34]

Louis Vuitton's asymmetrical "crystal pavilion" store in Singapore is consonant with the high-fashion merchandise inside.

Parking   Regardless of the design and image they choose, most stores must address the practical question of parking. Even the most beautiful building cannot get shoppers to visit it if the retailer fails to clear the walkways of leaves, snow, and ice. There must also be easy access from parking locations, and sufficient parking spaces to accommodate customers. Most local governments require developers to devote a certain amount of space to parking, and these requirements vary by type of retailer. For example, in Dallas, grocery stores must ensure that they have five parking spaces for every 1,000 square feet of store space, and clothing retailers must offer four

© Simin Wang/AFP/Getty Images

Landscaping enhances the image of the stores in malls.

© Rosa Irene Betancourt/Alamy Stock Photo

spaces for every 1,000 square feet, but movie theaters need provide only 0.3 space for every seat they host.[35] As discussed in Chapter 8, from an image perspective, the optimal number of parking spaces is difficult to determine. Too many empty spaces may indicate an unsuccessful retail location, whereas not enough spaces discourages customers from parking and shopping. As we noted previously, retailers must also offer sufficient accessible parking spaces to comply with the ADA.

Landscaping   Like so many retail decisions, whether, how much, and what kind of landscaping a retailer should seek depends on the type of store, its image, and in what type of location it has. The more hedonistic and expensive the merchandise in the stores, the more customers expect a reasonable level of landscaping outside. Also, stores located within regional malls, power centers, or strip centers have little control over external landscaping, although higher-end malls often create beautifully landscaped internal environments that are consistent with its tenants' image. Lifestyle centers, higher-end Central Business Districts, and Main Street locations also strive to maintain a well-landscaped appearance. At the other extreme, big-box stores like Staples and Walmart do not typically have opulent landscaping. To do so would be contrary to their image of have lower prices for their more utilitarian merchandise.

SPACE MANAGEMENT

Describe how to assign store floor space to merchandise departments and categories.

The space within stores and on the stores' shelves and fixtures is a scarce resource. Space management involves key resource decisions: (1) the allocation of store space to merchandise categories and brands, (2) the location of departments or merchandise categories in the store, and (3) the size of the store.

Space Allocated to Merchandise Categories[36]

Some factors that retailers consider when deciding how much floor or shelf space to allocate to merchandise categories and brands are (1) the productivity of the allocated space, (2) the merchandise's inventory turnover, and (3) the display needs for the merchandise.

Space Productivity   A simple rule of thumb is to allocate on the basis of the merchandise's sales. For example, if artificial plants represent 15 percent of the total expected sales for a hobby and craft retailer such as Michaels, then 15 percent of the store's space is allocated to artificial plants.

But as the discussion of marginal analysis for advertising allocations in Chapter 14 indicated, retailers should allocate space to a merchandise category on the basis of its effect on the profitability of the entire store. In practice, this recommendation means that Michaels should add more space to the artificial plant section as long as the profitability of the additional space is greater that the profitability of the category from which space was taken away. In this condition, the additional space for artificial plants will increase the profitability of the entire store. However, at some point it will be more profitable to not take away space from other categories.

Two commonly used measures of space productivity are **sales per square foot** and **sales per linear foot**. Apparel retailers that display most of their merchandise on free-standing fixtures typically measure space productivity as sales per square foot. In supermarkets, most merchandise is displayed on shelves. Because the shelves have approximately the same width, only the length, or the linear dimension sales per linear foot, is used to assess space productivity.

A more appropriate productivity measure, such as gross margin per square foot, would consider the contribution generated by the merchandise, not just the sales. Thus, if salty snacks generate $400 in gross margin per linear foot and canned soup generates only $300 per linear foot, more space should be allocated to salty snacks. However, factors other than marginal productivity need to be considered when making space allocation decisions. These factors are discussed in the next section.

In addition, retailers need to allocate space to maximize the profitability of the store, not just a particular merchandise category or department. Supermarkets often "overallocate" space to some low-profitability categories such as milk because an extensive assortment in these categories attracts customers to the store and positively affects the sales of other categories. Retailers might also overallocate space to categories purchased by their platinum customers—that is, those customers with the highest lifetime value.

Inventory Turnover   Inventory turnover affects space allocations in two ways. First, as discussed in Chapter 11, both inventory turnover and gross margin contribute to GMROI—a measure of the retailer's return on its merchandise inventory investment. Thus, merchandise categories with higher inventory turnover merit more space than merchandise categories with lower inventory turnover. Second, merchandise displayed on the shelf is depleted more quickly for items with high inventory turnover. Thus, more space needs to be allocated to this fast-selling merchandise to minimize the need to restock the shelf frequently and reduce stockouts. Many retailers, however, compensate for high inventory turnover items by assigning them more frequent deliveries so they don't take up so much space.

Display Considerations   The physical limitations of the store and its fixtures affect space allocation. Of course, store planners must provide enough merchandise to fill an entire fixture dedicated to a particular item. But in addition, a retailer might decide it wants to use a merchandise display to enhance its image. For Target to set itself apart as a source of high-quality home goods, it makes its display of private-label organic cotton sheets attractive and expansive. To really emphasize this offering, it even might overallocate space for the sheets and present a wide range of colors.

Location of Merchandise Categories

As discussed previously, the store layout, signage and graphics, and feature areas can guide customers through the store. The location of merchandise categories also plays a role in how customers navigate the store. By strategically placing impulse and demand/destination merchandise throughout the store, retailers increase the chances that customers will shop the entire store and that their attention will be focused on the merchandise that the retailer is most interested in selling—merchandise with a high GMROI. **Demand/destination merchandise** refers to products that customers have decided to buy before entering the store.

As customers enter the store and pass through the decompression zone, they are welcomed with introductory displays, including graphics. Once through the decompression zone, they often turn right (in Western cultures) and observe the prices and quality of the first items they encounter. This area, referred to as the **strike zone**, is critical because it creates the customer's first impression of the store's offering. Thus, retailers display some of their most compelling merchandise in the strike zone.

After passing through the strike zone, the most heavily trafficked and viewed area is the right-hand side of the store because most people turn right when come into a store. By this point in their journey through the store, customers have become accustomed to the environment, have developed a first impression, and are ready to make

Grocery stores often place produce after customers pass through the decompression and strike zones because of its visual/color appeal. It gets a shopper's mouth watering, and the best grocery store customer is a hungry one.

purchase decisions. Thus the right-hand side is a prime area for displaying high-GMROI merchandise. For example, supermarkets typically locate the produce section in this area because produce appeals to the shoppers' senses. The visual/color appeal of all the different produce—bright oranges, deep reds of tomatoes and peppers, rich greens of zucchini and kale—gets a shopper's mouth watering, and the best grocery store customer is a hungry one.

Impulse Merchandise   The prime store locations for selling merchandise are heavily trafficked areas such as 10 feet beyond the entrance on the right side of the store and areas near escalators and cash wraps. In multilevel stores, a space's value decreases the farther it is from the entry-level floor. Thus, **impulse products**, or products that are purchased without planning, such as fragrances and cosmetics in department stores and magazines in supermarkets, are almost always located near the front of the store where they're seen by everyone and may actually draw people into the store.

Demand and Promotional Merchandise   Demand merchandise and promotional merchandise are often placed in the back left-hand corner of the store. Placing high-demand merchandise in this location pulls customers through the store, increasing the visibility of other products along the way. So supermarkets typically put items almost everyone buys—milk, eggs, butter, and bread—in the back left-hand corner. In department stores, children's merchandise and furniture, as well as customer service areas like credit offices, are demand or destination areas and thus located in lightly trafficked areas of the store.

Special Merchandise   Some merchandise categories involve a buying process that is best accomplished in a lightly trafficked area. For example, women's lingerie is typically located in a remote area to offer a more private shopping experience. Categories that require large amounts of floor space, like furniture, are often located in less desirable locations. Some categories, like curtains, need significant wall space, whereas others, like shoes, require easily accessible storage rooms.

Category Adjacencies   Retailers often put complementary categories next to each other to encourage unplanned purchases. Thus at the end of the cereal aisle, grocery shoppers often find an end cap filled with fresh bananas, and audio cables tend to hang on a display near the section featuring sound systems in an electronics store. Such displays help encourage cross-selling, as discussed in Chapter 5.

Another option is to contradict traditional placement schemes to surprise and excite shoppers. A well-known example places beer next to diapers, based on the observation that fathers making an emergency diaper run often late at night buy themselves a treat during the same trip. Consumer-goods companies also hope to exploit a "halo effect" created by the fresh produce aisle in supermarkets.[37] If their packaged goods appear next to healthy, fresh vegetables and fruit, consumers are more likely to associate those appealing traits with the manufacturers' products. But supermarkets are cautious about such moves because the quality of the fresh produce section is a real competitive advantage. These critical trade-offs remain a constant challenge for grocers.

Location of Merchandise within a Category   As discussed in Chapter 4, most purchases in food, discount, drug, and many category specialists are either based on limited problem solving or habitual decision making. As such, retailers have a very short time, often a matter of a few seconds,

© David A. Tietz/Editorial Image, LLC

Retailers like Whole Foods display complementary categories such as apples and cheese next to each other to encourage unplanned purchases.

to get their attention and induce them to grab an item for purchase. Retailers use a variety of rules to locate specific SKUs within a category.[38] For instance, supermarkets and drugstores typically place private-label brands to the right of national brands. Because Western consumers read from left to right, they will see the higher-priced national brand first and then see and possibly purchase the lower-priced, higher-margin private-label item on the right that looks similar to the national brand. Produce departments in grocery stores are arranged so that apples are the first item most customers see because apples are a very popular produce item and can best initiate a buying pattern.

Supermarkets typically display merchandise on four shelves, with the most profitable merchandise on the third shelf from the floor. The third shelf attracts the most attention because it is at eye level for adults. Merchandise that appeals to a smaller group of customers is often displayed on the top shelf because reaching for the items requires significant effort. Heavy, bulky items are stocked on the bottom shelf for safety reasons.

However, when purchase decisions are influenced by shorter consumers, positioning merchandise on the lower shelves might be more effective. For example, children may influence breakfast cereal purchases when accompanying their parents to the supermarket. Thus, the second shelf from the floor might be a prime location for the most profitable cereal brands.

EXHIBIT 16–5
Grocery stores are experimenting in their produce departments with unconventional product placements.

Exhibit 16–5 illustrates some innovative merchandise placement options with which some grocery stores are experimenting. Specifically,

1. Place the dairy section near the front of the store so it is associated with fresh produce.
2. Place other premium products in the produce section since it makes them sell better.
3. Redesign carts to have a second shelf for fragile items and have holders for flowers and coffee.
4. Have a small milk refrigerator near the front door to better compete with convenience stores.
5. Use wood and other natural materials to induce a "farm-fresh" image.
6. Group ingredients necessary for a particular recipe, such as tomatoes, basil, and mozzarella cheese.
7. Place some organic products together and others throughout the produce section to experiment with how they sell best.
8. Place bananas at the back of the produce department to get customers to walk through the entire department.
9. To simulate farmers' markets, add some low shelves so customers can see through the department and locate various-colored items adjacent to each other for visual appeal.

Marks & Spencer in the United Kingdom uses a planogram system developed by SAS to develop a layout that maximizes space productivity.

Some tools that retailers use to make decisions on the positioning of items in a category are planograms, virtual-store software, videotapes of consumers, and spatial recognition systems as they move through the store.

Planograms   A **planogram** is a diagram that shows how and where specific SKUs should be placed on retail shelves or displays to increase customer purchases. The locations can be illustrated using photographs, computer output, or artists' renderings. In developing the planogram, the retailer needs to make the category visually appealing, consider the manner in which customers shop (or the manner in which it

© Marcin Rogozinski/Alamy Stock Photo

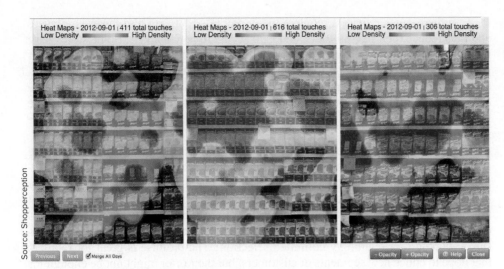

Source: Shopperception

Using Microsoft Kinect sensors, firms like Shopperception create heat maps of shopper interactions with the products (touches, pickups, and returns). The red represents the hot zones where shoppers touch the most, yellow less, and blue not at all.

would like customers to shop), and work to achieve its strategic and financial objectives. Planograms are also useful for merchandise that doesn't fit nicely on shelves in supermarkets or discount stores. Most specialty apparel retailers provide their managers with photographs and diagrams of how merchandise should be displayed.

Virtual-Store Simulation   Virtual-store simulations are another tool used to determine the effects of placing merchandise in different areas of a store and evaluating the profit potential for new items.[39] In these simulations, customers sit in front of computer screens that depict a store aisle. Retina-tracking devices record the eye movements of the customers. When the customers push forward on a handle, similar to the handle on a shopping cart, they progress down the simulated aisle. Customers can virtually reach forward, pick an item off the shelf, look at the packaging, and then place the item in the virtual cart. These virtual shopping trips allow retailers and their suppliers to develop a better understanding of how customers will respond to different planograms.

Videotapes of Consumers and Spatial Recognition Systems   Another research method used to assess customer reactions to planograms involves tracking customers in actual store environments. Traditionally, retailers would videotape customers' movements, but Microsoft's Kinect sensors are providing a less intrusive option. Discretely embedded in aisles, the sensors provide three-dimensional spatial recognition. Thus, retailers can unobtrusively track the amount of time people spend in front of a shelf, which products they touch or pick up, the products they return to shelves, and finally what they add to their carts to purchase.[40] The data gathered can be used to improve layouts and planograms because they can identify causes of slow-selling merchandise, such as poor shelf placement. By studying customers' movements, retailers can also learn where customers pause or move quickly or where there is congestion. This information can help them decide if the layout and merchandise placement is operating as expected, such as whether new or promoted merchandise is getting the attention it deserves.

Determining Store Size

A key space management decision is deciding how big the store should be. With the rise of online shopping, the scarcity of prime retail real estate in some markets, especially urban locations, and the associated high rental costs, retailers are coming to find that bigger is not always better. Improvements in supply chain management, such as quick response inventory systems described in Chapter 9, enable stores to decrease their size but still provide sufficient inventory levels.

With their smaller spaces, retailers likely pay less rent, can hire fewer employees and thus reduce their payroll costs, and gain access to new markets. Some stores have reduced the amount of merchandise to the extent that they operate more like showrooms that allow customers to touch, feel, and in the case of apparel, try on merchandise. But when it comes to purchasing from a limited store inventory, customers are encouraged to go online. The number of SKUs available online at stores like Home Depot, Staples, J.Crew, and Restoration Hardware far surpasses their in-store selection.

There are also negative effects of smaller stores, and most of those focus on the customer. Customers face reduced selection, decreased comfort, and little entertainment. Smaller formats mean there is less room for fancy dressing rooms, entertaining digital displays, or wide aisles that facilitate browsing. The potential outcomes suggest a broader question: Are modern consumers—time-pressured, price-sensitive, and computer-savvy—likely to embrace these smaller-format stores that cannot offer one-stop shopping or a seemingly unlimited selection? The promise is great for retailers that hope to entice new segments of customers, but their offer might not be enough for the average consumer.

While this section explored how retailers manage the precious and scarce resource of space in their stores, the next section looks at the "softer side" of managing a store—visual merchandising.

VISUAL MERCHANDISING

LO 16-4

Illustrate the best techniques for merchandise presentation.

Visual merchandising is the presentation of a store and its merchandise in ways that will attract the attention of potential customers. This section examines issues related to the presentation of merchandise, and the following section explores more sensory aspects of the store's environment. It begins with a review of the fixtures used to display merchandise and then discusses some merchandise presentation techniques.

Fixtures

Fixtures refer to the equipment used to display merchandise. Their primary purposes are to do so efficiently and attractively. At the same time, they define areas of a store and direct traffic flow. Fixtures work in concert with other design elements, such as floor coverings and lighting, as well as the overall image of the store. For instance, in stores designed to convey a sense of tradition or history, customers automatically expect to see lots of wood rather than plastic or metal fixtures. Wood mixed with metal, acrylic, or stone changes the traditional orientation. Apparel retailers utilize the straight-rack, rounder, and four-way fixtures, while the principle fixture for most other retailers is the gondola.

The **straight rack** consists of a long pipe balanced between supports in the floor or attached to a wall (Exhibit 16–6A). Although the straight rack can hold a lot of apparel, it cannot effectively feature specific styles or colors. All the customer can see is a sleeve or a pant leg. As a result, straight racks are often found in discount and off-price apparel stores.

A **rounder**, also known as a **bulk fixture** or **capacity fixture**, is a round fixture that sits on a pedestal (Exhibit 16–6B). Although smaller than the straight rack, it's designed to hold a maximum amount of merchandise. Because they are easy to move and efficiently store apparel, rounders are found in most types of apparel stores. But, as with the straight rack, customers can't get a frontal view of the merchandise.

A **four-way fixture**, also known as a **feature fixture**, has two crossbars that sit perpendicularly on a pedestal (Exhibit 16–6C). This fixture holds a large amount of merchandise and allows the customer to view the entire garment. The four-way is harder to maintain properly than is the rounder or straight rack, however. All merchandise on an arm must be of a similar style and color, or the customer may become

(A) Straight rack

EXHIBIT 16–6
Types of Fixtures

(B) Rounder

(C) Four-way

(D) Gondola

confused. Due to their superior display properties, four-way fixtures are commonly utilized by fashion-oriented apparel retailers.

A **gondola** is an island type of self-service counter with tiers of shelves, bins, or pegs (Exhibit 16–6D). Because they are extremely versatile, they are used extensively, but not exclusively, in grocery and discount stores to display everything from canned foods to baseball gloves. Gondolas are also found displaying towels, sheets, and housewares in department stores. Folded apparel can be efficiently displayed on gondolas as well, but because the items are folded, it's even harder for customers to view apparel on gondolas than it is on straight racks.

Presentation Techniques

Some presentation techniques are idea-oriented, item and size, color, price lining, vertical merchandising, and tonnage merchandising.

Idea-Oriented Presentation   Some retailers use an **idea-oriented presentation**—a method of presenting merchandise based on a

Using idea-oriented presentation techniques, retailers group individual items to show customers how they can be used and combined.

As the name implies, White House/Black Market takes color presentation to an extreme by predominately displaying and selling white and black clothing.

specific idea or the image of the store. Individual items are grouped to show customers how the items could be used and combined. Women's blouses are often displayed with skirts and accessories to present an overall image or idea. Also, furniture stores display a combination of furniture in room settings to give customers an idea of how it would look in their homes. This approach encourages the customer to make multiple complementary purchases.

Item and Size Presentation   Probably the most common technique of organizing stock is by style or item. Discount stores, grocery stores, hardware stores, and drugstores employ this method for nearly every category of merchandise, as do many apparel retailers. When customers look for a particular type of merchandise, such as breakfast cereals, they expect to find all items in the same location. Arranging items by size is a common method of organizing many types of merchandise, from nuts and bolts to apparel. Because the customer usually knows the desired size, it's easy to locate items organized in this manner.

Color Presentation   A bold merchandising technique is organizing by color. For instance, Ralph Lauren stores often have entire collections in one color hue, all merchandised together. White House/Black Market women's apparel stores take color presentation to an extreme—most of its merchandise is black, white, or a combination of the two.

Price Lining   **Price lining** occurs when retailers offer a limited number of predetermined price points and/or price categories within another classification that are merchandised together. This approach helps customers easily find merchandise at the price they wish to pay. For instance, men's dress shirts may be organized into three groups selling for $49, $69, and $99 (see Chapter 13).

Vertical Merchandising   Another common way of organizing merchandise is **vertical merchandising**. In this approach, merchandise is presented vertically using

Vertical displays like this one in a Uniqlo store generate more sales than similar merchandise with a diagonal display.

walls and high gondolas. Research has shown that a vertical display generates more sales than similar merchandise with a diagonal display.[41] Customers shop much as they read a newspaper—from left to right, going down each column, top to bottom.[42] Stores can effectively organize merchandise to follow the eye's natural movement. Retailers take advantage of this tendency in several ways. Many grocery stores put national brands at eye level and store brands on lower shelves because customers scan from eye level down. In addition, retailers often display merchandise in bold vertical bands of an item. For instance, you might see vertical columns of towels of the same color displayed in a department store or a vertical band of yellow and orange boxes of Tide detergent followed by a band of blue Cheer boxes in a supermarket.

Tonnage Merchandising   As the name implies, **tonnage merchandising** is a display technique in which large quantities of merchandise are displayed together. Customers have come to equate tonnage with low price, following the retail adage "Stock it high and let it fly." Tonnage merchandising is therefore used to enhance and reinforce a store's price image. Using this display concept, the merchandise itself is the display. The retailer hopes customers will notice the merchandise and be drawn to it. For instance, grocery stores often use an entire end of a gondola (i.e., an end cap) to display six-packs of Pepsi.

CREATING AN APPEALING STORE ATMOSPHERE

To provide a rewarding shopping experience, retailers go beyond presenting appealing merchandise. **Atmospherics** refers to the design of an environment by stimulation of the five senses.[43] Many retailers have discovered the subtle benefits of developing atmospherics that complement other aspects of the store design and the merchandise. Therefore, they use lighting, colors, music, scent, and even flavors to stimulate customers' perceptual and emotional responses and ultimately affect their purchase behavior. Research has shown that it is important for the atmospheric elements to work together—for example, the right music with the right scent.[44]

LO 16-5

Understand how retailers can create a more appealing shopping experience.

Lighting

Good lighting in a store involves more than simply illuminating space. Lighting can highlight merchandise and capture a mood or feeling that enhances the store's image. Retailers also are exploring ways to save energy with technologically advanced lighting. Having the appropriate lighting positively influences customer shopping behavior.[45]

Retailers use lighting to highlight merchandise and set the mood for their customers.

© JTB Photo/Getty Images

Highlighting Merchandise   A good lighting system helps create a sense of excitement in the store. At the same time, lighting must provide an accurate color rendition of the merchandise. It also allows the retailer to focus spotlights on special featured areas and items. The key determinant appears to be achieving an appropriate level of contrast, which helps attract visual attention.[46] Using lighting to focus on strategic pockets of merchandise trains shoppers' eyes on the merchandise and draws customers strategically through the store. Nike, for example, uses a lot of contrast and shadows, highlighting the merchandise but not necessarily the architecture.

Mood Creation   Retailers use lighting to set the mood for their customers. Ralph Lauren stores and boutiques in department stores use low levels of light to coordinate with their overall ambience of resembling a townhouse. With their lesser concern about atmospherics, full-line discount stores, food retailers, and category specialists tend to brighter and more energy-efficient LED lighting.

Color

The creative use of color can enhance a retailer's image and help create a mood. Warm colors (red, gold, and yellow) produce emotional, vibrant, hot, and active responses. Fast-food restaurants like Wendy's and McDonald's use warm colors since they tend to influence customers to eat fast and leave. Cool colors (white, blue, and green) have a peaceful, gentle, calming effect and appear to induce abstract thinking, leading customers to view products more favorably. Thus brick-and-mortar stores may want to use these more relaxing colors of the spectrum.[47] Although these trends are common, colors can have differential impacts, depending on various consumer traits such as their culture (e.g., in the East, white is a color of mourning, whereas in the West, it often implies purity), their age, and their gender.

Music

Music can either add to or detract from a retailer's total atmospheric package. Most shoppers notice music playing in stores, and nearly half of them say they will leave if they do not like the selections being played.[48]

Fortunately, unlike other atmospheric elements, music can be easily changed. For example, some retailers use a system that allows different types of music to be played at certain times of the day. It can play classic rock music in the morning when its customer base is older and adult contemporary in the afternoon for a 35- to 40-year-old age range customer. For its West Coast stores, it wants modern rock in the morning and Caribbean beats in the afternoon. And in Texas, it's country music all day, every day. Retailers also can "zone" music by demographics, playing more Latin music in stores that attract a higher Hispanic population.

Retailers also can use music to affect customers' behavior. Music can control the pace of store traffic, create an image, and attract or direct consumers' attention. For instance, Abercrombie & Fitch uses its famously loud club music to help keep its image "fresh." It believes that younger customers are able to withstand the loud music longer than older customers, thus attracting and keeping customers in its stores that are in line with its brand image.[49] In general, slow is good. A mix of classical or otherwise soothing music encourages shoppers to slow down, relax, and take a good look at the merchandise.

Scent

Smell has a large impact on a customer's mood and emotions. In conjunction with music, it can increase customers' excitement and satisfaction with the shopping experience.[50] Customers in scented stores think they spent less time in the store than do those in unscented stores. Scents thus can improve customers' subjective shopping experience by making them feel that they are spending less time examining merchandise, waiting for sales help, or checking out.

Our sense of smell is the strongest of all human senses and the closest sense linked to memory and emotion. Research suggests that the use of scent creates an overall store atmosphere that influences shopping behavior. Therefore, a growing number of retail chains use scents to draw and keep customers in their store longer. Before implementing scent branding, retailers need to educate themselves on the basic understanding of the six scent families, referred to as the "primary colors" of ambient scenting. The six scent families are as follows:

- **Citrus,** which is rejuvenating and stimulating and the best match for brands looking to deliver a high-energy atmosphere.

- **Floral,** as often found in expensive fashion boutiques and fine jewelry stores, because these scents tend to range from innocent and sweet to sophisticated and exotic.

- **Outdoorsy,** well suited for outdoor activity outfitters or eco-friendly stores, in that the scents are described as refreshing, clean, and nature-inspired.

- **Fruity,** which is bright, uplifting, youthful, and anxiety-reducing, making a good fit for specialty fashion retailers.

- **Ozonic** or airy, fresh, subtle, and light scents, perfect for stores with small spaces that want to emphasize or signal a less crowded, more open atmosphere.

- **Gourmand,** associated with food, which creates a homey setting for specialty food shops and kitchenware retailers.

The intensity level of the scent is nearly as important; an overly strong fragrance can send the customer quickly out the door. Fortunately, though, most stores can control that intensity with the touch of a button, using the cutting-edge scent delivery technology available in the market.

Source: Richard Weeing, "Crafting the Perfect Ambient Scent for Your Stores via the Six Scent Families," *Retail Customer Experience,* March 11, 2014.

Retailers also use different essences in different departments, suggesting they have a general understanding of the scent classes detailed in Retailing View 16.3: baby powder in the baby store, suntan lotion in the bathing suit area, lilacs in lingerie, and cinnamon and pine scents during the holiday season.[51] Some high-end retailers such as Saks Fifth Avenue and Nordstrom utilize their own unique scents. Yet these apparel retailers are not the only ones to use this atmospheric tool. Goodwill Stores now disperse the scent of honeysuckle and sweet orange in an attempt to make its retail sites more appealing.[52]

When New Balance spread into China, it aimed for a (Western) nostalgic sensory experience to introduce the U.S. brand. Thus, not only did the stores feature wooden floors and 1950s pop music, but they also smelled like wood and leather. Even pop singers get in on this scent action. During her California Dreaming tour, Katy Perry appealed to young fans by spreading the scent of cotton candy throughout the stadiums she played.[53]

Taste

It is a little more difficult to appeal subtly to consumers' taste buds. However, many department stores are reintroducing an old-fashioned offering to appeal to shoppers: the store restaurant. The option to grab a bite without leaving the store encourages customers to linger longer and enjoy their shopping experience more. Café SFA at Saks Fifth Avenue offers a stellar view of Rockefeller Center, while Bergdorf Goodman's BG Restaurant shows off Central Park. And for those shoppers who must have a $36 lobster club sandwich to complete their shopping expedition, Fred's at Barney's New York is the place to go.[54]

Taking a somewhat different approach, Kellogg's has opened its own café in Times Square, featuring dishes made with its cereal products. Emphasizing the feeling of nostalgia that cereal can bring adult consumers, the café is designed to have a retro environment: countertop seating and a wall of red kitchen cabinets that help remind customers of eating Kellogg's brand cereal at their kitchen counters as children.[55]

Kellogg's Café has an exciting environment, but it really appeals to its customers' sense of taste.

© Brendan McDermid/Reuters/Alamy Stock Photo

Just How Exciting Should a Store Be?

Retailers such as Cabela's, REI, Bass Pro Shops, and Barnes & Noble attempt to create an entertaining shopping environment by viewing their stores as theatrical scenes: The floor and walls constitute the stage and scenery; the lighting, fixtures, and displays are the props; and the merchandise represents the performance. This creation of a theatrical experience in stores has resulted in the combination of retailing and entertainment. In contrast, retail chains such as Costco and Home Depot successfully use minimalist, warehouse-style shopping environments, but create excitement in other ways, such as giving away food samples and hosting do-it-yourself classes.

Does providing an exciting, entertaining store environment lead customers to patronize a store more frequently and spend more time and money during each visit? The answer to this question is: It depends.[56]

The impact of the store's environment depends on the customer's shopping goals. The two basic shopping goals are task completion (utilitarian), such as buying a new suit for a job interview, and recreation (hedonic), such as spending a Saturday afternoon with a friend wandering through a mall. When customers are shopping to complete a task that they view as inherently unrewarding, they prefer to be in a soothing, calming environment—a simple atmosphere with slow music, dimmer lighting, calming scents, and blue-green colors. However, when customers go shopping for fun, an inherently rewarding activity, they want to be in an exciting atmosphere—a complex environment with invigorating smells, fast tempo music, bright lighting, and red-yellow colors.

What does this mean for retailers? They must consider the typical shopping goals for their customers when designing their store environments. Grocery shopping is typically viewed as an unpleasant task, and thus supermarkets should be designed in soothing colors and use slow background music. In contrast, shopping for fashion apparel is typically viewed as fun, so an arousing environment in apparel retail outlets will have a positive impact on the shopping behavior of their customers.

The level of excitement caused by the environment might vary across the store. A consumer electronics retailer might create a low-arousal environment in the accessories area to accommodate customers who typically are task oriented when shopping for print cartridges and batteries, and it might create a high-arousal environment in the home-entertainment centers that are typically visited by more pleasure-seeking shopping customers.

Finally, retailers might vary the nature of their websites for customers depending on their shopping goals. For example, research suggests that Amazon should serve up complex, high-arousal websites with rich media to customers who indicate they are browsing but provide simpler, low-arousal sites for customers looking for a specific book.[57]

SUMMARY

LO 16-1 Identify the critical issues retailers need to consider when designing a store.

To design a store, retailers must consider their main objectives: (1) implement their strategy, (2) influence customer buying behavior, (3) provide flexibility, (4) control design and maintenance costs, and (5) meet legal requirements. Because few store designs can achieve all of these objectives, managers make trade-offs among objectives, such as providing convenience rather than encouraging exploration or vice versa.

LO 16-2 List the advantages and disadvantages of alternative store layouts.

Regardless of the type used, a good store layout helps customers find and purchase merchandise. The grid design is best for stores in which customers are likely to explore the entire store, such as grocery stores and drugstores. Racetrack designs are more common in large upscale stores, such as department stores. Free-form designs are usually found in small specialty stores and within the departments at department stores. In-store signs help customers locate merchandise and provide information, including pricing. Although relatively expensive and requiring continuous maintenance, digital signage is dynamic and attracts customers' attention. Feature areas are designed to get customers' attention and include freestanding displays, mannequins, end caps, promotional aisles or areas, walls, dressing rooms, and cash wraps. Stores' exteriors, particularly windows, entrances, exterior signage, store design, parking, and landscaping, are important issues that impact customers' propensity to go to and enter a store.

LO 16-3 Describe how to assign store floor space to merchandise departments and categories.

Space management involves three decisions: (1) allocating store space to merchandise categories and brands, (2) locating departments or merchandise categories in the store, and (3) determining the appropriate store size. To determine how much floor or shelf space to allocate to merchandise categories, retailers might consider the productivity of the allocated space (e.g., using sales per square foot or sales per linear foot), the merchandise's inventory turnover, its impact on store sales, and display needs. In addition, by strategically placing impulse and demand/destination merchandise throughout the store, retailers can encourage customers to shop the entire store and focus their attention on merchandise that the retailer wants to sell most.

LO 16-4 Illustrate the best techniques for merchandise presentation.

Signage and graphics help customers locate specific products and departments, provide product information, and suggest items or special purchases. Digital signage has several advantages over traditional printed signage, but the initial fixed costs have made its adoption slow. Feature areas are designed to get customers' attention. They include freestanding displays, mannequins, end caps, promotional aisles or areas, walls, dressing rooms, and cash wraps. Finally, various types of display racks and shelving are more or less appropriate for different types of merchandise.

LO 16-5 Understand how retailers can create a more appealing shopping experience.

Retailers employ various forms of atmospherics—lighting, colors, music, scent, and even taste—to influence shopping behaviors. The use of these atmospherics can create a calming environment for task-oriented shoppers or an exciting environment for recreational shoppers.

KEY TERMS

atmospherics, *451*

boutique layout, *435*

bulk fixture, *448*

call-to-action signage, *436*

capacity fixture, *448*

cash wrap, *439*

category signage, *436*

center store, *433*

checkout area, *439*

demand/destination merchandise, *443*

digital signage, *436*

end cap, *438*

feature area, *437*

feature fixture, *448*

fixtures, *448*

four-way fixture, *448*

free-form layout, *435*

freestanding display, *437*

gondola, *449*

grid layout, *432*

hedonic benefit, *428*

idea-oriented presentation, *449*

impulse products, *444*

loop layout, *434*

mannequin, *437*

planogram, *446*

point-of-purchase (POP) counter, *439*

GET OUT AND DO IT!

1. **CONTINUING ASSIGNMENT** Go into the physical store location of the retailer you have chosen for the continuing assignment, and evaluate the store layout, design, and visual merchandising techniques employed. Explain your answers to the following questions:

    (a) In general, are the store layout, design, and visual merchandising techniques consistent with the exterior of the store and its location?

    (b) Is the store's ambience consistent with the merchandise presented and the customer's expectations?

    (c) How do the store's layout, design, and visual merchandising support the following objectives: (1) implements the retailer's strategy, (2) builds loyalty, (3) increases sales, (4) controls costs, and (5) meets legal requirements?

    (d) To what extent are the store's layout, design, and merchandising techniques flexible?

    (e) How does the store utilize atmospheric elements such as color, lighting, music, and scent? Are these uses appropriate given the store's merchandise and target market?

    (f) Is the store's design environmentally friendly? If yes, please describe. If no, how could it become more "green"?

    (g) Are the fixtures consistent with the merchandise and the overall ambience of the store? Are they flexible?

    (h) Evaluate the store's signage. Does it do an effective job of selling merchandise?

    (i) Has the retailer used any theatrical effects to help sell merchandise?

    (j) Does the store layout help draw people through the store?

    (k) Has the retailer taken advantage of the opportunity to sell merchandise in feature areas?

    (l) Does the store make creative use of wall space?

    (m) What type of layout does the store use? Is it appropriate for the type of store? Would another type of layout be better?

    (n) Ask the store manager how the profitability of space is evaluated (e.g., profit per square foot). Is there a better approach?

    (o) Ask the store manager how space is assigned to merchandise. Critically evaluate the answer.

    (p) Ask the store manager if planograms are used. If so, try to determine what factors are considered when putting together a planogram.

    (q) Are departments in the most appropriate locations? Would you move any departments?

    (r) What method(s) has the retailer used to organize merchandise? Is this the best way? Suggest any appropriate changes.

2. **INTERNET EXERCISE** Go to the home page of CoolHunters (**www.thecoolhunter.net**). Look at examples posted in the store subpage (under the design tab). How can this information of latest trends assist with store layout, design, and visual merchandising?

3. **INTERNET EXERCISE** VMSD is the leading resource for retail designers and store display professionals, serving the retail industry since 1869 (then called Display World). Go to its web page at **http://vmsd.com**, and develop a list of three or four items that describe the latest trends in visual merchandising.

4. **INTERNET EXERCISE** Go to the home page of Envirosell (**www.envirosell.com**). How does this marketing research consulting firm support retailers by collecting consumer information to assist with store layout, design, and visual merchandising?

DISCUSSION QUESTIONS AND PROBLEMS

1. One of the fastest-growing sectors of the population is the over-60 age group. Customers in this group may have limitations in their vision, hearing, and movement. How can retailers develop store designs with this population's needs in mind?

2. Assume you have been hired as a consultant to assess a local discount store's floor plan and space productivity.

Look back at Chapter 6 and decide which analytical tools and ratios you would use to assess the situation.

3. What are the different types of design that can be used in a store layout? How does the layout impact the types of fixtures used to display merchandise? Describe why some stores are more suited for a particular type of layout than others.

4. A department store is building an addition. The merchandise manager for furniture is trying to convince the vice president to allot this new space to the furniture department. The merchandise manager for men's clothing is also trying to gain the space. What points should each manager use when presenting his or her rationale?

5. As an architect for retail space, you are responsible for Americans with Disabilities Act compliance. How would you make sure that a store's retail layout both meets accessibility requirements and enables the company to reach profitability objectives?

6. What are the advantages and disadvantages of offering virtual dressing rooms from the retailers' perspective?

7. Complete the following table by briefly describing how the different retail formats could use each of the areas listed to enhance the store's image and atmosphere.

Area	Drugstore	Clothing Store	Music Store	Restaurant
Entrance				
Walls				
Windows				
Merchandise displays				
Cash wrap				

8. How can signage and graphics help both customers and retailers? Consider the following types of retail formats that you likely have visited in the past: discount store, department store, office superstore, and card and gift store. Describe which retail formats have implemented the best practices for coordinating signs and graphics with each store's image and which formats should improve this aspect of their store layout, design, and visual merchandising.

CHAPTER ENDNOTES

1. Nicholas Knight, "Bergdorf Goodman's Glistening Rennovation," *T Magazine,* September 1, 2016.

2. Barry Samaha, "Bergdorf Goodman Unveils Its Renovated Main Floor in Time for New York Fashion Week," *Forbes,* August 29, 2016.

3. Ibid.

4. Ainsley O'Connell, "Newly Renovated, Bergdorf Goodman Courts the Ladies Who Instagram," *Fast Company,* September 16, 2016.

5. Ibid.

6. Simona Botti and Ann L. McGill, "The Locus of Choice: Personal Causality and Satisfaction with Hedonic and Utilitarian Decisions," *Journal of Consumer Research* 37 (April 2011), pp. 1065–1078; Uzma Khan and Ravi Dhar, "Price-Framing Effects on the Purchase of Hedonic and Utilitarian Bundles," *Journal of Marketing Research* 47, no. 6 (2010), pp. 1090–1099; Eileen Bridges and Renée Florsheim, "Hedonic and Utilitarian Shopping Goals: The Online Experience," *Journal of Business Research* 61 (April 2008), pp. 309–314.

7. George Anderson, "Shopping at Wegmans on a Sunday Afternoon," *RetailWire,* June 27, 2012.

8. "An Overview," Wegmans, https://www.wegmans.com/webapp/wcs/stores/servlet/CategoryDisplay?storeId=10052&identifier=CATEGORY_2441; Michael Hess, "Could This Be the Best Company in the World?," *CBSNews.com,* September 13, 2011; "America's Largest Private Companies," *Forbes,* November 16, 2011.

9. "Taking Sustainability to New Heights," www.walmartgreenroom/com, October 15, 2012; "No Matter the Season, Our Energy Commitment Is Always On," www.walmartgreenroom.com, September 28, 2012.

10. Kendall Goodrich and Rosemary Ramsey, "Are Consumers with Disabilities Receiving the Services They Need?," *Journal of Retailing and Consumer Services* 19 (January 2012), pp. 88–97; Cynthia R. Jasper and Paul Waldhart, "Retailer Perceptions on Hiring Prospective Employees with Disabilities," *Journal of Retailing and Consumer Services* 19 (January 2012),

pp. 116–123; Stacey Menzel Baker, Jonna Holland, and Carol Kaufman-Scarborough, "How Consumers with Disabilities Perceive 'Welcome' in Retail Servicescapes: A Critical Incident Study," *Journal of Services Marketing* 21, no. 3 (2007), pp. 160–173.

11. See, for example, *EEOC v. Cottonwood Financial, Ltd.,* No. CV-09-5073-EFS (E. D. Wash.), 2012; *Disabled in Action of Metropolitan New York, Inc. et al. v. Duane Reade, Inc.,* U.S. District Court, Southern District of New York, Civil Action No. 01 Civ. 4692 (WHP), 2004; *Californians for Disability Rights v. Mervyn's,* Superior Court of California, No. 2002-051738 (RMS), 2003; *Shimozono, et al. v. May Department Stores Co. d/b/a Robinsons-May,* Federal Court, Central District of California, Case No. 00-04261 (WJR), 2001; *Access Now, et al., v. Burdines, Inc.,* Federal Court, Southern District of Florida, Case No. 99-3214 (CIV), 2000.

12. Roger Thorne, "Handicap Requirements for Retail Stores," *eHow,* www.ehow.com/list_6110547_handicap-requirements-retail-stores.html; ADA Accessibility Guidelines for Buildings and Facilities, www.access-board.gov/adaag/html/adaag.htm; Michael Barbaro, "Department Stores Settle Disability Lawsuit," *Washington Post,* February 9, 2005, p. E02.

13. James M. Kerr, "How Appealing to Women Has Helped the Home Depot," *ManagementIssues.com,* October 3, 2014.

14. Paco Underhill, *Why We Buy: The Science of Shopping* (New York: Simon and Schuster, 2000).

15. Herb Sorensen, *Inside the Mind of the Shopper* (Upper Saddle River, NJ: Pearson Education, 2009).

16. Bernice Hurst, "Is Fresh Killing the Center Store?," *RetailWire,* March 6, 2015.

17. Linda Winick, "Could a 'Breakfast Aisle' Revitalize the Grocery Center Store?," *RetailWire,* October 12, 2016.

18. Dhruv Grewal, Anne L. Roggeveen, and Jens Nordfält, "Shopper Marketing: Role of In-Store Marketing," in *Review of Marketing Research,* Vol. 12, Dhruv Grewal, Anne L. Roggeveen, and Jens Nordfält, eds. (Bingley, UK: Emerald Group, 2014; Jens Nordfält, Dhruv Grewal, Anne L. Roggeveen, and Krista

Hill, "Insights from In-Store Experiments," in *Review of Marketing Research,* Vol. 12, Dhruv Grewal, Anne L. Roggeveen, and Jens Nordfält, eds. (Bingley, UK: Emerald Group, 2014).

19. Anne L. Roggeveen, Jens Nordfält, and Dhruv Grewal, "Do Digital Displays Enhance Sales? Role of Retail Format and Message Content," *Journal of Retailing* 92 (March 2016), pp. 122–123.

20. Roggeveen et al., "Do Digital Displays Enhance Sales?"; Raymond R. Burke, "Behavioral Effects of Digital Signage," *Journal of Advertising Research* 49 (June 2009), pp. 180–186.

21. Roggeveen et al., "Do Digital Displays Enhance Sales?"

22. Len Lewis, "Making Signage a Cinch," *Stores,* May 2012; Sandy Smith, "The Big Picture," *Stores,* August 2011; Len Lewis, "Dynamic Displays," *Stores,* February 2011.

23. Anika Lindström, Hanna Berg, Jens Nordfält, Anne L. Roggeveen, and Dhruv Grewal, "Does the Presence of a Mannequin Head Change Shopping Behavior?," *Journal of Business Research* 69 (February 2016), pp. 517–524.

24. Grewal et al., "Shopper Marketing: Role of In-Store Marketing"; Nordfält et al., "Insights from In-Store Experiments."

25. Alicia Fiorletta, "Rebecca Minkoff Unveils Connected Store of the Future," *Retail Touch Points,* November 14, 2014; "Rebecca Minkoff Connected Store Demo," *eBay,* November 12, 2014, https://www.youtube.com/watch?v=6G3JIyG_GeY.

26. "Rebecca Minkoff Empowers Millennial Shoppers," *Think With Google,* August 26, 2015, https://www.youtube.com/watch?v=1i4KpNAY8uY.

27. Daniel Terdiman, "At Demo, Virtual Dressing Rooms Promise Big Sales," *CNet,* February 28, 2011.

28. F. Lange, S. Rosengren, and A. Blom, "Store-Window Creativity's Impact on Shopper Behavior," *Journal of Business Research* 69, no. 3 (2015) pp. 1014–1021; Britta Cornelius, Martin Natter, and Corinne Faure, "How Storefront Displays Influence Retail Store Image," *Journal of Retailing and Consumer Services* 17, no. 2 (March 2010), pp. 143–151.

29. JoAnne Klimovich Harrop, "Window Displays Create Interest, Merchants Say," *TribLive,* May 19, 2011.

30. "Jigsaw Westfield Store by Checkland Kindleysides, London, UK," *Retail Design Blog,* January 7, 2016.

31. Nick Statt, "Apple Just Revealed the Future of Its Retail Stores," *The Verge,* May 19, 2016.

32. Paco Underhill, *Why We Buy: The Science of Shopping,* 3rd ed. (New York: Simon and Schuster, 2009); Mindy Fetterman and Jayne O'Donnell, "Just Browsing at the Mall? That's What You Think," *USA Today,* September 1, 2006.

33. Sherri Geng, "IKEA: Modularizing Design and Value," *Harvard Business School,* December 8, 2015, https://rctom.hbs.org/submission/ikea-modularizing-design-and-value/; Rafiq Elmansy, "Guide to IKEA's Sustainable Design Strategy (Part 2)," *Designorat,* http://www.designorate.com/ikea-sustainable-design-strategy-part2.

34. Virginia Duran, "17 Architecturally Amazing Fashion Stores," *Virginia Duran: Art, Architecture, Graphic Design,* November 7, 2013, https://duranvirginia.wordpress.com/2013/11/07/17-architecturally-amazing-fashion-stores/; "Louis Vuitton in Singapore/FTL Design Engineering Studio," *Arch Daily,* October 2, 2012, http://www.archdaily.com/277610/louis-vuitton-in-singapore-ftl-design-engineering-studio.

35. "Parking Requirements," http://www.houstontx.gov/planning/DevelopRegs/docs_pdfs/parking_req.pdf.

36. Chase C. Murray, Debabrata Talukdar, and Abhijit Gosavi, "Joint Optimization of Product Price, Display Orientation and Shelf-Space Allocation in Retail Category Management,"

Journal of Retailing 86 (June 2010), pp. 125–136; Jared M. Hansen, Sumit Raut, and Sanjeev Swami, "Retail Shelf Allocation: A Comparative Analysis of Heuristic and Meta-Heuristic Approaches," *Journal of Retailing* 86, no. 1 (March 2010), pp. 94–105; B. Ramaseshan, N. R. Achuthan, and R. Collinson, "Decision Support Tool for Retail Shelf Space Optimization," *International Journal of Information Technology & Decision Making* 7, no. 3 (2008), pp. 547–565.

37. Sarah Nassauer, "A Food Fight in the Produce Aisle," *The Wall Street Journal,* October 20, 2011.

38. Pierre Chandon, J. Wesley Hutchinson, Eric T. Bradlow, and Scott H. Young, "Does In-Store Marketing Work? Effects of the Number and Position of Shelf Facings on Brand Attention and Evaluation at the Point of Purchase," *Journal of Marketing* 73 (November 2009), pp. 1–17.

39. "Growth Funds for Virtual Store specialist InContext," *Daily Research News Online,* October 26, 2016, http://www.mrweb.com/drno/news23460.htm; Edward Franczek, "Virtual Stores Drive Real Sales," http://www.greenbookblog.org, December 13, 2011.

40. Ronny Max, "7 Technologies to Track People," *Behavior Analytics In Retail,* July 1, 2015, http://www.behavioranalyticsretail.com/7-technologies-to-track-people/; "In Retail Stores, Research Tool Uses Kinect to Track Shoppers' Behavior," *Retail,* December 29, 2011.

41. Grewal et al., "Shopper Marketing: Role of In-Store Marketing."

42. Abhijit Biswas, Sandeep Bhowmick, Abhijit Guha, and Dhruv Grewal, "Consumer Evaluation of Sale Price: Role of the Subtraction Principle," *Journal of Marketing* 77, (July 2013), pp. 49–66; Grewal et al., "Shopper Marketing: Role of In-Store Marketing"; Nordfält et al., "Insights from In-Store Experiments."

43. The concept of atmospherics was introduced by Philip Kotler, "Atmosphere as a Marketing Tool," *Journal of Retailing* 49 (Winter 1973), pp. 48–64.

44. Aradhna Krishna, "An Integrative Review of Sensory Marketing: Engaging the Senses to Affect Perception, Judgment and Behavior," *Journal of Consumer Psychology* 22 (2012), pp. 332–351; May Lwin, Maureen Morrin, and Aradhna Krishna, "Exploring the Superadditive Effects of Scent and Pictures on Verbal Recall: An Extension of Dual Coding Theory," *Journal of Consumer Psychology* 20, no. 3 (2010), pp. 317–326.

45. Jens Nordfalt, *In-Store Marketing,* 2nd ed. (Sweden: Forma Magazine, 2011); Aradhna Krishna, *Sensory Marketing: Research on the Sensuality of Consumers* (New York: Routledge, 2009).

46. "Latest Findings on Ideal Lighting for Retail Stores," http://lighting.com/ideal-retail-lighting-for-stores/.

47. Tom Ryan, "The Purchasing Power of Om," *RetailWire,* November 7, 2011.

48. Giada Pezzini, "7 Reasons Why You Should Play Music in Your Store," *LS Retail,* April 12, 2016, http://www.lsretail.com/blog/7-reasons-play-music-store/; "Retail Customer Experience: Consumers Tune Out Stores Playing Annoying Music," *RetailWire,* November 14, 2011.

49. Humayun Khan, "How Retailers Manipulate Sight, Smell, and Sound to Trigger Purchase Behavior in Consumers," *Shopify,* April 25, 2016, https://www.shopify.com/retail/119926083-how-retailers-manipulate-sight-smell-and-sound-to-trigger-purchase-behavior-in-consumers.

50. Charles Spence, Nancy M. Puccinelli, Dhruv Grewal, and Anne L. Roggeveen, "Store Atmospherics: A Multisensory

Perspective," *Psychology & Marketing* 31, no. 7 (2014), pp. 472–488; Dhruv Grewal, Anne L. Roggeveen, Nancy M. Puccinelli, and Charles Spence, "Nonverbal and In-Store Communication in the Retail Environment: An Introduction," *Psychology & Marketing* 31, no. 7 (2014), pp. 469–471.

51. Eric Markowitz, "How Cinnamon Smells Will Save Holiday Sales," *Inc.,* November 3, 2011.

52. Lauren Covello, "Reaching Out to Customers, through Their Noses," *FOXBusiness,* October 13, 2011.

53. Jane Sutton, "Scent Makers Sweeten the Smell of Commerce," *Reuters,* December 19, 2011.

54. Dick Scanlon, "Lingerie on 6; Lobster on 9," *The New York Times,* December 29, 2011.

55. Margaret Harney, "Kellogg's Opens Cereal Cafe Concept Store in New York," *Design:Retail,* September 14, 2016.

56. Velitchka Kalchteva and Barton Weitz, "How Exciting Should a Store Be?," *Journal of Marketing,* Winter 2006, pp. 34–62; Benjamin Yen and P. C. Yen, "The Design and Evaluation of Accessibility on Web Navigation," *Decision Support Systems* 42, no. 4 (2007), pp. 2219–2235.

57. "Tips on Improving the Checkout Process," www.e-consultancy.com, July 1, 2010.

CHAPTER 17 | Customer Service

LEARNING OBJECTIVES

After reading this chapter, you should be able to:

LO 17-1 Identify how retailers balance customer service through personalization versus standardization.

LO 17-2 Explain how customers evaluate a retailer's customer service.

LO 17-3 Indicate the activities a retailer can undertake to provide high-quality customer service.

LO 17-4 Articulate retailers' service failure strategies.

© Bryan Bedder/Getty Images

A fancy envelope arrives in the mail: You have been invited to a wedding, or maybe a benefit gala, or a formal work engagement. It promises to be an unforgettable evening, and whatever the occasion, you want to look your very best and live up to the formal dress code implied by the invitation. But really, who can afford designer duds for a one-time party experience?

That's where Rent the Runway makes itself invaluable. For prices ranging from about $70 to $150, shoppers can select some of the latest designs from haute couture brands and rent them for a special event, then return the outfits and accessories after they have finished with them.[1] The convenient service promises to deliver the items quickly and reliably, to ensure that each customer is outfitted just as she prefers for whatever fun she has scheduled.[2]

But as every consumer who has ever ordered something online knows, sometimes it's hard to decide on which piece, in what size, will actually fit. For

Rent the Runway, this inherent challenge of online retailing represents a potential threat to its very existence and service promise. A dress that does not fit quite right will not satisfy its customers. Most customers place their order less than a week before the event for which they need the rental fashions. And those events tend to be fancy, high-profile events, such that the customers expect to look their very best in a luxury designer gown. If it cannot get women outfitted and looking great in time for the event that prompted them to place an order in the first place, even if the retailer is not at fault, then those customers will be left dissatisfied.

Faced with these high service demands, Rent the Runway is adopting several innovative service approaches. For example, it has long allowed customers to order multiple sizes of the same outfit, to make sure that one of them will fit. They also can request two different options in the same order, for a flat added handling fee.

But when panicked customers realized only too late that the bodice of a dress was too tight or that the hem trailed on a particular skirt, these options and the company's extensive customer service assistance by phone were insufficient. Noting that customers already were contacting it through Snapchat, to share pictures and videos, Rent the Runway decided to encourage customers to upload pictures or videos of themselves, how they move, and what kinds of clothing they like to the corporate site. In the meantime, it recruited a pool of models from among its own employees. Approximately 250 workers from the customer service department at its corporate headquarters have agreed to help and offer themselves as sort of living mannequins, with varied body types that generally offer matches with customers' bodies. Thus, when the customer uploads a video, provides her body type information, and explains what she's looking for, the company solicits the assistance of a model with a similar body type. This model then tries on the chosen outfit and offers a review of minor details that might make a difference, such as how easy it is to sit in a skirt or how low the neckline falls.[3] The customer and customer service representative then engage in a conversation, covering the customer's detailed questions and concerns. The plan is for service representatives to spend about 10 minutes with each customer, ensuring that the product ordered is the best option for this shopper.

As customers grew more familiar with the service, their expectations grew too, such that they wanted designer fashions not just for special events but for their daily lives. The cost of renting individual items was prohibitive though, so Rent the Runway innovated a new, Unlimited service.[4] For $139 per month, shoppers can receive packages with three clothing items at a time. When they return the items, they receive the next products on their list, similar to Netflix's initial mail-order model. The service helps working women rotate their wardrobes efficiently (without demanding a time-consuming trip to the mall) and at a reasonable cost,[5] while still enabling them to avoid the "throwaway" sensibility of fast fashion.[6] Once a customer has joined the Unlimited service, her body type, designer preferences, and other personalized factors are saved, such that Rent the Runway can offer recommendations for fit and highlight new arrivals that might appeal.

If Rent the Runway can keep up its communications and conversations with all of these customers, in all of these channels, for all of these purchase occasions, it seems poised to achieve even higher levels of satisfied—and well-dressed—customers.

Customer service is the set of activities and programs undertaken by retailers to make the shopping experience more rewarding. These activities increase the value customers receive from the merchandise and services they purchase. Some of these services are provided by store and call-center employees interacting directly with customers, while others are provided by the design of the retailer's store and/or website.

Many stores differentiate their retail offerings, build customer loyalty, and develop sustainable competitive advantages by providing excellent customer service. Customer service provides a strategic advantage because good service is important to customers, can be difficult for competitors to duplicate, keeps customers returning to a retailer, and generates positive word-of-mouth communication, which attracts new customers.[7] Unfortunately, the flip side is also true: Poor service by retailers increases negative

©John Patriquin/Portland Press Herald via Getty Images

L.L.Bean has developed a sustainable competitive advantage by devoting considerable time and effort to developing an organizational culture that stimulates and supports excellent customer service.

word of mouth in addition to reducing future visits. Customers are turned off by rude and ill-informed retail service personnel, frustrated by a lack of available personnel to answer their queries, and irritated by website inadequacies, such as confusing navigation or a lack of human interaction.[8]

All employees of a retail firm and all elements of the retailing mix can provide services that increase the value of merchandise to customers. For example, employees in the distribution center contribute to customer service by making sure the merchandise is in stock at the retailer's stores. The employees who choose store locations and design their interiors contribute by improving the customers' experience, both in terms of getting to the store and finding merchandise once they are in the store.

The challenge of providing consistent, high-quality service offers an opportunity for retailers to develop a sustainable competitive advantage. For example, L.L.Bean has devoted considerable time and effort to developing an organizational culture that stimulates and supports excellent customer service. Competing stores would love to offer the same level of service but find it hard to match L.L.Bean's performance—an asset that L.L.Bean has built over the past 75 years. In a recent experiment to test customer service provisions, one consultancy noted that though Best Buy offered the best shipping service, and Burberry was best when it came to product returns, L.L.Bean was tops overall, praising the retailer for making sure that callers could reach a live representative within 30 seconds on average.[9]

BALANCING CUSTOMER SERVICE: PERSONALIZATION VERSUS STANDARDIZATION

LO 17-1

Identify how retailers balance customer service through personalization versus standardization.

To develop a sustainable customer service advantage, retailers offer a combination of personalized and standardized services. **Personalized service** requires that service providers tailor their services to meet each customer's personal needs. Successful implementation of the personalized service relies on sales associates or the "personalization" offered by the retailer's electronic channel.[10] **Standardized service** is based on establishing a set of rules and procedures for providing high-quality service and ensuring that they get implemented consistently. The effectiveness of standardized services relies mainly on the quality of the retailer's policy, procedures, and store, as well as its website design and layout.

Customers might prefer different types of service on different buying occasions, even with the same retailer. As we discussed in Chapter 4, the consumers' buying process depends on their past experiences and the risk associated with the purchase decision. Thus, the level of customer service and personalized information desired from sales associates varies for different buying situations. Most consumers have significant knowledge and experience shopping for most products sold by supermarkets, convenience stores, and general merchandise retailers. These retailers tend to emphasize standardized service rather than the more costly and informative personalized face-to-face service. For example, more than two-thirds of grocery retailers in the United States now use self-checkout lines.[11]

Personalized Service

Personalized customer service is less consistent than standardized service. The delivery of personalized service depends on the judgment and capabilities of each service provider. Some service providers are better than others, and even the best service providers can have a bad day. In addition, providing consistent, high-quality personalized service is costly because well-trained service providers or sophisticated computer software generally are needed to implement the service.[12]

Fifty years ago, managers and employees in local stores knew their customers personally and offered recommendations of products that they thought their customers would like. This personal touch has all but disappeared with the growth of national chains that emphasize self-service and lower costs. Barneys New York is an exception. It is known in New York, the other markets it serves such as Los Angeles, San Francisco, Chicago, and

© tdub303/E+/Getty Images

To enhance the connections that salespeople in stores make with their customers, Barneys and other retailers have equipped salespeople with tablets that can be used to identify regular shoppers and help them check out immediately using Apple Pay.

Boston, and throughout the high-fashion world for its cutting-edge fashions for men and women. But consistent with its merchandise offering, and associated high prices, its customers have come to expect exceptional customer service. In its effort to perpetuate this reputation, Barneys constantly works to expand its service offerings. For example, to enhance the connections that salespeople in its stores make with their customers, it has equipped them with iPads that the salesclerks can use to identify regular shoppers and help them check out immediately using Apple Pay. With Barneys' mobile app, the retailer also seeks to provide more information, such as updates, announcements of store openings, fashion advice, and alerts about where to find products of potential interest to customers. Moreover, Barneys is expanding its product delivery capabilities to be able to provide same-day shipping, for a $25 fee, to customers in Manhattan or Brooklyn who order by noon. As the retailer leverages such modern-era technology and digital options, it demonstrates its continued commitment to the service aspects that have enabled its long and successful history.[13]

Another version of personalization relies on the combination of recommendation engines with a database of customer transactions. The Internet has made vast amounts of information on products and retailers available to consumers, and recommendation engines are a response to this information overload. At the appropriate moment—generally when you're about to make a retail purchase—the engine subtly makes a product suggestion. Amazon was the pioneer of automated recommendations, but the service has now been adopted by other retailers. For example, the Wine.com site offers customized pages for customers. Once they log onto the site, customers receive recommendations based on their past purchases and their interests.[14]

Standardized Service

Standardized, particularly automated services improve the speed and reliability of the retail interaction for customers. But this form of customization is also distinctly impersonal. Without any access to customers, retail employees cannot improve their experience, ensure their satisfaction, distinguish the retail store, or even provide simple human interactions. If consumers visit public spaces to interact with others, self-service technologies are unlikely to meet their needs. And if every store has the same technology, they cannot differentiate themselves in the same way that a great retail employee does automatically.[15]

Retailers standardize the service they offer to increase the consistency of their service quality and avoid the costs of paying the more skilled service providers required to effectively personalize customer services. For example, McDonald's and other quick-service restaurants develop and strictly enforce a set of policies and procedures to provide an acceptable, consistent service quality. The food may not be

IKEA effectively uses standardized services through its signage, information on displays, and merchandise.

considered gourmet, but it is consistently served in a timely manner at a relatively low cost throughout the world. McDonald's also is testing the use of about 10,000 touch-screen ordering systems in Europe to determine if customers will embrace them. If so, customers would be able to create any personalized customization option they prefer—rather than having to explain the complex ratio of pickles-to-onions that they want to a staffer at the counter—by using a standardized, automated tool.[16]

Store or website designs and layout also play important roles in the delivery of standardized service (see Chapter 16). In some situations, customers do not want to use the services employees provide. They know what they want to buy, and their objective is to find it in the store or on the website and buy it quickly. In these situations, retailers offer good service by simply providing a layout and signs that enable customers to locate merchandise easily, having relevant information on display, and minimizing the time required to make a purchase.

IKEA uses a standardized, self-service approach with some unique elements to attract customers who expect the traditional personalized approach commonly used in furniture retailing. Every product available is displayed in more than 70 roomlike settings throughout the 150,000-square-foot warehouse stores. Customers don't need a decorator to help them picture how the furniture will go together. Although IKEA uses a "customers do it themselves" approach, it also offers some services that traditional furniture stores do not, such as in-store child care centers, restaurants serving fast food, and extensive information and displays about the quality of the furniture. In many stores, sales associates use tablets with specially designed applications to enhance their interactions with customers. Yet, IKEA still maintains its self-service focus: An app enables users to browse through IKEA products on their smartphones, download a store map, and locate items on their shopping list in the store.[17]

In the following section, we discuss how customers evaluate the quality of customer service and what retailers can do to alter the actual and perceived levels of customer service.

CUSTOMER EVALUATIONS OF SERVICE QUALITY

LO 17-2

Explain how customers evaluate a retailer's customer service.

When customers evaluate customer service, they compare their perceptions of the service they receive with their expectations. Customers are satisfied when the perceived service meets or exceeds their expectations. They are dissatisfied when they feel that the service falls below their expectations.

So, when retailers attempt to differentiate their offerings by developing a reputation for outstanding customer service, they need to consider both the perception of the actual service offered and the expectations of their customers.

Perceived Service

Customers' perceptions of a retailer's customer service depend on the actual service delivered. However, because services are intangible, it is difficult for customers to evaluate the service offered by retailers accurately. Customers are often influenced by the manner in which employees provide the service, not just the outcome.[18] Consider the following situation: A customer goes to return an electric toothbrush that is not working properly to a retailer with a no-questions-asked, money-back return policy. In one case, the employee asks the customer for a receipt, checks to see if the receipt shows that the toothbrush was bought from the retailer,

Great customer service is always a priority at Nordstrom.

examines the toothbrush to see if it really doesn't work properly, completes some paperwork while the customer is waiting, and finally gives the customer the amount paid for the toothbrush in cash. In a second case, the store employee simply asks the customer how much he paid and gives him a cash refund. The two cases have the same outcome: The customer gets a cash refund. But the customer might be dissatisfied in the first case because the employee appeared not to trust the customer and took too much time providing the refund. In most situations, employees have an important impact on the process of providing services and thus on the customer's eventual satisfaction with the services.

Five customer service characteristics that affect perceptions of service quality are reliability, assurance, tangibility, empathy, and responsiveness.[19] Fashion retailer Nordstrom is renowned for its customer service. Let's look at how it addresses each of these five service characteristics.[20]

Reliability   **Reliability** is the ability to perform the service dependably and accurately, such as performing the service as promised or contracted or meeting promised delivery dates. To ensure service reliability, new Nordstrom salespeople go through training and extensive mentoring by managers and seasoned salespeople. Employees are trained to give their customer the best service possible every time based on the cardinal rule: "Use good judgment in all situations."[21] Good judgment at Nordstrom involves such issues as the following: Always check with the alteration department before promising a pick-up date. Don't answer any questions you don't know the answer to. Check with someone if you don't know the answer. Inaccurate information only frustrates customers.

Assurance   **Assurance** is the knowledge and courtesy of employees and their ability to convey trust and confidence. Trust and confidence are particularly important at Nordstrom, where merchandise can be relatively expensive and customers rely on the good taste and fashion judgment of its sales associates. When a customer asks "How do I look in this dress?" she doesn't always want to hear, "Great!" She wants a truthful answer that shows knowledge of the products and fashions, as well as an eye toward what is best for her. If the customer is sold something that, upon reflection, does not meet her needs or look good on her, Nordstrom may lose her as a customer forever. Thus, looking out for what is best for the customer is the best strategy for long-term customer retention.

Tangibility   **Tangibility** is associated with the appearances of physical facilities, equipment, personnel, and communication materials. Nordstrom has always prided itself in providing a modern, but classic ambience with wide unobstructed aisles. It maintains a consistent image throughout all the touch points with its customers including Nordstrom Rack, its catalogs, and other media like Facebook, Twitter, YouTube, and an array of fashion and photo-sharing sites.[22]

Empathy   **Empathy** refers to the caring, individualized attention provided to customers. Nordstrom attempts to hire people that are knowledgeable about fashion. But equally important, they must love helping others. To aide in the empathy dimension of service quality, Nordstrom provides salespeople with CRM software that tracks customer information such as preferences for brands and sizes and describes what was purchased in the past. Sales representatives often proactively call customers to alert them to new shipments of their favorite brands. If a customer's favored salesperson is unavailable when she comes in, another salesperson can access her record to better provide that famous individualized attention.

Responsiveness   **Responsiveness** means to provide customer service personnel and sales associates that really want to help customers and provide that service promptly. Customers don't have to go looking for salespeople to ring up a sale. Nor do salespeople disappear when a customer appears with a bag full of returns. Personnel are always eager to help at Nordstrom, and the retailer continues to find new ways to become more responsive. For example, it is experimenting with curbside pickup services for alterations. Whereas in the past shoppers who needed their pants hemmed or their jackets taken in had to come into the store multiple times—once to select the clothing, possibly again to be fitted by the tailor, and then a third time to retrieve their altered items—today they can pull up outside the store, call or text a dedicated number, and simply wait to have their newly altered clothes brought directly to the car. Whether they are picking up an online order or an alteration, customers also can contact in-store employees to announce that they have arrived, so that staffers know when to head out the doors with the pickup items.[23]

   Another way that Nordstrom achieves excellent service is by promptly solving customers' problems, because it empowers its employees. For example, a Nordstrom shoe sales associate decided to break up two pairs of shoes, one a size 10 and the other a size 10½, to sell a hard-to-fit customer. Although the other two shoes were unsalable and therefore made for an unprofitable sale, the customer purchased five other pairs that day and became a loyal Nordstrom customer as a result. Empowering service providers with a rule like "Use your best judgment" might cause chaos at some stores, but it speeds the sales transaction at Nordstrom.

Role of Expectations

In addition to the perceptions of the actual service delivered, expectations affect the judgment of service quality. Customer expectations are based on a customer's knowledge and experiences. For example, on the basis of past experiences, customers have different expectations for the quality of service offered by different types of retailers. Customers expect a traditional supermarket to provide convenient parking, be open from early morning to late evening, have an intuitive layout, position and display products so they can be easily found, and offer a fast and pleasant checkout experience. They do not expect the supermarket to have store employees stationed in the aisle to offer information about groceries or show them how to prepare meals. When these unexpected services are offered, and the services are important to them, then customers are delighted—the retailer has significantly exceeded their expectations. However, when the same customers shop in a specialty food store like Whole Foods Market, they expect the store to have knowledgeable employees who can provide expert information

With the growing recognition that approximately two-thirds of the decisions about home improvements are made by women, Home Depot has initiated what some observers call an "about-face" in its effort to appeal more effectively to female consumers, as well as compete better with its main rival, Lowe's. This radical change in direction consists of several key initiatives.

First, Home Depot is renovating its stores. Once the aisles purposefully embraced a sort of construction site feel, with wheeled pallets and jumbled displays of nuts and bolts. But new renovations will start with better lighting and cleaner product displays. In addition, greeters at the entrance will now be posted to help people find what they need.

Second, the greeters are not the only nod to improving customer service. Devices mounted in stores will enable shoppers to check prices or find particular items, without having to seek out an employee. At the same time, Home Depot is providing more training to employees, encouraging them to provide better and more effective assistance to those shoppers who might be less familiar with hardware and home improvement projects.

Third, new product lines feature familiar names such as Martha Stewart and expand the inventory mix to include more décor and convenience items for the household. The idea is to enhance the shopping experience for the entire family because it carries items for parents of either gender, as well as small projects for kids.

Fourth, if shoppers want to install their new purchases on their own, Home Depot offers do-it-yourself workshops in

As part of its strategy to appeal more to women, Home Depot offers do-it-yourself workshops in stores, as well as online video tutorials.

stores, as well as online video tutorials. If they want to have the product installed by professionals, Home Depot provides a list of qualified, rated subcontractors available for the work. Thus the retailer is hoping to become the source for all its customers' home improvement needs, from the smallest project to the largest remodeling.

Source: James M. Kerr, "How Appealing to Women Has Helped The Home Depot," ManagementIssues.com, October 3, 2014.

and courteous assistance. At Home Depot, customers might have grown to expect a sort of warehouse of pallets, but as Retailing View 17.1 notes, the retailer hopes to attract female customers with better, more comprehensive services, as well as a cleaner and better organized environment.

Some examples of unexpected positive service experiences are:

- A restaurant that sends customers who have had too much to drink home in a taxi and then delivers their cars in the morning.

- A jewelry store that cleans customers' jewelry and replaces batteries in watches for free.

- A men's store that sews numbered tags on each garment so that the customer will know what goes together.

Customers are also interacting with companies using various technologies. Retailers that do not offer omnichannel services are not favorably viewed. Customers still expect good service, which is defined by companies' responsiveness, flexibility, dependability, ease of access, apologies, or compensation when necessary. But now they expect this level of service even when people are not involved. The activities that retailers take to close the gap between customer expectations and perceptions of the actual service delivered are discussed in the following sections.

THE GAPS MODEL FOR IMPROVING RETAIL CUSTOMER SERVICE QUALITY

LO 17-3

Indicate the activities a retailer can undertake to provide high-quality customer service.

When the customer's perception of the service delivered by a retailer fails to meet the customer's expectations, a **service gap** results. Exhibit 17–1 illustrates four gaps that contribute to the service gap:

1. The **knowledge gap** reflects the difference between customers' expectations and the retailer's perception of those customer expectations. Retailers can close this gap by developing a better understanding of customer expectations and perceptions.

2. The **standards gap** pertains to the difference between the retailer's knowledge of customers' perceptions and expectations and the service standards it sets. By setting appropriate service standards and measuring service performance, retailers can close this gap.

3. The **delivery gap** is the difference between the retailer's service standards and the actual service it provides to customers. This gap can be reduced by getting employees to meet or exceed service standards through training and/or appropriate incentives.

4. The **communication gap** is the difference between the actual service provided to customers and the service that the retailer's promotion program promises. When retailers are more realistic about the services they can provide, customer expectations can be managed effectively to close this gap.[24]

Knowing What Customers Want: The Knowledge Gap

The first step in providing good service is knowing what customers want, need, and expect and then using this information to improve customer service.[25]

When retailers lack this information, they can make poor decisions. For example, a supermarket might hire extra people to make sure the shelves are stocked and organized so that customers will find what they want. But the supermarket's service perceptions

EXHIBIT 17–1   Gaps Model for Improving Retail Service Quality

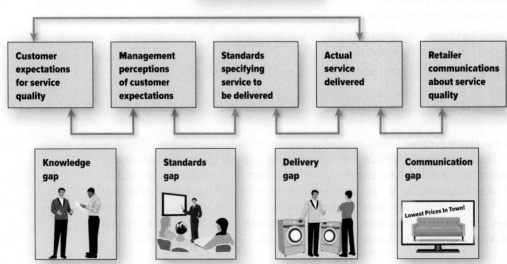

may not improve because the supermarket did not realize that its customers were most concerned about waiting in the checkout line. From the customer's perspective, the supermarket's service would improve if the extra employees were used to open more checkout lines rather than to stock shelves.

Retailers can reduce the knowledge gap and develop a better understanding of customer expectations by undertaking customer research, increasing interactions between retail managers and customers, and improving communication between managers and the employees who provide customer service.[26] Retailers use a variety of approaches for assessing customer perceptions and expectations of customer service.

Social Media   Retailers can learn a lot about their customer expectations and perceptions of their service quality by monitoring what they say about the retailer's offering and the offerings of competitors on their social networks, blogs, review sites, and what they are posting on sites like YouTube and Flickr. Numerous retailers have started to use a technique known as **sentiment analysis** to assess the favorableness (or lack of favorableness) in their customers' sentiments by monitoring these social media. Scouring millions of sites with sentiment analysis techniques provides new insights into what consumers really think. Retailers plugged into this real-time information can become more nimble, allowing for quick changes, such as product rollouts, new advertising campaigns, or responses to customer complaints. For example, when Target suffered a major data breach, it relied on its extensive sentiment analysis capabilities to listen closely to customers' questions and concerns. The resulting insights into some negative consumer sentiments led the retailer to develop a careful response. It avoided its usual quirky advertising, temporarily halted promotions of its social responsibility, and stopped pushing its branded credit cards. By gauging customers' sentiments, Target realized that these sorts of communications could easily backfire among people who had been harmed by the data breach, so it quickly shifted its techniques until it could regain their confidence and positive perceptions.[27]

Surveys, Panels, and Contests   Many retailers survey customers immediately after a retail transaction has occurred. For example, airlines, automobile dealers, hotels, and restaurants give customers surveys, encourage them to take an online survey, or call them on the phone to ask them questions about their service experience, such as how helpful, friendly, and professional the employees were.

Although some retailers use surveys as just described, others conduct interview panels of 10 to 15 customers to gain insights into expectations and perceptions. For example, some store managers meet once a month for an hour with a select group of customers who are asked to provide information about their experiences in the store and offer suggestions for improving service.

When Domino's undertook a massive revamp of its image, it focused largely on customer feedback. Pizza connoisseurs had long complained about its cardboard crust and use of canned tomatoes. The delivery chain improved its quality, but to enhance people's expectations, it needed to find out if customers really thought its food was better. Rather than traditional surveys, Domino's sponsored a photo contest: Take a picture of your pizza right after it arrives and upload it to a website. Great-looking food shots helped convince others that Domino's was providing a quality product. Problematic shots helped Domino's identify service concerns. And if customers' pictures ultimately appeared in ads, they earned cash prizes.[28]

Interact with Customers, Either Directly or through Observation   Owner-managers of small retail firms typically have daily contact with their customers and get accurate, firsthand information about them. Some managers go through the receipts from each day and select customers who have made particularly large or small purchases. They call these customers and ask them what they liked or did not like about the store. These customer contacts not only provide information but also indicate the retailer's interest in providing good service. Because the responses can be linked to a specific encounter, they also provide a method for rewarding employees who provide good service and correcting those who exhibit poor performance.

In large retail firms, managers often learn about customers through reports, so they may miss the rich information provided by direct contact with customers. Disney offers a stellar example of a large firm that constantly interacts with customers to learn about them and their preferences. For example, through careful observation, Disney learned that visitors to its parks will carry a piece of trash approximately 27 paces before dropping it on the ground. So the entertainment conglomerate made sure to place trash receptacles every 27 paces throughout its parks. In its consulting with other service providers, Disney has suggested ways they can interact better, too.[29]

Customer Complaints   Complaints allow retailers to interact with their customers and acquire detailed information about their service and merchandise. Handling complaints is an inexpensive means to isolate and correct service problems.[30] Catalog and Internet retailer L.L.Bean keeps track of all complaints and reasons for returned merchandise. These complaints and returns are summarized daily and given to customer service representatives so that they can improve their service. The information is also used by buyers to improve vendor merchandise.

Although customer complaints can provide useful information, retailers cannot rely solely on this source of market information. Some customers express inappropriate biases in their complaints, related more to the person providing the service than the level of service actually provided. Other customers simply like to complain, regardless of whether the service was good or bad, or whether a service failure was due to the actions of the frontline employee or a situation outside of her or his control.[31] Also, dissatisfied customers typically do not complain directly to retailers that fail them; they just stop shopping there. However, the validity of customer complaints may be improving as customers turn to blogs, review sites (e.g., Yelp), retailers' own online review systems, and customer service messaging systems more frequently. These methods of interacting with retailers can be useful, because they tend to feature very frank comments, compared with information gathered through more traditional research methods.

Feedback from Store Employees   Salespeople and other employees in regular contact with customers often have a good understanding of customer service expectations and problems. This information can improve service quality if the employees are encouraged to communicate their experiences and the information is collected and analyzed in a systematic way that can be used by higher-level managers.[32]

Using Customer Research in a Timely Manner   Collecting information about customer expectations and perceptions is not enough. The knowledge gap diminishes only when retailers use this information in a timely manner to improve service. Reporting the July service performance in December makes it hard for employees to reflect on the reason for the reported performance. Finally, feedback must be prominently presented so that service providers are aware of their performance. For example, at a major hotel chain, the front-desk personnel's performance feedback is displayed behind the front desk, while restaurant personnel's performance feedback is displayed behind the door to the kitchen. The next section reviews several approaches for reducing the service standards gap.

Setting Service Standards: The Standards Gap

After retailers gather information about customer service expectations and perceptions, the next step is to use this information to set standards and develop systems for delivering high-quality service. To close the standards gap, retailers need to (1) commit their firms to providing high-quality service, (2) define the role of service providers, (3) set service goals, and (4) measure service performance.

Commitment to Service Quality   Service excellence is achieved only when top management provides leadership and demonstrates commitment. Top management must be willing to accept the temporary difficulties and even the increased costs associated with improving service quality. This commitment needs to be demonstrated to the employees charged with providing the service.

Top management's commitment sets service quality standards, but store managers are the key to achieving those standards. Store managers must see that their efforts to provide service quality are noticed and rewarded. Providing incentives based on service quality makes service an important personal goal, so rather than bonuses based only on store sales and profit, part of store managers' bonuses should be determined by the level of service provided.[33] For example, some retailers use the results of customer satisfaction studies to help determine bonuses.

Defining the Role of Service Providers   Managers can tell service providers that they need to provide excellent service but not clearly indicate what excellent service means. Without a clear definition of the retailer's expectations, service providers are directionless.

The Ritz-Carlton Hotel Company, winner of multiple Malcolm Baldrige National Quality Awards, has its "Gold Standards" printed on a wallet-sized card carried by all employees. The card contains the hotel's motto ("We Are Ladies and Gentlemen Serving Ladies and Gentlemen"), the three steps for high-quality service (warm and sincere greeting, anticipation and fulfillment of each guest's needs, and fond farewell), and 12 basic rules for Ritz-Carlton employees, including "I build strong relationships and create Ritz-Carlton guests for life" (No. 1) and "I am proud of my professional appearance, language, and behavior" (No. 10).[34]

The golden rules for Zappos are a little different, reflecting its market and the customer expectations of an online retailer versus a luxury hotel. But the goal of excellent customer service is the same. That is, Zappos may sell shoes, apparel, and accessories, but it really has built its business on its superb service. The company's core values stress that customer satisfaction is more important than cost cutting; that message permeates every single aspect of its operations. The goal is to "wow" each customer in every interaction. Instilling such values in every worker begins with the interview and training process. During training, which lasts up to five weeks, all new employees are required to work in the call center. Anyone who thinks the assignment is beneath them is paid for his or her time and shown the door. Trainees are not given a script or a time limit for calls. Instead, workers are urged to creatively solve problems, even if customer satisfaction means doing something a little "weird," like buying shoes from a competing retailer for a customer in distress—and even footing the bill for their delivery. Zappos's shopping procedures are also designed to please. Customers are encouraged to order multiple sizes and colors of an item, so they can touch, feel, and try on prospective purchases. Returned goods ship free for up to a year. And Zappos likes to impress customers with speedy delivery, so it ships items faster than its website indicates. Customers who use the Zappos app get free next-day shipping and earn VIP points for other rewards. Employees who meet Zappos's unconventional customer service standards are rewarded. Its most common salaried job, fulfillment center process manager, is paid more than $32,000 a year, and the company has been on *Forbes* "100 Best Companies to Work for" for seven years.[35]

Setting Service Goals   To deliver consistent, high-quality service, retailers need to establish goals or standards to guide employees. These goals should be based on customers' needs and expectations, rather than the expediency and efficiency of the business's operations. For example, a retailer might set a goal that all monthly bills are to be mailed five days before the end of the month. This goal reduces the retailer's accounts receivable but offers no benefit to customers.

According to a recent study, shoppers who contact retailers through electronic channels expect rapid responses: within about 6 hours for both e-mail and Facebook, and within 1 hour for Twitter. But only about 20 percent of today's retailers have the capacity and ability to respond to customer requests through Twitter, and a little more than half even have operations in place to respond through Facebook. Even when they have these capabilities in place, retailers are not using them very effectively. For example, a customer tweeting a complaint or request for support would wait an average of 31 hours for a response. This 30-hour wait is significant, especially considering that failed customer service on a social media platform is nearly tailor-made for going viral. Therefore, retailers may need to develop new standards related to social media responsiveness, to ensure they meet customers' demands.[36]

Employees also must be motivated to achieve service goals. To do so, retailers must set goals that are specific, measurable, and participatory—in the sense that the employees participated in setting them. Vague goals—such as "Approach customers when they enter the selling area" or "Respond to e-mails as soon as possible"—don't fully specify what employees should do, nor do they offer an opportunity to assess employee performance. Better goals would be "All customers should be approached by a salesperson within 30 seconds after entering a selling area" or "All e-mails should be responded to within three hours." These goals are both specific and measurable. Employee participation in setting service standards also leads to better understanding and greater acceptance of those goals, whereas store employees tend to resent and resist goals arbitrarily imposed on them by management. See Chapter 15 for more about goal setting. Retailing View 17.2 considers some problems and solutions associated with setting standards for the time customers wait to be served.

Measuring Service Performance   Retailers need to assess service quality continuously to ensure that goals will be achieved. Many retailers conduct periodic customer surveys to assess service quality. Retailers also use **mystery shoppers** to assess

17.2   RETAILING VIEW   Using Analytics to Reduce Wait Time at Kroger

Shopping for groceries is rarely considered a pleasant task. But what makes the experience so odious? As Kroger found out when it asked customers, the answer is often the long checkout lines. To help alleviate the problem, it began analyzing customer data to find an answer to a simple question: What would happen if it could open up a lane exactly when needed? The answer was that it could significantly improve customer satisfaction. So Kroger developed QueVision.

QueVision combines infrared sensors over store doors and cash registers, predictive analytics, and real-time data feeds from point-of-sale systems to calculate how many registers are needed and what the actual wait times are, all in real time. Wait times appear on a screen at the front of the store. The overall goal of the combined system is to ensure there is never more than one person ahead of any shopper in the checkout line.

This technology has been so successful that it has cut the average wait time for customers from more than 4 minutes to less than 30 seconds. QueVision also has had some unexpected positive consequences, in the form of happier employees. Friendly associates are really important for defining customer-oriented metrics. Although the math might not have predicted it, the cashier friendliness metric, as measured by customer surveys, has improved throughout the company by approximately 24 percent. Shorter lines make customers happy, and when employees encounter happy customers, they're happier too. Kroger also uses its QueVision data in more detailed simulations. It has correlated enough data to

Customers' satisfaction decreases if they have to wait in checkout lines too long or if they feel others who arrive later are checked out before them.

keep people moving in the front of stores, including checkout lines, even in stores with unusual layouts. QueVision data also have helped Kroger evaluate new shopping systems, such as self-checkout.

Source: "About Kroger," http://www.thekrogerco.com/about-kroger; Laurianne McLaughlin, "Kroger Solves Top Customer Issue: Long Lines," *InformationWeek*, April 2, 2014, http://www.informationweek.com/strategic-cio/executive-insights-and-innovation/kroger-solves-top-customer-issue-long-lines/d/d-id/1141541?page_number=1.

their service quality. These professional shoppers visit stores to assess the service provided by store employees and the presentation of merchandise. Some retailers use their own employees as mystery shoppers, but most contract with an outside firm to provide the assessment.

The retailer typically informs salespeople that they have "been shopped" and provides feedback from the mystery shopper's report. Some retailers offer rewards to sales associates who receive high marks and schedule follow-up visits to sales associates who prompt low evaluations.

Meeting and Exceeding Service Standards: The Delivery Gap

To reduce the delivery gap and provide service that exceeds standards, retailers must give service providers the necessary information and training, empower employees to act in the customers' and firm's best interests, provide instrumental and emotional support, provide appropriate incentives, improve internal communications, and use technology.

Give Information and Training   Service providers need to know about the retailer's service standards and the merchandise it offers, as well as the customers' needs. With this information, employees can answer customers' questions and suggest products. This knowledge also instills confidence and a sense of competence, which is needed to overcome service problems.

Because Steve Jobs believed "Good artists copy; great artists steal," Apple stores have used the Ritz-Carlton model to train its employees. Staffers in Apple stores are encouraged to greet and say farewell to customers warmly. They are taught to "own" each customer interaction, even if it is not their specific job. In addition, Apple personnel are encouraged to anticipate needs, even if the customer doesn't express them. A PC user who keeps stopping by the store might need some encouragement about how easily Apple will help him convert his files, for example.[37]

Taking inspiration from the popularity of Apple stores, BMW is completely changing the car-buying experience for its customers too. Rather than staffing huge cadres of salespeople who sit in individual showroom cubicles, it has begun hiring "product geniuses" to explain the technology in its automobiles to customers. In eliminating the balloons and banners that have traditionally marked the carnival-like atmosphere of automotive dealerships, BMW instead seeks to instead create an environment that is more digital and hands-on, with in-store technology and regional fleets that allow customers to find cars to test drive easily.[38]

Service providers also need specific training in interpersonal skills. Dealing with customers is hard—particularly when they are upset or angry. All service providers, even those who work for retailers that provide excellent service, encounter dissatisfied customers. Through training, employees can learn to provide better service and cope with the stress caused by disgruntled customers. Specific service providers typically get designated to interact with and provide service to customers. However, all retail employees should be prepared to deal with customers.[39]

Empower Service Employees   **Empowerment** means allowing employees at the firm's lowest levels to make important decisions regarding how service will be provided to customers. When the employees responsible for providing service are authorized to make important decisions, service quality improves.[40] When they are not, even the best employee winds up being stymied in his or her efforts to please the customer. In call centers, this problem seems particularly acute. A customer who calls in with a product complaint and encounters a polite, respectful, professional service employee who lacks the authority to issue a refund or mail out a replacement is not a satisfied customer. In this case, though, the fault is the company's, not the employee's.[41]

Although airlines aren't typically known for customer service, Southwest Airlines encourages its employees to go above and beyond for its customers. For example, when a family was seeing off their father for a six-month deployment, Southwest employees allowed the family to go with him to the gate and even allowed them to go on the plane to say goodbye.[42]

However, empowering service providers can be difficult.[43] Some employees prefer to have the appropriate behaviors clearly defined for them. They do not want to spend the time learning how to make decisions or assume the risks of making mistakes. For example, a bank found that when it empowered its tellers, the tellers were afraid to make decisions about large sums of money. The bank had to develop decision guideposts and rules until tellers felt more comfortable.

In some cases, the benefits of empowering service providers may not justify the costs. If a retailer uses a standardized service delivery approach like McDonald's, the cost of hiring, training, and supporting empowerment may not lead to consistent and superior service delivery. Also, studies have found that empowerment is not embraced by employees in different cultures. For example, employees in Latin America expect their managers to possess all the information needed to make good business decisions. The role of employees is not to make business decisions; their job is to carry out the decisions of managers.[44]

Provide Instrumental and Emotional Support

Service providers need to have **instrumental support** (appropriate systems and equipment) to deliver the service desired by customers. Customers in need of an oil change expect and get a quick turnaround at Jiffy Lube because the entire operation, including the service personnel, equipment, and layout of the building, is designed to get customer's vehicles in and out in a "jiffy."

In addition to instrumental support, service providers need emotional support from their coworkers and supervisors. **Emotional support** involves demonstrating a concern for the well-being of others. Dealing with customer problems and maintaining a smile in difficult and stressful situations can be psychologically demanding. Service providers need to maintain a supportive, understanding atmosphere and attitude to deal with these demands effectively.[45] When "The customer is always right" is a business mantra, service employees also tend to feel as if they have to accept the cliché that their job is to "grin and bear it." Instead, retail employers should recognize just how stressful customer interactions can be, as well as assess the resulting effects on their employees' morale and performance.[46] Companies use various methods to reduce the stress that their service employees experience. Physical activity often helps relieve stress, so many employers offer fitness clinics or yoga classes. To tend to emotional stressors more directly, other retailers install entertainment/media rooms or provide massages in stores. Companies also can offer coaching on how to deal with the abuse meted out by angry customers. For example, call-center employees are encouraged not to take insults personally, fix problems, avoid engaging in arguments, and try to find the root issues of callers' complaints.[47]

Provide Incentives

As discussed in Chapter 15, many retailers use incentives, like paying commissions on sales, to motivate employees.[48] If service personnel feel incentivized and satisfied with their rewards, they likely offer improved productivity. But commissions on sales also can decrease customer service and job satisfaction while motivating high-pressure selling, which leads to customer dissatisfaction. Therefore, incentives should aim to improve customer service more effectively. When American Express started training and incentivizing its sales staff to engage customers, it empowered them by eliminating sales scripts or time limits on calls. It also radically changed the compensation system. Incentive pay is now based on customer satisfaction feedback. The result was a 10 percent increase in customer spending on American Express products, as well as a 5 percent bump in revenue.[49]

Improve Internal Communications

When providing customer service, frontline service providers often must manage a conflict between customers' and their employer's needs.[50] For example, retailers expect their sales associates to encourage customers to make multiple purchases and buy more expensive items;[51] customers are looking for the best value choices that fit their needs. Sales associates therefore may be conflicted between meeting corporate and customer goals.

Retailers can reduce such conflicts by issuing clear guidelines and policies concerning service and explaining the rationale for these policies. For example, training should teach employees to apologize for a service failure, even if the failure was caused by someone else in the organization or was a result of something the customer did. It is difficult for many people to apologize for something that is not their fault. But if employees realize that an apology for a service failure can help retain the customer, they should also recognize that it is necessary and therefore apologize for any service failure.

Conflicts can also arise when retailers set goals that are inconsistent with the other behaviors expected from store employees. For example, as we discussed in Chapter 15, if salespeople are expected to provide customer service, they should be evaluated and compensated on the service they provide, not just the sales they make.

Finally, conflicts can arise between different areas of the firm. A men's specialty store known for its high levels of customer service has salespeople who promise rapid alterations and deliveries to please their customers. Unfortunately, the alterations department includes two elderly tailors who work at their own speed, regardless of the workload. From time to time, management must step in to temper the salespeople's promises and reallocate priorities for the tailors.

Use Technology   Retailers have been actively engaged in implementing a vast variety of technology tools in their stores and websites to help their customers.[52] Retailing View 17.3 considers the implications of the arrival of futuristic service

---

RETAILING VIEW   Service-Providing Retail Robots   17.3

For shy or introverted shoppers who find the prospect of interacting with salesclerks unpleasant, one of Sprint's Japanese divisions may have just the answer: robots that can help people complete their entire sales transaction. The remarkable and technologically advanced Pepper robots are vaguely humanoid in their design, but they are programmed solely and specifically to provide service to customers seeking help in making a purchase.

Although Pepper is available for various retail and service uses (including banks, hotels, and hospitals), at the SoftBank Sprint store, the robots greet people as they enter the stores, explain how the various phones work and what features they offer, and make suggestions about which products and plans make the most sense for customers. Then they complete the transaction, enabling the customer to walk out of the store with a new phone and plan, without ever speaking with another person.

Pepper's software enables it to recognize not just human speech but bodily movements too. It is programmed to gauge the emotion expressed in human voices as well, to ensure that its responses are appropriate and matched with the shopper's needs. The robots have proven highly popular already, such that the manufacturer is having trouble keeping up with demand.

There's no reason to expect that demand to slow, either. Many consumers appear to appreciate the efficiency of working with a robot, which can access vast amounts of information and is not subject to any sort of emotional responses, even if the retail transaction becomes difficult. Research also has shown that many of the tasks that sales and service people currently provide could be automated. For example, one study indicated that nearly half of the functions currently provided

Sprint's Japanese divisions use Pepper robots to greet people, explain how the various phones work and what features they offer, and make suggestions about which products and plans make the most sense for customers.

mostly by human cashiers could easily be automated. Doing so would clearly lead to cost benefits for retailers, while potentially appealing even more to customers. It would, at the same time, eliminate many entry-level jobs that are important to those holding them and to the economy in general. And for every customer who appreciates the efficiency of dealing with a machine, there will be another that craves the personal human interaction. Only time will tell how this technology versus humanity battle will turn out.

Source: Tom Ryan, "Will Humans Shop at a Store Run Mostly by Robots?," *Retail-Wire,* February 1, 2016.

robots in retail locations. But more widespread technologies already in place include self-scan checkout stations, web-linked kiosks, service personnel equipped with iPads, various types of apps, digital displays, online agents, and QR codes. These technologies help customers find and learn more about products and services offered. They also enable faster and more efficient payment. For the service personnel, these technologies improve their ability to offer good service to customers, including up-to-date product information and access to merchandise available from an online channel if it is not in stock at the store.[53]

Communicating the Service Promise: The Communication Gap

The fourth factor leading to a customer service gap is the difference between the service promised by the retailer and the service actually delivered. Overstating the service offered raises customer expectations. Then, if the retailer fails to follow through by improving actual customer service, expectations exceed perceived service, and customers are dissatisfied. For example, if an apparel store advertises free alterations, and then informs customers that it is free only on full-priced items, customers shopping the sales racks may be disappointed. Raising expectations beyond what can be delivered might bring in more customers initially, but it can also create dissatisfaction and reduce repeat business. Disgruntled customers may then write negative online reviews or use social media such as Twitter to express their dissatisfaction. The communication gap can be reduced by making realistic commitments and managing customer expectations.

Realistic Commitments   Promotion programs are typically developed by the marketing department, whereas the store operations division delivers the service. Poor communication between these areas can result in a mismatch between a promotional campaign's promises and the service the store can actually offer. For example, after very successfully promoting its Black Friday sales online, Best Buy attracted far more sales than it was expecting but allowed back-ordering of many products, promising they would arrive in time for Christmas. Two days before Christmas, customers received notifications that products they had purchased online as far back as November would not be delivered in time for the holiday. Consumer backlash was immediate and intense, including designations of the retailer as "The Grinch That Stole Christmas." Although it apologized through select media outlets, it failed to communicate through Twitter or Facebook—two vehicles the chain had used to create the initial demand.[54]

Managing Customer Expectations   How can a retailer communicate realistic service expectations without losing business to a competitor that makes inflated service claims? At CVS, customers can download a mobile app that tells them when their prescriptions are ready, lists the wait times at the local MinuteClinic, allows them to make an appointment with the clinic staff, and sends them alerts 30 minutes before their appointment. Thus the drugstore avoids annoying customers by making them wait and also clears its aisles of frustrated, ill, waiting shoppers.[55]

Another solution to managing customers' expectations about their wait time relies more on personalized rather than standardized service: When checkout personnel chat with customers, those customers perceive the time in the queue as shorter.[56]

Information presented at the point of sale also can be used to manage expectations. For example, theme parks and restaurants indicate the waiting time for an attraction or a table. Online retailers tell their customers whether merchandise is in stock and when customers can expect to receive it. Providing accurate information can increase customer satisfaction, even when customers must wait longer than desired.

Sometimes service problems are caused by customers. Customers may use an invalid credit card to pay for merchandise, not take time to try on a suit and have it altered properly, or use a product incorrectly because they fail to read the instructions. Communication programs can inform customers about their role and responsibility in getting good service and give tips on how to get better service, such as the best times of the day to shop and the retailer's policies and procedures for handling problems.

SERVICE RECOVERY

LO 17-4

Articulate retailers' service failure strategies.

The delivery of customer service is inherently inconsistent, so service failures are bound to arise. Rather than dwelling on negative aspects of customer problems, retailers should focus on the positive opportunities the problems generate. Service problems and complaints are an excellent source of information about the retailer's offering (its merchandise and service). Armed with this information, retailers can make changes to increase their customers' satisfaction.[57]

Service problems also enable a retailer to demonstrate its commitment to providing high-quality customer service. By encouraging complaints and handling problems, a retailer has an opportunity to strengthen its relationship with its customers. Effective service recovery efforts significantly increase customer satisfaction, purchase intentions, and positive word of mouth. However, postrecovery satisfaction generally is less than the satisfaction level before the service failure.[58]

Most retailers have standard policies for handling problems. If a correctable problem is identified, such as defective merchandise, many retailers will make restitution on the spot and apologize for inconveniencing the customer. The retailer will offer replacement merchandise, a credit toward future purchases, or a cash refund.

In many cases, the cause of the problem may be hard to identify (did the salesperson really insult the customer?), uncorrectable (the store had to close due to bad weather), or a result of the customer's unusual expectations (the customer didn't like his haircut). In these cases, service recovery might be more difficult. The steps in effective service recovery are (1) listen to the customer, (2) provide a fair solution, and (3) resolve the problem quickly.[59]

Listening to Customers

Customers can become very emotional about their real or imaginary problems with a retailer. Often, this emotional reaction can be reduced by simply giving customers a chance to get their complaints off their chests. Store employees should allow customers to air their complaints without interruption. Interruptions can further irritate customers who may already be emotionally upset. It becomes very hard to reason with or satisfy an angry customer. Customers want a sympathetic response to their complaints. Thus, store employees need to make it clear that they are happy that any problem has been brought to their attention. Satisfactory solutions rarely arise when store employees have an antagonistic attitude or assume that the customer is trying to cheat the store. Store employees should never assume they know what the customer is complaining about or what solution the customer is seeking.[60] As we mentioned previously, more customers are posting their concerns and complaints on blogs and microblogs. In response, Nordstrom conducts sentiment analysis on all of the reviews of its products. This has allowed it to better understand its customers' experiences. For example, when looking through reviews Nordstrom noticed that although customers were giving the products high ratings, there were complaints about shipping. It was even able to break it down to which zip codes were being affected most with damaged boxed. Furthermore, it could also use this information to determine that customers expected nicer boxes for higher-end products.[61]

When resolving customers' problems, service representatives should listen to customers, provide a fair solution, and resolve the problems quickly.

© Rosalrene Betancourt/Alamy Stock Photo

Providing a Fair Solution

Customers like to feel that they are being treated fairly. They base their perceptions of fairness on how they think others were treated in similar situations and with other retailers. Customers' evaluations of complaint resolutions thus are based on distributive fairness and procedural fairness.[62] **Distributive fairness** is a customer's perception of the benefits received compared with his or her costs in terms of inconvenience or monetary loss. What seems to be fair compensation for a service failure for one customer may not be adequate for another. So, service providers probe customers to determine what would help resolve their issue.

Procedural fairness is the perceived fairness of the process used to resolve complaints. Customers typically feel they have been dealt with fairly when store employees follow company guidelines. Guidelines reduce variability in handling complaints and lead customers to believe that they are being treated like everyone else. But rigid adherence to guidelines can have negative effects. Store employees need some flexibility and empowerment capabilities to resolve complaints, or customers may feel they had no influence on the resolution.

Resolving Problems Quickly

Customer satisfaction is affected by the time it takes to get an issue resolved. So, empowering the first contact employee to move quickly to solve a problem increases customer satisfaction. When customers get referred to several different employees, they waste a lot of time repeating their story. Also, the chance of conflicting responses by store employees increases.

Although resolving customer complaints promptly generally increases satisfaction, if the complaints are resolved too abruptly, customers might feel dissatisfied because of the lack of personal attention they received. Retailers must recognize the trade-off between resolving the problem quickly and taking the time to listen to and show concern for the customer.[63]

SUMMARY

LO 17-1 Identify how retailers balance customer service through personalization versus standardization.

Customer service provides an opportunity for retailers to develop a strategic advantage through two basic strategies: personalized or standardized customer service. The personalized approach relies primarily on sales associates. The standardized approach places more emphasis on developing appropriate rules, consistent procedures, and optimum store designs.

LO 17-2 Explain how customers evaluate a retailer's customer service.

Customers evaluate customer service by comparing their perceptions of the service delivered with their expectations. If their perceptions are lower than their expectations, customers are dissatisfied. If their perceptions are better than their expectations, they might be satisfied or even delighted.

LO 17-3 Indicate the activities a retailer can undertake to provide high-quality customer service.

To ensure excellent service, retailers need to close the gaps between the service they deliver and the service that customers expect. To reduce the gap, they need to know what customers expect, set standards to provide the expected service, provide support so that store employees can meet the standards, and realistically communicate the service offered to customers.

LO 17-4 Articulate retailers' service failure strategies.

An effective service recovery requires (1) listening to the customer, (2) providing a fair solution, and (3) resolving the problem quickly. Then retailers must use the information gained from customer complaints and learn from their recovery efforts to prevent service failures in the future.

KEY TERMS

assurance, *465*

communication gap, *468*

customer service, *461*

delivery gap, *468*

distributive fairness, *478*

emotional support, *474*

empathy, *466*

empowerment, *473*

instrumental support, *474*

knowledge gap, *468*

mystery shopper, *472*

personalized service, *462*

GET OUT AND DO IT!

1. **CONTINUING ASSIGNMENT** Go to a local store outlet of the retailer you selected for the continuing assignment and describe and evaluate the service it offers. What service is being offered? Is the service personalized or standardized? Ask the store manager if you may talk to some customers and employees. Choose customers who have made a purchase, customers who have not made a purchase, and customers with a problem (refund, exchange, or complaint). Talk with them about their experiences. Also ask employees what the retailer does to assist and motivate them to provide good service. Then, write a report describing your conversations in which you make suggestions for improving the store's customer service.

2. **INTERNET EXERCISE** Scandit has created a mobile application to increase the speed of the checkout process by enabling customers to scan the products they want to purchase and pay for them on their smartphones. Visit the website (**www.scandit.com/products/mobile-app-suite-retail/self-checkout/**) and review both the application and the provided checkout process. How useful is this application for retailers? What sorts of retailers seem most likely to adopt it?

3. **INTERNET EXERCISE** Visit **www.amazon.com** and shop for a best-selling book. How does the website help you locate best sellers? How does the customer service offered by this website compare with the service you would get at another book retailer's website or in a brick-and-mortar bookstore?

4. **GO SHOPPING** Go to a discount store such as Walmart, a department store, and a specialty store to buy a pair of jeans. After visiting all three, compare and contrast the level of customer service you received in each of the stores. Which store made it easiest to find the pair of jeans you would be interested in buying? Evaluate the perceived service experience in terms of reliability, assurance, tangibility, empathy, and responsiveness. Does the service quality match the store format? Explain your response.

DISCUSSION QUESTIONS AND PROBLEMS

1. Both Nordstrom and McDonald's are noted for their high-quality customer service, but their approaches to providing quality service are different. Describe this difference. Why has each of these retailers elected to use its particular approach?

2. Have you ever worked in a job that required you to provide customer service? If yes, describe the skills you needed and tasks you performed on this job. If no, what skills and abilities would you highlight to a potential employer that was interviewing you for a position that included customer service in the job description?

3. Consider customer service at IKEA. How does this retailer utilize a self-service model to gain a competitive advantage over traditional furniture stores?

4. Assume you're the department manager for menswear in a local department store that emphasizes empowering its managers. A customer returns a dress shirt that's no longer in the package in which it was sold. The customer has no receipt, says that when he opened the package he found that the shirt was torn, and wants cash for the price at which the shirt is now being sold. The shirt was on sale last week when the customer claims to have bought it. What would you do?

5. Consider a situation in which you received poor customer service in a retail store or from a service provider. Did you make the store's management aware of your experience? To whom did you relay this experience? Have you returned to this retailer or provider? For each of these questions, explain your reasons.

6. Gaps analysis provides a systematic method for examining a customer service program's effectiveness. Top management has told an information systems manager that customers are complaining about the long wait to pay for merchandise at the checkout station. Taking the role of the systems manager, identify potential problems that may be occurring with each gap, and suggest how the gap should be closed.

7. How can retailers provide high-quality personalized service? Use an optometrist's office that also sells eyeglass frames and fills prescriptions for contact lenses as your example. How does this retailer's service compare with the service provided by 1-800 CONTACTS?

8. Consider a recent retail service experience you have had, such as a haircut, doctor's appointment, dinner in a restaurant, bank transaction, or product repair (not an exhaustive list), and answer the following questions:
   (a) Describe an excellent service delivery experience.
   (b) What made this quality experience possible?
   (c) Describe a service delivery experience in which you did not receive the performance that you expected.
   (d) What were the problems encountered, and how could they have been resolved?

CHAPTER ENDNOTES

1. "How Rent the Runway Works," https://www.renttherunway.com/how_renting_works.

2. "Who We Are," https://www.renttherunway.com/pages/about.

3. Hilary Milnes, "Rent the Runway Snapchats Customers the Right Fit," *Glossy,* August 15, 2016.

4. Clare O'Connor, "Rent the Runway to Hit $100M Revenues in 2016 Thanks to Unlimited Service," *Forbes,* June 15, 2016.

5. Cara Kelly, "Rent the Runway Unlimited Is a Game Changer," *USA Today,* March 23, 2016.

6. Megan Willett, "I Spent $150 a Month Renting Clothes and Now I'm Never Going Back to Fast Fashion," *Tech Insider,* April 29, 2016.

7. Roland Rust and Ming-Hui Huang, "Optimizing Service Productivity," *Journal of Marketing* 76, no. 2 (2012), pp. 47–66; Robert Cooperman, "Value over Profit," *T1D,* May 2010, pp. 58–62; Dhruv Grewal, Ram Krishnan, and Joan Lindsey-Mullikin, "Building Store Loyalty through Service Strategies," *Journal of Relationship Marketing* 7, no. 4 (2008), pp. 341–358; Valarie Zeithaml, Leonard Berry, and A. Parasuraman, "The Behavioral Consequences of Service Quality," *Journal of Marketing* 60 (April 1996), pp. 31–46.

8. Susan Reda, "Driving Shoppers Crazy," *Stores,* June 2012.

9. Mallory Schlossberg, "25 Retailers with the Best Customer Service," *Business Insider,* November 30, 2015.

10. Kwiseok Kwon, Jinhyung Cho, and Yongtae Park, "How to Best Characterize the Personalization Construct for E-Services," *Expert Systems with Applications* 37 (March 2010), pp. 2232–2240.

11. Raymond D. Jones, "Self-Checkout—What Should Drive the Retailer Decision?," *RetailWire,* April 25, 2012.

12. R. Di Mascio, "The Service Models of Frontline Employees," *Journal of Marketing* 74, no. 4 (2010), pp. 63–80.

13. Hilary Milnes, "How Barneys Is Digitizing Its New York City Flagship Store," *Digiday,* February 15, 2016.

14. "Wine.com Launches Advanced Personalized Recommendations to Enhance Shopping Experience," *MarketWire.com,* May 15, 2012.

15. John Lofstock, "Finding the Right Balance between Automation and People," *RetailWire,* May 23, 2016.

16. Ibid.

17. http://www.ikea.com/ms/en_CA/customer-service/about-shopping/free-ikea-apps/index.html; Ashley Lutz, "IKEA's Strategy for Becoming the World's Most Successful Retailer," *Business Insider,* January 15, 2015; http://www.ikea.com/ms/en_US/the_ikea_story/the_ikea_store/ikea_for_children.html; "IKEA Canada Just Made Shopping Easier," *MarketWatch,* May 1, 2012; "The Secrets of a Successful Store," *Retail Week,* January 13, 2012; "At IKEA, Kids Play in Free Day Care as Parents Shop in Peace," *Orlando Sentinel,* July 15, 2009; Bo Edvardsson and Bo Enquist, *Values-Based Service for Sustainable Business: Lessons from IKEA* (Oxford, UK: Routledge, 2008).

18. J. van Beuningen, Ko de Ruyter, and Martin Wetzels, "The Power of Self-Efficacy Change during Service Provision: Making Your Customers Feel Better about Themselves Pays Off," *Journal of Service Research* 14, no. 1 (2011), pp. 108–125.

19. Dwayne Gremler, Mary Jo Bitner, and Valarie A. Zeithaml, *Services Marketing,* 6th ed. (New York: McGraw-Hill, 2012); A. Parasuraman, V. A. Zeithaml, and L. L. Berry, "SERVQUAL:

20. Am Lyman, "Nordstrom—Great Service for over 100 Years Best Company for 25 Years," Great Place to Work Institute, 2009; www.nordstrom.com.

21. Ashley Lutz, "Nordstrom's Employee Handbook Has Only One Rule," *Business Insider,* October 13, 2014, http://www.businessinsider.com/nordstroms-employee-handbook-2014-10.

22. David Hatch, "Nordstrom in Fashion with Social Media, Mobile Tech," *U.S. News Money, Business, & Economy,* May 15, 2012.

23. George Anderson, "Nordstorm Kicks Its Omnichannel Strategy to the Curb," *RetailWire,* May 5, 2015.

24. The discussion of the gaps model and its implications is based on Valerie Zeithaml, Leonard Berry, and A. Parasuraman, "Communication and Control Processes in the Delivery of Service Quality," *Journal of Marketing* 52 (April 1988), pp. 35–48; Valerie Zeithaml, A. Parasuraman, and Leonard Berry, *Delivering Quality Customer Service* (New York: Free Press, 1990); Doen Nel and Leyland Pitt, "Service Quality in a Retail Environment: Closing the Gaps," *Journal of General Management* 18 (Spring 1993), pp. 37–57.

25. Ann Thomas and Jill Applegate, *Pay Attention! How to Listen, Respond, and Profit from Customer Feedback* (Hoboken, NJ: Wiley, 2010).

26. C. R. Lages and Nigel F. Piercy, "Key Drivers of Frontline Employee Generation of Ideas for Customer Service Improvement," *Journal of Service Research* 15, no. 2 (2012), pp. 215–230.

27. Natalie Zmuda, "Target's CMO Navigates Marketing Post-Security Breach," *Advertising Age,* March 14, 2014.

28. Ira Teinowitz, "Naked Pizza: Domino's Launches Ad Campaign Using 'Real' Photos," *Daily Finance,* July 7, 2010.

29. Brooks Barnes, "In Customer Service Consulting, Disney's Small World Is Growing," *The New York Times,* April 21, 2012.

30. Anne L. Roggeveen, Michael Tsiros, and Dhruv Grewal, "Understanding the Co-Creation Effect: When Does Collaborating with Customers Provide a Lift to Service Recovery?," *Journal of the Academy of Marketing Science* 40, no. 6 (November 2012), pp. 771–790; James C. Ward and Amy L. Ostrom, "Complaining to the Masses: The Role of Protest Framing in Customer-Created Complaint Web Sites," *Journal of Consumer Research* 33 (September 2006), pp. 220–230.

31. Knowledge@Wharton, "The Feedback Loop: More Data Doesn't Always Mean Better Customer Service," April 23, 2014.

32. Cristiana R. Lages and Nigel F. Piercy, "Key Drivers of Frontline Employee Generation of Ideas for Customer Service Improvement," *Journal of Service Research* 15, no. 2 (2012), pp. 215–230.

33. Z. Ma and L. Dub, "Process and Outcome Interdependency in Frontline Service Encounters," *Journal of Marketing* 75, no. 3 (2011), pp. 83–98.

34. The Ritz-Carlton, "Gold Standards," http://www.ritzcarlton.com/en/about/gold-standards; "Organizational Culture Must Be Lived Every Day," April 1, 2015, http://ritzcarltonleadershipcenter.com/2015/04/organizational-culture-is-lived-every-day/.

35. http://www.zappos.com/zappos-apps; http://www.zappos.com/shipping-and-returns; "100 Best Companies to Work

A Multiple-Item Scale for Measuring Consumer Perceptions of Service Quality," *Journal of Retailing* 64, no. 1, (Spring 1988), pp. 12–40.

For," *Forbes,* http://fortune.com/best-companies/2015/zappos-com-86/; "The Customer Service Strategies behind Zappos's Success," *Sharpen,* September 9, 2016; Susan Heathfield, "20 Ways Zappos Reinforces Its Company Culture," *The Balance,* June 28, 2016, https://www.thebalance.com/zappos-company-culture-1918813.

36. Tom Ryan, "Why Is Social Media Not Working for Customer Service?," *RetailWire,* November 9, 2015.

37. Carmine Gallo, "How the Ritz-Carlton Inspired the Apple Store," *Forbes,* April 10, 2012.

38. Christina Rogers and Joseph B. White, "BMW Tosses Salesmen for 'Geniuses,' " *The Wall Street Journal,* February 19, 2014.

39. Valarie Zeithaml, *Delivering Quality Service* (New York: Free Press, 2010).

40. Josh Bernoff and Ted Schadler, *Empowered: Unleash Your Employees, Energize Your Customers, and Transform Your Business* (Boston: Harvard Business Press, 2010).

41. Anthony Leaper, "How to Fail Your Call Centers," *Forbes,* May 13, 2012.

42. Carmine Gallo, "Southwest Airlines Motivates Its Employees with a Purpose Bigger Than a Paycheck," *Forbes,* January 21, 2014.

43. Kimmy Wa Chan and Wing Lam, "The Trade-Off of Servicing Empowerment on Employees' Service Performance: Examining the Underlying Motivation and Workload Mechanisms," *Journal of the Academy of Marketing Science* 39, no. 4 (2011), pp. 609–628.

44. Jyh-Shen Chiou and Tung-Zong Chang, "The Effect of Management Leadership Style on Marketing Orientation, Service Quality, and Financial Results: A Cross-Cultural Study," *Journal of Global Marketing* 22 (April 2009), pp. 95–107.

45. Jason Colquitt, Jeffery LePine, and Michael Wesson, *Organizational Behavior: Improving Performance and Commitment in the Workplace,* 2nd ed. (Burr Ridge, IL: McGraw-Hill, 2010); Felicitas M. Morhart, Walter Herzog, and Torsten Tomczak, "Brand-Specific Leadership: Turning Employees into Brand Champions," *Journal of Marketing* 73 (September 2009), pp. 122–142.

46. Guy Winch, "The Last Bullying Frontier," *Psychology Today,* March 31, 2011.

47. Roberto L. Bacasong, "Overcoming Call Center Stress," *Article Base,* March 21, 2008.

48. Alicia A. Grandey, Lori S. Goldberg, and S. Douglas Pugh, "Why and When Do Stores with Satisfied Employees Have Satisfied Customers?: The Roles of Responsiveness and Store Busyness," *Journal of Service Research* 14, no. 4 (2011), pp. 397–409.

49. "Want to Improve Customer Service? Treat Your Employees Better," *Knowledge@Wharton,* March 14, 2012.

50. Todd Arnold, Karen E. Flaherty, Kevin E. Voss, and John C. Mowen, "Role of Stressors and Retail Performance: The Role of Perceived Competitive Climate," *Journal of Retailing* 85 (June 2009), pp. 194–205.

51. S. Li, Baohong Sung, and A. Montgomery, "Cross-Selling the Right Product to the Right Customer at the Right Time," *Journal of Marketing Research* 48, no. 4 (2011), pp. 683–700.

52. Leonard L. Berry, Ruth N. Bolton, C. H. Bridges, J. Meyer, A. Parasuraman, and Kathleen Seiders, "Opportunities for Innovation in the Delivery of Interactive Retail Services," *Journal of Interactive Marketing* 24, no. 2 (2010), pp. 155–167; Zhen Zhu, Cheryl Nakata, K. Sivakumar, and Dhruv Grewal, "Fix It or Leave It? Customer Recovery from Self-Service Technology Failures," working paper, 2012, Babson College; Peter C. Verhoef, Katherine N. Lemon, A. Parasuraman, Anne Roggeveen, Michael Tsiros, and Leonard A. Schlesinger, "Customer Experience Creation: Determinants, Dynamics and Management Strategies," *Journal of Retailing* 85, no. 1 (2009), pp. 31–41.

53. Clemens F. Köhler, Andrew J. Rohm, Ko de Ruyter, and Martin Wetzels, "Return on Interactivity: The Impact of Online Agents on Newcomer Adjustment," *Journal of Marketing* 75, no. 2 (2011), pp. 93–108.

54. "Consumers Calling Best Buy the Grinch That Stole Christmas," *Ad Age,* December 22, 2011.

55. Jonah Comstock, "CVS MinuteClinic App to Get New Wait Times, Remote Scheduling Features," *Mobile Health News,* December 10, 2015.

56. Ana Swanson, "What Really Drives You Crazy about Waiting in Line (It Actually Isn't the Wait at All)," *Washington Post,* November 27, 2015.

57. Stefan Michel, David Bowen, and Robert Johnston, "Making the Most of Customer Complaints," *The Wall Street Journal,* September 22, 2008.

58. Roggeveen et al., "Understanding the Co-Creation Effect"; M. Gabbott, Y. Tsarenko, and M. Wai Hoe, "Emotional Intelligence as a Moderator of Coping Strategies and Service Outcomes in Circumstances of Service Failure," *Journal of Service Research* 14, no. 2 (2011), pp. 234–248.

59. Heiner Evanschitzky, Christian Brock, and Markus Blut, "Will You Tolerate This? The Impact of Affective Commitment on Complaint Intention and Postrecovery Behavior," *Journal of Service Research* 14, no. 4 (2011), pp. 410–425; Chihyung Ok, Ki-Joon Back, and Carol W Shanklin, "Mixed Findings on the Service Recovery Paradox," *Service Industries Journal* 27 (September 2007), p. 671; Celso Augusto de Matos, Jorge Luiz Henrique, and Carlos Alberto Vargas Rossi, "Service Recovery Paradox: A Meta-Analysis," *Journal of Service Research* 10 (August 2007), pp. 60–77.

60. Hui Liao, "Do It Right This Time: The Role of Employee Service Recovery Performance in Customer-Perceived Justice and Customer Loyalty after Service Failures," *Journal of Applied Psychology* 92 (March 2007), p. 475.

61. Nicole Laskowski, "Nordstrom Digs into 5-Star Customer Reviews and Finds a Shipping Problem," *SearchCIO,* July 2014, http://searchcio.techtarget.com/feature/Nordstrom-digs-into-5-star-customer-reviews-and-finds-a-shipping-problem.

62. Cengiz Yilmaz, Kaan Varnali, and Berna Tari Kasnakoglu, "How Do Firms Benefit from Customer Complaints?," *Journal of Business Research* 69, no. 2 (2016), pp. 944–955.

63. Kimmy W. Chan, Chi K. Yim, and Simon S. K. Lam (2010), "Is Customer Participation in Value Creation a Double-Edged Sword? Evidence from Professional Financial Services Across Cultures," *Journal of Marketing* 74, no. 3 (2010), pp. 48–64.

Cases

Case Number	Case Name	1	2	3	4	5	6	7	8	9	10	11	12	13	14	15	16	17
																CHAPTER		
1	Making Macy's Meaningful: Moves by the Retail Chain to Maintain Its Competitiveness			✓	✓	✓												
2	Find "Good Stuff Cheap" at Ollie's Bargain Outlet	✓	✓			✓											✓	
3	Tractor Supply Company Targets the Part-Time Rancher	✓	✓			✓		✓										✓
4	Build-A-Bear Workshop: Where Best Friends Are Made	✓	✓			✓												
5	Blue Tomato: Internationalization of a Multichannel Retailer			✓		✓												
6	Staples, Inc.			✓														✓
7	Remixing a Green Business: The Green Painter				✓								✓					
8	Ashley Stewart				✓	✓												
9	The Decision-Making Process for Buying a Bicycle				✓													
10	Home Depot: Opportunities and Challenges in China					✓												
11	Parisian Patisserie "Maison Ladurée" Goes Global					✓												
12	Retailing in India: The Impact of Hypermarkets	✓				✓												
13	Diamonds from Mine to Market					✓				✓			✓					
14	Starbucks's Expansion into China					✓												
15	Tiffany and TJX: Comparing Financial Performance						✓											
16	Choosing a Store Location for a Boutique							✓										
17	Hutch: Locating a New Store								✓									
18	Avon Embraces Diversity															✓		
19	Sephora Loyalty Programs: A Comparison between France and the United States										✓							
20	Attracting Generation Y to a Retail Career															✓		
21	Active Endeavors Analyzes Its Customer Database										✓							
22	Mel's Department Store under New Management													✓				
23	Developing an Assortment Plan for Hughes											✓						
24	Preparing a Merchandise Budget Plan											✓						
25	Kroger and Fred Meyer: Sourcing Products in a Global Marketplace												✓					
26	American Furniture Warehouse Sources Globally												✓					
27	How Much for a Good Smell?													✓				

continued

Case Number	Case Name	CHAPTER																
		1	2	3	4	5	6	7	8	9	10	11	12	13	14	15	16	17
28	See It! Scan It! Buy It! Shortening the Path to Purchase with Mobilibuy's Technology			✓													✓		
29	Promoting a Sale															✓			
30	Target Marketing with Google AdWords			✓												✓			
31	Diamond in the Rough																✓		
32	A Stockout at Discmart																		✓
33	Customer Service and Relationship Management at Nordstrom																		✓
34	Zipcar: Delivering Only as Much Driving as You Want																		✓
35	A Musical Quandary in an Italian Restaurant																	✓	
36	Yankee Candle: Product Management and Innovation				✓	✓													
37	Interviewing for a Management Training Position	✓																	

CASE 1   Making Macy's Meaningful: Moves by the Retail Chain to Maintain Its Competitiveness

In 2016 Macy's holiday sales dropped over 2 percent, spurring the closing of over 60 stores in 2017 and at least a total of 100 stores in the coming years. Faced with these surprising sales declines and threats to its status as the leading department store brand, Macy's has developed a multipronged strategy, seeking to leverage its existing advantages as well as some new retail options. Three key efforts reflect its expansion as an omnichannel retailer, its pursuit of relevant target customers, and its partnerships with other retail sources.

First, Macy's has a great online presence, and it simultaneously has adopted in-store technologies that help customers find the items they want, design fashionable outfits, make payments more easily, receive discounts, and even have their purchases delivered if they so choose. For example, with large Look Book displays, consumers interact with a sort of digital catalog in the store, finding fashionable ideas, ways to extend their existing wardrobes, and images from forward-thinking fashion icons. Touching the screen enables them to check the availability of various colors and sizes as well as receive more detailed information about items that are of interest. The POP (point-of-purchase) terminals in Macy's stores similarly are touch screens that provide extensive inventory information, though they are more functional than fashionable. These smaller kiosks indicate which colors and styles are available and also identify which items have prompted the most Facebook likes or customer favorite rankings.

When it comes time to pay, Macy's is working to make the process easier and quicker by installing Apple Pay capabilities throughout its network of stores. As one of the earliest adopters of this new technology, Macy's is seeking to appeal to Apple fans who love to use their iPhones for nearly everything. With Macy's Wallet and the Shopkick app, customers have two methods to receive coupons and special offers. Once downloaded, the Shopkick app requires people to opt in, and then, as they enter a Macy's store, reminds them to open it so that they can receive personalized notifications. It tracks their move-

ments through the store, so that a shopper in the outerwear department receives a discount offer on gloves rather than cosmetics, for example. The Macy's Wallet program is similar, except that it is unique to this retailer and links to consumers' loyalty cards. A shopper who has earned a percentage-off offer, on the basis of her or his prior purchases, thus no longer needs to worry about forgetting and leaving the paper coupon at home rather than bringing it on the current shopping trip.

Finally, using a crowdsourced delivery service called Deliv, Macy's offers customers the option of making their purchases in the store, then having them delivered to their homes, such that they no longer have to lug heavy packages through the mall.

However, according to one analyst, the inventory in Macy's stores is often messy and seemingly overstocked, without sufficient on-duty personnel to keep the experience moving along nicely. Thus, it might need to reorient its focus more on people and less on technology to maintain its high level of customer experience. As we discussed in an earlier chapter, to compete with Amazon, which continues to wow customers with its innovations, rapid delivery options, successful appeal to consumers, insurmountable product and service selection, and effective pricing, Macy's must leverage its multiple channels and exploit its omnichannel potential to its full extent.

Second, Macy's had determined that it needs to pursue those elusive young shoppers known as Millennials. Accordingly, it has implemented a $400 million renovation effort for its flagship New York City store, testing out various options that might attract more of the market of shoppers between the ages of 18 and 35 years. The basement level is newly designated "One Below," and it offers a notably different shopping experience. In addition to merchandise designed to appeal to Millennials, it provides services such as blow-drying stations, jean embroidering, and watch engraving. Shoppers can use a 3D printer to create their own custom jewelry, and a touch screen wall allows them to take high-quality selfies. These tests, if successful, are likely to spread to other locations as well. In the meantime, Macy's is opening more off-price stores, seemingly following the successful lead of Nordstrom with its Nordstrom Rack stores.

These moves reflect the conventional wisdom about what Millennials want. In particular, studies show that these young consumers tend to devote their spending more to personal or digital services than to apparel. They also suffer higher levels of debt, mostly due to student loans, and earn less on average than previous generations have. As a result, they generally seek lower-priced options for their fashion choices. This preference puts them in direct contrast with the previous big cohort of shoppers—namely, the Baby Boomers. The consumers in this age group, as they start to retire from the workforce, exhibit strong spending patterns and have enviable levels of discretionary income and time. From this perspective, some observers suggest Macy's might be going after the wrong age demographic—unless Baby Boomers like selfie walls too.

Third, noting the success enjoyed by Best Buy when it opened dedicated stores within the stores, which reflect its strong relationships with vendors and ability to offer the kind of variety its customers demand, Macy's entered into a partnership with Best Buy but flipped their roles. That is, as the host location, Macy's opened several Best Buy operations within about a dozen of its department stores. The mini–Best Buys take up about 300 square feet of space and offer tablets, smartphones, smartwatches, audio devices, and accessories. As in traditional Best Buy stores, Samsung has a strong presence. Staffing the in-store stores will be Best Buy personnel, ready to answer shoppers' questions about high-tech devices.

Best Buy's recent resurgence, as well as Macy's willingness to innovate, has contributed to the new initiative. In addition, Macy's notes that customers are seeking more variety in the items available to them, whether to purchase for themselves or as gifts. By adding the latest and coolest electronics gadgets—whether as tools to help people shop or as an expanded variety for consumers to purchase—Macy's seeks to ensure that it is a shopping destination for virtually anyone.

Sources: Christopher Mele, "Macy's Will Cut 10,000 Jobs after Poor Holiday Sales," *The New York Times*, January 4, 2017; Alexander Coolidge, "Hate Checkout Lines? Macy's Can Help," *Cincinnati Inquirer*, October 3, 2014; Ken Lonyai, "Rivals Need to Up Customer Experiences to Compete with Amazon," *RetailWire*, January 12, 2016; Marina Nazario, "Macy's Has a Master Plan to Capture the Most Difficult Customers," *Business Insider*, October 3, 2015; George Anderson, "Best Buy to Open Shops Inside Macy's Stores," *RetailWire*, September 9, 2015.

This case study was written by Elisabeth Nevins, Effectual Editorial Services.

DISCUSSION QUESTIONS

1. **What is Macy's plan to attract Millennials?**

2. **How is Macy's positioned in the fashion market? Who are its main competitors, and how well does it compete against them?**

3. **Who are Macy's target markets? With which targets is it winning, and with which is it losing? Why?**

4. **Perform a SWOT analysis for Macy's.**

5. **Do you shop at Macy's? Why or why not?**

CASE 2 Find "Good Stuff Cheap" at Ollie's Bargain Outlet

Ollie's Bargain Outlet describes itself as "one of America's largest retailers of closeouts, excess inventory, and salvage merchandise." It offers drastically reduced prices that attract hordes of customers to hunt for treasures, prompted by the brand's urgent slogan that "when it's gone, it's gone."

As a regional player, Ollie's is headquartered in Harrisburg, Pennsylvania. In 2004, it operated 30 stores in the Mid-Atlantic region of the United States. Since that time, though, it has been on an aggressive growth trajectory, with 219 stores and counting. It went public in 2015, a move that fueled the pace of its expansion even more. It also has been opening stores to the south and west, such that it now has stores in 16 contiguous states. Its ambitious goal is to reach to 950 stores across the United States in the coming years.

BACKGROUND AND RETAIL STRATEGY

Ollie's positions itself as a hybrid of an off-price and an extreme value retailer. However, it is formally classified as a miscellaneous retail store (SIC 5999) rather than an extreme discounter, because it offers an ever-changing assortment of merchandise. Similar concepts leveraged by Big Lots, Ross Dress for Less, and TJX Companies (i.e., T.J. Maxx, HomeGoods, Marshalls, and Sierra Trading Company) all feature aggressively priced merchandise, designed to sell a lot of discontinued goods or overstock items from other retailers and manufacturers. Another similarity among these retailers is their comparative lack of fastidiousness, compared with department and specialty stores, when it comes to displaying merchandise neatly. If a customer happens to move a garden hose to the tools section, the retailer does not worry too much because the next

customer who encounters the hose might think that she or he found the last one and move to buy it quickly.

To support this retail strategy, Ollie's highly experienced buying team procures an ever-changing assortment of merchandise, mostly fast-moving consumer goods, housewares, books, toys, tools, and do-it-yourself building materials. (The vast list of the different types of merchandise offered at Ollie's is available on the company's website: www.ollies.us/ what-is-ollies/store-departments/.) Vendors of all sorts willingly sell their wares through Ollie's, because the win–win situation helps them liquidate their excess merchandise. The excess might be leftovers from a previous season or inventory remaining due to excessive purchases, as well as poorly selling items, products with out-of-date labeling or packaging, or items that have suffered some minor damage. Ollie's buys merchandise that is not quite fit to sell at higher-end stores and offers the vendors favorable conditions. For example, it pays vendors in cash and does not demand return privileges.

The buying team also leverages its long-standing relationships with hundreds of manufacturers, wholesalers, distributors, brokers, and retailers worldwide. It selectively chooses from among a broad range of brand name and discontinued products, then passes the savings from the opportunistic deals it negotiates on to customers, such that it can offer prices as much as 70 percent below department and specialty stores' levels. Approximately 70 percent of Ollie's merchandise features national brand names; private-label and unbranded stock constitute the remaining 30 percent. Furthermore, the retailer makes an explicit point to not depend on any single supplier for more than 5 percent of its inventory.

MERCHANDISING

Merchandise placement in stores changes according to how the inventory fits best, rather than being assigned to predetermined locations, as in a typical department or home improvement store. If the buying team purchases a large amount of a particular type of merchandise (e.g., laundry detergent with old labels, patio furniture overruns, discontinued Paula Deen cookware, about-to-expire K-cups), Ollie's stores clear out an area toward the front, near the entrance, and present massive table displays. In addition, handwritten signs, drawn with thick markers and often faded over time by sunlight, hang in the windows to harken the arrival of recent shipments of priced-to-sell merchandise. Toys account for one of Ollie's biggest categories, especially around the holidays; Ollie's also earns a disproportionately high amount of its sales during the holiday period.

A CUSTOMER STORY

Roger and Emmy Brogan live on the moderate incomes they earn as a mechanic and hair stylist, respectively. They have two children: Jason, 7, and Jessica, 5. The kids constantly clamor for new toys, and the pressure is heating up as the holiday season approaches. Roger and Emmy struggle to make ends meet, let alone buy the little extras for the children. Having lived their entire lives in central Pennsylvania, the Brogans are very familiar with Ollie's Bargain Outlet.

Knowing that the store offers "good stuff cheap"—and they mean all kinds of stuff—the Brogans make a visit to Ollie's for a family shopping trip in early December. They encounter a vast and changing assortment of consumer goods, from books to carpet remnants to kitchenware to snacks. They fan out across the aisles, looking for bargains. Brightly colored red, yellow, and black signs seek to draw their attention through funny wordplay, such as "Buy something just for the halibut."

Although Emmy finds a treasure-trove of deeply discounted merchandise, including potato chip flavors that she cannot find in local grocery stores and health and beauty supplies from a previous season, the children are disappointed that they cannot find the latest toys and gadgets. Still, Jason is soon distracted by an old-school Battleship game that he and his friends can play for hours on end, and he admits that retro board games are pretty cool. Jessica also discovers a collectible

doll that she knows would look pretty on her dresser. In the meantime, Roger finds a wrench to round out his tool chest, and the parents consider how nice new laminate flooring would look to help them upgrade the worn-out carpeting in the house they purchased a few years back.

After 45 minutes of trolling the store and checking out one another's finds, the family members congregate near the checkout stations to review their combined basket before making their final decisions. The game and doll make the cut. Emmy purchases beauty supplies that she knows will appeal to some of her customers, but Roger decides against the wrench. He worries a little that he won't be able to find that exact design again in the future, but he and Emmy really want the flooring, so he decides to remove the wrench from the shopping basket and put the money toward this big home improvement project. Emmy agrees with this notion and decides to skip the snack foods for now.

After paying, the family members leave the store smiling, feeling satisfied that they got some great deals. Everybody found something that appealed to them, and if any of their purchases are not quite right, the family feels confident knowing that the store's return policy allows them to return the products for a refund within 30 days, as long as they keep the receipt.

Sources: David Thomas, "Good Stuff Cheap," *Jackson Sun*, May 11, 2016, www.jacksonsun.com/story/money/business/2016/05/11/good-stuff-cheap/84203556/?from=global&sessionKey=&autologin=); David Thomas, "Sun Sits Down with Ollie's Outlet CEO," *Jackson Sun*, July 2, 2016, www.jacksonsun.com/story/money/business/2016/07/02/mark-butler-ceo-ollies-bargain-outlet/86345334; United States Securities and Exchange Commission, "Amendment No. 1 to Form S-1 for Ollie's Bargain Outlet Holdings, Inc.," June 22, 2015, www.nasdaq.com/markets/ipos/filing.ashx?filingid=10292768; Zoominfo, "Ollie's Bargain Outlet," 2016, www.zoominfo.com/c/Ollie%27s-Bargain-Outlet/45859974.

This case was written by Lexi Hutto, Millersville University of Pennsylvania.

DISCUSSION QUESTIONS

1. Perform a SWOT analysis for Ollie's. If you were able to invest in Ollie's, would you? Why or why not?

2. Describe Ollie's target markets. How are they similar? Different?

3. Compare Ollie's retailing strategy to Macy's and to Marshall's.

CASE 3   Tractor Supply Company Targets the Part-Time Rancher

Tractor Supply Company (TSC), a large and fast-growing retailer with more than $6 billion in annual sales and more than 1,500 stores in 49 states, was the inventor of the "do-it-yourself" (DIY) trend. Its origins date to 1938, when Charles E. Schmidt Sr. established a mail-order tractor parts business. After the success of his first retail store in Minot, North Dakota, he opened additional stores to serve the needs of local farmers. But eventually TSC's sales stagnated because small farms and ranches were being acquired by large farming and ranching corporations. These large agricultural firms buy supplies and equipment directly from manufacturers rather than through local farm supply stores like TSC.

TARGET MARKET

Since the early 1990s, TSC has targeted a growing group of people interested in recreational farming and ranching. Called "sundowners," "U-turners," "hobby farmers," "rural-politans," "micropolitans," "gentlemen farmers," and "ex-urbanites," these people have turned to farming to escape the hubbub of urban and suburban life. They are drawn to what they believe is a more private, stress-free, simpler lifestyle. They typically live on 5 to 20 acres in a rural community outside a metropolitan area, where they work at a full-time profession, and use some of their earnings to keep their farms in operation. Many of them are the sons and daughters of traditional production farmers and inherited the family farm and decided to keep it running. Today less than 10 percent of TSC's customers classify themselves as full-time farmers or ranchers, and many of its customers do not farm at all.

RETAIL OFFERING

The typical TSC store has 15,000 square feet of inside selling space and a similar amount of outside space used to display agricultural fencing, livestock equipment, and horse stalls. The company tries to locate stores in the prime retail corridor of rural communities, two or three counties away from major metropolitan areas. Fifty percent of its stores are in previously occupied buildings.

The typical store stocks 16,000 to 20,000 SKUs, using a combination of national and private-label brands. TSC constantly tests new merchandise programs in its stores. For instance, based on a successful test of expanded clothing and footwear categories, TSC doubled the size of these areas of the store and added more lifestyle clothes and workwear for both men and women.

TSC stores are designed to make shopping an enjoyable experience and, at the same time, maximize sales and operating efficiencies. Their environment allows plenty of space for individual departments and visual displays. Informative signs assist customers with purchasing decisions by delineating "good, better, best" qualities, pointing out their "everyday low-pricing" policy, and providing useful information regarding product benefits and suggestions for appropriate accessories.

TSC emphasizes customer service. The company tries to hire store employees who have farming and ranching backgrounds. Its training programs include (1) a full management training program, which covers all aspects of its operations; (2) product knowledge modules produced in conjunction with key vendors; (3) frequent management skills training classes; (4) semiannual store managers' meetings, with vendor product presentations; (5) vendor-sponsored in-store training programs; and (6) ongoing product information updates at its management headquarters. This extensive training, coupled with a management philosophy that stresses empowerment, enables store employees to assist customers in making their purchase decisions and solve customer problems as they arise. Store employees wear highly visible red vests, aprons, or smocks and nametags. TSC uses a variety of incentive programs that provide the opportunity for store employees to receive additional compensation based on their team, store, and/or company performance.

While TSC creates a "hometown farmer" shopping experience for customers, there is nothing "small-town" or "laid back" about its operations and use of technology. Its management information and control systems include a point-of-sale system, a supply chain management and replenishment system, a radio-frequency picking system in the distribution centers, a vendor purchase order control system, and a merchandise presentation system. These systems work together to track merchandise from the initial order through to the ultimate sale.

TSC has a centralized supply chain management team that focuses on replenishment and forecasting and a buying team that selects merchandise, develops assortments, and evaluates new products and programs. Almost all purchase orders and vendor invoices are transmitted through an electronic data interchange (EDI) system.

MISSION AND VALUES

Despite changes to TSC's retail strategy in the past 78 years, its mission and values have remained constant. The company's mission and value statements appear on its website, on cards handed out to all employees, and on the walls of every store. According to TSC management, the first discussion with new employees centers on the firm's values and mission because the firm steadfastly maintains that "being a great place to work enables the company to be a great place to shop and invest."

Sources: Tractor Supply Co., Annual Report 2015; www.tractorsupply.com.

This case was written by Barton Weitz, University of Florida, and Jenny Esdale.

DISCUSSION QUESTIONS

1. What is Tractor Supply Company's growth strategy? What retail mix does TSC provide?
2. Why and how has TSC's target customer changed over time?
3. How does TSC's retail mix provide the benefits sought by its target market?
4. How vulnerable is TSC to competition? Why is this the case?
5. Why does TSC place so much emphasis on training employees?

CASE 4   Build-A-Bear Workshop: Where Best Friends Are Made

Modern consumers want good value, low prices, and convenience, but they also appreciate a great shopping experience. Build-A-Bear Workshop usually locates its more than 400 stores in malls worldwide. It generates more than $377 million in annual sales by offering customers the opportunity to make their own stuffed animals, complete with clothing and accessories.

In 1997, Maxine Clark came up with the idea for Build-A-Bear Workshop and opened a storefront in St. Louis. She had plenty of experience in the corporate side of retailing, having worked for Payless ShoeSource and May Department Stores. Clark left corporate America on a mission to bring the fun back to retailing. Currently, the company has sold more than 70 million furry friends.

The bear-making process consists of eight steps, Choose Me, Hear Me, Stuff Me, Stitch Me, Fluff Me, Dress Me, Name Me, and Take Me Home. The stores mirror the chain's name: Customers, or builders, choose an unstuffed animal and, working with the retailer's staff, move through eight "creation stations" to build their own bear (or other animal). At the first station, the Stuffiteria, children can pick fluff from bins marked "Love," "Hugs and Kisses," "Friendship," and "Kindness." The stuffing is sent through a long, clear tube and into a stuffing machine. A sales associate holds the bear to a small tube while the builder pumps a foot peddle. In seconds, the bear takes its form. Before the stitching, builders must insert a heart. The builders follow the sales associates' instructions and rub the heart between their hands to make it warm. They then close their eyes, make a wish, and kiss the heart before putting it inside the bear. After selecting a name and having it stitched on their animal, builders take their bears to the Fluff Me station, where they brush their bears on a "bathtub" that features spigots blowing air. Finally, they move to a computer station to create a birth certificate.

Bears go home in Cub Condo carrying cases, which act as mini-houses complete with windows and doors. In addition to serving as playhouses, the boxes advertise Build-A-Bear Workshop to the child's friends. "[You] could buy a bear anywhere," says Clark, chief executive bear. "It's the experience that customers are looking for." The experience isn't limited to the stores themselves. The retailer's website, www.buildabear.com, embraces the same theme, with a section where users can access games, activities, and videos.

Customers pay about $25 for the basic bear, but they can also buy music, clothing, and accessories. To keep the experience fresh, Build-A-Bear Workshop regularly introduces new and limited-edition animals. Clothes and accessories are also updated to reflect current fashion trends. Outfits for the bears complement the owner's interests and personalities with themes such as sports, colleges, hobbies, and careers. Some children and their parents hold in-store birthday parties, with music playing from the store's official CD. To ensure customers enjoy a great experience every time they visit, all sales associates attend a three-week training program, and the firm offers incentive programs and bonuses. The inventory in the stores changes frequently, with different bear styles arriving weekly. Build-A-Bear Workshops also feature limited-edition and seasonal merchandise, such as a Beary Businesslike Curly Teddy for Father's Day; mummy, wizard, and witch bears for Halloween; and a Sweet Hugs & Kisses Teddy for Valentine's Day.

In 2013, responding to the changing interests of children, Build-A-Bear announced a sweeping upgrade to its retail stores. Clark noted that developments in digital technology have changed how kids play: "[In 1997] children were playing board games. Now they're playing games online. . . . Kids are being bombarded with the next new shiny objects. But they've always loved teddy bears and that's not going to change."

Because the stores are a mix between the product (the teddy bear) and the experience of creating the teddy bear, the new design incorporates several digital upgrades. To help determine appropriate changes, the company enlisted several children, termed "Cub Advisors," and their moms for advice on the changes they would like to see in the stores.

Based on this research and advice, the stores underwent a massive redesign. Starting at the storefront, signage has been incorporated with Microsoft Kinect technology that enables kids to play with the signage before entering. The use of digital signage allows stores to highlight sales and new products, as well as several holiday themes. The revamped "Love Me" station allows kids to give their stuffed animals personalities at an interactive table using emoticons, which are pictorial representations of a facial expression like a happy face. The "Hear Me" station has a touch screen that allows customers to choose and load prerecorded music and animal noises, or record their own voice. The "Stuff Me" station offers the option to add custom scents such as bubble gum, cotton candy, and chocolate chip and has been redesigned to resemble a cotton candy machine. Finally, kids can wash their bears in a digital bathtub at the "Fluff Me" station. In an effort at contingency planning, "low-tech" options are being designed that can be put over the digital stations if computers act up.

Sources: www.buildabear.com; Krystina Gustafson, "Build-A-Bear Isn't Just a Store Anymore," *CNBC*, June 4, 2015; Sandy Smith, "Integration Specialists," Stores, January 2013; Tom Ryan, "Build-A-Bear Workshop Goes High-Tech," *RetailWire*, October 8, 2012.

This case was written by Barton Weitz, University of Florida; and Jenny Esdale, Brandeis University.

DISCUSSION QUESTIONS

1. **Is the Build-A-Bear Workshop concept a fad, or does it have staying power?**
2. **Describe the target customer for this retailer.**
3. **What can Build-A-Bear Workshop do to generate repeat visits to the store?**

CASE 5   Blue Tomato: Internationalization of a Multichannel Retailer

I. THE HISTORY OF BLUE TOMATO: A BRICK-AND-MORTAR RETAILER

When Blue Tomato started, it was at the initiative of Gerfried Schuller, a former European snowboard champion who opened a snowboarding school in 1988 and then launched a small store for snowboarders in Schladming, an Austrian ski resort, in 1994. By the end of 2012, Blue Tomato had opened eight brick-and-mortar stores throughout Austria and Germany and had expanded the variety of merchandise it sells, to include products for not just snowboarders but also surfers, skaters, and freeskiers.

In the summer of 2012, Blue Tomato was acquired by Zumiez Inc., a leading North American specialty retailer of action sports–related apparel, footwear, equipment, and accessories. Zumiez already operates more than 660 stores in the United States and Canada and maintains a web store (www.zumiez.com). Despite this acquisition, Blue Tomato has kept its headquarters in Austria, even as it seeks to meet its latest objective: to become the European leader in action sports retailing. To pursue this goal, the company has refocused its retail expansion strategy and opened new brick-and-mortar stores in Austria, as well as in its neighboring countries. Meanwhile, Blue Tomato runs 13 shops in Austria, 16 stores in Germany, and 1 store in Switzerland. Five of these shops are located in ski areas; the rest function in more urban locations.

II. EVOLUTION OF BLUE TOMATO INTO A MULTICHANNEL RETAILER

Before the acquisition by Zumiez, the number of brick-and-mortar stores that a small company like Blue Tomato could open easily was relatively limited, which meant its potential customer contacts were limited, too. Therefore, it expanded into the online realm in 1997, allowing Austrian customers to place orders 24 hours a day, seven days a week. By 1999, its first large-scale web store was online; in 2008 and in 2013, it relaunched its website (www.blue-tomato.com) to facilitate the product-ordering process and introduced several sophisticated buyer's guides designed to help customers locate just the right snowboard, boots, boot binding, snow gear, freeskis, avalanche equipment, wetsuit, and split-, skate-, long-, or surfboard. Furthermore, the website has been adapted for mobile devices (i.e., cell phones and tablets). For the company, the website relaunches were a great success, both times leading to sales increases. In general, Blue Tomato's web store has enabled it to attract new customers without investing in finding, building, or stocking new stores. In addition, it has been able to offer far more products online than it could stock in any single brick-and-mortar outlet.

In 2002, Blue Tomato expanded its multichannel strategy even further by publishing a new, printed snowboard catalog (with a print run of 130,000 in the first year) targeting convenience-oriented customers who avoid online shopping. This catalog has expanded to a print run of 400,000; in addition, the company offers not just the snowboard catalog but also a freeski catalog (with a print run of 120,000 in 2016), a back-to-school catalog with skate and streetstyle products (print run of 145,000 in 2016), and a summer catalog (print run of 380,000 in summer 2016). From 2013 to 2016, the company also published a printed style booklet twice a year (with a print run of 75,000 each) to give customers the opportunity to order the latest fashion trends. To distribute the catalogs, Blue Tomato uses direct mailings to selected customers, hands them out at events or in its stores, and promotes them in snowboard, freeski, skate, and surf magazines. Interested consumers also can request catalogs on the company's website, download them from its website, or view the pages online.

Although many of the company's sales come through its online orders, it relies on its brick-and-mortar stores to maintain close, direct contacts with its (potential) customers, in line with its overall corporate philosophy. To ensure direct customer contact and attract new customers, Blue Tomato also opened two test centers in ski resorts, which allow (potential) customers to try out new snowboards, boots, and bindings. The company hosts four snowboard schools in local ski areas, together with special events, such as its "Kids Days," during which children can attend its snowboard courses for free.

III. SYNERGIES ACROSS DISTRIBUTION CHANNELS

In addition to its individual strengths, Blue Tomato relies on the synergies it has created across its different distribution channels. Since 2010, it has installed media boxes, or kiosks, in its brick-and-mortar stores that allow consumers to look up personalized information about special offers in particular stores. They also can log on to their Facebook (or other social media) page, connect with their friends, and ask about how well the latest snowgear or streetwear suits them. Meanwhile, the company has added pickup and return services to its brick-and-mortar stores, enabling customers to order a product online

and pick it up or return it in their local store. Furthermore, customers can search for products in the printed or online catalogs and order them online, or vice versa. According to Blue Tomato, especially the printed catalogs have contributed to and extended its online business; the opportunity to view catalogs online might further boost its online sales.

IV. CHALLENGES COORDINATING DIFFERENT DISTRIBUTION CHANNELS

The main challenge of operating multiple distribution channels is for Blue Tomato to provide a consistent face to customers across all contact points. For example, it seeks to reinforce its commitment to customer service throughout its web store. To meet this challenge, it also standardizes all prices and communication. With regard to price, the company simply guarantees to offer the best price (within the EU). If a consumer orders a product on the telephone, after receiving a catalog, but the product is listed at a cheaper price on the website because the price dropped since the catalog was published, Blue Tomato charges the customer the lower price. Its return policy—customers can return products within 21 days—also is consistent in each channel. In terms of communication, Blue Tomato's devotion to snowboarding, skating, surfing, and freeskiing is manifested by employees in the brick-and-mortar stores, as well as through the events the company hosts. Beyond this content-oriented integration, the company's communication is formally integrated.

However, the product overlap across the different distribution channels is relatively minimal. Whereas the brick-and-mortar stores and catalogs offer limited merchandise variety and assortment, its website posts more than 450,000 products, from approximately 650 brands, available for purchase. This poor overlap might be a challenge for Blue Tomato in terms of reinforcing its retail brand image among customers.

V. INTERNATIONALIZATION

To initiate its internationalization moves, in 1997 Blue Tomato installed international shopping facilities on its website. The focus of these early internationalization efforts was on German-speaking countries (i.e., Germany and Switzerland) and German-speaking customers. The website thus was available only in German. This strategy represented an easy choice because the language barriers between different German-speaking countries are negligible, nor did Blue Tomato face many barriers in terms of export or customs regulations. Austria and Switzerland participate in stable exchange rates, and Austria and Germany already relied on a common currency (the euro).

But this internationalization process also has expanded, particularly in the catalog channel, in which catalogs are available in different languages (e.g., the snowboard catalog is issued in five languages, and the freeski catalog is offered in four). The relaunch of the company's website in 2008 also sparked advances in the internationalization process, because the web store was no longer restricted to German-speaking customers; today, it has been translated into 14 languages. Thus, customers from countries throughout the world can place an order with Blue Tomato. Its most important foreign markets remain geographically nearby, including Germany,

Switzerland, Scandinavia, the Benelux countries, Great Britain, and Spain, but it also has received orders from exotic destinations such as Hawaii, Hong Kong, and Argentina. Furthermore, Blue Tomato has earned the distinction of offering the largest selection of snowboards in the world on its website. As a result, 70 percent of its online orders come from foreign markets. Since 2011, its products are delivered to more than 100 countries.

Except from German-speaking countries, Blue Tomato's internationalization remained focused solely on its web store and its printed catalogs. In these channels, it relies on direct exports. Furthermore, regardless of the channel used to support the internationalization, it has maintained its standardization strategy with respect to prices charged and communication. That is, the online prices are the same for all customers in all countries, without any international price differentiation. The catalog layout also remains standardized, though the specific products included in each catalog issue vary slightly to reflect the varying appeal of certain brands in some international markets.

These eventual outcomes are not to suggest that the process of internationalization was easy. Blue Tomato has confronted several challenges, stemming largely from the complexity of the European market. Most countries in Europe are members of the European Union, but different legal conditions and tax rates arise in each member-state, and their cultural differences remain pertinent. Logistics costs and economic power also differ from country to country, with notable effects on the level of income of (potential) customers. Against this background, Blue Tomato decided to

undertake some foreign direct investment in its neighboring countries: By the end of 2012, the company had opened three brick-and-mortar stores in Germany. More direct investments have been made since the acquisition by Zumiez: 13 more shops have been opened in Germany, and in 2016, the first store in Switzerland has been opened.

Meanwhile, Blue Tomato ranks as the leading European multichannel retailer for board sports and related apparel. If it decides to expand its internationalization further by opening stores in other countries, it clearly will need to invest additional financial and personnel resources. Regardless of the strategy it might choose for such a foreign market entry, tackling more markets, with more widely variant national, legal, tax, and logistic characteristics, could make it more difficult for the company to continue with its strategy of standardization.

This case was written by Professor Thomas Foscht and Assistant Professor Marion Brandstaetter, both of Karl-Franzens-University, Graz, Austria.

DISCUSSION QUESTIONS

1. What strengths do the different distribution channels have from the company's perspective?

2. Which synergies has Blue Tomato created across different channels? What additional actions might it take to become an omnichannel retailer?

3. What key challenges remain for Blue Tomato in its efforts to coordinate these different channels?

4. Which challenges might Blue Tomato face as it expands its business activities internationally?

CASE 6   Staples, Inc.

Staples operates in the highly competitive office products market. The office supply category specialists, including Staples and Office Depot/OfficeMax, dramatically changed the landscape of the office supply industry. First, they greatly expanded the use of retail stores and Internet channels as means of distributing office supply products, capitalizing in part on the significant increase in the number of home offices. Prior to the mid-1980s, office supply customers primarily placed their orders through commissioned salespeople or catalogs.

Warehouse clubs, supermarkets, and full-line discount retailers also have begun taking market share away from the big two office supply retailers because of their ability to sell the bulk items at lower prices. Retailers such as Walmart and Costco offer low prices on office supplies, which forces the major office supply retailers to offer more than just products, such as extra services and greater customer service. The big two office supply stores have also expanded their business-to-business (B2B) efforts to sell to other companies, such as Wells Fargo or IBM. Staples Business Advantage, for example, offers a range of products and services to its B2B customers.

COMPANY BACKGROUND

Originally opened in 1986 by executive-turned-entrepreneur Tom Stemberg, Staples has reached sales of more than $25 billion. Staples also has been credited with pioneering

the high-volume office products superstore concept. By evolving its original mission of slashing the costs and eliminating the hassles of running an office to one of making it easy to buy office products, Staples has become the world's largest office products company.

To distinguish itself in this competitive industry, Staples strives to provide a unique shopping experience to customers in all its market segments. Central to maintaining customer satisfaction is developing strong customer relationship skills and broad knowledge about office products among all associates hired by the company. Therefore, Staples includes formal training as an integral part of the development of its associates.

Another truly important aspect of customer service is the availability of merchandise. In the office supply industry, customers have very specific needs, such as finding an ink cartridge for a particular printer, and if the store is out of stock of a needed item, the customer may never come back.

Staples uses various marketing channels to address the needs of its different segments. Smaller businesses are generally served by a combination of retail stores, the catalog, and the Internet. Retail operations focus on serving the needs of consumers and small businesses, especially through an in-store kiosk that enables customers to order a product that may not be available in the store and receive the product via overnight delivery. In-store kiosks allow them to choose to have the product delivered to their home, business, or local store. If a customer does not want to shop in the store, he or she can visit Staples.com to order required products and select from a much larger assortment. The typical Staples retail store maintains approximately 8,000 stockkeeping units (SKUs), but Staples.com offers more than 45,000 SKUs. This multichannel approach allows Staples to increase its productivity by stocking only more popular items in stores but not sacrificing product availability.

MULTICHANNEL INTEGRATION

Staples's overall goal has been to become the leading office products and services provider by combining its existing experience, extensive distribution infrastructure, and customer service expertise with web-based information technology. As a result, the integration of different channels of distribution into one seamless customer experience has been of particular interest to the company. Staples, like many other multichannel retailers, has found that many customers use multiple channels to make their Staples purchases and that sales increase when customers use more than one channel (e.g., customers who shop two channels spend twice as much as a single-channel shopper; a tri-channel shopper spends about three times as much as a single-channel shopper). Therefore, the greater the number of channels a particular customer shops, the greater the overall expenditures he or she is likely to make.

Staples faces several challenges in integrating its channels of distribution, though, most of which are related to its Internet channel. First, it must consider the extent to which the Internet may cannibalize its retail store sales. The most attractive aspect of the Internet is its potential to attract new customers and sell more to existing customers. But if overall sales are flat—that is, if online retailing only converts retail store sales to Internet sales—Staples suffers increased overhead costs and poorer overall productivity. Second, Staples must be concerned about the merchandise position of its retail stores compared with that of alternative channels. Because a retail store cannot carry as much merchandise as

the Internet channel, the challenge is to keep an appropriate balance between minimizing stockouts and avoiding the proliferation of too many SKUs in retail stores. Finally, Staples has to contend with price competition, both within its own multichannel organization and from competitors.

STAPLES'S ADDED SERVICES

Such competition means that Staples must continue to differentiate itself from other office supply retailers by adding extra value to office supplies, which themselves represent commoditized products. For example, its Copy and Print centers within all its stores enable customers to order print jobs and receive the help of an in-store print specialist. Customers can order their copies through the Staples website, then pick them up in-store or have them delivered.

Sources: www.staples.com; "Office Supply Stores in the US—Industry Report," *IBIS World*, March 23, 2010; 2015 Staples Annual Report; interview with Max Ward, vice president of technology at Staples; W. Caleb McCann, J. P. Jeannet, Dhruv Grewal, and Martha Lanning, "Staples," in *Fulfillment in E-Business*, Petra Schuber, Ralf Wolfle, and Walter Dettling, eds. (Germany: Hanser, 2001), pp. 239–252 (in German); interview with Staples's vice president of stores, Demos Parneros, and executive vice president of merchandising and marketing, Jevin Eagle.

This case was written by Jeanne L. Munger, University of Southern Maine; Britt Hackmann, Nubry.com; and Dhruv Grewal and Michael Levy, Babson College.

DISCUSSION QUESTIONS

1. Assess the extent to which Staples has developed a successful multichannel strategy. What factors have contributed to its success?

2. What are the advantages and disadvantages of using kiosks as part of its approach?

3. How should Staples assess which SKUs to keep in its stores versus on the Internet?

4. How do the Staples Copy and Print centers differentiate it from the competition?

CASE 7   Remixing a Green Business: The Green Painter

Healthy, sustainable communities operating as good stewards of the environment offer frameworks for collaborative efforts to determine how global warming and climate change affect the environment, including its effects on plants, animals, and humans, as well as on the infrastructure of the world economies. The United Nations has "stressed that the Sustainable Development Goals (SDGs) which are being formulated by Member States must address the environmental degradation that is threatening present and future generations." But the broad question "What is a sustainable environment?" can quickly become overwhelming, unless it is subdivided into manageable parts that then can be examined.

New Living is a unique home furnishing store located in one of the richest neighborhoods of Houston, Texas. It sells original furniture, designed to order, all made from recycled wood, along with environmentally responsible mattresses, fans, energy systems, and a mix of accessories, such as waxes, cleaning products, recycled gifts, and one-of-a-kind

art pieces. The great success of the retail arm led the company to expand into offering architectural services to families who were remodeling their homes to make them greener. Furniture designers and architects, hired by the retail firm, devised specialized custom furniture, such that New Living outfitted customers' homes with desks, unique bed frames, custom dining room tables and chairs, and children's furniture.

The company continued to enjoy success, creating demand for a new kind of product: nontoxic paint for healthy homes. According to Jeff Kaplan, the founder of New Living, a designation as nontoxic requires the absence of all chemicals like volatile organic compounds (VOCs), xylene, and formaldehyde that are found in the traditional paints sold in the conventional marketplace. Therefore, he launched The Green Painter in 2011, which prepares the basic paint, then delivers it to the retail store, which adds the custom colors desired by the customer. By leasing the space next door to

New Living, The Green Painter was able to provide stop-and-shop services to customers.

In addition to addressing his environmental goals, Kaplan hoped that The Green Painter would enhance sales and turnover at New Living. Specifically, his goal was to turn over the entire inventory six times per year, far faster than his current average of four times per year. By adding paint to his product line, he could encourage customers to revisit the store more often, and also appeal to contractors and painters in the Houston area. While researching the paint business, Kaplan recognized that female consumers generally choose the paint color, but contractors are the target market for the sale of high-quantity paints. A Hispanic workforce dominated the painters in Houston. During some test marketing, Kaplan also found that when he offered painters a free sample of the paint, they were skeptical of its quality because the nontoxic product had none of the traditional odor associated with paint. Rather than perceiving the lack of chemicals as a benefit, contractors and painters expressed skepticism and resistance.

Beyond the need to educate the workforce about nontoxic paint, some other early challenges included the need to develop a paint that was priced at the same level as traditional paints, to be able to market it effectively to painters and contractors. This breakthrough product could be produced in any color and was designed for use in hot, humid climates like Houston.

But even with all these advantages, Kaplan still struggled to establish a willing workforce of painters who would use his new paint products. As an entrepreneur, Kaplan ultimately came up with another experimental idea: create a new cadre of painters. He hired artists as painting contractors and certified them to use his products. The staff of 20 painters currently uses the healthy paint, and The Green Painter continues to recruit artists and others to join this "paint revolution" that aims to make sustainability accessible and affordable.

SUSTAINABLE PAINT

To be sustainable, paint needs to help protect ecosystems and maintain natural resources. Volatile organic compounds have been a primary focus, such that emerging technology has allowed for water-based formulas, light-reflective palettes, and sustainable graffiti removal systems, all of which support the production of paint with low or zero VOC levels. Various manufacturers, including Kelly-Moore Paints, Dunn-Edwards, and MetroPaint, also recycle their paints. As a national account manager for Kelly-Moore explains, "We make it known to our contractors and accounts that we are environmentally friendly and recycle. If they bring back their abundance of product, we remanufacture it."

The different manufacturers take different approaches to achieving sustainability in their paints. For example, Sherwin-Williams's Emerald line uses soybean and sunflower oils; the resin in the paint contains recycled plastic bottles. Other manufacturers include bio-based materials; some claim to be 100 percent natural. One product, Unearthed Paints, creates coatings, plasters, and finishes from clay, chalk, lime, and Italian marble, with vegetable casein protein used as the binding agent and mineral pigmentations.

THE GREEN PAINTER'S APPROACH

The mission of The Green Painter, from the start, has been to ensure sustainability that is accessible and meaningful for consumers. Kaplan describes his business history as similar to opening a Whole Foods grocery store in Houston, Texas, in 1970—challenging and thrilling at the same time. In particular, the original business plan simply did not work. Rather than selling everything available in the home furnishings store, New Living was selling out of custom furniture and related home products, leaving children's furniture, waxes, and energy systems on the shelves.

Thus in an early revision to the business, Kaplan began to focus on building the successful custom product line and eliminate those items that sold poorly or not at all. Without any totally green retailers to use as business models, the changes have represented a continuing experiment. Fortunately, The Green Painter had sufficient time and resources to make mistakes and take risks while still managing and minimizing the downsides. For example, Kaplan agreed to sell half of the shares of his business to 10 investors, giving him sufficient capital to expand.

Through the various experiments, The Green Painter has developed a clear sense of who its customers are: young, 20- to 40-year-old women with families who are committed to healthy lifestyles. The most recent innovations and introductions by the green retailer reflect this understanding. For example, New Living now offers custom-designed furniture made from reclaimed wood. To produce the unique designs, the retailer has incorporated its own wood shop. Then the stains produced and sold by The Green Painter provide the safe, tinted sealant for the desks, dining tables, end tables, bed frames, and unique designs. Each design is really a work of art, such that the store offers a gallery of artistically interesting pieces, priced at around $1,000 and up. In addition, New Living carries a small line of wood furniture made by an external manufacturer that also uses reclaimed wood.

Kaplan also believed that the introduction of a website and a catalog would expand the customer base. After talking with other business owners in the local area, he learned that they all suggested adding social media, which also would help link the products offered by his two business ventures, New Living and The Green Painter. However, in the months since the launch of The Green Painter website, the results have mainly been increased brand awareness, not heightened sales. A survey of customers showed that they want to see furniture ideas and products on the site, not paints. They prefer to see the paint colors in person and are more comfortable coming in to the brick-and-mortar store to buy them. Therefore, the website is undergoing a revision, dedicated more to marketing and with a greater focus on the products sold by New Living rather than green paint sales.

THE FUTURE AND SUSTAINABLE COMPETITIVE ADVANTAGES

This grand experiment has been a work of love, with a clearly focused mission. A new store recently opened in the Heights area of Houston, offering both The Green Painter store and a small New Living retail outlet. The expansion offers a fun place to shop. It also offers innovative service options. For example, people can bring in their old furniture and antiques to have them refinished or else work on the items themselves, with help from the design staff. With this option, Kaplan hopes to build up the green community of consumers; it also reflects the educational goals that have always been part of the retailer's business culture. Accordingly, New Living and The Green Painter was one of the first brick-and-mortar businesses in the country to receive certification as a benefit corporation (B Corp). A benefit corporation designation provides legal protection for the business (reduced director liability), expands stockholder rights, and provides increased access to private investment capital through an annual benefit report. The company must publicly report on its social and environmental performance using established third-party standards.

Currently, business profits reflect the following breakdown: about 30 percent from furniture, 30 percent from paint, 30 percent from mattresses, and 10 percent from design services. It also is negotiating with Whole Foods to offer the paint products in stores, which would expand the brand into vastly new markets. Although the model thus has achieved success, Kaplan and his partners continually seek new ideas to expand their green retailing business and offer the marketplace something special. The future of green retailing is still evolving; social entrepreneurs are at the core, suggesting the need for continuing education, at the university level, about sustainability and recycling concepts, as well as a value system for reasonable consumption. The future holds some green promise.

Sources: UN News Centre, "Sustainable Development Goals Must Address Threats to Environment—UN Officials," www.un.org/apps/news/story.asp?NewsID=44378&Cr=sustainable+development&Cr1=# (accessed March 16, 2013); Glidden Professional, "What Makes a Paint Sustainable: VOCs and Beyond," http://continuingeducation.construction.com/crs.php?L=222&C=759 (accessed February 26, 2013); Christopher Curtland, "Green Sustainable Paint Solutions: Whether Natural or Recycled, Green Paints Can Enhance Sustainability," July 24, 2012, www.buildings.com/article-details/articleid/14433/title/green%20sustainable%20paint%20solutions.aspx (accessed February 26, 2013).

This case was written by Marcella M. Norwood and Shirley D. Ezell, University of Houston.

DISCUSSION QUESTIONS

1. If you were starting a green business in the next five years, how would you design the business model? What lessons could you learn from The Green Painter?

2. Research current business practices being used in the food and retail industries in general and report practices that would help you develop your business.

3. Do a SWAT analysis for this business based on the information provided in this case.

CASE 8   Ashley Stewart

An auditorium full of graduate and undergraduate students was eager to hear what James Rhee, the CEO of Ashley Stewart, the largest plus-size retailer in the United States, would have to say. How did a middle-aged Korean American man turn around a struggling brand that catered primarily to African American women? But Rhee was accustomed to such questions and ready to answer them.

Founded in 1991, Ashley Stewart was named after two distinct style icons: Laura Ashley and Martha Stewart. The founder Joseph Stint sold his shares of the company in 2000. The following decades saw some challenges, such that the company filed for bankruptcy in 2010 and then reorganized again in 2014. But by that point, Rhee—inspired by the brand's promise and its connections to its customers—had resigned from his position on the board as an investor in the retailer to become its CEO. Today, Ashley Stewart maintains just shy of 100 stores in the United States and a global e-commerce platform, helping curvy women around the world find beautiful fashions that fit.

So how did a former high school teacher and hedge fund manager manage the success of a fashion brand?

INDUSTRY ENVIRONMENT AND ASHLEY STEWART'S POSITION

Approximately 67 percent of U.S. women wear sizes 14 to 34, yet many companies do not offer sufficient options for them. Sales of plus-size apparel thus account for only approximately $20 billion of the $108 billion apparel industry. Still, it is among the fastest-growing categories in fashion. Whereas once the fashion industry ignored this segment and focused almost exclusively on wearers of smaller sizes, today retailers cannot ignore this demand. Sales of women's plus-size apparel also increased almost 17 percent between 2013 and 2016.

Just like every other retail setting, women's fashions also have been influenced by the growth of the Internet. As the number of digital shoppers continues to increase, virtually every brand is seeking a space to establish itself in the digital world, to attract attention and expand its reach through traffic to either its website or its stores. At www.ashleystewart.com, for example, customers find bright colors and stylish models sporting the latest trends. With visually attractive lookbooks, the site also offers certain items exclusively to web shoppers every season.

But in the early 2010s, Ashley Stewart did not even have wi-fi at its company headquarters. Corporate decisions were mostly based on "gut" perceptions, rather than data. Its e-commerce platform was antiquated. Turnover among employees was high, and the corporate culture was described as fearful, leaving the brand without any real credibility. Following more than a decade of losses, the company seemingly had lost its way: Employees were angry, customers were annoyed, and investors had lost all hope.

But Rhee saw something in the brand. In his own words, he "loved the brand and everything it stood for. Ashley Stewart had been founded to provide plus-size fashion for women in boutique-like settings in urban neighborhoods across the United States. After listening to our customers, I came to realize that the brand stood for more than that—values like respect, empowerment, and joy. Despite the company's history of failure, I believed that the brand could capitalize on several macro-cyclical trends with a rein-vented business model."

A graduate of Harvard Law School, James Rhee had been a high school teacher and private equity investor, with no experience in the fashion industry. So he adopted a teaching-oriented philosophy and applied hedge fund policies to the effort to save the brand.

RHEE'S PHILOSOPHY

Rhee focused on a few core principles that led to the turn-around of the company. He relied on numbers and math, sought to reinvent the company culture, adopted a central focus on the core customer, encouraged continuous innovation, and—perhaps above all—prioritized kindness.

Rhee understood that customers would behave differently on different days, so Ashley Stewart's business model and algorithms would have to adapt to customers' varying behavior. Using sophisticated analytics and data, he improved the flow of goods through the supply chain, which also sped up the arrival of new fashions into stores. Furthermore, Rhee insisted on updated technology in all realms of the business, so that it could offer standardized IT and e-commerce operations. Preferring measures that could not be manipulated, Rhee focused on loyalty, returns on investment and capital, and time assessments. Moreover, "When we were re-writing all of the planning algorithms and business reports, the math and operational discipline was done at the level at which a blue-chip investment firm would operate."

These changes were also part of the reinvented culture, along with physical changes, such as knocking down all the walls in the corporate headquarters to encourage an open-door policy. The company stopped using virtually all its formal job descriptions. Instead, the goal was a culture that relied on mentoring and teaching, as well as a services-oriented approach. In response to the radical changes, approximately 40 percent of the employees at corporate headquarters left, but those remaining were dedicated to the new culture.

This new services-oriented culture also entailed a reinvigorated focus on the core customer, the "she" who is embodied in the very name Ashley Stewart. In every decision, Ashley Stewart considers what "she" might want and ensures it is respecting "her," such as through enhanced customer service and customer engagement. This "she" is critical to everything associated with Ashley Stewart and part of the reason Rhee even attempted the turnaround: "If this was a business that sold widgets or old expensive neckties for rich guys, I wouldn't have done this." This brand somehow had persisted for decades, without making any consistent profits. It was able to do so simply because "she" loved Ashley Stewart, which provided "her" with beautifully merchandised stores, where each customer is greeted by "Ms. Ashley," the store manager. Once customers found the stores, they stayed loyal to them; Rhee even recounts meeting three generations of women from one family coming together to shop in a place they felt comfortable and respected. With its segmentation and targeting focused primarily on African American plus-size women, Ashley Stewart also provided a safe space for a frequently marginalized population—another reason Rhee was drawn to the sinking brand. When he looked at customers in stores, he observed that their body language signaled more confidence, reminding him of how his mother, who emigrated from Korea, would exhibit pride and satisfaction when she walked into a Korean store. It was these emotions that he wanted customers at Ashley Stewart, the all-important "her," to feel when they walked into any store.

But a comfortable store is not enough to attract repeat visits by fashionable shoppers if it does not continually offer new looks. Ashley Stewart seeks to get new options in stores within six to eight weeks. Its assortment is extensive and includes clothing, swimwear, shoes, and accessories. Furthermore, noting that larger sizes were stocking out quickly, Ashley Stewart recently added sizes larger than the traditional plus sizes, 14 to 26. Many manufacturers charge retailers more for larger sizes, but Ashley Stewart refuses to pass on this additional cost to its customers, so the fast fashions also remain affordable for consumers.

Outside the stores, innovation also is the hallmark of Ashley Stewart's reinvented website. The brand refers to itself as a real person—that same "she" who is respected throughout the company. With this personalized phrasing, Ashley Stewart connects with other "Neighborhood Girls Gone Global," reminding them of how someone or something local can engage communities all over the world and succeed globally, such as when it promises, "With roots based in New York, my mission has always been to inspire you. . . . I want every woman to cherish her curves. After all, they're what make us sexy, confident, and fabulous. Ashley Stewart is a sisterhood, your best girlfriend next door. Join me—you fit in here." For its 25th anniversary, the retailer hosted a Rock the Block party in Brooklyn, a fun event that garnered more than 15 million social media impressions.

Its social media presence also is marked by its overriding philosophy of kindness, which Rhee calls the company's "core strategic pillar." For example, in a nationwide campaign, the #LoveYourCurvesTour, Ashley Stewart worked to connect with loyal customers by hosting fashion shows, model hunts, and shopping parties in Atlanta, Chicago, Philadelphia, Baltimore, Detroit, and New York. Encouraging women to celebrate their curves, the brand reaffirms its respect and appreciation for its customers. This appreciation also was evident in its #MOMspiration campaign, which encouraged customers to submit pictures of their mothers or daughters that depicted a meaningful memory they shared—perhaps one made while shopping at Ashley Stewart. In its philanthropic efforts, such as #ASGives, it also partners with charities that support local communities, raises money for cancer research, donates clothes and shoes, and grants need-based scholarships. Even in the midst of the company's bankruptcy and reorganization in 2014, Rhee insisted on introducing a generous charitable program during the holiday season, to remind the company of its need to stay true to its core values.

WHAT DOES THE FUTURE HOLD FOR ASHLEY STEWART?

By most accounts, Rhee's efforts at Ashley Stewart have been a huge success. The corporate culture is healthier. Sales growth has hit double digits over the past few years; e-commerce sales account for 35 percent of total sales. In addition to its robust sales, Ashley Stewart is widely recognized as one of the world's most engaging sites on social media, ranked among the top 10 in terms of its website's active engagement with customers through Facebook.

But the outlook is not all rosy. In its continued efforts to market the brand, Ashley Stewart has run up against rules imposed by Google's AdWords against targeting customers using terms that refer to their body type. Thus, any advertisement that promotes the brand as dedicated to curvy or plus-size women would be rejected from this popular and effective advertising channel. The policy has a respectful aim, yet for a retailer that relies specifically on body type to segment its market, it creates an impossible dilemma.

But facing an auditorium of interested students, James Rhee still predicts the continued success of the brand, as long as "she" continues to embrace the core principles that have gotten her to where she is today.

Sources: Shelly Banjo and Rani Molla, "Retailers Ignore Most of America's Women," *Bloomberg Gadfly*, May 10, 2016, www.bloomberg.com/gadfly/articles/2016-05-10/plus-size-could-save-retailers; James Rhee, "How I

Brought Ashley Stewart Back from Bankruptcy," *Harvard Business Review*, July 31, 2015; Marianne Wilson, "The Unlikely Champion of Ashley Stewart," *Chain Store Age*, April 20, 2016; Teresa Novellino, "After 2 Bankruptcies in 3 Years, a Reinvented Ashley Stewart Hits the Full-Figured Runway," *New York Business Journal*, June 22, 2015; "About Me," www.ashleystewart.com/aboutus.html.

This case study was written by Megha Mehta, Babson College; Elisabeth Nevins, Effectual Editorial Services; and Dhruv Grewal, Babson College.

DISCUSSION QUESTIONS

1. **What is Ashley Stewart's retail format?**

2. **Who is its target market? Could/should that target market be expanded?**

3. **What are its bases for sustainable competitive advantage?**

4. **Perform a SWOT analysis for Ashley Stewart. If you were a potential investor, would you invest in it? Why or why not?**

CASE 9   The Decision-Making Process for Buying a Bicycle

The Sanchez family lives in Corona, California, west of Los Angeles. Jorge is a physics professor at the University of California–Riverside. His wife Anna is a volunteer, working 10 hours a week at the Crisis Center. They have two children: Nadia, age 10, and Miguel, age 8.

In February, Anna's parents sent her $100 to buy a bicycle for Nadia's birthday. They bought Nadia her first bike when she was 5. Now they wanted to buy her a full-size bike for her 11th birthday. Even though Anna's parents felt every child should have a bike, Anna didn't think Nadia really wanted one. Nadia and most of her friends didn't ride their bikes often, and she was afraid to ride to school because of the traffic. So Anna decided to buy her the cheapest full-size bicycle she could find.

Because most of Nadia's friends didn't have full-size bikes, she didn't know much about them and had no preferences for a brand or type. To learn more about the types available and their prices, Anna and Nadia checked the catalog for Performance Bicycle, a large mail-order bicycling equipment retailer. The catalog was given to them by a friend of Anna's, who was an avid biker. After looking through the catalog, Nadia said the only thing she cared about was the color. She wanted a blue bike, blue being her favorite color.

Using the Internet, Anna located and called several local retail outlets selling bikes. To her surprise, she found that the local Kmart store actually had the best price for a 26-inch bicycle—even lower than Toys "R" Us and Walmart.

Anna drove to Kmart, went straight to the sporting goods department, and selected a blue bicycle before a salesperson approached her. She took the bike to the cash register and paid for it. After making the purchase, the Sanchezes found out that the bike was cheap in all senses. The chrome plating on the wheels was very thin and rusted away in six months. Both tires split and had to be replaced.

A year later, Anna's grandparents sent $200 for a bike for Miguel. From their experience with Nadia's bike, Anna and Jorge realized that the lowest-priced bike might not be the least expensive option in the long run. Miguel is very active and

somewhat careless, so they want to buy a sturdy bike. Miguel said he wanted a red, 21-speed, lightweight mountain bike with a full-suspension aluminum frame and cross-country tires.

Anna and Jorge were concerned that Miguel wouldn't maintain an expensive bike with full suspension. When they saw an ad for a bicycle sale at Target, they went to the store with Miguel. A salesperson approached them at an outdoor display of bikes and directed them to the sporting goods department inside the store. There they found row after row of red, single-speed BMX bikes with no suspension and minimal accessories to maintain—just the type of bike Anna and Jorge felt was ideal for Miguel.

Another salesperson approached them and tried to interest them in a more expensive bike. Jorge dislikes salespeople trying to push something on him and interrupted her in midsentence. He said he wanted to look at the bikes on his own. With a little suggestion, Miguel decided he wanted one of these bikes. His desire for accessories was satisfied when they bought a multifunction cyclocomputer for the bike. After buying a bike for Miguel, Jorge decided he'd like a bike for himself to ride on weekends. Jorge had ridden bikes since he was 5. In graduate school, before he was married, he'd owned a 10-speed road bike. He frequently took 50-mile rides with friends, but he hadn't owned a bike since moving to Riverside 15 years ago.

Jorge didn't know much about current types of bicycles. He bought a copy of *Bicycling* at a newsstand to see what was available. He also went online to read Consumer Reports's evaluation of road, mountain, and hybrid bikes. On the basis of this information, he decided he wanted a Cannondale. It had all the features he wanted: a lightweight frame, durable construction, and a comfort sports saddle. When Jorge called the discount stores and bicycle shops, he found they didn't carry the Cannondale brand. He thought about buying the bicycle from an Internet site but was concerned about making such a large purchase without a test ride. He then decided he might not really need a bike. After all, he'd been without one for 15 years.

One day, after lunch, he was walking back to his office and saw a small bicycle shop. The shop was run down, with bicycle parts scattered across the floor. The owner, a young man in grease-covered shorts, was fixing a bike. As Jorge was looking around, the owner approached him and asked him if he liked to bicycle. Jorge said he used to but had given it up when he moved to Riverside. The owner said that was a shame because there were a lot of nice places to tour around Riverside.

As their conversation continued, Jorge mentioned his interest in a Cannondale and his disappointment in not finding a store in Riverside that sold them. The owner said that he could order a Cannondale for Jorge but that they weren't in inventory and delivery took between six and eight weeks. He suggested a Trek and showed Jorge one he currently had in stock. Jorge thought the $700 price was too high, but the owner convinced him to try it next weekend. They would ride together in the country. The owner and some of his friends took a 60-mile tour with Jorge. Jorge enjoyed the experience, recalling his college days. After the tour, Jorge bought the Trek.

This case was written by Dan Rice and Barton Weitz, University of Florida.

DISCUSSION QUESTIONS

1. Outline the decision-making process for each of the Sanchez family's bicycle purchases.

2. Compare the different purchase processes for the three bikes. What stimulated each of them? What factors were considered in making the store choice decisions and purchase decisions?

3. Construct a multiattribute model for each purchase decision. How do the attributes considered and importance weights vary for each decision?

CASE 10   Home Depot: Opportunities and Challenges in China

The Home Depot, Inc. was founded in 1978 by Bernie Marcus and Arthur Blank who had a vision of one-stop shopping for the do-it-yourself (DIY) patron. In June 1979, the two pioneers brought this vision to reality when they opened the first two stores in Atlanta, Georgia. Over the years, the company has achieved stable growth and maintained leading market share in the home improvement industry. With almost 2,000 retail outlets across the United States and nearly 300 international stores—about 200 in Canada and 100 in Mexico—Home Depot has become the largest home improvement retailer in the world, offering a wide assortment of building materials, home improvement products, lawn and garden merchandise, and a diversified range of consultation, installation, delivery, and bulk inventory services both in-store and online for homeowners and professional contractors.

THE DO-IT-YOURSELF BUSINESS MODEL

From its inception, Home Depot has established a well-known business model centered on the DIY customer. The DIY customer consists of homeowners who purchase materials, tools, and appliances to complete projects and installations. To assist this customer group, the retailer offers a variety of educational workshops and project clinics to guide homeowners in the completion of their own work. The DIY model has worked well in the United States because it fits with the independent and individualistic characteristics of the U.S. culture. In addition, some people find pleasure working on their homes, and it is less expensive than hiring someone else to do it.

After two decades of success with the DIY model in the United States, the company deemed the model a strong candidate for greater endeavors, pursuing international expansion as a significant opportunity for growth. Home Depot expanded into Canada in 1994, and then into Mexico in 2001, both through the acquisition of local home improvement centers. Following its triumph in these two international markets, Home Depot started setting eyes on China—an exploding market with a population of more than 1 billion people. But soon the retailer found that the market was unreceptive to its entry. What happened in China?

INTERNATIONAL EXPANSION TO CHINA

In 2006, Home Depot entered China in order to corner the market in one of the world's fastest-growing economies. At the time, the Chinese home improvement market was booming, estimated at $50 billion, and had a stunning growth rate of 20 percent per year. Viewed as a young, underdeveloped, and underserviced market, China presented itself as a lucrative market with enormous growth opportunities. Hinging on its success in the domestic and international markets, using the same DIY model, Home Depot ventured into China through an aggressive acquisition of a local Chinese big-box home improvement retail chain, Home Way. Soon the company opened 12 Home Depot stores in the nation's northern corridor.

What Home Depot discovered, however, was that the same strategy that brought its success in the North American markets was the exact cause of its failure in China. Implementing the DIY model in the China market channeled a large gap between the services offered by Home Depot and the expectations held by the Chinese consumers for a home improvement retailer. The DIY culture that has sustained Home Depot in the United States is absent in China, and the accessibility to cheap and abundant labor stunted the receptivity of American-born DIY ethos. Chinese consumers' expectations of do-it-for-me rendered the retailer ill-positioned in the market.

As a result, after six consecutive years of struggle, Home Depot was forced to close all of its big-box stores in 2012. However, the company did not want to completely give up the China market. It maintained two small specialty shops in the city of Tianjin—a paint and flooring store and a home décor store. Claiming China "a market too big to ignore," Home Depot executives are searching for a new business model that might work for the China market.

THE EMERGENCE OF THE DO-IT-FOR-ME MODEL

Meanwhile, on its home front, Home Depot has discovered new opportunities as its domestic markets begin to shift from the dominant traditional DIY customer to include two growing customer groups: the do-it-for-me (DIFM) and the professional (Pro) customers. Home Depot's DIFM customers are homeowners who typically purchase products and installation completion services from the retailer. Home Depot currently has more than 100,000 professional subcontractors who perform over 2 million installations per year for DIFM customers. These numbers are projected to further increase as the U.S. housing markets are improving and populations are aging. The DIFM customers may hire third parties for installation services. The third-party providers are part of Home Depot's Pro customer group, including professional renovators/remodelers, general contractors, repairpeople, installers, small business owners, and tradespeople who purchase supplies from the retailer. Although Pro customers make up only 3 percent of Home Depot's customer base, they contribute to roughly 40 percent of the company's total sales. In contrast, Home Depot's DIY customers still account for about 60 percent of the company's total sales earnings, yet their percentage contribution to total sales growth is waning.

The shift in Home Depot's customer bases has steered the company to the services facet. In 2015, Home Depot acquired Interline Brands, Inc. to expand its service capacity. The $1.7 billion acquisition also helps Home Depot attract subcontractors with broader skill sets to optimize its service portfolio for DIFM customers. With the increasing demand for installation services, the concern becomes not only of capacity, but also quality. Since Home Depot serves as a general contractor for DIFM customers on installations, it incurs liabilities for its subcontractors. In order to maintain and improve customer satisfaction, the company needs to manage quality standards and strengthen quality assurance for services performed by its professional subcontractors. As such, Home Depot implemented a new interconnected retail and service framework, the three-legged stool strategy, in 2015. The emphasis is on providing a seamless and frictionless customer experience, curating the most comprehensive product assortment, and improving productivity and efficiency both in-store and online.

As Home Depot's service portfolio takes on drastic reformation for the first time in decades, the company is strengthening its position as a service retailer for its rising customer bases. In particular, the emergence of its DIFM model seems to inject a new possibility—Should the retailer reconsider full-scope operations in the China market? In order to answer the question, executives need to consider the broader market implications of China's current competitive arena and recent trends in regulatory, economic, and cultural environments.

THE HOME IMPROVEMENT AND FINISHING SERVICES MARKET IN CHINA

China's home improvement market can be summarized as three trends: (1) the privatization of the housing sector, (2) the growth in real estate development, and (3) the rising demand for building completion and interior design services.

China is the world's second-largest economy after the United States, with a middle-class population surpassing the entire population of the United States. Since the 1990s, the Chinese government has been moving to retire the socialistic public housing system, known as "Dan Wei," that was originally designed to evenly distribute housing to urban residents under a planned system. The deregulation of the housing sector and the extension of government protections have spiked private purchases due to boosted consumer confidence in homeowner rights. Over the past 20 years, private homeownership has risen from nearly zero to about 70 percent, and China now has one of the highest homeownership rates in the world.

As China is releasing its grip on government entities and taking great strides toward a market system, the privatization of the housing sector has opened the arena for domestic and international investment, promoting drastic growth in real estate development. The typical practice for developers in China is to sell residential properties as a hollow structural shell, with new owners left to design even the most basic finishing—flooring, carpeting, plumbing, tiling, painting, fixtures, and appliances—resulting in an immediate demand for building completion and finishing services.

The revenue of the building completion and interior design industry in China is almost $625 billion, and its annual growth rate is projected at 12.1 percent for several years. This industry consists of a substantial number of small players, with the top five home improvement retailers in China occupying merely 2.7 percent of the total market. Gold Mantis Construction Decoration Co. is the largest, with only 1.1 percent market share. The majority of players are domestic, privately owned companies that comprise 65.8 percent of the total market, with direct foreign investors accounting for only 5.1 percent of industry presence.

The competitive landscape shows that the current home improvement services market in China is fragmented and lacking strong leadership. The climate is favorable, and it could be an opportune time for Home Depot to enter and position as a leading service provider. However, based on their prior entry experiences in China, executives know that simply duplicating the service model in its domestic market will not prove effective. In order to maneuver within China's dynamic market, the company needs to assess the nation's complex environments and build an understanding of the underlying cultural and social drivers that shape how the Chinese set expectations and perceive services in the home improvement industry.

ENVIRONMENTAL COMPLEXITIES IN CHINA

The economic and cultural environment in China presents both opportunities and challenges for foreign entrants. China's economy is fast growing, but the country is experiencing a massive imbalance in economic development. Following China's reform, housing, industrial, and technological development has been concentrated in the most prosperous sectors along China's coastal regions, including Northeast China, the Beijing-Tianjin corridor, the Yangtze River Delta, and the Pearl River Delta. As cities on the coastal rim become increasingly congested, the result is a clearly segregated

EXHIBIT 1   Per Capita Income Disparity in China

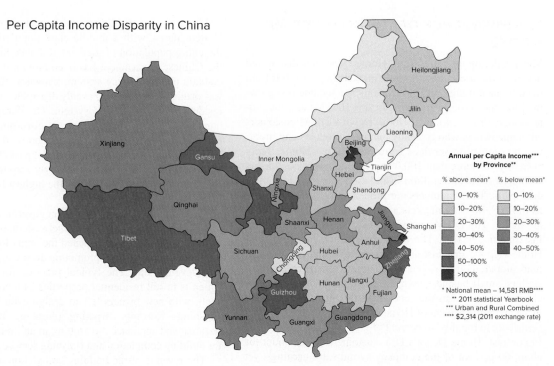

Source: Matt, Schiavenza. "Mapping China's Income Inequality," *The Atlantic,* September 13, 2013.

population, with the higher-income class residing in the urban areas and the lower-income class in rural and in-land regions. The disposable income of urban residents in these regions, on average, is more than triple that of those living in rural regions (see Exhibit 1). To further widen the class divide, the cultural intricacies also play a fundamental role.

The cultural environment defines consumer behaviors and expectations. The Chinese cultural intricacies exert broad influence on the attitudes and value perceptions of Chinese consumers, and these compounded forces in turn place pressures on foreign entrants. Examined through Hofstede's cultural dimensions, the Chinese culture is characterized by a low degree of individualism and a high degree of power distance. The collectivist culture emphasizes group identification; the self is only part of the whole. As a high power distance culture, the Chinese social system is structured with unequal distribution of power, distinctive order and authority, and the division of roles.

Furthermore, historically prevalent ideologies of Confucianism still widely affect societal perceptions of appropriate behavior in a hierarchical and role-abiding context. The ancient Confucian proverb states, "Those who work with their brain rule, those who work with their muscles are the ruled." These ideals significantly complicate the receptiveness of the Western concepts, particularly those rooted in the U.S. individualistic values, such as DIY. In the United States, Home Depot's primary market consists of people who are not carpenters, electricians, plumbers, or repairpersons but instead do home repairs and improvements during their spare time. In China, these are two distinctly separate identities. Social perceptions regarding DIY are clear—manual labor is the expected role of the working class. Middle- and upper-class populations would expect finishing work to be done for them. As such, Home Depot's DIY model was

ill-fitted to Chinese social and cultural expectations, while the new DIFM model that Home Depot is developing may show promise as a foundation for a new approach in the China market.

RECONSIDERATION OF CHINA

One decade following its misstep in China, Home Depot is reconsidering the market in order to regain first mover advantage. Its domestic rival, Lowe's, is considering tapping into China's growing home improvement industry. Home Depot's new focus on the DIFM model has significantly boosted its service capacity, and its two specialty shops in Tianjin have already given the retailer a foothold in the nation. Still, the intertwining of cultural factors, social stratification, and economic disparity require Home Depot to pay close attention to market expectations. If Home Depot wants to position itself as a service retailer in China targeting DIFM customers, the company will need to align its value proposition with customer expectations and meet the Chinese consumers' standard of service quality. The inability to identify and respond to customer expectations in a timely manner may adversely affect customer satisfaction, the demand for services, and the company's image in the market. Since the installation services for the DIFM clientele involve third-party subcontractors, Home Depot will also need to learn how to effectively manage the performance and service quality of its subcontractors in China.

After a harsh lesson learned through its initial entry attempt, Home Depot is carefully gauging market opportunities and challenges in China, as well as its new service strengths. Of all concerns, the most critical is to design an adapted DIFM model that can deliver products and services in a manner that is culturally sensitive to key markets amid the complexities in China's social, economic, and geographic environments. Many foreign entrants have learned the power of adaptation. For example, the Swedish furniture giant IKEA adds services to help Chinese customers assemble their furniture. KFC sells soy milk and egg tarts in its Chinese stores. McDonald's features "bubble tea," tea with tapioca balls in the bottom, on the menu. Building on it previous experiences, Home Depot executives are weighing the pros and cons, and pondering once again about the unresolved—how to successfully adapt its business models to China.

Sources: May Hongmei Gao, "Culture Determines Business Models: Analyzing Home Depot's Failure Case in China for International Retailers from a Communication Perspective," *Thunderbird International Business Review* 55, no. 2 (2013), pp. 173–191; Home Depot website, 2015 Annual Report, http://ir.homedepot.com/~/media/Files/H/HomeDepot-IR/documents/current-forms/hd-fy-2015-annual-report.pdf; Chantal Todé, "Home Depot Enters China with Home Way Acquisition," December 20, 2006, *Direct Marketing News*, www.dmnews.com/news/home-depot-enters-china-with-home-way-acquisition/article/93898/; Patti Waldmeir, "Home Depot Leaves Beijing, Closure Reflects Absence of DIY Culture in China," *Financial Times*, January 27, 2011; Laurie Burkitt, "Home Depot to Shut Seven China Stores, Take $160 Mln Charge," *Wall Street Journal*, September 14, 2012; Home Depot website, https://corporate.homedepot.com/; Xiao-xi Hui, "The Chinese Housing Reform and the Following New Urban Question," The 4th International Conference of the International Forum on Urbanism, 2009, Amsterdam/Delft, The New Urban Question—Urbanism beyond Neo-Liberalism, pp. 381–392; Steve Krin, "The Home Depot Considers Entering China," David F. Miller Center for Retailing Education and Research, University of Florida; IBIS World Industry Report, "Building Completion & Interior Design in China," August 2015, www.ibisworld.com/industry/china/building-completion-interior-design.html; Matt Schiavenza, "Mapping China's Income Inequality," *The Atlantic*, September 13, 2013, www.theatlantic.com/china/archive/2013/09/mapping-chinas-income-inequality/279637/; ITIM International, Geert Hofstede, "Comparison—China/U.S.," https://geert-hofstede.com/china.html; Laurie Burkitt, "Home Depot Learns Chinese Prefer 'Do-It-for-Me,'" *Wall Street Journal*, September 14, 2012.

This case was written by Erin Marie Hannigan and Ying Huang, University of Massachusetts, Lowell. Erin Marie Hannigan was an undergraduate student under the supervision of Professor Ying Huang.

DISCUSSION QUESTIONS

1. Discuss the elements of adaptability and global culture as they relate to successful global retailing. How should Home Depot adapt its business model and marketing strategy for success amid China's environmental complexities?

2. Perform a SWOT analysis to determine whether or not Home Depot should reenter the Chinese market. Exhibit 5–5, "Indicators of the Potential, Support, and Risk in International Markets," should be useful for pinpointing some of the issues to consider in your SWOT.

CASE 11 Parisian Patisserie "Maison Ladurée" Goes Global

Ladurée, a famous French pastry company known worldwide for its macarons, entered the U.S. market in 2011, which produced opportunities—but also challenges—for this company.

It all began in 1862, when Louis Ernest Ladurée created a bakery at 16 Rue Royale in Paris, where the most prestigious names in French luxury goods were already located. Ernest Ladurée's wife had the idea of mixing the Parisian café and pastry shop, which gave birth to one of the first tea salons in the city. At the beginning of the twentieth century, Pierre Desfontaines, second cousin of Louis Ernest Ladurée, first thought of taking two macaron shells (almond meringue cakes) and joining them with ganache, a creamy, smooth filling that gave birth to Ladurée's macarons.

This tea salon imbued with a refined atmosphere and charged with history seduced David Holder and his father, Francis Holder, founder of the Holder Group. The family would have lunch at the original Ladurée every Saturday. When they found out that the company was for sale by descendants of the Ladurée family, they bought it, having convinced the owners that they would preserve its heritage. David Holder likes to tell people that he woke up a sleeping beauty with their macarons. Indeed, macarons in general were not very popular at the time they bought the company in 1997.

Since then, Holder has run Ladurée more as a maison de mode rather than a pastry brand and wants to keep a sense of exclusiveness and luxury. Macarons are his most profitable pastry, which accounts for 40 percent of the sales revenues and comprises 70 percent of the takeaway sales. He boasts 18 subtle flavors, which change according to the season. In addition to its core range of macarons packed in pale mauve and pistachio boxes, Ladurée also retails its own pastries, coffee, chocolates, ice cream macarons, candies, perfumed candles, bath and body products, and fragrances.

Ladurée has successfully understood the challenge of satisfying the needs of a hip and global clientele and to position itself as haute couture of the food market. Since 1997, Ladurée has been expanding, first in four locations in Paris, where it sells 55,000 macarons a day. There is also one at Chateau de Versailles, boutiques and kiosks in Orly and Roissy airports, and a boutique in Saint-Tropez. There are currently 82 Ladurée stores in 27 countries. Around the world, each boutique sticks to the Parisian Ladurée signature style. The shops are done in pastel green with traditional decorative accents, mirrors, and dark wood, meant to showcase chocolates and tabletop items—and to respect the French tea salon tradition. Macarons and chocolates are made exclusively in Paris for all the Ladurée shops to protect the secret recipes. Different types of retail formats exist, from standalone retail locations featuring a small footprint, few seats, and excluding pastries and alcohol in Australia, for example, to larger tea salon sites, which are essentially stores within department stores, such as in Printemps in France and Harrod's in the United Kingdom, or within malls such as in the Centria Mall in Riyadh, the Saudi capital.

Ladurée opened its first Australian store in Sydney in July 2012 with its traditional French fit-out. While the company has eight baking facilities around the world, Australian products are frozen and shipped from Switzerland, where a production plant is located. David Holder was looking for production plant locations in the Middle East, in eastern Europe, and in Africa. The company chose Switzerland because of social peace, raw materials quality, and fresh air. Holder is not afraid to mention the Swiss-made origin of its macarons.

Ladurée entered the U.S. market in August 2011 by opening a shop on Madison Avenue in New York. Ladurée expanded to SoHo, on West Broadway at Broome Street, in the fall of 2012. This location boasts a retail shop and a tearoom plus a full-service restaurant with about 200 seats, private dining rooms, and a garden terrace. It hosts two chefs from France to prepare everything except the macarons and chocolates. Macarons are all flown in fresh from Paris. The other pastries, shipped from France, are stored in refrigerators.

After New York, Ladurée expanded to other American cities, such as Los Angeles and Miami. The retailer also opened stores in Hong Kong, Brazil, South Korea, Morocco, Qatar, and in well-known jet-set destinations Cannes and Megève. The Holder family never invests directly in countries where political, economical, or religious risk is possible. They own and operate their stores in France, the United States, Japan, and the United Kingdom; for all other locations, boutiques are owned by local franchisees.

Sources: www.laduree.com/; Carla Bridge, "Ladurée," *Inside Retailing*, May 25, 2012; Axel Tardieu, "Ladurée arrive à New York Par," September 7, 2011, http://frenchmorning.com/ny/2011/09/07/ouverture-de-la-premiere-boutique-laduree-a-new-york/; Anne-Laure Pham, "Ladurée ouvre boutique à New York," August 31, 2011, http://weekend.levif.be/tendance/culinaire/actualite-culinaire/laduree-ouvre-boutique-a-new-york/article-1195094843984.htm (accessed July 23, 2012); Catherine Dubouloz, "Nous avons d'importants projets de développement à l'international" and "À partir de l'automne 2011, les macarons de Ladurée seront produits en Gruyère," *Le Temps,* November 19, 2010; Mathilde Visseyrias, "Ladurée, l'autre pépite familiale," *Le Figaro*, December 17, 2010; Florence Fabricant, "Macarons and Ice Cream, Direct from Paris to the Upper East Side," *New York Times*, August, 30, 2011; Hannah Leighton, "Maison Ladurée to Open Soho Location This Fall," June 27, 2012, http://ny.eater.com/archives/2012/06/maison_ladure_opening_soho_location_by_fall.php; "Ladurée: A Clean Affair with Macarons!," *Arab News*, June 12, 2012.

This case was written by Sandrine Heitz-Spahn, Universite De Lorraine; and Michael Levy, Babson College.

DISCUSSION QUESTIONS

1. What is Ladurée's target market and retail strategy in the United States?
2. What are the key steps Ladurée has to go through when entering the American market?
3. Explain the reasons Ladurée owns its store in some countries and uses franchising with local licensees in others.
4. Which type(s) of retailing format(s) and location(s) is (are) best suited to match Ladurée's marketing strategy in the United States?
5. Could Ladurée sell its products online? Why or why not?

CASE 12   Retailing in India: The Impact of Hypermarkets

The history of India contains a wealth of change and alteration, and the modern era is no different as the country blossoms into a major player in the global economy. Sizable economic growth during the past decade, particularly in the retail sector, has changed the way Indian consumers behave. Although the size of the current Indian retail sector is impressive, its potential really speaks to what retailing will mean in the future. The retail market in India was approximately $600 billion in 2015, and by 2020 it will reach nearly $1 trillion. Furthermore, modern retailing (described shortly) is expected to expand twice as much as traditional retailing per year.

Before 2000, Indian consumers generally purchased many of their retail goods from local mom-and-pop stores called kiranas, which sold mainly provisions and groceries. Shopping at kiranas is easy and convenient because the small stores serve specific neighborhoods and establish personal relationships with their customers.

International retailers are slowly making their way into India. In the past, to enter the country they had two options: They could either set up a wholly owned subsidiary (WOS) in India, or they could enter a joint venture with an existing Indian firm. Until recently, India's government allowed foreign companies to open only single-brand stores, such as IKEA and Apple, in which the foreign company entered a joint venture with an Indian firm in which they owned no more than 51 percent of the Indian company they were partnering with. In 2012, India made dramatic changes to its laws regarding international retailers doing business in the country. Single-brand retailers are now allowed to retain 100 percent ownership of the subsidiary company (making them into wholly owned subsidiaries). India also eased its laws for multibrand retailers, though not as much as it did for single-brand retailers. Specifically, multibrand retailers are now allowed to open stores in India's 53 cities with populations greater than 1 million, provided that they retain no more than 51 percent ownership of the Indian firm they are entering the joint venture with, spend at least 50 percent of their investment capital on building supply chain infrastructure, and source a minimum of 30 percent of the manufactured goods they sell from small- to medium-sized local Indian companies.

Walmart and Tesco have opened hypermarkets in India, but doing so was not an easy process. Carrefour waited 10 years to open its first store in India as a result of the previous restrictions, and closed them all in 2014. The large store layouts and variety of merchandise force customers to spend more time in the stores, which in turn lead to more sales. The potential for hypermarkets in India sheds light on the country's changing retail landscape and the shopping habits of its consumers. The infusion of hypermarkets threatens to rob local store owners of their customer base.

Although this is good news for hypermarket and supermarket retailers, the changes in the laws are proving difficult to navigate. Walmart announced in September 2012 that it would open several retail stores in the next 12 to 18 months with partner Bharti Walmart, but Indian regulators quickly brought scrutiny to the partnership. In October 2012 it was announced that Walmart was being investigated for possible violations of the foreign investment laws, and by late November of the same year Walmart had suspended several of its employees, including its Indian CFO, until its own investigation was concluded. Clearly, although India is an excellent business opportunity, the road is rocky.

Currently, there are about 500 hypermarkets and 700 supermarkets in India. India has been experiencing a 20 percent annual growth in retail markets. Each new store opening may draw customers from 20 to 25 kiranas and fruit and vegetable stands, affecting more than 100,000 vendors. Most kiranas cannot compete with hypermarkets because these larger retail outlets create more efficiency within the supply chain. Much local produce in India currently is wasted because the country lacks sufficient infrastructure. Even as it progresses through rapid development, India still lacks some amenities that Westerners take for granted, such as refrigeration in retail operations. If a large retailer wants to open a hypermarket in India, it will have to invest capital to ensure freshness throughout the supply chain and help reduce waste. The Indian government is expected to spend $500 billion (U.S.) over the next few years to develop a world-class infrastructure, which should spur growth in the retail sector.

The lack of infrastructure underlies a related issue facing hypermarkets. Unlike in Western nations, India's rather poor roads and transportation systems do not allow retailers to locate on large plots of land on the outskirts of town because few consumers can reach them. Therefore, hypermarkets must look for retail space in more urban areas, which provide little available real estate. Buying up space from existing stores means displacing local corner shops already inhabiting that space, and this may prompt protests from Indian consumers and store owners who value the Indian tradition that the kiranas represent. Yet, larger retail outlets in India could have a dramatic impact on the economy, possibly creating millions of jobs in the next 10 years. Although many Indians may not appreciate the notion of hypermarkets immediately, their presence is likely inevitable.

Much of the impetus for the emergence of hypermarkets in India also comes from changes among Indian consumers. The country's younger generations are exposed to a host of innovative products that were unknown to their parents. They are far more receptive to new products and ideas. In addition, this segment of the population reflects the shifting age demographics; more than half of India's current population is younger than 25 years of age. With such a large percentage of younger consumers, it seems inevitable that India's cultural tastes will change. The strength and abundance of local kiranas has been a cultural mainstay, but they cannot efficiently offer Indians access to new and technologically advanced products. Because hypermarkets combine department stores and supermarkets, they carry product lines that local vendors cannot. They sell brand-name products at affordable prices, thereby enabling Indians to purchase a wide assortment of goods that they otherwise could not have.

This shift, from local mom-and-pop stores to more organized retail outlets, is happening very quickly in India. It is embraced by many consumers despite the cultural and legal considerations associated with hypermarkets. Furthermore, because hypermarkets offer potential benefits for both the economy and the national infrastructure, local governments generally support the arrival of a hypermarket. The ultimate target market, however, is not the government but the consumers, and just as in any country at any time, the challenge lies in understanding what those consumers want and how to get it to them.

Sources: Carrefour Group, "Carrefour Announces the Closure of Its Five Stores in India," Carrefour, July 7, 2014, www.carrefour.com/news-releases/carrefour-announces-closure-its-five-stores-india; http://gain.fas.usda.gov/Recent%20 GAIN%20Publications/Retail%20Foods_New%20Delhi_India_12-28-2015.pdf; "Retail Industry in India," India Brand Equity Foundation, November 2016; USDA, "India Retail Foods 2015 GAIN Report," USDA Foreign Agricultural Services, December 28, 2015; "Infra Red—India's Ambitious Development Plans Hinge on Attracting Private Capital," *The Economist*, July 8, 2010; "A Wholesale Invasion—a French Supermarket Chain Takes a Bet on India," *The Economist*, May 20, 2010; Armina Ligaya, "India Puts Squeeze on Hypermarkets," *The National*, September 16, 2009; "India—Tier I & II Cities May Have 300 Hypermarkets by 2011," RNCOS, August 13, 2009; www.ibef.org/industry/retail.aspx; "Coming to Market—Retailing in India," *The Economist*, April 15, 2006, p. 69; "Despite Growing Debt, the Indian Consumer Banks on Tomorrow," India Knowledge@Wharton, October 31, 2006; Ranjan Biswas, "India's Changing Consumers," *Chain Store Age*, May 2006; John Elliott, "Retail Revolution," *Fortune*, August 9, 2007, pp. 14–16; Amelia Gentleman, "Indians Protest Wal-Mart's Wholesale Entry," *The New York Times*, August 10, 2007; "Wal-Mart Enters India's Retail Market Amid New Rules," *CBCNews*, September 21, 2012; Vikas Bajaj, "India Puts Wal-Mart Deal with Retailer Under Scrutiny," *The New York Times*, October 18, 2012; Vikas Bajaj, "India Unit of Wal-Mart Suspends Employees," *The New York Times*, November 23, 2012; Angelo Young, "FDI in India Retail: Parliament Backs Delhi's Move to Let States Decide on Foreign Retail Competition," *International Business Times*, December 7, 2012; Rachit Vats, "Lure of the Hypermarket," *Hindustan Times*, April 22, 2012; "India: FDI in Single Brand Retail Increased to 100%," *International Law*, November 12, 2012.

This case was written by Todd Nicolini, while an MBA student at Loyola College in Maryland, under the supervision of Professor Hope Corrigan and Jenny Esdale, Brandeis University.

DISCUSSION QUESTIONS

1. How might a hypermarket located in India appeal to consumers and orient them to shopping in larger stores?

2. Is the Indian government's willingness to spend $500 billion to improve the nation's infrastructure good news for international retailers? Why or why not?

3. Identify the main changes that mark Indian consumers. How can international retailers learn more about India's youthful demographic?

CASE 13   Diamonds from Mine to Market

According to the American Museum of Natural History, a diamond is carbon in its most concentrated form. Because of their chemical makeup and crystalline structure, diamonds possess unique characteristics. They are the hardest known natural substance. These traits determine their status as the "king of gems," a reference to their vast popularity as jewelry and decoration.

The diamond supply chain consists of six steps: exploration, mining, sorting, cutting and polishing, jewelry design and production, and retail display. According to the website for De Beers, the producer of approximately 40 percent of the world's supply of rough or uncut diamonds, members of this extensive supply chain include geologists, engineers, environmentalists, miners, sorters, distributors, cutters, polishers, traders, manufacturers, exporters, and salespeople, who in turn employ vast technology and artistic and skill-related resources to discover, produce, and distribute jewelry-quality diamonds.

EXHIBIT 1   Description of the Four Cs for Diamond Quality

Cut	Cut refers to the angles and proportions a skilled craftsperson creates in transforming a rough diamond into a polished diamond.
	A well-cut diamond will reflect light internally from one mirror-like facet to another, dispersing it through the top of the stone.
	To cut a diamond perfectly, a craftsperson will often need to cut away more than 50 percent of the rough diamond.
	Cut also refers to the shape of a diamond: round, emerald, heart, marquise, or pear.
Carat weight	Carat is often confused with size, even though it is actually a measure of weight.
	The cut of a diamond can make it appear much larger or smaller than its actual weight.
	One carat is the equivalent of 200 milligrams. One carat can also be divided into 100 "points." A .75-carat diamond is the same as a 75-point- or a three-quarter-carat diamond.
Color	Most diamonds appear icy white, but many have tiny hints of color. Diamonds are graded on a color scale established by the Gemological Institute of America (GIA), ranging from D (colorless) to Z.
	Colorless diamonds are extremely rare and therefore very valuable.
	Diamonds are also sometimes found in colors: pink, blue, green, yellow, brown, orange, and, very rarely, red. These diamonds, called "fancies," are incredibly rare and valuable. These colors extend beyond the GIA color grading system.
Clarity	Diamonds, like people, have natural blemishes in their makeup. Minerals or fractures form these tiny faults, or inclusions, while the diamond is forming in the earth.
	When light enters a diamond, it is reflected and refracted. If anything disrupts the flow of light in the diamond, such as an inclusion, a proportion of the light reflected will be lost.
	Most inclusions are not visible to the naked eye unless magnified.
	To view inclusions, trained gemologists use a magnifying loupe. This tool allows experts to see a diamond at 10 times its actual size. Even with a loupe, the birthmarks in the VVS (Very, Very Slightly Included) to VS (Very Slightly Included) range can be extremely difficult to find. It is only when a diamond is graded "I" that it is possible to see the birthmarks with the naked eye.

The jewelry-quality designation refers to a particular rating according to four key elements of a diamond, better known as the 4Cs: cut, carat, color, and clarity. The De Beers Corporation introduced these criteria in 1939 to provide consumers with a reference for evaluating diamonds, as Exhibit 1 summarizes.

Before they reach showrooms to be evaluated on these criteria, diamonds have endured approximately 1–3 billion years of hot temperatures and intense pressures under the earth's surface. Production estimates from the World Diamond Council indicate diamond mining operations are in more than 20 countries, including Russia, Botswana, the Democratic Republic of the Congo, Australia, South Africa, Canada, Angola, Namibia, Ghana, Brazil, and Sierra Leone.

The world diamond supply is dominated by African countries, which generate between 60 and 65 percent (by weight) of current diamond production. Other key sources for diamonds span the globe, for example, the remote northern regions of Western Australia, which produce roughly 30 million carats (20 percent of global production) each year from both open pit and underground operations. These diamonds are known for the range of colors, especially pink stones.

Diamonds prompt significant competition, as depicted in the movie *Blood Diamond*, which portrays the gruesome conflict and violence in Sierra Leone over diamonds. In many countries, profits from diamonds go to fund civil wars that take millions of lives. To prevent such abuses, the Kimberley Process, an international diamond certification scheme, was established to abolish trade in diamonds that fund conflict. Since its launch in 2003, the Kimberley Process has become law in 75 countries and received backing from the United Nations. It requires that governments of diamond-producing nations certify that shipments of rough diamonds are not funding violence.

Even with a certification process, though, some diamonds continue to be smuggled out of African countries. Violent groups find ways to exploit the Kimberley Process to traffic in illicit diamonds. "Conflict diamonds continue to be certified in countries that are members of the Kimberley Process, legitimized by the very scheme which was designed to eradicate them." A contrasting report from the World Diamond Council claims that "because of the Kimberley Process, more than 99% of the world's diamond supply is from sources free from conflict."

When the international diamond industry agreed to implement a voluntary system of warranties, it promised consumers it could track diamond jewelry up to the point of sale. Invoices for the sale of conflict-free diamond jewelry must include a written guarantee of that status. To ensure the diamonds they purchase for their spouses, fiancées, or themselves are indeed sourced appropriately, consumers are expected to take some responsibility, such as asking a series of questions of the jeweler from which they are purchasing:

* What is the country of origin for the diamonds in your jewelry?
* Can I see a copy of your company's policy on conflict-free diamonds?
* Can you show me a copy of the written warranty from your diamond supplier stating that your diamonds are conflict-free?

Sources: "Blood Diamonds Are Still a Reality," Amnesty International, http://web.amnesty.org/pages/ec-230107-feature-eng; "Combating Conflict Diamonds," Global Witness, www.globalwitness.org/pages/en/conflict_diamonds.html; "Conflict Free Diamond Jewelry," Brilliant Earth, www.brilliantearth.com/conflict-free-diamond-definition; "Diamond Pipe," Antwerp Diamond Centre, www.awdc.be/diamond-pipeline; "Forever Diamonds," Gemnation, www.gemnation.com/base?processor=getPage'pageName=forever_diamonds_1; "Kimberley Process," www.kimberleyprocess.com/home/index_en.html; "The Argyle Diamond Mine," Argyle Diamonds, www.argylediamonds.com.au/index_whoweare.html; "The Four Cs," De Beers, www.debeers.com/page/guidance&layout=popups#author2.

This case was written by Hope Bober Corrigan, Loyola University, Maryland.

CASE 14   Starbucks's Expansion into China

BRAND HISTORY/GROWTH

Starbucks, an American-based coffee company, opened its first store in Seattle, Washington, in 1971. The mission for this coffee shop was to not only have high-quality coffee, but to create a more relaxed environment where customers could meet and converse with friends. In 1987, Starbucks consisted of 11 stores and 100 employees, with a dream of becoming a national brand. Starbucks coffee shops were opening throughout the United States with 1,015 stores by 1996. The Starbucks Corporation then set its sights on international expansion beginning in 1997, when the number of total stores was 1,412. In 2012, the company operated 17,003 locations, with 37 percent outside of the United States in 40 countries. Starbucks's financial performance showed an accelerated increase in revenue in the early 2000s because of the focus on international expansion.

Starbucks made the decision to concentrate in China in 1998, along with many other businesses. China is an emerging market because the middle class is in a state of constant growth, and companies want to capitalize on the opportunity the China market offers.

Starbucks quickly recognized that there were different cultures within China. Starbucks joined forces with three regional partners as a strategy to enter the emerging market and provide Chinese consumers with more localized products. In 1999, Starbucks launched a joint venture with Mei Da Coffee Company Limited in North China to open locations in Beijing. In this joint venture, both parties are equally invested in the project in terms of money and time. This was followed in 2000 with a joint venture in South China with Maxim's Caterers Limited. Starbucks also partnered with Uni-President in East China to further advance interests in Shanghai, Taipei, and Hong Kong.

Joining forces with Chinese business partners helped Starbucks gain insights into the tastes and preferences of local consumers. Entering a new market with established local partners enabled Starbucks to quickly learn about the different cultures in each individual region in China. It was not necessarily easy for coffee-centric Starbucks to grow its presence in a country that primarily drinks tea. Starbucks was faced with the challenge of creating a new marketing campaign that would revolutionize how the Chinese viewed and drank coffee. Total coffee consumption in China grew from 35.33 thousand metric tons in 2006 to 59.62 thousand metric tons in 2010 (see Exhibit 1).

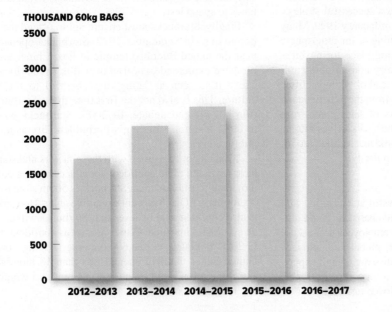

THOUSAND 60kg BAGS

EXHIBIT 1
China's Total Coffee Consumption

Sources: "Agriculture Consumption and Production," *China Country Review,* 2012, pp. 159–161; USDA, "Coffee: World Markets and Trade," USDA, June 2016, https://apps.fas.usda.gov/psdonline/circulars/coffee.pdf.

COMPETITIVE ADVANTAGE

Product

Starbucks is known for selling premium coffee products. However, in China, Starbucks realized that the global brand needed to appeal to local tastes. Starbucks elected to tailor the menu to match the preferences of the local culture. It began introducing beverages that included regional ingredients, such as green tea. Additional products created specifically for the Chinese market included white tea, black sesame green tea, Frappuccino blended crème, iced rice dumplings, and Starbucks moon cakes. In China, this allowed for customers to select from a wide variety of products to meet their needs.

Promotion

Starbucks used a smart market entry strategy to grow in China. The first step was to select high-visibility and high-traffic locations to project its brand image and attract loyal consumers. Starbucks maintained a strong brand identity and marketed it as a lifestyle "symbol" rather than just a logo. Starbucks wanted consumers to see the green circle Siren logo and to think of sophistication and the ability to afford "personal luxury." One reason this strategy is working is that Starbucks didn't seem to be a threat to the "tea drinking" culture. The company used innovative marketing to create new demand for coffee and the experience that Starbucks stores offer customers.

Price

Starbucks kept its corporate pricing strategy that utilized premium pricing to ensure the desired profit margin. Starbucks believes in the quality of its products. Many competitors cut prices in order to compete in the Chinese market. Starbucks believes this is a losing strategy because companies cannot afford to "out-cut" the local Chinese competitors.

Placement

Starbucks brought the "Western coffee experience" to the Chinese market. This experience was the ability to go somewhere with friends and acquaintances, relax, and drink some favorite beverages. This proved to be a successful strategy when Starbucks first opened in China in January 1999. Many competitors did not offer air conditioning or the atmosphere of Starbucks, which provides a meeting place for business executives and friends. Starbucks's very comfortable environment allows for dine-in service instead of taking a coffee or tea on the go. This is quite different from the experience in the United States, where the majority of sales come from takeout orders. The experience that Starbucks strives to give is not just the comfortable chairs, upbeat music, and chic interior, but the feeling of a more modern lifestyle.

Human Resources

Starbucks has been incredibly successful at recruiting and training employees. The company sends baristas (brand ambassadors) to all new stores and trains employees to preserve its brand integrity. This ensures that, globally, employees stay true to the Starbucks brand. Because the overall experience is what differentiates Starbucks from competitors, this is a critical component. Annual employee turnover rates of 30 percent or higher are common in China, but Starbucks's turnover rate is much lower due to its attractive compensation packages, career paths, and working environment. Starbucks's exceptional service contributes to its success in China. In interviews with people in Shanghai, the majority of the population stated that they preferred the taste of products from competitors, but that they continue to choose Starbucks due to a high level of service.

CHINA TODAY/FUTURE

Starbucks believes that there is still an opportunity to expand in China. As of 2015, Starbucks had more than 2,500 stores in 118 cities with numerous additional cities for future growth. Starbucks has been in China for 17 years and has laid a foundation for continued development. Belinda Wong was appointed Starbucks's China president in July 2011 and was promoted to CEO for China in 2016. Under Wong's leadership the first international roaster and reserve tasting room will open in Shanghai in 2017. With the projected growth in the Chinese market, Wong believes Starbucks will be able to continue to increase its market share.

Starbucks is not the only coffee company looking for continued growth in China. The market has attracted other businesses, such as British brands Costa Coffee and Pacific Coffee Company. Costa Coffee plans to expand to 700 stores by 2020. Starbucks also faces competition from McDonald's, Caribou Coffee, and Dunkin' Brands. Dunkin' Brands anticipates increasing its investment in China and recently announced that it will be opening 1,400 stores in China by 2035 as part of a deal with Golden Cup Pte. Ltd., which will run the Chinese expansion. Furthermore, to appeal to the Chinese market Dunkin' Brands has added pork donuts to customize the local menu.

In addition to increased competition, Starbucks also needs to pay careful attention to the average Chinese customer's income and discretionary spending. Chinese customers love the experience that Starbucks offers but may purchase only a coffee and spend all day in the store. However, a customer in the United States normally purchases coffee with a baked good. The Chinese consumer is more price sensitive and therefore tends to spend less.

Finally, Starbucks must ensure not to offend the Chinese population. In September 2012, Starbucks opened a store near the famed Buddhist temple in East China. Some people have expressed concerns over this store's location because it is seen as being disrespectful to the Chinese culture. This is also not the first time that a Starbucks location has created debate. In 2007, Starbucks was forced to close a store in Beijing's Forbidden City as a result of public outcries.

Wong is not concerned with these factors and stated, "We have never felt more confident about accelerating our growth momentum" after opening Starbucks's 500th store in Beijing. As former CEO and current executive chair, Howard Schultz is also confident and believes that Starbucks will continue to be successful in China. Critics are not as confident, however. In 2008, Starbucks closed 600 underperforming stores in the United States that had opened less than 18 months earlier. Time will tell if rapid expansion in China is a winning strategy for Starbucks.

Sources: www.starbucks.com; Reuters, "Starbucks Names Its First China CEO," *Fortune*, October 19, 2016; Julia Kollewe, "China Expansion Brewing for Costa Coffee Owner," *The Guardian*, April 26, 2016; Dunkin' Brand, "2015 Annual Report," February 18, 2016; Angela Chen, "Dunkin' Donuts to Open 1,400 Restaurants in China," *The Wall Street Journal*, January 8, 2015; "Agriculture Consumption and Production," *China Country Review*, 2012, pp. 159–161; "China: Brewing Up a Success Story," Thai Press Reports, March 5, 2012; "China Focus: Starbucks Outlet Near Buddhist Temple Triggers Debate," Xinhua News Agency, September 24, 2012; "Don't Get Excited about Starbucks' Chinese Expansion Just Yet," *Forbes*, May 4, 2012; "Greater China," News.starbucks.com, 2012, http://news.starbucks.com/about+starbucks/starbucks+coffee+international/greater+china; "Localization Fuels Starbucks' Success in China," *Business Daily Update*, February 14, 2012; Shaun Rein, "Why Starbucks Succeeds in China and Others Haven't," *USA Today*, February 10, 2012; Chris Sorensen, "Serving a Billion Latte Sippers," *Maclean's* 125, no. 17 (May 7, 2012), p. 41; "Starbucks Annual Report 1999–2011," Starbucks Investor Relations, http://investor.starbucks.com/phoenix.zhtml?c599518&p5irol-reportsannual; "Starbucks Believes That China Will Be Second Largest Market by 2014," News.starbucks.com, April 1, 2012; "Starbucks: Company Profile," www.starbucks.com/about-us/company; "Starbucks' Quest for Healthy Growth: An Interview with Howard Schultz," *McKinsey Quarterly* 2 (2011), pp. 34–43; Helen H. Wang, "Five Things Starbucks Did to Get China Right," *Forbes*, August 10, 2012; USDA, "Coffee: World Markets and Trade," United States Department of Agriculture Foreign Agricultural Service, June 2016, https://apps.fas.usda.gov/psdonline/circulars/coffee.pdf.

This case was written by Bethany Wise and Samantha Leib, MBA students at Loyola University, Maryland, under the supervision of Professor Hope Corrigan.

DISCUSSION QUESTIONS

1. Prepare a SWOT analysis based on the case to support Starbucks's expansion plans in China. Based on your SWOT analysis, what recommendations would you make to Starbucks's CEO with regard to the market development growth strategy for this country?

2. Give examples of how Starbucks was successful upon entering the China market. Please use the following videos to frame your response:

   - Starbucks grows coffee in China, Reuters video, available at: www.youtube.com/watch?v=BYSiGomkGdg
   - Starbucks in China, available at: www.youtube.com/watch?v=0A3rnWIEJY8
   - Starbucks wakes up to China, Reuters video, available at: www.youtube.com/watch?v=CgWJAouxorg

3. Compare Starbucks's U.S. and Chinese strategies. What are the similarities and differences? What generalities can you glean from this analysis to help the company expand into other global marketplaces? Please use the case and the following article to frame your response.

   - "Starbucks' Quest for Healthy Growth: An Interview with Howard Schultz," *McKinsey Quarterly* 2 (2011), pp. 34–43, www.mckinsey.com/global-themes/employment-and-growth/starbucks-quest-for-healthy-growth-an-interview-with-howard-schultz

---

CASE 15   Tiffany and TJX: Comparing Financial Performance

Charles Lewis Tiffany opened his first store in downtown Manhattan in 1837. Today, Tiffany & Co. operates as a high-end specialty retailer worldwide. It is mostly known for its exquisite jewelry, but also has additional luxury items in its product assortment. The Tiffany robin's egg "blue boxes" have become a ubiquitous status symbol, representing the company's brand quality and craftsmanship. Tiffany & Co. has a different strategy and marketing approach than other national retailers. Throughout its history, the company's mission has been to enrich the lives of its customers by creating enduring objects of extraordinary beauty that will be cherished for generations. Tiffany & Co. has accomplished this by crafting beautiful designs, using fine-quality materials and expert workmanship, and presenting those products to its customers at stores in high-end locations, within some department stores, and online.

TJX Corporation, on the other hand, consists of a mix of stores under the names of TJ Maxx, Marshalls, HomeGoods, and Sierra Trading Post in the United States (with additional stores under various names internationally). TJX strives to offer exceptional value through its four pillars of great fashion, brand, quality, and price. It works with a variety of national brands so that its merchandise assortments at these stores are ever changing. It is willing to purchase less-than-full assortments of items, styles, sizes, and quantities from vendors and pass on the cost savings to its customers. So that it doesn't have to completely rely on merchandise from national-brand vendors for its assortment offerings, TJX also offers private-label merchandise,

which is produced specifically for TJX only. It keeps moderately low inventory levels that helps produce relatively fast inventory turns while maintaining lower operating expenses, resulting in relatively higher net operating profit margins than its competitors (see Exhibit 1).

This case was prepared by Nancy J. Murray, University of Wisconsin, Madison.

DISCUSSION QUESTIONS

1. Calculate the following for both Tiffany & Co. and TJX using data from the abbreviated income statements and balance sheets in Exhibit 1.
   a. Cost of goods percentage
   b. Gross margin percentage
   c. SG&A expense percentage
   d. Operating profit margin percentage
   e. Net profit margin (after taxes) percentage
   f. Inventory turnover
   g. Asset turnover
   h. Return on assets (ROA) percentage

2. For a–h, compare and contrast the calculated financial figures for Tiffany & Co. and TJX, then analyze and discuss why the percentages and ratios differ for the two retailers.

3. Determine which retailer has the better overall financial performance.

EXHIBIT 1

2015 Financial Data
for Tiffany and TJX
(in thousands)

Sources: *TJX Annual Report, 2015;
Tiffany & Co. Annual Report, 2015.*

	TIFFANY & CO. (YEAR ENDING 1/31/2016)	TJX (YEAR ENDING 1/30/2016)
	Income Statement	Income Statement
Net sales	$4,104,900	$30,944,938
Less: Cost of goods sold	1,613,600	22,034,523
Gross margin	2,491,300	8,910,415
Less: SG&A expenses	1,731,200	5,205,715
Operating profit margin	760,100	3,704,700
Less: Interest expense	49,000	46,400
Other expense (income)	1,200	0
Net income before taxes	709,900	3,658,300
Less: Taxes	246,000	1,380,642
Net income after taxes	463,900	2,277,658
	Balance Sheet	Balance Sheet
Cash	$ 843,600	$ 2,095,473
Accounts receivable	206,400	238,072
Inventory	2,225,000	3,695,113
Other current assets	233,400	743,902
Total current assets	3,508,400	6,772,560
Fixed assets	935,800	4,137,575
Long-term assets	685,500	589,347
Current liabilities	729,900	4,402,230
Long-term liabilities	1,470,300	2,790,177
Stockholders' equity	2,929,500	4,307,075
Total Liabilities and Equity	$5,129,700	$11,499,482

CASE 16   Choosing a Store Location for a Boutique

Stephanie Wilson must decide where to open a ready-to-wear boutique she's been contemplating for several years. Now in her late thirties, she's been working in municipal government ever since leaving college, where she majored in fine arts. She's divorced with two children (ages five and eight) and wants her own business, at least partly to be able to spend more time with her children. She loves fashion, feels she has a flair for it, and has taken evening courses in fashion design and retail management. Recently, she heard about a plan to rehabilitate an old arcade building in the downtown section of her midwestern city. This news crystallized her resolve to move now. She's considering three locations.

THE DOWNTOWN ARCADE

The city's central business district has been ailing for some time. The proposed arcade renovation is part of a master redevelopment plan, with a new department store and several office buildings already operating. Completion of the entire master plan is expected to take another six years.

Dating from 1912, the arcade building was once the center of downtown trade, but it's been vacant for the past 15 years.

The proposed renovation includes a three-level shopping facility, low-rate garage with validated parking, and convention center complex. Forty shops are planned for the first (ground) floor, 28 more on the second, and a series of restaurants on the third.

The location Stephanie is considering is 900 square feet and situated near the main ground-floor entrance. Rent is $20 per square foot, for an annual total of $18,000. If sales exceed $225,000, rent will be calculated at 8 percent of sales. She'll have to sign a three-year lease.

TENDERLOIN VILLAGE

The gentrified urban area of the city where Stephanie lives is called Tenderloin Village because of its lurid past. Today, however, the neat, well-kept brownstones and comfortable neighborhood make it feel like a trendy enclave. Many residents have done the remodeling work themselves and take great pride in their neighborhood.

About 20 small retailers are now in an area of the village adjacent to the convention center complex, along with some vegetarian and nouveau cuisine restaurants. There are also 3 small women's specialty clothing stores.

The site available to Stephanie is on the village's main street on the ground floor of an old house. Its space is also about 900 square feet. Rent is $15,000 annually, with no extra charge based on the level of sales. The landlord knows Stephanie and will require a two-year lease.

APPLETREE MALL

This suburban mall has been open for eight years. A successful regional center, it has 3 department stores and 100 smaller shops just off a major interstate highway about eight miles from downtown. Of its 9 women's clothing retailers, 3 are in a price category considerably higher than what Stephanie has in mind.

Appletree has captured the retail business in the city's southwest quadrant, although growth in that sector has slowed in the past year. Nevertheless, mall sales are still running 12 percent ahead of the previous year. Stephanie learned of plans to develop a second shopping center east of town, which would be about the same size and character as Appletree Mall. But groundbreaking is still 18 months away, and no renting agent has begun to enlist tenants.

The location available to Stephanie in Appletree is two doors from the local department store chain. At 1,200 square feet, it's slightly larger than the other two possibilities. But it's long and narrow—24 feet in front by 50 feet deep. Rent is $24 per square foot ($28,800 annually). In addition, on sales that exceed $411,500, rent is 8 percent of sales. There's an additional charge of 1 percent of sales to cover common-area maintenance and mall promotions. The mall's five-year lease includes an escape clause if sales don't reach $411,500 after two years.

This case was prepared by Professor David Ehrlich, Marymount University.

DISCUSSION QUESTIONS

1. List the pluses and minuses of each location.
2. What type of store would be most appropriate for each location?
3. If you were Stephanie, which location would you choose? Why?

CASE 17   Hutch: Locating a New Store

In June, after returning from a trip to the Bahamas, Dale Abell, vice president of new business development for the Hutch Corporation, began a search for a good location to open a new store. After a preliminary search, Abell narrowed the choice to two locations, both in Georgia. He now faces the difficult task of thoroughly analyzing each location and determining which will be the site of the next store.

COMPANY BACKGROUND

The Hutch store chain was founded in 1952 by John Henry Hutchison, a musician and extremely successful insurance salesman. Hutchison established the headquarters in Richmond, Virginia, where both the executive offices and one of two warehouse distribution centers are located. Hutch currently operates 350 popularly priced women's clothing stores throughout the Southeast and Midwest. Manufacturers ship all goods to these distribution centers. They are delivered floor-ready, in that the vendor has attached price labels, UPC identifying codes, and source tags for security purposes and placed appropriate merchandise on hangers. Once at the distribution centers, the merchandise is consolidated for reshipment to the stores. Some staple merchandise, such as hosiery, is stored at these distribution centers. All Hutch stores are located within 400 miles of a distribution center. This way, as Abell explains, "A truck driver can deliver to every location in two days."

HUTCH FASHIONS

Hutch Fashions is considered one of the leading popularly priced women's fashion apparel chains in the Southeast. The stores carry trendy apparel selections in juniors', misses', and women's sizes, all at popular prices. The chain offers a complementary array of accessories in addition to its main features of dresses, coats, and sportswear. Located mainly in strip centers and malls, these shops typically require 4,000 to 5,000 square feet.

HUTCH EXTRA

Hutch Extra stores are primarily located in strip centers and malls. They bear a strong resemblance to Hutch Fashions. The difference is that Hutch Extra stores require less space (2,000 to 3,000 square feet) and cater to women requiring large and half-size apparel. (Women who wear half-sizes require a larger size but are not tall enough to wear a standard large size. In other words, a size 18½ is the same as size 18 except that it is cut for a shorter woman.)

HUTCH FASHIONS*HUTCH EXTRA

Although Hutch Fashions and Hutch Extra stores selectively appear as separate entries, the corporate goal is to position both as a single entity. The combination store emerged in 1986 and is now used for all new stores. The Hutch Fashions*Hutch Extra combination occupies a combined space of 6,000 to 7,000 square feet, with separate entrances for each entity. A partial wall separates the two frontal areas of the store but allows for a combined checkout/customer service area in the rear. These stores are primarily located in strip centers and can occasionally be found in malls. (Exhibit 1 shows a typical layout.)

EXHIBIT 1
Layout of Hutch Fashions*Hutch Extra Store

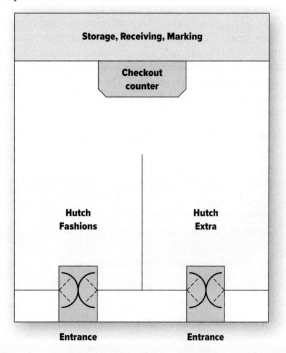

MARKETING STRATEGY

Customers

Hutch's target market is women between the ages of 18 and 40 years who are in the lower-middle- to middle-income range. Abell explains, "We don't cater to any specific ethnic group, only to women who like to wear the latest fashions."

Product/Price

Hutch positions merchandise and price levels between the mass merchandisers and the department stores. You won't find any bluelight specials or designer boutiques in a Hutch store. By avoiding direct competition for customers with the large discounters (Target, Walmart) and the high-fashion department stores and specialty shops, Hutch has secured a comfortable niche for itself. "Our products must be priced at a level where our customers perceive our products to be elegant and fashionable but not too expensive," notes Abell.

Location

Hutch stores are located throughout the Southeast and Midwest and must be within a 400-mile radius of a Hutch distribution center. Within this geographic area, Hutch stores are located in communities with a population range of 10,000 to 50,000 and a trade area of 50,000 to 150,000. These locations are characterized by a large concentration of people in the low- to middle-income brackets who work in agriculture and industry.

Hutch stores are primarily located in strip malls or strip centers—generally ones anchored by either a regional or national discount store (Walmart or Target). In addition, these centers contain a mix of several nationally recognized and popular local tenants. Hutch stores are primarily located adjacent to the center's anchor. Mall locations must be on the main corridor, as close to "center court" as economics (rent)

will allow. Abell remarked, "We don't care if it's the only center in the region. If the only space available is at the end of the mall, we won't go in there. Our plan is to be a complement to the anchor and to feed off the traffic coming to it. We may have a reputation for being picky and having one of the toughest lease agreements in the business, but it's one of the main reasons for our continued success."

DATA SOURCES

Abell is using several reports generated by Claritas to help him decide which location to choose for the next Hutch store. He has chosen reports that describe the 10-mile ring around each of the proposed locations. Exhibits 2 and 3 summarize these reports. They contain detailed population, household, race, income, education, and employment data, plus figures on retail sales and number of establishments. The reports also provide information about women's apparel sales and give a market index that estimates the annual per-person spending potential for the trade area divided by the national average (see Exhibit 3). Dalton's 99 index means that the spending potential for women's clothing is slightly lower than the national average of 100. Finally, Abell is using Claritas/UDS's PRIZM lifestyle reports. These reports contain numeric figures and percentages on the population, households, families, sex, age, household size, and ownership of housing. An excerpt from the report is given in Exhibit 4. Some of the cluster group names are described in Exhibit 5.

THE POTENTIAL LOCATIONS

Dalton

Dalton produces most of the carpeting in the United States. Consequently, carpet mills are the major employers in Dalton. Stainmaster carpeting has been putting a strain on the city's water supply. Stainmaster is said to require seven times the amount of water as regular carpeting and is rapidly becoming the largest proportion of carpeting produced. Expressing concern over market viability, Abell said, "If the Dalton area were ever to experience a severe drought, the carpet mills would be forced to drastically reduce production. The ensuing layoffs could put half the population on unemployment."

The proposed site for the new store is the Whitfield Square shopping center located off the main highway, approximately two miles from the center of town (see Exhibit 6). After meeting with the developer, Abell was pleased with several aspects of the strip center. He learned that the center has good visibility from the highway, will be anchored by both Walmart and Kroger (a large grocery chain), and has ample parking. Abell is also reasonably pleased with the available location within the center, which is one spot away from Walmart. However, he is concerned about the presence of two large outparcels in front of the center that would reduce the number of parking spaces and direct visibility of the center. (An outparcel is a freestanding structure at the front of a mall, commonly a fast-food outlet, a bank, or a gas station.) Other tenants in the center include a nationally recognized shoe store, a beauty salon, two popular restaurants (Chinese and Mexican), and McSpeedy's Pizza at the end of the center, as well as a Century 21 real estate training school in the middle.

		Dalton	Hinesville
Population	2017 projection	93,182	64,195
	2016 estimate	87,293	57,945
	1999 Census	79,420	49,853
	1990 Census	71,373	34,125
	% change, 1999–2008	9.9%	16.2%
	% change, 1990–1999	11.3%	46.1%
	In group quarters (military base) 2008	.9%	11.2%
Household	2017 projection	35,570	20,010
	2016 estimate	33,140	17,541
	1999 Census	29,340	14,061
	1990 Census	24,302	8,557
	% change, 1999–2008	12.9%	24.7%
	% change, 1990–1999	20.7%	64.3%
Families	2016 estimate	24,347	14,277
Race	White	92.0%	54.1%
	Black	4.9%	38.3%
	American Indian	0.2%	0.5%
	Asian or Pacific Islander	0.6%	3.1%
	Other	2.3%	4.0%
Age	0–20	31.2%	40.2%
	21–44	37.1%	47.0%
	45–64	21.7%	9.2%
	65+	9.9%	3.4%
	Median age	33.7	23.9
	Male	32.5	23.6
	Female	35.0	24.6
Household size	1 person	21.0%	15.2%
	2 persons	32.3%	26.6%
	3–4 persons	38.1%	45.7%
	5+ persons	8.7%	12.6%
Income	Median household income	$30,516	$23,686
	Average household income	$40,397	$28,677
Sex (% male)		49.1%	55.8%
Education	Population age 25+	49,298	22,455
	No high school diploma	41.0%	15.5%
	High school only	28.6%	41.2%
	College, 1–3 years	19.1%	29.7%
	College, 4+ years	11.3%	13.5%
Industry	Manufacturing: nondurable goods	42.3%	7.2%
	Retail trade	12.6%	23.3%
	Professional and related services	13.3%	21.4%
	Public administration	2.2%	20.0%
Retail sales ($ thousands)	Total	**$706,209**	**$172,802**
	General merchandise stores		
	Apparel stores	$26,634	$9,339
Retail establishments	General merchandise stores	12	3
	Women's apparel stores	21	8

EXHIBIT 2
Population and Competitive Profile, 10-Mile Ring from Centers of Dalton and Hinesville, Georgia

	Area Sales ($ mil.)	Area Sales per Capita	U.S. Sales per Capita	Index (area sales ÷ U.S. sales)
Dalton	$18.01	$206.26	$207.65	99
Hinesville	$8.97	$154.74	$207.65	75

EXHIBIT 3
Sales Potential Index for Women's Apparel

EXHIBIT 4 PRIZM Neighborhood Clusters

PRIZM Cluster	Population, 2017	Percentage of Population	PRIZM Cluster	Population, 2017	Percentage of Population
Dalton			Mines & Mills	7,694	8.8
Big Fish, Small Pond	4,727	5.4%	Back Country Folks	4,293	4.9
New homesteaders	6,030	6.9			
Red, White & Blues	31,123	35.7	**Hinesville**		
Shotguns & pickups	8,881	10.2	Military Quarters	45,127	77.9
Rural industrial	12,757	14.6	Scrub Pine Flats	3,476	6.0

EXHIBIT 5 PRIZM Lifestyle Clusters

Big Fish, Small Pond

Small-town executive families; upper-middle incomes; age groups 35–44, 45–54; predominantly white. This group is married, family-oriented, and conservative. Their neighborhoods are older. Best described as captains of local industry, they invest in their homes and clubs and vacation by car in the United States.

Rural Industrial

Low-income, blue-collar families; lower-middle incomes; age groups <24, 25–34; predominantly white, high Hispanic. Nonunion labor found in this cluster, which is comprised of hundreds of blue-collar mill towns on America's rural backroads.

Mines & Mills

Older families; mine and mill towns; poor; age groups 55–64, 65+; predominantly white. Down the Appalachians, across the Ozarks to Arizona, and up the Missouri, this cluster is exactly as its name implies. This older, mostly single population with a few children lives in the midst of scenic splendor.

Shotguns & Pickups

Rural blue-collar workers and families; middle income; age groups 35–44, 45–54; predominantly white.

This cluster is found in the Northeast, the Southeast, and the Great Lakes and Piedmont industrial regions. They are in blue-collar jobs; most are married with school-age kids. They are churchgoers who also enjoy bowling, hunting, sewing, and attending car races.

Back Country Folks

Older farm families; lower-middle income; age groups 55–64, 65+; predominantly white. This cluster is centered in the eastern uplands along a wide path from the Pennsylvania Poconos to the Arkansas Ozarks. Anyone who visits their playgrounds in Branson, Missouri, or Gatlinburg, Tennessee,

can attest that these are the most blue-collar neighborhoods in America. Centered in the Bible Belt, many back country folks are hooked on Christianity and country music.

Scrub Pine Flats

Older African American farm families; poor; age groups 55–64, 65+; predominantly black. This cluster is found mainly in the coastal flatlands of the Atlantic and Gulf states from the James to the Mississippi Rivers. These humid, sleepy rural communities, with a mix of blacks and whites, live in a seemingly timeless, agrarian rhythm.

New Homesteaders

Young middle-class families; middle income; age groups 35–44, 45–54; predominantly white. This cluster is above-average for college education. Executives and professionals work in local service fields such as administration, communications, health, and retail. Most are married; the young have children, the elders do not. Life is homespun with a focus on crafts, camping, and sports.

Red, White & Blues

Small-town blue-collar families; middle income; age groups 35–54, 55–64; predominantly white, with skilled workers primarily employed in mining, milling, manufacturing, and construction. Geocentered in the Appalachians, Great Lakes industrial region, and western highlands, these folks love the outdoors.

Military Quarters

GIs and surrounding off-base families; lower-middle income; age groups under 24, 25–34; ethnically diverse. Because this cluster depicts military life with personnel living in group quarters, its demographics are wholly atypical because they are located on or near military bases. Racially integrated and with the highest index for adults under 35, "Military Quarters" like fast cars, bars, and action sports.

Source: PRIZM/Claritas.

Hinesville

Like Dalton, Hinesville has one major employer, the Fort Stuart army base. Abell recalls that popularly priced stores generally do very well in military towns. In addition, Fort Stuart is a rapid-deployment force base. Because the United States currently is involved in a number of international activities, Abell is concerned with a comment by a Hinesville native: "If these guys have to ship out, this place will be a ghost town." The location under consideration is the Target Plaza at the junction of State Route 119 and U.S. Highway 82 (see Exhibit 7). The center is anchored by Target and a grocery store that is part of a popular eastern U.S. chain. The two anchors are located side by side in the middle of the center. The spot available in the center is a 6,800-square-foot combination of three smaller units immediately adjacent to

Target. Other tenants in the center include a bookstore, a waterbed store, a shoe store, an electronics retailer, a yogurt store, a video store, and a movie theater.

This case was written by Michael Levy, Babson College.

DISCUSSION QUESTIONS

1. How do the people living in the trade areas compare with Hutch's target customer?

2. How do the proposed locations, including the cities, tenant mix, and the locations within the malls, fit with Hutch's location requirements?

3. Which location would you select? Why?

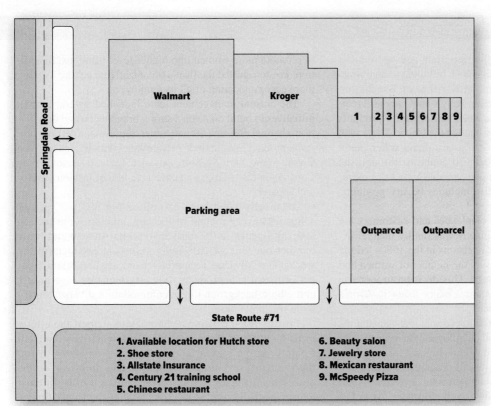

EXHIBIT 6
Whitfield Square
Shopping Center,
Dalton, Georgia

Springdale Road

Walmart   Kroger

1 2 3 4 5 6 7 8 9

Parking area

Outparcel   Outparcel

State Route #71

1. **Available location for Hutch store**   6. **Beauty salon**
2. **Shoe store**   7. **Jewelry store**
3. **Allstate Insurance**   8. **Mexican restaurant**
4. **Century 21 training school**   9. **McSpeedy Pizza**
5. **Chinese restaurant**

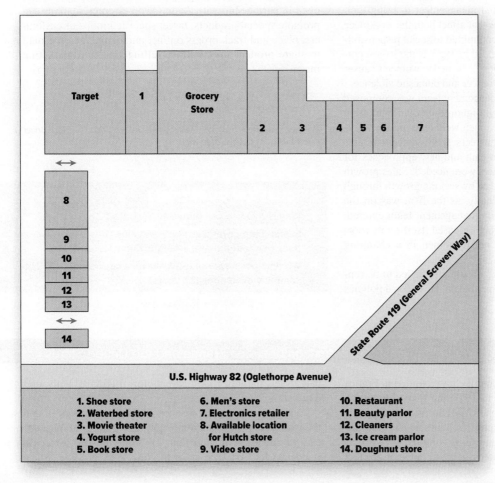

EXHIBIT 7
Target Plaza, Hinesville,
Georgia

Target   1   Grocery Store

2   3   4 5 6   7

8

9

10

11

12

13

14

State Route 119 (General Screven Way)

U.S. Highway 82 (Oglethorpe Avenue)

1. **Shoe store**   6. **Men's store**   10. **Restaurant**
2. **Waterbed store**   7. **Electronics retailer**   11. **Beauty parlor**
3. **Movie theater**   8. **Available location**   12. **Cleaners**
4. **Yogurt store**   **for Hutch store**   13. **Ice cream parlor**
5. **Book store**   9. **Video store**   14. **Doughnut store**

CASE 18   Avon Embraces Diversity

Women have always played an important role at Avon, a leading global beauty firm that has $6 billion in annual revenue and is 130 years old. Mrs. P. F. Albee of Winchester, New Hampshire, pioneered the company's now-famous direct-selling method. Women have been selling Avon products since 1886—34 years before women in the United States won the right to vote! As the world's largest direct seller, Avon markets to women in more than 70 countries through the efforts of more than 6 million independent Avon sales representatives. Avon's merchandise includes beauty products, fashion jewelry, and apparel.

Although most of Avon's employees and customers are women, until recently the company was run by men. However, a series of poor strategic decisions in the 1980s led the company to increase aggressively the number of women and minorities in its executive ranks. This decision to increase diversity among its managers was a major factor in Avon's improved financial performance.

Today, Avon is recognized as a leader in management diversity. Sixty percent of Avon's employees are women, and multiple members of its board of directors are women. The company also has undertaken various programs to ensure that women and minorities have opportunities for development and advancement. In the United States and elsewhere, Avon has internal networks of associates, including a parents' network, a Hispanic network, a black professional association, an Asian network, and a gay and lesbian network. The networks act as liaisons between associates and management to bring their voices to bear on critical issues that affect both the workplace and the marketplace. Avon is committed to social responsibility. The Avon Foundation, founded in 1955, is the largest corporate philanthropic organization dedicated to women's causes globally and focuses on breast cancer and domestic violence.

In the 1970s, Avon's top management team was composed solely of men. Avon essentially ignored its own marketing research that indicated more women were entering the workforce and seeking professional careers. It also failed to realize that cosmetic needs were changing and new approaches for selling products to its customers were needed. Sales growth slowed, and the company reacted by seeking growth through unrelated diversifications. Finally, as the firm was on the brink of bankruptcy, a new top management team entered. Led by CEO Jim Preston, Avon refocused itself on its roots and developed strategies to reach women in a changing marketplace.

Preston realized that Avon's customers needed to be represented in the senior management team. He enacted policies to promote more women into higher-level positions. In addition, Preston shifted the firm's organizational culture to being more accommodating of all its employees.

The current management team launched several growth initiatives to build on Avon's strong brand name and distribution channel through its customer representative network. Avon product lines include private-label brands such as Avon Color, Anew, Skin-So-Soft, Advance Techniques, and Avon Care. Avon also markets an extensive line of fashion jewelry and apparel.

Avon sells more than 125 million lipsticks per year, or 4 lipsticks every second of the day, making Avon the top seller of lipstick in the mass market. Its Anew brand is the number-one line of anti-aging skin care products in the world. The Advance Techniques hair care line offers high-performance hair products for every hair type, age group, and ethnic background to accommodate a diverse, worldwide consumer base.

Finally, Avon is using technology to support the efforts of its 6 million independent sales representatives. An electronic ordering system allows the representatives to run their businesses more efficiently and improve order-processing accuracy. Avon representatives use the Internet to manage their business electronically. In the United States, Avon representatives use an online marketing tool called youravon.com, which helps them build their own Avon business by selling through personalized web pages developed in partnership with Avon. Avon e-representatives can promote special products, target specific groups of customers, place and track orders online, and capitalize on e-mail to share product information, selling tips, and marketing incentives.

Sources: www.avoncompany.com; Avon Annual Report, 2015; www.avonfoundation.org.

This case was written by Barton Weitz, University of Florida; and Hope Bober Corrigan, Loyola College, Maryland.

DISCUSSION QUESTIONS

1. Why is Avon so committed to diversity?
2. Select another retailer that also values diversity. How does this commitment affect its financial results?
3. What values have helped Avon be a successful company even after 125 years?

CASE 19   Sephora Loyalty Programs: A Comparison between France and the United States

Sephora is a beauty products retail chain founded in France by Dominique Mandonnaud in 1970 and owned today by Moët Hennessy Louis Vuitton (LVMH), the world's leading luxury goods group. Sephora's self-service environment carries classic and emerging brands as well as Sephora's own private label across a broad range of product categories, including skin care, color, fragrance, body, and hair care.

Sephora has a strong presence in several countries around the world. It operates approximately 2,300 stores in 33 countries worldwide, with more than 430 stores in North America. It opened its first U.S. store in New York in 1998. Since

2006, Sephora stores are also found inside some JCPenney stores. These stores, smaller than normal with approximately 1,500 square feet, feature the signature Sephora look and an edited assortment. The company launched its Internet retail store in the United States in 1999 and Canada in 2003, which is Sephora's largest North American store in terms of sales and selection of products and brands.

U.S. LOYALTY PROGRAM: SEPHORA BEAUTY INSIDER

In 2007, Sephora launched a customer loyalty program in the United Stated called "Sephora Beauty Insider." When customers sign up for the program, they become a Beauty Insider and receive a loyalty card. Beauty Insiders earn perk points for purchases, both in-store and online. For every one dollar spent, one Point is added to the customer's Beauty Insider balance. The rewards for these points are given at six levels: 100, 500, 750–2,500, 3,000–4,500, 5,000–15,000, and 20,000 or more. Insiders don't have to use their points once they hit 100. Instead, they can choose to accumulate points. At the 100-point level, the reward is a sample-sized product. The 500-point-level reward is a limited-edition collection of four to five sample-sized products offered exclusively to Beauty Insiders. Sephora typically displays four to five frequently changing rewards at the point of sale for the 100- and 500-point perks. Higher-point perks typically include high-end and full-sized products and full makeovers and other experiences. These rewards are not available at Sephora inside JCPenney stores, even if customers accumulate their points there. Beauty Insiders also receive invitations to Beauty Insider–only events. On Sephora's Insiders account on the Internet, customers also receive special offers on products not available to the general public. Finally, every Insider receives a free birthday gift each year. Last year's gift was a sample NARS lip pencil duo, custom-designed to wish customers a happy birthday. Insiders can get the birthday gift either by visiting a store or by ordering online within 14 days of their birth date.

In 2009, Sephora launched V.I.B. [Very Important Beauty Insider], a premium level for its U.S. Beauty Insiders. V.I.B. status is conferred on customers who spend at least $350 per year at U.S. and Canadian Sephora stores (including Sephora. com and Sephora inside JCPenney locations). The benefits for V.I.B.s, in addition to the regular Beauty Insider benefits, include deluxe samples, exclusive monthly perks and gifts, access to prereleased products, event invitations, a 10 percent savings welcome offer, special discounts, and a free makeover. V.I.B.s are required to requalify each year by purchasing at least $350 worth of products.

FRENCH LOYALTY PROGRAM

Sephora is the leading perfume and cosmetic chain in France, despite fierce competition. Sephora's French loyalty program, launched in 2003, offers special products, exclusive information, and an all-access pass to personalized beauty products available in Sephora stores nationwide and on its website. It consists of three levels—White, Black, and Gold.

In an attempt to start a relationship with its customers, the White card is offered to anyone who asks for it in the store or applies on the Internet website. It is the first level of the customer relationship. After four purchases or 150 points on the Internet website or in a store, a 10 percent discount coupon is given for the customer's next purchase.

Furthermore, when customers have at least four purchases during a year, or spend a minimum of 150 € a year, they automatically receive the Sephora Black card, which is the middle-level program. Sephora Black customers get a 10 percent discount coupon either after four purchases or with every 150 points earned (1 point earned for 1 € spent). They also have access to specific and personalized rewards, such as invitations to special Sephora events, a sample-sized birthday surprise, updated information on the latest in beauty innovation, and personalized offers based on customers' skin type or makeup style.

The Gold card, which is the premium-level program, is dedicated to customers who purchase a minimum of 1500 € a year. In addition to the Black card benefits, Sephora Gold customers get access to exclusive private sales, a full-sized birthday gift of the customer's choice either in-store or online, free shipping on Sephora's website, free access to the Sephora's in-store Beauty Bar once a month (customers get made up and advised by Sephora's specially trained salespeople), an e-newsletter with exclusive beauty news, a special telephone line, a dedicated in-store salesperson or personal shopper, and access to the Sephora Gold boutique, where they can choose among several limited-edition Sephora Gold gifts in exchange for 1,000 points. Since 2012, Gold card holders must purchase a minimum of 700 € to requalify. If they drop below 700 €, they receive the Black card instead.

Sources: www.sephora.com; www.sephora.fr; http://hittingpan.tumblr.com/post/4962507405/7-reasons-for-joining-sephoras-beauty-insider; http://savingslifestyle.com/2010/08/sephora-beauty-insider-rewards/; Astrid de Montbeillard, "Sephora," *Relation Customer Magazine* 86 (April 1, 2010), www.relationcustomermag.fr/Relation-Customer-Magazine/Article/SEPHORA-37070-1.htm.

This case was written by Sandrine Heitz-Spahn, ICN Business School; and Nancy France and Michael Levy, Babson College.

DISCUSSION QUESTIONS

1. Identify the benefits for a company to implement a loyalty program.

2. What are the design characteristics of an effective loyalty program?

3. What are the benefits of having a tiered loyalty program such as Sephora's?

4. Describe Sephora's loyalty program design characteristics in both countries. What are the main differences? Which loyalty program is most effective at developing customer loyalty? Why?

5. Are both Sephora's French and American premium programs worth what they spend to reward customers? Why do both programs have a limited time validity and a specific requirement regarding the amount spent per year?

6. Could the premium loyalty program implemented in France be adapted to the U.S. market? Explain.

CASE 20   Attracting Generation Y to a Retail Career

THE DIVA BRAND

Diva is a specialty retail store focused on fast-fashion jewelry and accessories. The brand's origins are in Australia, but recent years have seen rapid international expansion, and the brand now has stores in America, Russia, and Europe. Diva is predominantly located in shopping centers, with some stores in high-street locations, and is always positioned in/around apparel fashion clusters. The stores are clean, simplistic, and brightly lit, reflecting their fast-moving, funky, and vibrant product range targeted at the youth market (predominantly 15- to 25-year-old females). Diva's positioning sees it as the only fashion jewelry/hair accessory specialist retailer in Australia.

Due to Diva's recent expansion, staff numbers have grown significantly. However, Diva is confronted with the problem of attracting and retaining experienced and talented people, particularly from Generation Y. In an attempt to counteract this problem, Diva has implemented several internal talent policies to provide a point of difference and be an employer of choice, including:

- Training plans/workshops to fill skill gaps.
- Career development program for top store managers.
- Leadership development program for top regional managers.
- Increased salary package offers for certain roles to attract talent/skill.
- Global expansion, with new offers of career progression.

GENERATIONAL DIFFERENCES IN THE WORKFORCE

As a result of key demographic and lifestyle issues such as aging populations, declining fertility, delayed retirements, rising labor participation rates, and higher life expectancies, there is a demographic trough in the Asia Pacific workforce, in which there are soon to be smaller proportions of younger-aged members and larger cohorts of mature-aged workers. This is further compounded by a shrinking talent pool and the fact that retail is not perceived as a career of choice by the adult population, who has limited sight of career path opportunities "beyond the shop floor."

Although research acknowledges the pertinence of this issue in retailing today, it remains unclear how to effectively manage generational diversity in the workplace. This is not a new issue; however, wider age groups are culminating in less segregated work arrangements. In the past, older staff undertook senior managerial positions, while younger workers assumed front-desk or field positions. However, today it is common to see staff members from all age groups working together on projects, with senior employees managing across several generations or younger employees managing older generations. It is important to note that, if managed poorly, intergenerational impacts can cause conflict for employers and among employees, hampering workplace productivity and morale.

Retailers, as well as organizations from many other industries, therefore need to identify and adopt the best approaches in attracting and retaining staff across all retail functions, optimizing the experiences of mature-aged workers while capitalizing on the potential of young employees. This involves understanding each generation and its unique perspectives, communication styles, and working styles in order to provide tailored support. Each generation holds different perspectives of work, including the definition of an attractive working environment, leadership qualities, and preferred team playing approaches, and has an individual information processing style. For example, Generation Y believes in having fluid work patterns and influencing job terms and conditions. Conversely, the baby-boomer generation regards work as a primary security in life, while Generation X values a balance between work and life.

GENERATION Y

Born between 1981 and 2000, members of Generation Y were one of the key segments of focus for Diva given their sheer numbers and prospective employment in retail as recent or upcoming workforce entrants. While organizations have had time to understand baby boomers and Generation X-ers, determining the needs of Generation Y-ers has been challenging, especially given their vastly different values. This is particularly important given the significant career opportunities that exist for Generation Y in retailing. In better understanding the unique career motivations, perceptions, and aspirations of Generation Y, a number of focus groups were conducted with university students who were studying a business major and currently working in retail and high school students who were studying retail-related subjects and currently working in retail or interested in doing so.

In terms of perceptions of working in retail, our research found that retail is simply not viewed as a career of choice by Generation Y. This is primarily due to the feeling that retail involves "just being a checkout chick," has limited or no career paths "beyond the shop floor" and is therefore a short-term employment solution, and has difficult conditions at times (e.g., long hours, repetitive tasks, low salaries). A related concern was that the retail industry is not generally perceived as prestigious in the eyes of the general public.

Despite such issues, there were a number of motivators (other than financial) for working in retail for Generation Y, such as improving one's social life and extending friendship circles, gaining work experience while studying, and following a particular passion (i.e., fashion). Generation Y-ers also reported a variety of career aspirations that were generally consistent with the courses or subjects they were studying. Despite the fact that few listed retail as their number-one career option, a strong desire was found for a career that could be facilitated by the retail industry, such as marketing, human resources, or buying.

Focused on self-improvement, Generation Y-ers also expressed enjoyment in working for organizations that provide constant learning environments; they want to be involved in the organization's vision and mission, desire mobility and flexibility in the workplace, and seek instant gratification. Members of Generation Y also thrive on systematic feedback and value positive reinforcement at accelerated rates, as compared to previous generations. This is the primary reason that Generation Y questions starting at the bottom of the organizational ladder, having developed a strong desire for rapid career progression from years of high-level education.

This case was written by Sean Sands and Carla Ferraro, Monash University, Australia.

CASE 21   Active Endeavors Analyzes Its Customer Database

Active Endeavors is an outdoor apparel and accessory retailer located in Iowa City, Iowa. The store is locally owned and has been in business for 13 years, and it has a reputation for high quality and product innovation. Its target market is high-income individuals with an interest in outdoor activities and travel.

Ken Stuart, the founder of the store, has felt pressure on profit margins and increased competition, especially due to the emergence of the Internet. He tries to remain on top of competition by offering new products and a wide and deep assortment, but he thinks there might be an opportunity to increase the store's market position by utilizing a transactional database of its customers. The store has the customers' transaction records, which include customer name and address, transaction date, products and quantity purchased, and purchase price. He is thinking of using the transactional database to design and target a direct mail campaign designed to increase traffic.

Ken analyzed the customers' past purchase behavior using the RFM analysis and classified the customers into six groups (Exhibit 1). The cutoff figures for the classifications were unique to the store. He is now contemplating the customer profile and what to do with it.

This case was written by Eddie Rhee, Stonehill College.

EXHIBIT 1   Customer Classification Based on Purchase History

Customer Group	Recency	Frequency	Monetary
1	Purchased within the last 3 months	Purchased 4 or more times	Purchased $337.63 or more
2	Purchased within the last 3 months	Purchased once	Purchased $18.90 or less
3	Purchased between the last 3 months and a year	Purchased 4 or more times	Purchased $338.63 or more
4	Purchased between the last 3 months and a year	Purchased once	Purchased $18.90 or less
5	Purchased more than a year ago	Purchased 4 or more times	Purchased $337.63 or more
6	Purchased more than a year ago	Purchased once	Purchased $18.90 or less

CASE 22   Mel's Department Store under New Management

Working for Mel's, a midsized department store chain, Elise Wickstrom recently was promoted to department manager of the Children's Department. Elise was excited about the opportunity but knew it would be a challenge because this department was not just apparel, but included toys and shoes, each having very different sales plans and margins. She was eager to show management that she was the right person for the job!

HISTORY

Mel's Department Store had struggled under previous management as the proliferation of larger chains continued. This really hurt Mel's business because these larger conglomerates had increased buying power with vendors, allowing them to constantly underprice Mel's. The Internet also played a role in Mel's deteriorating business. The ability for the consumer to easily compare prices as well as the convenience of shopping 24/7 were hard for Mel's to match. Mel's then began to also cut prices to stay competitive. Margins eroded, and business sales did not increase.

New management recently took over, giving Mel's a makeover. The lighting and layout for each store was improved. The outer façade of locations was painted and updated. With these improvements and fresh thinking, the chain also changed its assortment, including fresher looks and more unique goods. In addition, it retrained the entire workforce and now not only encourage a high level of customer service, but also gives bonuses for such behavior. Mel's hope is that these changes will decrease price pressures and allow it to increase its maintained markup percentages.

CHILDREN'S DEPARTMENT

Under this new plan, Elise has been asked to adhere to the initial and maintained markup percentages described in the following table:

	Initial Markup %	Maintained Markup %
Soft goods/apparel	60%	34%
Shoes	54%	33%
Toys	45%	25%

Elise just received her first shipment from FUNWEAR, her largest girls' vendor of unique jeans for kids. Its handpainted designs and jeweled enhancements were adorable and were a real traffic driver in the department. This vendor pre-marks all items for Mel's, allowing Elise to get them from receipt to selling floor quickly. At first glance, Elise wanted to ensure that the tags were correct. Here is how the invoice read:

	Item Description	Retail (on tag)	Cost
200 units	prewashed jeans	$30.50	$16.00
100 units	jeans jeweled	$43.75	$17.50

This case was written by Beth Gallant, Professor of Marketing, Brand Solutions Consulting.

DISCUSSION QUESTIONS

1. Given the soft-goods targets, are these marked correctly? If not, what should the initial retail price be to obtain her 60 percent minimum initial markup percentage?

2. By noon another shipment arrives. This time it is from SNEAK HERS, delivering her preholiday sneakers. Elise notices that the high tops do not have tags and need to be priced for the floor. She has her associate calculate the retail price. The invoice indicates the cost is $8.75. What should the initial retail price be, given her markup target?

3. Elise has been analyzing her sell through and saw that the "hot" T-shirts from back to school have not been moving, and she has sweater shipments due in the next two weeks. She decides to mark down the T's to make room for the anticipated shipment. The cost of the T's was $2.25, and they were on the floor at a 62 percent markup. If Elise takes a 33 percent markdown, what is the new selling price?

4. After six weeks passed, Elise analyzes her sales of the FUNWEAR prewashed jeans. Of her original 200 units this is what she found:

   - 50 units sold at the original retail
   - 34 units sold at a 38 percent markdown
   - 116 units sold at a 44 percent markdown

   What was her average maintained markup percentage? Did it meet her goals? Explain how this was possible.

5. Using the information in question 4, explain to management the possible reasons multiple markdowns could have been taken and why we compare to plan.

6. FUNWEAR is a long-time vendor of Mel's. It provides markdown dollars to help defray the lost gross margin dollars. Why would it provide this money to Elise?

7. Seventy-five toy trains were bought for the toy area at $3.50 each and were then priced at $10.00 each. Elise is running a department promotion and wants to reduce the price of the trains. To what can she reduce the retail price in order to meet her maintained markup goals?

8. Mel's wanted to create unique assortments and increase customer service. How does this strategy allow for better markup percentages? How are these related to perceived value?

CASE 23   Developing an Assortment Plan for Hughes

A well-established, medium-sized department store in the Midwest, Hughes satisfies consumers' needs by featuring popular names in fashion for the individual consumer, family, and home. It tries to offer a distinctive, wide assortment of quality merchandise with personalized customer service. The customer services include personal shoppers; credit through in-house charge, American Express, and Visa; and an interior design studio. Hughes's pricing policy permits it to draw customers from several income brackets. Moderate-income consumers seeking value and fashion-predictable soft goods are target customers, as are upscale customers with a special interest in fashion.

The department store is implementing new marketing strategies to prepare for continuing growth and expansion.

Hughes's merchandising philosophy is to attract the discerning middle-market customers, who make up 70 percent of the population, as well as sophisticated, fashion-conscious consumers who expect to buy high-quality, brand-name merchandise at competitive prices.

One portion of Hughes's buying staff is responsible for the Oriental rug department within home furnishings. The open-to-buy figure for this classification within the home furnishings division will be based on last year's sales history (Exhibit 1).

It has been projected that a 15 percent increase over last year's sales volume can be attained due to Oriental rugs' continued popularity. This year's open-to-buy for fall/winter will be $66,200.

The buying staff will be making its purchases for fall/winter in Amritsar, India, a city known for top-quality carpets. Ghuman Export Private Ltd. of Amritsar, Punjab, India, is the manufacturer the buyers will contact. Exhibit 2 shows information about Ghuman to use in the decision-making process.

EXHIBIT 1
Previous Year's Fall/Winter Sales Results for Oriental Rugs

Sales Volume Markup	$120,000 51.5%			
	Size	Percentage of Sales	Fabrication	Percentage of Sales
	3′ × 5′	20%	Silk	15%
	4′ × 6′	40	Cotton	25
	6′ × 9′	15	Wool	60
	8′ × 10′	10		
	9′ × 12′	15		

This case was written by Ann Fairhurst, Indiana University.

EXHIBIT 2
Ghuman's Wholesale Price List

Size	FABRICATION		
	Silk	Wool	Cotton
3 × 5′	$ 400	$ 250	—
4 × 6′	700	500	$200
6 × 9′	850	700	275
8 × 10′	1,200	1,000	350
9 × 12′	1,400	1,300	500

Colors: Background colors available are navy, burgundy, black, and cream.

Quantities required for purchase: No minimum orders required.

Payment plan: Payment can be made in American dollars or Indian rupees. Letter of credit needs to be established prior to market trip.

Delivery: Air freight—10 to 14 days delivery time; cost is usually 25 percent of total order.

Ocean freight—39 days plus inland time is necessary; cost is usually 8–10 percent of total order.

Customer loyalty: Loyalty to customers is exceptional. Damaged shipments can be returned. Ghuman's philosophy is to help the retailers obtain a profit on their product lines.

DISCUSSION QUESTIONS

1. **Work up a buying plan to use when purchasing merchandise from Ghuman's.**
2. **How should Hughes distribute the allotted open-to-buy dollars among the available sizes, colors, and fabrics?**
3. **Because it is dealing with an overseas manufacturer, how should Hughes address additional costs, such as duties and shipping, that need to be covered by the allocated open-to-buy dollars?**

CASE 24   Preparing a Merchandise Budget Plan

B-G is a specialty department store chain headquartered in Dallas. The stores are upscale and generally cater to upper-middle-class and well-to-do customers. They are generally located in the more affluent suburbs and downtown central business districts throughout the United States. By offering high-quality merchandise and a high level of service, they are able to promote and maintain customer loyalty. In addition, B-G has its own charge card and a very liberal return policy. Jim Morris is a buyer for men's sportswear. His merchandise manager has asked him to prepare a six-month merchandise budget plan for his department covering the months March through August.

Last year, sales for sportswear during the same six-month period were $1 million. Due to increased advertising, inflation, and a general increase in demand for sportswear, a 19 percent increase in sales is expected for this year. Also, Jim anticipates an additional 10 percent increase in the percentage of sales in March due to an increase in demand. The demand increase, due to forecasted unseasonably warm weather in March, will be offset by decreases in April and May of equal amounts, so total sales will be unchanged. Sportswear has traditionally maintained a high level of profitability, with a gross margin of 48 percent.

The following are the monthly sales percentages for the last three years:

	March	April	May	June	July	August
2014	10%	22%	26%	20%	13%	9%
2015	10%	19%	25%	22%	14%	10%
2016	10%	20%	24%	18%	18%	10%

The expected GMROI is 350 percent, and the forecasted ending stock level is 100,000. Total annual reductions average about 14 percent of total net sales. The breakdown of this figure is 60 percent for markdowns, 35 percent for employee discounts, and 5 percent for shortages. The distribution of reductions is as follows:

	March	April	May	June	July	August
Reductions	15%	20%	20%	15%	15%	15%

Unfortunately, the historical record of stock/sales ratios was temporarily misplaced during a recent office move. However, Jim has access to the National Retail Federation's (NRF's) guidelines on this type of store and department. B-G has a slightly higher than average inventory turnover; therefore the NRF figures must be adjusted.

	March	April	May	June	July	August
NRF	2.50	1.80	1.55	1.70	1.90	2.55

This case was written by Michael Levy, Babson College.

Planning Data

SALES FORECAST $ _____

Planned GMROI = $\dfrac{\text{Gross Margin}}{\text{Net Sales}} \times \dfrac{\text{Net Sales}}{\text{Inventory Costs}}$

$= \dfrac{\$}{\$} \times \dfrac{\$}{\$}$

$\dfrac{\text{Sales}}{\text{Inventory Costs}} \times (100\% - \text{GM}\%) = \text{Inventory Turnover}$

$X \times \% = X$

$12 \div \text{Inventory Turnover} = \text{B.O.M. Stock/Sales}$

$\div X = X$

Forecasted Ending Inventory $

The Plan

Markdowns	%	$
Discounts +	%	$
Shortages +	%	$
Total Reductions	%	$

		Jan	Feb	Mar	Apr	May	Jun	Jul	Aug	Sept	Oct	Nov	Dec	Total (Average)	Remarks
% Distribution of Sales by Month	1													100.0%	History/Projection
Monthly Sales	2														Step (1) × Net Sales
% Distribution of Reductions/Mo	3													100.0%	History/Projection
Monthly Reductions	4														Step (3) × Total Reductions
B.O.M. Stock/Sales Ratios	5														Adjusted by Mo. Sales Fluctuations
B.O.M. Stock ($000)	6													(Forecasted End Inventory)	Step (2) × Step (5)
E.O.M. Stock ($000)	7														EOM Jan = BOM Feb
Monthly Additions to Stock ($000)	8														Steps 2 + 4 + 7−6 Sales + Reductions + EOM−BOM

CASE 25 Kroger and Fred Meyer: Sourcing Products in a Global Marketplace

The Kroger Company is among the largest food retailers in the United States, and operates more than 2,700 stores under nearly two dozen store-brand names. These stores include conventional grocery stores, convenience stores, and approximately 240 supercenters. One of these store-brand names is Fred Meyer Inc., a chain of more than 130 supercenters located in Oregon, Washington, Alaska, and Idaho. Fred Meyer has been sourcing products overseas for more than 30 years, and Kroger recognized this expertise early on when it acquired Fred Meyer in 1999. Now all general merchandise buying is done by the merged staff at Fred Meyer's Portland, Oregon, headquarters. This location also houses the Kroger Logistics group, and virtually all of the products imported for Kroger's stores are handled in some way by this office.

The cost savings realized by retailers who source products in other countries, especially Asia, have made the logistics function essential to competing in today's cost-conscious marketplace. The investment in the infrastructure to support the complex processes involved in importing products is more than offset by the savings in the cost of the products. This infrastructure is very intricate and uses the services and talents of many specialized personnel. But the costs are not only present in staff salaries, office space, and other tangible investments; the costs also include the lengthy time importing merchandise can take due to the complexity of the processes. This case study follows the steps involved in sourcing products from Asia and bringing them to market. Your challenge will be to estimate the time that is necessary to do this successfully.

The process begins with the Kroger buyer who decides to buy a specific product. Imagine that the objective is to find a small collection of lamps for the back-to-school season next year. The Kroger buyers for general merchandise now buy for all the banners under which Kroger operates. This enables them to coordinate buys and make decisions that create the greatest amount of synergy. They have shopped the domestic markets; have paid attention to catalog, newspaper, and online advertising; and have been presented with ideas from various lamp importers. They have settled on three styles: two desk lamps and a floor lamp, with price points of $9.99 and $19.99, and they have made commitments for substantial quantities of these lamps to supply the anticipated demand for the stores.

The buyer has been in partnership with the product merchandiser in the Kroger product development group throughout this initial stage of this process. It is at this point that they hand off the sourcing of the lamps to the product merchandiser, who takes the next step of finding a source to manufacture them. Kroger works very closely with Li and Fung, a "global consumer products sourcing company managing the supply chain for high-volume time-sensitive consumer goods." It also relies on U.S. importers for identifying factories in Asia. The product merchandiser uses these contacts to solicit quotations for the lamps. Each potential supplier is sent specifications for the products: visuals, dimensions, colors, packaging, target delivery dates, approximate quantities, required testing, and any other available details. The suppliers are given approximately two weeks to create and submit samples and fill out the detailed paperwork known as quotation sheets. These documents specify to all parties involved what, when, and how all actions are done.

Once the quotation sheets and samples are received, the product merchandiser and Kroger buyer meet to assess and review the various submissions. The factors that influence their decision include product quality, vendor reliability, and product cost. All three of these must be seriously evaluated; if one of them is lacking, the whole program is at risk. In fact, decisions are often made to commit to a vendor with higher prices if there is a high degree of confidence in that vendor's quality and reliability.

When the supplier is chosen, the next step is the creation of purchase orders (POs). Factories do not generally start the acquisition of raw materials and other supplies for manufacturing a product until they have a firm financial commitment from the retailer. This is a very complex process that involves a number of behind-the-scenes support personnel. The Kroger buying team writes purchase orders that are reviewed by the Kroger Logistics group and given to the Bank of America, which processes the payment to the manufacturer.

The creation of the PO sets the actual production and shipping process in motion. During this process, the Kroger Logistics group monitors the purchase order at every step in the supply chain. The Geo. S. Bush Company, a customs broker and provider of international trade services, provides several employees on site to ensure that all U.S. government regulations are complied with. This involves four main agencies: U.S. Customs and Border Protection, the Food and Drug Administration, the Department of Agriculture, and the Consumer Products Safety Commission. Failure to comply with the requirements of these agencies can cause lengthy slowdowns in delivery and possible fines, so Bush ensures that all paperwork is complete five days before the arrival date of the products.

Concurrent with the creation of the purchase orders, the packaging design process begins. These lamps will be packaged in full-color boxes. The vendor will provide the package templates known as die lines for the boxes that will be needed for these lamps. The graphic designs are generally done in-house by Kroger using predesigned brand templates to ensure consistency of graphic elements with other Kroger products and color execution. When color proofs of the designs are created, they are circulated to the buyer as well as the merchandise manager to whom the buyer reports. As soon as the necessary approvals are secured, the package designs are sent electronically to the supplier. Closer to the delivery date, the supplier will be required to provide samples of the packages printed overseas to ensure the design has been executed properly by the printer. Because of the complexity of this process, finalizing packaging can sometimes take as much time as manufacturing the product.

Another step in this process that has become increasingly important is product testing. Products that pose a danger to consumers and are distributed by a retailer can result in physical harm and lawsuits and/or legal penalties that total in the millions of dollars. To avoid any such situation, importers must understand the possible ways in which different materials and manufacturing designs can cause harm, as well as the many laws in all 50 states that regulate the safety of products.

When the chosen supplier has received the purchase order and the payment arranged by the bank, the actual manufacturing of the product can begin. This entails acquiring the necessary raw materials, packaging, and scheduling the production. The factory has committed to the lead time specified on the purchase order—usually a minimum of 90 days—and it must coordinate with many different suppliers in order to fulfill this commitment. Any number of obstacles can be encountered at this stage of the process, so strong communication among all involved parties is essential to ensure that shipping deadlines are met. One of the services that an agent such as Li and Fung provides is inspection of the factory at different intervals. Domestic importers often offer these inspections as well. The inspection will not only ensure timely delivery and product quality; it will also ensure that compliance standards (safety, child labor, environmental impacts, etc.) are not violated.

The next step is to arrange for transporting the merchandise. Because lamps are a fairly bulky product, it is not difficult to reach quantities that fill entire containers. Fully loaded containers ensure that handling will move seamlessly from the factory door, to the freight forwarders who load vessels in the Asian port, into the port of entry in the United States, on through customs inspections, and finally to a distribution center. Also, the per-unit transportation cost is significantly lower when full, rather than partial, containers are used. When every connection in the supply chain is functioning properly, shipments from the Pacific Rim to the West Coast can reach port in less than three weeks.

A lamp program such as this is very likely planned to be featured in one or more advertised events in both Fred Meyer and the other Kroger banners. Print advertising for the entire Kroger chain requires significant lead times for photography, production, and printing. The printed copies should be complete and awaiting distribution around four weeks in advance of the planned advertising date. Any delay in the supply chain that might cause the product not to be received early enough could result in advertising without having the advertised product—an unfortunate outcome that disappoints customers.

When these lamp orders from Asia arrive on the West Coast, they are separated into Fred Meyer and Kroger orders. The Kroger merchandise is "trans-loaded" and three 40-foot containers are loaded into two 53-foot rail cars and sent east to Kroger distribution centers. This step adds approximately two weeks to the Kroger stores' lead time but reduces the shipping costs substantially. The Fred Meyer portion of the order is directed from the port to the Fred Meyer cross-docking distribution center in Chehalis, Washington. The bar codes on the lamps enable them to be placed on a conveyor belt, received by laser scanners, and then mechanically routed to the correct loading point at the ends of the conveyor system. Several merchandise containers can be received and ready to load on trucks within a matter of several hours. From that point, the lamps will be headed for the stores in the Pacific Northwest, Alaska, and California.

This case study describes the best-case scenario for the importing process at Kroger and Fred Meyer. There are many possible complications that might arise at these stages: production, shipping, customs, port-of-entry, distribution center

processing, and domestic transportation arrangements. These complications might add from two weeks to two months to the lead time. Only the intense focus by the teams at Kroger, Bank of America, Li and Fung or other importer, Geo. S. Bush Co., the manufacturer, the manufacturer's suppliers, the freight forwarders, and customs agents will enable this time to be as short and cost-effective as possible.

Sources: D. Gallacher, assistant vice president, Kroger Logistics Imports, and G. Parsons, vice president, product development, Kroger, interviewed August 2, 2012; Geo. S. Bush Co. Inc., www.geosbush.com/ (accessed December 17, 2016); Li and Fung, Ltd., www.lifung.com/eng/; The Kroger Co., Shipping Manual (n.d.), www.thekrogerco.com/.../general-merchandise-vendor-shipping-manual; The Kroger Co., Quote Sheet. (n.d.), www.thekrogerco.com/vendors-suppliers/import-vendors.

This case was written by Mary Manning, Portland State University.

DISCUSSION QUESTIONS

1. **What factors would you list that need to be evaluated in making a decision to source products overseas? Make a list of pros and cons, and explain what the pressures are that impel manufacturers and retailers to not source products domestically.**

2. **Based on the information given, how long do you estimate it will take to import these lamps? Create a set of target dates for each step in this process that will enable these products to arrive in time for the planned advertising date and selling period.**

3. **What areas of expertise do the various members of the product development team have? What are the possible communication issues that might arise between them?**

4. **There are several opportunities for questionable ethical situations to arise in the importing of products. What do you think the weak points might be? Where in the process is there the potential for unethical actions to occur?**

CASE 26   American Furniture Warehouse Sources Globally

The year 1975 saw the tail end of a recession that came on the heels of the 1973 Arab oil embargo, the fall of Saigon, and the resignation of Richard Nixon. That same year, Jake Jabs took over the American Furniture Company in Denver, Colorado, renamed it American Furniture Warehouse (AFW), and started turning it into a high-volume discount home furnishings retailer. Jabs responded to concerns that resonated with consumers in a tough economy: tighter pocketbooks, job insecurity, rising energy costs, a growing number of households as baby boomers branched out, and greater receptivity to generic products. Jabs was an experienced furniture retailer and had operated his own furniture manufacturing concern. Unbeknownst to Jabs at the time, global sourcing would become a more prominent way for his company to stock its showrooms.

Fast-forward to the present. Consumers' tastes change at a faster clip. They have higher standards than ever, and they demand bargains. As an inherently frugal man, Jake Jabs loves to give the public good value while keeping overhead low.

Eighty-five-year-old Jabs is the CEO and he employs no executives. No titles of vice president or executive vice president are anywhere in sight. The company is family-owned and is not beholden to stockholders demanding that high profit margins or quarterly objectives be met. Without pressure from such entities, AFW has continued to grow and thrive with year-over-year sales increasing an average of 10 percent since the mid-1980s. Jabs obsessively trolls for ideas on how to keep prices low, quality high, and merchandise current.

People from all over the western United States visit AFW's megastores and the rest of the U.S. population in the lower 48 can buy its merchandise online. Jabs aspires to become "the Amazon of the furniture business." They are intrigued with the values and constantly ask that AFW open a showroom near them. To date, AFW has preferred to remain a regional player, although it recently expanded into the Phoenix market with three stores. Its buys are based on the preferences and trends of Colorado customers.

Some of the many tenets to which AFW subscribes include striving to offer the lowest prices and the best guarantee, employing a no-pressure sales staff, having the best displays and selection, employing a careful delivery staff that works seven days a week, providing outstanding product information and customer service, and repairing merchandise on site rather than shipping anything back to the manufacturer.

In the 41 years AFW has been operating, it has forged strong vendor relationships worldwide. In fact, AFW sources goods from 30 different countries. Its major trading partners include Malaysia, Indonesia, China, Vietnam, and Mexico. It has a buying office in Asia. Its reputation has matured to the point where vendors travel up to 250 miles to bring samples to a foreign AFW buying office. AFW's small buying staff maximizes its time by having vendors come to buyers at specified dates and times; buyers no longer have to make arduous trips through countries such as China. Instead, they spend their time efficiently visiting stateside wholesale market centers and trade shows and working out of the AFW buying offices the majority of the time.

One of the dilemmas AFW has been grappling with centers around setting guidelines under which it will make time to see a new vendor. AFW's reputation is well known, and vendors clamor to get appointments with Jabs and his team on their limited market and trade show visits.

Many factories in developing countries have lower cost structures than those closer to home, often due to less stringent government regulations, lower pay, and fewer benefits for workers. Foreign factories often specialize in manufacturing one or two items well rather than constantly changing what product is on the assembly line, as is often the case in the United States. The one- or two-line process is less flexible but more cost-effective.

Because AFW sells so much, it is able to buy in volume. It directly imports full containers of merchandise. Its buying staff travel the world looking for the best deals. As a result, buyers are often able to negotiate prices 30 to 60 percent less than competitors' prices for comparable merchandise. This is due in part to the size of the order and the manner in which it is shipped. AFW sometimes pays in advance to get a better price, and it has a policy of always paying on time—a value factories respect and reward. Jake Jabs is exploring other ways in which AFW can differentiate itself in the buying process.

An example of how AFW has applied creative problem solving to reduce cost unfolds through its decision to build its own chairs, saving dramatically on freight costs. A garden-variety hardwood dinette chair can be manufactured abroad and the pieces assembled at AFW for much less than the cost if it were shipped already assembled. Typically, 1,000 assembled dinette chairs fit in a standard-sized container. AFW buys 4,000 identical chairs in pieces and fits them in that same container. It pays its domestic workers roughly $2 per chair to assemble them and can sell each chair at retail for less than what other retailers pay for the same chair at wholesale.

Yet another manifestation of its creative solutions to cost-reduction: AFW takes delivery on blanket-wrapped merchandise rather than carton-wrapped. Not only are the blankets reusable, but not putting the merchandise in cartons in the first place can save as much as 5 percent on the total purchase price. Once merchandise arrives at one of two distribution centers, it is placed into storage and samples are immediately shipped to the showrooms.

AFW makes it a policy not to return merchandise to a factory. If something is broken, its staff of 120 trained service technicians can repair just about any furniture problem they may encounter, often for pennies. Because of its no-return policy, if it makes a buying error, AFW will mark down the item and not repurchase it. With no returns to process, vendors sell to AFW for up to 15 percent less than to other retailers for that reason alone.

Artisans in Mexico make and sell accessories to AFW by the truckload. Recently, the accessories buyer was in Mexico at the invitation of the Mexican government. She was advising a group of artisans on what to create to appeal to the Colorado market. Because AFW buys items in bulk, it saves up to 50 percent over what competitors pay for similar items. Jake Jabs would like to replicate this sort of activity in other product categories in other countries.

In its Artists of the West program, Jabs developed an innovative way to sell art. Select artists earn commissions of up to $1,000 a month when their original paintings and other artwork are reproduced and sold in the mass market at under $100.

AFW takes chances on new, upstart vendors that other retailers may not have discovered. There are risks and rewards to this strategy, but AFW has found the rewards outweigh the risks, on balance.

Sources: Jake Jabs, *An American Tiger: An Autobiography* (Denver, CO: 2000); conversation with Jake Jabs, October 9, 2009, in Parker, CO; "At Age 83, Furniture Mogul Jake Jabs Still Leading by Example," *Pueblo Chieftan,* February 22, 2015, www.chieftain.com/business/3351394-120/jabs-furniture-colorado-state (accessed November 12, 2016); "Jake Jabs Discusses the Success of American Furniture Warehouse," *Fox News,* Denver, November 2, 2016, http://kdvr.com/2016/11/02/567160/ (accessed November 12, 2016).

This case was written by Lexi Hutto, Millersville University of Pennsylvania.

DISCUSSION QUESTIONS

1. Factories in many developing nations have lower cost structures, but that is often attributable to fewer benefits and lower wages for workers. What are the ethical trade-offs for retailers and shoppers when merchandise is sourced from countries in which labor practices fall short of standards Americans deem acceptable? Do shoppers really care about workers halfway across the globe, or are they more concerned about how many dollars are flowing out of their own pockets?

2. The world is our marketplace. AFW employs global sourcing, uses many negotiating tactics, and shifts channel tasks to keep its costs as low as possible. Enumerate the tactics AFW uses to keep its prices low. What other strategies and tactics could a furniture retailer use to hold the line on retail prices?

3. What criteria should AFW use when deciding whether to see a new vendor? How might it apply some of its best practices with its biggest vendors to new, smaller vendors? What strategies or innovations could it employ to stretch the productivity of its buying staff?

CASE 27   How Much for a Good Smell?

For the past two Christmas seasons, Courtney's, an upscale gift store, has carried a sweet-smelling potpourri in a plastic bag with an attractive ribbon. Heavily scented with cloves, the mixture gives a pleasant holiday aroma to any room, including the store.

Two years ago, the mixture cost $4.50 a bag. Courtney's (the only store in town that carried it) sold 300 pieces for $9.50. Courtney's supply ran out 10 days before Christmas, and it was too late to get any more.

Last year, the manufacturer raised the price to $5.00, so Courtney's raised its retail price to $9.95. Even though the markup was lower than that in the previous year, the store owner felt there was "magic" in the $10 ($9.95) price. As before, the store had a complete sellout, this time five days before Christmas. Sales last year were 600 units.

This year, the wholesale price has gone up to $5.50, and store personnel are trying to determine the correct retail price. The owner once again wants to hold the price at $10 ($9.95), but the buyer disagrees: "It's my job to push for the highest possible markup wherever I can. This item is a sure seller, as we're still the only store around with it, and we had some unsatisfied demand last year. I think we should mark it $12.50, which will improve the markup to 56 percent. Staying at $10 will penalize us unnecessarily, especially considering

the markup would be even lower than last year. Even if we run into price resistance, we'll have to sell only 480 to maintain the same dollar volume."

The owner demurs, saying, "This scent is part of our store's ambience. It acts as a draw to get people into the store, and its pleasant smell keeps them in a free-spending state of mind. I think we should keep the price at $9.95, despite the poorer markup. And if we can sell many more at this price, we'll realize the same dollar gross margin as last year. I think we should buy 1,000. Furthermore, if people see us raising a familiar item's price 25 percent, they might wonder whether our other prices are fair."

This case was prepared by David Ehrlich, Marymount University.

DISCUSSION QUESTIONS

1. **What prices caused Courtney's new charges?**
2. **Which price would result in the highest profit?**
3. **What other factors should Courtney's consider?**
4. **What price would you charge, and how many units would you order?**

CASE 28   See It! Scan It! Buy It! Shortening the Path to Purchase with Mobilibuy's Technology

Brick-and-mortar retailers struggle to keep up with shoppers' changing needs and dynamic buying habits. Many consumers expect to migrate easily across channels and devices, buy conveniently and quickly, and have products literally at their fingertips. Online retailers like Amazon thus are opening physical stores; offline retailers are adopting in-store digital technology to enhance customers' experience. Such omnichannel offerings are no longer distinctive advantages but necessary offerings. By 2019, pure online retail sales (e-tailers) are expected to account for at least 13 percent of total retail sales, while brick-and-mortar retailers are projected to lose 20 percent of their current selling space.

One dramatic change in shopper behavior patterns is the increase in consumer usage of mobile phones in searching and purchasing products online. Smartphone penetration rates continue to soar and the number of smartphone users worldwide is expected to surpass 2.5 billion in 2018. Shoppers use their mobiles to compare prices, access information, receive instant feedback from their social networks, and purchase products online. However, on the path to purchase, users are experiencing roadblocks such as the complexity of mobile shopping, relatively poor product image quality, inaccessible product information, difficulty making comparisons among products, and the task of clicking through many screens to get from product search to the actual purchase.

To address these ubiquitous challenges and increase retailers' advertising conversion rates, an Israeli start-up firm called Mobilibuy, founded in 2014, promises an innovative solution: a mobile app that can shorten and simplify the mobile shopping process. Specifically, Mobilibuy's cloud-based technology converts advertisements (such as in magazines,

brochures, and television commercials and on billboards) into virtual points of sale, using 99.9 percent accurate image recognition technology.

Consider, for example, a consumer who views a retailer's ad for a product she wishes to buy. If the retailer has adopted Mobilibuy's technology, the ad will display a "scan and buy" message, to notify consumers that it is scannable with either the retailer's app or (if the retailer doesn't offer its own app) with Mobilibuy's app. After downloading the relevant app, the consumer scans the advertised product, similar to a QR code, and is directed to an app-internal page for that particular product, where she can buy it with a single click. In case a retailer didn't adopt Mobilibuy's image recognition technology, a consumer who scans an unsupported ad will get a message notifying her that the ad is not recognized by the app. Mobilibuy's technology does not support scans of live people or products (i.e., scanning a product in a retail store or a person wearing cool jeans).

THE MOBILIBUY PROMISE

Mobilibuy's technology promises benefits for both retailers and consumers. Retailers provide their customers with a simplified path to purchase experience and increase the conversion rate of their advertising. Consumers can enjoy a quick, simple mobile purchase process, as well as improved opportunities of spontaneous purchase on the go.

Retailers

Retailers often seek to leverage their existing media assets and convert various advertising efforts and touch points with consumers into virtual sales, so that they can sell products anywhere and anytime. Mobilibuy's value for these retailers, especially those that offer their own mobile app, is to shorten and simplify the path to product purchase. Moreover, retailers that use Mobilibuy's technology benefit from additional and affordable touch points with consumers. These contacts serve as virtual points of sale and as such are expected to trigger new mobile purchases and increase conversion rates from advertisements, thus improving the effectiveness of advertising campaigns.

Consider, for example, a retailer that wants to enhance its marketing campaign for its winter collection. Mobilibuy's technology can be embedded into the retailer's own application, such that it pairs a relevant advertisement with the pertinent product page in the retailer's app, making the advertisements scannable and shopable. The consumer observes an ad that displays a "scan and buy" message using the retailer's app. She scans the ad and is instantly directed to the matching product page, which provides her with relevant product details, price information, and indicators of availability. Rather than having to search through the retailer's extensive app or website for the advertised product, by using the "scan and buy" feature embedded in the retailer's app, the consumer can instantly purchase a product in an advertisement, without requiring any search effort.

Retailers who don't use their own app can refer consumers to download and scan their advertisements with Mobilibuy's app. One complication of depending on Mobilibuy's app is that the retailer has to create an ad hoc product page, match it with its scannable advertisement, and put them onto Mobilibuy's platform, instead of using the information-rich product pages already existing on the retailer's own app, assuming the retailer has one.

Virtual Aisle Extension   Another feature of the Mobilibuy solution is that it acts as a virtual aisle extension. Physical retailers inherently have restricted shelf space and can display only a finite amount of inventory. With the Mobilibuy platform, they can extend their shelf space virtually, such as by creating in-store displays with images of products that might not be stocked in the store but are available for purchase online. Imagine a consumer who seeks a distinctive silver kettle, whereas the store stocks only more popular colors, such as black and white kettles. The retailer can place a small flyer or shelf tag of the silver version next to the display of black and white kettles in the store. With Mobilibuy's app, the consumer can scan this image, purchase it with a single click, and have the product delivered the next day. Similarly, the platform can facilitate the purchase of products that might be temporarily out of stock at that particular store. Instead of going to another retailer to search for the desired product, the consumer can simply scan the image/bar code of the missing product and complete the purchase on the spot.

Actionable Data Analytics   Marketers often struggle to measure the impacts of their advertising campaigns accurately. The Mobilibuy platform offers another important benefit in this realm, in that it provides retailers with accurate, unique, actionable data that they can use to analyze their

offline advertising effectiveness. Specifically, these data feature valuable information about shopper behavior and purchase characteristics, such as the location of the scan (i.e., where the consumer saw the advertisement), the timing of the purchase, the shopper's profile (which he or she provided to Mobilibuy upon registering on the platform), and the specific purchased items. Because the system recognizes the source and also location of the scanned image (e.g., catalog, brochure, billboard, television), it offers marketers a unique opportunity to test different versions of a campaign and learn which products, visuals, and media work best to trigger immediate sales, classified by location, timing, and message framing. The retailers on the platform pay Mobilibuy a monthly fixed fee or a commission per purchase. In return, they receive not only the primary sales functionality but also ongoing access to their sales data.

Consumers

Mobilibuy's app is designed to appeal to Millennials and Generation Z users, who grew up in a digital world. Most of them (86 percent) own a smartphone, and they use them extensively. For example, Millennials represent 15 percent of U.S. consumers but almost 60 percent of U.S. online mobile shoppers. In addition, as frequent social network visitors, they have considerable influence over the purchase decisions of their peers.

Consumers who wish to use the "scan and buy" feature on their mobile devices must first register their accounts and provide personal (e.g., shipping address) and payment (e.g., credit card number) information. Once they have registered, users can scan any advertisements that are supported by Mobilibuy's technology (using either the retailer's app or Mobilibuy's app if the retailer hasn't integrated Mobilibuy's app into its own system) and then buy rapidly and easily. The "scan and buy" feature offers an opportunity for consumers to make instant and spontaneous purchases that consequently could change the purchase process they go through. For example, by using the "scan and buy" feature, consumers could be encouraged to skip product information search or product comparison to alternatives. Such ease of use should keep consumers happier, as well as more satisfied with the retailer with which they interact through the "scan and buy" feature.

Consumer Education   In spite of the potential advantages of the "scan and buy" feature for consumers, as with any new technology, Mobilibuy and partnering retailers must invest significant resources in creating awareness to the app, and convince consumers to use it. Even if the app reaches high awareness, consumers might experience usage and psychological barriers such as having to learn how to operate the app, perceiving the automatic "scan and buy" feature as being risky (economically or functionally), or simply not being convinced that the app actually offers them significant added value.

Evidence from App Pretest

A test of Mobilibuy's app in the United Kingdom focused on the 2016 football (soccer) season. A top UK football team printed more than 10,000 small catalogs that featured its select merchandise. Fans could scan and buy from the booklets, using Mobilibuy's app, and then could either pick up their purchased products at the team's stadium or have them sent to their homes. The results showed that the app triggered a significant increase in purchases by fans at the game, and then continued to exert positive effect afterward. People who took the printed booklet home with them continued to purchase products using the app, even weeks after the game at which the booklet had been distributed.

Sources: P. Heckmann, M. Kesteloo, B. Schmaus, and R. Huisman, "Cross-Channel Integration in Retail: Creating a Seamless Customer Experience," Strategy&, www.strategyand.pwc.com/media/file/Strategyand_Cross-Channel-Integration-inRetail.pdf; "Worldwide Retail Ecommerce Sales Will Reach $1.915 Trillion This Year: Double-Digit Growth Will Continue through 2020, When Sales Will Top $4 Trillion," August 22, 2016, www.emarketer.com/Article/Worldwide-Retail-Ecommerce-Sales-Will-Reach-1915-Trillion-This-Year/1014369; "2 Billion Consumers Worldwide to Get Smart(phones) by 2016: Over Half of Mobile Phone Users Globally Will Have Smartphones in 2018," December, 2014, www.emarketer.com/Article/2-Billion-Consumers-Worldwide-Smartphones-by-2016/1011694; "Mobile In-Store Research: How In-Store Shoppers Are Using Mobile Devices," Google Shopper Marketing Council, April 2013, www.marcresearch.com/pdf/Mobile_InStore_Research_Study.pdf; "PayPal Mobile Research 2014/2015 GLOBAL SNAPSHOT," 2014, www.paypalobjects.com/webstatic/en_US/mktg/pages/stories/pdf/paypal_mobile_global_snapshot_2015_2.pdf;

Monica Anderson, "Technology Device Ownership," Pew Research Center, 2015, www.pewinternet.org/2015/10/29/technology-device-ownership-2015/; S. Ram and J. N. Sheth, "Consumer Resistance to Innovations: The Marketing Problem and Its Solutions," *Journal of Consumer Marketing* 6 (1989), pp. 5–14.

This case was written by Danna Tevet, Tel Aviv University; Michael Levy, Babson College; and Moti Levy, Mobilibuy.

DISCUSSION QUESTIONS

1. Taking the perspective of the retailer, what are the advantages and disadvantages of adopting each of the Mobilibuy functionalities? As a retailer, would you adopt the Mobilibuy system? If so, for which feature?

2. a. What are the advantages and disadvantages of Mobilibuy's technology for consumers? As a consumer, would you download the app? Explain your decision.
   b. How can Mobilibuy, and retailers who adopt its technology, encourage the app's download and usage by consumers?

3. How could the app affect consumers' decision-making process?

CASE 29   Promoting a Sale

A consumer electronics chain in the Washington, DC, area is planning a big sale in its suburban Virginia warehouse over the three-day Presidents' Day weekend (Saturday through Monday). On sale will be nearly $2 million worth of consumer electronics products—50 percent of the merchandise sold in the store. The company hopes to realize at least $900,000 in sales during the three days. In the retailer's past experience, the first day's sales were 50 percent of the total. The second day's were 35 percent, and the last day's, 15 percent. One of every two customers who came made a purchase.

Furthermore, the retailer knows that large numbers of people always flock to such sales, some driving as far as 50 miles. They come from all economic levels, but all are confirmed bargain hunters. You're the assistant to the general merchandise manager, who has asked you to plan the event's marketing campaign. You have the following information:

1. A full-page *Washington Post* ad costs $10,000, a half-page ad costs $6,000, and a quarter-page ad costs $3,500. To get the maximum value from a newspaper campaign, it is company policy to run two ads (not necessarily the same size) for such events.

2. The local northern Virginia paper is printed weekly and distributed free to some 15,000 households. Ads cost $700 for a full page and $400 for a half page.

3. To get adequate TV coverage, at least three channels must be used, with a minimum of eight 30-second spots on each at $500 per spot, spread over three or more days. Producing a television advertisement costs $3,000.

4. The store has contracts with three radio stations. One appeals to a broad, general audience aged 25 to 34 years. One is popular with the 18-to-25 age group. The third, a classical music station, has a small but wealthy audience. Minimum costs for a saturation radio campaign, including production, on all three stations are $8,000, $5,000, and $3,000, respectively.

5. Producing and mailing a full-color flyer to the store's 80,000 charge customers cost $10,000. When the company used such a mailing piece before, about 3 percent of recipients responded.

This case was written by Professor David Ehrlich, Marymount University.

DISCUSSION QUESTIONS

1. Knowing that the company wants a mixed-media ad campaign to support this event, prepare an ad plan for the general merchandise manager that costs no more than $40,000.

2. Work out the daily scheduling of all advertising.

3. Work out the dollars to be devoted to each medium.

4. Justify your plan.

CASE 30   Target Marketing with Google AdWords

Australia's oldest retailer evolved from Appleton and Jones in 1835 to David Jones in 1838. Today, David Jones, or simply DJs, has dozens of department stores, predominantly in Australia's capital cities. Similar to many retailers, and despite having a mail-order business since the late 1800s, DJs suffered a few missteps with its online presence in the early 2000s. Now, however, the David Jones website, davidjones.com.au, is integral to DJs's daily operations.

Chris Taylor, a recent university graduate, manages DJs's online presence. Thanks to its successful website and changing media habits, David Jones is considering online advertising to drive targeted traffic to the website. Given the prominence of Google and sponsored search, Chris would like to test Google AdWords.

Starting late last century, search engines began to develop interactive advertising models based on user interests, such as keywords typed into a search engine. The concept-sponsored search aligns online advertisements with search engine queries. In sponsored search—also known as paid search, keyword advertising, pay-per-click (PPC) advertising, and search advertising—advertisers pay for search engine traffic to their websites via link-based ads that search engines display in response to user queries. Thus, if a user searches Google using the keyword *retailers*, AdWords ads that mention "retailing" would appear. If the user clicks on an ad, the user then goes to a specific web page—the landing page—on the advertiser's website.

As the leading search engine, Google has driven developments in sponsored search beyond search engine results. In addition to placing advertisements on Google and affiliated search engine results, such as AOL.com and Ask.com, advertisers can place AdWords on other websites. Via its content network, Google dynamically matches ads to a web page's content and pays the website owner if a visitor clicks on the ad. Google's content network includes millions of websites in more than 100 countries and 20 languages, such as the British travel site Lonely Planet and the French television channel M6. In the United States, for example, the *New York Times* earns revenue by placing AdWords on its web pages. Thus, advertisers can place AdWords on search engine results and on the millions of websites in Google's content network.

AdWords are simple text-based ads with four lines of copy predominantly in the right-hand column and at the top of Google search results. The first line, or headline, has a maximum of 25 characters. The next two lines and the final line with the website address have a maximum of 35 characters each. Two sample AdWords advertisements for David Jones are shown in Exhibit 1. The copy is identical except for the first half of the third line, "Great holiday specials" versus "Expanded holiday hours." The ad on the left should interest value-conscious market segments, while the one on the right should attract consumers seeking after-hours shopping.

In addition to its simple and nonintrusive nature, AdWords's advantages over traditional advertising such as print or television include better segmentation and more direct targeting. Advertisers select the keywords and the geographic location of the person doing the search. For geographic segmentation, David Jones might want its ads to appear only for people in a key source market such as Sydney or Melbourne.

To target consumer interests, David Jones could use keywords such as *Christmas, holidays, shopping,* and *retailers*. But these keywords could be too expensive because they are so generic. Although generic terms may attract clicks on an AdWords advertisement, many of these clicks may be from random rather than targeted David Jones web shoppers. Unlike a cost-per-thousand model based on impressions, this contextual advertising based on keywords charges advertisers on a cost-per-click basis. Chris and her team want to pay for targeted clicks.

To minimize paying for unwanted clicks, online advertisers also include negative keywords such as cheap or free. Including the negative keyword *cheap* alongside the keywords *Christmas* and *shopping* means that no AdWords ads will show on search results for users keying in the three keywords *cheap, Christmas,* and *shopping*.

Furthermore, advertisers bid on the cost per click in a dynamic auction. When many advertisers bid on generic terms such as *Christmas* and *shopping*, this drives the cost up for these keywords. Thus, clever advertisers bid on specific phrases such as *Christmas shopping* rather than on *Christmas* and *shopping*.

Chris and her team use three Google websites to understand and determine applicable content network websites, keywords, and estimated keyword costs:

- Google AdWords Glossary (https://support.google.com/adwords/topic/3121777?hl=en&ref_topic=3119071, 3181080,3126923)
- Google Content Network (https://adwords.google.com/home/how-it-works/display-ads/)
- Google Keyword planner (https://adwords.google.com/home/tools/keyword-planner/)

Because AdWords accounts are easy to set up and manage, the testing possibilities are many. Major considerations that Chris and her team would like to test include:

- Appropriate keywords, keyword phrases, and negative keywords
- Geographic segmentation
- Advertising copy and appeals
- Keyword pricing
- Google's content network
- Landing page alignment with the AdWords copy

The final point—the landing page—leads to a key aspect of David Jones's online presence, its website. As davidjones.com.au illustrates, the website serves many target markets and offers many products. For example, online visitors may find information on store events, employment, publicly traded stock shares, and registration for e-mail alerts and bridal registries, as well as traditional department store products such as clothing. Effective AdWords align the advertising copy with the landing page. That is, the advertisement directs consumers to a relevant web page rather than to the David Jones home page at davidjones.com.au. The left-column ad in Exhibit 1, which focuses on holiday specials, would take visitors to a landing page with holiday specials. Similarly, the right-column ad in Exhibit 1 would take visitors to a landing page featuring expanded holiday hours.

This case was written by Jamie Murphy, Murdoch Business School, Australia; Meghan O'Farrell, Google; and Alex Gibelalde, Google; and Jenny Esdale.

EXHIBIT 1
Sample AdWords

Christmas at David Jones	Christmas at David Jones
Convenient major city locations	Convenient major city locations
Great holiday specials; visit now	Expanded holiday hours; visit now
DavidJones.com.au	DavidJones.com.au

DISCUSSION QUESTIONS

1. On the basis of your review of the David Jones website davidjones.com.au, use examples to explain how different sections of the home page serve different audiences. What other audiences would you suggest David Jones serve via its website? Why?

2. On the basis of your review of the David Jones website, davidjones.com.au, design three separate AdWords advertisements.

CASE 31   Diamond in the Rough

Ruth Diamond, president of Diamond Furriers, was concerned that sales in her store appeared to have flattened out. She was considering establishing a different method for compensating her salespeople.

Diamond was located in an affluent suburb of Nashville, Tennessee. Ruth's father had founded the company 40 years earlier, and she had grown up working in the business. After his retirement in 2008, she moved the store into an upscale shopping mall not far from its previous location, and sales boomed almost immediately, rising to just over $3 million in five years. However, once it reached that sales volume, it remained there for the next three years, making Ruth wonder whether her salespeople had sufficient incentive to sell more aggressively.

Diamond's staff was all women, ranging in age from 27 to 58 years. There were four full-timers and four part-timers (20 hours a week), all of whom had at least three years of experience in the store. All of them were paid at the same hourly rate, $14, with liberal health benefits. Employee morale was excellent, and the entire staff displayed strong personal loyalty to Diamond.

The store was open 78 hours a week, which meant that there was nearly always a minimum staff of three on the floor, rising to six at peak periods. Diamond's merchandise consisted exclusively of fur coats and jackets, ranging in price from $2,000 to more than $14,000. The average unit sale was about $12,000. Full-timers' annual sales averaged about $500,000, and the part-timers' were a little over half of that.

Diamond's concern about sales transcended her appreciation for her loyalty toward her employees. She asked them, for example, to maintain customer files and call their customers when new styles came in. Although some of them were more diligent about this than others, none of them appeared to want to be especially aggressive about promoting sales.

She began to investigate commission systems and discussed them with some of her contacts in the trade. All suggested lowering the salespeople's base pay and installing either a fixed or a variable commission rate system. One idea was to lower the base hourly rate from $14 to $12 and let them make up the difference through a 4 percent commission on all sales, to be paid monthly. Such an arrangement would allow them all to earn the same as they currently do.

However, she also realized that such a system would provide no incentive to sell the higher-priced furs, which she recognized might be a way to improve overall sales. So she also considered offering to pay 3 percent on items priced below $5,000 and 5 percent on all those above.

Either of these systems would require considerable extra bookkeeping. Returns would have to be deducted from commissions. And she was also concerned that disputes might arise among her people from time to time over who had actually made the sale. So she conceived of a third alternative, which was to leave the hourly rates the same but pay a flat bonus of 4 percent of all sales over $1 million and then divide it among the salespeople on the basis of the proportion of hours each had actually worked. This "commission" would be paid annually, in the form of a Christmas bonus.

This case was written by Professor David Ehrlich, Marymount University, and Jenny Esdale.

DISCUSSION QUESTIONS

1. What are the advantages and disadvantages of the various alternatives Ruth Diamond is considering?
2. Do you have any other suggestions for improving the store's sales?
3. What would you recommend? Why?

CASE 32   A Stockout at Discmart

Robert Honda, the manager of a Discmart store (a discount retailer similar to Target and Walmart) in Cupertino, California, was surveying the Sunday morning activity at his store. Shoppers were bustling around with carts; some had children in tow. On the front side of the store, a steady stream of shoppers was heading through the checkout counters. Almost all the cash registers that he could see from his vantage point were open and active. The line in front of register 7 was longer than the other lines, but other than that, things seemed to be going quite smoothly.

The intercom beeped and interrupted his thoughts. A delivery truck had just arrived at the rear of the store. The driver wanted to know which loading dock to use to unload merchandise. Honda decided to inspect the available space before directing the driver to a specific loading dock. As he passed the cash registers on his way to the rear of the store, he noticed that the line at register 7 had gotten a little bit longer. The light over the register was flashing, indicating that the customer service associate (CSA) requested assistance. (At Discmart, all frontline personnel who interact with customers are called CSAs.) As he passed by the register, he could not help overhearing the exchange between what seemed to be a somewhat irate customer and the CSA. The customer was demanding that another item should be substituted for an item that was on sale but currently out of stock, and the CSA was explaining the store policy to the customer. Normally, during a busy time like this, Honda would have tried to help the CSA resolve the situation, but he knew that the truck driver was waiting to unload merchandise that was needed right away on the floor. Hence, he quickly walked to the rear of the store.

After assigning the truck to a docking bay for unloading, Honda headed back toward the front of the store. On the way back, he ducked into the break room to get a Coke and noticed that Sally Johnson, the CSA who had been at register 7, was on a break. Sally had been on the Discmart team for about a year and was considered a very capable employee who always kept the store's interests at heart.

Robert: Hi Sally, I noticed that you had quite a line in front of your register earlier today.

Sally: Hi Robert. Yes, I had a very irate customer, and it took us awhile to resolve the issue.

Robert: Oh really! What was he irate about?

Sally: We are out of stock on the 100-ounce Tide Liquid Detergent that was advertised in our flyer and was on sale at 20 percent off. I offered the customer a rain check or the same discount on the same size of another brand, but he kept insisting that he wanted us to substitute a 200-ounce container of Tide Liquid Detergent at the same discount. Apparently, Joe Chang [the assistant manager] had told the customer that we would substitute the 200-ounce size.

Robert: Did you point out to the customer that our sale prices are valid only while supplies last?

Sally: I did mention this to him, but he thought it was strange that we ran out of stock on the morning of the first day of the sale.

Robert: Well, I guess you should have gone ahead and given him what he wanted.

Sally: As you know, our point-of-sale systems allow me to make adjustments only on designated items. Since the 200-ounce sizes were not designated as substitutes, I had to request a supervisor to help me.

Robert: I am glad that you got it resolved.

Sally: Well, the customer got tired of waiting for the supervisor, who was busy helping another customer, so he decided to take a rain check instead. He seemed quite dissatisfied with the whole episode and mentioned that we should stop running these TV ads claiming that we are always in stock and that we guarantee satisfaction.

Robert: I do hate it when they run these ad campaigns and we have to take the heat on the floor, trying to figure out what those cowboys in marketing promised the customer.

Sally: Well, my break is nearly over. I have to get back.

Honda pondered the encounter that Johnson had with the customer. He wondered whether to discuss this issue with Joe Chang. He remembered talking to him about inventory policies a couple of days ago. Chang had indicated that their current inventory levels were fairly high and that any further increases would be hard to justify from a financial perspective. He mentioned some market research that had surveyed a random sample of customers who had redeemed rain checks. The results of the survey indicated that customers by and large were satisfied with Discmart's rain check procedures. On the basis of this finding, Chang had argued that current inventory levels, supplemented with a rain check policy, would keep customers satisfied.

This case was prepared by Kirthi Kalyanam, Retail Management Institute, Santa Clara University.

CASE 33   Customer Service and Relationship Management at Nordstrom

Nordstrom's unwavering customer-focused philosophy traces its roots to founder Johan Nordstrom's values. Johan Nordstrom believed in people and realized that consistently exceeding their expectations would lead to success and a good conscience. He built his organization around a customer-oriented philosophy. The organization focuses on people, and its policies and selections are designed to satisfy people. As simple as this philosophy sounds, few of Nordstrom's competitors have truly been able to grasp it.

A FOCUS ON PEOPLE

Nordstrom employees treat customers like royalty. Employees are instructed to do whatever is in the customer's best interest. Customer delight drives the values of the company. Customers are taken seriously and are at the heart of the business. Customers are even at the top of Nordstrom's so-called organization chart, which is an inverted pyramid. Moving down from the customers at the top of the inverted pyramid are the salespeople, department managers, and general managers. Finally, at the bottom is the board of directors. All lower levels work toward supporting the salespeople, who in turn work to serve the customers.

 Employee incentives are tied to customer service. Salespeople are given personalized business cards to help them build relationships with customers. Uniquely, salespeople are not tied to their respective departments but to the customer. Salespeople can travel from department to department within the store to assist their customer, if that is needed. For example, a Nordstrom salesperson assisting a woman shopping for business apparel helps her shop for suits, blouses, shoes, hosiery, and accessories. The salesperson becomes the "personal shopper" of the customer to show her merchandise and provide fashion expertise. This approach is also conducive to building long-term relationships with customers, because over time, the salesperson comes to understand each customer's fashion sense and personality.

 The opportunity to sell across departments enables salespeople to maximize sales and commissions while providing superior customer service. As noted on a *60 Minutes* segment, "[Nordstrom's service is] not service like it used to be, but service that never was."

 Despite the obsession with customer service at Nordstrom, ironically, the customer actually comes second. Nordstrom understands that customers will be treated well by its employees only if the employees themselves are treated well by the company. Nordstrom employees are treated almost like the extended Nordstrom family, and employee satisfaction is a closely watched business variable.

 Nordstrom is known for promoting employees from within its ranks. The fundamental traits of a successful Nordstrom salesperson (e.g., commitment to excellence, customer service) are the same traits emphasized in successful Nordstrom executives.

 Nordstrom hires people with a positive attitude, a sense of ownership, initiative, heroism, and the ability to handle high expectations. This sense of ownership is reflected in Nordstrom's low rate of shrinkage. Shrinkage, or loss due to theft and record-keeping errors, at Nordstrom is under 1.5 percent of sales, roughly half the industry average. The low shrinkage can be attributed in large part to the diligence of salespeople caring for the merchandise as if it were their own.

Employees at all levels are treated like businesspeople and empowered to make independent decisions. They are given the latitude to do whatever they believe is the right thing, with the customers' best interests at heart. All employees are given the tools and authority to do whatever is necessary to satisfy customers, and management almost always backs subordinates' decisions.

In summary, Nordstrom's product is its people. The loyal Nordstrom shopper goes to Nordstrom for the service received—not necessarily the products. Of course, Nordstrom does offer quality merchandise, but that is secondary for many customers.

CUSTOMER-FOCUSED POLICIES

One of the most famous examples of Nordstrom's customer service occurred in 1975 when a Nordstrom salesperson gladly took back a set of used automobile tires and gave the customer a refund, even though Nordstrom had never sold tires! The customer had purchased the tires from a Northern Commercial Company store, whose retail space Nordstrom had since acquired. Not wanting the customer to leave the Nordstrom store unhappy, the salesperson refunded the price of the tires.

Nordstrom's policies focus on the concept of the "Lifetime Value of the Customer." Although little money is made on the first sale, when the lifetime value of a customer is calculated, the positive dollar amount of a loyal customer is staggering. The lifetime value of a customer is the sum of all sales and profits generated from that customer, directly or indirectly. To keep its customers for a "lifetime," Nordstrom employees go to incredible lengths. In a Nordstrom store in Seattle, a customer wanted to buy a pair of brand-name slacks that had gone on sale. The store was out of her size, and the salesperson was unable to locate a pair at other Nordstrom stores. Knowing that the same slacks were available at a competitor nearby, the salesclerk went to the rival, purchased the slacks at full price using petty cash from her department, and sold the slacks to the customer at Nordstrom's sale price. Although this sale resulted in an immediate loss for the store, the investment in promoting the loyalty of the happy customer went a long way.

Nordstrom's employees try to "Never Say No" to the customer. Nordstrom has an unconditional return policy. If a customer is not completely satisfied, he or she can return the new and generally even heavily used merchandise at any time for a full refund. Ironically, this is not a company policy; rather, it is implemented at the discretion of the salesperson to maximize customer satisfaction.

Nordstrom's advice to its employees is simply, "Use good judgment in all situations." Employees are given the freedom, support, and resources to make the best decisions to enhance customer satisfaction. The cost of Nordstrom's high service, such as its return policy, coupled with its competitive pricing would, on the surface, seem to cut into profit margins. This cost, however, is recouped through increased sales from repeat customers, limited markdowns, and, if necessary, the "squeezing" of suppliers.

Nordstrom's vendor relationships also focus on maximizing customer satisfaction. According to former CEO Bruce Nordstrom, "[Vendors] know that we are liberal with our customers. And if you're going to do business with us, then there should be a liberal influence on their return policies. If somebody has worn a shoe and it doesn't wear satisfactorily for them, and we think that person is being honest about it, then we will send it back." Nordstrom realizes some customers will abuse the unconditional return policy, but it refuses to impose that abuse back onto the vendors. Here again, the rule of "doing what is right" comes into play.

Nordstrom's merchandising and purchasing policies are also extremely customer-focused. A full selection of merchandise in a wide variety of sizes is seen as a measure of customer service. An average Nordstrom store carries roughly 150,000 pairs of shoes with a variety of sizes, widths, colors, and models. Typical shoe sizes for women range from $2\frac{1}{2}$ to 14, in widths of A to EEE. Nordstrom is fanatical about stocking only high-quality merchandise. Once when the upper parts of some women's shoes were separating from the soles, every shoe from that delivery was shipped back to the manufacturer.

This case was written by Alicia Lueddemann, the Management Mind Group; and Sunil Erevelles, University of North Carolina, Charlotte.

DISCUSSION QUESTIONS

1. What steps does Nordstrom take to implement its strategy of providing outstanding customer service?

2. How do these activities enable Nordstrom to reduce the gaps between perceived service and customer expectations, as described in Chapter 17?

3. What are the pros and cons of Nordstrom's approach to developing a competitive advantage through customer service?

CASE 34   Zipcar: Delivering Only as Much Driving as You Want

The expectation that your car will be waiting at the curb every morning got hard-wired into many Americans, with the growth of the auto industry. But that expectation has gone haywire for many city dwellers, who have been frustrated by the soaring costs and parking pressures that confront modern drivers. For them, Zipcar, the world's leading car-sharing company, offers the pleasure of driving without the hassles of ownership.

The Cambridge, Massachusetts–based company rents self-service vehicles by the hour or day to urban residents who prefer to pay for just as much driving as they absolutely need. Car sharing eliminates issues related to parking shortages; overnight parking restrictions; or soaring gas, insurance, and tax bills. That promise resonates well with consumer expectations on many fronts, especially among

Zipcar's primary urban customers, the large segments of college students who also enjoy the service, and even suburbanites who just work in the city.

Still the company's biggest growth obstacle may be Americans' inability to envision life without a car. To push an attitude shift, Zipcar makes the car-sharing experience as easy as possible, with just four simple steps:

1. Join the network.
2. Reserve your car online or from your smartphone.
3. Unlock the car with your Zipcard.
4. Drive away.

Today the car-sharing network offers more than 50 makes and models of cars, and has more than 950,000 members and 12,000 vehicles in major metropolitan areas and college campuses throughout the United States, Canada, United Kingdom, Spain, Austria, France, Germany, and Turkey. With so many locations, the company could bring convenient car sharing to a far larger market; it estimates that 10 million residents, business commuters, and university students now live or work just a short walk away from an available Zipcar.

Zipcar also is banking on more than shifting attitudes. Emerging trends due to the economic downturn and changing buying habits have helped spur growth. On average, automobiles consume 19 percent of household incomes, yet many cars stand idle for 90 percent of each day. Drivers seeking a less expensive and less wasteful alternative thus might save up to 70 percent on their annual transportation costs

Zipcar's service model also fits in with the emergence of on-demand, pay-per-use options, such as Netflix for movies, iTunes for music, and e-readers for books. Moreover, the popularity of mobile shopping and the growing expectation that they can order anything, anywhere, anytime from their smartphone have made urban young adults and college students two of Zipcar's most fervent member groups. For these "Zipsters," ordering up a set of wheels on the go is far more appealing than being saddled with car payments.

A strong urban public transportation system also helps make car sharing more attractive. That's why Zipcar started off in high-density urban areas such as Boston, New York, and Washington, DC, with their great public transportation systems already in place. Wherever subways and buses work, car sharing can extend the transit system's reach. By locating cars near transit route end-points, travelers gain an easy extension on subway or bus schedules to their final destinations.

Finally, the logic of car sharing works well in settings marked by increased urbanization. According to the United Nations, cities will contain 66 percent of the world's population by 2050. Many of these areas already face congestion, space demands, and environmental threats from crowding too many gas-driven vehicles into a small, population-dense space. Zipcar CEO Scott Griffith estimates that every Zipcar would replace 15 to 20 personal cars. Thus, some cities even work with Zipcar to identify and secure parking spaces close to subway stops and rail stations. New York and Chicago also rent Zipcars for municipal workers so they can shuttle more efficiently across city locations during their workday. Zipcar also provides fleet management services to local, state, and federal agencies.

Car sharing could translate into a $10 billion market globally. Cities in Europe and Asia are well primed for car sharing by virtue of their strong rail systems, heavy reliance on public transit, and widespread adoption of mobile and wireless technologies.

Such growth requires strong logistics, and Zipcar is backed by a corps of fleet managers and vehicle coordinators who track, schedule, and oversee vehicle maintenance; proprietary hardware and software technology that helps it communicate with drivers and track vehicles; and a large fleet that includes hybrid vehicles for fuel efficiency, as well as minivans to appeal to families who want to take a trip to the beach.

These behind-the-scenes moves aim to make Zipcar's service simple, convenient, and reliable. But failures are inevitable, as one customer's experience showed. The customer went to pick up his designated vehicle at the time and place reserved for him, but he discovered no car there. The Zipcar representative told him that it might be out, being serviced or cleaned, or it could have been delayed by another driver running late. But such excuses did little to alleviate the frustration of being stuck with no transportation.

Learning of his predicament, Zipcar tried but was unable to find another car in close proximity. Therefore, it quickly authorized the customer to take a taxi and promised to reimburse him up to $100. Although the "free ride" did not altogether mitigate the stress and inconvenience of the service failure, Zipcar's response showed him that the company was committed to doing right by him, even if that meant sending business to a competitor, the taxi company.

The considerable dimensions of a global car-sharing market are already emerging. Zipcar's 16-year experience and first-mover position in the market positions it well to compete. But the race to dominate is sure to intensify, especially as traditional car rental companies with great name recognition, such as Hertz and Enterprise, move into the marketplace. Whether Zipcar can maintain its space in this market depends mostly on its ability to meet its own standards for customer service—simplicity, convenience, and reliability—consistently and effectively.

Sources: www.zipcar.com; United Nations, "World's Population Increasingly Urban with More Than Half Living in Urban Areas," July 10, 2014; April Kilcrease, "A Conversation with Zipcar's CEO Scott Griffith," GigaOM, December 5, 2011; U.S. Securities and Exchange Commission, "Zipcar S-1 Filing," June 1, 2010; JPMorgan SMid Cap Conference, December 11, 2011; Courtney Rubin, "How Will the IPO Market Treat Zipcar?," *Inc.*, June 2, 2010.

This case was written by Laurie Covens; Dhruv Grewal and Michael Levy, both at Babson College; and Jenny Esdale.

DISCUSSION QUESTIONS

1. Using the five dimensions of service quality (reliability, assurance, tangibility, empathy, and responsiveness), evaluate Zipcar.

2. Compare Zipcar's service quality performance with that of the most recent car rental service (e.g., Avis, Hertz) that you may have used.

3. How well has Zipcar handled service failure situations? What could it do to improve recovery efforts?

CASE 35   A Musical Quandary in an Italian Restaurant

Jake recently received a promotion to manage one of the Italian restaurants that his family runs, hoping one day to be a franchise owner himself. The Mike's Restaurant chain, a local franchise in Ontario, Canada, started out as a single sandwich shop more than 50 years ago, but it has grown into a budding franchise success story, with close to 100 locations. The chain offers various Italian-themed dishes, including pizzas, subs, and pastas, along with famous breakfast platters. The restaurant that Jake has begun managing caters to young adults in a small city of 40,000 people.

As he starts making his mark on the restaurant, Jake faces what might seem like a relatively minor decision: What music should play in the background? Jake has always assumed that music can stimulate diners and ultimately affect their dining behavior, as well as their overall restaurant experience. But which kinds of music might have which effects?

Jake decided to bring up the topic with some other restaurant owners, who consistently advised him that patrons prefer restaurants that play authentic, culturally oriented music. That is, he should play Neapolitan music, to be consistent with the theme of the restaurant. He likes the ambiance of a nearby Rainforest Café, which uses rainforest-themed music and tropical animal noises to create consumer experiences that are consistent with its overall image. Los Colibris, one of the best rated Mexican restaurants in the city, also regularly plays Mexican music in the background. With this in mind, Jake starts to think that perhaps adding Italian music to his restaurant's musical portfolio would benefit its popularity and sales.

But most of the people who visit his restaurant are young adults, many of whom appreciate and enjoy modern, pop music. To cater to these patrons, who already regularly dine at the restaurant, Jake thinks perhaps he should play the "Top Billboard" playlist, which his customers likely will enjoy, rather than trying to match the theme of the restaurant. He consulted a few research studies, which suggest that retailers should match their music with their target market's preferences. Furthermore, pop music tends to be upbeat (i.e., faster tempo), which can increase listeners' arousal and excitement. Such arousal might mean that patrons who are listening to music spend less time at their tables, because the beat propels them, unconsciously, to take more bites per minute and consume their drinks faster. Such an outcome could be beneficial, in that Jake could turn the tables faster and seat more patrons, but it also might leave diners feeling rushed and unlikely to enjoy high-margin menu items, such as desserts and espressos.

Jake really wants to make the best choice for his restaurant and his patrons. Deciding on what music to play may seem like a simple task, but Jake needs to contemplate the pros and cons of both options carefully before moving forward. Should the music in the restaurant be consistent with its general theme (e.g., Neapolitan, Italian), or should he play music geared toward the types of genres that his patrons tend to prefer (e.g., pop music)?

Sources: C. T. S. Tsai and P. H. Lu, "Authentic Dining Experiences in Ethnic Theme Restaurants," *International Journal of Hospitality Management* 31, no. 1 (2012), pp. 304–306; J. Duncan Herrington and L. M. Capella, "Practical Applications of Music in Service Settings," *Journal of Services Marketing* 8, no. 3 (1994), pp. 50–65; C. Caldwell and S. A. Hibbert, "The Influence of Music Tempo and Musical Preference on Restaurant Patrons' Behavior," *Psychology & Marketing* 19, no. 11 (2002), pp. 895–917; N. Guéguen and C. Jacob, "Sound Level of Background Music and Alcohol Consumption: An Empirical Evaluation," *Perceptual and Motor Skills* 99, no. 1 (2004), pp. 34–38.

This case was written by Mathew Catangui and Seung Hwan (Mark) Lee, Ryerson University.

DISCUSSION QUESTIONS

1. How does music add value to businesses?
2. What type of music would you recommend that Jake play in his restaurant?
3. Identify other retail settings in which music influences consumer behavior.

CASE 36   Yankee Candle: Product Management and Innovation

Yankee Candle Company (YCC) is a leading designer, manufacturer, wholesaler, and retailer of premium scented candles in the giftware industry. The core product lines for YCC are scented candles and candle accessories. The premium-quality scented candles are offered in over 150 fragrances. Almost all candles are produced on-site at the advanced manufacturing facility in Whately, Massachusetts. Candles are made by master chandlers (candlemaking experts) who oversee a complex manufacturing process with strict quality control standards. As well as creating the candles themselves, YCC builds competitive advantage through expertise in formulating the scents that make up "the fragrance experience." According to information on the YCC website, master perfumers develop the fragrances, which are then rigorously screened, reviewed, and tested. The scents are unique compared to competitive products in that they maintain intensity through the life of the candle. In short, quality control of the candles and fragrances ensures premium products that provide high value to customers in the form of a true scent, long burn time, and consistency of fragrance over the life of the candle.

Candles are available in clear or frosted glass Housewarmer jars, Sampler votive candles, wax potpourri Tarts, pillars, tapers, and tea lights. Related products are flameless fragrance products (sprays, electric air fresheners), car fresheners, and candle accessories (decorative lids for the jar candles); taper holders; pillar and jar bases; matching jar shades, plates, and sleeves; votive holders; and tea light holders.

HISTORICAL SUMMARY AND PRESENT-DAY SITUATION

During its 40-year history, the company grew from an entrepreneurial family business started by Mike Kittredge to a publicly traded company in 1999. Craig Rydin joined YCC in 2001 as CEO. Under his leadership the company flourished; sales climbed higher than ever in company-owned stores and through the wholesale channel. Rydin was instrumental in establishing the partnerships with mass retailers including Bed Bath & Beyond and Linens 'n Things.

In February 2007, YCC went from a publicly traded firm to a private corporation. Madison Dearborn Partners LLC acquired YCC for $1.4 billion, and it was delisted from the New York Stock Exchange. By the end of 2008, sales were approximately $700 million and continued steadily upward for the next four years. In 2012, YCC booked $56.3 million in profit in on sales (up 7.4 percent) to $844.2 million, according to regulatory filings.

In September 2013, consumer products company Jarden Corporation acquired YCC for $1.75 billion in cash. "Jarden isn't a household name but owns dozens of well-known brands including Crock-Pot slow cookers, Rawlings baseball equipment and Sunbeam home appliances. The collection appears hodgepodge but reflects a strategy of buying leading brands in specialized niches, and expanding sales." Jarden Corporation, and its collection of consumer brands which includes YCC, was purchased in 2016 by Newell Rubbermaid Incorporated for $15.4 billion.

In the earnings call of October 28, 2016, Newell Brands CEO Mike Polk commented that YCC is a strong addition to the consumer brands portfolio. He cited strong point-of-sale momentum in the United States and double-digit sales growth in Europe.

PRODUCT MANAGEMENT AND INNOVATION AT YANKEE CANDLE

Success at YCC over time is due, in large part, to the ability to successfully manage existing products and support innovation of new products. Innovation in product development is an ongoing cross-functional effort to keep merchandise offerings new and fresh for consumers. For example, in March 2016, YCC launched four new tropical fragrances to support the #MyMargarita sweepstakes promotion. This effort, to connect customers to good memories and experiences through fragrance, is consistent with the Paradise Collection and Full Bloom lines launched in 2013.

Another new product/service innovation in 2015 involved updating the YCC web platform to support personalization of candle products. Customers can design a personalized candle in three steps (choose the holder, choose the fragrance, and upload a photo for the label).

In addition to innovation, careful management of product strategy is a key success factor at YCC. In December 2016, YCC president and CEO Hope Margala issued a product recall notice for six items in the Luminous Collection. Customer feedback about candle jars cracking while the candle is lit motivated the recall.

YCC has enjoyed success through innovation in its use of multichannel distribution. To date, YCC operates over 500 company-owned retail (brick-and-mortar) stores nationwide. YCC sells direct to consumers via its online store (yankeecandle.com) and by direct-mail catalog orders. In 2001, top management at YCC began cultivating partnerships with mass retailers to carry limited product selections.

Partners include retail giants such as Target, Walmart, and Bed Bath & Beyond. The wholesale distribution channel is equally important in the multichannel mix. This is a network of approximately 19,100 independent stores that sell YCC products across the United States. Many of these stores are small businesses with Hallmark and other gift-related franchises. For all of these retail and wholesale channels, products are YCC-branded goods.

All of the sources of product management and innovation success mentioned heretofore are in the consumer marketplace. An exciting innovation for YCC is its work in a new division for commercial customers, Scent Systems. "Many businesses are embracing scent as an integral part of their brand communications." said Hope Margala, in a 2015 YCC Press Release. To deliver the right fragrance impressions for experiential branding, YCC has paired with an app creator to allow B2B customers to monitor the brand environment using handheld mobile devices. For example, a hotel brand may work with YCC to custom design and develop specific scents for its rooms, lobby, conference facilities, and other areas. The scent becomes part of the brand identity. According to the website (http://www.ycscentsystems.com/), Yankee Candle's Scent Systems is targeting five market segments for potential customers: retail, hospitality, health care, gaming, and real estate.

Sources: Maureen Farrell, "Jarden Founders Seek New Venture," *The Wall Street Journal,* September 23, 2016; ProQuest website, www.proquest.com/ (accessed December 26, 2016); Serena Ng, "Corporate News: Yankee Candle Agrees to $1.75 Billion Deal—Jarden, Owner of Sunbeam and Rawlings Brands, Set to Acquire Retailer from Private-Equity Owner Madison Dearborn," *The Wall Street Journal,* September 3, 2013; "The Yankee Candle Company, Inc.: Yankee Candle Scent Systems App Creator Rocket Farm Studios Awarded 2016 MITX IoT Award," *Marketing Weekly News,* June 11, 2016; Yankee Candle Company Press Release, "Yankee Candle Escapes to Paradise with New Margaritaville Collection," March 29, 2016; Yankee Candle Company Press Release, "Yankee Candle Launches New Scent Marketing Division," June 9, 2015; Yankee Candle Company Press Release, "Yankee Candle Launches Online Tool to Create Personalized Photo Candles," October 6, 2015.

This case was written by Elizabeth J. Wilson, Suffolk University.

DISCUSSION QUESTIONS

1. Examine the Newell Brands website (http://www. newellbrands.com/). How does Yankee Candle create value for Newell Brands? (*Hint:* Evaluate Yankee Candle using SWOT analysis to answer the question.)

2. Refresh your memory about marketing strategy by doing an online search of "BCG growth share matrix." Then go to http://www.ycscentsystems.com/ to learn more about Scent Systems and the ScentIlligent approach to experiential branding. Is this new strategic business unit (SBU) for Yankee Candle likely to be a star, question mark, or dog in terms of the BCG growth share matrix? Explain your answer.

CASE 37   Interviewing for a Management Trainee Position

1. Assume the role of the college recruiter for a national retail chain that is reviewing résumés to select candidates to interview for a management trainee position. Which of the three résumés on the following pages do you find effective? Ineffective? Why? Which applicant would you select to interview? Why?

2. Update your résumé and prepare for an interview for a manager training program with a large lumber and building supply retailer. This full-time position promises rapid advancement on completion of the training period. A college degree and experience in retail, sales, and marketing are preferred. The base pay is between

$35,000 and $45,000 per year, plus a bonus of up to $7,000. This retailer promotes from within, and a new manager trainee can become a store manager within two to three years, with earnings potential of $100,000 or more. The benefits package is generous, including medical, hospitalization, dental, disability, and life insurance; a 401(k) plan; profit sharing; awards and incentives; and paid vacations and holidays. Your résumé should include your contact information, education and training, skills, experience and accomplishments, and honors and awards.

3. Role-play a practice interview for this position. In pairs, read each other's résumés, and then spend 20 to 30 minutes representing each side of the interview. One student should be the human resource manager screening applicants, and the other should be the candidate for the manager training program. As the human resource manager, ask appropriate questions of the applicant, such as the following:

* Why are you applying for this position?
* What are your strengths and weaknesses for this position?
* Why should this organization consider you for this position?
* Why are you interested in working for this company?
* What are your career goals for the next 5 to 10 years?
* Describe your skills when working in a team setting.
* What questions do you have about the company?

This case was written by Cecelia Schulz, University of Florida.

Marti L. Cox

xxxx@ufl.edu, (xxx) 3xx-xxxx
123 Your Street, Apt. 301
Gainesville, FL 32605

OBJECTIVE
Seeking a marketing internship utilizing leadership experience, strong work ethic, and interpersonal skills with a focus in product planning.

EDUCATION

Bachelor of Science in Business Administration	May 2017
University of Florida, Gainesville, FL	GPA 3.69
Major in Marketing	

LEADERSHIP

Student Government

Theater Nights Chair	Jan. 2016–Present
Emerging Leaders Conference Executive Assistant	Sept. 2015–Present
Student Integrity Court Justice	May 2015–Present
Banquet Cabinet Assistant Director	May 2015–Present
Innovate Party House Representative	Jan. 2015–April 2015
Homecoming Supper Staff	Jan. 2015–Present
Assistant Director of Jr. Pan-Hellenic	Dec. 2014–Present
Jr. Pan-Hellenic Executive VP Int. Relations	Sept. 2014–Jan. 2015

Philanthropy

Intramural Soccer—Captain	Oct. 2016–Present
Intramural Basketball—Captain	Sept. 2015–Present
Member since Aug. 2003	Jan. 2015–Present

HONORS

Savant UF Leadership Honorary	Oct. 2015–Present
Sandra Day O'Connor Pre-Law Society	Sept. 2015–Present
Alpha Lambda Delta Honor Society	Inducted March 2015
Phi Eta Sigma Honor Society	Inducted March 2015

COMMUNITY SERVICE

Mentor to First-Year Students for SG Mentor/Mentee	Sept. 2015–Present
Basketball on Wheels Volunteer	Sept. 2015–Present
Dance Marathon Dancer	Jan. 2015–March 2015
After-School Gators Volunteer	Jan. 2015–April 2015
Pillows for Patriots Service Project Volunteer	Sept. 2014–Dec. 2014

WORK EXPERIENCE

Senior Customer Service Associate, Videos-R-Us, Tampa, FL	Jan. 2013–Aug. 2014
Secretarial Assistant, Law Firm, Mount Dora, FL	June–Aug. 2013

References available upon request.

Tina Acosta
123 Your Street #335
Gainesville, FL 32608
(727) xxx-xxxx
lxxx@ufl.edu

OBJECTIVE
To integrate my financial and business background with my creative and artistic skills in a fast-paced industry

EDUCATION

University of Florida	International Baccalaureate Program
Warrington College of Business	St. Petersburg High School
Bachelor of Science in Finance	Focus in Theater, English, and History
Minor in Spanish	Graduation 2013
Graduation: May 2017	GPA: 4.0
GPA: 3.73	

RELEVANT CLASSES
Retail Management, Study Abroad in Spain, Business Finance, Managerial Accounting, Problem Solving Using Computer Software, Debt and Money Markets

EXPERIENCE

Abercrombie & Fitch—Gainesville, FL, Brand Representative (October 2015–Present)
- Oversee customer service on the sales floor.
- Maintain and update the sales floor design.
- Handle purchases and returns at the register.
- Prepare shipments and the floor for an internal audit.
- Promote the brand name for the women's fashion line.

Olive Garden—St. Petersburg, FL, Server (April 2014–August 2014)
- Used a computerized food and beverage ordering system.
- Maintained the management's expectations through customer service.
- Interacted with customers.
- Memorized an extensive menu and recommended foods satisfying customers' needs while maximizing the restaurant's profits.

Sacino's Formalwear—St. Petersburg, FL, Sales Representative (August 2012–August 2013)
- Managed incoming and outgoing shipment responsibilities.
- Organized financial paperwork.
- Oversaw customer service on the sales floor.
- Headed the formal wear department for young women.

SKILLS
Proficient in Spanish
Office Suite: Word—Document Formatting, Letters, Tables, Flyers, and Macros
　　　　　　　 Excel—Spreadsheets, Formulas, and Graph Database Analysis, Functions, and Simples Macros
　　　　　　　 PowerPoint—Professional Presentations

HONORS
Third place in the preliminary competition for the University of Florida's Center for Entrepreneurship and Innovation
Florida's Bright Futures Scholar
University of Florida Dean's List Student 2014

Richard Kates
xxxxxx@ufl.edu

123 Your Street #164
Gainesville, FL 32608
(352) xxx-xxxx

123 8th Ave. N.
Tampa, FL 33713
(813) xxx-xxxx

Objective	Seeking a position utilizing marketing, management, and organizational abilities, as well as interpersonal skills.

Education

Marketing Major
University of Florida
Minor in Mass Communications
GPA 3.7

May 2017
Gainesville, FL

Experience

Entrepreneur/CEO, Long River PC, LLC   August 2013 to Present
- Helped create and currently manage a new software company based in South Florida.
- Helped develop revolutionary program that aids people who are visually impaired.
- Research and develop multiple original nondisclosure as well as noncompete agreements.
- Responsible for hiring, funding, managing, and controlling progress of almost a dozen private software engineers.
- Report to and allocate funds of angel investors.

Server, Carraba's, Gainesville, FL   April 2015 to Present
- Help train new employees through shadowing and demonstration.
- Serve over 70 guests per day, and ensure customer satisfaction and attentiveness.
- Achieve multiple top sales, as well as winner of "Perfect Check" contest.

Usher/Security/Technician, Ben Hill Griffin Stadium, Gainesville, FL   August 2013 to August 2015
Pool/Health Club Attendant, Don Cesar Resort, St. Petersburg, FL   May 2012 to August 2014

Leadership

Executive Board Member, Varsity Tennis Team Social Chair
University of Florida, August 2014 to Present
Organize, plan, and finance all tennis team social events. In charge of planning large events, gatherings at home and away meets, coordinating the activities of over 60 members.

Executive Board Member, Fisher School of Accounting
University of Florida, January 2015 to May 2015
Aided in revision and draft of new official Fisher School of Accounting Council's by-laws.
Drafted a new 5-year program for the expansion and direction of the new Fisher School including member growth, activities, graduate prerequisites, and facility uses.

CHAMPS Mentoring Volunteer Program
Gainesville, FL, January 2015 to Present
Meet with an "at risk" elementary school student 2 hours per week each semester to spend quality time encouraging the child's healthy growth and development.

Affiliations

Phi Eta Sigma Honor Society, Member active 2013 to Present
Florida Tennis Team, Fall 2013 to Spring 2015; Varsity Fall 2014 to Spring 2015
Team Florida Cycling, Spring 2015 to Present
Student Alumni Association Member, Fall 2014 to Present
American Marketing Association, Member Fall 2015
International Business Society, Fall 2015
Business Administration College Council, Fall 2015 Member-at-Large
The Entrepreneurs Club, Fall 2015

Skills

Computer-fluent in Microsoft Word, Excel, PowerPoint, Explorer, and Media Player; Spanish-fluent

References

Available upon request.

ABC analysis An analysis that rank orders SKUs by a profitability measure to determine which items should never be out of stock, which should be allowed to be out of stock occasionally, and which should be deleted from the stock selection.

accessibility (1) The degree to which customers can easily get into and out of a shopping center; (2) ability of the retailer to deliver the appropriate retail mix to customers in the segment.

actionability Criteria for evaluating a market segment scheme indicating what the retailer should do to satisfy its needs.

add-on selling Selling additional new products and services to existing customers, such as a bank encouraging a customer with a checking account to apply for a home improvement loan from the bank.

advance shipping notice (ASN) An electronic document received by the retailer's computer from a supplier in advance of a shipment.

advertising Paid communications delivered to customers through nonpersonal mass media such as newspapers, television, radio, direct mail, and the Internet.

affordable budgeting method A budgeting method in which a retailer first sets a budget for every element of the retail mix except promotion and then allocates the leftover funds to a promotional budget.

analog approach A method of trade area analysis also known as the similar store or mapping approach. The analysis is divided into four steps: (1) describing the current trade areas through the technique of customer spotting; (2) plotting the customers on a map; (3) defining the primary, secondary, and tertiary area zones; and (4) matching the characteristics of stores in the trade areas with the potential new store to estimate its sales potential.

anchor A large, well-known retail operation located in a shopping center or Internet mall and serving as an attracting force for consumers to the center.

artificial barrier In site evaluations for accessibility, a barrier such as railroad tracks, a major highway, or a park.

asset turnover Net sales divided by total assets.

assets Economic resources, such as inventory or store fixtures, owned or controlled by an enterprise as a result of past transactions or events.

assortment The number of SKUs within a merchandise category. Also called *depth*.

assortment plan A list of merchandise that indicates in very general terms what should be carried in a particular merchandise category.

assurance A customer service characteristic that customers use to evaluate service quality; the knowledge and courtesy of the employees performing the service and their ability to convey trust and confidence.

atmospherics The design of an environment through visual communications, lighting, colors, music, and scent to stimulate customers' perceptual and emotional responses and ultimately to affect their purchase behavior.

autocratic leader A manager who makes all decisions on his or her own and then announces them to employees.

automated retailing A retail channel that stores merchandise or services in a machine, then dispenses them to customers who provide cash or a credit card.

backhaul Trips that trucks make to return to distribution centers after delivering merchandise to stores.

backup stock The inventory used to guard against going out of stock when demand exceeds forecasts or merchandise is delayed. Also called *buffer stock* or *safety stock*.

backward integration A form of vertical integration in which a retailer owns some or all of its suppliers.

bait and switch An unlawful deceptive practice that lures customers into a store by advertising a product at lower than usual prices (the bait), then induces the customers to switch to a higher-price model (the switch).

bargaining power of vendors A characteristic of a market in which retailers are so dependent on large, important vendors that their profits are adversely affected.

barriers to entry Conditions in a retail market that make it difficult for firms to enter the market.

base of the pyramid The 25 percent of the world's population at the lowest end of the global income distribution, with combined spending power of approximately US$5 trillion. Also known as the *bottom of the pyramid*.

base stock The inventory that goes up and down due to the replenishment process. Also known as *cycle stock*.

basic merchandise Inventory that has continuous demand by customers over an extended period of time. Also known as *staple merchandise*.

behavioral interview An interview technique used for selecting employees in which candidates describe how they have handled actual work situations in the past.

benefit segmentation A method of segmenting a retail market on the basis of similar benefits sought in merchandise or services.

big-box store Large, limited-service retailer.

billboard Outdoor advertisement that is generally large and appears adjacent to and above roads or highways.

black market The availability of merchandise at a high price when it is difficult or impossible to purchase under normal market circumstances; commonly involves illegal transactions.

block group A collection of adjacent census blocks that contain between 600 and 3,000 people that is the smallest unit for the sample data.

blog (weblog) A public website where users post informal journals of their thoughts, comments, and philosophies.

bottom of the pyramid (BoP) The 25 percent of the world's population at the lowest end of the global income distribution, with combined spending power of approximately US$5 trillion. Also known as the *base of the pyramid*.

bottom-up planning When goals are set at the bottom of the organization and filter up through the operating levels.

boutique layout A store design, used primarily in small specialty stores or within the boutiques of large stores, that arranges fixtures and aisles asymmetrically. Also called *free-form layout*.

brand loyalty Indicates customers like and consistently buy a specific brand in a product category. They are reluctant to switch to other brands if their favorite brand isn't available.

breadth The number of different merchandise categories within a store or department. Also known as *variety*.

break-even analysis A technique that evaluates the relationship between total revenue and total cost to determine profitability at various sales levels.

break-even point quantity The quantity at which total revenue equals total cost and beyond which profit occurs.

breaking bulk A function performed by retailers or wholesalers in which they receive large quantities of merchandise and sell them in smaller quantities.

breaking sizes Running out of stock on particular sizes.

buffer stock Merchandise inventory used as a safety cushion for cycle stock so the retailer won't run out of stock if demand exceeds the sales forecast. Also called *backup stock* or *safety stock*.

building codes Legal restrictions describing the size and type of building, signs, type of parking lot, and so on that can be used at a particular location.

bulk fixture A round fixture that sits on a pedestal. Smaller than the straight rack, it is designed to hold a maximum amount of merchandise. Also known as a *rounder* or *capacity fixture*.

buyback A strategy vendors and retailers use to get products into retail stores, either when a retailer allows a vendor to create space for goods by "buying back" a competitor's inventory and removing it from a retailer's system or when the retailer forces a vendor to buy back slow-moving merchandise. Also called a *stocklift* or *lift-out*.

buyer Person in a retailing organization responsible for the purchase and profitability of a merchandise category. Similar to category manager.

buying process The stages customers go through to purchase merchandise or services.

buying situation A method of segmenting a retail market based on customer needs in a specific buying situation, such as a fill-in shopping trip versus a weekly shopping trip.

call-to-action signage In-store displays placed strategically to encourage customers to engage with the retailer through quick response codes.

capacity fixture A round fixture that sits on a pedestal. Smaller than the straight rack, it is designed to hold a maximum amount of merchandise. Also known as a *rounder* or *bulk fixture*.

cash and cash equivalents Currency, checks, short-term bank accounts, and investments that mature within three months or less.

cash wrap The place in a store where customers can purchase merchandise and have it "wrapped"—placed in a bag. Also called *point-of-purchase (POP) counter* or *checkout area*.

catalog channel A nonstore retailer that communicates directly with customers using catalogs sent through the mail.

category captain A supplier that forms an alliance with a retailer to help gain consumer insight, satisfy consumer needs, and improve the performance and profit potential across the entire category.

category killer A discount retailer that offers a narrow but deep assortment of merchandise in a category and thus dominates the category from the customers' perspective. Also called *category specialist*.

category management The process of managing a retail business with the objective of maximizing the sales and profits of a category.

category signage Signage within a particular department or sector of the store; category signs are usually smaller than directional signs. Their purpose is to identify types of products offered; they are usually located near the goods to which they refer.

category specialist A discount retailer that offers a narrow but deep assortment of merchandise in a category and thus dominates the category from the customers' perspective. Also called *category killer*.

cause-related marketing campaign Commercial activity in which businesses collaborate with a charitable organization to market a product or service for their mutual benefit.

census A count of the population of a country as of a specified date.

census block An area bounded on all sides by visible (roads, rivers, etc.) and/or invisible (county, state boundaries) features that is the smallest geographic entity for which census data are available.

center store The middle of each aisle in a grocery store or other store using a grid layout. Contains less compelling and exciting products, though ones that consumers still require such as cereal or detergent.

central business district (CBD) The traditional downtown business area of a city or town.

channel migration A customer practice in which customers search for information from a retailer's channel, then purchase in a different channel maintained by a competitor.

chargeback A practice used by retailers in which they deduct money from the amount they owe a vendor.

chargeback fee The fee that retailers require vendors to pay when the provided merchandise does not meet the terms of the purchase agreement.

checking The process of going through goods upon receipt to make sure that they arrived undamaged and that the merchandise received matches the merchandise ordered.

checkout area The place in a store where customers can purchase merchandise and have it "wrapped"—placed in a bag. Also called *cash wrap* or *point-of-purchase (POP) counter*.

cherry picking Customers visiting a store and buying only merchandise sold at big discounts or buying only the best styles or colors.

chief executive officer (CEO) The executive responsible for overseeing the operations of the entire firm.

chief financial officer (CFO) An executive that works with the CEO on financial issues such as equity-debt structure and credit card operations.

chief marketing officer (CMO) An executive that works with staff to develop marketing, advertising and other promotional programs.

classification A group of items or SKUs for the same type of merchandise, such as pants (as opposed to jackets or suits), supplied by different vendors.

click-through rate (CTR) The number of times a customer clicks on an online ad, divided by the number of impressions.

closeout (1) An offer at a reduced price to sell a group of slow-moving or incomplete stock; (2) an incomplete assortment, the remainder of a line of merchandise that is to be discontinued and so is offered at a low price to ensure immediate sale.

collaborative planning, forecasting, and replenishment (CPFR) A collaborative inventory management system in which a retailer shares information with vendors. CPFR software uses data to construct a computer-generated replenishment forecast that is shared by the retailer and vendor before it's executed.

commercial bribery A vendor's offer of money or gifts to a retailer's employee for the purpose of influencing purchasing decisions.

common area maintenance (CAM) The common facilities maintenance that shopping center management is responsible for, such as the parking area, providing security, parking lot lighting, outdoor signage for the center, advertising, and special events to attract consumers.

common area maintenance (CAM) clause Shopping center real estate contract clause that assigns responsibility for maintaining common areas, such as parking lots and sidewalks.

communication gap The difference between the actual service provided to customers and the service promised in the retailer's promotion program. This factor is one of the four factors identified by the gaps model for improving service quality.

communication objectives Specific goals for a communication program related to the effects of the communication program on the customer's decision-making process.

community shopping center An attached row of stores, usually with onsite parking in front of the stores. Also known as *convenience, neighborhood,* or *strip shopping center.*

comparable-store sales growth The sales growth in stores that have been open for over one year. Also called *same-store sales growth.*

comparison shopping A type of shopping situation whereby consumers have a general idea about the type of product or service they want, but they do not have a well-developed preference for a brand or model.

compatibility The degree to which the fashion is consistent with existing norms, values, and behaviors.

competitive parity method An approach for setting a promotion budget so that the retailer's share of promotion expenses is equal to its market share.

competitive rivalry The frequency and intensity of reactions to actions undertaken by competitors.

complexity The ease with which consumers can understand and use a new fashion.

composite segmentation A method of segmenting a retail market using multiple variables, including benefits sought, lifestyles, and demographics.

congestion The amount of crowding of either cars or people.

conscious marketing Entails a sense of purpose for the firm higher than simply making a profit by selling products and services.

consideration set The set of alternatives the customer evaluates when making a merchandise selection.

consignment shop A store that sells used merchandise and reimburses the individual customers who provide the items only after they sell.

consumer direct fulfillment A supply chain system in which retailers receive orders from customers and relay these orders to a vendor and then the vendor ships the merchandise ordered directly to the customer. Also called *drop shipping.*

continuous replenishment A system that involves continuously monitoring merchandise sales and generating replacement orders, often automatically, when inventory levels drop below predetermined levels.

convenience shopping When consumers are primarily concerned with minimizing their effort to get the product or service they want.

convenience shopping center An attached row of stores, usually with onsite parking in front of the stores. Also known as *neighborhood, community,* or *strip shopping center.*

convenience store A store that provides a limited variety and assortment of merchandise at a convenient location in a 2,000- to 3,000-square-foot store with speedy checkout.

conventional supermarket A self-service food store that offers groceries, meat, and produce with limited sales of nonfood items, such as health and beauty aids and general merchandise.

conversion rate Percentage of consumers who buy the product after viewing it.

cookies Computer text files that identify visitors when they return to a website.

cooperative (co-op) advertising A program undertaken by a vendor in which the vendor agrees to pay all or part of a promotion for its products.

copycat brand A brand that imitates the manufacturer's brand in appearance and trade dress but generally is perceived as lower quality and is offered at a lower price.

copyright A regulation that protects original works of authors, painters, sculptors, musicians, and others who produce works of artistic or intellectual merit.

corporate social responsibility (CSR) Voluntary actions taken by a company to address the ethical, social, and environmental impacts of its business operations and the concerns of its stakeholders.

cost of goods sold (COGS) The fee the retailer pays a vendor for merchandise that the retailer sells.

cotenancy clause A clause in a leasing contract that requires a certain percentage of a shopping center be leased, while others name specific retailers or types of retailers that are to remain open.

counterfeit merchandise Goods that are made and sold without permission of the owner of a trademark, a copyright, or a patented invention that is legally protected in the country where it is marketed.

coupons Documents that entitle the holder to a reduced price or X cents off the actual price of a product or service.

cross-channel retailing A type of marketing channel in which customers use multiple channels to make purchases, such as when they receive an e-mailed coupon, download it onto their smartphone, and then go to a store to redeem the coupon and buy the product.

cross-docking distribution center Items are unloaded from the shippers' truck and within a few hours reloaded onto trucks going to stores. These items are prepackaged by the vendor for a specific store, such that the UPC labels on a carton indicate the store to which it is to be sent.

cross-selling When sales associates in one department attempt to sell complementary merchandise from other departments to their customers.

cross-shopping A pattern of buying both premium and low-priced merchandise or patronizing expensive, status-oriented retailers and price-oriented retailers.

crowdfunding Method of raising money to support a particular project by convincing a large group of people to donate money, often in relatively small amounts.

culture The meaning and values shared by most members of a society.

cumulative attraction The principle that a cluster of similar and complementary retailing activities will generally have greater drawing power than isolated stores that engage in the same retailing activities.

current assets Cash or any assets that can normally be converted into cash within one year.

customer lifetime value (CLV) The expected contribution from the customer to the retailer's profits over his or her entire relationship with the retailer.

customer loyalty Customers' commitment to shopping at a store.

A customer relationship management (CRM) A business philosophy and set of strategies, programs, and systems that focus on identifying and building loyalty with a retailer's most valued customers.

customer service The set of retail activities that increase the value customers receive when they shop and purchase merchandise.

customer spotting A technique used in trade area analysis that "spots" (locates) residences of customers for a store or shopping center.

cycle stock The inventory that goes up and down due to the replenishment process. Also known as *base stock*.

data mining Technique used to identify patterns in data found in data warehouses, typically patterns that the analyst is unaware of prior to searching through the data.

data warehouse A huge database comprised of purchase data collected at the point of sale.

delivery gap The difference between the retailer's service standards and the actual service provided to customers. This factor is one of the four factors identified by the gaps model for improving service quality.

demand/destination merchandise Products that customers have decided to buy before entering the store.

democratic leader A store manager who seeks information and opinions from employees and bases decisions on this information.

demographic segmentation A method of segmenting a retail market that groups consumers on the basis of easily measured, objective characteristics such as age, gender, income, and education.

department A segment of a store with merchandise that represents a group of classifications the consumer views as being complementary.

department store A retailer that carries a wide variety and deep assortment, offers considerable customer services, and is organized into separate departments for displaying merchandise.

depth The number of SKUs within a merchandise category. Also called *assortment*.

destination store A retail store in which the merchandise, selection, presentation, pricing, or other unique feature acts as a magnet for customers.

digital signage Signs whose visual content is delivered digitally through a centrally managed and controlled network and displayed on a television monitor or flat-panel screen.

direct investment The investment and ownership by a retail firm of a division or subsidiary that builds and operates stores in a foreign country.

direct mail Any brochure, catalog, advertisement, or other printed marketing material delivered directly to the consumer through the mail or a private delivery company.

direct selling A retail format in which a salesperson, frequently an independent distributor, contacts a customer directly in a convenient location (either at a customer's home or at work), demonstrates merchandise benefits, takes an order, and delivers the merchandise to the customer.

direct store delivery (DSD) A method of delivering merchandise to stores in which vendors distribute merchandise directly to the stores rather than going through distribution centers.

dispatcher A person who coordinates deliveries from the vendor to the distribution center or stores or from the distribution center to stores.

distribution center (DC) A warehouse that receives merchandise from multiple vendors and distributes it to multiple stores.

distributive fairness A customer's perception of the benefits received compared to their costs (inconvenience or loss) when resolving a complaint.

diversification growth opportunity A strategic investment opportunity that involves an entirely new retail format directed toward a market segment not presently being served.

diverted merchandise Merchandise that is diverted from its legitimate channel of distribution; similar to *gray-market goods* except there need not be distribution across international boundaries.

dollar store Small, full-line discount store that offers a limited merchandise assortment at very low prices. Also called *extreme-value retailer*.

drawing account A method of sales compensation in which salespeople receive a weekly check based on their estimated annual income.

drop shipping A supply chain system in which retailers receive orders from customers and relay these orders to a vendor and then the vendor ships the merchandise ordered directly to the customer. Also called *consumer direct fulfillment*.

drugstore Specialty retail store that concentrates on pharmaceuticals and health and personal grooming merchandise.

durable goods Merchandise expected to last for several years, such as appliances and furniture. Also known as *hard goods*.

duty A tax placed by a government on imports. Also known as a *tariff*.

dynamic pricing Charging different prices for the same offerings, depending on the time, season, customer, or level of demand. Also known as *individualized pricing*.

e-mail A paid personal communication vehicle that involves sending messages over the Internet.

editing the assortment Selecting the right assortment of merchandise.

80–20 rule A general management principle where 80 percent of the sales or profits come from 20 percent of the customers.

elastic In a pricing context, when a 1 percent decrease in price produces more than a 1 percent increase in the quantity sold.

electronic data interchange (EDI) The computer-to-computer exchange of business documents from retailer to vendor and back.

emotional support Supporting retail service providers with the understanding and positive regard to enable them to deal with the emotional stress created by disgruntled customers.

empathy A customer service characteristic that customers use to evaluate service quality; refers to the caring, individualized attention provided to customers, such as personalized service, sending of notes and e-mails, or recognition by name.

empowerment The process of managers sharing power and decision-making authority with employees.

end cap Display fixture located at the end of an aisle.

engagement An employee's emotional commitment to the organization.

Equal Employment Opportunity Commission (EEOC) A federal commission that was established for the purpose of taking legal action against employers that violate Title VII of the Civil Rights Act. Title VII prohibits discrimination in company personnel practices.

Equal Pay Act A federal act enforced by the Equal Employment Opportunity Commission that prohibits unequal pay for men and women who perform equal work or work of comparable worth.

ethics A system or code of conduct based on universal moral duties and obligations that indicate how one should behave.

event sponsorship A type of marketing communication for which corporations support various activities usually in the cultural or sports and entertainment sectors.

everyday low-pricing (EDLP) strategy A pricing strategy that stresses continuity of retail prices at a level somewhere between the regular nonsale price and the deep-discount sale price of the retailer's competitors.

exclusive brand A brand developed by a national brand vendor, often in conjunction with a retailer, and sold exclusively by the retailer.

exclusive dealing agreement Restriction a manufacturer or wholesaler places on a retailer to carry only its products and no competing vendors' products.

exclusive-use clause A clause in a lease that prohibits the landlord from leasing to retailers selling competing products.

extended problem solving A buying process in which customers spend considerable time at each stage of the decision-making process because the decision is important and they have limited knowledge of alternatives.

external sources (of information) Information provided by the media and other people.

extreme-value food retailer A supermarket offering a limited number of SKUs. Also called *limited-assortment supermarket.*

extreme-value retailer Small, full-line discount store that offers a limited merchandise assortment at very low prices. Also called *dollar store.*

extrinsic reward Reward (such as money, promotion, or recognition) given to employees by their manager or the firm.

factory outlet Outlet store owned by a manufacturer.

Fair Labor Standards Act A federal law, enacted in 1938, that sets minimum wages, maximum hours, child labor standards, and overtime pay provisions.

fair trade Purchasing practices that require producers to pay workers a living wage, well more than the prevailing minimum wage, and offer other benefits, like onsite medical treatment.

family brand A product's brand name associated with the company's name. Also called an *umbrella brand.*

fashion A type of product or a way of behaving that is temporarily adopted by a large number of consumers because the product, service, or behavior is considered to be socially appropriate for the time and place.

fashion leaders Initial customer adopters of a new fashion. Also known as *innovators* or *trendsetters.*

fashion merchandise Category of merchandise that typically lasts several seasons, and sales can vary dramatically from one season to the next.

feature area Area designed to get the customer's attention that includes end caps, promotional aisles or areas, freestanding fixtures and mannequins that introduce a soft goods department, windows, and point-of-sale areas.

feature fixture A fixture with two cross-bars that sit perpendicular to each other on a pedestal. Also called a *four-way fixture.*

fill rate The percentage of an order that is shipped by the vendor.

financial risks The risks customers face when purchasing an expensive product or service.

fixed assets Assets that require more than a year to convert to cash.

fixed costs Costs that are stable and don't change with the quantity of product produced and sold.

fixed-rate lease A lease that requires the retailer to pay a fixed amount per month over the life of the lease.

fixtures The equipment used to display merchandise.

flash sale site An online off-price retailer that sends e-mails to registered members, announcing the unique deals available for a limited, specific time.

floor-ready merchandise Merchandise received at the store ready to be sold, without the need for any additional preparation by retail employees.

focus group A marketing research technique in which a small group of respondents is interviewed by a moderator using a loosely structured format.

food desert Area that lacks ready access to affordable fresh fruits, vegetables, dairy, whole grains, and other healthful foods, as might be provided by grocery stores or farmers' markets.

forward integration A form of vertical integration in which a manufacturer owns wholesalers or retailers.

four-way fixture A fixture with two cross-bars that sit perpendicular to each other on a pedestal. Also called a *feature fixture*.

franchising A contractual agreement between a franchisor and a franchisee that allows the franchisee to operate a retail outlet using a name and format developed and supported by the franchisor.

free-form layout A store design, used primarily in small specialty stores or within the boutiques of large stores, that arranges fixtures and aisles asymmetrically. Also called *boutique layout*.

freestanding display Fixtures or mannequins that are located on aisles and designed primarily to attract customers' attention and bring customers into a department in stores using a racetrack or free-form layout.

freestanding insert (FSI) An ad printed at a retailer's expense and distributed as a freestanding insert in the newspaper. Also called a *preprint*.

freestanding site A retail location that is not connected to other retailers.

freight forwarders Companies that purchase transport services. They then consolidate small shipments from a number of shippers into large shipments that move at a lower freight rate.

frequent-shopper program The set of activities designed to identify and build the loyalty of the retailer's most valuable customers. Also called *loyalty program*.

fringe trading area The outermost ring of a trade area; includes customers who occasionally shop at the store or shopping center. Also called the *tertiary trading area*.

fulfillment center (FC) Similar to a distribution center, but instead of shipping to stores, it ships directly to customers.

full-line discount store Retailer that offers a broad variety of merchandise, limited service, and low prices.

generic brand Unbranded, unadvertised merchandise found mainly in drug, grocery, and discount stores.

gentrification A process in which old buildings are torn down or restored to create new offices, housing developments, and retailers.

geodemographic segmentation A market segmentation system that uses both geographic and demographic characteristics to classify consumers.

geofencing Offering localized promotions for retailers in close proximity to the customer, as determined by phone location technology.

geographic information system (GIS) A computerized system that enables analysts to visualize information about their customers' demographics, buying behavior, and other data in a map format.

geographic segmentation Segmentation of potential customers by where they live. A retail market can be segmented by countries, states, cities, and neighborhoods.

gondola An island type of self-service counter with tiers of shelves, bins, or pegs.

graduated lease A lease that requires rent to increase by a fixed amount over a specified period of time.

gray-market goods Merchandise that possesses a valid U.S. registered trademark and is made by a foreign manufacturer but is imported into the United States without permission of the U.S. trademark owner. Also called *parallel imports*.

green A marketing strategy that promotes environmentally safe or beneficial products or services.

green sheen The disingenuous practice of marketing products or services as being environmentally friendly with the purpose of gaining public approval and sales rather than actually improving the environment. Also called *greenwashing*.

greenwashing The disingenuous practice of marketing products or services as being environmentally friendly with the purpose of gaining public approval and sales rather than actually improving the environment. Also called practicing *green sheen*.

grid layout A store design, typically used by grocery stores, in which merchandise is displayed on long gondolas in aisles with a repetitive pattern.

gross leasable area (GLA) Total floor area designated for the retailer's exclusive use, including basements, upper floors, and mezzanines.

gross margin The difference between the price the customer pays for merchandise and the cost of the merchandise (the price the retailer paid the supplier of the merchandise). More specifically, gross margin is net sales minus cost of goods sold. Also called *gross profit*.

gross margin (in %) Gross margin divided by net sales expressed as a percentage.

gross profit The difference between the price the customer pays for merchandise and the cost of the merchandise (the price the retailer paid the supplier of the merchandise). More specifically, gross profit is net sales minus cost of goods sold. Also called *gross margin*.

habitual decision making A purchase decision involving little or no conscious effort.

hard goods Merchandise expected to last for several years, such as appliances and furniture. Also known as *durable goods*.

health and safety laws Regulations that hold that employers must provide every employee with an environment free of hazards that are likely to cause death or serious injury.

hedonic benefit Shopping for pleasure, entertainment, and/or to achieve an emotional or recreational experience.

hedonic need A need motivating a consumer to go shopping for pleasure.

high-assay principle A resource allocation principle emphasizing allocating marketing expenditures on the basis of marginal return.

high/low pricing strategy A strategy in which retailers offer prices that are sometimes above their competition's everyday low price, but they use advertising to promote frequent sales.

holding inventory A major value-providing activity performed by retailers whereby products will be available when consumers want them.

horizontal price fixing An agreement between retailers in direct competition with each other to charge the same prices.

house brand Products developed and marketed by a retailer and available for sale only by that retailer. Also called *store brand*, *private-label brand*, or *own brand*.

hypermarket Large (100,000–300,000 square feet) combination food (60–70 percent) and general merchandise (30–40 percent) retailer.

idea-oriented presentation A method of presenting merchandise based on a specific idea or the image of the store.

identifiability A criteria for evaluating market segments in which retailers must be able to identify the customers in a target segment for the segmentation scheme to be effective. By identifying the segment, it allows retailers to determine (1) the segment's size and (2) with whom the retailer should communicate when promoting its retail offering.

illegal discrimination The actions of a company or its managers that result in a number of a protected class being treated unfairly and differently than others.

impressions The number of times an advertisement appears before a customer.

impulse buying A buying decision made by customers on the spot after seeing the merchandise. Also called *unplanned purchasing*.

impulse products Products that are purchased by customers without prior plans. These products are almost always located near the front of the store, where they're seen by everyone and may actually draw people into the store.

in-depth interview An unstructured personal interview in which the interviewer uses extensive probing to get individual respondents to talk in detail about a subject.

incentive compensation plan A compensation plan that rewards employees on the basis of their productivity.

income statement A summary of the financial performance of a firm for a certain period of time. Also called a *statement of operations* or *profit and loss (P&L) statement*.

individualized pricing Charging different prices for the same offerings, depending on the time, season, customer, or level of demand. Also known as *dynamic pricing*.

inelastic In a pricing context, when a 1 percent decrease in price produces less than a 1 percent increase in the quantity sold.

information search The stage in the buying process in which a customer seeks additional information to satisfy a need.

initial markup The retail selling price initially placed on the merchandise less the cost of goods sold.

inner city Typically a high-density urban area consisting of apartment buildings populated primarily by ethnic groups.

innovators Initial customer adopters of a new fashion. Also known as *fashion leaders* or *trendsetters*.

input measure A performance measure used to assess the amount of resources or money used by the retailer to achieve outputs.

instrumental support Support for retail service providers such as appropriate systems and equipment to deliver the service desired by customers.

intangible assets Nonphysical assets such as patents and goodwill.

integrated marketing communication (IMC) program The strategic integration of multiple communication methods to form a comprehensive, consistent message.

intellectual property Property that is intangible and created by intellectual (mental) effort as opposed to physical effort.

internal sources (of information) Information in a customer's memory such as names, images, and past experiences with different stores.

Internet retailing A retail format in which retailers communicate with customers and offer products and services for sale over the Internet.

intertype competition Competition between retailers that sell similar merchandise using different formats, such as discount and department stores.

intratype competition Competition between the same type of retailers (e.g., Kroger versus Safeway).

intrinsic reward Nonmonetary reward that employees get from doing their jobs.

inventory shrinkage An inventory reduction that is caused by shoplifting by employees or customers, by merchandise being misplaced or damaged, or by poor bookkeeping. Also called *shrinkage*.

inventory turnover Net sales divided by average retail inventory; used to evaluate how effectively managers utilize their investment in inventory.

irregular Merchandise that has minor mistakes in construction.

job application form A form a job applicant completes that contains information about the applicant's employment history, previous compensation, reasons for leaving previous employment, education and training, and references.

job description A description of the activities the employee needs to perform and the firm's performance expectations.

job enrichment The redesign of a job to include a greater range of tasks and responsibilities.

joint venture In the case of global expansion, an entity formed when the entering retailer pools its resources with a local retailer to form a new company in which ownership, control, and profits are shared. More generally, any business venture in which two or more firms pool resources to form a new business entity.

just-in-time (JIT) inventory system Inventory management system that delivers less merchandise on a more frequent basis than traditional inventory systems. The firm gets the merchandise just in time for it to be used in the manufacture of another product or for sale when the customer wants it. Also called *quick response (QR) inventory system*.

keystoning A method of setting retail prices in which retailers simply double the cost of the merchandise to obtain the original retail selling price.

knockoff A copy of the latest styles displayed at designer fashion shows and sold in exclusive specialty stores. These copies are sold at lower prices through retailers targeting a broader market.

knowledge gap The difference between customer expectations and the retailer's perception of customer expectations. This factor is one of four identified by the gaps model for improving service quality.

labor relations laws Regulations that describe how unions can form and how companies must respond to them.

labor scheduling The process of determining the number of employees assigned to each area of the store at each hour the store is open.

lead time The amount of time between recognition that an order needs to be placed and the point at which the merchandise arrives in the store and is ready for sale.

leader pricing A pricing strategy in which certain items are priced lower than normal to increase the traffic flow of customers or to increase the sale of complementary products.

leadership The process by which a person attempts to influence another to accomplish some goal or goals.

level of support A measure used in inventory management to define the level of support or level of product availability; the number of items sold divided by the number of items demanded. Service level should not be confused with customer service. Also called *service level.*

lifestyle Refers to how people live, how they spend their time and money, what activities they pursue, and their attitudes and opinions about the world they live in. Also called *psychographics.*

lifestyle center A shopping center with an outdoor traditional streetscape layout with sit-down restaurants and a conglomeration of specialty retailers.

lifestyle segmentation A method of segmenting a retail market based on how consumers live, how they spend their time and money, what activities they pursue, and their attitudes and opinions about the world they live in.

lift-out A strategy vendors and retailers use to get products into retail stores, either when a retailer allows a vendor to create space for goods by "buying back" a competitor's inventory and removing it from a retailer's system or when the retailer forces a vendor to buy back slow-moving merchandise. Also called a *buyback* or *stocklift.*

limited problem solving A purchase decision process involving a moderate amount of effort and time. Customers engage in this type of buying process when they have some prior experience with the product or service and their risk is moderate.

limited-assortment supermarket A supermarket offering a limited number of SKUs. Also called *extreme-value food retailer.*

live chat Technology that enables online customers to access an instant messaging or voice conversation with a sales representative in real time.

locavore movement A movement focusing on reducing the carbon footprint caused by the transportation of food throughout the world.

loop layout A type of store layout that provides a major aisle to facilitate customer traffic that has access to the store's multiple entrances. Also known as *racetrack layout.*

loss leader An item priced near or below cost to attract customer traffic into the store.

low-price guarantee policy A policy that guarantees that the retailer will have the lowest possible price for a product or group of products and usually promises to match or better any lower price found in the local market.

loyalty program The set of activities designed to identify and build the loyalty of the retailer's most valuable customers. Also called *frequent-shopper program.*

m-commerce Internet channels accessed through tablets, smartphones, or other handheld devices. Also known as *mobile marketing, mobile commerce,* or *mobile retailing.*

Main Street The central business district located in the traditional shopping area of smaller towns, or a secondary business district in a suburb or within a larger city.

maintained markup The amount of markup the retailer wishes to maintain on a particular category of merchandise; net sales minus cost of goods sold.

mannequin Life-size representation of human bodies, used to display apparel.

manufacturer's brand A line of products designed, produced, and marketed by a vendor. Also called a *national brand.*

marginal analysis A method of analysis used in setting a promotional budget or allocating retail space, based on the economic principle that firms should increase expenditures as long as each additional dollar spent generates more than a dollar of additional contribution.

markdown The percentage reduction in the initial retail price.

markdown money Funds a vendor gives the retailer to cover lost gross margin dollars that result from markdowns and other merchandising issues.

market basket analysis Specific type of data analysis that focuses on the composition of the basket (or bundle) of products purchased by a household during a single shopping occasion.

market expansion growth opportunity A strategic investment opportunity that employs the existing retailing format in new market segments.

market penetration growth opportunity An investment opportunity strategy that focuses on increasing sales to present customers using the present retailing format.

market weeks Market weeks, often located in wholesale market centers, are a specific period of time in which buyers meet with vendors in their showrooms.

markup The increase in the retail price of an item after the initial markup percentage has been applied but before the item is placed on the selling floor.

markup percentage The markup as a percentage of the retail price.

mass-market theory A theory of how fashion spreads that suggests that each social class has its own fashion leaders who play a key role in their own social networks. Fashion information trickles across social classes rather than down from the upper classes to the lower classes.

merchandise budget plan A plan used by buyers to determine how much money to spend in each month on a particular fashion merchandise category, given the firm's sales forecast, inventory turnover, and profit goals.

merchandise category An assortment of items (SKUs) the customer sees as reasonable substitutes for one another.

merchandise group A group within an organization managed by the senior vice presidents of merchandise and responsible for several departments.

merchandise inventory The goods the retailer invests in and holds in stock, to enable customers to find what they want in the right place at the right time.

merchandise kiosk Small, temporary selling space typically located in the walkways of enclosed malls, airports, train stations, or office building lobbies.

merchandise management The process by which a retailer attempts to offer the right quantity of the right merchandise in the right place at the right time while meeting the company's financial goal.

merchandising planner A retail employee responsible for allocating merchandise and tailoring the assortment in several categories for specific stores in a geographic area.

metropolitan statistical area (MSA) A city with 50,000 or more inhabitants or an urbanized area of at least 50,000 inhabitants and a total MSA population of at least 100,000 (75,000 in New England).

microblog A short version of a blog, such as Twitter.

micropolitan statistical area (µSA) A city with only 10,000 inhabitants in its core urban area.

mission statement A broad description of the scope of activities a business plans to undertake.

mixed-use development (MXD) Development that combines several uses in one complex—for example, shopping center, office tower, hotel, residential complex, civic center, and convention center.

mobile commerce Internet channels accessed through tablets, smartphones, or other handheld devices. Also known as *mobile marketing, M-commerce,* or *mobile retailing.*

mobile marketing Internet channels accessed through tablets, smartphones, or other handheld devices. Also known as *mobile commerce, M-commerce,* or *mobile retailing.*

mobile retailing Internet channels accessed through tablets, smartphones, or other handheld devices. Also known as *mobile marketing, mobile commerce,* or *m-commerce.*

mobile task management Technology consisting of a wireless network and a mobile device that receives demand notification and enables a speedy response. This allows the associate closest to the ordered item to physically pull it and verify its availability.

model stock plan A list of fashion merchandise that indicates in very general terms (product lines, colors, and size distributions) what should be carried in a particular merchandise category; also known as a *model stock list.*

multiattribute analysis A method for evaluating vendors that uses a weighted average score for each vendor, which is based on the importance of various issues and the vendor's performance on those issues.

multiattribute attitude model A model of customer decision making based on the notion that customers see a retailer or a product as a collection of attributes or characteristics. The model can also be used for evaluating a retailer, product, or vendor. The model uses a weighted average score based on the importance of various issues and performance on those issues.

multichannel retailing Selling merchandise or services through more than one channel.

multiple-unit pricing Practice of offering two or more similar products or services for sale at one price. Also known as *quantity discount.*

mystery shopper Professional shopper who "shops" a store to assess the service provided by store employees.

national brand A line of products designed, produced, and marketed by a vendor. Also called a *manufacturer's brand.*

natural barrier A barrier, such as a river or mountain, that impacts accessibility to a site.

neighborhood shopping center An attached row of stores, usually with onsite parking in front of the stores. Also known as *convenience, community,* or *strip shopping center.*

net income Calculated as: Operating profit margin − Other income or expenses − Interest − Taxes. Also called *net profit margin.*

net profit margin Calculated as: Operating profit margin − Other income or expenses − Interest − Taxes. Also called *net income.*

net profit margin (in %) Refers to profit after taxes, interest income, and extraordinary gains and losses a firm makes divided by its net sales expressed in percentage terms.

net sales The total number of dollars received by a retailer after all refunds have been paid to customers for returned merchandise.

noncurrent assets Assets that are not likely to be converted to cash within one year.

North American Industry Classification System (NAICS) Classification of retail firms into a hierarchical set of six-digit codes based on the types of products and services they produce and sell.

objective-and-task method A method for setting a promotion budget in which the retailer first establishes a set of communication objectives and then determines the necessary tasks and their costs.

observability The degree to which a new fashion is visible and easily communicated to others in a social group.

odd pricing The practice of ending prices with an odd number (such as 69 cents) or just under a round number (such as $98 instead of $100).

off-price retailer A retailer that offers an inconsistent assortment of brand-name, fashion-oriented soft goods at low prices.

omnicenter A combination of mall, lifestyle, and power center components in a unified, open-air layout.

omnichannel retailing Coordinated multichannel retail offering that ensures a seamless customer experience across all the retailer's channels.

1-to-1 retailing Developing retail programs for small groups or individual customers.

on-the-job training A decentralized approach in which job training occurs in the work environment where employees perform their jobs.

open-to-buy The plan that keeps track of how much is spent in each month and how much is left to spend.

operating expenses Costs, other than the cost of merchandise, incurred in the normal course of doing business, such as salaries for sales associates and managers, advertising, utilities, office supplies, and rent. Also called *selling, general, and administrative (SG&A) expenses.*

operating expenses (in %) Operating expenses divided by net sales expressed in percentage.

operating profit margin The gross margin minus the operating expenses.

operating profit margin (in %) The gross margin minus the operating expenses divided by net sales expressed as a percentage.

opportunities and threats analysis Assessments of features of the environment that might positively or negatively affect the retailer's performance.

opt in A customer privacy issue prevalent in the European Union. Takes the perspective that consumers "own" their personal information. Retailers must get consumers to explicitly agree to share this personal information.

opt out A customer privacy issue prevalent in the United States. Takes the perspective that personal information is generally viewed as being in the public domain and retailers can use it in any way they desire. Consumers must explicitly tell retailers not to use their personal information.

order point The amount of inventory below which the quantity available shouldn't go or the item will be out of stock before the next order arrives.

organization structure A plan that identifies the activities to be performed by specific employees and determines the lines of authority and responsibility in the firm.

outlet center Typically stores owned by retail chains or manufacturers that sell excess and out-of-season merchandise at reduced prices.

outlet store Off-price retailer owned by a manufacturer or a department or specialty store chain.

outparcel A building or kiosk that is in the parking lot of a shopping center but isn't physically attached to a shopping center.

output measure Measure that assesses the results of retailers' investment decisions.

outsourcing Obtaining a service from outside the company that had previously been done by the firm itself.

own brand Products developed and marketed by a retailer and available for sale only by that retailer. Also called *store brand*, *private-label brand*, or *house brand*.

parallel imports Merchandise that possesses a valid U.S. registered trademark and is made by a foreign manufacturer but is imported into the United States without permission of the U.S. trademark owner. Also called *gray-market goods*.

partnering relationship Long-term relationship in which partners make significant investments to improve both parties' profitability. Also called *strategic relationship*.

percentage lease A lease in which rent is based on a percentage of sales.

percentage lease with a specified maximum A lease that pays the lessor, or landlord, a percentage of sales up to a maximum amount.

percentage lease with a specified minimum The retailer must pay a minimum rent no matter how low sales are.

percentage-of-sales method A method for setting a promotion budget based on a fixed percentage of forecast sales.

perceptual map A graphic depiction of customers' images of and preferences for retailers.

perpetual inventory An accounting procedure whose objectives are to maintain a perpetual or book inventory in retail dollar amounts and to maintain records that make it possible to determine the cost value of the inventory at any time without taking a physical inventory.

personal selling A communication process in which salespeople assist customers in satisfying their needs through face-to-face exchange of information.

personalized service A customer service strategy that requires service providers to tailor their services to meet each customer's personal needs.

physical risks The risks customers encounter when they believe using a product or service could impair their health or safety.

pick ticket A document that tells the order filler how much of each item to get from the storage area.

planned location Shopping centers for which management enforces policies governing store operations, such as operating hours. The shopping center management also maintains the common facilities such as the parking area and is responsible for providing security, parking lot lighting, outdoor signage for the center, advertising and special events to attract consumers, and so on.

planner Employee in merchandise management responsible for the financial planning and analysis of the merchandise category and, in some cases, the allocation of merchandise to stores.

planogram A diagram created from photographs, computer output, or artists' renderings that illustrates exactly where every SKU should be placed.

point-of-purchase (POP) counter The place in a store where customers can purchase merchandise and have it "wrapped"—placed in a bag. Also called *cash wrap* or *checkout area*.

point-of-purchase (POP) display A display that is positioned where the customer waits at checkout. This area can be the most valuable piece of real estate in the store because the customer is almost held captive in that spot.

point-of-sale (POS) terminal A cash register that can electronically scan a UPC code with a laser and electronically record a sale.

point-of-sale (POS) signage Signs placed near the merchandise they refer to so that customers know the price and other detailed information.

pop-up store Store in a temporary location that focuses on new products or a limited group of products.

positioning The design and implementation of a retail mix to create in the customer's mind an image of the retailer relative to its competitors.

postpurchase evaluation The evaluation of merchandise or services after the customer has purchased and consumed them.

power center Shopping center that is dominated by several large anchors, including discount stores (Target), off-price stores (Marshalls), warehouse clubs (Costco), or category specialists such as Home Depot, Office Depot, Dick's Sporting Goods, Best Buy, and Toys "R" Us.

power perimeter The areas around the outside walls of a supermarket that have fresh merchandise categories.

predatory pricing A method for establishing merchandise prices for the purpose of driving competition from the marketplace.

premium A type of sales promotion whereby an item is offered free of charge or at a bargain price to reward some type of behavior, such as buying, sampling, or testing.

premium store brand A branding strategy that offers the consumer a private label at a comparable manufacturer-brand quality, usually with a modest price savings.

preprint An advertisement printed at the retailer's expense and distributed as an insert in the newspaper. Also called a *freestanding insert (FSI)*.

price bundling The practice of offering two or more different products or services for sale at one price.

price elasticity A measure of the effect a price change has on consumer demand; percentage change in demand divided by percentage change in price.

price lining A pricing policy in which a retailer offers a limited number of predetermined price points within a classification.

pricing optimization software A type of software program that uses a set of algorithms that analyzes past and current merchandise sales and prices, estimates the relationship between prices and sales generated, and then determines the optimal (most profitable) initial price for the merchandise and the appropriate size and timing of markdowns.

primary trading area The geographic area from which a store or shopping center derives 50 to 70 percent of its customers.

private-label brand Products developed and marketed by a retailer and available for sale only by that retailer. Also called *store brand, house brand,* or *own brand.*

procedural fairness The perceived fairness of the process used to resolve customer complaints.

product availability A measurement of the percentage of demand for a particular SKU that is satisfied.

product placement A type of retail communication whereby retailers and vendors pay to have their product included in nontraditional situations, such as in a scene in a movie or television program.

productivity In a human resource context, it is sales generated per employee.

productivity measure The ratio of an output to an input determining how effectively a firm uses a resource.

profit and loss (P&L) statement A summary of the financial performance of a firm for a certain period of time. Also called an *income statement* or *statement of operations.*

prohibited-use clause A clause in a lease that keeps a landlord from leasing to certain kinds of tenants.

promotional aisle Area aisle or area of a store designed to get the customer's attention. An example might be a special "trim-the-tree" department that seems to magically appear right after Thanksgiving every year for the Christmas holidays. Also called *promotional area.*

promotional area Area aisle or area of a store designed to get the customer's attention. An example might be a special "trim-the-tree" department that seems to magically appear right after Thanksgiving every year for the Christmas holidays. Also called *promotional aisle.*

promotional signage This signage describes special offers and may be displayed in windows to entice the customer into the store.

protected class A group of people, such as women or minorities, who are treated differently or discriminated against, such as when a qualified woman does not receive a promotion given to a less qualified man.

psychographics Refers to how people live, how they spend their time and money, what activities they pursue, and their attitudes and opinions about the world they live in. Also called *lifestyle.*

public relations (PR) A retail communication tool for managing communications and relationships to achieve various objectives, such as building and maintaining a positive image of the retailer, handling or heading off unfavorable stories or events, and maintaining positive relationships with the media.

public warehouse Warehouse that is owned and operated by a third party.

pull supply chain Strategy in which orders for merchandise are generated at the store level on the basis of demand data captured by point-of-sale terminals.

push supply chain Strategy in which merchandise is allocated to stores on the basis of historical demand, the inventory position at the distribution center, and the stores' needs.

quantity discount The policy of granting lower prices for higher quantities. Also known as *multiple-unit pricing.*

quick response (QR) inventory system Inventory management system that delivers less merchandise on a more frequent basis than traditional inventory systems. The firm gets the merchandise just in time for it to be used in the manufacture of another product or for sale when the customer wants it. Also called *just-in-time (JIT) inventory system.*

quota Target level used to motivate and evaluate performance.

quota bonus plan Compensation plan that has a performance goal or objective established to evaluate employee performance, such as sales per hour for salespeople and maintained margin and turnover for buyers.

racetrack layout A type of store layout that provides a major aisle to facilitate customer traffic that has access to the store's multiple entrances. Also known as a *loop layout.*

radio frequency identification (RFID) tag A technology that allows an object or person to be identified at a distance using radio waves.

rain check When sale merchandise is out of stock, a written promise to customers to sell them that merchandise at the sale price when it arrives.

reachable A requirement of a viable market segment that the retailer can target promotions and other elements of the retail mix to the consumers in that segment.

rebate Money returned to the buyer in the form of cash based on a portion of the purchase price.

receiving The process of filling out paperwork to record the receipt of merchandise that arrives at a store or distribution center.

reductions Includes three things: markdowns; discounts to employees and customers; and inventory shrinkage due to shoplifting, breakage, or loss.

reference group One or more people whom a person uses as a basis of comparison for his or her beliefs, feelings, and behaviors.

reference price A price point in the consumer's memory for a good or service that can consist of the price last paid, the price most frequently paid, or the average of all prices customers have paid for similar offerings. A benchmark for what consumers believe the "real" price of the merchandise should be.

regression analysis A statistical approach for evaluating retail locations based on the assumption that factors that affect the sales of existing stores in a chain will have the same impact on stores located at new sites being considered.

related diversification growth opportunity A diversification opportunity strategy in which the retailer's present offering and market share something in common with the market and format being considered.

relevance In an advertising context, how helpful the ad message is for a customer searching for information.

reliability A customer service characteristic that customers use to evaluate service quality; the ability to perform the service dependably and accurately, such as performing the service as promised or contracted or meeting promised delivery dates.

resale store Retailer that sells secondhand or used merchandise.

resident buying office An organization located in a major buying center that provides services to help retailers buy merchandise.

responsiveness A customer service characteristic that customers use to evaluate service quality; the willingness to help customers and provide prompt service, such as returning calls and e-mails immediately.

retail analytics The application of statistical data analysis techniques to improve retail decision making.

retail brand community A group of customers who are bound together by their loyalty to a retailer and the activities in which the retailer engages.

retail chain A firm that consists of multiple retail units under common ownership and usually has some centralization of decision making in defining and implementing its strategy.

retail channel The means by which a retailer sells and delivers merchandise to customers.

retail community A group of consumers who have a shared involvement with the retailer.

retail format The retailers' type of retail mix (nature of merchandise and services offered, pricing policy, advertising and promotion program, approach to store design and visual merchandising, and typical location).

retail format development growth opportunity An investment opportunity strategy in which a retailer offers a new retail format—a format involving a different retail mix—to the same target market.

retail market segment A group of customers whose needs will be satisfied by the same retail offering because they have similar needs and go through similar buying processes.

retail mix The combination of factors used by a retailer to satisfy customer needs and influence their purchase decisions; includes merchandise and services offered, pricing, advertising and promotions, store design and location, and visual merchandising.

retail strategy A statement that indicates (1) the target market toward which a retailer plans to commit its resources, (2) the nature of the retail offering that the retailer plans to use to satisfy the needs of the target market, and (3) the bases on which the retailer will attempt to build a sustainable competitive advantage over competitors.

retailer A business that sells products and services to consumers for their personal or family use.

retailer loyalty Customers like and habitually visit the same retailer to purchase a type of merchandise.

retailing A set of business activities that adds value to the products and services sold to consumers for their personal or family use.

return on advertising investment (ROAI) Sales revenue minus advertising costs, divided by advertising costs.

return on assets (ROA) Net profit after taxes divided by total assets.

reverse auction Auction conducted by retailer buyers. Known as a *reverse auction* because there is one buyer and many potential sellers. In reverse auctions, retail buyers provide a specification for what they want to a group of potential vendors. The competing vendors then bid down the price at which they are willing to sell until the buyer accepts a bid.

reverse supply chain The process of moving returned goods back through the supply chain from the customer, to the stores, distribution centers, and vendors.

rounder A round fixture that sits on a pedestal. Smaller than the straight rack, it is designed to hold a maximum amount of merchandise. Also known as a *bulk fixture* or *capacity fixture*.

rule-of-thumb method A type of approach for setting a promotion budget that uses past sales and communication activity to determine the present communications budget.

s-retailing Conducting purchase transactions through a social media site. Also called *social retailing*.

safety stock The inventory used to guard against going out of stock when demand exceeds forecasts or merchandise is delayed. Also called *backup stock* or *buffer stock*.

sales per linear foot A measure of space productivity used when most merchandise is displayed on multiple shelves of long gondolas, such as in grocery stores.

sales per square foot A measure of space productivity used by most retailers since rent and land purchases are assessed on a per-square-foot basis.

sales promotion Paid impersonal communication activities that offer extra value and incentives to customers to visit a store or purchase merchandise during a specific period of time.

same-store sales growth The sales growth in stores that have been open for over one year. Also called *comparable-store sales growth*.

sample A type of sales promotion; a small amount or size of a product given to potential customers as an inducement to purchase.

satisfaction A postconsumption evaluation of the degree to which a store or product meets or exceeds customer expectations.

scale economies Cost advantages due to the size of a retailer.

scrambled merchandising An offering of merchandise not typically associated with the store type, such as clothing in a drugstore.

search engine marketing (SEM) Methods that marketers use to improve the visibility of their websites.

search engine optimization (SEO) Designing website content to improve the positioning of the site on search engine results pages.

search engine results page (SERP) The results a search engine lists in response to a user query.

seasonal merchandise Inventory whose sales fluctuate dramatically according to the time of the year.

secondary trading area The geographic area of secondary importance in terms of customer sales, generating about 20 to 30 percent of a store's sales.

sell-through analysis A comparison of actual and planned sales to determine whether early markdowns are required or more merchandise is needed to satisfy demand.

selling, general, and administrative expenses (SG&A) Costs, other than the cost of merchandise, incurred in the normal course of doing business, such as salaries for sales associates and managers, advertising, utilities, office supplies, and rent. Also called *operating expenses*.

sentiment analysis Assessments that monitor social media to determine how customers view the firm.

service gap The difference between customers' expectations and perceptions of customer service to improve customers' satisfaction with their service.

service level A measure used in inventory management to define the level of support or level of product availability; the number of items sold divided by the number of items demanded. Service level should not be confused with customer service. Also called *level of support*.

service retailer Organization that offers consumers services rather than merchandise. Examples include banks, hospitals, health spas, doctors, legal clinics, entertainment firms, and universities.

sexual harassment Unwelcome sexual advances, requests for sexual favors, or other verbal or physical conduct with sexual elements.

share of wallet The percentage of total purchases made by a customer in a store.

shopping center A group of retail and other commercial establishments that is planned, developed, owned, and managed as a single property.

shopping center property management firm Company that specializes in developing, owning, and maintaining shopping centers.

shopworn Merchandise that looks damaged because it has been on display for a long time and customers have been handling it.

showrooming A practice in which customers visit stores to interact with a physical product and receive sales assistance, then purchase it through a less expensive channel, such as online.

shrinkage An inventory reduction that is caused by shoplifting by employees or customers, by merchandise being misplaced or damaged, or by poor bookkeeping. Also called *inventory shrinkage*.

single-channel retailing Selling merchandise or services through only one channel.

SKU rationalization program An analysis of the potential benefits a retailer could achieve by adding or deleting specific items from its assortments.

sliding scale lease A part of some leases that stipulates how much the percentage of sales paid as rent will decrease as sales go up.

slotting allowance Fee paid by a vendor for space in a retail store. Also called *slotting fee*.

slotting fee Fee paid by a vendor for space in a retail store. Also called *slotting allowance*.

social media Media content distributed through social interactions. Three major online facilitators of social media are YouTube, Facebook, and Twitter.

social retailing Conducting purchase transactions through a social media site. Also called *s-retailing*.

social risks The risks customers perceive when they believe purchasing a product or service will affect how others regard them.

soft goods Merchandise with a relatively short life span, such as clothing or cosmetics.

special event Sales promotion program comprising a number of sales promotion techniques built around a seasonal, cultural, sporting, musical, or other event.

specialty shopping Shopping experiences when consumers know what they want and will not accept a substitute.

specialty store A type of store concentrating on a limited number of complementary merchandise categories and providing a high level of service.

Spending Potential Index (SPI) Compares the average expenditure in a particular area for a product to the amount spent on that product nationally.

spot A local television commercial.

stakeholders The broad set of people who might be affected by a firm's actions, from current and prospective customers, to supply chain partners, to employees, to shareholders, to government agencies, to members of the communities in which the firm operates, and to a general view of society.

standardized service A customer service strategy that is based on establishing a set of rules and procedures for providing high-quality service and ensuring that they get implemented consistently by service providers.

standards gap The difference between the retailer's perceptions of customers' expectations and the customer service standards it sets. This factor is one of four factors identified by the gaps model for improving service quality.

staple merchandise Inventory that has continuous demand by customers over an extended period of time. Also known as *basic merchandise*.

statement of operations A summary of the financial performance of a firm for a certain period of time. Also called an *income statement* or *profit and loss (P&L) statement*.

stock-keeping unit (SKU) The smallest unit available for keeping inventory control. In soft-goods merchandise, an SKU usually means a size, color, and style.

stock-to-sales ratio Specifies the amount of inventory that should be on hand at the beginning of the month to support the sales forecast and maintain the inventory turnover objective. The beginning-of-month (BOM) inventory divided by sales for the month. The average stock-to-sales ratio is 12 divided by planned inventory turnover. This ratio is an integral component of the merchandise budget plan.

stocklift A strategy vendors and retailers use to get products into retail stores, either when a retailer allows a vendor to create space for goods by "buying back" a competitor's inventory and removing it from a retailer's system or when the retailer forces a vendor to buy back slow-moving merchandise. Also called a *buyback* or *lift-out*.

stockout A situation occurring when an SKU that a customer wants is not available.

store advocates Customers who like a store so much that they actively share their positive experiences with friends and family.

store brand Products developed and marketed by a retailer and available for sale only by that retailer. Also called *private-label brand, house brand,* or *own brand*.

store maintenance The activities involved with managing the exterior and interior physical facilities associated with the store.

store-within-a-store An agreement in which a retailer rents a portion of retail space in a store operated by a different, independent retailer.

straight commission A form of salesperson's compensation in which the amount paid is based on a percentage of sales made minus merchandise returned.

straight rack A type of fixture that consists of a long pipe suspended with supports going to the floor or attached to a wall.

straight salary compensation A compensation plan in which salespeople or managers receive a fixed amount of compensation for each hour or week they work.

strategic alliance Collaborative relationship between independent firms. For example, a foreign retailer might enter an international market through direct investment but develop an alliance with a local firm to perform logistical and warehousing activities.

strategic profit model (SPM) A tool used for planning a retailer's financial strategy based on both margin management (net profit margin) and asset management (asset turnover). Using the SPM, a retailer's objective is to achieve a target return on assets.

strategic relationship Long-term relationship in which partners make significant investments to improve both parties' profitability. Also called *partnering relationship*.

strategic retail planning process The steps a retailer goes through to develop a strategic retail plan. It describes how retailers select target market segments, determine the appropriate retail format, and build sustainable competitive advantages.

strengths and weaknesses analysis A critical aspect of the situation audit in which a retailer determines its unique capabilities—its strengths and weaknesses relative to its competition.

strike zone The area in a retail store that customers pass through after the decompression zone where retailers display some of their most compelling merchandise.

strip shopping center An attached row of stores, usually with onsite parking in front of the stores. Also known as *convenience*, *neighborhood*, or *community shopping center*.

structured training program Training that teaches new employees the basic skills and knowledge they will need to do their job.

subbrand Part of a branding strategy in which a product's brand name is associated with the description of the product, such as Frosted Flakes, where the family brand is Kellogg's.

subculture theory A theory of how fashion spreads that suggests that subcultures of mostly young and less affluent consumers, such as motorcycle riders and urban rappers, have started fashions for such things as colorful fabrics, t-shirts, sneakers, jeans, black leather jackets, and surplus military clothing.

substantial In relation to a market, one that offers enough profits to support retailing mix activities.

supercenter Large store (150,000 to 220,000 square feet) combining a discount store with a supermarket.

supply chain A set of firms that make and deliver a given set of goods and services to the ultimate consumers.

supply chain management The set of approaches and techniques firms employ to efficiently and effectively integrate their suppliers, manufacturers, warehouses, stores, and transportation intermediaries to efficiently have the right quantities at the right locations, and at the right time.

sustainable competitive advantage A distinct competency of a retailer relative to its competitors that can be maintained over a considerable time period.

SWOT analysis An assessment of the retailer's internal and external environment, as represented by strengths, weaknesses, opportunities, and threats.

tangibility A customer service characteristic that customers use to evaluate service quality; it is associated with the appearance of physical facilities, equipment, personnel, and communication materials when a service is being performed.

target market The market segment(s) toward which the retailer plans to focus its resources and retail mix.

tariff A tax placed by a government on imports. Also known as a *duty*.

team incentive Sales incentive based on the performance of a group, department, or the store as a whole.

tertiary trading area The outermost ring of a trade area; includes customers who occasionally shop at the store or shopping center. Also called the *fringe trading area*.

theme/festival center A shopping center that typically employs a unifying theme that is carried out by the individual shops in their architectural design and, to an extent, their merchandise.

thrift store A retail format offering used merchandise.

ticketing and marking Procedures for making price labels and placing them on the merchandise.

tonnage merchandising A display technique in which large quantities of merchandise are displayed together.

top-down planning One side of the process of developing an overall retail strategy where goals are set at the top of the organization and filter down through the operating levels.

trade area A geographic sector that contains potential customers for a particular retailer or shopping center.

trade show A temporary concentration of vendors that provides retailers opportunities to place orders and view what is available in the marketplace.

trademark Any mark, work, picture, or design associated with a particular line of merchandise or product.

traffic flow The balance between a substantial number of cars and not so many that congestion impedes access to the store.

transformational leader A leader who gets people to transcend their personal needs for the sake of realizing the group goal.

trendsetters Initial customer adopters of a new fashion. Also known as *fashion leaders* or *innovators*.

trialability The costs and commitment required to initially adopt a fashion.

trickle-down theory A theory of how fashion spreads that suggests that the fashion leaders are consumers with the highest social status—wealthy, well-educated consumers. After they adopt a fashion, the fashion trickles down to consumers in lower social classes. When the fashion is accepted in the lowest social class, it is no longer acceptable to the fashion leaders in the highest social class.

trust A belief that a partner is honest (reliable, stands by its word, sincere, fulfills obligations) and benevolent (concerned about the other party's welfare).

turnover In a human resource context, the number of employees who voluntarily leave their job, divided by the number of positions in the firm.

tying contract An agreement between a vendor and a retailer requiring the retailer to take a product it does not necessarily desire (the tied product) to ensure that it can buy a product it does desire (the tying product).

umbrella brand A product's brand name associated with the company's name. Also called a *family brand.*

universal product code (UPC) The black-and-white bar code found on most merchandise; used to collect sales information at the point of sale using computer terminals that read the code. This information is transmitted computer to computer to buyers, distribution centers, and then to vendors, who in turn quickly ship replenishment merchandise.

unorganized retailing Collections of small, independent retailers, especially common in emerging economies.

unplanned location Freestanding and urban retail locations that lack any centralized management to determine which stores locate in them or how they operate.

unplanned purchasing A buying decision made by customers on the spot after seeing the merchandise. Also called *impulse buying.*

unrelated diversification growth opportunity Diversification in which there is no commonality between the present business and the new business.

unsatisfied need The condition that arises when a customer's desired level of satisfaction differs from his or her current level of satisfaction.

urban decay The process by which a previously well-functioning area falls into disrepair.

urban sprawl Expansions of residential and shopping center developments into suburban or rural areas, beyond urban centers.

utilitarian benefit A motivation for shopping in which consumers accomplish a specific task, such as buying a suit for a job interview.

utilitarian need A need motivating a consumer to go shopping to accomplish a specific task.

VALS (values of lifestyle survey) A tool used to categorize customers into eight lifestyle segments. Based on responses to surveys conducted by SRI Consulting Business Intelligence.

value Relationship of what a customer gets (goods and services) to what he or she has to pay for it.

variable costs Costs that vary with the level of sales and can be applied directly to the decision in question.

variety The number of different merchandise categories within a store or department. Also known as *breadth.*

vending machine A nonstore format in which merchandise or services are stored in a machine and dispensed to customers when they deposit cash or use a credit card.

vendor-managed inventory (VMI) An approach for improving supply chain efficiency in which the vendor is responsible for maintaining the retailer's inventory levels in each of its stores.

vertical integration An example of diversification by retailers involving investments by retailers in wholesaling or manufacturing merchandise.

vertical merchandising The presentation of a store and its merchandise in ways that will attract the attention of potential customers.

visibility Customers' ability to see the store and enter the parking lot safely.

visual merchandising The presentation of a store and its merchandise in ways that will attract the attention of potential customers.

warehouse club A retailer that offers a limited assortment of food and general merchandise with little service and low prices to ultimate consumers and small businesses.

wholesale market A concentration of vendors within a specific geographic location, perhaps even under one roof or over the Internet.

wholesale-sponsored voluntary cooperative group An organization operated by a wholesaler offering a merchandising program to small, independent retailers on a voluntary basis.

wholesaler Firms that buy products from manufacturers and resell them to retailers.

word of mouth Communications among people about a retailer.

zone pricing Charging different prices for the same merchandise in different geographic locations to be competitive in local markets.

zoning The regulation of the construction and use of buildings in certain areas of a municipality.

COMPANY INDEX